STATE AND LOCAL GOVERNMENT: A CASE BOOK

State and Local Government: A Case Book

Edited by *EDWIN A. BOCK*

Published for
The Inter-University Case Program
by the UNIVERSITY OF ALABAMA PRESS

1963

Library of Congress Catalog Card Number 59-11736

printed and bound by birmingham printing company
birmingham, alabama

Contents

THE CHIEF EXECUTIVE AND HIS AIDES

HOW MUCH TO SPEND? WHO WILL PAY?

ADMINISTRATION IN LOCAL GOVERNMENT

Introduction

THE RECENT publication of *Essays on the Case Method*[1] and the growing use of case studies in political science make it unnecessary to tax the reader with a methodological introduction as his price of admission to the 25 cases that follow. Nor will it be necessary to initiate him with an account of the fifteen-year history of the Inter-University Case Program, which has produced these cases primarily for the political science departments of nearly seventy participating colleges and universities.

The purpose of this collection is easily stated. It has been prepared to meet the expressed demand of professors in the state and local government field who regularly use ICP cases and who find it inconvenient to teach with ten to twenty separate studies. Several of the cases in the book have been teaching favorites from the time they emerged from the editorial desks of my predecessors, Harold Stein (1948-1953) and Paul Ylvisaker (1953-1954). Some of these older cases have been revised and brought up to date. Fifteen of the cases have appeared in the ICP-University of Alabama Press monograph series within the last five years. Three are 1963 publications.

Introducing a collection of case studies calls for a few words on at least two matters: (1) their accuracy and completeness, and (2) the claims made for their representativeness, if any.

Accuracy and Completeness

The reader will be helped in estimating the accuracy and completeness of the cases if he is familiar with the ICP's pattern of case preparation. Once a subject for a case study is chosen, the effort begins with the selection of a writer. He is usually a political scientist, and, before he is commissioned, consideration is given to such factors as: (a) his research and writing ability; (b) his ability to see the theoretical and scientific implications of the different aspects of the process that is to be portrayed; (c) his prospects for interviewing the principal actors and for studying files and corroborating documents; (d) any intellectual or occupational involvements that might inhibit his ability to produce a factual, complete account. The writer of an ICP case is usually told that he is expected to prepare an accurate narrative of government action that also conveys to the reader the contemporary strategies and perceptions of the principal characters. If possible, we refrain from selecting as writers persons whose approach to the people in a city hall would be either unbendingly zoological or quiveringly touristical. We seek writers who can achieve a blend of scientific curiosity, governmental sophistication, and sympathetic personal understanding.

A case writer's first drafts are usually circulated to the officials who appear prominently in his account. These officials are invited to point out inaccuracies, omissions, neglected nuances, or disagreements with the factual statements advanced by the other actors. Early drafts are also reviewed by specialists and by the twenty members of the ICP Executive Board, who bring to bear a wide range of government and academic experience. The finished case, which often embodies the contributions of many persons, is thus the product of a good deal of striving for accuracy and for tolerable completeness. Yet anyone familiar with public affairs—or human affairs of any other variety—will appreciate how many obstacles stand in the path of achieving, one or two years after an event, a perfectly accurate and complete literary re-creation of it. Therefore, it is appropriate to repeat here the caution that appeared in the ICP's recent collection of cases for the first-year course in American Government:

> although care may be taken to make cases complete

[1] Edwin A. Bock, ed.: *Essays on the Case Method* (International Institute of Administrative Sciences, Brussels, 1962). Available in English and French editions. English language copies may also be obtained from the University of Alabama Press or from Public Administration Service, Chicago.

and accurate, no case can achieve perfection. No case writer can know everything about any particular process. Memories are faulty, motivations are not entirely conscious, and sometimes the writer must depend on an unrepresentative document that happens to be the only source available to cover a particular point in a case. The reader has the right to expect the Case Program to strive for perfection, and the Case Program has the duty to warn the reader that perfection is impossible.[2]

Representativeness

The cases in this collection portray situations, atmospheres, processes, and tactics that form some of the real stuff of American state and local government. They are not, however, case studies of those routine matters whose disposal, in large quantities by lower officials following prescribed patterns, constitutes much of the unpublicized daily grind of government.

An effort has been made to include in the collection case studies about a variety of problems confronting state and local governments. But no claim is made that these 25 cases are representative of the most important problems or of all the major aspects of the governmental processes in the fifty states, the 3,050 counties, the 34,403 municipalities and townships, and the 14,424 special purpose districts that were reported in the *Statistical Abstract of the United States* for 1962. Attempts simply to develop the categories needed to measure this extra-federal universe face an obstreperous diversity of local and regional situations—differences in publics, traditions, culture, economics, geography; differences in prevailing attitudes about roles and styles of government; differences in governmental structures and political environments. Sometimes these differences turn out to be merely formalistic camouflage or variations in nomenclature: beneath are all the familiar forces and strategies and styles of behavior that one has observed in one's own city or state. On the other hand, some apparent uniformities, as A. H. Smith observed in *Village Life in China,* are

> found on investigation to be subject to surprising variations, not only in parts of the empire remote from one another, but in those which are separated by but a short distance.[3]

Many expected uniformities and unexpected differences in local government processes have turned up in the review of early drafts of these cases by members of the ICP Executive Board situated in different parts of the country. Sometimes a reviewer's insights and hunches, based on experience with local governments in his area, have helped the writer in another region of the country to uncover some elements or transactions that he had previously overlooked. On the other hand, there have been instances when a draft from one section of the country has run into strong criticism from reviewers in another section. And sometimes painstaking additional research has shown that the writer was correct in his original expostulation that "things just don't work that way [down/out/up/over] here."

Connection with Comparative Government Studies

These experiences suggest more than the already-evident conclusion that it would be foolhardy to claim any sort of representativeness for 25 cases. They raise the question of whether the particular mixture of uniformities and differences that prevails in the universe of American state and local government does not qualify this world for the research attention and theory-building effort of comparative government scholars, who today tend to direct their attention abroad. Opposed to the many dissimilarities that confront the international comparative scholar, the differences that the researcher has to contend with at home are less extravagant, less monumental, and at times less gaudy. The sheer number of factors that have to be contrasted or compared is less overwhelming. Domestic comparative studies may offer the feasibility of finer understanding, more delicacy, greater precision. And—no ironic symbolism intended—they do not require an additional language or, in most districts, Kaopectate.

If the comparative method in political science, with its current international emphasis, achieves the payoff that many hope for, and only slightly fewer expect, it should have fruitful repercus-

[2] Edwin A. Bock and Alan K. Campbell, eds.: *Case Studies in American Government* (Prentice-Hall, Englewood Cliffs, N. J., 1962).

[3] Edinburgh, 1899, p. 226.

sions in the American state and local government field. There would then arise the double question: what can the comparative study of the governments of different countries contribute to our understanding of the varieties of governmental processes within the United States? And what contribution will comparative American studies be able to make to the larger comparative government world? If domestic and international comparative government studies were considered part of a single intellectual continuum, each portion might benefit from the particular insights and research advantages of the other.

The cases in this volume also raise a question for those interested in economic development, "institution-building," "planned social change" and similar processes whose names carry the ring of urgency and action from the world of technical assistance and national uplift. Have we fixed our research sights so that, like the guns of Singapore, they train only out across the sea and cause us to ignore the land behind us? Don Price once suggested, not wholly in fun, that a possible law of government life could be summed up in the sentence: "It's easier to be liberal a long way from home." The officials depicted in the following cases are worthy of the attention of those interested in development precisely because they are dealing with change while immersed in the glutinous mass of local interests and sensitivities. Any impulse to vigorous action is subject to being worn smooth by the stream of daily face-to-face relationships with fellow citizens and fellow officials who are likely to be personally affected. Nevertheless, change is effected and its impacts do get adjusted, to the accompaniment of unending conversations in the office, on the street, or at home. The home telephones of officials in some of the cases that follow ring late into the night with calls from exercised citizens. Some of the officials are buttonholed by irate neighbors about official matters when they venture out into their front yards for some week-end gardening. Their wives and children feel the pressures when former friends or playmates begin to treat them distantly. In short, these cases, and the United States local government world from which they are drawn, may have suggestive material for the political scientist whose primary interest is why an Asian village headman moves so slowly to replace a polluted well with a good new one. Conversely, an understanding of the situation of the village headman may help us see in fuller perspective the involved process by which our governments deal with new problems, like air pollution, in our own villages.

The Arrangement of Cases

ICP cases designed primarily for teaching are chaste in presenting authors' opinions and conclusions. This is deliberate, and is done to permit the instructor the widest freedom and the student the greatest incentive to form his own initial ideas. Similarly, the arrangement of cases in this volume is one that has seemed suitable for this particular collection. It is not to be taken as our choice of the "one best" sequence of cases for a fancied ideal state and local course. Experience to date suggests that instructors who like to teach with case studies also like to arrange them to fit their personal pedagogical strategies and styles. To assist readers in selecting appropriate cases from the collection, a partial index is offered at the end of the Introduction.

Acknowledgments

From 1947 to 1957 the Inter-University Case Program was supported by grants from the Carnegie Corporation of New York; from 1957 to 1963 by grants from the Ford Foundation. Since 1951 the Program has also received annual fees from more than seventy participating universities and other institutions.

During its fifteen-year history, the Program has benefited heavily from the intellectual contributions of members of its Executive Board. A complete list of Board members appears on the following page.

The Inter-University Case Program is also indebted to Professor James B. McMillan, former Director of the University of Alabama Press, and to Mrs. Eunice H. Payne, Acting Director of the Press, for assistance in publishing this volume.

Edwin A. Bock

The Maxwell School, Syracuse University

THE CPAC POLICY COMMITTEE
(1948-1951)
AND
THE EXECUTIVE BOARD OF THE INTER-UNIVERSITY CASE PROGRAM
(1951-1963)

Index

(Cases with useful peripheral relevance are shown in parentheses.)

STATE

SPECIAL METROPOLITAN PROBLEMS

SPECIAL DISTRICT

CITY

COUNTY

SUBURBAN

* * * * * * * * * * * *

BUDGET/FISCAL/TAX

BUREAUCRACY/CIVIL SERVICE

CHIEF EXECUTIVES (ELECTED)

(a) Governors

Commuters vs. Black Ball Line
Florida Flood Control District
Florida Milk Commission
Governor Freeman and Minnesota Budget
Seattle Seeks a Tax
Shredded Wheat Property
Taxing Southern Railway in Alabama
(County Buys Dunwoodie Golf Course)
(Van Waters Case)

(b) Mayors

Appointed by the Mayor
City Manager Tries to Fire Police Chief
Defending Hill Against Metal Houses
Mayor and the Fire Chief
Philadelphia General Hospital
Seattle Seeks a Tax
Trenton Milk Contract

COMMUNICATION

California State Personnel Board
City Manager Tries to Fire Police Chief
Defending Hill Against Metal Houses
Demotion of Inspector Goldberg
Golden County Extension Agent
Hanover Builds a High School
Lonesome Train in Levittown
Massachusetts Department of Conservation
Philadelphia General Hospital
Trenton Milk Contract
Van Waters Case

COMMUNITY CONTROVERSY

Commuters vs. Black Ball Line
Defending Hill Against Metal Houses
Demotion of Inspector Goldberg
Golden County Extension Agent
Hanover Builds a High School
Lonesome Train in Levittown
Mayor and the Fire Chief
Moses on the Green
Trenton Milk Contract

EDUCATION

Hanover Builds a High School
Lonesome Train in Levittown
Michigan Athletic Awards Rule
(Governor Freeman and Minnesota Budget)

EXECUTIVE LEADERSHIP

(a) by Legislators

Hanover Builds a High School
Promotion of Lem Merrill
Seattle Seeks a Tax
Trenton Milk Contract

(b) Non-elective Officials

City Manager Tries to Fire Police Chief
Demotion of Inspector Goldberg
Florida Flood Control District
Florida Milk Commission
Mayor and the Fire Chief
Moses on the Green
Philadelphia General Hospital
Van Waters Case

HEALTH AND WELFARE

New York City Health Centers
Philadelphia General Hospital
(Florida Milk Commission)
(Trenton Milk Contract)

HUMAN RELATIONS

Appointed by the Mayor
California State Personnel Board
City Manager Tries to Fire Police Chief
Defending Hill Against Metal Houses
Demotion of Inspector Goldberg
Florida Flood Control District
Florida Milk Commission
Golden County Extension Agent
Hanover Builds a High School
Lonesome Train in Levittown
Mayor and the Fire Chief
Moses on the Green
Philadelphia General Hospital
Promotion of Lem Merrill
Trenton Milk Contract
Van Waters Case

INTEREST GROUPS

(a) External

Commuters vs. Black Ball Line
Defending Hill Against Metal Houses
Demotion of Inspector Goldberg
Florida Milk Commission
Golden County Extension Agent
Hanover Builds a High School
Lonesome Train in Levittown
Massachusetts Department of Conservation
Mayor and the Fire Chief
Michigan Athletic Awards Rule
Moses on the Green
New York City Health Centers
Taxing Southern Railway in Alabama

(b) Government Agencies or Officials, As

California State Personnel Board

LAY BOARDS OR COMMISSIONS

LEGISLATIVE BEHAVIOR

PERSONNEL

PLANNING AND LAND USE

POLICE AND FIRE

POLITICS AND PARTIES

RACIAL/RELIGIOUS MINORITIES

REGULATION/ADMINISTRATIVE LAW

REORGANIZATION

SCIENCE, GOVERNMENT AND

SPECIALISTS, PROFESSIONALS IN GOVERNMENT

Authors of the Cases

EDWIN A. BOCK is Director of the Inter-University Case Program and Professor of Political Science at Syracuse University.

PAUL B. CROOKS studied at Harvard. He has been a County Agricultural Agent and has served as an Extension Supervisor of the Agricultural Extension Service in Indiana.

ROBERT T. DALAND has taught at the University of Alabama and the University of Connecticut. He is currently on leave from the Department of Political Science at the University of North Carolina to serve as research co-ordinator for a University of Southern California AID project in Brazil. He gathered material on Westchester County while he was a post-doctoral fellow of the New York Metropolitan Region Program at Columbia University.

JOHN DE GROVE is an Assistant Professor in the Department of Political Science of the University of Florida.

VALERIE A. and CHESTER B. EARLE are both former staff members of the University of Alabama's Bureau of Public Administration. Mr. Earle is now Associate Professor, School of Government and Public Administration, The American University. Mrs. Earle is Associate Professor of Government, Georgetown University.

THOMAS H. ELIOT is Chancellor of Washington University, St. Louis. He served as Executive Director of the Massachusetts Special Commission on the Structure of State Government. He also has held several positions in the federal government and served one term as a member of the House of Representatives.

THOMAS FLINN participated in Minnesota politics during the events described in his case study. He holds a Ph.D. degree from the University of Minnesota, and is now a member of the Department of Government of Oberlin College.

ROBERT GOLEMBIEWSKI took a Ph.D. degree from Yale and later taught at Princeton. He is now Assistant Professor of Management, College of Commerce and Business Administration of the University of Illinois.

WILLIAM J. GORE was a member of the Department of Political Science, University of Washington at the time this case was written. He later taught at the University of Kansas and at Cornell University. He is now Associate Professor, Department of Political Science, Indiana University.

GEORGE KANTROWITZ did his graduate work at Michigan State University and is presently working with the Jewish Welfare Board, Toronto, Canada.

HERBERT KAUFMAN is Associate Professor of Political Science at Yale University. His earlier experience includes two years with federal agencies in Washington, and a year as a special consultant for the Mayor's Committee on Management Survey, New York City.

JOHN B. KEELEY, formerly with the Department of Social Sciences of the United States Military Academy, is a Captain in the United States Army.

WILLIAM N. KINNARD, JR. was Assistant Professor of Finance and Real Estate at the University of Connecticut at the time this case was originally published.

JOHN J. LOGUE is Assistant Professor in the Department of History and Political Science at Villanova University. He was formerly a member of the Department of Political Philosophy and the Social Sciences at Fordham University.

JOSEPH F. MALONEY taught in the Department of Political Philosophy and the Social Sciences at Fordham University at the time this case was written. He is now executive director of the Massachusetts Transportation Commission.

BEATRICE MARKEY, co-author of *The Mayor and the Fire Chief,* was a research associate in the

School of Public Administration of the University of Southern California. She is now on the faculty of the University of Hawaii.

Louis Menand III is dean of Bradford Junior College. He was formerly an Assistant Professor in the Department of Government at Dartmouth College and, at one time, worked in organization and methods analysis for the United States Bureau of the Budget.

Howard F. Miller is Assistant Professor of Political Science in the Maxwell School of Syracuse University. He served in the New York State Budget Commission from 1956 to 1958, first as administrative deputy, and later as deputy director. He holds a Ph.D. degree from Harvard University.

Frederick C. Mosher is Professor of Political Science at the University of California at Berkeley. He has served as personnel technician in the Los Angeles City Civil Service Department, as assistant director of personnel in UNRRA, and as assistant chief, Division of Foreign Service Planning, Department of State. In 1962 he served as Staff Director of the Committee on Foreign Affairs Personnel in Washington, D. C.

William K. Muir, Jr. is a member of the New York State Bar Association and was formerly associated with the New York firm of Davis, Polk, Wardwell, Sunderland & Kiendl. He is now an Assistant in Instruction in the Department of Political Science at Yale University, where he is also a doctoral candidate.

Robert L. Peabody is now a member of the Department of Political Science, Johns Hopkins University. He was formerly a research fellow at the Brookings Institution. Before that, he was a municipal research assistant and governmental research associate of the University of Washington. He holds a Ph.D. degree from Stanford University.

Mariana Robinson is a research assistant at the Institute of Governmental Studies at the University of California at Berkeley.

Glendon A. Schubert, Jr., now Professor of Political Science at Michigan State University, was formerly Chairman of the Political Science Department at Franklin and Marshall College. He is the author of numerous articles and books. One article, "Legislative Adjudication of Administrative Legislation" in *Journal of Public Law,* VII:1 (1958) contains additional background on "The Michigan Athletic Awards Rule."

Frank P. Sherwood is Professor of Public Administration at the University of Southern California.

Evelyn Shipman has had a career with the federal government, most recently in personnel training in the Bureau of Reclamation, Department of the Interior. She is the wife of Professor George A. Shipman of the University of Washington.

Corinne Silverman, former Associate Editor on the ICP staff, has written several ICP case studies, including *The Little Rock Story*. She has also been chief assistant to Samuel Lubell.

Helenan Sonnenburg, now Mrs. David M. Lewis, is an Assistant Instructor in the Department of Political Science at Michigan State University.

Harmon Zeigler is Assistant Professor of Political Science, Emory University. He was formerly with the Department of Political Science at Florida State University.

CLOSE TO THE PEOPLE

"The only argument with an east wind is to put on your overcoat."

James Russell Lowell

Defending "The Hill" Against Metal Houses

William K. Muir, Jr.

Introduction

ONE MARCH AFTERNOON in 1953, three ocean-going tugs docked at a wharf in West Haven, Connecticut. Each towed a heavy wooden barge on which rested three weather-beaten, prefabricated houses, 20 x 48 feet in dimension and one story high. One by one, the nine houses were lifted onto waiting trucks and hauled to a vacant lot on the western outskirts of New Haven.

In the ensuing weeks scores more of these houses were delivered in similar fashion to the same New Haven lot. The new owners of the houses were meanwhile making necessary preparations for the construction of a low-rent housing development for 130 families. Each one of the pre-fabs was to be used to shelter two families.

The houses stood on that lot—unused—until 1956. Why they were never used is the subject of this case study.

The Setting

THE METAL HOUSES had been brought to New Haven from New York, where they had been in use since 1946.

This was their history: At the end of World War II there was an urgent nation-wide housing shortage. New York City resorted to a temporary housing program for veterans and their families. "The city provided eight vacant tracts in the Bronx, Brooklyn, and Queens, and suitably graded and prepared them; the federal government supplied and paid for installation of a variety of surplus prefabricated structures, the most familiar of which was the Quonset hut."[1] Despite certain immediate drawbacks—the structures were cramped and drafty and often leaked—the program partially succeeded in stemming the critical need by sheltering 8,600 families in eight projects. As the years passed, however, the projects became more and more of a problem. The houses "were not intended to stand more than three to five years."[2] Wretched maintenance increased the rate of deterioration.

One of the projects was located in Queens, not far from LaGuardia Airport. The houses here were not of the predominant Quonset variety. They were "metal houses," 20 x 48 feet, and 10 feet high, with a pitched roof. The walls consisted of a thin, riveted metal (usually aluminum or galvanized iron), insulated by weatherproof, fire-proof material. The flooring consisted of linoleum, insulation, and a supporting network of two-inch steel girders. The roofing was also metallic and thinly insulated. The huts were cellarless, but were raised off the ground by cinder blocks.

Each metal house contained two tiny apartments. A doorway at each end of the structures served as the single entrance to each apartment. Immediately to the left of the doorway was the kitchen, roughly twelve by nine feet, containing some shelf space, a small Frigidaire, and a gas cooking stove. In the living room, across the hallway from the kitchen, the dining room table swung from the wall out into the room. There was barely room for more than a small couch and two chairs. Toward the center of the duplex unit was a tiny bathroom, crammed with shower facilities, a toilet, and a washstand. Further down the hall, were two bedrooms, one six by nine feet, one nine by eight feet.

1 New York City Housing Authority, *18th Annual Report, 1951,* pp. 26-27.

2 *Ibid.,* p. 27.

The outside walls were thin but well insulated; the partition separating the two apartments, however, was a thin piece of plastic board, a quarter of an inch thick. It insured neither quiet nor privacy. Each side of the house had six overhead windows. The windows were hinged along the bottom and opened down and into the house.

Assured that a federal low-rent housing program would be continued, the New York Housing Authority made plans to close all the temporary projects during 1951. Since the Queens project "generally provided the most difficult expensive maintenance problems,"[3] the Authority closed it first. The Authority offered the metal shacks for sale at $75 each. They were purchased in time by two brothers named Lebov, who were junk merchants, and were shipped across the Long Island Sound on barges to New Haven, Connecticut, where they became a part of this story.

New Haven

The Lebov brothers intended to use the homes again as low-rental dwelling units. New Haven had a housing shortage. According to its Housing Authority's 1953 report, 22,918 people, or roughly fourteen percent of the families in New Haven, lived "in overcrowded, improperly heated, insanitary or structurally unsafe buildings." Meanwhile two developments aggravated the situation. First, a rerouting of one of the main highways through the city had expelled 200 lower-income families from the eastern part of town; second, plans to demolish a slum area in the center of town were delayed by inability to relocate the many families involved.

Federal housing projects had been seriously curtailed for several years by Congressional restrictions. Private building had not filled the gap between need and availability, and construction was too costly to help those who could afford only low rents. The dilemma of New Haven was posed by its housing director: "I do believe that private initiative should come into the low-rental field; I understand why it cannot."

[3] New York City Housing Authority Release, August 27, 1951.

It was toward the homeless and inadequately housed low-income families (many of them Negro because their race as well as their poverty made finding a home more difficult) that the Lebovs beckoned with their metal houses.

The Hill

New Haven is an old city. Over the centuries it has spread from its original center, the famous "nine squares," first circling about the harbor; then, with the introduction of the automobile, beginning to project northward, eastward, and northwestward. The area south of the nine squares is peninsular, bounded on the west by the West River, which serves as the city limits, and on the east by the harbor shore. This is the area known as the Hill.

The Hill is a maze of intersecting and multi-directional thoroughfares. Its side streets, like those of any neighborhood developed in the pre-automobile era, are narrow, discontinuous, and irregular. Industry and homes stand in close and unhealthy juxtaposition. Along the main thoroughfares tenement-type dwellings house laborers, who pay low rents for their overcrowded, dilapidated flats.

Despite its general deterioration, the Master Plan of the City of New Haven pointed out that the Hill "appears to be a well-knit neighborhood around a center, including Prince Street School, St. Anthony's Parochial School, and B'nai Israel Synagogue." Such a consideration is significant in light of one of the assumptions of the report: "That the existence of a cohesive neighborhood and the full utilization of its resources is the major force, regardless even of the physical condition of the dwellings, which can retain the population in a given locality, hence stabilize and even improve real estate values, and provide the incentive for development and redevelopment."

The Triangle

The profusion of main arteries divides the Hill into many natural, uniquely shaped, smaller communities. It was in one such community, a triangular-shaped section, less than half a square mile in area, that the action of this story began.

The Triangle—as we shall call the neighborhood—is formed by the intersection of Washington and Columbus avenues; the base of the Triangle is the Boulevard, an ironic misnomer for a gutted, cinder roadway. Projecting almost perpendicularly from the Boulevard are three pleasant residential streets, Adeline, Frank, and Truman, and these run parallel with Washington Avenue. West of the Boulevard, and directly at the foot of the three stop streets, the New Haven junk merchants stored the prefabricated metal houses, which had just come from Queens, in full view for the whole neighborhood to see.

In 1953 a little over half of the nearly 3,000 inhabitants of the Triangle were Italian, with Irish, Germans, and Poles comprising the rest. There were some Jewish families, many of whom owned homes at the east end of Truman Street. A few Negro families had moved into the poorer part of the area (Adeline Street), but their intrusion had caused little acrimony.

The men of this community are skilled and semi-skilled workers, with a few white-collar clerks, waiters, and salesmen. Many of the homes are privately owned; some are well painted and clean. Physically Truman Street is the most attractive of the four main roads. Sturdy and beautiful elm trees hang over the street, and Truman School occupies a block at its western end. Some of the homes on Adeline, Frank, and Washington are insubstantial wooden buildings. Interspersed, too, between some of the homes are small tenements, a few housing as many as six families.

In the Triangle there were two distinguishing landmarks significant for this story. The first was the Emergency Housing Project for Veterans, erected after the war by the federal government. It consisted of fourteen drab, gray barrack buildings, which stood for seven years just south of Columbus Avenue. In time the city took over the administration of the project. In January, 1954, the New Haven Health Department submitted a report to the Mayor proposing their demolition and gave as reasons:

> it is isolated from other residential zones . . .
>
> a portion of the land upon which it is built is filled land . . .
>
> the salt water marsh is extremely close to the buildings . . . though "the project is fenced off from the undeveloped areas (to the rear), the fence has not been maintained properly and the children living there climb under, over, or through it readily; . . . and the West River is an attraction for some of the children during the summertime . . ."
>
> a great hazard to life and limb is the traffic on Congress Avenue . . .
>
> Heavy traffic noise should be avoided in residential areas so as not to interfere with sleep and relaxation . . .
>
> the lack of community facilities within easy walking distance . . . there are no opportunities for community development . . .
>
> a heavy rat infestation . . .
>
> overcrowding . . .
>
> advanced deterioration . . .

The degeneration of these barracks made the neighborhood wary of any kind of emergency housing.

A second landmark is the Eastern Machine Screw Corporation. Founded in 1910, this factory created the neighborhood surrounding it. Many of the old families of the community obtained their first employment there as immigrants from Italy.

The depression hit the factory hard; not until 1935 did it begin to re-employ at pre-1929 levels. The community still remembers the poverty and degradation it endured. Today, a home symbolizes material security to its people.

The factory provided the community a center for disseminating information. Though only 22 of the factory's 300 and more employees came from the Triangle itself, its small size gave opportunities to the lavatory sweep from Washington Avenue, the expediter from Truman Street, the secretary from Barclay, and the die operator from Adeline to talk to each other daily if anything of importance occurred in the neighborhood. Also, an unusually successful relationship between management and labor over the years had generated a spirit of trust among the employees. Thus, the shop hierarchy was ready to be transposed to political organization. The shop's expediter did become the spokesman of the Triangle's citizens, and an assistant foreman, along with one of his ablest young workmen, was chosen to be part of the movement's leadership when the Triangle became more formally organized.

The People

Met on the street, the people who live in the Triangle are unassuming, monosyllabic, garrulous. Observed, they are noisy, excitable, petty. Known, they are proud, cultured, compassionate, and cheerful.

An alderman once gave this impression of them: "The only reason why I would vote to oppose the metal houses would be to keep the poor people who would have to rent them from living with that riffraff." Perhaps two closer looks will alter such an impression.

The Possidente family came from Italy fifty odd years ago. In 1912 they moved to New Haven, built and settled in the very house they live in now. Possidente went to work for the Eastern Screw Corporation to support his large family. He worked hard, became foreman, and grew to be friends with the owners of the shop. In 1937 he died. Though Mrs. Possidente was, and still is, unable to put together a coherent English sentence, she has since that time succeeded in sending all her ten children through high school. Her four boys have graduated from college. While raising her own family, Mrs. Possidente assumed responsibility for the eight children who lived next door. Their mother died in 1933.

Another woman, Mrs. Virginia Gambaccini, worked as a waitress and cook and sent her son through the University of Connecticut, where he graduated with highest honors in 1952.

These are the kind of people who live in the Triangle: cautiously proud of what they have accomplished and determined that their children, if not they themselves, shall have a decent home, healthy environs, and a chance to prosper.

The Lebovs

In the Triangle, at the foot of Truman Street, the Lebov brothers had established their junk business. They were unpopular, for with junk come rats and dirt. The brothers were young and exceedingly rich, with a reputation for cupidity. Before 1953, their business activities had aroused a few citizens of the Triangle enough to ask the law to interfere. The fact that the Lebovs were Jewish did nothing to allay the suspicions of the predominantly Roman Catholic neighborhood.

When the New York Housing Authority offered the metal homes for sale as scrap, the Lebovs eyed the possibilities of their re-use. The Lebovs' lawyers checked the New Haven Building Code to find any regulation against such housing. There was none. From the railroad the brothers purchased a site which at that time was no more than a piece of marsh land directly behind the Emergency Housing Project.

Fortified with legal advice and a priority to purchase the metal houses, possessed of a land site, engineering details, architectural layouts, and the $96 fee, the Lebovs entered the New Haven office of Building Inspector Falsey on February 24, 1953, and secured a license to erect 65 of their homes. The homes, according to their plans, were to be arranged in eleven rows of six houses each, with a roadway separating every two rows, allowing each family access to a street. A playground was situated adjacent to the homes.

The Lebovs had seen to it that every regulation was satisfied; the west side of the Boulevard was zoned for industry, and such a zone allowed the erection of any kind of structure. The Building Inspector granted the permit with no stipulations other than that the buildings be erected six feet apart with forty feet separating each row.

Miss Mary Grava

But if the city officials did not balk at the Lebov housing project, Miss Mary Grava did.

Miss Grava was fifty years old, a spinster with an over-active thyroid. Her home occupied the northeast corner of the Barclay and Truman Street intersection. On the northwest corner stood the Lebovs' tawdry brick building, emitting smoke and smells and sounds of clanging scrap metal. Diagonally across from Miss Grava's home was the Eastern Machine Screw Corporation, and directly across Truman Street was the school.

Miss Grava had lived on Truman Street all her life. The home she occupied was built by her father nearly half a century ago, and with his death, she became custodian, looking after her epileptic and tubercular sister and serving as domestic for her younger bachelor brother, Joseph. There were many Gravas on the Hill. Three lived near Mary's home, and still another worked in the shop. A fifth owned the local hardware store. The Gravas were respectable and well-known; they had been the first residents of Truman Street.

Miss Grava did not like the prospect of the metal homes development. They were dirty and a blight to look at. In her estimation, they would attract riffraff. They meant the possibility of disease, crime, and bodily harm. They meant lowered real estate values. Her sense of security was outraged.

Political Activity

SEVERAL DAYS after the first few metal houses appeared in New Haven, a group of workers at the Eastern Machine Screw Corporation took a lunch hour stroll down to the Lebovs' lot to scrutinize them closely. A Lebov laborer was busy repairing one. The strollers approached him. No, the Lebov man volunteered, the houses were not to be junked; the Lebovs were going to put up a large housing development a few hundred yards up the river.

Back at the shop word spread quickly: Slums . . . Negroes . . . riffraff . . . crime . . . dirt . . . property values. When the workers went home that night, they carried the news. Miss Grava heard it from her brother, Joseph. Immediately she determined to try to kill the threat to the neighborhood.

Miss Grava knew her alderman, Mr. Slavin, slightly, and phoned him. Slavin apologized; he had not seen the houses, but he promised to call a fellow alderman, Mr. Montalto, and together they would inquire down at City Hall. He would phone her back.

He did not need to, for Miss Grava barraged the alderman with at least one phone call a day for the next month. The investigations of the two aldermen revealed that the Building Inspector had approved the development and had granted the Lebovs a license.

Slavin and Montalto

Under Miss Grava's constant promptings, Slavin and Montalto combed the city charter to find what powers the Board of Aldermen had in dealing with such a case. It was an arduous task for them, for both had little schooling. Slavin was a milkman—a political novice, serving his first term. His inexperience in political fields had led him to call on Montalto for help. The latter's nickname was "Happy." He was a salesman—garrulous, carefree. His delights were beer, television, maintaining his tidy little home, and politics. Since his election in 1948, he had survived three narrow victories. Re-election depended upon protecting the interest of his ward, and the ward showed the benefits of his concern. For a working class area, it received unusual attention from the city. Trees were carefully pruned; curbs were painted; the garbage was collected regularly. The community was happy with Happy Montalto. Being an alderman meant a great deal personally to both Slavin and Montalto. They welcomed and sought out any opportunity to procure an extra vote.

While the aldermen were busy on the political front, Miss Grava conferred with her neighbor and good friend, Carl Camilloni. Camilloni, who was a bachelor and a few years her junior, worked in the factory. Miss Grava took care of his invalid mother, cleaned his house, and did his marketing. Camilloni encouraged Miss Grava during the whole campaign against the Lebovs. Without his support, she might have given up when the fight seemed hopeless.

March and April passed fitfully for Miss Grava, while Montalto and Slavin looked for legal means to halt the housing project. The two aldermen ultimately conceived an amendment to the already overloaded city charter. The sense of it was to prevent houses of "unusual materials," especially metal, from being erected in New

Haven until the City Plan Commission and the Board of Aldermen had granted their separate permissions.

On May 4, Montalto and Slavin read their amendment at a meeting of the Board of Aldermen for the first time. (Since the Board consists of 33 aldermen and usually meets but once a month, it handles most of its work in small, specialized committees. The Board as a whole tends to give great weight to the research and decision of the committees.) The Slavin-Montalto amendment was directed to the Committee on Legislation, where it would have, as required, a public hearing.

Prospects were high. Montalto was a good friend of the members of the committee, and, anyway, it was a matter of custom and etiquette that no alderman should be opposed in matters which concerned the welfare of his ward.

The Board of Zoning Appeals

Toward the end of April the Lebov brothers, in hopes of selling more metal houses, erected a sample house, fully furnished, in a pleasant and quiet neighborhood a few blocks north of Congress Avenue along the Boulevard. The house looked so well in its new environment that the Lebovs went to the Building Inspector to get another permit for a development of metal homes in this less industrial locale.

The Building Inspector was unable to grant such a permit since the new area was zoned for residence, and the plans for the houses did not fulfill some of the requirements for such a zone. The Lebovs were told that they had to get a waiver of the zoning restrictions from the Appeals Board before a license could be granted. The Lebovs prepared a request to the Board of Zoning Appeals, and the hearing was set for May 26.

Miss Grava, her brother Joseph, and Mr. Camilloni appeared at the hearing. So did thirty or more residents of the invaded community. Four aldermen, among them Montalto and Slavin, were present, officially representing the complaints of the citizens against the Lebovs.

The legal question involved the amount of space between the metal structures. The plans of the brothers did not satisfy the minimum required distance. The attorney for the Lebovs, Alexander Winnick, stated the reasons for the lack of distance between the homes.

The four aldermen then testified against the project. The Chairman of the Zoning Board listened patiently and then asked for the hands of those who opposed the houses. Forty-five were raised.

The persuasiveness of the arguments can be gauged by the minutes of the Zoning Board's executive session:

> The appeal was considered. The Board found that the establishment of these metal houses would create a slum area that would affect the welfare of the neighbors in the vicinity and would interfere with the enjoyment of the property by actual occupants; that the type of property as described would not conform with the type of property in the vicinity, and therefore would decrease the value of these properties and operate as a detriment to these people in the vicinity; that there was no evidence of hardship to warrant a waiver of the zoning requirements. Hence, in view of the above, motion to deny this appeal was made . . . and said motion was passed unanimously.

The Lebovs had lost their chance. They decided to arrange their plans differently to satisfy the zoning requirements, but the owner of the property which the Lebovs had hoped to lease, a Mr. Mariani, had attended the meeting and had seen enough. He decided not to lease.

The meeting provided Miss Grava with an insight into the effectiveness of the various arguments which were presented. It also gave her confidence that administration officials could be persuaded to see the undesirability of these houses. In addition, the meeting introduced two new aldermen to the problem of the metal houses. One of them was Irving Horowitz, formerly a state representative. Though sometimes mistrusted on the Board, he was wise in the ways of politics, and his counsel to the less experienced Montalto and Slavin was a major factor in the subsequent campaign.

Miss Grava knew what the victory meant. The Lebovs would have to return to the original site at the foot of Congress Avenue. There was, however, nothing to do until the public hearing of the Montalto-Slavin amendment, scheduled for June 8, and as days crept by, the impatient Miss Grava became more querulous than ever, keeping up a drumfire of telephone calls to her alderman. Moreover, she talked to her neighborhood—and talk was a powerful weapon. She stimulated her brother Joseph and her neighbor Camilloni to maintain interest among the employees at the factory. She found a useful ally in Miss Anne Battistella, who lived in the neighborhood south of Washington Avenue. Miss Battistella owned three or four houses in the area. She carried on an anti-Lebov crusade with fervor.

Another friend was May Dietle. Her husband, Carl, was expediter at the Eastern Machine Screw Corporation and a natural leader. He was a friend of the owners of the factory, quite intelligent, and much aroused by the Lebovs' plans. Miss Grava and Mrs. Dietle never let his temper simmer down.

A loquacious postman carried the Misses Grava's and Battistella's news of the metal houses to all the residents while making his tours. Miss Grava herself was everywhere, dropping words of warning, or the latest rumor of some alleged Lebov malfeasance, in stores, on street corners, from her front porch, or on the telephone.

The Hearing

June 8 at last brought the hearing of the Committee on Legislation. Again Miss Grava and her brother attended the meeting. Slavin read the amendment and was informed that an addition to the city charter was not necessary, since Article 225 already provided the Board of Aldermen power "by ordinance . . . to regulate . . . the density of population and the location and use of buildings."

The committee was composed of three sympathetic aldermen. One, Guida, was a real estate man, and the other two were lawyers. The chairman, Reynolds, was a young Democratic attorney, and the other member, Henry Istas, was the Republican with most years of service on the Board. Their sympathies for Montalto and Slavin were reinforced that evening by the opinion of the director of the City Plan Commission, who in executive session described the undesirability of all metal homes in general.

Winnick and the Lebovs also appeared at the meeting. Seeing the opposition, Winnick stated that his clients were going to relent and would erect the houses several hundred miles away from New Haven. But his clients did not relent. One week later, construction began on the development, and within 24 hours, Chairman Reynolds had filed with the City Clerk a resolution demanding that the license be revoked.

By request of a majority, the Board of Aldermen convened a special meeting on June 26. The meeting lasted fifteen minutes. Discussion centered around a newly-found charter provision. Section 50 read:

> The Board of Aldermen shall have power by majority vote of all the members thereof . . . to enact . . . orders, resolutions, or ordinances . . . for any of the following purposes: . . . 1) to provide for the health of the city and to prevent and summarily abate nuisances of any kind . . . 2) to prevent nuisances and summarily abate the same at the expense of the person maintaining them; to prevent the erection or use of any building within said city for the purpose of carrying on therein any trade, manufacturing, or business, which in the judgment of said Board of Aldermen, shall be prejudicial to the public health, or considered an unnecessary annoyance to those living or owning any property in the vicinity . . .

Under this provision the aldermen felt that the Board could pass a resolution declaring the houses "nuisances" and revoke the license. (Montalto's and Slavin's original resolution was rendered superfluous by this discovery, and it was dropped and forgotten.)

Two aldermen had reservations. Norton Levine, the Democratic majority leader, felt the Board was going beyond its authority, and a young friend of his, Edward Marcus, agreed. They moved to request the opinion of the Mayor's legal adviser, the Corporation Counsel. The tone of the meeting was overwhelmingly in Montalto's and Slavin's favor, however.

By requesting the advice of the Corporation Counsel, Marcus and Levine involved Republican Mayor Celentano and his Counsel, George DiCenzo, in an embarrassing situation. As Levine and Marcus were careful to point out to the newspapers, if the Mayor agreed with the majority of aldermen, then it followed that all temporary housing units in New Haven should be demolished. Since there were already numerous temporary units in the city, and the housing situation was becoming every day more critical, either way he decided, the Mayor was bound to lose some votes.

Preparations for the Meeting

A new resolution, written by Montalto and Slavin and declaring the metal house development a "nuisance," awaited the Board's action at its next regular meeting, July 6. The twelve days that elapsed before that meeting were stormy days for the Triangle and the aldermen however. The Lebovs began to fight back. On June 28, the *Evening Register* printed this story:

> The Lebovs allowed a reporter to inspect one of the houses on the Boulevard yesterday. It was midday and the sun was beating on the closed house. It was cooler inside the insulated house than it was out. The unit was newly painted. There are four rooms and bath in each of the duplex buildings. There is block tile on the floors of the bedrooms. The bathroom and kitchen fixtures are new. The Lebovs said that new kitchen and bathroom equipment will be installed in all units.
>
> There are ample electric plugs, ceiling lights. There are automatic sprinkler system outlets in the kitchen and living room. The buildings are 48 feet long and 20 feet wide, so each living unit is 24 feet by 20 feet.

It was almost the last piece of favorable publicity the Lebovs got. At that time, however, apparent *Register* support of the brothers damaged the Triangle's confidence.

The worst was yet to come. On July 3, DiCenzo gave his opinion:

> The Board of Aldermen does not have the legal power to order abatement of existing metal houses on the ground that they constitute a nuisance. . . .
>
> Ordinarily, buildings are not nuisances *per se,* and public authorities cannot by mere declaration make that a nuisance which is not such in fact. . . . The reasons for these fundamental rules of law are obvious, for if this Power existed in public authorities, it could also well amount to a taking of property without due process of law. There appears nothing in the aldermen's resolution to indicate any of these facts, nor does anything appear in the resolution that tends to show that the 'existing metal houses' are a nuisance in fact.
>
> A building must be a NUISANCE IN FACT to be validly declared one.

The day before the July 6 meeting, an *Evening Register* reporter wrote an article which produced the moment of greatest demoralization for Montalto, Slavin, and the Triangle:

> FIGHT WANING
> IN MOVE TO BAR
> METAL HOMES
>
> MANY ALDERMEN CHANGE
> POSITIONS AFTER OPINION
> BY DICENZO
>
> . . . Several aldermen said today it would be 'senseless' to give an affirmative vote to the pending resolution in view of DiCenzo's unqualified opinion that the aldermen would be exceeding their authority and, if they do approve it, would probably be overruled by the Courts. On the basis of DiCenzo's decision these aldermen have decided to vote against the resolution and may recruit sufficient support in caucus prior to the meeting to defeat it.

Montalto and Slavin were frantic. They felt that failure to take positive action would be disastrous. Slavin suggested that the situation called for a meeting of all the friendly and wavering aldermen, in order to renew the strength of the coalition. The two men telephoned every alderman. To each they explained their case at length, answering all questions, and scotching the rumor that aldermen could be sued individually if they voted against the Lebovs. Would the aldermen come to a meeting at Montalto's Goodfellows' Club above the Howard Theater that evening and talk the matter over? Some refused. To Nathan Portnoy, it was a "prejudicial meeting." Marcus and Levine were not interested. Others couldn't come in from out of town. But 25 did appear that evening, and over beer, Henry Istas carried the day. DiCenzo's opinion was only an opinion, he reminded his colleagues. Istas' prestige and legal acumen meant a great deal.

At least one, Cohen, voiced a dissident sentiment. He was going to tomorrow's meeting to vote against the revocation of the permit. Others, too, left the meeting still undecided. But Alderman Horowitz gave advice and promised his support, which was especially reassuring to Montalto, who looked with idolatry on Horowitz's parliamentary skill.

Monday, July 6, was a hot, humid summer day. Men worked at half speed over their desks or their machines. The afternoon temperature climbed into the nineties. The windless calm and the enervating heat gave no hint of what was to happen.

Miss Grava had hardly moved all day. The strain of the campaign to alert the neighborhood had sapped much of her energy. The blow of DiCenzo's decision had overwhelmed her emotionally, and the oppressive weather had worn her down physically. She had wanted to go to the Board meeting that night, but it just seemed too hot. Toward mid-afternoon, she heard a timid knock at her front porch door. Standing at the screen door was one of her neighborhood cousins. She had a message for Mary. On Lines Street, she said, there was a lady who was urging people to attend the meeting that night to support the Montalto-Slavin resolution. Miss Grava's cousin was talking about Mrs. Gambaccini, who, worried by DiCenzo's opinion, had contacted Miss Battistella. The two middle-aged women had spent the whole previous night calling friends, seeking advice. One of the people they had reached was the wife of the President of the Board of Aldermen. She had emphasized the importance politicians place on the intensity of interest aroused by an issue. The President's wife thought that popular pressure at the meeting would be extremely effective. Mrs. Gambaccini, who had to work the next day, had asked Miss Grava's cousin to pass the word on to her neighbors. Eventually the news had come to the ears of the excitable Miss Grava.

The message had its effect. Miss Grava leaned over the fence and asked Camilloni if he was going to the meeting. He thought he might. Then Miss Grava called Mrs. D'Angelo on Frank Street, and soon after Mrs. D'Angelo's children were scurrying up and down the street, telling the neighbors to get down to the evening's meeting. May Dietle was telephoned, and she immediately began calling her friends. Everyone suddenly seemed eager to attend the meeting to balk the Lebovs.

The Meeting

By eight that evening, the aldermanic chambers were flooded with over 200 people. Shirt-sleeved and sweating in the roasting City Hall, they were a vexed and humorless and leaderless mob. They posed for pictures and peered into and out of windows. Those who could not edge their way into the chambers crawled along the fire escapes.

Meanwhile the aldermen had retreated upstairs to the caucus rooms. One of the Board's unwritten rules of procedure was that an important question was never debated in public if it could be avoided. Democratic and Republican members reached their decisions separately in partisan caucuses. Then the minority party chairman was allowed to barter with the majority leader for as much compromise as his "position of weakness" could obtain. After the agreements were made, the aldermen would proceed to the public aldermanic chambers and give a *pro forma* ratification to the decisions.

The people of the Triangle did not understand why the aldermen were not holding their meeting in public, and the aldermen were even more reluctant than usual to leave the sanctuary of the caucus rooms to face such mob vehemence. After two hours, Anne Battistella and Mrs. D'Angelo had had enough. Fearing that their neighbors, their patience exhausted, might leave before the aldermen arrived, Miss Battistella assumed the President's chair and quieted the crowd so that Mrs. D'Angelo could read a petition. The people were signing when the aldermen, at last, descended from their caucuses and tried to get into the hall.

A harried policeman attempted to usher the people out. The aldermen tried to get in. The people wanted to be where the aldermen were, and there was only one narrow doorway. In this melee the meeting finally began.

The caucus apparently had produced little agreement among the city fathers, for Horowitz, certain that even the most doubtful alderman would vote for the resolution rather than extemporaneously debate in public, wanted to take the issue to the floor. Montalto was the first to speak. He received great acclaim which was quelled by the sympathetic but distraught sheriff. The crowd quieted, and Montalto, exhilarated by the applause, denounced the metal houses as "a menace to the health, safety, and welfare of the people of New Haven." Istas was even more outspoken: "While millions are being spent on slum clearance, this project would create one." When he commented on DiCenzo's legal opinion with a curt "How naive can one be?" the enthusiasm of the crowd knew no bounds. Horowitz, too, spoke for the resolution.

When the resolution was put to a vote, all but three aldermen supported the measure. Marcus and Levine remained steadfast in their opposition, and so did a third, Portnoy; but several doubtful legislators had been won over. The resolution, with the Board's approval, was now sent on to the Mayor, where no veto was anticipated.

The initial battle had been won. The aldermen did not get home until late that night. The crowd, excited by their success, swarmed about asking them questions and congratulating them.

Consolidation

MISS GRAVA had extraordinary political sense. From the first, she seems to have understood that approval of the Montalto-Slavin resolution was not victory. Lawsuits and political changes-of-mind were always dangers. A broader base of support for the Triangle's position was what was necessary. Influential citizens, many thousands of voters, the whole city government—these were the factors that would ultimately defeat the Lebovs.

Mrs. Robert Cook

And so Miss Grava began to look for help outside the Triangle. She called the chairladies of the Republican and Democratic Women's leagues, but their determination to avoid any part of the metal house controversy more than equaled her desire to get their help. The split between the aldermanic board and the Building Inspector was embarrassing to the Republicans, and the Democrats felt they could best maintain the political initiative if they remained critical neutrals.

Failure to obtain party support led Miss Grava to call Mrs. Robert Cook, one of the directors of the New Haven League of Women Voters. Mrs. Cook was in her fifties, widowed, respectable, and intelligent. She had maintained a law practice for thirty years.

The New Haven League of Women Voters had several weaknesses. It had become involved in a struggle to change to a city manager form of government, a battle which it subsequently lost. The issue had divided its membership. An even more fundamental weakness recognized by its leaders was that a large proportion of the League's members came from the exclusive St. Ronan's-Prospect Hill part of New Haven society.

Miss Grava, then, for several reasons found a willing listener when she called Mrs. Cook. First, the confusion and lack of "review" and "co-ordination" in the city government, which seemed to Mrs. Cook to have brought about the metal houses problem, was an example of governmental incapacity under the "antiquated" New Haven charter. Second, Miss Grava represented the other side of the tracks. If the League of Women Voters could aid the people of the Triangle, it might obtain some new members from these lower income groups. (Actually, despite Mrs. Cook's considerable contribution, neither Miss Grava nor any of her helpers ever took an interest in the League's affairs.)

Mrs. Cook was sincerely interested in the problem of the people in the Triangle. Her legal background qualified her to provide advice on the technicalities in the case. She calmed Miss Grava when rumors circulated that the Lebovs could sue those citizens who opposed them. She provided constant encouragement. And she offered funds to pay a lawyer's fee when the case had to be taken to court.

Richard Lee

Richard Lee had been the unsuccessful Democratic candidate for Mayor in 1951. Although he was not an alderman, Miss Grava telephoned him soon after the July 6 success. He listened patiently to Miss Grava's plaints and on Sunday, July 12, he and his wife drove down to the area and looked at the houses. Conversant with the process of government, Lee was able to give some advice to the Triangle about pressure-group tactics. The substance of the several phone conversations he had with Miss Grava focused on three questions.

Where was the Triangle most likely to be attacked? The most vulnerable point in the Triangle's coalition, Lee warned, was the aldermanic board. It was impossible to be certain what would happen if the Mayor vetoed the resolution. Montalto had succeeded in rallying his Republican colleagues against the Lebovs, but to oppose the Mayor was another matter. DeVita, the Republican minority leader, had never opposed Mayor Celentano. It was his responsibility to achieve what the Mayor wanted. Another alderman was a great friend of Celentano, and it was probable that he would not oppose him if there was to be a fight. In addition, those aldermen who had remained doubtful until they saw the size of the pressure group at the meeting might change their minds. Finally, the opposition of Marcus and Levine had to be brooked and contained.

What counter-measures could be employed by the Triangle? Obviously, the pressures had to be kept up, perhaps more systematically. All hearings had to be attended and each alderman reminded again of how many and how intense were the people who opposed the Lebovs. This meant organization—to formalize the pressure, to make it more constant.

Where was the Triangle likely to be most successful? The appearance of the houses down in the area was the Triangle's strongest point. Publicity was necessary: newspapers, television, radio.

Carl Dietle

Miss Grava and Miss Battistella both had realized at the July 6 meeting that intimidation by a leaderless mob was not desirable for long-run political pressure for two reasons: a mob's behavior always frightens the public, and the newspapers had described the Triangle's pressure group as unruly, ill-mannered, and irrational. Second, as Lee had pointed out, a mob's energies are too volatile; it was doubtful if so large a force could be gathered for later meetings. The Triangle group had to have leadership when it took part in public debates. The Triangle's "public" leader must be respected, articulate, well-informed.

Carl Dietle was, the ladies thought, the perfect man. He was well-liked. He worked in the Eastern Machine Screw Corporation as an expediter, an extremely high position, and the president of the factory would be sure to give him afternoons off if Dietle had to attend important meetings.

Dietle's wife, May, was a close friend of Mary Grava. The two women discussed the need for Carl's help, and then May went to her husband, suggesting that since he was an important man in the community, he should play an important role in the fight against the Lebovs. He agreed.

Thereafter, whenever two or three aldermen were gathered together, whether it was to discuss buildings or sewers and sanitation or lighting, Dietle appeared and pleaded the cause.

Dominic Grava

Saturday morning, July 11, Miss Grava was visited by her brother, Dominic. She was nervous and upset and poured forth her problems to him.

Dominic Grava was 63. He was prosperous, intelligent, kindly, and shrewd. He, among all the Gravas, had left the Hill behind and had moved out into the more affluent environs of Westville. A neighbor of Mayor Celentano, he had known him since he was a boy; had befriended him, disciplined him, and served as a godfather to him. When Grava retired, the Mayor had placed him on the Capital Projects Programming Commission for the city. It was a position of high prestige.

Despite his success, Grava's ties with his old neighborhood remained strong. He was a landlord of several houses in the Hill area. Also there persisted the memories of his childhood life with his immigrant parents. He still owned a store situated less than a mile from the Triangle. His sons managed it.

Grava understood pressure groups. He had participated in a successful one in 1946. Ironically, its objective had been to prevent the erection of temporary barracks in the City Point area for veterans' housing right after the war. Instead, the government placed the barracks off Congress Avenue, where they remained to plague the Triangle.

Grava was impressed by the urgency of opposing the Lebovs. He immediately volunteered to help. He made an excellent leader because he could command without arousing suspicion or envy. Also, the presence of a man from Westville in the movement gave a certain ring of authenticity to the cause.

The Hill Civic Association

Three of Miss Grava's confidants—Lee, Cook, and Grava—urged that there be some formal organization of the neighborhood. Mary Grava was suffering from overworry and exhaustion. She did not want the full responsibility of opposing the houses. An organization could get better publicity. Furthermore, it was desirable for legal purposes. The community knew the Lebovs would take matters to court in order to get their way. That they might sue an individual citizen seemed a real possibility, and the threat of it had had a divisive effect in the neighborhood. An association, however, would protect individuals against such lawsuits. Moreover, organization represented to the politician a number of voters who appeared to be one-minded about the issue.

Dominic Grava planned the Association and outlined to his sister what should be done. He emphasized the importance of having officers who represented different geographical areas of the community, various age groups, and as wide a sprinkling of nationalities and faiths as possible.

Miss Grava phoned Anne Battistella, the first step to attain geographical distribution. They agreed that a male Battistella cousin should be president and that the treasurer should be an interested young mother named Nellie DiLeonardi, who happened to be in the Battistella home when Miss Grava next invited Mrs. D'Angelo to be vice president. She accepted and suggested her younger sister, Lucille Possidente, for the secretary's job.

Grava felt the slate was too heavily weighted with Italians. The president was asked to resign almost before he had accepted. In his place the Gravas settled on a Jewish resident of Truman Street named Leonard Platnick. Neither knew him, but he had been seen at the aldermanic meetings. The choice was confirmed by Battistella.

A board of directors was also selected. Three were obvious choices: Grava as chairman, and Dietle and Battistella. To fill out the five-man Board, there was the Jewish Mrs. Sherman Geller and a young employee at the factory, Orlando Balbusti.

The Association's officers publicly waged the Triangle's war, presiding at all public functions and attending the aldermanic meetings. Grava, however, dominated the thinking and planning. He arranged to hold a community meeting on July 27. Montalto suggested bringing several key aldermen to it. Lee managed to rent the school for the evening.

In the afternoon of July 27, Dietle broadcast from a sound truck an appeal to the residents to come to the first meeting of the Hill Civic Association. So many of the Triangle attended on that hot July evening that the school auditorium was unable to accommodate them all, and the meeting was transferred to the playground. The officers were ratified; the aldermen spoke; and Platnick outlined Grava's program of action: maintaining pressure at all government meetings, getting publicity, generating sympathetic public opinion, and finally, securing a lawyer.

During the meeting, one of the aldermen, Guida, had approached Grava with the suggestion that the Association seek the services of a lawyer named Joseph Koletsky. When Grava asked others for advice on the suggestion, almost all felt that if Koletsky would work for a reasonable price, he was an ideal choice.

The selection of Koletsky brought about conflict, however. Platnick, in his role as president of the Association, had presumed to obtain the legal services of a personal friend, a young lawyer from West Haven. The August 4 meeting of the officers of the Hill Civic Association was a strained showdown between Grava and Platnick and shortly afterward Leonard Platnick resigned.

That week, Dietle, who succeeded to the presidency, and the two Gravas called on Koletsky. Koletsky demanded a fee of $1,000, to be paid in advance. He apparently hoped this would be a prohibitively high price.

The next day, when Mrs. Cook heard from the discouraged Miss Grava the outcome of the meeting, she was delighted that Koletsky had been obliging enough even to quote a fee, and one that to her seemed so small. She phoned Grava and offered to pay as much of the $1,000 as was necessary. Grava advised, however, that it would be much more effective if every willing resident of the neighborhood contributed to a general fund.

Five days later, August 12, the Hill Civic Association informed Koletsky that it would gladly meet his fee and presented him with a check for the full amount. More than $1,000 was collected through careful planning and hard work in less than a week from an economically poor community. Over 600 families were approached in door-to-door collection, and in the Triangle 36.7% contributed. Through a systematic and elaborate process of collection outlined by Grava, any suspicion of dishonesty was prevented.

Obtaining the services of Joseph Koletsky as legal counsel was a major achievement, for Koletsky was regarded as one of the shrewdest, cleverest, and most imaginative lawyers in New Haven. He was a truly flamboyant figure, with a flair for dramatizing causes.

The Board of Aldermen

All the while the Hill Civic Association was being formed, Montalto and Slavin were busy seeking extra newspaper coverage and conferring with the Mayor and all the departments involved. But the pressure group was merciless in pestering the two aldermen, and the Montaltos began leaving town early Saturday mornings to escape the constant telephoning of Misses Grava and Battistella. The little plot of grass in front of the alderman's home, the tidy garden, and the well-painted front porch fell victims of neglect, for any appearance by Montalto out-of-doors brought swirling about him a wave of neighbors' questions concerning the metal houses.

What was gratifying for the two aldermen was the apparently final crystallization of aldermanic support behind the people of the Triangle. First, Republican leader Henry DeVita issued a statement that he categorically opposed DiCenzo's opinion. His support meant there would be no break in his party's unanimous opposition to the Mayor if the latter decided to veto the resolution. Second, Levine and Marcus, who supported the Lebovs, had personally alienated some of their Democratic colleagues.

A third factor in causing the Board to give more enthusiastic support to the Montalto-Slavin resolution was Nathan Portnoy's opposition to it. Portnoy was an obese, emotional, demagogic alderman. The targets of his abuse were always stereotyped villains. In 1953, for example, he attacked the electric company for its failure to put its whole wiring system underground when a severe ice storm disrupted power lines.

In the metal houses case, Portnoy did not pass up his opportunity to attack another major villain of the city, the University. After the war, in order to shelter veterans and their families, Yale was forced to build two Quonset hut colonies. Both villages were eyesores, but both were privately maintained and policed by the University.

On July10, Alderman Portnoy made this statement to the evening newspaper:

> I am preparing a resolution . . . which declares Yale University's Quonset hut colonies . . . a 'nuisance' and directing their immediate evacuation and demolition. . . . I will press for passage of my resolution if the Board succeeds in its plans to block the erection of the metal houses on the Boulevard. . . .
>
> I am going to find out who is sincere and who isn't sincere on this housing question. If they are really opposed to metal houses, let's get rid of the Quonset huts. . . . I want to find out if the aldermen are really opposed to metal housing or are motivated by some other reason—or fear.

Whatever its other effects, Portnoy's statement cemented the Montalto and Slavin forces.

The fourth factor was the continuing influx of metal homes through the months of April, May, and June, until there were about 160 in the Lebov lot. On July 11, an advertisement appeared in both the daily papers:

> MEET YOUR NEED WITH A USED QUONSET HUT . . . Ideal for sheds, shops, garages, stands, liv-

ing quarters, etc. Easily and quickly re-erected. $695 FOB Truck . . . .

Each alderman was aware that if the Lebov development succeeded in the Triangle, similar colonies could be "easily and quickly re-erected" in his own ward.

The Mayor's Veto

Soon after, hopes that the Mayor would approve the resolution collapsed. On July 10, Mayor Celentano, Counsel DiCenzo, the fire inspector, health director, building inspector, and housing director met in executive session in the Mayor's office. The officials agreed that the action taken by the Board was out of order; that the building inspector had not been negligent in his duties; and that the Corporation Counsel had taken the right and proper legal stand.

The Triangle nevertheless maintained good morale. Mrs. D'Angelo and Miss Battistella carried from door to door the petition to the Mayor. To the 300 signatures previously collected, there were added several hundred more. The children of the Triangle showed their distaste for the houses by making nocturnal forays through the Lebovs' lots, smashing windows and destroying the flooring. Not a house escaped their systematic abuse.

When the Mayor's veto was made public on July 15, the leaders of the Triangle were more determined than distressed. The Mayor's veto message was a pithy, politic note. He armed his disapproval of the aldermanic resolution with the following reasons:

1) The Board of Aldermen is without power and does not have the authority by declaration to make that a nuisance which is not a nuisance in fact.

2) The Building Inspector feels 'the houses satisfy all legal requirements of the building code.'

3) The Fire Marshal . . . writes me, 'I am of the opinion that the project should not be considered as constituting a fire hazard.'

4) The Director of Health . . . states to me '. . . I see no real health hazards in this housing project.'

5) I have reliable information that the need for rental housing in the city is still far from being met by the amount of newly created facilities of this type. Most of the rentals are far beyond the means of the average renting family even in the moderate income group. The impending action of the Highway Commissioner in the relocation of Route 1 will further add to the need for rental housing in the city. All of these factors cannot be overlooked in considering the action of your honorable board.

A diplomatic paragraph at the end of the letter served to place much of the community wrath on DiCenzo.

I am mindful of the feeling of many of the people who signed the petition to me, urging me to give the action of the Board my approval. . . . I do understand the concern of many of these people and I feel that to some degree at least the actual situation has been misrepresented to them. Nevertheless, it is my duty to uphold the laws and ordinances of the city, no matter how sympathetic I may feel towards a particular group or groups. It is still my duty and wish to uphold the law.

The last paragraph was to have a latent effect. It gave the aldermen an opportunity to override the Mayor without giving him a personal rebuff. The whole letter gave the Mayor room to change his mind.

A Bipartisan Caucus

When the veto letter was received, Montalto and Slavin decided to call another special meeting. O'Connell, DeVita, and Horowitz encouraged them. The three veteran politicians warned that aldermen who might not want to embarrass the Mayor would express their opposition by not attending future meetings. Since a two-thirds majority of the whole Board, 22 votes, was necessary to override the Mayor's action, absence was the same as casting a negative ballot.

Some did not appear, but 26 aldermen did attend the special meeting. So did 300 citizens from the Triangle. Guided by Dietle, their generally calm behavior at this session contrasted favorably with their previous excursion to City Hall. The procedural byways of the Board were more familiar to them; their patience was less taxed by the inevitable hour and a half wait while the legislators caucused upstairs.

To keep the issue clean of "party politics," the leaders had decided to conduct a bipartisan caucus. It opened peaceably. The Republican Istas and the Democrat Guida took over the leadership of the Mayor's loyal, but insistent, opposition. To consider Mayor Celentano's veto, unanimous consent had to be obtained. Otherwise, according to the usual procedure, the

Board would have to wait to take a final vote until the next meeting. Unanimous consent was probably impossible. Levine, for one, wanted indefinite postponement of the whole issue. But it was not Levine who prevented unanimous consent. It was Irving Horowitz, the parliamentarian who had helped the Triangle's cause so much, who unexpectedly arose to insist that consideration was impossible until the Mayor's veto letter had been printed in the *Journal*. Why he, who had engineered so much of the action to revoke the license, changed his mind at this moment, no one knows. By 9:30 all hope for agreement had vanished, and the aldermen began to move out of the hot caucus room. Slavin, distressed and not really certain of what had happened, went excitedly from one alderman to another imploring each one to take action.

The Triangle, expecting a smashing victory, cheered the entrance of the aldermen. Applause turned into bewilderment when the Board resolutely by-passed all discussion of the Mayor's veto.

Portnoy tried to make a speech advocating the demolition of all emergency housing, but the crowd burst out with boos, and he sat down. Guida, hoping that the intensity of the crowd's disapproval would have a coercive effect on Horowitz and Levine, asked for a recess just before adjournment. He could not persuade the two, and the meeting was adjourned.

The Lebovs' Last Stand

The Lebovs and their supporters launched two counterattacks before the next meeting of the Board of Aldermen. First, one of the pro-Lebov aldermen, Marcus, exploited his colleagues' fears of individual legal action. He released to the newspapers a letter he had sent to Corporation Counsel DiCenzo requesting an answer to the following question:

> In view of the fact that the Board of Aldermen has received your legal opinion which sets forth the illegality of the action of the Board, will those members of the Board [who disregard the opinion] have so abused their discretion as to have waived their legislative immunity and hence subjected themselves to being made parties of any lawsuits?

The Lebovs' second tactic was to accuse the Triangle, through newspaper statements, of "racial discrimination." This was a weak point in the Triangle's public position. Opposition to the metal houses at a time when housing for low-income families, many of them Negroes, was badly needed, did not seem ethically wholesome to many citizens of New Haven. There were, for example, several liberal and dedicated Protestant clergymen who carried on the Oak Street Christian Parish in the midst of the city's worst slum area. Plans for development of Oak Street had been delayed by the urgent need to relocate the hundreds of Negro families living in the area. The need for low-rent housing was crucial to the success of this slum-clearance project. One of the Oak Street ministers was present at several of the Board meetings. The fervor of the opposition of the people of the Triangle made him determined to investigate for himself. After seeing the houses, however, he concluded that they were not a suitable solution to the housing problem.

There were many New Haven citizens, however, who did not bother to look at the houses and who were impressed by the Lebovs' charges of discrimination. Admittedly, much of the motivation of the people in the Triangle was a desire to keep Negroes out. The Catholic priests at St. Anthony's Church were open in admitting that fact about their parishioners. The Lebovs, therefore, had hit a vulnerable spot.

The effect of the Lebovs' attack, however, was somewhat blunted by a letter from the federal government to the Urban Redevelopment Agency. The URA is a federal enterprise, set up in most of the nation's largest cities and concerned with the making over of blighted areas. The agency in New Haven was working hand-in-hand with the City Plan Commission and it had been intensely interested in the problem of the metal houses because of the likelihood of their deteriorating into a new slum. Sympathetic to opposition to the houses, it had forwarded to Henry Istas the letter from Washington which urged all cities to take steps to prevent the propagation of slum areas. The letter further warned that cities which did not do so would be deprived of federal aid for housing and slum clearance. Its effect was to undercut the Lebovs' claims to legitimacy.

By the August 3 meeting, the issue was no longer in doubt. The aldermen caucused, the two parties in separate rooms this time, but the mood was conciliatory and confident. A telegram, sent from Mexico City by one of the Possidente children, had started the meeting off in a good-humored vein. It read:

BOARD OF ALDERMEN, NEW HAVEN, CONN. BE NOT AFRAID. UNSHEATH THE BLOOD-STAINED SWORD OF DEMOCRACY. DO NOT SURRENDER THE HILL.

WILLIAM POSSIDENTE

When at last the caucuses broke up and the Board convened, the Montalto-Slavin resolution to revoke the permit was read for the last time, and it was adopted over the Mayor's veto, 25 to 2, with Alderman Portnoy abstaining. Amid cheers and good-natured back-slapping, the president of the Board adjourned the meeting.

The Problem of Joseph Koletsky

The Lebovs immediately retaliated. Within a few days, subpoenas had been served on the aldermen. The Lebovs summoned for suit the whole Board, both as a legislative body and also as individuals. (They wanted $70,000 damages and a court order to allow them to continue their development.)

Koletsky had been hired by the Hill Civic Association, but he now found himself in the awkward position of representing no litigant. The Lebov Corporation was suing the city, not the Hill Civic Association. Koletsky could only appear as a friend of the court, a legal position which provided him opportunity to give testimony to help the court arrive at a decision. He testified, however, at the sufferance of the judge, and what he said or advised could be disregarded or halted if the judge pleased to do so.

It was necessary, then, that Koletsky be allowed to defend the city in the trial. In order to get the city government to ask him to serve as defense counsel, Dominic Grava and Koletsky adopted the strategy of focusing on the Board of Aldermen. If the separate summonses of all the aldermen were handed over to Koletsky, then he could represent them, officially, in court. Since the administration already provided the Corporation Counsel's office to represent the city in all litigation, such action would mean another clash with the Mayor and another affront to DiCenzo, but the task had to be undertaken.

Montalto and Slavin sought out each alderman for his help. The inconsistency of DiCenzo's position—to defend a cause he had already adjudged wrong—was clear enough to most of the aldermen; still, some were afraid that their legislative immunity would be jeopardized if they split themselves away from the protection and majesty of the city administration.

With Montalto and Slavin running up against some opposition, the women of the Hill Civic Association went to the telephone again and began calling their friends in other wards. The telephone calls did not cease until, on August 23, seventeen aldermen, a bare, but sufficient, majority, had turned their summonses over to Koletsky.

Early in September two special Board meetings were called. The result was a resolution that the Board, as a legislative body, be represented by a man "owing no duty to the executive branch of the City Government or any department whatever." The issue was beclouded by a controversy over the payment of Koletsky, who at last resolved the matter by writing a letter to the Board, stating that "I have determined that I will not accept any moneys whatsoever from any of you . . . for my legal services. . . ." The Mayor could not reasonably oppose such action, and the Board in October adopted a resolution naming Koletsky as their defense counsel in the litigation.

As late as April 1, 1955 Koletsky had succeeded in postponing any action by the courts. With the passage of months, the metal houses were reaching such a state of deterioration that it was becoming more and more doubtful if the Lebovs could, victors in the suit or no, use them for a housing development.

Moreover, delay in court action erased one of Winnick's more effective points, namely, the contention of "racial prejudice." In the middle of November, 1953, one of the leaders of the National Association for the Advancement of Colored People, Dr. Harold Flemming, heard of the Lebov case. He sent a letter to Winnick, posing several questions:

> 1) Is it the purpose of the Lebov Co. to sell or rent such houses, if erected, to Negroes? . . .
>
> 2) When and how was it first brought out that there might be opposition to Negro families moving into the area?

Winnick was unable to answer the questions in any specific way without losing some friends. If he said that there were going to be Negroes moving into the area, the indignation of the Triangle would be even further aroused, and what was more, it would be made painfully clear that the Lebovs were blatant liars, for they had insisted all along that only old white people would live in the houses. If, on the other hand, the attorney said that Negroes would be prevented from coming in, he would not only lose the support of the NAACP, but also undercut his own court case. As a result he ignored the NAACP letter. Flemming, angered by Winnick's attitude, visited the site to investigate the houses, and expressed indignation that anyone would think of putting any human beings into such buildings. With this argument vitiated, the Lebovs had little protection against the charges Koletsky now released to the press:

> The Lebovs have through the public press, radio and T.V. impugned the integrity and the motives of the Board of Aldermen, and of the now 750 voters whom I represent, who are simply protesting for decency in housing, be it for poor or rich, white or Negro.
>
> What monetary motives or money profits have the Board of Aldermen or my clients to gain in their anxiety to protect the City and themselves from business inroads throwing shack metal houses on dump lands, unfit for any race. Where are they false, etc.?
>
> On the other hand, the Lebovs are certainly not in this business of cheap, unfit, unsanitary metal housing for any benevolent, altruistic purpose. Nor are they emulating Abraham Lincoln, when they purr hypocritically in the public press about race discrimination. We charge that the Lebovs and they alone are out for a cool money profit in dollars and cents, and shall so allege in Court, and they cannot hide behind a smoke screen, inciting race discrimination. I give this statement in defense of my clients, and to avoid any public disorder . . . .
>
> My clients will not be intimidated.

The Administration Changes Its Mind

WITH KOLETSKY safely established as legal counsel for the aldermen, the Triangle sought to isolate the Lebovs from their last vestige of support, the Administration. With one minor exception, it was singularly successful.

The Fire Inspector

The first city official to withdraw his approval of the Lebovs' project was the fire inspector. He had advised the Mayor that the metal homes were fire-proof. A few days after he had rendered his opinion one of the houses was seen spewing flames and smoke. The fire department arrived in time to douse the white-hot framework with some cooling waters. A picture of the skeleton of the house appeared in the evening paper with the following description:

> This twisted frame was all that remained of one of the buildings in the controversial Lebov project off the Boulevard after a fire of unknown cause this morning.
>
> The flames feeding on wooden flooring and partitions created such an intense heat that the metal walls were bent out of shape.

This unusually thorough refutation of the fire inspector was the work of a person described in the newspapers which reported his arrest, as "an arson bug." It was suggested that he had been challenged by the alleged invulnerability of the metal houses to fire.

The Director of Health

It was inconceivable to the residents of the Triangle that anyone might consider the metal houses as conducive to good health. Furthermore, the dump was a health menace by itself, with the infestation by rats, its spring flooding, and its proximity to the dirty river. To the women of the Triangle, especially, the disease argument was an incontrovertible one, and the decision of Dr. Batelli, the Director of Health, that the project would present no real health hazards, outraged them.

Miss Grava called him several times with no success. He was sympathetic, but he was not going to change his mind. Montalto and Slavin called a meeting of the aldermanic Sewers and Sanitations Committee on July 31. They subpoenaed all the police, health, and fire statistics available and then invited Dr. Batelli to appear. He sent one of his lieutenants. The hearing accomplished nothing, but the women of the Triangle had a chance to vent their fears and imprecations upon Dr. Batelli's assistant.

Despite this failure, Miss Grava was not through. She sent a letter to the State Board of Health in Hartford, pointing out some "misrepresented facts" about the metal houses case and casting not a few aspersions upon the integrity of Batelli. The reply from Hartford was disappointing. The last paragraph read:

> The construction of housing projects according to State Law is in the hands of the Local Authorities in the 169 cities and towns of the State. I see no reason why the questions that you raised cannot be adequately met in planning housing [sic] and we understand that the New Haven Health Department is giving full consideration to the sanitary aspects of the proposals.

Miss Grava was put out by the response, but, as a matter of fact, the Health Director played no further part for or against the Lebovs.

The Mayor

Mayor Celentano, in July, had been so determined in the defense of the Lebovs that even the persuasive efforts of his friend, Dominic Grava, had been unable to shake his resolution. The passage of months changed the Mayor's mind. Election time was approaching, and the Mayor was acutely conscious of the need for votes. Celentano had won the 1951 election with a majority of two votes out of more than 60,000 ballots. The Hill had supplied him with a large enough majority to cushion his less successful efforts in other parts of New Haven.

In October, when the 1953 campaigning was beginning to increase in intensity, the Mayor, accompanied by DiCenzo, visited the Truman Street School. Celentano's administration took great pride in, and due credit for, the development of New Haven's school system. For the campaign the Mayor arranged to give several speeches, especially staged for television, from atop the steps of some of the schools, including the one on Truman Street. The site of the telecast was within easy range for Miss Grava. Though the opening moment of the television program was imminent, she ran out of her home and began to scold the Mayor in a shrill voice. Quick action by a few men in the Mayor's party prevented a televised scene.

Miss Grava was removed to a safe distance by a policeman, but the incident seemed to have some effect. Next week the Mayor presented a statement to the press. He wanted to make it clear, he said, that under no circumstances would he ever allow the Lebov houses to come into the city. He wished also to explain that his veto had been motivated by a desire to keep the Board from being sued, and, from this time forth, he, the Mayor, would take all legal steps to oppose the houses.

Corporation Counsel DiCenzo

Of all the city officials, none was so thoroughly hated by the leaders of the Triangle as Corporation Counsel DiCenzo. In addition to his interpretation of law, he had attempted to find the least controversial way out of a difficult legal and administrative tangle by upholding the Lebovs' position.

The neutralization of his opposition came about in two ways. One day in early August, a young priest visited the sick mother of Miss Grava's good neighbor, Mr. Carl Camilloni. Before saying goodbye, he had been guided down to the Lebov lot to see the condition of the metal houses. The young padre gave assurances that he would talk to Father Guido, his superior, about the houses to prepare him for Miss Grava's telephone call later that day. Father Guido greeted her call with some sympathy; he knew DiCenzo, and he promised to see what he could do. That same afternoon Father Guido and DiCenzo were seen at the dump, looking over the houses together. For the Corporation Counsel, it was his first view of the run-down structures.

The second way was perhaps more effective. When DiCenzo accompanied the Mayor to the Truman Street School for the telecast, he stood across the road while Celentano spoke. Miss Grava, frustrated in her initial charge upon the Mayor, now turned on Mr. DiCenzo. She rained blows on him. "Crook," she cried, "crook, you dirty crook," and in near hysterics, she leveled a stream of accusations. DiCenzo backed away. "I promise you those houses will never go up in the city," he said hastily. Quickly calmed, Miss Grava assembled witnesses, to whom DiCenzo ignominiously repeated his new view.

A week later DiCenzo sent a letter to every voter who had placed his or her name on the July petition to the Mayor.

> I have received many inquiries from residents in the Boulevard area concerning the proposed erection of . . . metal houses . . . by the Lebov Corporation. Many of the people believe, from the opinion which I gave the Board of Aldermen in July, that I, in some way, approve of the erection of these houses.
>
> This impression is entirely wrong. I am opposed to the development of this kind of project.
>
> The question which was presented to me by the Board of Aldermen and on which I rendered an opinion, was whether the Board could legally declare the houses to be a nuisance and thereby prevent the issuance of a building permit for the erection of the houses. I answered the question by stating that in my opinion the Board of Aldermen could not legally declare something to be a nuisance which in fact did not yet exist. That is the law.
>
> After studying this question I have come to the conclusion that the Lebov Corporation which had proposed to erect these houses had not proceeded in accordance with the law and that, therefore, regardless of the prior action of the Board of Aldermen or the Building Inspector, that corporation cannot proceed with the erection of these houses.
>
> The State Statutes forbid a plotting or subdivision of land, such as is called for in the plans for the erection of these houses, without prior approval by the City Plan Commission, and since this approval has not been obtained from the City Plan Commission these metal houses cannot be erected.
>
> I will resist the development of this metal house project in this area by every legal means.

Conclusion

Shortly before the November election, the Lebovs sold some of the property in the Triangle on which they had originally planned to build their development. This news along with the capitulation of the Mayor and DiCenzo quieted those in the Triangle who had been temporarily stirred to political activity.

The law suit against the aldermen was postponed again and again. The finale to this case came with the announcement in August 1956 by the Lebovs that they were junking the metal houses. Although no formal announcement was made, the law suits were also junked.

Chronology

1953:

Feb. 24: Lebovs obtain license for housing project from New Haven building inspector.

Apr. 26: Lebovs rebuffed by Board of Zoning Appeals.

June 8: Committee on Legislation holds public hearing.

June 15: Lebovs give orders to go ahead with development.

June 17: Notice filed with city clerk that houses are a "nuisance."

June 26: Special aldermanic meeting.

July 3: Corporation Counsel gives opinion to newspapers that aldermen have no authority to revoke license.

July 5: Informal session of the aldermen at the Goodfellows' Club.

July 6: Aldermanic meeting; Montalto-Slavin resolution is passed.

July 10: Mayor meets in executive session with his department heads.

July 15: Mayor vetoes the aldermen's resolution.

July 20: Special aldermanic meeting; veto discussed but not overridden.

July 27: Hill Civic Association meets publicly in Truman Street School yard; Leonard Platnick elected president.

Aug. 3: Mayor's veto is overridden.
Miss Grava sends letter to State Board of Health, Hartford.

Aug. 6: Revocation of license by the building inspector.

Aug. 11: Platnick resigns as president of Hill Civic Association.

Aug. 14: Winnick serves legal papers for Lebovs against city.

Aug. 16: Hill Civic Association asks Koletsky to serve as *amicus curiae.*

Aug. 31: Aldermen adopt resolution to ask Koletsky, not DiCenzo, to defend them in court.

Oct. 21: DiCenzo's letter renounces the Lebovs.

Nov. 2: Election day in New Haven.

Mid-November: NAACP letter to Winnick.

Moses on the Green

John B. Keeley

Moses on the Green

ROBERT MOSES, the renowned Commissioner of the Park Department of the City of New York (to cite the one of his many posts from which he draws an annual salary) has often been roundly criticized for projects designed to better the welfare of the city as he sees it, but he has seldom been thwarted in his perseverance with such projects. This story relates one occasion when Moses did not finally succeed in getting what he started out to obtain. It is the story of an attempt by his Park Department to convert a little less than half an acre of Central Park into a parking lot for the Tavern-on-the-Green restaurant. This privately-owned restaurant is a concession granted by the Park Commissioner and is located on Park land.

The area in dispute consisted of rocky, hilly ground with a scattering of trees and grass. Opposition to the plans for the parking lot sprang from a relatively small group of people living on the north-south avenue known as Central Park West in the vicinity of West 67th Street. Although the cross streets shade off rapidly into a low-income area as one walks west, the apartment buildings lining Central Park West are peopled with well-to-do residents, many from the arts and the professions. The objections to the Park Department plan which are crucial to this story came from a group of mothers whose children played in the area proposed for the parking lot. The mothers' activities do not carry the story to its end, nor was it primarily in consideration of their interests that the city later reversed its stand. Moses is not the whole of the city government, either. Nevertheless, without the mothers and without Moses there would be no story.

In a metropolitan area as built up and as densely populated as New York City, the introduction of any new project is likely to dislocate and discomfit some citizens, even though it may be undertaken for the benefit (often in the long run) of others. The sense of hurt on the part of those who are inconvenienced or deprived by projects such as slum clearance or the construction of a highway is intense and immediate, whereas the many future individual beneficiaries may feel only relatively small satisfaction if, indeed, they think of it at all. This is a characteristic situation that frequently troubles a government official who desires to introduce a change or an improvement. Looking at it abstractly, he has a choice of a number of strategies. He may, on the one hand, seek to win over those who will be harmed by a new project, or he may seek to arrive at some pattern of accommodation, possibly providing alternative satisfactions or facilities. On the other hand, he may ignore immediate protests, put down his head, and butt his way through to completion of the project.

By 1956, the year of this case, Robert Moses had a national reputation as an administrator who had successfully carried through many major improvements (highways, parks, slum-clearance projects, and the like) by overriding neighborhood groups and others who stood in their way. In New York he was widely regarded as an "irresistible force," and his reputation at the time of this case had recently been fortified by a major victory over local groups trying to stop his new Bronx Expressway from coming through their neighborhoods.

Moses had long been a significant figure in New York politics, both city and state. Ever since 1919, when Governor Alfred E. Smith appointed him Chief-of-Staff of the New York State Reconstruction Commission, Moses had been continuously occupied with city and state administrative posts. A man with an independent income, he had tried for elective office only once, in 1934, when he ran for Governor of New York on the Republican ticket. He was defeated by Herbert H. Lehman who won with a record 800,000 majority. When Mayor Fiorello LaGuardia appointed him New York City Park

Commissioner in 1934 Moses already held the chairmanships of four commissions and independent authorities. The list of commissions and authorities—most of them dealing with parks and highways—on which Moses has served, many of them simultaneously, stretches out for a good-sized paragraph in *Who's Who,* and Moses has been chairman of most of them. Although a Republican, he had continued as New York City Park Commissioner, gathering other posts along the way, through a succession of mayors, including Fusionist La Guardia, Democrat William O'Dwyer, Independent Vincent Impellitteri, and Robert F. Wagner, Jr., the Democratic Mayor when the Tavern-on-the-Green incident became news.

Moses' reputation extends beyond that of being able to ward off citizen pressures against major improvement projects. Those who attack him frequently find themselves on the defensive before his acid public comments. Public or private officials who differ with Moses ruefully recall the lash of his wit or the sting of finding out that he has carried his case over their heads, behind their backs, or around their flanks. In 1956 Moses' reputation discouraged officials as well as neighborhood groups from expecting to emerge successful or unscathed from a conflict with the Park Commissioner, the City Construction Co-ordinator, the Chairman of the Triborough Bridge Authority, the Chairman of the New York State Power Authority, or any of the other titles Moses held.

This case is unusual because Moses lost, but he lost not to a group of outraged mothers but because the mothers found an ally with an eye for the jugular as sharp as Moses' own. The mothers' case was also strengthened because they were battling not only against Moses but for a "cause" dear to the hearts of many New Yorkers, the cause of "saving Central Park." Surrounded by skyscrapers and concrete, New Yorkers traditionally rally in behalf of Central Park's trees and grass. In the 100 years of the Park's life (the city owes Central Park's existence to the foresight of the poet William Cullen Bryant) many plans to appropriate portions of it for various purposes have been defeated by an aroused public. There is a private Park Association in New York, which has as its purpose the improvement and protection of Central Park. (One of its prominent officers at the time of this case was Mrs. Arthur Hays Sulzberger, wife of the publisher of the *New York Times.*) Only a few months prior to the Tavern incident Moses himself had suffered a minor setback when he attempted to establish a recreation area especially for the aged in a rugged portion of the Park known as the Ramble. His proposal drew immediate and stout protests from groups of bird watchers and nature lovers who wrote furious letters to the newspapers pointing out that the Ramble for some obscure ornithological reason attracted a wider variety of birds than any other section of the city.

The Mothers March on the Bulldozers

The story begins with a notice in the *New York Times* on January 18, 1956. It stated merely that the Park Department was planning to convert a portion of Central Park in the vicinity of West 67th Street into additional parking space for the Tavern-on-the-Green as part of a larger improvement program for the restaurant. The announcement did not provoke any particular reaction; several people living in the neighborhood later recalled having seen the notice but at the time gave it no more than a passing thought.

Three months later, Mrs. Stuart Davis, a resident of the neighborhood, was walking her child in the vicinity of the proposed parking lot. She noticed a number of men, blueprints in hand, examining the area. When she questioned them she was told that construction of a parking lot would begin later in the week. She was greatly concerned and spread the news to other strollers in the Park. Several of them sat down immediately to draft a petition of protest. They struggled with the opening sentences for a while, and then they decided they would need more help and organization. Mrs. Davis called a friend, Mrs. Arnold Newman, the wife of a prominent photographer. Mrs. Newman, whose two boys used the area, was equally upset and promised to consult her husband. A rudimentary neighborhood organization quickly formed.

The Newmans played a crucial role in these early stages. Since Newman, in contrast to most of the other men, worked as well as lived in the neighborhood—his studio was only a block from the Park—he was a natural choice as the neighborhood leader. His studio became the nerve center of the organization, and information was communicated largely through the Newmans.

The mothers of the neighborhood felt strongly about the proposed parking lot because they had long found the area a convenient place to stroll, push their baby carriages, and exercise their children. On one side, the area was next to a formal playground reserved for children of eight years and younger. Mothers with families "on both sides of eight" could supervise their children's play in both areas from benches in the formal playground.

A few days later, on April 11, a letter of protest was sent to Commissioner Moses signed by 23 residents of the Central Park West area, including many of the neighborhood's more prominent members such as writers Fannie Hurst and Ludwig Bemelmans. One of the signers, a former employee of the *New York Herald Tribune,* gave the contents of the letter to the *Tribune,* which printed it. The other signers were not aware of his actions and later sent a letter to Moses apologizing for this premature disclosure.

Moses answered the letter of protest on April 17. The area had never been a play area, he said, and the parking facilities for the Tavern were to be much smaller than those allotted to restaurants in other city parks. He defended New York's play facilities for children and suggested that the protestors take a guided tour of the park system: "You might even find something to be proud of."

Moses sent his response to the five leading daily papers in the city. The Commissioner may have felt he would silence his opposition with a trenchant, public reply; if so, he was mistaken. Almost any public dispute in which Robert Moses is involved is news in New York City. Overnight the residents of West 67th Street found themselves front-page material.

Meanwhile, between the time of the neighborhood's protest on April 11 and Moses' answer on the 17th, there had been other developments. On the 13th, some 23 mothers, three fathers, and eleven children met under the canopy of the Tavern-on-the-Green, braving a spring rain, to protest Moses' actions. Newman was in charge, and distributed petitions addressed to Moses and Mayor Wagner which had been prepared by him, his wife, Mrs. Davis, and Fannie Hurst. The group set to work with a will. The mothers canvassed the neighborhood during the next ten days or so, collecting signatures from the neighborhood residents, posting the petitions in apartment building elevators, and stopping Park strollers. Before they were done, they had several thousand signatures from an area running roughly from West 65th Street to West 71st Street, and from Central Park West two blocks west to Broadway.

Trial by Combat

On Tuesday, April 17, Moses made his first show of strength. A bulldozer was sent to start construction. The neighborhood was ready for it, warned by a "look-out" whose apartment faced the Park. The bulldozer was met by fifty mothers, two poodles, and fifteen children (ten in baby carriages), all of whom stood, sat, or, in the case of the poodles, barked in front of it. The contractor withdrew the bulldozer and replaced it with two men with shovels. They made little progress on the rocky ground.

The "look-out" did more than signal the alarm. He called a friend, City Councilman Stanley Isaacs. Isaacs, a Republican-Liberal, was in a sense an interloper, since his bailiwick is the east side of Manhattan. But Isaacs, a City Councilman since 1941, has long been accustomed to defend minority causes, frequently finding himself the lone Republican on the New York City Council. He went to the Park immediately and told the mothers he would do everything possible to prevent construction of the parking lot. That day he sent a letter of protest to Mayor Wagner, saying "not even the Lord High Park Commissioner should be allowed to destroy Park beauty for the benefit of a commercial enterprise."

The next day a delegation from the neighborhood went to see Deputy Mayor John J. Theobald with the request that work on the project be held up pending further study. Theobald promised to see what could be done, but the delegates left with a sense of frustration. They felt that Theobald, new to his position and to City Hall—he was on leave from the Presidency of Queens College—was not the man to challenge Robert Moses. In fact, Theobald had telephoned Moses and had been persuaded that Moses' stand was correct.

While the group was meeting with Theobald, Moses announced to the newspapers that work on the project would recommence the following day, April 19. But no equipment appeared on the 19th, and instead Moses stated that he would wait out the opposition. The neighborhood was elated at this apparent victory. Newman announced: "It appears we have Moses stopped cold." But on Friday, April 20, a small piece of construction equipment appeared on the scene. Mrs. Newman, however, had organized a watch system in the Park during the daylight hours, and the equipment was blocked by two women and a child.

On Monday, April 23, Moses denied a request by James Boland, Democratic City Councilman for the area, that a public hearing be held before continuing construction. Boland, together with the Democratic district leader, Louis Okin, and several other residents of the neighborhood, also went to Theobald. The Deputy Mayor attempted to calm the group by advising them "to have patience and confidence, particularly in the light of the past record of our Park Commissioner in providing and maintaining such outstanding, fine recreational facilities." He pointed out that the proposed parking lot would be reserved as a playground until 5:00 p.m. and that it would serve as an ideal area for bicycling and roller skating. When the delegation left Theobald's office, it discovered that the Deputy Mayor had already informed the press that he supported Moses' position.

Although there had been no activity in the Park for several days, Moses was far from stopped. About 1:00 a.m. the morning of April 24, the Police Department received a complaint that "someone is chopping down trees in the Park." A policeman, sent to investigate, discovered an eight-man squad of Park Department employees erecting a four-foot snow fence around the disputed area. At 6:00 a.m. Newman received a phone call from the *New York Post* telling him of the fence, and this report was confirmed a few minutes later by the "look-out." The Newmans were at the Park about 7:30 a.m., just as construction equipment to level the area was arriving. The rest of the neighborhood gathered more slowly. By 9:00 a.m. some thirty workmen were busy, aided not only by the bulldozer but by a power shovel, two dump trucks, pneumatic drills, a chain saw, and numerous pickaxes, shovels, ropes, and hatchets. Twenty-five policemen guarded the area. The watchers restricted themselves for a time to denouncing the project as "official vandalism," but the women grew emotional when the bulldozer pulled down a tree. At this sight they charged the fence, halted only by a human chain of policemen. Tears flowed, and impassioned speeches were made.

The newspaper coverage of this "coup" was broad and sympathetic, and the mothers' fight for their playground became a *cause célèbre*. The newspapers were receiving and printing many letters like this one which appeared in the *Times:*

> If parking space for taverns on the green is more important to Robert Moses than the green of the parks, why does he not admit it openly and call himself by his true title: Parking Commissioner for New York City?

Later that day Boland and Isaacs introduced a resolution in City Council calling on the Mayor to "take such steps as may be necessary to prevent the destruction of part of Central Park." The resolution was referred to the Committee on City Affairs, which set hearings for the next day.

Moses had effectively countered the obstructive tactics of the mothers. If the Park were to be "saved," action of another sort would have to be taken and promptly. In only a few days the bulldozers would so alter the ground that no victory by the mothers could restore the area to its natural state.

The Case Goes to Court

On April 25, the day following the erection of the snow fence, Louis N. Field, an attorney, announced that he would request New York Supreme Court Justice William Hecht to sign a preliminary injunction "to prevent irreparable damage" to the Park. Field, it developed, had been retained by Stanley Friedberg and Norma Rosen to bring a taxpayers' suit against Moses and Wagner. Friedberg, father of four children, had become interested in the activities of the neighborhood group and had attended at least one of the meetings. However, in instituting suit he had acted without consulting the rest of the neighborhood. The group was not completely happy about his move, since it had planned action along similar lines itself, but now that the case was in court there was little that could be done about it. Judge Hecht ordered a halt to construction activity on April 26, pending hearings for an injunction to be held the next day before New York Supreme Court Justice Samuel Hofstadter. From this point the fate of the play area was to rest largely in other hands than those of the neighborhood protestors.

The taxpayers' suit was based on the claim that construction of the parking facilities in question was "illegal, unlawful and unauthorized by law and is a violation of section 383 of the New York City Charter." (This section concerns the alienation of park property.) The project, Field claimed, was outside the power of the Commissioner, and, he alleged, would result in "great, substantial, and irresponsible damage to the taxpayers, citizens and residents of the City of New York."

If the case were to be won solely on its legal merits at least one of these contentions would have to be proved. However, Field focused his argument before Judge Hofstadter not on these legal points but on the propriety of the operation on public land of a restaurant such as the Tavern-on-the-Green. He emphasized the fact that the restaurant operated as a night club when the rest of the Park was not normally in use by the citizenry. Waving a Tavern menu, Field said that the prices were extremely high—a hamburger and a beer cost more than $4.00. With these prices, Field continued, the Tavern was serving a relatively restricted clientele and thus did not have the characteristics of a restaurant intended to serve the general public.

The attorneys for the city were quick to point out the discrepancy between the legal bases of the plaintiffs' claim and the facts presented. From the legal standpoint, the plaintiffs did not appear to have a particularly strong case. The City Charter grants the Commissioner of Parks broad powers over the administration and development of public property under his control. He is specifically authorized to "maintain the beauty and utility of all parks . . . and to institute and execute all measures for the improvement thereof for ornamental purposes and for the beneficial uses of the people of the city."

However, for the moment the legal issues were not joined, for Judge Hofstadter granted a temporary injunction on May 2, halting all operations until a formal trial, saying that he did not concern himself with the legal basis for the city's action. Rather, he held, "It is a sufficiently grave question whether a half-acre of park land, shrubbery, and trees . . . may be sacrificed to a contemplated use of compounded dubiety, i.e., more parking space . . . for an enlarged cocktail lounge of a plush restaurant." (Hofstadter had spent a quarter hour or so earlier that week tramping around the disputed site, accompanied by mothers, children, newsmen with cameras, lawyers, city officials, and spectators attracted by the crowd.)

The case was ordered to trial for May 4. The city obtained several delays in the trial date and then finally decided to appeal the temporary injunction granted by Judge Hofstadter. Its appeal was heard by the five-member Appellate Court on May 22, and rejected on June 5. The city attorneys maintained that the Appellate Court had given as little consideration to the legal aspects of the case as had Judge Hofstadter earlier.

In the intervening weeks, opposition to the project had become more widespread. Several organizations such as the Citizens' Union, the Southern New York Baptist Association, and the Americans for Democratic Action, had condemned Moses' action. Moses, for his part, held firm. He left on May 2 for a short vacation in Spain, asking the newsmen who saw him off why no one had mentioned all of the new trees the Park Department was planting on Third Avenue. He returned several weeks later. To reporters who greeted him at the ship he remarked that those opposing him were a "small, noisy minority" consisting largely of "childless women howling about their non-existent children."

Isaacs Locates the Jugular

Meanwhile, Councilman Isaacs had become increasingly interested in the nature of the financial relationship between the city and the Tavern, feeling that these financial arrangements, while completely legal, were extremely favorable to the Tavern operators. The Tavern was owned by the city and operated on a concessionary basis. The concessionnaire paid slightly more than five percent of the gross receipts to the city as rent, except that a provision in the agreement permitted him to deduct eighty percent of the cost of any capital improvements he made that were approved by the Park Department. As a result of this clause, the city in recent years had averaged only 1.5% of the gross receipts. The parking lot was $30,000 item in a total improvement program for the Tavern of $536,100. Under the eighty percent proviso the city would have paid $448,880 of this in the form of reduced rent.

Isaacs pressed for a full investigation of these arrangements, urged on by the refusal of the Park Department to furnish certain figures until the Mayor intervened. Isaacs continued to offer resolutions in Council calling for an investigation, and the resolutions continued to be buried in the Council committees.

Although Isaacs never got his investigation, he had opened up the whole question of the city's system of granting concessions. So when, on May 20, Mayor Wagner publicly upheld Moses' authority to order the Tavern project (although not justifying the project itself), he also added that it might "be better all around" to have the Park Commissioner responsible to the City Board of Estimate on matters of granting concessions. (This had been Isaacs' proposal to the Council.) Wagner also urged the Council to support Isaacs' resolution to investigate the financial arrangements.

For Moses the unrest over the parking lot was broadening into a possible attack on his general powers as Park Commissioner.

The Mayor Decides

When its appeal of Justice Hofstadter's temporary injunction was denied, the city had three choices: it could (1) appeal the temporary [1] injunction to a still higher court; (2) agree to a date for a trial on the merits of a permanent injunction; or (3) drop the whole matter, letting the injunction stand. The Mayor decided on the third course.

The Corporation Counsel had advised against either of the first two courses. The city attorneys felt, on the basis of the two unfavorable decisions already received, that regardless of the legal merits of the city's position, the dominating factor was public sentiment, and the evidence was that the public was vociferously against the Tavern project. Furthermore, if the case were taken to court for trial and the city lost, the defeat would be a "bad" precedent which might encourage more litigation against the city's concessionary system.

At first Moses maintained that the city was legally right and that it should take the dispute to trial. However, the summer wore on with no further statements from any of the parties. The dispute had largely dropped from public sight when, on July 18, Moses stated that the city would take over the paving contract for the site and build a playground for children aged eight to thirteen. In Moses' words, this was a "sensible solution." Mayor Wagner, at a press conference that same day, said he did not know who had determined the exact form of the city's decision, but he thought it had been worked out between Moses and Peter C. Brown, the Corporation Counsel. The Mayor also noted that he had "informally" suggested the playground idea to the Board of Estimate a week earlier in an executive session. Isaacs expressed "great joy" at the news but said he would continue to press for an investigation of the financial arrangements between the Department and the Tavern.

Epilogue

On April 26, 1957, the Park Department announced the formal opening of the new playground. The issue over the city's concessionary arrangements had not yet been laid to rest.

[1] There was no "final" injunction, and could be none without a trial on the merits; but the temporary one would stand until then, unless set aside in an interlocutory appeal.

Isaacs continually pushed in City Council for acceptance of a resolution which would severely limit the power of individual commissioners to grant concessions, and introduced several bills to amend the City Charter to this effect. As of January, 1959 none had succeeded, but Isaacs maintained that as long as he remained on the City Council he would not allow the matter to be forgotten.

By announcing the decision to build the playground instead of a parking lot, Moses did much to restore himself in the public's eye. However, the incident, aside from having given the Commissioner a "bad press," dented his reputation for invincibility, a fact which some observers felt might serve to encourage other groups of citizens who found themselves in the way of one of Moses' improvements.

Golden County and Its Extension Agent

Paul B. Crooks

Golden County and Its Extension Agent

BRIEFLY, THIS IS THE STORY of how Golden County's new Agricultural Extension Agent—in a display of initiative and shrewd manipulation which some may question—overcame local indifference and the opposition of elected County Councillors to build what he regarded as a minimum program of Extension activity. The data for this account were obtained from an academic study prepared by the County Agent himself; no other sources were consulted.

The county agent demonstration program developed early in the twentieth century before the United States Department of Agriculture sought—and before Supreme Court decisions allowed it to exercise—authority to conduct development programs directly with farmers. Several states employed county demonstration agents to encourage farmers to adopt improved practices before the passage of the Smith-Lever Act in 1914. The Act authorized grants-in-aid to state agricultural colleges to support extension programs. Even before the Smith-Lever Act was passed, county agents had helped encourage the development of local co-operating committees—sometimes the sequence was the other way around—which became known as farm bureaus. By 1920 these bureaus had formed state federations, and a national organization, the American Farm Bureau Federation, was formed. The Farm Bureau became the largest of the farmers' organizations. In many states the Farm Bureau contributed part of the state's matching contribution necessary to obtain federal funds for extension work. In most states the Farm Bureau strongly influenced the amount appropriated by the legislature for this purpose. In the state in which Golden County lay, there was no organic connection between the state Farm Bureau and the state Extension program. There was a Farm Bureau in Golden County, but there were many farmers who did not belong to it.

The Extension system is a joint venture of federal, state, and county governments. The key position in the system is the one occupied by the state Extension officials, who usually make their headquarters in the state land grant colleges. Collectively they hold the balance of power in negotiations with Washington, even though they depend heavily on federal grants-in-aid. Individually, they exert a controlling influence over Extension policy and personnel within their respective states.

It is at the local level that one finds the symbol of the entire system—the County Agent, whose services as a technical missionary among local farmers are jointly directed and paid for by all three levels of government.

The Extension Office in Golden County was a generation old when the fourth agent to serve it retired and presented county officials with the problem of finding a replacement. The retiring agent was M. T. Brown, whom the community had known for 25 years as a genial soul, an able organizer, a man with the best interest of the community at heart. But he was not a builder, much less a crusader or pioneer. Never during his long tenure had he reached for the stars, and when he retired he left to his successor only what he had inherited: a one-man office, an elementary program of extension work, and barely enough of a budget to make ends meet each year.

Aside from limitations of personality and the modest nature of his ambitions, Brown had been hampered by his lack of technical training—he was not an agricultural college graduate. He had been stymied even more by the grudging attitude toward extension work which prevailed among members of the elected County Council. Some of this feeling was personal. Chairman Vernon Todd, for example, could not forgive Brown for allying himself closely with the Farm Bureau and for helping organize a Bureau cooperative which had cut into the business of Todd's own grain elevators.

For the rest of it, the Council's animus was the "plain orneriness" of a conservative and tax-minded rural board whose members had been long in office. From the beginning of Extension work in the County, 33 years before, the Council had refused to contribute toward the Agent's salary or in any way to encourage the expansion of local staff and facilities. Each year it had pared its Extension appropriation to a minimum which covered only a portion of the Agent's office expenses.

Legally, the Council was under no obligation to do more. The fact that it did not showed that it was a good deal more tight-fisted than the governing bodies of most other counties in the state. Under state statutory provisions every county was free to decide how much money—in addition to the monies made available by state and federal governments—it would contribute toward the Agent's salary and (beyond a prescribed minimum) toward the remaining costs of the local Extension program. Salary and expense appropriations varied depending upon the interest and generosity of each county council, and, as the following case indicates, upon the ability of each county agent to generate local support. The average county added about $1,000 annually to the Agent's salary.

The New Agent Is Chosen

M. T. Brown retired from office on June 30, 1947. His last act was to set in motion machinery for selecting his replacement. Even this was rusty. It consisted of a committee long ago appointed by Brown—now revived and restored as Golden County's Extension Committee. The Committee had never met or operated in regular fashion, but since its members were Brown's personal favorites there had seemed little point in consulting them formally on a program which went unchanged from year to year.

As a preliminary and necessary move toward naming Brown's successor, the Committee conferred with Extension officials at the state's Land Grant College. The law of this particular state holds that all Extension Service personnel are staff members of the Land Grant College. Their appointment rests officially with its Board of Trustees, acting upon recommendation of the State Extension Director and the President of the College. The County Extension Committee's part in the appointment of an Agent is, therefore, extra-legal and advisory, although as a matter of policy and good public relations, the College permits a county to choose from among those candidates the College deems qualified.

The members of the Extension Committee of Golden County were told on this occasion that they could not hope to obtain a qualified Agent without some appropriation by the county toward his salary. The Committee took heed and soon afterward submitted a request to the County Council for an emergency appropriation of $500. The request was granted.

Representatives of the College then recommended William Cox, assistant Agent in another county, as an approved candidate for the job. Cox was a native of the state and a graduate of its Land Grant College; some years before embarking on his Extension career he had been employed as a vocational instructor in agriculture. He was young, energetic, and skillful at getting people to think and act as he thought best.

On June 21, 1947 Cox arrived in Golden County for his interview with the Extension Committee. He was well briefed on the local situation. He had talked with Brown during the past two years at district Extension meetings. He had also checked with state officials, one of whom had come along to introduce him. In his own mind he had settled the terms on which he would accept the Golden County appointment.

His session with the Committee was not quite what he had expected. After waiting outside while the state representative and the Committee discussed his qualifications, he went before the Committee and waited for questions which never came. To fill the void, Cox began asking questions of his own, inquiring about local conditions, the nature of the county's Extension program, functions of the various township committees, and so forth. The answers he received were mostly of the "don't know" variety. Realizing that the Committee was not very well informed and that he was apparently in a favorable bargaining position, Cox proceeded to outline his own position. He would accept the

Committee's offer if made, he said, but only if he were satisfied that:

1) the appropriation for the Agent's salary would be continued on a regular basis, and the amount increased;
2) he would be given an assurance of support for the development of a strong Extension program in the County;
3) he would not be expected to attend meetings "just to warm a seat."

By this last condition, Cox hoped to make clear that if appointed he would not be drawn into the same close attachment to local pressure groups, including the Farm Bureau, which in his judgment had proved a ball and chain for his predecessor.

After making his statement Cox retired from the room. An hour and a half later he was called back and congratulated on his appointment. It was not until later that he was told the ensuing debate had had nothing to do with his appointment. The Committee had almost immediately voted for him unanimously and had then turned to the more controversial question of whether a carnival should be included in the next 4-H show.

Cox Sets his Course

Cox began work as County Agent on July 1, 1947, determined to build as he had promised. His ambition was to achieve a full program of Extension activity, similar to the standard program with which his technical and administrative training had made him familiar. With this model before him, he set out systematically to reproduce it in Golden County.

His first move was to get acquainted with the members of the Extension Committee which had appointed him. He found that its chairman had held office for 25 years—there was, in fact, no procedure for holding an election to replace him, had there been any wish to do so. The incumbent was Norman Taylor, a close friend of the former agent, a charter member of the Farm Bureau, and an elected member of the County Council. Though still a prominent citizen, he had lost ground with the years. As one of his colleagues described him:

> Taylor liked to run everything. . . . He had been a community leader but gradually he lost his leadership as he gained in wealth and lost friends. He would not stand hitched on any issue, but would go in the direction of the most pressure. He was the only Democrat on the Republican County Council and was ineffective. He had started to become childish and dominating.

Cox decided that if Taylor was not the stalwart upon whom he could build permanently, at least he was a man who was open to suggestion and could be worked with temporarily. The Agent soon made a practice of consulting Taylor before each meeting of the Extension Committee —working out a detailed agenda for him (Taylor was a poor chairman) and suggesting ideas which Taylor invariably would accept and present as his own.

Taking a longer view, Cox then singled out two other members of the Committee, John Davis and James Alward, who, he felt, could be counted on to carry his program. He began to encourage these two to move toward positions of leadership. Both men—Alward in particular —were prominent in the Farm Bureau and were active over a wide front of community affairs.

Having oriented himself and set his course, Cox lost no time in getting started on the development of a model group of activities. For this he needed the proper staff, and this in turn depended on securing adequate funds. First he sought an increase in the regular County appropriation.

A Larger Appropriation

The Extension Committee, when first convened after Cox's appointment, had agreed to meet regularly and to hold an annual election of officers. Equally important, the Committee decided to press for increases in the county's Extension appropriation, from \$500 to \$820 annually toward the Agent's salary, and from \$65 to \$100 per month for secretarial help.

Two more meetings of the Committee were held before its proposed budget was submitted to Council. On each occasion Chairman Taylor seemed possessed of a wealth of new ideas. Among them was his suggestion that it might be wise, since he was the sole Democrat on the County Council, for the Committee to have three of its Republican members appear before the Council when the new budget was presented. His suggestion was approved. Two of the delegates chosen were John Davis and James Alward.

Before the County Council met for its budget session in December, Cox struck up an acquaintance with the county chairmen of both the Republican and Democratic parties, and managed also to introduce himself to all the county councilmen. When the time came, the Council allowed the increase in funds and adopted the Extension budget without a dissenting vote.

But Heaven was not yet. A budget enacted by the County Council had one more hurdle to clear before going into effect: approval by the County Tax Adjustment Board. This body was composed of the Chairman of the County Council, the Mayor of the county's largest city, a representative of the township trustees, and four additional members named by the Judge of the Circuit Court. By law, the Tax Board's review was limited to one of two actions: it could either accept the budget as presented or reduce the budget on a percentage basis. It could not reduce or delete individual items.

On this occasion the Tax Board of Golden County ignored its statutory limitations and deleted entirely the appropriation for the Agent's salary and mileage expenses. No vote was taken; no reasons recorded. Only one member expressed himself: he viewed the office as a waste of time and money and was "all for throwing the damn thing out anyway."

Within 24 hours County Agent Cox had consulted his statute books and had satisfied himself that the Tax Board had overstepped its authority. He had also learned that an appeal could be made to the State Tax Board. He suggested to Norman Taylor that an emergency meeting of the Extension Committee be called to record a protest vote and to organize support for an appeal.

At the meeting each Committee member agreed to appear at a hearing before the State Tax Board and to bring with him a carload of neighbors. James Alward was chosen to speak for the delegation.

The day of the hearing arrived with more than 100 Extension sympathizers on hand. Alward, tall and distinguished, spoke convincingly, going beyond the legal issue (with facts supplied him by the Agent) to contend that the items which had been deleted from the budget were ones sorely needed to bolster the county's Extension program.

David Earl, Golden County's Auditor, took it upon himself to state the case for the opposition, implying, though his official position as secretary rather than member of the Council gave him no right to do so, that he spoke for the County Council. This body, he said, had never before appropriated money for the Agent's salary and should not do so now; taxes were high enough as they were.

Earl's comment brought a sharp rejoinder from Alward. He accused the Auditor of having successfully exerted pressure in the past on Agent Brown to buy Extension supplies on county contract rather than through the Land Grant College where materials of better quality could be purchased at prices seventy percent lower. Cox, similarly pressed by Earl, had refused to go along, and Alward implied that Cox's resistance had prompted Earl's attack on the Extension program.

Earl did not reply. After some deliberation, the State Tax Board decided to reinstate the deleted items.

New Leadership, Stronger Organization

In December 1947 the County Extension Committee held its annual organization meeting, the first and most important item of business being the election of officers. County Agent Cox favored the re-election of Taylor as Chairman, thinking that his long service merited the honor of at least one real election, and remembering as well that Taylor was still a friendly and active member of the County Council.

In his other suggestions on Committee officers, made informally to Taylor and other key members, Cox was concerned with securing stronger, more effective leaders. He proposed:

for vice-president: Robert Knowles, 40, a Land Grant College graduate, successful farmer, active in community affairs; a Republican.

for secretary-treasurer: Mrs. Arthur Ellis, officer in the county Farm Bureau, mother of seven children, wife of the County Production and Marketing Administration chairman; a Democrat.

as directors: John Davis and Mark Grimes, both successful farmers; the first a Republican, the second a Democrat. Also, Mrs. Stephen Holt, president of the County Home Economics Club; a Republican.

These suggestions were duly accepted, the result being that half of the Committee's officers were now Republicans, half Democrats. Cox had thereby secured another of his objectives: an Extension policy group bipartisan in fact and in appearance.

A further change in local officialdom took place shortly afterward. At the next county election, Auditor Earl was defeated by a candidate more favorably disposed toward Extension work. Cox deliberately refrained from playing an active part in the campaign, but he did discuss possible alternative candidates with the chairmen of both parties at the time nominations were being considered.

Funds for a Stronger 4-H Program

Cox's next move in the direction of his model program was designed to bring 4-H Club work in the county up to par. In the preceding year Golden County's percentage of 4-H members completing their projects had been the lowest in the state. To improve the situation Cox needed extra staff; and for extra staff he would need more money.

Rather than ask for another salary appropriation from the county, Cox decided to ask help from the state. He conferred with the Director of Extension and obtained a pledge from him that the state would pay the salary of a part-time 4-H Club leader if the county would provide enough money to cover travel expenses.

Now bearing gifts, Cox was willing to risk another visit to the keepers of the county purse. He met with the Extension Committee, stressed the need for improving 4-H work, and recommended that it ask the County Council for an emergency appropriation of $280 for travel expenses. His recommendation was accepted. Members Alward, Knowles, and Mrs. Ellis brought the Committee's request before the County Council, and it was granted without opposition.

This was February 1948. A month later, Golden County hired its first 4-H Club Agent to work during the busy season of each year, from March through August.

Starting a Home Demonstration Program

Point four of Cox's program called for an expansion of staff to include a Women's Home Demonstration Agent. Again Cox faced knotty problems of finance. This time the solution was not so easily reached.

In the first place, Cox had no alternative but to ask the County Council for a further salary appropriation. The new Agent would be a full-time staff member, and as in the case of Cox himself, only the basic part of her salary would be covered by state and federal funds. Her mileage expenses would also be a charge on the local exchequer.

In the second place, there was a shortage of qualified people to fill the post. The state could not guarantee to provide a candidate, and the county would very likely have to conduct a search of its own. The danger in this was a double one: if asked to choose among local candidates, the Extension Committee would probably be under pressure to name some local favorite of uncertain qualifications.

In his own mind, Cox had already decided on a candidate, Mrs. Dorothy Finch, a Land Grant College graduate now employed as a teacher of home economics in one of the local high schools. The fact that her father was Chairman of the Democratic Party in a strongly Republican county was admittedly a problem, but Cox thought her ability justified the risk. Mrs. Finch agreed to take the job if it were offered to her and to keep her discussions with Cox a matter of confidence until he had won the consent of the Extension Committee and of the Home Economics Club Council.

Cox planned his strategy carefully. He visited several of the women leaders in the county, attended meetings of their clubs, and—without suggesting he had already decided on a candidate—discussed ways and means of obtaining a Home Demonstration Agent. He emphasized that an Agent could be appointed if the women were really interested and if the County Council were to make an appropriation for the Agent's expenses and for part of her salary.

The women were interested. They said so quite definitely at a joint meeting of the Extension Committee and the Home Economics Club Council which was held in June of that year, 1948. Their argument was that the women of the county were as much entitled to help from the Extension Service as were the men. Allowing as how they were, the Extension Committee voted to request $540 for the Demonstration Agent's salary and $360 for her mileage expenses.

The request was later incorporated into the budget which the Extension Committee then prepared. County Agent Cox gracefully vetoed the suggestion that a request be made for an increase in his own salary, but he did not object to an appeal for an additional $300 for travel expenses, and that figure was added to the budget.

Although he was interested in the details of the budget, during this time Cox was engrossed in making certain that the County Council, and later the Tax Board, would accept it. The County Fair in August had helped—everyone agreed that the 4-H exhibits were better than they had ever been before. But Cox knew that there was a more direct route to public and official support than through the County Fair.

Much earlier he had marked the "grey-haired Sage" of the Circuit Court as a man of influence; and he had begun resourcefully to cultivate the Judge's friendship. The Judge liked to "fish, eat, and drink a beer now and then," and Cox made a point of inviting him "to do the things he liked to do." By budget time, 1948, the Agent and the Judge were close companions, and the Judge had demonstrated his confidence in Cox by asking him for advice on his own forthcoming appointments to the 1948 County Tax Board. Cox at first refused to commit himself, but after a time offered his friend a list of ten "suggestions." The four persons appointed by the Judge were all taken from Cox's list: John Davis, Mrs. Stephen Holt, and two other members of the Extension Committee.

In September 1948 the new budget was accepted by the County Council and was straightway approved by the County Tax Board.

The Crisis of 1949

Mrs. Finch took up her work as Home Demonstration Agent as soon as the new budget went into effect. With Cox's firm but tactful support, her appointment had been safely engineered through the Extension Committee.

As the new Agent, she found acceptance slow. Much of the resistance she encountered was the inevitable reaction of farm housewives to a young college graduate whose job it was to suggest new and better ways of doing things. But there were also hints of politically-inspired resentment: apparently there was no overlooking the fact she was the daughter of the county's leading Democrat. Cox continued to think highly of Mrs. Finch's work, and he publicly attributed the success of girls' 4-H work to her efforts. But feeling persisted.

Aware of this feeling but not greatly disturbed by it, County Agent Cox was absorbed in the task of strengthening the Extension program. The election of Extension Committee officers, held in December, had produced the organizational changes he wanted: Norman Taylor—still cordial but more disorganized than ever—had given way as chairman to Robert Knowles, who was younger and far more effective. Other officers remained as before, except for the appointment of a representative from the County Home Economics Council to serve as an additional member of the Board of Directors.

Further gains were the friendly contacts Cox had by now established with the editors of the six weekly and two daily newspapers in the area. Any items he wished to have published were readily accepted and given a prominent place in the local news.

When his Extension Committee met in June 1949 to consider the next year's budget, Cox felt that Extension's position in the county was secure enough to venture an appeal for more funds. The entry for secretarial pay was therefore raised by the Committee from $100 to $135 per month; general expenses (office supplies and telephone) by $600 for the year; and the county's share of the Agent's salary from $820 to $1,280. Other items were left untouched, among them the salary and expenses of the Home Demonstration Agent.

The members of the County Council met for their budget session in September. On the first day of their deliberations they listened without any signs of hostility while officers of the Extension Committee presented the new requests.

Thinking all was well, no one appeared for the Extension Committee on the following day when the Council was scheduled to vote the final budget. That morning, however, the old opposition which for so many years had cowed former Agent Brown emerged from its two-year quiet and broke into a bitter tirade against those who supported the appropriations for a Home

Demonstration Agent. County Council Chairman Vernon Todd led the opposition, joined by a brother-in-law and two other members. Their stand was summed up in Todd's remark that "the money spent for a Home Agent is wasted, and the women know more than she knows anyway."

When the Council adjourned for lunch, Chairman Todd dropped in to see the County Agent to tell him he thought "the boys" would not go along with the whole budget. But he added that he would do all he could to get the rest of the budget passed, since he was sure the men of the county wanted to keep Cox, even if the women weren't so enthusiastic about their own special Agent. Before leaving, Todd suggested that Cox appear before the Council during the afternoon session.

Cox immediately went to find Norman Taylor. Taylor assured him that everything was all right and that he would set things in order with the help of his friend, Councilman Calvin Hesler. Observing that Taylor was in an advanced state of confusion, Cox was not wholly convinced. But there was no time to arouse other Extension support, so Cox proceeded to the meeting alone, fearing the worst.

Discussions were resumed. Chairman Todd, turning to the County Agent, reported again that "the boys" questioned the necessity for the lady Home Demonstration Agent, and asked Cox for his opinion. Cox replied that the decision to hire the Home Agent had been taken at the request of the women of the county, and he added that he thought Mrs. Finch was doing an excellent job.

Todd is then reported to have said: "Well now, Mr. Cox, I believe the boys will go along with everything in this budget except the woman's appropriation. If you'll agree to that I think I can get the rest of your appropriation through. Will that be satisfactory with you?"

Cox said that he would be grateful for any appropriation, but he felt very strongly that the women of the county deserved a Home Agent, and he was sure they would take vigorous exception to the proposal.

There was a pause. Then, indicating he thought nothing further could be done, Norman Taylor moved that the budget be adopted, except for the items covering the salary and expenses of the Home Demonstration Agent. Calvin Hesler seconded the motion, and the motion was carried.

Protest and Recovery

Cox "thanked" the Council, then left the meeting and immediately telephoned the members of the Extension Committee. The protest which followed is described in his own words:

> A disgruntled group met and swore vengeance on the members of the County Council. It was voted to resubmit the request for the Home Agent appropriation at a special session of the County Council and to let the women do their own talking at the session. It was also decided that it was time to elect some new Council members.
>
> The special council session was held in late October starting at 9 a.m. Seventy-three women from every part of the County were assembled in the council room at 8:30. The councilmen filed into the meeting, took their seats around the council table, and opened the meeting. Only one man, an attorney appearing on an appropriation request for the Veterans Service Officers, was in the audience. The remainder were seventy-three women with fire and determination in their eyes.
>
> Mrs. Holt stated the purpose of the women's appearance before the council, why they felt that a Home Agent was essential to the welfare of the County and that they would appreciate favorable action by the council members. Several other women spoke supporting Mrs. Holt. The "fireworks" started when Mrs. Volney suggested that Mr. Taylor and all the other council members tell why they had voted against the appropriation. The following discussion then ensued:
>
> *Mr. Taylor:* I didn't vote against Mrs. Finch.
>
> *Mrs. Cunningham:* That's not the way I heard it. I heard that you even made the motion.
>
> *Mr. Taylor:* I never did any such thing. I have always supported the Extension Service.
>
> *Mrs. Newman:* Isn't there a record of that meeting?
>
> *Mr. Schuler* (County Auditor): Yes, we keep official minutes of all meetings.
>
> *Mrs. Newman:* Those records are public property. Bring them out and let us see them.
>
> [Mr. Schuler produced the records for inspection.]
>
> *Mrs. Newman:* See there! Mr. Taylor did make the motion and Calvin Hesler seconded it.
>
> *Mr. Taylor:* Those records are wrong. I never did any such thing.
>
> *Mr. Schuler:* Are you calling me a liar and saying I falsified those records?
>
> *Mr. Taylor:* I never made any such motion.

Mrs. Webster: Someone is more than an ordinary prevaricator.

Mrs. Newman: Why did you second the motion, Mr. Hesler?

Mr. Hesler: It's nothing but the lowest element that makes scenes and stirs up trouble like this.

Mrs. Caldwell: Well! This is the first time I ever knew I was one of the lower element.

Mrs. Jones: So it's the lower element that elected you Councilman, was it?

Mrs. Smith: You fellows had better remember that there's an election coming up next year.

Mr. Todd: This discussion will get us nowhere. What would happen to the state and federal funds paid on the Home Agent's salary if the county appropriation were not made?

Mr. Fabert: Get Mr. Cox up here. He'll know.

[*Cox's account continues*] I was then called to the meeting and I stated that it was necessary that the County appropriate mileage in order to retain funds from state and federal sources. Without mileage the Home Agent's services would be discontinued January 1 when the appropriation in effect terminated. I also stated that a salary appropriation was necessary to meet wage competition and to have a Home Agent.

Cox then left the meeting. For the next hour nothing happened. The Council refused to vote in the presence of the women, and the women refused to leave until the Council had voted. The deadlock continued until hunger forced both parties to recess for lunch.

During the recess, in a move which clearly revealed that by now everyone recognized the fact that Cox was the lion under Extension's throne, one of the less partisan members of the Council went to the Agent's office. He told Cox that if he would "call off the women" the Council could be persuaded to sit down and settle the matter with, say, three of the women's representatives. The Agent said he would try. Shortly afterwards he returned with Mrs. Holt's promise that she would do what she could to restore peace and order. It was then agreed the women would limit their representation that afternoon and send only the officers of the Home Economics Council.

The whole issue was resolved quickly and peacefully when the Council reconvened. After conceding that the women were entitled to their rights, the moderating member of the Council moved that the appropriation in question be granted. Hesler seconded the motion, and a majority which included Taylor voted for it. Chairman Todd and two others abstained from voting.

Securing an Assistant County Agent

During the twelve months which followed peace and progress prevailed. The 4-H Fair was larger and grander than ever; the Extension Committee pioneered by developing one of the first Long Range County Programs in the state; the budget for 1950 met no opposition (one of the Councilmen remarked he didn't want "those women" in his hair again); and all the officers of the Extension Committee were re-elected to serve another year.

All the while, County Agent Cox was moving steadily toward his next objective: the appointment of a full-time Assistant County Agent. His first task was to stir up interest in the appointment. This he did in a general way by "discussing the matter" with 4-H leaders, Extension Committee members, parents, and others, and by mentioning that state and federal funds would again be forthcoming to pay the major part of the bill.

Whenever he could, he also argued from particular cases, though admittedly he did what he could to prod these cases into line. For example, he had noticed that the County (Poor) Farm was being managed very badly from an agricultural point of view. The Farm was losing money every year. Cox had also noticed that the Commissioners who ran the Farm were a powerful group politically. Therefore when, conveniently, he was asked to replan the operation of the Farm and thereafter to use the Farm for demonstration purposes, the Agent agreed—adding, however, that he would need additional staff to keep from falling behind in his other work. He suggested the appointment of an Assistant Agent, and predicted that the increased earnings of the Farm would more than offset the added cost to the county of employing the new Agent.

Satisfied with the response to his suggestion, Cox urged his Committee to adopt a bold approach in preparing its next budget. Again his advice was followed. Requests were made:

for new appropriations, making it possible to appoint an Assistant Agent and another full-time secretary; for increased appropriations, to provide salary raises for the County Agent, the Home Agent, and the office secretary; and a further levy for office expenses.

The total budget for 1951 called for a county appropriation of slightly under $7,500—five times the amount available to Extension in the years before Cox began his work as Golden County's Agricultural Agent.

With this much at stake, Cox and his Committee prepared with extreme care for their budget session with the County Council. Representatives of the Committee visited each member of the Council individually, and then to make doubly certain of political support, they paid calls on the County Farm Commissioners and the County Chairman of the Republican Party. This time when the County Council met to consider the budget, Extension forces were present in strength on both days of the Council's deliberations.

Their reward was to see the new budget passed without dissent.

Winning Over the County Council

After three years of adroit maneuvering and hard work, the building of Golden County's Extension staff was nearly complete. One final objective remained: to make sure that Extension would have the continued support of the County Council. This last objective was secured by ballot in the 1950 county elections. Four members of the Extension Committee, joined by the father of the Extension office secretary, entered the race as candidates for County Council. All five were successful in the November elections.

Chairman Todd, too, survived the election; but in a probably wise and generous move, Extension forces made it unnecessary to use their majority on the Council against him. At their annual meeting in December, they elected Todd a member of the Extension Committee.

Conclusion

Agent Cox had now obtained the funds and staff he deemed necessary to conduct an adequate Extension program for Golden County—though he knew well what everyday grief there would be in perfecting and administering that program.

Looking back over the long campaign, Cox was fully aware that for an administrator he had assumed an exceptionally aggressive and dominant role. He was not an elected official. Yet he had manipulated local interests, he had not hesitated to develop and guide policy, and in the end he had engineered the community-wide support which his program now enjoyed.

He had acted—to use his own phrase—"on the theory that manipulation is permissible, providing it is not obvious." He was convinced that under the circumstances he had had no alternative—except, of course, to follow the discredited example of his predecessor and wait quietly while time and the contrariness of local politicians erased his vision of a stronger Extension program.

Postscript

The year 1959 found Cox in the position of State Supervisor of County Agents.

'The Lonesome Train' in Levittown

Joseph F. Maloney

Introduction

IN 1954 AND 1955 the residents of a vast housing development in a suburb of New York, many of whom were participating for the first time in a public school system, confronted a contentious problem: whether a cantata entitled "The Lonesome Train," which had been described by a church publication as "loaded with Communist propaganda," should be banned as instructional material. The controversy was fought out in School District 5, which contains two-thirds of the large development known as Levittown, Long Island, New York.

This story centers on the efforts of the Superintendent of Schools of District 5—and the efforts of his key staff aides—to work out a solution which would maintain for the public school system the confidence of a community already sharply divided on such educational matters as the need and cost of proposed school plant expansion, the utility of the form of report card in use, the degrees to which Hanukkah and Christmas should be celebrated and explained in the school programs, and the "progressiveness" of the District's educational procedures.

During the "Lonesome Train" controversy, the Superintendent, his aides, and many of the members of the Board of Education wanted to uphold the right of professional educators to use the teaching materials they thought appropriate. The reader may decide for himself whether the Superintendent acted wisely in exercising what initiative he had in a community that was working itself up to a high pitch of excitement. The case also describes the roles of the local Board of Education and of the State Department of Education in the "Lonesome Train" matter. The question of the appropriate administrative responsibility of these latter two bodies is raised by the course of events to be described. Finally, the case portrays the actions of citizen groups, particularly church organizations, in the continuing public school controversy.

Thirty miles from Manhattan, midway in the Long Island suburban county of Nassau, Levittown in 1947 was just a section of potato farms with a population of several hundred people. By the end of that year builder William J. Levitt had plowed under the potato vines and had begun to build low-cost houses. By 1951 the former farm land had a bumper crop of 17,500 homes. (The basic house consisted of two bedrooms, a living room, one bath, a large kitchen, and an unfinished attic—all on a 60 by 100 foot plot.) By 1957, 82,000 people were living in Levittown. In the early fifties turnover was exceptionally high, partially because of the sale of rental units, but by 1956-57 the rate of house sales in Levittown had declined to near the national average of one in seven.

Levittowners had more in common than homes that looked identical. The average adult had had fourteen years of schooling. The average primary annual income of family heads in 1955 was estimated at $5,000. Over eighty percent of the new homeowners had come from rented houses or apartments, two-thirds of them from New York City. They were inexperienced in dealing with many of the problems of new suburbia, especially the problem of managing their own school system. In New York City the Board of Education is appointed by the mayor, the school budget controlled by the city government, and there is no separate school tax. In Levittown, as in most of the 2,000 local school districts in the state (which are guided and loosely supervised by the State Department of Education, headed by a Commissioner), the taxpayers actually control the school system by annual and special District meetings and through an elected Board of Education. The seven Board members are nominated by petition and are elected for staggered three-year terms in early May when the annual school district meeting and budget referendum also take place. Every adult resident who owns property in the District or has a child in its public schools may participate in the election and the meeting.

In 1939 District 5 had one school and a school population of forty. In 1956 it had fourteen schools and 12,000 pupils. The average family in the development had three children, and over fifty percent of the 82,000 in Levittown were under seventeen, compared to the national average of 24.3%. In 1945, District 5 had a school tax rate of 73 cents per $100 of assessed evaluation, and assessment for tax purposes averaged 44 percent of real value. In 1956, the tax rate was $4.74.

Many Levittowners felt that the school budget was rising beyond the financial capacity of the community. As a group, the citizens of District 5 were intensely concerned with their children's education. School District meetings, School Board elections, and referenda on school questions aroused great interest. But most of the families were spending $200 a year for their schools even though state subsidies met about half of the educational expense. When other real estate taxes (also rising) were added to the school tax, the total real estate tax levied on the average Levittown home was over $300 a year, or more than six percent of the average gross family income. Nearly all Levittown homes had been purchased with high G.I. or F.H.A. mortgages, leaving little room in family budgets for additional expenses. Many who had moved to Levittown from city apartments had not anticipated that local taxes would consume such a great portion of their weekly wages.

There was a further economic squeeze. Half the wage earners in Levittown worked in New York City, and commuting fares on the Long Island Railroad were rising. Many of those who did not work in Manhattan were employed in nearby aircraft plants or in industries which did contract work for them. In 1954, many of these plants cut down on overtime work, and the loss of extra pay was felt in many Levittown homes. Some heads of families took on second jobs, some wives went to work, and many families were conscious that they could keep their mortgaged homes only by sacrifice.

Two Groups

Their economic problems led many Levittowners to conclude that "unnecessary frills" in the public school system should be cut to a minimum. This was only one aspect of a deeper division over Levittown school affairs. One group of residents pressed for ever-increasing quality in local public education. These residents were known as "the majority" because they supported the policies of the members of the Board of Education who were in the majority from July, 1954 until July, 1956. A number of supporters of the "majority" viewpoint formed the District 5 Education Association which enthusiastically and vocally pressed for improvements in public education. Although the Educational Association was associated in the public mind with the majority members of the School Board, its recommendations were frequently rejected, and from the standpoint of securing improvements in the school system the Parent Teachers Associations were generally more effective.

The minority group felt that the three R's, as well as discipline, were being neglected in favor of "progressive education." Its members saw "progressive education" as based on "John Dewey's pragmatism," which they felt did not sufficiently emphasize moral training; they believed that the majority gave insufficient weight to the tax cost of its educational policies. A small citizens' group (it had twenty to thirty members admitted by invitation only), the Parents Association for Education, spearheaded and mobilized the civic protest of citizens who emphasized economy and the dangers of insufficient moral training.

Religious Cleavages

The split over School District 5's policies was complicated by the fact that an estimated sixty percent of Levittowners were Roman Catholic.[1] Many had been educated in parochial schools, and there were no parochial schools in the development. Parochial schools outside the development were crowded and expensive even if a vacant desk could be found. Both factions numbered prominent Catholics and non-Catholics among their leaders, but many of the more active members of the E.A. were Jewish (it was estimated that about half of the 50 to 100 Levittowners who annually paid $1.00 dues to E. A. were Jewish), while Catholic leaders were prominent in the P.A.E. of the minority group. (Most

[1] The Jewish population of Levittown is estimated at ten percent by a writer in the Nov. 18, 1957 issue of *Congress Weekly* published by the American Jewish Congress.

of the Jewish members of the community seemed to support improvements and progressive educational methods even if these were costly.) On the other hand Albert Dumont,[2] the Chairman of the Board of Education and the leading spokesman for the majority view, was a Catholic—in fact, a former member of a Catholic religious order of teaching brothers. He had been a member of the E.A. but resigned when he became a Board member.

Many of the leaders of the minority group justified their criticisms on the basis of their own parochial school background. Some argued that in the parochial schools of their youth the nuns had handled classes of forty and fifty students without any disciplinary problems. Hence, they argued, the public schools in Levittown could save money by having larger classes. (In 1954 Levittown classes averaged about thirty pupils each.) Their parochial schools had not had so many bands, clubs, and other educational frills—yet they themselves were well educated in the three R's. Furthermore they felt that the moral training and discipline that had been so prominent in their own parochial school education was simply not present in the Levittown public schools.

Both factions had strong personalities among their members, and basic issues were frequently muddied by personal attacks. Some vigorous members of the E.A. accused the minority of attempting to turn the public schools into parochial schools in everything except the clothes of the teachers and the legal formalities. "Beat the Catholic bloc" became the slogan for some of the extreme members of the E.A. Some of the minority group countered with the accusations that the E.A. was controlled by atheistic Jewish leftwingers bent on subverting the children from being moral, disciplined Americans into being amoral, radical internationalists. These accusations and counter accusations added a bitter undercurrent to community consideration of school problems.

There were a few Catholic teachers and school administrators in the Levittown school system who at one time had studied for the priesthood but who, for various reasons, had not taken the final vows. These former seminarians, who desired to improve the public school system in which they worked, were alarmed at the intensity of feeling being generated in the community, and were not happy at the thought that the people of Levittown would view as typical of Catholic thinking the extremist attacks being made by some of the Catholics in the community. They sought the advice of a priest in the community who was familiar with the problems of suburbia and who was professionally trained in community relations.

The priest advised them that ordinarily most of the higher-educated and more sophisticated Catholic suburbanites were not active in the usual local parish lay societies. Most Levittown Catholics, he said, had only recently acquired middle-class status. The unanticipated higher costs of home ownership coupled with the expenses of commuting or the end of overtime pay were contributing to anxiety that their new social position might be lost. Since the ever-increasing taxes for public schools were such a large part of the economic burden, economy in the public schools had become a symbol for many of them of social self-preservation.

The priest also advised the former seminarians that a number of sociological studies indicated that because Catholics had frequently been charged with putting their church before their country, many had swung to extremist positions on "internal security" to prove that they were foremost in the defense of the "American way of life." In more than one district in Long Island, and perhaps in other parts of the country, the priest went on, this combination of conservatism on economic matters and extremist enthusiasm for exposing so-called left-wing propaganda had been most noticeable in attitudes on school affairs. It was these Catholics who were most disturbed who tended to become most active in the local parish societies. They received far more attention than their more liberal-minded coreligionists who tended to ignore the emotional outbursts of the "hyper-sensitive" lay society leaders.

As the hope for a calmer Levittown, the priest saw two possibilities: one was that the continuing process of public education through discussion of

[2] The names of all the local figures in this case have been changed. "John Johnson," the Superintendent of District 5 at the time of this controversy, is now a New York State official and has declined to discuss the "Lonesome Train" incident.

community problems would dissipate the emotional vigor of the extremist attacks; the second hope was that eventually both Catholics and non-Catholics would recognize the unrepresentative character of the Catholic extremists.

The Superintendent from Ohio

If a school district in New York State is sufficiently large and meets other qualifications, it has its own superintendent of schools who is a professional educator appointed by the local board of education. The Superintendent of Schools of District 5, John Johnson, was the only administrator in the school system of the young community who had held a position of comparable responsibility before coming to Levittown. Prior to his selection in the spring of 1954, he had been a superintendent in Ohio, where he had successfully initiated and supervised the integration of Negro and non-Negro teachers in a public school system.

The Board of Education had unanimously selected Johnson as Superintendent. Subsequently there were some disagreements between the Superintendent and the Board of Education. However, the majority members and Johnson confined their differences to the issues, and Johnson tried to make recommendations only when he anticipated approval. The majority group never criticized the Superintendent in public, and the community gained the impression that there was complete harmony between Johnson and the Board majority.

Although conscious of the desirability of the professional schoolman remaining aloof from community disputes, Johnson could not avoid being identified with the Board of Education majority in the eyes of the minority group. The minority saw as proof for this association the facts that Johnson was not a Catholic, and that he had taken some of his graduate work (one course) at Columbia University's Teacher's College, the supposed spawning ground of [John] Deweyism and "progressive education." (Actually, Johnson himself had once privately remarked that Levittown was trying to obtain a higher quality of public education than it could afford but that as Superintendent he felt he had to go along with the majority drive for better education and higher budgets.)

Some members of the minority also opposed Johnson because he refused to fire the District's business manager, James Dorsey. Fred Gerber, a leading minority member of the Board, and other prominent minority leaders of the P.A.E., were opposed to Dorsey because of a number of conflicts with him on School District business matters. They made no secret of their determination to remove him from the school system. Johnson frequently defended his business manager and his other professional assistants when the minority attacked them at open Board meetings. A newcomer to New York State, Johnson found it necessary to lean heavily on Dorsey in matters of finance.

Some of the leading members of the minority were in the fall of 1954 out to "get Johnson"; an ultra-conservative Catholic group was opposed to the school system's "progressive education" program which Johnson apparently supported; and both of these elements were opposed to the Board majority with which Johnson had become identified. A substantial bloc of opposition was building up against Johnson as the "Lonesome Train" controversy began.

"Snake in Suburbia's Garden"

ALBERT TROUT, a local merchant involved in many community activities, had gained the reputation of being a level-headed, intelligent community leader. He was identified with some of the more conservative groups in Levittown. He was president of the local Republican club, and had been one of the chief promoters of the slate of conservative ("minority") School Board candidates which had been defeated in the May, 1954, elections.

In early October, 1954, Trout received phone calls from several people, asking for his comment on the use of a "leftist" phonograph record in the public schools. None of Trout's first callers could give him any specific information about the record or its contents. Finally a man called who was able to present Trout with a copy of the October, 1954 issue of *The Catholic World,* a monthly magazine of modest circulation, published by the Missionary Society of St. Paul the Apostle in the State of New York. (Neither Trout nor the man who gave him the magazine was a Catholic.)

The issue featured an article titled "Snake in Suburbia's Garden." The article labeled a recorded cantata called "The Lonesome Train"[3] as "so patently loaded with Communist propaganda that even a tyro in Communist lore could detect it."

The article was an account of an unsuccessful attempt of a Citizens' Committee in suburban, upper-class Scarsdale, N. Y., to have "The Lonesome Train" banned from the public schools there. The Citizens' Committee of Scarsdale had supported its charges with citations from testimony before various Congressional investigating committees.

The *Catholic World* article noted that Millard Lampell, who wrote the text of the cantata, had invoked the Fifth Amendment in 1951 and 1952 when questioned on Communist party membership by the U. S. Senate Subcommittee Investigating Infiltration of Radio, Television and the Entertainment Industry. Another witness before the Senate Internal Security Subcommittee, Vincent W. Hartnett, a self-styled "private expert," had made a special study of Communist penetration in the entertainment industry. According to the *Catholic World* article, "Mr. Hartnett went on to fill some five pages with testimony regarding Mr. Lampell's extensive connections with Communist fronts and causes." Another witness identified Lampell as a fellow member of the Communist Party about the time "The Lonesome Train" was written. The article went on to note that the subcommittee report signed by Senators Eastland, McCarran, and Watkins described Lampell as a "hard-core Communist."

Earl Robinson, who wrote the score for the cantata and for "Ballad for Americans," had been listed, reported the article, "as an identified Communist in the 1952 annual report of the House Committee on Un-American Activities."

The second half of the magazine article was an analysis of the contents of "The Lonesome Train"—the special train that carried Lincoln's body back to Springfield for burial. Said *The Catholic World:*

> The essential thesis of the cantata is that the great and good Abraham Lincoln was the champion of one class of people, those whom the Communists claim to represent, the masses, the workers, the farmers. They, according to Communist propaganda and 'The Lonesome Train', were Lincoln's friends and he was theirs and only theirs.
>
> This is the class struggle emphasis of Communism. It is basic to Communism. Mr. Lampell identifies Lincoln with it. . . .
>
> But, what about businessmen, industrialists, and property owners? They're part of the people too. They helped to save the Union for which Lincoln fought the Civil War. Their sons marched in the ranks, fought in the field, suffered and died. What

3 See Appendix for excerpts from the text of "The Lonesome Train."

about them? Weren't they Lincoln's people too? No, not in the Communist interpretation of American history; not in 'The Lonesome Train' either. There, they are the enemy, Lincoln's enemy, the enemy of Lincoln's people, and the enemy of freedom.

In 'The Lonesome Train', while others mourn for the martyred Lincoln, *they* rejoice. You can't have any sympathy for *them*. They're the *enemy*. The businessmen, industrialists, and property owners are the enemy. This is the class struggle emphasis of Communism. . . .

Albert Trout was not altogether convinced on the basis of this article that the use of the cantata presented a serious danger to Levittown school children. Still, he was aware that the use of the record could stir up a controversy, and he wanted to prevent any further growth of community ill feeling. He set out to discover how the record of "The Lonesome Train" was actually being used.

Neither a friendly assistant principal nor one of the District's specialists in audio education recalled the record offhand. Finally they discovered that it was being used not because of its substantive content or as an aid in the teaching of social studies but as an "auxiliary optional" aid in teaching music appreciation. It was being used occasionally in kindergarten and the lower three grades to teach small children the many different ways of using music. The cantata had funeral music, march music, gay music, folk-dance music, all cited as examples of how music could be used to tell a story.

Although reassured that the use of "The Lonesome Train" was not in itself a serious threat to the children, Trout still believed that some effort should be made to prevent the development of a community controversy. On October 11, Trout visited School Superintendent Johnson to discuss the matter. Trout and Johnson had become acquainted through their activities as members of several community groups and considered each other good friends.

Trout gave the superintendent the October issue of *The Catholic World* and told him that he had received phone calls from several people asking about the District's use of the record. Johnson thanked Trout for the friendly warning and told him that he would ban the use of the record while he made further inquiries.

That same day, Johnson dictated two memoranda, one to the Curriculum Co-ordinator of District 5, James Donohue, and the other to the head of the Department of Instruction of the N. Y. State Education Department in Albany.

In his memo to Donohue, Johnson mentioned the criticism of "The Lonesome Train" which had appeared in *The Catholic World,* and told him that ". . . the article inserts some quotations from the record which, if they are accurate, are in my judgment quite inflammatory. I am not prepared to say that they are communistic by design, but then many things are so without being so designed."

Johnson asked Donohue to find out which schools were using the record and to request their principals ". . . on my behalf to cease the use of it for the present until we have had an opportunity to request a review of the material by the state commission established for that purpose. When we have received the report of the state commission we will be delighted to report back to the principals affected."

The state commission to which Johnson referred had been established by the Board of Regents to pass on any formal complaints from individuals that textbooks in the public schools violated Section 704 of the N. Y. State Education Law. This section forbids the use of any text that contains "any matter or statements of any kind which are seditious in character, disloyal to the United States or favorable to the cause of any foreign country with which the United States may be at war."

In his letter to the head of the State Education Department in Albany, Superintendent Johnson said:

A group of citizens in our community have called to my attention a critique in the October issue of *The Catholic World* of a record currently being used in some schools here and which is entitled 'The Lonesome Train'. I would very much appreciate your securing for me any reports that may have been prepared on this record, the specific instructional materials list from which this record must have been chosen.

This information will be greatly appreciated. We do not anticipate any serious difficulty about the record, and we do not intend to follow the policy of simply eliminating instructional materials because someone has complained of them. If, however, it develops a serious question about the influence of any instructional material is justified, I expect to learn

> this from responsible sources and take the necessary action at the local level.

Four days later, on October 15, before the Superintendent had received an answer from Albany, another Levittowner, Peter Reilly, picked up the October issue of *The Catholic World* and was impressed by the contents of the "Snake" article. He immediately wrote Superintendent Johnson protesting the use of the record. On October 20 Johnson wrote Reilly:

> Some weeks ago, upon reading the criticism of 'The Lonesome Train' in *The Catholic World,* we asked those schools which were using it to cease its use and referred the material to the Commission set up by the State Board of Regents for their evaluation of it.
>
> We shall not make use of the material while this evaluation is in progress and, if the evaluation supports the evidence indicated in your letter, no further use whatever is anticipated. We are certainly concerned that all materials used in the education of children be highly loyal in tone and nature. We will not hesitate to remove from circulation any materials which cannot meet these standards.
>
> Thank you for your thoughtfulness.

On November 1, 1954 the head of the Department of Instruction in the State Education Department replied to Johnson's inquiry:

> Please forgive my delay in responding to your letter in regard to 'The Lonesome Train'. I have tried to obtain from our Audio Visual Education people some slant on this recording. As you know, we do not recommend or approve textual material or material in any form for use in the schools. The responsibility for such selection rests with the [local] Board of Education. We do have a Textbook Commission which will receive proper communications with respect to textual material, but I am not certain that this commission would deal with recordings. Questions of the kind raised are certainly difficult to deal with. I expect to hear the recording soon, but as a member of the Education Department, I would not feel free to give you an official opinion as to whether it is or is not satisfactory instructional material in the schools.

Although he had written both his Curriculum Co-ordinator and Peter Reilly that he was referring the record to the Textbook Commission, Johnson never did so, possibly because he may have been advised that the Commission would probably not acknowledge jurisdiction over phonograph records. (As of September 1956 the Textbook Commission had received only two formal complaints from the entire state. Neither came from Levittown or concerned "The Lonesome Train.")

Still seeking guidance, Superintendent Johnson consulted the Superintendent of Schools in Scarsdale, where "The Lonesome Train" had first been attacked. Johnson also had at least two phone conversations with Alexander Kingston, the Assistant Commissioner of Education in Albany. Johnson concluded from these conversations that he was without any authoritative precedent.

On November 17, Johnson presided at a conference of school principals and other administrators concerned with the fourteen schools in School District 5. "The Lonesome Train" was one of the many subjects discussed, but it was neither the main subject nor the one over which the group spent the most time. When Johnson raised the topic of the cantata, several of the principals remarked that they had heard the record more than once and could not recall any objectionable aspects. No one at the meeting raised the question of possible community controversy. Only the educational value of the record was considered. Johnson mentioned that some objections had been raised to the use of the record, but it was noted that the record had been approved four years earlier and had been used in District schools since then without any question arising.

The administrators suggested to Johnson that the District should support the judgments of its professionals. They recommended that the District establish a policy of resisting arbitrary pressure for removing any teaching material that had been approved by professional educators.

Johnson approved the recommendations of his administrators and directed that the record again be made available for use at the option of individual teachers. His action was taken without any public announcement and without any private notice to either Albert Trout or Peter Reilly. Since Trout in occasional friendly conversations with the Superintendent raised no further question about "The Lonesome Train," Johnson felt he had no cause to fear unpleasantness from this quarter. And Peter Reilly was not an active "joiner" of civic groups nor was he widely known in the community.

Letters to the Editor

FOR EIGHT MONTHS there was no mention of "The Lonesome Train" in Levittown. This is not to say that all was peaceful in the School District or that sensitivity to leftist subversion in the schools had lessened. In June the local press had published an extensive letter from one William O'Brien denouncing the proposed hiring of school psychologists and dental hygienists as "fostering the plan that is now afoot to advance socialized services." These were family matters, wrote Mr. O'Brien. To allow them to become community matters, "would produce an erroneous sense . . . of morals."

In July 1955 a mild public explosion about a related matter brought the question of the cantata to public notice. A summer recreation teacher had mimeographed and distributed to his charges some parodies of the then popular song, "Davey Crockett." The parodies had been composed and repeated by some of the children. One verse ran:

His feet are biggest of them all.
His feet are squarest of them all.
He's ahead of us all—at leading retreat.
The reason is simple—he's got the biggest feet.
Davey, Davey Crackpot—scared of the wild frontier.

On July 28, Mrs. Sally Vitale, a local housewife, wrote Johnson a letter which she also distributed to the two local weekly newspapers. Mrs. Vitale protested that Davey Crackpot conformed with the Communist Party efforts to distort the picture of American heroes. "What element in our community," she asked, "would be interested in perpetrating this brazen attempt to undermine our children's respect for a patriotic figure and for everything for which he stood?" (Another Levittown resident, Mrs. Patrick Kelley, wrote: "Perhaps the teacher responsible considered this under the heading of good clean fun but I consider it a brazen attempt to destroy a patriotic symbol.")

Mrs. Vitale also wrote in her letter that several months previously the children in District 5 had been taught a song "written by two communists and used at Communistic celebrations." Mrs. Vitale noted that the cantata had been denounced as Communistic by *The Catholic World*. The weekly paper carrying Mrs. Vitale's letter described the song as a "cantata which describes the story of Abraham Lincoln's funeral train," all but naming "The Lonesome Train."

The parodies and the letters to the editor were soon widely discussed by local residents in coffee sessions, car pools, commuter trains, at parish organization meetings, and in the local newspapers. The Superintendent's office quickly issued an apology and announced that there would be no further disrespect for Davey Crockett. Two investigations—one by Johnson and another by Mrs. Vitale and her friends—disclosed that the summer recreation teacher who had collected, revised, and published the doggerel verses was a regular teacher with tenure in the Levittown system. He was noted for his devotion and skill with his pupils and was one of the most active Catholic laymen in the District and in his own parish.

Although one of the weekly newspapers received five letters the next week protesting the parody, Davey Crockett ceased to be the issue, and "The Lonesome Train" became the center of controversy. In response to the complaint recorded by Mrs. Vitale and to other complaints, Johnson defended his authorization of the use of the record in a statement to the press:

> I wrote to the State Department inquiring whether or not the song or authors were subversive. They replied that they had no evidence to support any claim of subversion against the song. I then talked to Alexander Kingston, a representative of the State Education Department who specializes in handling matters of this sort, and he reiterated that he had no evidence to support any claim about the song. I will not remove the music books from our program unless I determine that they are detrimental to our school.

On July 31, 1955 Mrs. Vitale wrote Johnson another letter, recapitulating some of the highlights of the article in *The Catholic World.* She also included a list of several organizations, labeled subversive by the California Tenney Committee, with which either the author or composer had been connected, as members or sponsors.

The next day, Superintendent Johnson wrote Mrs. Vitale:

> I have read and studied your letter of July 31st concerning the Lonesome Train. I am referring your letter to our department of instruction for study and examination.
>
> Thank you for your kindly interest in the schools and your deep concern for real Americanism which all of us who work in the schools heartily share.

On the same day, Johnson sent a memorandum to Donohue, the District's Curriculum Coordinator:

> I am enclosing with this memorandum Mrs. Vitale's letter concerning the Lonesome Train. I have not to this date replied to the letter but you can see here is at least the germ of another storm in connection with this single item of instructional material. It has always been and still is a fundamental principle that I will not remove materials of instruction unless in the judgment of the professional staff they are detrimental to children.
>
> Once again, I refer the matter to your judgment and to that of the professional staff and guarantee you that your judgment will in all cases be supported to the full.

Mrs. Vitale did not wait to hear the results of the examination by Johnson's department of instruction. On August 6, she wrote the Superintendent again to tell him that she had just received a letter from Alexander Kingston, the Assistant Commissioner of Education, which apparently contradicted Johnson's press statement that Kingston "had no evidence to support any claim of subversion against either the authors or the song." Kingston said in his letter to Mrs. Vitale that his office had never been asked about the song or its authors.

As Mrs. Vitale wrote Johnson:

> I am ... disturbed at a quotation attributed to you by the Levittown *Tribune* in which you are alleged to have stated that you wrote to the State Education Department inquiring whether the authors or the cantata were subversive. In addition, you are quoted by the same paper as saying you talked to Mr. Kingston, a representative of the State Education Department and a specialist in handling matters of this sort. You are further quoted as stating the State Education Department and Mr. Kingston had no evidence to support any claim of subversion against either the authors or the song. My disturbance results from the fact that I have in my possession a letter from Mr. Kingston, Associate Commissioner, State Education Department in which he states, "To the best of my knowledge, no opinion has been requested from this office regarding this matter in any way and no opinion has ever been written concerning Mr. Earl Robinson and Mr. Millard Lampell."
>
> I'm sure that the interest you have shown in this matter will address itself to this apparent contradiction.

Superintendent Johnson was beginning to feel that "The Lonesome Train" could develop into a major community controversy. So were the members of the Board of Education, some of whom expressed to Johnson strong dissatisfaction with the way the situation was being handled. They said they believed Johnson had been wrong in banning the record when the first complaint had come to his office. This immediate banning without even a preliminary investigation, they felt, seemed to imply that Johnson did not believe the District's professional educators were competent to select teaching materials.

Some members of the Board majority had even broader criticisms. They were annoyed because they had learned of the complaints about "The Lonesome Train" eight months after the original inquiry, and then only through the newspapers. They complained that the Superintendent should have consulted them when the issue first arose and certainly when the record was restored to the shelves. If they had been consulted, they argued, they could have assisted Johnson in handling the dispute, and their assistance might have drawn the sting from any subsequent publicity.

These Board members told the Superintendent that they would have recommended different actions at a number of stages. In the first place, they would not have recommended restoring the cantata merely because there had been no adverse information or opinion from the State Education Department. It had been their experience that the Education Department officials were apt to fall back on legalism on difficult occasions, and, unless one was familiar with the way the State Education Department operated, confusion was almost inevitable. Kingston had been telling the truth when he wrote Mrs. Vitale that "no opinion has been requested," and "no opinion has ever been written" about "The Lonesome Train," for Kingston had not received a *formal* petition from Johnson on the cantata. If one wished to obtain *informal* guidance from the State Education Department, the Board members explained to Johnson, such verbal assurances as Johnson had received were sufficient. But if one wished to have an opinion on record, the only really reliable course was to obtain a written opinion by formally filing and then pressing an appeal. It was usually not worth bothering with such a lengthy procedure, they told Johnson, and such questions as the "Lonesome Train" issue were often most peacefully settled by diplomacy at home rather than by getting involved in exchanges with Albany. "You are new to New York State," they reminded the Superintendent, "and we could have helped you learn the ropes."

These Board members believed that Johnson had erred in restoring the phonograph record to the shelves without any explanation or notice to the two taxpayers who had taken the trouble to complain about it. When Mrs. Vitale and others in the District made a public controversy over the restoration of "The Lonesome Train," both Albert Trout and Peter Reilly told their friends that this was precisely the kind of community controversy they had been trying to prevent by their warnings to Johnson. The Board members warned Johnson privately that he must exercise more diplomacy. Johnson took their advice and promptly sent a copy of Mrs. Vitale's second letter to Albert Dumont, the President of the Board of Education, who had been one of Johnson's consistent public supporters. The Superintendent wrote Dumont that all the statements he had made about his conversations with Kingston were "exactly true," but that he "did not wish to continue the discussion via the newspapers." Dumont concurred.

A few weeks later, on August 16, Johnson wrote Kingston reminding him of their telephone conversation about "The Lonesome Train" and asking him to describe the mechanism established by the State to handle such questions. Two days later, Johnson visited Kingston, and the Albany official confirmed their first conversation about the information on the cantata. However, the only written confirmation of their discussion was a letter written by Johnson on August 22, thanking Kingston for the interview.

For many members of the community, the only clear written record was the letter Mrs. Vitale had received from Kingston which said that no opinions had been sought from his office about the song or its authors.

On September 1, another Levittowner, Mrs. Trackson, wrote an open letter to Johnson in the local weekly. She asked Johnson to publish his correspondence with the State Education Department, and concluded by saying, "We, in Levittown, do not like to be in the position of not having complete confidence in our administrators."

The editor of the weekly did not wish to publish the letter without a counter statement from Johnson and called the Superintendent a half an hour before press time for comment on Mrs. Trackson's letter. Johnson told the editor that any letter received by District 5 could be seen by the taxpayers on request, and also explained to the editor that his discussions with Kingston had been *oral.*

The September 1 issue of the newspaper carried Mrs. Trackson's letter and the editor's account of Johnson's reply, but since there was no explanation of the State Education Department's distinction between a formal ruling and an informal opinion, some vocal members of the community stated that there were grounds for withholding confidence from the School District's administrators.

A Policy Is Made

BOTH SUPERINTENDENT JOHNSON and Curriculum Co-ordinator Donohue agreed that it was important to set up some standard procedure for dealing with questions about the suitability of teaching materials—a procedure which would minimize community friction and at the same time maintain professional standards.

After considerable thought and consultation with his associates, Donohue suggested that a board, composed of members of the District's professional staff, be set up to review any questioned teaching materials. This review board would give its opinion to the Superintendent, who would make the final determination.

Johnson accepted the suggestion but made one change: the review board would include some lay representation from the community. Accordingly, Donohue set up the Review Board with himself as chairman and with the Supervisor of Audio-Visual Education, the Supervisor of Music, three school principals, and one teacher whose duties involved the optional use of the questioned material. The non-professional community member was to be the President of the District's P.T.A. Council.

The professional members of the Review Board volunteered their services with the understanding that this would be another administrative committee whose report as usual would be addressed solely to the Superintendent. Any subsequent action would be the responsibility of the Superintendent.

Inadvertently, Johnson's press release on the establishment of the Review Board stated that the report of the Board would be "presented to the Board of Education and a full report will be made to the party or parties who raised the objections." In the midst of many other pressing matters, neither the Superintendent nor any of the professional members of the Review Board noticed the serious discrepancy between the procedure described in Johnson's release to the newspapers and the previous understanding that the report was intended only for the Superintendent.

The following week there was considerable discussion of the Review Board at the Board of Education meeting. Several taxpayers spoke from the audience. The Board President and others objected to the inclusion of non-professionals on the Review Board. As a result, the P.T.A. Council President was removed from the Review Board by the Board of Education.

This move was not well regarded by some in the audience. One local weekly reported:

> In full discussion following the executive session [Alberto] Menoti was the most verbal of the spectators arguing in favor of lay representation on the Review Board. He expressed the belief that confining the review personnel to the teachers would "throw too much responsibility on them," that since teachers and administrators originally chose or passed on instructional material, they were not in a favorable position to review its merits later. . . .

The Review Board convened and began its investigation of the "Lonesome Train" complaints. While it was deliberating, the Social Action Committee of the South Nassau Unitarian Church issued a statement to the local weekly newspaper saying that it believed "the public schools can function best for the benefit of the children if they are directed by professionals, properly chosen, who are free to do their work without hindrance from pressure, individual, or group."

The Unitarians' release stressed as a matter of principle that the children should be exposed to divergent views, and said that "any exclusion of such material because of the political, religious, or racial background of the author or artist is completely undemocratic. To so exclude for these reasons would be tantamount to admitting a lack of confidence in democracy."

The proclamation by the Unitarians struck a responsive chord in one portion of the community, although it did not still the anxiety of the other portion. Many of the Catholics who were worried about subversion in the schools were critical of "free thinkers," and to them the Unitarians in town *were* "free thinkers."

Those who welcomed the Unitarians' statement were dismayed by a similar defense of the School District's administrators by the local branch of the American Labor Party.[4] Those who had not found the Unitarians' stand reassuring felt their doubts even more justified by the A.L.P.'s participation.

Anxieties were heightened by another incident involving the Board of Education. At a late September meeting, the Board of Education, on Johnson's recommendation, had authorized the Anti-Defamation League of B'nai B'rith, a Jewish community organization, to conduct a Workshop on Human Relations in a Levittown high school. The workshop had been planned by teachers, parents, and representatives of the Anti-Defamation League as an in-service program to assist the teachers in understanding and combating the causes of prejudice and intolerance. With full parental approval, a few school children were selected to participate in a panel discussion. Although intended for the teachers, the public was invited to attend as an afterthought when it became apparent that the workshop was generating community discussion. Fred Gerber, who had already attracted community attention as the spokesman on the Board of Education for more economy in the school budget, objected to the workshop: "I don't like the title 'Human Relations'—I'd like to ask them if they'll let their daughter marry a colored fellow and see what they'll say."

A flock of emotional letters appeared in the press. After the workshop had ended, dissatisfaction was expressed by members of some community organizations, including lay Catholic organizations. At least one or two Catholics vocally complained that the children who participated in a panel discussion of the problems of mixed marriages had not been concerned with the religious and sacramental aspects of sex and family life. Three or four of the more active members of the local Catholic lay societies expressed fears that the forum had been held partly to weaken the role of religion and the family in the social structure.

The Review Board members, deliberating on the suitability of "The Lonesome Train" while these events were taking place, found that they agreed on a number of principles. They agreed first, that they wished to protect the public educational system from arbitrary external censorship while at the same time preserving public confidence in the professional competence and patriotism of the District's administrators.

The Review Board members also agreed that to take a strong stand on the basis of "academic freedom" (or the grammar school equivalent) would increase community dissension.

Three of the Review Board's members were Catholic and were aware that criticism of Johnson and his staff was being voiced at the meetings of the Catholic parish societies. The criticism followed the lines that Johnson and his administrators were lax about promoting the proper moral atmosphere in the schools and were indifferent to the possibility of left-wing efforts to subvert school children. The Review Board members did not accept these criticisms (actually, four of the six members of Johnson's central staff and four of the eight principals were Catholic), but they judged that community feeling was so strong that no matter what the Review Board decided controversy would continue.

The members of the Review Board also agreed that as professional educators, they should remain free to give their honest and best advice to the Superintendent without becoming involved individually in the public controversy. Although they agreed on all these points, however, they could not agree on the central purpose of their assignment: determining the suitability of the cantata.

In an effort to solve its problems, the Review Board asked that its membership and the individual opinions expressed be kept secret. Anonymity was sought for two reasons: first, since the professionals could not reach unanimous agreement, they did not want to set themselves up

[4] The American Labor Party, originally founded in 1936 in N. Y. by labor leader David Dubinsky and others as an independent liberal party, was deserted in the middle forties by many of its original founders and supporters (who then formed the Liberal Party) as it became progressively dominated by extreme left-wing and Communist members. After the 1954 election, the A.L.P. lost its status as a recognized political party in New York because of its failure to attract the legal minimum of votes necessary for continued inclusion on the state ballot.

against one another and the Superintendent in a public controversy; second, they did not want to create a precedent to hamper future similar committees.

The Superintendent, the Board of Education, and the local press co-operated, and only the name of the Review Board's chairman, Curriculum Co-ordinator Donohue, was ever again mentioned in public in connection with the cantata. Of course, any citizens who badly wanted to know the names of at least five Review Board members could find them in the back numbers of the weekly paper that described the appointment of the Board.

In the last week of October 1955 the Review Board submitted a report to Johnson giving the two interpretations which had come out of its discussions, but without disclosing which members favored which view and without classifying either opinion as majority or minority. In a meeting with the Superintendent, the Review Board members assured him that they felt the final professional decision in the District was properly his, and, as his professional assistants, they would all support him regardless of differences of opinion within their midst.

Johnson publicly announced a slight delay pending his own analysis of the report, and after three weeks of study, on November 19, he sent each member of the School Board a copy of his own report on "The Lonesome Train." He asked each member to keep the contents of his report in strict confidence until after it had been read publicly at the evening meeting of the School Board the following Monday, November 21.

At 8:30 on the morning of the 21st, School Board member Fred Gerber went to the District's administration offices and demanded the text of the Review Board's report and a summary of the individual opinions of the members of the Review Board. Johnson emphatically declined to give Gerber the information.

That evening, Johnson summarized the divergent opinions of the Review Board. One opinion was that "the cantata, heard in its entirety by children and not torn to shreds by adults, is of value and interest when used as supplementary enrichment material." The reasoning behind this was

> one does not mold a democratic individual by hiding from him all that is written or sung or painted by persons of other political persuasions; that any questionable message the recording might seem to adult minds to contain is read into isolated phrases by those seeking to prove a point in the present ideological conflict. . . .

Johnson continued with his report by saying that the other opinion was that " 'The Lonesome Train' carries a message that will unfavorably influence the minds of children, and that is not done by poetical accident but by definite design."

Johnson described these Review Board members as concluding

> We cannot interpret freedom of speech so broadly that we will permit our classrooms to serve as avenues to the minds of children for subversive materials composed by those who have been clearly and directly related to causes and activities in organizations which have been classified as subversive by branches of our state and federal government. The message in the cantata is clearly intended to be and is communist propaganda.

Johnson then made his own recommendation: the record should still be used at the teacher's option, but

> each copy of the recording which is used in our schools [should] be accompanied by a statement of the specific quotation in the recording which is under question and the specific quotation from Lincoln's writings which sets the recorded quotation right factually, and that all teachers using the recording be requested to accompany any use of the recording with a clear statement delineating the distorted material and the factual material which sets the record straight.

Johnson's opinion was that the record would serve a useful purpose if it were used with an accompanying explanation by the teacher showing how any quotations had been distorted. It would "assist growing minds to develop the attitude of inquiry and critical evaluation when confronted with other people's opinion," and would be useful for children of the seventh grade and above. There was no mention of the record being used for the music appreciation classes of the lower grades.

The Board of Education adopted the Superintendent's recommendation, but made it mandatory for the teacher to point out the alleged distortions when using the record. The vote was four to two, with Fred Gerber in the minority.

Reaction

FRED GERBER was not satisfied with the actions of the Superintendent and the majority of the Board of Education, and he again asked to be given the text of the report of the Review Board. Again Johnson refused his request. This refusal was approved by the same four "majority" Board of Education members who had formally adopted Johnson's report on the cantata.

In upholding Johnson's refusal to attempt to identify the Review Board members and their opinions, the Board of Education majority was affirming what it regarded as a fundamental principle of administration. These Board members felt that the recommendation to the Board of Education was the Superintendent's, not the Review Board's. They argued that the relationship between the Superintendent and the Review Board was a professional relationship requiring mutual confidence. To disclose the individual opinions of the members of the Review Board would impair this confidential professional relationship and, the majority thought, would probably destroy the ability of the Superintendent to get advice freely from his assistants on controversial matters. Preserving such a professional relationship was of much greater importance to Johnson and to the Board of Education majority than the disposition of "The Lonesome Train."

The policy on the use of the cantata adopted by the Board of Education did not quiet the community. The local press received and published a new flock of letters. Johnson and the Board majority were attacked from both sides. Some letters protested the decision to permit "Communist propaganda" to be used in the schools, while others protested the decision to label the cantata as a distortion, claiming that such "prejudgment by those in authority" would hinder "genuine criticisms" and independent evaluation by the students.

Fred Gerber was not content with the Board's rejection of his demand for the names and opinions of the review committee members. He and a local attorney, John O'Donnel, filed petitions to the State Commissioner of Education in early December, with O'Donnel also serving as Gerber's attorney. They appealed to have the record banned from the school as subversive material, and demanded that the names and opinions of the Review Board's members be disclosed. On December 5, State Commissioner James E. Allen stayed the use of the record by the District pending his decision.

Such appeals to the Commissioner of Education follow a long procedure. The petition is answered formally by the defendant, oral hearings are held, and written briefs are presented. After delays sometimes longer than common to most courts, the Commissioner of Education hands down a decision accompanied by appropriate orders. The dissatisfied party can petition the Commissioner for a review, repeating the above procedures, or he can petition the Supreme Court of the State of New York for a review on questions of law.

Gerber's central theses were that he was illegally denied the Review Board's report and that it was illegal for Johnson to refuse to show anyone the Review Board report and his correspondence with the Scarsdale Superintendent (which the Scarsdale Superintendent had asked Johnson to keep in confidence). He also contended that since the record was "Communist propaganda," its use would "deny Christians and Jews and people of other religious beliefs" equal protection of the law because they could not similarly propagandize in the public schools. This discrimination, Gerber claimed, was a fundamental violation of the New York and federal constitutions.

The District in its answering brief replied that "a staff report is not considered to be a public record within the meaning of . . . the Education Law and therefore need not be made available for public inspection." The District, however, submitted copies of the Review Board's report. Aside from identifying the chairman, the District did not identify the Review Board members and did not disclose any of their individual opinions.

While the appeals were before the Commissioner, the local press received many more letters on the issue, and a number of citizens' committees sprang up—many of them short-lived, and almost all with overlapping membership.

Support in the local press for the Superintendent and the Board of Education came from various individuals and organizations, including the Center Island Jewish School of nearby Hicksville and the Executive Council of the Levittown Teachers Association, although there was some dissent in the latter body about its public stand.

Somewhat to the embarrassment of the Board, the local branch of the American Labor Party continued its vocal defense of Johnson. The position of the Superintendent and Board majority was also not bolstered in the minds of the opponents of the cantata when the New York Civil Liberties Union submitted a brief to the Commissioner opposing Gerber on the grounds of "academic freedom."

Board of Education President Dumont did not attempt to influence public opinion in either direction, feeling that proselytizing would be improper while the matter was before the Commissioner in semi-judicial form.

At about this time, Dumont, who was himself a practicing Catholic, received a request from the Holy Name Society of one of the two local Catholic parishes for a copy of the record and the text of the cantata. He was subsequently informed that these had been used as the basis for a lengthy discussion at a meeting of the Society. The discussion was led by William O'Brien, one of the strongest critics of the Board majority and the moving spirit of the P.A.E., whose letter protesting the employment of psychologists and dental hygienists has been described above. The Society passed a resolution demanding that the cantata be banned.

The School Board Election

The Commissioner's decision on Gerber's appeal was still pending when campaigning began for the May School Board elections. Neither Dumont nor Gerber was up for re-election. Six candidates filed for the three vacancies, three representing the "majority" viewpoint and three publicly committed to support Gerber's "minority" outlook. Two of the three "majority" candidates were incumbents who had been appointed by President Dumont to fill vacancies caused by resignations. All three "majority" candidates were endorsed and supported by the District 5 Educational Association. Two were Jewish; the third was not a Catholic.

Opposing these three "majority" candidates were the three "minority" candidates endorsed by the P.A.E. and by O'Brien and Gerber. All three were Catholic; one was an incumbent Board member who had attained his seat two years earlier by running as an independent—without either E.A. or P.A.E. support. These "minority" candidates and their zealous supporters stressed the issues of socialism, communism, atheism, and juvenile delinquency along with the need for greater economy, for tighter school discipline, and for keeping teachers' salaries and other costs down partly by increasing the number of students per class.

For years the supporters of the "minority" position had accused the "majority" supporters of being spendthrifts so far as the District's schools were concerned. But in this election the "majority" candidates and Board members and their supporters were also accused of being leftwingers or, at the very least, of being "soft" on possible communist subversion of the children in the District's schools.

There were strong religious undertones to the campaign. Some adherents of the minority camp circulated pamphlets saying: "Don't be a rubber stamp for Johnson—vote 'No' for Milty, Stanny, and Joey." (The first names of the majority slate candidates were Milton, Stanley, and Joseph.) These pamphlets were attacked as anti-Semitic in tone by some of the E.A. adherents.

Two of the minority candidates and many of the most enthusiastic supporters of the minority (or the "Gerber-pledged") slate were active in the lay societies of the leading Catholic parish in Levittown. While the local Catholic parishes and their organizations took no official position in the election, they did provide a strong nucleus and informal meeting places for the minority side's campaign. Parish societies discussed the elections off the record; members urged one another to vote for the "Gerber candidates"; and the priests told their parishioners from the pulpit that now they had the chance to do something about the school conditions about which they had been complaining.

The Tablet, the official newspaper for the Brooklyn Diocese which then included Long Island, published letters from one of the Gerber candidates in which he gave his interpretation of the Levittown school situation. *The Tablet* also published biographies of the three Gerber candidates, all of whom were Catholics. Several of the local Catholic priests directed the attention of their parishoners to *The Tablet* for enlightenment on the school elections, with one priest reminding his listeners from the pulpit that three Catholics were running.

The three candidates supporting Gerber were elected by very narrow margins, indicating that Catholics had voted on both sides. While the "left-wing" issue was important, most observers agreed that it was subordinate to the "economy" issue in affecting the vote.

In the first week of July, six months after Gerber and O'Donnel had filed their appeal, State Commissioner Allen rejected their petitions. Allen held that the use of the record, accompanied by correction by the teacher of distortions, "is not subversive." The Commissioner added that perhaps the Board might consider "whether it desires to have any instructional material . . . which requires explanation. . . ." Without ruling on the propriety of withholding the names and opinions of the Review Board members, the Commissioner said he saw no useful purpose in ordering their disclosure.

At the first meeting of the new Board, in July 1956, Fred Gerber was elected President of the Board of Education, and the Board immediately banned the "Lonesome Train" record by a vote of four to three.

Many of Johnson's supporters, however, did not feel "defeated." The Commissioner had sustained the action of the former Board majority; they were "tired" from so much fighting; and, as one member put it, the song "wasn't very good anyway."

One of the new members of the Board moved to censure the Review Board members for "refusing to stand up and be counted," but the new majority was not eager to start its term of office by creating a rift with the professional educators. The motion was defeated and, in fact, the new Board passed six to one a motion praising the nameless members of the Review Board for their work.

During the summer, State Commissioner Allen appointed Johnson to a high state post, a sign of the recognition Johnson had earned in professional education circles.

But peace did not come to Levittown.

On October 11 the new board majority voted to establish a committee composed of two representatives from each of Levittown's veterans' organizations to review any educational material that might be questioned. This action was immediately denounced as un-American by two of the groups, the American Veterans Committee and the Jewish War Veterans. The other veterans' groups remained silent, and eventually the whole matter died for lack of any organizational support.

The District was even more aroused when an elementary principal wrote the parents of each of her pupils that they should send their children to church regularly so that they would have a better moral character. When this was questioned as a possible violation of constitutional separation of church and state, many who raised the question were accused of being opponents of morality. The bulletin of one of the local Catholic parishes expressed its approval of those majority Board members who had voted to sustain the principal, while a local interdenominational group of clergymen expressed its disapproval of such a use of school authority.

While these events were taking place, Gerber appealed again to the Commissioner to have the earlier decision reversed and "The Lonesome Train" formally banned by the State. In February 1957, the Commissioner again rejected Gerber's appeal, and Gerber petitioned the State Supreme Court to reverse the Commissioner. (In June 1957, the Supreme Court denied Gerber's appeal because it had been filed months after the legal deadline for such an action.)

The supporters of the former Board majority were convinced that election of the Gerber slate posed a serious threat to the quality of public school education in the District. Repeatedly they organized hundreds of Levittowners to attend the School Board meetings to support the appropriate Board members. They started in the fall of 1956 to organize the campaign for the May 1957 elections.

In the May 1957 campaign Gerber filed for former Board President Dumont's seat to give the voters a clear choice between the leaders of the two sides.

The Dumont team supporters developed a large organization of over 500 members just for the election, while about half of Gerber's 1956 supporters abstained from campaigning.

An anonymous telephone campaign was started by some Levittowners, who accused the Dumont team of "softness on communism." One enthusiastic Gerber-team supporter told several people that the Dumont team candidates were all "Commies with a capital C."

Other Levittown Catholics were determined to try to prevent the parishes from once again being the center of election activity. Sixty-three Catholics signed a letter which was hand-delivered to each of the local Catholic priests. The delivery was timed to occur late in April, shortly before the monthly meeting of the lay societies and just before the election.

This letter noted that the current school election had again provoked some Catholics to participate in a telephone and word-of-mouth campaign and to cast aspersions upon the religious integrity and patriotism of some of their fellow Catholics. The letter went on to note that educational methods used in the schools were being labeled socialistic, un-American, and anti-Christian, even though these same methods had been accepted and in some instances instigated by Catholic educators. The letter maintained that attempts to answer such accusations had been met with renewed accusations of agnosticism and communism. The use of such tactics by Catholics against Catholics was declared by the signers to be unjust and un-Christian.

Partly as a result of the letter, the Catholic lay societies refrained from electioneering in the 1957 campaign. Dumont defeated Gerber by a record-breaking vote of 6,700 to 3,300, with Dumont's two fellow candidates also defeating the two Gerber associates by a similar two-to-one margin.

Thousands of Levittowners participated in the annual District meeting. The Board modified the budget slightly, in line with the suggestions of the Dumont group to reject the budget as too high.

The effects of the "Lonesome Train" controversy were still apparent in Levittown in 1957. Even after the Dumont team victory of that year some of the District's professional educators were looking for posts in a calmer environment. The vacant position of superintendent could not be filled for more than a year.

Appendix

Excerpts from "The Lonesome Train" by Earl Robinson and Millard Lampell

WOMAN (ALTO:) There was a silence in Washington town,
When they carried Mr. Lincoln down.

CHORUS: A lonesome train on a lonesome track,
Seven coaches painted black.

. . . .

BALLAD SINGER: They tell a story about that train,
They say that Lincoln wasn't on that train;
When the train started on its trip that day,
Lincoln was in Alabama, miles away!

. . . .

BALLAD SINGER: Just a pulpit and some wooden benches,
Abe Lincoln on the last bench away in the back,
Listening to the sermon,
Listening to the singing.

. . . .

NEGRO PREACHER: We got a new land, my dear friends, we got a new land!
Ain't no riding boss with a whip,
Don't have no backbiters,
Liars can't go, cheaters can't go,
Ain't no deputy to chain us,
No high sheriff to bring us back!

. . . .

NARRATOR: From Washington to New York people lined the tracks.

. . . .

At lonely country crossroads there were farmers
And their wives and kids standing around for hours;
In Philadelphia, the line of mourners ran three miles!

But some wanted him dead for a long, long time.
A cotton speculator turned away from the coffin, saying,

SPECULATOR: "All right boys, the drinks are on me!"

CHORUS: For there were those who cursed the union,
Those who wanted the people apart;
While the sound of the freedom guns still echoed,
Copperheads struck at the people's heart!

BALLAD SINGER: (SPEAKS)
I've heard it said that when that train pulled into New York town,
Mr. Lincoln wasn't around.
(SINGS)

. . . .

Lincoln was down in a Kansas town
Swinging his lady round and round!

CALLER: (FADING IN)
Swing your maw, swing your paw
Don't forget the gal from Arkansas

CHORUS: (MEN AND BALLAD SINGER)
When young Abe Lincoln came to dance,
Those Kansas boys didn't have a chance!

. . . .

BALLAD SINGER: Some in the north and some in the west
And some by the President's side
They cursed him every day that he lived,
And cheered on the day that he died!

NARRATOR: Yes, they cheered.
The Copperheads...
A New York Politician who didn't like Lincoln.
An Ohio business man who didn't like Negroes.
A Chicago newspaper editor who didn't like people!

GIRL ALTO: (SINGS SOFTLY)
You couldn't quite tell where the people left off.
And where Abe Lincoln began.

. . . .

LINCOLN: (SPEAKS)
Until all men are equal, and all are free
There will be no peace,
While there are whips and chains,
And men to use them,
There will be no peace;
After the battles,
After the blood and wounded,
When the chains are smashed,
And the whips are broken,
And the men who held the whips are dead!
When men are brothers and men are free,
The killing will end, the war will cease,
When free men have a free men's peace!

. . . .

MAN'S VOICE: Mr. Lincoln, isn't it right that some men should be masters and some should be slaves?

LINCOLN: "Brother, if God intended some men to do all the work and no eating,
He would have made some men with all hands and no mouths."

. . . .

WOMAN'S VOICE: Well, I say, America for Americans. What happens on the other side of the ocean, shouldn't be any skin off our backs. Right, Mr. Lincoln?

LINCOLN: "Well I'll tell you, ma'am. It seems to me the strongest bond of human sympathy, outside your family, of course, should be the one uniting all working people of all nations, tongues and kindreds."

. . . .

CHORUS: A lonesome train on a lonesome track
Seven coaches painted black.
Abe Lincoln had an Illinois face,
And he came out of a pioneer race,
He knew how hard the fight would be
And he liked the idea of being free!

. . . .

Freedom's a thing that has no ending.
It needs to be cared for, it needs defending!
FREEDOM!

Commuters vs. the Black Ball Line

Washington Purchases the Puget Sound Ferries

William J. Gore and Evelyn Shipman

Introduction

ON JANUARY 1, 1951, the ferry system serving the Puget Sound area in the State of Washington was transferred from private to public ownership and operation. The flag of the Black Ball Line, after dominating Puget Sound waters for half a century, gave way to the Washington State Ferry System.

The transfer came after nearly ten years of public controversy ranging from the acrimonious to the explosive. During this period, and as late as 1957, there were conflicting concepts of just what the underlying issue really was. In broadest terms this is a story of the clash between public desire for improved transportation across Puget Sound and the unyielding yet unacceptable realities of economic cost. In this sense, the story of the fight between two of Washington's governors and the head of the Black Ball Ferry Line is a product of basic transit problems which may be found in many metropolitan areas, signified by protests against rising fares and sometimes by simultaneous demands for better service through public ownership and subsidy.

Historically, ferries met a vital need of Puget Sound communities, just as ferries were once integral to the San Francisco Bay area. They began to fall short of service acceptable to Puget Sound users as the automobile came into increasing use, as the highway system was refined and enlarged, and as the pace of commuting and travel accelerated. A collision between clientele and ferry system operator was probably inevitable. But such a collision need not lead to state ownership. It did not, for example, in New York where the state sought to revive the crippled Long Island Railway by authorizing it to raise rail fares. The ferry issue in Washington, however, scarcely broke the surface before citizens' groups, *ad hoc* commuter bodies, organized labor, farm groups, and business leaders became involved. They made it and kept it a major political issue. "The government" had to do something, they insisted. Government—city, county, and state—had to take cognizance of these demands. According to where one sat, the question varied from one of private enterprise vs. creeping socialism, of businesslike management vs. state subsidy and operation of a public service, of an uncomplicated demand by an outraged clientele for better service at pre-war prices vs. the realities of post-war costs, or of an issue blown up for reasons of political expediency. All of these viewpoints, and many refinements of them, were present. The object of this study is to describe how public policy was formed on this thorny and not uncomplicated problem.

The Black Ball Ferries

THE PUGET SOUND BASIN is a gentle land of meadow and forest, in pleasant contrast to the dramatic peaks of Mount Rainier and Mount Baker on one hand and the arid, treeless plains in western Washington on the other. The basin lies between the Cascade and Coast mountain ranges, extending about 100 miles south from the Strait of Juan de Fuca and Canada. Puget Sound is about 80 miles long and 25 miles wide; its numerous arms form a fine natural harbor system, and more than 300 islands dot its expanse. Seattle is the largest city on the Sound. It is the center of a metropolitan area of over 1,000,000 people.

The Alaska gold rush of the 1890s found Seattle a frontier settlement and left it a major port

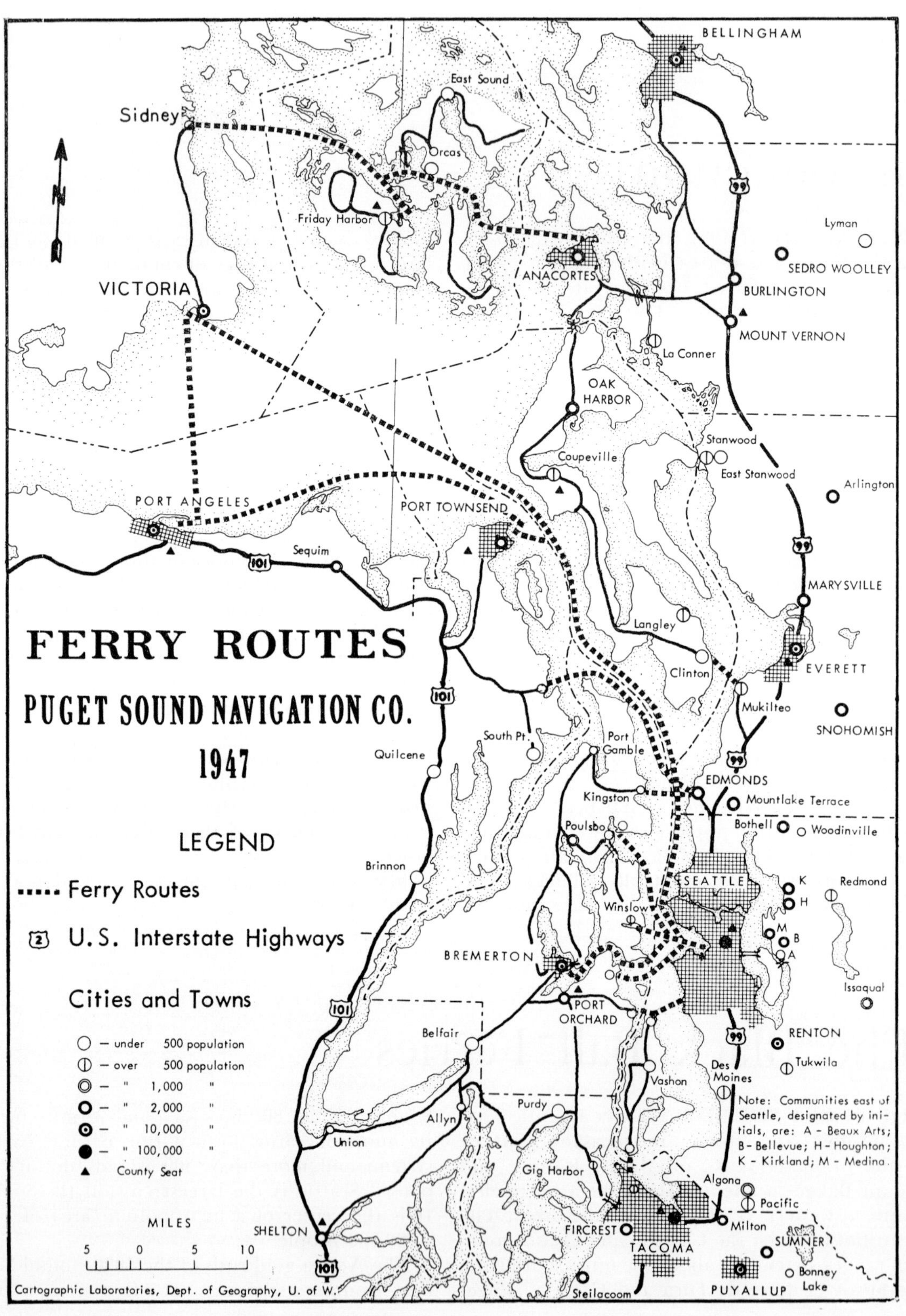
FERRY ROUTES
PUGET SOUND NAVIGATION CO.
1947
LEGEND
Ferry Routes
U.S. Interstate Highways
Cities and Towns
— under 500 population
— over 500 population
— " 1,000 "
— " 2,000 "
— " 10,000 "
— " 100,000 "
County Seat
MILES
5 0 5 10
Cartographic Laboratories, Dept. of Geography, U. of W.
BELLINGHAM
East Sound
Sidney
Orcas
Friday Harbor
ANACORTES
VICTORIA
Lyman
SEDRO WOOLLEY
BURLINGTON
MOUNT VERNON
La Conner
OAK HARBOR
Coupeville
Stanwood
East Stanwood
Arlington
PORT ANGELES
PORT TOWNSEND
Sequim
MARYSVILLE
Langley
Clinton
EVERETT
Mukilteo
SNOHOMISH
South Pt.
Port Gamble
Quilcene
EDMONDS
Kingston
Mountlake Terrace
Bothell
Woodinville
Poulsbo
Brinnon
SEATTLE
Redmond
Winslow
BREMERTON
PORT ORCHARD
Issaquah
Belfair
RENTON
Tukwila
Vashon
Des Moines
Purdy
Allyn
Union
Note: Communities east of Seattle, designated by initials, are: A - Beaux Arts; B - Bellevue; H - Houghton; K - Kirkland; M - Medina.
Gig Harbor
Algona
Pacific
Milton
SHELTON
FIRCREST
TACOMA
SUMNER
Bonney Lake
Steilacoom
PUYALLUP

city. Its economy, based on agriculture and timber, flourished and expanded. Water transportation was essential. The land was honeycombed with small waterways in addition to the two major bodies of water, Puget Sound and twenty-mile long Lake Washington that lay along both sides of Seattle's string of hills. Settlement tended to concentrate on the waterfront, and most movement of both people and goods was by boat.

In 1896, as the gold rush was subsiding, a man named Peabody appeared upon the Seattle scene. He descended from a sea captain named Marshall, who had figured in the pre-Revolutionary War merchant trade between the American colonies and England. Some years after the Revolution, Marshall and three associates, observing that there were no scheduled trans-Atlantic sailings from the young America, acquired four ships, and, doing business as the Black Ball Line, inaugurated regular runs between New York and Liverpool. Civil War blockades brought an end to this enterprise, but the family shipping tradition survived. The Peabody who migrated to Seattle was quick to appraise Puget Sound transportation needs, and the Puget Sound Navigation Company was founded by him in 1900. Flying the Black Ball flag,[1] it operated around the Sound, touching at numerous points in Washington and in British Columbia to the north.

The line prospered with the area. The ferries, friendly and dependable, were a social institution as they plied their leisurely runs along the coast. Many Seattle residents built summer homes and even year-round residences on the Sound's islands, with assurance of comfortable commuting between home and Seattle by ferry. Not a few of them had private docks where the ferries stopped on signal. By 1913, the volume of this business caused the company to have six new steamers built.

But in the next decade, the pattern changed. World War I brought the automobile to dominance. Little "coasters" became obsolete. The company acquired a new fleet, one capable of transporting cars. By so doing, it placed itself sufficiently ahead of highway development so that the capacity of its fleet remained adequate for some ten years. Not until 1930 did the auto traffic entering the ferry terminals begin to strain the capacity of the Black Ball fleet.

The 1920s also brought changes in Puget Sound traffic patterns that affected ferry operation. Roads and highways were fast being built, and the demand for coastal water transportation fell off sharply. The north-south runs of the "coasters" were rapidly becoming superfluous. The need was for east-west, or cross-Sound, runs by large car ferries.

During the 1920s also, a new figure succeeded to the leadership of the Puget Sound Navigation Company. With the death of Peabody Sr., his son, Captain Alex M. Peabody became Secretary of the company and three years later, President.

Alex Peabody had inherited the family marine tradition. He had been to sea as a World War I Navy captain (and ever after retained both the title and the aura of authority), and was representing a ship brokerage company at the time his father died. He was, and is, a large-framed man with a forceful bass voice and a strong personality. Impatient with formalities, Peabody had a deep dedication to the free enterprise system. Many Seattleites who knew him saw in Peabody, with his homburg, his prominent if not meticulously-groomed mustache, his expensive cigars, and his individualism, some resemblance to the captains of industry of earlier days.

Captain Peabody soon found that underlying the problems of Black Ball management was a Basin-wide transportation problem that required for solution a dozen or more large, speedy automobile-carrying ferries. But traffic volume would not support construction of enough of these vessels to meet the problem. The Captain balanced on the horn of this dilemma for ten years before San Francisco attacked its own ferry problem by constructing in 1937 the Bay Bridge and thereby released a substantial portion of the Southern Pacific ferry fleet. Peabody bought. Eight of the second-hand vessels were delivered in 1937 and placed in immediate service; four were added in 1938, and five in 1941-42. The company's investment was only a fraction of what it would have had to pay to build new vessels, and Peabody gained a reputation for astute financial management.

[1] The line was incorporated as the Puget Sound Navigation Company, and this was properly its name for as long as it operated on the Sound. Because of the flag, however, the name "Black Ball" early came into common usage. Wherever it appears in this text, it refers to the Puget Sound Navigation Company.

Between 1935 and 1937, strikes idled the ferries from time to time, inconveniencing most commuters and irritating some of them immensely. In 1937, under the pressure of complaints from the public, the State Department of Transportation (charged with regulation of the rates of public transport franchise holders) undertook an examination of the line's operating costs, revenue needs, and fare structure. The outcome was a rate revision agreed to by company, Department, and commuter representatives. The revision took into account not only current costs but the trends anticipated in that pre-war time. During these negotiations Peabody also secured a "closed" (exclusive) "certificate of convenience" from the state to carry freight between Seattle and Bremerton, largest city in Kitsap County and site of the Puget Sound Naval Shipyard.

World War II traffic generated commuter patterns most favorable to the ferry system. The recently-acquired equipment was adequate to cope with the war traffic, and the company entered a very profitable period. Mushrooming employment at the Naval Shipyard in Bremerton brought mass commuting of foot passengers between Seattle and Bremerton. Rationed gasoline curtailed automobile movement, especially on the unprofitable outlying ferry runs. Traffic concentrated in the Seattle terminal where the company could handle it most effectively. Intensified shipyard activity also brought a booming freight business. The revenue picture was, on the whole, so favorable that Peabody assented to Navy and local requests that he reduce fares on the Seattle-Bremerton run to facilitate shipyard recruitment. These reductions, made on a yearly renewable basis, eventually amounted to about thirty percent.

In almost every respect the climate of wartime ferry operations was friendly. The public reacted favorably toward Black Ball because it was, they felt, doing the best it could within the limits of a war economy. Substantial increases in traffic brought concomitant increases in the number of trips on the large-volume runs, so wartime service was in one respect better than pre-war service. For his part, Captain Peabody was at pains to meet the commuters' needs, if not in style and comfort then with safety and convenience.

The end of the war brought an immediate change in the *rapport* between the line and its clientele. Subtle cracks began developing immediately. Black Ball patronage fell off sharply as production in the Navy yard was drastically cut back. Puget Sound's defense-based economy was brought to a climactic, if temporary, halt by wholesale termination of Boeing contracts (for the Superfortress bomber) and similar terminations throughout the rest of the area. It was inevitable that there would shortly follow talk of reducing the number of trips on several of the most heavily-traveled ferry routes.

Black Ball could ill afford the cessation of hostilities, for this portended the re-emergence of its difficulties of trying to survive in an economy built around the gasoline engine. It faced the depressing prospect of an even greater volume of automobile traffic, further geographic dispersion of its patronage, higher operating costs, and a public demand for a level of services beyond what revenues alone would support.

But the storms of acrimonious feeling which were soon to explode against Black Ball and Captain Peabody were not just economic and technological in origin. They represented the release of an accumulation of wartime strains and stresses triggered by the forbidding expectation of local economic crisis.

The average Seattleite was looking forward to a breather. As the war ended, he anticipated letting down a bit and living the good life of the Northwest: skiing, a hike up to a trout-filled lake, a Sunday afternoon ride on the ferry, trips to the family "summer place," a spin in someone's boat.

Black Ball confronted an even more explosive, though as yet unarticulated, public expectation. The attitude of the public toward Black Ball in the thirties had been dour and even threatening. Early in the war public attitudes had changed. But 1946 showed that the commuter had merely called a truce "for the duration." When Captain Peabody announced a reduction in the number of trips on the Fauntleroy-Harper-Vashon run in May, 1946, the pre-war grumble suddenly reappeared as a menacing growl—brought on by the clash between the reality of a possible reduction in service and the public's expectation not only of a sustained level of service, but of increased trips by modern, stylish, and comfortable vessels.

Without appreciating the extent of public expectations, Captain Peabody, in December 1946, took two actions to adjust to the increasing rate at which traffic was falling off. Two days after Christmas he announced that the company would shortly apply to the Department of Transportation, as a rate regulator, for rate increases to cover wage increases. Three days later he served notice that the full pre-war passenger rates—almost forgotten by many members of the public as they accepted the voluntary wartime reductions—would be restored on New Year's Day of 1947.

Government Is Involved, 1947-1948

BY THE BEGINNING OF 1947, people of the Puget Sound Basin generally perceived cross-Sound transportation as a problem with some urgency about it. Ferry-users took up and vigorously discussed random dissatisfactions with Black Ball's service; Chambers of Commerce, service clubs, and similar organizations registered the dissatisfaction, and protests of these groups commanded attention at all levels of government in the state. Since the geographical area of controversy encompassed several counties and municipalities, and especially because only the state had legal power over the company's operations, public pressure was directed particularly to the state and the administration of Democratic Governor Mon C. Wallgren.

At this time, Governor Wallgren was nearing sixty. He had been elected to Congress in 1932 and served in the House until 1942, when he was elected to the Senate. In 1944, he defeated incumbent Republican Arthur Langlie for the governorship.

Mon C. Wallgren had been a political figure in Washington state politics for more than a generation. Rigorous party discipline is unknown in Washington state. Political leaders tend to build personal alliances with the leaders of such interest groups as the Grange, the American Legion, the State Chamber of Commerce, and the trade unions as well as with independently powerful business, labor, and farm leaders. The typical Washington voter tends to regard himself as a political independent rather than as a party-line voter.

Wallgren thrived in this political environment. He was unruffled when opponents characterized his espousal of liberalism as New Dealism. He was proud of his part in the Roosevelt era and believed his election as Governor demonstrated the popularity of the liberal viewpoint in the state.

Easygoing, his heavy frame built along classic Scandinavian lines, Wallgren believed several other things about state politics. He felt that his constituents were of several minds about government in general and state government in particular. While they would support the nation's most generous welfare program for the aged, the blind, and the children of broken families, they would not give approval to plans for the effective supervision and control of the state's forest lands and timber—a matter much closer to their pocketbooks. Some part of his effectiveness as a political leader, Wallgren believed, stemmed from the fact that, after his commitment to liberal political principles, his second commitment was to the will of the people as he could ascertain it. Such a commitment came naturally to Wallgren after his many years of legislative experience. The Governor was skilled in the practice of sending up "trial balloons," or revealing his own programs at about the pace that strong public sentiment was forming behind them.

During 1946, many persons the Governor saw, both in his office and socially, registered complaints about Black Ball, and these he accepted with the good-humored patience developed during his years as a Representative and Senator. That this dissatisfaction was widespread among people living around the rim of Puget Sound was clear. The fact that a number of the community leaders Wallgren knew personally raised this matter gave it something of the status of a community problem that deserved his concern if not his immediate attention. And from all of these contacts the Governor gathered that the central point of the matter was that the public hoped the state's Department of Transportation would force Black Ball to increase its level of service but not its fares.

Puget Sound was, however, only a portion, if an important one, of the state, and the Governor, while considering the matter and discussing it informally with his top associates, refrained from overt action. He had not yet enough evidence to convince him that he was confronted here with more than a passing irritation. Besides, he had several pressing major policy issues to deal with. These included rebuilding the state's highway system, which had been neglected during the war, and stimulating the state's economic development against the post-war economic readjustment which was expected to be painful sooner or later.

The Company Asks for Higher Fares

January 1, 1947 saw the restoration of pre-war passenger rates on Puget Sound Navigation Company ferries. At this time, too, the company was negotiating wages with the Inland Boatmen's Union which represented most "above-decks" personnel. On January 9, the Union formally rejected a company offer of a ten percent wage increase, demanding instead an increase of $36 a month and a six-day week. It gave notice of intent to strike if these demands were not met. On January 14, the company tentatively accepted. January 16, in accordance with Captain Peabody's earlier warning, the company applied to the State Department of Transportation for what amounted to a thirty percent increase over the pre-war fares then being charged.

This application was approved on a contingent basis pending a complete study of company finances. Increased rates were to go into effect February 15. In announcing the Department's action, Director Paul Revelle said: "Should the increase ultimately allowed be less than 30%, Black Ball should be prepared to refund the difference paid by commuters in the interim, and should post a bond which will insure its capacity to refund." (See Appendix Two for a detailed account of the manner in which the Department made its study and for a description of the way the rates were determined.)

The moderate tone of Revelle's response found no public counterpart. The Chamber of Commerce of Vashon Island, one of the important island communities served by the ferries, mirrored popular reaction when it stated: "We condemn the proposed ferry rate increase as suicide and apt to reduce residence on Puget Sound islands to summer vacation status." Many individual commuters and shippers spoke in even stronger terms, frankly rebellious at the prospect of paying "tribute" for a service with which they were dissatisfied at best. Announcement by the Vashon Chamber of plans to organize a group to oppose the rate increase was enthusiastically received; most people regarded it as a move long overdue.

On February 11, the Vashon Chamber sponsored a meeting of representatives of civic groups from Bremerton, Bainbridge Island, Port Angeles, and other cities around the Sound. Captain Peabody was invited to state his position to this unsympathetic group, and he did. He urged them to recognize the economic reality of his company's situation; it was operating at a monthly loss of $125,000; quite possibly it could not have survived without the restoration of the pre-war rates six weeks before. This explanation did not influence the assembled community leaders. To them Peabody appeared as an unyielding company spokesman "playing the blues." They were almost unanimous in their belief that Peabody could provide better service at less cost if he only tried. To a public which believed Black Ball had made millions during the war, Peabody's comments on economic realities and losses lacked credibility. Those at the meeting agreed to form a permanent council of Olympic Peninsular civic, business and farm groups to press their views. As a first move, they decided to organize an automobile caravan to the state capitol at Olympia to dramatize their demand for suspension of permission for increased ferry rates.

The caravan was not successful in forcing the state administration into the fray. There were long delays in getting off, lack of agreement on what to say and who was to say it, and finally pleasant talks with numerous officials all of whom professed jurisdictional inability to act conclusively. In every other respect the expedition was a striking success. Press coverage was full and often flamboyant. The gist of the reporting was that the Vashon Islanders were finally going to do something about the ferry line. At this news, groups, clubs, and associations of all kinds in communities around Puget Sound began to devote meetings to discussions of the "ferry problem."

It is not without significance that the initiative came from Vashon Island. The top rank of the leadership of the Seattle metropolitan area lived in three exclusive residential sections inside or near the city limits and was not dependent upon the ferries for commuting. Captain Peabody, but not the Democratic Governor, moved freely *socially* among these leaders. He was one of them. He shared their interests—some of them tangibly. At this point, these leaders shared Peabody's view that the public did not understand the problems of businessmen and that the agitation would sooner or later pass away.

The NWCC Is Created

Vashon Island is one of the very desirable residential spots in the region. Among its residents were a dozen substantial citizens who stand just below the top group of 60-100 leaders of the metropolitan area. In general, these people were younger and more aggressive than those in the top leadership stratum. Affiliated with these Vashon Island leaders were a larger number of local businessmen whose economic future depended on the Island being a year-round community rather than just a summer colony and a week-end resort. During the winter they invested their time in the commuter project. Vashon Island Chamber of Commerce became the initial organizational mechanism for mobilizing these sources of opposition to fare increases. The community itself was loosely structured, but it was in the formal councils of the island community that the consensus evolved that something "drastic" had to be done. Initially, in the absence of agreement on just what should be done, various groups started their own projects. Shop owners, real estate brokers, and some of the Island's professional men organized the Olympia caravan. Another group, including some of the more substantial citizens of the Island, sought to determine what top leaders in the metropolitan area felt could be done and whether other groups around the Sound would be interested in forming an area-wide organization. The activity of this group set off a wave of discussions in communities all around Puget Sound. Less than two weeks after the caravan to Olympia, representatives of many of these groups met and formed the Northwest Washington Community Council.

The caravan had highlighted the fact that the State Department of Transportation had statutory authority only to review and regulate Black Ball's activities. Thwarted by this limitation, some of the most vociferous citizens were demanding that the state take over the ferry system. This was considered to be at best the view of a few "hot-heads," but some Vashon lawyers joined by some colleagues from the mainland formulated a bill which would authorize the Department of Highways to operate a ferry system. NWCC formally presented this bill to the Legislature which was then in session. This bill authorized the state to purchase vessels and operate a ferry system.

In general the bill was sympathetically received. But it encountered some resistance from rural eastern Washington legislators. Their constituents were not directly concerned with Puget Sound water transport, and they feared the enabling legislation might be a first step toward a state ferry operation subsidized by gasoline tax revenues which would otherwise have been used for highway construction. A compromise bill, passed February 26, 1947, authorized the creation of special districts empowered to operate ferries. This bill was endorsed by the State Grange and other farm groups.

The Legislature did more. A special committee of the House of Representatives examined the record in the rate increase matter and, after being informed that the Department of Transportation would require about four months to make its study of the company books, stated its conclusion that "the Department . . . acted wisely in permitting a temporary 30% increase in rates." The day after the passage of the special ferry district bill this committee recommended that the State Highway Director study the feasibility of state operation of ferries on routes where rates were inequitable.

Thus NWCC, in existence only two weeks, could claim concrete achievement in the Legislature. It had also issued and obtained much publicity. It had won enthusiastic response from civic groups around the Sound, and claimed to represent 150,000 ferry patrons and Olympic Peninsula residents; shortly it was to claim the support of 48 civic organizations. The principle that state government should protect the commuter-shipper interest had been stated, and the Legislature had accepted its legitimacy. The climate of opinion was sympathetic to government officials who could and were disposed to intervene in the matter. Finally, the ferry issue had been pushed up near the top of a hypothetical list of major policy problems requiring prompt governmental attention.

This seemed a creditable record. Even so, Captain Peabody has said: "Up to this time, this outfit was more in my hair than a threat to my company." Two factors prevented NWCC from realizing its full potential of influence. First, it was a confederation of groups. Some of its leaders had less status than various individuals in its member groups and were consequently limited in their plenipotentiary roles. A second and more apparent deficiency was that NWCC had reached no real agreement on a solution to the ferry problem. Its membership was united in a strong drive to resolve the problem permanently, and this enthusiasm triggered a concomitant public expectation. But within NWCC were adherents for a variety of solutions ranging from closer state regulation of Black Ball on the one hand to the elimination of ferries by great cross-Sound bridges on the other.

Events soon impelled NWCC's members to agree on something, if only temporarily. On February 28, the ferries were tied up from noon until 7:00 p.m. Two weeks' notice of this stoppage had been given by the Marine Engineers' Union of "below decks" personnel who had not been covered by the January negotiations. No strike occurred, but the episode was regarded by the commuting public as symbolic of the trouble suffered from the ferry system, company and unions alike. This atmosphere of grievance (unaffected by Captain Peabody's protestations that the company was "taking it on the chin for something the union did") caused NWCC to offer a tentative solution: "We propose to place the ferries under the Washington Tollbridge Authority.[2] We believe no legislative authorization is necessary to carry out this program."

With the Legislature adjourned, little could be done until the Department of Transportatio completed its examination of PSNC's financia situation. Meanwhile, labor demands had bee met, fares sixty percent above 1946 rates wer being charged, and commuters took such comfor as they could from the refund coupon accompanying each ticket which symbolized potentia state intervention.

In early May, Revelle announced that his Department's investigation was nearing completion and a public hearing on the Company's application for a thirty percent increase above pre-wa rates was set for June 4. Response to this announcement put both Revelle and Captain Peabody on notice that the hearing would not be perfunctory negotiation between company an Department. On May 17, NWCC filed with th Department a Petition to Intervene (as a forma participant) in the hearing. Informally, NWCC leaders declared that they proposed to demonstrate that Captain Peabody was taking ruthles advantage of a captive public. Peabody countered with an assertion that he welcomed th opportunity to put the company's position o record and to acquaint the public with "the economic realities of water transport on Puge Sound."

Peabody's role as a victim of circumstances wa to be prejudiced in the public view before thi opportunity was granted him. On May 2 Revelle ordered him to come before the Department June 2, two days in advance of the hearing to explain why Black Ball had not fully complie with the order authorizing a temporary rate increase. Specifically, the company was charge (1) with disregarding the stipulation that i should set aside the extra income received fron the tentative increase pending final establishmen of new rates, and (2) with failure to post a bon to insure its capacity to make whatever refun was directed. Neither Peabody's bearing at th hearing nor his testimony suggested compunction at the implied criticism. He asserted tha his company had no choice but to use the additional revenues; the alternative would have bee to cease operations. With respect to the bonc

[2] An independent, corporation-type agency of the Stat of Washington. It had built and operated several su cessful toll bridges, notably the Lake Washington floatin bridge.

he held there had been a misunderstanding; the company would post it promptly upon formal notice from the Department as to the proper procedure.

The Public Hearing

The public hearing on the rate increase request opened in the Seattle City Hall on June 4, as scheduled. Stewart Krieger, who, as chief accountant of the Department of Transportation, had directed the investigation of Black Ball's finances, was at hand with several staff assistants and the long-awaited report. Captain Peabody, his accountants, and his legal counsel were ranged against the law firm representing NWCC.

For several days proceedings were confined to consideration of the line's financial position. Krieger took the stand first. His 253-page report sketched the company's corporate and financial organization, and described its property, operating revenues, taxes, depreciation reserves, and, finally, its "Operating Income and Rate of Return."

On the basis of these data, Krieger made positive replies to several key questions. Of the level of service, he said: "If the present schedules were reduced, it would bring about more frequent instances of cars being left on docks (which now occurs during peak hours on Sunday) and result in further inconvenience to the public. Unless carefully planned, any curtailment of present service should not be considered." Expanded service, he testified, would necessitate purchase of more vessels.

With respect to company earnings, Krieger cited the Department's finding that net earnings on capital investment dropped from 14.1% in 1945 to 10.9% in 1946. Inquiry brought out the fact that the company had paid no dividends from 1930 to 1940, and an average four percent per year in the period 1940-47.

Krieger pointed out that the Department's investigation had disclosed that six of the company's twelve routes had operated at a loss in 1946.[3] He suggested that this indicated that the thirty percent rate increase applied for "was justified and should be allowed to stand."

[3] Seattle-Bainbridge, Seattle-Victoria, Mukilteo-Columbia Beach, Seattle-Suquamish, Bremerton-Point White, and Tahlequah-Point Defiance.

On the third day, the hearing dealt with the question of the rate at which the company was depreciating vessels (both steel and wooden), terminals, office equipment, and motor vehicle equipment. It was a popular allegation that Peabody had built his fleet from "scrap vessels at scrap values" but was depreciating them on the basis of their full original cost (in the 1920s) and, worse still, that he sought to depreciate at 1947 replacement value. If the useful life of a wooden vessel was thirty years, an estimate upon which company and Department agreed, the company was building an excessive reserve by annually setting aside one-thirtieth of the $500,000 initial (1920) cost of such a vessel, instead of one-thirtieth of the $100,000 that the company had, on the average, paid for it.[4] NWCC suggested pointedly that some part of this depreciation fund could probably be found in dividends to stockholders. In rebuttal the company contended, and Krieger's staff agreed, that replacement costs of vessels would be double or triple initial costs, even at the same specifications, and these specifications were inadequate in terms of current needs. Most of the fleet, of post World War I vintage, had been designed to carry from forty to sixty automobiles of the dimensions of the Ford Model A.[5] The traffic density of the late 1940s called for "floating parking lots," capable of carrying two or three times that number of the longer, wider modern cars. Five hundred thousand dollars would hardly buy one.

Elaborating his position, Krieger pointed out that the examiner's recommendation that the full thirty percent rate raise be allowed did not follow from any single finding in the investigations but from the pattern of the whole problem. Because no one knew just what the profile of future traffic levels would be, it was not possible to state that the company would cease to exist if the raise were refused. But if, as Peabody expected, the present trends in ferry usage persisted, it was obvious that the company could not survive as a self-supporting enterprise.

This was, however, a moot question. The pub-

[4] See Appendix Two for details.

[5] Automobile passengers frequently had difficulty getting out of their cars when the auto deck of one of these vessels was fully loaded. Vehicles were so closely parked that doors could be opened only twelve or fourteen inches.

lic was dissatisfied with "scrap vessels." If there was a demand for "floating parking lots with plushy cocktail lounges, running every fifteen minutes instead of on the hour," the public would have to expect to pay for them and the rate increase Peabody requested was modest enough.

If Krieger was satisfied with the facts the investigation had uncovered, NWCC was not. Its facts were the feelings and convictions of its clientele, not figures or charts. A Seattle dairy products distributor was called to the stand. He testified that almost a third of his business was in Kitsap County and that increased ferry rates would "result in additional costs which would lower my return," with the clear implication that he would not, because he could not, tolerate this kind of a curb on his business. A Puget Sound Naval Shipyard employee stated that a "raise in rates actually means a reduction in our earnings." Like hundreds of other shipyard workers, this man was unwilling to see his earnings reduced to fatten, as he believed, the pockets of Black Ball stockholders. The Secretary of the Bremerton Council of Metal Trades Unions—a group of unions representing the critical skills in the shipyard's operations—appeared to state the Council's position: "The people are entitled to ferry service. If the Puget Sound Navigation Company cannot afford to provide us with transportation at a reasonable cost, the State must take over." Next, Thomas Revelle, (brother of the Director of the Department), a real estate broker on Vashon Island, appeared and declared that property values on the Island had declined since the imposition of the temporary fare increase because otherwise willing buyers found transportation costs excessive. Many others testified, all rejecting Krieger's findings and demanding that the existing rate level be frozen.

The hearings ended with disagreement clearly outlined: the public demanding a denial of the application for rate increase, and Black Ball insisting that continued service required it.

Revelle Issues an Order

Revelle, Kreiger, and their staff returned to Olympia to review the situation. Pressure from NWCC was constant and substantial throughout this period. Consultations with other top officials in the administration showed widely divergent views; there was no firm administration policy on the matter. Persons who had access to Revelle because of his previous involvement with the Democratic Party continued to exert such influence as they could on his review of the situation. Though they expressed general sympathy with the "little man," they all had different—frequently vague—solutions to suggest. Revelle reported to Governor Wallgren and discussed the situation with him. Both were impressed with the gap between the financial data and the sentiments of the public. Wallgren was impressed with the commuter's needs; yet the facts established by his own examiners could not be dismissed. He told Revelle to exercise his own best judgment and assured him that he would support his decision.

On July 3 Revelle issued a formal Departmental order:

(1) Allowing Black Ball a ten percent increase over the January (or pre-war) rates. (This reduced by two-thirds the increase allowed in his temporary order of February 15.)

(2) Stipulating that the company make appropriate refunds to all ferry patrons presenting valid refund coupons.

From the public this order received a generally favorable reaction. In the order Revelle noted he was allowing the company a 6.04% return on cash investment (assuming minimal depreciation rates), and this was regarded as equitable by those who believed the company was entitled to a measure of financial relief. The modest increase did not, at the same time, offend those who held the prevailing conviction that the ferry operation had been highly remunerative over the years at the expense of commuter and shipper—the customers for whom they felt the company was neglecting to provide first-class service even when (they assumed) funds were available. The favorable public reaction also reflected gratification that an agency of government was sufficiently concerned with the public interest to intervene on behalf of a segment of the citizenry which felt it was powerless to protect its own interests.

The company's initial reaction was one of surprise. Captain Peabody thought the Krieger report substantially justified the company's position, and he had expected that Revelle's decision would be principally influenced by it. He was not in the least disposed to accept the order as a fair and just compromise, but, upon receipt of the order, said, "We'll be swamped Monday with rebate applications. All we can do is tell the people we're not going to make the refunds until after this is settled in court."

By this time Peabody's concern for his company's financial well-being was matched by his concern for the fundamental issue as he saw it: whether an agency of government was to be allowed to intervene between a business and its clientele. In his view, he had been saddled with a confiscatory rate structure as a result of his customers' political pressure upon the rate-making agency. He was convinced that NWCC, as the primary pressure group, had exerted its influence without caring whether it put the company out of business by so doing. Some basis for his conviction may be found in the statement of a Bremerton businessman (member of NWCC) about this time: "It isn't good for one individual to have the control Peabody has over this town. I wish Peabody would throw in the sponge and let the state take over." Another businessman said: "We are not getting our money's worth. I favor state control." The Mayor of Bremerton declared, "People here are tired of the Puget Sound Navigation Company using the [heavily traveled] Bremerton route to subsidize other Puget Sound runs."

On July 21, Black Ball's attorneys filed with the Thurston County Superior Court both a Writ of Review, for judicial examination of all aspects of the matter, and a Writ of Supersedeas, for a stay of the effect of the order until they could prepare and present their case demonstrating that the order had the effect of confiscating company property. On July 23, they filed with the Department of Transportation a petition for rehearing on the original application. On the NWCC side, Vashon attorney Charles Law applied on July 28 to the State Supreme Court for a Writ of Prohibition, which would restrain the company from continuing to collect fares at the level allowed by Revelle's temporary order of the previous February. The Supreme Court refused to intervene. On the same date, Thurston County Superior Court heard the company attorneys, accepted the legitimacy of their plea, and granted the company a Writ of Supersedeas against the Departmental order until the court could make a complete review of the law and the fact involved.

Peabody Threatens to Halt Service

While these legal negotiations were going on, both parties engaged in a diversionary skirmish from which the company emerged less confidently. On July 17, when company stockholders met and authorized legal action, Captain Peabody announced that if the court did not set aside the Departmental order by August 3 the company would tie up the ferries. NWCC promptly countered this threat with a resolution to the State Tollbridge Authority demanding that the state operate the ferries if such a suspension of service occurred. It urged the state, further, to begin an immediate exploration of ways of purchasing the ferry system. This led company counsel to issue a statement that the ferries would not be tied up, whatever the outcome of the court action.

The contest seemed to be at a temporary impasse, but neither side was idle while awaiting the Superior Court hearing in December. NWCC leaders addressed themselves to Governor Wallgren in a series of conferences, and apparently succeeded in impressing him with the breadth and depth of public opinion as they represented it. On August 4, he stated for publication that the state might be forced to enter the ferry business. NWCC leaders took this as an affirmation of their emerging position. September 1, as though to demonstrate the "economic realities" of its plight to Bremerton commuters, the company removed one ferry from the Bremerton-Seattle run. Later in September, a group of Vashon Island residents, encouraged by NWCC but upon their own initiative, organized a ferry district under the legislative authorization of the previous March. This group took its action by vote of 326 to 38, stating ". . . if Black Ball's fare increase goes through, we think we can operate our own ferry more economically . . . ," but ". . . state purchase smells of creeping socialism."

Top Leadership Is Aroused

These surface eruptions began to be reflected in the community as a whole. Two years had passed since the matter had initially flared, but now as the ferry situation festered into a major and urgent problem, the leadership of the community modified its stance. Where initially the matter was considered one of those passing flare-ups which only temporarily disrupt public equanimity, it had now attained such a momentum and intensity that some members of the top strata of community leadership felt their intervention might be needed to find a solution. They began to search for an answer.

The people involved were the heads of the city's largest manufacturing and retail establishments, its largest and most responsible labor unions, owners and instrumental officials of the local newspapers, a number of professional men, and a handful of top political figures. These same people were also those responsible for the leadership of the United Community Fund, the Friends of the Library, and the Symphony Association. They were the prime movers behind the Municipal League and other "good government" organizations. Some of them were also key figures, mostly behind the scenes, in the two political parties. They represented, in short, a fluid reservoir of leadership through which most of the stable civic and community groups were led, and, incidentally, through which their activities were co-ordinated in a loose way. Their common pursuits, on both the professional and avocational sides, brought them into frequent contact with each other. In addition, nearly all of them were members of the Rainier Club and met there for meals or other occasions. Finally, most of them also maintained an active membership in either the Chamber of Commerce or the Central Labor Council, or, in a few cases, both. Peabody and Wallgren both participated actively in the discussions of some of the cliques and subgroups of this top strata of community leadership. The NWCC official leadership was not included in this circle.

Since the membership of this circle penetrated every group, firm, agency, and association in the community, information began to pour in as the ferry question came under more and more discussion, and these men came face to face with the dilemma Wallgren and Revelle had confronted several months earlier. They came, likewise, to the conclusion that the problem, in these terms, was insoluble. Something of their thinking is reflected in a by-line article by Ross Cunningham, Associate Editor of the *Seattle Times*—himself a member of this top strata of community leadership and in a sense a spokesman for them. Cunningham knew both Wallgren and Peabody well, and his treatment of the problem in the *Times* was as much motivated by his desire to provide some basis upon which these men might "get together" as it was to lay out the boundaries of the problem for the public.

Would State Operation Help?

Cunningham first reminded readers that, during the rebuilding of the Tacoma Narrows suspension bridge, the state had operated a small ferry across that narrow neck of water. The operation had lost $150,000 to $200,000 annually, the deficit being made up from gasoline tax revenues. Based upon his examination of the facts, he warned that the state, if it took over the PSNC operations, would probably be faced with an annual deficit of approximately $2,000,000. He suggested that it was unrealistic to expect to repair this loss from gasoline tax revenues; eastern Washington legislators were united in their opposition to use of the ear-marked gasoline tax funds for any purpose but highway construction. An alternative form of state operation, purchase and rehabilitation of the ferry system through funds derived from the sale of bonds, would still necessitate rates adequate to retire the bonds. On balance, Cunningham concluded, the ferry system, whether in private or public hands, had to be supported by the public, and higher rates were almost inevitable in either case as traffic volume diminished and operating costs increased.

Captain Peabody had spent many hours discussing the ferry matter with Cunningham and was pleased to see him take a stand consistent with the facts of the situation as he saw them. But if NWCC or the public were any nearer to accepting the "economic realities" Peabody and the *Times* publicly espoused, they gave little evidence of it, for on December 16, as Superior Court hearings opened, NWCC leaders declared their confidence in their position. The company's statements were less optimistic. A company attorney announced that an annual operating loss of $112,720 was anticipated even if the full increase of thirty percent over the 1937 rate base was allowed; at the ten percent increase, the deficit would amount to $770,600 a year.[6] This prospect would compel the company to cease operations despite its reluctance to do so. NWCC reiterated its charges that a monopoly sought to exploit further the captive commuter public.

The Superior Court hearing was concluded December 19; the court directed both parties to file briefs within twenty days.

The new year found Black Ball again in labor negotiations. On January 1, 1948, Captain Fox, business agent of the Inland Boatman's Union, received a letter from Captain Peabody which read, in part:

> . . . present rate schedules are insufficient for the company to meet a shifting labor cost. The Department of Transportation has ordered these rate schedules reduced and this order is being reviewed by the Superior Court. . . . Until adequate rate schedules are authorized by the Department of Transportation, it is necessary that wage costs be reduced to enable the company to continue to operate. . . . We hereby give notice . . . of our desire for a downward revision of wage costs to be made effective by reduction of wage rates and an increase in hours of employment paid at straight time rates.

Captain Fox, a short, aggressive man and a militant unionist who had fought with Peabody for twenty years to establish the rights of labor, shot back: "There is not a chance in the world that we would accept either wage reductions or do away with the 40-hour week. . . . It isn't our responsibility to see that the company has adequate rates. This is up to the state. On the basis of our study, we think that Peabody got a helluva bum deal from the state when they only granted him the 10% increase."

The business agent of the Marine Engineers' Union received the same letter, and made a similar statement: "[We know that] . . . Peabody is in a tough spot. But it isn't up to the unions to subsidize management, which he is, in effect, asking us to do."

6 On December 30, the company board of directors authorized Peabody to attempt to negotiate a loan of $2,000,000 to complete payment for a new vessel constructed for the Canadian run, and to provide a temporary cushion against operating losses.

The Court Rules Against Black Ball

Contracts of both unions provided for a thirty-day notice prior to opening wage negotiations. In this instance, negotiations were not instituted, for the Superior Court acted four days before the notice period expired. Action came in the form of a memorandum opinion, issued in advance of the formal opinion:

> I believe the Department, in determining the rate base in this case, has followed a correct and lawful procedure, and that part of the order will be affirmed. It is as much the duty of the Department to protect the customers . . . the rate payers . . . as it is to protect the interest of the company. If it shall finally be determined that the rate now enforced by the company is in excess of the lawful rate, the customer who has paid the excess should, in all fairness and equity, be repaid.

The court stated further that, upon the evidence, the company's claim for a thirty percent rate increase appeared to derive from a depreciation allowance based upon replacement costs of vessels. On this point, the court in effect agreed with NWCC, taking the position that actual cost, not replacement cost, was the proper basis for calculating the depreciation factor.

NWCC leaders were fully satisfied with this opinion. They regarded it as a further endorsement of their point of view, and it would accomplish the one objective accepted by the entire NWCC membership: to force the company to operate at "reasonable" rates.

Captain Peabody was not disposed to assent. A week after the memorandum opinion was handed down, he notified Governor Wallgren that the rate reduction and refund provision supported by the court would leave the company with a deficit in excess of $200,000 for 1947 and, on the basis of the company's projection, nearly $1,000,000 for 1948. Accordingly, he said, the state should be prepared ". . . to lease the company's vessels and facilities to the Washington Tollbridge Authority under terms and conditions which will insure a reasonable return on the property and continuation of the company's operations."

This letter brought statements from the Governor, and from two of his department heads as well. Wallgren labeled Peabody's proposal "silly," adding, "We are not taking over the ferries on a temporary basis. If we had wanted to do that, we would have taken them over during the war when they were making money." Revelle, regarding Peabody's statement as preliminary to a threat to suspend operations, reminded the public that state law did not permit a public utility to abandon service without permission of the state. The Director of Highways, less certain of the state's power to force the company to operate against its will, stated, after consulting his counsel, that the Tollbridge Authority would "probably take over operation of the Puget Sound Navigation Company if forced to do so."

The Captain Sets a Deadline

Revelle was concerned, since Peabody had told Editor Cunningham that "they might as well know I'll tie up those boats if they try to push this through," and Cunningham had passed the word along when he saw Wallgren. Peabody, though capable of a tactical threat, was not posing. He called a full meeting of the stockholders and proposed tying the vessels up at the end of the month. Some stockholders opposed any interruption of service, but the majority supported Peabody. It was decided to stop operations as of midnight Sunday, February 29. On February 15, 700 employees of the company received their notices.

When the company's intention was made public Revelle promptly and emphatically repeated, in a press release, his earlier assertion: "I don't believe the Puget Sound Navigation Company can legally cease to operate without the state's permission. As far as I am concerned, the company does not have that permission." He was, he added, prepared to go to court to force the company to continue operating. Governor Wallgren directed Revelle and the Attorney General to invoke all legal means of compelling the company to carry on ferry service. He said, however, that he realized there was a question of the state's authority to enforce this requirement. He added: "The state should have the power to condemn property for the inventory price, less depreciation. I think it is very silly that franchises should be issued in such a manner that it would be possible to hold a knife at the state's throat."

Peabody had gone too far as far as Revelle was concerned. His desire was that the Department of Transportation should treat all clients with scrupulous fairness and promptness. Revelle was generally considered to have supervised his comparatively small staff well before the ferry problem loomed up. And when his staff representatives, the Governor, and he himself had decided to examine and review Black Ball rates, he had made carefully explicit his intention that the review should be professionally competent, impartial, and just. He was proud that the review was generally accepted as fair and objective.

But Revelle felt that Peabody had tried to make his staff, his Department, and himself the issue. Peabody's attempt to personify his difficulty as stemming from "bureaucratic bungling in Olympia" and "proponents of creeping socialism" was irritating to Revelle. Wallgren sympathized with his associate but was more irked because the center of the storm of public opinion generated by Peabody's threat to tie up the system was clearly moving toward a demand for a final solution by the state administration.

The impact of Peabody's threat permeated every corner of the controversy. If the Captain reasoned that the average commuter would rather pay the higher fare than risk the inconvenience of disrupted ferry service, he was only partially accurate in his anticipation of the patrons' reactions which to him were always unpredictable. Reactions ranged from those who held that this was only a tactic which Peabody would not dare to carry off, to those who felt that the thing had gone too far and that some third party must be found immediately to settle the differences between the company and the Department, to those who uttered epithets, characterized Peabody as a tyrant, monopolist and worse, and swore to swim both ways if they had to rather than to capitulate to his demands. Some commuters began to look for new homes on the same side of the water as their work, and the trickle of prospective clients in island real estate offices virtually ceased.

What Can the State Do?

NWCC was strangely silent during this period. It was not, however, inactive. Delegation after delegation went to Olympia to consult with the

Governor, Revelle, the Director of Highways, and Assistant Attorneys General in an attempt to find some legal means of forcing Peabody to his knees or at least to continue operations.

Wallgren and Revelle consulted with these delegations, both as a means of plumbing their intentions and of seeking political support for some future move which would cope with the problem. They found NWCC representatives in belligerent, aggressive moods, but running off in several directions at the same time. NWCC, it appeared, was neutralized by its own inability to mobilize a clear majority behind one concrete line of action. At this time, many NWCC adherents spoke loudly of the state taking over the whole ferry operation, but to the seasoned Governor their words did not have a foundation in an understanding of the full consequences of state operation. Besides, he was not himself committed to the principle of state ownership unless there was absolutely no other avenue of solution, and this was far from certain at this time.

Other NWCC representatives demanded that Wallgren exercise his legal powers as Governor and protect the public from "the awful Captain," assuming that the Governor surely must have sufficient powers if he would but use them. To these the Governor explained his "knife at the throat" statement, and pointed out that the Legislature had not anticipated that someone would try to blackmail the State of Washington and had not specifically provided him with the power to seize the ferry system.

A growing number of NWCC members had committed themselves to ridding Puget Sound of Peabody, and while they might not be in favor of state ownership in principle, they now came to it reluctantly as a last-ditch means of defeating the Captain. But this group was not in control of the organization at this time. It was the moderates, the "let's take it one step at a time and not rush into anything" boys, as one pro-purchase leader put it, who held control—diffuse as it was.

These moderate leaders of NWCC and their influential neighbors, who were their means of access to the top strata of community leadership "downtown" on the mainland, were still assessing the situation. Aware that their authority and influence within the NWCC was limited largely to articulating the case against Peabody, they were searching for some resolution to the problem which was consistent with their own and their followers' ideology. To most of these men, "free enterprise" and "creeping socialism" meant just what they meant to Captain Peabody. Further, there was some concern about allowing the problem to become a political football, lest it never be resolved. Third-, fourth-, and even fifth-party intermediaries were intensely active between NWCC and Black Ball during this time. Peabody seemed quite reasonable, frequently sympathetic, with old friends with whom he had had business dealings over the past twenty years, but he was firm. To the proposal that he set back the date for a tie-up, he pointed out that he had already waited longer than he should have and that the company could not survive. To the proposal that he sit down with community leaders, who would then talk with Wallgren, he asked if this would change in any way the economic realities which were the heart of the problem. Nothing availed. Peabody would not or could not compromise. Time passed, and the termination of service was now imminent.

In an attempt to bring in a different kind of third party, State Senator Jack Rogers, chairman of the Legislature's Interim Committee studying the problem, offered to mediate between the company and the Department. At the same time, NWCC leaders went back to Olympia asking that something be done to provide for the continuation of ferry service. Wallgren was amenable, but said the matter was formally in Revelle's hands and *he* was very irritated with Peabody. The Attorney General was prevailed upon to ask Revelle to appoint a citizen board to review and, if possible, resolve the issues. Revelle was still adamant and stepped past the point of no return by saying, "Rate-making is a legislative function which has been delegated by the Legislature to my Department. It is clear that I have no authority to select a group of laymen to advise upon such a complicated situation as the making of rates for the ferry companies."

Up to this point the city as a whole had been interested but did not really believe that both sides would, in the end, carry through their threats. There was some basis for this feeling in that both the Department and Black Ball had been confidently telling associates that they were sure the other side would back down if the thing "comes right down to the wire." The public interest, they assumed, demanded it. But now the die appeared to be cast, and suddenly something that had been interesting reading became something that had to be settled. The tie-up could not be allowed to happen; it didn't make sense, said the average citizen.

On February 24, Black Ball employees demonstrated their loyalty to Peabody by presenting the Attorney General with a petition signed by 540 workers asking that the rate order be removed, and stating their conviction that the thirty percent increase was essential.

The Attorney General stated only Revelle could do this but that he was preparing to petition the court for a temporary restraining order, prohibiting cessation of service by the company. The next day Revelle, at an NWCC-sponsored meeting in Bremerton, stated that he was wholeheartedly in favor of compromise, but "the law doesn't allow any compromise. . . . Peabody is a law violator." The Director of Highways, also present at this meeting, assured the group that the state was actively exploring means of acquiring ferry equipment. "We can't tell what we've done because we can't tilt our hand to Peabody. But we have plenty of cards up our sleeves, and will play them when and if Peabody moves."

The Highway Director's statement made some commuters enthusiastic. Less volatile observers wondered where this equipment was, where the state would get the crews to operate it, and where it would get the funds and authority. They were relying more on the action they hoped the court would take in forcing Black Ball to continue operation. Previous actions of the court had been sympathetic to the commuters' cause.

In Olympia, Governor Wallgren was quoted as saying that imminent insolvency, in the full legal sense, threatened the company. (No notice was taken of the fact that this seemed to substantiate Peabody's claims.) A Seattle attorney then suggested that the company be compelled to place itself in receivership. A temporary receivership, he suggested, could carry on the ferry operations, to be succeeded by a permanent receiver directed to "wind up and terminate the company's business and sell its assets." Here was a course of action NWCC could have sponsored, but its leaders, irritated with Peabody's stubbornness and egged on by the rank and file now up in arms against Peabody, sat on their hands. Revelle indicated he would not object to establishment of a receivership, and Wallgren added that he had reason to believe that a receiver could, without difficulty, obtain a certificate to operate the ferries. The court had not yet acted, however, and everyone waited.

On February 28, the state's petition for a restraining order was heard in Thurston County Superior Court. The state, represented by an Assistant Attorney General, contended that the company had not requested the Department of Transportation to rehear its application for a rate increase and thus had not exhausted its channels of relief; it should be required to continue operations until all possibilities of recourse had been explored. Company attorneys submitted that a petition for rehearing had been filed July 23; that an application to borrow $1,000,000 had been filed; that an application to borrow $2,000,000 had been filed January 1; and that in none of these matters had the company received so much as an acknowledgment from the state.

> The Department [of Transportation] has been pushing this company around to the limit. It has pushed us to the very brink. And now it has come to court and asked the court to push us over. If this court will look into the facts, it will find that it has never seen more injustice done to a public service corporation than has been done to this company.

The court handed down a memorandum opinion:

> It is conceded that a public service corporation may not abandon its operations without a proper showing of just cause. It is also conceded that the company cannot be compelled to continue to operate at a great loss. The evidence in this case shows that the respondent cannot operate except at a loss, and cannot operate at all by reason of its financial difficulties. Under the law and the facts, the petition for mandate will be denied.

In his review of the facts, the Judge said:

> The company is not able to borrow any more money from the bank. It has no money or means of securing money to pay for fuel or labor or maintenance, for each of which items it now owes a considerable amount.[7] The evidence further shows that there is a decided decline in the travel between the points

7 The court apparently accepted the company's contention that it had exhausted the operating resources provided by the $2,000,000 January loan.

served by the ferry company as compared to travel existing at the time of the hearing before the Department.

An announcement from Captain Peabody followed promptly:

It is with the utmost regret that the company is forced to discontinue its operation as previously announced. This is the result of the utter collapse of the regulatory functions of the Department of Transportation. The court has found . . . that under the rates fixed by the Department of Transportation the company is unable to operate except at tremendous losses.

Suddenly the public, community leadership, and NWCC realized that a tie-up was almost upon them—without any alternative that could be implemented in time to prevent disruption of ferry service.

At this point, Governor Wallgren asserted himself. Elections were a year and a half off, and the party was holding its annual Jefferson-Jackson Day dinners. Wallgren was addressing the Seattle gathering as a probable candidate for re-election when he first disclosed a firm policy on the ferry problem:

If you will have a little patience and put up with inconveniences, I will try to help you get rid of this monopoly. I'll try to clean it up once and for all. . . . We should have this [state operation] even if it means subsidizing the operation. If this is the only way we can get reasonable transportation, then I'm in favor of state ownership. It is more than a question of ferry operation. It works into the entire development pattern of this state.

That Wallgren expressed the sentiments of most of those immediately involved in the problem, there is no doubt. From those not immediately involved, there was no active opposition. The Governor had committed his administration to a policy.

But to those attuned primarily to the economic as opposed to the political rhythm of the region, the tie-up portended serious consequences. The commuter would suffer mostly inconvenience, but cross-Sound business might not recover for several years. With a conviction born of necessity, certain of the most influential leaders of the community prevailed on Wallgren and Peabody to make one last try to resolve the issue. They hoped that if Wallgren and Peabody could get together even at this late hour, the exigencies of the situation might produce some compromise; or at least some temporary agreement might be evolved which would support continued ferry operation by Black Ball.

Accordingly, a meeting was arranged for the evening of February 29. Peabody, his top assistants, and his counsel drove to the Governor's office in Olympia where they sat down around a large table with Wallgren, Revelle, and his top staff. The discussion was restrained, but nothing was gained but a review of the arguments which had been so fully developed during the past two years. No common ground had been identified in a low-pressure climate, and now any concession either man made would have been perceived as backing down, especially if he made a move toward compromise which was rejected by the other side. Peabody and his associates left the meeting in time to arrive back in Seattle before midnight, and the Captain personally gave the order to cease operations at that time.

The Ferries Stop

There followed nine days of confusion and sometimes chaos. Some passenger transport on the Sound was provided through various makeshifts. The Navy moved its shipyard employees by LST; NWCC and certain community groups were able to charter vessels for at least partially scheduled operation. Many commuters used their cabin cruisers to get themselves and their friends across the Sound and back, and for several days the whole thing was something of a lark taken in good humor. On the whole, a substantial number of commuters were getting to work either by these means or by "staying in town." But virtually no freight was moving, and the vessels pressed into passenger service offered few comforts and no convenience. Moreover, their service was costly; the fares charged were well above those of the company at the time of the tie-up. The idle company ferries, rolling at anchor, took on a new desirability seen in a new perspective.

The state and the company remained adamant. The Department of Transportation canceled the company's franchise and certificate of convenience and necessity. With the franchise surrendered, many astute NWCC leaders believed that their victory over Peabody would be complete if they could provide an acceptable substitute ferry service in a reasonable time.[8] But how to provide such service? The vessels and the docks were owned by the company; Peabody was declaring that he would not hesitate to sell the vessels to systems outside the Puget Sound area if he found buyers.

One possibility was introduced when Governor Wallgren received from the Attorney General an opinion to the effect that the Washington Tollbridge Authority had the power to acquire company equipment and facilities by condemnation, if this was necessary to provide ferry service. The Governor announced that condemnation proceedings would be instituted if the company was not prepared to sell its equipment to the state at a reasonable price.[9] Out-maneuvered by state officials, Peabody filed an application with the Department of Transportation for a new certificate covering domestic operations only (he proposed forming a new company to carry on Canadian operations) and providing a rate schedule thirty percent higher than the one in effect, on a temporary basis, at the time the system was shut down. Revelle emphatically rejected this application: "... proposed fares and rates [are] 69 percent higher than the 1937 rates. Peabody has got to learn that if he is going to do business in this state, he must conform to the law just as all other citizens."

Peabody remarked blandly, "There is nothing to prevent the Department from putting the company to work tomorrow by approving the application."

State Ownership Reassessed

Local government jurisdictions, which had heretofore been outside the controversy becaus of the state's concern with it, now began to fee strong home pressures to get the ferries int operation while company and state worked ou their differences. The Executive Secretary of th State Association of County Commissioner quoted the Commissioners of King, Island, Ska git, and Jefferson counties as believing resident of those counties to be unwilling to have th state enter the ferry business. Snohomish Count Commissioners, on the other hand, were "willin to help the Governor acquire the ferries, provid ing we can be assured that operating expense from the boats will be taken from gas tax reve nues, thus assuring reasonable rates." Th County Commissioners (who had the responsi bility for building and maintaining the urba highway network), found excruciating the possi bility that a state-operated ferry system migh drain off gasoline tax revenues earmarked fo roads. They needed much more road money tha they presently had, not less.

Six days after the ferry tie-up, Governor Wall gren advanced a positive proposal. "The state,' he said, "definitely is going into the ferry busi ness." He had consulted with Edgar Kaiser, so of the wartime shipbuilder. Kaiser estimate that his Swan Island yards in Portland, Oregon could build eight new ferries in six months at cost to the state of approximately $20,000,000 The Governor suggested that this cost be fi nanced from bonds to be retired from fares.

Forces favoring state ownership were discour aged. The more concrete the proposal to imple ment state ownership, the more violent seeme the reaction against it. Seattle investment expert maintained that bonds could not be markete until the ferries were operating and until i could be demonstrated that rates were hig enough to pay off the bonds. One expert pointe out that if PSNC had been losing money with $2,000,000 debt, the state would have to impos an astronomical rate schedule to retire the con templated bond issue. Industrial and labor lead ers united in criticism of constructing new ferrie outside the State of Washington. The Mayo of Bremerton said, "The whole bunch seems t be grasping at straws. Building new ferries i going to take a long time. Black Ball has th ferries; someone has got to get Black Ball and th state together. The service we are getting now

[8] It later appeared that, even at this time, their position was more favorable than they realized. A reputable report of the company's condition when it stopped operations indicated that Peabody had less than $6,000 in the bank and owed $2,000,000 plus a separation payroll of $500,000.

[9] Legal opinion was not unanimous on this point. Several lawyers commented that, since PSNC was a Nevada corporation, condemnation action would have to be taken through the federal courts, and it might be as long as three years before a decision was obtained. This approach was thus of questionable feasibility unless other ferries could be used in the interim; and if other ferries were available, there was no need for PSNC vessels.

under the emergency set-up, is lousy." The Mayor of Port Orchard, on the other hand, was inclined to support the Governor: "The present arrangement would be very difficult to undergo for six months, but I think we could stand [it]. Anything to get away from Black Ball. If we could break Black Ball's monopoly, the rates would take care of themselves." A vice-president of the Bainbridge Chamber of Commerce seemed to express the prevailing view when he said, "We would be very slow to welcome Black Ball back. Whether we want state operation is something else again. We'd want to know the plan. One thing is certain, I think; we can't wait six months for ferries. There must be some kind of emergency service. Bainbridge can't exist without ferry service much longer."

Conceding that his trial balloon had been punctured, the Governor was at a loss. The public appeared to be angry, but it would not yet support remedial action. Wallgren critics, on the other hand, held that the situation demanded bold, forceful leadership and action. The Governor, they said, had shown himself unequal to the problem.

Again, from the center of this ferment, a clique of community leaders came to the fore. Wallgren felt that he had some potential solutions but public opinion was not yet sufficiently solidified to support bold action. NWCC, so aggressive and so effective as a negative force, had found it could not muster consensus on any positive course of action; its *ad hoc* status did not appear to provide the organizational mechanisms for developing a response of this quality.

Peabody alone had elaborated a clear and well-defined position, and it was from this point that a self-appointed group of community leaders—several business men and lawyers—began its efforts. The state administration was beyond the influence of these men, but local county and municipal officials were not. They were approached to determine their willingness to develop some interim arrangement. They were more than willing to do anything they could. Next, Peabody's counsel was approached. He checked with the Captain, who reiterated his desire to get the whole system back in operation.

The Ferries Are Leased

Without quite knowing how, the idea of a lease suddenly emerged from these discussions and immediately Peabody was invited to a County Commissioners meeting on March 8. At this meeting the King County Commissioners asked Peabody if he would be willing to operate his ferries under lease to the County, and if so, at what rates. Peabody replied that he was anxious to have ferry service restored, to alleviate the problems resulting from the tie-up. He would welcome the lease arrangement; his only request was that the terms allow him a fair return on his investment. He proposed the rate schedule for which he had applied, a few days before, to the Department of Transportation, i.e., rates approximately thirty percent higher than those being charged prior to the tie-up. He agreed that after thirty days of operation at these rates he would open his books to the County for complete examination. The rate schedule might then be modified either upward or downward as indicated to assure the "reasonable return." On this basis a contract was signed between the Captain and the King County Commissioners subject to cancellation at any time by either party. On March 9, the company ferries were again traveling their routes. The rates had, in effect, been removed from the purview of the state; the law provided for no state supervision of a county operation. The Commissioners certified, however, that they would withdraw from the operation ninety days after receiving notification from the state of its readiness to institute ferry service.

The action of the Commissioners was applauded throughout the Puget Sound Basin. Private cruisers on the springtime chop of the Sound had proved to be a poor substitute for the squat, lumbering ferry boats. Shippers' representatives pointed out to cross-Sound outlets that the added expense of trucking their goods up from Portland directly was not necessary in the light of this arrangement which could be used as long as the problem persisted. Wallgren and Revelle now had time and hence room to maneuver in.

One of the implications of this action was not lost to either Wallgren, as titular Democratic party leader, or to his Republican opponents. The dominantly conservative business leaders of the community had worked out an acceptable alternative with the dominantly Republican county commissioners first. Both the state Republican leader and Arthur Langlie, potential Republican gubernatorial candidate, saw the possibility of an effective campaign issue in this. So did the incumbent Governor.

The State Acts

Partly with the political necessity for action in mind, but mostly because the Governor was now beginning to take action, the Washington State Tollbridge Authority moved to develop a state ferry system. The decision to delegate this responsibility to the Tollbridge Authority instead of to the Highway Department reflected the administration's acceptance of the political difficulty of making any move which threatened, even potentially, the sanctity of the gas tax funds earmarked for the Highway Department. The Department of Transportation, though having dealt with water transportation, was a regulatory agency. TBA had considerable experience in moving traffic across water over the bridges it built and operated for the state.

Another potential solution was supported by a small but vocal minority which found the TBA intervention highly acceptable. Why, these citizens said, at first to themselves and later publicly, should there not be bridges across the Sound? Nearly everyone had ridden the floating bridge[10] across Lake Washington. Why should there not be a similar, but longer, bridge across the Sound? They were shortly to ask the TBA to study the feasibility of such a project.

But now the TBA was proposing the construction of six 100-car and four 60-car ferries at a cost of $8,000,000. A Seattle firm was retained to submit plans for these vessels in 45 days. Governor Wallgren stated that the ferries, ancillary dockage, and one bridge could be built for $12,000,000 to $15,000,000. He proposed that the funds be obtained from the sale of bonds, these to be retired through a rate structure equivalent to that effective in 1946.

The rapidly growing tendency to blame the Governor for lethargy, and even incompetence was halted. These critics were virtually silenced by Wallgren's additional statement that, in the interest of providing a reliable basis for developing a comprehensive plan for state operatio and ownership, the state had contracted with th Gilman firm of Chicago, transportation consu tants. The firm was to make a survey of wate transport on the Sound and prepare a plan for self-supporting ferry system, within 1946 rate providing for an equivalent or even superior leve of service to that offered by Black Ball. Th generally favorable response which these an nouncements evoked was seen by the Governor' aides as an indication that he had taken the ma ter out of the hands of "the Seattle interests, and at the same time had placed Captain Pea body back on the defensive.

A Chamber of Commerce-sponsored poll o some three thousand Kitsap County residents in dicated that 85 percent of them now favore maintaining the lease arrangement until the Gil man study was completed. If the Governor sav the Gilman study as a means of taking some o the political heat out of the issue, his step ap peared well timed.

In April the Wenatchee Chamber of Com merce, reflecting the interests of agricultura eastern Washington, passed a resolution opposin any use of highway funds for a state ferry opera tion on Puget Sound. Later in the month, Cun ningham, in another by-line article, suggeste that the Governor's position on the ferry questio would in all probability become an issue in th November elections.

A New Commuter Group Coalesces

Meanwhile, what was to become a familia controversy was developing around the interin ferry service. On May 1, Captain Peabody re ported that his company had lost more tha $5,000 in its first month of operation under th King County lease. Any rate reduction was ac cordingly out of the question.

The commuter anger generated by this an nouncement did not find expression throug NWCC; leadership of that organization had nov altered somewhat and tended to accept the eco nomic necessities of Peabody's current situation especially since his contract was a temporary one But to many commuters there was no middl ground. Reports circulated that Peabody's oper ating expense statement included a six-digit fig ure that was in fact being applied to compan

10 A bridge which rests on huge floating caissons of concrete extending ninety feet into the water.

indebtedness, and that rates could be substantially lowered if the County Commissioners would only "crack down." The Commissioners responded to this allegation with a reminder that Peabody talked of suspending service again if rates were reduced. Despite this threat, a second commuter organization was formed in late May. This group called itself the Puget Sound Ferry Users Association. It announced that its objective was to obtain adequate, low-cost, uninterrupted ferry service. It termed the arrangement between King County and Peabody "one-way," and called for the negotiation and enforcement of a new and lower set of rates. On June 10, the County Commissioners ordered a thirty percent rate reduction, effective at the end of the next thirty-day period, but this did not satisfy PSFUA. It contended that the 1937 rate base plus ten percent allowed by the Department of Transportation was the maximum acceptable standard. Captain Peabody asserted that he would have to suspend operations unless the Commissioners modified their order or unless King County made up the difference between the rates ordered and his stated minimum.

At a PSFUA-sponsored meeting, one of the Commissioners declared that the only real alternative to the existing rate schedule was for the County to withdraw from the operation. A spokesman for the Association replied: "Why don't you get out of the ferry business and let us fight our own battles? It's summertime now, and we'll manage to get back and forth. If Peabody wants to quit because of rate reduction, let him quit." At this, the crowd cheered. The reaction drew from one observer the comment that, while NWCC had learned the importance of dependable ferry service at almost any cost, PSFUA seemed unaware of it.

The emergence of PSFUA was evidence that the heterogeneity which was NWCC had been too much to force into one mold. After its initial successes, the leadership of NWCC had grown continuously more divided. One of the major divisions was between the shopkeeper-commuter segment and the community leader-shipper segment. As it happened, there was a tendency to represent this roughly as a Democratic-Republican division—with the former tending to identify with the Governor. But the crucial split was between the alternative of state ownership on the one hand and more effective regulation of Black Ball on the other. Peabody had succeeded in winning some support from the latter group, to the dismay of the proponents of state ownership—who ultimately seceded to found the PSFUA.

Despite PSFUA pressures, the County Commissioners later withdrew their rate reduction order and, in conference with Captain Peabody, settled for a July schedule amounting to the 1937 rates plus sixty percent. This was a six percent reduction. PSFUA bitterly criticized both Peabody and the Commissioners, and renewed its demand for a drastic cut.

Except for the skirmishes between PSFUA and the Commissioners, the ferry problem lay dormant, reflecting tacit public acceptance of the Governor's decision to call in the Gilman firm, with its presumed professional competence and objectivity.

The Gilman Report

In mid-June, the Gilman consultants gave the Governor a private preliminary report. It recommended the expenditure of $18,000,000 on a combination bridge and ferry system, and stated that bonds in this amount could be retired from fares somewhat lower than the 1937-plus-sixty percent rate currently being charged. In a letter to Captain Peabody the consultants commented: ". . . we have not expressed any opinion whether the ferry system should be publicly or privately owned and operated, but have stated that out-of-pocket expenses would be about the same whether the system was operated by the present company or by a public agency. . . . Our figures also show that operation with proposed new boats would be more expensive than with present boats." The Governor and top TBA officials began considering the administrative implications of the report. At the same time the Governor spent considerable time with PSFUA leaders listening to their concerns and explaining the fixed limits within which he had to work.

On June 30 the King County Commissioners, under strong pressure from PSFUA leaders, discussed the possibility of condemning ferry system property in King County and conveying it to the state. One Commissioner believed that, in this way, vessels and docks could be acquired for much less than $18,000,000. All the Commissioners stated that they now favored state purchase of the system, but only if the Governor made it clear that no highway funds would be diverted to the ferry operation. Captain Peabody's response to a report of the Commissioners' discussion was a prompt announcement that the ferry system was not for sale. Informally, competent observers were quoted as considering it doubtful that any public jurisdiction could acquire the property by condemnation so long as Peabody was willing to provide service.

The Gilman report, as the formal document submitted by the consultants was generally known, was released to the public on July 6. The earlier informal recommendation of a combination bridge-ferry system to be financed by a bond issue was unchanged. In an appraisal of public expectations with respect to the ferry system, the report formally stated a premise that the public generally and opinion leaders among commuters and shippers had only begun to perceive. Ferry users, the report said, had come to assume that one could take an automobile and travel by highway from one city to another at any time of the day or night in one continuous, uninterrupted trip. They had come to think of ferry routes as cross-Sound highway extensions, and expected to traverse the Sound with no more delay or inconvenience than they experienced on highways. In reality, the report asserted, only bridges could provide this convenience. Accordingly, the consultants recommended that five existing ferry routes be replaced by bridges. But since bridge costs would have to be met from tolls, a volume of traffic sufficient to retire construction bonds would have to be generated by eliminating several additional ferry routes and funneling their traffic across the bridges. This was the only long-range approach to the problem that would meet the demands of commuters, the report said. For the time being, however, use of ferries would have to continue.

The Gilman report had a many-sided impact on the situation. That, in the professional opinion of the engineers, there *was* a good deal that *could* be done was received with relief by a public which had become somewhat disenchanted with its lay leadership.

In the headquarters offices of Black Ball, the Gilman report was received with enthusiasm and an air of vindication. Again the "facts had bee[n] laid out on the table and twice our belief tha[t] we are doing as good a job as can be done unde[r] existing conditions has been vindicated," Blac[k] Ball officials said.

NWCC, now presenting itself as the "moder[-]ate" group, felt that the report supported its po[-]sition that PSNC operations should be continue[d] under more careful state supervision. Some da[y] bridges would have to be built—the Gilman re[-]port substantiated this—and, of course, thes[e] would be TBA bridges; but until that time, s[o] long as Peabody's operation had come off wit[h] such a clean bill of health from Gilman, it wa[s] prudent to assume that he could operate his tir[-]ing vessels more cheaply than new state-buil[t] ones. Besides, he would probably run a more ef[-]ficient system than the state.

PSFUA leaders, aware of the broad outline[s] of the report before its release, stated that th[e] report demonstrated state ownership and opera[-]tion was in fact feasible and that they propose[d] to work toward the implementation of the Gil[-]man proposals.

Wallgren Tries to Buy the Ferries

To the Democratic administration and th[e] Governor, the report was a mixed blessing. Sinc[e] it had treated primarily the economic and engi[-]neering facets of the problem, and since it ha[d] stated that operation with Peabody's vessels woul[d] probably be less costly than use of new vessels, the impasse over the purchase of Black Ball equipment was prolonged and made harder to resolve. Further, the Governor felt that the re[-]port provided tangible materials for those who sought to make the ferry problem a political issue. But the positive contributions from the Governor's viewpoint were substantial. State op[-]eration had been found economically feasible; a professionally competent group of experts had documented this. On a different plane, the re[-]port had helped greatly to transform the violent thinking of March into calmer, more rationally-oriented opinions focused not primarily upon who was right and who was wrong, but on the elemental problem itself, on the various aspects of the feasibility of improving ferry service on the Sound. There was now, Wallgren felt, a climate of opinion in which he might be able to evolve a program acceptable to most of the interests involved.

That the Governor had yet to develop public agreement on a solution was made evident to him when, at their July meeting, the Commissioners of Southern Puget Sound counties publicly announced that the only permanent solution to the cross-Sound transport problem was a system of bridges. But, they said in a resolution transmitted to the Governor, ". . . ferry rates are at heights which are already stagnating our communities. While we compliment you on the long-range approach to the ferry problem, we urge you to find an immediate solution to this emergency."

Wallgren had been moving toward just this objective. He had engaged Allyn and Company, Chicago investment bankers, to try to negotiate purchase of the Black Ball equipment. On July 12 an Allyn representative disclosed that he had been meeting with Black Ball officials as the Governor's representative. A company spokesman corroborated that a deal might be arranged. The Governor himself stated, "If there is no deal because of price or refusal of the company to sell, we shall proceed with the building of new ferries, providing the financing firms work out a satisfactory program."

But the Captain had by no means given up hope. The Governor, Peabody held, was mistaken if he thought he was supported by anything approaching broad agreement on the central issue. The issue? Whether a majority agreed that it was appropriate for the State of Washington to go into the ferry business at the behest of a vocal minority when a competent consultant firm had indicated that the existing system could do the job just about as well. Cunningham, over his by-line, seemed to agree with Peabody, suggesting that for his own political well-being, the Governor had best come up with a workable solution before the November elections. The people wanted action. What had begun as a conflict between a public service corporation and its clientele was evolving into a major political issue.

A Price Is Agreed Upon

No one was more aware of this than Wallgren. While Cunningham was writing his article, the Governor was closeted with PSFUA representatives. Under his tutelage they had become aware of the possibility that the problem might emerge as a campaign issue. They came away from the meeting believing that if the problem were thrown into the partisan political arena, further delays would be inevitable. They hoped that by publicizing their own reasoned program for state ownership massive public support would be attracted quickly; the ferry issue would thus not become a "political football."

Just two weeks later, the executive board of PSFUA publicly endorsed state ownership of the ferry system on these conditions:

1. The Tollbridge Authority should operate the system;
2. The system should be self-supporting;
3. The system should impose no obligation upon the taxpayer;
4. It should include all of the routes on Puget Sound;
5. Only one bridge, Agate Pass, should be built from the ferry bond issue;
6. The fares should be favorable to the public.

The PSFUA added that, according to its estimates, the Tollbridge Authority would have netted a $14,000,000 profit if it had been operating the system from 1937 to 1946.

About this time, a member of Black Ball's board of directors disclosed that a minority group of stockholders had approached the Governor several weeks previously with an offer to sell the system for $7,500,000. However, Captain Peabody was opposed to sale on any terms. In early August, the state offered the company $5,500,000 for all its vessels, docks, and equipment except that part related to its international activities. The company asked $5,975,000 cash. The state countered with a proposal to pay $2,000,000 in cash and the balance in revenue bonds. This proposal was rejected. The state then offered to pay the full price in cash if financing could be arranged. The company gave the state an option to buy the system on these terms, subject to stockholders' approval. On August 30, stockholders endorsed the arrangement. PSFUA promptly endorsed it also. The Governor breathed easier.

This respite was short, for former Republican Governor Arthur Langlie, defeated by Wallgren four years earlier and again a candidate for the office, did not accept the agreement and said so. Certain that there had been impropriety (an incorrect assumption, he admitted ten years later) Langlie declared that the proposed purchase of the ferry system should be investigated by the Legislature before any further action was taken. He believed that the ferry operation should be undertaken by the state, he said, but he had serious reservations about the way in which Wallgren was going about it. He was especially critical of the "secret negotiations" that had been reported. A Republican-oriented committee of the Legislative Council announced its intention to hold hearings on the impending transaction. This committee wanted to ascertain, it stated, whether more boats were being purchased than were actually needed and whether the state could in fact operate the system at rates lower than the company charged. It also wanted to review the details of the bond arrangement.

Wallgren replied that both Langlie and the legislative committee were seeking political advantage, not the public interest. He pointed out that two of the three members of the committee were Langlie associates; one of them had been his 1944 campaign manager, the other was his current King County campaign manager.

Meanwhile, the legal implications of state acquisition of the ferry system were yet to be fully unraveled. On September 21, the State Tollbridge Authority appeared before the Supreme Court seeking a Writ of Mandamus directing the Secretary of State to issue the bonds with which the state proposed to purchase the ferry system. This was a test action, entered into by friendly agreement between the parties to the transaction. It aimed at resolving a possible legal question about the state's authority under existing law. Its primary purpose, however, was to forestall the private legal action that the Langlie forces were rumored to be preparing to block completion of the transaction. The Washington Taxpayers' Association, participating as a friend of the court, pointed out that if the decision were negative, or if it were delayed, the state's option to purchase the ferry system would expire, and the probability was that the company would demand a higher price if negotiations were reopened.[11] The court acted swiftly, but, in effect, negatively. It held that the question had been brought prematurely, before a real legal question had developed. This opinion avoided direct reference to the question of the state's authority, but it was generally agreed that another attempt to raise the question would evoke a clearly negative opinion. Wallgren supporters grumbled that the judge was known to be friendly toward Langlie.

Langlie now made the ferry issue central to his campaign. In a statement typical of many he made, he said:

> Peabody saw the handwriting on the wall. He had taken his company through the lush war years, and now he was confronted with decreasing traffic and rising costs with the resulting financial losses. . . . Step by step he goaded the state into one vulnerable position after another, until finally he had an excuse to take the ferries off the runs. Peabody had the state where he wanted it, and the public was all riled up and demanding action. Wallgren immediately started making wild promises to relieve the pressure, and every time he opened his mouth the state was deeper in the hole.

The last straw, Langlie added, was the finding that the state lacked the authority to enter into these negotiations in the first place without additional legislation. Peabody was enraged but silent.

Election day was imminent. Poltical charges and countercharges on the ferry issue became more and more heated, although the ferry issue was by no means the dominant issue in the gubernatorial campaigning. PSFUA and a number of other commuter and civic groups in western Washington affirmed and defended Wallgren's position. But they observed with alarm that support for Langlie's point of view was mounting ominously in eastern Washington, where citizens had been consistently suspicious of potential threats to highway funds.

Langlie was elected. Meanwhile, the state's option to purchase the ferry system expired.

[11] It was also disclosed that the contemplated price was $912,382 under the latest appraised value of the property.

Langlie Seeks a Solution, 1949-1951

THE PROBABLE IMPACT of the Republican victory upon the ferry situation was variously construed by the Puget Sound public in the days immediately following the election. But there was no lessening of pressure for solving the problem.

By the time Wallgren turned over the Governor's office to Langlie, the ferry issue had been extensively discussed. Political parties, newspapers all over the state, chambers of commerce, labor unions, granges, and other groups had expressed their views many times over. A mass of information about the "economic realities" of Sound transport had been virtually forced upon the public. In the face of it, many citizens, some NWCC leaders among them, found their initial conceptions and preconceptions weakened and even transformed. By inauguration time, too, several alternative approaches to the problem had either been attempted (as with enforcement of arbitrarily established rates, leases to counties, and suspension of ferry service) or realistically examined (as with construction of Sound bridges or new and competing ferry systems). Each of these alternatives, by fairly general consent, had been discarded as unworkable. In the campaign, both candidates had supported state purchase.

As Langlie took over, then, there was fairly wide agreement upon the propriety and feasibility of state purchase of PSNC equipment and facilities. The expiration of the state's option to purchase PSNC facilities was only a temporary obstacle; the company's willingness to sell was on the record. Captain Peabody might still be reluctant, but there were indications that several Black Ball stockholders were determined to salvage their investment by selling out to the state if it offered a fair price.

Governor Langlie appeared to appreciate the advantageous position of his administration on the ferry issue. Then in his fifties, an attorney by profession, he had, like Wallgren, spent much of his adult life in the public service. Unlike Wallgren, whose experience had been heavily legislative, Langlie had served primarily in an executive role. It was a role, he noted later, that suited him more than a legislative one. As Mayor of Seattle (1938-40), as Governor (1940-44), he had tested and refined a conception of executive leadership that was different from Wallgren's. Where "good government" was concerned, it was not part of his philosophy to await an overwhelming public mandate for action. His record suggested a ready aggressiveness to institute new policies, reorganizations, and even new programs in the cause of "good government." And his support of these efforts seldom wavered, though several of them had only the most passive public support. Langlie had developed effective working relationships with a dominant segment of the state's business leadership. He was now unquestioned leader of his party. And accordingly his influence with the Legislature was considerable.

As he took office in 1949, Langlie was firm in his commitment to a state ferry operation. His campaign statements had clearly endorsed ridding the Sound of the Black Ball ferry system. He publicly labeled Wallgren "blundering and gullible," and, as if to emphasize his pivotal position, he labeled Peabody a "robber baron."

"Creeping Socialism?"

In taking this position, Langlie anticipated that he might be criticized by those in his party who would equate state operation with "creeping socialism." "State purchase," one conservative Republican had said, "would amount to prostitution of Republican principles for political gain." The Governor-to-be did not doubt that most people around the Sound wanted PSNC displaced. But how to convince his more conservative colleagues? As a first step he adopted the point of view that the ferry system was properly a public utility, to be operated in the public interest—not for profit.

The ferry issue had been a ticklish campaign issue for Langlie to handle, and it was still delicate. Langlie knew that to the typical voter in eastern Washington a stand on his part against state ownership would have had some appeal. But he also knew that to the Puget Sound Basin resident—especially to the nominal Democrat and the Independent whose votes had accounted for his victory—he was now generally committed to state purchase. This was not, however, a view held so widely among his friends—and in some cases principal financial supporters—among the top strata of community leaders. Most of them had been irked by the ferry tie-up, feeling that Peabody had gone too far or that he had clearly placed private interest above the public's interest. But few of them were so violently opposed to Peabody that they would not prefer some arrangement that would provide an alternative to state ownership. Langlie's attacks on Peabody's irresponsibility were genuine and in character. He had been appalled during his first term as Governor with Peabody's alleged failure to develop out of the fat war traffic a capital fund for post-war improvements in the service. During his first term also Langlie had joined Naval officials in insisting that Peabody cut his fares. To Langlie, men like Peabody were bringing the free enterprise system into disrepute "even though in some ways I admire the old buccaneer." With these thoughts in mind, determined to take the ferries over, Langlie set about attempting to convert the reluctant, right-wing Republican business leadership of the community to his point of view.

Peabody was incensed that a candidate wearing Republican colors should launch against him what he considered to be such calumny. If the man were in favor of free enterprise, if he opposed creeping socialism, how could he attack one who stood, above all else, for these values long precious to Republicans? Through mutual acquaintances Langlie was well aware of Peabody's ire. He proposed that they should meet face to face in front of the influential Committee on Transportation of the Chamber of Commerce, each to present his case. Peabody accepted the challenge, assuming that if all of the facts were laid on the table for a third time, his point of view would prevail again.

They met, and the discussion was heated but gentlemanly. Though Peabody had superior knowledge of the facts of cross-Sound ferry operations, Langlie carried the day and most of the committee. He thereby neutralized the potential opposition of the business community before it could form, for the Transportation Committee was looked to by many of the members of the Chamber as a source of leadership on this kind of question.

Two Bills

When the Legislature convened in January, 1949 Langlie immediately submitted an enabling bill which would provide the state with full powers to establish and conduct ferry operation. He was promptly visited by a delegation of labor leaders. They represented not only the three unions involving Black Ball personnel; the selection of delegates reflected state labor strategy to break the previous barrier against union membership among state employees. The callers sought assurances that if a state-operated system materialized, employees would retain the right to belong to unions, to bargain with the state, and to strike for increased benefits. These leaders offered support for a bill enabling state purchase in return for gubernatorial support for a bill protecting their right to bargain collectively with the state.

A bill recognizing the right of ferry employees to continue dues-paying membership in a union and establishing a Marine Employee Commission to function as an arbitrator in any labor-management controversy was introduced in the House with Langlie's overt consent and support. (Langlie's ferry bill was introduced in the Senate.) There was quiet co-ordination of these bills as they were processed through both houses so that the labor bill was always just one step ahead of the enabling bill—testimony to labor's power. The Governor signed both bills on March 12, 1949. While the labor bill did not specifically prohibit strikes, union leaders had agreed to forego the use of the strike as a bargaining device for the foreseeable future if the Marine Employee Commission was set up. From the commuters' standpoint, the Governor had secured a substantial protection against future disruption of service.

These positive moves on the part of the state

brought action from Captain Peabody. Black Ball's critical financial situation had been alleviated during the period of operation at the higher rates provided by the county leasing arrangement, and the company's debts had been substantially reduced. If Captain Peabody's enterprise had flagged while financial pressures were strong, it was now restored in full. He was still intent upon retaining the ferry operation, and was prepared to throw such political and financial resources as he had into another major campaign.

A Bid for Free Enterprise

Peabody made two simultaneous moves. On April 2, 1949, he proposed to the King County Commissioners a plan for a twenty-year lease arrangement to continue Black Ball operation of vessels and facilities. The other move came through NWCC. On May 1, speaking as a private commuter committee of interested citizens, certain NWCC "moderates" publicly proposed that:

1. Black Ball continue the ferry operation under contract to the Tollbridge Authority;
2. Black Ball create a vice-presidency to supervise rates;
3. A permanent advisory body be established to monitor PSNC's operations in the name of the public and its interests;
4. Wage recommendations of the Gilman Report be adopted;
5. Gilman and Company be retained to make periodic (perhaps semi-annual) checks on rates in relation to traffic volume and profits;
6. Rates be adjusted every six months to assure minimum cost to the commuter consistent with survival of the company;
7. Unions agree to a no-strike clause, similar to the agreement made with the state.

Governor Langlie spent little time in contemplation of this proposal. He rejected it the day after it was made, stating that he would direct the Tollbridge Authority to acquire the Black Ball system for state operation. As though to dispel any possible doubt about his intent, he made a further statement on May 10 in which he said that Black Ball was on its way out as a ferry operator, even under a lease arrangement. "It is apparent," he added, "that the public has lost confidence in Captain Peabody's operation of the ferry system. The relationship over a period of years has been such that ferry users themselves no longer have confidence in his ability or desire to operate the ferries in the best interests of the area served." Langlie was supported by leaders of the PSFUA.

A Legal Reversal

A legal development late in May suggested that the State Supreme Court, at least, felt that there was some legal basis to Black Ball's claim that it was being crucified for the public's benefit. The Court refused to affirm the Superior Court decision upholding the Department of Transportation's rate reduction order. The Supreme Court held that there was reasonable basis for taking further evidence and for reviewing the Department's rate determination.

This development was gratifying to Peabody but of little practical advantage since the company's situation had now advanced far past the problem of rates alone. The Department of Transportation had been reorganized as one of Langlie's earliest official actions. Because he needed to gain control of the Department and because he believed it had been too susceptible to "political" pressures, the Governor had replaced its key officials, Revelle among them, and had reconstituted it as the Public Service Commission. The Commission was now more independent of the Governor and also less potent. Langlie had, however, continued Wallgren's practice of using the state Tollbridge Authority as his primary staff instrument in analyzing and dealing with the ferry problem.

Despite the unfavorable court action, the state, early in the summer of 1949, appeared well on the way to having brought Peabody to a point where he had only one choice:—to sell to the state. But a sudden illness removed the Governor from the scene until after the beginning of the new year, and the force went out of the administration's drive. So far as the public was concerned, the problem seemed to be at a standstill—or, more precisely, at a standoff. The Governor's assistant began to work behind the scenes, seeking to provide a means for direct negotiation with Black Ball. At first Peabody displayed a determination to resist any settlement with the

Langlie regime. But the defeat he had suffered before the Transportation Committee at Langlie's hands was a symbol of an underlying difficulty which was finally undermining the Captain's capacity to "bounce back." Once before Black Ball stockholders had agreed to the sale of the company's properties. They were still agreed upon the principle of reducing their operations to the international run. Now Peabody told them that the Governor sought to confiscate the company. He asked for their support that he might resist this effort to the end.

With the Governor on the side lines, with his more tractable, more pleasant (to Peabody) assistants handling things, and with the conviction that the public, the Legislature, the administration, and the commuter groups were committed to the displacement of Black Ball, Peabody found that his stockholders were hedging on their commitment of support. Several of them believed that now, while Langlie was off-stage, was the time to make a vigorous attempt to work out an agreement with the state.

Bargaining

As summer gave way to autumn, Black Ball found itself involved first in informal talks with administration representatives and later in what amounted to formal negotiations with TBA representatives. TBA leaders felt that the company was not really in a mood to try to work out a sale on reasonable terms and broke off the negotiations early in the winter. The Authority stated that Black Ball was not showing good faith and that TBA would not talk again unless it was understood that the purchase price must be less than what Wallgren had accepted. Peabody was intransigent, Authority spokesmen said; the state would simply have to acquire equipment from other sources.

A month later the state took the first step toward this end. It purchased the four vessels and the facilities of the Vashon Island Ferry District for $130,350. A rumor spread that the state was changing its strategy; it would force Peabody out of business one route at a time. Peabody, by his public silence, appeared to see advantage in this, and indeed he might. At the rate structure which the Commissioners had allowed, he could amortize much of his properties in the event that bargaining dragged on for five or ten more years

Within a week there was a reaction agains this strategy. A spokesman for Vashon resident told the press that King County Commissioner were demonstrating more interest in preservin the company by their lease arrangement than i serving the taxpayers' interests. Then PSFUA petitioned the new Public Service Commissio to seize jurisdiction over Black Ball rates, regardless of the fact that the lease was with Kin County. In January, 1950 the King Count Commissioners renewed their lease with Blac Ball at the existing rates. The renewal reminde the public that Langlie had been in office a year and that the impasse continued.[12] Th PSFUA complained about the delay.

In this atmosphere, the on-again, off-again negotiations between the state and company gener ated more and more heat. Peabody charged i March that the state was attempting to cheape Black Ball by offering to purchase the entir system at the unjustifiably depressed figure o $3,332,000. Langlie countered that Peabody wa garbling the issue by suggesting that the stat was attempting to acquire the system at less tha a fair value. A month later Langlie stated tha his hopes of buying the system were dwindling the state would not go beyond an offer o $4,983,000, while Peabody persisted in talking o a price between $9,000,000 and $12,000,000. I June Langlie disclosed that he was appealing b direct mail to the Black Ball stockholders, of fering to buy their stock at a par value tha would bring the total consideration for the sys tem to $3,900,000. A stockholders' meeting i July recorded a resolution that "the officers an directors of the PSNC be instructed to continu to take any and all actions which in their judg ment are necessary to protect the substantial asse value of the company."

Agreement on a Bridge

A few days later Langlie, now nearly recovered stated his own view of the problem: "I am con vinced . . . that the development of the Puge Sound area must be facilitated by the construc

12 Langlie said later that around this time he considere having the state purchase Black Ball shares—becoming a minority stockholder. This possibility was rejected as o doubtful constitutionality.

ion of a bridge or a series of bridges to afford wenty-four-hour service that eventually would ecome toll free. The studies of . . . the Washngton Tollbridge Authority indicate that such project is entirely feasible. . . . The ferry boat roblem is being developed with a view to its eing replaced by the construction of bridges."

Behind the public bickering lay the fact that he two principals had now come to a fundanental agreement on the long-range nature of vater transport across Puget Sound. Bridges were he solution. This was what Peabody had long naintained. While he agreed that the projected ridges were technically feasible, he did not feel hat the volume of cross-Sound traffic was yet ufficient to make bridges economically feasible. His view was that ferries were essential as an nterim solution. In eight or ten years anticiated population increases would bring potential raffic volume to the point where bridges could e built and maintained through tolls. Langlie, e held, would soon see this, too.

Ross Cunningham was pleased to hear of the Governor's statement. He had been the Governor's Executive Assistant in a previous term and ad felt that Langlie was vulnerable if he did ot work toward the only long-range solution— system of bridges. He had first seen the necesity for bridges in his frequent talks with Peaody while covering the development of the issue or the *Times,* and he had gradually documented his necessity to his own satisfaction from the Gilman Report and other independent economic nd engineering studies. Since he had tried many imes to prevail upon Langlie, on a friendly basis, o accept this point of view, he felt that the roblem was a whole step nearer solution when he Governor took a public stand to this effect.

How to Make Peabody Sell?

The company and the state continued to skirnish, each trying to maximize its bargaining poition. The state moved toward developing oprations on a second route. Peabody sought to utflank this move. He purchased shore lands t a point where an access bridge would ultinately be essential. Langlie denied him access o these lands by refusing him permission to uild a road across state-owned lands behind his hore tract. Peabody then purchased a tract comprising both shore and access lands, 150 feet south. Langlie refused permission to relocate the state's highway to provide a way of getting to this tract. So went the beginning of winter.

As Cunningham continued his coverage of this sparring, he felt that neither side could take decisive action, yet neither side could disengage itself from commitments previously made (in an essentially different climate of opinion) to move toward a modified position in keeping with the moment. Langlie could not afford to disrupt the whole Sound economy with another suspension of ferry service—even if he had been disposed to. But without risking another tie-up, he could not force Peabody to agree to a sale price consistent with commitments made during and after his campaign. The weight of public opinion effectively blocked Peabody from any real attempt to re-establish Black Ball on the Sound. But if he tried to improve his bargaining position with the state by tying up his equipment—without overt aggravation—he risked loss of his best potential purchaser. In any case, until his company's debts were fully repaid, he could not afford to let his craft lie idle. Cunningham tried adroitly to demonstrate to both sides that this state of affairs would in the end be harmful to almost everyone. But he had little feeling that either of the two protagonists was persuaded.

The Threat of Regulation

Langlie moved to break the impasse by other means. He had adopted the position of a patient observer while the various members of his staff and his official family had attempted to negotiate with Black Ball's management. He had, he believed, made concessions without any being offered in return by the company.

Now he proposed to take the matter of control of ferry rates to the courts for decision. His assistants did this, through the Attorney General's office, and in July the Superior Court handed down its verdict. Its opinion: that the Public Service Commission had always had jurisdiction over Black Ball rates and schedules on the basis of the statute which established its predecessor, the Department of Transportation. Although Peabody contended that the state had no such jurisdiction so long as the county lease was in effect, the stalemate was broken.

The negotiations, which had never been completely broken off by either side, suddenly became more fruitful. It was commonly held that Peabody had now completely given up hope of salvaging his domestic operations and sought only a just sale price. Even so, the situation remained essentially unchanged for another six months while basic agreement on price matured.

Black Ball issued its last blast on December 13, 1950. It demanded, in its usual emphatic terms, that King County cancel its contract with Black Ball when the lease came up for renewal in January. The County Commissioners deferred action on this demand, but stated that the county was willing to withdraw from the ferry business if the Public Service Commission approved.

On December 30, Governor Langlie announced that the state and the company had come to terms. For $4,900,000, the state was to receive virtually all the equipment and facilities used in PSNC's domestic operations. The company retained for its Canadian run the fine, large vessel built just after the war and several smaller vessels to be used to expand Canadian operations. PSNC was to continue its Puget Sound operation, under county contract, through May 1951. It was relieved of any obligation to make fare refunds.

The Washington Tollbridge Authority issued, during May, $6,500,000 worth of bonds. The proceeds were used to pay Black Ball and to begin rehabilitation of vessels and dock facilities.

The transfer took place quietly and on schedule. At 3:00 a.m., June 1, 1951 the State of Washington began operating ferries on Puget Sound.

Postscript

A CROSS-SOUND transportation system as convenient, reliable, and economical as the public demanded in 1947 was not created by state purchase of the ferry system. (See Table of Fares, Appendix One.)

It remains the view of both state and private traffic specialists that unhampered auto traffic across the Sound can only be provided by a comprehensive system of costly bridges. The first of these bridges will become economically possible, on the basis of present traffic projections, about 1967. The rest of the network of bridges will probably be completed in the following two or three decades.

Appendix One

SAMPLES OF FERRY RATES ON PUGET SOUND

Passengers	1937	6/1/38-2/15/47	2/16/47-2/29/48	3/9/48-6/30/49	7/1/49-5/31/51	6/1/51-7/15/52	7/16/52-1/9/55	1/10/55-3/31/57	4/1/57-1958
Seattle-Bremerton (heaviest commuter)	$.42	$.45	$.59	$ .75	$ .65	$ .65	$.60	$ .65	$ .70
Fauntleroy-Vashon (Seattle connection for Vashon traffic)	.20	.20	.26	.25	.25	.25	.25	.30	.30
Anacortes-Friday Harbor (weekend tourist)	.70 (est.)	.70	.91	1.20	1.00	1.00	.90	1.00	1.10

Automobiles	1937	6/1/38-12/21/41	1942-12/31/46	1/1/47-2/15/47	2/16/47-2/29/48	3/9/48-6/30/48	7/1/48-6/30/49	7/1/49-5/31/51	6/1/51-7/15/52	7/16/52-1/9/55	1/10/55-3/31/57	4/1/57-1958
Seattle-Bremerton (heaviest commuter)	$1.00	$1.10	$ .80	$1.10	$1.43	$1.85	$1.65	$1.55	$1.55	$1.50	$1.60	$1.80
Fauntleroy-Vashon (Seattle connection for Vashon traffic)	.70 (est.)	.70	.50	.70	.91	.90	.90	.90	.90	.90	1.00	1.10
Anacortes-Friday Harbor (weekend tourist)	2.15 (est.)	2.15	1.55	2.15	2.80	3.65	3.30	3.00	3.00	2.80	3.00	3.30

Appendix Two

ADDITIONAL TECHNICAL details of the rate-setting practices of the Department of Transportation may be of interest to students of regulation. In general, relations between the company and the Department in 1947 and 1948 were a bit ragged, but not so much as to disrupt free exchange of information. A number of professionals and officials in the Department were well aware that the company was entering a difficult period and were predisposed to be sympathetic to the formal presentation of C. R. Lonergan, company counsel.

Early in 1947 Lonergan appeared before Transportation Department Director Paul Revelle and others and maintained that wages had risen rapidly since the 1937 rates had been set; that traffic was falling off rapidly; that the company had suffered substantial losses in November and December, 1946 and January, 1947; and that there was no reason to anticipate reversal of these conditions. The company, he said, faced a crisis and was forced to ask for an immediate thirty percent rate increase on all routes. He documented each of these contentions with charts and tables prepared by company officials.

Departmental accountants, carefully checking and reviewing these documents, stated that so far as they could determine, the picture thus presented was accurate. They added, however, that it would be questionable procedure to establish a new rate structure from company representations alone; the 1937 rates—for example—had been based upon a comprehensive departmental survey of company finances. In the light of this, Revelle and his associates decided to grant the thirty percent increase temporarily and to make it contingent upon the full department analysis of PSNC finances.

Though the company was given immediate and somewhat unprecedented relief, the Department sought to protect the commuters' interests by including the following three conditions in its formal order.

1. All the funds obtaining from the temporary increase should be impounded in a single bank account.
2. The company should provide a bond which would guarantee whatever funds the company might be forced to withdraw from said account.
3. Every ticket sold at the increased rate should be accompanied by a refund tab, the value of which would be established by the Department if less than the initial thirty percent increase were eventually determined upon.

Three Issues

The order was issued early in February to be effective on February 15, and the company had the refund tabs printed immediately. On February 16 the new rates were put into effect. Shortly after this, a staff of thirteen departmental accountants arrived at Black Ball headquarters to begin their investigation and were given the assistance of five company accountants to act as guides—and perhaps as interpreters upon occasion. Ten weeks later they presented their findings in a report running just under 300 pages.

After a general survey, this investigation settled down to a rather careful analysis of several crucial, interrelated issues:

1. Integrated system vs. route-by-route analysis, and independent consideration of the international routes.
2. Valuation—original cost vs. book vs. replacement.
3. Definition of a fair rate of return.

For years Bremerton residents had complained that the revenue from their patronage not only subsidized all of the other routes but kept the whole operation solvent. The volume of traffic on this run was by far the heaviest. Further, said Bremerton spokesmen, this run had a very stable traffic load in comparison to any of the other routes in the system. Not only was the Bremerton resident paying for part of the costs of the rest of the system, but he was paying dead overhead costs resulting from the capricious traffic patterns of other routes.

These contentions had been successfully disregarded by Black Ball. Now the Department undertook a careful analysis which tended to bear out the Bremerton case. The Bremerton route generated ten times more revenue than seven other routes—half the system. Expenses per traffic unit were well below those of any of the other domestic routes. The operating ratio—the relation of route expenses to route revenues—was far below that of any other route save one. And rate of return—one measure of profit—was very high. On the other hand, the fact remained that six of the twelve routes were in the black and six in the red. Bremerton could not maintain that it was subsidizing the whole system, nor could it maintain that the typical Bremerton patron was contributing substantially more to the whole system than the typical San Juan Islands patron (who was likely to be a tourist).

Regardless, said the Department, the welfare of the state as a whole demanded that the whole system be considered in setting rates because Black Ball basically was involved in moving people from the Seattle metropolitan area out into the hinterland across the Sound and back. If more people went through Bremerton than some other terminal points, this was to Bremerton's benefit. In fact, said the Department, "if the Bremerton-Seattle route were operated by a company other than [Black Ball] . . . such company would have added to its operating expenses the complete overhead expenses, administration, management, maintenance, etc., in addition to the investment in and expenses of standby vessels. . . . There is . . . a definite relationship between all the routes and a parity of rates must be maintained." The Department added that this is what the courts insisted upon anyway, and cited thirteen cases to this effect.

However, said the Department, "The Seattle-Victoria route of the company, we believe, should be segregated from the rest of the system for rate-making purposes." Initially this recommendation was a means of overcoming difficult accounting problems. It was taken up by the company as a means of salvaging something from the situation and finally supported by the commuters as they came to accept the unit-system concept.

Valuation

Valuation was the technical problem around which the investigation soon focused. All parties to the controversy were agreed that the company should receive sufficient revenues to continue its existence. These revenues should cover all direct and indirect costs of operating the vessels and facilities including the replacement of vessels and docks, the repayment of its debts, and the payment of a reasonable dividend to its stockholders. They were also agreed that the company should receive sufficient revenues from all routes to continue the existing level of service on all routes (with the exception of the removal of one vessel from the Bremerton run).

This agreement actually could be translated into a formula for setting the rate structure, for if agreement could be reached upon the total amount of income which the company would require to continue in existence, and if there were general agreement that the Department's analysis of the distribution of system costs between routes was reasonable as it existed, then the problem could be settled by taking agreed-upon traffic projections and increasing rates evenly until they would generate the required annual need.

It was in this context that the valuation problem became the first real issue between the Department and the company. The company maintained initially during the investigation and finally in the hearings that the valuation should be so established that it enable the company (a) to replace existing vessels, and (b) to raise the standard of service by providing faster, cleaner, and larger vessels. In short, replacement value should be the only basis of valuing the company's properties—a replacement value which took full account of future needs.

A Difference of Five Million

The Department, however, held that the courts had clearly indicated that the basis for valuation in rate-making was to be a "fair and just balancing of the interests of investor and consumer." Further, said the Department, the total impact of the burden of costs is more important than any technical question of systematic valuation. It noted that three bases were available: original cost, book value, and replacement value. It estimated original costs of the property currently in use by the company at $10,242,489. The book value, however, was only $4,480,821. The Department declined even to take cognizance of replacement cost but informally accepted the company's estimate that it was several times original value. The difference of more than $5,000,000 in these figures would show up as important percentages in the cost of an individual ticket.

[The difference of five million can be accounted for through a discussion of the concepts of book value, original value, and replacement value, and can be illustrated using two ferry boats. The *Enetai* was purchased by Black Ball from Southern Pacific for $55,000. A total of $10,158.13 was spent towing her to Seattle. A new Busch-Sulzer diesel engine was installed for $149,197.72. She was then re-outfitted and redecorated at a cost of $196,487.88. This brought her cost on the books of Black Ball to $410,843.73. But if one took account of the original price that Southern Pacific had paid for her, and added the investments of both Southern Pacific and Black Ball, the total came to $671,658.71; the difference in these two figures reflected the $250,000 loss Southern Pacific took on each of the ferries it sold. The replacement value of the *Enetai,* however, was calculated at somewhere between two and three times original cost, or about $2,000,000. Where new engines were not installed, the difference is even more striking. The $79,755.45 book value of the *Illahee* compares with its original cost of $548,826.05.]

The Department concluded that in this case use of the original value "would result in requiring the rate payers to pay rates which would return a fair return on an amount greatly in excess of what the company had actually invested in the property. . . . It would result in the rate payers providing the capital whereby a new fleet of vessels will eventually be acquired by the company, i.e., the stockholders, through the rates which the patrons pay in order to assure fair return on this inflated rate base. . . . That the rate payers are not required to furnish . . . revenues to provide capital for the public utility is a fundamental rule of public utility regulation. The obligation to furnish capital is the utility's obligation."

During the investigation, Departmental accountants and company personnel agreed on life expectancies for each of the company's vessels. With this in hand, then, (and with upkeep and replacement tables for non-floating facilities), it was a simple matter to estimate precisely the replacement factor to be included in the total annual revenue needs.

The Department and the company also agreed upon the need for a working capital fund of $213,603.74.

This led to the calculation of total revenue needs of $4,380,745.33 which reflected the sum of projected operating expenses (given the agreement upon costs and future traffic patterns), a depreciation factor, and a working capital factor. There remained the question of a fair rate of return on the company's investment.

The company valiantly maintained that its return should reflect the need for a growing service, and that its risks were relatively great since no one knew what traffic patterns were going to be five years hence.

Its position was damaged, however, by the contentions of its critics that more than $2,000,000 had been squandered in the new Alaska vessel *Chinook,* that it had never tried to provide modern, efficient ferry vessels anyway, and that it would soon be put out of business by the bridges everyone hoped would be built. Therefore, the critics maintained, it did not require many new vessels.

The Department pointed out that the company's monopoly secured it from the competitive risks which most firms faced and that its other risks were simply part of any business operation. It also pointed out that the courts had recently accepted five percent as an adequate return on the investment of a telephone company and that it saw little difference between Black Ball and a telephone monopoly. "The rate of return which we will allow in this case is in excess of 6% (6.04). We find this to be a fair rate of return upon the fair value of the property of [the company] used and useful in rendering public service."

This decision added $283,740.95 to the total already justified as required revenue, bringing the grand total to $4,664,486.28 to be raised from the revised rate structure. Said the Department, "[this] will enable the company to pay an annual dividend of 4 percent on the intra-state portion of its common stock based upon the [allocation of inter- and intra-state facilities] in the amount of $118,137 and leave a balance of $165,603.95 for accumulation in the surplus account. . . . This amount added to the $250,000 allowance will enable the company to replace the existing fleet in forty years which we deem exceedingly more than ample for the needs of the company."

Rates were adjusted sufficiently to provide for revenues to cover the established revenue requirement, and with minor adjustments between routes, these approximated ten percent for all classes of traffic.

THE LAY BOARD: THE DIFFICULTY OF BEING IN THE MIDDLE

"Egad, I think the interpreter is the hardest to be understood of the two."

Sheridan

The Mayor and the Fire Chief:

The Fight over Integrating the Los Angeles Fire Department

Frank P. Sherwood and Beatrice Markey

Editor's Note

This case was originally written early in 1954 while the desegregation controversy in Los Angeles was still raging. Fire Chief John Alderson was not then available for interview. And he has since written in a letter: "At that time numerous requests of this nature were reaching my desk from would-be researchers to would-be magazine and feature writers. . . . I was under specific instructions from the Board of Fire Commissioners to make no public statements and was not permitted to even speak in a public Commission meeting unless asked a direct question by the Commission."

Chief Alderson has been good enough to review successive drafts of this case and to suggest certain additions and corrections. The inclusion of Mr. Alderson's remarks at points in the draft should not be taken as an indication that he necessarily agrees with every sentence in the present version, although it deserves to be noted that he does not take exception to any statements of fact.

Introduction

TO TAKE DEPARTMENTAL administration out of politics and to provide a buffer of civic-minded laymen between mayors and the career department heads, many U. S. cities, most conspicuously Los Angeles, rely on semi-autonomous commissions composed of laymen who usually are appointed by successive mayors to overlapping terms. In Los Angeles these lay commissions are supposed to set policy and to administer departmental programs particularly in the fields of recreation, planning, libraries, and the protective and welfare services.

The interposing of lay commissions between himself and the top career officials of city departments has weakened the power of the Mayor of Los Angeles. The general public expects him to exercise complete command of the city administration and to play a dominant role in policy formation. Since his actual authority is far short of what the public thinks it is, how to bargain, plead, and coerce in order to fulfill policy commitments becomes one of the Mayor's biggest problems.

This case study describes the bargaining, pleading, and coercing undertaken by Mayor Norris Poulson to get the Board of Fire Commissioners to accept for the Fire Department a policy of desegregation that was opposed by the Fire Chief. In describing the competition between the Fire Chief and the Mayor to see who could win the support of the fire commissioners for his own policy, this case may encourage the reader to reflect on the pros and cons of lay commissions and sensitize him to the peculiarities of administration under this system.[1]

[1] Chief Alderson dissents: "There was never any competition by the Fire Chief to win the support of the Fire Commissioners for his own policy. . . . The Fire Chief can set no policy. . . . The Commissioners . . . who are alleged to have supported me did so . . . merely because they had reached certain conclusions from observing operations of the Department." The reader may judge for himself.

Mayor Poulson felt that the law required integration. John Alderson, the Fire Chief and General Manager of the Fire Department—a career official who had won a national reputation for raising the Department to peak efficiency—felt that integration would damage the morale of his force, since much of a Los Angeles fireman's life is spent in the close community of the fire house. The reader himself may attempt to assimilate into one decision the qualitatively different legal, moral, political, administrative, and managerial arguments that arise in this case. He may wish to consider, too, a problem which this case barely touches: namely, given the decision to integrate—and the ruffled feelings aroused in the decision-making process—how could the policy have been introduced with the least damage to departmental morale and with the best chance of winning acceptance from line personnel?

The reader may also detect in the Los Angeles story more than the ordinary amount of irony and human unpredictability to be found in public affairs. Mayor Poulson, having defeated his predecessor, Fletcher Bowron, widely known as a "reform mayor," in a bitter campaign in 1953 involving public housing and the teaching of UNESCO material in the public school system, was a man of whom advocates of both civil service reform and desegregation expected little. As a Republican congressman, he had voted against the Fair Employment Practices Bill. On the other hand, Chief Alderson, a former Rhodes scholar who had worked closely with the former Mayor, was widely admired as an efficient career official, not least by many of the same Los Angelenos who feared the advent of Poulson. Yet, as this story relates, Poulson came to feel that the Fire Department should be desegregated, and Chief Alderson, fighting to preserve both his Department's morale and his managerial discretion as a career administrator, opposed both desegregation and the Mayor. The reader may wish to recapitulate in his own mind the subtle as well as the broad implications of this story for determining what should be the relationships and the relative responsibilities of top career administrators and elected officials.

Some readers may need to be reminded that California's constitution requires that local government elections be non-party. These provisions have been strongly bolstered by tradition. Both in primary and general elections for local government posts, party identifications of candidates are not stated on the ballot or in campaign literature or, in practice, in newspaper, radio, and television accounts of campaigns for city offices. Local primary elections serve to weed out the top two candidates from a larger body of aspirants, none of whom carry party labels. The top two contenders oppose each other in the general election. In the election fight of 1953 between the incumbent Mayor, Bowron, and the victorious challenger, Poulson, both men were in fact Republicans, but in the California tradition of non-party local elections this affiliation was no more publicized than the fact that the former had been past president of the American Municipal Association while the latter was a member of the Lions Club. And both men were mindful that California tradition obliged them, on assuming city office, to act the way non-party, popularly elected political officials should act. Members of the City Council acted in the same tradition. Hence, this case offers the reader the somewhat unusual spectacle of a hot minority issue being disputed with almost every means at the disposal of the disputants except the political party.

The Setting

AS THE WARMTH OF JULY, 1953, began to descend on Los Angeles, expectancy pervaded the corridors of City Hall. Only weeks before, a bitter mayoralty campaign had been concluded. A man who had been in office so long that few city employees could remember his predecessor had been soundly defeated by Norris Poulson, a relatively unknown congressman from the city's northeast section. Fletcher Bowron, the retiring Mayor, had been the reform candidate of 1938. To many Los Angelenos he was the man who had brought good government to the city, and in all parts of the sprawling metropolis people were pondering the meaning of his defeat. Had this been a vote against the elaborate career service developed since 1938? Were politics once again to dominate City Hall? A bitter controversy over public housing had so over-shadowed other issues during the campaign that none of the 30,000 employees who served the city were quite sure what the future held.

Mayor Poulson's position was complicated by the fact that the departmental general managers held *permanent* civil service status. They were removable only for cause—good cause, to be demonstrated in a legal proceeding. While they served formally under citizen commissions interlayered between the Mayor and themselves, they would necessarily have to be key members of the new Poulson team—the Police Chief, the Fire Chief, the Health Director, the Personnel Director, and the like. How loyal would they be? How closely were they tied to the policy and personality of the former Mayor? How much change did the citizens expect? Newspaper reports to the effect that various department heads were slated for removal intensified the atmosphere of suspicion in City Hall.

Not all the problems facing the Mayor had been debated in the campaign. One of these problems was a highly volatile issue: racial segregation in the Fire Department.

Throughout Mayor Bowron's last four-year term both the National Association for the Advancement of Colored People and the Los Angeles Urban League, which had seen segregation eliminated from other city departments including the Police Department, had begun fighting for desegregation in the Fire Department. Little progress had been made in convincing Chief Alderson, but in 1953 most of the officers of the NAACP personally supported incumbent Mayor

Bowron. They decided to withhold public action in order not to give challenger Poulson another issue for his campaign. However the NAACP wrote a letter to both candidates warning that it would attack segregation in the Fire Department after the election. Each candidate replied, promising to fight segregation if he should be elected, and the issue had little effect on minority group support of either candidate during the campaign.

Although the racial issue was not raised, the campaign did strain the relationship between new Mayor Poulson and Fire Chief Alderson. The Chief had been one of Bowron's most trusted department heads. While the Chief did nothing publicly to indicate his attitude, some of the leading Poulson supporters questioned Alderson's neutrality, and many expected the new Mayor to attempt to remove Alderson. When Poulson met Alderson after taking office he told him plainly that he deeply resented the Fire Chief's participation in the campaign. He added, however, that because of his respect for Alderson's professional competence, he had no plans for a change in Fire Department leadership, so long as the Chief behaved himself.[2]

In this environment the NAACP made plans to carry out its fight against segregation. On August 17, 1953, a group of citizens inspired by the NAACP signed a "Petition Concerning Racial Discrimination and Segregation in the Fire Department." Addressed to Chief Alderson and the citizen Board of Fire Commissioners, the petition alleged that:

1. Negroes are not appointed to vacancies in the Fire Department unless vacancies occur in one of two Negro stations, Nos. 14 and 30.
2. Negroes are not permitted to transfer from these two stations to other stations in the city.
3. Negroes are precluded from promotions excepting as vacancies in the higher ranks may occur in these two stations.
4. These circumstances constitute discrimination contrary to the constitutions and laws of the state and the nation, in that equal protection of the laws is being denied the Negro firemen.

Receipt of the petition was reported to the August 27, 1953 meeting of the Board of Fire Commissioners, which set the matter for hearing on October 8. A copy of the petition was also sent to Mayor Poulson. In a letter to the President of the Board of Fire Commissioners, dated September 14, the Mayor reviewed the claims of the petitioners and then said:

> I would appreciate you and the fellow members of your commission investigating immediately the allegations of this petition. *If they are true, I am sure that you will agree that such practices are abhorrent in a democratic nation such as ours. I trust that your board will take such summary action as may be necessary to completely eliminate any such unfairness.*
>
> If there is any way in which my office can be helpful in implementing the requests contained herein, I would appreciate your calling upon me. Further, I would be grateful on hearing from you as to what disposition your board makes of the subject matter of the petition referred to. [Emphasis added.]

The Mayor's letter appeared to set forth a broad policy line: no racial discrimination in the Fire Department.

The Position of the Mayor in Los Angeles

A closer look at the organization of the Los Angeles municipal government will be helpful at this point.

In Los Angeles, as in nearly all major U. S. cities, the separation of powers principle is observed. The Council is the legislative agency of the city, the Mayor the chief executive, and the line between these two entities is sharply drawn when it is convenient or politically advantageous for either side to do so. At other times the line becomes fuzzy to the point of providing a smokescreen behind which the Council can withdraw from touchy matters when it finds it expeditious to do so. It found it expeditious to withdraw in the Fire Department segregation case. The Council did not have to enter the fracas. It did not.

Within the executive branch the battle over integration was promoted by the "weak mayor" structure of Los Angeles' city government. The Mayor, as chief executive officer, has no direct lines of authority over his departments. Instead

[2] In commenting on this case, Chief Alderson agrees that many persons assumed that Mayor Poulson would remove him. However, he maintains that persons in Los Angeles who believed that he had supported the Bowron campaign were misinformed: "To this day I do not know how my son voted. I made no statements, contributed no money, asked not one voter to vote or to vote for anyone."

he must work through commissions, which, according to the charter, "supervise, control, regulate, and manage" the various departments. The major features of this type of organization can be seen in the following chart:

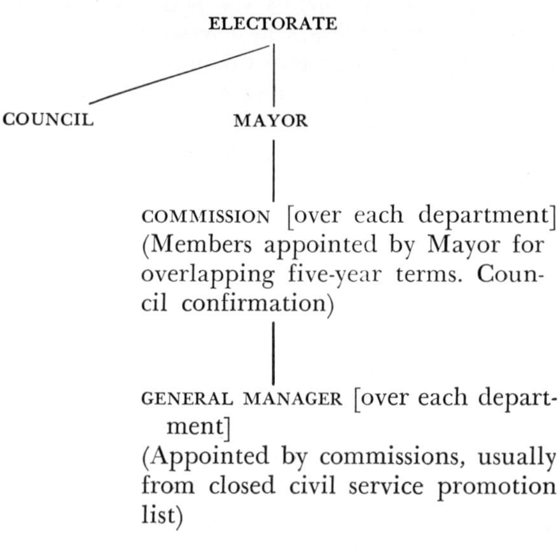

The Mayor's authority over the commissions is limited by three conditions: (1) Service on a commission is for five years, rather than at the pleasure of the Mayor. (2) Terms are staggered; one vacancy occurs each year. (3) Appointments and removals of commissioners are subject to confirmation by a majority of the Council. The Mayor may remove a commissioner for any reason, but the traditional jealousy between the Council and the Mayor has made confirmation of such removals highly unpredictable. As a result, the Mayor's removal power is seldom exercised.

With the exception of the Board of Public Works, which functions on a full-time basis, the commissions generally meet once each week for a few hours. Members are paid a small sum per meeting for attendance. While many persons wish to serve on such bodies, leading citizens often decline appointments because of the time required and the contentious atmosphere which frequently characterizes commission work. Also, many civic leaders live outside the city limits and are not eligible. The Mayor is generally limited in his choices for appointment by (1) the scarcity of interested candidates, and (2) political obligations of councilmen whom he seeks to help.

Under the commissioners are the operating departments of Los Angeles' city government. The general manager of each major department reports to its commission and operates under the terms of Section 79 of the City Charter, which says:

> The Board may issue instructions to the General Manager of its department concerning his exercise of any of the powers conferred upon him by the Charter. Failure on his part to comply with such instructions or incompetency, dishonesty, discourtesy or neglect of duty on his part as determined by the Board of his Department shall constitute adequate grounds for his removal by said Board.

Although the power of the commissions over the general managers would seem to be absolute, in practice such power is seldom exercised. Civil service protection extends to and includes the general manager's position. Removal is not a simple matter. In addition, there is a system of closed promotions, which tends to limit access to top departmental jobs to persons who have come up through the ranks. On the other hand, the leadership of the general managers and other members of the career service has, in the opinion of most knowledgeable experts, done much to increase the managerial effectiveness and the moral tone of the Los Angeles city government over the past twenty years. (Chief Alderson is frequently cited as an outstanding example in this connection.)

Almost without exception, the career officials recognize the limitations under which they operate and regard the commission form of government as outmoded. These attitudes of the general managers and members of the career service are promoted, to a marked degree, by community opinion of the commissions. The General Manager of the Police Department, for example, has extremely high status in the community. The President of the Police Commission usually is virtually unknown, as are all other commission presidents.

Mayor Bowron's predecessor (before 1938) usually confined his management relationships to the commissions, which functioned in fact as administrative heads. Bowron himself tended to by-pass the commissions and to rely on the general managers for administrative leadership. Also, the commissions languished considerably during the war when many of the citizens interested in public service turned their energies to enterprises of the federal government.

When Norris Poulson succeeded Bowron as Mayor in July, 1953, the prevailing mayor-general manager intimacy was amended somewhat to suit the personalities involved. In some instances the Bowron pattern was followed, but in others, as in the Fire Department where personal antagonism had already developed, the new Mayor dealt primarily with the commission. Thus, in the Fire Department the Board of Fire Commissioners was in a new and prominent role at a time when the integration dispute began.

The Nature of the Fire Service

In the United States as a whole the emergence of the fire service as a professional, full-time occupation has been a comparatively recent development. Throughout the 19th century most of the nation's cities depended on volunteers. Volunteer companies were frequently the bulwark of a city's political machine as well as the nucleus of many social activities. This heritage together with the assumption that anyone can be a fireman has fostered in many U. S. cities an acceptance of political appointments to, and political use of, the fire department. Fire fighting, which consumes fifteen to twenty percent of the average city budget, has been slow to gain public acceptance as a career civil service profession. Perhaps for this reason, firemen, compared with other municipal employees, sometimes appear to be somewhat on the defensive, to associate largely with one another, and to share more intensely occupational group attitudes.

The Los Angeles Fire Department

In Los Angeles the first full-time paid fire crew was hired in 1885, only fourteen years after the formal establishment of a volunteer department. The Fire Commission was established that same year. Under Alderson, who became Chief in 1940, the Los Angeles Fire Department became a model department with a Class I rating by the National Board of Fire Underwriters. Its operation in 1955 cost the city approximately $15,000,000 and required a force of about 2,800, nearly all uniformed personnel.

The following table shows the various ranks in the Fire Department at the start of 1953. (By 1954 there were 81 Negro firemen.)

	WHITE	NEGRO
Fireman	1727	55
Auto Fireman	252	9
Engineer	181	4
Captain	287	6
Battalion Chief	36	0
First Ass't. Chief Engineer	15	0
Deputy Chief Engineer	1	0
Chief Engineer	1	0

Since Los Angeles firemen are in the city's civil service system, their recruitment, examination, and promotion are handled by the Civil Service Commission, limiting the Fire Department's participation in the personnel process to two areas:

1. After lists of eligibles have been established, the Department may choose from the top three, the so-called "rule of three." Only when an individual waives his priority position may the Department reach farther down for a man.
2. In promotions to Captain and above, examinations have been in two parts: written (sixty percent) and oral (forty percent). The Civil Service Commission's practice has been to ask senior fire officers to serve on the oral boards, a system followed also in the Police Department.

While these procedures have by all accounts resulted in the selection of an efficient force, the disparity between the percentage of Negroes employed as firemen and their proportion in the population as a whole was conspicuous to the NAACP. The 1953 special census showed that Negroes comprised ten percent of the city's population, while only about three percent of the Fire Department was Negro.

To Chief Alderson the reason for the disparity between whites and Negroes was obvious: "The facts are," he wrote later, "the Negro cannot compete, principally because of requirements for a high school diploma. The Negro population of Los Angeles consists in the main of an influx from the Deep South which started during World War II. Most of these people are not high school graduates." Alderson also charged that "over 50 percent of the Negro firemen had been appointed by the administration previous to Bowron's entirely illegally—in some cases being jumped over white men on eligible lists as many as 300 to 400 places when the City Charter limits choice to the first three names only." The Chief made this charge on several occasions, including Commission meetings, and no one ever denied it.

The Department's promotion system was also criticized by the NAACP. Its leaders noted that although Negroes had been on the Fire Department since 1909, none had risen above the rank of Captain, the highest grade to be found in a single station.

While in 1955 most Los Angeles firemen were scattered in some ninety stations throughout the city, many were assigned to headquarters duties such as departmental administration, fire prevention, arson investigation, rescue service, fire communications, and supply and maintenance. Since 1940 Chief Alderson had placed five Negro firemen in the Fire Prevention Bureau and three in the Supply Maintenance Bureau. An eight-hour day was observed in each of these bureaus. In the Training School, which was begun by Alderson, there was no segregation: the men worked, ate, and slept together for a nine-week period. It was the prospect of immediate integration in the fire houses that was worrying the Chief and the commissioners.[3]

Throughout the nation, the fireman who works on the shift system averages about 67 hours per week at his fire station, much of it waiting for fires to occur. (In Los Angeles, the average fireman might expect to fight two fires in a week.) The shift system, 24 hours on and 24 hours off, is more common than the eight-hour day. This schedule is followed in all Los Angeles stations where extra days off reduce the work week to 62 hours. A number of large cities, notably Boston, New York, Philadelphia, Seattle, and Phoenix, have changed to the eight-hour day with the total work week varying between 42 and 48 hours. How prevalent the eight-hour day will ultimately become is still difficult to predict. It is said to involve about a fifty percent increase in costs, and on that count alone resistance to its adoption has been very strong in most communities. The eight-hour day, forty-hour week is also opposed by firemen on the 24-hour shift system for two reasons: (1) many are able to take part-time jobs on their "off-days" and, (2) many fear that the eight-hour day will lead to integration of fire with police departments.

The use of the 24-hour shift instead of the eight-hour day greatly complicates race relations. The firemen who spend 24 hours together in the fire house must live with one another on terms of much greater intimacy than is the case with the eight-hour day men. In most instances, eating and recreational arrangements in the fire house are made on a group basis. Bedding is a personal responsibility, but there is a great deal of clubbing together for recreation in the fire house.

Thus, in Los Angeles in 1953 nearly half of all the hours in a fireman's week were spent socializing and sleeping with people whose ties to him, while essentially occupational, had come to assume the qualities of kinship. The integration issue led many to inquire: how important was a harmonious social life in the fire house to the morale of the fireman? And how was this type of morale related to efficiency?

[3] The Chief later maintained that interracial association in the Training School was the key to peaceful integration in the fire houses in the long run: "In a period of less than five years the great majority of the uniformed force . . . would have become accustomed in that nine weeks to working with and accepting the Negro. . . ."

The Conflict

MAYOR POULSON'S LETTER of September 14, 1953 stating his opposition to racial segregation in the Fire Department created little public stir. It was not even mentioned in the daily newspapers. There was only a slight reaction in the four-story Fire Department headquarters building on Hill Street, a few blocks from towering City Hall.

From the Mayor's point of view, the lack of public interest was a stroke of fortune. He was not sympathetic to the aims of the NAACP, had voted against FEPC in Congress, and was now thinking of the problem primarily in legal terms, in contrast to his earlier feeling that it was essentially a political matter. He did not want to stir emotions. He wanted racial integration carried only to the point necessary to avoid any legal action against the City.[4]

Thus the Mayor's dutiful letter was received and perfunctorily announced by the Board of Fire Commissioners' President Howard Callanan at the September 17 meeting. There were no comments. The Board had set a public hearing on the NAACP petition for October 8.

After transacting routine business in the unpretentious headquarters of the Fire Commission, the Board adjourned to the Department auditorium for the 22nd item, the hearing on Poulson's letter. There the commissioners were arrayed around a long table on stage, and Chief Alderson sat down with the audience, which included NAACP attorneys and representatives.

The backgrounds of the members participating in the hearing that morning varied widely. President Callanan was an undertaker, a prominent Catholic layman. He had been appointed by the former Mayor in 1943 and had been chairman of the Board since 1949. The other Bowron appointee, Cyril R. Rothmund, was a businessman from San Fernando Valley. His service on the Board had begun in 1946. Both Callanan and Rothmund had submitted *pro forma* resignations, as is customary but not obligatory when a new mayor takes office. No action was taken on their resignations. They remained in the Mayor's desk ready for him to use.

Seated with old-timers Rothmund and Callanan were an attorney who specialized in property management, an executive of the Fox West Coast theater chain, and the Dodge-Plymouth dealer of a suburban community. Their names were, respectively, Richard Yeamans, W. H. Lollier, and C. F. Joscelyn.

[4] Chief Alderson comments: "It became a common remark in and around Commission meetings that if the Mayor would make his policy clear it would be followed. Privately he spoke one way and publicly another. He repeatedly encouraged me at first to oppose integration and then, to go very, very slowly."

Yeamans and his wife had been active in Poulson's campaign. His appointment to the Fire Commission was interpreted as a reward for personal services. Lollier's commissionership was the one which the city's theater owners had come to regard as their own. Their link with the fire service was close, and they had virtually succeeded in establishing in the minds of others as well as their own the principle that one man on the commission should always represent the theater owners. Well-known to politicians, theater executive Lollier had turned out to be a "natural" for that vacancy.

Poulson's third appointment, Joscelyn, was a product of the niceties of legislative-executive relationships. While he happened to be a fire "buff" with a strong interest in the Department, his major qualification had been advocacy of his candidacy by Councilman Harold Harby. The Councilman was unpredictable, outspoken, aggressive—a force with which the new Mayor had to reckon. Joscelyn's appointment was consequently seen as an attempt by Poulson to put uncommitted Councilman Harold Harby in his debt.

At this first hearing on the segregation issue, NAACP attorneys claimed that segregation was illegal and recited the specific charges of discrimination in their petition. President Callanan retorted, denying that the Department had ever practiced discrimination. Chief Alderson stated: "For the last ten years, at least, no Negro has been passed over or denied appointment. Negroes have had equal treatment with whites in all respects." The Chief further emphasized his right under the Charter to make appointments, promotions, and transfers "for the best interests of all the people of Los Angeles."

As the hearing moved on routinely, most of the commissioners demonstrated strong sympathy for Alderson's position. The NAACP attorneys were refused the opportunity to question Chief Alderson about his statements and were told in effect that they had not made their case. They were asked to present additional specific evidence of the alleged discrimination at the Board's next meeting.

The Community Joins the Conflict

The conflict was now out in the open. President Callanan and Chief Alderson had in effect answered the Mayor's letter by denying the existence of segregation or discrimination, and the majority of the Board indicated sympathy with the Chief's position.

The hearing also set in motion political and social forces determined to win the controversy. Saying that its case *had* been proved, the NAACP refused to submit further evidence. Not by coincidence, 39 of the 81 Negroes in the Fire Department requested transfers the day of the NAACP announcement. The others were not so willing to enter the fray actively on the NAACP side.

Meanwhile, public support was being rallied behind the Fire Department. The person of the General Manager, Chief Alderson, came through clearly as the symbol around which those favoring the *status quo* sought to converge. A resolution was adopted by the City Council praising Alderson for his "inspiring leadership and demonstrated skill" in building the city's nationwide reputation for superior fire-fighting techniques and fire-prevention methods. The Fire Commission itself adopted a resolution praising Alderson for reducing the number of fires through "an extraordinary campaign of fire prevention and house-to-house inspection."

Letters and petitions urging no change in racial policies were circulated in the fire houses; and the *Los Angeles Daily News,* the city's Democratic newspaper which had supported Bowron in the mayoralty campaign, published the following pro-Alderson editorial:

> Chief Engineer John H. Alderson of the Fire Department has suddenly found that one of his pet causes has boomeranged. The former Rhodes scholar, who trained for the ministry, is the victim of a cheap political trick which masquerades as a drive to eliminate segregation in the Fire Department and the blocking of promotions for Negro firemen. . . .
>
> Alderson got in bad with Mayor Norris Poulson and public housing foes when he protested the insulting tactics used by Congressman Clare Hoffman and his investigators during their questioning of ex-Mayor Fletcher Bowron who was a voluntary witness at a hearing held here. Alderson, as a private citizen and on his own time and at his own expense, sent protest telegrams to Vice President Richard M. Nixon, Senator William Knowland, and Representative Joe Holt. That Alderson should dare exercise his own freedom of speech was something unheard of among the anti-public housing groups and newspapers. *When Poulson succeeded Bowron, Alderson was among the first marked for removal. . . .* [Emphasis added.]
>
> Shortly after the election, Mayor Poulson and his anti-public housing pals whetted their axes for Chief Alderson. It is extremely significant that Alderson has been deluged with fifty-four transfer requests from the city's eighty-one Negro firemen [sic]. Before that and during the past fourteen years, Alderson had not received one transfer request from a Negro fireman. . . .
>
> Chief Alderson's long-range plans call for full assimilation of Negro firemen within six years, during which time he plans to intensify his continuing educational program. Now, he unhappily finds that, due to political axe-wielding, his whole plan has been set back fourteen years—the exact amount of time it has taken him to lay the foundations for it.

The NAACP fought back, charging that battalion chiefs were circulating anti-integration petitions on government time. The NAACP lawyers denied the existence of a "Get Alderson" campaign or any relationship between the segregation issue and public housing. They stated:

> We learned in the course of trying to secure a *Daily News* retraction that the writer of the editorial was a close friend of Alderson and had written many articles praising Alderson's conduct of the Fire Department. We believed then, and we believe now, that the editorial was inspired by the Chief and that he furnished the garbled "facts" which were used to apologize for his racial policy. At no time had the NAACP or its lawyers made any demand for the removal of the Chief.

The Commissioners Delay Action

Action *around* the Board was more intense than *within* it. The Board itself promised an "early decision," and the Chief was instructed to submit a report with recommendations for the disposition of the petition. Otherwise, meetings were routinely held in November. There was among the commissioners no sense of urgency or high concern because there was no "follow up" pressure from the Mayor, a fact which led some Board members to believe that Poulson had no strong convictions in favor of desegregation. Aside from one thirty-minute session held before a formal meeting, no special caucuses were called to discuss the problem. The commissioners were following the habits of the past; they were expecting Chief Alderson to come up with an answer.

Thus, the Chief was the central character at the December 10 meeting, which was witnessed by a capacity audience. Called upon by the Board President to make a report on the petition, Alderson again categorically denied that there had been "any discrimination whatsoever in the appointment of the men, in the promotion of men, in the training of men, or in the treatment of men in this Department for many years." He pointed out that the issue had been raised by sources outside the Fire Department and that in his memory "no request for transfer other than to the Fire Prevention Bureau and special assignments was ever received by the Administrative Office from members of the negro[5] race until the issue was raised by the filing of the petition." In conclusion, Alderson said:

> I respectfully recommend that your Board stand on Section 78 of the City Charter and that we continue to appoint, promote and transfer employees of the Department for the best interests of all the City of Los Angeles.

The Chief's report carried the day. It was adopted as the report of the commission with only Yeamans dissenting. In its resolution accepting Alderson's policy, the Board said that the matter would be reviewed from "time to time and that the Board desired to assure the people . . . that the policy will be carried into effect for the best interests of all the people. . . ." The resolution concluded with a statement of confidence in the "policies being pursued under the present General Manager, John H. Alderson, of the Fire Department."

Chief Alderson had been given a vote of confidence.

The Mayor Confers

Four months had elapsed since the NAACP petition had been presented and three months since the Mayor had written his letter. Yet nothing had been changed. The commission, in effect, told both the NAACP and the Mayor that there was no segregation and no discrimination, that present policies would be continued. The next move was up to the NAACP and the Mayor. Although the Mayor's letter had appeared to side with the NAACP, he made no move to persuade the commissioners to do anything more.

The NAACP pondered its next action. Its attorneys reported:

> We have reached a complete impasse. Chief Alderson had said in no uncertain terms that he intended no change in his policies. The Board had backed him up. The Mayor had been silent since his original statement. We came to the reluctant conclusion that we had no option but to file suit. Before doing that, we decided to appeal to the City Council to deny funds for defense of such a suit by the City Attorney on the grounds that . . . "racial segregation is so at variance with the public policy of this city."

On December 17 such a letter was sent to every member of the City Council, the Mayor, the City Attorney, the Board of Fire Commissioners and Chief Alderson. The letter included this statement: "This policy of racial segregation did not originate with John H. Alderson . . . but it has been refined and implemented during his term of office." The NAACP attorneys wanted to be firm in their opposition to the Chief, they said, but at the same time they wanted to be fair.

The letter aroused slight councilmanic interest, for there was little inclination to fight battles that the legislators believed to be in the sector of the chief executive. However, it brought a quick response from the Mayor, who wrote that he had arranged a meeting with the commission on "the first available date, January 7," and concluded: "Shortly thereafter, I hope to have something additional to add to this acknowledgment."

It has proved difficult to reconstruct a definitive and mutually agreed-upon account of the January 7 meeting in the Mayor's office. The Mayor, the Fire Chief, and the commissioners all left the meeting with different understandings of what agreements had been reached. The meeting opened with the Mayor's deputy reading a copy of Poulson's first letter to the commissioners. The Mayor then proposed to the

[5] The extreme sensitivity required of the administrator in dealing with racial issues is illustrated here. The Chief did not capitalize the proper name Negro throughout the basic one-and-one-half-page document, as the NAACP was careful to point out in its report. While this would seem to be a small matter, colored people are highly sensitive about it. They consider such a failure a slight to the race, pointing out that the word Caucasian is always capitalized. The Mayor's letters always carefully capitalized Negro, as did the Los Angeles newspapers.

commission and the Chief that he, the Mayor, issue a statement promising that any improper practices would be corrected.

The Mayor recalls that Alderson was the principal antagonist and that the Chief said there was no reason for such a statement. There were no improper practices. The only public announcement required was one in which Alderson's position as Fire Chief was re-stated and his responsibility for assignment of personnel was reaffirmed.

Alderson's recollection is that he was not "the leader of the opposition" but rather one of several persons present who protested the Mayor's suggestion. The Chief recollects that all the commissioners except Yeamans argued "at length" against the proposal. Alderson felt also that he and the commission had merely been brought to the Mayor's office to approve a statement that had already been prepared.

After considerable debate during which several amendments relaxing the firmness of the Mayor's statement were proposed and accepted, Chief Alderson said nothing further. This was interpreted by Poulson and his aides as a reluctant acceptance, and the meeting was adjourned on a note of desperate optimism, with only Yeamans having clearly stated support for the Mayor's position.

Immediately the press was called in. The Mayor read the statement in which he said that some present practices were improper but that a sudden change in these long-standing practices might seriously impair the efficiency of the Department. Therefore, he said:

> . . . in an effort to conform with my firm policy of securing fair and equal treatment for all, the Board of Fire Commissioners has decided that there should be, commencing within the next six months, a gradual correction of these practices. In the interest of unity and my overall responsibility to all our citizens of whatever racial origin, I have acceded to this program of gradual correction of these policies.

The ink was hardly dry on the newspapers carrying the Mayor's statement when four members of the commission told reporters that they had agreed to nothing. Chief Alderson said he had accepted no proposal of gradual change in "six months, or in two months, or in one year. . . ." He would continue to follow the policies laid down for him by the fire commissioners, not by the Mayor. "I reported to them three weeks ago," he said, "that I considered the policy a fair one and was told then to continue to follow it."

The rebuff by the commissioners and Alderson left Poulson in a difficult position. Possessed of little administrative power, and having to work through citizen commissions serving for a fixed term, there was no dramatic action that he could take. To order the commission to adopt his policy violated tradition and would, he felt, unquestionably result in mass resignations. The political consequences of mass resignations he could not foresee, but they seemed hazardous. Therefore, to the Mayor, ordering the commission to obey was not an answer. Alderson himself was untouchable. Not only was he protected by civil service, but he was following the orders of his appropriate authority, the commissioners.

The Mayor knew his limitations, but the public did not. The picture presented in the newspapers was clear cut: a subordinate defying his boss. How was Poulson to avoid creating an image of himself as weak and vacillating? It was obvious that further debate in the public press would serve only to emphasize his limited power. Before Poulson decided his next step, however, the NAACP acted. It captured the headlines the next morning, January 9, with an indirect threat of litigation unless a specific integration program was adopted. Gratitude was expressed to the Mayor, and the letter to him included this paragraph, which was well publicized:

> We join you in the hope that this matter can be adjusted without resort to litigation, but we are dismayed by the statement of Fire Chief John H. Alderson that he has made no agreement to end his segregatory practices and his reiteration of his formerly voiced intention to maintain the very practices that are the subject of negotiations.

Pressing the attack (and thus taking the Mayor off a very uncomfortable hook), the NAACP filed a petition with the Superior Court of the County of Los Angeles to take depositions from Alderson and all the fire commissioners. While the NAACP action made it unnecessary for the Mayor to decide what initiative he should and would take, Poulson had no part in its timing. In fact, the NAACP would have taken the same steps even if Alderson and the commissioners had unanimously agreed to sign Poulson's statement, for the NAACP lawyers had decided that even the Mayor's statement offered possibilities of temporizing and hence was not sufficiently encouraging to warrant lessening their pressure. As one NAACP attorney commented, "It is the implementation and not the adoption of such a policy that takes time."

Thus the NAACP's intervention worked to the Mayor's great political advantage. He was relieved of the necessity of answering Alderson, and he escaped involvement in the NAACP attack. Chief Alderson and the commissioners were left to stand alone, while Poulson for the first time in his life found himself inferentially allied with the NAACP. Seen in retrospect, these events of early January, which started out so blackly for Poulson, deeply affected all subsequent events in the case. In the first place, the personal differences between the Mayor and the Chief became a public matter. The Mayor and his advisers felt that there was a conflict, although Alderson has always denied that he was challenging the Mayor, maintaining that he was simply obeying the Board and the regulations. Secondly, the fight was no longer over an abstract legal principle in which the Mayor himself had relatively little interest. And third, the NAACP and the Mayor were now on the same side. The NAACP, no longer suspecting that the Mayor was secretly abetting the Chief, directed the full brunt of its attack at Alderson and the commission.

Alderson Testifies

On January 29 the presiding Judge ordered Alderson and all fire commissioners to appear and give depositions before a Superior Court Commissioner. Various court delays occurred, and it was not until March 9 that the Chief began his testimony. Depositions were taken over a two-month period. Board President Callanan, who had been ill, finally appeared April 27. While stenographic records were kept of the testimony, these have never been transcribed. The newspaper accounts furnish the only available public record of the statements made.

Chief Alderson, the first witness, spent two days on the stand. He said that 75 of the 81 Negroes were assigned to two stations. While it was not a Department policy to refuse graduation to Negro rookies if there was no vacancy at these two stations, he could not recall when a vacancy did not exist at one or the other for Negro graduates. In cross examination by NAACP attorneys, Alderson was quoted by the *Herald-Express* as saying that he believed in racial segregation. Other specific questions and answers recorded by the newspapers during the two-day session follow:

The Los Angeles Times:

Q: "Is it by accident or design that only Negroes have been assigned to the two stations in question?"

A: "It is not an accident. The practice has my complete consent and approval, and no one has imposed this policy on me."

The Daily News:

Q: "Why have two requests for transfers by Negro personnel been denied?"

A: "Such requests are always denied if anyone outside the Department intervenes."

The Herald-Express:

Q: "Would Chief Alderson see that racial segregation was ended in six months?"

A: "No."

The commissioners underscored Alderson's statements. Lollier, Joscelyn, and Rothmund were reported as saying that they approved existing policy and practices; and, according to the *News,* they said that nothing had been done about Poulson's letter. Yeamans, the lone member of the commission who was clearly opposed to the Department's policy, stated before the Court Commissioner, "Firemen are assigned to their stations on the basis of race."

President Callanan, appearing late in April after his illness, put the capstone on Board testimony. The *Herald-Express* reported these points in Callanan's testimony:

1. He believed in segregation.
2. All Negroes were assigned to two stations.
3. Eighty percent of the colored firemen had asked for transfers, but they had been turned down because the whites didn't want them.
4. Seventeen hundred white firemen had sent letters to Alderson threatening to resign if Negroes were assigned to their stations.
5. The Fire Commission did not intend to change its policy, despite Poulson. "I think," he said, "it works out for the best interests of the Department and the city."

6. The present policy of segregation was not discrimination, "because the two stations in question have better than average buildings and facilities."

Approximately nine months had now elapsed since the Mayor's letter of September 16, 1953. It was apparent that neither the commission nor the Chief was planning any basic change in policy and practice. The Mayor's letter and his later personal plea were being ignored.

As a consequence, the NAACP reasserted its threat of court action. In a letter to the Mayor, written shortly after the completion of Chairman Callanan's testimony, Attorney Loren Miller requested a conference to discuss the problem. Acknowledging the Mayor's good faith in the matter, Miller commented:

> We are convinced from the sworn testimony of your Board of Fire Commissioners and Fire Chief Alderson that there is neither a desire nor an intent to make any change in the long standing segregation policies practiced in the Fire Department. And, as we said in our letter of January 9, 1954, "We are firm in our conviction that such a practice runs counter to applicable state and federal statutory and Constitutional requirements and to the public policy of this city and state." If we are right in that contention, we have the duty to seek a reversal of present policies in the Fire Department.

Meanwhile, events were occurring in Washington that strengthened the hand of the NAACP. Arguments had been completed on the famous school segregation cases. On May 17, 1954 the opinions in *Brown et al* v. *Board of Education* and *Bolling* v. *Sharpe* were delivered by Chief Justice Earl Warren, who said:

> Classifications based solely upon race must be scrutinized with particular care, since they are contrary to our traditions and hence constitutionally suspect. As long ago as 1896, this Court declared the principle 'that the Constitution of the United States, in its present form, forbids, so far as civil and political rights are concerned, discrimination by the General Government, or by the States, against any citizen because of his race.'

While the Supreme Court decision was restricted to segregation in the schools, its moral force seemed to reach far beyond this single activity of government. No one, of course, knew the lengths to which the Court might carry its newly enunciated doctrine, but the implicatio was clear that any discrimination based on rac alone would be subjected to the most searchin examination. In Los Angeles, the NAACP' threat of legal action now seemed to have rea teeth in it.

What Is Legal?

The Fire Commission responded quickly t the legal development. Early in June, Commis sioner Yeamans proposed a resolution askin the City Attorney for a ruling on present prac tices, since, to quote from the resolution, "th United States Supreme Court has recently ren dered certain decisions construing the rights o Negroes," and since "certain groups have as serted that the assignment of Negro firemen ir the Los Angeles Fire Department may violat rights, as being discriminatory and restricting promotion possibilities. . . ."

The resolution passed unanimously. The City Attorney immediately asked the commission whether assignments were made on the basis o race alone. If so, what were the administrative reasons for such action? At their June 25 meet ing the commissioners decided that despite Al derson's view the answer to the City Attorney' first question was "yes." Alderson was asked t prepare a reply setting forth the administrative reasons for such assignments.

The Alderson report was issued July 1. H was sharply critical of the commission's resolu tion requesting an opinion from the City At torney. Since he had made personnel assign ments for the past fourteen years "without defi nite direction from the Board of Fire Commis sioners," Alderson believed that he was "bes qualified to state on what basis assignments have been made." He emphasized that assignment were not based on race alone; the fact that six Negroes were in other Bureaus proved it. H concluded:

> The City Charter gives to the General Manager of a Department the right to transfer and assign employees subject to the rules adopted by the Board. To my knowledge, the Board of Fire Commissioners has never adopted a rule or issued an order concerning the transfer or assignment of any member of this Department. *Every transfer and assignment which I have made during my term of office has been based*

not on race but on what in my considered opinion was best for the morale of the department, the efficiency of the department and the benefit to the people of the city that the department serves. If I became convinced that transfer of members from Stations 30 and 14 to other stations was for the benefit of the department and the people of this city, I would make those transfers without question.

. . . In the final analysis, the decision will be made, unless I receive orders from the Board to the contrary, based on (1) the efficiency of the department, (2) the effect on the member who is making the request, and (3) finally and most important, the effect on the service rendered to the people of this city. [Emphasis added.]

Alderson's statement received wide and prominent newspaper coverage. He buttressed it by a threat to resign. The *News* said he would "leave forthwith if the Fire Commission insists on taking over assignment of personnel, transfers, and other functions now under his control." To the *Herald-Express,* on the same date, he declared:

I am not going to remain as Chief if the power of transfer of personnel is taken from me. I believe I've had some small part in building a first-rate Fire Department in Los Angeles, and I will not remain to see it torn down to a second, third, and fourth rate department.

The commission was caught in a cross-fire that had been made more intense by the Supreme Court decision. A hasty action might send one of the nation's most highly regarded chiefs into a martyr's retirement. Who could predict the consequences for the city? On the other hand, a failure to face the facts might invite legal disaster at a later date. Tension once more gripped the small Fire Commission meeting room. A second vote was taken on the question, "Are firemen assigned on the basis of race alone?" "Yes," said the commission in a three to two vote, with Callanan, Yeamans, and Lollier in support and Rothmund and Joscelyn opposed.

Callanan agreed with the Chief about the undesirability of integration; he disagreed that segregation was not a basis of departmental assignments. Yeamans had picked up Lollier's vote for his pro-integration stand, while Callanan, Rothmund, and Joscelyn were still allied with the Chief on the basic issue. While the Supreme Court decisions undoubtedly affected Lollier, more immediate and more subtle social factors had worked on him to change his mind. Lollier and Yeamans met frequently socially outside the commission meetings. They came from the same Los Angeles community, were members of the same Legion club, and participated in various other social activities together. Looking back, another member of the Fire Commission stated that from this point on Lollier took his signals from Yeamans, the Mayor's supporter on the integration issue.

The Mayor now had two of the five votes on the commission. July 1 provided him an opportunity to make it three with the expiration of President Callanan's term. The search for a successor had been going on for several months, but in the end the Mayor turned to an old acquaintance, a supporter of his mayoralty campaign. He appointed Milton Brock, a well-known contractor and builder. There was no preliminary interview in which the Mayor stated his policy and asked Brock to agree to it if he wanted to serve on the Board. Brock himself said that he would not have accepted the position on those terms. He wanted to remain free to make his own decisions. And since like most citizens he had not followed the integration issue closely enough to have formed a firm opinion, he said he would have been completely unwilling to make a commitment if the Mayor had asked him. The Mayor's only opportunity to sound out Brock occurred at a social event where Poulson asked Brock how he felt about colored people in the city government. Brock said he had no strong prejudices one way or the other, that everyone essentially had a right to a fair opportunity. With this as his only glimpse into Brock's attitudes, the Mayor appointed him to the pivotal position on the commission.

The calculated aloofness of the City Council members to the entire affair evidenced itself in the confirmation proceedings. Brock appeared before the body but the only question asked was how he thought he would like the "hot seat." Approval of the Mayor's appointment was unanimous.

Nearly one year after his basic policy statement, Mayor Poulson appeared to be in control of the Fire Commission. He was in a position to take more aggressive steps.

Poulson Acts

Poulson now publicly criticized Alderson for even suggesting that his authority for assignment of personnel was under attack. He told reporters: "Nothing of that nature had been said or implied by myself or members of the Fire Commission. . . ." The *News* quoted the Mayor as declaring: "The Commissions set policy, and the General Managers of the Departments then carry out the policy. The Fire Department is no exception." Further, the Mayor said that he doubted that the integration of 81 Negro firemen with 2,500 whites would result in a "third or fourth-class" department.

In a letter addressed to the commission early in July the Mayor reported on a personal study he had made of the progress of racial integration in fire departments in Washington, D. C., and in Baltimore. Both were "working successfully." The Mayor concluded:

> I feel this information which I have obtained may be of some assistance to your Honorable Body. Your action of several weeks ago requesting an opinion from the City Attorney relating to this question of integration in our Fire Department was noted by me, and I approvingly interpreted this request as a positive step by the Commission in line with our agreement of last January 7 calling for a "gradual correction, commencing within the next six months, of unsatisfactory policies in personnel assignments originating more than 20 years ago."
>
> I am hopeful that the remarks attributed to Chief Alderson do not really reflect his true opinions or beliefs or those of the members of the Commission. I trust that the Commission will proceed to take other positive, well-reasoned steps leading to a solution of this entire matter.

Hardly had the commission met on July 8 to consider the Mayor's letter when Poulson exploded another bombshell. He acted on the resignation of Bowron-appointed Cyril R. Rothmund which had been in his desk for over a year. While Rothmund had been appointed by the former Mayor, he had actually supported Poulson for the mayoralty. Only the dismissal of Alderson himself could have created a greater stir.

The next morning Alderson was shown in the *Times* shaking hands with Rothmund,[6] while in adjoining columns Rothmund was castigating the Mayor. Said Rothmund: "The whole thing is politics on the part of the Mayor, and I want no part of it." Although he had no proof, he wondered if Poulson had not made some campaign promises that "led to all this." He charged the Mayor with personal coercion, saying that he had been ordered by Poulson's representative to vote "correctly" at the July 1 meeting or face removal. Instead, as noted above, Rothmund had sided with Alderson. A few days later came the "acceptance of his resignation."

In retrospect, it appeared that Rothmund's position on desegregation had not arisen from any deep-seated racial prejudice. Nor did he have any social or political relationships with other members of the commission that coerced him into voting with the majority. "I never saw them before I got in the elevator going to the fourth floor," he reported. Nor did his strong support of the Chief arise out of any personal warmth for Alderson: "He was often arrogant, and I had many clashes with him." What Rothmund loved was the efficiency of the Fire Department, and what he hated was "politics." Like oil and water, the two could not be mixed. Rothmund summed up his position:

> When Chief Alderson took over in the 30's, politics had already come into the department. He has eliminated it and brought a No. 1 rating to the department. We should keep that rating and not change our policies. A winning team like the Yankees doesn't change when it's ahead.

To succeed Rothmund the Mayor quickly appointed Robert A. Day, a young oil company

6 Chief Alderson explains the news photograph in this way: "Commissioner Rothmund announced during the meeting that his resignation had been accepted and a successor appointed, which was news to me. He made a statement critical of the Mayor and expressed admiration for the manner in which I had conducted my office. The room was filled with news photographers, television cameras, and news reel cameras. When the meeting adjourned Rothmund shook hands cordially with the other four Commissioners, wished them good luck, turned to me, extended his hand and wished me luck. This apparently was photographed by some photographers or many photographers present. . . . I had no control over the arrangement or composition of the front page of . . . [any Los Angeles] newspaper."

executive. The situation surrounding Day's appointment raised the question in the minds of some reporters whether Rothmund was actually removed because of his voting or because a place on the commission was desired for Day. The new member was in a sense a volunteer, a type of volunteer that Mayor Poulson could not afford to ignore. Day's father-in-law, who had suggested his appointment to Poulson, was William Keck, President of the Superior Oil Company. This firm had been one of the largest contributors to the Republican Party, and Keck himself was a potent influence in state and local politics.

With Day, Poulson did not even attempt the polite, off-handed screening on the racial question he had pursued with Brock. At a pre-appointment meeting, he and Day talked only in very general terms. Day's great personal interest in the fire service was expressed. But as to the big issue before the commission, the Mayor did not directly seek to discover what his new appointee's attitude would be.

Legal Decisions

As the controversy over the Rothmund dismissal spluttered into mid-July, investigation into the legal aspects of the problem was proceeding on two fronts. The City Attorney was readying his opinion, in response to the Fire Commission's resolution. The state Attorney General, at the request of a Negro assemblyman from a northern California district near San Francisco, was also preparing an opinion. The guiding role of the NAACP in the dispute was again evident.

On July 20 the first of the legal opinions was issued. It came from the City Attorney's office, and it did little to resolve the problem. It was clear from the legal precedents, said the City Attorney, that assignments could not be made on the basis of race alone. However, this restriction should not prevent the exercise of a reasonable discretion in personnel assignments, for it was quite proper that people should work where their efforts would result in the most efficient operation. Hence, the real question raised, according to the City Attorney, was whether or not the reasons for assignment were good and sufficient enough to disprove the claim that such assignment was on the basis of race alone. "The facts as presented to us," he declared, "are such that this question cannot be answered categorically. . . ." He pointed out that the commission's original resolution failed to give reasons for the assignment policy. He noted the Chief's July 1 report that assignment was not on the basis of race alone, and the later three to two vote by the commission flatly contradicting the Chief's statement. "This, of course, presents a factual conflict which we are unable to resolve. We are not a fact-finding body," the City Attorney observed. The opinion continued:

> In view of this conflict in the evidence presented to us, we cannot make a determination as to whether or not the practices referred to in said resolution are in violation of the Constitution or laws of this State or of the United States. As to violation of any decisions of the appellate courts of this State, or of the United States, we know of no decision directed to the Board of Fire Commissioners, the Fire Department, or the Chief Engineer of said department, or any officer thereof, upon this matter.
>
> . . . It appears to us that the problem with which you are confronted is one to be resolved by administrative decision.

The New Commission Acts

Of the old Alderson supporters, only Commissioner Joscelyn remained when the Board met to consider the City Attorney's opinion. It was he who now took the leadership; for it had become apparent to him, Joscelyn confided to Commissioner Brock, that some changes were inevitable. He therefore proposed that Chief Alderson submit, within six weeks, recommendations as to the manner in which "Negroes *could* be integrated gradually . . . with the least disruption possible in the Department, namely in morale and efficiency." Furthermore, the resolution emphasized that it had been and was now "the policy of this Commission and the Fire Department that personnel are assigned and promoted without regard to race, creed or color."

The Joscelyn proposal was not easy to disagree with. On the other hand it committed the commission to nothing. It asked only for suggestions as to how integration *could* take place. The possibility of achieving a unanimity of action, however, captivated the Board, and the resolution was adopted without a dissenting vote.

There was no question which one of the two principal protagonists, Alderson or Poulson, found the new order most acceptable. The Chief quickly said that he considered the resolution quite appropriate. It simply asked a question. It was "not an order or interference. . . . All they want to know is how I think integration could be done if the Board decided to do it. . . ." Mayor Poulson, on the other hand, was disturbed. He declined to comment to reporters, but he had hoped for a much stronger action from the new commission. Newspapers reported that "city hall sources" agreed that this had been a victory for Chief Alderson.

Other events occurred late in July. In a *Daily News* feature story a Negro fireman attacked the composition of oral interview boards in promotion examinations for captain and above. He pointed out that such boards were composed of chief officers of the Fire Department, who " . . . know they cannot give a Negro a top grade, because under present policy there would be no place to assign that man. . . ." It was a restatement of an old complaint, but it kept the atmosphere crackling.

By this time the NAACP attorneys had reviewed the City Attorney's opinion and concluded it was inadequate. As a consequence, they forwarded a well-documented statement of case particulars to the state Attorney General's office. The NAACP said that the opinion had failed to consider certain precedents fully. It was quite irrelevant, they declared, to be concerned with the administrative reasons behind assignment policy. A factual determination of the existence of racial discrimination could be made "on the basis of the patterns and practices over a period of years." In short, it was enough to know that Negroes were to be found at only two of the 88 stations and that only seven of the 81 Negroes in the Department had other assignments.

Another July event kept temperatures boiling. Only a few days after Alderson had been directed to report within six weeks on integration procedures, he indicated that his major policy recommendations would be three in number:

1. Negroes will be assigned to white stations if there are no vacancies at the Negro stations.

2. When a Negro passes a promotion examination, he will be appointed. Thus, he will be given the opportunity to command whites.

3. No Negro will be turned away or discriminated against on the entrance examination.

The Alderson report drew strong and varied comment. The new Board President, Yeamans, objected to the report, stating: "It represents no change at all; and if he brings in a program like that, it will not be satisfactory to me, personally." Joscelyn liked it. "If I were assigning personnel, which I am not," said Joscelyn, "I would do it this way." Lollier and the other new member, Brock, refused comment. Of greatest interest, however, was the attitude taken by new member Day. On his first real opportunity to disclose his stand on the integration issue he made his position clear. He was squarely behind the Fire Chief and his proposals. The Mayor's failure to effect any kind of prior understanding with his latest appointee thus left the Board split three to two on the race issue. The Mayor had played all his trumps. All the appointees were his, and yet the best he had done was to create an almost evenly divided Board. Alderson was far from beaten.

August became the month for pressure group activity as the commission, the Mayor, and other interested parties awaited the formal presentation of Chief Alderson's full program for racial integration. "The [Chief's] announced recommendations . . . are an insult to the intelligence of any fair-minded American," said the president of the Los Angeles Urban League. "To allow such a situation to continue would make a mockery of our highly regarded democratic processes," the secretary-treasurer of the Greater Los Angeles CIO Council commented to the press. On the other hand, 500 members of the Pacific Coast Inter-Mountain Association of Fire Chiefs meeting in Long Beach adopted a resolution deploring the attacks on Alderson and asserting that personnel matters must be the responsibility of the Chief and that he should not have any interference in dealing with them. The Fire Chiefs did not mince any words:

> . . . the Pacific Coast Inter-Mountain Association of Fire Chiefs expresses its complete and studied confidence in Chief John H. Alderson as a Fire Department administrator; that we deplore the political attacks upon the Los Angeles Fire Department; that

we advise the people of Los Angeles that if the present situation is allowed to develop further or continue that the best fire fighting and prevention organization in the nation will be demoralized and that the public safety will be jeopardized.

We urge upon the Mayor of Los Angeles that he cease and desist in his attack upon the Fire Chief from his announced intentions to strip the Fire Chief of certain administrative powers.

Also in August the formation of a Fact-Finding Committee of four Fire Department captains and one auto-fireman was announced.[7] On August 19 the committee appeared before the commissioners with a petition signed by 1,885 firemen requesting that no final decision be made on racial integration before December 2, 1954, when the committee planned to present a report on racial integration in other departments throughout the nation. The report was to be based on a survey financed by contributions from members of the Fire Department. Since September 2 had already been set as the date for their hearing of the Alderson report, which they still hoped would provide an answer to the problem, the commissioners refused to make any commitments. However, they did indicate privately that they would give the fact-finding study full consideration when received. Thus encouraged, the Fact-Finding Committee immediately readied a questionnaire to 275 cities with populations over 43,000 and prepared for a cross-country tour that would take it to eighteen of the nation's leading cities.

The activities of these various interest groups did not seem materially to affect the attitudes and strategy of either the Mayor or the commissioners. The deep-seated opposition of the firemen themselves had long been apparent. So too was that of the extremist groups such as the United Neighbors. While the extremist organizations were active (their members appeared at commission meetings and distributed a considerable amount of propaganda) none of the major participants wanted to develop an alliance with them. On the other side of the fence, labor groups began to join the NAACP, the Urban League, and the County Conference on Community Relations in support of integration.

To judge from their own recollections, the most influential pressures on both the Mayor and the commissioners were unorganized. They came at social affairs, business luncheons, and on other occasions where downtown businessmen cornered one of the officials and urged that the dispute be resolved. And since Chief Alderson was held in high regard by the people the Mayor and the commissioners met at luncheons, most of the settlements suggested were on his terms. In the recollections of the officials, the arguments were mainly ideological; there was little attempt to bring other types of influence to bear on the participants.

Alderson Reports

Chief Alderson submitted his report to the Board on September 2. It was filed by the commissioners without discussion since they wanted time to digest it before making a public commitment. Actually it contained little that was new. Its eight pages did *not* embody the requested plan for integration. The Chief flatly said that complete integration under conditions present in Los Angeles had not worked satisfactorily "in any department in the United States." Under the 24-hour shift system the station is the fireman's "home," where he sleeps, eats, and lives. "It is not a place, in my opinion, to experiment with social experiments," Alderson affirmed.

The day on which the commission next met, September 16, was one of much activity. The commissioners took their stand on the Alderson report; the state Attorney General issued his opinion on segregation in the Fire Department; and 25 Negroes, charging discrimination in promotion examinations, appeared before the City Civil Service Commission.

Reflecting a new unity, the commissioners unanimously adopted a resolution expressing deep disappointment with the Chief's report. It was termed "unsatisfactory . . . void of any worthwhile constructive suggestions as to the matter involved." The Chief was ordered to submit a new report containing a plan of operation for "assignment of personnel, whereby there may be integration of personnel in the Fire

[7] Chief Alderson comments: "Almost overnight a loose organization sprang up to which more than 2,400 members contributed morally and financially to oppose forced integration."

Department without regard to race, creed, and color . . . by September 30." Meanwhile, over at City Hall 25 Negro firemen were complaining to the Civil Service Commission. One, Jacob H. Addison, said he had proof that the Chief's own representatives had acted to keep Negroes off eligible lists. He said that he had placed second in a written promotion examination, and another Negro twelfth. Neither were among the 43 men certified for promotion. "The Negro is just a pawn moved by city officials for their own selfish interest," the *News* quoted Addison.[8]

In this explosive atmosphere the state Attorney General's opinion caused only a slight ripple. It was couched in restrained legal language. But its eighteen heavily-documented pages lent great weight to the Mayor's contention that segregation, as practiced in the Fire Department, was illegal. Maintenance of segregated Negro fire houses by a city, the Attorney General said, was prohibited under both the state and federal constitutions. His legal arguments, which incidentally agreed very closely with the position of the NAACP lawyers, may be summed up in the following quotations:

> In view of this State's policy against racial discrimination, it is not likely that any responsible official of this State or of a city would admit that his action in personnel management matters is based solely on race. However, where, over a long period of time there appears a systematic exclusion of members of a certain race from the opportunity and privileges accorded to others similarly situated, the court will conclude that the action is attributable to racial discrimination rather than to the lawful exercise of discretionary authority.
>
> If Negro firemen have been systematically assigned only to firehouses already entirely manned by Negro firemen and regularly have been denied transfers to other firehouses, the courts will conclude that the administrative officer is acting upon assumptions concerning the racial group characteristics of Negroes. Such action is not permitted. . . .
>
> The legislative policy of this State regarding discrimination which we deem to be merely an expression of the fundamental principles set forth in the State Constitution and the Fourteenth Amendment, is such that considerations regarding morale and efficiency are irrelevant. Efficiency cannot be achieved at the expense of the constitutional rights of the employees. It must be secured in other ways. The action of the National Guard, on public works, in labor unions, in state civil service, and in places of public accommodation, indicates a general legislative determination . . . that public services of the State and municipalities are to be conducted on a non-discriminatory basis even if segregation of personnel on a racial basis may be considered more convenient or efficient.

At the next commission meeting, September 30, Chief Alderson took a somewhat different approach. He did not pursue the point that assignments had been made on the basis of efficiency rather than race. He did not argue again for his right to assign personnel. On the contrary, he cited the Charter provision that final authority rested with the Board of Fire Commissioners. He then proceeded to confound his accusers by building his case largely around a definition of integration. There was integration, he said, in appointment of personnel, in training, in civil defense, in athletics, in fire fighting, and in command at fires. That to him meant integration existed in the Department. "If the Board of Fire Commissioners have a different definition of integration than I do, then I believe that they should frankly and in a straight-forward manner define what they believe integration to be."

He then told the fire commissioners, "If it is

[8] The charge of discrimination on promotional exams was not new. Addison himself had made his claims to the Civil Service Department staff five months earlier, and at that time the Department undertook a careful analysis of the experience of Negroes and whites in the oral and written portions of the captain's examinations over a ten-year period. The Department analysts found no pattern. On the whole, the Negroes did about the same on the written as on the oral examinations.

The Civil Service Department staff recommended to *its* Commission that there be no change in policy, i.e., oral boards continue to be composed of five superior officers of the Fire Department. Such a policy was adopted February 18, 1954. But as a result of the Addison matter and certain other events, the Commission fourteen months later reversed itself, saying on May 6, 1955:

"The Commission adopted the motion to have a complete citizen board to conduct the oral examination portion for fire captain, because the Commission concluded that this is necessary in order to perpetuate the democratic principles of government which this administration is attempting to continue and practice. . . . The Commission feels that this principle should apply not only to the Fire Department but to all City Departments."

our policy to transfer Negroes from Stations 30 and 14 to every station throughout the city, do believe that I am entitled to know that and o be advised in order that I may advise you as o what procedure I will follow." Thus, Alderson put the issue squarely to the commissioners. The real question was what to do about the wo Negro fire stations. No one could actually prove discrimination in entrance or promotional exams; and Alderson, as he said, had made trides toward integration in other aspects of he Department's work. The key problem had inally been identified: did the commissioners actually want to break up the Negro stations?

The Mayor Lays Down the Law

The Alderson report seemed to catch the commission unawares. President Yeamans suggested more public hearings in October, saying, "We're still groping for some type of workable plan."

Then the Mayor stepped in again. On October 5, in a letter to the Board, he came right o the point:

1. There is no need for public hearings. ("You are not a legislative body.")

2. Break up the two Negro fire stations. (" . . . segregation on the basis of race alone s illegal and . . . the existence of two fire staions staffed wholly by Negroes constitutes segregation.")

3. If the Chief fails to go along, fire him. "If the Chief Engineer refuses or fails to comply . . . replace him with a man who does not egard himself as above the laws of our city, tate and nation.")

A further public statement issued two days ater pronounced Poulson's fourth point:

4. If you don't take action on the question, ou will be removed as commissioners. (To the *News:* "I will then ask the City Council to approve the removal of any commissioner or commissioners who are blocking an orderly concluion of this matter. . . .")

The atmosphere was tense when the Fire Commission met on October 8. About 350 offduty firemen converged on headquarters and overflowed the Fire Department auditorium to which the hearings had been moved. Doorways nd halls were blocked, and attorneys from the NAACP never did get into the chamber. The police were called to stand by "just in case." Both Alderson and the commissioners urged the members of the jostling crowd to "keep their heads" and "be as quiet as possible."

As the meeting finally got under way, one and one-half hours later, Lollier was in the chair in order to allow President Yeamans to introduce a resolution. Brock was in Europe, so only four commissioners were present. The commission quickly reversed its previous decision to hold more public hearings. Yeamans reviewed legal opinions and court decisions. Then he said:

> The present situation as it exists must be changed. I propose to offer an instruction which cannot be misunderstood. If our country is going to stand, we must be a democracy and act like one.

At this time Yeamans introduced the critical resolution: break up the two Negro stations. Assign no more than two Negroes to any single station.

Poulson's most recent appointee, oil executive Robert Day, spoke into the microphone. The issue was not integration, he said, but how it was to be accomplished. He still wanted "cleancut recommendations" from the Chief, and he wanted to hear from the Fireman's Fact-Finding Committee which had "traveled throughout the country studying the problem" and would have a report ready by October 14. He proposed that the resolution be tabled until then. Enthusiastic applause from the audience of firemen was still echoing when Commissioner Joscelyn assumed the floor. He said that the commissioners had "been harangued by representatives of the NAACP," and that failure to hear the Fact-Finding Committee would be "the greatest double-cross we could commit." Again, there was prolonged applause and cheering.

Chairman Lollier asked for a second to President Yeamans' resolution and got none. He declared it tabled. Then there was a vote on Day's proposal of postponement. It was a tie with Day and Joscelyn in support, Yeamans and Lollier opposed. The stormy session concluded with no decision. It was quite clear that the return of Commissioner Brock, rather than the fact-finding report, was essential if a decision was to be made. After the meeting, quotations from the central characters in the dispute were

The commission deliberates. A *Los Angeles Times* photograph, taken at a critical meeting of the commission, shows some of the principal participants in the racial integration controversy. From left to right are Fire Chief Joh H. Alderson and Fire Commissioners W. H. Lollier, Milto J. Brock, Sr., C. F. Joscelyn, and Richard K. Yeaman

liberally reported in the city's newspapers.

Chief Alderson reported that considerable pressure had been put on him by rank and file firemen to stay on the job, "notwithstanding the outcome of this." He said that he had not changed his opinion in "any way," that he did not intend to retire, that he intended to "fight," and that they "might as well have a showdown." A fund of $500,000, to be subscribed by policemen and firemen, was reported in the making to aid the Alderson "fight."

There were jabs at the Mayor. He was threatened with recall by the "Police and Fire Recall Committee," the composition of which was never really identified. One commissioner rid culed the Mayor's threat to remove the con missioners saying, "He can't get eight votes i the City Council." The Mayor was attacked i the *Daily News* for failing to contribute "cal administrative judgment" to the situation. Th editorial further declared:

> He [Poulson] bullyragged the Fire Commission by threatening dismissal of those members who refused to meet his deadline for integration of Negro and white personnel. Poulson's temper tantrum merely complicated the problem he says he wants to solve.

The NAACP attorneys, unable to make the statement at the hearing itself, released a pr posal to the press. Theirs was a three-point program, its key provision: break up the two Negro fire stations.

The next meeting of the Fire Commission on October 14, one week later, was largely perfunctory. Brock was not expected back by that time, and Day had gone to Japan. The meeting, which Brock incidentally did attend, was convened only to receive the fact-finding report. Before a crowd of 400, mainly firemen, the Fact-Finding Committee presented a 27-page document containing a review of the race relations in a variety of departments across the country. Perhaps its most striking finding was the small degree to which Negroes had been utilized in the fire fighting service and hence, the relative uniqueness of the type of problem Los Angeles was experiencing.[9]

The report mingled fact and emotion. The data on racial relations in the various fire departments were couched in neutral language; but the recommendations, pitched at a highly subjective level, spoke of "the natural barriers that exist between the negro [sic] and white races"; of "the fallacy of the example and conclusions contained in the Attorney General's opinion"; and of "rival political factions" currying the favor of the "negro [sic] bloc as the balance of power." The report concluded:

> This Fact Finding Committee, representing and expressing the will of over 98% of 2400 men of the Los Angeles Fire Department, exclusive of negroes, therefore recommends and urges that the Board of Fire Commissioners unequivocally reject *forced* integration of negroes and whites in the same fire stations as a policy which we firmly believe would be inimical to morale and efficiency and not in the public interest.

Thus, the "will" of the white firemen was stated by someone other than Alderson. Change might be inevitable, but the white firemen did not want anything "forced" upon them. The report, with its recommendations couched in such language, did not strengthen the firemen's case in the minds of some key observers. It caused Alderson's staunch supporter, the *News,* to change its attitude. In biting words, the paper editorialized:

> No fair-minded reader of the report on integration of the Los Angeles Firemen's Fact-Finding Committee can come to any conclusion but that from beginning to end it is an unabashed effort to uphold the discredited doctrine of white supremacy.
>
> This is demonstrated by the fact that the report has absolutely nothing to do with the purpose for which the fact finders were permitted time by the Fire Commission to make their recommendations.
>
> The purpose was to discover how other cities had carried out integration of white and Negro personnel in their fire departments, and to find out if this experience would be helpful in formulating an integration program for Los Angeles, inasmuch as this already had been decided upon.
>
> But instead of making a constructive effort to find how best to formulate a local program, the fact finders openly rebelled against the integration policy and concluded that the racial barriers complained against should be perpetuated.

A Policy?

The Fact-Finding Committee report became just one more of a long list of documents accumulating in the commission file. The time was approaching for a decision. The Mayor had let it be known that he had set November 1 as a personal deadline for action. Thus, when Milton J. Brock arose shortly after 9:00 a.m. on October 28 to present a resolution, the crowd of more than 100 sensed that a decision was at hand. Commissioner Brock's proposal in a nutshell: break up the Negro fire stations, but do it gradually.

Brock's motion, which, incidentally, was written by Yeamans, was almost an anti-climax. The tempo had been sustained over so many months that the realization a decision was at hand brought calm rather than disturbance. The firemen were silent as the Secretary read the resolution. Commissioner Joscelyn protested weakly that the Board should await Commissioner Day's return from Japan. Alderson sat quietly. There seemed little point to prolonging the dispute. Brock, Yeamans, and Lollier supported the motion; Joscelyn opposed. It said in part:

> This Board reiterates its stand that the assignment of the Negro fire-fighting personnel exclusively to Stations 14 and 30 is not in accord with the policy of this Board, and is considered to be a discriminatory assignment of such personnel, and therefore, not lawful.

[9] A 1953 Report of the Los Angeles Urban League showed that only 62 of the nation's 16,000 municipalities employed Negro firemen.

> This order constitutes an instruction to the General Manager . . . that he is hereby instructed, ordered and directed to initiate a gradual transfer of a part of the personnel now stationed at Stations 14 and 30 to such other stations in the city of Los Angeles as he may deem to be in the best interests of the people of the city and this department, regardless of race, creed, or color.
>
> The Chief . . . shall be, and he is hereby instructed, ordered, and directed to appoint, transfer, assign and promote personnel of this department without regard to race, creed, or color.

Nearly fourteen months after his first letter to the Board the Mayor was now able to say, "The mission has been accomplished." Whether or not the action deserved the Mayor's enthusiasm, it was generally agreed that the commission had at long last established a policy framework within which administrative action could be taken and for which the Chief could be held accountable. The NAACP, though regretting the "no time limit" provision, saw the resolution as a "clear mandate for 'fair play' in employment." Chief Alderson said somewhat ominously that when the resolution's legality had been checked, he would comply "in my own way."

Aftermath

THIS STORY OF fourteen months of attempted policy making by the Fire Commission ends with the adoption by the commissioners of the Mayor's policy. The events have raised in the minds of some observers a number of questions about the role of the citizen commission or board which is given top administrative responsibility. One of the underlying reasons for making lay commissions the administrative heads of Los Angeles departments, some observers noted, was to provide bodies which could make decisions combining both policy elements and administrative elements. But the commissioners were dependent on either the Chief or the Mayor for information; they were without a staff organization of their own; and they were able to devote only a modest amount of time to Fire Department affairs. One question suggested by the desegregation issue was whether a part-time lay board could play an independent role or whether it was inherently so weak and unsupported that it had inevitably to gravitate to the administrative orientation of the Chief or to the policy-political orientation of the Mayor.

Implementing the Policy

The commission faced a similar dilemma—although the commissioners did not appear to be aware of it when they finally voted for the desegregation policy—in the implementation of desegregation. Were they to content themselves with enunciating policy and leave it to Chief Alderson to carry out integration in his own way and at his own pace? Or was it up to the commission to see that the policy was speedily implemented, to compete with the Fire Department bureaucracy by concerning itself with individual assignments, and to develop its own independent information sources about the daily happenings of the large Department?

The preceding questions assume—as did the commissioners and the Mayor—that Chief Alderson would continue in office. Some questioned whether they were realistic in expecting a senior career official, accustomed to public and professional recognition—a man who had involved himself heavily in arguing against a policy—to make a complete about-face and to carry out zealously and speedily the delicate task of implementing a new policy which he had branded unworkable. By retaining Alderson the commissioners seemed to assume that the making of integration policy was quite separate from its implementation. They seemed to accept completely the concept that the civil service career official will devote himself wholeheartedly to administering a policy he has argued against in the policy-making process. They seemed to believe that the Chief still had sufficient room for maneuvers to carry out the new policy in co-operation with both the embattled firemen and the suspicious NAACP.

The two years following the commission's decision turned out to be struggle and turmoil for all concerned. Chief Alderson's disbelief in the integration policy seemed to some commissioners to become even more apparent as the period of implementation began. He pointed out that integration was to be a "gradual process." Two months after the Board's decision the Chief took a first step by transferring two Negroes to an all-white station. Two months later, two more were transferred, but almost immediately one asked to be returned to the all-Negro station. No white personnel was transferred to the all-Negro stations.

The emotions stirred during the policy fight in the fall of 1954 reached an even higher pitch the following spring. One captain resigned with a public attack on the Chief, alleging that Alderson was waging a subtle war against those white firemen who wanted integration to work. Another white fireman, a temporary captain who had supported integration, was disciplined for "falsifying records."

It is still difficult to evaluate the charges and counter-charges of the period. But even by a cautious estimate it appears that Alderson did little to foster among the rank and file a climate of co-operation and understanding. The Negroes were apparently treated as outcasts, and the white firemen who clearly affirmed their support of integration fared no better. By May, 1955 it was obvious to the commissioners that the program was hopelessly stalled. Something had to be done.

Three New Appointments

The three majority members of the Fire Commission resigned on the ground that they had been "unable to obtain co-operation" from the Chief. They did not claim he was insubordinate. They did not say he should be fired. They simply attested to their inability to handle the situation. Alderson had bested the Board.

This time, Mayor Poulson made certain to strengthen his position and that of the Board. In filling the three vacant commissionerships, he consulted privately with religious and lay leaders of the Catholic, Jewish, and Protestant congregations of the city. Certain of their support, he asked representatives of each of the three groups to suggest a nominee for commissioner. These three men became the new commissioners. As Joscelyn's term expired, the Mayor made a fourth appointment, an insurance man. The Mayor knew in advance that his fourth appointee would support the integration policy just as he knew he could count on the three other appointees because they informally represented the three religious congregations which favored integration.

Appointment of the new commissioners did not appear immediately to change the fundamental problem. The commissioners assumed that Alderson would remain as Chief. As the months of 1955 wore on, the commissioners and the Chief battled endlessly. Finally, five Negroes were transferred to white stations in the San Fernando Valley section. Threats against them followed instantly, and accusations, hazings, and bad feelings became a regular feature of life at these stations. There were charges that the fire-fighting capacity of at least one of the Valley stations had seriously deteriorated. Finally, without consulting the Fire Commission in advance, Chief Alderson in December summarily transferred all colored firemen back to their previous stations. He wanted, he said, to avoid "bloodshed by outside interests."

The Chief and the Commission Part

This final cancellation of all integration efforts was to be the Chief's last gesture. Worn and harried by the pressures of the previous years, he had informed the commission on November 1, 1955 that he wished to retire from his position not later than January 1. Thus by the time his order was issued moving the Negro firemen back to the all-Negro stations, the wheels had been set in motion for the appointment of a successor. The Civil Service Commission had announced that an examination would be given on December 17. Yet the commission, meeting hurriedly on December 15, adopted an order relieving the Chief of his duties "immediately" on grounds of insubordination.

Charges were filed with the Civil Service Commission, and a hearing was scheduled for December 23. However, the question of Alderson's pension and other rights was never involved, for he was covered under an act which permitted no cancellation of these privileges regardless of the reason for separation. Since there were no retirement questions at issue and since the appointment of a new chief was imminent anyway, the Fire Commission ultimately dropped the charges, and after two postponements the hearings were terminated. As of January 1, 1956 Alderson's long and active association with the Los Angeles Fire Department came to an end.

Shortly after Alderson's retirement, Assistant Chief William L. Miller, Lt. Commander, U. S. Naval Reserve, was appointed to the position Alderson had held for approximately fifteen years. Miller pleaded for time to deal with the integration question, and everyone was glad to give it to him: the Board, the newspapers, even the NAACP. A calm settled in, and two weeks after he assumed command, Chief Miller sent eight white firemen who said they favored integration into one of the all-Negro stations. By September, 1956 all Negro firemen had been assimilated and were working in 17 of 91 stations in the city. There were no all-Negro stations.

As of January 1958 it was still too early to write *finis* to the racial integration problem in Los Angeles, however. The basic policy of mixed stations was approximately two years old, but charges of discrimination, hazings, and unfair treatment of the Negroes continued to sprinkle the newspapers.

The Florida Flood Control District

John De Grove

The Setting

THIS IS THE STORY of the relationships between the executive officer of the Central and Southern Florida Flood Control District and the members of its governing Board who were appointed successively by four different governors over a seven-year period. Although legislation provided for a Board of five members with overlapping three-year terms, the seven-year period (1949-1956) described here saw each new governor fill the Board with his appointees. The turnover in Board personnel, which reflected the different political factions behind newly-elected governors, posed serious problems for the executive officer, W. Turner Wallis.

The major problem, as Wallis saw it, was the difficulty in maintaining continuity of policy and administration in a $360,000,000 water control project covering 15,000 square miles in seventeen counties in the lower Florida peninsula. A part of this problem was that the turnover in Board members also affected Wallis' influence and initiative with his Board. Finally, since the changing Board members were the appointees of different political factions Wallis also faced the basic problem of survival in his post.

The Area and Its Water Problems

Florida, with 30,000 lakes, has more inland water than any other state. The Central and Southern Florida Flood Control District contains the portion of the state with the heaviest rainfall.

The most dramatic natural feature of the Flood Control District area is Lake Okeechobee, a roughly circular body of shallow water of about 730 square miles. Stretching southward from Okeechobee lie the Everglades with thousands of acres of rich muck and peat soil that man has been attempting to drain for agricultural use since the 1880s. North and east of Okeechobee are the Kissimmee and St. Johns Rivers—the former flowing south into the Lake, and the latter flowing north from headwaters northeast of the Lake. The state's subtropical climate produces two seasons—wet and dry. In the wet season, the seventeen-county area of the Flood Control District is spotted with large and small lakes, and marshland abounds. Although the region subdivides naturally into four drainage areas, it is for all practical purposes a single drainage basin, since during periods of high water the various watersheds are joined in floods that cover the entire region. Unlike floods in other states, where a river basin overflows and the water rushes down a valley, the flood waters in Florida spread over the flat terrain and stand covering the ground for days or weeks, with devastating effect on land and property.

The original approach to Florida's water problems, conceived in the 1840s and first attempted in the 1880s, was to attempt to drain the area around the Lake and in the Kissimmee Valley for extensive farming. Although the drainage works never prevented floods during periods of unusually heavy rain, they carried off water too rapidly during dry periods. Flood-drought cycles became the rule. The flood problem was further complicated by the threat of hurricane winds blowing Lake Okeechobee's waters over the farming communities along its southern shores. Such floods drowned several hundred persons in 1926 and some three thousand in 1928.

A serious problem was created by the extensive drainage system. During the long dry spells, the drained muck and peat soils of the Everglades caught fire and burned for months at a time. These fires destroyed thousands of acres of soil and spread a thick smog over the east coast tourist centers. An even greater menace was oxidation which affected the organic soil when it was drained. The resulting "soil subsidence" meant that every year a part of the precious topsoil was lost forever — literally burned away by the processes of nature.

The needs of the rapidly growing tourist

counties—Dade (which contains Miami), Palm Beach, and Broward increased in population from 387,000 in 1940 to 694,000 in 1950 and to 1,360,000 in 1959—soon pointed up the inadequacy of the prevailing policy. The drainage efforts were gradually lowering the fresh water table, while municipal water requirements were rising. Many unique flora and fauna of the region were threatened with extinction, and many areas were being closed to hunting, fishing, and boating at a time when the growth in urban and tourist population was creating a demand for large recreation areas.

The lowering of the fresh water table also posed a threat to agricultural areas. As the fresh water table was lowered, salt water intruded, ruining land for farming.

The task of reclaiming the Everglades was first undertaken by the Internal Improvement Fund and the Everglades Drainage District, each with identical ex-officio boards composed of the governor, attorney general, treasurer, comptroller, and commissioner of agriculture.[1] From 1906 to 1928 the two state agencies spent about $18,000,000 installing a basic system of drainage canals and levees in the Everglades. Federal agencies played only a minor role during this period.

After the collapse of the Florida land boom in 1926, no significant additions were made to the drainage system until 1950 (with the exception of flood control levees around Lake Okeechobee constructed by the United States Army Corps of Engineers). However, by the late 1930s there was general recognition that simple drainage was creating more problems than it was solving, and that a solution to the area's water problems demanded a multi-purpose approach.

Acting on this new appreciation, the various state and federal agencies with responsibility for the water problems of the area undertook to remedy some of the deficiencies of past water control efforts. In the 1930s, under the leadership of the National Resources Planning Board, these agencies launched a joint program for collecting and analyzing data aimed at providing at least some foundation for future programs. The bulk of the work was performed by the Soil Conservation Service of the Department of Agriculture and the United States Geological Survey of the Department of the Interior.

[1] Each of these was an elected official. The governor was not elected on a party slate.

The importance of the data collection project was headlined when in September 1947—an unusually wet year—a tropical hurricane struck the lower Florida east coast, dumping large amounts of rain on the already water-soaked area. The resulting flood was one of the worst in the history of south-central Florida. More than 3,000,000 acres of land were under water, some for as long as six months, and extensive urban areas along the lower east coast were flooded for weeks. Damage was estimated by the Corps of Engineers at $59,000,000. The survey data which were available by that time were quickly compiled into a report by the Corps, and a comprehensive water control plan was submitted to Congress. Hearings held before the Senate Public Works Committee in May 1948 featured a united emergency plea by state interests and the support of the Corps of Engineers and the Bureau of the Budget. The project was approved for inclusion in the Flood Control Act of 1948, but only its first phase was authorized for construction. This meant that until 1954, when the second phase came due for authorization, no primary works would be constructed north of Lake Okeechobee. Corps and state witnesses stressed the fact that the plan had not been devised as one that could be divided into phases, but they agreed that the emergency situation warranted accepting the limited authorization if that was all Congress was willing to grant.

The New Plan and Its Limitations

The plan stressed overall water control rather than drainage, flood control, or any single element of water-resource development. Although flood control, reclamation, and land enhancement accounted for virtually all of the benefits claimed by the Corps of Engineers in its justification before Congress, the plan also provided for storing surplus waters, preventing overdrainage and salt water intrusion, permitting added agriculture and urban development, improving navigation, conserving fish and wildlife, and raising the water table in the area. The plan called for about 780 miles of levees, 492 miles of canals, numerous pumping stations, spillway structures, and culverts—all to be constructed by the Corps of Engineers with the co-operation of the state. These major works were considered the primary structures needed in the area. Additionally, a secondary network of local drainage canals and smaller works was to be built by local interests, both private and public. The secondary network would be ineffective without the primary works; conversely, the primary works would not be totally effective unless the secondary works were built. The federal government's responsibility was limited to the primary projects, and even for these the state would have to provide financial assistance.

Florida's efforts to meet its share of this giant water control program resulted in the adoption of several important new laws during the 1949 session of the State Legislature. One of these statutes created the Central and Southern Florida Flood Control District. The District was authorized to "cooperate with the United States or with this state, . . . with any county, district or other governmental agency, and to enter into and make such cooperative agreements or commitments as the governing board . . . may determine to be necessary . . . ." The extent of the District's authorized co-operation was not defined, but it included, at the least, cash contributions to the primary works at a rate which would be determined by Congress; the providing of lands, easements and rights-of-way; and the assurance to the United States that the state would assume responsibility for (a) all damages resulting from construction or operation of the works, and (b) perpetual maintenance and operation of the completed works.

There were already in existence several units called "sub-drainage districts." These drainage districts were formed when a group of landowners within a county voted to put themselves under the control of several of their members, designated by vote of the group. By a system of self-taxation, these districts could arrange for whatever water control measures the group voted to pay for. The new legislation explicitly contemplated that drainage districts would play a part in constructing the necessary secondary works. What was not spelled out was the role that the Flood Control District should play in encouraging the formation of new drainage districts or in assisting the existing districts to plan and construct levees, canals, and other works.

The new primary program was financed jointly by the federal and state governments. Congress appropriated annually the federal government's portion of the authorized funds. The state's contribution to the construction costs of the federal project was appropriated by the Legislature to the Flood Control Account of the General Revenue Fund, which was administered by the State Board of Conservation. Money was disbursed from this account, however, on request of the Flood Control District, which requested specific amounts to be paid directly by the Board to the Corps of Engineers. The State Legislature authorized an additional amount each biennium for land acquisition and relocation of roads and utilities.

The Flood Control District itself had independent taxing power. The state enabling legislation authorized the District to levy an ad valorem property tax of not more than one mill across the board on all property in the District. Unlike the state contribution to the federal government for the primary program, this money could be spent on any project approved by the governing board; it comprised the District's only flexible source of money.

The Program Gets Underway

Construction began in January 1950. Several years of operation brought to light serious limitations in the original project design. First, detailed studies soon revealed that the hastily devised plan was inadequate. The original inadequacy was increasingly magnified by a phenomenal boom in the population and economic development of the urban counties in the District. In addition, construction fell drastically behind schedule—the Corps of Engineers had underestimated the length of time it would take to complete the necessary detailed planning. For the first few years the Corps was not able to use the full amount appropriated by the state. This, plus a persistent confusion about the nature of the project, and an economy drive by the Eisenhower administration, caused Congress to grow increasingly reluctant to appropriate federal matching funds. In 1954 it appropriated no funds at all. The State Legislature was equally reluctant to continue appropriating funds which, unused, reverted at the end of the year to the general fund. At the prevailing rate of construction, the project, originally scheduled for completion within ten years, would not be finished until the turn of the century. Price increases and design changes meant that the original estimated cost of the first phase, $70,000,000, grew to more than $100,000,000 by 1956. The estimated total cost of the original plan had been about $280,000,000. Project revisions and inflation raised this to $360,000,000 by 1957. The contribution to the primary works from state units, which paid fifteen percent of the actual construction costs[2] and furnished all lands needed for the project, rose to about 35 percent of the full cost of the program.[3] Land in Dade County which would have been free (or at most $500 an acre) if work had proceeded on schedule was selling for $3,000 an acre eighteen months later by the time the planners were able to pin-point the land that would have to be bought for rights-of-way for the canals of the primary project.

During the first eight years of its existence, the Flood Control District (FCD) faced a series of policy problems. First, should it confine its ac tivities only to its share of responsibility for th primary projects? Second, for what part of th secondary network of engineering works shoul it be responsible? Third, in view of the laggin federal construction, should the state agency de velop emergency works? Fourth, should the Dis trict undertake directly or sponsor indirectl other phases of the multi-purpose water pro gram?

A further policy question plagued both th Corps and the FCD during the period: to wha extent should modifications be made in the pla to remedy both the original inadequacies and th new problems brought on by delayed construc tion? To what extent did modifications need t be authorized by Congress? The Corps of Engi neers was already being criticized by congression al committees for the degree of discretion it ha exercised on other projects, and on several occa sions the recommendation had been made tha the Corps be relieved entirely of its civil func tions in the water resource area. The Corps ha become cautious in the extent to which it woul modify plans, and this caution was reflected i the Florida project. The burden fell on the stat agency first to decide whether modification wa desirable, and second, if it was, to attempt t secure Corps agreement.

This then was the policy and administrativ framework in which the FCD's chief executiv officer, W. Turner Wallis, operated. These wer the continuing problems which furnished th setting for the story of the relationships betwee Wallis and the governing Board of the FCD.

[2] This was raised to twenty percent in 1954.

[3] Detailed breakdowns were these: state-local government units paid 15% of the cost of work included in the original (1948) authorization, 20% for the remainder of the original project authorized in 1954, and 27½% for the first of many anticipated additions. Additionally, the Flood Control District provided the necessary highway and highway bridge relocations and bore most of the cost of operation and maintenance of project works. Estimates of the total state-local share range from 35 to 55%.

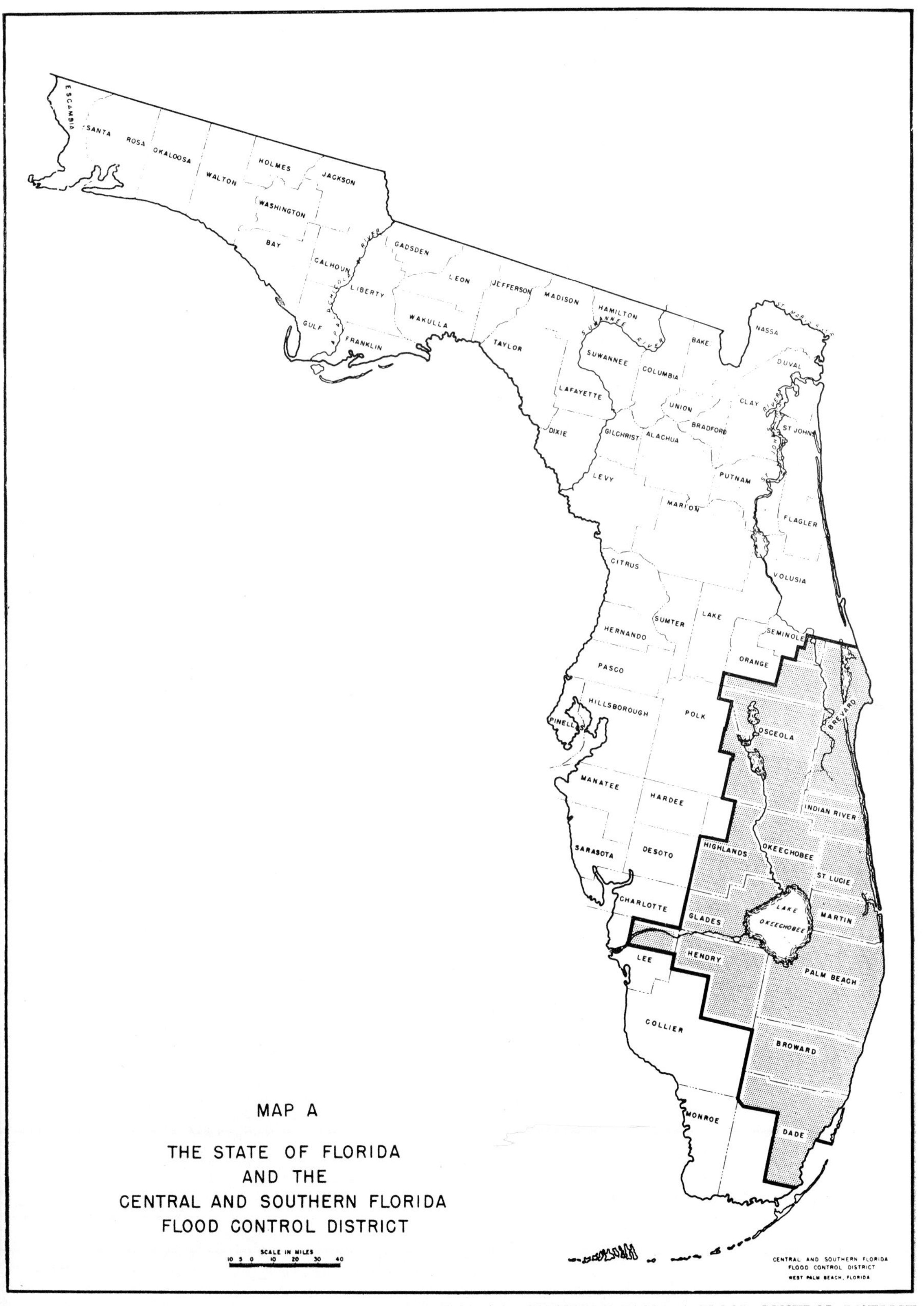
ESCAMBIA
SANTA ROSA
OKALOOSA
WALTON
HOLMES
JACKSON
WASHINGTON
BAY
CALHOUN
APALACHICOLA RIVER
GULF
LIBERTY
FRANKLIN
GADSDEN
LEON
WAKULLA
JEFFERSON
MADISON
TAYLOR
HAMILTON
SUWANNEE RIVER
SUWANNEE
COLUMBIA
BAKER
NASSAU
ST MARYS RIVER
DUVAL
LAFAYETTE
UNION
CLAY
BRADFORD
ST JOHNS RIVER
ST JOHNS
DIXIE
GILCHRIST
ALACHUA
LEVY
PUTNAM
MARION
FLAGLER
CITRUS
VOLUSIA
LAKE
SUMTER
HERNANDO
SEMINOLE
ORANGE
PASCO
HILLSBOROUGH
PINELLAS
POLK
OSCEOLA
BREVARD
MANATEE
HARDEE
INDIAN RIVER
SARASOTA
DESOTO
HIGHLANDS
OKEECHOBEE
ST LUCIE
CHARLOTTE
GLADES
LAKE OKEECHOBEE
MARTIN
LEE
HENDRY
PALM BEACH
COLLIER
BROWARD
MONROE
DADE
MAP A
THE STATE OF FLORIDA
AND THE
CENTRAL AND SOUTHERN FLORIDA
FLOOD CONTROL DISTRICT
SCALE IN MILES
10 5 0 10 20 30 40
CENTRAL AND SOUTHERN FLORIDA
FLOOD CONTROL DISTRICT
WEST PALM BEACH, FLORIDA

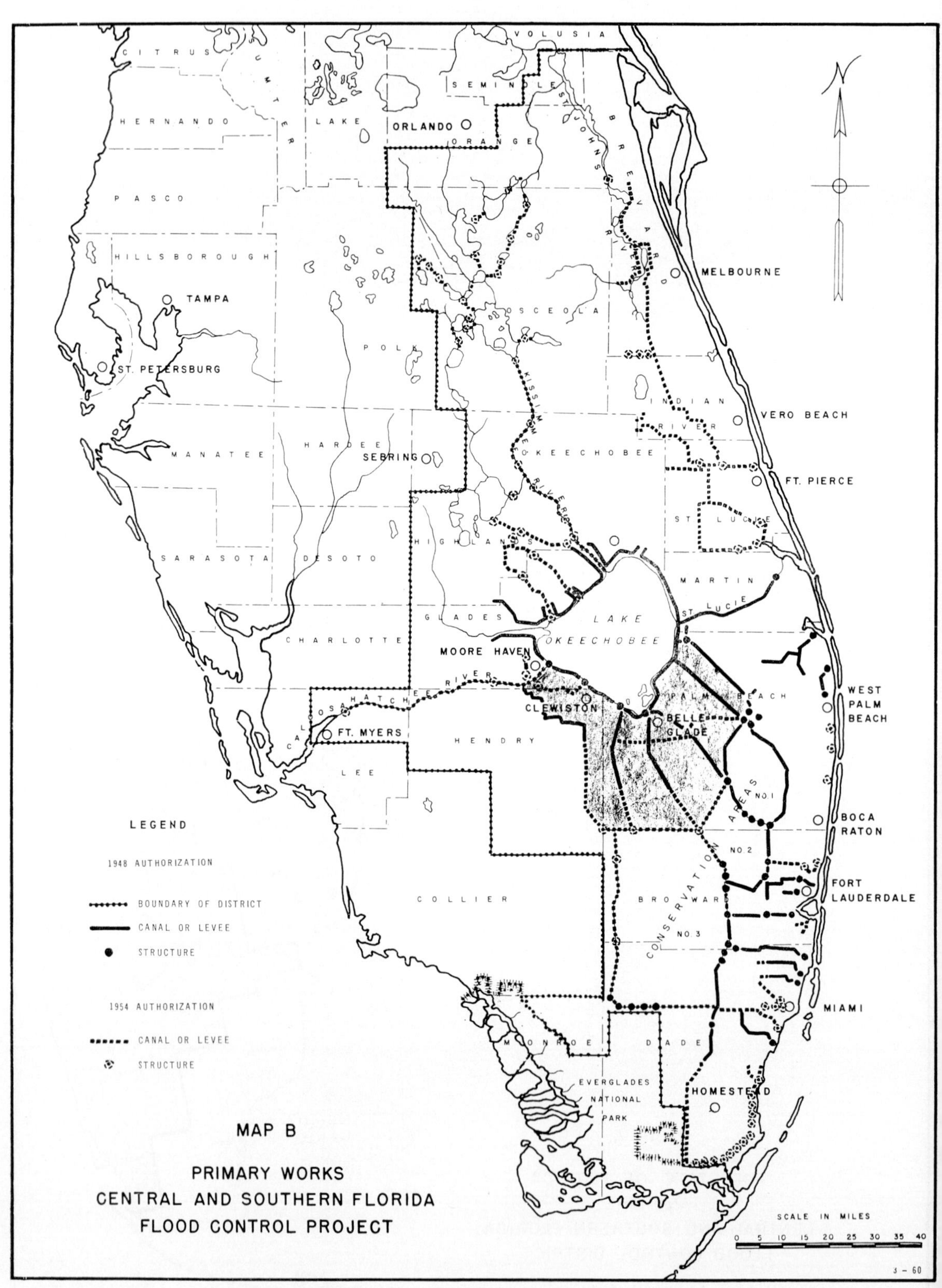

CENTRAL AND SOUTHERN FLORIDA FLOOD CONTROL DISTRICT

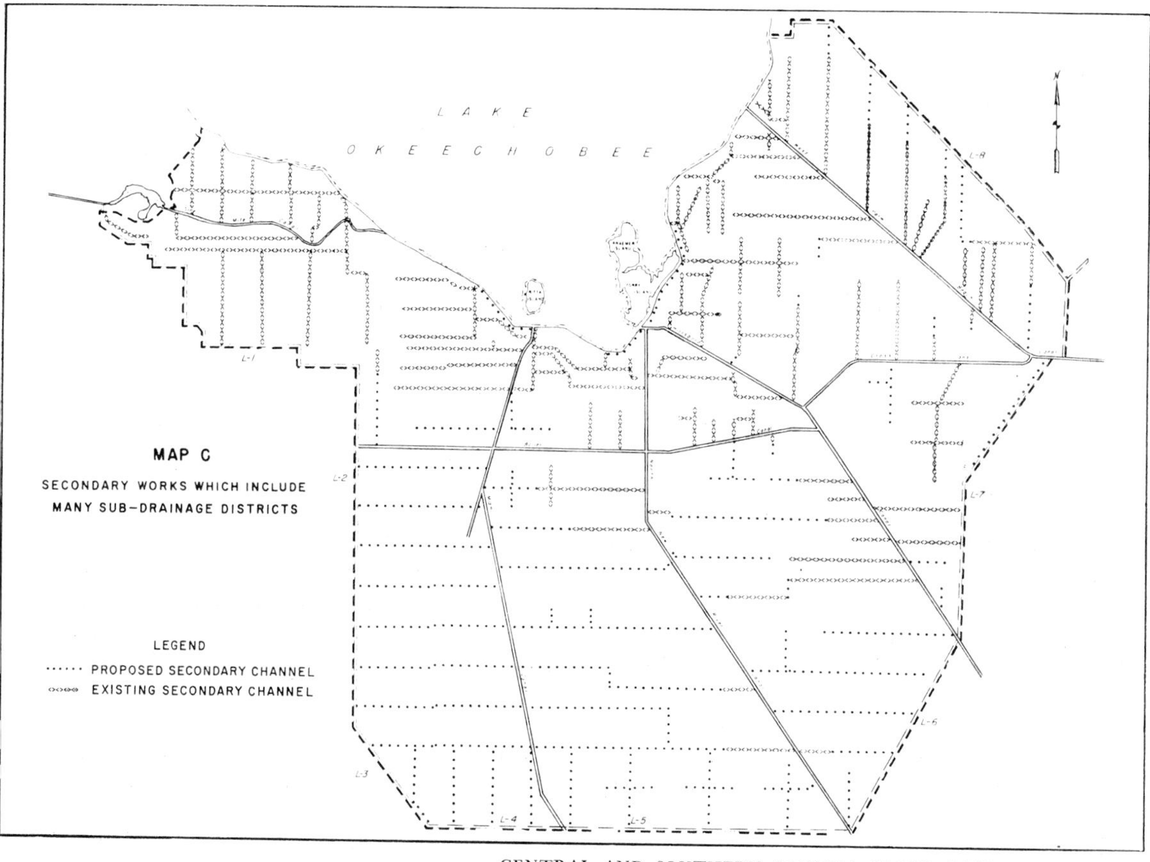

CENTRAL AND SOUTHERN FLORIDA FLOOD CONTROL DISTRICT

Map B (facing page) shows the FCD primary works. The solid lines and dots represent the canals, levees and structures authorized in 1948. The dotted lines and broken circles represent the works authorized in 1954.

Map C is a detail map of the shaded area shown on Map B. This area map encompasses many sub-drainage districts, and shows the extent of the proposed and existing secondary channel system.

Wallis and Governor Warren's Board

W. TURNER WALLIS served as the chief executive officer of the Flood Control District from its establishment in 1949 until 1956. He was a colorful and controversial figure who had been associated with efforts to develop a water control plan for central and southern Florida since the 1920s. Wallis had served as engineer and financial consultant for the Everglades Drainage District, for various sub-districts in the area, and he had for a time managed a large ranch in the Everglades. His many friends, and even some of his enemies, considered him one of the most knowledgeable men in the state in the field of water-resource development. He had at times a somewhat abrasive manner and was given to making blunt statements.

Wallis' appointment as District secretary-treasurer and chief engineer grew out of a number of events. Congressional approval of the 1948 comprehensive water control plan called for prompt state action during the 1949 session of the Legislature. The task of drafting state legislation setting up the District was given to Fred C. Elliot, secretary and engineer of the Internal

Improvement Fund, the state's land control agency. Elliot immediately enlisted the help of his long-time friend and professional associate, Wallis. The two had worked closely in supporting the project in Congress.

The spring preceding the 1949 legislative session had been enlivened by the Democratic primary elections in Florida.[4] The gubernatorial contest featured four strong candidates—Fuller Warren, Dan McCarty, Colin English, and W. A. Shands. Warren and McCarty drew the most votes, and a run-off primary was held.

Warren, a native of northwest Florida, had run a surprisingly strong race for governor in 1940 and had served in the State Legislature. He drew some backing from supporters of United States Senator Claude Pepper. Warren laid much stress on his status as a "man-of-the-people," although he did raise some of the specific issues faced by a rapidly growing state.

McCarty, a member of a wealthy Ft. Pierce citrus and cattle family, had served as speaker of the lower house of the Florida Legislature. He had been elected to that post at the age of 29, after two previous terms in the house. McCarty built his campaign almost entirely around the need for "clean government" and a more "business-like" approach to the conduct of its affairs. He received solid support from the Junior Chamber of Commerce element in Florida politics.

The contest between McCarty and Warren in the second primary was spirited. Warren won by only two percent—a margin of about 23,000 out of 576,066 votes cast. While his greatest strength was in northwest Florida, he also ran a strong race in other sections of the state. Thus, although his largest majority occurred in populous Duval County (Jacksonville) in northeast Florida, where the victory margin was some 18,000 votes, Warren also carried Hillsborough (Tampa) and Polk counties, in the central Florida area. McCarty supporters were bitterly disappointed by the defeat, and watched through a veil of suspicion as Warren conducted the state's affairs.

Wallis had supported Shands in the first primary, and upon his elimination he supported McCarty in the run-off primary with Warren. Despite Wallis' support of his opponents, Governor Warren approved the Flood Control District Board's selection of Wallis as secretary-treasurer and chief engineer, partly because of his long professional service in the water control field, and partly because of the support of Fred Elliot, who commanded the respect of many people close to Warren.

Warren's appointments to the Flood Control District Board illustrated some of the peculiarities of Florida government. Florida politics were characterized by shifting Democratic factions which rarely had roots in policy differences. The transient nature of factional organizations was intensified by a constitutional prohibition against a governor succeeding himself after serving one four-year term. Thus a candidate for governor assembled an organization to put him in office, but this organization tended to disintegrate once he was elected. There was thus no political organization in the state with any degree of permanence and hence no party "position" on matters of public policy.

The role of the governor was further weakened by Florida's system under which every other major state administrative officer was elected and *could* succeed himself. To achieve his purposes, therefore, the governor often had to develop his own sources of power in competition with his cabinet members. His patronage power offered the governor one means of marshaling support for his program.

Patronage was a problem as well as an opportunity to Florida governors, who had to make appointments to over 100 statewide boards and to almost numberless local boards. There was almost no time in the tenure of a Florida governor when he was not considering an immediate appointment to some specific board. Given this situation, the governor could give his personal attention only to major board appointments such as the State Road Board or the State Racing Commission. For the rest he tended to rely almost completely on his political advisers in the various sections of the state. Once boards were appointed, it was impossible for the governor to exercise even the most cursory supervision over their activities. He himself served in an ex-officio capacity on about 35 state boards in addition to performing his many other duties as chief executive. The result was that he could give his sustained attention to no more than a handful

[4] Victory in the Democratic primary in Florida assured victory in the fall general election.

of major boards. The others were of concern only in the event of a major controversy.

In the case of the Flood Control District Board, the various governors making appointments during the 1949-1956 period had little contact with the Board once it was appointed. Most of the political factors governing appointments were the same for all the governors involved. These dictated that for the Flood Control District Board the typical member should be the campaign manager, or otherwise a very close political supporter, of the governor in the county from which he was appointed. FCD Board membership was not generally considered a stepping stone to further political office. However, since the agency was authorized to let construction contracts (other than those for the primary project) and to buy and sell land, its work directly affected the economy of much of the state, and its Board members thus were in strategic and influential positions.

When Governor Warren made his appointments in 1949, his campaign manager for Palm Beach County was asked what position he wanted. He chose to be the attorney for the Flood Control District Board. The new attorney, Wareing Miller, received a retainer of $12,800 annually in addition to extra fees for much of the work he did for the Board. Governor Warren's knowledge of water problems and of the Flood Control District was limited, so Miller was given a free hand in selecting a proposed slate of Board members. He arranged a meeting of the county campaign chairmen in the District's seventeen counties, out of which came the recommendations to Warren for the Board positions. There were several statutory requirements: each of the five members of the Board had to be an owner of real property in the District and had to be a resident of the District. In addition, there could be no more than one member from any one county. The statute also provided for three-year staggered terms.

Of the five men chosen, two had managed the Warren campaign in their counties, one had served as campaign office manager in the City of Miami, one had been the "right-hand man" of a county campaign manager, and one had been a close friend of Governor Warren when they were both students at the University of Florida.

Four of the five original Warren appointees retired during the first year. Some served only a few months. Most of their replacements, on the other hand, served for the remaining three years of the Warren administration. In all, Warren appointed eleven members, all of whom were named either because of their efforts in Warren's campaign, because of their personal friendship with the Governor, or on the strong recommendation of the outgoing Board member. Political support of Warren did not appear as important a motive in the replacement appointments as in the original ones. One of the replacements had not supported Warren at all and was named mainly at the insistence of an outgoing Board member who, though he had quarreled with Warren, retained enough influence with the Governor to name his successor.

Of the eleven Warren appointees, only one was engaged in any form of agriculture at the time of his appointment. Three were in the real estate and insurance field, three were lawyers, one a "professional politician," one a county official, one the manager of an ice plant, and one a physician.

The Wallis View

The first Board met on July 14, 1949 and adopted an organizational structure providing two top administrative posts—general manager and secretary-treasurer-chief engineer. Wallis received the latter position, and Stacy Rogers, close friend and political supporter of Governor Warren, was named to the post of general manager. Ordinarily this would have been the top administrative post. However, through an informal arrangement between Wallis, Rogers, and the Board, it was agreed that Rogers' task would be to secure for the District the political support at the state capital that it needed to begin operations on a sound basis. For the most part, Rogers used his political power and influence with the Governor to help keep the patronage wolves from the District's door. Rogers made many friends for the District both in the state and in Washington. The division of labor between him and Wallis worked smoothly. When the District was well launched, Rogers was put on a consulting basis, and finally he retired from District work altogether. The division of duties between the two placed the responsibility and power for administering the District squarely in the hands of W. Turner Wallis.

From the beginning of his service as chief executive officer, Wallis took a broad view of what the FCD's responsibilities should include. His long association with past efforts to solve the water problems of the region had made him intensely aware of the limitations of a drainage-flood control focus. Almost everyone agreed that the primary works would provide only the basic skeleton—as vital as that was—and that local works would be needed to make water control fully effective. Wallis resolved to do everything possible through the FCD to encourage the development of the subsidiary network of local works. The FCD could promote the formation of local drainage districts to undertake the task; or it could itself construct emergency works; or it could persuade the Corps of Engineers to expand the original primary works plan.

Wallis saw the comprehensive water control project as an opportunity to undo some of the unfortunate results of decades of inadequate developmental efforts. In addition it represented to him a golden opportunity to seize the initiative and develop a truly complete water control plan, beyond even the scope of the federal-state project adopted as a result of the 1947 flood.

Wallis was encouraged in this broad-gauge concept by the form of the Florida legislation, which he had helped draw up. The statute created the flood control district:

> 1) To cooperate with the United States in the manner provided by Congress for flood control, reclamation, conservation and *allied purposes* [emphasis added] in protecting the inhabitants, the land and other property within the district from the effects of a surplus or a deficiency of water. . . .
>
> 2) To plan, construct, operate and maintain works of the district. . . .
>
> 3) To determine, establish and control the level of waters to be maintained in all canals, channels and reservoirs owned and maintained by the district.

The key section of the statute defined the "District's works" as those

> set forth in the plan comprising the project as authorized by the Congress, and such other works and facilities as the governing board may deem necessary for augmenting, and making more effective use of the works set forth in and as shall be provided under such plan. The district may acquire or take over for operation and maintenance such works of other districts as the governing board may deem advisable under agreement with such districts.

Thus, as Wallis saw it, by interpreting broadly the words "allied purposes," or by laying stress on the FCD's statutory authority to do whatever necessary to make more effective use of the works, the FCD was empowered to do practically anything it chose in the water control area. And as a public corporation with a life of 99 years, it had a potential flexibility not enjoyed by a regular state agency. These were the foundations on which Wallis built his broad conception of the District's role in promoting and directing the development of water resources.

Wallis Has Free Rein

Wallis' view was not challenged by the Warren Board members. The first Board faced a monumental assignment. The Flood Control District was new and complicated in form; the scope of the project was immense; the variety of technical expertise required to understand more than a small segment of the project was beyond the experience of most laymen. As it happened, the majority of the Warren Board appointees knew little of the details of water problems in the area when appointed to the Board, and none of them could devote full time to gaining an education in water control. During the first year the turnover of members was so rapid that few Board members were able to gain familiarity with the project. Wallis, on the other hand, had had several decades of experience in almost all aspects of water control problems in the area, and his reputation was respected by the members of the Warren Board. Thus, the pattern of staff-Board relations in these crucial early years became one in which the Board followed the guidance of Wallis, the permanent staff director, in shaping District policies.

Actually, Wallis did not seriously contemplate the possibility that the Board would disagree with his broad concept of the project and of the FCD's responsibility. He felt the question of what the FCD should or should not do had been settled by the Legislature: as he saw it, the Legislature had decided the FCD should do anything possible to solve the water problems. Moreover, Wallis was not the type of administrator who spent long hours mulling over the problem of his relations with Board members. He was an engineer, faced with the enormous task of organizing a huge and complicated project. If he thought at all about what the role of a good board should be, he considered it one which would leave him entirely free to make all administrative decisions, and hopefully, one which left him free to determine major policy as well. The Warren Board fitted these criteria perfectly: it gave Wallis free rein.

As Wallis saw it, there was no reason to fear organized opposition to the District's efforts to go beyond mere co-operation with the Corps in constructing the primary works. Most of the counties in the District were controlled by farming or ranching interests; and Wallis reasoned that since they would receive greater benefits from the program if the FCD began constructing local works, they would offer no significant resistance.[5] Every other major group concerned with the project stood to gain, Wallis felt, from the implementation of his broad interpretation of the statute. Fish, wildlife, and recreation groups would benefit directly; real estate developers could anticipate additional acreage with sufficient drainage for residential and industrial development.

Wallis had been badly disappointed by one action of the Legislature while it was discussing the enabling legislation in 1949. The draft bill prepared by Elliot and Wallis would have allowed the FCD to levy taxes in proportion to the benefits to be realized by the taxpayers. The Legislature, dominated by representatives of the rural sections of the state that would benefit most from the FCD, had threatened to kill the entire enabling bill unless that provision was removed, and the sponsors had finally agreed. Thus, the FCD received its money instead from an ad valorem tax. Clearly, most of the ad valorem tax would come from the urban coastal counties, although rural areas would receive most of the direct benefits. Wallis continued to hope (vainly, as it turned out) that the Legislature would change its mind and substitute a tax power based on benefits received.

[5] South of Lake Okeechobee were the farms which raised subtropical fruits, sugar cane, and the vegetables which supplied a good portion of the nation's winter needs; north of the Lake were citrus groves and cattle ranches.

Building Support

With the full support of the Warren-appointed Board, Wallis plunged into the job of giving life and direction to the new agency. His first concern was co-ordinating the efforts of the many agencies, federal, state, and local, involved in the plan. His often blunt and impatient manner did not seem to affect his ability to work well with officials of other agencies. To speed the flow of vital data, he quickly broadened old and initiated new co-operative agreements with a number of state and federal agencies. The Corps of Engineers was not ready to start construction immediately. There was still a great deal of advance planning to be done before the first structures could be built, and the added data were badly needed to make the planning complete.

Wallis also moved to encourage grass roots support in the state. In order to deal more effectively with local areas in the District, and to build support for the broad program, he sponsored the formation of county water conservation and flood control committees. Eventually his work resulted in the establishment of committees in eleven of the seventeen counties in the project area. Wallis aimed to have represented on these committees every agency or group with an interest in water control. Most of the committees included the county agent or Soil Conservation Service district representative; cattle, farming, and citrus interests; wildlife groups; municipalities; chambers of commerce; real estate interests; and newspaper representatives.

The county committees came to serve mainly as vehicles for communicating to the District local wishes about the drainage and reclamation portion of the project. In this respect the committees were of aid to Wallis in dealing with one of the more serious problems in developing the overall plan. It took the Corps longer than anticipated to bring its studies to the point where actual construction could begin, and, as the program lagged further and further behind, there were insistent demands from local interests either for a stepped-up federal program or for the Flood Control District itself to deal with pressing water problems ahead of schedule. Most of these demands were articulated through the county committee system, and during the Warren administration (1948-1952) Wallis developed a program of emergency works construction. There were two categories of such works: first, projects which were originally part of the primary federal-state plan but which the Flood Control District would construct ahead of schedule; second, projects which were not included in the primary plan but were considered necessary "to prevent damage by floods or to provide better regulation and conservation of water." Many of the projects in this second category were part of the proposed secondary local system. The total estimated cost of the emergency program was about $3,350,000 of which about two-thirds, Wallis estimated, would be reimbursable as part of the Corps-state primary plan.

The emergency works program became a subject of political dispute in the third year of Governor Warren's administration. In a vigorous attack in 1951 a *Miami Herald* columnist characterized the program as a "political pork wagon," basing his charge largely on the claim that one particular large canal would benefit only fifteen landowners. The columnist also argued that the function of one of the disputed projects was merely to pacify those areas that had received no benefits in the District's first two years of operations. Furthermore, he warned, the state might not be credited by the federal government for money spent in developing parts of the primary plan ahead of schedule.

Wallis reacted vigorously. He defended the projects as having been chosen on the basis of maximum benefit for the funds invested; the District, he insisted, would almost certainly be credited with the bulk of the expenditures as part of the primary projects. Never one to step softly, Wallis branded as "deliberate misstatement and misrepresentation of facts" reports that the District operations were politically motivated, and he countercharged that the *Herald* articles were themselves politically motivated. One *Herald* staff member had been secretary of one of the committees sponsoring action after the 1947 flood. At that time, of course, neither Wallis nor the Miami newsman knew that the benefit assessment system of FCD taxation, which both favored, would be rejected by the Legislature. When the ad valorem tax was adopted, over Wallis' opposition, the *Herald* representative took the position that since the tax structure was inequitable, he would oppose any but the most narrow interpretation of the powers of the District. The broader the role of the District, he felt, the more money would be drawn from Dade County. The *Herald* had periodically stressed the fact that metropolitan Dade County paid about two-thirds of the total ad valorem levy but received fewer benefits from water control than the farm-ranch counties.[6]

In at least one respect, the *Herald* critic was correct: Wallis did see the emergency works program as a device to satisfy those areas of the District in which no work had been done. He feared that if all work was completed in one area before starting in another, the area which had already received the benefits would lose interest in supporting the remainder of the project. And the first phase—the only one then authorized by Congress—called for primary works construction only in areas south of Lake Okeechobee.

The bitter attacks of the *Miami Herald* and the equally bitter rebuttals by Wallis and the Flood Control District Board caused Wallis to be identified politically as a supporter and defender of the Warren administration. And Warren had not enjoyed a term of office free from controversy. While he had gained much support, especially by his vigorous program to eliminate off-track betting, he had been hurt by the hearings and reports of a special congressional committee headed by Democratic Senator Estes Kefauver of Tennessee. Among other charges, the committee reported that Warren had "allowed the power of his office to be used by the Capone syndicate in its successful effort to muscle into Miami Beach gambling." Warren flatly denied any connections with the various criminal activities under committee investigation, but the charges remained to be exploited by Dan McCarty, the defeated contender of 1948 who was trying again in 1952 for the governorship.

6 The emergency works program drew fire from yet another quarter. The recreation and fish and game groups feared that the project works would be constructed with benefits to the farmers and ranchers uppermost in mind, to the detriment of the needs of recreation. But interest groups other than the directly represented agricultural forces never managed to marshal sufficient strength to force significant modifications of the agricultural orientation of the plan during the period covered by this case (1949-1956).

Wallis Clashes with a New Board

DAN McCARTY defeated Brailey Odham in the 1952 spring primary, and succeeded Warren as Governor in January 1953. Where Warren had appealed to the rural element in Florida politics, McCarty drew his support from the urban areas and from large corporation-type farmers. He typified the successful young businessman element in politics; he was dedicated to "cleaning up the mess" created by the "professional politician" by bringing a business approach into government. This moderate-progressive faction in Florida politics avoided either conservative or liberal extremes, especially the latter.

Wallis knew that McCarty supporters considered him to be a "Warren man," his open support of McCarty in the 1948 primary notwithstanding. He was anxious to establish a precedent of smooth transition so that the continuity of the operations of the Flood Control District would be insulated from changes of governors. Therefore, after McCarty won the election (but before he assumed office) Wallis suggested to the Board that it hire as general manager Bartlet Arnold, a resident of Ft. Pierce, the McCarty family's home town, and a close friend of the McCarty family. Wallis' primary concern was to try to preserve the staggered-board provision in the FCD's enabling legislation, and Arnold agreed that if he became general manager he would seek Dan McCarty's assurance that the Board members appointed by Warren would be permitted to serve out their terms—although, of course, McCarty would not be bound to reappoint them. Arnold was hired as general manager late in 1952.

However, the McCarty forces were skeptical of anything which had been in favor during the Warren period. Many McCarty supporters were convinced that the Warren-appointed FCD Board had used the District to advance partisan interests, chiefly by padding the District's payroll with patronage employees. Hearty denials by Wallis were given little heed since he was labeled a Warren supporter. Criticisms of him ranged from the charge that he had actively participated in some of the allegedly existing practices to the charge that he had at least acquiesced in them. Within six months after McCarty's inauguration, four new members had been appointed to the FCD Board; one Warren appointee was carried over.[7]

Wallis was convinced that this almost completely new Board had come about because of an unexpected occurrence: only a few weeks after his inauguration in January, 41-year-old Dan McCarty suffered a heart attack. He never really recovered from the seizure, and that September he died. During this nine-month period, the affairs of state did not proceed in quite the orderly fashion that might have prevailed had the elected Governor been completely healthy or in full command of his strength. Dan's younger brother, John, took over many of the Governor's commitments and duties. If Arnold had indeed approached Dan McCarty, it was more than likely, Wallis felt, that the Governor's possible agreement to retain the Warren Board had not been communicated to those who were helping the ailing Governor bear his load.

The four members appointed by McCarty came from three major geographic subdivisions of the District: Dade County, Lake Okeechobee, and the Kissimmee Valley. The carryover member was from the east coast area south of West Palm Beach. All members, including the carryover, had worked actively in McCarty's 1952

[7] The biennial sessions of the Legislature made it easier for a new governor to clear the decks than, perhaps, those who drafted the FCD enabling legislation had intended: appointees often had to wait a year or more for confirmation of the State Senate if their appointment had been made between sessions. If a gubernatorial election intervened, the new governor could simply decide not to present the held-over names for confirmation and by this inaction he created vacancies which he could fill.

campaign. (Three of the appointees had been campaign managers in their respective counties.) All were acquainted with the Governor, and three were close personal friends. One Board member was a large-scale farmer in south Dade County, one a rancher in the Okeechobee area, one operated a migrant labor camp in the Everglades, one managed a large ranching and citrus operation in the Kissimmee Valley, and the carryover member was in the real estate and insurance business. The one member carried over had managed Warren's campaign in 1948 in his county, but he later became a strong McCarty supporter and worked hard for him in the 1952 campaign. He was kept for three reasons: (a) because McCarty had a clear majority on the Board; (b) because the carryover member pledged himself to go along with the views of the majority in appointing a new Board attorney; and (c) because he had the strong support of the McCarty group in his home county.

The McCarty Board was complete by June 1953. J. Abney Cox, a wealthy landowner from Dade County, was elected chairman by his fellow Board members.

By this time the FCD's staff had grown to a sizeable number. The FCD had started out in 1949 with only a handful of employees and with a few rooms in an office building. Its main need at that time had been for planning personnel. As the Corps of Engineers passed the planning stage and began construction, the District hired people to handle the land acquisition program and to arrange for rights-of-way. The FCD mushroomed out room by room, although appropriations for new space and personnel always lagged behind requirements.

Wallis himself had spent a good deal of time outside the offices, arranging the various intergovernmental co-operative programs, making speeches to acquaint engineers and other technical people with the overall project, and building local committee support for the District.

The Board Curbs Wallis

The McCarty Board cast a discontented eye on the District's operations. Among all members, in varying degrees, there was a feeling of general disapproval of the Warren administration. Their reactions to Wallis varied. One Board member felt he should be fired outright; he saw Wallis as a Warren man who had contributed funds to McCarty's 1952 opponent. Two Board members, including Chairman Cox, felt strongly that Wallis' powers should be curtailed. Cox did not agree that Wallis' trouble stemmed from any political affiliations. He felt, instead, that Wallis had been given too free a rein by the Warren appointees, and that his policy-making powers had thus been too great. It was the responsibility of the Board, he felt, to make policy. Moreover, Cox felt that the large size of Wallis' salary was improper: Wallis was being paid $18,000—more than the Governor's salary at that time.

The two other Board members were less opposed to Wallis. One was the carryover member; the other was the member from the Kissimmee Valley, who happened not to be as closely allied politically to McCarty as were the two who opposed Wallis more strongly.

Three of the four Board members who opposed Wallis agreed with his supporter in one respect: Wallis' knowledge and experience in the project were unmatched. The problem, they felt, was establishing a pattern of relationships which would "curb" Wallis while preserving his contributions on matters that were not disputed policy questions.

Wallis, on the other hand, felt that the opposition to him stemmed primarily from his identification with Warren politically—an identification which he felt was not justified. He also believed that much of the opposition was being stirred up by the new board attorney, Robert Tylander, a close friend of the McCarty family who had managed the Governor's campaign in Palm Beach County. Tylander, Wallis felt, resented Wallis' strong efforts to retain the attorney who had served during the latter part of the Warren administration. Wallis had regarded that attorney as exceptionally competent.

There was still another source of friction, in Wallis' view. Second in command to Wallis in the engineering department was Lamar Johnson. Since the 1920s Johnson had been a close associate of Wallis in efforts to develop the water resources of central and southern Florida. He had first served under Wallis on a survey crew in 1922, then finally succeeded him as head of the Everglades Drainage District when Wallis resigned that position in 1945. As head of the

Everglades Drainage District, Johnson had been a leading competitor of Wallis for the Flood Control District post. Their long-standing friendship did not survive Wallis' appointment, although Johnson accepted a position subordinate to him in the FCD. By the time the McCarty Board took office, Wallis felt Johnson had begun to work against him.

As soon as the McCarty Board held its organization meeting in June 1953, it moved to take specific steps to curb Wallis' power. The McCarty Board created a new staff organization pattern. Wallis would henceforth share responsibility for the administration of the District with the general manager, Bartlet Arnold, and with a new chief engineer. At the June 12, 1953 meeting of the Board, it was resolved:

> . . . that Mr. Lamar Johnson be named Chief Engineer of the Flood Control District and that he assume complete responsibility for the Engineering activities of the Board, and that his responsibilities include the liaison work necessary with the Corps of Engineers and other Federal, State, and local agencies pertaining to problems in this field and that he be responsible for recommending policies in the engineering field to the board.

The directive of June 12 removed from Wallis' control the task of co-ordinating District activities with those of other state and federal agencies, an area in which the McCarty Board felt he had exceeded his authority by committing the Board to policies without proper prior consultation. It also modified the former arrangement, under which all roads had led to Wallis, by giving Arnold and Johnson direct access to the Board. The McCarty Board then moved quickly to curtail Wallis' remaining power as Secretary-Treasurer by appointing special Board committees on administration and operations. The major purpose of these committees was to enable the Board to keep a close check on the affairs of the District in general and the activities of Wallis in particular.

Perhaps the clearest expression of the distrust of Wallis came in a Board regulation that one or more members of each appropriate Board advisory committee would henceforth accompany members of the staff at "significant public meetings and at important conferences." The purpose of the latter provision was to prevent Wallis from committing the District to broad programs of action in co-operation with other agencies without prior Board approval. The McCarty Board was convinced that Wallis' alleged inability to say no to anybody about anything resulted in his going about the District making promises that could not be fulfilled, leaving to Chief Engineer Lamar Johnson the task of informing the individual or groups concerned that the District could not deliver on the commitments.

Basic Policy Clashes

There was a further source of tension—this one perhaps more fundamental than the clashes of personalities. The project was far behind schedule, and the McCarty Board members and Wallis could not agree on what course the District should follow as a result.

The project was behind schedule partly because the Corps of Engineers had underestimated the length of time needed to complete the planning and engineering of works. Also, from the very first year, Congress had been appropriating much less than the original authorizations had permitted. However, even with relatively low appropriations, the end of a fiscal year often found the Corps turning back unexpended funds. There was also continued criticism from the House Appropriations Committee that Florida's contribution of fifteen percent was too low, and that the entire project was really a land reclamation project benefiting a few farmers rather than a bona fide water control or flood control project. At home, the Florida Legislature, which met every two years, had been appropriating funds biennially to match expected federal contributions. When, year after year, federal funds were not utilized or the federal appropriation fell below the authorization, the funds appropriated by the state reverted to the general fund. The Florida Legislature was beginning to feel that this was, at the least, an inefficient way to do business.

The McCarty Board members felt one partial remedy was for the District to concentrate on speeding the primary projects. As a result of policies initiated under the Warren Board, the District was spreading its present efforts too thin, they argued. Wallis, however, was not prepared to back pedal after his many efforts to get a successful broad program started. Furthermore he saw no logical reason for the approach proposed by the McCarty Board. He felt that continuing support for the project depended in part on making a start on some project works ahead of Corps construction dates. He also felt that rapid economic and population growth in many areas of the District made it necessary to develop local (secondary) works simultaneously in order to safeguard life and property.

However, Wallis did not make a sustained effort to convert McCarty appointees to his point of view. He believed that he had to choose between spending most of his time playing what he considered would be a futile diplomatic game with the McCarty Board or doing his job as a top administrative officer in the District. In addition, he considered it a waste of time to attempt to explain intricate engineering considerations to Board members: the result, he felt, would be to confuse them further. His view of their intellectual capacities and of their public responsibilities did not ingratiate Wallis with the already skeptical and critical members of the McCarty Board.

The organizational changes and continuing friction between Wallis and the McCarty Board made it virtually impossible for Wallis to pursue effectively the various programs developed during the Warren regime. He saw this as a setback to the project. The McCarty Board members, on the other hand, considered they had accomplished their objective—to shape District policy as they considered advisable. The friction between Wallis and the Board grew. Wallis grew increasingly indignant at what he considered stubborn refusal of the McCarty Board to support his goals. The McCarty Board became more and more determined to exercise its policy-making powers by sharply restricting the powers of the executive officer.

The McCarty Board did not repudiate the emergency works activity, although it did develop more specific and more stringent criteria for evaluating both emergency works and secondary system applications from county committees or other local representatives. Wallis considered this hypocritical on the part of the McCarty Board members, suspecting that both programs were being continued in order to promote pet projects in certain Board members' home territories. He felt that the emergency works program had "gotten out of hand," and that many projects not justifiable on a true emergency basis were being constructed. The division of authority adopted by the McCarty Board made it difficult for Wallis or anyone else to exercise co-ordinated control of such activities.

Thus, the atmosphere of mutual distrust and suspicion grew. Before the clash reached any resolution, Governor Dan McCarty died, and the stage was set for a new Flood Control Board to be appointed.

The Johns Board

UNDER FLORIDA LAW, Charley E. Johns, as president of the Senate, became Acting Governor upon the death of Governor McCarty, and he was inaugurated on September 29, 1953. But Johns was soon deeply embroiled in the bitterest of quarrels with the supporters of McCarty, including members of various state boards appointed by the late Governor. When Dan McCarty had suffered his first heart attack the preceding February, reporters had quoted Johns as saying that he would follow McCarty's policies if he succeeded to the office. On October 1, at Johns' first press conference as Governor, reporters pressed him for his intentions. Johns declared that so far as acting against illegal gambling was concerned he intended to "follow out Dan's policies to the letter," and that he also intended to follow through McCarty's program of economy and of cutting back unnecessary employees.

Many McCarty supporters interpreted this to mean that McCarty appointees would be retained. They felt betrayed when, two weeks later, Johns suggested that many of McCarty's major appointees offer to resign. A day or so later, on October 15, John McCarty announced that there would be a candidate in the next gubernatorial race who would be pledged to carry out his brother's program. Johns came back with a heated statement that he had originally asked for resignations in order to ensure that he would have loyal officials, but that with John McCarty as a potential contender he felt even more justified in removing department heads who might be torn in their loyalties. Johns' replacement of McCarty appointees proceeded, and McCarty supporters seethed.

Florida law, however, did not permit Johns to serve out the late Governor's full term. A special election was scheduled for the spring of 1954. Johns announced his candidacy, and a legal battle sprang up, with Johns contending that the constitutional provision against a governor succeeding himself did not apply to his special circumstance. In December 1953 the State Supreme Court upheld Johns' position, and the campaign was underway. John McCarty did not run, but he supported Johns' principal opponent, LeRoy Collins.

Sometime during the campaign Johns was visited by one of his ardent supporters, a West Palm Beach attorney. The attorney called to Johns' attention the fact that not only were McCarty appointees still filling the Flood Control District Board, but that the Board attorney's job, which then carried an annual stipend of about $10,000, was also in the hands of a McCarty man. He made it clear that he wished the job for himself. The Acting Governor agreed that there had been an oversight, and he turned his attention to appointing a new FCD Board.

Collins defeated Johns in the May 1954 primary. He was to assume office in January 1955, and it seemed clear that any of Johns' appointees still requiring senatorial confirmation then would probably be disappointed. Johns, however, continued to fill the various state boards with his own appointees. By the August 13, 1954 meeting of the FCD, Johns appointees formed a majority of the Board membership, most of them destined to serve only until Collins was inaugurated as Governor and replaced them.

The Board Is Appointed

Johns held over one McCarty FCD Board member, Elgin Bayless, from the Kissimmee Valley area. One top McCarty aide felt that Bayless was the Board candidate about whom the late Governor McCarty had had the most hesitation. On the other hand, another McCarty administrative assistant later held that both Bayless and his wife were extremely valuable political allies, since they were known and liked all over the state, and that McCarty had had full confidence in Bayless. Bayless' carryover may have been related to the fact that he subsequently "gave his loyalty" to Johns in his campaign against Collins. Bayless himself confirmed his support of Johns, noting that he had long been a close friend of both McCarty and Johns. He was named board chairman during the Johns regime.

Acting Governor Johns' approach to making appointments to various boards in the state was not always characterized by careful study. It was reported that the first person to get to him, or to be suggested to him by a supporter, often got the job. Actually, of the four District Board members appointed by Johns, only one was active in a major way (county campaign manager) in his subsequent gubernatorial campaign. Two others supported Johns but were not particularly active campaigners. They both attributed their appointments to the intercession of strong Johns supporters in their respective areas. The fourth had supported McCarty in 1952, and he supported Collins in the run-off race with Johns. This latter Board member, upon hearing of Johns' intention to appoint him, called the Acting Governor to say that some mistake in identification must have been made. Johns replied that there was no error and that he wished him to serve. The Board member continued to support Collins (though not actively), and Johns found it "a hard thing."

The Johns Board was at least superficially similar to the McCarty Board in its agricultural orientation. One member was a large-scale fruit and vegetable farmer in south Dade County; another was a rancher in the Caloosahatchee Valley area;[8] another was a retired road construction contractor who owned land in the Caloosahatchee Valley; and the final member appointed by Johns was the advertising director of a West Palm Beach newspaper.

[8] The Caloosahatchee River runs from Lake Okeechobee west to the Gulf of Mexico.

There were close political ties between Johns' men and the forces of former Governor Warren in the Flood Control District area. For example, a man who had served as Board chairman during Warren's term was offered a Board post by the Attorney of the Johns' Board. (He refused because it was not for a full term.) A Warren Board member from the Miami area became the head of a District Miami office authorized by the Johns Board. A number of Warren Board members also supported Johns in his unsuccessful bid for the final two years of the McCarty term.

Wallis found the ten months of the Johns Board a brief era of harmonious relationships. In September 1954 the new Board set up a committee to review the District's personnel and management arrangement. This review resulted in a sweeping reorganization which ended the triple-headed administrative structure that had prevailed during the McCarty period. The authority and responsibility for administering the affairs of the District were concentrated in the post of Executive Director-Secretary-Treasurer, and Wallis was named to fill the position.

Four Board members supported the change without reservation. The fifth member, Bayless, approved the reorganization in principle, but he was not enthusiastic about Wallis receiving the new job. This was not a reflection on Wallis' technical competence, for Bayless had served for many years as land agent for the Internal Improvement Fund, and he had long admired Wallis' knowledge of water problems in central and southern Florida. In Bayless' mind it was a question of whether this was the position in which Wallis would be most useful to the project. Actually, most McCarty Board members had been disappointed with the three-headed arrangement even before the Johns Board took office, but their plan to reconcentrate responsibility in one administrative officer had not included giving Wallis the post.[9]

The FCD Is Attacked

During the period from August 1954 to June 1955, the "lame duck" period of the Johns Board, the FCD Board continued to carry out the work of the District. During that time, also, a bitter dispute concerning patronage flared into the open.[10] Shortly after the Johns Board reorganization, Lamar Johnson, District Chief Engineer under the McCarty Board, abruptly resigned his position with the District. Johnson gave an interview to the *Miami Herald* in which he stated as the reason for his resignation the "changes in personnel and procedure made by appointees of the administration of Acting Governor Charley Johns." The *Herald* reported that the policy changes referred to by Johnson included: (1) the order making Wallis "final authority" under the Board on all Flood Control District matters; and (2) a change in the status of Bartlet Arnold, involving a lessening of his authority. When Wallis had made it clear that he intended to be boss in fact as well as name of the entire District staff, including the engineering division, Johnson had resigned. In addition, Johnson was much more sympathetic than Wallis to the McCarty Board's more restricted conception of the District's responsibilities. The Johnson resignation was at least partially responsible for the *Miami Herald's* subsequent attacks on the District under the Johns administration.

The articles in the *Herald* and several other state newspapers accused the Johns Board of al-

[9] The Johns reorganization was not finally adopted by the Board until January 1955, the same month Governor Collins took office. The Board at that time issued a statement of policy that left no doubt that W. Turner Wallis was to be the chief administrator of the District: "The Chairman informed the staff that the Board will henceforth look to the Executive Director and Secretary, Mr. Wallis, to implement the policy decisions of the Board; keep the Board informed of the status of all District programs and projects; direct the efforts of the entire District Staff; represent the Board in public meetings when directed by the Chairman, and, in addition, all salary increases or changes in classification resulting in a salary increase be cleared through Mr. Wallis and reported to the Board at the next meeting."

[10] Up to 1955 there had been no state merit system plan. A system was adopted in 1955, but implementation was slow and for several years each agency improvised its own personnel plan. All had to struggle with the problem of political patronage. With the possible exception of salaries (higher during the Warren Board period) the personnel practices and problems of the Central and Southern Florida Flood Control District were characteristic of other Florida resource development agencies. Up to 1960 the District had not been brought under the state merit system, and patronage was a difficult problem.

lowing the District to be loaded with patronage employees, with the result that many professionally trained people had left the District (an obvious reference to Johnson). The *Herald* charged that the alleged demand of Acting Governor Johns for hiring large numbers of patronage employees had robbed FCD of two top engineers, neither of whom had been replaced.

Wallis quickly produced a reply to the *Herald* articles in a memorandum of March 25, 1955, in which he strongly condemned "certain misstatements of fact concerning political patronage under this Board." After summarizing the charges that had appeared in the *Herald,* Wallis sought to refute them one by one.

Wallis also prepared for the FCD Board a memorandum which clearly outlined his views on the *Herald* articles, the patronage problem, and the relative merits of the McCarty-Johns boards. The memorandum bitterly condemned the *Miami Herald* for printing as straight news a story that gave "obvious evidence of incompetence, negligence, or deliberate harmful intent." It continued:

> It is true that top-echelon personnel within the state agencies are often changed with changes in administration. And it is incontrovertibly true that members of the legislative and executive branches of government occasionally use their influence on behalf of friends and supporters or persons for whose capabilities they have high regard.
>
> The propriety of this type of activity is questionable. If it is a matter of throwing out experienced, competent people to replace them with inexperienced people, it is a wasteful practice. If it results in building better government by replacing poor personnel with good, the same end should perhaps be achieved without political overtones. If it is a matter of firing competent people or creating unnecessary jobs to provide sinecures for misfits, it is of course reprehensible.
>
> There is no question that political pressures affecting the manning of a state agency create grave problems for those who direct it, and insecurity for those who work for it. Hence it is comforting to note that the present [Johns] board's early adoption of a firm stand against the practices of hiring "strictly from politics" has meant that less consideration was given to political pressures in employment since last July than in the McCarty administration. It is to be hoped that this policy can be continued and made more binding.
>
> It is true that there are persons on the FCD payroll who were hired on the basis of political recommendations during the McCarty administration. They are still there because they also proved that they had ability. And there are some "political appointees" from the Warren administration who are still on the payroll for the same reason. It is safe to say that the total number of patronage appointees from all administrations does not exceed 10-15 percent of present District employment, and that neither past nor present political endorsement gives them immunity from being fired if they fail to perform their duties in a creditable manner.

To Wallis the heart of the matter was that under the Warren and Johns boards he enjoyed the full power to hire and fire, and thus he was able to keep the patronage problem firmly under control. Under the McCarty Board the power to hire and fire had been divided between the three top administrative officers. In the case of both the Warren and Johns boards, an agreement between Wallis, key Board members, and the Governor apparently limited sharply the practice of dumping patronage employees on the District.

Wallis' Programs Proceed

The Johns Board depended as heavily on Wallis in matters of policy and administration as had the Warren Board. Its members believed that they should function chiefly to support Wallis when he needed help. Johns Board members were keenly aware of their unfamiliarity with the details of the complex project and of the probability that they would not serve long enough to master them. Therefore, they looked primarily to Wallis for leadership. And Wallis was delighted to have the lead once again.

The District was facing serious financial problems, in addition to its usual clutch of responsibilities. Congress had authorized no federal funds at all for fiscal 1954, partly because $3,750,000 was as yet unexpended by the Corps, partly because of House Appropriations Committee opposition to the project, and partly because of the Eisenhower administration's drive to cut the budget for fiscal 1954. During that year the Corps had operated entirely on carryover funds. The FCD, along with other interested state and local agencies, was deeply occupied during 1954 with presenting the District's case to Congress. In the immediate sense this took the form of securing congressional approval for the Corps to use almost $3,000,000 in accumulated surplus state funds during fiscal 1955 in order to speed construction on the project. In addition, the first phase authorization had run out, and there was a substantial threat that Congress would increase the percentage of the District's contribution. The second phase authorization, approved in 1954, did not specify what the local share should be, and the District and Corps representatives were working constantly on presentations before the Bureau of the Budget and congressional committees.

During this year Wallis moved quickly, with full Board approval, to renew work on the programs begun during the Warren period. Several policy statements were adopted restating and expanding the District's intention to follow a broad approach to its responsibilities in the project. Specifically, Wallis pushed the development of new programs in the areas of recreation and in the secondary system of canals, dikes, and project works. A master plan was developed to promote a maximum use of the District's waters for hunting, fishing, and general recreation.

Wallis also saw a chance to insure a more rapid and comprehensive development of a secondary works system for the District by integrating it with the small watershed program authorized by Congress in 1954. (Since soil conservation districts, the usual sponsors of small watershed projects, lacked authority to levy taxes and condemn land, the FCD hoped to correct these deficiencies by promoting the use of its sub-districts as sponsors for these projects.) Under this program, the Department of Agriculture's Soil Conservation Service was authorized to co-operate with local agencies in constructing local flood control works, provided the local agency involved assumed half the cost of construction and full responsibility for maintenance. The District, mostly through Wallis, had lobbied actively in Washington for the watershed legislation, and Wallis had been instrumental in moderating the opposition to the bill of Florida's Democratic Senator Spessard L. Holland. Once the legislation was approved, Wallis developed a series of proposals which provided for leadership, including financial aid, on the part of the FCD in applying the new law to central and southern Florida. He relied on a section of the FCD's enabling legislation which provided for the formation of subdistricts within the FCD. These were to be under the direction of the FCD Board and could be authorized to raise funds through taxation. By the end of the Johns Board's service, preliminary approval had been given for District co-sponsorship of two watershed projects.

Wallis and the Collins Board

BY JUNE 11, 1955 Governor LeRoy Collins had completely replaced the Johns Board with five nominees of his own.[11] There was a close connection between the Collins Board and the McCarty administration. J. Abney Cox, Board chairman during the McCarty period, was appointed to the same post by Governor Collins. Robert Tylander

[11] The vacancies were made possible by the fact that Elgin Bayless, first appointed by McCarty and kept on by Johns, was belatedly discovered not to live within the District's boundaries and was thus disqualified as a Board member. The other four Johns appointees had never been confirmed by the Senate, so Collins simply did not submit their names for confirmation when that body convened.

One of the Collins appointees later distinguished between Collins' and Johns' actions in replacing the FCD Board members by commenting: ". . . a duly elected . . . Governor of a state should be expected to appoint loyal men to high political positions who reflect his views, and the logical place to find such men is among his friends. Sound public administration requires that the appointive power of a Chief executive be made responsible to the peoples' will. It is regrettable that one Acting Governor (Charley Johns), who was never elected by the people of Florida, [presumably as Governor, since Johns had been elected to the Legislature] saw fit to insist upon the resignation of this and other Board memberships . . . The succeeding Governor (Leroy Collins) would have and should have been seriously criticized had he continued in office these unorthodox 'lame duck' appointments. . . ."

was named Board Attorney, the same post he had held under Dan McCarty. Brian McCarty, brother of the ex-Governor, was named to the Board from the upper east coast area.[12] Cox, McCarty, and Tylander were all close personal friends and strong political supporters of Collins, and all had worked actively in his campaign against Johns. David G. Click of Clewiston (representing the Everglades Agricultural Area) was also a friend of Collins and had managed his campaign in Hendry County. Neither the West Palm Beach nor the Kissimmee appointee was as close to the Governor as the other Board members were. Neither had supported his campaign as actively. Both were appointed largely on the recommendation of the Collins organizations in their counties.

Board-Staff Friction

There were a number of factors in the new situation making unlikely a continuation of the peaceful staff-Board relations of the Johns period.

First, the new Board was inheriting a chief executive officer in whom its individual members, to one degree or another, lacked full confidence. The District and Wallis were now stalked by the ghosts of past political struggles launched during the Warren administration and intensified during the McCarty and Johns periods. To a greater or lesser extent, each of the Collins Board members viewed Wallis as a supporter of Warren and Johns. At the same time most Board members had great respect for his technical competence; but there was a general feeling that this ability had not been channeled properly in the past.

Added to these circumstances was the fact that the District had been functioning for six years, long enough for Board members, as District residents who had been concerned with its progress, to be at least somewhat familiar with its problems. It is possible that almost any FCD Board appointed at this time would have become more active in District affairs than had previous Board members. There was still another factor—in the nature of the men whom Governor Collins appointed to replace the Johns Board. Most were successful businessmen.[13] This in itself did not set them apart from former FCD Board members; what did was that their business enterprises did not require their constant attention. Almost all of them could (and did) devote much of their time to their Board responsibilities. The Collins Board was thus a "working Board" to a very great extent. Its members spent a good deal of time on District affairs and grew familiar with many detailed problems.

Furthermore, it was not likely that there would be a repetition of the unusual circumstances of the past six years which had seen four different governors and a whirling turnover of Board members. Assuming a Collins victory at the next regular election in 1956, the new Board members could look forward to serving their full three-year terms.

The Collins Board was determined to assume full responsibility for shaping policy. Wallis might have admitted that in any showdown the final word on policy belonged to the Board; but he was irritated by the Board's encroachment on an area which he felt was clearly *his*: the internal administration of the District's offices.

The members of the Collins Board had been shocked on the occasion of their first visit to the FCD. They felt the District offices were in chaos: office personnel appeared to be crowded on top of one another; files seemed in disorder; employees did not seem to know precisely what their responsibilities were; and there was no consistent pay scale. Their impressions of the District offices and operations had convinced many of the new FCD Board members that Wallis, knowledgeable as he was, was a poor administrator. The Board voted at its October 14 meeting to

12 Collins and his administrative staff viewed the geographic factor as of crucial importance in making board appointments. During the Collins administration an attempt was made to represent Dade County, the Everglades Agricultural Area, the West Palm Beach area (since District headquarters were located there), the upper east coast area (north of West Palm Beach), and the Kissimmee Valley. This left several areas, such as the Caloosahatchee Valley, Broward County, and the upper St. Johns River Valley without direct representation. In deciding whom to appoint, Governor Collins leaned heavily on one individual, or on a very small group of key men, in each county concerned.

13 Three of the Board members owned and operated very large farms or ranches; the fourth owned a bottling plant; and the fifth, a hardware store.

study and review the FCD's personnel system. One of the Board members, David Click, was a former Commander in the United States Naval Reserve. Among the posts he had held was that of a special assistant to the Under-Secretary of the Navy, and he was especially expert in Navy personnel problems. Click spent nearly three weeks of almost uninterrupted work devising a new personnel system for the FCD, and after careful discussion the Board adopted the new system in May 1956.

Wallis resented the Board's incursion into administrative detail. He and some of the other staff members felt that the Board was overlooking the fact that the FCD was not a business which had been in operation for many years: it was a government agency, started only six years before the Collins Board took office. The personnel had expanded from 34 in 1950 to about 50 in 1953, and to about 100 in 1954. The responsibilities of the District had been proliferating each year. The original six or seven office rooms had long since been outgrown, and room by room the FCD had expanded, always several rooms and employees behind its actual needs. At the time of the Collins Board appointment the FCD offices were actually divided between two office buildings—an administrative arrangement which added to the appearance of chaos and one for which Wallis was not to blame. The staff was kept wholly occupied with coping with the "crash needs" of the ever-changing situation. To Wallis it seemed that there had never been a quiet moment during which the staff could straighten out files, records, or job classifications. Click, on the other hand, did not agree that the District had been faced with organizational problems of greater complexity than those of many other governmental units with which he was familiar.

The Collins Board Takes Control

The Board's initial response to its dissatisfaction with FCD affairs was to move immediately to establish its control of overall policy. The major policy question, it felt, was the extent to which the District should engage in projects other than the primary works. At the first meeting of the new Board in June 1955 a policy statement was issued that

> the Central and Southern Florida Flood Control District was created for the primary purpose of expediting the program of water control for central and southern Florida as authorized by the Federal government in cooperation with the State of Florida. Any activity of this district not directly connected with the authorized Federal program will be extremely limited.

In this and other statements the Board was sharply critical of its predecessor's programs for emergency works and secondary systems. There were several reasons why the Board took the stand it did. None of these reasons represented an attack on secondary or emergency works as inherently bad; nor did the Board feel that the District would overstep its legal authority in pursuing the broad approach. Rather, the major reason was that most of the members believed that District participation in secondary and emergency programs threatened the primary project by depriving it of needed funds and energies. All manpower and financial resources, the Board felt, had to be concentrated on the primary project so that the District could successfully obtain the necessary rights-of-way and conservation area land, provide the required cost-sharing funds, and operate and maintain primary system works economically and effectively.

Wallis countered this argument by holding that the District did, in fact, possess the fiscal resources to take an active part in something other than the primary project. He noted that the great financial problem for the District had been the slow rate at which *federal* matching funds for the project had been appropriated. This lag resulted in a state FCD surplus of several million dollars, and in 1955 the state had actually advanced the federal government almost $3,000,000 to help speed the work. As for the ad valorem levy, Wallis pointed to the steadily rising property valuations in the District that had increased the District's tax income from $390,000 in 1950 to over $2,000,000 in 1956.[14]

The second major rationale advanced by the Collins Board was that while some participation in non-primary works was no doubt desirable, or perhaps even necessary to meet the needs of the

[14] In 1957 the Collins Board partially removed this argument by lowering the millage rate from one mill to three-fourths of a mill. It thus reduced the District's income by about 25 percent, or $500,000, annually.

area adequately, there was no way to keep such programs from getting out of hand. Much of the activity during the Johns period, the Collins Board members felt, had been political boondoggling designed primarily to oil the Johns political machine. One of the major ways to avoid such distortion of the goals of the FCD, the Board felt, was to stick purposefully to the primary works. It was preferable, in the Board's eyes, to participate in no such secondary work rather than to get involved in some work that was not justified. Not only would this course avoid possible boondoggling, but it would avoid the more innocent but equally dangerous mistake of lulling sub-drainage districts into inactivity by having the FCD construct local works in their territories.

The Board also felt that having the FCD construct some secondary works but not others would inevitably create resentment, and that the best way to maintain harmony in the District was to treat all equally by showing no preferences at all and constructing no local works. And overall, most of the Collins Board members were inclined to feel that it was desirable to seek measures which promoted economy and a lowered tax rate.

Wallis disagreed almost completely with the reasoning of the Board. The FCD, he felt, could not continue to draw taxes from an area without giving it something for its money; if the primary works plan did not call for any construction for four or five years (as was the case in parts of the Kissimmee and upper St. Johns River areas) it was a wise expenditure of District funds to construct some primary works there on an everyday basis ahead of schedule. In addition he felt there were numerous engineering arguments for speeding secondary works in any region where local sub-drainage districts had not yet been formed.

But the major clash between the Board and Wallis centered on the co-operative programs Wallis had developed: the small-watershed program and District development of a master recreation plan. The Board's June policy statement meant the end of them. The central argument of the Collins Board was that the District did not have the funds to undertake such broad programs. Wallis did not agree. In the case of the small-watershed program, the local areas had indicated their willingness to submit to a special assessment tax covering the local half of the construction costs. Federal legislation required that maintenance and operation costs of small-watershed projects would have to be met by local drainage districts. However, Wallis (to encourage participation and because he regarded maintenance costs as trifling compared with the FCD's tax income) had committed the FCD to pay these costs for the local districts. The Warren Board's reversal of policy, Wallis felt, would severely strain the former close working relationships between the FCD, the Soil Conservation Service, and the District-sponsored county flood control and water conservation committees that had developed the plans with the understanding that the District would participate.

The Collins Board stood firm. Naturally, most Board members felt, other state, local, and federal agencies would be delighted to shift a financial burden from their budgets onto that of the FCD. And, they felt, in a situation where inactivity would mean the flooding of personal property, property owners themselves would quickly assume the responsibility for local works.

The disagreement as to whether there would be a financial drain on the FCD by participating in the small-watershed program was never resolved. Moreover, Wallis never took the time to explain his point of view fully to the Board. In part this was because he lacked the patience necessary for such sustained effort. While he recognized that there was a basic disagreement (apart from political differences) on what District policy should be, he felt that no amount of persuasion or reasonable argument would convince either himself or the Board that the other's view was correct.

And so, Wallis and the Collins Board found themselves at loggerheads over the basic policy question of the scope of the District's powers and responsibilities. The Board resolved to curtail Wallis' "free-wheeling" by reinstating the committee system of the McCarty era, designed to enable Board members to keep a closer watch on Wallis.

The Board finally decided that Wallis should not continue in the top post, although most of the members did not want to lose his extensive knowledge and experience. Wallis was told that as soon as the Board found a successor he would be relieved of his job. The search continued for a few months. In May 1956 Wallis collapsed from ulcer complications. While he was convalescing, the Board created the post of director of planning and research and offered the job to Wallis with no reduction in salary. Wallis accepted the position, and he was replaced as executive director.

Wallis served in this new post for about six months, and on January 1, 1957 he left the FCD completely to become deputy head of the Internal Improvement Fund.

The Flood Control District continued in its efforts to speed the Corps and the project; Wallis soon was working full time as consultant in water control problems for a multitude of agencies, private groups, and communities—often in direct conflict with the FCD and its new policies.

Wallis himself felt that the tempestuous history of the FCD suggested the moral that it is incumbent on an administrative head to devote a good deal of time and energy to educating and placating Board members if stability of policy is to be attained.

Other observers have expressed the belief that (1) with shifting political factionalism and the lack of continuity of party policy; and (2) with the organizational structure of the FCD, political and policy conflicts were inherent in the situation. They felt that stability of administration would have been difficult to achieve regardless of the personalities and accidents involved during Wallis' term.

The Reorganization of Philadelphia General Hospital

Mariana Robinson and Corinne Silverman

ntroduction

N MARCH 12, 1952, ten weeks after the new emocratic administration had been installed to perate the city under a new Charter, six "rep-sentative" citizens of Philadelphia met in the rnate, ballroom-size reception room outside the xecutive offices of Mayor Joseph S. Clark, Jr. 'hey were waiting for the Mayor and his new ommissioner of Health to induct them as mem-ers of the new Board of Trustees of the Phil-delphia General Hospital (PGH).

After a brief wait during which some trustees et some of their colleagues for the first time, n aide ushered them around a conference table one of the inner offices. There entered Mayor lark, characteristically intense and haggard. e was accompanied by his new Health Com-issioner, who was to be an ex-officio member f the Board of Trustees.

After shaking hands all around, Clark pro-eeded to tell his appointees his concept of their sponsibilities for Philadelphia's municipal hos-ital, the fourth largest general hospital in the Jnited States. He gave each trustee a copy of e new City Charter which created the Board f Trustees as a layer between the hospital staff nd the city administration. He noted that there ere ambiguities in the Charter provisions—for xample about the relative responsibilities of the ealth Department and of the PGH trustees.

The choice that had confronted Mayor Clark implementing this section of the new Charter as whether he should appoint a weak Board of 'rustees who would become, in effect, instru-ents of his Health Commissioner, or whether e should appoint a representative group of ustees and encourage them to act independ-ntly. Clark had decided that the Charter indi-ated the latter course. He appointed six rep-esentative citizens—"a Strong Board." Half ere Republicans, but all six had participated his reform mayoralty campaign.

That afternoon around the table, Clark told the trustees that although the Charter placed the PGH Board under the Department of Health, he wanted them to be an independent body. At the same time, he went on to remind them that one of his prominent campaign promises had been to improve the quality of medical care in the municipal hospitals. He asked them to keep this objective foremost in their minds. It was their responsibility, he said, to choose an Executive Director of PGH and to see that the patients got the best possible care—with no discrimination on the basis of race, creed, or political influence. This was a reform administration, he reminded them, and in only four years time the voters would judge whether or not it had kept its promises.

(Reform had been in the air in Philadelphia for several years, following a series of scandals raw enough to shock complacent upper and upper-middle class Philadelphians into working for civic improvement along with the renascent Democratic forces. Clark had encouraged many influential and established Philadelphians, including, significantly for this story, quite a few doctors, to work for Charter reform and to contribute advice and more tangible support to his Democratic campaign. The new Charter had been adopted the previous April. Victory in the November elections had put Clark in the Mayor's office and the Democratic party in control of the City Council on January 1, 1952.)

Briskly, Clark told the trustees that he wanted all their meetings to be public and open to the press. He allowed that there might be a need for an occasional executive session, but he told them that he wanted to run his administration "in a goldfish bowl." Thanking the six for their willingness to serve, Clark returned to his private office to cope with the many problems awaiting Philadelphia's first Democratic mayor since 1884.

The trustees lingered long enough around the

table to decide that they would wait to elect a chairman until their next meeting which, they agreed, would be held at PGH. Business concluded, the six citizens chatted as they moved to the coat racks in the waiting room. They were beginning to form the relationships that they conceived members of a board of trustees should have with one another. These conceptions varied, since three of the six had never before served as trustees of anything and had had no previous experience with hospital administration.

One of the three new to a trustee's role was *Joseph Schwartz,* 50, manager of the AFL local of the Knit Goods Workers, International Ladies' Garment Workers' Union (ILGWU). In his work with the ILGWU, Schwartz—shrewd, hard-hitting, but soft-spoken—had gained a reputation as a skillful negotiator. Sometimes characterized as "a lone wolf" in Philadelphia politics, he had worked with the independent citizens group for Clark in the 1951 campaign. His appointment reflected Clark's desires (1) to have represented on the PGH Board a labor official and (2) to give recognition to Schwartz for his service in the reform movement.

A second trustee was *Ted Schlanger,* a Warner Brothers executive who had contributed to Clark's campaign. *Tanner Duckrey,* the third appointee new to a trustee's role, was a Negro and a District Superintendent of Schools. His service on the fifteen-man Charter Commission had brought him to the attention of two of Clark's closest advisers who considered him conscientious, intelligent, well-respected, but not particularly aggressive. It was because of his presumed lack of the latter quality that Duckrey was appointed a PGH trustee rather than to the post he aspired to on the new Human Relations Commission. So far as Clark and his advisers could tell at the time, the PGH Board was less likely to be involved in intense controversy.

Closer to Clark socially were the three members who *had* had previous experience as trustees and who enjoyed some familiarity with medical or hospital matters: *George Clark* and *Alfred Scattergood,* both bankers, and *Mrs. David Remer,* wife of a financial adviser, and board member or professional official of a number of social agencies in the city. Clark had wanted someone on the PGH Board who would link public health with voluntary agencies, and Mr Remer filled the bill. At the time of her ap pointment she was on the budget staff of th Philadelphia Community Chest, a position sh retained throughout her tenure as PGH truste Mrs. Remer had served previously as a membe of the Board of the City House of Detentior She was acquainted with more of the PGH tru tees than were any of her colleagues. She ha worked with Alfred Scattergood and Tanne Duckrey in various community activities; an she knew George Clark socially.

George Clark, the banker, a close, first cousi of the Mayor, had served on the Board of Chil dren's Hospital since 1939. He had urged hi cousin to appoint to the PGH Board only ex perienced people. Specifically, he had urged hin to appoint his friend Alfred Scattergood. Scat tergood was a retired banker in his seventies mentally acute but slowing down physically Respected and influential, he had been activ in many community charities and came from on of Philadelphia's old Quaker families. He ha served on the Board of Managers of the Pennsyl vania Hospital and had been President of th Board of the Friends' Hospital for nine years Unknown to Clark or his aides was the fact tha whenever Scattergood served as chairman or pres ident of a board or committee, this grave an courteous man followed the practice of delayin decision until everyone felt a genuine "sense o the meeting."

Neither Mayor Clark back in his office no any of the trustees bidding goodbye to one an other in front of the city hall imagined tha within a year they would all be embroiled in violent controversy with the medical staff o PGH, a controversy that would finally erupt ir cutting accusations, glaring headlines, and frus tration and embarrassment for almost all con cerned; a controversy that would divide the trus tees and that would raise the question of the ex tent to which the trustees were obliged either t act independently or to carry out the medica program (and the campaign promises) of th new administration.

The trustees were vaguely aware that one o Mayor Clark's campaign statements had callec for improving the quality of medical care a PGH by relating its volunteer medical staff mor closely with the five medical schools in Philadelphia. Neither they nor the Mayor foresaw that the effort to carry out this campaign promise would place the PGH trustees in the midst of a conflict between, on the one hand, the volunteer medical staff of PGH, anxious to defend its traditional autonomy, and, on the other hand, the Mayor, his Health Commissioner and the rest of the city administration.

The controlling leadership group of the PGH medical staff was to initiate all-out resistance to affiliation with the medical schools because it did not want to relinquish any of its power to the medical schools or, for that matter, to "City Hall," toward which, over a hundred years, it had built up an attitude of distrust and a tacit policy of bartering some political accommodation on "non-essentials" in return for virtual autonomy in determining medical standards and administering medical care.

Indirect parties to the controversy were the deans of the five local medical schools, who favored the Mayor's plan since it would insure clinical teaching facilities for their growing enrollments and would also, they believed, improve the quality of medical care at PGH.

The Background

IN CHOOSING THE TRUSTEES he did, Mayor Clark was following, in part, the recommendations of the framers of the new City Charter, and, in part, his own inclinations.

Those who had written the Charter had decided that a lay board was preferable to a professional one, although no definite restriction was written into the Charter. In general, it was anticipated that a Board of Trustees would help to remove the Hospital from party politics, would bring the Hospital closer to the citizens of Philadelphia insofar as the trustees were representative of them, and would tend to humanize hospital operation as a result of the trustees taking a personal interest in it.

Before the Mayor appointed his Board, he had received a list of suggested trustees from some of the medical staff members of PGH. The names on this list were those of doctors, not laymen. Clark had been discussing the question of trustees with his recently-appointed Commissioner of Health, Dr. James Dixon, and although Dixon was new to Philadelphia and could not, of course, suggest any specific names, he and Clark were in agreement that the trustees should be laymen.

Both Clark and Dixon felt that previous city administrations had let PGH run down and that there might be a clash between the Hospital personnel and the new reform administration. Dixon foresaw a possible clash between professionalism on the one hand and civic necessity on the other. Hence he preferred the buffer that lay trustees could provide.

Clark had more general reasons for preferring a lay Board of Trustees, summed up in the old saw which he liked to use: "Keep the experts on tap, not on top." He also wanted a Board which would include representatives of the kinds of citizens most likely to use a free city hospital.

Clark felt he had appointed a Board which could be said to be a cross-section of Philadelphia: he had put business on the Board in the person of George Clark; labor was represented by Schwartz; community voluntary and social welfare organizations were represented by Helen Remer; the Negroes, who comprised about sixteen percent of Philadelphia's voters, were represented by Duckrey. Business in politics was represented by Schlanger, medicine by Dr. Dixon. Alfred Scattergood could be said to represent business, the community as a whole, and moderation.

The Charter Provisions

Although the trustees as a group were starting a new institution, some of them had general ideas of the problems they might have to face in the future.

Tanner Duckrey, for example, remembered

the many discussions concerning the PGH Board of Trustees among his colleagues on the Charter Commission. The decision to create a Board of Trustees within the Department of Health had carried by a single vote. The belief that creation of such a board would provide the best form of administration reflected the thinking of many in the field of public health. A Board of Trustees was strongly recommended after a survey of the Hospital made in 1948 by the U. S. Public Health Service. It was advocated at the time the Charter was framed by people familiar with state hospitals having such boards. A minority of the Charter Commission had opposed establishing a board on the ground that the device had not proven administratively successful in public institutions.

The medical staff of Philadelphia General Hospital unsuccessfully opposed the inclusion of a Board of Trustees in the new Charter. One of the doctors on the staff, Dr. Winifred B. Stewart, attended meetings of the Charter Commission in an effort to block this provision. Up to that point, the Hospital was, at least theoretically, under the jurisdiction of the city Health Commissioner who appointed the Hospital Director. Actually, the medical staff of the Hospital, working in co-operation with the Hospital Director, had often been able to go directly to the City Council to try to obtain what it needed. Dr. Stewart and her associates on the medical staff at PGH feared that if the Charter Commission inserted a Board of Trustees between the Hospital Director and the city administration, the trustees might become the actual governing body of the Hospital.

The Commission overruled Dr. Stewart and included a Board of Trustees in the new Charter but in a somewhat ambiguous manner. By one provision, the Board of Trustees was set up within the Department of Health and made responsible for "day-to-day operations" of PGH, notwithstanding the fact that provision was also made for an Executive Director of the Hospital who was to be appointed by the trustees and to serve under them. At the same time, however, the Commissioner of Health was charged with responsibility for "formulation of overall City policy" in the medical field, including policy affecting hospitals. His Department was responsible for the PGH budget appropriation, and the Charter required the PGH trustees to account to the Health Department for all expenditures. In addition to their responsibility for "general supervision of hospitals," the trustees of PGH were, according to the Charter, responsible for "satisfactory hospital conditions . . . proper care of patients, proper staffing of hospitals" and for determining policy in regard to them.

Before the trustees had convened at City Hall for their first meeting, Clark, his Managing Director (Robert K. Sawyer), and Health Commissioner Dixon had discussed the question of whether some agreement should be reached between the city administration and the trustees as to the specific functions and responsibilities of each. Such an agreement was not attempted. The three men concluded that the trustees should have a free hand, since that appeared to be the intent of the Charter. In Clark's letter of appointment to the trustees he said: "Although the Charter placed the Board under the Department of Health . . . the Board exercises its powers and performs its duties as an independent agency."

The Board Learns About PGH

All the PGH trustees had to acquaint themselves with the Philadelphia General Hospital.

Many hospitals are, to some degree, teaching hospitals, with double tasks of providing (1) medical care for patients and (2) facilities for clinical teaching of medical school students. Some hospitals follow a form of the "closed staff" principle where, for example, the entire medical staff is composed of members of the faculty of a medical school or their appointees. Generally, in this situation, the dean of the medical school appoints the chiefs of the hospital's services and these chiefs select their subordinates. (A "service" is a subdivision within a medical field—as for example a unit of forty beds in General Medicine, or a number of beds in Surgery.) In other hospitals, a medical school might assume responsibility only for certain services in the hospital, while the hospital staff itself and not the medical school would remain responsible for patient care and teaching outside these services.

Philadelphia General, in contrast, had always worked on an "open staff" principle. The members of its medical staff did not have to be simultaneously on the faculty of a medical school, and there had never been any formal connection between the Hospital and the schools. In actual practice, most—though not all—of the members of the PGH medical staff also held medical school appointments. In some cases a faculty member of one of Philadelphia's five medical schools received an appointment to the PGH staff; in other cases the medical schools, in order to gain access for their students to the Hospital patients, took onto their faculties staff members of PGH.

In the area of medical care, PGH, like most other hospitals, had a very few salaried physicians and relied upon a large voluntary medical staff of around 500 physicians and surgeons who received for their services the prestige of the appointment, opportunities for teaching and research, and altruistic satisfaction. There were about 180 interns and residents who, although responsible for daily patient care in the Hospital, were there primarily for training.

Before the appointment of the trustees, the ultimate responsibility for patient care and for teaching and training at PGH rested with the members of the voluntary staff, and the influence of the medical schools, although substantial, was indirect. The Department of Health supposedly exercised a check against irresponsibility directly and through the Hospital Director, which it appointed. But in the eyes of many on the PGH medical staff, city administrations through the years had failed to meet their responsibilities. Staff members frequently recollected that they or their predecessors had had to fight for the Hospital's welfare against what they considered to be the neglect, indifference, or active interference of the "city politicians." As a result, the medical staff of Philadelphia General Hospital had developed a tradition of resentment toward City Hall along with a strong spirit of devotion to the Hospital.

One of the first things the trustees found out about PGH was that they had been appointed to govern an organization which in a sense had long had no real boss outside itself. Medical staff members and members of other staffs (nurses, technicians, and clerical personnel, for example) were responsible to the Executive Director of the Hospital in administrative matters and to the Medical Board, at least in the first instance, in medical matters. Each medical staff member at PGH was appointed to one of its departments as a chief or assistant chief or as a consultant. The governing body of this medical staff was the PGH Medical Board, which consisted of all chiefs of departments and divisions. Membership came automatically to full chiefs and numbered around 108. The working body of the Medical Board was its Executive Committee consisting of its elected officers, representatives of each department, the Executive Director of the Hospital, and the Commissioner of Health.

The PGH Medical Board was governed by its own bylaws, approved under the old system by the Director of Public Health and under the new City Charter by the Board of Trustees. Standing committees were appointed annually by the president of the Medical Board. Nominations for appointments to the staff and for internships and residencies originated within the staff departments and were sent to the Executive Committee. Under the new Charter, the appointments themselves were to be made by the Board of Trustees. Formerly, the Medical Board had had virtually a free hand in making staff appointments.

The Mayor's Program

In his campaign platform, Clark had favored as one point in a ten-point program for better public health services:

> closer cooperation between the Department of Health and the five medical schools to provide better medical services for the city and its hospitals, and better training opportunities for the students of the medical schools.

Clark, as a candidate, had come to this view after discussions with a number of local doctors. He felt he had received the best advice from a group of medically eminent and socially respectable Philadelphia medical men, and he followed their advice with no hesitation. Clark was not aware at the time that his advisers were doctors whose motives on this matter were viewed with suspicion by some members of the medical staff at PGH. These PGH staff members had felt for a long time before Clark appeared on the scene that the local medical schools wanted to "take over" the Hospital; they saw Clark's campaign plank as one step in that direction.

Between the time of Clark's election in November, 1951 and the appointment of his trustees in March, 1952, the Mayor's campaign plank had been given a little more substance by the new Commissioner of Health.

Clark had appointed Dr. James B. Dixon as Commissioner on the advice of a committee composed, for the most part, of the same group which had advised him on his campaign public health policy. These doctors had met with Clark at his home several times and had come up with three recommendations, one of them Dr. Dixon. Dixon was the first choice of Clark and of new Managing Director Sawyer partly because his experience included service in a reform administration in Denver. Majority opinion of Clark's five-man committee was that there was no qualified man in Philadelphia and that an outsider with no political connections in the city was preferable anyway.

While no specific qualifications other than a medical degree were stipulated by the Charter, Clark's advisory committee wanted a man experienced in both public health and hospital administration. Dr. Dixon held a degree in hospital administration from Columbia University, was a Diplomate of the American Board of Preventive Medicine and Public Health, and had had experience in both fields. He was well disposed toward medical school affiliation with public hospitals, having worked out such an arrangement at Denver.

Dixon was informed before his appointment of the Mayor's commitment to closer co-operation between PGH and the medical schools. It became his responsibility to develop policies and programs for PGH. What neither he nor the Mayor knew, and what the PGH trustees did not learn until after their appointment, was that PGH had gone through a bitter battle five years earlier on the same issue of medical school affiliation, and that the medical staff of the Hospital was still nursing the wounds of that earlier struggle.

The Old Battle Scars at PGH

In 1945 PGH had been in one of the periodi crises that had marked relationships between th city administration and the Hospital since 173 The Department of Health was weak and exe cised little control over the Hospital. The PG medical staff felt funds were seriously inad quate and that political appointments to nor professional posts were impeding effective ope ation.

Dr. Russell S. Boles, who had been contir uously on the staff for 33 years, was presiden of the PGH Medical Board in 1945. After severa fruitless efforts by the Medical Board to get th city administration to correct deficiencies a PGH, Boles and three other members of th Medical Board had sent an open letter of protes to Mayor Bernard Samuel. The staff, in Boles opinion, was doing a magnificent job, but wa hampered by conditions it was powerless t change.

It was his concern over these conditions tha prompted Boles in 1946 to suggest formal affil iation with the medical schools of the city. Hi motive was to "rescue the patients from Cit Hall." There was the feeling in some quarters for example, that some patients were pressed t pay their bills, while others were not. It de pended, it was believed, on whether the patien knew the right ward leader. Or, it was com plained, some patients were allowed to stay sev eral days, others only for a day or so. Again th length of stay hinged, some thought, on whethe the proper telephone call had been made fron the proper person in ward politics. Dr. Bole was convinced after a personal study of larg public hospitals with medical school affiliation that PGH would be improved by the direct par ticipation of medical schools in the medical car program. Hospital standards would be pegge to medical school standards. The schools, more over, would provide a stabilizing element in th Hospital and would have more weight with th city government than the staff in obtaining wha was needed by the Hospital. During 1946, there fore, Boles initiated several informal discussion between the deans of the medical schools an the staff of the Hospital.

Boles did not develop his ideas in detail, but he had in mind the type of affiliation practiced in other city hospitals. Bellevue, in New York City, for example, has four divisions. One division is staffed by Cornell Medical School, which is responsible for appointments, teaching, and patient care in its portion of the hospital. Another division is staffed similarly by Columbia School of Physicians and Surgeons; the third by New York University Medical School; and the fourth by New York University Graduate School of Medicine. Boles conceived of dividing PGH's medical services (in the sense of units of beds) among the five Philadelphia medical schools. The idea was tagged "vertical services."

Dr. Pascal F. Lucchesi, whom Mayor Samuel prevailed on to become Chief of the Bureau of Hospitals and Superintendent of PGH—a civil service post—in March, 1946, agreed that the Hospital was then in need of improvements. However, neither he nor many on the medical staff believed that vertical services would be in the best interests of the Hospital. They argued that the Hospital's quality of medical care would suffer through the disruption of the harmony and unity of the institution. Affiliation with five medical schools, they argued, would introduce medical politics and school rivalries into a Hospital that had long been united by an intense *esprit de corps*. Competition would replace co-operation in care of patients, in teaching, and in research. Patients might no longer be shared for teaching purposes, and research programs that utilized the Hospital's entire resources might be restricted to those services run by a single school.

Fearing the possibility of the establishment of a system of vertical services in the Hospital, some members of the medical staff organized to take control of the Medical Board. At the annual election of officers in the spring of 1947 (at which time Dr. Boles himself was not a candidate for re-election) this group elected an "opposition" slate of candidates that won by 63 to 9 over the candidates presented by the regular nominating committee. The winning faction in 1947 kept control of the Medical Board and was "in power" when the new trustees took over in 1952. Dr. Winifred B. Stewart was a prominent spokesman for this dominant, anti-vertical services group.

As a result of the 1947 Medical Board election, the Boles proposal for closer affiliation with the medical schools died on the vine. The merits of the case for and against vertical services were obscured by strong personal factors. The Medical Board, the outvoted proponents sometimes charged, would have lost some of its autonomy and some of its power if the medical schools had been allowed to participate directly in Hospital affairs, particularly in the selection of the staff. Some proponents also hinted broadly that one or two of the opponents (but none of those named in this chapter) opposed medical school control because their professional status in the eyes of the medical schools was marginal.

The opponents, for their part, did not believe in the good faith of proponents of vertical services. The plan, they said, was essentially an effort by the Medical School of the University of Pennsylvania to get control of the Hospital. The Penn Medical School, located next door to PGH, was the oldest and second largest in the city and already had more teaching services at PGH than did any of the four other schools. (That is, more members of the faculty had individual appointments at PGH and vice versa.) Dr. Boles was a member of the Penn faculty, and some of his opponents circulated the rumor that he had been offered a promotion in return for putting through the vertical services plan at PGH. The other four schools were held to be merely protecting their own interest by participating with Penn in discussions of the plan. This rumor was emphatically denied by Boles and by an officer of the University of Pennsylvania's Medical School.

Boles' opposition, having gained control of the Medical Board, changed the rules. The president's (Boles') term of office, formerly unlimited, was limited to three years; the Executive Committee, instead of being appointed by the Medical Board's president, was elected by departments in the Hospital; and the method of appointment of chiefs and assistant chiefs was revised with nominations originating in departments instead of the Executive Committee. These changes were viewed by the group that effected them as ensuring more democratic government of the medical staff. By those on the medical staff who were out of power, they were seen as a means of perpetuating control by the winning faction.

Two important convictions were established by the 1947 dispute in the minds of the doctors in the winning faction: (1) that Penn Medical School was pulling strings to get control of PGH for its own ends; and (2) that since control ought to remain undiminished where it was—in the Medical Board—any effort to alter fundamentally the status quo should be vigorously opposed. These attitudes were deep-seated by the time Clark's campaign began and by the time the new trustees assumed office in 1952. Many who in 1947 had strongly opposed closer affiliation with the medical schools were still on the PGH medical staff in 1952-53. For them the Mayor's new plan was Round Two of the same old battle.

Clark Decides to Appoint A New Hospital Director

Dr. Pascal F. Lucchesi, who had been appointed Executive Director of PGH by Mayor Bernard Samuel in 1946 following the Medical Board's public letter of protest, was something of a hero in South Philadelphia—a local boy who had built a solid career in hospital administration and public health.

Adept at public relations, Dr. Lucchesi had many friends among the professionals in both parties and among the newspaper men, who always found him eager to keep them abreast of medical developments in the city hospitals.

Mayor Samuel had to persuade Lucchesi to accept the PGH post. The doctor attached several conditions to his acceptance; he insisted that there must be no political interference by city government, no interference from the Director of Health, and full support of his policies for the Hospital from Samuel. Samuel agreed to these stipulations and kept his word.

In the absence of a strong City Department of Health, Lucchesi worked independently. He found the Hospital in as bad shape organizationally as he had expected; the only department which had any strength was Nursing. Morale was "terrible." For a time, every problem came over his desk and all decisions were made by him, but slowly responsibility was delegated to department heads.

In 1947 he encouraged the changes made in the rules of the Medical Board. He opposed Dr. Boles on vertical services because he believed that the Hospital would suffer from medical school politics if the plan was adopted. On the other hand, he was convinced that medical school teaching services were good for the Hospital, providing high quality of patient care. He therefore encouraged these services, sometimes reallocating them among the schools, sometimes organizing new ones. But instead of formal relationships with the medical schools, Lucchesi parceled out the services by personal agreements with the deans.

Lucchesi resigned his position in September 1951, to be effective January 8, 1952 (just after Clark's administration took office). He later became Executive Vice-President and Medical Director of the Albert Einstein Center in Philadelphia at an increase in salary.

Clark first asked Lucchesi to continue at PGH but later changed his mind. While Clark respected his record at PGH, Lucchesi had been a Samuel appointee, and Clark was publicly committed to cleaning up the conditions that prevailed under the outgoing administration. Clark had a vague impression that PGH was a "mess." Lucchesi, Clark told his advisers, had done well in a bad situation, but the Hospital was in need of a thorough overhaul which could best be accomplished by a new director. And Lucchesi was not an "expert" in the narrow sense. He had years of experience in hospital administration but no degree in that subject.

Dixon's Appointment at Penn

Another piece of background that the new trustees were not aware of as they began their administration of PGH was that the *manner* of Clark's appointment of Dr. Dixon as Health Commissioner had reopened many latent suspicions at the Hospital. Dixon had been quite content as Health Commissioner of Denver, and the salary that Clark could offer in Philadelphia was only $12,000. It is not uncommon in the municipal public health field to make arrangements to supplement civil service salaries to make city posts attractive to able medical men. These additional arrangements usually take the form of a part-time appointment, with nominal duties, to the faculty of a nearby medical school. Clark was eager to get a highly qualified man for the health commissionership, and it was arranged that the University of Pennsylvania Medical School would offer Dixon an appointment at an annual salary of $3,000. Dixon accepted the city post and the Penn appointment, and shortly after he assumed his duties Clark also obtained from the City Council an increase in Dixon's city salary from $12,000 to $15,000. Dixon's two salaries thus amounted to $18,000.

The Penn appointment for Dixon stirred suspicion in some Philadelphia medical circles. To the medical staff of PGH the appointment seemed a subsidy offered by Penn to obtain influence in the Health Department. The leaders of the PGH Medical Board who felt that Clark and the University of Pennsylvania doctors were out to take over PGH identified Dr. I. S. Ravdin of the Penn Medical School as the *eminence grise* behind Clark's public health program. Ravdin, a chief at Penn and an outstanding surgeon who was later to gain national attention by operating on President Eisenhower, had been one of the medical men to whom Clark had turned for advice in drawing up his campaign statement. Although he was not dean of the Penn Medical School and although he was never involved in this case in any official capacity, Ravdin was influential both at Penn and in Philadelphia medical circles because of his professional reputation, and he was an open and ardent supporter of medical school affiliation with PGH.

The deans of the medical schools, after the Mayor's election, had notified him of their interest and willingness to co-operate with the new administration in public health. They were not, however, represented on the committee for recommendation of a Commissioner of Health, nor were they consulted. This circumstance did nothing to allay suspicion of Penn's alleged effort to dominate PGH for its own teaching advantage.

Dixon's Preliminary Work

When Dixon took office as Commissioner of Health in January, 1952, he faced the task of reorganizing the Department of Health and extending its program as well as the job of overseeing, at the high policy level indicated by the new Charter, the operations of PGH, the cost of which took up about 85 percent of the Health Department's budget. Lucchesi had left PGH, and a new Executive Director had to be appointed. It would be three months before the new trustees would be appointed. There was no specific set of plans for carrying Clark's campaign idea into reality. At this point in January, the initiative on the PGH front passed directly to Dixon.

Dixon's appraisal of the Hospital led him to believe that it was in an unstable condition, approaching a crisis in medical care. As he saw it, the voluntary medical staff was almost disorganized. The resident and intern staffs—the younger men—rather than the voluntary medical staff, were taking the responsibility for patient care. Dixon also believed that some medical staff members at the Hospital were not giving enough time to attending patients.

Dixon believed that from an administrative standpoint he was faced with three alternatives: (1) abandon the idea of free medical care by the city; (2) put in a salaried staff; (3) prevail upon the medical schools to participate more directly and responsibly in the medical care program. Clark's campaign statement had selected the third alternative, and Dixon was in full accord.

If PGH could be made a complete teaching hospital, Dixon felt, its standards of medical care and teaching would be improved and stabilized by medical school standards. In Dixon's opinion—which was shared by a sizable number of Philadelphia medical men—the Hospital's need of help from the medical schools was as great as, or greater than the schools' need of the Hospital's teaching facilities. Dixon proceeded in the belief that good teaching and good patient care go together. The objective of medical teaching is to train doctors in the art of giving good patient care. Therefore, the better the training, the better the care the patient receives. Moreover, a teaching physician must of necessity give his best to both students and patients, and he must also be at the Hospital regularly.

Having determined upon a course of action,

Dixon started in February (a month before the trustees were appointed) to explore its feasibility. The question was whether the need for ward beds for teaching purposes was great enough among the five medical schools so that they would be willing to cover the needs of the Hospital in daily patient care. Dixon saw this as a bargaining situation, trading teaching facilities for a stable and improved medical care program. Dixon felt he was handicapped in his bargaining by the fact that the city had no funds for a substantially increased ancillary staff to make his proposition more attractive to the medical schools. Moreover, each school had its own hospital as its first responsibility.

Dixon initiated several meetings with the deans of the schools to explore the situation. The deans responded favorably; they felt that the schools could staff the Hospital adequately if it became a complete teaching hospital.

At this early stage of consultation, Dixon had no precise ideas about the way in which affiliation might be accomplished. He expected to proceed with caution. He advised the deans that affiliation might take a unique form at PGH and that two or three years might be needed to bring it about.

At one meeting arranged by Dixon early in 1952, a committee of the deans met with leaders of the Medical Board of PGH to talk over the question of affiliation. The meeting reached a general agreement, or so Dixon thought at the time. Both Dr. Winifred Stewart, leader of the 1947 fight against vertical services, and Dr. David Kramer, then president of the PGH Medical Board, were present at the conference. They raised what seemed to Dixon to be normal and proper reservations for people in their position. Although he gathered it would be difficult to win their enthusiasm for any specific form of affiliation, there seemed to Dixon to be agreement on the principle that affiliation could improve PGH care.

Had Dixon known of the intense opposition put up in 1947 against the vertical services form of medical school affiliation by that section of the PGH Medical Board led by Dr. Stewart and her associates, he might have interpreted the discussion at the conference more pessimistically. As it was, he felt that long and careful negotiation could work out a form of medical school affiliation that PGH medical staff members would accept. They might accept with some displeasure, but Dixon foresaw nothing that could completely obstruct affiliation. The deans favored it. It was, after all, the Mayor's policy. It was Dixon's policy. The Mayor appointed the PGH trustees, Dixon being one of them ex officio. Dixon and the trustees would appoint the new PGH Director. The PGH Medical Board had a traditional independence, but even if Dixon had known the intensity of this feeling of autonomy, and of the suspicion of City Hall built up in PGH during a hundred years, he could have assured himself that this feeling had no place now that there was in City Hall a reform administration dedicated to improving the quality of patient care. A Board of respectable, and to some extent representative lay citizens, all of whom had supported the Mayor's campaign, would now oversee the Hospital and would presumably support affiliation to improve medical care.

This, then, was the situation that existed that day in March 1952, when Mayor Clark first received his new trustees in City Hall.

The Trustees Select a Director

AT THEIR FIRST MEETING in Mayor Clark's outer office, the trustees had decided to hold their next meeting at the Hospital the following week. The intervening period was marked by phone calls and conversations between City Hall and various trustees on the question of who would serve as Chairman of the Board. Efforts were made to persuade George Clark, the Mayor's banker cousin, to take the chairmanship, but he declined. He favored Scattergood, the elderly and respected Quaker who was a banker as well as a trustee and board member of several community organizations and philanthropies, including a hospital. Scattergood did not want to take the post but eventually was persuaded. He was elected at the trustees' next meeting.

Seeking to familiarize themselves with their new responsibility—and with one another—the trustees met once a week at first and soon twice a week in a conference room at the Hospital. As Mayor Clark had requested, their meetings were open to the press, and reporters often sat in. Irritating to newspaperman Pierre Fraley, science editor of the *Philadelphia Bulletin,* was the trustees' practice of following the public meeting with a private meeting at which, so Fraley thought, the "important" matters were taken up. Fraley recognized that the trustees were probably meeting in private in the early stages in order to learn something about each other. But the newspaperman, who had already heard much about the affiliation proposals and the reactions to them by the Hospital's medical staff, felt that these private meetings opened the trustees from the beginning to accusations of "plot hatching." Dr. Stewart and her associates on the medical staff at PGH, already suspicious of the Mayor as a "captive of Penn," were trying to size up the trustees and to find out which of the Mayor's appointees were "in Penn's corner." The private meetings by the trustees were soon discontinued, however, and the press attended regularly many of the Board meetings.

The Medical Board of the Hospital pressed its case early with the trustees. One of the trustees recalled, "All in good faith, we wanted to work co-operatively together. But we hardly had our uniforms issued when we were invited to a dinner of the Medical Staff. I no sooner got there than I realized we were in a hornet's nest. The doctors clustered around us and started to ask us 'Are you for vertical services or not?' We were in no position to have any opinion about it at all."

Fraley went to the second official meeting of the trustees—the first meeting held at PGH. He probably knew more about the issue of vertical services than any of the trustees did at this time, and he too set out to determine just where they stood.

Posing one of the extreme alternatives to trade unionist Schwartz, he asked whether the medical schools were going to take over PGH. "Over my dead body!" replied Schwartz.

Scattergood responded to Fraley's question in a restrained manner, saying that the trustees were going to look into everything very carefully and study the whole problem thoroughly. He answered Dr. Stewart in the same way when he was interviewed by her in these first few weeks. His attitude was neutral, and he took the position that the problem required study.

The trustees spent most of their time in the first four months getting acquainted with the range of problems involved in the supervision of the Hospital and had no formal Board discussion of the question of affiliation until July. They gave top priority to the selection of an Executive Director for the Hospital.

The Deans and the Doctors Confer

Meanwhile, proceeding under Dixon's impetus, the Medical Board of PGH and the Committee of Deans of Medical Schools were holding a series of conferences, ostensibly seeking some area of agreement. In reality neither side appeared willing to compromise.

At the first meeting in March the deans expressed the belief that the services at PGH could be improved if the deans had the privilege of deciding which of their faculty members should become chiefs. They also pointed out that if they had this authority over their staff members, they could see to it that rounds were made more conscientiously than some members of the staff appeared to be making them. The Medical Board members replied that patient care at the Hospital was as good or better than that given in any of the schools' hospitals, but that better care could be given if more money were available. They admitted that a few chiefs had performed their duties somewhat casually, but counter-argued that these same physicians were equally remiss in the schools' hospitals, and that if the deans could not control these men there, how could they expect to improve the situation at PGH? The meeting ended inconclusively.

The Medical Board called a special meeting of the PGH medical staff for April 17. The Medical Board itself met on April 7 and passed a resolution stating that it was the consensus of the medical staff that it should maintain its independent stand, with willingness to co-operate with the deans in furnishing teaching facilities for the students, interns and residents. At the April 17 meeting of the medical staff there was much discussion but no vote, the great majority speaking against vertical services, according to Dr. Stewart.

A second meeting of the Medical Board committee and the deans took place on May 20. At this meeting the committee of the Medical Board stated that it was willing to arrange for security (tenure) of services and to set up what services the schools might need. But the committee insisted that the Medical Board would retain the power of appointment within the framework of the Hospital and would not consider giving the power of appointment to the deans. The deans refused this alternative to the vertical services idea. In the face of this stalemate a small subcommittee consisting of two deans (Dr. John M. Mitchell of Penn and Dr. George A. Bennett of Jefferson) and two Medical Board members (Dr. Stewart and Dr. Kramer) was appointed to try to reach agreement and report back to the main committee.

These further discussions accomplished nothing except to make plain a wide difference of opinion. Dr. Stewart believed that the deans were holding out for a five-way division of the Hospital with power to appoint the chiefs of services. This degree of control the Medical Board was determined not to relinquish to the schools. The deans, on the other hand, believed that the Medical Board was equally unyielding; that, in fact, it would settle for nothing except the status quo in the Hospital.

By summer each side had come to feel that further negotiations were futile, and each looked elsewhere for support for its view. The deans had Dixon and City Hall on their side. The Medical Board continued its efforts to win adherents among the trustees.

Stalemate

In July, 1952, officers and members of the Medical Board met with the trustees. Presei from the Hospital again were Drs. Kramer an Stewart with three other physicians. At th meeting Kramer and Stewart repeated their ol jections to the vertical plan system. Kramer sai that by dividing the Hospital into five section each controlled by a medical school, authorit would pass from the Medical Board to the dean This, Kramer said, would tend to destroy th unity of the Hospital.

Dr. Stewart argued that if PGH were divide up, "the medical director would probably hav only authority over the janitors as all the a thority would be in the hands of the medic school."

Trustee George Clark replied to this by sayin that under the City Charter all authority reste in the Board of Trustees.

The Trustees Select an Executive Director

The trustees had been working on the sele tion of an Executive Director for the Hospita since their second meeting in March. At firs there was some discussion about whether th Director should be a doctor. George Clark firs pressed for a lay administrator, saying that fe doctors were good administrators. They get to involved with individual patient problems, h argued, and are not inclined to be cost consciou However, Clark came around to what becam the unanimous view of the Board that the PGH situation required an Executive Director wh was a doctor. By then the Board had caught th flavor of the medical staff's opposition, and th trustees felt that since the doctors were bound t resent lay trustees telling them how to run th hospital, there was no need to build up un necessary antagonism by appointing a lay d rector.

In selecting an Executive Director the truste leaned heavily on the judgment of Health Com missioner Dixon. On request, Dixon gave h opinion that under the new city organization th PGH Executive Director would be the executiv of the trustees for managing the Hospital an for formulating and carrying out the progra approved by the Board of Trustees.

Dixon and a number of specialists in the fiel

of hospital administration drew up a list of possible candidates. Also, the position was advertised on the civil service lists. The trustees were flooded with candidates.

Dixon did most of the screening, being guided by the desire of the Board and by his own preference for a person with a strong administrative background. He narrowed the list down to less than a dozen, and these were carefully considered by the Board. The most promising men were interviewed by the Board. The name of Dr. August H. Groeschel (pronounced Grow-shell), with whom Dixon was acquainted, was on a list of those who "have been suggested or have expressed an interest in the post," and in April Scattergood and Dixon went to New York to interview him.

Scattergood and Dixon talked with Groeschel at his home and explained the plans that had been developed. Dixon made it clear that the mission was to bring about some kind of formal affiliation with the medical schools. He was pleased with Groeschel's reaction. Groeschel was enthusiastic about the idea and was a firm supporter of the principle of medical school affiliation.

Groeschel had studied hospital administration at Columbia where the affiliation principle had been strongly advocated. He had held positions at University Hospital in Philadelphia (affiliated with the University of Pennsylvania) and with New York Hospital (affiliated with Cornell Medical School) and felt this system worked successfully. Dixon, who was looking for a leader to give the trustees direction and support on the affiliation question, felt "we had in Groeschel a man with a rare sense of program."

In June, Groeschel went to Philadelphia to be interviewed by the rest of the trustees. They asked him about his stand on the principle of medical school affiliation, and he again expressed his enthusiasm for the idea. On his side, Groeschel made every effort to assure himself that the trustees also favored affiliation for PGH. He could find no trustee opposition to vertical services.

During the interview, Groeschel was intensively questioned about his attitudes on staff appointments for minority group members. Schwartz and Duckrey especially were concerned with keeping the Hospital and its medical staff free from racial or religious discrimination in appointments. They asked Groeschel if he had ever worked at a hospital with Negroes or Jews on the staff; whether the New York Hospital had limitations on Negroes or Jews on its staff; whether Groeschel, a Catholic, had a preference for Catholic doctors in making appointments.

After the interview the Board appeared satisfied that Groeschel was its man. Indeed, George Clark, for one, was so enthusiastic that he told Dixon, "If you land Groeschel, I'll buy you a box of cigars because it will be the most wonderful thing that ever happened to the Hospital!"

Groeschel was also interviewed by City Managing Director Sawyer and by Dr. John P. Hubbard, the Vice President of the Board of Health. (Hubbard, a member of the Penn Medical School faculty, had been on the committee to advise Mayor Clark about appointing a Commissioner of Health.) With these men, as with Dixon, Groeschel's advocacy of medical school affiliation weighed in favor of his appointment.

At the same July 8 meeting at which the Board met formally with Drs. Stewart and Kramer to discuss vertical services, the trustees ratified Groeschel's appointment as Executive Director of PGH. Because of his commitment at New York Hospital, Groeschel was unable to take up his duties until November 1, but he did attend several meetings of the Board of Trustees in the meantime.

Groeschel Gets 'The Go-Ahead'

In August, three months before he moved to Philadelphia, Groeschel took his family on a brief seashore vacation in Ocean City, a south Jersey resort town frequented by Philadelphians. One day he left his family sitting on the sands and went for a swim. When he returned, he found Mrs. Groeschel greatly disturbed.

"Do you see those people sitting right over there?" she asked, pointing to a group sitting several yards away. "They have been talking about you! They all seem to be doctors from Philadelphia. That one on the right just said, 'I give him eight weeks and then he'll be out!' Then the one right next to him said, 'Oh no, he won't last eight weeks. He'll be out before that!' "

The incident unnerved Mrs. Groeschel considerably. She had not been enthusiastic about pulling up their New York roots and disrupting the children's education. (The Groeschels had five children, ranging in age from three to seventeen.) When she saw that not only was the family moving to a relatively unfamiliar city but also to a post with unfriendly surroundings, her reservations deepened. Since Groeschel was eager to take on the new job, Mrs. Groeschel agreed to go ahead but she did so with a reluctance that was never ameliorated as long as the family remained in Philadelphia.

Groeschel was looking forward to the PGH directorship as his first opportunity to be top man in a civilian hospital. It would be his first time to work directly under lay trustees.[1] It was also his first experience working for a city department of health. He did not believe that heading a public institution would be substantially different from directing a private hospital.

Between the time of Groeschel's appointment and his arrival in November, the Philadelphia situation had changed, in some respects crucially.

On June 26, the Board of Health had presented recommendations on affiliation to the trustees of the Hospital. The Board of Health, a seven-man body, had been established by the Charter to serve in an advisory capacity to the Department of Health, and had been requested by the Department to advise on policy making and broad program planning for the Department. Dixon had worked carefully with Mayor Clark in picking Health Board members. George Clark and Mrs. Remer served on both boards, as, of course, did Dr. Dixon. The letter from the Board of Health, read to the trustees at their September meeting, recommended

> . . . that the Trustees should establish relationship with the medical schools of the community to assure the maintenance of high professional standards and providing the best available medical care to the hospital patients.
>
> . . . .
>
> The Board of Health is of the opinion that satisfactory standards cannot be maintained unless some element of responsibility be placed upon medical schools for medical staff regardless of what mechanism is designed. However, to do this, the ultimate responsibility for staffing should not and, in fact, cannot pass from the Board of Trustees of Philadelphia General Hospital.

Dr. Dixon Leaves

Of more moment to Groeschel was the departure of Health Commissioner Dixon. Dixon had not served in the armed forces during the war, and in Denver his job had been given an essential classification. He was not afforded this exemption in Philadelphia, however, and became subject to the draft. He was then 35 years old. In October, 1952, one month before Groeschel was due to arrive, Dixon was drafted for two years service with the U. S. Public Health Service in Washington.[2] He was put on leave from the Department of Health, and Dr. Norman R. Ingraham, a deputy commissioner, was made Acting Commissioner.

Acting Commissioner Ingraham was a dermatologist who had been a career official in the

[1] Groeschel, then 44 years old, was a native of Jersey City where his father had been a restaurant owner. He had received his B.A. from Holy Cross and graduated from the Columbia Medical School. After interning in New York City he started private practice in 1934 in Sussex, N. J.

In 1941 he went into the Army as a Squadron Surgeon and from 1942 until he was released from service in 1945, he served in the Officers' Candidate School of the Medical Administration Corps. He moved up rapidly. By 1943 he was an Assistant Commandant, responsible only to the Commanding General of the post and to the Surgeon General's office in Washington. In May 1945 he was made commanding officer of the hospital ship *Larkspur,* where he remained until his discharge in October.

Back in civilian life, he attended the Columbia School of Public Health, wanting to continue his career in medical administration. Completing his course at Columbia in June 1946, he went to the University of Pennsylvania Hospital as Administrative Assistant. After ten months at Penn he became Assistant Medical Director of the Hospital Insurance Plan of Greater New York, and in November 1948 he became Assistant Director of New York Hospital.

[2] Some Philadelphia Democrats stoutly maintained that the drafting of Dixon was the result of complaints to Washington made by irritated Philadelphia organization Republicans.

Department of Health for many years. He held appointments on the faculties of both the School of Medicine and the Graduate School of Medicine at Penn. He was also on the Medical Board of PGH where he had interned. He had been a member of the PGH medical staff since 1933.

Ingraham succeeded also to Dixon's position on the PGH Board of Trustees. He was quite friendly with the PGH staff members and remained so throughout the controversy. He saw himself as a moderator rather than an aggressive innovator like Dixon. He said of himself that his policy was to try always "to be everybody's friend," and that he "never made enemies until it was absolutely necessary to make a break."

Groeschel arrived at PGH deprived of the backing of Dixon who had been responsible for developing and promoting the plan for medical school affiliation. Ingraham was inclined to leave the initiative in this matter to Groeschel and the trustees. He took virtually a neutral position on the affiliation question and avoided becoming directly involved in the controversy.

With Dixon absent, Groeschel relied heavily on the prospect of trustee support. He worked closely with the Board in all matters concerning the Hospital. He also consulted Mayor Clark directly on several occasions, an act Ingraham construed as going over *his* head and ignoring normal administrative channels, since PGH was in the Department of Health.

Low Morale at PGH

The hospital that Groeschel took over in November was, as he saw it, in a bad way. Some of the problems flowed from the disruption in top leadership. Dr. Alfred C. LaBoccetta, Director of the Philadelphia Hospital for Contagious Diseases, had been asked by Dixon to serve as Acting Director after Lucchesi left in January. LaBoccetta had had to divide his time between the two hospitals. The resignation of two additional top men on the Hospital's administrative staff further handicapped PGH operations.

There were also problems of personnel and procurement. These were affecting all city agencies, but they temporarily crippled the Hospital. The two new city departments, Procurement and Personnel, had been set up by the Charter, and it took them some time to get procedures operating smoothly. All city supplies—including drugs—had to be obtained through Procurement, and all employees had to be processed by the Personnel Department. The latter requirement involved determining job classification, examinations, new pay levels, and the like. Both the procurement and personnel procedures took time and caused some fumbling and confusion. PGH employees were worried and insecure in their jobs; requisitioning of supplies for the Hospital nearly broke down. The situation in the Hospital approached chaos, and there was a bad slump in morale. In addition, some members of the medical staff were worried about the affiliation proposal, feeling that it implied criticism of their ability and loyalty and reflected unfavorably on their work in the Hospital. On this matter, Dr. LaBoccetta had played a scrupulously neutral role, viewing his temporary job as a holding operation.

It was during this chaotic interim period that Dr. Erna L. Boroush, a second-year resident who became Assistant Medical Director in July, assumed increasing responsibility for the running of the Hospital. She and one other of the paid staff under LaBoccetta were carrying much of the administrative load when Groeschel arrived. She was considered able, conscientious, deeply concerned for the welfare of the Hospital, and somewhat high-strung.

When Groeschel arrived at PGH the staff looked to the new Director to rescue the Hospital from its difficulties and to restore order and security. But these feelings were mixed with resentment and sadness over the loss of Lucchesi. There was resentment against the new city administration and the new Charter, which were seen as causes of most of the current problems and uncertainties. And Groeschel, being a new appointment, was, in the eyes of the staff, partly identified with—or viewed as a product of—the new state of things.

As he took office on November 1, Groeschel had one basic objective: to make the Hospital outstanding in every department—patient care, research, education, medical staff, administration, and personnel. He had identified three major means of achieving this goal. One was to improve immediately the administrative structure of the Hospital. Second, he would seek to improve services and personnel, and to eliminate the special privileges and perquisites (obtainable through political influence) that had, he had been told, long been common at PGH. Third, he would press for affiliation with the medical schools which he believed would improve all of the Hospital's medical programs.

Shortly after Groeschel arrived he had a long conference with Dr. Stewart on vertical services. The conversation was taken down verbatim by Groeschel's secretary with Dr. Stewart's consent. During this interview Dr. Stewart recounted the episode of the 1946-47 defeat of vertical services and summarized her reasons for opposing medical school affiliation. Groeschel did not state his own position at this interview.

Soon after the Groeschel-Stewart conference, several staff members including Dr. Stewart came to see Groeschel about vertical services. They wanted to know where he stood. He told them that he favored the proposal and intended to support it.

Groeschel believed from the start that the opposition faction in the Medical Board would fight him by every available means and would defeat medical school affiliation if it could no matter what the Mayor wanted or what Groeschel's own position was. He felt that the Stewart faction was "laying for him," and he made no attempt to win this faction over or to conciliate it. He determined not to discuss his plans frankly with anyone until he had had a chance to identify the real friends and enemies of the affiliation plan. Groeschel did not seek assistance in identifying enemies and allies from Acting Commissioner Ingraham who knew PGH and its history intimately. He construed Ingraham's own outward cautious neutrality as masking a lack of enthusiasm for affiliation. Ingraham, somewhat irritated by Groeschel's failure always to move through Health Department channels and by the new Director's occasional direct communication with Mayor Clark, was further displeased when Groeschel did not consult him about who was on what side in PGH medical staff factions. He determined that his course should be not to offer advice unless Groeschel asked for it. And Groeschel, construing Ingraham's silence as possible hostility, never did.

The Trustees Split

IN NOVEMBER, the trustees officially placed on their agenda the question of how to get the best care for Hospital patients. They asked Groeschel to prepare a report on affiliating the medical schools with PGH services. (The trustees themselves never used the medical staff's phrase, vertical services.) Accordingly, he began in December, 1952, a series of negotiations with the deans, the medical staff of PGH, and the PGH trustees. His effort to arrive at a form of affiliation that would be agreeable to these three parties was to continue to June, 1953.

Groeschel was certain when he came to Philadelphia that the trustees wanted medical school affiliation with PGH. Dixon and Scattergood had emphasized this matter when they interviewed him in New York, and he had made his enthusiasm clear at the interview with the trustees in Philadelphia. In addition, Mayor Clark had told Groeschel after his arrival in November that the trustees were all in agreement with him (Clark) on the question of affiliation.

Of all the trustees, George Clark had been the first confirmed believer in affiliation. Scattergood and Mrs. Remer had come to favor it shortly after they became trustees. But it became disconcertingly clear to Groeschel in the latter part of December that the other three trustees—Schwartz, Duckrey, and Schlanger—had serious reservations. Schwartz in particular wanted proof that affiliation would benefit PGH. To offer some evidence, Groeschel invited the trustees to sit in on a session at which prospective interns were being interviewed. He wanted the trustees to see at first hand one of the medical personnel problems that affiliation would solve. He asked each intern why he wished to come to PGH. Half of them answered that they knew that at PGH they would have a free hand in dealing with patients. This, Groeschel felt, illustrated the problem. Men just out of medical school needed supervision. They *shouldn't* have a free hand. But this argument did not move Schwartz or the other two doubtful trustees, and so Groeschel invited the Board members to go through the Hospital at any time and talk to any members of the staff. "But don't talk only to people with a vested interest in keeping the medical schools out," he added.

Schwartz quickly accepted this invitation and started in January to hold independent conferences with many of the doctors at PGH and with the deans of the medical schools. Schwartz's lifetime of trade union experience had accustomed (some said "addicted") him to bargaining, infighting, and intramural conflicts. He had come onto the Board with no specific knowledge about the PGH situation except that there was a basic conflict between the medical schools and the medical staff over control of patient care. Schwartz knew where Mayor Clark stood. He was prepared to admit that even though Clark had given the trustees no specific instructions on this matter when they were appointed (beyond urging them to be independent and to provide the best care possible regardless of race, creed, or politics), the Mayor probably assumed that Schwartz shared Clark's point of view on affiliation. One thing Schwartz was quite clear about: neither the Charter nor the Mayor expected the trustees to be "just a bunch of dummies." He felt it was the responsibility and the right of each individual trustee to investigate affiliation and other questions independently. Groeschel, working for the first time directly under a Board of Trustees, had given him an invitation to investigate, and there was no firm hand from the chairman of the trustees to hold him back. So Schwartz started on his independent conferences with all parties.

Discrimination Becomes an Issue

Schwartz did not trust the medical school deans as a group. He felt they were running "closed unions," admitting to their schools and staffs only "members of the club." He was convinced that the medical schools were operating with stiff quotas for Jews and Negroes, and as he discussed the problem further with the anti-affiliation members on the PGH staff (who had been probing for months to find trustees who could be won over) his conviction deepened that it would be disastrous to allow the deans to "take control."

Having failed earlier to influence the deans, the city administration, or Groeschel, the PGH group led by Dr. Stewart now found a possible source of disagreement that might split the trustees. These members of the PGH Medical Board were not especially concerned about the question of discrimination, but now that they had found an argument that struck a responsive chord, they pressed the possibility of medical school discrimination on the two Jews (Schwartz and Schlanger) and the one Negro (Duckrey) on the Board of Trustees. Clark, in appointing trustees "representative of Philadelphia," had unwittingly created a miniature of the social conflicts of the city.

Schwartz's worries that alleged racial or religious discrimination in the medical schools might carry over to the services the schools would control at PGH led Duckrey to feel a similar apprehension, and later Schlanger came to share it, too. Both Schwartz and Duckrey were liberals and both knew of friends or relatives who had tried to get into medical school and who had been rejected. They believed that often these rejections were made because the medical schools enforced quotas for Jews and Negroes, and they were convinced that the same type of discrimination was applied in appointments to medical staffs.

Duckrey was active in Republican politics. Having served on the Charter Commission he knew that the new Charter assured every citizen equality of opportunity and he wanted that principle preserved in the staffing of PGH. Rather than give control of Hospital services to the medical school deans, he wanted to keep control in the hands of those entrusted by the Mayor to carry out the Charter, the trustees. PGH, he felt, had not had a long history of equal opportunity. For decades Negro nurses and interns had not been employed there. Within the past decade the situation had begun to change, largely, he felt, through the work of Dr. Lucchesi. He did not trust the medical schools to continue this trend if they were given control over the Hospital's services.

Duckrey wrote into the first draft agreement with the deans a section intended to prevent discrimination:

> In any relationship with any of the medical schools of the area, it should be clear that the several medical schools involved must demonstrate in their procedures and practices in the selection and upgrading of the staffs of the schools involved, that there are no discriminatory practices against people because of race, color, religion or national origin that will now or hereafter affect the employment, upgrading or conditions of work of any qualified man or woman in the various professional or non-professional activities of the Philadelphia General Hospital.

Schwartz became passionately devoted to preventing any discrimination at PGH. He sometimes referred to the alleged discrimination in medical schools as "Hitlerian." This sense of moral necessity coupled with a desire to be something more than a rubber-stamp trustee, led him to oppose Groeschel, who felt that Duckrey's provision plus the assurances of the deans afforded sufficient guarantee against possible discrimination. At one meeting of the trustees, Schwartz told Groeschel that he personally would settle for something a little less than perfection in medical care if he could be certain that there would be no discrimination. At this, Groeschel, after noting that as a Catholic he was himself a member of a religious minority group, replied: "I didn't come down here to solve the social problems of Philadelphia. I came to make PGH the best hospital possible."

Describing his activities years after the event, Schwartz said: "I had a concept of power relationships, and I was always looking for the balance of power in my union work. I did the same thing as a trustee." Seeking for the balance of power in the trustees' negotiations with the deans in the period between January and June, Schwartz felt that the trustees as laymen could not confidently determine whether a doctor was being kept out or kept down on grounds of medical qualifications or on grounds of race or religion. He concentrated on the question of who should make the recommendations for appointment and determined to set up the agreement with the medical schools in such a way that the deans would have as little power as possible. He sought a system of checks and balances between the medical schools and the Hospital so that the trustees would always have controlling power.

Apart from his dedication to the principle of no discrimination, it seemed to some of the other trustees that Schwartz, the self-made man from South Philadelphia, got satisfaction out of driving a hard bargain with the medical school deans. Another trustee recalls that Schwartz seemed to be a suspicious person by nature. "He was always afraid someone was going to pull something. . . . He was always on the lookout for 'a racket'." Another trustee saw Schwartz as "a keen and able person. He had directness and fortitude that quite early made its mark on the trustees. He was certainly dedicated to the best interests of the Hospital."

As Groeschel and Schwartz intensified their arguments over negotiations with the deans on an affiliation agreement, they began to distrust one another. Apart from differing with Groeschel over the reliability of the deans' assurances on discrimination, Schwartz came to feel that Groeschel lacked understanding in handling people. In his efforts to bring some order to the administration of the Hospital, Groeschel since his arrival had issued numerous directives announcing changes in operating policies. Some members of the staff, uneasy from the start about their future and about the Hospital's autonomy, resented the changes, particularly Groeschel's practice of announcing them in directives. These staff members felt that there should have been prior consultation with the staff to discuss any proposed changes. As Schwartz conferred with members of the Hospital medical staff on his independent investigation, these dissidents complained to him. Schwartz sympathized with them. He felt Groeschel's policy showed lack of understanding of the techniques of "democratic leadership."

"You just don't treat people that way," he said. "If you have an idea you want to get across you don't just tack a notice on bulletin board number six. You call a meeting and everybody discusses the question. Your problem is to lead the discussion in such a way that the same suggestion you have in your desk drawer comes out from the group. Then they will back it."

Scattergood's Role

In the Board's discussion of affiliation between January and June, 1953, set as it was in a conflict between Schwartz (supported by Duckrey and Schlanger) and Groeschel, Alfred Scattergood, the elderly Quaker chairman of the trustees, assumed a pivotal role. It was clear at the outset that the proponents of affiliation had a majority. Scattergood himself, George Clark, Mrs. Remer, and Acting Health Commissioner Ingraham were prepared to vote for affiliation. But Scattergood was by temperament and experience unwilling to force a decision on anyone or to use high-pressure methods to resolve a difference of opinion. He had told his fellow trustees at the start that he preferred reaching a meeting of minds instead of resolving questions by a vote. In practice this meant deferring action when there was evidence of a strong difference of opinion, in the hope of achieving consensus or unanimity. And in the January to June period, Scattergood's policy meant that the PGH staff group led by Dr. Stewart had unlimited time to build up opposition to the program of affiliation and unlimited opportunity to exploit the tendency of Schwartz, Duckrey, and Schlanger to be suspicious of agreements of any kind with the medical schools.

As chairman, Scattergood was inclined to discussion and compromise—not only among the trustees but between the deans and the Medical Board of PGH. Even though he himself favored the plan of affiliation, he believed it was more important to reach a satisfactory solution than to push through a plan vehemently disliked by the PGH staff and by several of the trustees.

Negotiations with the Deans

Groeschel understood it was his responsibility to pursue the study of affiliation. Some start had to be made, and he felt one logical way was to develop a plan or proposal to be used as the basis for discussion by all parties concerned. The controlling faction of the medical staff had made it clear that it was unalterably opposed to affiliation, and, Groeschel felt, no proposal could be expected from that side. There remained the medical school deans. Accordingly at the Board of Trustees meeting in early December, 1952, Dr. Groeschel requested authority to discuss affiliation with the deans and to develop a proposal acceptable to the deans and the trustees which could be used as a point of departure in negotiating with the PGH Medical Board. The Board of Trustees voted unanimously to authorize Groeschel to proceed with the discussions with the deans.

Groeschel drew up the first plan for affiliation and circulated it as a confidential memorandum to the Dean of the University of Pennsylvania Medical School and the Dean of Jefferson Medical College. It was essentially a summary of notes from a meeting held on December 30 between Groeschel and the two deans, and it included Tanner Duckrey's section on nondiscrimination.

Labeling the memorandum "confidential" raised at least temporary suspicion on the part of the deans of the other medical schools who were alert to any effort by Penn to increase its teaching services at PGH. By making the memo confidential Groeschel also irritated some of the reporters on the PGH "beat" who viewed the city hospital as "city property" and its administrative details as open to the public.

The first official plan which developed from these notes and from numerous conferences between Groeschel, the deans, and the Medical Board of PGH, was presented by Groeschel to the trustees on March 3. It was labeled the First Draft of the Deans' Plan.

Just at this time, there was a change in the composition of the Board of Trustees. George Clark, who had been serving on both the Board of Health and the PGH Board of Trustees, felt that he was devoting too much time to public affairs. He resigned from the PGH Board, remaining on the Board of Health. He was replaced by J. Peter Williams, a banker and a close friend of both George and Joseph Clark. Along with Scattergood and Mrs. Remer, Williams favored affiliation with the medical schools.

The Deans' Plan—First Draft

On March 7, 1953, the deans met with the trustees to discuss the plan as it stood then. The initial plan was divided into seven basic elements.

The first provided for a five-way participation in all the departments of Blockley (the older name for the main division of PGH).

Section two provided for the assignment to the school departments of a number of full and part-time clinicians whose salaries would be paid by the schools. These salaried physicians (the exact number would be determined by negotiation between the Dean and the Executive Director) were to be responsible for the day-to-day supervision of medical care. A large non-salaried staff of visiting physicians and surgeons was to be maintained as before, and each staff member would be required to visit the Hospital every week day for a period of six months out of the year, more time than had been required.

Section three, covering the mechanism for appointment, became a chief bone of contention. This first draft provided that the schools were to nominate all members of the salaried and non-salaried staff as well as the resident doctors. The medical school nominations would go to the Executive Committee on the PGH Medical Board which would recommend appointments to the Board of Trustees. (Interns would continue as before to be selected by the Intern Committee of the PGH Medical Board.)

Section four provided for the medical school representatives to be ex-officio members of the Hospital Medical Board's Executive Committee.

Section five dealt with the integration of the existing staff into the proposed organization. Almost all members of the PGH medical staff held faculty positions, and it was anticipated that all current members would be retained in their positions. The details were to be worked out by each school with its own staff members.

Section six guaranteed to the schools adequate space for research and teaching.

Section seven was Duckrey's anti-discrimination clause.

At the conference on March 7 members of the Board of Trustees raised questions on three points: appointment procedures, the status of current staff members, and possible discrimination.

The deans said they wanted only the power to nominate, not appoint staff members. Schwartz objected to the draft as it stood. He insisted that vacancies should be widely advertised, and the deans agreed that applications for staff positions would be received from all qualified physicians. The deans also agreed to strengthen the guarantee continuing current staff members in their positions. On salaried positions, however, the deans insisted that they should have control over the physicians who were to train their students, and the best that could be agreed on in the minutes was that "it was assumed that many details would have to be worked out in good faith, and with full cooperation of all parties concerned." The minutes also included this summary:

> Dr. Ingraham expressed the opinion that the majority of individuals on the Medical Board of Philadelphia General Hospital desire affiliation with the medical schools. The small groups which seem to be opposed happen to be articulate and aggressive and [he] stressed the importance of finding the proper method of working out a desirable proposal. However, discussion brought out the fact that many of the present medical staff do not look forward to the supervision which would come with closer tie-up with medical schools, as they are now working on their own authority. But it was again emphasized that the Board of Trustees will have to decide which type of medical service is best for the patient.

The trustees decided to meet with the Executive Committee of the Medical Board to discuss the proposal, and the meeting was set for March 18. At this meeting, a second draft of the deans' plan was to be presented to them—the first official presentation of the proposal.

The Opponents Take to the Press

On March 15 the *Philadelphia Inquirer* carried a story in which Dr. Stewart attacked the first draft of the deans' plan. This news story marked the opening gun of an extensive publicity campaign by the faction on the PGH Medical Board opposing affiliation with the medical schools. Several newspapermen in Philadelphia noted, as the controversy wore on into the spring and summer, that Dr. Stewart and her colleagues prepared regular press releases to present their side of the story to the Philadelphia public. The newspaper campaign turned out to be a one-sided affair, since Groeschel, the deans, and Chairman Scattergood had no thought of replying with counter-releases or declarations. They did not believe that the medical school affiliation issue was one that should be fought in the newspapers.

In the March 15 story Dr. Stewart charged that the deans had used smear, pressure, and politics to "soften" the Hospital for seizure. As a result of their campaign, she went on, the Hospital was demoralized and the staff suffered from anxiety, which in turn was reflected in the patients.

She repeated the arguments which she had been presenting ever since the issue of vertical services was first raised in 1947, opposing the five-way division proposed in the new plan, pointing out that almost all of the chiefs were already faculty members of the schools and the Hospital was already extensively used for teaching. With the medical staff, she declared, patient care was the first consideration while the schools were primarily interested in teaching. Proof of the quality of the Hospital could be found, she said, in the fact that PGH had four times as many applicants for internship as it could accept, while other hospitals were unable to fill their quotas.

No one answered these charges publicly. A spokesman for the Deans' Committee said that they preferred not to make any statement on the accusations at that time. Groeschel stated that the trustees were studying the quantity and quality of medical care at PGH and in this connection were considering the question of establishing formal affiliations with the medical schools. No decision had been reached and further study was necessary, he added.

Dr. Stewart's story appeared just three days before the meeting of the trustees and the Medical Board, and a day before the annual meeting of the PGH Medical Board. At the Medical Board meeting two resolutions were presented. One, offered by Dr. Stewart, opposed vertical services, stating "we are unwilling to surrender the control of the Philadelphia General Hospital to the medical schools." The other, offered by Dr. Boles, was a simpler statement, with minor variations, of the general proposal for vertical services. After heated discussion both resolutions were turned down. Action was deferred until a written proposition could be received from the deans.

Groeschel Gets 'The Go-Ahead'

By this time it was clear to the officials in City Hall that serious trouble was brewing. The division on the Board of Trustees was also clear. Ingraham and City Managing Director Sawyer were keeping in touch with the developing situation. At one conference in February on Health Department programs Groeschel was counseled to slow down on the affiliation plan and to proceed with caution.

Acting Commissioner Ingraham, who had assumed a moderating role, left the initiative to Groeschel and the trustees. Managing Director Sawyer was leaving responsibility to the Department of Health, and, in the Board of Trustees, Scattergood was trying to achieve a compromise satisfactory to all parties.

Sometime in March, Groeschel attended a dinner party with Mayor Clark and, pulling him aside, discussed the whole situation with him. He explained the disagreement among the trustees and between the deans and the Medical Board, and told Clark that, as he saw it, there were two alternatives. One would be "to go straight ahead and push right into it. There will be an explosion, but maybe we can ride it through. Or we can take it easy, let up the pressure now, and maybe take two or three years, but we could probably get it through by then."

Mayor Clark told Groeschel to go straight ahead, saying that on an issue as important to his program as public health reform, he couldn't afford to wait two or three years.

A Second Draft

The second draft of the deans' plan incorporated Schwartz's plan for wide advertisement of vacancies. Now all applications received would be forwarded to the medical schools on whose service the vacancy existed. The medical school was to evaluate all candidates as qualified or unqualified and return *all* applications to the Hospital. Men considered qualified would be listed in order of capability. These lists were then to be examined by a screening committee which represented the trustees, the medical school involved, the Medical Board, and the Executive Director. The Medical Board would then consider the nominations and forward them to the trustees for appointment.

These changes in the appointment procedure were moving in the direction of Schwartz's thinking. His aim was to soften, or if possible eliminate, the medical schools' influence in the appointment procedure, but in any case to make sure that no application was dropped along the way.

Another revised section guaranteed that every staff member would have the opportunity to retain his position. Safeguards against discrimination were tightened, and appeal procedures were added.

At a joint meeting of the trustees with the Medical Board on March 18, a number of physicians spoke against the plan. Among them were Drs. Stewart and Kramer, joined by Dr. Harrison Flippin who supported their position vigorously throughout the controversy. Dr. Stewart gave a historical sketch of the controversy over vertical services from 1946 through the abortive attempt by their committee to reach agreement with the deans in 1952. Dr. Boles spoke in favor of affiliation. Several physicians expressed a desire to study the revised deans' plan in writing and to meet with the deans for discussion. The trustees agreed.

Meanwhile, Mrs. Remer had been growing increasingly concerned about the intransigency of the Hospital medical staff, especially about the continued appearance before the trustees of only a few members of the Medical Board, almost all of whom spoke against affiliation. She talked with a friend of hers who was a surgeon connected with one of the medical schools—*not* the University of Pennsylvania—and who was also on the PGH staff. She asked him if he agreed with the position of the Stewart-Kramer-Flippin group.

"Of course I don't," he answered.

"Then why don't you speak up?" she demanded. "Why is it that all we hear are these few shrill voices?"

He answered, "I don't want to have anything to do with medical politics! I have enough to do carrying out my responsibilities as a surgeon."

She asked him how many other doctors at PGH felt the same way, and he said, "Count up how many people you've heard from—five, six, a dozen? There are about 480 other doctors on the staff. There's your answer."

On April 1, the trustees and the representatives of the Medical Board met again. The deans' plan had been circulated in advance to all members of the medical staff. It was entitled "Official Proposal" and superseded preliminary drafts.

This draft varied in some details from the second draft. One change was the exclusion from the plan of the ancillary service departments (Radiology, Anaesthesiology, Laboratories, Physical Medicine and Cardiology). They were to continue as they were, and to be available to all the schools for teaching purposes.

The provisions for nomination and appointment were the same except that the position of the Medical Board was strengthened. Now when the applications were returned by the schools, they would go first to the Medical Board, and then to the screening committee. From there the applications were to go to the trustees for appointment.

That some staff members were still jittery about whether they would be able to stay at the hospital if the plan were adopted was reflected in a change in the language referring to them. Instead of reading that they would have the "opportunity to continue," the plan now read that they "will continue" in their positions, and this statement appeared in the first section of the plan instead of the fifth.

At the April 1 meeting, Dr. Stewart attacked both the second and third drafts saying that "it is a deliberate attempt to confuse the staff as well as the Board of Trustees. The medical schools intend to take over the power of appointment."

The Medical Board spokesmen presented a list of objections to the deans' plan prepared by Dr. Charles Rupp, Secretary, and an alternative plan prepared by Dr. T. Montgomery. This plan offered the schools extended facilities for teaching and security of services but reserved the privilege of nomination to the Medical Board. The schools could pay the staff members as they saw fit.

In the next few days, Groeschel wrote detailed criticisms of the statements of Dr. Rupp and Dr. Montgomery, and of one made by Dr. Flippin—directing his correspondence to Schwartz whose independent researches and negotiations had led Scattergood to designate him as Chairman of the Medical Affairs Committee of the Board of Trustees. Groeschel took a strong position in favor of affiliation. He was emerging as the main spokesman for vertical services, and in the minds of those opposed to the plan, as an ally of the deans.

The deans also sent individual comments on Dr. Montgomery's proposal, and a number of letters from members of the staff were now coming to the trustees, some favoring, some opposing the deans' plan.

On April 8, the meeting requested by the Hospital staff was held. The trustees, the Executive Committee of the Medical Board, and the Deans' Committee discussed point by point the deans' plan, with the deans answering questions. The deans attempted to demonstrate that their plan would not disturb the position of authority of any member of the medical staff. Following this meeting the plan was again re-drafted in an attempt to bring it closer to the thinking of the medical staff.

One of the letters received by Chairman Scattergood from a medical staff member commenting on the atmosphere of this meeting read as follows:

> The main difficulty at the present time is the lack of faith in each other of the three parties concerned, i.e., the administration, the staff and the Deans. I was present when the members of the staff drew up criticisms to the last Deans' proposal. I felt that they were almost paranoid in their search for hidden meanings in it and told them so. However, I was amazed to find the Deans just as paranoid in criticizing Dr. Montgomery's proposal. This latter, to me, seems to give the Deans practically everything they want except the fact that it was not suggested by them. If to it was added the suggested proposal of the Deans in choosing the permanent staff, I think it would be an ideal compromise.
>
> Many of us have looked forward . . . to improvement of Blockley [Philadelphia General Hospital] under the present regime. However, we are disappointed that the staff has not been more frequently asked for suggestions to accomplish this. . . . Blockley needs help from the medical schools . . . but can't this be accomplished in a spirit of compromise and without destroying . . . the "Spirit of Blockley"?

The plan was modified slightly after the April 8 meeting. An extra step was added to the nominating procedure. Lists of qualified and unqualified applicants were now to be returned by the medical schools to the chiefs of service of the department where a vacancy existed for their recommendations before going on to the Medical Board. This version became the "Official Proposal of the Deans' Committee with Amendments Suggested."

On April 22 another joint meeting was held by the Board of Trustees with the deans and the service chiefs from the PGH Division of General Medicine. Officers of the Medical Board also were present. The purpose of the meeting was to discuss the manner in which the provisions of the deans' plan would be applied to the Division of General Medicine, if accepted by the Board of Trustees.

During the discussion, the same division of opinion was apparent. Although the mechanics of application were talked over, much time was spent arguing the merits of vertical services, the quality of patient care in the Hospital, and who should have the power of nomination. Dr. Stewart expressed the opinion that further negotiations would have little effect. She preferred that the Board of Trustees make the decision. The Hospital had been deteriorating and they could not delay. Chairman Scattergood expressed the thought that they were so close to a settlement that he did not want to force the issue at this point. Dr. Boles wanted the proposal acted upon that day; he saw no reason for further extensive negotiations.

It was decided that a small committee should be appointed to work out a final proposition. Dr. Charles L. Brown (Dean of Hahnemann) and Dr. Kramer (President of the Medical Board) were chosen as co-chairmen. Schwartz pointed out that the trustees could only give consideration to their thinking, and that the decision was up to the trustees.

The Medical Affairs Committee (Schwartz and Duckrey) of the Board of Trustees met April 29. Schwartz suggested changes in the appointment procedure of the deans' plan and in the bylaws of the Medical Board. The trustees at their meeting April 30, accepted these changes. They were beginning to take decisive steps toward drafting a plan of their own that would represent a compromise of the conflicting attitudes that had been expressed to that time.

Schwartz's proposal for the nomination procedure was that two steps be dropped. Applications received at the Hospital would go neither to the medical school nor to the chief of the school service at the Hospital but instead directly to the chiefs of all services in the department. From there they would take the same course as in the deans' plan. Schwartz's proposal was identical with the already existing machinery for nominations except for retaining one new step proposed by the deans: namely, that recommendations go from the Medical Board to an advisory committee before being acted upon by the Board of Trustees. This advisory committee was the only group in which the medical schools would be directly represented.

The trustees added one modification to Schwartz's plan: that the medical schools receive duplicate lists of applicants at the time they were sent to the chiefs.

No change from the existing procedure would be made in the appointment and assignment of residents.

Schwartz Explodes a New Proposal

The trustees believed they were at last reaching an agreement among themselves. Accordingly, following their April 30 meeting, Dr. Groeschel drew up the Initial Draft Plan of the Board of Trustees of Philadelphia General Hospital for the Organization of the Medical Staff of Philadelphia General Hospital. This version included those portions of the deans' plan relating to the five-way division of services, the appointment of salaried clinician-teachers, and the retention of all staff members. It also incorporated the proposals offered by Schwartz on nomination procedures and changes in the bylaws and regulations of the Medical Board.

This apparently final plan, which guaranteed security to all staff members and allowed the medical schools almost no voice in nominations, would have caused little change in the status quo. Its major departure from existing conditions was to provide more salaried staff at the expense of the medical schools. Most of the debated points had been altered to suit the Medical Board. Things seemed to be settled.

On May 5 Scattergood, Williams, Mrs. Remer and Ingraham were shocked when Schwartz circulated his own plan to counter the one drawn by Groeschel.

The trustees met on May 7, in an atmosphere of deep discouragement, to consider this new proposal. Schwartz stated that the deans' proposal was unacceptable to him since the splitting of services that had been proposed was not satisfactory. Services should belong neither to the individual doctor nor to the school, but to the Hospital. He had been satisfied with the agreed changes in appointment procedure, but the Board at its earlier meeting had taken no action as to the dividing up of services. Schwartz said:

> It has been intimated that the care of patients is far from satisfactory. It has therefore been suggested that the only way to get good care is by affiliation with the medical schools. I do not share that viewpoint. . . .
>
> I believe that the Medical Staff of Philadelphia General Hospital was given inadequate consideration, administratively and policy-wise, by the Board of Trustees. Undue attention was given to the organization of "vertical services" as the great panacea. So little time was devoted in seeking out deficiencies in the existing setup and arranging consultations for improvement in the services.
>
> I firmly believe that the only way the Board of Trustees can maintain absolute day-by-day control of the medical services is by assigning responsibilities to its own selected Medical Staff operating under the supervision of the Trustees. Assigning the Hospital services to the schools, no matter how the Medical Staff is selected, places responsibility and control in the school, not in the Hospital.

Schwartz's plan provided that the trustees might grant service privileges to any of the medical schools, the service to be under a chief designated by the trustees. The schools were to be bound to accept the human rights provision in the City Charter, to agree to the employment of an adequate number of paid clinicians designated by the trustees, and to agree to abide by the rules and regulations of the Medical Board. The schools were to have no part in the nomination or appointment procedure, except that one representative of a medical school would be on the advisory committee of the Board of Trustees to review the recommendations of the Medical Board.

Affiliation Is Abandoned

Robert K. Sawyer, Managing Director of the City, was present at this May 7 meeting of the Board. The day before, after Schwartz's proposal had been received, Groeschel, Harold Schneidman (City Public Relations) and Sawyer had conferred, and Sawyer had agreed to attend the trustees' meeting as a representative of City Hall.

Groeschel insisted that Schwartz's plan was unacceptable. Schneidman gave his opinion that Schwartz and Duckrey were trying to defeat vertical services by using Scattergood's desire for unanimity as a wedge. He noted that the opposition group led by Dr. Stewart benefited from any delay and that daily it was strengthening its position before the public by its newspaper releases.

Sawyer pleaded that negotiations proceed as rapidly as possible. Observing that some members of the Board seemed to have crystallized their opinions, he urged the trustees to make a quick decision on what they were going to do about affiliation and then to get on with the business of the Hospital. However, he added: "We do not want this change unless we have a unanimous or almost unanimous decision of the Board to effect it." He cautioned that the Executive Director might be placed in an untenable position by the Board's decision, and urged the trustees to give consideration to the long-term effect for PGH.

Dr. Groeschel stated that the Board had been kept informed at every stage of the discussion and at no time was he given the impression that the deans' proposal as such was entirely unacceptable. He believed and had stated from the start that affiliation with the medical schools would provide the best care to the patients. He had proceeded in good faith with full knowledge of the Board.

A motion expressing complete confidence in the integrity of the Executive Director was unanimously carried.

The deans' plan for affiliation was abandoned at this meeting. The substitute policy suggested was to grant services under contract to the schools for a stated term. There would be no five-way division. A subcommittee consisting of Trustees Williams, Ingraham and Duckrey was appointed to draft an acceptable proposal for the Board.

Mayor Clark had not personally intervened to resolve the differences between the trustees. As late as April 30 he had refused Sawyer's request, instigated by Groeschel, that he take some action with the trustees. Clark told Sawyer the trustees were well aware of his stand on affiliation.

Sawyer, aware that the newspaper publicity was making affiliation a potentially embarrassing matter, favored affiliation but was principally concerned with breaking the stalemate. After the May 7 meeting he recorded his uneasiness about the attitude expressed toward Groeschel during the meeting. He believed that Groeschel would need public support from the Mayor, since, as he put it, Groeschel was "way out in front on this thing at our request."

Opposition Continues

The original deans' plan was so watered down with compromises that there seemed little left for the Medical Board to criticize. Opposition from PGH, however, continued as strong as ever, possibly because the opponents felt that Groeschel could reopen the question at any time. The opposing faction believed Groeschel, the deans, and the Mayor still intended to take away from the Medical Board the autonomy it had enjoyed. Members of this group said in effect "Yes, the final plan gives no power to the schools, but it could be an entering wedge. The schools will continue to try to gain control." They were fighting a possibility.

Explosion and Resignation

SIX DAYS AFTER the May 7 meeting the *Evening Bulletin* carried a front-page streamer headline over a story that Dr. Erna Boroush (the young Assistant Medical Director of PGH who had been appointed during LaBoccetta's "caretaker regime") had resigned and had charged Dr. Groeschel with neglecting his hospital duties because he was spending most of his time lobbying for vertical services. Dr. Boroush further charged that at least two deaths had occurred at PGH due to insufficient supervision and untrained personnel. She also complained that inadequate equipment led to inadequate care of patients. She declared that Groeschel had succeeded in a deliberate attempt to demoralize the hospital staff; had made no effort to understand the Hospital's problems; and had not consulted with the staff. She asked for a full investigation by the Board of Trustees.

Dr. Boroush had not been directly involved in the dispute over affiliation. At the time she resigned, she stated that she had not made up her mind on the issue. Her administrative position would not have been directly affected by the change. (As Assistant Medical Director she had worked closely at first with Dr. Groeschel, but in March Dr. F. Lloyd Mussells had become Medical Director of the Hospital and Dr. Boroush's immediate superior.) Dr. Boroush told reporters she had become increasingly disturbed by continuing deficiencies in the Hospital which she attributed to Dr. Groeschel's neglect and indifference. Whatever became of affiliation, she believed these daily problems were of first importance and should have had first call on the Director's time.

Dr. Boroush had decided to resign at the beginning of May. She had talked over her problem with Trustee Duckrey more than once and told him her decision. At that time she did not know personally the members of the medical staff who were strongly opposed to affiliation although, of course, she knew who they were. She did, however, tell Dr. Stewart of her intention to resign. Dr. Stewart advised her against resigning on the grounds that she could do more for the Hospital by staying, but Dr. Boroush held to her decision.

A few days before the story broke in the *Evening Bulletin,* Dr. Boroush left a note of resignation as of July 1, on the desk of Dr. Mussells. Shortly after this she talked with Mussells on the telephone. Mussells reported the gist of the conversation to Groeschel. The latter interpreted what Mussells told him as meaning that Dr. Boroush had attempted to persuade Mussells to support the anti-affiliation faction in return for that faction's support of Mussells for Executive Director after Groeschel was dismissed. Dr. Boroush telephoned Scattergood and told him of her decision and also sent him a letter confirming it.

Dr. Stewart advised Dr. Boroush that if she resigned she should, for the good of the Hospital, tell the newspapers why. According to Dr. Boroush a reporter from the *Bulletin* telephoned her and asked for her story. Scattergood, Groeschel, and some City Hall officials got wind of the impending publicity. Scattergood and Groeschel went to Pierre Fraley at the *Bulletin* and tried unsuccessfully to persuade him not to publish the story.

On May 13, the day the story broke, the interns' organization and the resident physicians at PGH sent a public letter to Mayor Clark endorsing Dr. Boroush's stand:

> Should the current Hospital administration fail to achieve an acceptable resolution of the conflict which now threatens the welfare of the Hospital and its patients, then it is our request that the resignation of the current Executive Director be requested.

Mayor Clark Jumps In

Without consulting his Managing Director, his Health Commissioner, the trustees, or the city public relations office, Mayor Clark responded immediately. He did not remove the dissident trustees; he did not tell the trustees to discharge any of the PGH dissidents. He plunged directly into the newspaper war. The day the story broke Sawyer had arranged with the Mayor that Clark would wait until Scattergood had issued a statement supporting Groeschel before he (Clark) would issue a brief statement supporting Scattergood. Clark, angered by the May 13 publicity and by the interns' letter, did not wait for Scattergood's statement. He put himself publicly at the head of the forces supporting Groeschel against the Stewart faction:

> It is unfortunate that a small group of disgruntled physicians on the medical staff of Philadelphia General Hospital have been able to use young and relatively inexperienced Dr. Erna Boroush as one of the pawns in their vicious "get Groeschel" movement It is equally unfortunate that you young interns and residents . . . should also lend yourselves to a movement so clearly against the public interest. . . . The conditions Dr. Boroush complained of . . . over the heads of her superiors and in violation of her obligations to them existed, as you well know, at the time you and your colleagues received your appointments. . . . None of them are of Dr. Groeschel's making and you know it.
>
> Dr. Groeschel has my full support in his efforts to remedy the deplorable administrative and medical conditions he found at the Hospital on his arrival last November. I am particularly proud of his efforts to remove both partisan and medical politics from all operations at the Philadelphia General Hospital.
>
> The public is entitled to know that the ringleaders in this skillfully organized plot to secure Dr. Groeschel's dismissal are Doctors Harrison F. Flippin, Winifred B. Stewart, and Anthony Sindoni, Jr. Their purpose is to turn back the clock and maintain the medical empire they built up under the previous administration. Since you and your colleagues owe your appointments at Philadelphia General Hospital to the little group which these three ringleaders dominate, it is perhaps only human that you should be willing to further their aims. But you should know that the present administration intends to build from the ground up for the first time a really high class medical and administrative service at the Philadelphia General Hospital . . . the job will be done by Dr. Groeschel with the support of the Board of Trustees of the Philadelphia General Hospital and the Mayor whether or not the little group of recalcitrants named above cooperates.
>
> . . . the public charges which Dr. Boroush and your group have so recklessly made will be fully investigated; but I can assure you that the old days of medical and partisan politics are gone at the Philadelphia General Hospital and that Dr. Groeschel has a clear mandate from this administration to put the institution back on its feet.

(Some of Clark's closest advisers, reading the statement the next day, felt that the Mayor had acted hastily albeit heroically. As one of his cabinet officials told Clark some days later when he had a chance to see him, if the Mayor wanted to affect the PGH situation he should have fought administratively and not through the press. Clark, the adviser told him, should have removed the trustees who were aligned with the Stewart faction against Groeschel. He could thereby make certain that the trustees would sever the PGH appointments of the dissident members of the medical staff. If Clark was not prepared to move thus drastically, his adviser held, he should not fight the issue in the press for this forced the dissident group to revolt not only against Groeschel but against the Democratic city administration. Clark countered that the intention of the Charter was that the trustees should be independent of City Hall.[3] He admitted that his newspaper defense of Groeschel had been almost an instinctive reaction of anger, but added that he would not change his action if he had it to do over again.)

On May 14 Philadelphia papers also carried the following charges and countercharges: The PGH Graduate Nurses Association issued a statement endorsing the stand of the interns and residents; Republican Councilman Lord called for a full investigation of maladministration at PGH to be made by the City Council; Dr. Groeschel issued a statement denying Dr. Boroush's charges. He regretted that the Hospital's troubles "have been seized upon as a

[3] It was also true that the trustees had never been told by anyone up to this point that the city administration's interpretation of the Charter was that they had the power to sever the appointments of dissident voluntary physicians on the PGH medical staff. Some trustees stated later that they felt it unlikely that the Board under Scattergood would ever have exercised such power. Others have questioned whether such a severe tactic would not have "kicked back" by bringing a hostile public reaction.

vehicle for attacking the administration of the Hospital in a spirit of bitterness, and in an attempt to discredit the so-called vertical services plan, with which they are not even remotely connected"; The Executive Committee of the PGH Medical Board passed and issued a resolution requesting the trustees to table Dr. Boroush's resignation pending a full investigation; Trustee Schwartz expressed the opinion that a public investigation should be made; The Board of Trustees, through Chairman Scattergood, expressed complete confidence in the integrity and ability of Groeschel. Scattergood regretted that Dr. Boroush had based her charges on the very conditions which the present administration of the Hospital was working so earnestly to correct. He stated that Groeschel had improved conditions a great deal—more than Scattergood had at first believed possible in view of the complexity of the problems.

The Trustees Meet

On May 15 the Board of Trustees met with City Managing Director Sawyer, City Solicitor Abraham Freedman, City Public Relations Advisor Harold Schneidman and Dr. Groeschel. Groeschel requested that an investigation be made for the sake of his reputation as a hospital administrator. The conferees decided to hold an inquiry which would be conducted by Dr. Ingraham and Trustees Scattergood and Williams. No action was taken on the resignation of Dr. Boroush. A statement was issued to the press that an inquiry would begin on May 18.

Dr. Boroush now found herself the focus of a violent public controversy. She believed she had performed her clear duty, but was distressed by the consequences which she felt would affect the Hospital adversely. She telephoned Scattergood to tell him she was sorry for all the trouble she had incited, although she said she was glad she had acted. She went on to say that it was her own act, hers alone.

She then turned to Dr. Stewart and the anti-Groeschel faction of the Medical Board for support and advice. They advised her to retain as counsel Lemuel B. Schofield. Schofield was a well-known Philadelphia criminal lawyer and a substantial owner of the then Republican newspaper, the *Daily News*. Acting on Schofield's advice, Dr. Boroush refused to appear at the May 18 meeting of the Board of Trustee's special committee, implying that the reason for her refusal was her feeling that Mayor Clark and Scattergood had prejudged the case. She asked that the investigation be conducted before a committee of City Council. Following her refusal to appear, the trustees accepted her resignation.

City Council President, James A. Finnegan, who was also the Chairman of the Democratic Party in Philadelphia, announced a few days later that the Council was not planning to investigate the Hospital because it did not consider itself qualified to investigate a subject as technical as medical administration. Since the Democrats controlled the Council, this was final.

Dr. Lucchesi now responded to the Mayor's open letter to the interns, which he saw as an attack upon his administration of the Hospital. He defended his record and the Hospital staff, reminding the Mayor that Clark had originally invited him to remain at PGH. Clark replied through the press that had Lucchesi remained at PGH he would have given him the same support he was giving Groeschel. Clark referred to "the dead hand of mediocrity which was the trademark of the politically dominated system under which the city suffered for so many years. The same thing has been true in the Health Department in general and Philadelphia General Hospital in particular," Clark went on. "To state the obvious fact is no criticism of you."

In the next week statements on Dr. Boroush's charges, on Dr. Groeschel, on medical school affiliation, and on hospital administration in general appeared from many doctors, some in, some out of PGH. They were in newspaper stories, not letters to the editor. Dr. Stewart replied to Mayor Clark's statement:

> There is a plot involving the fate of Philadelphia General Hospital but the ringleaders are not members of the Philadelphia General Hospital staff, but are Dr. Ravdin and other faculty members of the Medical School of the University of Pennsylvania who are planning to include the annexation of the Philadelphia General Hospital in the extensive program of the University of Pennsylvania Medical School. The Mayor and the Deans of the other four medical schools are the "pawns used by the ringleaders" to gain their objectives.

The same week, three Republican councilmen threatened to hold an independent investigation, unless all sides were given an opportunity to be heard fairly before the Board of Trustees.

Role of the Press

Immediately after the Boroush story broke, both Scattergood and Schwartz had issued public statements, but after that the trustees—with the exception of Schwartz—acted as a group, issuing only one statement. The medical school deans maintained a complete silence on the ground that they had no official connection with either the Hospital or the Administration.

Of the three Philadelphia newspapers, the Republican tabloid *Daily News* was the only one which took an editorial position on the controversy, and it was unremitting in its attacks on Groeschel and the city administration. The *Evening Bulletin* and the *Inquirer* did not take editorial stands on affiliation, and their news stories presented relatively balanced accounts. However, neither Groeschel nor Scattergood could overcome their conviction that this was not an issue to be settled by statements to the press. The end result was that the city administration's case made a poor showing in the press, and the arguments for affiliation did not get as wide coverage as did the statement of the foes of vertical services.

Judging by letters to newspaper editors (only one was published) and to the Mayor's office (a total of six were received), the controversy was over the heads of the general public and limited to the professional groups involved. But it was believed at City Hall that the public was gaining the impression that something was wrong at PGH and that this was in some way being charged to the new city administration which, on the whole, had a positive, reforming reputation at this time.

The Trustees Investigate

On May 26 Dr. Boroush appeared before the Board of Trustees with Schofield present as her lawyer. The hearing was not public, but the press was admitted. Dr. Boroush amplified her charges. The trustees were inquiring but courteous. Her record at the Hospital was mentioned and her courage and sincerity were commended. She explained the circumstances of her resignation. Scattergood called her actions disloyal. Dr. Boroush countered that she had been disloyal to the administration but loyal to the Hospital. She was questioned as to why she had said, "this is my own act." She answered that it was because of the immediate response of the Hospital's staff organizations in her support, which might have been misunderstood.

Dr. Boroush requested that for the sake of the Hospital, the press releases be edited. But it was too late for that, since news of the hearing had been continuously relayed to the papers during its course.

Except for a brief statement by Dr. Boroush that she had not made up her mind on vertical services and that the affiliation issue had nothing to do with her charges against Groeschel, there was no reference to the issue which had engrossed trustees and staff during the past year. The trustees were determined to keep the affiliation issue out of the hearings.

The trustees met June 1 and decided further hearings should deal specifically with the charges made by Dr. Boroush. Schwartz and Ingraham were appointed to determine who should be heard and to arrange the order and procedure of hearing. The next hearing was set for June 8.

The Funeral of Vertical Services

The report of the special committee of the trustees on affiliation (Dr. Ingraham, Trustees Williams and Duckrey) was made and unanimously accepted by the Board on June 4. It was prefaced with a public statement which said that

> . . . the committee has unanimously agreed that the so-called "vertical system" is not the best answer to the particular problems of Philadelphia General Hospital. The committee therefore has urged the full Board to reject the "vertical service" concept.
>
> In the opinion of the committee, the provision for equal division of the Hospital's services among the medical schools which appears to be an essential part of the plan, is not a realistic and workable system. In addition we believe that there should be an opportunity for independent services which are not affiliated with any school. . . .
>
> Therefore, the special committee recommends that

> the cooperative method of participation by the medical schools which is now in effect . . . be maintained and strengthened through the formalizing of the understanding presently existing.

The committee recommended that individual contracts be made between the trustees and the medical schools for teaching privileges on specific services. The trustees would extend teaching privileges to any or all of the schools on this basis, and they in turn would be required to render adequate medical supervision of day-by-day care at all times. Although Schwartz accepted this substitute proposal, he considered it a defeat for his point of view.

Thus was the vertical service plan formally buried. The unanimous vote constituted recognition of defeat, and did not reflect any change in the opinions of those trustees who had favored affiliation. These trustees maintained privately that although they were abandoning the form, they were not dropping the concept. Formal affiliation lived on as a goal to be effected piecemeal by contracts.

The new plan was approved by a formal resolution of the PGH Medical Board on June 10.

The Investigation Continues

Five more hearings on Dr. Boroush's charges were held in June and July. The trustees heard several physicians at PGH criticize specific actions of Groeschel's, but also heard an impressive series of statements supporting the Executive Director.

At one hearing on June 26, for example, when six members of the Hospital staff gave details of shortages, overcrowding, and lack of facilities at PGH, none criticized Groeschel. Medical Director Mussells commended Groeschel for the "splendid job he is doing. In my dealings with him I found him to be extremely fair and just. I have complete faith in his ability."

At the final hearing on July 1 Groeschel was given the opportunity to answer all charges. He made a formal statement in which he sketched the highlights of the situation at PGH when he arrived: the transition period in city government, and the lack of a full time director for ten months; the new Board of Trustees; the new Charter; the difficulties with personnel and supplies, and the anxiety and insecurity of the employees and the medical staff; the confused area of authority between the Health Department and the trustees.

He then listed the many accomplishments of his eight months of administration, which included solution of the anesthesia problem by the establishment of a new service; improvement in the research program; and development of a capital program for improvements at Blockley Division, PGH, amounting to $2,000,000 over three years.

Groeschel was questioned on each charge against him. In many cases he had taken action on problems brought to him that Dr. Boroush was not aware of. Many other snarls and delays were due to difficulties with other city departments. "We are not the masters of our own household here," Groeschel reminded the trustees.

He maintained, on the charge of failure to make TB ward rounds more than once, that this was not his job. As an administrator it was his role to delegate responsibilities to his subordinates and to exercise judgment as to which problems were most urgent where there were too many to deal with at once.

On his staff relations, Groeschel explained that his discontinuation of administrative board meetings, an action criticized by many in the Hospital, was due to his feeling that they accomplished very little, and to the tremendous overload of work on the Hospital's short-handed staff. He had set up a new system of administration as soon as possible. He regretted that he had not had more time to confer with more people and felt now that he had underestimated the psychological importance of the administrative board meetings. But he had never refused to see anyone, although he had been so busy that he was not always immediately available to those who wished to see him. This situation had improved as all the other problems were alleviated. He believed the staff was now working smoothly, with clear lines of responsibility, good communications, and adequate and regular department meetings. Morale, he felt, had improved a great deal with the decision against affiliation, and it had been the long uncertainty which had been the chief demoralizing element.

In the 138 pages of the transcript of this one hearing, Groeschel answered most of the charges of neglect brought against him, to the satisfaction of the city administration and of a majority, if not all, of the trustees.

Groeschel Exonerated

On July 28, the Board of Trustees issued the following statement:

> The attention of the Board of Trustees of Philadelphia General Hospital having been directed to certain published comments reflecting criticisms of the administration of the Hospital, the Board has made a thorough inquiry into the matter during the past two months.
>
> All of the testimony given by many of the members of the medical and administrative staffs has been recorded. It contains many helpful suggestions which we believe will be valuable in correlating, consolidating and improving administrative procedures at the Hospital and will prove a further benefit to the citizens of Philadelphia.
>
> After completing this exhaustive investigation, we affirm our confidence in the administration of the Hospital.

Mayor Clark said he "was delighted" at the findings. Dr. Groeschel said, "I am gratified by the expression of confidence by the Board of Trustees in my administration."

But this statement, issued by the trustees with Groeschel's name conspicuously missing, was the result of some behind-stage compromises effected partly by the City Solicitor's office. Several much longer statements had been discarded because Schwartz and Groeschel's other opponents on the Board of Trustees thought them too favorable to Groeschel, or because the other trustees objected to any real criticisms of Groeschel's administration.

Schwartz and his allies on the Board were persuaded to withhold their critical opinions, but refused to endorse Groeschel by name. None of the trustees was really satisfied with the statement as issued. Scattergood was unhappy about its weakness but feared the possibility of a minority report if the majority supporting Groeschel insisted on a stronger one. Williams and Mrs. Remer shared Scattergood's disappointment. Schwartz and Duckrey weren't satisfied. Schlanger, although personally opposed to Groeschel, was reported to feel a political obligation to support the Clark administration.

Schwartz, who disliked Groeschel, did not credit Dr. Boroush's charges against him. He said he believed that Groeschel was an "excellent administrator." But Schwartz believed that Groeschel was in league with the University of Pennsylvania's alleged effort to get control of PGH and that he had "sold out to the deans." To Schwartz this constituted disloyalty in an employee of the Board and it was because of this, not because of Groeschel's performance as an administrator, that Schwartz wanted Groeschel ousted. He consequently refused to endorse a stronger trustee statement supporting him.

When the trustees' statement was ready for release, the City Solicitor's representative timed it to miss the *Evening Bulletin* which he felt had been hostile, and gave it to a reporter he considered more friendly on the morning *Inquirer*. Groeschel's name, so conspicuously lacking in the statement itself, was headlined in the story reporting his exoneration. Mayor Clark followed this with his statement of gratification, also naming Groeschel. Groeschel's opponents were chagrined by the maneuver. Subsequent reports in the *Evening Bulletin* of dissension among the trustees were hardly noticed.

By the time the final statement was made the PGH situation had cooled off. The affiliation plan was considered defeated by its PGH opponents. The Mayor, Dixon, and the pro-affiliation trustees believed that it would be best to forget affiliation plans for a year or so, but they did not consider that the events of May-July, 1953 had settled the question permanently. Rather, they saw their defeat as a temporary setback in a long-range campaign.

Solution by Contract?

In June, Trustee Williams had been requested to work out a contractual procedure whereby the trustees could arrange for the medical schools to supervise some of the PGH services. Williams and the City Solicitor's office sought to work out a basic contract that would conform with city laws and regulations. This contract went through six drafts but the final form was not accepted by the trustees in December because of opposition from Schwartz. A draft submitted to the deans met with an unfavorable reception because it required the schools to employ and pay salaries to Hospital staff members they would have had little control in appointing. This was the same disagreement that had occurred in the affiliation negotiations.

At a board meeting December 29, 1953, Schwartz emphatically rejected the sixth draft of the proposed contract form on the grounds that it deviated seriously from the June 4 "doctrine." Williams replied that the trustees had made a statement rather than formulated a doctrine, and that the deans had, in any case, rejected that form of contract. He believed the deans' argument had considerable merit: the Hospital was refusing to delegate responsibility for medical care and at the same time demanding that the schools bear the expense of providing such care.

A representative of the City Solicitor's office stated that this sixth draft appeared to delegate appointment procedure to the medical schools, since a person could not be appointed to a medical school service as a practical matter if that person was not going to be a faculty member of the school in question. He concluded that this delegation was contrary to the City Charter.

Schwartz said that the Hospital had already bent entirely too much in the direction of the medical schools. The meeting ended in a stalemate. Scattergood stated there would have to be further discussion. Those trustees who were anxious to formalize relations with the medical schools felt that Schwartz was obstructing a resolution of the problem. He in turn was angry at Williams for making concessions to the deans.

Dr. Groeschel Resigns

In October 1953, when the Boroush investigation had been concluded and the attempts to work out a contract system were proving as frustrating as the earlier affiliation negotiations, Groeschel was offered a position as Associate Director of New York Hospital.

Groeschel felt isolated and bruised by his eleven months in Philadelphia. His enthusiasm for the absorbing job had died. Moreover, in view of the strong opposition, he believed tha medical school affiliation would never become reality and that therefore it would be impossibl to achieve for PGH the highest possible stand ards of medical care, teaching, and research. H felt he had learned that the director of a cit hospital needs not only professional skill but political aptitude that he did not have.

Then, too, Mrs. Groeschel had not enjoye living in Philadelphia. Both felt a sense of isola tion. Philadelphians, they concluded, were no quick to admit outsiders into their society Groeschel's old friends made at his earlier sta at the Penn Medical School had kept their dis tance of necessity to avoid further accusations o a Penn plot to take over PGH. The Groeschel had not been able to form close friendships wit any of the PGH staff, particularly among th group that regarded the Executive Director a an enemy. The Groeschel children, too, had fel the impact of the controversy, hearing thei schoolmates discuss their parents' reactions t newspaper stories. These stresses contrasted t the quiet social and family life the Groeschel had enjoyed in New York when he had not hel a municipal medical post. All in all, Groesche felt it was time to go.

Groeschel decided in December to accept th New York offer. Before he made his decisio known to the New York people—and before any one in Philadelphia knew he was even consider ing such a move—he received an invitation t lunch with Trustee Peter Williams.

Williams told Groeschel that Clark wanted t find out whether Groeschel thought he coul work with Schwartz. Schwartz's term on th Board was terminating soon, and Clark wante to reappoint him if Groeschel thought workin relations would improve.

Groeschel told Williams that he didn't car whom Clark appointed since he was going bac to New York in any case. When Clark heard o this he called Groeschel in and attempted t persuade him to remain but Groeschel stuck t his decision.

In January, 1954, Mayor Clark had the task o appointing some new PGH trustees. Mrs. Reme had resigned in September 1953 for personal rea sons. Scattergood told Clark he did not desir reappointment. And Clark decided that h would not reappoint Schlanger. There was, finally, the problem of whether or not to reappoint Schwartz. Clark did not want to depart from his concept of having the trustees both independent and to some extent representative of the groups and classes in the city that turned to PGH for medical care. But he had seen the results of a completely independent Board.

To fail to reappoint Schwartz would cause some unpleasantness and would remove labor representation from the trustees. Clark also appreciated Schwartz's initiative and his dedication to PGH even though it led him to oppose affiliation. Nevertheless, the Mayor decided he would have to drop Schwartz. He called Schwartz into his office and told him that he was not sure whether Schwartz had been given a two or four year appointment. "What difference does this make?" replied Schwartz. "Let's assume that my appointment ran out a few minutes ago."

"O.K.," said Clark. "I'm not going to reappoint you."

Clark had hoped he could replace Schwartz with a representative of labor, but after Schwartz's severance was reported in the papers, the directors of labor's League for Political Education went on record as opposing vertical services at PGH. They voted to support the position of Joseph Schwartz and stated: "In view of the existing circumstances, the Board will not recommend AFL participation on the Board of Trustees." CIO officials joined the boycott.

By March 1954, Clark had appointed three new trustees, two of whom were personal friends who could be depended on not to fight City Hall. Filling the vacancies left by Scattergood and Schlanger were Recreation Commissioner Frederick R. Mann and John M. Patterson, an unofficial member of the Mayor's circle of advisers. Mrs. Townsend Munson replaced Mrs. Remer. Peter Williams, whom Clark had appointed to fill the vacancy created by the resignation of George Clark, was made Chairman of the Board. Of the original trustees, only Tanner Duckrey remained.

When the Mayor announced his appointments, the *Daily News* ran a final editorial on this phase of the PGH controversy. The Mayor, the *Daily News* complained, was packing the Board of Trustees so he could steal the city hospital.

1958 Postscripts

BY 1958, Joseph Clark had been succeeded as Democratic Mayor of Philadelphia by Richardson Dilworth, who retained Dixon as his Commissioner of Health. Dr. Mussells, who had succeeded Groeschel, was Executive Director of PGH, and J. Peter Williams was still Chairman of the Board of Trustees. (Dr. Winifred Stewart was dead.) Dixon and Williams, after consultation with Dilworth and with his support, had devoted more than a year to working out a new plan for medical school affiliation, this time with a unanimous Board of Trustees. (Tanner Duckrey, too, had died.) On March 2, 1958, Dilworth issued a statement to the press announcing the new plan under which the University of Pennsylvania and Temple University medical schools would assume exclusive control of medical student training at PGH. This new arrangement was termed by the Mayor "absolutely essential to improve the medical care at our city hospital." The *Evening Bulletin* quoted Dilworth as saying that the change "means that for the first time there will be a formal affiliation between Philadelphia General Hospital and the medical schools which provide services at the city hospital." The Mayor said that a special committee of the trustees had found the condition of medical services at PGH under the five-school arrangement "unstable because of competing interests." He also noted "wide variations in the quantity and quality of the services provided." The PGH trustees, Dilworth was quoted as saying, were convinced that under the five-school arrangement they lacked sufficient control of patient-care policy and that the hospital was not sufficiently staffed with full-time doctors to enable its Executive Director to exercise responsible control.

The Mayor's announcement came as a surprise to the PGH Medical Board, which went on record the next day as being opposed to the affiliation plan. Division chiefs were asked to hold meetings with their staffs to inform them of the sweeping nature of the new scheme.

By March 8, the medical staff had begun a steady drum fire of press statements in opposition. The *Inquirer* reported on March 8 that the staff was charging that patients at PGH would become "human guinea pigs" under the new arrangement; it said a "storm of protest" was sweeping PGH, and that more than ninety percent of the 500 doctors and interns were against the change. The *Inquirer* also quoted an unnamed trustee as reportedly telling the medical staff: "We made this move without consulting you because we knew you would object."

On March 15 the *Inquirer* gave prominent treatment to a report that PGH staff members had charged that Commissioner Dixon had violated principles of "conflict of interest" because he was also "on the payroll of the University of Pennsylvania." The newspaper quoted an unnamed medical staff member as saying that "Dr. Dixon is leading the undercover move at City Hall to negotiate the give-away." It also reported that a group of medical staff members had suggested that Dixon had persuaded Dilworth to support the new plan without advising him that the medical staff opposed the move or that "involuntary medical experimentation will become the standard practice with PGH patients."

On March 17 the boards of Hahnemann, Jefferson, and Women's Medical Colleges announced that they would seek reconsideration of the new plan which would exclude them from participating in patient care and student training at PGH. The same day at a mass meeting c medical staff members at PGH, a resolution wa adopted, 71 to 18, asking the Mayor to reque the trustees to cancel immediately the arrang ment with the University of Pennsylvania an Temple University.

In a letter to the editor of the *Inquirer* o March 20 Mayor Dilworth defended Commi sioner Dixon, the trustees, and the new arrang ment. "The decision," he said, was "not that c any one person. The original recommendatio was made by a subcommittee of the Board c Trustees of PGH after full consultation wit Dr. Mussells, the very fine Executive Director c PGH, and Doctor Dixon. It was then adopte unanimously by the Board of Trustees after thorough investigation of the facts. I was pe sonally present at the meeting of the board wher this decision was made."

In another statement, Dilworth also attacke those on the medical staff who had supporte the resolution against the new plan:

> It is high time the staff learned that the PGH is not their private preserve. . . .
>
> Unfortunately, the staff is still under the thumb of a small clique of political doctors who wormed their way into the hospital a good many years ago and virtually took it over.
>
> They have since taken the attitude that it is their private sanitorium. . . . They got away with this for a good many years because in the old days, any time the Board attempted to interfere with their possession of the hospital they threatened to expose some of the political shenannigans going on at PGH, to which they were willing to close their eyes as long as they had their way. . . . I have no doubt that if this little group of doctors had its way there would be no trustees.

The controversy continued through April, bu the Mayor, Dixon, and the trustees held thei position, and as 1958 ended the new plan of a filiation was going into effect.

Hanover Builds a High School

Louis Menand III

Introduction

THIS IS THE STORY of how the citizens of the small town of Hanover, New Hampshire dealt with the need for a larger high school. It is a case study of citizens coping with a problem that faced many United States cities and towns at mid-century: how to provide school facilities for the swelling number of children—facilities that met rising public standards of education but were at the same time within the means of the local taxpayers.

Hanover was too small to have any professional, elected office-holders. For governmental matters it relied primarily on citizen boards and committees whose decisions were subject to debate and ratification at annual town meetings and school district meetings. In a community where almost everybody knew almost everybody else—and where it was easy to get an intimate neighborly opinion about a person one didn't know—the people who served on the School Board or on the Town Finance Committee or as selectmen were not regarded—nor did they see themselves—as anything more than citizens taking a turn at the offices that had to be filled if there was to be any local government at all.

Hanover would have interested Jean Jacques Rousseau, because its annual Town, Precinct, and School District meetings gave the whole body of citizens an *opportunity* to participate in making the final decisions on governmental matters and because the town was sufficiently small so that these governmental matters had been discussed privately among townspeople before the annual meetings were held. But even Rousseau, who believed that this type of direct expression of community will was the best of all governmental arrangements, would have quailed at the prospect of 2,000 adults undertaking to decide not only whether a new high school should be built but all the major technical details including cost, classroom space, location, curriculum, population projections, and what kind of gymnasium and domestic science facilities to construct.

Actually, the Hanover high school decision started to be made—as many public decisions were in Hanover—without a great deal of public discussion. The initiative was taken by the elected School Board which appointed an advisory citizens committee to formulate detailed plans and present these, with price tags, to the citizens. When opposition developed, a large number of people in the community became actively involved in the issue, with some citizens making independent investigations to support or oppose the School Board's presentations. With one transient exception, there was a strong inclination on the part of the interested public to make its own choice rather than to leave the matter to experts. As community controversy intensified, more aspects of the high school plans and more questions of educational policy were exposed to public discussion, and the range of choices seemed to widen. The road to community decision was tortuous. There were detours as new possibilities were advanced and debated. There were horseshoe turns as citizens or board members changed their minds and switched to new plans. A choice was finally approved at a school district meeting, leaving the question of whether this lengthy decision-making process had been successful in terms of achieving broad public participation and in terms of yielding a conclusion that met, in good time, the realities of Hanover's educational problem.

A Small Community

Hanover is a small community, the home of Dartmouth College and of the Hitchcock Clinic and Hospital which provide medical service for a large region of northern New England. In 1954 its population was about 4,100, excluding the 3,000 students in the College and three associated graduate schools. The town's growth had been slow and without striking impact upon its institutions and resources. In 1920 Hanover had 2,200 people; in 1950, 3,800. For more than a

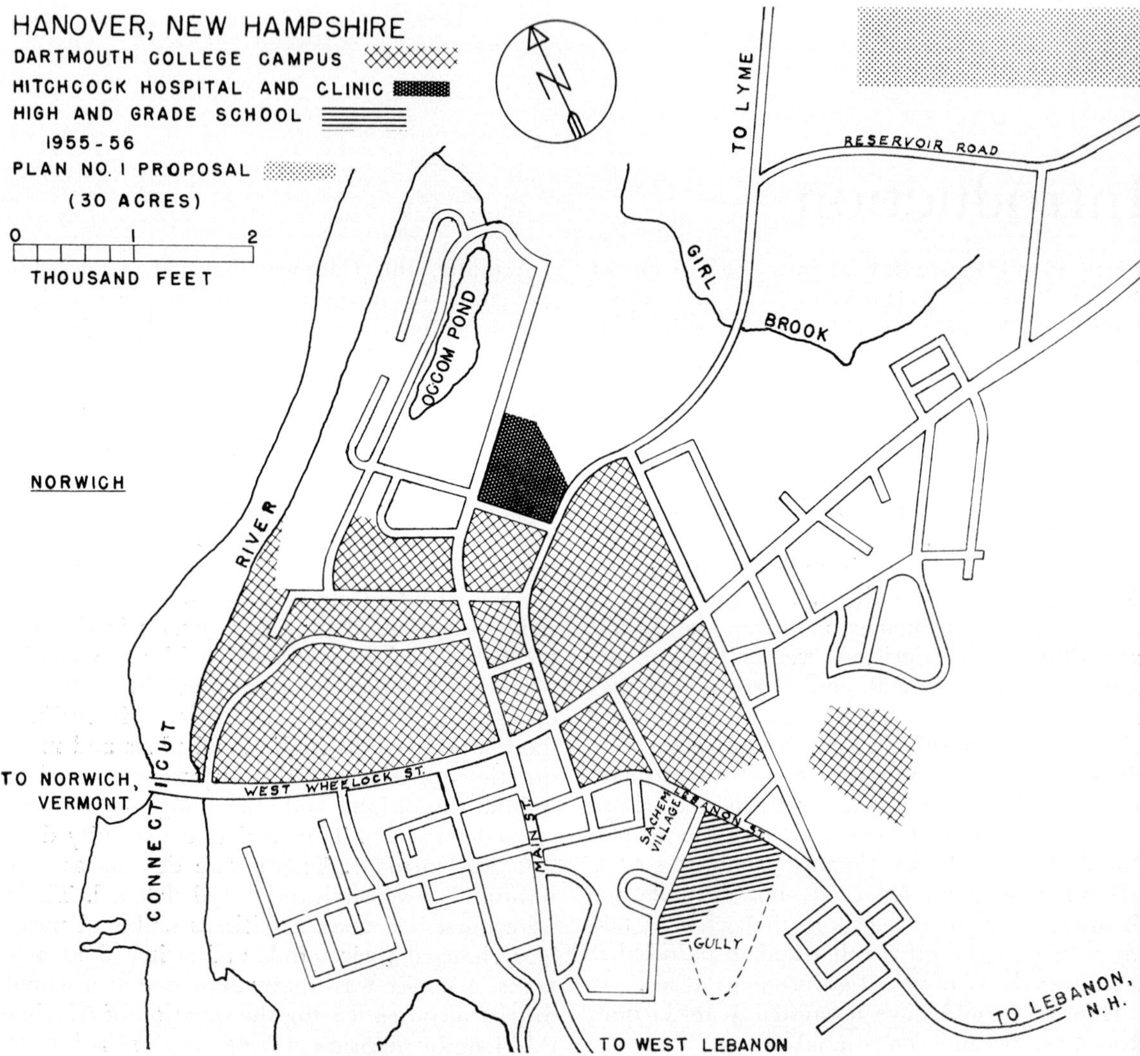

century the rate of growth had been far below that of the United States as a whole. Except for a construction firm, a winter sports equipment distributor, and a printing establishment, the only commercial activities were retail stores clustered within a short block and a half on or near Main Street.

The pattern of community affairs for generations had been set by the College and more recently also by the medical center. Only a few professors and doctors lived outside of Hanover. On the other hand, the majority of the nonprofessional employees of the College and Hospital made their homes in nearby towns where housing costs and taxes were lower. The majority of the 400 College faculty and administratio officials owned their own homes in Hanover, bu a substantial proportion, principally younger o newer members of the group, occupied College owned rental properties. Only about 100 resi dents of Hanover were employed outside of th town. These included a few successful merchant from neighboring localities who had been at tracted by the social opportunities of a colleg community.

Hanover tastes, including aspirations for it public schools, were high. In its own region o New England it enjoyed the reputation of pos sessing unusual resources and advantages. Ye the community was far from wealthy. While few people of means, including some alumni of the College, had settled in the town, life was geared to the more modest incomes of the College families and the Main Street merchants.

Hanover was governed by the traditional town form peculiar to New England. The three officers of the town government, the selectmen, were elected for staggered three-year terms at Town Meeting in March. They had general administrative duties, assessed property, and levied taxes approved at the Town Meeting. Hanover, under an option open to it, had also created a precinct, a village within the town, whose elected commissioners, three in number, administered certain highway, fire, and other functions in the heart of what might be called "downtown" Hanover. The governing authority of the precinct was the Precinct Meeting, held annually a few days after Town Meeting, and usually less well-attended. There were, then, two governing bodies for the community of Hanover, the Town Meeting and the Precinct Meeting. Usually elections of town selectmen and precinct commissioners, for which nomination was made in open meeting, were uncontested, selection of the nominees being made by informal arrangements before the meetings.

In addition to these two governing units there was a third unit, the School District, which was coterminous with the town. Its nine School Board members were elected for staggered three-year terms at the School District Meeting held annually in March during the same week as the Town and Precinct meetings. Interest in school affairs was usually much higher than in town or precinct issues. The school budget was more than twice that of the other two units combined. Candidates for the School Board declared in advance, and vacancies usually were contested. The executive officer of the school system was the Superintendent, who served not only the Hanover School District but also three smaller districts in neighboring towns, the four districts comprising a supervisory union. Actually the Superintendent put in most of his time on Hanover business, and for many years the incumbent had resided in Hanover.

Role of Dartmouth College

Hanover had little town-gown cleavage. While it was customary for members of College families to serve as town selectmen, precinct commissioners, and School Board members, they were joined in these responsibilities (and in the leadership of the local churches and other community enterprises) by merchants, doctors, farmers, and their wives. Inevitably, however, the interests and actions of the College played an important and at times a dominant role. The College, for example, owned and operated the only hotel. Even excluding the campus proper, it was the largest holder of real estate. Along with the precinct it was the principal stockholder of the waterworks, a private corporation, and it still owned several of the sewers in the community. While College administrators and town fathers usually worked well together, the relationship was not entirely without tension. The same was true of relations between the Hospital and town officials. Many residents believed that the two institutions, largely tax exempt, should make a greater direct contribution to the costs of providing public services, even though the College in 1955 carried about eighteen percent of the total town tax load.

Partisan politics played a relatively small part in the management of local public affairs. Candidates for local office were elected on a nonparty ballot. Traditionally the community had been overwhelmingly Republican, but it regularly voted for the more progressive of Republican candidates when given the opportunity in primaries. Recently the Democratic Party had come to life under the leadership of several younger members of the College faculty. School matters, however, were completely divorced from party politics. While some of the individuals in the high school controversy were active in their respective parties, they took no part as party leaders.

Of Hanover's total voter registration of 2,400, roughly 900 were professionals or administrators (or their wives) associated with the College or the medical center. Over the years Hanover had drawn on its educated citizens to think through its educational, social, and governmental problems. Yet, by and large, the community was open and unrigid. Geographically, it was small and compact. The post office, motion picture theater, bank, and bookstore were within a short walk of each other, bringing people into frequent face-to-face meetings. Families came together at school, church, summer swimming pond, and winter ski slope. Any member of the College faculty of more than a few years standing was known to the Main Street merchants; usually relationships were on a first-name basis. There were some recognizable groups which met each other on easy and friendly terms. Newcomers were somewhat apart from long-time residents. Professors were somewhat apart from the doctors and merchants, but not so far apart that they did not speak, and many were on close terms. The elderly and retired people tended to keep to themselves. But there were no highly structured neighborhoods; rather there were status groups or friendship groups that one came to know. Practically all of the principals in this story, as in other public affairs in Hanover, were personally acquainted with each other, many of them intimately. They had mutually circulating families and knew each other well enough to have definite expectations of each others' attitudes and responses on social matters. Usually these expectations were accurate, but the need to arrive at a community decision on high school improvements led to disagreements that, temporarily at least, ruffled social relationships and at times caused pain and surprise when expectations of how friends would react were disappointed.

Enrollment Pressure

By 1954 the Hanover high school was badly crowded. The small laboratories were inadequate, the library practically nonexistent, the gymnasium outdated and too small. The cafeteria facilities doubled as home economics class space. The extent of future increases in the Hanover school population was uncertain in 1954, although a study made in 1949 projected an increase which would make existing facilities outmoded by 1960 and totally inadequate by 1965.

The high school building had been completed in 1935 when the population of Hanover itself was about 3,200. Pupil enrollment in 1935-36 had been 348 for grades seven to twelve. By 1950 it had risen to 357 and by 1955 to 413. The school authorities declared that 400 was the building's top capacity. There was a feeling current in Hanover that the high school building was too small. What had to be determined was what kind of facilities to construct and where.

The 1950 Elementary Program

In 1950 Hanover had voted $285,000 for an expanded elementary school after a campaign led by the then School Board Chairman James Cusick, a Dartmouth professor. In 1949 Cusick had alerted the rest of the Board to the number of war babies reaching school age. An advisory committee had been set up, consisting of Cusick, the Superintendent of Schools, the Principal of the Hanover grade school, and three other townspeople. Cusick had also organized an independent citizens group to keep up a constant flow of public discussion. Cusick himself had been an untiring speaker at numerous local social and service club meetings.

In 1950 cost-conscious citizens had looked to a report from the Town Finance Committee for guidance on how to vote on the Advisory Committee's expansion proposals for the elementary school. The Hanover Finance Committee was modeled after so-called budget committees authorized for towns by New Hampshire law. These non-partisan committees were designed to give general citizen control over the expenditures of town, precinct, and school tax monies, and they scrutinized in closed sessions the annual budgets of all three bodies. The budget committees were composed of the finance members of the town selectmen, the precinct commissioners, and the School Board. Six additional persons were appointed by the Town Moderator to represent the citizens, making a Finance Committee of nine. In some towns the budget committee had to give its formal approval of proposed budgets before they could be presented to the voters in annual meetings, but in Hanover the Finance Committee was purely advisory, and its reports on the three budgets, while important to the citizens, were not in any sense binding. Usually the Committee's advice was followed; its report became an important piece of information the people used in making up their minds.

Before the annual School Meeting in 1950 the Finance Committee had been given the school budget with the proposed expansion figures included. The School Board had been represented on the Hanover Finance Committee by John Stebbins, then chairman of the School Board's finance committee. The Hanover Finance Committee had been in an economy mood. Its members were inclined to think that the expansion proposals were too elaborate and costly and that twelve additional elementary classrooms were too many. They had suggested the deletion of two. As they proceeded one night to change the architects' drawings, a member from the School Board's finance committee had phoned Cusick who had hurried from bed to rescue the two classrooms. Cusick had been able to save the essential character of his building plans, but had had to agree to the elimination of two classrooms.

The new elementary school plans, as modified, had been approved at the annual School District Meeting in March 1950 by better than a two to one vote.

The Holyoke Studies

By 1952 it was apparent that the grade school expansion was only the beginning of the School Board's planning. The high school had been neglected consciously in 1950, although it was generally realized and often noted that "something must be done about it." But who was to do it? How much would it cost? What kind of instruction should be included? When must a new building be ready? These were questions that plagued the new chairman of the School Board, John Stebbins, when he assumed office in 1952. Stebbins had had four years' service on the School Board. A midwesterner, he had attended Princeton University and Yale Law School, but he had settled in Hanover following his marriage to the daughter of a much-respected Main Street merchant. Sociable but taciturn, Stebbins practiced law in the nearby manufacturing town of Lebanon in association with U. S. Senator Norris Cotton. His four children attended the Hanover schools.

As he reviewed his experience with the Cusick elementary school expansion campaign, Stebbins was struck with the heavy burden Cusick himself had carried,[1] and he came to the conclusion that as many persons as possible should be associated with planning for the high school. Stebbins determined he would take the initiative, but he did not want to be the central figure. For one thing, he did not believe that the Board chairman should become heavily involved in public debate on controversial school building issues. For another, planning the high school curriculum was bound to be more complicated than the elementary school work of 1950.

Stebbins adopted the assumption of the Cusick committee report that *"a school building should be built around a well-thought-out educational program, rather than that a hastily-conceived building should come first, and the vital activities of education forced into it afterward."* With the advice of Professor A. O. Davidson, an educational consultant who taught education at Dartmouth, Stebbins proposed starting with a study of the curriculum by the citizens of the community. Davidson's experience had led him to believe strongly in committing a large part of the community to planning for future education programs. The final decision would rest with the Board, of course, but citizen participation in discussion and in drawing up reports, Davidson felt, was an invaluable way of enrolling large numbers of persons in the project.

The Board was able to initiate the kind of curriculum study it wanted. In May 1952 it enlisted the services of John Holyoke, a well-known physician attached to the Hospital Clinic. In addition to himself, Holyoke's committee consisted of six persons, including a member of the School Board, the Principal of the high school, and the Superintendent of Schools, who had headed the curriculum study for the elementary school with success.

The composition of the Holyoke Committee reflected the fact that in Hanover it had been customary for the medical, merchant, and College families to provide leadership and to serve on the various boards and committees that dealt with community matters. They set the tone, and in a sense they ran the town, subject to formal or informal expressions of disapproval from the entire community. It had been this way for many years. Much of what was done was said to be done for the common good, and there was rarely organized opposition to challenge this assumption.

[1] Cusick retired from the Board in 1953.

The terms of reference for Holyoke's committee were broad enough to warrant subcommittees on health, vocational guidance, industrial arts, home economics, vocational education, agricultural education, extracurricular activities, practical life problems, creative arts, the library, and audiovisual aids. Over 100 persons became involved.

The studies of the separate subcommittees were ready for discussion by October 1953, and during the fall and winter several open meetings were held at which Holyoke, along with the various members of his committee, explained the importance of the studies and answered questions. Community interest in the report was high, and copies of the studies were made available at the local bookstore, a spot visited daily by many to pick up the Boston or New York newspapers. On March 15, 1954, almost two years after it had been appointed, the Holyoke Committee submitted its final report to the School Board. As became apparent later, however, the committee itself did not digest the separate topical reports, nor did it attempt to relate them to each other or to establish priorities. It did not produce a concise statement of educational aims. Indeed, the Holyoke Committee disbanded without producing a final written report; the separate subcommittee studies remained as the sole documentation of its labors.

Masland and the BAC

WITH THE HOLYOKE studies in hand, the School Board decided to begin the preliminary negotiations with the community on the high school building itself. At the annual School District Meeting of March 1954, Stebbins secured authorization for a Building Advisory Committee to be supported by an appropriation of $1,500. On March 30, 1954 the Board met with Dr. Holyoke to draw up a list of building needs stemming from his committee's studies. It was at this meeting that the Holyoke studies were for the first time translated into building requirements. These were:

1. Classroom facilities to provide adequate space to service the present curriculum. This must include repairs to the present high school building.
2. Space for an adequate guidance program.
3. Enlarged shop facilities.
4. An adequate cafeteria and kitchen; space for a health program.
5. An adequate gymnasium and locker-room facilities.
6. Provision for audiovisual facilities; for music; and for speech.

The understanding reached at the March 30 meeting was the Board's basis for subsequent planning of the school building. Soon thereafter, Dr. Holyoke accepted an appointment in the Pacific Northwest.

In April and May, Stebbins and the Board pored over names of individuals who might head the Building Advisory Committee (BAC). The Board was looking for a "cross section" limited to professionals, merchants, and housewives. Stebbins decided not to include himself on the Building Advisory Committee, feeling that such a committee should work independently of the Board.

Unanimous choice for the chairmanship was John W. Masland of the Government Department at Dartmouth College. Masland accepted with hesitation. He insisted on making certain conditions. He was working on a research project which he was loath to slight, and he asked if he could set a deadline of January 1, 1955 as his reporting date, with the presumption that after that he would be freed from responsibility for plans presented to the Board. Masland also agreed to the slate of names that had been drawn up for his committee. Thus, as constituted by the Board, the committee, in addition to the chairman, included a Main Street merchant and a proprietor of a small store and service station, both of whom had grown up in Hanover and attended the local schools; a physician attached to the Clinic; a woman prominent in community affairs; and one member of the School Board. The School Superintendent and the High School Principal also were named as members.

Masland had moved to Hanover in 1946 after having served in the federal government and at Stanford University. He was the father of four school-age children and a property owner. Like Stebbins, he had come from another area but had married a Hanover girl, the daughter of an administrative officer of the College who himself had at one time been active in town government. The previous winter Masland had been asked by the School Board to make a study of school organization, following the illness of the subcommittee chairman who had been charged with this task. This had been Masland's first direct association with school or other public affairs, and the task had been accomplished quickly and without public notice. Masland was chosen for the chairmanship of the BAC in part because he counted as a neutral on school matters in the minds of the community and in part because he had a reputation among his friends for organizing ability and for delivering on any assignment he undertook.

The Cost Limit

On June 1 the Board met with Masland and the members of the BAC. Stebbins outlined the job facing the committee, noting the six categories of needs that had been developed by the Board and Dr. Holyoke in March. Stebbins did not give the BAC written terms of reference; he relied instead on an oral discussion. He also spent a few minutes explaining the financial status of the School District. As of 1950 New Hampshire ranked forty-seventh among the 48 states in per capita state expenditures for local school districts. What state aid was available to local school districts was based on an ability-to-pay theory, which meant that towns like Hanover (with fairly sound property tax resources in relation to the number of pupils) got little from Concord.

Under New Hampshire law the borrowing capacity of a local school district was set at five percent of its assessed valuation, less veterans' exemptions. Thus, on its current assessment, Hanover could borrow about $325,000 for new construction.

The prevailing notion of BAC members at the end of the meeting with Stebbins was that their mission was to plan a new high school building that cost no more than $325,000 but that achieved the six priorities abstracted from the Holyoke report. It was agreed that the report should be submitted to the School Board by December.

Masland left the meeting with the impression that his responsibilities would end with submission of the final report. Stebbins, on the other hand, felt the Masland committee would probably help sell the product to the town at the 1955 School District Meeting. The other members of the BAC were equally divided between viewing their job as a planning operation, and as a planning *and* selling task.

Masland felt he had a big job to pull together the many strands of thought in the Holyoke studies and still come up with a meaningful building report. He soon sought out Cusick who, on the basis of his elementary school planning experience, asked questions about the sharing of responsibilities between the BAC and the Board which Masland could not answer. On the public relations side, Cusick urged that citizen meetings be organized soon to get the selling campaign started. He advised Masland to be prepared to meet the objections of economy-minded citizens, and recommended early consultations with the Town Finance Committee to forestall what had happened to the elementary school plans in 1950. In general, Cusick urged Masland to assume the leadership responsibilities he, Cusick, had assumed in 1949-50.

It was not until August 17 that Masland was able to convene a preliminary meeting of the Building Advisory Committee. By this time he began to perceive a lack of continuity between the Holyoke curriculum studies and the responsibilities of the BAC. No member of the Holyoke Committee was included in the BAC. In addition, William Bragner, the new High School Principal, had just arrived in town. The superintendency also had been vacated recently, and the new Superintendent would not reach Hanover until October.

For the August meeting Masland prepared a written statement of the six priorities outlined by the School Board at the joint meeting on June 1. This list, it will be recalled, was headed by adequate classrooms and space for a guidance program. Next came the shop, the cafeteria and health program, and the gymnasium. Audio-visual facilities, music, and speech came last.

At its first meeting the BAC decided (1) to ask the four architectural firms practicing in Hanover to appear before the BAC early in September, and (2) to inquire about the leadership and organization of the Town Finance Committee.

The BAC met three times in September to discuss the priorities of the Holyoke report, to set up a work schedule, and to hear presentations from the three local architectural firms who desired to compete. At the third September meeting Masland took what he called a "sense of the meeting" and announced that Hudson and Ingram had been chosen—the same firm that had designed the old schools.

How Much to Spend?

In its early discussions the BAC discovered a gap between the priority needs listed by the School Board and the $325,000 expense limit. BAC members had been told by the Board that there was a legal possibility that the School District could borrow up to eight percent of its assessed valuation under certain circumstances, but the BAC had understood that it should plan within the regular five percent limit. Masland and his colleagues concluded, therefore, that the Board would have to eliminate some of the priorities or exceed the five percent limit.

The degree to which $325,000 could cover the priority items depended not only on the amount of facilities desired but also on the number of children expected in the classrooms as well as in the gymnasium. The BAC reviewed the school population study of 1950, but it decided it needed its own study for the high school. Mrs. Margaret Sperry, a member of the committee, was assigned the task of studying the population problem and reporting as soon as possible. She co-opted Mrs. Rose Mather, not on the BAC, as co-worker. The two ladies interviewed College and Hospital officials on anticipated growth of those institutions. Their researches extended over much of the working life of the Masland committee, a fact which later led Mrs. Mather to note plaintively that her figures were used to justify decisions rather than as aids in making decisions.

In its meetings in September and October, the BAC worked with tentative population figures extracted from Cusick's 1950 study. Masland asked the Principal for an estimate of future classroom needs and was told that nine or ten new classrooms would be required. If this estimate were correct, the additional classrooms would take up a large part of the money available.

A New Gymnasium?

On September 28 the BAC surveyed the existing high school in company with the architects. All members came away convinced that either a formidable job of alteration would have to be done or an entirely separate high school would have to be built. Even if a new school were erected, the old building would require considerable repair.

The gymnasium presented a major problem. A gym adequate for both boys and girls, with proper locker-room facilities, would mean a totally new gym structure either in a new high school or attached to the present building. This would also mean a considerable financial outlay, which, coupled with the classrooms needed, would probably far exceed the budget limits given to the BAC.

The visit to the high school highlighted another problem. Back in 1953, Masland had prepared for the Holyoke study a report on the organization of the schools. After study and consultations with the officials of the State Department of Education, Masland had recommended that Hanover retain the so-called six-six arrangement with the elementary school including grades one to six and the high school grades six through twelve. Masland thought Hanover could not afford and would not require a separate junior high school and the six-three-three organization. Masland had not heard whether his report had been accepted by the School Board, but he now operated on the assumption that the BAC should consider the six-six organization as Board policy. This assumption was not questioned by the other members of the BAC.

During October the BAC discussed the population, organization, and gymnasium problems. On October 19, Hudson and Ingram presented preliminary plans for building additions to the present high school within the $325,000 figure. They used the population estimates from the

1950 Cusick report updated by the High School Principal's estimates, since Mrs. Sperry and Mrs. Mather were still collecting data. The preliminary suggestions of the architects convinced the BAC that it would be impossible to fulfill the six-point Holyoke priorities within the budget limit that the School Board had set. Nevertheless, the architects were instructed to prepare a plan which would incorporate all of the Holyoke recommendations, including a new gymnasium.

A New Superintendent

In October a new Superintendent of Schools joined the BAC. The Superintendent who had lived with Cusick through the elementary school campaign of 1950 had resigned during the summer of 1954. The new Superintendent, Arthur Pierce, had long association with schools in New England and was a former Dartmouth student. He came to Hanover directly from a tour of duty with the Air Force as a consultant on manpower training. Pierce arrived to find the BAC developing its new plans. He became concerned at the inadequate preparation of data on the meaning of the Holyoke report and on the number of classrooms needed. He prepared a two-page brief of the Holyoke report and a statistical breakdown of the use of classrooms based on existing and projected enrollments. His conclusion from these data was that nine classrooms would be needed in addition to the other special-purpose areas. Pierce was impressed with the Holyoke studies and assumed that the community understood their meaning and generally accepted their findings, particularly those advocating new facilities for shop and for physical education.

The BAC Seeks a Higher Limit

The architects' new plans demonstrated that inclusion of the gymnasium was not possible within the $325,000 figure set by the five percent limit. What to do? For several weeks BAC members examined alternative plans. Then one of the members, Dr. John Milne, expressed vigorously his conclusion that the gymnasium should not be dropped. The community itself should be given the opportunity to determine whether it wanted the gym. Dr. Milne urged the BAC to ask the School Board for authorization to go to the full eight percent limit or $600,000. This the BAC agreed to do. Masland called Stebbins and asked for a joint meeting.

When the BAC met with the Board on November 16, Masland reviewed his committee's deliberations and then passed out a mimeographed statement listing various alternatives along with Hudson and Ingram's cost estimates. The BAC had concluded, Masland said, that the Board should be informed of all the facts and asked to make the choice. The BAC wanted instructions, but its members made clear their hope that the higher figure would be authorized.

The members of the Board were shocked. The BAC was asking for 100 percent more money. Board members reserved decision. Masland felt somewhat impatient with the Board at this point. He felt it might have given the Holyoke studies more thought, particularly in relation to the $325,000 limit. Had the Board itself thought this matter through it could have spared the BAC the agony of three months of struggle against an impossibly low cost limit.

Several days later Superintendent Pierce informed Masland that the Board had thought long and hard about the increased figure and had given its approval for the BAC to go ahead and plan with a $600,000 limit. Masland instructed the architects to proceed. On November 23, the Board, the BAC, and the architects met with Paul Farnum from the New Hampshire Department of Education. The architects' sketches were examined. State laws of financing were discussed, and Farnum said nothing to the group that was discouraging.

The members of the BAC now felt that they were heading into the home stretch. Building plans, providing for all of the requirements set forth by the Board five months before, were now in the making. The next task, presenting the final recommendations to the Board and the community, was almost at hand.

On November 30 the BAC spent most of its meeting discussing public relations. Mrs. Katherine Larmon, member of both the Board and the BAC, was to act as go-between for the two groups. However, it was agreed that no public relations campaign could take place until the School Board approved whatever plan the BAC proposed and until there had been an opportunity to meet with the Town Finance Committee.

The Board Approves

During early December the architects worked with the BAC in refining the plans. By the end of December the BAC was ready to report, and on December 28 the School Board gave its approval to the architectural drawings and cost estimates as working plans. The plans were in two parts. The first part, costing $40,000, involved replacement of the roof and the boiler plant of the existing high school building. The second was the new building program. It included: a new classroom addition to be used for the junior high grades costing $245,000; a new gymnasium costing $225,000; and additional alterations to the old building and equipment costing $135,000. With an extra amount for new roads, landscaping, and the like, and for a contingency fund, the new program came to about $660,000. Adding the $40,000 for the immediately needed roof and boiler repairs, the total cost to the community would be about $700,000.

A legal obstacle had to be hurdled before the School District could go beyond the five percent debt limit, which the plans certainly did. The special provision in the state law, under which a school district could petition the Governor for permission to borrow up to eight percent of its assessed valuation, was due to expire on December 31. On January 3 Chairman Stebbins phoned one of the state representatives from Hanover, Dr. David J. Bradley, to ask if he would file a bill in the Legislature giving Hanover permission to borrow up to eight percent. Bradley answered that he would be glad to, and he subsequently did file a bill which was ultimately passed.

An Opposition Forms

EARLY IN JANUARY, Masland and Mrs. Larmon worked to ready the BAC's report for distribution at a public meeting sponsored by the Parent Teachers Association on January 19. It was assumed that the annual School District Meeting would take place during the middle of March and that the School Board and the BAC had until then to prepare the community for the vote.

Masland had agreed to serve until the BAC report had been filed. He told Stebbins that he wanted to finish up by the end of January. But Stebbins was vague about releasing Masland from his duty, and the upshot was that Masland found himself committed to seeing through the selling phase that would end, it was expected, at the March school meeting.

Members of both the School Board and the BAC were concerned about the possible influence of the Town Finance Committee. Masland, recalling Cusick's advice, looked upon the Finance Committee as a source of trouble. He feared that the interest in economy of certain of the members would overshadow their possible concern for educational needs. He had hoped, therefore, to have preliminary conversations with the Committee during the autumn, but he had found that it had not yet organized itself. With time pressing, nothing more was done until January, when Jack Manchester, a successful local merchant who was chairman of the School Board's finance committee, called the other members of the Town Finance Committee, of which he also was a member. Manchester was able to set January 10 as the date for the hearing. It would be closed to the public; Finance Committee hearings traditionally were.

Among the nine members of the Finance Committee was John Meck, Treasurer of Dartmouth College, the chief College official concerned with relations between Dartmouth and the town. Masland phoned Meck before the Finance Committee meeting to explain why he had been unable to discuss the Building Advisory Committee proposals with College officials privately in advance.

The BAC presented its proposals to the Finance Committee aided by charts, drawings, tables on population trends, plans for the additions, and figures on the costs of the additions.

The meeting went amicably. Meck asked if the BAC had considered the possible use of Sachem Village, a tract of land immediately adjacent to the high school property which was owned by the College and on which were temporary World War II housing units. Masland answered that Sachem Village had been discussed but that since it was now being used and since the BAC's plans did not call for the use of that land, the subject had been dropped. The meeting ended with the Finance Committee taking the proposed building budget under advisement.

A 'Leak' to One Newspaper

Three days before this meeting, a leak in the press had caused some flurry in the School Board and in the BAC. A reporter for the *Valley News,* the regional daily newspaper, had obtained a story on the BAC report from the architect. The architect discovered that he had violated secrecy in giving the story, and Masland attempted unsuccessfully to dissuade the newspaper from running it. He felt that it should not be publicized prior to the meeting with the Finance Committee. The same day, the assistant editor of the *Hanover Gazette,* the local weekly, called Masland and asked for an advance story. She was informed that no information would be given out before the Finance Committee meeting. Masland added that he would brief the *Gazette* before the public meeting on January 19. The coincidence of the leak to the *Valley News* and the refusal of an advance to the *Gazette* alienated at least one staff member of the latter. The *Valley News* was edited by two liberal Dartmouth graduates in their thirties. It had been started after World War II. The *Hanover Gazette,* on the other hand, was *the* established weekly paper in Hanover.

About 300 persons turned up for the PTA open meeting on January 19. Masland had charts with him and had prepared mimeographed statements on population, building needs, and costs which were distributed to the audience at intervals during his presentation. After he had outlined the program "with care and thoroughness," as the *Valley News* commented the following day, Masland turned the meeting over to Manchester who filled in the important details on costs. The *Valley News* reported, "The cost sheet came last and apparently left the local taxpayers so stunned [by the $700,000 figure] there were only two questions from a normally articulate crowd after an hour and a half of explanation." After the meeting, Board and BAC members alike commented to one another on the paucity of questions. Masland had anticipated a real grilling and was alarmed at the audience apathy. What did all of this mean? Why not more questions? Where were the usually loyal opinion leaders?

The *Valley News* editorial the next day commended the Board. It said the meeting was:

> . . . a fine example of the care and forethought which that town has devoted to public education. . . . The taxpayer-voter's responsibility to decide what expansion will be done at the high school is made easier to fulfill by the careful, orderly six-year period of study and preparation which have gone into the proposals. He may be sure that there are few, if any, aspects which have not been considered in drawing it up. . . .
>
> This chain of events shows promise of achieving completion with new construction *before*—as is often not the case—pupils are obliged to sit two in a seat or attend in shifts.

On February 2, at the weekly Rotary luncheon, Masland discussed the high school plans with one of the town's businessmen who was a member of the Finance Committee. His probing and slightly hostile questions on costs and on the need for a new and expensive gymnasium gave Masland some clue about the trend of local opinion. The questions raised by the businessman were being asked by others. In January the *Gazette* had carried an advance story on the January 19 open meeting under the headline "How Big—How Much." On February 3, the *Gazette* asked in its editorial column for advice as to what editorial stand the *Gazette* should take.

Criticism of the Gym

On February 8 and 14 the League of Women Voters scheduled sessions in several Hanover homes for discussion of the school plans. Masland and the BAC members looked forward to these meetings as a way of talking with opinion leaders in town.

The outcome of the LWV meetings was not anticipated. Although BAC members came armed with architects' drawings, they found themselves in the midst of debates not on building plans but on curriculum and educational programs. At one meeting, for example, the assistant editor of the *Gazette,* the wife of a College physicist, asked why a new quarter-million-dollar gymnasium was necessary? This line was picked up by Dr. David Bradley, the town's State Representative, who had agreed to introduce the bill authorizing borrowing up to the eight percent limit. Masland found himself arguing against Bradley's contention that the winter sports opportunities in Hanover minimized the need for an indoor physical education program. This and similar criticism of the recommendations for a shop during the four League meetings exposed BAC members to a kind of criticism for which they were not prepared. They felt that the shop and gymnasium were necessary to meet the priorities derived from the Holyoke studies which, it was assumed, had general community support. Even though the Holyoke priorities had never been formally stated, the School Board had approved them and the educational program they implied. The educational program, BAC members felt, was the School Board's responsibility, but yet they found that they had to defend the program if they wished to win support for their building proposals.

On February 15, the day after the second of the LWV meetings, the BAC recommended minor cuts in its plans to bring the total cost, including the separate repairs to the existing building, exactly within the eight percent debt limit set by the state. The cut for new construction, alterations, and equipment was from $660,000 to $600,000. The cut was made known at the next closed joint meeting of the Finance Committee with the BAC and the Board, which took place on February 18. To the surprise of the school representatives one Finance Committee member charged deception on the part of the Board for changing figures in the middle of the community discussion. This charge angered Stebbins, and was an indication of rising tension. Masland explained at length the reasons for cuts and denied any deception on the part of the BAC or on the part of the Board. Finance Committeeman Meck also commented on several matters, notably the extensive plans for a new gymnasium and the proposed cafeteria, citing information he had gathered in connection with the College's building studies. The meeting ended with the members of the Finance Committee revealing little enthusiasm for making an early recommendation to the community.

On February 17, an editorial in the *Gazette* questioned the need for a quarter-million-dollar high school gymnasium in a town the size of Hanover. Physical education, the editorial pronounced, could be taught in the fields and hills of the surrounding countryside, and, after all, baseball, football, hockey, skiing, track, tennis, and golf would have to be played outside a gymnasium.

The BAC had struggled with the question of the gym as far back as early September when it had been suggested that the gymnasium be offered as a separate package. This plan had been rejected because the other building plans were physically related to the gymnasium. The old gymnasium was to be made over into a new shop. In addition, the School Board itself had specifically approved the inclusion of the gymnasium plans in the proposal and had agreed that the entire addition should be presented to the community as one unit. But throughout February and March not only the *Gazette* writers but others in Hanover strongly criticized such an expensive addition to the school plant. Up to this time Masland and other BAC members had expected opposition on the grounds of cost. They were not prepared for the indirect attack on their plans by way of the school program. Least of all had they expected attacks from the younger professional families and League of Women Voter members, to whom they had looked for support. As the weeks passed citizen discussions increased in number and in intensity. The sides were slowly forming. There had not been a serious public difference in Hanover since 1948 when a heated discussion had occurred in a town meeting over a proposal to fly the United Nations flag in front of the Precinct Building.

An Uncertain Element

At the same time that the gymnasium and shop issues were being discussed, an additional and somewhat confusing element was thrown into the controversy. In December, Masland had learned from the Dean of the Faculty that a federal agency might locate in Hanover, but he had been advised that the possibility was too remote to consider. In a letter to the Sperry-Mather population study group, which was quoted in the BAC report made public in January, the Dean made no mention of this possibility. Mrs. Sperry noted in her report that the "effect of these [faculty retirement and replacement] changes on the future population of the high school, or of the grade school, is extremely difficult to estimate. We decided not to adjust our projections upward because of them, and to that extent our projections may be underestimates." Underestimates they turned out to be, for on March 3 the *Hanover Gazette* carried an announcement that the U. S. Army's Snow, Ice, Permafrost Research Establishment might locate in Hanover under Dartmouth College auspices but as a non-taxpaying federal agency. SIPRE, as the organization came to be known, was a research adjunct of the Army Engineers. The community reacted immediately to the possibility of the SIPRE installation. How many people would it bring with it? How many students would enroll in the Hanover schools? What about the validity of the Sperry-Mather population report? How adequate now was the estimate of nine classrooms?

By the time of the open meeting scheduled for March 9, sponsored by the PTA and established for the purpose of letting citizens question the BAC and the Board, there was a growing antagonism toward the plans as a whole. But no opposition leadership had emerged.

College Land?

The meeting opened with Masland once again explaining the plans. After his presentation, questions were raised from an audience of about 150 persons. Several dealt with the need for an expensive gymnasium. One asked whether Sachem Village, the College rental property adjacent to the high school, had been considered to augment the land on which the school buildings were situated. Board Chairman Stebbins replied that the School Board had not been offered the land by the College.

Two days later, on March 11, Meck wrote Stebbins saying that while it was true that the School Board had not been offered Sachem Village, the College had not been asked to offer it by the Board. He went on to say that within a year the College would know definitely what it wanted to do with the Sachem Village site. The best current guess was that it would *not* have a major place in the College's plans. In order not to upset the people living in the temporary housing on the Sachem site, Meck asked Stebbins to keep the contents of the letter confidential. Meck also revealed in a conversation with Stebbins and Masland that the College had employed a firm of consulting architects to assist in the preparation of a long range master development plan. Until this task was accomplished, the future of the Sachem site would remain uncertain.

On the same day Meck's assistant sent a memo to Stebbins outlining his estimates of the number of children SIPRE would bring to Hanover. This information came two days too late for use at the March 9 meeting. Although the SIPRE issue remained unsettled, the BAC concluded that the additional children could be handled within the plans that had been developed.

The Finance Committee Delays

The Finance Committee remained a focus of attention for Stebbins and Masland. At a joint meeting of the Finance Committee with the School Board and the BAC on March 22 Mrs. Ruth Colton, a member of the Finance Committee and wife of a College administrator, presented (1) a proposal for postponing consideration of the plans, (2) a proposal for a new committee to be appointed by the Board and (3) a proposal for holding a meeting in the fall after the community had been polled on the outstanding issues posed by the plans.

The Colton propositions were discussed, but the Chairman avoided bringing them to a vote. Other members of the Finance Committee (most of them heavily taxed property owners and businessmen) raised questions on program, layout, the gymnasium, and other matters, indicating a deep concern with costs. The long and at times heated meeting ended without an indication of what the Finance Committee would report. Toward the end of the meeting the Finance Committee sounded out the School Board on the desirability of postponing the annual School District Meeting (scheduled for April 12) to give the Finance Committee more time to discuss the proposals and to hold an open hearing with the community. Under state law the School District Meeting had to be held within a certain period, but there was no rule against holding part of the school meeting on April 12 and postponing action on the BAC plans until an adjourned meeting at a later date. It was agreed to hold the meeting as scheduled but to devote the last part of the meeting to an open discussion so the Finance Committee could sample community opinion. An adjourned school meeting on the high school plans would then be held on May 18.

Masland now told Stebbins that, with the final vote postponed until May 18, he could not serve much longer. He had been granted a leave of absence from teaching for the spring term and was anxious to get on with his research. But Stebbins, whose law practice limited the time he could devote to school matters, prevailed on Masland to continue. Masland did not want to leave Stebbins in the lurch. Also, despite his protests, Masland was intrigued with what he was doing.

On March 30, the BAC met to consider some criticism of the gymnasium, cafeteria, and other structural items made by Meck and by the College's business manager, who was an engineer. The latter two had been surprised, if not shocked, at the extravagant allowance of space per student in the cafeteria, many times the space in the College cafeteria. After consultation with the architects the BAC redesigned the gymnasium, reduced the size of the cafeteria, added two classrooms from the released space, and modified the part of the building addition facing the main thoroughfare to make it more attractive. These were technical changes but they did involve abandoning a basement under the gymnasium which had originally been devoted to a music room and other purposes.

The Gazette Questions

This action of the BAC was not announced for another few days, but on the following day, March 31, the *Gazette* carried two editorials on the BAC proposals.

On February 20, Masland had invited David Hewitt, the editor, and Mrs. Hull, his associate, to his office to talk about the building plans. This interview followed by three days an article in the *Gazette* which had asked why the community was not permitted to make a choice between two plans, with and without the enlarged gymnasium. Masland hoped to answer this query. Using the architect's drawings, he tried to explain why the complete plan was not separable in this manner. The published report of the interview in the next issue of the paper showed that the editors rejected his reasoning. Accordingly, Masland concluded that further approaches to the *Gazette* would be fruitless. Almost all the weekly's editorials were mildly hostile and raised the major questions that faced the Board and the citizens.

In a long editorial on March 31, the *Gazette* ticked off the various questions it felt had not been answered. It began:

> The "all-or-nothing" idea of the package plan makes it impossible to vote down any part as a unit without disapproving the whole plan. This the School District must decide. . . .
>
> The School District, as a voting body, never formally accepted the recommendations of the Holyoke Committee, therefore any plans based primarily on that committee's findings could very possibly be unacceptable to a majority of voters.

This editorial troubled Masland and Stebbins because much of the wording was similar to that in Mrs. Colton's proposals to the Finance Committee on March 22. They began to sense the formation of organized opposition. The reference in the second paragraph of the editorial suggested to the School Board that some individuals thought educational policy should be voted on by the School District. The *Gazette* confirmed this suspicion when it noted: "There is a real question in the minds of many people as to the educational policy and philosophy we are committing ourselves to in complete acceptance of the proposed expansion plans as outlined." It listed curriculum, cafeteria, scheduling, land use, population figures, teacher salaries, teacher consultation, community use of school building, and the division of the schools as items it thought needed public discussion.

Opposition from Bradley

A week or so later the BAC and School Board

were guests at an open meeting held in the high school auditorium. Masland felt this would be another opportunity to explain the proposals and answer questions. Up to now no real identification of the opponents of the BAC plans had been made. The annual town and precinct meetings had been held, and there had been no mention of the $640,000 school proposals. Hostility was in the air, but it was strangely ineluctable.

At the PTA meeting, Dr. David Bradley spoke for economy and against hasty approval of BAC proposals. With his speech Bradley became the leader of the opposition. His speech, in a sense, formalized the opposition and gave those who were doubtful a position to which they could attach themselves. Bradley asked several pointed questions on costs and related matters and announced that he would shortly make available alternate plans or proposals which would go a long way toward reducing the proposed costs of the addition. Masland sensed that Bradley was articulating the feelings of some younger College and medical faculty families who were concerned about school costs and who questioned the extension of the school program in physical education and non-college preparatory subjects such as woodwork shop. Masland felt that these latter subjects should be available for children who would not go on to college educations and for college-bound children who were interested in them.

Bradley was a relative newcomer to Hanover as a resident. A 1938 Dartmouth graduate, he had taken medical training and had served in the Navy during World War II as a medical officer. In 1946 he had participated in the atom bomb tests conducted at Bikini. Subsequently, while serving as a resident in surgery in San Francisco, he had written about this experience in a book, *No Place to Hide,* which soon became a national best seller. He then became deeply interested in the World Federalist movement and decided to give up medicine in order to devote all of his time to lecturing and writing. After several years of work with the United World Federalists, Bradley had moved to Hanover in 1952, buying a home in a short time and settling down to a career of writing and active interest in public affairs. In the summer of 1954 he had served on a state committee on educational matters and from this experience had become convinced of the need for a vigorous attack on the financial and other plights of the schools. In 1954 he had been elected one of Hanover's four representatives in the New Hampshire Legislature, polling the largest vote. Bradley was the father of five children, school age and younger.

In pursuit of his interest in schools, Bradley had placed in the Warrant for the Hanover Town Meeting in March of 1955 a proposal to take the sense of the meeting about the desirability of the state levying a sales tax in order to aid school districts. He had pleaded his cause eloquently in the Town Meeting, and his proposal had been voted on favorably.

Masland knew Bradley socially; the two families were close, and the children were often together. Mrs. Masland and Mrs. Bradley were, like Mrs. Stebbins, members of families that had deep roots in Hanover. Elizabeth Bradley was a member of a Manchester, New Hampshire family long prominent and respected in state and College affairs. Her father was a leading member of the New Hampshire Bar and an influential trustee of the College. Although Bradley and Masland began working at cross purposes on the school issue, there seemed to be no lessening of family ties. This was also true of the close relations between the Stebbins and the Bradleys. Nonetheless, Masland was surprised and somewhat piqued to see that Bradley was opposing the plans. He had expected hostility to the school plans to come from the local merchants and the elderly citizens who had no children, not from young College families with whom the Bradleys associated socially.

Standing up at the PTA meeting, Bradley spoke for economy and objected to Masland's statement that Hanover was not large enough to justify the expense of a separate junior high school on Sachem Village property. Bradley noted that low-cost grade school units were being built in the state in the range of from $250,000 to $300,000. In the words of the *Gazette* news story, he "summarized the doubts and hesitations of people who dislike adding two or three wings to a 20-year old building in confined space."

Another speaker who criticized the plans was Mrs. Colton, the member of the Finance Committee who already had questioned the building recommendations in private sessions. She questioned the taxpayer's ability to pay for the school expansion. As noted above, Mrs. Colton's husband was on the College administrative staff. She herself was active in community and church affairs. The Coltons had recently sold their home outside of the precinct but in the town, and had bought property directly in the precinct where taxes were somewhat higher. The Coltons never took a stand against expansion but were concerned with value for dollars spent. They represented the articulate citizens who questioned their own ability to pay more.

At the PTA meeting in early April Chairman Stebbins was pressed to tell why the voting was being postponed until the middle of May. He answered that the Board was in possession of certain "confidential information" which might change the picture before May 18. What this information was he did not reveal, but he had in mind a possible contribution from the College to the town.

Two days after the PTA meeting, the *Gazette* ran a signed editorial entitled "This Is Our Job" in which it explained that "we are not trying to defeat the school building plan that has been developed by the school building advisory committee, either editorially or through our news columns. What we are and have tried to do is to present all sides of the picture, ask pertinent questions which are related to the problems of an expanding school population; in short, do the things we believe to be the duties of a free press." These words were prompted, according to the editorial, by a question from a member of the School Board as to whether the *Gazette* was attempting to "crucify" members of the Board.

School District Meeting, April 12

According to the *Gazette,* 309 of 2,193 eligible voters of the School District turned out on April 12 to vote on the annual school budget, to elect new School Board members, and to discuss the proposed plans with the School Board and the Finance Committee. The early part of the meeting was the annual School District Meeting in which three School Board members were elected and the budget was passed. In a League of Women Voters questionnaire submitted earlier in the week each of the five School Board candidates had expressed approval of the BAC proposals.

In the discussion on the school budget it was revealed that an increase in the teacher salary schedule was being proposed and that a committee composed of teachers, School Board members, and members of the community would be named to study the whole teacher salary question. The salary question was raised again later in the evening after the open meeting got underway. Two professors of economics said that it might be better to put a really large amount into salaries rather than into a fancy new building. Manchester, Chairman of the School Board Finance Committee, responded that even if drastic salary raises were enacted, something would have to be done about the inadequate building anyway.

In discussing the school plans, more questions were raised on SIPRE, Sachem Village, gym facilities, and other matters. Bradley talked about neighboring school districts which were building schools at a much smaller cost than that proposed for Hanover. This seemed to make a considerable impression on the audience.

If it was the cost the building opposition was going to stress, Masland felt he would have to stress quality. He questioned the quality of the buildings cited by Bradley, and suggested that inferior quality would mean greater annual maintenance cost. Robert Allen, an associate of George Colton in the College administration, asked about the possibility of building a junior high school, separating older from younger students, and saving in this way. Masland replied that the BAC had considered separate facilities and a possible six-three-three plan for the twelve grades but had discarded it as being unfeasible. He told the audience that the Board had agreed with this decision.

On his way out of the hall Masland invited Bradley to meet with the BAC two evenings later. Bradley accepted.

The day preceding the meeting with Bradley Masland and architect Ingram studied possible costs of a school addition on the Sachem Village site, preparing themselves for questions that Bradley and others might raise.

To complicate Masland's dealing with Bradley and the others who were seriously questioning the proposals, word got to Masland that Ingram had told Robert Allen that the school addition could be constructed for something like $100,00[illegible] less than the BAC proposed. Allen told this to Masland by phone, and a quick check with Ingram showed that in response to Mrs. Bradley's questioning, Ingram had suggested that with some major alterations there could be considerable saving. He did not mean that the same thing could be had for $100,000 less. Allen's call to Masland indicated that Allen's information was coming from Bradley and that Allen associated himself with Bradley's unfavorable comparison of the Hanover proposals with new school construction in other parts of the state. In particular, the new school being built in Littleton, a town to the north, was being cited as an example of low-cost building. Masland was getting irritated. After a telephone conversation with an officer of the State Department of Education he concluded that the comparisons suggested by the opposition were not for similar facilities. On April 14 he wrote Mrs. Bradley about the Littleton comparison and enclosed a statement of comparative costs and comparative space values being obtained in the two districts. In her response Mrs. Bradley rejected the conclusions and asked if the BAC had taken into account the possibility of a mental hospital being erected in Hanover, bringing more families to the community. The BAC had in fact heard such a rumor and had satisfied itself that it was groundless.

Bradley and the BAC

On April 14, Bradley met with the BAC. He described two complaints which he said had led him to oppose the proposed plans. First, he questioned the wisdom of adding to the twenty-year-old building a wing or two which cost much more than the building itself. Second, he questioned the decision of the BAC in not presenting proposals for a separate junior and senior high school. Underlying this objection was Bradley's general disapproval of the way subcommittee reports of the Holyoke Committee had been accepted as dicta by the BAC. It was important, he felt, to stir the community into full consideration of some of the recommendations. Masland responded that evidence indicated that Hanover could not support a separate junior high school; and he wondered from Bradley what the trend in New Hampshire was on separate schools in towns of comparable size.

Bradley then questioned the sincerity of the School Board in announcing new teacher salaries at the meeting of April 12. He wondered whether this decision to raise teacher salaries was not taken and made known in an attempt to forestall the developing opposition to the expensive high school addition. Superintendent Pierce retorted with some heat that the salary question had been decided in the fall long before there was any community deliberation on the proposed high school plans. These exchanges between Bradley and the BAC resolved nothing. Bradley was determined to show up what he considered cost fallacies and to push for a separation of junior and senior high facilities. These were his two major issues, and he was later to enjoy the support of the other young taxpaying families who wanted no unnecessary tax increase. Getting full value for money spent—that was the rallying point of the opposition. From this point on, little more was said about the school program, including the need for a larger gymnasium.

Two days after the meeting, Masland received from Bradley a letter which began: "Getting punchy?" That letter crossed one in which Masland asked Bradley to give him as much concession on the schools as Bradley received on matters of state legislative policy and in particular on the sales tax proposal about which he was knowledgeable. A week or so later Bradley wrote Masland a long letter:

> The [BAC] plan may well be approved. If not I see no great harm resulting. The least that could happen would be simply that a restudy proved the plan to be right and then you would have everybody behind you. If something else turns up that seems to be better I think we should all be glad of that.

Perhaps more revealing of Bradley's basic feelings on the issue was this portion of his letter:

> It is entirely right for the Committee to have decided on the plan it thinks is the best. It is no less right, since the purpose of the plan is to spend a large chunk of the town's money, for people to question the plan severely. I recognize that there is such a thing as false economy; there is also true economy. This would appear to be the only difference between us. You can justify your larger expenditure in terms of what you get; I can justify my lesser expenditure in terms of what I would be satisfied with. Certainly the nearer we approach the legal debt limit of the District the more prudent it behooves us to be.

From this point on, communication between the BAC and Masland on the one side and Bradley and his group on the other was through letters to the local press. The Masland and Bradley families remained friendly, but there was some strain, and school business was not discussed.

The Gully

Masland now felt that there was only one issue remaining. Could a separate junior or senior high school be built in Hanover for something less than $600,000? Involved in the answer to this was the availability of land around the high school building itself. Immediately behind the building was a large gully which might serve if filled in or if terraced in some way. But short of taking over Sachem Village, apparently there was no land for a separate building except the athletic field itself.

To prepare himself on this question Masland wrote the state education officials in Massachusetts and Connecticut to find out their experience with separate high schools in communities comparable to Hanover. He also prepared some additional data on the added costs of the junior-senior high proposal, discovering from data prepared by Superintendent Pierce that an additional $20,000 a year in operating costs would be involved. Further he had the High School Principal make a survey of the athletic field. Principal Bragner reported later that the athletic field could not be spared for a building. With Ingram, Masland tramped through the gully. The architect said that filling the gully for a playing area or a building would cost too much money.

On April 18 the Finance Committee had another meeting and failed to come to any recommendation to pass along to the town. By April 21 a "Battle of the Letters" had begun. Bradley and George Colton wrote to the *Gazette,* Colton comparing what Hanover was getting with what Littleton was supposedly getting for less. And Bradley returned to his argument that "we could, if we wished, build a good new high school for 300 pupils on land we now have for something close to $450,000. Logically, this would mean a division into junior and senior highs."

It now became apparent to Masland that the antagonists were going to press the theme "more for less." Masland believed that some voice other than that of the BAC should be raised in favor of the plans. He made up a list of prominent persons in the community who might rally around the School Board's banner and organize a drive similar to the 1950 Friends of Hanover Schools. He was unsuccessful. The people he approached indicated that they favored his plan, but some said they felt that no organized effort was necessary, while others expressed reluctance to become involved. A College professor and a Main Street businessman, both active in the Friends of Hanover Schools in 1950, sent a joint letter to the press supporting the BAC plan, and several other interested citizens did likewise. Masland felt that preparation for the vote should not resemble a political campaign, even though this was a political battle. He felt that subtle pressure applied by a group of interested citizens would do what a "political campaign" might do. Dining room talk, telephone conversation, and sidewalk chats were the principal and most effective means of communication in Hanover.

A Petition

The inability to organize an independent citizens group to support the BAC plan was all the more disconcerting to Stebbins and Masland because of the apparent success of the opposition in this respect. On May 2 they received duplicate copies of a petition asking that the School Board postpone voting on the plans and "support a further study taking advantage of certain possibilities which have not yet been tried." The letters were signed by George Colton speaking for twenty original signers, including the Bradleys and several medical men.

The petition was considered by many of its signers as a last resort, an attempt to forestall a vote, an attempt to gain time for a reconciliation of plans and proposals. Bradley, in particular, felt very strongly about the attitude of the BAC, as he saw it. He had strong views on the cleavage between "insiders" and "outsiders" in New England towns. He viewed the "cross-section" committees as government by "Gentleman's Agreement": boards selecting their successors, and operating with a tradition of doing things quiet ly, preferably without public debate and dispute. This procedure, he felt, had the effect of putting on the defensive those who legitimately wanted to question the proposed decisions if the questioners were not "on the team." He felt that BAC members tended to bristle at any questions; that they were no longer open-minded citizens but had an "official" position to defend. Bradley felt that neither the BAC nor the Board would seriously weigh any idea or proposal other than their own.

Stebbins and Masland, of course, were not fully aware of the way their opposition saw them. The petitions to them meant only further delay. They were convinced that they had a sound plan and that postponement would mean higher costs in the end. So Stebbins responded on May 5 saying that in fairness to the voters and the BAC, "we feel that the time has come to present this program to the School District."

Also on May 2 the Sachem Village issue took a new twist. Acting on the advice of its consulting architects, the College took the Sachem site totally out of the running as available land. This aided Masland's public discussions with Bradley, for now the BAC opponent had nothing but the gully to fall back on. On May 10, Masland and Bragner visited the school in nearby Lebanon, to see at first hand what Bradley had talked about in his letters. It seemed to them that the Lebanon school had been built as a grade school and was being used temporarily as a junior high school. Masland circulated a memorandum on this school to members of the Board and the BAC, asking them to speak up against Bradley's arguments. In the meantime, he heard from Massachusetts and Connecticut on their experiences with separate schools. He was pleased to note that they advised against such separate facilities in their own states for towns the size of Hanover.

On May 12 Dartmouth announced what Stebbins and Masland had been hoping for. The College had reached an agreement with the town fathers to make available a total of $40,000 in money, land, or services over the next four years. Presumably this gift was to be used either by the town, the precinct, or the School District. Masland and Stebbins had pushed Meck hard on this contribution, but they were surprised at the low figure; it amounted to $10,000 a year. Nevertheless it might help in the vote on May 18 by *seeming* to take some pressure off the taxpayers.

On the same day the long-awaited report of the Finance Committee was made available and printed in full in the *Gazette*. After a lengthy analysis the Committee concluded that the voters would have to make up their own minds as to whether the plans were the best and most economical. Chairman Charlotte Ford had decided on this general report rather than on pressing for a vote which she feared might be less than favorable to the School Board, even though such a vote would be only advisory to the citizenry.

On May 10 the School Board sent to all voters the final plans and accompanying statements which they were to consider on May 18. The same day, the *Valley News* in its editorial column asked for a postponement of the voting and a reconsideration of the plans. In January the *News* had lauded the Board for tackling the building issue before students had to sit two in a seat. In May the *News* commented that from the beginning in January

> the additions had a "rush, rush" air to them. It was intended they be constructed for fall, 1955. However, since then, without any specific announcement, the notions of timing have changed, and it is now proposed by the Board to aim for the opening in fall, 1956. The delay would seem to allow enough time so that the decision could be put off six months, and still have added facilities ready for high school pupils in September of 1956.

Two days later, the *Gazette* reaffirmed its opposition largely on the ground that $600,000 was too much.

School Meeting, May 18

On the eve of the May 18 meeting, in addition to a hostile press, the BAC confronted opposition not only from those citizens of Hanover who normally were expected to oppose school expansion but from the ranks of College and medical families who had children in school. What was more, the opposition had vocal and influential leadership for the debate that preceded the vote. In the last days before the meeting, the Coltons and Bradleys and their friends circulated their petition and secured 126 signatures. On the day before the meeting the *Valley News* carried on page one a statement prepared by the petitioners: "Our original hope—in the interest of preserving community harmony and in order to further the plans for the high school expansion—was that we might persuade the School Board to propose a further study." The purpose of the petition, they went on, was "to make clear that we were not just opposing but interested in further constructive suggestions. Our belief was and is that excellent school facilities could be provided at a substantial saving in money."

Masland and Stebbins, on their side, felt that all questions of fact had been answered either in open meeting or in letters to the newspaper. However, they were uncertain how the vote would turn out and what the turnout at the meeting would be.

As the Colton-Bradley petition picked up more signatures, Stebbins came to believe that a second battle might be necessary. Superintendent Pierce, who had been through building controversies in other towns, had been saying all through the spring that some school districts discussed plans for two or three years.

As the May 18 District Meeting got underway, Stebbins introduced Masland who explained the reasoning by which the BAC had arrived at the proposed plans. Mrs. Colton spoke in favor of postponement, George Colton spoke comparing other schools with Hanover's proposals, and David Bradley spoke in favor of economy. Charlotte Ford made an impassioned appeal for acceptance, speaking as a citizen and not as Chairman of the Finance Committee. Masland answered all opposition speakers, since no one else volunteered who possessed the facts on the Board side. Stebbins had associated himself completely with Masland, but it was Masland who was the authoritative voice in the meeting.

Balloting got underway on the question of approving the plans as submitted by the BAC. The total number of voters present represented 27 percent of the registered voters in Hanover, but that 27 percent approved the BAC plans 311 to 275. Only a simple majority was needed. The second vote, on the bond issue to raise $600,000, was then taken by secret ballot. Although 264 voted yes to 200 no, the necessary two-thirds majority required for a bond issue was not obtained. One hundred twenty people had gone home, not staying for the crucial second vote. Many later indicated that they were not aware of its importance. As the School District Moderator read the results, there was a hush in the hall. Immediately Stebbins asked for a ten-minute recess, and it was voted. He caucused with his Board backstage and on reconvening announced that the Board was going to ask for an appropriation of $7,000 to hire outside consultants. When he spoke the words $7,000 there was a dead silence, for the audience seemed to sense that $7,000 was only the beginning of more planning, controversy, and cost. Members of the Bradley group had talked about professional consultants before the final vote, but they had mentioned a $500 figure. The voters nevertheless approved the request and, after voting separately $42,000 for a new boiler and roof to the old high school, adjourned until January 10, 1956 when the Board would report on new plans.

The BAC had completed its work; the School Board was left to work out its problems. Masland flew to Colorado the next morning on his research project. On the way he stopped off in Chicago to visit with Russell Stearns, a close friend and member of the Board who had been on leave of absence for the year. Masland strongly urged Stearns to use his influence when he returned to Hanover to assure that the Board itself assumed leadership during the next phase.

More Studies, More Choices

AFTER THE MAY 18 vote, the School Board had $7,000 at its disposal and a mandate to report before January 10 with new building plans. It proceeded to find a consultant who could make precise population projections, who could design a structure which would suit Hanover's needs, and who could give to the planning the professional touch which the Bradley opposition felt had been lacking in the BAC's work. On July 20, the Board announced that a New York City educational consultant would survey the community and present recommendations to the Board and to the School District.

Although members of the School Board interpreted the May 18 bond issue vote as a defeat, they felt obliged to try a fresh approach and to see it through to community decision. But they did not interpret the May 18 vote as a mandate to come up with a less costly scheme or a curtailed educational program. Along with Superintendent Pierce they were still anxious to build an adequate gymnasium and to provide facilities for shop work, home economics, music, guidance, and other activities covered in the Holyoke reports.

On September 8 the Board met with the consultant for a preliminary consultation. In the same month the Board announced a rise in the school enrollment larger than the projections of the Sperry-Mather report.

During September and October the consultant made several trips to Hanover. On September 20 he discussed with the Board his suggestions for adding to the present plant. At this meeting one of the members asked the consultant what he would recommend if he could start from scratch without consideration of cost. His prompt reply was that he would start new construction on a large site away from the built-up community. The Board then suggested that he explore this possibility, but it had no further indication of what he would recommend until he appeared at a public meeting on November 1. (This was deliberately arranged, presumably so that the consultant could render the town an independent judgment.) The public had seen little of the New York expert, and many who attended the November 1 meeting were eager for their first glimpse of a professional educational consultant.

The Consultant's Choices

With 130 persons present the consultant made a detailed analysis of the national crisis in education and then proceeded to deal with Hanover's problems. He said the school population showed a net annual out-migration of about three percent, thus disagreeing with the Sperry-Mather figures of the preceding year. He also stated that there should be at least 25 acres for a combined high school and elementary plant and pointed out that the present joint piece of property was much too small. With all of these figures in mind he made two suggestions. The first was that the School District authorize a new school on new property for grades nine through twelve. The existing high school would then hold grades six through eight and administrative offices for the District. The existing elementary school would contain kindergarten through grade five. He called this new plan a "worthwhile endeavor" but "not a proposal you will readily accept because it is going to cost a lot of money." He felt it important that the community consider it, however.

His second proposal was similar to the BAC plan. It envisioned adding to a remodeled version of the present high school building. Costs for the two buildings: Plan 1 (new site) $751,-000; Plan 2 (alterations) $512,000. Once the figures were presented and the plans outlined, many questions were directed to the consultant. How much would this cost? What kind of gym would Plan 1 include? What classroom area in Plan 1? What about traffic congestion if Plan 2 were adopted? Under Plan 1, how far should the school be located from the center of town? Someone suggested that the costs of the two plans corresponded roughly to those of the BAC proposals, and Dr. John Milne of the former BAC rose to ask whether it was not likely that before the Board was through with the new Plan 1 it would cost $1,000,000. He received no answer.

The net effect was that the community was given two proposals and advised to think them over. The meeting was adjourned with a promise that an open meeting would be called soon to consider the proposals in more detail. Shortly thereafter Stebbins announced the selection of a site committee to be made up of members of the Board. The committee would prepare data on possible sites for the new school envisioned under Plan 1. He appointed to the Committee Jean Milne (wife of Dr. John Milne of the BAC) who had been elected to the Board the previous March; S. Russell Stearns,[2] professor of engineer-

[2] Stearns had been a member of the School Board since 1951, and had been very active in Board affairs before he took a leave in 1954-55.

ing, the man to whom Masland had spoken in Chicago; and Jack Manchester, still chairman of the Board's finance committee.

Under Stearns' direction the site committee proceeded to look over properties, consult with the town fathers, seek out the services of the Town Planning Board, and ask the public for suggestions about sites. On November 29, the day of the promised open meeting, the committee in company with the consultant visited fifteen possible sites. At the meeting Stearns was not able to do more than run through the list of sites and suggest that more time was needed to get appropriate data together. From the audience Mrs. Colton proposed that a straw vote be taken of those present at the meeting, and the result was overwhelming endorsement of Plan 1 in principle. To the Board members it seemed that here was a plan that excited the imaginations of the taxpayers and might have a chance of succeeding.

Following the straw vote for Plan 1 the site committee continued its work with vigor and pursued talks with the officials of the College.

On December 6, Stearns discussed with Dartmouth officials and the Chairman of the Hanover Planning Board some so-called Reservoir Road property one mile and a half north of the center of town, but beyond a deep ravine and open pastureland. This property consisted of about fifteen acres held by Dartmouth College and another fifteen acres held by the heirs to the Garripay estate. It was commonly known as the "Garripay north land."

On December 20, John Meck offered Dartmouth's fifteen acres to the School Board as part of the College's earlier offer of $40,000 in services and kind to the town. This was a boost to the Board, and as a result efforts were pushed to secure a figure from the Garripays. The figure set on January 10, was $36,000 for the fifteen Garripay acres. For $36,000, then, the School Board could have over thirty acres of new land on which to construct a new high school. In addition, the State Education Department gave approval to Plan 1, even though this proposal would annul the six-six school organization and substitute a five-three-four plan.

But on January 10, the date of the adjourned School District Meeting voted the previous May, the Board ran into a snag. Before an audience of 35 persons, David Bradley suggested that the Board look into the gully behind the present high school to determine definitely whether it was suitable for expansion as suggested by Plan No. 2. His suggestion came after two townspeople proposed that the gully could be developed to permit new playing fields enabling the present fields to be devoted to new classroom space. The Board found itself back on the track of Plan 2 or a modification of the original BAC proposals, and this at the suggestion of Bradley. Although Bradley's purpose was to dispose once and for all of the proposal to make additions to the present school, what he actually did, quite unintentionally, was to force reconsideration of the old BAC proposal and to activate interest in the less expensive of the two plans, thus laying the groundwork for another community division of opinion.

Sensitive to suggestions and particularly to Bradley's, the Board proceeded in its own thinking to re-survey the gully for Plan 2, while Stearns wrote letters to the Garripays and to the College confirming offers for the land, provided the School District voted the necessary appropriation for Plan 1. Thus both of the consultant's suggestions were being followed. On January 13 Stearns, Manchester, and a College geologist tramped through the gully and decided to ask for an appraisal of making it suitable for use. The figure was $100,000, but this was subsequently scaled down to $75,000. In later discussions, the $75,000 figure was the one used. Earlier the Town Planning Board had given some thought to using the gully for a road to by-pass Main Street, but on January 30 a member of the Planning Board said it had no objection to use of the gully by the School Board.

Comparative Costs

Stebbins now proceeded to work out in detail the costs of the two plans. On February 7 he presented his estimates to the Board. Both plans came to more than the $700,000 debt limit, and the Board expressed concern over its finances. Stebbins calculated that Plan 1 could cost as much as $1,612,000 in twenty years including interest payments. Masland, who had remained on the side lines up to this time, learned of these figures from Stebbins, and he and his former BAC colleague, Dr. Milne, began to discuss them privately about town. They argued that a separate school was fine in principle but that in the end it would be either too costly or substandard.

On February 13 a building committee of the School Board was appointed, presumably to think in terms of Plan 1 on the Garripay-Dartmouth land. Stearns was chairman; the other members were Mrs. Milne and Linwood Bean, a businessman. The new committee felt it needed additional data to evaluate both plans, and on February 21 the Board addressed a series of questions to the consultant in New York, among which were requests for evaluation of Stebbins' memoranda on comparative costs, estimates of the costs of bus transportation to the proposed new school, costs of administering the separate schools, costs of a sidewalk out to the new school, and costs of classroom spaces. The Board was being pressed privately and in its own deliberations to reconcile its reluctance to countenance a separate junior high school the previous year with its willingness to consider one now. It had countered the earlier suggestions by arguing that separate schools could cost too much and were educationally unsound for Hanover. Now the Board was tending to support separate schools under Plan 1. It wanted help from its consultant.

Superintendent Pierce had already asked the consultant about these items at a meeting in Atlantic City but had received little satisfaction. Again on March 8 Stebbins wrote the consultant, for by this time the Board felt the need to act. The annual School District Meeting had to be held before the middle of April, and the Board had not reconciled any conflicting views, nor had it any detailed drawings to recommend to the taxpayers. It was decided that the consultant should journey to Hanover to help in the developing crisis, although he told Pierce on the phone that he was "at a loss as to what additional 'close-up' the Board needed." He arrived on March 21, and told the Board he felt that a classroom breakdown for Plan 2 as sketched by Pierce was not adequate. The following morning he sat down in Pierce's office and drafted a new Plan 2. It became known as Plan 2A. Plan 2A, he felt, was an addition to the present high school which was in general comparable in cost and room facilities to the drawings for Plan 1.

By this time the advocates of expansion on the existing site had become active. Virgil Poling, the man who suggested use of the gully just behind the existing high school building, had prepared a model of how the gully could be used, and this was exciting some persons familiar with the proposals. Jean Milne, who had served on the site committee, became a particularly strong advocate of Plan 2A when it was presented to the Board. She had by now developed an intense concern over the school building situation. A talented writer, her interest in school matters, as the mother of four boys, had been stimulated further by her husband's activities on the BAC in 1955. She had run for the School Board in March 1955 at the suggestion of a neighbor, an older faculty wife. Together Jean and John Milne began to spend much time thinking and talking about the two building proposals.

Mrs. Milne's Choice

After reviewing Plan 2A, Mrs. Milne felt that here at last was a realistic proposal which would satisfy Hanover's educational needs and its financial capabilities over the long run. From that moment onward she advocated the additions to the present high school building and worked ceaselessly for their acceptance. As March waned and there was still no clear picture of what the Board would present to the populace, Stebbins worked to gather the necessary cost data so that the Board could make a realistic decision before the public meeting now scheduled for April 16.

In late March, Mrs. Bradley announced her candidacy for the School Board. She had fought to the end against the Masland proposals the preceding spring and would, if elected, join the Board at a time when a split within its membership must result in another public battle. However, the reaction of the community to her announcement was mild. Incumbent School Board members were reluctant to oppose her candidacy. Contrary to the usual practice, no other candidate filed for the single vacancy. (Mrs. Larmon and Manchester had filed for reelection).

As April opened, Dartmouth announced a new position on Sachem Village. It now offered to make available to the School District the Sachem Village property of three and one-half acres adjacent to the present school property *if* the Board decided to support Plan 2A. But the offer was not made public until the time of the School District Meeting on April 16. College authorities were reluctant to make any announcement which would appear to favor either side. At a meeting of the Board on April 11, attended by the Superintendent, the Principal, and the consultant, the Board in a straw vote recorded a seven to two majority for Plan 1 (the new high school on the edge of the town at a projected construction cost of more than $675,000). Linwood Bean and Mrs. Milne were a minority for Plan 2A (adding to the present building) which would cost less ($585,000) and provide less space. (Mrs. Bradley had not yet been elected.) At last there seemed to be a chance of united Board action backed by the public approval expressed in the straw vote at the public meeting of November 29.

A Board Divided

With the decision for Plan 1 tentatively made, Stearns took command of planning. As an engineer he was well qualified to organize the data for presentation of the Board majority position to the District Meeting. Class space, sidewalk construction to the proposed new school, athletic facilities, and transportation all had to be taken into account. Four days later, on April 15, the day before the annual School District Meeting and School Board election, the Board took a final and deciding vote. Mrs. Milne read a vigorous statement listing the reasons, principally relating to costs, why she advocated the extensions to the old building, and she was joined in this by Linwood Bean. When the voting took place, much to everyone's surprise the vote had shifted from seven to two to five to four for Plan 1. Mrs. Milne and Bean were now joined by Mrs. Dorothy Strong, widow of a former dean, and Clark Horton, a member of the College faculty who was about to retire from the Board. Mrs. Milne's arguments had brought them back to support of an integrated school on a single site, a position they had maintained in supporting the Masland proposals the year before. Horton, in fact, had assisted Masland in 1955 in preparing the case against a separation of the junior and senior schools, and he was now to work closely with Mrs. Milne, assisting in the preparation of data and the drafting of statements even after leaving the Board. Thus the Board went before the annual School District Meeting 24 hours later deeply divided as to the best plan to follow.

At the April 16 meeting the Board reported to the District and asked for an adjourned meeting on May 21 at which time a formal vote could be taken on the proposals. Stebbins reported the division on the Board but said that the Board would go ahead with Plan 1. There was considerable discussion from the floor about the cost of a mile and a half long sidewalk to the new school, whether Sachem would be lost to the District if Plan 2A were not accepted (it would be), and similar questions. It was apparent the audience was divided. At the end of the meeting it was announced that Mrs. Bradley had been elected to the Board to replace Clark Horton. This portended an additional vote on the Board for Plan 1, making the majority six to three.

Factions Square Off

After the District Meeting factions formed to support the various proposals. Mrs. Milne sought out the architects and personally worked over the plans for 2A. By April 24, a week later, she came up with even newer plans henceforth to be called Plan 2AR (revised). She had found room for more class space and was able to work out with the architects cost figures which were less than Plan 1. Her reworking excited a number of people and influenced some of the members of the Board majority. Some of the former supporters of the BAC recommendations were told of Mrs. Milne's plans, and they began to discuss them in turn among their friends. By this time, no one was paying much deference to the views of the New York consultant.

On the other side, Plan 1 proponents began to organize. Their spokesman on the Board was Mrs. Bradley and in the community her husband. Plan 1 proponents included the Coltons and many others who had sided with the Bradleys against the BAC proposals a year earlier. What now began to develop was an argument over the extent Hanover would grow during the next ten to twenty years. Would it remain a small town or grow to considerable size while servicing the localities around it? Would Congress—the Senate and House had not agreed at the previous session—vote appropriations for the Army Engineers SIPRE installation in Hanover? Were the consultant's low population projections more credible than the "hunch" of Board members that Hanover's population would increase? The Plan 2AR proponents appeared to argue that there would not be too considerable a gain in population. They believed that to expand present facilities within the town's modest resources was more rational than to commit the town to a new plant with the costs a new plant would involve. They felt that in spite of the limited amount of land adjacent to the present school, the Sachem site and the gully made future expansion feasible. (Stebbins was surprised to find that Plan 2AR would allow additional classrooms when needed.)

Similar arguments went on within the Board. Mrs. Milne continued to press for better figures from the Plan 1 majority to justify its position. Dr. Milne began lining up supporters for Plan 2AR; he even approached Stearns and Manchester. The situation became tense in the Board and perceptibly, now, in the community. The issue was forced by Mrs. Milne at a meeting of the Board on April 30. In a statement prepared with the assistance of Bean after consultation with Horton, she asked for facts and figures which the Plan 1 proponents had said would indicate the justice of their position. When these were not adduced in a manner that satisfied her, Mrs. Milne stormed out of the meeting. Arriving home in distress, wondering if she had done the right thing, she sought the counsel of the next door neighbor who had first urged her to run for the School Board. To her delight she not only received commendation for her independence, but found that she had won a convert to Plan 2AR! Out of this conversation came further meetings by Jean and John Milne with other friends and neighbors and the creation of an informal group that began to operate much as the Bradley-Colton-Allen group had done the year before. The group included Charlotte Ford, Chairman of the Hanover Finance Committee, who had recently been married to a faculty member who was chairman of the Town Planning Board.

The Board Reconsiders

School Board members Stearns and Manchester also now had doubts about Plan 1, largely as a result of the studies that Stearns had conducted on the costs of constructing and operating an entirely new school on a site far removed from the other units of the system. They conveyed their conclusions to Stebbins. The School Board chairman personally continued to favor Plan 1 as an ideal for Hanover, but he harbored misgivings about costs and about the feasibility of securing voter approval. Although a further switch on the Board appeared to be taking shape, these three individuals were reluctant to press the matter until all the facts were in. Superintendent Pierce, moreover, while reluctant to press his views heavily upon Board members, indicated that he continued to favor Plan 1. He had confidence in the advice of the professional consultant.

On the evening of May 2 the PTA planned another open meeting on the school situation. On this day there was much talk, both overt and covert, about the building issue. The consultant returned to the community for his last visit, and Mrs. Bradley gave a morning coffee at her home at which he presented the advantages of Plan 1 to faculty wives and other partisans of the cause. She also arranged for him to be interviewed on the local radio station. The program was sponsored by the League of Women Voters, and he was interviewed by a League member who had been in the Bradley-Colton group in 1955. Behind the scenes, Stearns and other Board members, worried about the rising costs of Plan 1, were putting their heads together. That evening before the PTA meeting, most of them met at the Bradley's for dinner. Several members of the Board drew Mrs. Bradley aside and declared that if she would support Plan 2AR it would be possible to go to the meeting with a unanimous recommendation. This she indignantly refused to do.

Thus at the PTA meeting the Board once more revealed itself as divided. Both plans were presented in outline. At the urging of the Plan 2AR proponents, Horton, the former Board member, read a statement which drew considerable applause. Masland, the former BAC chairman, also joined the open debate. He declared that although Plan 1 suggested exciting possibilities, the actual building that was proposed was unattractive and of limited utility. It was now clear that the sentiment for a new school on a new site that had been expressed months before no longer prevailed. Moreover, the formal majority of the Board was still on record in favor of Plan 1, a position that all but one of its members, Mrs. Bradley, no longer accepted as valid on a cost basis.

Soon after this meeting, the Board met again. Stebbins and Stearns were ready for a vote. There now were eight proponents of Plan 2AR and only one, Mrs. Bradley, for Plan 1. The Board had done an about face. Its own figures showed Plan 2AR cheaper to construct and to operate.

Decision

THE FINANCE COMMITTEE had been meeting with the Board to consider what advice it would give to the town. The composition of the committee had changed slightly since the year before, and several of the new members looked with favor on Plan 1, including one younger member of the College faculty who lived in the area north of town near the proposed new site. Mrs. Colton was still a member of the Finance Committee, and she favored Plan 1. But the others, including those who had been critical of costs in 1955, now appeared to favor Plan 2AR. Although more costly than the BAC proposal, Plan 2AR looked less expensive than going to a new site. During the period of Finance Committee meetings, the Town Planning Board was consulting with the school authorities preparatory to making a report to the community.

On May 7 the School Board met to approve the draft of its final report recommending 2AR. It had been decided to ask the voters to choose between the two plans. As now proposed in the report, Plan 1 would cost $808,000, Plan 2AR $707,000. Plan 1 provided for a single T-shaped building, with two classroom wings and a central section including a combined arts and crafts and homemaking room, and a combined cafeteria and assembly hall, and a gymnasium. Plan 2AR was similar in many respects to the BAC's proposals of the year before. Like them, it called for adding on to the existing building, although the positions of the principal units had been reversed. Plan 2AR also provided a larger cafeteria, a larger shop, and better space for music and other activities. These changes as well as higher construction costs, accounted for the higher price. Chairman Stebbins read to the Board the draft of a letter that he proposed to issue with the report, which said in effect that Plan 1 was still the better one or at least equally as good. In the face of the almost unanimous hostility of the Board the letter was torn up on the spot. The majority of eight was for 2AR and did not want any letter around which would suggest otherwise. The one agreement which was reached on the part of the entire Board was that all members pledged to work for whatever plan the town adopted. Mrs. Bradley agreed to this in spite of her last-ditch stand for Plan 1.

Once again the League of Women Voters arranged a series of informal meetings in private homes, as it had done in 1955. This time proponents of two plans were on hand. With the Bradleys and their associates on one side and the Milnes and theirs on the other, debate was heated, and feelings ran high. Chairman Stebbins and Board member Stearns, who had devoted a great deal of time to working over the alternate plans, did not participate in these discussions. They were meeting with the town fathers on the Finance Committee and the Town Planning Board. For the most part, it was the women who did the public debating, getting people out to the League meetings, telephoning each other about latest developments, and passing along reports and rumors as more and more people in town became identified with one plan or the other.

During these final days the battle raged on the phones, in the letter columns of the local papers, and in sidewalk conversations. Those who had been for the BAC recommendations were now for Plan 2AR and those, like Dr. Bradley, who had been in vocal opposition before, were now for Plan 1. Protagonists of both sides arranged for canvassers, paid for advertisements in the local newspapers, and in general raked over the battles of the previous eighteen months to argue their respective points. And Chairman Stebbins, having abandoned his notion that the Board itself should not propagandize for its position, asked John Masland to arrange a publicity and vote-getting drive to secure adoption of Plan 2AR. Some observers felt that a victory for Plan 2AR would be vindication of the BAC, for its plans had called for somewhat the same building construction although at a cost of $100,000 less. Stebbins this time wanted to leave no stone unturned to insure a two-thirds majority for Plan 2AR even though he personally favored Plan 1. It was of overriding importance, he felt, for the community to agree to some building plan so that construction could be started soon.

Bradley's continued opposition to the Board came about in part because the Board itself had changed its mind for 2AR. Bradley the year before had argued more for less; now he was arguing for a wholly new building the expense of which would top anything proposed so far. In 1956, unlike the year before, he made no criticism of the curriculum. His support of separate junior and senior schools was consistent, and in this he was more consistent than the Board. Throughout the spring he remained friendly with Stebbins, and at one point the Stebbins and Bradley families had a pleasant Sunday picnic together. What motivated Bradley apparently was an honest conviction that modernity, separation of ages in a junior and senior high school, and economy were best. That his convictions were genuine was never doubted by the Board members. They just did not understand him.

The Finance Committee Votes

The Bradleys, the Coltons, the *Valley News,* the believers in Hanover's growth, all threw their energies into the battle for Plan 1. The *Gazette* did not take an editorial position except to say: "It is your choice." The associate editor who had felt so strongly about the BAC plan in 1955 was no longer with the weekly, and her successor did not continue her fight. There had been eighteen months of argument and discussion, and the alignments were now clear. The College had offered to contribute land for either plan, fifteen acres if Plan 1 were adopted, and three and one-half acres next to the existing school site if Plan 2AR were adopted. Whichever plan won, the town would have to exceed its debt limit, and the arguments settled now on town growth, maintenance costs of a new building, and the alternative school organizations of five-three-four or six-six.

As the day of the School District Meeting approached, authoritative support came down on the side of Plan 2AR. On May 10, the eight to one recommendation of the School Board was announced. Shortly thereafter the Finance Committee lined up with the School Board by a vote of seven to two. One other member joined Mrs. Colton in the minority. On May 17 the Planning Board reported a six to one vote for Plan 2AR, and the majority issued a detailed analysis of the two proposals, and the population, land use, transportation, and cost factors supporting this recommendation. The majority report declared that Plan 1 would cost $100,000 more initially and $32,000 more each year to operate. One member submitted an equally detailed minority recommendation for Plan 1, basing his argument for a new site upon Hanover's potentials for growth. The School Board, Finance Committee, and Planning Board reports were given prominent coverage in the local press. The Planning Board reports were reproduced in full in the *Valley News.* The voters now had before them the recommendations of recognized community leaders who overwhelmingly favored Plan 2AR.

Two days before the final meeting, in response to inquiries, Chairman Stebbins revealed to the *Valley News* that the Board had received a letter from the consultant declaring that Plan 2AR would be inadequate in a short period of time. Stebbins, in a statement published in the newspaper, declared that although the Board respected the consultant it could not accept his judgment of this matter. "On the contrary, for the present and from the long range point of view, it believes that Plan 2AR will provide better education for the youth of Hanover." The same day the *Valley News* published a long editorial favoring Plan 1, emphasizing the necessity of looking ahead.

'Vote!'

The day arrived, May 21, 1956. Before the meeting the majority of the Board made one last public appeal in the form of a front page statement carried in the *Valley News*. "We are most concerned with the false impressions that have been given to the public in the last few days through the press and other printed material," the Board majority declared. "It is our duty to inform the voters of the Hanover School District and to recommend action on school matters." The statement then reviewed the planning activities of recent months and the reasons for the Plan 2AR recommendation. This plan, it was stated, was equal in facilities to Plan 1, and included a separate music room besides, but it cost $60,000 less. "Separate schools are not recommended for school populations in Grades 7-12 of less than 800 because of the necessary duplication of facilities and staff. Hanover High School grades 7-12 has 650 expected by 1969." The statement concluded with the warning that the delay of one year had cost Hanover $100,000.

In the evening the townspeople made yet another journey to the College's Webster Hall to talk about their school problems and for the second time in a year to vote whether to borrow up to the legal debt limit and then some for new school facilities. The largest town meeting in decades filled the Hall. The moderator, Professor Herbert Hill, explained that the voters would choose between Plan 1, listed at $808,000, and Plan 2AR at $707,000. Chairman Stebbins related the developments of the past four years, propounded the arguments for Plan 2AR (the first time he had done so publicly) and then asked Mrs. Bradley to present the case for Plan 1. Members of the community spoke feelingly from various vantage points. Plan 2AR was supported by Dr. Milne and others.

When Stebbins asked whether voting should start or be postponed for additional discussion, there was a vocal and physical response by the audience, for citizens surged toward the platform to stand in line to vote. The action of the townspeople seemed to say, "Let's vote and not argue any more." Even the warning voice of the moderator, asking people to stay to vote again on the crucial bond issue for which a two-thirds vote was necessary, even this was lost in the rush to vote.

First came the vote on the plans, and, after a secret ballot which took more than an hour as each individual was marked off on the check list, it was announced that 75 percent of those present, 631 to 206, favored Plan 2AR. At this point, James Cusick, chairman during the 1950 grade school controversy, asked for the floor. Although he had remained outside of public discussion of school building plans during the last two years, he had agreed to Stebbins' suggestion that he speak. Cusick made an eloquent plea for a spirit of common enterprise. He urged a big show of support for the bond issue and declared that in spite of tensions of recent weeks, the time had come for the community to pull together again in common support of the school program. He was enthusiastically applauded.

Next came the vote on a $667,000 bond issue. Stebbins explained that this amount was the maximum permitted under the eight percent debt limit and that the difference between this figure and the $707,000 cost of the new buildings, alterations, and equipment would be provided by direct appropriation. The vote on the bond issue showed that 91 percent of those present favored it.

Hanover had decided how to meet its high school building needs.

THE ADMINISTRATOR AND HIS PUBLICS

"Men seldom understand any laws but those they feel."

Halifax

The Demotion of Deputy Chief Inspector Goldberg

John Logue and Edwin A. Bock

The Demotion of Deputy Chief Inspector Goldberg

I.

THIS STORY describes the difficulties of high-ranking police officials who had the responsibility for enforcing the law on a controversial matter of public morals—and of the communication problem in a large police department when some top officials wished to encourage subordinates to exercise discretion in enforcing gambling laws against bingo games without at the same time putting the department in the position of "winking" at violations of the law. The climax of the story occurred in September 1954 when a Deputy Chief Inspector of the New York City Police Department was demoted by the Police Commissioner allegedly for failing to notify his superior that he was going to ask a Knights of Columbus Club to discontinue charitable bingo games. The Deputy Chief Inspector had begun asking religious and fraternal organizations to cease conducting bingo games only three weeks before. Bingo games violated the state law, but it had been the custom of police to tolerate them. The Deputy Chief Inspector had not begun a major effort to discourage the continuation of bingo games in his jurisdiction until shortly after he received from headquarters a routine copy of a citizen complaint.

This story is told in two parts. The first describes the background and the main outline of events leading up to the demotion of the Deputy Chief Inspector. The second and principal portion of the case consists of the first-person accounts of the Deputy Chief Inspector, his immediate superior, and the Police Commissioner. These accounts are excerpts from the court proceedings in a libel suit subsequently brought by the Deputy Chief Inspector against a daily newspaper. He sought redress because the newspaper had conveyed in some of its editions on a certain day the impression that his action in requesting the Columbus Club to discontinue bingo games was in effect insubordination and a challenge to the authority of the Police Commissioner. The jury found for the Deputy Chief Inspector. (The newspaper appealed. The appellate court offered the plaintiff the choice of accepting lower damages or of going through a new trial.) Much of the testimony concerned the question of what police department policy really had been and how it had been communicated. The reader should understand that none of the principal figures in this story have consented to be interviewed. It is based primarily on court testimony, records of a public hearing, newspaper accounts, and interviews with persons other than the principals.

The Setting

By 1954 there had been in New York City and in other parts of New York State more than three years of sporadic public controversy about the extent to which police should apply state lottery laws to bingo games sponsored by churches or fraternal organizations. The State Constitution clearly outlawed such games, and under Section 1370 of the Penal Law anyone who operated a bingo entertainment—the law did not distinguish between charitable and non-charitable purposes—was guilty of a misdemeanor and subject to two-year imprisonment and a fine of not more than $1,000 or both.

In the five boroughs of New York City, particularly in the Borough of Brooklyn (sometimes called "the city of churches"), it had been customary since the late 1930s for some religious, fraternal, and charitable organizations to conduct bingo games without police molestation except when public complaints required action. Somewhat similar policies were followed by law enforcement authorities in a number of other cities and towns in New York State, and one estimate in 1954 was that $25,000,000 a year was being raised by bingo games.

The year 1952 had brought great public interest in enforcement of gambling laws as a consequence of televised hearings of the Kefauver Senate Crime Committee which suggested links between gamblers and public officials in a number of large cities. There had been a major scandal in New York City. The wave of interest in the activities of professional gamblers and their dealings with public officials had elevated to greater prominence the question of what police should do about charitable bingo games. Many of the games in New York City and in other cities throughout the state were run by Roman Catholic parishes or lay associations.[1] A smaller number were run by other churches or synagogues and by fraternal and veterans' organizations.

Supporters of bingo maintained that its elimination would force church and charitable organizations to curtail many of their activities. (In some Catholic parishes bingo revenue met a portion of the parochial school budget.) They protested that the law had been passed before charitable bingo games had become common, and that the people who played and who operated the games were decent citizens—not professional gamblers. There were also some citizens who felt that gambling in general should not be illegal (pari-mutuel track betting had been legalized in the state) and that efforts to enforce gambling laws resulted, as in the case of Prohibition, in greater evils than would be caused by gambling itself.

On the other hand, many groups—particularly many Protestant church leaders—strongly condemned, on moral grounds, any form of gambling. Other critics of charity bingo held that the games constituted too great a temptation for the average person (and too great a drain on the household money of the lower and lower-middle class housewife). If bingo were allowed to continue, these groups asked, how could the line be drawn at any other form of gambling? Those who opposed bingo as morally wrong were joined by others who believed that as long as the law was on the statute books it was the duty of the police to enforce it under any circumstances; "winking" at bingo could foster disrespect for all law. The course for those who wanted to legalize "charitable bingo," these groups maintained, was to try to amend the law. This the supporters of bingo had attempted to do on several occasions without success. Some of them claimed that "upstate" (largely Protestant) rural communities were over-represented in the perennially Republican-controlled Legislature at the expense of big cities like New York and Buffalo which had large Catholic populations.

Protests mounted against bingo games in New York City, and in September 1952 Police Commissioner George Monaghan declared that bingo did, in fact, constitute "a violation of the law." The same day a Police Department official stated that "the Police Department enforces all the laws." Simultaneously it was disclosed that policemen were visiting churches, clubs, and other sponsors of bingo in the five boroughs of the city to ask them to close down. The Commissioner's action drew strong criticism from those parishes and organizations where bingo had been played for years without interference, and there were instances where attempts to close games in progress led to commotion or near riots on the part of the (predominantly female) devotees. The *New York Times* praised the Commissioner's action editorially, adding: "The Police Commissioner is not authorized to pick and choose among laws to enforce and laws to ignore."

Discretion in Law Enforcement

Despite the *Times'* statement, and despite the fact that the core of the formal creed of every police department is that its function is to enforce the law, some students of police administration have noted that in reality police must exercise discretion in law enforcement. It has been maintained that if policemen acted on their own initiative and arrested violators of the letter of every law the courts and jails could

[1] Prevailing Catholic moral teachings held that gambling in moderation was not morally wrong.

not cope with the flood of offenders, and police departments might have to include a substantial part of the population. Laws are sometimes vague or require interpretation on the part of the law officer, the most common example being a policeman's judgment when to charge someone with "disorderly conduct." Sometimes laws are allowed to remain on the statute books after they are outmoded. Legislatures occasionally prefer to rely on the discretion of the police rather than cope with the political difficulties of repealing laws or enacting new ones. (In New York City at the time of this case a law against all-night parking was seldom enforced, and a Sunday closing law was not vigorously enforced in certain orthodox Jewish neighborhoods, even though repeated attempts to legalize such Sunday sales had been defeated in the State Legislature.) Also, the limitation of its manpower imposes on a police department the need to establish certain priorities. Thus, alongside the basic creed that it is the duty of the police to enforce all laws, some experts lay the qualifying principle that a major duty of police administration is the formulation of departmental policies about which laws should be stringently enforced, which should be enforced moderately, and which should be enforced or investigated only, for example, upon receipt of citizens' complaints. (In practice, much of the work of a police department consists not of the exercise of police initiative in enforcement but in the following up of complaints from private citizens about alleged offenses of other persons.)

After Commissioner Monaghan's statement in September 1952 the controversy over police action against bingo games in New York City quieted down somewhat, and as it did the games were resumed.

The Jackman Letter of Complaint

On August 10, 1954 the following complaint was received at Police Headquarters:

> 109-07 112 Street
> Ozone Park 20, New York [City]
> August 9, 1954
>
> Police Commissioner, New York City,
> 240 Centre Street,
> New York, N. Y.
>
> Dear Sir:
>
> While the increase in crime, especially among the youth of our city is rightly giving the law enforcement officers much concern, one cause of the widespread lawless attitude is allowed to continue unopposed by the Police Department in practically all instances and only limited restraint is placed on it when law-respecting citizens of a community register complaints.
>
> Reference is made to the various illegal gambling devices operated in widely advertised bazaars run by churches and fraternal organizations for the purpose of raising money. In some of these bazaars crowds of children are influenced to take part in illegal chance games and lotteries, and are thereby taught to defy the law.
>
> If these institutions, which are supposed to inculcate high moral standards, are permitted openly to teach and practice disrespect for law by inducing old and young to engage in illegal gambling and lotteries, is it any wonder that respect for law is widely breaking down and crimes of every nature are on the increase?
>
> As a tax-paying citizen, I respectfully urge you to use the power vested in you to put a stop to this deplorable situation.
>
> Sincerely,
> (Signed) L. W. B. Jackman

Francis W. H. Adams, the Police Commissioner to whom this letter was addressed, had been appointed by newly-elected Mayor Robert F. Wagner nine months before. A Democrat, a Roman Catholic, educated at Williams College and Fordham Law School, Adams had previously served as U. S. Attorney; as Associate Public Member of the National Defense Mediation Board; and as a member of the U. S. Delegation to the Reparations Commission in Moscow. He had a reputation in the city as an able, civic-minded lawyer. Adams inherited a Police Department still somewhat shaken up by repercussions from a grand jury investigation in Brooklyn which in 1949 and 1950 had uncovered links between a number of police officials and a twenty-million-dollar-a-year bookmaking enterprise headed by Harry Gross. The investigation of the Brooklyn Special Rackets Grand Jury, under the Brooklyn District Attorney and Judge Samuel Leibowitz, had been followed by the resignations of a Police Commissioner, a Deputy Police Commissioner, and more than 100 policemen including the Chief Inspector and the Chief of Detectives. Departmental trials, following alleged revelations by Gross, led to dismissal of additional policemen in late 1952 and early 1953.

On assuming office in January 1954 Commissioner Adams had moved strongly and briskly to improve the Department. He had named as Chief Inspector (the highest uniformed official and the managing executive of the Department) the only officer who had graduated from the FBI Police Academy, 47-year-old Stephen P. Kennedy. Kennedy was jumped to the top post from the rank of Inspector over the heads of 21 Assistant Chief Inspectors and Deputy Chief Inspectors. (In New York City policemen rise from patrolman to sergeant to lieutenant and to captain after passing the required civil service examinations for those posts. Appointments to the successively higher ranks of Deputy Inspector, Inspector, Deputy Chief Inspector, Assistant Chief Inspector, and Chief Inspector are made at the discretion of the Commissioner who may also demote such higher officials back to captain if he wishes.) Stephen Kennedy, the new Chief Inspector, rapidly established a reputation as a conscientious, hardworking, and strict police officer. By means of evening courses he had finished high school, then college, and finally—in 1950 at the age of 44—law school.[2] Aided by Kennedy, Adams proceeded to tighten up police discipline and administration—sometimes with a zeal that drew protests from the Patrolmen's Benevolent Association. However, Adams won newspaper and civic acclaim, and his appointment was frequently linked with Wagner's appointment of other able Department heads as a reason for public satisfaction with the new city administration. The Mayor made it plain during the early months of his administration that he admired Adams and would support him completely.

In August 1954, when Jackman's letter of complaint turned up in the Commissioner's morning mail, bingo was still a touchy matter. It was not only that the gap between the letter of the law and the custom of bingo playing was uncomfortable for the police, or that in the judgment of some police officials efforts to close bingo games might lead to public disturbances by the thwarted players. Public announcement of *any* police policy on bingo might have intensified differences between major religious groups in the city. The possibility of such a flare-up was always present because at the political level bingo was still a controversial issue. Gubernatorial elections were three months off. Three-time Republican Governor Thomas E. Dewey was about to leave office, and Democratic leaders believed that their party had its best chance in years to win the governorship. The bingo issue in neighboring New Jersey had contributed, many thought, to the surprising victory of Democrat Robert Meyner in 1953. In New York both parties approached the bingo issue with care because of its religious overtones.

An observer could note also that a controversy on bingo violations might embarrass Commissioner Adams' campaign to increase the size of the Police Department, a move that would require public support for additional appropriations. On Sunday, August 1, Adams made a special TV and radio report to the public in which he pictured New York "on the verge of becoming a community of violence and crime." "The actual fact," he said, "is that the Police Department of this city is at least 7,000 men under strength today." He continued:

> Before this hot August Sunday is over, one of us in this city will have been murdered.
>
> Another of us will have died as the result of criminal negligence.
>
> Twenty-seven of our people will have been feloniously assaulted.
>
> Three women will have been raped.
>
> One hundred and forty of our homes and businesses will have been burglarized.
>
> The property which will be stolen from New Yorkers on this one day will amount to more than $140,000—enough to pay the salaries of 28 policemen for a year.
>
> Even in this brief half hour in which I talk to you, seventeen crimes will be committed in the City of New York—more than one every two minutes.

Later in August Adams announced that the Department would undertake an experiment to prove his contention that major crime in New York City could be controlled by substantially enlarging the police force. He revealed that

[2] In 1955 Adams resigned to resume private law practice, and Mayor Wagner appointed Kennedy Police Commissioner.

starting September 1 the police force in the 25th Precinct in Manhattan would be tripled, and he promised a public report on the outcome of "Operation 25" within four months.

Having emphasized the need for men to deal with major crime, the Department might lose public support by any move that would make it appear that it was deploying much of its manpower to close charity bingo games.

Goldberg Gets the Letter

Jackman's letter of complaint was one of thousands of public complaints on various matters received by the Police Commissioner each year. On August 12, two days later, the letter with an accompanying memorandum was dispatched routinely to the different borough commands. On August 17 Deputy Chief Inspector Louis Goldberg, commander of the Brooklyn Morals Squad, opened an envelope from headquarters containing a copy of the Jackman letter and a rubber-stamped message:

> The attached copy of communication is referred to you for investigation, appropriate action and report in duplicate on U.F. 49 not later than Sept. 1, 1954.
>
> STEPHEN P. KENNEDY
> Chief Inspector

The Chief Inspector's signature, too, was made with a rubber stamp.

A police official is required to investigate complaints similar to Jackman's, but according to testimony at the trial, complaints of bingo playing in Brooklyn had sometimes been handled by replying that the situation complained of had been investigated and no illegal gambling had been found. But Deputy Chief Inspector Goldberg did not handle this complaint—which came down from the Commissioner's office—in that fashion. He was at the time in a somewhat unusual administrative situation. A *New York Times* report described him this way:

> Louis Goldberg contradicts the typical stage portrait of a 'cop' in every particular. He is tall . . . speaks in a light tenor voice and gentle manner, and never swears . . . his face soft and florid. . . . He is a vegetarian who never drinks, smokes, or plays cards. As a bachelor, he lives with two sisters in an apartment at 1 Tennis Court, Brooklyn, and is said to have only two intimate friends. Virtually his only recreation is playing the piano. He once studied music at the New York Conservatory and became good enough to give a recital in Steinway Hall. . . . As a policeman he enforced the rigid letter of the law. . . .

Goldberg was regarded in the Police Department as incorruptible. Some also saw him as a naïve police officer who occasionally carried to extremes his respect for regulations. In 1942 he had testified against two fellow police officers at a departmental trial rising out of an earlier grand jury investigation of official corruption and gambling in Brooklyn. In that trial Goldberg alleged that one of the two officers had tried to persuade him to acquiesce in a system of accepting regular bribes so that gambling establishments in his district might continue to operate. According to Goldberg's testimony, the officer in question had tried to overcome Goldberg's refusal by stating: "Don't you know the okay was given down the line? Don't be a fool." His reply, Goldberg swore, had been: "If a person who is honest is a fool, then I am a fool!"

Sixty-one years old, Goldberg, when he received the Jackman letter from Police Headquarters, headed the special 122-man Brooklyn Public Morals Squad, charged with enforcing laws enacted for the protection of public morals including gambling laws, laws against prostitution, and drug and liquor laws. In the other boroughs of the City of New York and in the Borough of Brooklyn prior to the establishment of this Morals Squad, law enforcement of this type was carried on at the division level by plainclothes policemen who are, jurisdictionally, in the uniformed force and not in the detective force. (A division comprises several precincts, each of which is commanded by a captain. Divisions are responsible to the Borough Commander, an Assistant Chief Inspector, and the heads of Borough Commands are in turn responsible to the Chief Inspector at City Headquarters.)

However, in March 1953 the Brooklyn Grand Jury (the same one that had investigated charges of police corruption in the Gross case in 1949-50) had suggested taking plainclothes operations out from under the control of divisional commanders and setting up instead a special borough-wide squad under the direction of an officer at the Brooklyn Borough Headquarters.

Regardless of the law, large numbers of persons in New York and other cities like to gamble on horse races or to "play the numbers." Profits from such operations are enormous, and it is common for gamblers to seek to protect the continuity of their operations by offering bribes to plainclothes policemen and their superiors. The Brooklyn Grand Jury, the Brooklyn District Attorney, and Judge Leibowitz apparently reasoned that a squad operating out of Borough Headquarters, whose members had rotating assignments that did not coincide with the precinct or divisional jurisdictional areas, would be much harder—and exceedingly more expensive—to "fix" than a regular divisional plainclothes detail. Gamblers in a neighborhood would not have an opportunity to become familiar with any single plainclothesman. The Grand Jury accordingly recommended that the Police Department make such a shift in Brooklyn and in the other four boroughs of the city.

The Department was in a weak position as a result of the Gross affair. Police Commissioner Monaghan, then in office, accepted the Brooklyn Grand Jury's recommendation for a borough morals squad even though there was opposition to it at Police Headquarters on administrative grounds. This opposition grew as time went on. Some officials at City Headquarters believed that the Brooklyn Morals Squad was unsound police administration and had the harmful effect of further diluting the authority of divisional commanders in the borough, already weakened by special squads operating out of higher headquarters. This objection was reiterated from outside by the late Bruce Smith, a leading authority on police administration, in his New York Police Survey. Some police officials also felt a plainclothesman permanently assigned to a district would become more knowledgeable about it than would be possible under a system of rotating assignments designed to prevent gamblers from becoming too knowledgeable about the plainclothesman. It may also be surmised that officials at Headquarters did not relish interference in police administration by the Brooklyn Grand Jury, the Brooklyn District Attorney, and Judge Leibowitz.

Goldberg had testified before the Grand Jury and had made a favorable impression during these proceedings. Much of his experience had been in Brooklyn, and he was appointed to head the Morals Squad.

Early in 1954, shortly after he took office, Commissioner Adams expressed dissatisfaction with the small number of arrests made by the Brooklyn Morals Squad. In 1953 and 1954 a special squad from Police Headquarters raided certain minor gambling activities in Brooklyn. These raids were interpreted by a *Brooklyn Eagle* reporter as efforts to "show up" the work of Goldberg's Morals Squad. On his side, however, Goldberg retained the support of the Brooklyn Special Grand Jury, and the Brooklyn District Attorney.[3] He reported to them from time to time, and they expressed satisfaction with his work in dealing with gambling in the borough. On March 9, 1954 the Flatbush Chamber of Commerce awarded Goldberg its Gold Medal of Valor because of his cleanup of bookmaking, policy operations, and other gambling activities. Somewhat of a local hero, Goldberg was quoted as telling a reporter in March 1954 that the Brooklyn Morals Squad pattern of operation was "so superior to the old system that it is only a matter of time before it will be adopted in other cities."

There was, finally, a personal element. Chief Inspector Kennedy had worked under Goldberg on the Brooklyn Morals Squad. There had been differences of opinion between the two men and Goldberg testified later at a public hearing that at one point he had had to get confirmation from Headquarters of his absolute authority over the Squad to overrule an administrative improvement proposed by Kennedy. Although both men were strict disciplinarians and although both had reputations for absolute honesty, they did not conclude their association in Brooklyn, the *New York Times* later noted, on friendly terms. Goldberg was one of the 21 higher-ranking officials Kennedy had passed when he was elevated by Adams to the Chief Inspector's post. Stories describing how promoted officers have proceeded to make life uncomfortable or unbearable for former associates under whom they had served earlier are part of the organizational folklore of the New York

[3] The Special Grand Jury's term had been periodically renewed by Judge Leibowitz since it had been convened in 1949 to hear evidence of police corruption in Brooklyn.

Police Department. None of the principals in this case suggested in their later testimony that Chief Inspector Kennedy sought to use his top rank to chivvy Goldberg, although the day of his demotion Goldberg told reporters that he felt that it had not been caused by bingo or religion or politics, adding, "I have a pretty good idea that a personal issue is responsible." On the other hand, doubt about the superiority of a separate Morals Squad had existed at Headquarters before Kennedy became Chief Inspector. At any rate, there were factors that might have caused any official in Goldberg's position—even one with less sensitivity to regulations—to treat very carefully any orders from Headquarters, including the routine message that accompanied the copy of the Jackman letter.

Goldberg Acts

The court testimony below contains detailed accounts of what happened after Goldberg received the Jackman communication from headquarters. It is necessary here to sketch only the bare outline of events.

Because it dealt with gambling laws, the Jackman letter (with attached memorandum) was sent directly to Goldberg at Brooklyn Borough Headquarters and not through his superior, Assistant Chief Inspector David Condon, commanding officer in Brooklyn. After receiving it Goldberg directed members of his squad to begin a survey of bingo games. Later Goldberg notified Condon of the complaint, adding that he proposed to ask the proprietors of religious and charitable bingo games to co-operate by closing down. By this method, he informed Condon, he would avoid making summary arrests. Condon testified that he was somewhat puzzled by Goldberg's policy: bingo had been played unchallenged in Brooklyn for some time. Condon also testified that Goldberg's squad had investigated previous complaints of this sort and had reported "no gambling on the premises." Condon, a mellow man approaching the end of his police career, struck some who later heard him in court as a person who in his police experience had become intimately acquainted with a wide range of human weaknesses and eccentricities and who had long since learned to take people as they come.

Between August 23 and September 1 Goldberg and members of his squad visited between twelve and forty religious and fraternal organizations, asking them—always politely, as Goldberg later emphasized—to cease conducting bingo games. The practice of seeking the co-operation of citizens who are violating the letter of unpopular laws dealing with relatively small offenses is a common one in police departments throughout the country. It is considered a means of avoiding troublesome incidents. But the use of this technique on Brooklyn bingo games did not avoid trouble. By September 1 Goldberg's activities had been prominently reported in almost every New York newspaper. A number of Catholic citizens in Brooklyn and in other parts of New York City were upset, as were the congregations of a few synagogues whose games had been "voluntarily" closed at the request of Goldberg's men. Protests were made at Police Headquarters, while some commendatory letters and phone calls from opponents of bingo were received at Goldberg's office.

On the evening of September 1, after a conversation with Chief Inspector Kennedy, Assistant Chief Inspector Condon cautioned Goldberg about his activities on the bingo front and relayed, as he later testified, a warning from Kennedy: "You tell that fellow that he's not setting the policy of the Police Department. And if he attempts to set the policy of this Department, he'll find out what happens to him." The Chief Inspector's warning, according to one version in later court testimony, followed the public complaints that had been made to the Police Department and inquiries at Headquarters by the Catholic Chaplain of the Police Department. (Goldberg testified that Condon had transmitted to him a Headquarters verbal order that he was not to act against any bingo games operated by Catholic churches. A Police Department official had denied that such an order was ever given.) Goldberg responded to the relayed warning by asking Condon what the policy of the Police Department actually was. Condon told Goldberg repeatedly, he later testified, that the policy of the Department was plain although undocumented. At the same time, he added, he could not tell Goldberg not to enforce the law. Condon testified that Goldberg in one of their conversations asked him to put in writing the fact that the police should not enforce gambling legislation against charitable or religious organizations. Goldberg denied making such a request.

The afternoon of September 1, the Deputy Police Commissioner in charge of Community [i.e., Public] Relations met with reporters, and stories like the following (from the *New York Times)* appeared the next day:

> The Police Department, reversing the action of the chief of its Brooklyn Morals Squad, gave its blessing yesterday to bingo games that raise money for worthy causes and exclude professional gamblers.
>
> It was made clear at Police Headquarters that police officers were expected to wink, in those cases, at such violations of the state penal code, which proscribes lotteries, including bingo games where players pay for the chance to win prizes.
>
> It developed that Deputy Chief Inspector Louis Goldberg, who had warned several Brooklyn churches and synagogues to stop running bingo games, had made the 'mistake' of thinking that a recent memorandum from headquarters meant he was supposed to enforce the law strictly.
>
> In the absence of Police Commissioner Francis W. H. Adams, Deputy Commissioner Richard A. Dougherty, in charge of community relations, denied that any crackdown had been ordered on church or charity games that retained their 'amateur' status.
>
> 'The policy of the department has not changed,' said Mr. Dougherty.

As a result of stories about Dougherty's press conference, the Protestant Council of the City of New York (representing 31 denominational groups) issued a statement noting that it was "strange indeed" for the Police Department to appeal for proper enforcement in some areas of the law and at the same time to encourage "flouting and ignoring" of illegal bingo games. Goldberg was invited to address the Baptist Ministers Conference. The *New York Times* was moved to write a sarcastic editorial in support of Goldberg and in favor of dealing with bingo by legislative action rather than police discretion.

Following the Deputy Police Commissioner's news conference and the criticism it stirred up, many telephoned Goldberg's office to ask what the present policy of the Police Department was in regard to charitable bingo games. Was it to wink at bingo or was it to ask that games be closed? Goldberg had several talks with Condon who was, in a sense, beginning to feel fires from above and below. When Goldberg asked Condon what Police Department policy was, the latter referred him to the press release by the Deputy Commissioner and suggested he consult with Kennedy; but Condon steadfastly refused to put himself in the position of telling Goldberg that he should not enforce the law. For several days there was a lull in enforcement. Some bingo sponsors began to resume their games on the basis of newspaper stories about the Dougherty news conference.

The Letter About the Columbus Club

On Saturday, September 4, Goldberg received the following complaint addressed to him at Brooklyn:

> Taxpayer
> Bklyn, N. Y.
> Sept. 2, 1954
>
> Whom It May Concern:
>
> In reference to Bingo sure wish you would investigate the night of Columbus on Monday & Wednesday night—
>
> . . . .
>
> I have a sister who is a Bingo feind she goes as far as Jersey to play Bingo there is no night that she aint got a Bingo to go to and believe you me I feel sorry for her husband, and children as they are the ones who are neglected and they are husdrands of women like my Sister, who take there house money to used for Bingo.
>
> Know for a fact that the fellow on Monday night Plays right in with the Winner, As he knows Just Who had the number he calls; after all I sure wish you would send in a few good Plain Clothes Women who can not Be bought, Just to see how crocked the nights Bingo are, and also the Gambling that Goes on there with the Women and men Before Bingo—
>
> After all Women that really cant afford it Go there with hopes of winning but how can a Poor person win when the Game is in the Bag before it even starts—
>
> Why all Summer right on the Benches along Flatbush Ave from Plaza St. to Union St, some of the women would Play right there Cards in their Hands money on the Bench and Cops passed in Prowl Cars and never say a word, I know you would clean this thing up and soon, as I know if it go on any longer, Im going to get a Petition up and have it sent to the Police Commissioner and Im sure something would be done right away.

Homes are a hell with Bingo going on Children neglected, hungery, and let to do What they want while their Mother is of to some Bingo, Lets Clean this rotten Racket up, and soon

Taxpayer.

[It should be noted that none of the allegations about the Columbus Club were substantiated except the charge that bingo games were regularly held there.]

On the Labor Day weekend Condon learned from Goldberg's subordinates that he had ordered them to approach the manager of the Columbus Club, a large building in Brooklyn connected with the Knights of Columbus and the site of the Monday-Wednesday games referred to in the anonymous letter. He was to be asked to discontinue bingo at once. Worried about the public commotion that might attend the closing of one of the larger games in the borough without greater advance notice—some of the games at the Columbus Club were attended by more than a thousand people—Condon testified that he instructed Goldberg's subordinates not to act on this matter without consulting him.

Between Sunday, September 5 and Thursday, September 9 Goldberg and Condon had a number of other conversations. Their respective versions appear in the testimony. On Wednesday morning Goldberg told Condon that he planned to go ahead with his enforcement campaign. But their testimony conflicted as to the rest of this conversation. According to Goldberg's version he showed Condon the letter complaining about bingo at the Columbus Club, told Condon that he planned to visit the Columbus Club that afternoon to ask the management to discontinue, and heard Condon reply, "That's your job." Condon, on the other hand, testified that Goldberg did not show him the letter and did not tell him that he was going to visit the Columbus Club that day. Condon said that he feared that Goldberg might now close down some bingo game without sufficient notice and thereby precipitate an unnecessary disturbance. Therefore, said Condon, he now, for the first time, told Goldberg not to close down games without consulting him.

On Wednesday afternoon Goldberg went to the Columbus Club and personally asked the manager to discontinue that night's game, a benefit for a Catholic home for crippled children. The manager agreed. Goldberg then visited other bingo proprietors with the same request. Meanwhile the manager of the Columbus Club telephoned Assistant Chief Inspector Condon and described the difficulty of stopping patrons from turning up for that evening's program. Condon said that there must have been a misunderstanding. He told the manager not to call off the game for that evening but to announce that no further games would be played.

The newspapers, which had been giving much space to Goldberg's activities, got news of his Wednesday afternoon visit to the Columbus Club, of Condon's subsequent permission to the Club, and of the manager's announcement that future games were canceled. Some newspapers ran prominent stories on this sequence of events in their Wednesday evening and Thursday morning editions, one—in its early editions—interpreting Goldberg's action as a challenge to the Police Commissioner.

On Thursday morning, September 9, after the newspapers had been published, Chief Inspector Kennedy talked with Condon at Police Headquarters. The same morning he dispatched this memorandum to the Police Commissioner:

POLICE DEPARTMENT
City of New York
New York 13, N. Y.

September 9, 1954

Memorandum for THE POLICE COMMISSIONER:

At 9.35 a.m. this date, Assistant Chief Inspector David A. Condon, Commanding Officer, Borough Headquarters, Brooklyn, was present at the office of the Chief Inspector and stated that at about 10.30 a.m. on September 8th, 1954, he had had a conversation with Deputy Chief Inspector Louis Goldberg, Brooklyn Borough Headquarters, relative to the procedure to be followed in the enforcement of the laws relative to bingo games and instructed Deputy Chief Inspector Goldberg to consult with him before taking any action in connection with such games. Deputy Chief Inspector Goldberg informed Assistant Chief Inspector Condon that he would enforce all gambling laws and would obey no other order unless it was put in writing by Assistant Chief Inspector Condon. Despite this directive from Assistant Chief Inspector Condon, Deputy Chief Inspector Goldberg did visit several bingo games in Brooklyn and directed that they be stopped without further consulting Assistant Chief Inspector Condon.

On prior occasions Assistant Chief Inspector Condon had given similar instructions to Deputy Chief Inspector Goldberg and on no occasion did Deputy Chief Inspector Goldberg comply with instructions to confer with Assistant Chief Inspector Condon. On no occasion did Assistant Chief Inspector Condon inform Deputy Chief Inspector Goldberg or direct him not to enforce the laws relating to gambling.

In view of the fact that Deputy Chief Inspector Goldberg disregarded the instructions of his Commanding Officer, Assistant Chief Inspector Condon, relative to proper procedure in the enforcement of laws relating to gambling, his services are seriously impaired, and, therefore it is recommended that he, Deputy Chief Inspector Goldberg, be reduced in grade.

(Signed) STEPHEN P. KENNEDY
Chief Inspector

After conferring with other high Department officials that morning, Commissioner Adams approved Kennedy's recommendation for Goldberg's demotion and prepared the following statement which would soon be issued to the press:

Effective this date I am demoting Deputy Chief Inspector Louis Goldberg to the rank of Captain. I am taking this step because so long as I am Police Commissioner I do not intend to let anybody run the Police Department except myself.

Captain Goldberg has demonstrated a degree of insubordination which may not and cannot be tolerated. It must be clear always, both to the public and to the members of the Department, that it is for the Commissioner and the Commissioner alone to administer the Department. I have had occasion to make this clear before and I now make it clear again. Failure on my part to recognize this fact and failure to act upon it would constitute a tacit abdication of my duties as chief law enforcement officer of this city.

. . . .

The issue here is not bingo. It is rather and quite simply the question of who runs the Police Department. To allow this challenge to the Commissioner's authority to go unanswered would invite chaos in an organization in which discipline and proper respect for authority are absolute essentials.

While bingo in this case is irrelevant, I think it only proper for me to observe that I am and have been throughout my life dedicated to the proposition that all laws be enforced. This is as true with reference to the laws relating to bingo as to any others.

Speaking as a private citizen and not as Commissioner, however, I must frankly state that I do not think the present laws relative to bingo games held under the auspices of churches, synagogues, and philanthropic agencies, and free from any racketeering influences, are sound from any point of view. I believe these laws should be changed and I believe this to be an issue which should be carried to the people and decided by the people.

The situation is one in which vital social and health services provided to tens of thousands of children are now jeopardized. It is my private view that to prevent these fine institutions from giving the enormous help they do in the prevention of juvenile delinquency and in caring for our people is wrong. . . .

Finally, as Commissioner, I again wish to call attention to the ugly fact that crimes of violence and other serious crimes against person and property are rising rapidly in this city and that we are doing our best to cope with this situation with a force that is grossly inadequate. . . .

Goldberg started his day in Brooklyn by visiting a number of bingo proprietors on the way to his office. He asked them to call off future games voluntarily. He arrived at his office to find a large number of reporters anxious for a statement about the Columbus Club affair. About the same time that Kennedy was interviewing Condon at Police Headquarters, Goldberg in Brooklyn told reporters: "I am going to continue to enforce the law, and I ask all good people to co-operate." The *New York Times* reporter noted that "he had a list of 100 Catholic Churches and clubs, a few synagogues, veterans halls, and Protestant Churches where bingo or lotteries were regularly run" and he intended to ask sponsors of these games to close voluntarily.

At 11:00 a.m. Goldberg was ordered by telephone to report to Chief Inspector Kennedy at Police Headquarters across the river in Manhattan. On doing so, Goldberg testified, he was handed an unsigned typewritten note informing him that as of 4:00 p.m. he was demoted to Captain (a drop of three grades) and was being transferred to a civil defense detail. Goldberg stated that there was no further discussion between the two men.

The reporters and photographers were still present when Goldberg returned to his Brooklyn office. There he wrote out and read aloud a letter to Commissioner Adams requesting that he be allowed to retire from the force. Goldberg appeared profoundly affected to a reporter who quoted him: "This is my reward after 36 years of hard, faithful service to the people of New York . . . demotion and disgrace. . . . Nothing in the history of the Police Department has broken morale as much as my case. . . . I took an oath when I joined the Department to uphold and enforce the law. I have done just that throughout my career. And now, for having done my duty, I am penalized. The good people of this city and within the United States and other civilized nations are behind me."

Wrote a *New York Times* reporter: "The Inspector declared it was the duty of a police officer to take action when a letter of complaint was received. When asked about the charity aspect of the games he said . . . 'The Police Department doesn't make the laws. . . . We enforce the laws of the land.'" The *Times* report concluded: ". . . he never raided a charity bingo game until three weeks ago, but has refused to explain why."

That afternoon Commissioner Adams read his prepared statement to reporters. He indicated it had been cleared with Mayor Wagner. By evening the Mayor had stated that Adams had his complete support. He said the Commissioner saw it as a disciplinary matter. He added that he, too, favored legalizing bingo but stated that the law would be enforced while it remained on the books. In a radio interview that evening, Goldberg put his case to the people of the city. He summed up his feelings: "My performance of duty in compliance with directives has resulted not in commendation but in degradation. . . ."

All newspapers gave prominence to stories of Goldberg's demotion. Some criticized the Police Commissioner in editorials. Spokesmen on both sides of the bingo issue made strong public statements, and Goldberg was invited to address a number of civic associations.

The Foreman of the Brooklyn Grand Jury sent Goldberg a telegram: "It is deplorable to me that your loyalty, honesty, and devotion to your job has been rewarded by your being demoted and transferred for doing your sworn duty to enforce the law. Your position was therefore untenable and your resignation inevitable." The Protestant Council of the City of New York called the demotion "an amazing spectacle" and Goldberg's resignation "the City's loss." It said "law enforcement is the issue. Enforce this law as well as every other law." A Brooklyn rabbi said that "Goldberg has proved for thirty years his integrity and loyalty toward the maintenance of law and order." Roman Catholic leaders generally declined to comment. A spokesman for the Archbishop of Brooklyn indicated that the Brooklyn Diocese had not taken a stand on bingo and was leaving it up to the individual parishes.

The *New York Times* commended Goldberg for putting the Police Department "in an untenable position." Its editorial writer observed: "Mr. Goldberg chose to live recklessly. . . . He performed the great service of establishing the principle that the only fit place to change a law . . . is in the legislature." A lawyer who supported Goldberg contended that one moral to be drawn from the incident was that police officers above the captain level should have permanent civil service appointments (and not be promoted or demoted at the discretion of the Commissioner). Then, the lawyer pointed out, the Department would have had to prefer formal charges against Goldberg and hold a hearing before demoting him.

Republican leaders called the demotion "political expediency," but they did not ask for strict enforcement of the law by the city. Democratic leaders generally did not try to defend Goldberg's demotion but instead stressed their legislative solutions for the "absurd situation." Meanwhile, the Police Department began a major enforcement effort, closing down all bingo games. Some frustrated bingo enthusiasts chartered buses to take them to games in Suffolk County, Long Island, whose County District Attorney said that bingo there was a matter for local police action. In October, Goldberg called on Adams and his rank was restored. He did not accept the Commissioner's offer to let him withdraw his retirement papers. By 1957 the voters of the state had passed an amendment authorizing local option on legalizing charity bingo games.

II.

[These excerpts from the testimony of Messrs. Goldberg, Adams, and Condon are taken from the record of GOLDBERG VS. NEWS SYNDICATE ET AL., *1957, New*

York Supreme Court, Kings County, Judge Edward G. Baker presiding. Goldberg was represented by Morris K. Siegel and the Defendants by J. Howard Carter. To present the testimony in ascending order of rank Mr. Adams' examination appears last; he actually testified before Mr. Condon. In appraising such conflicts of testimony as exist, readers should note that witnesses are testifying about events that occurred some three years earlier.]

Excerpts from Testimony of Former Deputy Chief Inspector Louis Goldberg

Direct Examination by Mr. Siegel:

Q. Will you please tell us what ranks you held in the Police Department . . . and the period of time you held each of these ranks? ——The first ten years I was a Patrolman; February, 1928, I was promoted to the rank of Sergeant of Police; in 1932, I was promoted to the rank of Lieutenant; in 1940, I was promoted to the rank of Captain of Police; in 1947—June of 1947, I was promoted to Deputy Inspector of Police; and in 1950, I was promoted to the full rank of Inspector of Police; March 1st, 1953, I was promoted to the rank of Deputy Chief Inspector. . . .

* * * * *

Q. Now, what is the name, or title, of the squad that you had commanded since March of 1953? ——The Public Morals Squad, Borough of Brooklyn.

Q. What was the purpose . . . of the Public Morals Squad . . . ? ——To investigate and take appropriate police action on all complaints received concerning violations of the public morals law.

Q. What violations come under that category? ——Gambling, with all their ramifications, prostitution, drug violation, liquor violations, and other laws enacted for the protection of public morals.

Q. Now, was and is bingo still a violation of the lottery laws of the state of New York? ——Yes, sir.

* * * * *

Q. After receiving the letter addressed to the Police Commissioner and the memorandum from Chief Inspector Stephen P. Kennedy's office . . . what did you do with respect to this complaint? [several lines omitted] ——I notified my men of the complaint—the seriousness of it—and I caused a survey to be made of the entire borough of Brooklyn for the purpose of ascertaining locations where conditions as complained of in the letter existed.

I then had a talk with Assistant Chief Inspector Condon and I said, "Dave, in connection with the Attorney Jackman complaint on gambling, with all its ramifications, I feel that it would be a good idea that places of religious nature and fraternal organizations where these violations are found to exist, no summary arrests to be made, but we will ask the people to please discontinue violating the law."

* * * * *

Q. I see. Is that the time that you inaugurated that procedure in connection with the Jackman complaint? ——Yes sir.

Q. Can you tell us when you spoke to Chief Condon with respect to the Jackman complaint? ——Well, I received the complaint about the 17th of August, 1954. Perhaps within a week.

THE COURT: Well, did you tell us what he replied when you—

THE WITNESS: Yes, sir. Chief Condon said, "That's a very good idea, Lou. Fine. Carry on. Continue doing just that."

* * * * *

[*The following testimony was elicited prior to the above.*]

Q. Now, what were the instructions that Assistant Chief Inspector Condon gave to you September the 2nd, 1954. . . ? ——To continue enforcing the law as I had been doing at that time.

Q. Will you please tell us the conversation you had with Mr. Condon with respect to those orders? ——Yes, sir. On September 2nd, 1954, my attention was called to a newspaper article where Deputy Police Commissioner Dougherty of the New York City Police Department made a statement to the effect that policemen——

MR. CARTER: Wait a minute. I object to it, if the Court please.

THE COURT: Don't tell us what was in the article. Let that part stand in which the witness testified that his attention was called to a certain article.

Q. Yes. . . . I am not interested in the article so much. Would you please tell us the conversation you had with Assistant Chief Inspector Condon on September the 2nd, 1954? ——I asked Chief Condon if the statement in the newspaper dated September the 2nd, 1954, stating that policemen were expected to wink at bingo games was true. The newspaper further said that winking at bingo games was the policy of the Police Department. I asked Chief Condon, "Is that true? Is there such a policy?" He said, "I don't know of any such policy. I read the paper. I haven't received any orders to that effect."

I said, "Dave, I want to do the right thing. What am I supposed to do now? Are there any changes as to law enforcement?" He said, "I have received no orders to the contrary. Continue enforcing the law as you are doing."

Q. Did you later that day have another conversation with Mr. Condon with respect to bingo enforcement? ——Yes, sir.

Q. That was still on September 2nd, 1954? ——Yes, sir.

Q. Please tell us what the conversation was later that day? ——Later in the afternoon of the same day I went upstairs to Chief Condon's office. I informed him that people were calling me on the phone, others came in person, asking if the policy of the Department permitted bingo playing since the publishing of that article. I told the people that I had received no orders to the contrary. That I was not in a position to tell people to disregard a law; that I had no such authority. . . . I said, "Dave, now what are we going to do? People are asking me—shall they continue, shall they not continue? What shall I tell these people?" Again Chief Condon said to me, "Lou, I have received no further orders. You will continue doing as you are doing at the present time."

* * * * *

Q. Now, did you have occasion to visit the Columbus Club on September 8, 1954, in connection with bingo violations?

* * * * *

——Yes, sir.

Q. Before going to the Columbus Club on September 8, 1954, did you consult with your superiors? ——Yes, sir.

Q. When was that? ——That was the morning of September 8, 1954, about the hour of eleven a.m.

Q. And with whom did you consult with respect to the bingo violations at the Columbus Club? ——With Assistant Chief Inspector Condon.

* * * * *

Q. Now, tell us the conversation that you had with Chief Condon. . . . ——I said, "Dave, here is a letter which I had received, sent to me through the mail direct, complaining of card violations and bingo games at the Columbus Clubhouse." I gave him the letter. He read it and he returned it to me.

I then said, "Dave, do you recall about two weeks ago when you were down to my office and you said to me, 'Lou, I understand that two of your plainclothesmen were down to the Columbus Clubhouse and told them to discontinue playing bingo games.' And at that time, Dave, you told me let them continue today—" the exact date I do not recall. Dave said, "Let them continue playing the game today and this will be the last; they will not play after this."

I said, "Apparently, Dave, they did not discontinue playing bingo games, and this letter is the result of it." I said, "Dave, I will go there this afternoon and speak to the management and ask them to please discontinue violating the law." He said, "That is your job."

Q. And after leaving Chief Condon's office on September the 8th, 1954, did you proceed to the Columbus Club? ——Yes, sir.

* * * * *

Q. When you arrived at the Columbus Club did you have a conversation with anybody representing the Columbus Club? ——Yes, sir.

Q. With whom did you talk? ——Mr. Robert Halpin, the banquet manager.

Q. Now, tell us what the conversation was with Mr. Halpin? ——I introduced myself to Mr. Halpin. He took us into his office and I appraised [*sic*] him of the nature of the complaint that I had in hand. . . . I read to him the part which pertained to gambling at the Columbus Clubhouse, card playing and bingo. I said, "Mr. Halpin, I, as the Commander of the Public Morals Squad, had instituted a plan whereby fraternal organizations and religious organizations maintaining such violations, no summary arrests would be made, but we merely ask you people to please cooperate with the police authorities and discontinue the violations." Mr. Halpin was very cooperative—very fine gentleman—and he said, "Chief, I will discontinue, effective tonight, the playing of bingo."

Q. Was there a game scheduled that night? —— That was Wednesday. Yes, sir. Yes, sir.[4]

* * * * *

Q. Now, did you have occasion to talk to Chief Condon later that day? ——Yes, sir . . . on a telephone . . . perhaps between 8 and 9 p.m. . . . Chief Condon called me because I tried to get him, and when I could not, I left word and he called me.

I said, "Dave, Lieutenant Doyle from my office called me a short time ago and he is at present at the Columbus Clubhouse. Lieutenant Doyle said, 'Chief, the bingo game at the Columbus Clubhouse is in progress.' Lieutenant Doyle said, 'I asked Mr. Halpin why he did not keep the promise which he had made to Chief Goldberg.' Mr. Halpin said, 'When I promised Chief Goldberg that I will discontinue playing bingo effective tonight I was sincere. But Chief Condon has told me since to disregard Chief Goldberg's directions and continue that night.' "

---

[4] Later, under cross-examination Goldberg testified that Halpin had asked if that night's game could continue.

Q. What did you say? ——I said "I could not authorize you to violate the law."

Q. And by that did you want him to understand that his request . . . was being denied? ——I presume he understood it that way.

Q. That was the thought you were trying to convey to him? ——Yes, sir.

I said, "Dave, I called you to ascertain whether or not Mr. Halpin was telling the truth." Dave said, "Yes, I told him to play tonight." I said, "Thanks, Dave, for calling me." Dave Condon said, "Lou, tomorrow I am going to the office of the Chief Inspector and I will ascertain from him just exactly what do they want us to do in connection with the enforcement of the bingo laws."

Q. Did you authorize Lieutenant Doyle to permit the game to continue that night? ——Yes, sir. . . .

* * * * *

Q. All right. Now, the following morning, on September the 9th, 1954, were you requested by the Chief Inspector to appear at his office? ——Yes, sir.

Q. What time did you receive the request to appear at his office? ——About 11 or 11:15 a.m.

* * * * *

Q. And did you appear at his office? ——Yes, sir.

Q. And did you have a conversation with the Chief Inspector? ——Yes, sir.

* * * * *

Q. Please tell us what . . . Kennedy said to you and what you said to him? —— . . . Kennedy gave me a sheet of white paper with typewriting on it —no signatures. He said, "Police Commissioner Adams told me to give this to you to read. When you get through reading it, you will leave this office."

* * * * *

Q. Do you have that paper? ——No, sir. I asked him if I could keep it and he grabbed it out of my hands.

Q. Do you know what in substance the paper said? ——Yes, Sir. . . . It said that I was demoted to the rank of captain and transferred to the Civil Defense—the Office of Civil Defense.

Q. And when was that demotion to take place? ——Effective 4 p.m. that day.

* * * * *

THE COURT: . . . Tell me this, was there anything in the paper as to the reason why you were then demoted to the rank of captain?

THE WITNESS: No, sir.

THE COURT: In the paper itself?

THE WITNESS: No, sir. No, sir.

THE COURT: And Inspector Kennedy told you the reason, did he?

THE WITNESS: No, sir, he did not.

* * * * *

Q. Before you were demoted on September 9, 1954, did any of your superiors, including Commissioner Adams, tell you why you were being demoted? ——No, sir.

Q. Were any charges or complaints filed against you by any of your superiors for insubordination? ——No, sir.

Q. Were you given a hearing? ——No, sir, I was not.

* * * * *

Q. Under the rules and regulations of the Police Department, the filing of an application for a pension takes effect 30 days hence; is that right? ——Yes.

Q. During this 30-day waiting period after September 9, 1954, when you filed your application for retirement, did you have occasion to talk to Police Commissioner Adams? ——Yes, sir, . . . October 2nd, 1954.

* * * * *

Q. After your conference with Commissioner Adams, were you restored to the rank of Deputy Chief Inspector? ——Yes, sir, I was.

* * * * *

Q. . . . Mr. Goldberg, will you please tell us what your conversation was you had with Commissioner Adams on October the 2nd, 1954? ——Yes, sir. I asked Commissioner Adams why I had been unjustifiedly demoted to the rank of captain when I had performed my duty in compliance with the rules and regulations and the oath of office that I had taken upon appointment to the Police Department. Police Commissioner Adams said to me, "Why did you enforce the bingo laws?" I said, "Mr. Commissioner, I have been enforcing bingo laws for a long time; I was never told not to enforce them, neither by you nor by any of my superior officers." . . . I said I saw no reason why I should leave this department as a captain of police when I worked so hard and diligently to reach the rank of deputy chief. That my life has been destroyed by this unjustifiable demotion. He said, "We can get around that. We can get around to that." He asked me if I wanted to return to the department. I said, "No, Mr. Commissioner. A week from today, the 9th of October, 1954, my 30-day waiting period will have expired and I will have been fully retired from this department. My health has been injured beyond repair, and I feel that I will be unfit to continue the performance of my duties and I would rather stay retired."

Then Police Commissioner said to me that he will restore me back to my rank as Deputy Chief Inspector of Police.[5] I then said, "Mr. Commissioner, I had lost the difference in pay for 3 weeks that I had been in the rank of captain, and I see no reason why I should have lost any money at all because all that I did, Mr. Commissioner, was to enforce the laws of this state." And he said, "I will

[5] [So that Goldberg could retire at that rank.—Ed.]

return you the money that you lost." And subsequently the Police Department returned the money to me.

Cross Examination by Mr. Carter:

Q. Now, your retirement was voluntary, wasn't it? I mean, nobody forced you into it, did they? ——Well, using the police language, when a high-ranking officer is demoted, that is considered more or less . . . of an invitation to get out.

Q. And you accepted the invitation, I take it; didn't you? ——I retired. I had no invitation. I am only giving the jury and honorable Judge an opinion of a police officer with 26 years of police experience. I had no invitation. I wanted the job.

* * * * *

THE COURT: I think what you mean is this: That when a high-ranking officer, or one who has held a high rank, is demoted, it puts him in a sort of untenable position with people who have theretofore been his subordinates.

THE WITNESS: That's right.

* * * * *

Q. Let's go back for a moment to the time in 1953, when you were . . . made a Deputy Chief Inspector. Between 1953 and August, let's say—the middle of August, 1954, had you taken any affirmative action with respect to charitable bingo in Brooklyn? ——The Police Department?

Q. No, you. ——I?

Q. You. ——As a member of the Police Department, we do not decide and we are not censors to ascertain the origin of a bingo or any other gambling enterprise. Bingo is not and was not my main duty.

* * * * *

Q. What affirmative action had you . . . taken between March of 1953 and August of 1954 with respect to charitable bingo in Brooklyn? ——Well, the only time we enforce the bingo laws is when it was called to our attention.

Q. . . . Are you saying by that, Mr. Goldberg, that nobody called your attention to playing of bingo in Brooklyn during that period. . .? ——I would say very, very little, if any. . . . We had some activity. I wouldn't say none at all.

* * * * *

Q. Didn't you say on your direct examination . . . that it was your policy when you found that charity was involved not to make summary arrests?

* * * * *

——I said nothing of the kind. I said nothing about charity. I will repeat again, for the benefit of the Court and jury.

Q. And mine, too, if you don't mind. ——And yours. I did say, and I say again and again, that I have respect for authority. That I see no reason why I, as a law-enforcing agent, should take drastic action against religious or fraternal organizations. Because of that, I took it upon myself to show kindness, to show culture, to show refinement, to show appreciation for the institutions concerned, and I said we should not make summary arrests. The people are decent, the people are nice. I have no reason to arrest for such a condition. And because of that, and because of the respect that I have for the people of this community and for the institutions that I had made reference to, that I said we will not make arrests. I said nothing about charitable institutions. I am charitable to all people.

Q. Well, now, did you make summary arrests when you found bingo games were being run by professionals? ——I found no professionals. I found no professionals in my experience. In my experience I found no grounds, or reasons, for making summary arrests in connection with bingo.

Q. Now, do I understand from that, so we'll be perfectly clear, that between March of 1953 and August of 1954, you or your squad made no arrests for professional bingo; is that the fact? ——That's right, we made no arrest for bingo.

Q. And would your answer be the same if I asked the question with respect to charitable bingo? ——I couldn't answer the question when you mention charitable bingo. That was not within the scope of my position, I couldn't answer that question.

Q. Did the fact that the proceeds of these bingo games—did the fact that those proceeds were going to charity induce you to be nice to these people? ——I am nice to the most vicious criminal. I am a gentleman and always have been.

* * * * *

Q. Mr. Goldberg, commencing in the latter part of August of 1954, there was a sudden spurt of activity on your part in Brooklyn in connection with bingo; was there not?

* * * * *

——Yes, I would say there was.

* * * * *

Q. Well, now at or about this time the New York newspapers were writing stories about bingo in Brooklyn and your activities in connection with it, weren't they? ——Yes.

Q. At or about that same time, isn't it the fact that substantial citizens—not only of Brooklyn, but of New York City—were making inquiry of the Police Department and, more particularly, the Police Commissioner, as to what the official attitude of the Department was with respect to bingo? ——I don't know anything about that.

Q. Well, you were reading the papers, weren't you? ——Yes, I read the papers.

Q. Now, as a result of what you read in the newspapers on or about September 2nd and September 3rd, did you realize that—at least according to the newspapers—your activities and the activities of your squad in connection with bingo was causing widespread embarrassment to the Police Department? ——No. I was simply enforcing the law of the state of New York and performing my duty.

* * * * *

Q. . . . Now, prior to September 2nd, did you have any discussion with your superior, [Assistant] Chief Inspector Condon, relative to your activities in connection with bingo? ——Yes, sir. . . . Following the receipt of the complaint from Attorney Jackman.

Q. And that would be approximately August 17th, or thereabouts? ——A few days after.

* * * * *

Q. . . . Now is it the fact that you told your superior that 30 years ago some . . . police inspectors were brought up on charges and sentenced to jail for failing to enforce the laws? Did you tell that to Condon? ——Yes.

* * * * *

Q. When did you tell that to him? ——During a conversation that I had with him after I had received the complaint from Attorney Jackman.
[several questions omitted].

Q. Now, when you are told that to Condon . . . was that in reply to a suggestion made to you by Condon to consult with him prior to engaging in any more activities in connection with bingo? ——Well, Condon never told me to consult with him prior to any bingo or any law enforcement. Condon never told me to consult with him.

* * * * *

Q. Well, would you tell us then . . . what purpose you had in reminding Condon that 30 years before inspectors had gone to jail for failing to enforce the law? ——I had received a complaint from the Police Commissioner's office written to the Police Commissioner by an attorney named Jackman, with an endorsement thereon by the Chief Inspector for appropriate police action. . . . I went upstairs and I spoke with my immediate superior officer, Assistant Chief Inspector David Condon. . . . I showed it to Inspector Condon and he read it, and it is at this time that I said, "Dave, this man is complaining. He has a serious complaint." I said, "We have a new Police Commissioner. We must be very careful not to overlook any violations that are called to our attention. This letter of complaint was written to the Police Commissioner and it was sent to us with an endorsement by the Chief Inspector, where all kinds of violations have been mentioned, including lottery, which takes in bingo." And I said, "I am causing a survey to be made to ascertain where these violations take place," and I said, "We must enforce it religiously." I said, "We cannot overlook any violations because they may be within a religious place." I said, "Law must be enforced impartially and I would recommend that we follow that attitude." I said, "I recall when I was a young policeman that almost every police inspector was brought up on charges and, if my memory serves me correctly, they were sent to jail for a year less one day. . . ." And that was in my mind, and my thoughts always were to do the right thing by the people and for the people, without any prejudice, without any hatred, without any disrespect for authority. And Dave Condon agreed that I should do just that, and that was the policy that we adopted. And I continued by saying, "Dave, in places of religious institutions and fraternal organizations, we will not make a summary arrest, but we'll ask the people to please cooperate with the authority." And Dave agreed with me. . . . But with the permission of the Court, I want to say at this time that at no time did Dave Condon tell me not to enforce the law.

* * * * *

Q. Now, did you have a conversation with him on or about September 2nd? ——Yes, sir, I did.

Q. Now, did you seek out Inspector Condon on September 2nd, or did Condon seek you out? ——No, I went to speak to Inspector Condon.

* * * * *

Q. Now, I take it you had a reason for that, didn't you? ——Yes, sir.

* * * * *

Q. What was the reason? ——The newspaper article that I read that day in which Mr. Dougherty made a statement. The newspaper article of September the 2nd, in which Deputy Police Commissioner Dougherty made a statement in the press that policemen were expected to wink at bingo games.

* * * * *

Q. Now, if I understood you correctly yesterday, you testified, in substance, that when you saw Condon on or about September 2nd, he told you to continue enforcing the law? ——Yes, sir.

* * * * *

Q. . . . Was that the truth? ——That was not the complete answer. . . . Dave Condon told me not to enforce the law in certain places. He told me—I would like to complete this, your Honor.

THE COURT: Finish the answer.

THE WITNESS: It's of utmost importance. Dave Condon said to me, "Lou, I spoke to Chief Inspector Kennedy, and he told me to tell you that Monsignor Bracken, the Police Department Chaplain, has told the Chief Inspector that clergymen of the Catholic churches in Brooklyn had told Monsignor Bracken that since the bingo has been discontinued in the borough of Brooklyn, the churches were losing large revenue."

Dave Condon told me that "Stephen Kennedy told me to tell you, Louis Goldberg, that you should not enforce the law on bingo in Catholic churches if they play the game on their church property."[6]

I said, "Dave, let me get this straight. I want to do the right thing. I want to protect my job; I have a long time in the Police Department. But please tell me, Dave, assuming that there is a Catholic church on this corner that has a bingo game, and there is a non-Catholic church on this corner that has a bingo game, do I understand you, Dave, that we are to let this church—the Catholic church—violate the law and take action in this church?"

He said, "Lou, I know that isn't right, but the Chief Inspector told me to tell you to do that." I said, "Dave, your order will be complied with. I will tell my men just what you said."

* * * * *

Q. Well, now, Mr. Goldberg, didn't you tell this Court and jury yesterday . . . that . . . Inspector Condon . . . told you "continue to enforce the law?" ——That's right.

* * * * *

Q. . . . after the newspaper articles on September 2nd. . . . Didn't you say that? ——That's right. . . .

Q. Now, I am asking you when for the first time Condon told you not to enforce the law with respect to bingo in Catholic institutions? ——That was some time in August, 1954—latter part.

* * * * *

Q. Now isn't it a fact, Mr. Goldberg, that Condon made that statement to you after your activity in Brooklyn in connection with the banning of bingo had reached the stage where it was the subject of widespread comment in the press? ——I don't recall just when Dave Condon made that statement.

Q. . . . So that according to your present recollection, Condon made that statement to you after September 2nd or September 3rd . . .? ——No, not after September 2nd. No.

Q. Well, now, when you went to the Knights of Columbus to ban bingo, were you distinguishing between a Catholic church and a charitable organization? ——I did not go to the Knights of Columbus to ban bingo.

Q. Well, now, if Condon gave you those instructions, as you say, in August, you promptly proceeded to violate them, didn't you? ——I violated no orders.

* * * * *

Q. Well, when you received these instructions from Inspector Condon, whenever you received them, did you follow them? ——Yes, sir.

Q. Did you discontinue your efforts to ban bingo at Catholic churches? ——There was no such thing. I wouldn't use the word "ban" bingo. We asked them to please discontinue. I wouldn't use the word "ban." There is a big difference between ban and asking.

* * * * *

Q. Mr. Goldberg . . . I want to know . . . if you can tell me if you distinguish between the use of the word "ban" and "prevent"? ——Well, I am not qualified to give you an answer on anything like that.

Q. Are you sufficiently qualified if I changed the word "prevent" and "stop" and ask you if you distinguish between . . . "ban" on the one hand and "stop" on another? ——No, I couldn't answer that either because that has been shown in the Columbus Clubhouse. We asked them to please discontinue but they didn't discontinue. They continued playing nevertheless.

Q. We'll come to that. I am asking you—and if you don't understand this question, please so indicate. . . . After you received these instructions with respect to the Catholic churches from Inspector Condon, did you discontinue your efforts and the efforts of your squad designed to prevent bingo at those institutions? ——Well, I gave the instructions to my superior [*subordinate*] officers. And I might mention at this time, if your Honor will permit, that in my answer I omitted to say that I asked Dave Condon, at the time of that conversation we had, did he tell the Chief Inspector that we are not making summary arrests at religious institutions and fraternal institutions. He said no. I said, "Well, perhaps that's what the Chief Inspector meant, not to make summary arrests." Because when a complaint is received you must investigate. If the complaint is not sent to you, or you don't receive a complaint, you don't investigate. But you have to answer a complaint. And in order to answer a complaint, you investigate the complaint.

Now, as I understood that request for the Catholic churches to continue, that the complaints would have to be investigated under all circumstances, but we would not send policemen there, as we had been doing in other places, to check on them as to whether or not they played. But the complaint had

6 [*Editor's Note: On October 12, 1954, Commissioner Dougherty had issued a statement approved by Adams, containing a denial by Condon that he had ever received such orders from Kennedy or passed them on to Goldberg. A direct question whether he had ever received such orders was never put to Condon at this trial.*]

to be investigated, otherwise why did the Police Department send the complaint to me. It had to be investigated.

For me to make a false statement in answering that it was investigated and no action—and no violations was observed would be a false statement. And because of that we had to investigate. But I told Dave Condon, "Now, perhaps if Chief Inspector Kennedy had known of our plan that we will not make arrests—we were not making arrests at places of religious nature and fraternal organizations—then he would understand the situation."

But we made no arrests anyway. All we did—we asked the people to please discontinue, and we were performing our duty. And that is about the answer to that.

Q. Now, would you mind answering the question, please? Would you read it to him, Mr. Stenographer.

* * * * *

——Well, I instructed my men and my subordinate superiors. I gave them the information I received from Inspector Condon and told them not to proceed. But investigation of complaints had to be investigated. But we did not send policemen there at nighttime, or whenever the game would take place, for the purpose of observing or to see whether or not they continued playing.

* * * * *

Q. Now, when you got a complaint about bingo being played at a Catholic church and you or your men investigated, did you allow the game to continue? . . .

THE COURT: . . . Or did you suggest in a kind way to the people in charge that the game not be played? Add that to the question.

THE WITNESS: Well, after the request was made that the Catholic churches be permitted to play on Catholic church property, they were not in any way interfered with. I don't know of any case where churches, after that request, had been interfered with while the game was in progress.

* * * * *

THE COURT: Well, were there situations where, while the game may not have been in progress, you had information that a game was planned? ——Yes, sir.

* * * * *

THE COURT: Well, what would be your procedure. . . ? ——To interview and ascertain so you will be able to answer the report. But no action would be taken in connection with the game itself.

* * * * *

Q. Well, then to that extent, Inspector, you were carrying out to the letter the instructions you had received from Chief Condon, weren't you? ——I was enforcing the law.

Q. You say you were enforcing the law by allowing the game to continue because it was being run by a Catholic church? ——I was enforcing the law and I was obedient to the orders of my superior officers.

* * * * *

THE COURT: . . . I would like to ask this one question. I am a little bit confused.

You said that on September 2nd, you had a conversation with Inspector Condon in which he said, in substance, continue to enforce the law.

THE WITNESS: Yes.

THE COURT: Well, that direction by Inspector Condon, it seems to me, would have been inconsistent with what you say he told you in August, which was do not interfere if these games are being played in Catholic churches on church property.

THE WITNESS: Yes, sir.

Q. . . . Didn't you tell us . . . that Condon told you, his subordinate, that the Chief Inspector had told him, Condon, to tell you not to enforce the anti-bingo law in Catholic churches? ——That's right.

Q. So to that extent through the chain of command from the Chief Inspector to the Deputy Assistant Inspector to you, instructions were given that the anti-bingo law was not to be enforced in Catholic churches. . . ? ——In substance, yes.

* * * * *

Q. Did you say to Condon or anybody else, "Give it to me in writing and we'll see what we'll do about it."? ——I certainly did not.

* * * * *

Q. Now, did you ever discuss with anyone in the Police Department who was higher in rank than you and higher in rank than Condon—and I am referring particularly to the Chief Inspector, Stephen Kennedy, and Police Commissioner Adams—the instructions relayed to you by Condon not to enforce the anti-bingo gambling law in Catholic churches? ——I was never questioned by any one of the officers you mention.

Q. I didn't ask you, sir, if you were questioned about it. I asked you did you discuss those instructions with anyone in a rank above your own? ——No, I did not.

* * * * *

Redirect Examination by Mr. Siegel:

Q. Mr. Goldberg, just to clarify, just a few questions I would like to ask you.

Under the rules of the Police Department, do you have the authority to question a superior—your superior's orders? Do you have a right to question them? ——Well, I may ask for an explanation.

Q. But if an order is given? ——It's an order.

Q. Under the rules of the Department, must you obey it? ——Yes, sir.

* * * * *

Q. Now I want to ask this question: Did you receive any letters or telephone calls from some substantial citizens commending you upon your activity in connection with bingo violations after August 17, 1954? ——Yes, I received many commending me for my police action.

Q. Now, after August of 1954, or August 17, 1954, did you receive any complaint from any of your superiors with respect to your activities in connection with the enforcement of bingo violations? ——I received no complaints from my superiors to that effect.

* * * * *

Testimony of Former Assistant Chief Inspector David A. Condon

Direct Examination by Mr. Carter:

Q. When did you retire? —— . . . July, 1956.

Q. Now, as of July, 1956, how long had you been a member of the Police Department? ——38 years.

* * * * *

Q. How long had you known Deputy Chief Inspector Goldberg, approximately? ——Well, I know him since we're patrolmen together; we used to study —we didn't study together but we were going to school together. I knew him then, although we weren't exactly friendly at that time.

Q. That would go back, as of 1954, over a period of thirty years, about? ——At least, yes.

Q. Now, between, let's say, January 1st of 1954 and the middle of August of 1954, was there any activity by the men in your command with respect to the enforcement of the anti-bingo law where charities were involved? ——Not to my knowledge there wasn't, no.

Q. Have you any recollection of any so-called charity bingo games being stopped between January 1st, let's say, of 1954 and the middle of August of 1954? ——No.

Q. Now, to your knowledge, in the Borough of Brooklyn, during that period of time, were bingo games being played where the proceeds were for charitable purposes? ——Yes.

Q. Had you at any time received any instructions from Police Headquarters in Manhattan to enforce the anti-bingo laws in connection with those games? ——No, except once in a while we would get a complaint and just come over and we would answer it back and that would be all to it. See?

Q. Now, was Inspector Goldberg in your command during the period, say, from January 1, 1954 through September of 1954—or through August of 1954? ——Yes, he was.

Q. And to your knowledge, up to August 15, 1954, had Inspector Goldberg been taking any action to enforce the anti-bingo law? ——None that I know of.

Q. Now, between the 15th of August and let's say Labor Day, the 2nd or 3rd of September, 1954, was there Police Department activity in this borough in connection with charitable bingo? ——Yes. Inspector Goldberg had notified a number of people to discontinue their games.

Q. Were you as of that time, say in August, familiar with the activities of Inspector Goldberg? ——Yes.

Q. Have you any idea of the number of occasions in which Inspector Goldberg had stopped bingo games where the proceeds were for charity? ——I wouldn't know how many, just a number. They were calling me up.

Q. You say they were calling you up. Who was calling you up, for instance? ——Well, various American Legion posts and some of the churches and some representative synagogues called me up and I referred them to Inspector Goldberg's office until Monsignor Bracken called me up.

* * * * *

Q. What was the substance of these calls? —— They wanted to know if there was any change in the policy of running bingo games in the Borough of Brooklyn and I said that I didn't receive any such orders from Headquarters.

Q. And what had the policy been up to that point? ——Well, the policy had been to where they were run by charitable or fraternal or religious associations, it wasn't run by anybody outside and handled by themselves, we were not to interfere with them. That was the general attitude taken at the time.

Q. Did there come a time, as you say, when Monsignor Bracken called you up? ——Yes.

Q. Who is Monsignor Bracken? ——Monsignor Bracken is the Catholic Chaplain for the Police Department. He has the similar rank of Inspector within the Department.

Q. Now, approximately when did Monsignor Bracken call you? ——Almost, to be exact, I should think it would be about August 30th, the Monday before.

Q. And what was the substance of your conversation? ——He asked me if there had been any change in the policy of bingo and I said "Not that I know of." I said I didn't receive any word from Headquarters and I didn't get any telephone—any written orders about [it]. So he said to me, "You know they're stopping bingo games?" I said "Yes." . . . He said, "What is that about?" I said, "Well, Inspector Goldberg has decided they must be stopped."

Q. Yes? ——So I said, "I can't do anything about it because he maintains it's a violation of law, and I guess technically it was a lottery, distribution of property by chance. I can't tell him to let them go." So he said to me, "Do you think I would do any good by calling Jim Kennedy?" [James Kennedy was First Deputy Commissioner; no relation to Chief Inspector Stephen Kennedy.]

* * * * *

Q. As a result of the conversation that you had with Monsignor Bracken, did you talk to anyone in Police Headquarters who was superior in rank to you? ——Yes.

Q. Who? ——First Deputy Commissioner Kennedy, James Kennedy.

* * * * *

Q. Now, when did you talk with James Kennedy? ——I'm pretty sure, I'm almost positive the date was September 1st because there was a graduation—appointment of new recruits and I met him in the building there and spoke to him.

Q. What was the conversation you had with 1st Deputy Police Commissioner Kennedy?

* * * * *

——I said to him, "Monsignor Bracken told me that he spoke to you about this stopping of bingo games and that you told him to see Dave"—who was I—"about it." So Monsignor Bracken said, he said, "I didn't tell him that I had spoken to you already."

So when I saw him in the building, I asked him about it. He said, "Yes, what is that about?" I said, "Inspector Goldberg had decided that he's going to stop the bingo games." He said to me, "Go down and tell that to Steve."

Q. Steve who? ——He meant Steve Kennedy, the Chief Inspector.

I went down to see the Chief and he wasn't in, he was up with the Commissioner. So I waited at least an hour and he didn't come down. So I left a message with an Inspector in his office to give to him.

That afternoon—that evening around, well, around four, between four and five, Kennedy called me up, Steve Kennedy, Chief Inspector, and he said "I got your message." And I said "Yes." He said, "You tell that fellow that he's not setting the policy of this Department. And if he attempts to set the policy of this Department, he'll find out what happens to him."

MR. SIEGEL: May we have the date on that, please?

THE COURT: Can you tell us about when this conversation was?

THE WITNESS: I think the exact date is September 1st. . . . So I sent for Goldberg, he's downstairs, two floors below me—

Q. This is on the same day? ——Same afternoon, same night. And I told Goldberg what Kennedy had told me.

Q. Did you repeat that conversation to Goldberg? ——That's right. And he says to me, "What does that mean?" I says, "Well, I don't know, it means to follow the policy that's been going on." He says, "Does that mean that I'll let bingo run?" I says, "Well, I don't know. Whatever the policy was." I wasn't going to commit myself to Goldberg.

So he said, "Well, I don't understand the policy." "Well," I said, "why don't you go over and ask him? You know all of these people. You know Steve Kennedy, he worked for you, and you know the 1st Deputy, you know, find out what the policy is."

The next day, I think it was September 2nd, or something, [Deputy] Commissioner Dougherty, who was public relations man for Commissioner Adams, Public Relations Deputy Commissioner, issued a statement in the paper to the effect that I have stated before, that there was no change in the policy, that in religious and social and fraternal organizations where nobody was interfering with them, nobody was running it for them, it was run by themselves . . . and the proceeds were used strictly for their organization or church or religious institution, that we would not interfere with them.

Q. Now, after you had read that in the newspaper, did you have a further conversation with Inspector Goldberg? ——We had conversations back and forth about the things.

Q. Now, did you have any further conversation with Inspector Goldberg with respect to the policy of the Department? ——No, except that I—well, this happened on September 8th, I think that was the date they went down to the Knights of Columbus. I sent for Goldberg on something else.

So when he was through—when I was through with this investigation I had, another thing about some action he didn't take, I said to him, "Look, what's your policy now on the bingo?" He said to me, "Unless you give me an order in writing not to interfere with bingo or to permit bingo games to run, I'll stop them."

I says, "I'm not going to give you any such thing in writing at all." So I said, "Is that despite the policy of the Police Department?" He said, "What is the policy of the Police Department? I don't know." I said, "Well, it was Dougherty issued it for you [in his press release]. The policy has been going on for years, going on for a couple of years anyway. If there's any doubt in your mind, why don't you before you do these things go over and see somebody over there. Go over and see Dougherty and ask him what is the policy."

He says, "Give it to me in writing." I says, "I didn't get it in writing, I'm not going to give it to you in writing." And he left.

* * * * *

Q. And any time during the day of September 8, 1954, did Inspector Goldberg tell you in words or in substance, that he was going to visit the Knights of Columbus? ——No.

Q. Now, when for the first time did you learn that Inspector Goldberg had visited the Knights of Columbus and banned the game that was scheduled for that night? ——I guess it was when I was back to the office after being out in the afternoon, it was in the neighborhood of five o'clock, and there was a message there that Mr. Halpin of the Knights of Columbus, or Columbus Club, wanted to talk to me about something important. So I called him up and he told me that Goldberg had been there and told him that he could not run that game tonight.

"Well," I said, "I think you misunderstood Goldberg, because Goldberg and I had an understanding." And I did speak to him one day about it in the presence of a number of people, an understanding that he would give these people a chance to stop their games in view of the fact that they had been running so long.

And I said, I added, "I mentioned to Goldberg in view of the fact that you allowed them to run so long, that I think you should give them a chance." He agreed very willingly to that. There were a number of other people in the room at that time. That was some time previous.

So I said to him, "I think you misunderstood him. You don't have any chance to stop that game, so you run it tonight. You can run it. I don't think Goldberg will interfere with you. With the understanding that you announce to these people at night that this is the last time that will be played for this hospital. And that's all."

* * * * *

Q. Did you let it be known to whoever made inquiry of you that you had instructed Mr. Halpin to play the game that night on the condition which you have outlined? ——That's right; I told that to my office when they made the inquiry, sir.

Q. And did you officially give orders to your office that the game at the Columbus Club was to be run that night with the approbation of the Police Department? ——No, I told them I was allowing it to run in the interests of safety, that there would be a riot, there would be trouble if they try to stop it.

Q. In your experience as a police officer at that time of approximately 36 years, had that game been stopped that evening, how many policemen would have to be assigned there? ——Well, from experience we had out in Arcadia Hall, I think we would need fifty or sixty policemen there. There was something like approximately a thousand, all women.

THE COURT: Was that because they were women, you would need all those cops?

THE WITNESS: They would make more disorder with the screaming and hollering. I think there was quite a disorder after it was announced that they weren't going to play any more.

* * * * *

Q. Now, sometime later that evening, did you have a conversation with . . . Chief Inspector Stephen Kennedy?

——Yes, not about bingo.

Q. Was that a telephone conversation? ——Telephone conversation I received home around two o'clock in the morning.

THE COURT: This was on September 9th?

THE WITNESS: Yes.

Q. Now, what was the substance of that conversation? ——He said to me, "You had a policeman shoot his wife last night." I said, "Yes." He said, "Were you there?" I said, "No, I wasn't."

——And he said, "All right, be here tomorrow morning at nine o'clock."

Q. Were you at his office at nine o'clock the following morning? ——Right.

Q. Did you talk with him? ——Yes.

* * * * *

Q. Will you state in your own words, please, the substance of the conversation that you had with Chief Inspector Kennedy that morning? ——Well, he said to me, "What happened last night?" I said, "Well, I don't know." He said, "Over in the Knights of Columbus?" I said, "I don't know." I didn't even know at the time. So he said, "Did the bingo game go?" I said, "Yes, as near as I know, it went." He said, "Did Goldberg try stop the game?" I said, "Well, I don't know. I think he sent somebody down from what I hear and they found that I had given them permission and they left." He said, "Did he tell you he was going down?" I said, "No." That was about all.

Q. Was there any conversation between you and Chief Inspector Kennedy that morning with respect to an understanding or an arrangement that you had with Chief Inspector Goldberg with respect to his future activities in connection with charitable bingo?

* * * * *

——Yes, he asked me about the instructions I gave him and I told him that [*I had told Goldberg that*] he was not to change the policy. But I said [*to Kennedy*], "Goldberg insisted he was going to stop them. So I said, in trying to keep Goldberg out of trouble, really, I said, 'Before you go to stop any of these games, let me know ahead of time, will you? Because I'll notify Headquarters and see what we can do about it.' " I knew that Headquarters, from certain actions were getting very angry at these things and I was trying to tone Goldberg down to comply with the order that he got.

Q. Did you tell that to Stephen Kennedy? ——I told that to Steve Kennedy. . . . I remember he got a stenographer there and he was writing this memorandum to the Commissioner.

* * * * *

THE COURT: Now, have you told us all of the conversation?

THE WITNESS: As near as I know. It wasn't a long conversation. The conversation, in full, as I can remember, I went in and I thought I was going in about the patrolman, sir. . . . So he said to me . . . "Did Goldberg tell you he was going there?" [*to the Columbus Club*]. I said, "No . . . I told him, 'Don't take any action in these cases until you get in touch with me first.' "

* * * * *

THE COURT: Mr. Condon, you testified, as I recall it, that on the morning of September 8th, you suggested to the plaintiff Goldberg that before he took any action in any of these situations, he consult with you?

THE WITNESS: That's right.

* * * * *

THE COURT: Here is what I wanted to know from the witness; was your conversation with Goldberg in that respect in the nature of a direction or an order or was it merely a suggestion?

THE WITNESS: Well, I guess it was—I don't know what you would interpret it. Here's almost the words I used: "Before you take any action in these cases to stop any of these games, you had better get in touch with me so that I can notify Headquarters."

THE COURT: Did you consider that to be a direction from a superior officer to a subordinate not to do anything until he first consulted with you?

* * * * *

THE WITNESS: I considered it an order because it involved me that I would have to get help if he did. I said, "Before you do anything in these games, consult with me, let me know."

Q. And you considered that an order? ——I considered that an order in view of the fact that he was taking action which would require my attention to send men there to preserve order.

THE COURT: Will you tell me this: When Goldberg said to you, as you say, "What is the policy of the Department?" You knew what that policy was?

THE WITNESS: I had my idea of the policy, yes.

THE COURT: You knew what it was?

THE WITNESS: Yes.

THE COURT: Your answer to him, as I recall it, was, "Why don't you go and see Kennedy about it?"

THE WITNESS: That's right.

THE COURT: You were his superior?

THE WITNESS: Yes.

THE COURT: Why wasn't it the sensible thing to say, "Look, this is the policy and you know what it is."

THE WITNESS: Well, I don't know, not with Goldberg. I wouldn't tell him what the policy was.

THE COURT: What?

THE WITNESS: Not with Goldberg. I wouldn't tell him what the policy was, sir. In fact, I didn't positively know. The only information I had on the policy was what I had from custom and from what I read from Dougherty in the paper. And that's where he should get his policy, I thought, the same as mine. Nobody at Headquarters ever wrote the policy out for me. And I presumed the policy, and I wanted Goldberg to presume the policy the same as they did.

Policy is not a special order that they give or anything. It's just a custom that goes around and you have to find out what it is and comply with it. That's all.

Cross Examination by Mr. Siegel:

Q. Mr. Condon, you and Mr. Goldberg had been on the force for about 36, 38 years, is that right? ——Right.

* * * * *

Q. And what was Mr. Goldberg's reputation with respect to honesty and integrity? ——Oh, he had a wonderful reputation for honesty and integrity.

Q. And what was Mr. Goldberg's reputation with respect to faithfulness to duty? ——Very good, too.

Q. And what was Mr. Goldberg's reputation over these years that you knew him for being a disciplinarian? ——He was supposed to have a very good reputation—good reputation. But when he worked with me, he didn't—probably I kept him down; he didn't exact too much discipline.

* * * * *

Q. And Mr. Goldberg, in your opinion, always enjoyed the finest reputation as a police officer, is that right? ——Yes.

Q. And you never heard anybody complaining about Mr. Goldberg's activities as a police officer other than this situation that you are now talking about in September, 1954? ——Well, I don't know how to answer that. You see, Goldberg's attitude was he wanted to enforce things regardless of policy.

Q. I see. ——And there were certain instances like that where I would be called to Headquarters and told to tell Goldberg to—

Q. Now, you say with respect to enforcement of bingo regardless of policy, you say that you didn't approve of his actions, is that right? ——In enforcing bingo?

Q. Yes. ——I didn't care anything about it. It was Headquarters who didn't want him to enforce.

Q. I'm talking about you, Mr. Condon. You were his superior? ——That's right.

Q. Now, did you approve of everything he did as a police officer with respect to his conduct of the men and the enforcement of gambling other than this winking at bingo? ——I said I approved of everything, even the bingo.

* * * * *

Q. And the only objection you had with respect to Mr. Goldberg's activity is that he didn't tell you that he was going to the Columbus Club, is that right? —— . . . . That's right.

* * * * *

Q. . . . You are his superior? ——[several lines omitted] I was in charge of Brooklyn, yes. [several lines omitted]. The wording of the thing was read to me by Commissioner Adams. When he felt that I was not active enough in that, he brought me over one day and he read the order to me which read like this: Plainclothes staff in the Borough of Brooklyn will be under the head of a Deputy Chief, or something, under the immediate supervision of the Borough Commander. And Commissioner Adams says, "Who is the Borough Commander, is that you?" I said, "Yes." So he said, "What are you doing about it?" "Well," I says, "I can do as much as I can. I have everything else to handle besides that and I have a big staff. But that's how much they run to me, the same as any captain was under me."

* * * * *

Q. Now you said you had a talk with Commissioner Adams about the Public Morals Squad? —— Yes.

Q. And when was that? ——The early part of January . . . I think it was around January 13th.

* * * * *

Q. He was appointed a few days before that, is that right? ——January 1st. . . .

Q. The 13th you went to Headquarters in Manhattan to talk about Brooklyn . . .? ——Right.

* * * * *

Q. . . . Who else was at that meeting . . .? —— The Chief Inspector and the Chief of Staff.

Q. And did you talk about the Public Morals squad? ——Yes.

Q. And did Commissioner Adams then say that he was not satisfied with the number of arrests and the number of convictions in Brooklyn as far as gambling was concerned? ——He said he was not satisfied with the number of arrests.

* * * * *

Q. And he wanted more arrests by the Public Morals Squad in Brooklyn? ——Right.

* * * * *

Q. And at that meeting . . . didn't you say to Mr. Adams that Goldberg was doing a good job as head of the Public Morals Squad? . . . ——Probably did.

* * * * *

Q. Now if a Commissioner were to get [a] letter and send it on . . . how would that come to your office? ——Well, a letter on gambling wouldn't come to my office at all. . . . It would go direct to Goldberg's office in a sealed envelope.

* * * * *

Q. . . . Now I show you Plaintiff's Exhibits 2-A and 2-B [the Jackman letter and the transmittal memorandum] . . ? [several lines omitted] . . . You know why this has a memorandum on the back? It's gone to every borough so they had to make this one up, make a copy of it and put it on it and the copy is rubber stamped. . . . It didn't mean it was anything important. . . . They made up Kennedy's signature rubber stamped.

Q. So this letter was not important? ——No.

Q. So in your opinion, if a complaint like that was received by a Borough Commander or by Mr. Goldberg, he's to disregard this letter because it has no meaning whatsoever, is that right? ——No, I didn't say that. It doesn't have the importance that if Kennedy sent him the little note on that.

* * * * *

Q. Does it mean what it says when it says here, "The attached copy of communication is referred to you for investigation, appropriate action and report in duplicate . . . Signed, Stephen B. Kennedy, Chief Inspector" . . . ? ——Yes, you can put that on barking dogs, too, the same thing, same endorsement; a complaint of barking dogs or uncovered garbage cans, same endorsement.

* * * * *

Q. What was Mr. Goldberg supposed to do after he got this letter from the Chief Inspector's office, according to the rules and regulations of the Police Department? ——Investigate it.

Q. . . . And after he investigated it, what was he supposed to do . . . ? ——I guess what he was doing for the last year he was in there. . . . I did have out of my file when this investigation was going on seven or eight letters complaining of bingo and endorsed by Inspector Goldberg to the effect that there's no gambling in the premises.

Q. And he's supposed to say that there is no gambling in the premises? ——That's what he said on the others. I don't know what he's supposed to say here.

* * * * *

Q. Did you at any time tell Mr. Goldberg not to enforce bingo violations? ——Never did.

Q. Now after Mr. Goldberg started investigating the [Jackman] complaint . . . he told you what he was doing? ——He did.

Q. And you did not disagree with what he was doing, you approved it? ——Never did.

Q. You approved it? ——That's right.

Q. Now there came a time when some people telephoned you? ——Yes.

Q. And they complained about Mr. Goldberg closing down these places, is that right? ——They wanted to know why they had changed the policy, that's what they inquired.

Q. What was the policy of the Department with respect to bingo enforcement in August of 1954? ——Well, as near as I took it, it was that if it was charitable or religious or fraternal organization, that no people outside run it, and the proceeds were used entirely for that organization, that they were not going to interfere with it.

Q. Now where did you get that policy from? ——Well, it was by custom which you get policy and the custom was not to bother with it, by custom; and later in this particular case, it was issued by Dougherty in the newspapers.

* * * * *

Q. And did you know that it was not Commissioner Adams' policy not to enforce bingo? ——No, I didn't know that.

Q. Mr. Adams testified[7] that it was the policy of the Department at all times to enforce bingo violations. Do you disagree with that statement? ——No, I didn't say that. I said I didn't know. I just figured that it was allowed to be continued, sir.

* * * * *

THE COURT: In connection with this Columbus Club situation, did you consider the fact that Mr. Goldberg had not reported to you in advance of whatever action he took there was a violation of the order which you had given? ——I thought it was, yes, because there would have been—

THE COURT: Didn't you just say that you had told him that his duty was to enforce the law? ——Right.

THE COURT: In that situation, was he enforcing the law? ——He was, but it was enforcing the law under conditions which would cause a lot of disorder and trouble for something that had been allowed to continue for some time.

* * * * *

Q. Supposing I told you that Mr. Adams said that the policy of the Department was not to wink at bingo but to enforce? ——If Adams said it—I didn't count it as the policy.

7 [Commissioner Adams' testimony is presented here after Condon's so that the reader may see how things looked at successively higher levels in the Police Department. Adams' testimony on this particular point may be found below on pages 260 and 261.—Ed.]

Q. And you believed that the policy of the Department was to wink at bingo when you read it in the newspapers on September 2nd or 3rd, 1954? ——I had the opinion all year not to wink at it but not to bother with it as long as it's run for religious and fraternal organizations, I had that in my opinion all the time. I understood that was their policy.

Q. What was Mr. Goldberg's duty with respect to enforcing bingo if it came to his attention that bingo violation was being played at a particular place? ——I guess he would have to enforce the law.

Q. He would have to enforce it? ——That's right. When he told me he was going to enforce it, I said, "I can't tell you not to."

Q. Now, was that in compliance with the policy of the Department if he went out and enforced bingo? ——Well, I didn't think it was, but I wouldn't tell Goldberg not to do it. I didn't think it was the policy of the Department in those kind of institutions.

* * * * *

Q. You didn't have that officially from any source whatsoever? ——No.

Q. Now, when Mr. Goldberg received a complaint from a taxpayer to investigate bingo at the Columbus Club, was he required to follow up that complaint? ——Yes.

Q. And what was he supposed to do with that complaint? ——Whatever action—stop the bingo game.

Q. He was supposed to? ——Yes. As long as it had been going so long, I didn't want it to be stopped in any way that would cause disorder.

Q. Is there a duty on the part of a police officer to investigate a complaint? ——Yes.

Q. And if he doesn't investigate a complaint, is that a violation of the rules and regulations of the Police Department? ——Right.

* * * * *

Q. And if he were to enforce the law according to the complaint, would he be following the policy of the Department? ——In which particular case? You see, there are a lot of things that are allowed, certain laws that are just prohibited—they're violations because they're prohibited. So the Department turns and frowns on these things. They get the idea that it's a law that's not for the convenience of the citizen. I have in mind which Goldberg has very much in mind, the Sabbath law. The Sabbath law is widely open over in Brownsville, nobody complains. Over on the east side of New York, down this part of Brooklyn, you can't get anything on there.

The same way with the all-night parking. We used to—nobody told us, it was a regulation—serve four or five summonses each night. It was one of those laws where the administration figures it's just prohibited, it's for the convenience of the people, and in this it was supposed to be doing some little good.

This idea of not enforcing law does not apply to crimes themselves, just like larceny or robbery or anything like that. These are just laws that are violations because they are prohibited and for the convenience of the people they kind of allow them to go.

* * * * *

Q. Now, Mr. Condon, if Mr. Goldberg were to go to a place where it's run for charity and bingo is being played there, would he be violating the policy of the Department if he asked them to discontinue? ——I think he would be violating the policy as I understood it.

Q. As you understood it? ——As I understand it.

Q. And that policy came from your imagination? ——Principally from custom and the way they acted over in Headquarters. That's the only way you get policy. And furthermore, the fact that Kennedy gave me the instructions to give him, "Do not change the policy of this Department."

Q. Now, when you told Mr. Halpin . . . to play that night and after that you told him to discontinue . . . were you violating the policy of the Department? ——I think in a certain extent, it wasn't according to their wishes. But as long as my subordinate wouldn't go along with policy, I couldn't direct him to let them play.

* * * * *

Q. Now, let us get back to the time that you said you had a conversation with Mr. Goldberg with respect to bingo violations in August of 1954. When he first showed you the complaint from the Chief Inspector, did he tell you that he had made a survey of the number of places where bingo was being played? ——I think he told me he was sending out for a survey.

* * * * *

Q. Did he after the survey was made tell you, in words or in substance, "Now we've decided that it would be advisable not to make summary arrests in cases of charity or fraternal organizations, but just to warn them in a friendly, gentlemanly way," did he tell you that? ——No.

Q. And did you know at any time during the month of August that when his men went out, that they had requested in a very friendly and gentlemanly fashion to please discontinue bingo? ——Yes.

Q. He told you that? ——He did.

* * * * *

Q. And you agreed with the policy? ——That's right. In fact, I asked him, if he didn't get a chance, to notify the people or have the game started, in view of to prevent disorder, to let them play that particular game. That's how I come to give it to the Knights of Columbus that night.

Q. Did it ever come to your attention that Mr. Goldberg or any of his men stopped a bingo game when run by a charity at the time it was actually run? ——No. You see, I had asked Goldberg to agree to that. I went to his office one day and there were some people there—I can tell you two of them—and they got up and started to leave. And I said, "Don't bother, it's just going to be a minute." I knew two of them and I said to him, "Listen Lou"—of course I had to be careful—"in view of the fact that you let this bingo go so long without taking any action" —I was first giving it to Goldberg, see?

Q. When is this conversation? ——The month of August, before. I said, "In view of the fact that you let this go so long that it's almost become a custom, I wouldn't want to see any disorder in connection with the stopping of these games. Will you give these people a chance to notify the people that there will be no more games?" "Oh, yes," he said, "I certainly will." That's why I was surprised when Halpin called me up and told me. I said, "You misunderstood me."

Q. But you authorized him, you permitted him to go on and stop them . . .? ——Well, I let him go, if that's what you mean.

Q. You spoke to him every day and he told you what he was doing and what his men were doing and you permitted him to go on? ——Right.

Q. Now, you as his superior had the authority to prevent Mr. Goldberg from going out on bingo violations? ——No, I didn't.

Q. Why not? ——Because my impression is that bingo is a violation of law and I couldn't direct anybody, whether I was superior or not, to allow a violation of law to continue.

* * * * *

Q. Tell us about your conversation with Mr. Goldberg on September 2nd or 3rd, do you remember that, when the newspapers carried the story that the police were going to be required to wink at bingo? ——No, I just remember September 1st telling him there will be no change in policy, sir. Now, I don't remember the second or third day what happened.

* * * * *

Q. And what was that conversation you had with Mr. Goldberg? ——I gave him the message that the Chief Inspector gave me, which was, "Tell that fellow he's not changing the policy of this Department. That if thinks he can change the policy of the Department, he'll find out what will happen. This man upstairs is just the type of man who'll not let him run the policy of the Department."

I gave him that message as straight as I could.

Q. Did you ask the Chief Inspector what the policy of the Department was? ——No, sir, anymore than Lou asked me and I didn't think it was proper for me to tell him. I think policy is something you've got to find out for yourself.

Q. You weren't interested in asking the Chief Inspector what the policy was? ——No, because I thought I knew the policy.

* * * * *

Q. And you at no time told Goldberg what the policy of the Department was did you? ——He asked me. He said, "Give it to me in writing." I said, "I think . . . they don't want you to interfere with certain religious or fraternal or these other organizations who are running a bingo game by themselves, without any interference, without anybody else running it for them and the proceeds are used entirely for their benefit." He said to me, "Give it to me in writing." I says, "I won't give you anything in writing."

Q. You said to Mr. Goldberg "I think the policy is"? ——That's right.

Q. You weren't sure yourself what the policy was? ——That's right I'm not sure what the policy is.

Q. But you thought it was the policy? ——The policy. The way I come by policy is you've got to find out from the workings of the Department.

* * * * *

Q. Now you read in the paper the following day or two, Mr. Condon, after your conversation with Goldberg, that the policy of the Department was not changed, namely, the police were required to wink at bingo, isn't that so? ——Words to that effect, yes.

Q. Now did you have a conversation with Goldberg after you saw this article in the paper? ——Yes.

Q. And wasn't it at that time rather than the night before when Goldberg asked you what the policy of the Department was? ——No, Goldberg was always harping on the policy. He wanted me to put something in writing, to tell him not to let bingo run and I wouldn't do it. He often mentioned it. I said, "It's in the paper today for you, see? What the policy is." He said, "I don't take orders from the paper." I said, "Well, go over and see [Dougherty, Adams, or Kennedy]."

* * * * *

Q. Is a policeman required to follow the policy as stated in the newspaper? ——No. I had that policy before, but that was just a confirmation. That's what I thought it was when it was issued by the Police Commissioner's Deputy Commissioner on Public Relations. In fact, Kennedy had told me that he didn't want any change in policy. So there must have been some policy and I gave it to Goldberg.

Q. Is a policeman supposed to guess as to what he is supposed to do or is he supposed to follow the law? ——He's supposed to follow the law.

Q. Now when Goldberg spoke to you after this newspaper article of September 2nd or 3rd, 1954, did Goldberg tell you that he was going to continue on unless he got orders to the contrary, he was going to continue on whatever violations are found? ——Continue stopping bingo games unless he got an order in writing. . . .

* * * * *

Q. He told you what he was doing every day, didn't he? ——He would come up nearly every day, but it wouldn't be all about bingo. It would generally wind into bingo because Headquarters was after me on the bingo.

Q. Now did you have a conversation with him on September 8, 1954? ——Yes . . . I called him to the office to show him some other report that I was going to submit. The report was relative to his action in failing to suppress a certain condition.

Q. Was that with respect to bingo violation? ——No, some other, some gambling, and I wanted him to see this report because—and I told him when I gave it to him. I was sent from Headquarters to report there and pick up a communication, which is very unusual. That's why he was there.

* * * * *

Q. And will you please tell us the conversation you had with Mr. Goldberg that morning?

* * * * *

——You asked for the conversation. I said, "This is the report I'm submitting on that complaint, Lou," and I showed it to him and he read it. And I said, "Is that all right?" You know, to straighten it out for him. And I said, "I think they're a little peeved because they sent for me to come over and get this report." I'm trying to give Goldberg the feeling that everything wasn't right.

So then when he finished that he thought it was very nice and he thanked me for it.

And I said, "What do you intend to do about bingo, Lou?" He said to me, "Unless I get an order from you in writing telling me to allow bingo to go, I'm going to suppress it." Well, I just kind of laughed and I said, "Do you want me to tell you who told me that?" He looked at me. I said, "I'm wondering who you're looking for, you're looking for me or somebody else over in Headquarters? I'm not putting any such thing in writing." Because, as I testified here a number of times, I think bingo is a violation of the Lottery Law and I'm not going to tell anybody in person or especially in writing not to enforce the bingo law.

So he said, "Well, I'm going to enforce it." I said, "Well, do you intend to do that in view of what I told you about the policy of the Department?" He says, "I don't know the policy of the Department." I said, "Well, it was in the paper the other day for you, issued by Dougherty who is the Police Commissioner's Public Relations man." He said, "I don't take orders from the newspapers." I said to him, "Well, you don't have to. Why don't you go over and see Dougherty? Why don't you see Kennedy and ask them what they want?" Because it was my opinion Goldberg knew better than I do what they wanted. But I know he was just mixed up about it.

So he didn't say he would or wouldn't. I said, "I'll tell you what you do. Before you do anything more on these bingo games, before you go any place on this bingo, let me know what you're going to do."

So he got up and walked out and that was the last I knew until I got the call from the Columbus Club.

* * * * *

Q. Didn't Mr. Halpin—now remember very carefully, if you can, didn't Mr. Halpin on an occasion before September 8th tell you that Mr. Goldberg's men were there at the Knights of Columbus? That's before September 8th. ——Come to think of it, I think he might have, yes.

And isn't it a fact that Mr. Goldberg's men had visited the Columbus Club before September 8th and specifically on the 5th of September, 1954, isn't that a fact? ——I don't know whether he did or not.

* * * * *

Q. Mr. Condon, you just said that you had spoken two days before to two lieutenants of Mr. Goldberg's squad about the Columbus Club [when he was on his day off], is that right? ——That's right, I did.

* * * * *

Q. On the 6th you were talking about the Columbus Club, that was the only thing you were talking about? ——They came up and told me what place they were going to raid and on the grounds they were going to stop it. And I said to them, "You see, Headquarters didn't want it to be done." I was doing it for Goldberg's sake. I wanted him to come down to earth. I had Goldberg before when he would go off like this and I would bring him down to earth. And I knew they were getting peeved up there. I said, "Don't do anything about bingo until he sees me." And they may have went down there and told him.

* * * * *

Q. Now, what made you feel that he was going to change his attitude towards bingo enforcement starting on September 8th? ——From our conversation that morning, the conversation was entirely different, sir. On this morning, he was very indignant about it. He said to me that he will stop any bingo game unless I give him an order in writing. . . .

Q. And did you think that he suddenly changed his character that you had known about for 36 years, that he was going to be a wilful, insubordinate policeman? ——I didn't notice any change in character. I knew he was getting more insistent that he was going to enforce the gambling laws.

* * * * *

Q. And what is the attitude that you ascribe as being responsible for your sudden desire to have him report to you? ——I think I said three times when he asked me to put the thing in writing for him because that's a most unusual request to ask anybody, and especially to ask him to do something which you know yourself is probably a violation of law.

* * * * *

Testimony of Francis W. H. Adams

Direct Examination by Mr. Carter:

Q. . . . Are you the Francis W. H. Adams who was formerly Police Commissioner of the City of New York? ——I am.

Q. And when were you appointed to that office? ——January 1, 1954.

Q. And when did you resign? ——August 2, 1955.

* * * * *

Q. Now, approximately how many members were there of the Police Department of the City of New York when you took office? ——Something over 19,000.

Q. And then, as time progressed, was the personnel of the Police Department augmented? ——Yes.

Q. Now, in a word, from a disciplinary angle, how is the Police Department run? Is there sort of a chain of command or something similar to what you would find in the Army? ——Yes, the Police Department of this city or any other city is basically a military organization and the disciplinary functions are carried out normally through a chain of command. The difference perhaps between that and—well, it's basically the same thing. The final disciplinary power resides in the Commissioner.

* * * * *

MR. CARTER: May I have that Jackman letter, please? . . . Now, sometime between the receipt of that letter and let's say the 2nd of September of 1954, did you in your official position as Police Commissioner have occasion to be called by certain people with respect to the activities of the Department in connection with bingo? ——Yes, sir.

* * * * *

Q. Did they represent all segments of our so-called religious society in the City of New York?

* * * * *

——They represented all segments of our society, whether religious or not.

Q. And in general, what was the substance of their talks with you? ——There was a considerable concern for securing on one side proper compliance with the law and enforcement of the law, and on the other side, there was a considerable concern for the people who were from time to time engaged in this pursuit, because these were not lawbreaking people, and the concern was expressed which law officers share for the kind and nature of compliance with law which you are going to obtain because of the kind of people in the community who are involved.

And I recall that it was indicated that there was at that time a statute which made it unlawful to park an automobile on the streets of the city between the hours, I think of 7:00 A.M. and 12:00 Midnight for more than an hour or for more than three hours from 12:00 Midnight to 7:00 A.M. And that kind of law was not enforced and that the enforcement of it would do serious damage to property owners in the city.

It was that kind of concern that was expressed. And also, there was a concern expressed which I shared concerning the best method of securing compliance with the law so that it would not result in violence, physical damage, riots and the like. That's generally the kind of thing that was called to my attention from every part of the city.

Q. Now, were you receiving calls from what you might characterize as representative people, citizens of the City of New York in the top echelon, particularly from all religious segments with respect to the enforcement of the anti-bingo law in Brooklyn? ——Oh, yes.

Q. And in general, what was the tenor of the conversations that you had with these people? ——Well, my view was, of course, that any law must be enforced in accordance with the ability of the police to enforce it, in accordance with the requirements of the community and in accordance with the best method of securing compliance with the law, whether or not I personally agreed with the statute in case, it was my job to see to it that compliance should be secured. But as any police officer or police commissioner, it's necessary to see to it that compliance is secured in such manner that it is best for the entire community.

Q. Well, now, did you have calls from representative citizens of this community, particularly those in the religious segment of it, which objected to the activities of the Police Department in connection with enforcing the anti-bingo law? ——Oh, yes, of course.

Q. And would you say that those calls were numerous? ——Yes.

Q. And as a result of those calls, did you have occasion to discuss the anti-bingo enforcement with Chief Inspector Kennedy? ——Oh, yes.

* * * * *

MR. SIEGEL: May I have a date fixed, please?

* * * * *

Q. Would you say that they were in the area of the latter part of August, in the early part of September of 1954?

* * * * *

——Generally speaking, that is my best recollection.

Q. And what was the substance, if you recall, of those conversations? ——Well, the discussions were generally along the line that there were these laws. In general, it was necessary to secure compliance with the law. We discussed the fact that there were a great many people who were sincere, decent, law-abiding citizens who were engaged in this kind of misdemeanor and we did discuss the fact that they were misdemeanors and not felonies, and that the best thing to do would be to see to it that we could —how we could—rather, see how we could secure compliance and at the same time not do any serious damage to the community in general and also we were very much concerned about this, very much concerned about the fact that people who were engaged in this and engaged in it in the best of faith as far as they were concerned, might so resent it, that we would have a critical situation developing almost any place at any time which would have involved violence, possible riots.

It was reported to me that there were upon occasion large numbers of people who participated in these games, some of them coming from considerable distance. And we were concerned about the possibility of violence occurring if these games were suddenly shut down.

So we were trying to devise reasonable methods for accomplishing what obviously should be done.

Q. And did your discussions with the Chief Inspector center solely around the enforcement of the anti-bingo statute in Brooklyn as distinct from every other borough in the city? ——Oh, no, we discussed it throughout the city.

Q. Now, do you have any recollection of any Police Department activity during this period in question with respect to the enforcement of the anti-bingo statute in any borough other than the borough of Brooklyn? ——Oh, yes.

Q. Now, as a result of your talk with then Chief Inspector Kennedy, do you have any knowledge as to what instructions he, Kennedy, issued to the men under his immediate command with respect to it?

* * * * *

——Well, the general policy which I'm sure the Chief Inspector expressed through the chain of command was that we would endeavor to find out where the situations were existing and we would endeavor to secure compliance, and if compliance could not be secured voluntarily, then we would go forward with the necessary prosecutions.

Q. As of that time, was it a situation which you as Police Commissioner considered delicate? ——Very.

Q. Was it a situation that you in your official capacity felt had to be handled with circumspection? ——Yes, Mr. Carter, this was a situation which very definitely involved, whether rightly or wrongly, the emotions of a large segment of our population and it was my view and continues to be my view that part of the function of a Police Commissioner is to see to it that law and order is preserved and not to stimulate violence. And part of what I was trying to accomplish in this extraordinarily delicate situation was to see to it that what the law provided could be done and at the same time that it would not be an eruption caused in the community, particularly, because for the most part, these were decent, otherwise law-abiding people who were involved.

* * * * *

Q. I ask you if you can identify this document [Kennedy's recommendation for the demotion of Goldberg] for us . . . ——Yes, I recall this paper.

Q. Now, that paper which you have just perused, was that given to you in exactly that same form on the morning of Thursday, September 9, 1954 at Police Headquarters by Chief Inspector Kennedy? ——Yes, sir. I notice that I approved it on that date with my stamp and initials.

* * * * *

Cross-Examination by Mr. Siegel:

* * * * *

Q. When was the first time you ever met Mr. Goldberg? ——I don't know. I met a great many of the police officers of all ranks within the first few months after I came into the Department. . . .

Q. You wouldn't deny that you spoke to Mr. Goldberg in January, 1954, Mr. Commissioner? ——Certainly not.

Q. . . . Now, see if I can't refresh your memory. Did Mr. Goldberg enter your office with Assistant Chief Inspector Condon in January of 1954? ——Mr. Siegel, he may have. I cannot say either way.

Q. . . . And didn't you say to Mr. Goldberg in the presence of Chief Condon, "What's the purpose of this Public Morals Squad?" And Mr. Condon said to you at that time that this was organized as a result of the Harry Gross bookmaking case at the request and suggestion of the Brooklyn Grand Jury investigating rackets in the Police Department, would that refresh your memory? ——It does not. I will not say it did not happen, but I cannot say it did happen.

* * * * *

Q. Now, did you say this to these people, Mr. Goldberg and Mr. Condon: "I'm dissatisfied with the number of arrests in the Gambling Squad and I want more arrests," did you say that? ——I have no recollection of having said so to either of those gentlemen and I think it would be most unlikely that I would have said that because if I had . . . I would have said it to the Chief Inspector and to the first Deputy, not to the men in the lower ranks.

* * * * *

Q. Am I to understand that you were satisfied with the operations of the Gambling Squad under Mr. Goldberg's supervision? ——No, sir, I emphatically was not.

* * * * *

Q. You were not satisfied with the number of arrests made by the Public Morals Squad, is that right? ——You've got two questions here. I was not satisfied with the operation of the Public Morals Squad in Brooklyn because it was not a good police operation and it is not a good police operation in my opinion today.

* * * * *

Q. . . . Did you come to the conclusion anytime before September or October, 1954, that the Public Morals Squad was not operating properly according to your belief? ——I have said I don't think so and I'm trying to say that I think that took place later on in the spring of 1955.

* * * * *

Q. . . . Is a lottery part of the gambling laws which are prohibited by the State of New York, Mr. Commissioner? ——It's my recollection that it is.

* * * * *

Q. And bingo played for a consideration is also a crime under the laws of the State of New York under 1370 of the Penal Law? ——If you say it is. I don't recall the section.

Q. Regardless of what section, playing bingo for a consideration is a crime, isn't that so? ——That's right.

Q. And anyone who runs a game like that is guilty of a crime, is that right? ——That's right, sir.

* * * * *

Q. . . . During the period of your incumbency of office, had there been other police officers in other parts of the City of New York enforcing bingo violations? ——Yes, sir.

Q. So that Mr. Goldberg's squad was not the only squad in the City of New York that was enforcing bingo violations? ——That's correct.

Q. Now, what was the policy of the Department with respect to the enforcement of bingo violations on September 8, 1954? ——[several lines omitted] The policy was at that time to consider the fact that a number of religious institutions . . . of every faith had come to me and . . . to other officials of the city and were very seriously upset . . . because of the fact that decent, law-abiding people who were playing this game were being put in the position of, as they said, becoming criminals. And the policy was, considering that fact, and considering that it was a situation requiring an extraordinarily diplomatic approach to an explosive situation, to see to it within the limits of my own ability and the limits of the ability of the Department, that the law was enforced and that compliance with the law was obtained. But to do it in such a manner so that we would not create or further create a situation which, as I say at the time was actually explosive. That was the policy of the Department at the time.

Q. I repeat, was it the policy of the Department in September of 1954 to wink at bingo? Yes or no? ——No, sir. The policy of the Department at that time—and I would like to make this clear—was to, among other things, to keep itself informed as to what was developing in this situation so that adequate steps could be taken wherever necessary to bring these games to a close without in so doing causing decent people to be marked as criminals.

Q. So that you mean to tell us that the policy of the Department in September, 1954 was to enforce bingo violations, is that right? ——Yes, within the limits that I have described in the manner that I have described.

Q. I don't understand what limits you placed on it. Was the policy of the Department either to wink at bingo or to enforce bingo. Can you give us an unequivocal answer to that, please? ——The policy of the Department was not—I don't know what you mean by winking at something. The policy of the Department—

Q. You never heard of that expression, winking at bingo? ——Yes, but what I'm trying to say, Mr. Siegel, is that the policy of the Department was to take into consideration the fact that an extremely dangerous situation had been created and in the opinion of experienced professional members of the Department—and I do not say that I was ever more than an amateur—a situation had been created which was a very difficult situation. We felt, therefore, that while we were going to see to it that these laws were enforced, that we were going to see to it that it was done and that compliance was secured in a proper manner. If that answers your question, which I hope it it does.

Q. I'm afraid it doesn't. I'm going to get an answer from you, Mr. Commissioner, with all due respects. What was the Police Department or a police officer to do with respect to enforcing bingo violations in September of 1954, enforce the law? ——Yes, sir.

* * * * *

Q. . . . Now, I want you to answer this question, Mr. Commissioner: Mr. Louis Goldberg, as head of the Public Morals Squad, on September 8, 1954 walked in with two of his subordinates to the Columbus Club, 1 Prospect Park West, Brooklyn. He goes into the manager's office, he asks the manager, "Will you please co-operate with the Police Department and not run bingo that night?" The manager says he will co-operate with the Police Department and not run bingo that night. Was Mr. Goldberg carrying out the policy of the Police Department of the City of New York on that occasion? Yes or no? ——I would think so, yes.

Q. Yes. Now, did you read in the newspapers about Deputy Commissioner Dougherty making a statement to the press about winking at bingo, did you read that story? ——No, sir.

* * * * *

Q. . . . And of course, if such a statement were made by Deputy Commissioner Dougherty, that was without your knowledge or consent? ——That's right.

* * * * *

Q. [Reading from *New York Times* news story about Dougherty's statement] "At that time, after Commissioner Adams' office had been deluged with complaints of Goldberg's sudden activity, Deputy Commissioner Richard A. Dougherty and his official spokesman announced the policy of the Department has not changed." "Now, what was the policy of the Department at that time, Mr. Commissioner? ——I described it here. . . .

* * * * *

Q. Am I correct in saying that your policy was to enforce bingo violations . . . ? ——. . . what I tried to say . . . is that what we were trying to do in an extraordinarily difficult and explosive situation was to obtain compliance with the requirements of the law where we could, to prevent violations of the law, and in that sense and wherever we could to secure enforcement of the law. . . . It's not enough, Mr. Siegel, to put it simply as you do, that what we were after was merely to enforce the law, because as I indicated before, we could have enforced the law with respect to parking all over the city, but that was not the entire problem that faced the police.

Q. Did you know that Mr. Goldberg had never made an arrest in any case where there was a bingo violation called to his attention or to the attention of his squad, did you know that? ——I don't know anything about that one way or the other.

Q. Did you know that it was his policy to go into a prospective place such as a church or a synagogue or a fraternal organization and ask them in a gentlemanly way, "Please co-operate with the Police Department and not play bingo," did you know that was his policy? ——I do not know anything about his policy one way or another. Do you mean his personal policy?

Q. Yes. ——As distinguished from his duty as a policeman?

Q. No, I'm only concerned about bingo violations and the policy that Mr. Goldberg and his squad had adopted in September of 1954 to enforce bingo violations. ——I don't recall one way or another about that.

* * * * *

Q. Had you ever heard of any one incident where Mr. Goldberg or his squad, in attempting to enforce bingo violations, had created a riot or that there was violence . . . ? ——I had not heard of specific acts of violence, but it had been reported to me that there were situations developing in Brooklyn as well as elsewhere in the city where violence might well result.

Q. . . . but you don't know of any instances where there was violence or where there was a riot at a bingo party in the Borough of Brooklyn? ——No. What we were trying to do is prevent those situations from occurring.

* * * * *

Q. Now, under the rules and regulations of the Manual, insubordination is a serious offense by a police officer, is that right? ——It is indeed.

Q. And insubordination is subject to dismissal from the force at the Commissioner's request? ——It could be.

Q. It could be. And if the Commissioner were to dismiss an officer for insubordination, he would lose his pension rights, is that right? ——He probably would, yes.

* * * * *

Q. . . . in charges leading to dismissal from the force, there's a hearing provided under the rules and regulations of the Police Department? ——That is true.

Q. And he's given an opportunity to defend himself, is that right? ——In that nature, in that kind of a charge, yes.

Q. Now, you were acting upon the letter of Chief Inspector Kennedy, dated September 9th, Defendants' Exhibit F, when you ordered Mr. Goldberg's demotion, is that right? ——That's right.

Q. You relied wholly and completely upon the information contained in that letter, Defendants' Exhibit F, is that right? ——I relied upon that and upon conversation which took place with Chief Kennedy simultaneously which was substantially to the same effect.

* * * * *

Q. And after receiving this letter from Chief Inspector Kennedy which you approved ordering his demotion, you immediately gave this to the press, this information about demoting him, is that right? . . . ——I would say sometime that day, I couldn't say when.

* * * * *

Q. Now, did you speak to Chief Condon that morning before ordering Mr. Goldberg's demotion? ——No, sir.

Q. The only one you spoke to is Chief Inspector Kennedy? ——No, I am quite clear that I also conferred with James R. Kennedy, who then was and now is the First Deputy Commissioner; and I may be wrong but I think I also conferred with the Chief of Detectives, Thomas A. Nielsen, who is now the Chief Inspector; and I'm not sure about this, but I think I also conferred with Mr. Dougherty and I think also with Mr. Vincent L. Broderick, who was then Deputy Commissioner in charge of legal affairs. And I considered with all or some of the gentlemen that I have named the serious effect upon the Department of the conduct reported to me of Mr. Goldberg, and the serious loss of command and discipline which necessarily would result if we permitted that kind of conduct to go on.

At that point, you see, we had passed any question of bingo. We had a situation in a military organization where a subordinate officer had flatly refused to do what his commanding officer required him to do.

* * * * *

Q. Tell us what happened [at that meeting]. —— . . . The Chief Inspector reported to me that Assistant Chief Inspector Condon, in turn, had reported to him that Deputy Chief Inspector Goldberg had been properly instructed by Assistant Chief Inspector Condon to report to him when—and to consult with him in connection with these bingo games and what he proposed to do. That was a lawful, proper order for Assistant Chief Inspector Condon, who was his chief.

Deputy Chief Inspector Goldberg had flatly refused to follow the proper, lawful command of his immediate superior. Those facts were reported to me. And I may say that kind of situation—well, I'll withdraw that because that was—well, yes, that was considered by us, by me, that that kind of insubordination would immediately become widespread in the Department. It would be known that Deputy Chief Inspector Goldberg had been able to tell his superior that he wouldn't do what his superior reasonably required.

I realized that if that was permitted to continue past that day, I was no longer in command of that Police Department and I decided that something had to be done and it had to be done right then.

That's the story.

* * * * *

Q. You don't know of your own knowledge whether or not Goldberg was or was not insubordinate to Condon, do you?

MR. CARTER: I object to that. The record speaks for itself.

THE COURT: I will allow it.

——I relied upon the statements made by Assistant Chief Inspector Condon to the Chief Inspector to me.

Q. You're not answering my question. ——That's

whether or not I personally know it of my own knowledge? I do not.

Q. You do not know it of your own knowledge whether or not Goldberg was insubordinate to Condon, you don't know that of your own knowledge? ——Well, I'm not going to try to make metaphysical distinctions. I relied upon the facts as given to me.

* * * * *

Q. Now, did you, before demoting Mr. Goldberg, speak to him? ——No.

Q. And did you ask Mr. Goldberg whether or not he was or was not insubordinate? ——No.

Q. Did you, before demoting him afford him an opportunity to be heard as to his side of the story? ——No, sir.

* * * * *

Q. You testified on direct examination that there were some people complaining about enforcement of bingo violations. . . . Now, did you also receive visits from respectable citizens of all denominations and telephone calls and letters from people of all denominations asking for the enforcement of bingo violations? ——I would say I received some visits. But I would not say they comprehended all denominations. . . . It seems to me we had some mail but I don't think I had any visits. I might have, I'm not sure.

Q. This letter [Jackman letter] . . . you probably read it, to the best of your memory? ——I may have.

Q. . . . it would be the practice for you to order the Chief Inspector to take care of it . . . ? ——In the ordinary course a communication of that kind would go first to the Chief Inspector.

Q. Now, if the Chief Inspector were to forward this on to some of his subordinates with the memorandum, "Investigate, take appropriate action and report," what does that mean? ——Just what it says.

Q. Does that mean that you wanted an investigation made with respect to the complaint? ——Yes. You see, there's some—oh, I would hazard a guess, maybe twelve, fifteen thousand communications of this kind, a couple of thousand a week that come. . . . Some of them would come to my attention, some might not. Then they go down to the Chief Inspector's office and he sends them out. . . .

Q. When you forward it down to the Chief Inspector, you want this complaint investigated, isn't that so? ——Ordinary routine.

The Michigan Athletic Awards Rule

Glendon A. Schubert, Jr., Helenan Sonnenburg, George Kantrowitz

The Rule Is Broken

ON JUNE 9, 1953, three high school boys were awarded prizes in a golf tournament jointly sponsored by the Junior Chamber of Commerce and the *Daily Press* of the small city of Escanaba, Michigan. The prizes included shirts, ties, socks, and golf balls. Before accepting his prize, one of the boys asked whether it would violate the Awards Rule of the Michigan High School Athletic Association (MHSAA), which declared ineligible for high school athletics any student who accepted an athletic award worth more than $3.00.[1] The boy was assured that tournament officials had secured the approval of local school officials and of the office of the State Director of Athletics. Stories in the local newspapers had announced that the awards to be given the winners would remain within the limit set by the Michigan High School Athletic Association.

One of the winners was William LeMire, student at Escanaba High School. When his school principal heard of the incident he called LeMire into his office and told him he had violated the Awards Rule.

As this news spread quickly in Escanaba, a number of its most influential citizens expressed strong opinions that LeMire and the other two students should not be punished. Rather than make an unpopular decision, the principal asked the Executive Committee of the Michigan High School Athletic Association to call a special meeting to decide the case.

The principal's decision to push the case outside the boundaries of Escanaba was followed by successful efforts of the relatives and friends of the boys to publicize the case throughout the state. William LeMire's uncle was Mayor of Escanaba. He gave the story, as he saw it, to the editor of the *Grand Rapids Herald,* and it was played up in the *Herald* and two other papers in the same chain, the *Battle Creek Inquirer-News* and the *Lansing State Journal.* Nor did the boys' supporters stop at publicity. One of the members of the MHSAA Executive Committee later reported: "Because of the political and family connections of these boys . . . attempts were made to influence all the members of the Executive Committee through influential people in their local communities even before the cases had been heard."

By the time the Executive Committee convened, a similar violation by six boys from Hastings High School was reported. They had played in a summer softball league as members of a team sponsored by Orchard Industries and had accepted fishing rods manufactured by their sponsor. The Executive Committee decided to hear both cases at the same time.

The Executive Committee met in the offices of the MHSAA in the State Capitol building in Lansing on August 20. It consisted of four high school principals and school superintendents, who were officers of the Association, and the State Director of Athletics, the Association's executive officer. None of the boys was present, although some were represented, as were Escanaba and Hastings High Schools. Representa-

[1] The rule, as published in the MHSAA Handbook for the school year 1953-54, read as follows:

SECTION 10—AWARDS

Section 10(A)—A student who accepts from any source an award (merchandise, memberships, privileges, services, or money in any amount) for excellence in athletic performance shall be ineligible for further interscholastic athletic competition, except that the acceptance of a medal, ribbon, badge, plaque, cup, trophy, banner, picture, or ring having a value not to exceed three dollars ($3.00) shall not render him ineligible; nor shall the acceptance of the regular letter award of the school render him ineligible.

Section 10(B)—A student ineligible under this rule may not apply for reinstatement until the equivalent of one full school year of enrollment has elapsed following the date of his last violation.

tives of the Escanaba Junior Chamber of Commerce and the *Daily Press* attempted to assume full responsibility for any violation in the golf tournament, the former admitting that they had failed to check with any school officials about prizes. A representative of Orchard Industries said his company had been unaware of the rule and "accepted full responsibility for having caused the difficulty as far as the boys were concerned." However, school officials from Escanaba and Hastings testified that the boys had been informed of the Awards Rule, both in discussions and by MHSAA posters displayed on bulletin boards.

In the words of one of its members, the Executive Committee "tried for three hours to find a way out." But four months were to elapse before a "way out" was found. During this time, the problem was pushed to still higher levels, in the course of which it forced Michigan's new State Superintendent of Public Instruction into a political-administrative "no man's land" between schoolmen, favoring enforcement of the rule, and the public and the Legislative Committee on Administrative Rules, favoring leniency and suspension of the rule. To appreciate the State Superintendent's position—and how he got into it—it is necessary to know something about administrative rulemaking and the government of high school athletics in Michigan.

Rule-Making and the Legislature

During the 20th century one of the most prominent trends in government has been the growth of rule-making by executive departments, acting under authority delegated by legislative bodies. The general practice in the United States is to place primary reliance upon the courts for the review of administrative rules. In principle, such judicial review does not deal with the wisdom of the challenged rules but is concerned only with the legal sufficiency of administrative authority to issue these rules. Recently, a number of states, including Michigan, have turned to the supplementary device of legislative review of administrative rules, not necessarily limited to the question of legality, and providing a form of control believed to be more directly responsible to the people.

In Michigan the Administrative Code Act of 1943 provides that, with certain exceptions, a rule promulgated by any state agency can take effect only after it has been approved by the Attorney General "as to form and legality." It must then be filed with the Secretary of State and published by him in a quarterly compilation, or, in the event of emergency, it may be approved by the Governor and thus become immediately effective. In practice, about seventy percent of all rules proposed by state agencies are "emergency" filings.

The Legislative Committee on Administrative Rules was set up by an act of 1947 providing that all rules to which the Administrative Code Act of 1943 applies shall be submitted to the state legislature, which may abrogate them by concurrent resolution. The 1947 act authorized establishment of a Joint Legislative Committee on Administrative Rules, with authority to meet between sessions of the Legislature to consider rules which the Legislature has not already considered, and "to suspend until the next regular session of the legislature the operation of any rule not in conformity with the statute under which it was promulgated."

Only once in the six years following the 1947 act did the Legislature pass a concurrent resolution abrogating regulations of a state agency. This amounted to an almost complete delegation to the Joint Committee of the Legislature's power to review and abrogate rules. In 1951 an amendment to the earlier act provided that "any rule heretofore or hereafter suspended by the committee shall continue to be suspended until such rule is reinstated by the committee or is considered and approved by concurrent resolution of the legislature."

From its inception, in June, 1947, the Legislative Committee decided not to challenge administrative rules on its own motion, but instead to entertain complaints from the public against the rules of state agencies. It developed a procedure of a single open hearing with all parties (and frequently their attorneys) present, allowing cross-examination. After the open hearing came the executive session which representatives of the state agency or other interested persons might be invited to attend. The purpose of the executive session was to arrive at a decision, usually a compromise in which the gency agreed to reformulate the rule, making oncessions to the complainant along the lines roposed by the Committee. If an agency re- used to yield, the Committee could suspend the ule or—and this seemed to be a much more ersuasive sanction—leave the recalcitrant to isk the displeasure of committee members who 'ere strategically placed on standing commit- ees of the two houses, including both appro- riations committees. Many members of the egislature were re-elected and were noted for heir long memories; nor could any responsible dministrator forget that no committee of the enate had been discharged of a bill since 1911.

However, there were some doubts whether he 1947 act inaugurating legislative review of dministrative rules was constitutional. A 1947 ttorney General's opinion on the powers of the Committee contained an ominous passing allu- ion to this question. Doubts about constitu- ionality even bothered some members of the egislative Committee sufficiently to make them eluctant to risk a showdown on the question. Ience, the Committee followed a policy of cau- ion, seeking compromise decisions with the gencies against whose rules complaints were iled. Hence, too, the Committee's reliance upon ndirect and informal sanctions. Committee earings (especially executive sessions at which he agencies were represented) took on some of he overtones of a poker game, with both sides luffing at times, neither knowing for certain ow far it was wise or possible to go, either gally or politically.

upervising School Athletics in Michigan

The Superintendent of Public Instruction of Iichigan is an elected official. Clair L. Taylor, former high school teacher and administrator, ad succeeded to this post in June and had been n office less than two months when he attended he MHSAA Executive Committee meeting 'hich heard the Escanaba and Hastings cases.

A law of 1923 gave the Superintendent of ublic Instruction "supervision and . . . control ver the interscholastic athletic activities of all he schools of the state." In practice, control of igh school athletics remained largely in the ands of a state-wide group of school officials nown since 1924 as the Michigan High School Athletic Association. The MHSAA is not a state agency. Its income is derived solely from regis- tration fees collected from referees and umpires and from the profits from annual state basket- ball tournaments which it sponsors. Its expenses in 1953-54 were about $70,000, and its surplus is distributed at the end of each year to its member (public and parochial) schools. The State De- partment of Public Instruction provides MHSAA with office space in the State Capitol building and with a stenographer and other services.

MHSAA's charter provides for a thirteen-man Representative Council, made up of school su- perintendents and principals, and for an Execu- tive Committee, which includes the State Di- rector of Inter-Scholastic Athletics, MHSAA's full-time chief executive who is appointed by the Superintendent of Public Instruction with the advice and approval of MHSAA's Representa- tive Council. There have been only two Direc- tors of Athletics since 1924; the second, Charles E. Forsythe, has served as MHSAA's chief execu- tive since 1931. The Superintendent of Public Instruction, on the other hand, as an elected of- ficial, must normally be not only a professional educator but one with some flair for politics. The regulation of interscholastic athletics is one of his smaller responsibilities, and superintend- ents have been quite content to let the MHSAA handle this problem for them. The Director of Athletics, Charles Forsythe, has seen several su- perintendents come and go, and they tend to rely upon his advice in any decision respecting high school athletics.

Each year in July or August, the MHSAA publishes a *Handbook* containing codes for the administration of athletics. The code for high school and junior high school athletic compe- tition consists mainly of rules which have been adopted from time to time by the Representa- tive Council. Since MHSAA is not a state agency, any rule or amendment adopted by the Representative Council is transmitted to the Superintendent. If the Superintendent approves, he forwards it to the Attorney General and, usu- ally, to the Governor for "emergency" clear- ance before filing with the Secretary of State for publication in the *Supplement to the Adminis- trative Code*.

By 1953, both the Association and the Super- intendent had come to take this process so much for granted that sometimes a year or more elapsed between adoption by the Representative Council and publication in the *Supplement,* and some amendments that had been approved by the Representative Council and duly published in its *Handbook* had never found their way into the *Administrative Code.* In fact, very few high school coaches, principals, or superintendents had ever heard of the *Supplement to the Administrative Code.* The law schoolmen followed was printed in the *MHSAA Handbook.*

Violations of the rules were usually dealt with by the local school officials, although they frequently asked the Director of Athletics for advice. When local political pressure became too "hot," cases were taken to the MHSAA Executive Committee, whose decision, in practice, was usually final. It was customary, however, for the Director to inform the Superintendent of Public Instruction of the action taken by the Executive Committee, and the Superintendent almost always concurred. Rarely would the Superintendent personally hear an appeal from the decision of the Executive Committee, and therefore there were no established procedures spelling out the details of the relationship between the Superintendent and the MHSAA in such a case.

The Awards Rule first became a part of the *Administrative Code* in 1947, and a revision was published in a 1950 *Supplement* to the *Code.* About 35 cases arising under the Awards Rule had reached the Executive Committee by the end of the 1952-53 school year, and in all of these the decision of the Committee had been accepted as final.

The Superintendent's Dilemma

FOLLOWING ITS THREE-HOUR deliberation, the MHSAA Executive Committee concluded that the students had violated the Awards Rule. It declared them ineligible for further interscholastic competition. After the meeting adjourned, Superintendent Taylor sent this memorandum to Athletic Director Forsythe:

> August 20, 1953
>
> I have reviewed the decision of the Executive Committee of the MHSAA with reference to the eligibility of the following students of the Escanaba and Hastings high schools:
>
> . . . .
>
> I approve and endorse the decision of such committee.

The press reacted violently. For several days newspapers all over the state carried front-page stories and bitter editorials. Taylor and "his committee" were depicted as "zealots." The boys were described as innocent teenagers who had been misled by respectable adults.

A two-front assault was then opened by Dean and Siegel, attorneys for the Hastings boys. First, they filed a petition for a writ of injunction against Taylor with the Circuit Court for Barry County in which Hastings is located. Taylor did not want to fight the issue on this front. As he later remarked:

> It is my honest and conscientious judgment that the matter of high school athletics should not be settled in the courts of Michigan, and it would be far better to go to rather extreme lengths to settle the matter among ourselves before it is necessary for the courts to decide. In other words, let us always attempt to settle problems within our educational family.

Next, on September 4, Dean and Siegel filed a complaint with the Legislative Committee on Administrative Rules requesting suspension of the Awards Rule. On September 16, the Committee conducted an all-day open hearing in the Senate Chamber. Taylor, Forsythe, and the members of the MHSAA Executive Committee were present. The Hastings boys came with their attorneys, but the three boys from the Escanaba area appeared only through counsel. As Charles Semler, the president of the MHSAA, described the hearing:

> Anyone who wished to do so was permitted to make

statements. The hearing was not confined to the charges in the petition and the very right was attacked of the schools of the state to have any voice in the control of athletics through their elected representatives on the Council of the MHSAA.

The Legislative Committee Meets

The next morning the Legislative Committee held an executive session at which only the committee members and Taylor, Forsythe, and Semler were present. Hastings was within the district represented by a member of the Committee, Senator Hutchinson, who opened the proceedings by reading a proposed statement of the Committee's decision:

> . . . . Testimony before the Committee established that once a violation is recognized, the fixed penalty applies, there being no different penalty for the most flagrant and intentional violation than for an innocent violation.
>
> The Committee recognizes that the statutory authority under which this rule was promulgated broadly grants to the Superintendent of Public Instruction supervision and control over the inter-scholastic athletic activities of all the schools of the state. So broad a grant of authority cannot be any justification, however, for the promulgation and administration of a rule so inflexible in its penalty for violations as to admit of no consideration of mitigating circumstances, resulting in such harsh application in particular cases as to jar the sensibilities of the community. We are of the opinion that the legislature intended no grant of authority to act arbitrarily and with capriciousness. For this reason and others, we find that Awards Rule No. 10 is not in conformity with the statute under which it was promulgated and this Committee, therefore, has power to suspend its operation.
>
> We are mindful of the effects of immediate, outright suspension of this rule insofar as it would create a void into which all manner of commercialism might flow and we hesitate to order an immediate outright suspension without giving the Superintendent of Public Instruction necessary time to formulate and promulgate a rule in conformity with his statutory power. We recommend that the Superintendent of Public Instruction immediately formulate and promulgate a rule on the subject matter of awards which will provide in its penalty section a maximum penalty of suspension rather than a fixed penalty.
>
> If rules in conformity with the statute are promulgated without delay in conformance with this opinion we will withhold suspension of the present rule and we request the Superintendent of Public Instruction to show his compliance at the next meeting of this Committee which will be held on October 7, 1953.

Several members wanted Taylor to promulgate immediately a new rule such as was called for in Senator Hutchinson's draft. They assumed that a reinstatement clause which permitted violators to apply for reinstatement in less than a year's time would apply to the offenders from Escanaba and Hastings. These members proposed, therefore, to suspend the existing rule at once. But Senator Hutchinson did not think that the suspension of the rule would necessarily lead to a restoration of the boys' eligibility. Taylor agreed that nothing the Committee could do would bring about a reinstatement of the boys without his concurrence. He said, however, "I am willing to take under advisement a change in the rule."

As the hearing progressed, it was evident that the Committee might yet suspend the rule, and that some of its members were willing to use the threat of suspension to force Taylor to reconsider his decision in the cases at issue. Taylor finally asked: "You would like to say, then, that it was the order of the committee to say to the Superintendent of Public Instruction—'You go back and amend this rule under the threat that if you do not we will suspend it at the next meeting.'" Chairman Phillips demurred, protesting that the Committee had no power to force Mr. Taylor to do anything. Later, however, the same line of argument was resumed:

> *Senator Hutchinson:* . . . Since it is not in conformity with the statute this Committee could suspend it but . . . I think we should give the Superintendent of Public Instruction time to write a rule in conformity with the statute.
>
> *Senator Prescott:* Give them the right to reconsider the rule and have it comply with the statute.
>
> *Dr. Taylor:* I am unwilling to be coerced by your Committee.

Finally Taylor proposed the following statement of the Committee's position:

> *Dr. Taylor:* You have heard this testimony as this rule is applied and in your opinion the rule has been applied too drastically or harshly but to suspend this rule would create a void or impossible situation for the operation of our total athletic program until such time as a new rule could be promulgated and that you recommend to the Superintendent of Public Instruction that he do two things:

1. Arrange for a hearing with these boys or their representatives.
2. That you ask me to revise or rewrite this rule.

Senator Hutchinson: I might go along with that if you would permit the Committee to place certain emphasis on facts which would permit us to point out the manner in which the rule was too harsh.

Dr. Taylor: I would permit that.

A *modus vivendi* had been reached; the Committee deferred its decision on the complaint that had been filed with it, and Taylor scheduled a rehearing for September 28.

The Rehearing

The day before the rehearing the Representative Council of the MHSAA met and unanimously resolved to support the action taken by the Executive Committee in the Awards Rule cases, and commended "the firm supporting action taken by Superintendent Clair L. Taylor in his adhering to the original decision made by the Executive Committee which was concurred in by him." A resolution was also adopted suggesting that Taylor set up a committee for the "evaluation and study of the procedures for the administration of the interscholastic athletic program and the enforcement of eligibility rules" of the MHSAA.

At the rehearing Taylor personally questioned each of the nine boys (one had decided to accept the penalty). When it ended, he sat in his office alone and played the tape recording of the testimony over and over again, hoping to find some new evidence to justify a reversal. The next day he pondered without much enthusiasm a memorandum from the Assistant Attorney General assigned to the Department of Public Instruction. The memorandum pointed out that under Part B of the existing rule, a *student* who had been suspended could not apply for reinstatement until the equivalent of one full school year had elapsed following the date of his last violation, but that there was nothing in the rule to prevent the principal of his school from requesting reinstatement any time after suspension had taken place.

The Superintendent's decision remained a secret for about ten days. Then on October 8, the MHSAA Representative Council met again in Lansing, this time at Taylor's request. Taylor presented the schoolmen the following decision: (1) He could not reverse the earlier decision. No new evidence had been presented in favor of the boys; (2) Barring a change in the rule, the only way the boys could be reinstated was by petition from their respective school officials. Since this would "tend to establish a precedent by which any school wishing to do so could petition the Superintendent of Public Instruction . . . and I would be almost duty bound to grant reinstatement . . . I therefore deny the requests for reinstatement from the boards of education."

Taylor accepted the Representative Council's earlier suggestion that he appoint a committee of laymen and schoolmen to make a thorough study of all high school athletic rules. This case had shown him, he declared, that the Awards Rule "is not well understood and is very inflexible." He hoped that the new advisory committee which he would appoint would make recommendations to him by December 1. "If such a committee recommends a change in this penalty rule under which the boys have been declared ineligible, I will apply the new rule to them as soon as the change can be cleared through the Attorney General's office, the Secretary of State's office, and the Legislature and has become a part of the State Administrative Code."

After hearing Taylor's decision, the Representative Council reaffirmed its confidence in him. Taylor then designated Athletic Director Forsythe as chairman of the new State Advisory Committee on Interscholastic Athletics, and the Council chose Charles Semler and Albert L. Deal to represent it on the Committee.

The next day, October 9, Taylor sent individual letters to each of the athletes and released to the press a statement announcing his decision.

The Committee Suspends the Awards Rule

The Legislative Committee reacted swiftly. Chairman Phillips convened a special meeting on October 12 at which it voted to suspend the Awards Rule. The reasons given by the Committee in its statement to the press and in its order published in the *Administrative Code* included:

> We were led to believe by the Superintendent of Public Instruction that the obvious injustices in these cases could be rectified in a rehearing. Such a rehearing has not corrected the injustice.
>
> We have stated that we believe a rule so inflexible in its penalty for violation as to admit of no consideration of mitigating circumstances resulting in such admittedly harsh application in particular cases as to jar the sensibilities of a community is not in conformity with the statute under which the Superintendent of Public Instruction was granted general supervision and control of interscholastic athletic activities in this state.
>
> The Committee therefore finds that in order to prevent injustices arising from the application of this admittedly harsh and inflexible rule that said rule should be suspended.

No sooner had the Awards Rule been sus-ended than the MHSAA was dealt a blow from nother quarter. Shortly after the hearing be-ore the Legislative Committee, Representative erald W. Graves (not a member of the Com-iittee) had written to Taylor, requesting infor-iation concerning the MHSAA's creation, ac-ivities, and sources of revenue. Specifically, he anted to know who paid the Association's tele-hone, printing, and postage bills; whether the ssociation was paying the $3.00 per square foot ental charge for space in a state building as-essed against all state agencies; and who paid he salaries of the Association's employees. On receiving answers to his questions from Director Forsythe, Representative Graves next asked the Attorney General for an opinion on the legal status of the Association.

The day after the Legislative Committee suspended the Awards Rule, Graves received a letter from the Attorney General stating that the MHSAA, not being a state agency, "would be subject to the rental charges prescribed by Act 53 of Public Acts of 1952, if state office space is occupied by the Association."

The newspaper chain which had been vociferously supporting the suspended boys seized upon the Attorney General's opinion. Its newspapers headlined charges of diversion of public monies to support the activities of a "private" organization, as the result of collusion and conspiracy on the part of Superintendent Taylor and MHSAA officials.

To add to the MHSAA's woes, the office of the Director of Internal Revenue, U. S. Treasury Department, announced that an investigation was under way to determine whether MHSAA was entitled to exemption from federal taxes on the price of tickets of admission to the basketball tournament it sponsored. The investigation ultimately ended with a report favorable to MHSAA, but that action came too late to repair the political damage wrought at the time of the announcement.

The Superintendent's Solution

WEEK after the Legislative Committee sus-ended the Awards Rule, Taylor's newly-ap-ointed advisory body of schoolmen and lay-ien met in Lansing. For this group (formally nown as the State-Wide Committee on Inter-holastic Athletics) to recommend a modified ule under which he could reinstate the boys as now Taylor's only clear way out of a diffi-ult situation. However, just as every previous ffort at passing this case upward from local igh school jurisdiction had caused new contro-ersies, so was convening an advisory body to be ttended with more trouble for Taylor.

In addition to Director Forsythe as chairman, and Semler and Deal who were representing MHSAA, Taylor had appointed fourteen other members. Three of these were high school principals and two were superintendents of schools; these eight, plus Father MacEachin of East Lansing, who was to represent the parochial schools, appeared to give the schoolmen a majority on the Committee. The other eight members included: a businessman representing the Lansing Junior Chamber of Commerce; a member of the House of Representatives from a rural district near Lansing; a reporter for the *Battle*

Creek Inquirer-News, who was President of the state Sportswriters Association; Robert E. LeMire, the Mayor of Escanaba who had touched off the initial press campaign; a Protestant minister from Hastings; David Pence, the immediate Past President of the Michigan State Bar; Billy Wickens, the State Commander of the American Legion; and Francis P. Kelly, chief of the High School Athletic Officials section of the State Civil Service Commission.

A Split on the Advisory Committee

The Committee held sessions over a two-day period, apparently in an atmosphere of substantial harmony. Overwhelming majorities supported motions to affirm that athletics should remain under the direction of the Superintendent of Public Instruction; that the co-operative arrangement between the Superintendent and the MHSAA should continue; that a motion to recommend reinstatement of the violators of the Awards Rule should be tabled; and that an opinion should be requested from the Attorney General concerning the constitutionality of the suspension of the Awards Rule by the Committee on Administrative Rules. Five schoolmen abstained from voting on a motion that the State Director of Athletics should no longer be a member of the Representative Council of the Association, but this motion, too, was adopted by a vote of nine to one. It was tentatively agreed, by a unanimous vote, that the reinstatement clause should be amended to read: "A student violating the above rule [10A] shall be ineligible for a period of not less than one semester or more than one year from the date of his last violation." The Committee then adjourned, presumably to reconvene in a month for a final vote on the redrafted Awards Rule.

However, underlying conflict was far from resolved, as Taylor soon realized when he received a letter of resignation from Francis Kelly, stating that:

> In reviewing the work of the committee, it is my personal opinion that it not only failed to comply with the instructions in your appointed letter, but also refused to face the issue at hand, namely, the reinstatement of the 10 high school students who had been suspended under rule 10.

On the heels of this letter, Taylor received one from Mayor Robert E. LeMire of Escanaba:

> . . . I read, with interest, in our local newspaper about the resignation of Francis P. Kelly. Truthfully, I was contemplating doing the same thing. I honestly feel that you acted in good faith in forming this committee. I have discussed you with our mutual friend, John Lemmer [Escanaba Superintendent of Schools], and we both agreed that you were a man of integrity, that you felt badly over the severe penalty inflicted upon the boys, and that you wanted the situation remedied. However, I was somewhat disturbed when I learned that you had appointed Charles Forsythe as chairman of the committee. You and everyone concerned must agree that Charlie did not enter the committee meeting with an open mind, as all of his statements and actions clearly indicated that he was biased and prejudiced from the beginning. Further, the minutes of the meeting are not too accurate, Clair. For instance, a few minutes after Charlie finished his dissertation on the rules and the reasons for them, Russell Le Cronier, Superintendent of Schools at Mt. Pleasant, made a motion that the committee approve the *status quo* of the MHSAA. The said motion was readily seconded by another school member. The minutes fail to show that Mr. Le Cronier withdrew his motion after Mr. Rose [the Junior Chamber of Commerce representative], Mr. Kelly, and I objected strenuously to such a motion. As you must realize, passage of the said motion would have meant that the committee approved, in its entirety, the entire set-up. Further, the minutes do not show that Charles Forsythe stated the reason for the Awards Rule was to protect the schools which could not afford to give expensive awards, in competition with the schools which possessed more money. Needless to say I was absolutely shocked because it was my belief that the purpose of the Awards Rule was to teach the young men the spirit and benefits of amateurism in comparison to professionalism.
>
> Another matter that greatly disturbed me, Clair, was the fact that you neither have the right nor authority to hire or fire the director of the MHSAA. It is my understanding that in reality the MHSAA is an organization, separate and distinct from your office, that Charles Forsythe's salary is paid by the MHSAA, that the MHSAA is handling hundreds of thousands of dollars and that they need not account to anyone but the Council for the receipts and expenditures of the moneys, that all funds enter and leave the office of the director, and that the decision of the Council to declare these youngsters ineligible was not your decision, as you contend, but the decision of the director and his Council. . . .

The Superintendent Yields

Superintendent Taylor was getting it from all directions. The press was generally critical of his failure to reinstate the boys at once. The Committee on Administrative Rules was obviously displeased. Still pending was the court action in Barry County, seeking an injunction against Taylor, which, if granted, would have the effect of reinstating the suspended Hastings boys. On the other hand, any sign that he was thinking of reinstating the suspended athletes was certain to alienate the only solid support he enjoyed in the matter, that of the MHSAA schoolmen. And now, the Committee he depended upon to recommend a rule which would give him the grounds he needed for reinstating the athletes was about to make a recommendation which would leave them ineligible for three more months. Furthermore, the Committee appeared likely to fall apart before its final report was rendered. Taylor, an elected official, would have to choose between further offending the public and the Legislative Committee, on the one hand, and offending his professional clientele, the schoolmen, on the other. He took the latter course. With the resignation of the one member, he appointed two new members to the Committee: Representative Phillips and Senator Hutchinson, the Chairman and a member, respectively, of the Legislative Committee on Administrative Rules. There were now eight schoolmen (not including Chairman Forsythe) and nine "lay citizens" on the Committee. This should give a clear margin for speedy reinstatement.

The Advisory Committee Meets Again

Taylor himself was present at the second meeting of the Advisory Committee on November 23. All of the Committee members attended except lawyer David Pence. The Committee approved a revision of the *Handbook* providing that any student declared ineligible by either the Executive Committee or the Representative Council could be reinstated by the Committee or Council "provided new evidence is introduced as a result of further testimony or upon a re-evaluation of evidence previously submitted." A subsequent attempt to amend this motion by substituting "may be reinstated by the Superintendent of Public Instruction with or without the recommendation of the Executive Committee or Representative Council" lost decisively, with only Senator Hutchinson and Representative Phillips, the mover and seconder of the amendment, voting in favor of it.

The Advisory Committee now turned to redrafting the Awards Rule and finally reached the crucial reinstatement clause. Taylor had proposed that the period of ineligibility should be not less than three months nor more than one year, and that a recommendation concerning the length of ineligibility should be made in each case by the Representative Council to the Superintendent of Public Instruction. His announced reason for favoring a three-month minimum was that most high school sports were played for a period of three months or less rather than for a full semester of almost five months. Taylor was not unaware, however, that more than three months already had elapsed since the awards to the Escanaba and Hastings boys, who would be eligible for immediate reinstatement under such a clause if Taylor were to carry out his announced intention of "giving the boys the benefit" of any changes made in the Awards Rule. Taylor's proposal was put in the form of a motion by Rose of the Lansing Junior Chamber of Commerce; it was seconded by Representative Phillips.

Perhaps Taylor had taken too much of a gamble in depending on a Committee whose balance turned on a single vote. The absence of Pence, a layman, proved critical, because the motion lost by the casting vote of Chairman Forsythe. One schoolman and the minister from Hastings abstained from voting; the remaining public schoolmen, plus Billy Wickens of the American Legion, voted solidly against lowering the minimum to three months, the rest of the laymen and the representative from the parochial schools favoring it. Semler moved immediately to substitute a semester minimum, but before a vote could be taken Taylor interrupted.

The public school officials had lined up solidly and pointedly against Taylor and his proposal, and a showdown was at hand. He flatly told his Advisory Committee:

> The proposal which I made concerning minimum and maximum penalties is what I feel is fair and workable. I am sorry it wasn't passed. Since these rules are mine to administer when they become a part of the *Administrative Code,* I feel I must tell you that I shall submit my proposal to the Attorney General.

He added that he would submit the Advisory Committee's proposal for the first part of the rule, together with his own reinstatement clause, to the Attorney General and to the Governor for emergency approval so that "the high school students who have been ineligible under the old Awards Rule may be reinstated to interscholastic athletic competition at the earliest possible opportunity." As soon as Taylor had made his announcement, Billy Wickens left the room.

The legislators took immediate advantage of Wickens' absence. It was moved by Phillips, and seconded by Hutchinson, that Rose's motion for Taylor's penalty clause be reconsidered. This motion carried, seven to six, Chairman Forsythe not participating. The Rose motion was then passed by the same count.

Taylor promptly forwarded the text of the Awards Rule, as recommended by the Committee, to the Attorney General, who gave his approval on November 30. On the same day, the Governor signed the certificate to give it immediate effect. The new penalty clause read:

> E. A student violating Sections A, B, C or D of this rule shall be ineligible for interscholastic athletic competition for a period of not less than 3 months or more than 1 year from the date of his last violation. The period for which he shall be ineligible shall be recommended by the Representative Council or Executive Committee to the Superintendent of Public Instruction.

The basis of the emergency in this case was stated by Taylor to be "my desire to give the students involved in high school athletics immediate benefit of the awards rule." On December 1, the following telegram was sent to each of the suspended athletes:

> YOU ARE IMMEDIATELY ELIGIBLE FOR INTERSCHOLASTIC ATHLETIC COMPETITION IN ACCORDANCE WITH NEW RULE.

Taylor did not consult either the Executive Committee or the Representative Council of the MHSAA, though Section E might have been interpreted to call for such consultation. In the light of the existing rift between himself and the schoolmen, Taylor assumed that consultation would entail delay, if not further disagreement. The important thing to Taylor at this time was to reinstate the boys and get the whole controversy settled.

The Schoolmen Retaliate

Following his address to the annual business meeting of the MHSAA on December 3, Taylor was heckled by questions from the floor concerning the new Awards Rule. The schoolmen knew that they had been beaten on the issue of the reinstatement clause, and they knew that they had not been consulted on the recent reinstatement of the suspended athletes. The fact that the MHSAA had no status as a state agency and that the Superintendent of Public Instruction clearly had legal authority to adopt, amend, and enforce rules governing high school athletics in complete disregard of the Association, did not assuage the injured feelings of the group of educators who for years had been accustomed to exercising *de facto* superintendence of Michigan high school athletics.

The indignation of the professional educators was expressed by Charles Semler, MHSAA president, speaking December 2 at the concurrent Detroit meeting of the North Central Association of Colleges and Secondary Schools:

> The importance of this whole procedure cannot be measured merely in terms of the amount of penalty which may be imposed for any violation of the Awards Rule or any other rule governing athletic competition. The real issue at stake is, who shall govern high school athletics in Michigan? Shall they be governed in accordance with the laws of the State and the wishes of the schools of the State as expressed through their duly elected representatives to the Representative Council, or shall the rules be written at the instance of an interim Legislative Committee which, there is every reason to believe, has no constitutional authority to do so on the very simple but fundamental principle of American government that its action rescinding this rule, and attempt to write a new one, constitutes an administrative and judicial function which a Committee of the Legislature cannot constitutionally perform? Shall we continue to enforce rules governing athletic competition impartially and fairly through the elected representatives of the schools and the Superintendent of Public Instruc-

> tion or shall their enforcement depend on the amount of political and personal pressure any offender may be able to bring to bear? For the first time since any attempt was made to control high school athletics in Michigan (1895) we now have a rule which is not the result of the action or recommendation of regularly elected representatives of the high schools of the State. Since arriving in Detroit I have learned through the public press that Superintendent Taylor has reinstated all the boys concerned to immediate eligibility without consulting the Council of the MHSAA in spite of the fact that the new Awards Rule as adopted by him provides that penalties under it shall be recommended by the Council or Executive Committee of the MHSAA.
>
> If we follow the practice of yielding to political pressure and ignoring the wishes of the schools of the State in writing and enforcing athletic regulations, all the work which has been done in the last thirty years to make the athletic program an important and integral part of the educational program will be destroyed. . . . To submit to such political pressure will set a precedent which is capable of seriously impairing the administration of the entire education program.

The Attorney General Rules

A week after the schoolmen's meetings in Detroit, Representative Adrian deBoom, a former high school teacher, asked the Attorney General for an opinion on the constitutionality of the laws authorizing the Legislature to abrogate administrative rules, and authorizing the Joint Committee on Administrative Rules to suspend them. A motion approving such a request had been adopted by the State-Wide Committee on Interscholastic Athletics at its meeting on November 23, but the Superintendent of Public Instruction did not want to use legal procedures to settle his problems. However, on December 2 Semler again questioned the constitutionality of the Legislative Committee and lamented the fact that the Attorney General's opinion had not been asked. DeBoom's letter followed Semler's speech by a week.

It was not until February 11, 1954, that the Attorney General rendered his opinion. It concluded:

> This power to suspend the operation of a rule depends in the statute entirely upon a finding by the committee that such a rule is not in conformity with the statue under which it was promulgated. The determination of the question as to whether a rule is in conformity with the statute under which it was promulgated appears to be a judicial function. Not having the power to make such determination, the legislature cannot lawfully delegate such power to one of its committees. For this reason the provisions under discussion purporting to give a legislative committee power to suspend a rule for the reasons stated appear to contravene that provision of the Constitution under which the legislative power of the government may not perform judicial functions.

The Legislature was in the middle of its session when Millard's opinion was announced. Initial legislative reaction was mixed. It was suggested that the Committee on Administrative Rules might continue to sit in an "informal capacity," without legal power to suspend rules but exercising its powers of persuasion (reminding administrators that nonconformists might experience difficulty with the Appropriations Committee). Not a single legislator made a public statement in opposition to the Attorney General's ruling. Several privately expressed gratification, since some of the Committee's activities had embarrassed many of the legislators themselves.

It was something of a surprise then when on May 14, the last day of the regular legislative session of 1954, each house approved Senate Concurrent Resolution No. 53, providing for the continuation of the Legislative Committee during 1954 with no indicated change in its composition, powers, or function. According to the report in the *Lansing State Journal,* only "a handful of legislators" were on hand for the adjournment session, and approval was by voice vote.

Conclusion

The Legislative Committee on September 17 had recommended to the Superintendent of Public Instruction

> that he immediately promulgate such procedural rules as are required under the provisions of Act No. 197 of the Public Acts of 1952 and that his rules provide in substance that at any hearing involving the eligibility of an individual, such individual be entitled to be present at such proceeding and to present his case.

There was no question of the Department of

Public Instruction's legal obligation to formulate and publish such procedural rules, and, after a number of months, they emerged, were cleared by the Attorney General, given the normal emergency approval by the Governor, and became immediately effective on July 8, 1954, when they were filed with the Secretary of State. They were to apply in cases of appeals from the MHSAA that were heard by the Superintendent of Public Instruction, for there was no change in MHSAA's internal procedures for handling eligibility cases. The relationship between MHSAA and the Superintendent was formalized and classified for readers of the *MHSAA Handbook* by the appearance of a revision of Regulation VI, Section 3, in the 1954-55 edition:

> Appeals from actions of the Executive Committee or Representative Council shall be made to the Superintendent of Public Instruction.

The *Handbook's* Regulation VI, which otherwise deals with the membership and functions of the Executive Committee, is for the first time prefaced with a cautionary note:

> (NOTE: This Regulation is not a part of the Michigan Administrative Code. It has been adopted by the Representative Council of the Michigan High School Athletic Association.)

A concluding irony, however, occurred in July when, long after the controversy had died away, Taylor's department *re*-amended the reinstatement clause, replacing the three-month minimum with a "full semester" minimum.

Thus, the Superintendent of Public Instruction, faced with opposing demands from the public, the Legislative Committee, and the schoolmen—because, as he maintained, local school officials had refused to handle in the first place decisions that were rightfully theirs—had found a way out of a most difficult position. The Awards Rule had been changed to suit the Legislative Committee and to permit the boys' reinstatement, thus quieting the political and public controversy. Once this had been done, the schoolmen, who had lost on the question of the boys' reinstatement, were pacified by a second change in the rule, giving them the one-semester penalty period they wanted. By-products of the controversy were the improvements made in the Awards Rule and in appeal procedures. As a by-product, too, the constitutionality—or rather unconstitutionality—of legislative review of administrative rule-making had been ruled upon by the Attorney General. But the Legislative Committee continued to operate as if nothing had happened. A month after the Legislature adjourned, the State Department of Agriculture was hailed before the Committee to defend a regulation governing the sale and contents of milk.

The Van Waters Case

Thomas H. Eliot

The Commissioner Decides to Act

WHEN A NEW AND LITTLE-KNOWN department head distrusts an experienced and famous subordinate and disapproves of her policies, but can lawfully remove her only for "just cause," what happens? That is the subject of this study.[1] The events related here excited thousands of people in Massachusetts in 1948 and 1949. The Commissioner of Correction, Elliott E. McDowell, clashed with the Superintendent of the State Reformatory for Women, Miriam Van Waters, and, in an atmosphere of controversy and sensational publicity, made a series of decisions which largely determined the nature and the outcome of the conflict.

The struggle, however, was influenced not only by the Commissioner's official decisions but by his theory of the administrator's function, by his methods of dealing with his staff, and by the interplay of personalities. What might have been a fairly routine administrative problem became, instead, a fighting issue in which the decent reputation of the state itself was at stake.

The chief actors in the case were McDowell, Van Waters, and Frank A. Dwyer, Jr., Deputy Commissioner under McDowell.

McDowell, a graduate of Massachusetts Institute of Technology, was by profession a construction engineer. As such he had worked on the building of Norfolk State Prison Colony (for male offenders), and then for fourteen years had directed the "prison industries" program at that institution. He was elevated to the Commissionership of the Department of Correction in 1948. In speech and appearance, he gave the impression of being unaffected and direct, a good fellow and a good citizen. He had a heroic record in the first World War, and afterwards maintained a very active interest in veterans' organizations. His one-time deputy described him as "having more intestinal fortitude than any man I ever knew."

Van Waters was one of the best-known penologists in the country. Professionally trained at the University of Oregon and Clark University, she had served as Superintendent of the Juvenile Court Detention Home and Referee of the Juvenile Court in Los Angeles, as president of the National Conference of Social Work, and as the Wickersham Commission's specialist on juvenile delinquency. After she became head of the Reformatory at Framingham, Massachusetts, in 1932, her reputation continued to grow. She wrote several books; she was appointed as the one woman member of a United States delegation to a United Nations body studying delinquency; she was awarded the annual medal of the United Prison Association "for meritorious service." In speech articulate and precise, in appearance short, erect and dignified, she had a natural histrionic talent which added to the impact of her personality. She was the kind of disciplined, quietly forceful person who makes some bitter enemies and wins many devoted admirers.

Dwyer was a "self-made man" and conscious of that fact. He had been a member of the state police force, but when his friend, Charles F. Hurley, became Governor of Massachusetts in 1937, Dwyer served as one of his aides and found time to study law. He was admitted to the bar, but never practiced, for when Hurley was leaving office a place was found for Dwyer in the Department of Correction. Dark, earnest, and intense, Dwyer was a man of strong emotions and strong convictions, a believer in the observance of strict rules of conduct and compliance with the letter of the law.

[1] In this study, a number of inmates and former inmates of the Reformatory are given *wholly fictitious* names. No person having any such name is known to the author, the editor, or the publisher; and if any person exists who does have any such name, she is obviously *not* the inmate or former inmate mentioned herein.

Introduction

At midnight on January 11, 1949, Dr. Miriam Van Waters was removed from the position which she had held for seventeen years, that of Superintendent of the Reformatory for Women at Framingham, Massachusetts. The man who ordered her removal was the state Commissioner of Correction, Elliott E. McDowell, who had been in office for less than a year. Pursuant to the elaborate statutory procedure for the protection of state employees, McDowell accompanied his order with specific charges against Van Waters, and himself gave her a lengthy public hearing, after which he reaffirmed his decision. Van Waters then claimed her right to a hearing before a special impartial commission appointed by the Governor of Massachusetts. This commission found that some of McDowell's charges were not substantiated and that the remainder, even if true, did not constitute just cause for her removal. Accordingly, she was reinstated on March 12, 1949.

Such is the bare chronological outline of one of the fiercest conflicts ever to arise from the administrative decisions of an officer of the Commonwealth of Massachusetts. No political party or economic pressure group was fighting for advantage, no crime or corruption was charged. Yet for months the Van Waters case was major front-page news in Massachusetts, hotly argued in living room and on street corner. Through the long weeks of hearings before McDowell and the special commission hundreds of citizens sat and listened and often, improperly, hissed or applauded. The administrative action of the Commissioner made him a symbol—to some, a symbol of official responsibility and rectitude; to others, a symbol of reaction and devotion to red tape, if not of outright cruelty. Conversely many citizens found their eyes dazzled by the almost holy light which they thought they saw emanating from Dr. Van Waters, the far-seeing, kind and resolute helper of the oppressed, while many others shook their heads over her "lawlessness," and spread scandal about her by dark whispers and anonymous letters.

It was, all in all, a highly emotional affair, and had become such well before the climax was reached in the winter of 1949. Emotions, personalities, and professional viewpoints all helped to shape the events which led to that climax. Those events, which took place in the fourteen months prior to the removal order, cannot be usefully considered without a brief look at the background of both the protagonists and the institutions which they served.

Van Waters at Framingham

The Reformatory for Women was built nearly ninety years ago near the border separating the towns of Framingham and Sherborn, about twenty miles from Boston. It was not a walled prison but, in the beginning, a large building with barred windows standing in the center of a pleasant field close to farming country. Later additional buildings were added, frame cottages rather than the "security-type" prisons. Some of the extensive acreage was cultivated, a barn was built, and dairy farming became one part of the Reformatory routine.

In 1879, shortly after the main building was erected, the Massachusetts Legislature engaged in some penological pioneering, enacting a statute known as the Indenture Law. Under this law women sentenced to the Reformatory were permitted, if they wished, to work for pay as domestic servants in private homes, pursuant to contracts entered into between the employer and the Board of Prison Commissioners. When the Department of Correction was established in 1919, with general control over all of the state's penal institutions, the authority to make such contracts was transferred to the Commissioner of Correction.

Apparently the first Superintendent to make full use of the Indenture Law and even to disregard its restrictions was Mrs. Jessie C. Hodder, who headed the Reformatory from 1911 to 1931. Mrs. Hodder was a popular and "progressive" penologist, expounding the view that the Reformatory existed primarily for the purpose of rehabilitating the individual offenders who were sent there and practicing what she preached. Her successor, Miriam Van Waters, testified concerning Mrs. Hodder's regime as follows:

> She had residing with her a lifer who had complete charge of raising all the flowers. . . . Mrs. Hodder has personally taken women to church and to local

hospitals. . . . Women commonly went from the institution to save the crops of the farmers and to lend a hand at hay-making, apple-picking. . . . They worked in laundries. . . . They worked in the neighborhood whenever a request came and in the opinion of Mrs. Hodder it was a good plan for the rehabilitation of a person.

During the influenza epidemic of 1918, Mrs. Hodder "indentured" numerous inmates to assist in nearby hospitals even though their work was not "domestic" service within the meaning of the law. In the 1920s she had the confidence of Commissioner Sanford Bates and continued to use the indenture system, both for domestic service and for other useful employment. When Dr. Van Waters succeeded her on January 1, 1932 it was not surprising that the use of this system continued and gradually increased. Many new contracts were made, some of them for "day work" (under which the indentured woman returned to the Reformatory each night) and a considerable number for duties other than "domestic service."

The use of the indenture system and the readiness to permit some contact with the nearby community were symptomatic of the difference between Framingham and the various state institutions for male offenders. Illustrative of the atmosphere which Mrs. Hodder and Dr. Van Waters sought to create at the Reformatory was a sentence on the first page of a handbook given to each inmate on her arrival there: "Here you are a student, not a prisoner."

Of course, Framingham's inmate population was very different from that of the usual prison. Strolling through the Reformatory grounds, one would not be likely to see murderers or burglars or counterfeiters or arsonists. In 1948 there were, on the average, 363 inmates, not counting some sixty babies born to inmates, or a number of defective delinquents who were housed at Framingham because there was no room for them in more appropriate institutions. Of the ordinary inmates, more than eighty percent were serving sentences for misconduct involving sex or liquor, or, frequently, both.

A sympathetic, albeit reasonably critical, picture of the Reformatory at the time when the Van Waters case was coming to a head was drawn by a social worker who was employed there while preparing a doctoral dissertation. She wrote:

The Superintendent has tried to put her aims into effect by her program of individual counselling, group therapy, modified student government, and a full vocational, educational, health, psychological and religious program.

The chief aim of Hodder Cottage [a comparatively new and pleasant frame house, where about thirty inmates lived] is to teach the girls a new way of life, an individual respect for good work, clean sportsmanship, happy associations, and the use of leisure time. . . . The girls work, play, cry, laugh, and fight together. . . . Staff members may help the student to reestablish a relationship with her family. The girls, after their release, keep in touch with the staff members, frequently write, telephone, or visit. They feel that someone cares.

Day work is assigned on the basis of a conference. It is done on a highly individualized basis, and other students do not know all the factors that enter into a decision. The policy is not properly clarified, so that a large group of students and a vocal section of the staff feel that the granting of day work is on a basis of favoritism. This is one of the major "gripes" in the institution. . . . As with most other programs in the institution, it is an attempt to keep away from a stereotyped plan based on merits, rather than need.[2]

For sixteen years, under Commissioner Stearns, who had appointed her, and his successors, Sayre, Dillon, Lyman, and Doyle, Superintendent Van Waters enlarged and developed the "progressive" policies of Mrs. Hodder. Each Commissioner respected her; each gave approval to her major policy decisions. Each signed the indenture contracts which she proposed, even though some of these called for work other than domestic service and a few named Van Waters herself, or a member of her staff, as the employer. And more and more, Framingham became an admired show-piece in the eyes of modern penologists.

Winslow and McDowell at Norfolk

When Van Waters came to Framingham in 1932, the state was in the process of greatly ex-

[2]Excerpted from Gertrude King, "Use of the Findings of the Rorschach Test in Relation to Social Treatment," unpublished doctoral dissertation, Simmons College School of Social Work, 1948.

panding its facilities for male offenders at Norfolk, thirty miles away.[3] But the growth was accompanied by pain and controversy. In 1933, the "progressive" penologist who headed the Norfolk Prison Colony was removed and in his place Commissioner Dillon appointed a building engineer, Maurice F. Winslow. Soon Winslow appointed another building engineer, Elliott E. McDowell, as superintendent of prison industries at Norfolk. For fourteen years these men worked together at the Prison Colony. McDowell's viewpoint cannot be wisely considered or understood without some understanding of his long-time chief and friend, Winslow.

Although relatively untrained in prison administration when he took the top job at Norfolk, Winslow was a man of intelligence, energy, and force. He has been described by former staff members as despotic. He was a careful manager, and was credited with devising an air-tight system of checking the whereabouts of every prisoner every thirty minutes. At the same time, he did not subscribe to the old "vengeance and punishment" theory of penology. He was concerned about the men at Norfolk, some of whom acquired an admiration for him not altogether unlike the respectful devotion given by some of the Framingham inmates to Van Waters. Winslow and his staff, especially McDowell, helped to train inmates for future employment and aided them in finding jobs after release.

Winslow came into prison work with a feeling of high respect for law, and a tendency to insist on strict adherence to regulations. He had a natural capacity for leading men and a sharp distaste for political pressure and outside interference. Despite his comparative lack of background, he began almost at once to gain a good reputation as an administrator and penologist.

His lack of background, however, was perhaps the main reason for the violence of his reaction toward one sordid phase of prison life. In virtually every large prison, where persons of one sex are shut away from society for long periods of time, there is a considerable amount of overt homosexuality. Whether or not Winslow understood this, theoretically, before he took the job, it was only after he became Superintendent at Norfolk that he fully realized the harm that could be done by aggressive perverts. He was deeply troubled and put much thought and effort into trying to prevent the perversion of young men by old offenders. The suggestion that psychiatric advice was the best guide in dealing with homosexuals left him unconvinced. He came to believe that he could recognize homosexual tendencies when he saw them and that he had a serious responsibility for preventing perversion, or checking its spread, by strict measures of surveillance, segregation, and control.

In his first years in prison work, Winslow knew Van Waters only slightly, although he was aware of her reputation and her liberal penological views. Sometime in the late 1930s, however, a friend who had worked at Framingham told him a story that disturbed him: a story of laxness on the part of Van Waters and her staff, of their taking homosexuality lightly and making little effort to control it. Winslow's respect for Van Waters lessened and his doubts about her liberal policies increased. Contacts which he had with her during World War II, when he was acting as Farm Coordinator of the state, added to his suspicions. He believed that she deliberately withheld information from him and tried to mislead him. His critical opinion of her deepened into dislike and distrust.

It may be, too, as some suggest, that Winslow was envious of Van Waters' eminence. Hers was the national reputation, hers the institution which experts from all over the world came to visit. It is certain that he believed her to be an artful publicist, skillful in obtaining publicity for the favorable aspects of her program and in suppressing news that might tend to be discreditable.

Winslow made no particular secret of his doubts about Van Waters' policies. His subordinates at Norfolk including McDowell were aware of his attitude. Framingham's methods were rarely discussed at Norfolk staff meetings, but any casual mention of them was likely to be the occasion for a derogatory remark.

Through all this period the principals in the case, McDowell and Van Waters, met but rarely. On several occasions Van Waters requested

[3] There were three state institutions for mature, sane, male offenders in Massachusetts: the State Prison at Charlestown, the "Reformatory" at Concord and the Prison Colony at Norfolk.

Winslow to send McDowell, as a trained engineer, to Framingham to open sealed construction bids. Once McDowell visited Van Waters' home at the Reformatory, to take measurements for Venetian blinds which were being constructed in the Norfolk shops; and at this time he was apparently on friendly terms with her. But although in the same Department, they were running on different tracks which seldom coincided.

Appointment of Commissioner McDowell

Early in 1948 Governor Robert F. Bradford decided not to reappoint Commissioner of Correction Doyle, whose term was expiring. He offered the position to Winslow.[4] Winslow refused it, and suggested that McDowell be named instead. Bradford asked to see McDowell and shortly met with Winslow, McDowell, and Reuben L. Lurie, a prominent attorney and former chairman of the Parole Board. At this brief conference Winslow spoke up about Framingham. In the preceding months, from Parole Board members and Department officials, he had heard more stories about the Reformatory, tending to confirm his suspicions. In December and January he had read in the *Boston American*, a Hearst tabloid, a series of sensationally derogatory stories about favoritism, laxness, and worse, at that institution. Now Winslow told the Governor that very probably the new Commissioner would have a nasty job on his hands to clean up the mess at Framingham. Lurie, on the other hand, suggested to McDowell that it might be wise to do as former Commissioners had done and leave the Reformatory in the very capable hands of Van Waters. Bradford said nothing implying any commitment; McDowell said nothing at all.

On February 18, 1948, by Governor Bradford's appointment, McDowell became Commissioner of Correction. As he moved into his high-ceilinged State House office, he found a number of old acquaintances at work in the Department: several men formerly on the Norfolk staff, and another who had long had overall responsibility for industrial work in the state's penal institutions. Shortly he selected as Deputy Commissioner one staff member whom he did not know intimately but whose loyalty he could trust. This was Frank A. Dwyer, Jr.

Among McDowell's subordinates whom he saw daily in Boston, three never concealed their reservations about Van Waters. One, cool, precise, and accurate, was irritated by her customary insistence that her facts and figures were correct when, he believed, he could prove that they were not. Another scorned her policies and disliked her as an "intellectual." The third, Dwyer, had frankly expressed his disapproval of the indenture system. He was something of an expert on the state statutes and decisions concerning sentencing; when a court directed that a person go to prison, "there to be confined," it seemed to him virtually contempt of court to let that person out of the prison gates, and decidedly so when the departure was not plainly authorized by statute. Furthermore, Dwyer felt at least as strongly as Winslow about sex deviations. In dealing with Van Waters during his years in the Department, he had sensed that she did not share his abhorrence, and had been alarmed by the absence of "controls" at Framingham. Van Waters, in turn, was somewhat alarmed by Dwyer; to her, his direct, rather brusque manner seemed to show personal hostility.

Before the Investigation

Shortly before McDowell became Commissioner, his predecessor, Doyle, had approved a personnel requisition establishing a vacancy in the position of Interne at Framingham. A former inmate had actually begun to work in this position, on February 9, although the final "authorization form," prepared by the State Division of Personnel and Standardization, had not yet been signed. This signing was ordinarily a formality; the official who approved the requisition would naturally sign the authorization.[5] But on this occasion there was a change in com-

[4] Party politics apparently played no part in the appointment of Doyle's successor. McDowell was not an avowed member of any party; he had voted Democratic more often than not, but Bradford, a Republican, indicated no concern with his politics at all.

[5] By statute, appointments at the Reformatory were to be made by the Superintendent alone. However, McDowell was apparently unaware of this, and Van Waters, if she knew it, did not wish to raise the point; the Division of Personnel and Standardization forms all provided space for the Commissioner's signature, and the requisitions were regularly submitted to him.

missioners at the crucial moment; and the new Commissioner, McDowell, held up the signing of the authorization form.

He delayed because it was brought to his attention by one of his subordinates that the employee was a former inmate of the Reformatory. McDowell was inclined to disapprove of employing ex-convicts in penal institutions, and he wondered why Van Waters herself had failed to notify him of the appointee's criminal record.

On February 20, Van Waters came to Boston to talk with her friend, Lurie, at his law office, about certain pending legislation. At her suggestion Lurie called up McDowell and asked if he would be able to see her, as she would like to "drop in." Again the new Commissioner wondered. Why did Van Waters have Lurie call? Why didn't she just come in? They needed no introduction, after all.

When she arrived McDowell had on his desk the file concerning the former inmate. Van Waters explained to him her reasons for making the appointment and described the kind of work to which the appointee was assigned. "It would not work at Norfolk," observed McDowell, "to have an ex-inmate in charge of other inmates." He asked her to put her case in writing. Eventually, on March 4, the matter was closed by the Commissioner's letter which said in part: "After carefully examining your letter and the records of this Department re Patrice Rudolph, I am forced to the conclusion that it would be unwise for me to approve this appointment at present." The woman was dropped, and the salary that had already been paid to her was repaid to the State Treasurer by Van Waters personally.

The conference on February 20, illustrative though it was of one key difference in policy between the Commissioner and the Superintendent, had more historic significance. Van Waters, at the outset, congratulated McDowell and said that she wished to assure him of her loyalty and co-operation. McDowell's response was that "your cooperation is mandatory and your loyalty is to the Reformatory, in accordance with your oath of office."

According to Van Waters, McDowell in making this chilling reply "looked like a carven statue." According to McDowell, he spoke in a friendly fashion and was merely being accurate and matter-of-fact. But regardless of the manner in which he answered, the words were to weigh heavily against him a year later.

Within a week Van Waters, already uncomfortably aware of the new Commissioner's dislike of employing ex-convicts, had reason to be gravely concerned over his attitude toward the whole indenture system. On February 24 she attended a public hearing before a legislative committee that was considering a bill to abolish indenture. Frank A. Dwyer heartily favored this bill, and when Van Waters learned that he was to be appointed Deputy Commissioner, she assumed that Commissioner McDowell favored it also.

Upon her return to Framingham she took action to cancel an outstanding "day work" contract under which a number of girls had been working weekends at Seiler's restaurant, a large establishment in nearby Wellesley. She realized that their work there—cooking, waiting, cleaning, washing dishes, and the like—was not strictly "domestic service" within the meaning of the statute, and she assumed that McDowell would insist on a strict adherence to the law, strictly interpreted. Accordingly she notified the restaurant that the girls' services would have to be terminated on Sunday, February 29.

Andrew Seiler, informed by his Wellesley manager that the restaurant might be sadly short-handed on future weekends, promptly protested to Governor Bradford. The Governor's secretary telephoned McDowell and asked him to do what he could to straighten out the matter and give Seiler "some satisfaction." The Commissioner replied that he would not order the girls to continue at "that type of work," but would try to convince Seiler that no injustice was being done.

A Sudden Visit

Early next morning, February 28, without any advance notice to Van Waters, McDowell and Dwyer drove to Framingham. It was Saturday and Van Waters' secretary was off duty. The Commissioner and his Deputy suddenly appeared and demanded all outstanding day work contracts. They were not favorably impressed when Van Waters and her assistant superintendent took some time to find copies of all of these contracts in the files, and they were surprised that there was no contract with Seiler. (The contract had been made with Seiler's Wellesley manager personally.)

Then, as abruptly as they had arrived, McDowell and Dwyer departed. They went to Seiler's restaurant and explained to the manager that his employment of inmates was illegal because the work was not "domestic service." From the restaurant McDowell telephoned Seiler, making the same explanation. "We left," he said later, "with everybody satisfied about the termination."

There were three other small but revealing factors in this incident. When they visited the restaurant McDowell and Dwyer insisted on being shown the payroll records and examined the recorded deductions. Dwyer's distrust of the indenture system extended to its financial operation; he had heard critics refer to it as "penal servitude" and he was suspicious.

Second, on the day that the Governor's office called the Commissioner about Seiler's, one of the Department staff mentioned to him that the manager of Seiler's restaurant in Wellesley had a criminal record. If, in McDowell's eyes, it was dubious policy to employ ex-convicts as Reformatory officers, it was worse to indenture female prisoners to ex-convicts outside of the Reformatory gates. As his controversy with Van Waters developed, McDowell did not forget that she had permitted inmates to work for a man with a record—even though the manager had been "going straight" for many years, had earned a good reputation in Wellesley, and might well have been considered to be a good example of successful rehabilitation by the Commonwealth. Nor did the Commissioner hesitate to expose the facts about the ex-convict, who thereupon left town.

Third, while McDowell was waiting for the contracts to be gathered at the Reformatory, Van Waters spoke to him. She later testified: "I asked Commissioner McDowell to return soon as there were urgent matters of policy I wished to discuss with him in private—because although I did not say this to my Commissioner, my reason for needing to see him in private was that Mr. Dwyer's attitude toward me was so belligerently hostile and scornful that I could not present problems of policy effectively to the Commissioner in Mr. Dwyer's presence."

McDowell responded to Van Waters' invitation by spending most of March 8 at Framingham without Dwyer. The chief subject Van Waters wished to discuss with him was a major one at the Reformatory—the treatment and release of alcoholics. Under Massachusetts law alcoholics were given an indeterminate sentence with a one-year maximum; the Commissioner of Correction had authority to release them at any time during that one year. In the case of male alcoholics at Norfolk, release was customary at the end of six months, and sometimes it happened earlier. But for Framingham inmates there had been no six-months custom. Van Waters said that the alcoholic women "should wait until the institution authorities thought they should be released." This was because she had embarked on a vigorous program to help them, using the services of a special clinic at a Boston hospital and encouraging the growth of an Alcoholics Anonymous chapter at the Reformatory. Automatic release at the end of six months might, in some cases, interrupt real progress toward rehabilitation. Hence her desire for a flexible system.

The Commissioner had a friendly talk with her as they strolled around the grounds. He consented to her request that he should release alcoholics only on her recommendation, at least for the time being. But this was the last time that the Commissioner and the Superintendent ever talked together alone.

On April 7 McDowell and his Department's business agent stopped briefly at the Reformatory to instruct Van Waters about the desired procedure for submitting applications for indenture contracts. Van Waters had often sent to previous Commissioners, for their signatures, contracts already signed by the prospective employer. Now, however, McDowell decided to have applications signed by the prospective employer and submitted to him by the Superintendent. The applicant would then be examined by one of his staff before any final contract was drawn up.

Only nine days later, however, McDowell departed from this new procedure by initiating an indenture contract, signing it in blank, and forwarding it to Van Waters with instructions that an inmate was to be indentured immediately to Mrs. J. Alan Hodder. This housewife had employed indentured inmates before, and her husband was a member of the State Legislature.

McDowell made one more friendly visit to Framingham that spring. That was on the annual "Prison Industry Day," when he spoke to an assembly of inmates. *Harmony News,* the inmates' newspaper, reported him as saying that he didn't have much experience with women offenders but that the institution existed to better the condition of the inmates and that he would do everything possible[6] to accomplish this end.

But as spring came the seeds of controversy were sprouting fast. The *Boston American* was smoldering after its series of articles on Framingham. It was willing to give the Commissioner a little time, but only a little. McDowell may have been thinking merely about the employment of ex-convicts, indenture irregularities, and the coddling of alcoholics when, that April, he said at a United Prison Association luncheon that he intended to "straighten things out" at Framingham. Apparently he hoped to move slowly and steadily toward the establishment of a regime there which would conform strictly to the statutes, with adequate security and none of the "favoritism" alleged by the *American.* But his hand was forced, or so he seemed to believe. In early May he ordered an investigation of the Reformatory, and by so doing plunged his administration into a highly-charged emotional maelstrom.

The Dwyer Investigation

In the preceding November, an inmate named Antonette A. DiBenedetto[7] had died at the Reformatory. Her body was found hanging in her room shortly after lunch, when the "barn group" of which she was a member was preparing to go back to the cow-barn for its regular afternoon job.

The girl's parents later inquired as to the cause of her death, insisting that she was not a suicidal type. They enlisted the interest of their state Senator, Michael A. LoPresti, who let reporters on the *American* know that he was questioning the statements of the medical examiner and the Reformatory officers that "Toni" DiBenedetto had killed herself. A rumor spread that she had been murdered by a fellow-inmate, a girl who had allegedly received favored treatment at Framingham. As a result of sensational publicity two investigations were made. The District Attorney of Middlesex County made a brief inquiry and decided that the death was by suicide. LoPresti, however, insisted that J. Paul Doyle, the Commissioner of Correction who preceded McDowell, should investigate further.

Accordingly in early February, 1948, just before his term expired, Doyle sent his Deputy Commissioner, Daniel J. McDevitt, to Framingham. McDevitt, a Boston politician, was highly regarded by some Department officials, including Van Waters, but he had no training in investigative work. He filed a brief report with Doyle on February 6 stating that he had "reviewed the records" and interviewed the head farmer at the Reformatory. He quoted from letters indicating that at two other institutions where she had been confined, Toni DiBenedetto had been resentful and bitter and had had a bad effect on other inmates. He concluded that she had committed suicide.

After McDowell took office, LoPresti, the DiBenedettos, their attorney, and the *American* refused to let the matter drop. Finally on April 30 the Senator and the girl's parents came to McDowell's office. They insisted on a further investigation; they claimed that they had heard credible stories that Toni had either been murdered by a fellow-inmate or had been driven to suicide by her. McDowell had already read the report filed by McDevitt (who was no longer with the Department) and had found it totally unimpressive. As he put it, "It wasn't very complete and not very satisfactory. I just sat on it, waiting for something to happen, and of course it did. The family of the girl and a State Senator wanted further investigation, so I had to make further inquiry into the matter to satisfy them, and of course they are entitled to satisfaction."

On May 3 McDowell telephoned Van Waters telling her that he was sending Dwyer to investigate. Van Waters replied that the case had

6 McDowell later insisted that he was misquoted. According to him, he promised to "do everything possible *within the law*" to improve conditions.

7 This name is the single exception to the fictitious names given for any inmates mentioned in this study.

already been investigated twice, but McDowell said that Dwyer was coming anyway, and should be given an office in which to conduct interviews. He told the *American:* "You can rest assured that the investigation by Mr. Dwyer will be a thorough one."

The Interviews

The next day, May 4, Dwyer went to Framingham. Van Waters was not present, but to her deputy, Margaret O'Keefe, Dwyer stated that he would conduct all interviews alone with only a stenographer (from McDowell's office) present. He interviewed first girls in the barn group who had worked with Toni.

The inmate who headed the group, Margot Chauvier (described in Dwyer's notes as "mannish type . . . wears slacks . . . deep voice"), was the supposedly "favored" inmate who had figured in the ugly rumors of foul play in Toni's death. She told Dwyer that she had found Toni hanging when she called her to go to work after lunch. She denied, in answer to Dwyer's questions, that she had been overly friendly with Toni or had ever beaten her up. Dwyer told her that he had contrary information and severely informed her that this was a serious matter and that he did not think that she had been telling the truth.

To the other girls in the group Dwyer put many leading questions, some relevant to Toni's death but others apparently concerned with another subject: "Did the Chauvier girl approach you?" "Haven't they approached you around here?" "Did you hear of them having a fight?" "Did you hear of trouble with Margot?" "Did you ever see anyone caught? . . ." Much of it was the kind of questioning that may go on at a police station, late at night, but would never be allowed in a court of law. A typical sequence went as follows:

Q. Did you ever see her [Margot] do anything to her [Toni]?
A. No.
Q. Did she?
A. I don't know.
Q. Where did they do these things?

Of the five barn-group girls Dwyer interviewed at the outset of his investigation, two made statements that were damaging to Margot Chauvier. One was admittedly vague. The other, however, stated that "the kids told me" that Margot had beaten up Toni the night before the suicide. This inmate went further, giving Dwyer terminology that was new to him as she informed him that she "wasn't mixed up in the 'doll racket,'" the inmates' phrase for pervasive perversion. This girl was obviously trying to be helpful to Dwyer: she made guesses as to how Margot might have killed Toni and suggested the names of special friends of Margot who "might tell you something." With respect to her remarks concerning homosexuality, Dwyer questioned her in great detail.

On May 7 Dwyer went to the New Bedford House of Correction to interview a former Framingham inmate, Bettey Gallane, who had been a member of the barn group with Toni the previous summer. She had been transferred to New Bedford because "I couldn't stand it up there [at Framingham]." This girl told Dwyer that she had been Toni's best friend, and, with no urging from Dwyer, she expanded on the subject and named other inmates and many of the highest officers of the Reformatory as "being in love with each other." Another girl at New Bedford ["I asked for a transfer; they gave me a runaround up there"] said that she had left the barn group because Margot "made it tough for me." She gave to Dwyer an undated love letter beginning "Dear Margot" and signed "Toni" which she said she "happened to pick up from the floor" the month before Toni died.

While at Framingham, Dwyer personally examined the room where Toni died and concluded that no murderer could have killed her and escaped from the room. Returning to Boston, he told McDowell this; but he also emphasized that he had obtained information which went far beyond the DiBenedetto case—information that raised serious questions about the whole Reformatory. Promptly McDowell decided to expand the scope of the investigation to include "conditions not conducive to proper management of the Reformatory and not in compliance with the laws of the Commonwealth and the 'Rules and Regulations for the Officers and Employees of the Reformatory for Women,' and of such a nature as to endanger the welfare of those confined." On Monday, May 10 he issued a press release stating that while Dwyer's investigation had shown the DiBenedetto girl to have committed suicide, "certain conditions have been brought to light and will be further investigated and eliminated."

On Dwyer's advice, also, McDowell on May 15 ordered the transfer of Margot Chauvier to East Cambridge jail and arranged that she should not be interviewed there except with his permission. Apparently he feared that pressure was being brought on Margot by Reformatory officials to keep her from telling any story damaging to the Reformatory. At Framingham, however, it was feared that Margot was probably being coerced into fabricating a more damaging story. The transfer was duly publicized in the *American,* which quoted McDowell as saying: "I gave that order for the purpose of separating this girl from her associates at the Reformatory. This order was issued so that she could be better interrogated, separate from the institution, without that influence to bother us in the questioning." There was no transcript of any subsequent interview with Margot, however, attached to Dwyer's eventual report.

For the rest of May Dwyer worked hard and long. He questioned 53 inmates and former inmates, 23 members of the Reformatory staff, and six other persons. At these interviews the only persons present were Dwyer, the person being questioned, and Dwyer's female stenographer. Dwyer was an experienced policeman. In his days on the state police force some had called him a "tough cop." His approach was direct and hard-boiled. The witnesses, of course, were not sworn; and their stories varied widely. He asked them about favoritism; about Margot having keys to many rooms; about particular inmates being indentured to staff officers and living in the staff home, but not performing any domestic service. Some of them told him stories (usually hearsay) about liquor in the institution. Many described trips with staff officers for ice cream or to the movies or to a "Chinese restaurant" in the nearby town.

Dwyer never let go of the subject which had caused him to ask that the scope of his inquiry be broadened. From a number of inmates, usually by the use of leading questions, he drew the opinion that a dozen or more women were involved in the "doll racket." Two of the officers agreed that there was some homosexuality at the Reformatory; one pointed out that it was an evil prevalent in penal institutions generally and the other gave a rather interesting answer: "In a place like this where girls are shut away from normal interests, it is natural for them to become attached to each other. I don't think it is as impure as some suggest."

All through the interviews with inmates Dwyer drew on what one girl had told him and sought corroboration from others. As a result he asked a number of inmates questions that reflected on the Reformatory officers: "What have you on Miss White? . . . What do you hear on Miss Brown? . . ."

While Dwyer was investigating, McDowell stayed in the background except for transferring Margot Chauvier to East Cambridge and taking one other administrative action. This involved inmate Thelma Atwell, whom Dwyer interviewed on May 14. She told Dwyer that Margot had beaten Toni and that "a lot goes on around here," adding a specific charge against a particular officer. Four days later Van Waters had Thelma interviewed by a state psychiatrist, Thelma having requested to be released on parole. That night Dwyer requested McDowell to order her release and McDowell did so on May 19. Immediately Dwyer interviewed her again. She was picked up for drunkenness again a few days later. (The psychiatrist's report, incidentally, indicated that she was a highly psychotic individual, of dubious veracity, but McDowell never asked to see it.)

From Van Waters' standpoint the effect of the investigation was tragic and devastating. On May 8, in answer to a query from the *American,* she said that she did not believe that girls' statements about "brutal beatings . . . were the free, spontaneous utterances of those to whom they were ascribed." Later she testified about the Dwyer investigation as follows: "In all my thirty years of work in Federal, county, or state institutions, I have seen nothing so disastrous on the morale. . . . A girl would report in tears that she had been asked what she described as a 'revolting question' about an officer then employed at the institution. This would be followed by another sobbing girl who said she had been asked a revolting question about some other employee. Within two or three days, the moral reputation of some eleven women holding key positions . . . had been questioned. I only know that they came in with a feeling of horror and revulsion, or else with the idea that the authority of the staff was about to be undermined. Since some questions related to Negro and white officers and . . . inmates, and since it is very difficult in any institution to avoid factions, rumor, and gossip, I felt myself about to be confronted with what might develop into a race riot. Then, some girls, fearing a sudden unexplained release or transfer, and others who thought they might be able to get one and be sprung from the institution—all made it a scene of unwarranted terror."

In contrast to her feelings were Dwyer's own reactions, transmitted by him orally to the Commissioner and later summed up in his report as follows: "A thorough investigation is most difficult, in that . . . there has been intimidation of inmates interviewed, by institution personnel, in the questioning of certain inmates as to what was said in the interviews and in some cases causing inmates, after being interviewed, to be examined by State experts for the examination of insane prisoners; . . . by the refusal by certain institution personnel to talk when interviewed and the hostility of others. . . ."

Van Waters Is Questioned

The interrogation of Van Waters herself on June 1 concluded the investigation. McDowell and two of his stenographers accompanied Dwyer. The Commissioner began by explaining why he had reopened the DiBenedetto case, and then said: "The reason I am here today is, not that I do not have confidence in Mr. Dwyer, but I did not think he should talk with you without my being present. You are the number one person and the key person here." Van Waters' reply was, as she later recalled, an earnest plea to call off the investigation because of the harm it was doing to the institution and the inmates, although none of these remarks were recorded. McDowell answered merely that she should answer Dwyer's questions.

Dwyer then began the questioning, asking about the rules and regulations and any changes therein "in the past six or seven years." Van Waters appealed to McDowell: "I don't think I should be questioned about my proceedings under [former] commissioners. Everything that I have done has been done with the knowledge and approval of my commissioner." But McDowell replied that "as a matter of justice, plain justice to the people, I have a right to inquire into any matters which have taken place in the past."

Van Waters said: "I was appointed by Governor Ely and Commissioner Stearns. At that time my instructions were to do everything that I thought fit to modernize the institution and to work for rehabilitation." McDowell answered, "That is certainly my policy"—and thereafter, except for two very brief interjections, he was silent throughout the ensuing hours of interrogation. He left at lunch time; but Dwyer questioned Van Waters for most of the afternoon.

Dwyer's questions ranged widely, and most of them were staccato, jumping from one subject to another. Some, to use Van Waters' phrase, were "repulsive" but these, again, were justified by Dwyer as checking up on whether Van Waters herself had heard the stories which a few of the girls had told to him. There were many questions about the number of girls taken to restaurants and shows; questions, too, as to girls whose "special treatment" resulted in their having pleasanter rooms than most of the other inmates. Frequently, Dwyer asked whether named pairs of inmates had homosexual relationships, and demanded "yes" or "no" answers. Van Waters was unwilling to give categorical replies. She tried to explain that in such matters she relied largely on psychiatric guidance and staff discussions. Finally Dwyer asked: "Were you ever told that [Toni] was very much in love with Margot Chauvier?" To this the Superintendent replied: "Well, all this you see makes it so difficult for an honest person to answer. With all the rumors that go around, I think I had better just not say anything. I have told you my policy. They all [reports of homosexual tendencies] go before a [staff] conference at which these things are discussed."

Throughout the Dwyer investigation the *Boston American* had been running a sensational series about the Reformatory. Dwyer was not making his interviews public but from other sources the *American* was learning "facts" about Van Waters. Some of this information presumably came from the Commissioner's office: for instance, on May 4 the paper reported, "it was learned that Dr. Van Waters asked the Department of Correction to approve the immediate appointment of an inmate about to be discharged, as a Reformatory staff member. This request was turned down." (This story, headed, "Charge Ex-Convicts Sherborn Aides,"[8] was obviously a version of the difference of policy made clear on February 20.) On May 6 Senator LoPresti referred to "the first witness Dwyer interviewed," alleging that Van Waters had sought to have her paroled. On May 12 the *American's* story, headed "Sherborn Girls Forced to Work for Ex-Convict," obviously referred to day work formerly done at Seiler's restaurant; that the manager of the restaurant was an ex-convict was not generally known, but it was known to a few officials in the Department.

The *American* printed two stories of particular interest to McDowell. On May 18 it reported that "Sherborn Rule [had been] Branded Disgrace" by a former chairman of the state Parole Board, Ralph W. Robart. Robart was an old acquaintance of McDowell, active with him in the Army and Navy Legion of Valor, of which Robart had been national commander. Two days later an unnamed "master of a Massachusetts jail" was quoted as saying that "shameful conditions have been allowed to flourish [at Framingham] . . . cliques, favoritism, freedom to come and go, titles held by some inmates, one student interne carrying keys. . . ."

McDowell did not fool himself that Van Waters welcomed the investigation. She had originally objected to it and though she made no formal protest at its extension, McDowell was aware that it was causing resistance. In mid-May Governor Bradford told him that he had received protests about it; McDowell replied that Dwyer had been given a tough job to do and was doing it and ought to be allowed to finish it. He understood the Governor to answer that it was his policy to let the various commissioners run their departments and that he knew that Dwyer was a good man at getting evidence.

The Commissioner assumed that Van Waters had many friends and admirers, highly-placed and influential. Doubtless it would not have surprised him at all had he learned that as early as June 3, before Dwyer had filed his report, a vice president of the National Association for Mental Hygiene, in New York, was writing to a Massachusetts leader in that organization: "I have just learned that an effort is being made to undermine the program of the Women's Reformatory at Framingham. From what I can learn Mr. Dwyer . . . has been contacting Dr. Van Waters' staff to try to show that 'moral turpitude' exists among the staff. . . . It would indeed be a tragedy . . . if the progressive program in operation at Framingham should be frustrated by the kind of irresponsible investigation which I understand is under way." To McDowell, had he known of it, this letter would have been evidence to confirm his strong belief that, instead of co-operating, Van Waters and her friends resented his effort to "straighten things out" and were trying, already, to build up pressure against his methods and policies.

The Dwyer Report

The next step was the issuance of a "directive" by the Commissioner on June 7. Dwyer's formal report was not filed until June 17. All through his investigation, however, Dwyer had discussed his findings almost daily with McDowell and the latter's directive stemmed largely from these discussions. As Dwyer's report was in the main the direct product of his investigation, it is logical to consider the report now, and later examine the directive, which opened a new phase of the controversy.

Dwyer's report was in two parts. The first dealt with the DiBenedetto case. Dwyer wrote that "as a result of interviews with inmates, it has been ascertained that the subject was involved in a homosexual relationship with inmate Margot Chauvier," and as supporting evidence quoted in full the letter beginning "Dear Margot" and signed "Toni." However, Dwyer continued, there was no discrepancy in the stories told by several inmates and officers of the position of Toni's body when it was found in her

[8] The Reformatory is located on the border of Framingham and Sherborn and in the early days of the Van Waters controversy was referred to as "Sherborn" almost as often as "Framingham."

oom with the door virtually barricaded. Clearly o murderer could have hanged the girl, arunged the barricade, and got out of the room. Dwyer, therefore, found Toni's death to have een by suicide—cause, "not definite."

Part II of the report, concerning "conditions ot conducive to proper management . . . and hich endanger the welfare of those confined," as much more extensive. While it had many ıb-headings and dealt with a wide variety of ıbjects, these can be reasonably grouped into x categories: (1) privileges of inmates; (2) cononing of homosexuality; (3) violations of rules nd regulations; (4) violations of indenture atute; (5) employment of ex-convicts; (6) misellaneous.

(1) Dwyer reported that "special privileges" or some girls, such as taking them to a Chinese estaurant, the movies, and the like, constituted nequal treatment and lowered inmate morale. urthermore the Superintendent, by permitting sentenced prisoners to be outside of the initution as described above," had violated the w and the orders of the courts—had indeed made a mockery of the sentence of the courts f the Commonwealth." Dwyer also wrote that these special privileges have also been a cause or confusion in the mind of the person priveged as to the purpose of her imprisonment s has been stated in the case of Tillie McDerıott when she stated 'I have gone out nights alf a dozen times, shopping and to the show r something. I have felt very funny when sitng in the show because I always felt that I as supposed to be in jail!' "

(2) In a section entitled "Homosexualities" Dwyer declared that "homosexual practices had ccurred at the Reformatory within the past w years," and said that the Superintendent's lack of knowledge" of this fact was "incompreensible." "I find," wrote Dwyer, "that because f a lack of proper segregation, innocent young ımates have been approached by perverts, to e involved in the 'doll racket.' " He described ıe "doll racket," explained the terminology in se and declared that "little or nothing [was] eing done to control or keep such practices at a ıinimum." He named two officers, implying ıat they were perverts and of one of them sayıg that "it has been alleged by inmates" that ıe had been "involved in homosexual acts." He flatly charged Van Waters with "not having told the whole truth when asked questions pertaining to homosexual tendencies of inmates."

(3) Dwyer cited six violations of the Rules and Regulations Governing the Officers and Employees of the Reformatory—departmental rules which had been issued in 1923 and last amended in 1926. The violations were:

1. A copy of the Rules had not been given to every officer;
2. Keys had been entrusted to prisoners;
3. Inmates' money and valuables had not been held by the institution authorities;
4. Former inmates had been allowed to visit the institution;
5. The Reformatory librarian had failed to perform her duty when she refused to answer Dwyer's questions;
6. The prescribed oath of office had not been taken by every officer.

(4) Dwyer reported that a number of inmates had been indentured, not for domestic service in private homes but to the Superintendent and other responsible officers of the Reformatory. These girls, for pay, did various things: caring for babies in the institution, stenographic work, going to secretarial school, and the like. "I find," Dwyer wrote, "that the employment of those released on 'indenture' . . . has had a bad effect on the morale of some officer personnel, and in the case of inmate morale, in view of the fact that some of those indentured receive money for their work, are allowed to live in the staff home, and that certain inmates were known as having been involved in the 'doll racket,' and they resented that fact that they, the inmates, are supervised by persons serving sentences for serious crimes." He also reported in detail the case of one indentured domestic servant who had told him that she had mixed and served highballs at a dinner party given by her employer; and he declared that "it has been found" that as a result of allowing inmates to do domestic day work, liquor had been smuggled into the institution.

(5) The names and police or court records of sixteen present or recent employees of the Reformatory were listed in the report. "I find that there are presently employed at the Reformatory the following persons who have served sentences of imprisonment," Dwyer began, and at the head of his list was Margaret O'Keefe, Assistant Su-

perintendent, Van Waters' second-in-command for the last ten years. "The importance of 'proper personnel' in penal institutions exceeds all other factors," wrote the Deputy Commissioner. "... Certain of its [the Reformatory staff's] members are not of the calibre and type of officer that the administration of a penal institution requires."

(6) The Dwyer report also included some personal observations of the investigator as to the state of the classification and casework files, the policing of the grounds, the safeguarding of drugs, and the cleanliness of the kitchen, and one item that did not directly reflect his investigation—the placement of babies born at the institution. The Commissioner of Public Welfare and his subordinate, the Director of the Division of Child Guardianship, had called on McDowell and Dwyer in early June, raising questions as to the Reformatory's methods of placing babies in foster homes and even its legal authority to do so, which seemed to them to overlap or conflict with theirs.

Dwyer's conclusion was revealing. He mentioned that a mimeographed "Handbook for the Newcomer to Framingham" was given to each inmate when she arrived and that on its first page was written: "Here you are a student, not a prisoner." Wrote Dwyer: "I find that ... the statement 'You are a student, not a prisoner,' is a misstatement of fact, in that the official name of the institution is the Reformatory for Women at Framingham, and the legal status of a person sentenced by the courts of the commonwealth is that of a prisoner. Respectfully submitted. . . ."

When Dwyer filed his report, together with a carefully indexed volume of interviews, McDowell read it. He was already fairly familiar with its contents, and he was not a lawyer. A casual reference to the interviews seemed to him to substantiate his Deputy's findings, despite Dwyer's warning that the investigation had only "scratched the surface." Had McDowell carefully checked Dwyer's statements with the supporting evidence, he might have been more hesitant about accepting the report and using it as a basis for future action.

For instance Dwyer stated flatly that a homosexual relationship existed between Toni and Margot Chauvier. Yet among his "exhibits" he included a report by Dr. Henry M. Baker, State Expert for Examination of Insane Criminals about Margot Chauvier that appeared to contradict Dwyer's findings. Dr. Baker reported to Van Waters that he examined Margot on Ma 11, 1948 and concluded: "She reveals no symptoms of mental or nervous disease.... She is now connected with the Alcoholics Anonymous and has a better insight and plans for her future. There is no evidence of homosexuality ... She is a suitable person for parole consideration."

In the same way, McDowell might have noticed that although Dwyer said that "little or nothing" had been done to control homosexual practices at the Reformatory, he had omitted any references to what Van Waters had said about the matter. To be sure, he had given her little opportunity. He had once asked what means were used for segregation of inmates "with a record of homosexuality," and Van Waters replied: "I bring it before a medical board—physician, psychiatrist, psychologist, social worker, and chaplain." Instead of seeking to elicit a full explanation, Dwyer then asked "Are any known homosexual inmates in charge of a group of other inmates?" Thus, McDowell might have wondered whether Dwyer's "finding" on this point would really stand up under attack. However, he would doubtless have agreed with the finding, for he was ready, like Dwyer to use common sense and objective evidence rather than psychiatric opinions. Beyond question, a quick reading of the transcripts of Dwyer's interviews gave an utterly sordid and horrifying impression. McDowell had worked in prison administration for fourteen years, was well aware of human frailty and somewhat skeptical about human virtue, and knew si when he saw it.

The Directive of June 4

After the interrogation of Van Waters o June 1, McDowell talked at length with Dwyer and then personally drew up a fairly lengthy directive, dated June 4. Believing that the matter might still be settled by simple administrative action, the Commissioner decided to make this directive, if possible, a communication only between Van Waters and himself. Accordingly he took it personally to Framingham on June

Van Waters was not in the main building at the moment, so McDowell put the document in a sealed envelope and left it at the front desk with instructions to deliver it immediately to the Superintendent.

This directive, in McDowell's view, went very far toward "straightening things out" at Framingham. It effectively reversed policies which had been pursued at the Reformatory for nearly forty years. It terminated those indenture contracts whereunder inmates were indentured to the Superintendent and other Reformatory officers, including one of the chaplains. It directed that inmates should be strictly confined within the bounds of the Reformatory—no more outings, no more trips to restaurants. It forbade the Superintendent to allow former inmates to visit the institution voluntarily. It ordered her to refuse admission to "voluntary" inebriates. It required her to send to the Commissioner "by return mail" lists of: (a) personnel who had formerly been inmates with the life history of each such employee; (b) personnel who were "working out of classification," that is, performing duties different from those named in their official job descriptions, with an explanation of each discrepancy; and (c) facilities for the receipt and housing of inebriates and drug addicts voluntarily entering the Reformatory.[9] Finally, in a sweeping clause, it ordered her to comply with all of the Rules and Regulations issued in 1923, as amended in 1926.

McDowell, shocked by what Dwyer had told him and exposed to pressure from the *Boston American,* was acting promptly and firmly. His directive, however, appeared to go further than he really intended. In prohibiting voluntary commitments, McDowell did not examine the statutes; if he had he would have seen that they gave the Superintendent sole authority to decide whether to accept inebriates who sought, voluntarily, to be confined at the Reformatory. As for compliance with all of the rules, the latter were in many particulars out of date; for instance, they required all inmates to wear uniforms although no uniforms had been provided—or appropriated for—for many years.

[9] By statute such persons could, in effect, commit themselves to the Reformatory for brief periods if the Superintendent was willing to admit them.

However, the directive achieved McDowell's immediate purpose, which was to serve notice on Van Waters, first, that the Commissioner was running the Department; second, that the Commissioner insisted on strict compliance with the letter of the law; and third, that the Commissioner intended to eliminate "special privileges for individual inmates." Much later McDowell recalled that when he wrote the directive he hoped that Van Waters would comply in a spirit of teamwork and co-operation and that all further controversy would thus be avoided.

On June 28 McDowell transmitted Dwyer's report to Governor Bradford, saying that "it is my considered judgment that decisive action must be taken at once respecting the administration of the Reformatory for Women. Proper remedial action would appear to be within my legal authority." Whether he was alluding to his June 4 directive or whether he was hinting that stronger action was called for (e.g., the removal of Van Waters) is not clear.

Van Waters responded immediately to McDowell's directive, sending to the Commissioner the information which he had requested, and with one minor exception carrying out his other orders where that was possible. McDowell was acquainted with staff members at the Reformatory and he had good friends at the United Prison Association. Very soon he heard that his directive was bitterly resented at Framingham.

The directive did not restore harmony—yet the Commissioner did not go further. The Legislature was moving into the picture. Framingham was a "hot potato." McDowell grew a bit cautious. He decided to wait and see.

The Waiting Period

Actually nearly seven months elapsed between the date of McDowell's directive to Van Waters and her removal. Throughout that period the Commissioner went to Framingham only twice. On July 28 he and his business agent, at Van Waters' request, conferred with her and the Reformatory's medical advisers. The Commissioner and the Superintendent disagreed as to the proper interpretation of relevant statutes, and Van Waters deferred to her superior. In late November he paid a short visit to the Reformatory, accompanying a "survey team" from the Division of Personnel and Standardization.

His other activities with respect to the Reformatory were few and far between. Van Waters sent him about twenty applications from nearby housewives for day work indentures, but he made no reply and did not act on them. (Mrs. J. Alan Hodder, the Representative's wife, remained the only successful applicant.) In early September he conferred with Anne Gladding, the Reformatory's "child placement worker," who for several years had been finding homes for babies born at Framingham. McDowell asked her to write to him the reasons why her position was necessary or desirable, what legislation would be required to make it legal, and what qualifications the incumbent should have. She complied, writing him a long letter. In it she stated her belief that the position was legal under existing statutes and suggested that if he had any doubt about it he might ask for an opinion from the Attorney General. McDowell did not acknowledge this letter nor did he ask for an opinion.

Also early in September McDowell sent to Van Waters a written request for the names and job descriptions of interns employed at the Reformatory on a year-to-year basis. She complied, pointing out that some of these contracts were coming up for renewal, including one with Irene Tower, an aged ex-inmate with a long record. Late in October, McDowell talked with Van Waters on the telephone. The Superintendent told him that Irene Tower was 88 years old and bedridden: she was of some use in that in taking care of her, girls who had aged mothers or grandmothers would get some experience in nursing the aged. McDowell agreed that "it would be a downright shame to practically drive her out," and formally approved her reappointment on November 2.

That was the sum of the Superintendent's contacts with Framingham in the "waiting period." He ordered no further investigation. When he finally removed Van Waters, all of the charges related to the period prior to June 7. Yet sometime during those seven months, McDowell made his final decision. Why?

According to the Commissioner, his hand was forced. He delayed in order not to interfere with an impending legislative "probe"; he acted because he was under violent attack and had to move, virtually in self-defense. Van Waters' supporters dispute this interpretation. In any event in order to understand the atmosphere in which the decision was eventually made, we must briefly survey the developments in the summer and fall of 1948.

They began almost as soon as Dwyer had finished his investigation. Senator LoPresti, on June 9, filed a resolve in the Senate for the establishment of a special commission to "make an immediate and thorough investigation of the conduct of the Reformatory for Women . . . with a view to making such changes in the law as may seem advisable for improving conditions. . . ." The wording of the resolve was mild enough but LoPresti's speech on its filing was not. He spoke of "unbelievable conditions . . . indescribable in language with which decent people are familiar." McDowell neither supported nor opposed LoPresti's measure. It was adopted on June 16, and subsequently the special commission was appointed: five Representatives, three Senators, and three persons named by the Governor. (All of the Governor's appointees knew and admired Dr. Van Waters.) The chairman was Senator J. E. Callahan. It was election year, the primaries were in September, and Callahan faced a tough fight for renomination. Although the commission was directed to file its report by December 1, 1948 he was too busy campaigning to call it together and commence the investigation before the primary. Then he was defeated, went off for a rest, and lost interest. Several other legislative members also became "lame ducks" in September and were not eager to have the commission meet. Only by pressure from Governor Bradford was the commission activated briefly, in November, a few weeks before it was to expire under the terms of LoPresti's resolve.

Support for Van Waters

Meanwhile, however, Van Waters' friends and opponents were not idle. The directive of June 4, the whisperings about the Dwyer report (which was never made public or shown to Van Waters), and the possibility of a legislative "probe" all stimulated the Superintendent and her supporters to take some action. Shortly after receipt of the directive, the United Prison

Association was urged to make an effort to get it rescinded; but the U.P.A. had concurred with Winslow in recommending McDowell for the commissionership, and its staff members were more friendly with him than with Van Waters. On July 27, however, Van Waters lunched with old friends in Boston and explained the difficulties under which she was laboring. They talked with other friends, and on their own account decided to try to form an organization which would have two major purposes: to defend Van Waters, and to work for statutory reforms consistent with her policies. In August letters were going to numerous citizens asking for both moral and financial support. Most active in the effort were LaRue Brown, a respected Boston lawyer, and his wife, Dorothy Kirchway Brown. The latter, a former president of the state League of Women Voters, had an unusually wide acquaintance both inside and outside Massachusetts. Furthermore she had a special interest in this controversy, for she was the daughter of Dr. George Kirchway, who had acted in 1915 as Warden of Sing Sing when the prison reformer, Warden Thomas Mott Osborne, was absent undergoing an ordeal not altogether dissimilar to that which Miriam Van Waters now faced.

The organization, "The Friends of the Framingham Reformatory" (generally known as "Friends of Framingham") did not try to make itself felt until late in the fall; in fact its leaders hardly met at all until late October. But already, with their advice, Van Waters had sought legal counsel. Brown steered her first to Edward O. Proctor, president of the State Bar Association. He agreed to represent her, but shortly thereafter his partner, Paul A. Dever, became a candidate for Governor, and Proctor asked Van Waters to excuse him. On his recommendation she retained an experienced trial lawyer, Claude B. Cross.

McDowell, meanwhile, was sitting tight and holding to the letter of the law. Typical was his handling of a request which he received asking that a Framingham inmate should be permitted, under supervision, to visit her home so that she could see her little son, who was dying of cancer. It was a hard decision for the Commissioner to make, but he stuck to his guns. "The law is specific in that the inmate can be released only to view the remains or attend the funeral," he said, and he rejected the request.

Headlines

In September, immediately after the primaries, the Van Waters case again burst into print. This time all of the Boston newspapers jumped into the fray, with the battle lines quickly forming: the Hearst tabloids, the *American* and the *Record,* on one side and the *Herald* and the *Traveler* (under single ownership) on the other. Portions of the Dwyer report somehow got into the hands of reporters on the *American* and the *Post,* and both printed excerpts. Every other newspaper promptly ran roughly similar stories.

McDowell said that he did not know how the leak occurred, nor would he comment on the Dwyer report. He said to the friendly *Christian Science Monitor:* "The information didn't come from this office; and I'm not interested in finding out where it did come from. All I know is that I released but one copy of the report and gave it to the Governor, who, I understand, gave it to the legislative commission to look at. I don't plan to do anything about it whatever at the present time." On the following day (September 14) the *Herald* quoted McDowell as saying: "I want to see the report of the special [legislative] commission before I make any decision."

LoPresti made the headlines when he formally requested the Governor to remove Van Waters "now that the information contained in the so-called secret report has been made public." The *American* demanded her head. The *Herald,* on the other hand, while initially calling for a "suspension of judgment," printed a long story by one of its best reporters, Catherine Coyne, sympathetic to the Van Waters regime. Miss Coyne pictured the conflict as one between philosophies of penology. "Whether the State Reformatory for Women should be strictly a penal institution," she wrote, "or should continue to pioneer new and admittedly experimental techniques for the regeneration of women offenders, including alcoholics, is boiling into one of the hottest controversies in the State administration." She described how McDowell's directive of June 4 had terminated the tie-up with the Peter Bent Brigham Hospital clinic for alcoholics and had prevented "rehabilitated" ex-inmates from returning to Alcoholics Anonymous meetings at the Reformatory. Of these ex-inmates she quoted an inmate as saying: "They came back and talked a language we understood. . . . They were well-dressed, they were sober, they were happy. And they were proving to us that we could do it, too."

The stories did not die down quickly, the *American* especially reminding its readers frequently of nameless evils at Framingham; but the presidential campaign was filling the front pages. As soon as the election was over, interest in Framingham was suddenly revived. LoPresti demanded that one member of the legislative commission, Reuben Lurie, disqualify himself as a Van Waters partisan.[10] The *American* attacked the legislative commission's delay. Then on November 13, for the first time, Van Waters took the offensive. Through her new attorney, Cross, she demanded a public hearing to refute the "bitter and baseless" attack on her and her staff.

It looked as though the legislative commission would never meet, for it was due to expire on December 1. McDowell's waiting period was nearing an end. He had still not finally made up his mind, but on November 9 he asked the Attorney General for a legal opinion as to whether the Superintendent came within the recently-enacted statute governing the removal of certain state employees and giving them a right to a hearing and appeal. The Attorney General replied that she did.

The Legislative Commission's Hearing

At last Callahan called his commission together. The members visited Framingham and had lunch there. "With the burned chicken, they gave us . . . coffee that tasted like dishwater," complained the indignant LoPresti. Finally the commission held a public hearing on November 22. In a way it was a mock trial: the commission furnished Van Waters with "specifications" taken verbatim from the Dwyer report dealing with violations of the rules as to keys, valuables, visits from ex-inmates, oaths of office, the alleged contumacy of the librarian, and trips to the movies and a Chinese restaurant. After an angry speech by LoPresti, Van Waters was called as a witness. Cross introduced her and then she made a lengthy statement, eventually answering each of the "specifications" taken from the report.

Her general defense was that everything she did had had the approval of the Commissioner of Correction at the time. She explained that some trusted inmates had been given keys when there was a staff shortage, but that she had ended this practice in 1947. She denied that the staff had improperly permitted inmates to retain "money and valuables." She could not answer for the librarian's alleged refusal to reply to Dwyer's questions. She said that when she was notified that officers had not taken an oath of office as prescribed by law, she had promptly, on June 8, had the oath taken by all of them.

When she finished her statement, the audience applauded so enthusiastically that Senator Callahan threatened to clear the room. The Friends of Framingham were not yet publicized, but they had effectively alerted Van Waters' admirers.

Members of the commission questioned her for hours. At least two or three were friendly. Lurie's questions, for instance, brought out that the dispute about ex-inmates or paroled inmates visiting the Reformatory was nothing new; the practice had been opposed nine years before by the Parole Board, but the objections had been overruled, and after an investigation of the Parole Board itself, two members of the Board had resigned. (One of those Parole Board members, incidentally, was Ralph Robart, McDowell's friend in the Legion of Valor.) There were hostile questioners, too, especially LoPresti. Throughout, Van Waters remained composed and good humored. Her testimony was clear and responsive. More than one newspaperman, skeptical when he arrived to cover the hearing, was persuaded that day that the Superintendent was a remarkable woman worthy of high respect. Several of the commission members were similarly impressed.

Only twice at the hearing was mention made of the explosive issue, the control of homosexuality. Toni's name was brought up, and the Superintendent said: "One of the tragedies of

[10] Lurie certainly admired Van Waters; but he had also recommended McDowell to Governor Bradford.

this is that through the press, a subtle imputation has come that this girl was a sexual deviate, and a victim of another. Our records, our physicians, our psychiatrists do not show that this girl suffered that unfortunate deviation. . . . Abnormalities are medical problems; they are not within my province except as administrative and what doctors and psychiatrists and psychologists tell me to do. . . . An examination is made, recommendations and findings are made in writing, and the staff and I follow them." She was asked: "Surely you have an opinion that might be equal if not better than most of these psychiatrists?" and she answered: "I wouldn't act on it." Finally LoPresti challenged her: "You would be surprised to know that they [persons with homosexual tendencies] were on your staff, wouldn't you?" She answered calmly: "It isn't so."

McDowell sat in the audience throughout the hearing, since the commission had requested his presence. During the luncheon recess he stood alone in the corridor smoking a cigarette, and to an acquaintance who came up to him, he remarked, shaking his head: "I wish this business had never happened. I'd like to have things go along the way they are." He did not testify; the commission heard nobody except Van Waters. When they finished with her, it was 5:15, and they adjourned. Later they issued a virtually meaningless report, recommending that another special commission be named to carry on the investigation.

The existence of this rather futile body had had a considerable effect on McDowell's course. It had served as a reason, if not the only reason, for postponing action. It had stimulated, and made him aware of, a substantial amount of sometimes vociferous support for Van Waters and hostility toward him. It might have warned him, too, that in any public hearing after removal Van Waters would be a dangerous antagonist, but if it did he did not take the warning. By December 16, 1948 his mind was made up. He would remove the Superintendent.

Removal

In the first week of December, McDowell sought out his old acquaintance, Paul A. Dever, who had been elected Governor and would succeed Bradford on January 3, 1949. He told Dever that he was contemplating dismissing Van Waters. Dever, unwilling to be drawn prematurely into the controversy, replied merely that he would expect each department head "to do his duty as he saw it." Rumors of impending removal began to spread. On December 6, the *Herald* ran a front-page story saying that McDowell would remove the Superintendent "in a few days," and McDowell did not flatly deny the story. He said simply that he had not told anyone that he was going to remove her. The following day another *Herald* story declared that "former State Commissioners of Correction and a large committee of citizens and clergymen were marshalling today to fight for retention" of Van Waters. This was the first identifiable public reference to the Friends of Framingham, but McDowell knew that the organization was becoming active. Not everyone approached on behalf of the Friends of Framingham, any more than everyone in the United Prison Association, was sympathetic to Van Waters. McDowell was not kept in the dark concerning the activities of the opposition.

On December 16 the Commissioner attended a luncheon meeting of the Legion of Valor. His old friend Robart, in a brief speech, shouted that "the situation [at Framingham] is one of the filthiest conditions imaginable." McDowell rose and said in his usual matter-of-fact manner: "I agree that the conditions are similar to what he described." Then he announced that he would "recommend action to Governor Bradford today." He had made up his mind. He had the legal authority to order removal, and he would exercise it. He met Winslow casually that afternoon and told him that he was going to act. "Are you certain you can make it stick?" asked Winslow. "I'm certain I can," replied McDowell.

He still hoped, however, that he could obtain full backing of the Governor, although Bradford gave him little encouragement. In a brief conference, the Governor counseled delay. He announced to the press that "there are no new developments, and I have complete confidence that, should the Commissioner consider the best interests of his Department and the Commonwealth to require him to take any steps at the present time, he will bring them to my attention."

McDowell chafed at the bit. Two days after Christmas he insisted on a further conference with the Governor. By now Bradford's term had only seven days to run. He pointed out that if Van Waters were immediately removed and she appealed, her case would be heard by an impartial commission appointed by Governor Dever. In a press release Bradford said: "It seems obvious that to initiate ouster proceedings in the last week of an outgoing Governor's administration, which will come up for review within the first two weeks of the incoming administration, presents a situation which is not fair to either Governor, to the Commissioner, or to the ousted official. Commissioner McDowell has agreed to postpone removal action until after the new administration has taken office."

The Commissioner continued his preparations. With Dwyer's help he drew up a list of charges. Personally he examined, line by line, the 128 typed pages of Van Waters' testimony before the legislative commission, inserting challenging questions on the margin in his neat, legible hand. On January 7, 1949 in a letter to which were appended 27 charges, he notified Van Waters that she would be removed from office at midnight on January 11.

His detailed reasons for the removal were, of course, set forth in the charges. But what was McDowell's own analysis of the causes of his action? In a sympathetic story in the *Christian Science Monitor* a month later "sources close to the Commissioner" were quoted as stating those causes. (What those "sources" said is almost exactly what McDowell himself said in private conversation four years later.)

> . . . Mr. McDowell would have preferred, and at first planned, to handle his differences with Dr. Van Waters within the Department of Correction and without resorting to discharge. He consistently refused therefore to comment to the press concerning the administrative affairs of the Reformatory.
>
> He personally took his directive to Framingham on June 7, in an effort to keep the matter strictly between himself and Van Waters. Despite these precautions, within 24 hours the officials at the United Prison Association were getting telephone calls from members around Greater Boston protesting about the contents of the supposedly confidential directive.
>
> From then on, there was constant publicity on what became popularly known as the "Van Waters Case," and Dr. Van Waters made it known that she would contest any effort by the Commissioner to oust her. Those in the confidence of Mr. McDowell say that these tactics virtually forced him either to dismiss Dr. Van Waters or to abrogate his job as Commissioner.
>
> He chose to discharge her. By so doing, he made himself the target of charges that he was a reactionary official, that he was opposed to enlightened penology, that he was the tool either of Frank Dwyer, his deputy, or Maurice Winslow (Superintendent of Norfolk Prison Colony), his close friend and former superior, and finally that he either was trying to empty the position of Superintendent of the Reformatory to give it to a friend or was the instrument of politicians who wanted the job as a plum.[11]

The last paragraph of the foregoing quotation is significant. Whether or not he was unjustly the victim of unfair charges, McDowell felt that he was. The "great and powerful," the well-to-do, the corporation lawyers, that organ of respectability the *Herald,* and leaders of the clergy were lining up against him. He was the one who had taken action, but he felt himself to be on the defensive.

The Charges and the Answers

For the purpose of convenience and conservation of space, the 27 charges are summarized here, and each charge is followed by a summary of the formal answer of Van Waters, which was prepared with the advice of Cross, her attorney, and his assistants. The answers were delivered to McDowell on January 11.

> 1. *Charge:* Failure to comply with statute, by permitting prisoners [sic] to go to the movies, and the like; by negligently permitting a prisoner to escape; by permitting a prisoner to go to a secretarial school; and by allowing a room in the Reformatory to be used by a private shoe manufacturer, who employed prison labor there.
>
> *Answer:* Trips outside of the Reformatory were a practice approved by each former Commissioner, and

[11] It has been suggested by supporters of Van Waters that she was disliked because of her insistence on financial honesty in the Reformatory's dealings—her alleged refusal, for instance, to sign receipts for supplies prior to actual delivery. However, there is no evidence that any financial corruption or refusal to condone it was a factor in the controversy. Neither is there any evidence that McDowell wished to give the superintendency to any particular person.

were discontinued under McDowell; the "escape" was that of a properly indentured inmate; the inmate attending secretarial school did so under an indenture permit approved by the then Commissioner; and Commissioner Doyle initiated and approved of the shoe manufacturing project in 1945 and 1946.

2. *Charge:* Circumvention of the sentences of the courts, by permitting prisoners to go outside of the Reformatory; the courts' "mittimus" directed the Superintendent to "confine and control" the convict, and to keep her safely "in custody in the Reformatory."

Answer: Emphatic denial.

3. *Charge:* Failure to comply with statute in not having all Reformatory employees take an oath of office.

Answer: The oath was taken immediately after receipt of the directive of June 4.

4. *Charge:* Failure to comply with statute in not having a question in the visitors' book at the Reformatory as to whether the visitor had ever been convicted of a felony.

Answer: The correction was made upon receipt of the directive; prior to that time the omission had not been noticed. Even McDowell and Dwyer had signed the book without raising any question about it. "It has always puzzled me to know what is to be done if a person desiring to make a visit answers this question in the affirmative, as the statute is silent on that point."

5. *Charge:* Former inmate, in whose psychiatric report was a statement indicating sexual perversion, was permitted to visit the institution and for several days to share a room with a "lifer."

Answer: Grossly unfair. The former inmate had married, and was devoted to church work. She made frequent visits. In a spirit of devotion and helpfulness, she stayed with the "lifer" when the latter was greatly depressed. "This visit was of notable benefit to the inmate."

6. *Charge:* Former inmates, including some with homosexual tendencies, were permitted to attend social functions at the Reformatory.

Answer: The practice of allowing former inmates to attend such functions was approved by former Commissioners. No such visits since receipt of the directive of June 4.

7. *Charge:* Violation of rules in that a copy of the rules was not given to each employee.

Answer: Not enough copies available for everyone, but rules often discussed at staff meetings, and after June 7 everyone was instructed to study the copies in the office.

8. *Charge:* Violation of rules in that inmates had keys.

Answer: This was necessitated by staff shortage during the war, but use of keys by inmates was materially restricted in December 1947.

9. *Charge:* Violation of rules in that inmates were permitted to retain valuables.

Answer: Only wedding rings or family keepsakes; otherwise no valuable rings or watches retained.

10. *Charge:* Violation of rules in that former inmates were allowed to visit without personal approval of the Superintendent.

Answer: Denial, "so far as I am aware."

11. *Charge:* Failure to comply with Commissioner's directive in that (a) an inmate thereafter had keys, (b) employees were not reassigned to duties within their classifications, and (c) there was no reply to the request for a list of facilities for persons desiring voluntary commitments.

Answer: (a) One inmate, who by order of the Commissioner had to move from the staff home to the main building, could be placed only in an annex and needed a key to the bathroom.

(b) A full list of jobs and classifications was sent to the Commissioner on June 8, with an explanation of cases where variations existed and with a request for the Commissioner's recommendations. "Not having heard anything, I had during the past seven months assumed full compliance on my part with your directive."

(c) The information was promptly furnished: "I received no intimation" that it was not full compliance.

12. *Charge:* Impairment of good order and security and failure to provide exemplary and constructive influence by the employment of former inmates and other ex-convicts, including the Assistant Superintendent and the aforementioned 88-year-old Irene Tower.

Answer: No Commissioner questioned these appointments when they were made. No rule or law forbade them. "Moreover, I have believed it conducive to the highest morale of the institution to employ certain rehabilitated persons, who by their example prove the value of the system of correction."

13. *Charge:* Four inmates were improperly indentured to Reformatory officials and two of them unlawfully paid out of the inmates' "canteen fund."

Answer: They were not paid out of the "canteen fund." The indenture contracts, approved by former Commissioners, were canceled by the Commissioner's directive of June 4.

14. *Charge:* Failure to prevent the continuance of homosexual relationships, and placements without giving due weight to reports of homosexuality: both leading to fights, to a desire by paroled inmates to

return to the institution, and to renewed unnatural relationships after release.

Answer: "Each officer is requested to report in full all evidence of behavior of homosexual nature, or of suspicion of such . . . to the classification conference. . . . Examination by the psychiatrist is then routine procedure. . . . Utmost care is taken to prevent unwholesome attachments." Fights arise from a variety of causes. The Superintendent cannot know the desires of paroled inmates nor be responsible for the conduct of former inmates.

15. *Charge:* Failure to segregate inmates with recorded homosexual tendencies.

Answer: This was done by the classification committee subject to psychiatric guidance.

16. *Charge:* Favoritism toward inmate Margot Chauvier.

Answer: Denial. [The answer included a partial case history of the inmate.]

17. *Charge:* Usurpation of powers of the Commissioner in that in many instances the Superintendent negotiated indenture contracts, and got inmates to sign them, which contracts bore the signature of former Commissioner Lyman but were not executed until long after he had left office.

Answer: The indenture contracts were signed by the Commissioner.

18. *Charge:* Violation of statute in that inmates worked as restaurant waitresses or in laundries without any written contract.

Answer: This work was done pursuant to indenture agreements signed by the Commissioner.

19. *Charge:* Inmates were indentured to persons outside Massachusetts.

Answer: This was pursuant to indenture agreements signed by the Commissioner.

20. *Charge:* Violation of statute in that inmates were indentured for other than domestic work.

Answer: This was pursuant to indenture agreements signed by the Commissioner.

21. *Charge:* An inmate on day work served liquor at her employer's home and was driven back to the Reformatory at 9:00 p.m. by the employer's son.

Answer: No knowledge. Instructions to employers require that a woman must return inmate before 4:45, and warn against easy access to liquor.

22. *Charge:* Illegal indenture of an inmate to work for pay made directly to her, enabling her to buy liquor and bring it into the Reformatory.

Answer: Contract was terminated upon discovery that she had violated it by failing to pay the money over to the Reformatory for her account.

23. *Charge:* Failure to provide proper supervision in that inmates worked on the delivery truck, or as automobile mechanics, under the sole supervision of a male employee.

Answer: Emphatic denial that this was not proper supervision. "I do not understand . . . that you charge any of the male employees with improper conduct."

24. *Charge:* Failure to provide adequate staff on night shifts.

Answer: The Reformatory has been understaffed for years, despite the Superintendent's repeated requests for increases in the budget.

25. *Charge:* Assignment of employees to duties outside the scope of their official job classifications.

Answer: The whole list, with the reasons for the discrepancy, was furnished the Commissioner in June, 1948; and "I concluded by asking you: 'May we have your recommendations?' None has been received."

26. *Charge:* Unauthorized establishment of a "division of child placement" at the Reformatory and the placing of children in homes without adequate investigation.

Answer: The division has been approved by Commissioners since it was established in 1934. Well-qualified child placement worker has placed 202 children in homes in eight years without complaint.

27. *Charge:* Wasting the resources of the Commonwealth, in permitting non-employees to live at the staff home or eat in the staff dining room.

Answer: Not conscious of waste. Members of the Department of Correction, visiting superintendents, study groups from foreign countries, social workers, and the like, are treated as guests, but per capita feeding cost is lower than at other state institutions.

The Hearing and the Appeal

FOLLOWING the procedure outlined in the statutes, Van Waters promptly demanded a public hearing before the Commissioner, and McDowell immediately set it for January 13 at the State House. He asked the outgoing Attorney General,[12] Clarence Barnes, for legal assistance, and Barnes assigned Assistant Attorney General George B. Rowell. McDowell and Rowell, however, decided that the proceeding could not be exactly a trial, as it was not an adversary proceeding between contesting parties; after all, the Commissioner who had removed his subordinate was now going to preside over a hearing to determine whether she should have been removed. They agreed that Rowell should be present, ready to advise McDowell on points of law, but that the evidence supporting McDowell's charges should be brought out by Dwyer.

The hearing lasted eighteen days, and the transcript of the record, exclusive of exhibits, fills 2,257 pages. McDowell was performing one of the most difficult of a Department head's functions: he was presiding at a quasi-judicial hearing in which his own prior decision was being questioned. Most of the time he tried to act like a judge, though he was careful to refer to himself not as a judge but as the "presiding authority." Sometimes, especially in the last days of the hearing, he acted like a lawyer, taking over from Dwyer the task of cross-examining some of Van Waters' witnesses. And all the time, when he was not presiding, he was the executive head of his Department, fighting for his reputation, planning strategy, making decisions.

Van Waters Testifies

His task was made immeasurably harder by Van Waters, her attorney, and her friends. The Superintendent herself was the first witness and a most effective one. She underwent examination by Dwyer for nine and one-half days. All through that period, she dominated the hearing room and seemed to be in complete command. For a good part of the time on the witness stand she stood, dramatically erect. This disconcerted both McDowell and Dwyer; again and again they asked or even urged her to be seated and again and again she answered: "Thank you. I will stand up." Almost every day she saw and seized an opportunity to score with the press and to set the friendly audience cheering.

Much of her scoring was at the expense of the dogged Dwyer. Thus she managed to convey the impression that Dwyer was brutal by saying of one ex-inmate, "It is cruel that this woman, completely rehabilitated and released from all supervision, should have this incident brought up here"; and that he was tricky, when she told of his interview with her at Framingham on June 1, 1948 saying: "Occasionally Mr. Dwyer would say [to the stenographer] 'You need not take that.' Finally I appealed to you, Mr. Commissioner, and said 'Unless you take every word I say, I will say nothing,' and you said 'Let her talk.' "

She briskly laughed at his prudishness, as in the following colloquy:

> Q. Would you give to the recorder the crime for which that inmate was committed to the Reformatory for Women? . . .
>
> A. The offense for which she was sentenced was cohabitation.
>
> Q. *Please!* I asked you not to—
>
> A. Well, it sounded so mysterious, I thought I would say it. A five year sentence for cohabitation.

When Dwyer asked her if she believed that the Commissioner of Correction had any power to direct her to permit private manufacturing at the Reformatory in disregard of the statutes, she answered: "Sir, I have never doubted the

[12] By a quirk in the Massachusetts Constitution, the Attorney General's two-year term runs from and to January 20, nearly three weeks after a new Governor is inaugurated.

power of my Commissioner to give me any orders or instructions whatsoever." The audience applauded. And when he asked her about the sentence in the handbook for new inmates, "Here you are a student, not a prisoner," she read the handbook's whole first page, an eloquent message of encouragement for the fallen and downhearted, of Christian love and hope. Much moved, the audience cheered again. Even more impressive, and typical of her ability to give answers that were not responsive but were effectively impressionistic, was her reply to a question about whether an inmate who went home for an evening accompanied by a Reformatory officer was being "safely kept" at the Reformatory in accordance with the court's sentence. Ignoring the legalistic implications of the question, Van Waters read a letter from the inmate:

> Dear Dr. Van Waters,
>
> Verbal or written thanks are most inadequate to express what my family and I feel after our wonderful evening. We are really on our way now. I say "we" because my family has been and will be with me through everything. I have been refired with ambition again to really do something for them. Thank you with all my heart, Doctor.

If Van Waters was an able and astonishingly durable[13] witness, her attorney, Cross, was skillful both as lawyer and as showman. As a lawyer he was pitted against Dwyer, who had never tried a case in his life. Cross had a good deal of fun at Dwyer's expense; as Dwyer put it later, "They thought they could get this Irishman mad and make him lose his head." Cross did not succeed in doing that, although his hectoring began as soon as the hearing opened. Dwyer's first question to Van Waters was: "Prior to January 11 at midnight, were you the Superintendent of the Reformatory?" Cross promptly interjected "You will have to speak up louder, Mr. Dwyer. Pacing up and down, we cannot hear you."

It was to McDowell, however, that Cross was most insulting. This, too, began in the first few minutes of the opening session. As Dwyer began to question the witness, Cross addressed the chair: "I would like to know under what numbered reason [charge] this question is directed and I think I am entitled to an answer." McDowell replied: "Mr. Cross, you are not entitled to an answer to that question. Proceed, Mr Dwyer." "Well," said Cross loudly, "that is about the treatment that I expected." For several days Cross's conduct was frequently discourteous to the Commissioner. "I think you got your ruling confused; you'd better consult Mr. Rowell again." . . . "Who made this note on this folder? It was made by a man in your Department. . . . outrageous!" . . . "Are you [McDowell] through? That is the most outrageous conduct that I have ever seen!" . . . "This buffoon exhibition. . . ."

On the fourth day, McDowell finally took some notice of these tactics. "Mr. Cross," he said, "I believe that a lawyer of your experience and ability must know that your conduct at this time would not be tolerated in a courtroom. This, as you know, is a quasi judicial hearing—" Cross interrupted at that point, but for several days thereafter his conduct at the hearing was more restrained.

On the fourteenth day, however, there was a final flare-up. Because of other professional engagements on the morrow, Cross had asked to have that day's hearing extend into the evening, and McDowell had agreed. In the afternoon, the questioning concerned letters written by an inmate to an ex-inmate on parole; the ex-inmate's father had found these epistles and brought them to the Parole Board. Cross objected; McDowell overruled him. Then the attorney burst out: "Well, if you are determined to drag it in, go ahead, but I think people are shocked at any such attempt to drag in by the heels something that you know and Mr. Rowell knows is highly inadmissible." The crowd booed McDowell, who whispered to Rowell for a moment and then, saying, "The hearing will be adjourned until 10 o'clock tomorrow," rose and walked grimly toward the door. The situation was made to order for Cross. The *Herald* reported: "With Defense Counsel C. B. Cross accusing McDowell of 'breaking your word,' more than 800 persons rocked Gardner Auditorium by standing up, whistling, hooting, and yammering at the Commissioner. McDowell stalked out, however."

[13] In all, she testified for twelve days, most of the last three under questioning by Cross and, to a lesser extent, McDowell.

Public Opinion

Cross knew what he was doing all through the hearing. He did not dream of logically persuading the Commissioner to reinstate his client. He sought to arouse public opinion. And here he was greatly aided by the Friends of Framingham, who formed the enthusiastic nucleus of the crowd that filled the hearing room day after day. The audience was partisan and vocal. McDowell pleaded frequently for order but he could not enforce it, for by law he had to hold a "public" hearing. He could "stalk out," but he would have to come back again. Again and again Cross played on the audience, eliciting their boos or cheers; once, when the response was somewhat belated, McDowell remarked drily: "Well, you finally got the applause you wanted, Mr. Cross." Not until the eighth day did the attorney join McDowell in asking the crowd to remain quiet.

It was not only the crowd at the hearing that presented difficulties. The public was aroused. The *Herald* and the *Traveler* were printing editorials on the front page declaring that "McDowell and Dwyer must go"; even the usually disinterested *Globe* was clearly favoring Van Waters. And every evening when McDowell returned to his office, the piles of unanswered mail were more huge.[14] There were petitions with hundreds of signatures, and resolutions from civic and religious organizations all over the state, all urging reinstatement. Typical of McDowell's mail are the following excerpts:

> [From a minister]: The only real charge that Mr. Dwyer has been able to level at Dr. Van Waters is that she had applied Christian principles to scientific casework.
>
> * * *
>
> I was horrified yesterday by the disclosure that you did not allow an inmate to visit the bedside of her dying son.
>
> * * *
>
> How can you, and a man of the caliber of Frank A. Dwyer, stand in judgment of a woman with the brains, education, and training that Dr. Van Waters has?
>
> * * *
>
> [From a former staff member]: Dr. Van Waters inspired in her staff not only a fine cooperative spirit but a deep loyalty to her progressive ideas for rehabilitation.
>
> * * *
>
> I took a position as deputy probation officer in Los Angeles. Dr. Van Waters was then our Juvenile Court referee, and a more human, understanding woman was never born. She was given a great testimonial dinner when she left.
>
> * * *
>
> [An anonymous postcard]: Did you ever hear of Joan of Arc?

There was plenty of anti-Van Waters mail, too, a good part of it anonymous and some of it unprintable. McDowell got unsigned cards and letters saying:

> I feel that it is my duty as a former inmate to tell you confidently that this Van Waters woman is a low-down filthy woman.
>
> * * *
>
> How about the girl who beat the Benedetto girl to death? Does she go scot free? To probably visit Van Waters . . . degenerate filth. . . .
>
> * * *
>
> She so mentle. She has no shame.

But there were somewhat more impressive signed communications, too:

> [From a former staff member]: It has always been a matter of surprise and concern that she has been allowed to remain at Framingham so long.
>
> * * *
>
> [From the widow of a judge]: To me, a lay person, the basic question in the entire case is: Did Miss Van Waters act contrary to the statutory law governing the administration of the Reformatory? By her own admission she did this in many instances.

Sensational newspaper publicity kept public interest at a high pitch. "Three hundred inmates are backing up Dr. Van Waters, with a pledge of allegiance," declared the *Traveler*; and shortly afterwards appeared a poem by an unnamed "20 year old inmate," dedicated to Van Waters and including the lines "When God made the angels, God made you, and sent you down to us." Every day, in almost all the Boston newspapers, the hearing was the lead story.

Once in a while through those trying days McDowell got some encouragement. On January 27 the Massachusetts Chapter of the Army and Navy Legion of Valor passed a resolution praising him and condemning "the Communist

[14] The Governor had to have extra stenographic help at this time to keep up with his correspondence on the Van Waters case.

and Nazi-like tactics of the adherents and sympathizers of the former Superintendent. . . . Among the publicized sympathizers are the names of individuals and organizations who are parties to a plan to overthrow our government itself." Even in the *Herald* he found something pleasing; that paper's political columnist, W. E. Mullins, pointed out that the statutory system, not the Commissioner, had created the odd position of judge, jury, and prosecutor which he filled at the hearing and added that "upon learning the facts about Framingham, McDowell, being a conscientious career man, was shocked. His attitude was aggravated by Deputy Commissioner Dwyer, who has never cared for Dr. Van Waters because of her haughty and patronizing treatment of him and his associates."

In the mail he found a few heartening letters. An old associate wrote him: "You and Deputy Commissioner Dwyer have been despicably slandered in the Boston press, in what is only the path of duty, however distasteful it must be to you who must perform it." Another letter said: "All through the hearings I have marvelled that any man could react as you have towards the 'Friends of Framingham Reformatory' who deserve by reason of their rudeness, booing, etc. to be called by much less polite terms—hoodlums, per example."

McDowell's Procedural Decisions

In this stormy atmosphere McDowell had some difficult procedural decisions to make. Cross from the beginning had been demanding that evidence be related to some specific charge. Eventually he had his way—but not until McDowell had weakened his own position with the public by answering Cross's objection that "you ought to at least stay within the charges" with the unfortunately-worded statement: "We are not concerned with charges." More important was Cross's complaint that Van Waters could not testify accurately if all the records, especially the case folders of individual inmates, were kept away from her. McDowell showed his natural inexperience in handling this objection, too, and received little or no help from Rowell. At the end of the first day the Commissioner told Cross: "Those records will be made available during the hearing . . . before Dr. Van Waters leaves the stand." Cross objected vehemently, with such an obviously good reason that the newspapers could not miss it. Yet not until three afternoons later did McDowell reverse himself and agree that each evening Cross should be furnished with the names of inmates whose records would be the subject of the next day's questioning and should have access to their folders at Framingham.

After two uproarious days at the Gardner Auditorium in the State House, McDowell suddenly decided to move the hearing to Framingham. Over Cross's objections, he adjourned to meet the following day in a large basement room in the staff home at the Reformatory. Apparently his only purpose was to get away from the crowd, although the Van Waters supporters suspected that he planned to call inmates to testify. No inmates testified, but neither did McDowell escape from the public clamor. A twenty-mile trip was nothing to the Friends of Framingham. The basement room was crowded with 150 spectators and hundreds of other people shouted outside, many of them finally signing a protest against what they called "unconstitutional methods." After one exhausting day McDowell moved back to the Gardner Auditorium.

Another issue for the Commissioner to handle was raised acutely at the session at Framingham. On the preceding days Dwyer had asked questions about several individuals, naming them. But now when Dwyer asked about inmates working at Seiler's and began to name them, Van Waters pleaded: "Couldn't we use numbers up here on the Reformatory grounds where people are entitled, as wards of the State, to protection?" McDowell said nothing and Dwyer persisted: "Will you answer the question, please?" "But," begged the witness, earnestly, "couldn't we use numbers instead of names?" The audience cheered and McDowell insisted on silence, whereupon the crowd chanted, "Give us numbers! Give us numbers!" A few hours later Rowell found the right answer in a procedure whereby the inmate's name was written down and shown to the recorder but was not publicly mentioned; but by this time the afternoon papers were on the streets, and McDowell faced more criticism.

All through the hearings there were mutter-ings and rumors concerning the Dwyer report and the investigation which had preceded it. Should the report be put into evidence, and if not, why not? On January 21, the eighth day, Cross raised the question publicly. "We have repeatedly asked for an opportunity to see that report. We have been refused for some seven months. . . . You showed it to two unofficial people. . . ."[15]

McDowell replied: "I am perfectly willing to have the report produced here and put in evidence, and also the statements of all the witnesses interviewed by Mr. Dwyer." But Cross apparently did not wish to see the report so ardently after all. He immediately read an affidavit from an ex-inmate, to the effect that she had had a bad hangover when Dwyer interviewed her; and then he shouted: "I don't know what is in it, but any man who will go out and take statements . . . from a drunken woman, I don't want to see the report." McDowell might have surmised from this about-face, that Cross really preferred to leave the report alone; but if any such idea occurred to the Commissioner, he failed to act on it. The Dwyer report did not become part of the record.

As for the substance of the testimony at the hearing, most of it naturally followed the lines indicated in the charges and the answer. Dwyer frequently introduced excerpts from individual inmates' case folders, including some psychiatrists' opinions; soon Cross was insisting that the whole chronological history of the inmate be read aloud. One unexpected witness turned up, brought to the hearing by Senator LoPresti. She was Gloria Barlotta, who had allegedly served liquor while performing "day work" as a waitress in a Framingham doctor's home. She made rather lurid charges concerning the "doll racket" and the failure of the authorities to control it, but wilted completely on Cross's cross-examination, answering in a barely audible mutter: "Gee, I don't know. . . . It is beyond me. . . . God knows. . . ." Dwyer called no inmates.

Four Bits of Testimony

Four bits of the testimony are worth recording here. The first provided a neat illustration of a basic difference between the Commissioner and the Superintendent:

> *Dwyer:* What is your standard practice in dealing with inmates who had crushes on each other?
>
> *Van Waters:* People are individuals. People are not masses. People are not numbers. Each one must be handled according to a plan based on her individual needs and nature. [Applause.]

The second was a letter written to Lurie by an inmate in September 1948, when Lurie was a member of the legislative commission:

> As the time draws near for the expiration of my two-year sentence, I feel that I should try to express what she has done, not only for me, but for hundreds of unfortunate girls who have lost their way. In various "wondrous ways" Dr. Van Waters helps them to find it again. . . . I was told that I was a hopeless alcoholic. Dr. Van Waters doesn't know the meaning of the word hopeless and I have never heard it used in this institution.

The third was Van Waters' own testimony about the effect of the directive of June 4. "It was not the orders I received," she said, "that upset the institution so much. For thirty years I have been a government employee. I am used to taking orders and obeying them without any delay. But never in my life have I been given a set of orders without some question from my superior as to the possible outcome and effect upon women and children whose lives they concern." Shortly thereafter McDowell himself questioned her about the actual results of the directive. Had it stopped classification and research, group therapy, religious services, medical care, psychiatry? Van Waters acknowledged that the first three had not been affected. But as to medical care she said that since June 7, inmates could not go out for surgical fittings or for visits to the dentist. And with respect to psychiatry, she ignored the directive and answered bitterly, thinking of the public hearing itself: "I doubt if psychiatry in the Reformatory for Women will be practiced for many a long year to come in the way that it was, because of the violation of confidential statements made by inmates to doctors."

The fourth was the capstone of Cross's design for the defense. He had called four former Commissioners, all of whom had praised Van Waters and taken full responsibility for what they had allowed her to do. He had called Catholic and Protestant chaplains, leading law-

[15] Employees of the United Prison Association, friendly to McDowell.

yers, and a bishop to testify to her good reputation. Now to the stand came Austin H. MacCormick,[16] executive director of Osborne Association and widely reputed to be the leading penologist in America. Said MacCormick, who had directed a study of the Reformatory a few years before, "I would say that Framingham, because of its utilization of technical processes in the climate of kindliness and genuine interest in the welfare of the women, has made a notable contribution not only to Massachusetts, but to America and the world. . . . To a much greater extent than most institutions, the Framingham Reformatory attempted to study the women who were sex deviates or might be, and help to straighten them out. . . ." In the audience, Van Waters listened, and her eyes filled with tears as he concluded: "Dr. Van Waters is one of the finest human beings I ever knew. She is absolutely tops in character, personality, inspiration, ideas, and everything else."

The final full day of the hearing was anticlimactic. There had been rumors that when Cross finished, Dwyer would produce a "surprise witness." Van Waters' friends thought that it would be Margot Chauvier, still incarcerated at East Cambridge jail. Instead, it was a handwriting expert who testified that former Commissioner J. Paul Doyle's signature on an indenture contract was forged. There was no evidence as to who might have forged it, or why, and Doyle himself, under oath a few days before, had identified the signature as his own. It is very hard to see what McDowell and Dwyer expected to gain by this testimony; but it is clear that they were convinced that the signature was forged. McDowell had said earlier that "there is no question raised about Dr. Van Waters' character," but he meant only that the *charges* raised no such question. Aside from the charges, he had his own opinion.

McDowell's Decision

Now McDowell had his first opportunity, or at least the first which he had taken advantage of, to express publicly his views on the major issues. While Dwyer and the Assistant Attorney General, Rowell, were going over the record making notes on the evidence sustaining each individual charge, the Commissioner planned to make an effective presentation of the general principles involved. He asked his former chief, Winslow, to draft a few pages; and, through an intermediary, sought oral suggestions from the Harvard Law School criminologist, Sheldon Glueck. Professor Glueck's chief point was that it was poor administrative practice for a subordinate to fail to work harmoniously with a Commissioner who had the ultimate responsibility. But although McDowell used some "ghosted" paragraphs, the first quarter of his decision was primarily his own. He dictated the final version of the remainder, too, though his Deputy and his legal adviser worked with him in preparing it. There was no question in the Commissioner's mind that virtually all the charges had been sustained and that just cause for removal had been amply shown.

Most of the 36-page decision (which was in the form of a letter to Van Waters) dealt with the numbered charges, but it was in the first quarter of the document that McDowell expressed his deeper feelings. "Before proceeding to the findings on the specific charges," he wrote, "I deem it germane to the issue as a whole to point out certain general matters. . . .

> The main issue appears to be whether a superintendent who persistently disregards the laws of the Commonwealth and disregards instructions of the Commissioner of Correction should remain in office. . . .
>
> Another fundamental issue is whether the effort to rehabilitate certain selected inmates should be attempted by allowing extra special privileges and by subjecting other inmates to deleterious influences. One case in point is a girl whose past record showed many strong indications of homosexuality. In order to build up this girl's self-confidence she was assigned a position of responsibility and given control over a group of inmates. This may have been a sincere and well meaning effort at rehabilitation of this selected girl, but it certainly was not prudent treatment for the girls under her supervision. . . . This case is cited chiefly to show the differing penal philosophy between you and me. I believe that all inmates should have an equal chance at rehabilitation and that none should suffer from extra privileges given another. . . .
>
> Long experience with the treatment of criminal

[16] Second in command (under T. M. Osborne), Portsmouth Naval Prison, 1917-19; former Assistant Director, United States Bureau of Prisons; Commissioner of Correction, New York City, 1934-40.

offenders has convinced me that our society is rendered a distinct disservice by conducting our penal institutions on the basis of vengeful punishment. . . . Advances in, and the greater opportunity for the use of medicine, psychiatry, psychology, social work and religious treatment should be extended to all possible at the reformatory. The present difficulty concerns the administration of the reformatory and not the penological thoughts behind it. Under an administrative policy where the superintendent on her own part and subordinate officers upon the order of the superintendent take inmates, committed by court warrant to be detained at the reformatory, away from the premises of the reformatory for social interludes, it seems to me that the guards become the servants. . . .

I would not arbitrarily condemn the practice [of "social interludes"] as unworthy; it might prove a contribution to modern penal treatment. . . . But I do deny your right to use it as a rehabilitative implement unless and until the laws are amended. . . .

From these introductory pages McDowell could not exclude what he had been feeling, as well as thinking, especially what he felt about Cross, the Friends of Framingham, and Van Waters herself.

My conduct of the hearing was not facilitated by the repeated demonstrations by the audience. . . . The propaganda campaign directed against me and my Deputy Commissioner by you and some of your adherents accounted for much of the unruliness. . . . The actions of your counsel in attempting to confuse me during the hearing, his slurring remarks concerning me and my Deputy Commissioner, and his discourtesy in turning his back to me in order to read documentary evidence to the audience, added to my difficulties in conducting the hearing. Notwithstanding, a full, fair and impartial public hearing was conducted. None of the vexations connected with the hearing have been considered by me at any time following their immediate occurrence, so that they have in no wise colored my judgment. . . .

Once or twice McDowell hit out directly at Van Waters, though he acknowledged that she had a "good reputation and adequate background," and had "accomplished much good in a number of cases." "The Reformatory for Women has a long tradition in an enlightened correctional policy," he wrote. "One has only to remember . . . your distinguished, but modest predecessor, the late Mrs. Jessie C. Hodder. . . . Laws and regulations are made to be obeyed by all citizens. There is not one law for great penologists and another for everyone else. . . . You have succeeded in giving the impression that you regard the law as sufficient in regulating the behavior of the common herd, but that you and other professionally trained people are superior to the law. . . . The oath of office is required of penal employees by the General Laws. It was made to appear to me that not only did you ignore this mandate imposed on you by law, but that you held it frivolously. . . . Such an attitude for the head of a penal institution is unseemly. . . . You disregarded them [the rules] as old and outmoded. I cannot but conceive this as approaching anarchism in its sense of a society made orderly by good manners rather than by law."

When McDowell, Dwyer and Rowell went over the 27 charges, they agreed that almost all could be sustained, usually with little or no discussion appearing in the opinion. There were a few exceptions. On charge 13, McDowell admitted that there had been no improper use of the "canteen fund." Under charge 12, McDowell found that the evidence fully supported the charge as to some employees, and as to three others showed that the employment of an ex-convict, while not impairing good order and security, failed to provide an exemplary and constructive influence at the Reformatory. (One of these three was the aged Irene Tower, whose reappointment had been approved by McDowell himself.) In one instance, however, the Commissioner reluctantly decided to backtrack. The case of the assistant superintendent, Margaret O'Keefe, had received wide publicity and aroused public sympathy. McDowell and Dwyer were being sharply criticized for dragging into public view her juvenile misfortunes of twenty years before, which in fact did not include any "criminal record." In that one instance, therefore, the Commissioner's decision found that the charge was not sustained.

McDowell's decision reiterated that there was no question as to Van Waters' good reputation, yet in it he indicated his own difficulty in believing all of her statements. She had testified that after receiving the directive on June 7 she had promptly written a requested letter concerning facilities for persons seeking "voluntary commitment." Unable to find this letter in his files, McDowell flatly found that she had not complied with his request. In discussing one of the former inmates whom Van Waters had employed, he pointed out that this woman's own case folder included a fairly recent statement that her "living should be carefully supervised, especially because of her homosexual tendencies"; and he concluded: "I am amazed that before me you testified that no officer with homosexual tendencies had been appointed by you to the Reformatory staff."

His professed "amazement" was a natural reflection of the differences between his whole approach—and Dwyer's, too—to the problem of homosexuality in penal institutions, and that of Van Waters. They used the same words but their meanings were different. Wrote McDowell: "It should not be necessary to observe an inmate in an overt homosexual act before preventive steps are taken. . . . Experienced penologists can frequently determine from study of an inmate's prior record, from development of over-affectionate 'crushes,' from interception of 'mash' notes, from complaints of other inmates . . . that certain individuals are likely to have homosexual tendencies." This was McDowell's emphatic opinion. Equally emphatically, Van Waters believed that a layman could not "determine" the probability of any such tendency without competent medical and psychiatric testing and advice.

McDowell gave short shrift to the Superintendent's argument that what she did had the approval of prior Commissioners. Realistically, he placed the blame on Van Waters even though the legal responsibility rested with the Commissioner. "This indenture," he wrote of one case where the inmate did not perform domestic service, "was planned and suggested by you and you caused this girl to be released from the premises of the Reformatory for Women with full knowledge that the Commissioner's action was illegal." And in another instance: "You wilfully and with full knowledge that such contracts were in violation of law released inmates . . . to go out to work at industrial, laundry, restaurant, and other employment. I find that the fact that the then Commissioner in most instances signed the indenture contract does not and cannot excuse your personal violation in releasing the prisoner and your effort to circumvent and defy the law."

The decision—"you stand removed"—was issued on February 11, 1949. Promptly, in accordance with the statute, Van Waters appealed to Governor Dever. Promptly, Dever selected the three-member impartial commission whose decision, under the law, would be final.

The Impartial Commission

The Governor wanted to have on the commission a woman, a prosecutor, and a well-known judicial figure or the equivalent. He found the woman in Mrs. Caroline Putnam, a leader in Catholic charitable work, and wife of a man well-known in the political and industrial life of the state. The prosecutor, an old friend of Dever's, was Robert Clark, Assistant District Attorney of Norfolk County. For the key post of chairman the Governor named Erwin B. Griswold, Dean of the Harvard Law School.

This commission instantly commanded public respect. It was a highly intelligent group, generally well-informed although without any expert background in penology. None of the members had an axe to grind. The chairman, Griswold, was a forceful man of serious mien, who could be impressively stern when necessary. There would be no more high-jinks, no more "yammering."

Above all, this trio was impartial. They had not prejudged the case. Yet as the hearings went forward, McDowell and Dwyer felt that perhaps they had prejudged it after all. They thought that Mrs. Putnam, at times, seemed not to be paying attention to their side of the case as closely as they would have liked. They noticed that Griswold had a note book in front of him but almost never wrote in it. They feared that these were indications that the case was "in the bag." They had a deep suspicion of the opposition, which seemed to them to be a combination of the radicals and the rich. Certainly Mrs. Putnam was "high society," and presumably the head of the Harvard Law School might lend an ear to the intellectuals and the wealthy. Thus they rested their hopes almost wholly on Clark.

Certainly, they felt, they were "sold down the river" by the new Attorney General, Francis Kelly. After telling them that to assist them he would appoint Rowell, who was familiar with the case, Kelly changed his mind. Shortly before the impartial commission met, he named one of his better known assistants, Bernard J. Killion, who went over the case with them for many hours. When the first public hearing opened, however, they were suddenly informed that Killion would not be able to represent the Commissioner; instead, an elderly lawyer, Henry P. Fielding, would appear. McDowell lost patience and declared that he would have no lawyer at all; he would try the case himself. Griswold was reluctant to let this hasty decision stand and urged a brief postponement and a conference. After further discussion it was agreed that Dwyer would present the evidence and examine the witnesses, with Fielding available to give legal advice and to deliver the closing argument. This came as a shock to Dwyer, who had not expected that he would do the examining.

Furthermore, as Dwyer told McDowell, it presented a difficult problem concerning the Dwyer report. Dwyer had expected to testify, and had considered having the Dwyer report introduced in evidence through him. Now, however, he was to be the attorney; and he was unable to see how the document might be introduced. McDowell had always kept his copy of it under lock and key. Perhaps he had some doubts as to whether it would "stand up" if it were introduced and served as a basis for cross-examination by Cross. Furthermore, it included names of inmates and officers. Neither the Commissioner nor his deputy, therefore, made any extra effort to "put it in." Cross made a point at the hearing that the report had been kept from him. In view of his earlier performance he may have had his tongue in his cheek when he complained about this; but it made an impression on Griswold and his colleagues.

One serious policy question confronted McDowell and Dwyer. Should they call inmates and ex-inmates to testify? Dwyer said he could get forty whose testimony would be useful. But McDowell worried about the effect of the resulting publicity on these women and especially their families; and Dwyer, remembering Cross's cross-examination of the Barlotta girl, was reluctant to make others face a similar ordeal. Perhaps both men wondered a little, too, whether the girls' stories really would be impressive when subjected to cross-examination, and also whether evidence of the existence of a "doll racket" would by itself sustain the charges against Van Waters. Not the existence of perversion but failure to control it was the charge. To sustain that, the Commissioner could show from the records that persons with reported homosexual tendencies had been given responsible positions directing the work of other girls.

Furthermore, McDowell was by no means resting his case on this one point. He was convinced that the evidence would prove that his subordinate had deliberately and wilfully flouted the law. That should be enough.

The hearing lasted nine days, with a tenth for the concluding arguments. At its first meeting the commission decided that it would have to try the case *de novo* rather than rely on the transcript of the record before McDowell. It was willing to accept any of that recorded testimony if the parties so agreed and a little time was saved thereby. The statute being silent as to whether the commission's hearing should be open to the public, the commission decided to hold a public hearing if either party so requested. McDowell would have preferred privacy, for then it might have been more practicable to summon inmates to testify, but Cross promptly made a demand for the hearing to be public.

Dwyer called Van Waters as the first witness. This time she was on the stand the better part of four days. For one full day, Dwyer questioned her about homosexuality at the Reformatory—her knowledge of specific instances and her action upon receipt of information. The names of inmates were given in writing to the witness and to the commission, but were never mentioned orally.

Once again Dwyer, and McDowell sitting near him, listened to Van Waters question the meaning of words: "The term homosexual tendency has to have definition and since there are, at least in my observation, five possible interpretations. . . ." Once again they heard her explain her method of bringing all reports of homosexuality before a professional board. And once again they shook their heads in disbelief when they heard her deny any suspicion, on her part, that certain pairs of inmates were involved in homosexual attachment. Months before, one of these very girls had answered Dwyer's direct question by saying: "Could be; I'd prefer not to answer that yes or no."

In subsequent testimony, to be sure, Van Waters readily stated that certain other girls did have homosexual tendencies and offered to describe the treatment given in each case.

Dwyer's examination ended with several hours of questions concerning, chiefly, indenture contracts, trips away from the Reformatory, and visits to the institution. Then Cross took over, cross-examining his own client. Now Van Waters had an opportunity to talk at length, explaining her methods and beliefs and illustrating her remarks by specific references to rehabilitated inmates. She defended the frequent employment of ex-inmates. Cross asked her about her first contact with McDowell after his appointment as Commissioner. She merely said: "I offered my congratulations and pledged the loyalty of myself and the institution, expressing the hope that the Commissioner would visit us soon," and then mentioned the difference of opinion about the employment of a recent inmate. It was McDowell himself who would tell the full story of that conversation.

Dwyer continued to put in his case, calling several witnesses to testify about the placing of babies born at the Reformatory. Then he swung back to the old subject. A Reformatory officer testified that she had caught Toni and Margot Chauvier together one night in May 1948. She said that she had not made any written report of the incident but had mentioned it to one of the Reformatory research workers in the morning. On cross-examination, Cross brought out that the research worker, at the McDowell hearing, had flatly contradicted her story.

Dwyer's next witness, a nurse, gave evidence that was helpful not to McDowell but to Van Waters. She testified to catching two inmates together in the hospital and reporting the incident to the head nurse. On cross-examination she said that the two girls were promptly removed from the hospital and placed in separate quarters, a psychiatrist was immediately summoned and a classification board meeting held.

This testimony concluded the sessions in Boston; the Gardner Auditorium being unavailable, the commission met thereafter in the handsome courtroom at the Harvard Law School in Cambridge. Now, for the first time in all the proceedings, Commissioner McDowell took the witness stand. After he had briefly outlined his experience he testified sketchily concerning the Dwyer investigation and report. Then Dwyer asked a question which Dean Griswold described as "neither proper nor relevant," but the answer was revealing. "As a result of this [Dwyer] investigation did you feel that there was cause for the removal of Dr. Van Waters?" McDowell replied: "I did."

That ended the very short direct examination, and Cross took over. He was polite and deliberate. McDowell was not surprised. He felt that the opposition's strategy was to picture him as Dwyer's well-meaning dupe—to demonstrate their scorn of Dwyer but act respectfully towards him. (To him, and to Dwyer, this picture seemed absurd.)

But the cross-examination, while polite, was deadly for soon it reverted to the first talk he had had with Van Waters in the Commissioner's office, on February 20, 1948. A year and a week had passed, but he remembered it well and he told the commission exactly what he remembered. She had congratulated him and offered him her co-operation and loyalty. In reply, "I said that co-operation was mandatory and that loyalty was due not to a Commissioner but to the Reformatory for Women in accordance with her oath of office."

Two members of the commission simply stared at him, but the third, Clark, spoke up with amazement in his voice. "I did not get that.... You said that when she came in to congratulate you?" "That is right." . . . "You made this answer when she congratulated you?" "I did."

From that time on, McDowell's hopes sank. He had counted considerably on support from Clark, a prosecutor who knew the score. Now Clark seemed shocked by his testimony. McDowell continued to testify in a tired, low voice, so that shortly Chairman Griswold requested him to speak up and enunciate more clearly.

Cross hammered him hard concerning his failure to communicate with Van Waters after his directive of June 4, especially on two points. First Van Waters had concluded her letter of reply with a question: "May we have your recommendations?" Second, McDowell charged her with failing to comply with the directive.

Q. Did Dr. Van Waters ever receive your recommendations?

A. No.

Q. What reason do you give us for not saying or doing anything about it . . . ?

A. In the meantime, I had a report concerning the institution. I did not think my question was answered there and certainly would not be answered by making recommendations. . . .

Q. Did it occur to you, you ought to tell Dr. Van Waters you hadn't considered it [her letter] full compliance?

A. No.

Q. It never occurred to you?

A. No.

And Cross took him all through a colloquy at the earlier hearing in which the Commissioner had finally said that "there is no question raised about Dr. Van Waters' character." McDowell declared that that was still his position, "oh, definitely."

After all the evidence was in, the commission recessed for a day while final arguments were prepared. Dwyer and McDowell, especially the former, worked late into the evening writing a hard-hitting, vigorous speech for Fielding to deliver. The elderly Assistant Attorney General accepted it with thanks and took it with him to Cambridge for the final session of the commission.

Then the blow fell. After Cross had argued, Fielding arose. He left Dwyer's draft on the table beside him and made a wholly different kind of argument. Specifically he praised Van Waters and sympathized with her difficulties. Still, he said, however noble her motives, she had broken the law; and because she had broken it the Commissioner had just cause to remove her.

Now, if Fielding was not as familiar with the details of the case as he might have been, he was an astute observer of the judicial mind at work. He had sensed, correctly, that the commission members admired Van Waters' character and her ability, and were disturbed by some of the Commissioner's procedures in dealing with her. Accordingly, he pitched his argument in a minor key and addressed himself solely to the point of technical violations of the statutes and the rules.

To McDowell, however, it seemed like rank treachery. With difficulty he remained silent. At last Fielding finished, the commission adjourned, and Van Waters herself came over to shake Fielding's hand. It was too much. Stolid and self-controlled throughout the weary weeks in the public glare, McDowell finally exploded. Leaping to his feet, he shouted: "This is a cause for justifiable homicide!" As he moved toward Fielding, Dwyer hurried after him calling: "Now, don't say anything to him." "The hell I won't," roared the Commissioner, "I'll tell him exactly what I think!" But the loyal Dwyer took his arm and steered him toward the door. McDowell regained his composure and on the following day wrote a handsome letter of thanks to Fielding.

Decision of the Impartial Commission

Dean Griswold and his colleagues spent a week considering the case and preparing their decision, which they presented to the Governor on March 11. Unanimously they held that no "just cause" had been shown for removal, and therefore, in the language of the statute, they "reversed the decision of the appointing authority." The denizens of the Reformatory burst into a gay celebration as soon as the news was made public. Van Waters received it quietly and gravely, at Cross's office, and then returned in sober triumph to Framingham.

McDowell heard the news unemotionally. He had expected the result. But when he began to read the commission's opinion, he found it hard to keep calm. Parts of the decision angered him, other parts shocked him. Some of his friends felt more bitterly than he did. Especially they were amazed that Clark, a prosecutor, could have signed this document. They assumed that Griswold was the chief author.

The decision disposed of most of McDowell's 27 charges by dividing them into ten general groups:

(1) Brief trips away from the Reformatory were not illegal; "no court has ever held the Superintendent, or any other similar official of the Commonwealth, to be in contempt of court for allowing such visits." Nor did they constitute favoritism; they were carefully planned parts of the rehabilitation program.

(2) Private manufacture at the Reformatory was arranged for by Commissioner Doyle, and Van Waters' part in it "was at most an irregularity (and we are not sure it was that.)"

(3) The charges concerning homosexuality were wholly unproved. The evidence showed that no known means of dealing with this problem were omitted or neglected at the Reformatory. Visits by former inmates were specifically allowed by the Rules, and they were properly permitted by Van Waters.

(4) The use of keys by inmates up until late 1947, did violate the Rules; but it was approved by former Commissioners, and did not constitute just cause for removal.

(5) Van Waters sought faithfully to comply with the directive of June 4, except for the excusable use of a bathroom key by an inmate.

(6) No law or Rule forbade the employment of prior inmates. "The evidence also showed that the appointment of such persons, carefully selected, and in proper numbers, might be a constructive influence in the conduct of the Reformatory."

(7) "The development of the indenture system by Dr. Van Waters grew out of prior practice." All contracts were signed by the Commissioner in office at the time; the basic responsibility was theirs.

(8) There was insufficient evidence to support the charge of under-staffing the night shift. "It also appeared that Commissioner McDowell has not provided any increased personnel since Dr. Van Waters' removal."

(9) The fact that employees worked outside of their classification was not just cause for removal. "If this were a ground for removal, it seems likely that every responsible employing officer in the service of the Commonwealth would find his position in peril."

(10) Child placement work was essential at the Reformatory, and was carefully and faithfully done. "Dr. Van Waters would have failed in her responsibility if she had not made provision for this work. To charge that she committed an offense by doing it seems to us strange indeed."

But the commission went further than this. Its decision appeared to McDowell to reflect unjustly on his good faith and that of Dwyer. Worse, it expressed what seemed to both men to be an astonishingly anarchistic philosophy of law.

The criticisms of the Commissioner and his Deputy were sprinkled through the decision. McDowell's remark about "loyalty and co-operation" was quoted. The Dwyer investigation received vague but adverse comment: "There are various episodes in connection with this investigation which did not create a favorable impression on the Commission." The unexplained failure to introduce the Dwyer report in evidence was mentioned.

The commission questioned whether McDowell's directive to furnish certain information "by return mail" was "a proper order." It said that McDowell's charges as to the employment of the Assistant Superintendent and Irene Tower were "irresponsibly made," for he had withdrawn his criticism of the former and approved the employment of the latter. And, finally, it dismissed the charges numbered 3, 4, 7, 9, 10, 16, 21, 23, and 27 as "trivial and captious." "Indeed," said the commission, "their chief importance appears to the Commission to be found in the light they cast on the general basis of the Commissioner's action."

All of this was unpleasant reading for McDowell, but it was the *obiter dicta* concerning the effect of statutes and regulations that really surprised him. It was one thing for Griswold (McDowell was sure that the Dean drafted the decision) to describe the old rules as "archaic and obsolete in a number of respects"; but it was quite another for him to say, in connection with the use of keys by inmates: "A rule is not a statute. Within considerable limits it is the function of such an officer as the superintendent of a reformatory to exercise judgment and discretion. One of the tasks and responsibilities of any senior administrator is to know when to relax the rules. Anyone who is engaged in any field of public administration knows that practices often develop more rapidly than rules can be changed to meet them."

While the commission agreed that indenture contracts for other than domestic service were not lawfully made, it continued: "No institution can be static. Development will occur despite individual administrators and despite rules and regulations and even statutes. Many bits of progress in the law have come about because the practices get ahead of the law and it has been necessary to change the law to catch up with what is being done. . . . We say this not to agree with the construction of the law adopted by Dr. Van Waters and prior Commissioners, but to show that what was done is constantly and necessarily being done in many administrative organisms, both governmental and private. If the things being done were not authorized by the statute, it was Commissioner McDowell's privilege to direct that they be terminated. This he did, and Dr. Van Waters complied."

Reading these words, McDowell felt as strongly as ever that his course had been right. His enemies chorused that he must resign. He did not resign. He served until his term expired. And at Framingham he was still the ultimate boss. Governor Dever sought to mediate, inviting McDowell and Van Waters to lunch with him; but the experience had been too bitter and the differences too deep. Van Waters kept her job but McDowell's directive stood. Not while McDowell was Commissioner would he condone at Framingham practices which had developed more rapidly than the rules could be changed to meet them, nor would he abrogate those rules which he believed were sound.

Editor's Postscript

Miriam Van Waters was due to retire three years later, in October 1952, when she became 65. However, she appealed to the State Retirement Board, and with the approval of the new Commissioner and of Governor Dever she was allowed to continue at Framingham for an additional five years.

In November 1956 Van Waters became seriously ill, and although she recovered she went on sick leave until her official retirement a year later. During that year, and in the months immediately following her retirement, a new series of charges was levied against Framingham and against the entire Massachusetts prison system. It appeared that the Van Waters hearings of 1949 had left suspicion in the minds of at least several Massachusetts legislators.

The Joint Legislative Committee on Penal Institutions voted to investigate Framingham and all state prisons in August 1957, following lurid charges about conditions at Framingham by an escaped inmate who had been arrested in Louisiana and was fighting extradition. The same month the *Boston Traveler* printed an interview with Van Waters in which she denied as "untrue and ridiculous" a number of stories including one that an inmate had regularly entertained men at the Reformatory and another that dope and liquor were passed around there. "I have never seen a homosexual at Framingham," she was quoted as saying. "To my knowledge there are none there." Framingham inmates rallied to the defense of Van Waters, and reporters learned that they regarded the escapee's charges as biased and unfounded. Van Waters offered to remain at Framingham after her retirement, but this suggestion was never mentioned by the press again. Shortly before retiring, she was given a testimonial dinner on October 15, attended by hundreds of persons, many eminent, including Mrs. Eleanor Roosevelt and New York City Commissioner of Correction Anna Kross.

Early in January 1958 an official at Framingham who had unsuccessfully applied to succeed Van Waters was quoted by a *Boston Herald* reporter as stating that immorality at Framingham was "even worse than it has been painted." A few days later, a minor employee at the Reformatory was arrested and charged with allegedly harboring and making pornographic films. The next day the *Herald* reported that a former Framingham correction officer, unnamed, had resigned suddenly. A policeman had taken her to a police station along with a recent Framingham parolee after seeing them in a parked car. The same week the Commissioner of Correction held a press conference and stated that the Framingham situation had troubled him since he had taken office in May 1957. The Reformatory was run down physically (due, presumably, to limited budget appropriations); "disrespect for officers was particularly marked with Dr. Van Waters on sick leave"; and evidence had come to him from the Federal Bureau of Investigation that one or two officers had had improper relations with inmates.

One day later, January 8, the Joint Legislative Committee convened a press conference. Charges made about Framingham included: that there was excessive use of barbituates; that there was a high escape rate; that the rate of return of inmates was 57 percent; and that inmates were allowed unsupervised visits by men in their cells. The Committee investigator (he was a former FBI agent and had been assisted by two state troopers) said he had found evidence of homosexuality but that it was probably not disproportionate to that existing in other institutions. Reported the *Herald:* "The committee found that prostitution did exist on the grounds, that staff members were aware of it and did not report it to proper authority."

The Chairman of the Joint Legislative Committee concluded by saying that the Committee's charges dealt with incidents which occurred in 1956, and that it was not intended to blame Van Waters or her administration. At this point one member of the Committee interjected: "If this gives Dr. Van Waters a clean bill of health, I want no part of it." Another Committee member said immediately that he held the same sentiment.

The Friends of Framingham met after the Committee press conference. The Reformatory chaplain and its staff physician challenged the accuracy of the charges, saying that the investigators had interviewed only the guards and inmates and had not consulted with the higher officials. The Friends denied charges and offered statistics of their own. It was also pointed out that the Committee investigators had allowed no opportunity for rebuttal or for cross-examination. The Committee announced it was continuing its investigation, and the Friends of Framingham indicated they would continue to defend the institution against unfair attacks, although, the *Herald* reported, a number of former Friends had deserted the cause. The Governor and the Commissioner of Correction found the situation still too highly charged to appoint a successor to Van Waters four months after she retired, and it was plain that the charges and countercharges of the Van Waters case of 1949 had planted, or reflected, divisions of feeling in Massachusetts that were still troublesome almost ten years later.

Reorganizing the Massachusetts Department of Conservation

Thomas H. Eliot

Introduction

IN 1952, the Massachusetts Special Commission on the Structure of the State Government, generally known as the "Baby Hoover" Commission, made an unsuccessful effort to reorganize the State Department of Conservation through legislative action. The failure of the attempt raises questions as to whether the Commission, and especially its Executive Director, Thomas H. Eliot, erred in making decisions concerning both the proper organization of the Department and the use of tactics in the face of concerted opposition.

The situation in Massachusetts in 1952 was such as to make the kind of questions faced by the Commission of general applicability. The same type of problem may confront reorganizers in other states at other times. Particular local factors, such as one-party domination or personal opposition to a Governor, were conveniently absent. Although it was established in 1949 as the result of a message from Governor Paul A. Dever, a Democrat, and although Eliot, its first Executive Director, was a former Democratic Congressman, the Massachusetts Commission was bipartisan in composition and nonpartisan in spirit. To a degree that was praiseworthy and surprising, considering the hot party contest in the state (with the Democrats having a small majority in the House and the Republicans an even smaller one in the Senate), the Commission ignored considerations of partisan advantage. The Governor, while generally endorsing the Commission's aims, did not intervene strongly in behalf of any particular proposals. Thus the Commission lacked the benefit of vigorous political support, but at the same time it escaped the handicap of partisan opposition. Baby Hoover Commissions were the rage in over a dozen states in 1949. Many of the legislators who voted to organize a Massachusetts Baby Hoover Commission that year probably regarded it as more a public relations gesture than anything else. A few thought that it might do some good, while some of the Commission members were determined that it should. By 1952, after it had been at work for two years, the Baby Hoover Commission had won a fair measure of respect in the Legislature and a generally favorable press, and it had made few enemies.[1]

For the 1952 session of the Legislature, the Commission prepared reports on five major departments, accompanying each one with legislation to carry out the recommendations in the report. Of these five departments, the one which seemed most obviously in need of reorganization was the Department of Conservation. As that report began to take shape, in the summer and fall of 1951, it appeared to Eliot and his staff that it would be easy to make a persuasive case for reorganization. Only one organized group could be counted in the opposition, and if necessary, that group could be placated. Furthermore, unlike most department heads, the Commissioner of Conservation himself was clearly in favor of having the Department reorganized along the lines suggested by Eliot and agreed upon by the Commission.

Yet, while other Baby Hoover bills prevailed over the bitter protests of department heads, the reorganization of the Conservation Department was defeated in 1952. This study presents the story of that losing fight, analyzing the factors which produced defeat, and asking whether, had any one of a number of decisions been made differently, the final result would have been victory.

The Baby Hoover Commission

The Massachusetts Commission, during the 1951-52 period considered here, consisted of thirteen men, four of them representatives and four

[1] In the 1952 session of the Legislature, out of twenty Baby Hoover bills, ten were enacted. Several were "lost in the shuffle" at the end of the session and were hastily referred back to the Commission for further study; aside from the Conservation measures discussed herein, the only major proposal rejected by the House of Representatives was one which would have attached the Massachusetts Commission Against Discrimination to the Department of Education.

senators. Of the non-legislative members appointed by the Governor, one had been a representative and two had served in both houses. The Commission was supposed to have fourteen members, equally divided between the parties, but the resignation of a Republican public member in September 1951 created a vacancy which remained unfilled. By this time, however, the nonpartisanship of the Commission had already become well-established; and the equality between the parties was effectively maintained by the appointment of a public member, Frank Vorenberg, who although a registered Democrat, regarded himself as an independent voter and was commonly so considered.

The Commission was unpaid, and the task of directing its research work was entrusted to Eliot, its Executive Director. Eliot had a small full-time staff, and he also called upon a number of expert consultants, who served on a per diem basis. At the outset, the Commission decided that it would be impolitic to try to present a single report covering the entire state government. It was believed that any such report would be doomed to failure, because each interest group opposing a particular recommendation would probably join forces with all other similar interest groups and successfully attack the whole report. Therefore, the Commission decided to bring out a series of separate reports, each with draft bills attached, keeping in mind throughout a general view of the whole picture so that recommendations affecting more than one department would not conflict with subsequent proposals by the same Commission.

Including, as it did, a preponderance of legislators, the Commission was acutely aware of the need for legislative support. At one of its very first meetings it had heard a high state official express the cynical opinion that all that this Commission should do was to copy the language of reports made in earlier years and resign itself to having its reports gather dust in the archives. There was a very general skepticism in the state administration, in the Legislature, and among the public concerning the possibility of any successful reorganization of any department. Experience in Connecticut, where a sweeping reorganization report had been rejected by the Legislature in 1950, increased this skepticism.

To build up support for the Commission's recommendations, therefore, Eliot proposed that an effort be made to establish a broad-based Citizens' Committee along the lines of the National Committee for the Hoover Report. But the Commission's Chairman, Chester A. Dolan, Jr., rejected this suggestion, and he was supported by a majority of his colleagues. They felt that if any leading citizens were recruited to head a Citizens' Committee, they would either be well-known partisans with many political enemies in the Legislature, or they would be persons carrying little weight with the Legislature, despite their possible distinction in professional or business life. Furthermore, they were fearful of criticism if the Commission or its staff actually stimulated the creation of any such pressure group. Finally, the Connecticut experience showed that a committee of this sort could easily melt away once specific recommendations were made; and indeed, in Massachusetts, some prominent individuals who were vocal in their enthusiasm about the establishment of the Commission became quickly silent or hostile when their own ox was gored by any Baby Hoover bill.

The idea of a Citizens' Committee was therefore dropped. From that point on, Eliot sought a wide base of general support chiefly through the press, which was largely favorable, and through two half-hour television programs in the winter of 1952. In addition, the state branch of the National Committee for the Hoover Report made its regular weekly radio program available from time to time to the Commission; and Eliot, his assistant (and successor) William A. Waldron, and some members of the Commission also made numerous speeches to luncheon clubs and other groups. The use of all these publicity media unquestionably created a generally favorable atmosphere which affected the Legislature when the Baby Hoover bills were brought up.

The opposite side of the same shield was the elimination, where possible, of enmity arising from the misunderstanding or fears of department and bureau chiefs and state personnel. The Commission promptly adopted and publicized a policy of not affecting the rights of any civil service personnel, justifying this position by pointing out that in recent years the regular personnel turnover in Massachusetts had exceeded fifteen percent, so any reduction in personnel permitted by reorganization could take place quickly through not filling vacancies. This satisfied the civil service workers. There remained the question of dealing with the higher placed appointive officials.

At Waldron's suggestion, and upon the urging of both Waldron and Eliot, the Commission adopted an elaborate and time-consuming procedure. For each of its major reports, the work began with the preparation of a staff memorandum, which stated the facts and asked numerous questions but contained no specific recommendations. This staff memorandum, after being revised by the Commission, was then sent to the heads of the various state agencies affected. Each of them was invited to sit down and discuss it with the Commission. Thereafter, the same or a revised staff memorandum was sent to a group of unpaid "advisers" who were citizens with some special knowledge or interest in the field being studied. They, too, met with the Commission and expressed their views.

The staff memorandum was then rewritten in the form of a tentative report which was given to the press together with an announcement that the Commission would hold a public hearing on the tentative report. After the public hearing, the Commission met again, and made further revisions before filing its formal report with the Legislature.

It was this procedure which was followed in the case of the preparation of the report on the Department of Conservation. It was supposed to allay the opposition of appointive officials and to satisfy private citizens that they had had a chance to be heard and to participate. In this case, apparently, it did neither.

The Department of Conservation

For many years, the Massachusetts Department of Conservation had been a subject of widespread criticism. It was hardly a Department at all, but rather a conglomeration of several different agencies, each of them jealous of its prerogatives. Its history was marked by internal conflict and duplication and by a significant lack of any affirmative program to develop the state's natural resources.

Nominally, the head of the Department was the Commissioner of Conservation, appointed by the Governor. But although the statutes appeared to give the Commissioner control of almost all of the Department, no Commissioner, for many years, had been able effectively to exercise any such control. This was primarily because the Commissioner did not have the power to appoint or remove the directors of the divisions in the Department. These officials were, instead, named by the Governor for fixed terms. Furthermore, the substantive laws conferred various powers upon the division directors, exclusive of the Commissioner. To a very considerable degree, therefore, the last few commissioners of conservation in Massachusetts had felt themselves to be little more than figureheads.

By statute, there were five divisions in the Department—Marine Fisheries, Parks and Recreation, Forestry, Law Enforcement, and Fisheries and Game. All but the last were supposed to be under the control of the Commissioner. Until 1948, the Division of Fisheries and Game was also at least nominally under his control. In that year, however, the Legislature established a new agency, the Fisheries and Game Board, and entrusted it with the responsibility for the administration of the Division of Fisheries and Game. The Board, an unpaid five-member body appointed by the Governor for staggered terms, appointed the director and other officials of the Division of Fisheries and Game. That division was financed by appropriations from an earmarked Inland Fisheries and Game Fund, into which were placed all the receipts obtained by the sale of hunting and fishing licenses.

The Division of Parks and Recreation was responsible for operating a number of state-owned recreational areas, several of them located within the boundaries of state forests. The Division of Forestry was responsible for the state forests and for the administration of a potentially lucrative forest-cutting program which remained ineffective. The Division of Marine Fisheries administered the laws with respect to shellfish and deep sea fishing. In the Division of Law Enforcement were two groups: conservation officers, exclusively occupied in enforcing the inland fish and game laws, and coastal wardens, whose only duties were those concerning the prevention of illegal digging, catching or processing of clams, lobsters, and similar marine life. One-half of the salaries of the conservation officers was paid out of the Inland Fisheries and Game Fund.

The Commissioner of the Department was Arthur T. Lyman, Jr., appointed by Governor Robert F. Bradford, a Republican, in 1948 to serve for a five-year term. He was an experienced public servant, having previously been Commissioner of Correction by appointment of Governor Joseph B. Ely, a Democrat. As indicated, he had to exert whatever influence he could chiefly through persuasion, rather than through any real authority. With two of his division directors he was on close and friendly terms; with the head of the Division of Law Enforcement, a man with a political background who has since retired to seek political office, Lyman dealt at arm's length. Between Lyman and the director of the Division of Forestry there was open and obvious hostility. That director, Raymond J. Kenney, was himself a former Commissioner of Conservation, and he appeared ready to resist anything which he considered interference with his prerogatives as division chief.

Early in Lyman's term as Commissioner, the Fisheries and Game Board was established and the Division of Fisheries and Game was removed from the Commissioner's control. Lyman did not appear to resent this, but rather welcomed it, as he disliked the constant pressure exerted by various sportsmen's groups in connection with the administration of the fish and game laws.

This was the Department which the Baby Hoover Commission, among its other duties, sought to reorganize in 1952.

The Staff Memorandum

The staff memorandum on conservation was prepared under Eliot's direction largely by Melvin Zurier, a young Harvard graduate who had worked the previous summer for a special commission investigating the Milk Control Board of Rhode Island. The consultant on the project was Professor Arthur A. Maass of Harvard, who had taken part in the Hoover Commission's work in Washington and had headed the task force on natural resources in the Connecticut reorganization program. Most of the interviewing was done by Zurier, and some by Maass and Zurier together, with Zurier writing full reports on the facts found. Eliot put these reports together into a preliminary memorandum, while Maass, separately, prepared a full report of his own. Eliot believed that some of Maass' suggestions were too drastic to be politically practicable, but he drew on others substantially in revising the preliminary draft and preparing the staff memorandum used for discussion. It was completed on August 27, 1951.

In view of what later transpired, it is interesting to concentrate here on only a few of the questions raised by the staff memorandum. The final battle, many months later, concerned four substantive issues: (1) whether the Department should continue to be headed by a Commissioner or instead should be under the general direction of an unpaid five-member board; (2) whether the Division of Fisheries and Game should remain under the Fisheries and Game Board, or should instead become an integral part of the Department, its director to be appointed by the Commissioner; (3) whether the Department's law enforcement activities should be entrusted to conservation officers trained and equipped to enforce all of the conservation laws instead of only segments of them; and (4) how a unification of two divisions, those of Forestry and Parks and Recreation, could be effected.

The first of these questions was not raised in any way by the staff memorandum. Neither Eliot, nor Zurier and Maass, nor members of the Commission, gave any serious thought to establishing a board or commission to direct the Department. Shortly before this staff memorandum was prepared, the Commission had filed its report on the Department of Education. The members had rather reluctantly agreed to leave that Department under the direction of the Board of Education, but they had publicly explained that this was the "exception that proved the rule" and had reiterated their belief that ordinarily an operating department should be headed by a single individual. Far from getting rid of the Commissioner and replacing him with a board, the staff memorandum asked whether the Commissioner should not be given greater power—especially, the power to appoint and remove his division directors.

In connection with the Division of Fisheries and Game, the staff memorandum suggested that "it would seem that there is an excellent opportunity for the Commonwealth to realize a savings by making the Division of Fisheries and Game part of the Department of Conservation," with the director of the division to be appointed by the Commissioner, and the Fisheries and Game Board (an unpaid body) to be retained only in an advisory capacity, without administrative responsibility. These suggestions were made in extremely tentative form, the memorandum also including arguments for a continuation of the system in effect since 1948 when the Fisheries and Game Board was established and placed in charge of the Division of Fisheries and Game.

The development of a "multipurpose" staff of conservation officers, a key proposal in the Maass report, was not mentioned in the staff memorandum. It suggested instead that possibly the law enforcement officers in the Law Enforcement Division should be assigned to the particular operating divisions with which their major duties were connected. Thus, the conservation officers enforcing the Fish and Game laws might be assigned to the Division of Fisheries and Game, and the coastal wardens to the Division of Marine Fisheries.

Finally, the staff memorandum did raise the question of a merger of the Division of Forestry with the Division of Parks and Recreation, and implied that if this merger were effective, the head of the new division should be appointed by the Commissioner.

The staff memorandum was sent to the Commissioner of Conservation, to the Chairman of the Fisheries and Game Board, to the heads of two departments affected by other recommendations which do not concern us here, and to Senator Edward Stone and Representative Fred Blake, the Senate and House chairmen of the standing Committee on Conservation.[2] A dinner meeting of the Commission was arranged, to which Commissioner Lyman, Senator Stone, and Representative Blake were invited, but only Commissioner Lyman attended.

Lyman, not at all surprisingly, gave an affirmative answer to the question of whether the Commissioner should appoint the division directors. (At no time, at that meeting, was there any suggestion of having the Department headed by a board.) He expressed some reluctance at having the Division of Fisheries and Game directly under his control, because he believed that this would make him the subject of ceaseless pressure from rival sportsmen's groups; but he agreed that the integration of the division was logical and justifiable. With respect to law enforcement, he suggested (as had Maass) that the officers in the Division of Law Enforcement should enforce all the conservation laws. Rather mildly, he argued that the work of the Division of Forestry was sufficiently different from that of Parks and Recreation to justify the continuation of two separate divisions, but he indicated his readiness to go along with a recommendation for consolidation.

Shortly thereafter, Eliot held a long conference with Senator Stone. (Neither at that time, nor later, did Representative Blake respond to repeated invitations to confer with Eliot or with the Commission.) Senator Stone was deeply interested in the Department and said that he strongly favored giving the Commissioner authority commensurate with his responsibility. Most of this discussion, however, related to the Department's activities in destroying the gypsy moth by aerial spraying, a subject which was mentioned in the staff memorandum and subsequently became an important part of the report.

At the end of September 1951, the Fisheries and Game Board and the heads of the other departments concerned were invited to meet with the Commission. Throughout its existence, attendance at the meetings of the Baby Hoover Commission had been unpredictable; and unfortunately, on that particular day, there was only one member of the Commission present, Representative Howard Whitmore, Jr., of Newton. It was probably also unfortunate that the other department heads were heard first and talked a long time so that the members of the Fisheries and Game Board had to wait in an outer office for over an hour. When they came into the meeting they were obviously dismayed by the fact that only Whitmore and Eliot were present. However, they talked freely, the Chairman of the Board, Matthew M. Coyne, being the chief spokesman. They found no fault whatever with any factual statements in the staff memorandum. They did oppose vehemently any possible suggestion that they be deprived of administrative

2 In Massachusetts, most standing committees of the Legislature are joint committees, senators and representatives sitting together.

responsibility or that the Director of Fisheries and Game be appointed by the Commissioner instead of by themselves. In the main, they gave an accounting of their stewardship and urged that no change be made. They expressed no opinions with respect to the rest of the memorandum. After Eliot and Whitmore had listened, with few interruptions, for 55 minutes, Eliot asked in a moment of silence whether Mr. Coyne or his colleagues had anything further to say. Coyne declared himself satisfied, and the conference was concluded.

Before preparing the tentative report, Eliot personally had further conferences with several advisers whom he invited to discuss the staff memorandum with him. (The Commission itself was holding regular meetings on other subjects, and in view of the difficulties of obtaining substantial attendance, Eliot decided that these extra conferences might as well be held by him alone, although on each occasion he informed the Commission members and invited them to attend.) For present purposes, the only conference with advisers that was relevant was one with Robert Livermore, then president of the Massachusetts Fish and Game Association. Livermore emphatically opposed any change in the Fisheries and Game Board and the Division of Fisheries and Game. He said that for the first time within memory sportsmen were united in supporting the official program of these bodies. He said that prior to 1948 the director of the division was appointed by the Governor and was a political figure subject to political pressure. The establishment of the Board with administrative responsibility, Livermore said, had removed politics from the whole area of wild life management.[3] He said that he would approve of integration of the division within the Department of Conservation only if the Department itself were headed by a similar nonpolitical board. He told Eliot that both he and many other leaders of sportsmen's organizations were thoroughly sold on the idea of a board and would be happy to see the Department of Conservation headed by a board, but that if it was not headed by a board he would fight to keep Fisheries and Game independent of the Department.

[3] Livermore's thesis had wide support; actually Eliot was also of the same view that the situation in the division had improved since 1948; but, as will be seen, he did not share Livermore's further conclusions about the proper permanent organization of the division and the Department. *Ed.*

The Tentative Report

Eliot then wrote a draft of the tentative report and submitted it to the Commission for consideration. Now for the first time he raised the question which later turned out to be basic—namely, whether the Department should be headed by a Commissioner or a board. Eliot's draft assumed that it would continue to be headed by a single Commissioner, but he reported his conversation with Livermore and suggested that the matter be considered. When asked for his own views, Eliot said that he would prefer to have a single Commissioner. Several members of the Commission, especially Whitmore, echoed this as being consistent with a fundamental principle of administrative management.

Eliot's draft also raised squarely the question of whether the Division of Fisheries and Game should be integrated and the Fisheries and Game Board either abolished or made an advisory unit. Both he and the Commission members were in agreement that "to create a real Department, capable of developing a unified Conservation program with maximum efficiency and economy," all divisions should be under the Commissioner. "The work of the Division [of Fisheries and Game] should not, functionally, be kept separate from that of the Department of Conservation. To keep it separate is to impair the possibilities of achieving the maximum results from a real Conservation program. . . . To insist that the Division remain wholly independent of the Department of Conservation is to assume that the management of wild life areas should be undertaken separately from the management of parks and forests—some of them the very woods and streams where the wild life abounds."

This tentative recommendation was the subject of prolonged discussion at the Commission meeting on October 18, 1951. The question was, in part, a political one. The eleven members of the Commission who were or had been members of the Legislature were acutely aware of the potentialities of the sportsmen as a pressure group. Several of them recounted instances of large numbers of hunters and fishermen coming to hearings, buttonholing legislators in the corridors, and "putting on the heat" in connection with various measures. It was obvious to all that the sportsmen would vociferously oppose the tentative recommendation. Nevertheless, the tentative recommendation stood. It stood largely because the Commission members agreed with Eliot, first, that it was a sound recommendation in itself, and second, that the Commission had more to gain than to lose by making it. The Commission members themselves were unwilling to appear subservient to any pressure group. Eliot believed and said, furthermore, that as a tactical matter it would be sensible to make the tentative recommendation, because if the opposition should prove to be too fierce, the Commission could still gracefully withdraw from its position. By such withdrawal, he assumed, the sportsmen would be mollified.

Thus after prolonged deliberation, but without dissent, a basic decision was taken: namely, to recommend in the tentative report that the Division of Fisheries and Game be brought under the Commissioner of Conservation, with the Fisheries and Game Board becoming an advisory body. A concession was made in the form of giving the Fisheries and Game Board the right to nominate a list of six persons, from which the Commissioner would select the director of the division.

The tentative report, as drafted by Eliot and approved by the Commission, specifically provided for the multi-purpose conservation officers urged by Maass. This was agreed to with little discussion. Furthermore, the tentative report proposed a new, combined Division of Parks and Forests. In discussing this part of the tentative report, Commission members did raise a question as to what would become of the directors of the two divisions which would be merged. One of these directors, Kenney, had wide political contacts in the state and especially in the State House. While the fact that he might have some political influence was noted, however, no one on the Commission urged that any special provision be made for him. This was partly because the Commission, as a matter of policy, consistently refrained from dealing in personalities and chose to abide by its fixed rule of protecting civil service employees, but of disregarding the claims, political or otherwise, of officials outside of civil service.

The tentative report was then adopted and made public, and the Commission held a hearing on it on November 2, 1951. Of the four questions considered here, only one was emphasized at the hearing—the tentative recommendation with respect to Fisheries and Game. No witness urged that the Commissioner be replaced by a board; nobody discussed the expansion of the functions of the conservation officers; and there was no opposition to the merger of the Division of Parks and Recreation with the Division of Forestry, nor to having the head of that division appointed by the Commissioner.

Commissioner Lyman himself spoke in favor of almost the entire tentative report, but he "reluctantly opposed" the proposals with respect to the Division of Fisheries and Game. He implied that integration, in the face of the fierce opposition of the sportsmen, might well be self-defeating.

More surprising was the statement made by Coyne, Chairman of the Fisheries and Game Board. Instead of discussing the issues presented by the tentative report, Coyne attacked the Commission and its staff. He complained about Zurier's youth; he complained, quite incorrectly, that neither he nor the chief of the Division of Fisheries had been more than perfunctorily interviewed, and that the hatcheries and game farm had not been visited; he complained that he and his fellow board members had not been given a hearing by the Commission. Eliot corrected him with respect to interviews with officials and visits by Zurier and Maass to the division's installations, and he pointed out that Coyne had said everything he had to say at the Commission meeting on September 24. To this, of course, Coyne could and did reply that only one member of the Commission was present. Eliot's rejoinder was to ask Coyne whether despite all the alleged shortcomings of the Commission and its staff, there were any factual misstatements in the tentative report. Coyne admitted that he had found none.

A number of other speakers stuck to the issue more closely. Representing various rod and gun clubs, they reiterated Livermore's earlier point to the effect that a "nonpolitical" Fisheries and Game Board had in three years succeeded in establishing a program which they could all support. These sportsmen claimed to represent many thousands of persons, although less than 100 attended the hearing. The showing was sufficiently impressive, however, to make Eliot believe that the time had probably come to retreat, especially with Commissioner Lyman siding with the sportsmen on this issue. In a brief conference after the hearing, Eliot found the members of the Commission ruefully agreeing that in its final report the Commission should recommend leaving the Fisheries and Game setup alone. They said that this reversal was absolutely necessary if the whole conservation report was to have a good chance of success in the Legislature. Eliot then assured them that he could draft a final report which would thus reverse the Commission's position but which would at the same time save its face.

The Opposition Organizes

Nobody was surprised, when the tentative report was issued in October, to find sportsmen's clubs protesting the proposal to change the status of the Division of Fisheries and Game. Eliot was a little startled, however, to discover, first, that the "alarm" was actually sent to the sportsmen's organizations by Coyne, the Chairman of the Fisheries and Game Board, and second, that many of the rod and gun columns in the daily papers of the state simply reprinted, verbatim, handouts apparently prepared by one man in Boston, without any independent evaluation of their fairness or accuracy.

To be sure, prior to the public hearing on November 2, 1951, the newspaper stories were reasonably accurate, although hardly unbiased. "Trapper Bill" in the Fish and Game column of the *Lawrence Eagle* on October 29, 1951 noted a forthcoming meeting of the State Council of Sportsmen's Clubs, Massachusetts Federation of Sportsmen's Clubs, and Middlesex and Norfolk County Leagues to "talk over the report," and said that at the hearing the following Friday, sportsmen's groups, individuals, and the like, in opposition to this proposed reorganization, "should be on hand to register their opposition." Henry Moore, Rod and Gun Editor of the *Boston Herald,* about whom more will be heard later, ran a strictly factual column on November 2. The *Springfield Union,* on the same day, reported a sizable meeting of sportsmen's representatives as opposing the tentative report, and made an unexplained reference to "wholesale sabotage of the sportsmen's funds." Several of the "representative sportsmen" at the meeting mentioned in this story were themselves rod and gun editors of various papers.

Widespread publicity was given to a statement by Paul White, then field secretary of Wild Life Conservation, Inc., opposing the tentative report. White said that when the Fisheries and Game Board was established "the sportsmen succeeded in divorcing fisheries and game policies from political control—under the Baby Hoover proposal, the Fisheries and Game Director would again be a political appointee, the only difference being that he would be named by the Conservation Commissioner instead of the Governor. Since the Commissioner himself is a political appointee, fisheries and game administration would be right back where it was three years ago, deep in the heart of politics."

Virtually all of this publicity, like virtually all of the arguments made at the hearing itself, was confined to the issue of whether the Division of Fisheries and Game should be brought under the Commissioner, or remain under a responsible Fisheries and Game Board. Thus far, the opposition seemed to be reasonable, and developments were just about what Eliot had expected. The first tip-off of a different kind of campaign —the kind of campaign that ultimately had much to do with the Commission's defeat—came in the "Sportsmen's Roundup" column in a relatively small paper, the *Lowell Sunday Telegram.* The writer of that column, one Ed Coughlin, wrote as follows: "The biggest proposed steal since the Brink robbery was uncovered this week by a few wide-awake sportsmen's leaders, and an innocent-appearing report of the Baby Hoover Commission was disclosed as the key the politicians had hoped to use in their raid on the lucrative but well-guarded treasury of the state's sportsmen's fund. Once again, the hunter and the fisherman had learned the only way to safeguard the money derived from their license fees is to handcuff the suction-cupped fingers of the slush fund grabbers." Coughlin referred to the tentative report as "highly secretive" and said that "it appears on the surface to be a fairly deliberate attempt to get the Division of Fisheries and Game back into politics."

This story was significant, despite its limited circulation. It stated three themes. The first of these, relating to the "steal" of the sportsmen's fund, was so far-fetched that it reappeared only infrequently. The other two, however—the charge of "secrecy" and the insinuation that the Baby Hoover Commission was nefariously interested in "politics"—were played over and over again in all parts of the state. Coughlin's column may well have given to the aforementioned Henry Moore the basic ideas upon which he framed the later publicity which was so effective in wrecking the reorganization plan.

One other factor in this early period could not be overlooked. That was the unity of the various sportsmen's groups. Historically in Massachusetts, these clubs and leagues had constantly been at war with one another, each wanting more fish for its own streams. The tentative report had the effect of uniting them, for in the main the sportsmen were well satisfied with the administration of the fish and game laws under the Fisheries and Game Board and were most sincere in their opposition to any change. In November, conservation, wild life, and outdoor groups formed a body called United Conservationists, with Paul White as director.

This unity, however, did not seem particularly significant at the time. It helped to persuade Eliot and the Commission to recede from their original proposal, but they assumed that once they had receded the opposition would cease. They did not realize that the tentative report had so stirred and united the sportsmen, or at least their official leaders, that the opposition would continue and grow more vehement as time went by. They did not see, at first anyway, that United Conservationists had come into existence primarily to fight the Baby Hoover Report and that the fight was therefore likely to continue regardless of how much the report was changed. They overlooked the fact that others before White had gained political reputations by successfully organizing opposition to proposed legislation.

The Rival Bill

On December 4, 1951 a small self-constituted steering committee of Republicans in the Massachusetts Legislature, including the President of the Senate and the Minority Leader of the House, issued a proposed program for the coming legislative session, due to convene in January 1952. In this policy statement, they urged the reorganization of the Conservation Department, and specifically proposed placing it under the direction of a five-man board instead of a single Commissioner. This was the first time that this suggestion had been publicly made, at least in 1951. It was followed immediately by the filing of a bill by Senator Christopher H. Phillips to carry out the proposal. United Conservationists were behind both the statement and the bill, White openly admitting that his group had drafted the measure. Senator Phillips was selected to introduce it because his uncle had been a conservation pioneer in Massachusetts and because, unlike Senator Stone, he was persuaded that a board should supplant the Commissioner.

These moves took the Baby Hoover Commission by surprise. Whitmore, although an assistant floor leader of the House, had not been consulted and was somewhat indignant. After conferring with some of his fellow Republicans, however, he understood that the program was not binding on the party and did not believe that it was necessarily a firm commitment to any particular details of policy. Eliot, engrossed at that time in rewriting the conservation report, drafting the conservation bills and preparing two other reports for early presentation to the Legislature, was inclined to shrug the matter off.

There were two things that he might well have done. The first was fairly obvious, and had he had more time, he probably would have done it. Arranging a prompt conference with Paul White and other spokesmen for the sportsmen's groups might have reduced the subsequent hostility to the Baby Hoover Report. Eliot knew, however, that it was most unlikely that the Baby Hoover Commission would advocate the establishment of a board to run the Department. He also thought that while White was committed to continuing the battle regardless, his supporters would be satisfied by the final report. Underestimating the intensity of the opposition, he did not see that much could be gained by any conference.

The other thing which Eliot or a Commission

member might well have done was something that did not occur to them. Not until months later, in fact, did it appear to be a matter of any real significance. It concerned the referral of bills to standing committees of the Legislature.

All of the Baby Hoover bills were filed in the House, and were automatically referred to the Committee on State Administration. Commission members, and especially Eliot, had worked many hours with that Committee, acquainting them with the overall objectives of the Baby Hoover Commission and with the details of its various bills. The Chairman of the Committee, Senator Ralph Lerche, was himself a member of the Baby Hoover group, and he relied heavily not only on Eliot, but also on Edward H. O'Brien, of Eliot's staff, for general assistance in the Committee's work as it pertained to the Baby Hoover reports.

Under the Massachusetts system, a favorable report from the Committee on State Administration was not enough to bring a bill before the House for action if the bill in any way related to the raising or spending of money. All of the Baby Hoover bills, after receiving favorable reports from State Administration, were automatically referred to the House Committee on Ways and Means. All of them, therefore, had to run a double gauntlet.

Each bill, of course, related to some specific function of the state government, and for each such function there was a separate legislative committee, such as the Committee on Education, the Committee on Conservation, the Committee on Labor, and the like. To send the Baby Hoover bills to one of these committees, however, would have meant that each measure would have had to run the gauntlet three times. Such an obstacle course was something to be avoided at almost any cost.

The Baby Hoover Commission attempted to work out a reasonable compromise by inviting the members of the appropriate standing committees to confer with it, and to sit with it at the time of the public hearing on its tentative report. These efforts evoked little or no response.

When Senator Phillips, on December 5, 1951, introduced his Conservation bill (Senate 73), the clerk of the Senate had to decide where the bill should be referred. If the bill had been introduced by a representative in the House, probably the House clerk would have referred it to the Committee on State Administration. He would have recognized it as a reorganization bill. The clerk of the Senate, however, had not had the job of referring any Baby Hoover bills. He did recall that four years before, the Committee on Conservation had studied the Department and introduced some bills looking towards its reorganization (including the establishment of the Fisheries and Game Board). It was natural for him, therefore, to refer the Phillips bill to the Committee on Conservation.

As soon as they heard of the introduction of the Phillips bill, Eliot, O'Brien, or some member of the Commission would have done well to hasten to the office of the Senate clerk and urge referral to the Committee on State Administration. Thus they might have avoided the complicating factor of intercommittee jealousy and conflict—although to be sure, the Senate clerk might still have sent the bill to the Committee on Conservation.

The Phillips bill was relatively short. It abolished the position of Commissioner and established a commission of five members, four of them to be appointed by the Governor with staggered terms. The fifth member was the Chairman of the Fisheries and Game Board, ex officio. This five-member commission was authorized to appoint an executive secretary to act as the chief administrative officer of the Department.

The only other change in the existing organization proposed by Senate 73 was the merger of the Division of Parks and Recreation with the Division of Forestry. The bill included a specific provision that the Director of Forestry—Kenney—should head the new consolidated division. No similar provision was made for the Director of Parks and Recreation.

The Final Report

On January 19, 1952 the Commission filed its report on conservation with the Legislature, together with seven bills drafted to carry out its recommendations.

Although Livermore's idea of heading the Department with a five-man board had by now borne fruit in a bill with apparently substantial support, the Commission's report did not raise this question at all. It did recommend that the directors of all divisions, except the Division of Fisheries and Game, should be appointed by the Commissioner. It changed the name of the Division of Law Enforcement to "Division of Conservation Services," and it recommended that the conservation officers in this division should be trained, authorized, and directed to enforce all conservation statutes and regulations. One-half of their salaries was to be paid out of the Inland Fisheries and Game Fund. The report expressly left the Division of Fisheries and Game alone, together with the Fisheries and Game Board. All of these recommendations were embodied in a bill entitled Appendix A.

The "face-saving" promised by Eliot was apparent in the Report's introduction as follows:

> There may come a time when a completely integrated resources program can be achieved. At present, however, the organized sportsmen of the State do not recognize the Conservation Department as 'their' department; they are mainly interested in only one of its functions, wildlife management. This particular function has been performed well in recent years. We cannot reasonably expect the sportsmen to accept a change in the existing organization unless and until they are convinced, by experience, that the rest of the Department is capable of running a scientific, constructive, coordinated program affecting all natural resources. The first necessary step, therefore, is to make it possible for the Department to do this.

Appendix B, attached to the report, was a bill providing for the establishment of a new Division of Parks and Forests formed by the merger of two existing divisions. No special provision was made for the continuation in office of the director of either of the merged divisions. The bill provided that the Commissioner should appoint the director of the new division.

Appendix C directed the Department of Conservation to embark on a state-wide aerial spraying program to destroy the gypsy moth and provided for the transfer of funds from the cities and towns to finance the program. The Commission estimated that this program would, within five years, bring about savings of approximately $900,000 annually to the taxpayers of Massachusetts. Aside from the merits of this recommendation, its inclusion in the report was doubly beneficial to the Commission. First, the proposal was dear to the heart of Senator Stone. Second, and more important, it gave the Commission a chance to talk in definite figures and make a reasonably accurate estimate of cash savings. All reorganization commissions are plagued by this problem—people seem to expect price tags to be placed on each structural change—but the wise and honest commission can seldom make an accurate estimate of just how much money can be saved by the merger of agencies or the reassignment of functions. Accordingly, Eliot had long since seized on the gypsy moth issue as one which would enable the Commission to speak of large savings when it made its conservation report public. Although the recommendation hardly pertained to the structure of the state government, Eliot justified its inclusion in the report because it was a recommendation for instituting "modern practices" of operation.[4]

Appendix D related to the Division of Marine Fisheries—the unit administering the laws with respect to ocean shellfish and deep sea fishing, as distinguished from sport on inland waters. In the main, this bill merely transferred numerous legal powers, such as those to issue licenses, from the division director to the Commissioner of the Department. It also provided for increases in license fees, which, the Commission said, would increase the state's revenue about $50,000 a year.

Appendix E made the Department of Public Works responsible for maintaining automobile roads in state forests. Appendices F and G concerned reassignment of functions, which aroused little controversy and need not be described here. The whole program was deliberately separated into seven legislative proposals in the hope that even if some were defeated, others would pass.

The report received fairly wide publicity in the state, hitting the front pages of several Sunday papers. All of the newspaper stories made it clear that the Fisheries and Game Board would continue unaffected. As the Associated Press story said, "The final report of the Commission proposes leaving the Fisheries and Game Division under its present Board direction." The

[4] Even this was a little far-fetched; the Resolve creating the Baby Hoover Commission mentioned "improvement of operational efficiency by . . . the introduction of sound management practices. . . ." However, no one at any time raised any question about the propriety of the recommendations.

Boston Sunday Advertiser story was more specific: "Completely reversing its Tentative Report of last October, the Commission advises a status quo, with the Division functioning under a Fisheries and Game Board as presently constituted. The reversal is the result of nearly unanimous and organized protests of sportsmen against the first proposal to return the Division to Conservation Department control." The Commission's own release, part of which was used intact by several papers, said: "The Division of Fisheries and Game should continue, for the present at least, to operate under the Fisheries and Game Board, which should appoint the Director of the Division."

The Battle Opens

The Baby Hoover Report's initial reception was generally favorable. The news editors gave it prominence; editorial writers praised it. (Throughout the rest of the controversy the editorial pages and the sports pages of Massachusetts newspapers were frequently on opposite sides.)

The report and the seven appended bills were referred to the Committee on State Administration. That Committee was devoting one day a week to consideration of the various Baby Hoover proposals, and Chairman Lerche fixed Tuesday, January 29, 1952 as the date for consideration of this particular report. Lerche, himself a member of the Baby Hoover Commission, was well aware of the fact that its recommendations had been revised since October in conformity with the requests of the organized sportsmen. He also recalled that substantially all of the opposition at the Baby Hoover Commission's hearing on November 2 had been directed at the proposal to alter the status of the Fisheries and Game Board and incorporate the Division of Fisheries and Game in the Department. This proposal having been abandoned, Lerche could see little or no purpose in holding another public hearing. He persuaded his fellow committee members to dispense with a hearing, pointing out that if any groups wished to offer new testimony, they would still have an opportunity to do so when the bill was considered by the House Ways and Means Committee.

Accordingly, on January 29, Lerche invited two people—Eliot and Commissioner Lyman—to sit with his Committee in executive session. At this session, Lyman stated his opinion several times that the Baby Hoover Report was "sound as a nut," and Eliot answered a few questions about the details of the various bills. After some perfunctory discussion the Committee voted to report the whole matter favorably to the House, knowing that it would then be automatically referred to Ways and Means.

The Baby Hoover Commission as such had nothing to do with this procedure. Eliot, in fact, was very much surprised when he learned that only Commissioner Lyman and he were to attend the meeting. Apparently the organized sportsmen had not been invited nor even notified that any meeting was to be held. On that particular day they were concentrating on the forthcoming hearing of Senate Bill 73 before the Committee on Conservation, which was held the following day and was attended with enthusiasm by representatives of various wild life groups. The witnesses at the Conservation Committee hearing supported Senate 73 and opposed the Baby Hoover recommendations, although the latter were not before that Committee. The opposition was still harping on the idea that under the Baby Hoover proposals the status of the Fisheries and Game units would be altered; as the *Lowell Sun* reported, "Indications point toward the fact that Senate Bill 73, which was submitted by the sportsmen, will be enacted into law, thus continuing the Division [of Fisheries and Game] as it currently is."

It was several days before the sportsmen returned to the fight. Then, suddenly, on the front page of the *Boston Sunday Herald* of February 10, 1952, they fired away with both barrels. Henry Moore, publicity man of United Conservationists, Inc., and also Rod and Gun Editor of the *Herald,* wrote a blistering article headed "Outdoor Groups Act to Block 'Sneak' Conservation Bill."

Moore's article was designed to appeal to all possible opponents of the whole Baby Hoover Report. First it attacked the Commission by implication, saying that its plan "to reorganize the Massachusetts Department of Conservation under one-man control has been smuggled through the House and referred to the Ways and

Means Committee under the same cloak of secrecy which roused a storm of opposition when the report was first uncovered last summer . . . the Baby Hoover plan supporters are maneuvering to get their bill before the House, even though it is defeated, simply to block consideration of United Conservationists' own organization bill, Senate 73, which asks for the unpaid Commission form of streamlined reorganization unanimously endorsed by all interests involved."

Moore implied that the Fisheries and Game Board would be supplanted by a new board appointed by the Governor, saying that the Report "authorizes the Governor to name a five-man advisory board to the Fisheries and Game Division." Quoting Paul White, Moore said that the Baby Hoover plan "would nullify every gain made in the Conservation Department three years ago and turn it into a one-man-dictatorship . . . under control of one political appointee." The story described the five-man unpaid commission form of control as a proposal "advocated by conservation interests and made an integral part of the state GOP's twelve-point better government program."

Moore left few stones untouched. He sought to alarm the employees of the Department, saying that the Baby Hoover Report "gives the Commissioner the sole right to transfer any Department employee from job to job, place to place, or abolish their positions and transfer them to other state departments as he sees fit"—a thoroughly inaccurate statement. He pointed out that the Baby Hoover proposal for uniting all state lands under a Division of Parks and Forests would result in certain county commissioners being "stripped of their control" over state reservations in their counties. He charged that the Commissioner of Conservation would be given the right "to manipulate the state highway fund" because the Baby Hoover Report proposed that the Public Works Department, financed out of the highway fund, should be responsible for maintenance of automobile roads in state forests. Thus, in this one story, United Conservationists and the *Boston Herald* (which, editorially, had consistently been favorable to the Baby Hoover Commission's work) sought to discredit the Commission, condemn its plan for responsible management, and arouse the sportsmen, the state employees, the county commissioners, and the Public Works Commissioner against the report. The fact that the charges concerning the Fisheries and Game Board and the state employees were false was of no significance. Moore's story had the effect which he sought.

Ill and angry, Eliot drafted a long point-by-point reply, thought better of it, and instead sent a short letter to the *Herald*. He decided that the heart of the matter was the continuing mistaken belief that the Commission was seeking to abolish the Fisheries and Game Board. His brief letter, accordingly, dealt only with that point. Eliot wrote that Moore's article "was astonishing because it was based on a wholly false premise. It apparently assumed that the Commission was recommending a change in the status of the Division of Fisheries and Game and the Fisheries and Game Board. The fact is that no such change was recommended. The status of both the Division and the Board is unaffected by the Baby Hoover Report." In a reply in the *Herald* three days later, Moore said merely that Eliot "seems to have missed the main point" which, according to him, was that the Committee on State Administration had reported the bill without a hearing.

On February 15, Moore's column again charged that the Baby Hoover bill was a "legislative secret," and said that "it is believed to ask for a single, politically appointed Commissioner in absolute control of all department divisions except Fisheries and Game." The idea that the report was "secret" was, of course, absurd. While printed copies were not yet available, the Baby Hoover Commission itself had multigraphed several hundred copies and had sent them to all interested organizations, notifying them that additional copies were available.

Moore's columns were widely reprinted throughout the state. Other rod and gun editors came back into action, and White himself traveled about the state making speeches. When he could not attend himself, he sent messages carefully designed to stir up opposition in particular quarters. He wrote to the chairman of one of the local reservation commissions, saying, "I feel that I would not be fulfilling my job if I did not bring to your attention a certain section of the 'Baby Hoover Report' "—the section combining all state reservations under the new Division of Parks and Forests. In his letter to the Amesbury

Sportsmen's Club, reported in the *Haverhill Gazette,* he said that the "Baby Hoover bill calls for the curtailment of the existing department and would not be advantageous to sportsmen." He spoke to delegates from sixteen sportsmen's clubs in Franklin County, where the *Greenfield Gazette* quoted him as saying that the Baby Hoover bill could create a single Commissioner "with all power imaginable—a Conservation dictator—and no man knows enough about the whole field to undertake that job." He also repeated the false charge that the Fisheries and Game Board would be abolished and would be replaced by a brand new five-man board appointed by the Governor. In this particular speech, furthermore, he combined his attack on the Baby Hoover Report with criticism of a proposed budget cut, with which the Baby Hoover Commission had nothing to do, so that the story was conveniently headed "Conservation Department Change Threatens New Hatchery in Sunderland, Clubs Told."

Again and again, the same old charges were made. As late as March 30, the *Lowell Sunday Telegram* was describing the Baby Hoover Report as "the controversial bill which had been slipped into Committee by the Hoover Commission without benefit of public hearing" and was urging sportsmen to "protest the radical changes proposed for the presently smooth running Division of Fisheries and Games."

Meanwhile, although busy with other matters (the Baby Hoover Report on Education was given a public hearing on March 4, and its report on Public Safety was issued a few days later), Eliot was not ignoring the opposition to the Conservation Report. He continued to believe that most of it, at least as far as the rank and file of the sportsmen were concerned, was based on the mistaken belief that the Fisheries and Game setup would be changed. All of his counterattacks were aimed primarily at that point. He helped to prepare a speech delivered by Senator Maurice J. Donahue before the Hampden County Council of Sportsmen's Clubs on February 17. Donahue, a member of the Committee on State Administration, supported the whole report and pointed out that the Commission's recommendations did not affect the Division of Fisheries and Game. This seemed to have little effect, even at the very meeting where Donahue spoke. As the *Springfield Republican* reported it, the Senator was followed by the president of the State Council of Sportsmen's Clubs, who said, "We are very satisfied with the management of the Division of Fisheries and Game under the management of the present five-man Board and don't want to see any changes." According to the newspaper story, "he pointed out that the Commission's plan would affect the Division in many ways."

Eliot also assisted in preparing a speech by Senator Lerche before the League of Women Voters in Springfield on March 21. In this speech, Lerche said that he was "very disturbed by the various groups who wish to misinterpret the proposed Conservation reorganization," and he emphasized that the proposals would in no way modify the autonomy of the Division of Fisheries and Game.

On the same day Chairman Dolan signed a vigorous statement denouncing the "confusing smoke screen of misinformation thrown up by the opponents of the Conservation Report." Eliot sent this statement to editors, with a personal letter referring to the frequent inaccuracies in their rod and gun columns. Receiving fairly wide publicity, this was about as effective a counterattack as could have been made at that time. Probably the Dolan statement would have been more effective if it had been printed on the sports pages instead of in the regular news columns. It not only reiterated the facts about the Commission's report, but it also made a pointed attack on the claims of supporters of Senate 73 that they were backing a nonpolitical bill. The Dolan statement said that while the Baby Hoover bills would remove four positions from gubernatorial control, Senate 73 would create four new positions to be filled by the Governor's appointees. It singled out as obviously political the provision in Senate 73 assuring Raymond J. Kenney, Director of Forestry, of continuation in office as the head of the new combined Division of Parks and Forests, and it said that, in providing that Fisheries and Game should be independent of the Department but that the Chairman of the Fisheries and Game Board should be a member of the Commission running the Department, the sportsmen were attempting to "have their cake and eat it too."

All during March, Eliot, speaking at luncheon clubs and other meetings, hammered home the point that the Conservation Report did not adversely affect the sportsmen's interests. During that month he talked privately with Governor Dever. When the subject of the Conservation Report was brought up, the Governor, with instinctive political prescience, immediately asked what role Kenney was playing in the controversy. Eliot replied that the present difficulties were chiefly caused by the opposition of the organized sportsmen. The Governor then said that the sportsmen were a truly powerful political group, so powerful that both parties sought to make special appeals to them in political campaigns. However, he promised to speak to the Democratic leaders in the House, including the Chairman of Ways and Means, generally in favor of the Report, inasmuch as it did not affect or hurt the sportsmen. However, Eliot understood him to imply that he might be reluctant to throw himself fully into the battle for the adoption of Baby Hoover Conservation bills if the latter ran into serious trouble.

The Ways and Means Committee held a public hearing on the Baby Hoover Report on April 1, 1952. Eliot, Lyman, Representative Johnson of Worcester, and four Baby Hoover Commission members spoke in favor of the seven bills. The opponents were more numerous. Senator Phillips, who had introduced Senate 73, made a reasonable argument in favor of the commission form of department direction, and indicated no opposition to any other phase of the Baby Hoover Report. A whole series of sportsmen's representatives opposed the Report, but at this hearing, before well informed legislators, their opposition was primarily in the nature of favorable comments on Senate 73. One and all, they urged that the Baby Hoover Report be sent to the Committee on Conservation for further study.

Indicative of the effectiveness of White's campaign was the appearance of several representatives from the western part of the state, who knew little or nothing about the details of the Report but wished to register their opposition. Each of them said he did not wish the Fisheries and Game organization disturbed. Each was speaking upon request of his local sportsmen's club.

Coyne, the Chairman of the Fisheries and Game Board, admitted that his own unit would not be directly affected by the reorganization. He now justified his opposition, however, by claiming that under the Baby Hoover bills a part of the inland fisheries and game fund would be diverted to pay the expenses of enforcing other conservation laws. This presumably referred to the recommendation that all conservation officers should enforce all conservation laws, with half of their salaries being paid from the fund. As Eliot pointed out, any small increase in the drain on the fund might well be matched by an increase in service, in more effective enforcement of the fish and game laws; but Eliot also said, and other Commission witnesses repeated, that this particular matter was of no great significance and that the Commission would readily support an amendment confining the use of the fund solely to the enforcement of fish and game laws.

The Ways and Means hearing was the scene of the first public appearance of certain other persons in opposition to the report. These included people alerted by Henry Moore's original article. Thus, a spokesman for the Public Works Department protested the bill making that Department responsible for maintenance of automobile roads in state forests, and several county commissioners spoke against the plan to have the state Division of Parks and Forests administer all state reservations. By far the most bitter testimony, however, was that offered by two division directors, Kenney and Alfred B. Cenedella, Director of the Division of Law Enforcement. If ever there was proof of the Commission's charge that the Department of Conservation was a "conglomeration of independent agencies," it was furnished here. Both Kenney and Cenedella, especially the former, occupied themselves in studiously insulting the man to whom they were supposedly responsible, namely, Commissioner Lyman. Kenney made a vehement defense of the status quo, while Cenedella picked up the argument that under the plan, state employees might be transferred and his division decimated. Kenney's opposition was not surprising, for his dislike of the Commissioner was well known. The vigor with which Cenedella spoke was, perhaps, explained a few months later, when he resigned to seek the Republican nomination for a political office.

The only important new development at the hearing was the emphasis laid by several witnesses on the need for referring the Baby Hoover bills to the Committee on Conservation. Several sportsmen and also Representative Howard Russel, a member of that Committee, urged that this be done. This was the first public indication that a new opposition force was gathering—namely, the legislators on the Committee on Conservation, who could be appealed to on the ground that their own prerogatives had been slighted. The effective exploitation of this appeal, as it turned out, was a major factor in the ultimate defeat of the Baby Hoover plan.

Efforts at Compromise

The pressure now was turned on the Ways and Means Committee. The chairman was visited at his home by a delegation of sportsmen who threatened him with defeat in the forthcoming election if he permitted his Committee to report the Baby Hoover bills favorably. When a speech by Eliot before the Boston Rotary Club was widely reported, quoting him as saying that the Division of Fisheries and Game would be unaffected, nearly 100 letters promptly reached the Governor and as many more went to the members of the Ways and Means Committee, disputing Eliot's statement and demanding that the bills be killed. A syndicated State House column, appearing in many newspapers, reported that although "the Baby Hoover Commission skirted any trouble with the sportsmen by proposing that the Fisheries and Game Division and its fund not be affected"; nevertheless "sportsmen saw red when they thought major alterations were being made in their pet function." This column also pointed out what Chairman Dolan's statement had revealed, that the sportsmen's own proposition was to give their representatives a "foot in the door" to control of the whole Department.

The rod and gun editors kept the pressure up. For instance, on May 1, the *Brockton Enterprise and Times* described the Baby Hoover bill as making the Commissioner of Conservation "the boss of the Division of Fisheries and Game," and on May 15 Henry Moore wrote bitterly about the Baby Hoover Report having been "sneaked into the Ways and Means Committee," having received only "token favor" but "overwhelming opposition of . . . half a million people."

Meanwhile, the Director of Forestry, Kenney, spoke to individual members of Ways and Means, urging first that the whole Report be pigeonholed, and second, that in any event, a special provision be inserted taking care of him. The Ways and Means Committee decided that Kenney's political strength was too great to ignore. They therefore agreed on an amendment to the bill taking care of Kenney. This amendment provided that the Director of the Division of Forestry would remain an employee in the Department, with no change in pay, for the duration of the term for which he was appointed. It did not satisfy Kenney, however; he objected that it did not specifically provide that he should be the head of the new Division of Parks and Forests, nor, he said, did it take care of him after his present term expired a year and a half hence.

In May, Waldron reviewed the whole situation with John M. Woolsey, a director of an old, established organization known as the Trustees of Public Reservations. Waldron believed that the Commission should "fight back" by causing the Legislature to be bombarded by letters favoring the Baby Hoover Report. Eliot viewed this suggestion very dubiously, partly because he was busy with countless other matters and partly because he did not think that letters from individual citizens, no matter how distinguished, would have much effect. His reluctance was increased when Commissioner Lyman poured cold water on the whole idea, saying that it would only serve to "stir the animals up." However, a letter was drafted, and a copy of it was sent to a few people known to be sympathetic to the Baby Hoover proposals. These few signed it, but Woolsey himself then wished to rewrite it entirely before signing it, and the project came to nothing.

Despite the sportsmen's pressure, and perhaps because of the generally favorable attitude of the Governor, Ways and Means favorably reported all seven Baby Hoover Conservation bills on June 10, 1952. The Committee acted unanimously. Moore sent out the alarm in his column, widely reprinted, and the pressure increased.

By this time, Eliot, O'Brien, and Fred Harrington, a popular Democratic representative and vice-chairman of the Commission, all believed that the major reorganization proposals had only a bare chance of passage. Eliot was thinking in terms of salvaging as many of the seven bills as possible. O'Brien and Harrington thought that with a few breaks in the luck, and an all-out fight, the major bills might pass the House, but even they could make no favorable predictions with respect to Senate action. Waldron, however, refused to accept any defeatist attitude. He urged Eliot to see the Governor and demand that the Governor come out strongly for the whole Report. This Eliot refused to do for several reasons. First, he believed that it would be futile, because the Governor had already indicated that he did not particularly desire to get into a brawl with the organized sportsmen. Second, he thought that even if the Governor did assume leadership, such leadership might result in the death of the bill in the Republican Senate. Furthermore, he was most unwilling to inject the Governor too far into any of the Baby Hoover battles because of the probability of incidentally arousing purely partisan opposition, especially as the gubernatorial election was only a few months away.

Waldron did not give up. In early June, in a radio debate, Eliot and the sportsmen's spokesman, White, had agreed that the only real issue was whether the Department should be headed by a single person or a five-member board. Waldron thereupon proposed that the sportsmen's leaders sit down with the Commission and try to work out a satisfactory compromise. He believed that the issue of commissioner vs. commission was relatively unimportant and was himself ready to advocate acceptance of the sportsmen's five-man board proposal if the rest of the program could be saved.

With Eliot's reluctant acquiescence, Waldron, at the Baby Hoover Commission's meeting on June 18, urged that this conference be held, and the Commission agreed to hold it. Several Commission members, therefore, met on Friday, June 20, with White, Woolsey, and representatives of the Conservation Council, a "holding company" of numerous organizations interested in wild life management. More or less self-invited, a number of legislators were also present—Senators Stone and Phillips, and several representatives serving on the Committee on Conservation. One of the latter, Representative Porter, said that he had drafted an amendment to the Baby Hoover bill to provide for a five-man board. It seemed possible that the Baby Hoover Commission members would agree to support this amendment if the sportsmen could assure them that, as so amended, the whole program would be supported. At this point White hastily backtracked. Although claiming that he was representing half a million sportsmen, he now said that he could not possibly speak for all the groups which belonged to his organization nor could he foreclose any of their individual members from opposing various parts of the Baby Hoover Report. Furthermore, he pointed out that Fred Blake, House Chairman of the Conservation Committee, was strongly opposed to any five-man board, and the Porter amendment might therefore be defeated, for Blake was influential. Whitmore, and especially Frank Vorenberg, of the Baby Hoover Commission, then spoke out vigorously against the commission form of control and in favor of retaining a single Commissioner. Thus the chance for any real compromise was lost.

Eliot, never hopeful of any satisfactory compromise, nevertheless now made one last effort to pull the chestnuts out of the fire. He suggested that the Porter amendment be carefully redrafted so that it would clearly pose the issue without causing an unnecessary number of changes to be made in all of the Baby Hoover bills and that it be introduced at the outset of the debate on the first bill. He expressed the hope that if the amendment was passed, the bills would then be enacted, and that if the amendment was defeated, the sportsmen would still get behind the bills and try again next year to supplant the Commissioner with a board. This proposal was greeted favorably by all present, and White, Woolsey, and Eliot spent the afternoon drafting the proposed amendment.

Over the ensuing weekend both White and Representative Porter changed their minds. Porter, who was a neighbor of one of the chief sportsmen's lobbyists at the State House, told Eliot on Monday that he did not see how he could possibly offer the amendment. Instead, he said, all seven bills should be referred to the Committee on Conservation for study during the forthcoming legislative recess, from July 1952 to

January 1953. Eliot promptly called White on the telephone and received the same information. Eliot then asked Porter if he was definite as to what he was going to do. Porter replied that someone had urged him to refer three bills (Appendices A, B, and D) to the Committee on Conservation, but apparently now "the idea was that all the bills should be referred." He said he had nothing against the four other bills, nor had he heard of any opposition to them.

As soon as Porter left his office, Eliot quickly called O'Brien, who was keeping a close watch on Baby Hoover legislation on the floor of the House. O'Brien then informed the clerk of the House that there were four bills (Appendices C, E, F, and G) which he understood were noncontroversial and might be passed even though they were not on the regular House calendar for the day. A few minutes later, these four bills duly received the requisite number of readings and passed the House without any debate at all. If this quick action had not been taken and they had come up at the same time as the three other bills, there is no question but that they would have all been sidetracked.

Defeat

The remaining conservation bills were on the House calendar for June 23, 1952. As soon as the first of the three bills was read, Representative Porter moved to refer it to the Committee on Conservation for study during the recess. Before the debate started, several Republican representatives reported that the Republican leadership had passed the word to vote for Porter's motion. By no means all of the Republican members, however, were ready to follow the leadership. The recalcitrants were besieged by lobbyists in the corridors—some by regular, registered and paid lobbyists, some by sportsmen, and some by frightened and angry state employees. Several employees of Cenedella's Division of Law Enforcement buttonholed Representative Johnson of Worcester, a well-informed proponent of reorganization, and claimed that passage of the bills would cost them their jobs. When he pointed out to them that this was not so, they argued that in any event it might mean they could be transferred. Johnson angrily retorted that if he were the director of the division he would transfer them to China, and he stamped back onto the floor of the House. Kenney divided his time between the lobby and the House gallery.

Four Republicans, only one of them a member of the Baby Hoover Commission, spoke forcefully in favor of the Baby Hoover bills, along with two Democratic members of the Commission. The first speakers in opposition were not particularly effective, for they were obviously incompletely informed and merely repeating what their local sportsmen's groups had told them. The program was doomed, however, when Representative Blake, a Democrat and the House chairman of the Conservation Committee, made a vigorous speech in favor of referring all three bills to his Committee. Blake had the respect of the members, especially as an authority on all matters pertaining to conservation. It was hardly necessary for several other members of his Committee, of both parties, to follow him to the microphone and echo his appeal.

The vote came up on motion to refer to the Committee on Conservation, and on a standing vote the House was evenly divided forty to forty. When the roll was called, however, the appeal of the Committee on Conservation, plus the pressure of Republican leadership on members who had missed the debate, helped to put the opponents of the Baby Hoover Report well into the lead. When the call was half completed, it was obvious that the bills were to be sidetracked and for the rest of the alphabet almost every Representative voted "Aye," including many Democrats from city districts. The final vote of 179 to 52 thus gave an exaggerated picture of the extent of the opposition. Once the Baby Hoover bills were surely defeated, it was easier for all concerned to vote against them and thus avoid recriminations.

To be sure, there were some recriminations of a very public sort. The *Boston Globe* and the *Springfield Union* editorially chastised the Legislature for its action. Ironically, this very chastisement—perhaps, too, a twinge of conscience—helped to get the next major Baby Hoover Commission Report, on Public Welfare through the House without opposition two days later.

THE CHIEF EXECUTIVE AND HIS AIDES

"The most important qualification of one who is high in the service of the state is his fitness for acting through others."

Sir Henry Taylor

A City Manager Tries To Fire His Police Chief

Frank P. Sherwood

Introduction

IN 1956, the year City Manager Singer fired Police Chief Black, or tried to, the population of the City of Valley had risen to about 25,000.[1] Within a two-hour drive from Los Angeles, Valley was the center of a large citrus farm area. The green orchards which dotted the hillsides south of the city relieved the semi-desert brownness of the landscape. Valley was also the site of a sizable college supported by a Protestant denomination.

For years, going back to World War I, Valley had held a reputation as one of Southern California's most pleasant and peaceful communities. Before 1940 its population had been composed of four main groups: citrus owners, and leaders of associated service firms (packing company owners and managers, and the like); downtown businessmen, realtors, and professionals; the college people; and the Mexican-American laborers. The town had always been heavily and quite seriously Protestant; the Baptist and Methodist congregations were two of the largest groups.

The Setting

Railroad tracks running from east to west bisected the community. High ground and hills rose to the south. With the exception of the college, which formed its own little enclave of green lawns and architectural confusion, the area north of the tracks was the poorer part of town. Here the houses were older, the people less well-to-do, less educated. Here one was more apt to find a Democratic voter. Also in this northern section was the Mexican-American community, predominantly Roman Catholic, which tended to be isolated socially from the rest of the city. Rising south of the tracks were the leading hotel, the banks (units of state chains, which appointed the local managers), the City Hall, and the business district. Also to the south was the country club, which had the reputation of being a gathering place for the prestigeful, the old families, and the better-off, although some of the more austere or fastidious among the eligible families chose not to frequent it. Still farther south, up in the hills, were the luxury homes.

By 1956 there had appeared a new element in Valley's population—one that could not be as neatly categorized as those that had been familiar for over forty years. Valley was gradually becoming a "bedroom city." The new people were the product of the rapid growth of the nearby Xerxes metropolitan area. They lived in Valley, but they worked close by in the larger urban centers. These new residents spread throughout the community. Many moved into housing developments on the north side. The wealthier ones erected homes up on the hills. Religiously, the newcomers seemed to include more Catholics and fewer Methodists and Baptists than the pre-existing population. Economically, socially, and politically it was not clear just where they would fit. Although Valley had often been regarded by outsiders as hostile to newcomers who might disturb the peace and order of its settled ways, the newcomers were absorbed without visible eruptions. Up to 1956 observers had not detected any real impact by the newcomers on the politics of the city.

Politically, Valley had always been a city of predominantly Republican voters. Xerxes, the county seat, a railway center with a population three times the size of Valley's, was a Democratic city, and since the mid-thirties the County Board of Supervisors and the county administration had usually been under Democratic control. California state law required non-party local government elections, but most informed people

[1] The names of persons and local jurisdictions used in this case are entirely fictitious. Because of the author's departure for an overseas assignment, portions of this case—particularly those dealing with the political background—have been prepared by the editor.

in Valley knew who the infrequent Democratic candidates for the City Council were and whether a Republican or a Democrat had been elected to speak and vote for Valley on the County Board of Supervisors.

By and large, Valley's citizens were not intensely interested in party politics or in city government. From the well-to-do citrus families there had usually come a leading element of support and influence in the Valley Republican organization, but much of the party work and many of the candidates willing to devote time to local government came from the ranks of the more established local businessmen, realtors, and professionals. Some of the downtown businessmen and professionals, meeting regularly and separately for luncheon in different local chapters of six different national service organizations (Rotary, Kiwanis, and the like), some of the country club people, some of the leading laymen in the church congregations, and the (Republican) publisher and editor of the daily *Valley Times* were usually aware of political and governmental events. But beyond this circle were the majority of citizens who seemed uninterested in governmental affairs as long as things ran smoothly and quietly—which up to the 1950s they almost always did.

The "Lemon Street Gang"

Among those who were quite well-informed, an almost legendary element in the city's political history was the Lemon Street Gang. Most people in Valley did not know of its existence, and among those who claimed to, its membership, its political influence, or even its continued existence were often guessed at or disputed. The men alleged to be in the group denied that such a group existed or that they worked together; they were just friends of long-standing and intimate acquaintance. But most insiders believed that the group operated informally and secretly to wield influence in local government and politics.

No hard evidence has been found that the Lemon Street Gang played any part in the events of 1956 that form the subject of this study, but some of the principal participants suspected that the Gang was active behind the scenes.

Actually, the group had started as an informal personal association of a half-dozen Valley war veterans—not sons of high-status families—after they had returned from military service in World War I. They had found it difficult to get jobs and discovered that they were not the only returning veterans who were not well-regarded by potential employers. They resolved to work together at influencing affairs in Valley to see that deserving veterans were taken care of, despite the unsympathetic attitudes of Valley's leading citizens and the existing Republican organization. Many of the men who were associated with the group proved to have considerable ability in politics and government. Some were sons of small tradesmen who, in the twenties, were far down from the top of Valley's informal social ladder.

Some members of the group organized a formal veterans organization that spread throughout the county and beyond. One of the leading members became an extremely effective precinct worker for the local Republican organization. The group bargained its voting influence in order to secure jobs for veterans in local and county government. The more jobs it obtained for veterans, the greater its political bargaining power became. Its leaders began to operate increasingly at arms length from the older, more conservative, and more socially established men who acted as leaders of the local Republican organization. Finally, in the middle thirties, one of the leading political figures in the group, dissatisfied with the recognition offered by the county and local Republican organizations, helped secure the election of the first Democrat as County Supervisor from Valley. He stayed on the Democratic side of the fence and formed the first Democratic organization in the city and in the county. During the Depression the political efforts of the Lemon Street Gang to win jobs for veterans were not disturbed by the fact that some were in the Democratic camp and others were Republicans. The members of the group moved below the level where the public tends to pay attention to politics (which in Valley was not deep) to place their protégés, using whatever means their ingenuity could devise. Most often, it was admitted, the men they placed in government jobs proved to have the necessary ability.

The Lemon Street group had its greatest successes in the thirties, when Valley operated under a modified commission form of government, which was then traditional in California. By 1945, some of the leaders in the original group had moved out of Valley to careers in county, state, and even federal government. In the early postwar years the remaining members of the group succeeded in getting the city to set up a veterans bureau with a paid staff. One of the leaders of the group helped to secure necessary Council support for Valley to accept an extensive public housing project, against the inclinations of several local realtors. The group also allegedly secured the appointment of an extraordinarily able and dedicated man to serve as director of the housing project. Some of those who benefited from these projects—including the Mexican-Americans—were alleged to be sufficiently appreciative to vote as the group's leaders suggested when the Lemon Street men wanted to muster support behind some particular local candidate or issue.

The Introduction of a City Manager

The postwar period also brought to Valley a growing pressure from civic-minded citrus families, professionals, and local businessmen in favor of more efficient municipal government under centralized management. A public services director was appointed in 1946 and given many of the powers of a city manager. Under the leadership of Mayor Cassius Bolt, a temperate and respected local businessman who was a deacon in the Methodist congregation, the council-manager plan was adopted by Council ordinance in 1949. Bolt had been moved to devote time to local government by a sense of duty. He took no part in local political party organizations, although, like most respectable people in the city, it was assumed that he voted Republican in state and national contests. Among those strongly supporting the plan was Councilman Antrim Heald, one of the few Democrats ever elected to the Council. Heald was a planing mill owner and a leading figure in the local Democratic organization. Widely-respected, Heald was not connected with the Lemon Street group, although one of the leaders of that group remained active in the Democratic organization and presumably helped to get votes for Democratic candidates in elections.

It was believed by some of the leading supporters of the council-manager plan that during the 1950s the leaders of the Lemon Street group found the existence of a city manager a threat to their continued influence in local government—particularly in the placement of protégés. Hence it was believed by the council-manager adherents that any event that appeared to embarrass the manager or hinder the success of centralized management in local government had been caused by the secret manipulations of the Lemon Street Gang. It appeared to some outsiders that by the mid-1950s the Lemon Street Gang had lost influence and, to some extent, had lost interest in municipal affairs. The movement of some of the group's members to higher echelons of government, the increasing age of those who remained, and the fact that city jobs were no longer as highly sought after as they had been during the Depression were all reasons for less intense involvement in local affairs. But when they wanted to, the remaining Lemon Street men could produce votes and could use extensive personal connections. And there was some evidence that the group was still sufficiently interested to fight selected rear-guard actions against the advance of unsympathetic city managers. Its members still mobilized occasionally to support certain Council candidates who were personally sympathetic, Republican or Democrat. And it resisted efforts of city managers and "good government" supporters who sought to turn certain elective posts such as city treasurer into positions filled by managerial appointment. Whatever it actually did or did not do, whether it was still intensely active or declining in influence and interest, or even whether it still existed as a group, the Lemon Street Gang was still seen in the 1950s as a potent harassing force, working secretly and deviously for patronage and against city manager government. It was seen this way only by those few insiders in Valley who supported manager government and who were sufficiently acquainted with local affairs to have heard of the Gang's alleged activity. Since the friends who reputedly made up the Lemon Street Gang never acknowledged publicly that they worked together, much less had an organization, it was hard to tell just what the truth was.

The Early Days of Manager Singer

JACK SINGER became Valley's third City Manager in July 1952. He was a lean six-footer in his mid-thirties who had formerly been manager of a smaller California city. He had become a manager by progressive municipal experience rather than by a university education for the profession. He had once served as an elected town clerk and had become quite an expert in sewage problems. (Valley was about to undertake a sewage project at the time.) Singer heard of the opening in Valley at a district meeting of city managers. Attracted by what he knew of the city, he applied even though the salary offered was below that prevailing in cities of similar size. He was selected.

In talking with his predecessor, Singer found that Valley's council-manager system was reasonably typical for California. As state law prescribed, the City Council had five members elected at large. The Manager served at the pleasure of the Council. At variance with orthodox theory, however, was the Manager's limited power over appointments of department heads other than the City Treasurer and City Clerk, who were elected. In Valley these key administrative appointments were recommended by the Manager but required Council confirmation. Dismissal of these officials was handled the same way. From the Model City Charter standpoint, these requirements represented a significant infringement on the Manager's "right to manage." But Valley's Manager did have considerable discretion in personnel matters because there were no formal merit system, no civil service tenure, no written appeals procedures, no provisions for probationary service. The lack of these formal procedures and regulations broadened the power of the Manager over city employees, but it also placed heavier burdens on him, since he had no laws with which to justify his actions.

Singer's early conversations also yielded some consistent opinions about the style of administration that Valley's leading citizens felt suitable for their town. He was given to understand that Valley had its own quiet ways of community living and that it would not accept as Manager anyone who pushed for changes too strongly or too rapidly. He learned that one of his predecessors had aroused much personal opposition by being too severe in his rigid devotion to efficiency and management principles. He had been gruff with citizens and allegedly had not treated people in a friendly manner. Irritation with him had become so strong that several Council candidates known to oppose him (but not the manager form of government) had been elected. He had thereupon resigned to take another post. Getting on well with people had always been one of Singer's strongest qualities, and he gathered that this had been one of the things that had been given weight in his selection.

Singer came to value highly the advice he received from former Mayor Cassius Bolt who had been instrumental in passage of the Council-Manager Ordinance in 1949. Bolt had retired as Mayor, but he was still well-informed. From Bolt and from Councilman George Simpson, a well-to-do orange grower and real estate man, Singer learned that the manager form of government was safely established in Valley but that it was not immune from attack if a Manager did not perform acceptably.

Councilman Simpson, who had played a considerable part in the hiring of Singer, had lived in Valley most of his life and came from a local citrus-owning family. He was widely respected on all sides as an able, intelligent man. He held all the essentials for full membership in the community: long residence, conservatism, Protestant church affiliation, and prosperity. He had a firm commitment to the manager form of government, and he was critical of some of the men connected with the Lemon Street Gang.

Singer also learned about Hector and Homer Smith, the brothers who were publisher and editor, respectively, of the *Times,* Valley's only daily newspaper. It had to compete for local circulation with the *Xerxes Clarion,* the nearby metropolitan daily that inserted a Valley page in papers delivered there. The Smith brothers had inherited the *Times* from their father. Hector, the publisher, was active in Republican politics in the city and the county. Homer, the editor, was nobody's man, but was willing to give advice, orally or editorially, about almost any community matter. The brothers' policy was that any local controversy should be thoroughly aired, if not inflated, in the *Times* more rapidly and more extensively than in the competing Xerxes daily.

The Kelly Affair

According to Singer's comments in 1960, many of the problems of the Valley government of the fifties arose from events of the past. Valley had been like many other small communities—a government of privilege. Building regulations had been winked at for friends; various public utilities, such as street paving and water lines, had been installed to help the "right" people; and other favors had been financed out of public funds. This same general pattern had been found in the Police Department. "I think it is fair to say," Singer said, "that the appointment of Chief Jason Kelly in 1951 marked the first time that the law was *really* enforced in Valley."

Chief Kelly's appointment in 1951 had followed a heated community controversy about the effectiveness of the police. On that occasion hearings before the Council had been held, and the previous Chief had resigned. Some insiders alleged that he had been too susceptible to the wishes of the Lemon Street Gang. There was internal dissension, several policemen had resigned, and, said the *Times,* "public confidence had been shaken."

The new Chief brought a spirit of friendliness to the Valley police operation. "A good-natured Irishman," Kelly, who had retired as a Lieutenant from the force of the city of North Beach, particularly wooed the downtown business community and regularly dropped into the stores of local merchants to exchange pleasantries. When Singer took over as City Manager several months later, he and Kelly became fast friends. They mixed socially and were regular golf competitors at the country club. As Kelly made friends in the community and with top management, his Police Department settled into an easy routine. Kelly himself was not demanding. "There's enough sordidness in police work without making it tough on the boys," he once commented. He joked with his secretary, other girls in the office, and the members of the thirty-man force; and he found little interest or enthusiasm for the paper work of the operation.

Into this good-natured environment, however, trouble finally descended. It came not from the community but from some of the members of the Department, including the Deputy Chief. They criticized the "country club atmosphere," raised questions about the Chief's alleged relationships with his secretary, and charged that he was not giving full time to his job. These accusations were ultimately brought to public attention through two members of the Council in the late fall of 1954. The Chief first resigned, then agreed to stay when City Manager Singer's investigations led him to conclude that the attacks had been inspired by a few men in the Department. And behind these men, Singer felt sure, stood the Lemon Street Gang.

Singer and some councilmen, including Simpson, believed that the men who had instigated the charges against Kelly had been protégés of the Gang. Some of them had consulted with one of the best-known members of the Gang about their complaints and about how to present their charges. The two councilmen who had introduced the charges were also believed to be close to the Lemon Street group. One was Joe Rodriguez, the first Mexican-American and the first Catholic to serve on Valley's Council. Born in the Mexican-American section, he had moved to the richer south side. Rodriguez was a complicated person. He had a law degree, had been a school teacher, and was an escrow officer in a large Xerxes firm. Politically liberal, Rodriguez had generally allied himself with the interests of the less well-to-do and the less powerful in the community. Yet he was a registered Republican. Rodriguez' election in 1954 had caused some surprise. He had been supported strongly by a principal member of the Lemon Street Gang, who had been a personal friend of his father. Rodriguez had made much in his campaign of the fact that he was a World War II veteran. Soon after his election he became a critic of Manager Singer, whom he considered ineffective and "always doing what the downtown businessmen wanted."

The Councilman who had joined with Rodriguez in introducing the police charges against Chief Kelly was Mayor Crispin Lloyd, believed by Councilman Simpson and some others to have won a Council seat in 1952 because of the support of the Lemon Street Gang. Lloyd worked as a handyman in a local store.

Rodriguez and Lloyd were regarded by some local observers as two councilmen who were opposed to domination of city affairs by the Manager or by the well-to-do families of the south side. Often opposed to them were Simpson and Councilman Frank Jones. Jones was one of the largest property owners in the downtown business area. The fifth man on the Council was Ralph Jennings, professor of political science at the local college, whose faculty he had joined in 1949. Jones, Rodriguez, and Jennings had all been elected for four-year terms in April 1954. A Democrat and a liberal, Jennings, like Rodriguez, had run well in the public housing area, but he had received a good number of votes on both sides of town. He supported the council-manager system, but had voted with Rodriguez to elect Lloyd Mayor, while Simpson and Jones had abstained. Jennings saw himself as the "swing man" on the Council, with Rodriguez and Lloyd on one side and Simpson and Jones on the other. Jennings had not heard of the Lemon Street Gang until he became a Councilman. As time went on, he developed an increasing respect for Councilman Simpson, despite the latter's conservatism.

When Manager Singer opposed accepting the resignation of Chief Kelly at the meeting at which Lloyd and Rodriguez introduced the police statement of charges, both councilmen sought to override his suggestion. Nevertheless, the City Manager stood his ground, rejected the Chief's resignation, and stoutly defended Kelly. By a four-to-one vote, the Council went along with the Manager in refusing the resignation.

Shortly thereafter the Deputy Chief was demoted to Lieutenant and at least two other officers were fired. These actions against the individuals who were presumably the central figures in the attack on the Chief caused more disquiet in the community. It could not be ignored by the Council. At the insistence of Lloyd and Rodriguez, joined by a number of citizens including one of the Lemon Street leaders, the Council finally agreed to an investigation. The hearings were closed, but the press was invited and permitted to report in detail. One of the Lemon Street men contributed to pay for a lawyer for the discharged and demoted policemen. A citizens committee was also appointed to play a watchdog role and insure that procedures at the hearings were fair to both sides.

In the newspapers the community read of (1) the Deputy Chief's withdrawal of his original charges, (2) accusations that some officers had sought to force the Chief's secretary to lie about the closeness of her relationship with her boss, (3) allegations that the Chief's accusers had planned all succession arrangements favorable to themselves once the Chief had been forced to resign, and (4) evidences that the Chief had apparently not run a tight administrative organization. Emotion in the community was very high; the City Manager, his behavior, and the form of government he personified did not escape criticism from the defenders of the discharged policemen. It was clear that Singer had trusted Chief Kelly to run his own department. The Manager had not known much about what was happening in the Police Department until the investigation. (From this point on, he kept a close eye on it.) At the conclusion of the hearings one of the Council members emphasized that the only question with which the legislative body had to deal was whether it had lost confidence in the Manager because of the dismissals and other problems in the Police Department. If so, he should be fired. Otherwise the Council should sustain the Manager. In the vote that followed four councilmen supported Manager Singer. The fifth abstained.

On the surface the police problem was settled. Yet the effects remained. There were people in the community who felt that the prevarications of police officers could cut both ways. Was it not just as possible that the Deputy Chief and the other police officers had capitulated to the Manager and to the other leaders in order to hold their jobs?

Four months after what the *Times* called the "marathon police investigation," Chief Kelly left Valley to accept a position as Chief of Security in a private industrial organization at "twice the pay." His resignation was reluctantly accepted by City Manager Singer as of March 15, 1955, and the Manager's search for a new Chief began.

The Search for a New Chief

WILLIAM BLACK was a retired Lieutenant Commander in the Navy. In the spring of 1955 he was teaching at the University of Southern California, as a one year replacement for the University's professor of police administration who was in Iran. However, Black did not plan to stay in teaching and was interested in engaging in more active police work. When the Director of the University's Delinquency Control Institute told him about the opening for a Police Chief in Valley, Black was interested. He immediately dispatched a letter to Valley expressing his availability and thus became one of about thirty applicants for the post, which paid approximately $550 a month. The letter in which City Manager Singer acknowledged Black's application reported that there were no major police problems. Particularly striking to Black was the statement that "the present department is in top working efficiency, as the former Chief retired voluntarily to go into private industry." The letter, mimeographed and obviously sent to all applicants, was dated March 23, 1955.

By the time Black had heard about the opening and made his application, City Manager Singer had taken a number of steps to fill the vacancy created by Kelly's resignation. First he reviewed the personnel situation in the Department and decided that none of the officers in the organization "looked too strong." Since he was under no pressure to appoint a local person, Singer determined to recruit a new Chief on a California-wide basis. The absence of a formal civil service system meant that there was nothing to block such a recruiting program. Singer inserted an announcement of the vacancy in *Western City Magazine,* and wrote to a number of cities in California soliciting applications.

Because he recognized the appointment of a new Chief to be one of the most important steps he had taken in his more than four years in Valley, Singer was determined to make the selection system as foolproof as possible. Therefore, he appointed a Screening Board composed of the City Manager, the Assistant Administrative Officer, and the Chief of Police of three different cities in Southern California. Of the thirty applicants for the position, ten were interviewed by this Board at a meeting attended by Singer. Although several chiefs of smaller departments were among those screened, the professor from USC, William Black, was the unanimous choice of the Board. Singer, too, was greatly impressed. Black had strong recommendations from the University. He "interviewed well," and he seemed to be just the kind of person needed to compensate for Kelly's laxity in administrative routine. While the Manager felt some hesitation about Black because he had not had actual experience as a Chief of Police previously, members of the Board agreed that the professor's technical competence outweighed his lack of experience and made him first choice. Singer decided to recommend the appointment, which was tantamount to selection. Council confirmation had become, as in many other centralized management cities, largely perfunctory. Despite all the previous police problems, Council members did not actively involve themselves in the selection process for the new Chief. Jack Singer was being given a chance to run his own show without interference from the Council. Black was "his" man.

The new Valley Chief of Police first heard of his appointment in a telephone call from a reporter on the *Los Angeles Examiner,* asking for a comment. Then Manager Singer called Black to say that he had been hired and to ask when he could start. The date agreed upon was

June 13, 1956. After the hiring, Black journeyed to Valley to meet the Council. It was a friendly occasion. As Black recalled, he was particularly impressed with the words of Mayor Crispin Lloyd, who said, "We have made you Chief because we want a firm law enforcement program." It was the kind of statement Black was pleased to hear. It became a charter for his future actions. Crew-cut and muscular, active in amateur wrestling, Black had about his whole being an air of authority. He also had a strong commitment to the professionalization of the police and felt that too frequently police officers themselves failed to pay a proper respect to the important work they had undertaken. He viewed the police function as important to the maintenance of an organized society, as technically demanding, and as requiring the highest moral and intellectual integrity. William Black was now anxious to prove himself equal to the task.

The first day on the job, June 13, Black spent with Manager Singer, who also emphasized that he wanted a rigorous enforcement program. Much of the time on that day was spent in discussing the people in the city government and in the community. Singer for his part believed that he was introducing the newcomer to the mysteries and subtleties of the city government. He was anxious to keep Black from making an early slip. But as Black recalled the talk, the Manager produced a picture of the members of the Department taken in 1954 and talked about each man on the force. Particularly striking to Black was the fact that a number of the men in the photograph were no longer in the city's employment. At this time, he had little knowledge of the Kelly affair, and he was struck by the high attrition rate. Black says he left the meeting somewhat worried. He felt that Singer demonstrated a "suspicion of everyone who was not on his side."

The Rift Between Black and Singer

WILLIAM BLACK was Police Chief in Valley for just about a year. Nearly every event during that year was seen and interpreted differently by Black and Singer, and the passage of more years has not made any easier the assembly of a set of facts acceptable to both sides. From the day of their first meeting in June 1955 a gulf widened between the City Manager and his new Police Chief despite the fact that both men had every reason to desire a successful and satisfying relationship.

Singer's Background

Jack Singer was very familiar with the ways of the small town. He had had several years of successful experience as a Manager and as an elected City Clerk. Valley embodied a style of life he accepted, enforced, and understood.

Singer's particular view of the responsibility of the Manager seemed to be rooted more in the concept of responding to community expectations and wishes than to hewing rigidly to city manager professionalism. He saw the Manager as the *interpreter* of citizen and Council desires, which he was obliged to satisfy. This orientation, along with his background, led Singer to be more sensitive to the play of forces of power and influence than most city managers might have been. On almost any matter, Singer was acutely aware of his friends and enemies, and of the forces at play. He had, for example, argued strongly and successfully for Council action to carry out more street improvements in the poorer sections of town, and to do it wholly at city expense (with no street assessments), an unusual thing in Valley. On another matter, when a planning officer had aroused protests for pushing a plan some groups thought too rigorous and advanced, Singer had ordered the plan modified so that it was less perfect from a planner's standpoint but more acceptable to those affected. Since his arrival in 1952, Singer had been highly successful in carrying through city planning and capital development programs. He won community approval for such efforts, which were often neglected in other cities of Valley's size.

Within the city administrative hierarchy, Singer believed strongly in the Manager's right to manage. He expected to be held responsible for the functioning of the various departments, and he demanded the authority necessary to meet these obligations. This meant that each department head was distinctly his subordinate and that it was the Manager's prerogative to take whatever fact-finding steps appeared necessary to check on performance in these various units. Nevertheless, the Manager and the employees generally had gotten on well together. On the whole, Singer was proud of the governmental performance of Valley. Despite the events of the previous fall, he did not believe that there was a "mess" in the Police Department, but he knew that the Department was still much in the public eye.

Personally, Singer was happy in Valley. He liked the people and the community. His job, though carrying a compensation somewhat under that paid in other similar-size cities, still returned him a comfortable income. It was a pleasant life which he, his wife, and school-age children enjoyed. He belonged to the country club and to one of the Protestant congregations. Only a very substantial increase in salary could have moved him to another city.

Black's Background

Black's experience and outlook were different from Singer's. His police experience had come in Evanston, Illinois—some of it while studying at Northwestern University. He had had a long career in Navy security. While he had served in the Navy, on the Evanston Police Department, and in academic positions at Northwestern and at the University of Southern California, there nevertheless had been the tangible unifying thread of law enforcement. It was to the profession of law enforcement and its values that Black felt his basic responsibility, not to the city. As he explained later to an interviewer:

> We in police worry so much about how people are going to feel about what we do that we lose sight of our basic responsibility.
>
> In Valley there was a disrespect for the law. Thus the basic problem was the rebuilding of that respect for the laws of the community and the enforcers of those laws; then would have been the appropriate time to worry about public relations. It is also my conviction that in order to engage in law enforcement you must at times be harsh; but that doesn't mean it is ever necessary to be nasty.

This sense of the profession also seemed to permeate Black's perception of the Police Chief's role in council-manager government. As he saw his responsibility, it was to give the community the best possible law enforcement, judged by his professional standards. Political or community squabbles were matters for higher echelons.

Emerging Differences

Chief Black had been on the job only a few days when he began to see things that upset him. Within the Department, he found no written rules and regulations, inefficient procedures, and oddly arranged shifts. When he asked why things were being done in a certain way, Black said the men had no good answer. In addition he felt that morale was poor, the men inadequately trained, and their general appearance not up to his standards. Nor was Black satisfied with the deployment of the men. He found that the small Department was still using two men in patrol cars in the predominantly residential town. To Black this was a particularly indicative sign of ineffective management. Though a lot of old-timers still preferred two-man cars to the one-man variety, Black laid this resistance to a lack of knowledge of modern police doctrine. Thus the use of the old system in Valley not only revealed a great waste of manpower to him; it also meant that the Department had not had imaginative and progressive leadership in the past. For this failure he blamed not only the former Chief but also City Manager Singer.

In the community as a whole the general disregard of the law that was most striking to Black was in the traffic field. (Black's graduate work had made him something of a specialist in traffic problems.) "Nobody paid any attention to stop signs," he recalled. Speed limits were not observed, and there was no selective enforcement in those areas of the city where accidents were most likely to happen. Parking signs and restrictions were not properly obeyed. A good share of the central district's parking spaces were occupied by local merchants and professional people who "nickeled the machines to death."

Black's answer to these problems was tighter enforcement all along the line. He took a personal hand in sharpening procedures and organization, spending the greater part of his first ninety days writing a policy manual, the first the force had had. There were reassignments, new training programs, re-design of forms, and many other changes.

As a result of Black's policies, the men on the force began to hand out an increasing number of citations for parking and traffic violations. The effect of this stringency was magnified when the *Valley Times* began to print a column listing the names and addresses of those who had received tickets. The irritation of citizens at getting citations for driving and parking practices that had previously not drawn police action was exacerbated when their names and offenses were printed in the *Times* for their neighbors and all others to see. Black publicly congratulated the *Times* for initiating the column. As Black's campaign for better parking and traffic enforcement continued, some policemen carried tape measures and allegedly used them when issuing citations for drivers who parked a greater number of inches from the curb than the city ordinance permitted.

The Chief found another practice he opposed: the issuance of special treatment cards or badges to influential citizens. A request for such an item was made shortly after he came on the job, and he discovered that the practice had long been followed in Valley. Badges or cards had been issued since the twenties to large fruit growers to give them some authority in policing their groves, some of which were in remote sections. Black refused to issue more cards and called the others in. "In two months we picked up about 100. I don't know how many more we didn't get," he recalled.

While thus busily engaged, Black found he had no time to follow his predecessor's practice of visiting the merchants in the downtown business section. Nor did he have an interest in doing so. "I personally think the former Chief engaged in these kinds of activities to the detriment of law enforcement in Valley," Black said later. Some of the downtown businessmen were displeased with Black's policy of strict enforcement of parking meter regulations.

Criticism Reaches the City Manager

Criticisms of Black's approach to his new job almost immediately reached City Manager Singer. Irritation was expressed that he was not a friendly, jocular sort. More indignant were those who had run afoul of the new look in Valley's law enforcement activities. Most significant, however, were charges of increasing belligerence and antagonism on the part of police officers. Singer reported that much of the criticism was directed squarely at Chief Black, who was said to have been stopping people himself. He was accused of having an approach to violators which "was sadistic, officious, and out of proportion to the violations committed."[2] To these attacks Singer at first paid little attention; but the increasing volume of complaints caused him to move to the defense of the Chief by personally urging press and public leaders to help him across a "difficult period of adjustment."

Much of the difficulty, Singer felt, was that Black had not brought the community along with him. A new regime of law enforcement had suddenly descended on Valley without warning. In Singer's mind it was the Chief's responsibility to "sell" his program. He felt it was a mistake for Black to spend his time in his office. He urged

2 On this point Black has commented: "My officers leaned over backward and were so nice it was almost sickening to watch and listen to. *But* those who had previously talked their way out of arrests or used their influence could no longer do so. When this happened to them for the first time, they reported the officer as belligerent and antagonistic whereas he was nothing of the kind. Several investigations on my part proved this point. In one case an officer said, "No madam" and "Yes madam" only. She reported him to Singer as insulting. She treated the incident as a light joke until she saw she was going to get a ticket for a 50 mph violation; then she became indignant and insulting. To the law violator it might appear that the officer was sadistic, officious, and out of proportion to the violation committed, but it is the result of losing the immunity from arrest that caused the great flareup among a small group of special privileged people. With regard to traffic violations, I have seen every type kill an individual; therefore it is proper and justifiable to treat each violation the same, but with courtesy and firmness."

him to invite and accept speaking engagements, which the Chief said he did at the rate of two to three a week. Singer has reported he did not question the policy of firm law enforcement Black had inaugurated.

Even at this early stage, communications between the two men seemed to have been strained by two events. The first had to do with an order issued by Black prohibiting officers from discussing police business with anyone. This, he said, was a standard procedure for most police agencies and was included in his manual of rules and regulations which the City Manager approved. The intent was to keep data on investigations restricted to as few people as possible and was not really directed toward administrative matters. Insofar as the councilmen and the Manager were concerned, Black said he instructed his men to answer any questions but to let him know about such conversations, a procedure he felt was normal for any organization which had a formal chain of command.

The order was perceived in quite different terms by Singer. Since the Kelly incident of the previous year, Singer had taken a greater interest in the operation of the Police Department and had come to know a number of the policemen. Soon, however, he found that these men refused to talk to him, even those of long acquaintance. He was told Black had issued an order that the men were not to talk to Singer. If they did, they must report the conversation back to the Chief. The order irritated Singer greatly. Yet nothing was ever said to Black, and he did not realize how a directive which he considered routine had antagonized his superior.

At about the same time another incident occurred. In this instance it was Chief Black who felt he had been "used" by the City Manager to avoid political fire. Among his other duties, Black was the city's official poundmaster. It was a nominal title because one man in the employment of the Department did all the work. Up to that time dogs had run relatively free in Valley, and a considerable problem had been created. At the request of the Council, City Manager Singer drafted an animal regulation ordinance and gave it to the Police Chief to introduce at the Council meeting. He said it was within the police responsibility, and the proposed law would perhaps have more acceptance coming from that source. Although he knew that dog laws were almost always controversial, the Chief agreed, because "I really thought it was a good thing."

Then, "all hell broke loose." The citizens of Valley who had let their dogs run free for many years were up in arms. They accused the Chief of something worse than inhumanity—a hatred of dogs. "I took to riding the streets of Valley with my big setter to prove to people that I really loved animals." After much furor, the effort to pass the ordinance was abandoned. What upset Black was that never during the controversy did the Manager make a major public defense of the proposed ordinance.

Meanwhile, Black was making speeches as the Manager had suggested, but they seemed only to deepen the problem. Members of his audiences charged that the newcomer was too free in his criticism of their community. Although Black declares he had never used the word, a story spread among parents and school officials that he had typified Valley youth as "rotten."[3] His appearances before the local civic associations and clubs, according to the editor of the *Times,* probably did more to destroy his support in the substantial segments of the community than any other single factor.

Singer Gets More Complaints

By fall, three to four months after Chief Black had come to Valley, Singer was getting so many complaints that he had to take them seriously. There were many besides those who complained of harsh personal treatment by police enforcing traffic violations. A number of middle-class mothers told the Manager that Black's policies were making their children speak of policemen as enemies rather than as friends. They expressed concern that their sons were talking of stoning police cars, and compared this to the pre-Black days when, they said, police in patrol cars would often stop and chat with teen-agers, even those who had been in minor scrapes with the law. The

[3] Black has commented: "This was one of the false stories spread about town by the 'Hate Black' group. I never said this. Actually the man who started the rumor was never at the speech where it was supposed to have been said. He had been arrested previously for speeding—his first time as a local bigshot and was unable to get the officer to let him go."

mothers attributed the trouble to the tough manner used by the police with teen-agers since Black had assumed office.

Another complaint, Singer recalled some years later, had come from the officer who dealt with juvenile delinquents. Several months after Black arrived, this officer reported to Singer that the load of juvenile offenses was rising enormously. This was attributed to the increased stringency of police enforcement.

Singer also received complaints from local insurance men (who were often also realtors and who were one of the occupational groups active in following and influencing city affairs). Black, the Manager recalled later, "had tangled with insurance men who were trying to get the facts on traffic accidents. They needed information for their clients and for their reports to their companies. This sort of information is routinely made available to properly qualified investigators as provided in the Vehicle Code." Black, the insurance men had complained, had arbitrarily decided to withhold some of the data from them. Black's position was that certain items in the reports should be confidential; these were the things he withheld.

Singer also stated later that he had received some reports that Black had had difficulties with other police jurisdictions. The County Under-Sheriff had paid an unannounced courtesy call shortly after Black had arrived in Valley, but Black had been too busy to see him. A school safety patrol had taken the number of a private car that had gone through a crossing zone near the high school. The teacher in charge had forwarded the license number to Sacramento. It had turned out to be the number of a car of a member of the force, and this had led to Black being cautioned by a member of the State Highway Patrol. Black had complained to higher headquarters of the Highway Patrol, denying the charge and criticizing the pettiness of the action.

Another complaint, Singer recalled later, came from the parents of two girls of high school age who were exceeding the speed limit in town one night and were chased by a pair of off-duty policemen who were riding in a car with out-of-state license plates. The policemen sought to force the girls' car to the curb. The girls, allegedly not realizing these were policemen, went even faster and drove toward the deserted areas of town before they were stopped. Their girls, the parents complained to Singer, had been frightened almost to the point of hysteria.

These incidents and others arising from tougher parking and traffic enforcement came to Singer with increasing frequency. In the late fall or early winter, Singer recalls, a former Democratic councilman asked him how long he was going to keep the Police Chief. He suggested that if Singer delayed getting rid of Black, the public would force the Council to act. He allegedly told Singer that if Singer waited too long, public resentment might even cost the Manager his own job.

Black's View

If Valley's problem of adjustment to Black was difficult, so was Black's adjustment to it. He saw himself making compromises difficult for a man of his professional background and ethics to accept. There was the failure to book the homosexual son of a prominent citizen. "After the withdrawal of that complaint," he said, "I felt like I had a sin on my soul. So far as I know, that man is still walking the streets and is not even registered as a sex deviate. Whatever harm befalls him or others, I will certainly have to assume part of the guilt."

In another instance the wife of a prominent official of a nearby newspaper was charged with hit and run. Black said she had knocked down a brick wall with her auto and left the scene of the accident. Her license number was traced, however; and her attorney came to Valley to make a settlement. Black refused to negotiate. Later that same day, Black said he got a phone call from the City Manager asking him to delay arrest until the following day.[4] By that time the warrant had been withdrawn by the court and the Chief was left powerless in the situation. He never said anything further about it, but he often asked himself what would have happened if the offender had been a Mexican, rather than the wife of a prominent newspaper man. As one observer put it,

[4] One Councilman disagreed strongly with the Black story. He has noted: "This is Black's version, and an example of giving a sinister import to a fairly simple matter. Black considered any request for information to be an attempt to intervene."

Black had difficulty learning that there are "somebodies and nobodies" in every community. To that Black has agreed.

In January 1956 occurred the "Mr. X" case, which later received considerable attention because of its relationship to compromise and the community elite. Mr. X was a well-to-do citrus man, over sixty, and long influential in Valley. He had the same last name as one of the councilmen. It was alleged that he was driving drunk, had turned a corner and run head on into another automobile. As Black later reported, "Mr. X was drunk. He did not know who I was that night. He said he would get my job for this. He threw money around the street and said he ran Valley. . . ." Actually the arresting officer had been fearful that he was a councilman and had called both the Manager and the Chief when he got him to the station. Black says Manager Singer took a look in the window, said, "I don't know the man. . . . Do what you want with him." As a consequence the Chief gave the order to "treat him like any other drunk." At midnight an attorney for the drunken man came to the jail and asked to post bond for his release. While it was against departmental policy to free booked people before the following morning, the Sergeant was more aware of the standing of the man in the community than Singer or Black and so released him. Black said later that if he had been at the station, he would not have permitted the Sergeant to take such an action. At any rate, Black said that the next morning at 8:00 he got a call from the City Manager wanting to know what could be done about the case. According to Black, a city Councilman was reported as interested in seeing that the charges were either reduced or quashed. However, Black told Singer that the case was already out of his hands, charges having been filed, bail posted, and the man released. It was now up to the courts. The Chief thought that Singer was clearly irritated by this departure from routine and indicated he thought the steps had been taken to thwart any "arrangements." The man was found guilty and fined $350. Later, in public hearings, Singer disputed the Black version and called it a "classic distortion." He reported

> I was met in the parking lot and told that—sure enough, the man they held was not Councilman X. I was told also that the "Mr. X" they had in custody had been picked up drunk, abusive, and most certainly in no condition to drive. I told them to lock him up, and I drove home and went to bed. The next morning the man's family, worried and concerned, made inquiries. Among others, they asked Councilman Jones to find out what had happened to the man. Jones asked me, I got the information, and Jones relayed the facts to the family. There was no discussion concerning the disposition or handling of the case. To this day I have never met or talked to—nor could I recognize on the street—the man who was arrested and who—the next morning—pleaded guilty and paid a fine.

An incident occurring in March again dramatized the gulf growing between Manager Singer and his Chief. It involved a relatively minor traffic case in which the wife of a well-to-do professional man was arrested for speeding. Infuriating to her, however, was the fact that the citation was written outside her home. By the next morning she and her husband had called a number of neighbors, with the result that a delegation visited the Manager the following day to urge the Chief's resignation on the grounds that his men were rude and arrogant. "I was called into the City Manager's office," Black later reported, and "he was very much upset. He said he might have to ask me to resign. 'I had a committee visit me,' he went on, 'and they are upset about your enforcement program.'" Black said he thought the charge was probably untrue and asked that he be permitted to talk to the woman before any decisions were made. As a result of a later conversation with the woman, the Chief concluded that she was angry simply because she got a legitimate ticket. He informed Singer that he would take no disciplinary action against the officer. Although the Manager said nothing more, Black felt that his superior was not happy with the decision.

The Peters Case

However, it was the Peters case, which occurred later in March, that caused Singer to decide to dismiss Black. A police car in pursuit of an automobile speeding through town at seventy miles per hour collided with a vehicle driven by elderly Phil Peters, who was thrown on the pavement and killed. The police car was running without flashing light or siren, which was a violation of a state law specifying the use of such equipment "when necessary" in exceeding the speed limit. The police officer, said Black, had fastened his safety belt but had not yet had time to open up the various warning devices on the car. At the Coroner's inquest these facts were laid before the jury; and it was also discovered that the elderly man's driver's license had been suspended two years earlier. The jury concluded the police officer was not guilty of negligence. Valley's insurance carriers, however, did settle any possible claims by making a payment of about $3,000 to the widow.

During the Coroner's inquest on the Peters case, an official in the District Attorney's office told Singer that Black had been angry and had wanted to testify in the hearing that the officer was simply following the policy of the Department. Since such a policy would have been in direct violation of the state law, the official told the Manager, Valley would have been liable for a huge damage suit. This report was a shock to Singer, and a conference with Black on the matter did not ease his mind. As a result the Manager himself issued an order requiring the Department to conform to the state law. Singer later wrote on the importance of this incident to his final decision,

> I maintained hope that Black still could continue as chief and that in time he might come to wear this authority a little more comfortably, both for himself and for the people he was brought here to protect. But suddenly it was demonstrated that the community was actually threatened by the attitudes he held toward his job.
>
> I refer to the tragic death of Mr. Phil Peters out on Brookside Ave. Two conclusions were inescapable concerning the way that Black intended to carry out his job. One had to do with the quality of his judgment, and the other again—with his real attitude toward the citizenry of Valley. Under Black's direct and personal instruction, the police vehicle was violating both the laws of the State of California and the tenets of generally accepted good police practice. And in so doing was creating as great—if not a greater hazard to life and property than was the vehicle being pursued.
>
> Section 454 of the California Vehicle Code provides that whenever conditions required that a police vehicle be operated in excess of legal speed limits that the operator shall use both his red light and siren. Black had ordered that neither be used until the officer had clocked the speeder. Had Black, himself, been driving the fatal police car, he could and should have been booked for manslaughter.
>
> In discussing with him the possible liability the city had incurred by reason of this incident, Black's position was indefensible. The substance of his reaction is covered by the phrase, "Nothing to get excited about —if you're going to get convictions, you're going to have to take chances and somebody may get killed."[5]
>
> *As I sat there listening to him talk, I was forced into the realization that the city could no longer be exposed to the threat imposed by Black's inexperience, bad judgment and his persistent refusal to recognize human considerations in carrying out his job.* [Emphasis added.]

Chief Black has disagreed with Singer's understanding of the events surrounding the Peters case. He has denied, in the first place, the truth of the story told by the official of the District Attorney's office to Singer. Furthermore, he has declared he never issued such an order to the Department. "For heaven's sake, I certainly knew what the State law was," he has commented. He has pointed out that it was his custom to put all general Department orders in writing and that no such command was ever issued.

At the Coroner's hearing, Black said, the District Attorney had asked the defending police officer, "Do you usually run without a red light?" The man answered, "Yes, as do most other Departments." Chief Black said he was much concerned that his officer was leaving the impression that this was Departmental policy, whereas he was really trying to indicate that practice almost universally did not accord with the state policy. Therefore Black got up and asked the District Attorney, "Would you like to have me tell you what the policy is?" The District Attorney said no, and Black made no further remarks.

Problems of Communication

With so many points of conflict, it would seem appropriate to describe what the Manager did to alert Black to his deficiencies. Even here, however, there is dispute between Singer and Black. The Manager has declared that he tried regularly to counsel Black in meetings occurring

[5] Black's comment: "Here is what I really said. 'We could expect further and more deaths in the future if proper enforcement tactics are not carried out.' . . . I never said any such thing [as statement in the text above] to Singer; a man would be crazy to say anything like that . . ."

two or three times a week and lasting 30 to 45 minutes. The Manager did not feel, however, that the Chief ever really listened with an open or receptive mind. Whenever he raised questions or complaints, Singer said, the Chief either denied them or would retort, "Well, you either want a good law enforcement program or you don't." Furthermore, Singer felt that in their conversations Black never perceived that he might have made a mistake. The Manager kept no record of these conversations and was unable later to indicate precisely what was discussed on the various occasions.

Totally different was Black's perception of his contacts with Singer. He said that most of their business was not conducted orally but by written memo. The Chief revealed he also felt ill at ease in talking to the Manager because he kept a recording device in his office. The Manager had told him, Black said, that the recorder could be set in operation without a warning signal. Seldom, said Black, did they discuss the way he was performing his job, although in March 1956, after the angry housewife's delegation had paid its visit, Singer had told him, "These people have put so much pressure on me, I am afraid I am going to have to ask you to resign." Yet even in this situation, Black did not feel that he was being given any clear picture of where he might be making his mistakes. This, incidentally, was a point that Black made continually later in the controversy. He said that he had not knowingly disobeyed any of Singer's orders. If he had done the wrong thing, it was only because the Manager had not made clear to him what the policy was.

To some degree, at least, the channels through which City Manager Singer received his information affected communications between the two men. In almost every instance Singer had to rely on reports, rather than first-hand observations. These came from citizens, school officials, realtors, other policing agencies, and some members of the Police Department. It is possible, as Black contended, that these complainants were not in all cases unbiased; and it is also to be noted that the statements from other governmental agencies, such as the schools, could not be verified officially. These people refused to state their accusations publicly, a problem which became quite acute for Singer later in the case. As a consequence it was someone else's word against the Chief's. From Black's perspective, each of these reports meant that he was "called on the carpet" and decisions made before the facts were in. He did not think he was given the backing a subordinate might expect from his chief. The City Manager had so little confidence in him, or was so fearful of a mistake (and Black thought this was the real problem), that the Chief was never given the discretion and freedom from interference the job required.

Except for parking, where Singer did urge some relaxation, the level of enforcement was apparently never raised as an issue between the two men. Nevertheless, Black always felt this was the heart of the problem. He saw himself as a professional law officer—one who put effective law enforcement above all other considerations, and who, in so doing, inevitably had to alienate certain segments of the community. That was the price to be paid for a program that benefited the citizenry as a whole. Singer contended, on the other hand, that the problem lay not in *what* was being done but *how* it was being done. "You can have firmness with courtesy," as he put it. The Department led by Black was playing "cop" too much, and people were resentful not so much of the tickets they got as the way they were treated. Thus the grounds upon which Singer based the dismissal were elusive and difficult to pin down. Black's technical competence, industry, dedication, and general ability were not questioned; he was really not charged with insubordination. In Singer's view, Black's sin lay in certain subtle factors of attitude, approach and judgment, that distorted an otherwise sound program.

In his own mind, Singer was certain that dismissal of Black was the only answer. But how effectively could he communicate his reasoning to the City Council and the public? It was a question that began to answer itself the day William Black was dismissed.

The Leak About Black's Dismissal

WHILE THE CITY COUNCIL listened to a discussion of a supermarket re-zoning issue on the evening of May 1, 1956, Manager Singer's mind was already dwelling on what lay ahead that night. He had made up his mind to dismiss Police Chief Black and to ask the councilmen for their approval.

Singer's timing, which was later criticized, may have been connected with the fact that the April Council elections and the Council's election of the new Mayor were now over.

Singer had been particularly heartened by the April elections for two Council seats. George Simpson, his firm supporter, had been swept back into office, and his tireless antagonist, former Mayor Crispin Lloyd, had suffered a humiliating defeat. At the first Council meeting after the election, Simpson had been chosen as the new Mayor. Elected in place of Lloyd was a jeweler from the downtown business center, Andy Carter. He was so new on the Council—and to municipal government generally—that it was unlikely that he would raise any questions. The three continuing members of the Council, who had been elected to four-year terms in 1954, included Jones, the big property owner who usually voted with Simpson, and Jennings, the Democratic college professor, who had proved reasonable and who supported the manager system. That left the third continuing member, Joe Rodriguez, who had opposed Singer on the Kelly affair and who had never masked his disapproval of the Manager and many of his policies. Singer, like Simpson, thought he saw behind Rodriguez and the defeated Lloyd the influences of the Lemon Street Gang.

After the regular meeting Singer asked the five councilmen to go to his office for a closed personnel meeting.[6] Singer's expression, recalled one Councilman, indicated that he had a serious problem on his mind, but none of the legislators knew what it was. After they sat down, the City Manager told them perturbedly that he wanted to fire Police Chief Black. He recounted in some detail the events and complaints that had led him to his decision. "I have tried everything conceivable," he reported. "I have held one conference after another and gotten nowhere. I can see no alternative but to ask Black for his resignation. I want you to know about this and the reasons because I am going to need your support." Singer then suggested that Black be given an opportunity to resign. If he did not, he would be dismissed.

Simpson, Jones, and Jennings had expected that such a recommendation might be coming but had not known when. Rodriguez did ask some questions. Most of the time, however, he stared at the table in front of him. The others were clearly unhappy. "The last thing we wanted," one recalled later, "was trouble in the Police Department." Singer then asked if he had the Council's support. Two or three said, "Well, if it has to be, it has to be." There was no formal vote, and Rodriguez did not register his specific disagreement with the tacit decision. Singer went on to say that Black was out of town for the week, and it was important that the meeting be held in strictest confidence until he had had a chance to see him. The Manager did not want it to appear that he was firing the Chief while he was away. There was no further comment on this strategy, and the meeting broke up shortly after midnight.

The newcomer, Councilman Carter, the downtown jeweler, was not taken entirely by surprise. He had noted that "Bill [Black] was never around the community . . . and we had been accustomed to a man that was a part of the town."[7] Carter also said that even in his short tenure he had

[6] Under California law, only meetings of legislators having to do with personnel matters may be closed to the public and press.

[7] Carter meant, presumably, that Black did not socialize much with the downtown merchants in the Kelly pattern. Black lived in Valley in a north side development.

had a number of complaints about Black's way of doing things. There was more than one manner of arresting a person, the new Councilman said, and Black could not do it "like a gentleman." Nevertheless, it "came as a jolt to me that Black was to be fired. I didn't think he had been given enough of a chance," he concluded.

One Councilman's View

Simpson, Jones, and Jennings had been in closer touch with City Manager Singer and were more familiar with the problem. One of them explained his general understanding of conditions at the time of the meeting with Singer in this way:

> After Black was appointed, he began a vigorous campaign of traffic enforcement and put much pressure on the men for arrests. Once he took us Councilmen on a tour of the station and showed us a chart of the number of arrests each officer was turning in weekly. We were given to understand that he expected them to come through with a certain amount each week.
>
> No one was really antagonistic to any part of Black's program. It was the extreme pettiness that got them down, for example, the carrying of a tape measure to check on the distance of cars from the curb. People got to feeling that if they were caught in a violation, they would really get the book thrown at them. Black used to cruise around himself and seemed to take great delight in hauling someone down and giving him a tongue lashing. A prominent minister told me he had gone through this, that Black had started out, "Haven't you got better sense. . . ."
>
> I was getting quite a few complaints, and it got to the point where people were asking, "How long are you going to keep this guy around here?" I think we all tried to defend him, saying we wanted vigorous law enforcement. We either took that position or we said nothing when the complaints were made to us.
>
> I believe, too, that we were all aware of these problems. Two or three months after Black arrived, I remember encountering Mayor Lloyd, who asked me, "Are you getting a lot of complaints about this new Chief?" I answered I was. Lloyd's comment was, "Jack Singer's really pulled a boner on this guy."
>
> Actually, the Council was not filled in on Singer's day-to-day problems with Black, nor what efforts he was making to solve them. We were aware, however, that the Manager was holding meetings with the Chief in an attempt to straighten him out. As to how he was going about this, I don't think we considered it our problem.[8]

Thus, as of 1:00 a.m. Wednesday, May 2, it appeared that Singer's proposal to dismiss the Police Chief would have the rather strong support of at least three members of the Council. One was disposed to go along with some misgivings, and only one might be in direct opposition. The Manager had not attempted to present a full dossier of facts on Black that night. He had relied on the councilmen's general knowledge of the Chief's behavior and had pointed out that some of the more important causes of dismissal involved information and complaints whose sources could not be publicly identified. There was not a great deal of concern at the time as to whether a good public case for the dismissal would have to be developed. It was apparently hoped that Black would take the easy course and resign.

Any possibility of a tidy handling of the affair, however, reckoned without the reaction of Councilman Rodriguez. Since he commuted to Xerxes, he did not talk often with the other councilmen or with the Manager; and though his colleagues insisted he had been present, he did not remember that the Manager had ever discussed his problems with the Council before. As a consequence, Rodriguez could not escape the feeling that the "whole thing had been caused by a couple of big guys being arrested." Secondly, he was perhaps more mindful than his colleagues of the public response to a dismissal without reasons given. "Personally," he said, "I thought it was only decency that Black be given a chance to speak."

Councilman Rodriguez first made known his strong feelings the next afternoon in a discussion with Mayor Simpson. He said then that he would have "no part in firing Black." The Mayor was conciliatory and unperturbed, Rodriguez recalled. He told Rodriguez, "Black will resign, and that will be all there is to it."

The *Times* Breaks the Story

At 10:00 the next morning (Thursday, May 3) Rodriguez got a call from the *Valley Times*. Was

[8] Chief Black declares that these charges are essentially untrue.

it true, a reporter asked, that Black was being dismissed as a result of the Manager's recommendation to the councilmen at the closed session Tuesday night? The indignant Rodriguez replied, "Yes." (The reporter did not tell Rodriguez where he had gotten his information. Singer and others later suspected that it had come from former Mayor Crispin Lloyd, the Manager's long-time critic, and that Lloyd might have heard of the dismissal originally in personal conversations with Rodriguez, his former ally on the Council.)

The *Times* published the story that afternoon. Councilman Rodriguez was quoted at length:

> The City Manager asked the Council to agree on two proposals. (1) To ask the Chief's resignation and (2) an outright firing backed by the council if the chief refused to resign.
>
> On the basis of the facts presented to us, I cannot see sufficient reason for the move. The reason given was "poor public relations" on the part of the chief, but no particular facts to substantiate these reasons were presented to the council.
>
> I was unaware of any problems in the Police Department until the personnel session last Tuesday, and can say I was definitely shocked.
>
> In my opinion the law enforcement program we now have is commendable in many ways. I understand the morale in the police department is now as high as it ever has been. . . .
>
> Chief Black was highly recommended by the city manager as to background, character, police knowledge, and personality. Now, less than a year later, we are informed things are not as they were supposed to be at that time.
>
> I, for one, do not want to see another upheaval in the police department unless it is for the betterment of the community.
>
> There has been no written report of reasons presented to the council, and I think there should be. I further think that Chief Black should be given an opportunity to have his say.
>
> If the chief has failed in his duties, then the council has the right to know all the facts. Persons reporting unfavorably on his conduct should be identified and the facts investigated. The public and the chief should know what the reasons behind this are.

The *Times* reporter had also telephoned the news to Chief Black, who had been in Los Angeles for the week, serving as an official in the wrestling tryouts for the 1956 Olympic team. The *Times* quoted Black as having said on the telephone:

> For some time I have been well aware that a group of people who I know have been seeking to get me replaced. I wrote a statement to this effect last week, but in view of the fact that I was going to be out of town for seven days, I decided not to release it until I returned.

The *Times* story noted that City Manager Singer and other councilmen had had no comment for the press.

Publication of the story while Black was out of town put the Manager in a disadvantageous position. Rodriguez' decision to talk was viewed by his colleagues and the City Manager as an unpardonable breach of confidence. They felt he was basically responsible for the ensuing community conflict. Some erroneously believed at first that Rodriguez had been the person who had first leaked the story to the *Times* reporter. Why had Rodriguez confirmed the report? There were doubtless many reasons: his dislike for Singer and his opposition to the downtown business interests. But perhaps the most important was that he had felt no commitment to his Council colleagues to maintain a silence. He believed that Singer had purposely called the meeting late at night to rush through the dismissal. "I didn't know why they were taking the action, and it was too late to argue. I had to work the next day. I just didn't feel they could bind me to silence in such a casual and arbitrary way."

Some of those on the Manager's side felt that the *Times* should have killed the story and avoided plunging the community into another police controversy. The *Times* publisher later expressed a different view: "This wasn't the dismissal of a clerk-stenographer but just about the most important man in our government. Furthermore, it wasn't a question of *if* he was to be fired but *when*. He had alienated too many important publics in town to last. We were just doing our job." Moreover, some *Times* men pointed out later, the competing Xerxes daily might have published the story first if the *Times* had not.

Singer Sees Black

After Singer received his message from the newspaper, he hurriedly contacted Black, found he was too late, but went ahead and made a date to see the Chief at 4:30 p.m. in Hollywood. By noon he and his assistant were on their way to urge Black to resign.

The call from the *Times* that morning had not surprised Black. The developing pressure, particularly since the Peters case in March, had caused him to set down, before leaving for the Olympic trials, some of the reasons why he believed certain people in the community were trying to have him dismissed. He had written the statement for publication in the *Times* and had personally taken it to the editor. The two men had discussed its content and decided that it would certainly stir things up. But the editor suggested Black "hang on to it for awhile."

When Singer and the Assistant City Manager arrived at Black's Hollywood Knickerbocker suite about 4:00 p.m., little time was lost in getting down to the point. The Chief was shown the proposed resignation, which was typed on City of Valley stationery. Black's name was included, ready for signature. The text was,

> Personal reasons make it necessary that I submit my resignation as Chief of Police of the City of Valley, effective at the earliest possible date.

The Manager explained that it would be better all around if the Chief signed the statement. The city would avoid embarrassment and Black would not have the problem of a discharge on his employment record. Black then asked, "What if I don't sign it?" Then, the Manager said, he would have to institute dismissal proceedings. "What have I done wrong?" Black queried. Singer said there would be no point in such a discussion and urged him to resign. The meeting lasted about 45 minutes, with Black telling the Manager of "20 to 25" improvements that had been made in the Department. He suggested Singer was really submitting to pressure from a small group in the town. Singer said nothing. Ultimately, the Chief declared he would not sign the resignation. He wanted time to consider.

Statements in the Press

The *Times* the next day carried a banner headline that Black had been fired and was demanding a hearing before the Council. Three statements were given prominent display. The first was from City Manager Singer, who said:

> I regret sincerely the extremely unfavorable publicity that has been created by the ill-advised and premature release of information concerning the proposed resignation, or termination, of Chief Black at a time when he was out of town. . . . Because of the premature release of the information it was my desire to contact Chief Black in Los Angeles at his earliest convenience, in order to explain to him that I had no intention to handle the matter behind his back.
>
> Since Chief Black has decided that he will not submit his resignation, his termination papers are being processed today, because he has not come up to the expectations of the City Manager's office. . . .
>
> This office and the members of the City Council do not disapprove of a firm law enforcement program and firm police department discipline and there will be no efforts made to change these particular programs in any way.

The second statement was from Chief Black. It said in part:

> I now request a fair and impartial hearing before the City Council during which time the City Manager would have an opportunity to bring his charges and reasons for asking for a resignation or discharge.
>
> Also, it would give those persons who have charges to make against the Chief [an opportunity] to bring their cases openly before the City Council.
>
> I would also like to bring before the Council police officers so that they may testify as to the present conditions within the department. I am confident that the good people of this community and the members of the police department are desirous of having an honest and efficient administration of the police department. I believe that I have given them such an administration.
>
> I came to Valley to do the best job possible in good law enforcement at the request of the City Council and the City Manager. If the City Manager and present Council desired any change in that policy, or wished a new policy, I would have been most happy to have carried them out. . . .

The third statement came from former Mayor Crispin Lloyd, who made two basic points. The first was that the Council shared responsibility with the Manager for the firing of Black. Valley's elected representatives "have, and should have, a part in such decisions." The former Mayor's second point sounded a theme that was to re-echo in most pro-Black arguments throughout the remainder of the controversy: "We either will have impartial law enforcement, or we can again bow to the privileged few." Lloyd continued:

> . . . This action was taken without any opportunity for him [Chief Black] to present his side of the story or defend himself in any manner.
>
> To my knowledge, his only crime is the rigid enforcement of our laws—laws, in many cases, made by the City Council. Admittedly, Chief Black has made some mistakes, as will anyone endeavoring to satisfy the public regarding law enforcement.
>
> Valley is growing and the days of Sacred Cows are rapidly passing. These Sacred Cows are the ones making the strongest complaint. . . . Shall we have a chief of police willing to work and enforce our laws, or shall we have a coffee-drinking, hand-shaking figurehead who takes his office and duties with a detached attitude?

With the Lloyd and Black statements, the pro-Police Chief side assumed the offensive. Black hammered at a point that would recur many times. He had done what he was told. Without warning he was now fired and no specific reasons were given. The Lloyd statement represented a blanket refusal to let the Council off the hook. Since the ordinance required the Council to confirm all appointments and dismissals of department heads, Lloyd charged the Council with responsibility for making a full investigation. There was no question, too, but that Lloyd's raising of the fair and equal treatment question was quite a boon to the Black cause. As one Councilman later remarked, "How can you argue against fair and equal treatment? It's like sin and mothers. And the person who accuses you first has the big advantage. All you can do is deny the charge and claim you're not that bad."

On May 4 City Manager Singer appointed the Deputy Chief as acting head of the Police Department and ordered him to continue to follow the policies laid down by his predecessor. Over the weekend the councilmen were mum. Black was still in Hollywood officiating at the wrestling tryouts and due back on Monday. But the newspapers kept the story going.

Pressure for a Public Hearing

From this point on, the telephones in the homes and offices of the councilmen began an intermittent ringing that was not to cease for almost six weeks. The Black affair aroused citizen feeling as no previous civic matter ever had. The volume of telephone calls, sidewalk conversations, and efforts to register opinions with councilmen or their families was unprecedented. And so was the indignation and vituperation with which the citizens communicated their views to their elected representatives. As the Black affair grew hotter, the phone calls came at all hours of the day and night, and before the controversy ended, many of the councilmen felt considerable strain and fatigue.

At the beginning, the extravagant newspaper coverage and the charge that the Manager had acted because some unnamed, but presumably influential, people in Valley did not want tough law enforcement applied to themselves, made the whole affair "look rather sinister," one Councilman recalled. It indicated to him that people were always ready to believe the worst when it came to governmental matters. "Black," this Councilman said,

> was playing the part of the sincere, conscientious Chief who treated everyone fairly and never knowingly did anything wrong. By assuming this role, he made the rest of us seem as if we did not want such a person in the job. Though in my opinion it was never the issue, he made it appear that the real question was whether we wanted to support Singer's attempt to protect his "friends."
>
> There was no question about the impact of this approach. I got calls from constituents saying "We want you to know that we think it is a good thing to have active law enforcement. Lives can be saved that way."

On Monday Mayor Simpson and all the coun cilmen except Rodriguez declared that ther would be no public hearing. "We intend to b firm on this thing," he said. "A public hearin . . . accomplishes little . . . does much harm t the families of the principals involved . . . is to time consuming . . . is very expensive." Th situation was different, the Mayor declared, fro the "last Police Department flareup. At th time there were some charges of malfeasance i office." In addition to his oral remarks to r porters, the Mayor also issued a rather length statement, which, however, dealt more with th method taken by the Council in arriving at i decision than the reasons. Among the questio Mayor Simpson said he felt people were aski were:

> . . . whether this means a less active law enforcement program; whether the action taken was arbitrary and based on a snap judgment, or whether it resulted from some individual's encounter with local

law enforcement officers. To all of these, the answer is definitely NO.

1. All members of the Council and the City Manager have strongly supported the program of vigorous law enforcement and will continue to do so. . . . Good law enforcement, in the long run, is good public relations, not bad. . . .

2. While the Council had not been filled in on all details of existing problems until recently, the Manager informs us that he has discussed them repeatedly, and at length, with Mr. Black . . . the decision to take this action was made slowly and reluctantly. It was no sudden decision, and had no reference to any single specific incident.

3. A number of very fine technical improvements . . . have been made. . . . The problems, without going into unnecessary detail, have apparently been in the area of judgment, personal psychology, relations with other law enforcement agencies, relations with juveniles, etc.

There has been no malfeasance in office, merely a case of resolute incompatibility. It was never intended that the Chief should be dismissed in a manner to prejudice his future employment. . . . Unfortunately the unwise and premature disclosure, before the Manager had a chance to discuss the matter with the Chief, placed both of them in an awkward position. . . .

It is unhappily true that a small group of perennial trouble makers that enjoy behind the scenes activity in our community will seize upon a problem of this sort to exploit community division. Issues should not be decided in that setting. Every effort will be made to handle this fairly and properly, and we ask your patience and confidence. . . . [Emphasis added.]

That same day the *Times* published its first editorial on the "Chief Black Affair." It said that the community was deeply disturbed. Conceding that the Chief had been tactless and had moved too fast in his law enforcement program, the newspaper also noted the furor of the previous few days had revealed that a large number of people considered his performance "vigorous, firm, and impartial."

The majority of the Council and the manager made a mistake in the naive assumption that a highly controversial decision could be made on a Tuesday night, and not leak out before the anticipated Singer-Black conference six days later.

Having made that mistake the council was then unprepared for the public reaction that followed. All members except Joe Rodriguez have been placed on the defensive. They may have excellent reasons for supporting Singer against Black, but the public is unaware of them. They have placed themselves in the position of seeming to have bowed to pressures which they have not explained.

Far more than the council, the people are blaming the city manager. Perhaps it was all right for him to seek council approval of the firing of Black while the chief was out of town for a week. But it doesn't look like fair play to a lot of people.

They are holding the city manager to accountability for his judgment. Only a year ago, they observe, Mr. Singer found Mr. Black to be the best qualified candidate among many. Now he has reversed his opinion and fired the chief.

If he did not like the policies of the Chief of police, then why didn't he issue a different set of instructions, they want to know? Why wasn't Black given a chance to defend himself?

In the first round of the controversy, Mr. Singer has certainly lost, by failing to justify his position publicly. Mr. Black has proved to be an articulate champion of his own position. . . .

What the public wants now is information. . . .

The Council Agrees to Hear Black

Meanwhile, a woman whom Black "had never heard of" began to circulate petitions asking the Council that he be given a hearing. By midmorning of the first day the lady had obtained 43 signatures, and the *Times* printed each name and address. The petition asked that Black be given a chance to state all the facts "regarding his summary dismissal . . . and present to the people of Valley his admirable record in fulfilling his duty, and the just reasons for his reinstatement." The lady said that people were anxious to sign and some thought that the manner of the firing was "un-American." Although it never came out publicly, the circulation of the petition brought the issue of religion into the controversy. Though Black was a Protestant, the woman circulating the petition was a Catholic and most of the early signatures she obtained were those of Catholics. Hence there was some feeling that the Catholic people, who represented about twenty percent of the population and were growing in proportionate number, were using the problem to secure political power in the community.

Spurred by the newspapers, citizen interest grew in extent and in intensity. It was reported that City Manager Singer's home was visited by a mysterious prowler on Monday night and a rock with a threatening note attached was hurled through his garage window on the preceding evening.[9]

It was becoming increasingly clear to the Council members that their hope of avoiding some kind of public unfolding of the issue would be impossible. Five days after Black had been fired, on May 10, the Council passed unanimously a motion by Rodriguez to allow Black to appear before it at the next regular Tuesday meeting. Mayor Simpson said Black had never really been denied the right to appear at a regular meeting. However, he noted the Council "was, and still is, against a lengthy drawn out hearing such as we had a year ago."

Thus the Council bowed to a strong public sentiment. Councilman Jennings particularly felt that the Manager's public relations had been poorly handled. He believed that it was necessary under the circumstances for the City Manager to state as "fully and frankly" as possible his reasons for dismissing the Chief. Until this was done, Jennings did not believe the clamor would subside. Jennings had suggested this step to Singer, and Singer had agreed to prepare such a statement. The expectation that the Manager would have such a statement in time for the next Council meeting was one reason why Rodriguez' motion to grant Black "a fair opportunity to speak before the Valley City Council . . ." had been passed unanimously.

Singer Issues His Statement

The day before the Tuesday, May 15, hearing, City Manager Singer issued the statement Councilman Jennings had requested. It was not specific; rather it was an attempt to create the tone that Singer felt was important to an understanding of the reasons for the dismissal. A major portion of the statement follows:

> Tomorrow the former chief of police will have his say.
>
> He has asked why he was discharged. You, the people of this sensitive community, have asked also.
>
> I have been accused of protecting so-called Sacred Cows and yielding to political motives. Am I protecting anyone? Of course. And I fear I must always do so, public hearing or no.
>
> But I offer no protection to Sacred Cows or other vested interests. They not only do not ask my help, they do not need it. They hire legal counsel or go to a higher power than I.
>
> You ask to know why a man who has contributed much to the police administration of this city should be tossed aside. Was not his duty that of enforcing laws? Has he not done it more forcefully than any other chief Valley has had in past years?
>
> Very true. No one has argued that point. We did say, however, that he lacked "good public relations." This meant little to most of you.
>
> What we should have told you was that he lacks something far more important. That precious quality of human kindness . . . a genuine liking for people and an interest in you, as individuals.
>
> More high sounding talk? No, rather the reflection of the forlorn look in the eyes of those who have come away from a visit to the former chief, troubled and humiliated.
>
> These are not people of means and influence. These are people, who, because they lack means and influence, came to me since they had no other place to go. These are the little people. These are the ones who brought the downfall of ex-Chief Black.
>
> They came alone or in groups of two or three. They came apologetically, sometimes a little fearfully. They ask for no favors or relief from violations of the law. They came humbly, asking only for a courteous audience and perhaps an explanation. They had talked with Black. But he had lost himself in the hard printed words of written law. Laws which after all, were made by people, for people—not against people.
>
> Black's downfall came not from a lack of professional knowledge or ability. It came not from any one tangible incident. It came rather from those who spoke softly but from the heart. They cannot step forward and identify themselves "for investigation." They cannot, because they do not even know that their soft words were added month by month to many other soft words, eventually creating a roar which I could no longer ignore. They do not know this, these little people . . . and they never will unless they recognize themselves here.
>
> I did not fire William Black. Nor did the City Council. William Black fired himself.

This was the general situation, the City Manager reported. He went on to say more specifically that there was a "serious, growing friction" between the local schools, the insurance agents, the other law enforcement agencies, and the

[9] The note said: "You have lost the best chief of police you ever had or ever will have. You have made the worst mistake you ever will make. Now you can live with it. The window is nothing. Just wait."

Valley police, "caused by lack of cooperation or lack of judgment on the part of Mr. Black." Because of their "public positions," however, these agencies and their representatives could not speak openly. Singer concluded:

> Yes, other problems exist. In my humble opinion some still should not be discussed. However, you are interested in good government and you have asked, "Why has Black been discharged?"
>
> I have tried to briefly answer this and point out that the step was taken as much to protect the future of the people of this community as for what already occurred.

Black Dominates the Council Hearings

JUDGING BY THE TURNOUT and the mood of the people at the hearings the next day, Singer's statement had not quieted many citizens who were displeased with the dismissal of Chief Black. Councilman Jennings, who had publicly requested the statement, was not satisfied, either. "You couldn't answer those petition-happy people with high-sounding words. I was well aware of the great difficulties in getting the people who had complained about the Chief to come forward. But . . . I felt we had come to the point where much had to be spelled out and people identified if possible. . . . For example I talked to the school people too. They generally confirmed what the Manager had said to us, but 'couldn't get the schools mixed up in this.' Where did that leave Singer and us?"

The hearings, which began Tuesday, May 15, were "gruesome," as one Councilman put it. Originally scheduled for the Council Chamber in the basement of the City Hall, the appearance of some 300 people forced the removal of the session upstairs to the auditorium. The day was hot, 92 degrees, as some 250 found seats and the others stood around the walls. Chief Black appeared with his attractive wife and teen-age son and daughter. It was a pro-Black audience. Some 1,400 signatures had been obtained on the petitions asking for the hearings, and it looked as if a good number of the signers were present. None of the persons who had previously complained about Black to the Manager could be seen in the audience.

Mayor Simpson was in the chair flanked by all his colleagues except Jennings, who missed the session. The Mayor stated that the proceeding resulted from Chief Black's written request for a public hearing at the regular Council meeting. Black then took the floor and began to read a three-page prepared statement as City Manager Singer sat poker-faced. On this occasion, and in the hearings that followed, the Chief proved to be a highly effective speaker, capable of moving a large audience on his own behalf. Black declared, first, that he was not seeking reinstatement to his position. He said he was still Chief until action had been taken by the Council, "elected to that office to do the will of the majority of the people in keeping with city ordinances." He had refrained from performing his duties since his "illegal" discharge from office because he did not "wish to cause turmoil and upset among the people of Valley." Since no charges had been filed and he had been unable to confront his accusers, Black stated that his dismissal was a violation of the Sixth Amendment of the Constitution of the United States. "I am here to ask the people of Valley to make known to me, through the City Council, the reasons why I should be discharged from the police department," he said, concluding his typewritten statement amidst applause and cheers.

Black then suggested that a motion to restore him to office would be in order. Councilman Rodriguez said, "I so move." But the motion died for lack of a second. Later on Rodriguez tried a second time, but again there was no second.

Black's Speech

No longer reading from notes, Black started a lengthy speech in which he concentrated on four major points: (1) the improvements that he had brought about in the Department ("the first professional administration . . . the Valley police department . . . has ever had."); (2) his insistence on impartial enforcement of the law which had really lost him his job ("it was implied that I would have to adjust to 'the Hill' and to 'the other side of the tracks.' He [Singer] had the wrong man to talk to because I live on the other side of the tracks."); (3) a categorical denial that he failed to co-operate with other agencies ("falsification," he said, producing letters and calling witnesses from the California Highway Patrol and the Valley Police Department); and (4) a view of City Manager Singer as a nice but ineffectual person caught in the squeeze of pressures on his office. (He and Singer "had never had a harsh word" until the current trouble came up.) The witnesses Black called supported his statements, one former officer testifying that he, too, had been warned about the difference between the people on "the Hill" and those "on the other side of the tracks."

At one point in the session Councilman Rodriguez also hurled at Singer the charge that he was not informed equally with the other councilmen about the case. He said he had known nothing of Black's shortcomings before the meeting, and he read from the Manager's Handbook that administrators should "deal frankly with the Council as a unit rather than as individual members."

The meeting ran long over time, but Black was still not finished. The audience by this time was intensely and angrily pro-Black. No one on the Manager's side had commented to any extent. It appeared that the hearings might drag on indefinitely, exactly what the Council had originally sought to avoid. Three of the councilmen—Jones, Rodriguez, and Carter—said that under the circumstances they would not be prepared to vote until "all statements are made." Thus, the Council agreed to convene on Thursday at 3:00 p.m. to continue the hearing. Some young Black supporters moved toward the Manager with jeers as he and the councilmen sought to leave the crowded auditorium, but a newspaper man, fearing violence, headed them off.

The hearing had been a trying experience for City Manager Singer, mindful of the *Times* editorial suggesting that he too was on trial. He had spoken only once when he became angered by Rodriguez' comments, firing back that an example of the Manager's trouble in handling personnel was the hearing, which arose from premature release of information on Black's pending dismissal. "When the end of the meeting came," Singer recalled, "I really felt in physical danger. I'll have to give Black credit. He really stirred up the people in that room."

Singer Faces a Hostile Audience

On the second day of the hearings the atmosphere was, if anything, even more highly charged with intense pro-Black feeling. The crowd numbered at least 350 persons. "Black's supporters applauded him, and moves they considered fair or favorable to him, and were audibly hostile to City Manager Jack Singer," the *Times* reported. This time City Manager Singer was allowed to speak first by Mayor Simpson, even though Chief Black insisted that he still had the floor and should be allowed to continue.

Singer's delivery was mumbling and ineffective compared to the Chief's oratory. In his remarks the Manager was more specific in treating his reasons for dismissing Black. He stated his version of the problem with the schools, with the insurance agents, of the Peters traffic death, and of failures of co-operation with other law enforcement agencies. Against Black's observation the previous Tuesday that the Manager in Valley had too much power over employees who "lived in fear of their jobs" because there was no formal civil service system, Singer made a spirited statement in defense of the council-manager plan. He said

> Mr. Black was familiar with our form of government when he came here. The people of Valley adopted it by vote in 1948. I believe the city has progressed and prospered under it. I feel sorry that Mr. Black believes our form of government has done him an injustice.
>
> I am shocked to learn from Mr. Black that the department heads and the employees of the city government are constantly in fear of losing their jobs. I can only say that in my four years as city manager, I have dismissed but one department head . . . Mr. Black.

Singer declared that he did not propose to "refute, point by point," Black's allegations but called Acting Chief Ken Boyer and asked him about "discriminatory arrests." Boyer, who had been on the force nearly sixteen years, scoffed at the charge, saying he "never heard of it." Black, then getting permission to speak, asked if Boyer was ever present when Singer interviewed new officers. Boyer admitted he was not.

Jennings Sees a Way Out

During the hour or so that the hearings had been under way that day, Councilman Jennings had become increasingly concerned about where the whole controversy might lead. He felt the hearings were getting out of hand and that Black might want several more days to talk about his side of the case. The audience was becoming more inflamed, and no one could see any end to them other than increased passion and community discord. Moreover, Jennings was afraid of what Black would do when he had the chance to reply to the Manager's fumbling remarks. "I felt that Black, clever as he is, would tear into it."

Groping for a way out, Jennings recalled a conversation he had had the previous evening with the Reverend Richmond Jackson, pastor of the State Street Christian Church. The minister, who knew Black well and had provided spiritual guidance to him at times, was much disturbed by the affair. Like others, he felt the violent controversy was beginning to tear the community apart. He had talked to Black as he had to Jennings, about finding some more appropriate basis for mediation. Black had approved of Jackson's proposed intervention.

Jennings asked for the floor. Before asking Jackson to speak, Councilman Jennings first observed that there had been a "welter of charges, and counter charges, which are almost impossible to sort and prove or disprove. . . ." He then continued, "I am concerned by what this does internally to a community and by the problems that arise from it." Declaring that in such an environment the quest for a solution to the problem was futile, Jennings asked for a new approach, which would involve the application of Christian ethics to a social situation. He then asked the Reverend Mr. Jackson to speak.

Everyone was taken by surprise. Jennings himself did not know the details of the proposal Jackson would make.

The minister said the hearing as presently operating was dividing the community. There could be no satisfactory conclusion. He suggested a private conference between Black, Singer, the Council, with a committee of ministers attending. In such an atmosphere perhaps a real "Christian reconciliation" could take place:

> Christian reconciliation that would heal this hurt in the community would be my hope. If invited by the Council, I would be very happy to serve.

For the Jackson statement, the *Times* reported, there was "moderate applause." Councilman Jennings then offered a motion that "this Council invite Mr. Jackson, and four or five other ministers of this community, possibly one of the Catholic priests, in for that kind of a conference." The motion was interrupted from the floor on a point of order on the assertion that Black still had the parliamentary right to speak first. The Mayor said the Chief would be given time, and then Councilman Jennings asked Black for his reaction to the proposal. Actually, of course, Black had already given his approval to Jackson's idea. He later wrote, "I purposely feigned reluctance in not wanting to appear overly-enthusiastic. Jackson felt this was the way to bring Singer to terms. . . ."

According to the *Times,* Black replied:

> "This puts me on the spot. I think it is unfair at this moment." He then interpreted it as a move that would cause him to lose the floor. He said that the city manager had not said anything new in his prepared statement. Then he said he would have to agree that Jackson did have a point.
>
> Looking toward the full-house audience, he said, "I don't know what these people came here to hear. I think they want to know more of what goes on in this community."
>
> This touched off loud applause which continued until the mayor rapped the gavel to restore order.
>
> The Mayor asked Black if he would agree to concluding his remarks in a "reasonable time" and then go "into the personnel session with the ministers. . . ."
>
> Black said Mr. Jackson had an excellent thought, although the proposal came prematurely in the hearing. . . .

Close to "Mob Rule"

Chief Black then resumed his speech. He refuted a number of the points in Singer's statement, talked of a "whispering campaign" by people "who don't have the guts to say those things directly to me." He spoke mainly to the audience, intermittently firing sharply barbed accusations at the City Manager. At one point cries of "fire Singer" were heard from the audience, as the intensity of feeling brought the affair close to "mob rule." Black concluded, saying, "I am forced to the conclusion that some persons are bringing pressure on some members of the city, or city council, or that they have committed themselves to someone. That is the reason for your stony silence. Whatever shackles are binding you, throw them away." The Chief sat down to loud cheers and long applause.

It was then after 5:00 p.m., and a procedural wrangle began. Mayor Simpson said the Jennings motion had been seconded and was before the house. To Councilman Carter's comment that the motion might lead to interminable hearings, the audience shouted, "Vote now." Soberly Jennings said he still felt that Christian social ethics should be applied, adding that the aim would be "to resolve the problem," but with the Council making the final decision. However, Councilman Rodriguez was cheered loudly when he asked for "one last attempt to settle this question, openly, fairly, justly, here in this open meeting as we were elected to do." He saw no reason why Black and Singer could not get along together, and he asked Jennings to withdraw his motion so he could move "for the last time, that we reinstate Black." But he added he would have to go along with the Jennings motion if there were no other choice.

Jennings said the Jackson approach was the only answer and insisted on his motion. The *Times* then described the final events of the afternoon:

> . . . A call for the question brought shouts of "no, no" from the audience. Rodriguez then defended his colleagues saying that they were in a tough spot and deserved the consideration due to members of a deliberative body.
>
> "If Black would cooperate would Singer forgive and forget?" Rodriguez asked, and sought an answer from each.
>
> Black said, "Yes." Singer said he would prefer the Jennings-Jackson approach and added that Rodriguez was out of order, a motion being before the house.
>
> Jennings, asked if the conference would be open to the press, replied, "Yes—that was included in the motion."
>
> . . . At 5:23 the Jennings motion was put to a roll call vote and was carried unanimously, all members being present and voting.
>
> The hassle involving Black and Singer having been referred, in part, to a committee of ministers, the *Times* inquired about their religious affiliations. Both Black and Singer said they are Protestants.

Although the motion was carried unanimously, the degree of support was not as strong as might have been assumed. Not only was Rodriguez strongly opposed; Mayor Simpson also was unsympathetic to the approach. He did not like the idea of "mixing church and state" and wanted to get "hardboiled" and make a decision to dismiss the Chief. Since he was chairing the meeting, however, Simpson did not put forth his views aggressively.

Thus, after over five hours of meetings, Black's blistering attacks had so excited the community that the Manager and the Council were now clearly on the defensive. Moreover, Singer felt that the reconciliation proposal had lost ground for his position. As he recalled his uncomfortable feeling later, "This just compounded the already existing community feeling that Black and I were engaging in some kind of personal fight. The real principles were being lost sight of. I should have refused to go along. But how do you object to being prayed over?"

In a "Spirit of Christian Reconciliation"

THE NEXT NOON four Protestant ministers met immediately after lunch and hastily drew up the ground rules for the session, which was to begin in two hours with the Council, the Manager, and the Chief of Police. Besides the Reverend Mr. Jackson, the others were pastors of the First Methodist Church, the First Baptist Church, and the Lutheran Church. They were a completely informal body, nominated by no official process, and participating only to create the atmosphere in which Singer and Black might patch up their differences. When the meeting began, these four were joined by the pastor of Valley's Second Baptist Church (a Negro) and two Catholic priests.[10]

The four Protestants developed three principles, which they suggested should govern the tense conference. These were later accepted by the other clerics.

> 1. We propose as a basis for our participation in this conference that we are not going to express a judicial opinion as to the right or wrong action of this case, due to our lack of evidence.
>
> 2. Having no authority in this government, we are unwilling to be responsible for acts which are of necessity the sole responsibility of the duly elected governing officials.
>
> 3. As representatives of some of the religious groups in this community, we are willing to express a concern for the total welfare of the community, and realizing that the final judgment rendered by the Council will leave many persons disappointed, that whatever decision is arrived at by his duly elected Council, it be accepted by the citizens of this community and that we live up to the ideals of brotherhood and understanding through it.

That afternoon, May 18, 1956, all the members of the Council, the ministers and priests, Singer and Black, and members of the press gathered in the small parish house room of the First Evangelical Lutheran Church. The atmosphere was greatly different from the two previous public meetings. "Affirming the presence of God," the group carried on its discussion amicably over a four-hour period. Members of the clergy and the councilmen did the talking. Black and Singer, sitting only two chairs apart, said very little. When they did talk, they spoke quietly and did not argue. Both men, admitting they had made mistakes, stated their grievances in rather general terms. Singer held that the Chief had attacked his honesty, character, and judgment. Black insisted he was fired without specific charges and without an opportunity to confront his accusers.

The councilmen particularly took the opportunity to express their positions and to confront Black with some of their own questions and grievances. Mayor Simpson said that, based on complaints told him, Black had acted unwisely at times, was dogmatic and belligerent in his approach, and rubbed people the wrong way. "These are some of the intangibles," he said. "That's why we tried for a closed hearing right from the start." He said Valley was a "sensitive town."

Councilman Fred Jones, who had said little earlier, declared that he heard many compliments for Black's program. However, he had also been kept aware of the difficulties the Manager said he was having. ". . . When Singer said that he could no longer keep Black subordinate, I agreed. . . . If Singer and Black can agree—then Singer must remember he must have assurance from Black that he will submit himself to constituted authority. . . . If we put him [Singer] in a position where every employee went to the people, it would be untenable."

Councilman Andy Carter also took advantage of the occasion to express his criticism of the Chief. He reminded the group that the problem with the insurance agents had not been resolved. Carter then asked:

> If Singer ordered you to work, do you feel in your heart that you could work with the City Manager and the Council? Would you try your best to keep from creating a situation such as we have had? And further, would you throw open your office doors and try to be a likeable citizen?

Black answered, "Yes, sir." Carter then went on:

> We would want to know that you would not only obey orders but would do so willingly, not grudgingly. You inferred at the hearing that my idea for downtown parking was to give four hours. It actually was for only two hours in the courtesy parking plan. Suppose it doesn't work? If our local Lions club is willing to furnish the nickels and if the Council does act on it, would you instruct your department willingly to go along with these clubs? Maybe it isn't a good plan,

10 Black had a strong basis of support in this last group. He had earlier consulted with the Catholic fathers at the church in the Mexican-American community as to the availability of a good young Mexican-American for police service. The Department had one Mexican-American at the time, and Black had given him a more responsible assignment in traffic. The Chief had also talked to church people in the small Negro community about the possibility of putting on a Negro officer. He felt at the meeting that these representatives of the minority groups were basically in sympathy with him.

maybe it won't work, but if a civic group wants to do something, and you don't want to, then it would be time to resign.

To this Black responded, "I did not say I was opposed to the plan. I was only trying to point out some things. I will certainly do what the Council asks." The Chief, one Councilman later recalled, "was more humble than I ever saw him."

Among the clerics, the general tendency was to emphasize their community responsibility to the actors in the drama. However, one of the Catholic fathers—he came from the nearby estate of a religious order and at least two councilmen had no idea who had invited him—was particularly vigorous in insisting that a decision be reached that would restore Black to duty. Directing many of his remarks to Manager Singer, the priest was sufficiently scathing to cause one Councilman to suggest that he had been "briefed" by Black supporters. Singer was saved from answering the father's query whether he would put Black back to work "tomorrow morning" by several who said that the purpose of the meeting was not to force a decision on the Manager. Black thought Singer would have reinstated him had he not been interrupted by the ministers.

At 6:00 p.m. the meeting broke up. Black said he thought the meeting had been fair. Singer announced the session was "wonderful" but "some things have gone unanswered which I feel must be answered. I don't think the breach can be healed in four hours. There are some things I must do and some you must do." Then, apparently swept up by the "spirit of Christian reconciliation," Singer added, ". . . I now hold a totally different position than when I first came here. I trust we'll clear up every point. I know I certainly will try." On this basis the two principals decided to meet two days later, Monday, May 21, to search out a possibility of resolving the bitter dispute.

The immediate reaction of the community was enthusiastic. One of the councilmen said he had felt "the presence of God at the meeting. Sometimes I lost the feeling but it kept coming back." A reporter for the Xerxes daily enthusiastically reported that the session "bared some souls" and the "new approach" appeared to offer its own "happy ending." The *Times* also provided a happy version of the affair. Black and Singer were shown together in earnest conversation, and six smiling ministers were posed in another picture. Over the pictures the *Times* ran a bold headline, "Black May Be Restored As Chief."

The Monday Morning Conference

Actually, City Manager Singer did feel that the reconciliation meeting had had an effect on him, not perhaps as great later as he had thought at first. Over the weekend Singer was reasonably certain that Black would be reinstated. "The pressure was terrific," he has said, "and it was clear that the only possible villain in the reconciliation picture would be me if I failed to make peace with Black." His only price for a reversal of his decision, Singer said, was some acknowledgment of human frailty by Black: "If Bill would only say he had made some mistakes and would try to correct things, I thought I could get along."

However, as soon as the pair started talking in City Hall on Monday morning, the City Manager said he realized that Black had not changed. The meeting opened with Singer reviewing some of the problem areas that needed correction. Black took notes. On all the critical issues, however, the Chief refused to concede that he had made any errors. "Actually it was his attitude more than what he said," Singer recalled. "I just had the feeling that if there were going to be any changes made at all, I would have to make them. I couldn't buy that. After about two hours, and when I realized the complete hopelessness of the situation, I just said, 'Well, Bill, I guess that's about all.' " At that time Singer did not indicate to Black that he had no further hope of reconciliation.

According to Black's report of this meeting, the moment he walked into the Manager's office Singer said: "I agreed last Friday to a reconciliation, but since then I have talked to certain people and I am not going along." According to Black, the session from that point on was dominated by Singer, who pointed out problem areas and indicated what he would expect of the Police Chief. However, Black perceived these points as "nothing of real importance—little individual things."

At the conclusion of the session the two men issued a statement to the press. Singer said, "We have covered a great deal of ground regarding our own personal reconciliation and we are now in the process of discussing the problem as it exists as a result of the activities during the past two weeks." Black agreed that Singer's comments were "fair and correct," and they both said they would "probably" meet again that same afternoon to continue discussions. Actually, nothing had been said about a future meeting. There was no conference that afternoon or the next day.

It was the following day (Wednesday) at 11:15 that City Manager Singer made public his decision to oppose the return of Black. He summoned the Chief to his office, as well as press representatives, and made the announcement. Black said only, "O.K." and had no comment for the press. As soon as Singer finished, the Chief left. In a statement written in advance of Singer's official announcement, Mayor Simpson declared that a meeting of the Council would be called to "bring the Black matter to a conclusion at the earliest possible time." However, Councilman Carter was in Monterey for the rest of the week attending a conference for new legislators sponsored by the League of California Cities.

Singer's statement was biting and direct:

> It was proposed that Mr. Black and I might attempt some sort of reconciliation. What sort of "reconciliation" I am not sure. I have met in good faith with Mr. Black. This meeting only made it more clear to me that this issue had nothing to do with any personal reconciliation. Reconciliation has nothing to do with the problem of Mr. Black's qualifications to be Police Chief for all the people of Valley.
>
> I have nothing personal against Mr. Black. . . .
>
> Nothing that has happened . . . has in any way changed that condition. It is even more evident to me (and I am sure it is to the people and their Council) that Mr. Black is incapable of being the Chief of Police of the City of Valley. The Council has been able to verify all of the reasons which I gave them in support of my recommendation for dismissal.
>
> It has been, and still is, the responsibility of the Council to act on my recommendation for the dismissal of Mr. Black. I have again notified the Council that I wish their action as soon as possible.

Chief Black Is Rehired

BY THE TIME COUNCILMAN Andy Carter had gotten back to Valley from the Monterey meeting of new city legislators, he was convinced that it would be an error to fire Black. He was deeply disappointed at City Manager Singer's insistence that his action be upheld. With Councilman Jones, he later reported, he went to the Manager's office "with tears in my eyes" and "practically got down on my knees" begging Singer to keep Black on the job.

Finally, Councilman Carter decided that the Council would have to take the initiative itself. He proposed that the City Manager be required by Council action to take back the Police Chief for ninety days. If, in that time, Black failed to work out, it would be agreed in advance that the Council would support the dismissal. Something had to be done, Carter felt, to prevent the complete disintegration of community morale and pride.

(By this time the charges of Black and the leaders of the Black petition movement—charges that the firing had been the result of the desire of people on the south side for special treatment—were cutting deep crevices of controversy and suspicion into Valley's customary cohesiveness and orderliness. This was beginning to worry some leading citizens more than the issue of the dismissal of Black.)

Carter frankly admitted that he had changed his mind. Even though he had investigated Singer's charges and felt they had been substantiated, he nevertheless believed that Black's voiced willingness to change at the reconciliation meeting entitled him to another chance.

Excited by the prospect that his compromise would remove the Council from a very uncomfortable hook, Carter consulted with all his colleagues except Rodriguez. He talked with Mayor Simpson for a considerable part of the day. Carter heard the Mayor say he did not think he would "go for it"; but he still felt the Mayor was not completely negative. Actually Mayor Simpson thought he had been arguing against the proposal. He told Carter to see what the others said. "We were in such a turmoil," Simpson recalled, "I didn't want to discourage anybody." While Jones agreed to go along, Councilman Jennings found the idea completely unsatisfactory and reported that his conversation with Carter went something like this:

Carter: "I have talked to George Simpson and I think I have a plan which should be satisfactory to everybody. I will move that Black be reinstated for ninety days. If he doesn't work out in that time, he can be dropped."

Jennings: "Andy, do you realize what you're doing? What you are proposing in effect is to fire Singer."

Carter: "No, I don't want to do that."

Jennings: "You are voting no confidence in the Manager and you are voting to dismiss him."

But Carter protested that his proposal cast no reflection on the Manager and would not affect his position in the least. "While at Monterey," he said, "I came to realize that not only must the councilmen back up their City Manager, but also our City Manager should back up his Council."

Carter Moves A Ninety-Day Trial

The Council meeting was announced late on Monday, May 28. Scheduled for 5:00 p.m., it was 4:00 before the date was given to the public. Nevertheless, about thirty spectators quickly assembled and were present as the deliberations began. Some of them were city employees. Black, who knew nothing of the Carter compromise, later said he thought sure this would be the time when the firing would be made official. Action started quickly when Carter introduced his motion that Black be given another chance and be restored to duty on a ninety-day probationary basis. It was Councilman Jones, sitting next to Carter, who seconded the motion, supported by Rodriguez. The plan had a majority.

Even though the decision was clearly made, it did give most of the councilmen an opportunity to read into the record some of their attitudes toward the whole affair. The most intense was Jones's reaction. The large property owner had been a strong supporter of the Manager. He said he felt that Singer was completely justified in his action. "Black," he said, "has failed from a public relations standpoint. . . . He was abrupt and not well received. . . . Here at home, I've found people have complained. I, too, agreed that Black should go."[11]

Nevertheless, Jones said he was "amazed, actually amazed" that the people who had complained to Singer about Black now refused to come forward and state their positions publicly. This failure had been particularly irritating to the nervous Jones, who had been subjected to anonymous threats and, under the barrage of constant telephone calls, felt himself under terrific pressure. He was, as one of his colleagues said, "boiling mad." As a consequence, Jones said, "I told these people who were against Black that they should come and stand beside me, not behind me. These people apparently haven't felt that this was important enough to stand by Singer. This morning I talked with Singer. I knew his position. He must have the respect of all department heads and employees. I said I'd not ask him to take Black back. I would be willing to take action over his head. . . ." In short Jones was angry enough at the lack of support given the Council by the pro-Singer people in town to put Black back.

The third member of the majority, Joe Rodriguez, was not completely satisfied with the motion. He saw no reason why Black should be placed on probation. "Black," said Rodriguez, "has successfully refuted the charges made." He suggested that if Black went on probation, Singer should too. At this, the *Times* reported, the small pro-Singer audience cried, "No!"

Councilman Jennings also had his say. He read a three-page statement in which he declared that the Police Chief had "handled facts loosely in the hearings and artfully managed to give a sinister implication to a number of things which were not sinister and even questionable." Jennings characterized Singer as honest and conscientious. "Independent" investigations indicated that the "Manager did have grounds for his decision"; but both Manager and Council had handled their public relations poorly.

Then Jennings emphasized his underlying theme. By its action, the Council would either support or undermine council-manager government in Valley. He said:

Realistically, our only choice now is to either confirm

[11] Chief Black says Councilman Jones once told him, ". . . use me as a reference any time."

> the discharge of Mr. Black or perhaps in effect force the resignation of the City Manager and Assistant City Manager (and possibly lose some other valued city employees as well). We are not supposed to decide whether as individuals we would have acted in identical fashion. Reduced to the basic issue, the Council must decide whether it believes the Manager had any reasonable grounds for his action. If he did, we confirm; if he did not, we ask his resignation. Whether or not we might have preferred another approach, it seems clear that he had grounds. I certainly could not honestly and conscientiously conclude that Mr. Singer had no reasonable basis for his decision.

Singer Threatens to Resign

Before the vote was taken, Singer asked for his chance to talk. He said that the "basic facts in the Black case have not been altered. . . . I feel that I must urge the City Council to ratify the recommendation that Mr. Black be terminated." Failing this, he said the Council could order his own termination and accept the responsibility for a decision he did not wish to be "associated with." After applause for Singer's statement died down, the question was called, and Carter's motion for a ninety-day reinstatement passed by a three to two vote. The pro-Singer audience felt the defeat keenly. After the vote, a number of city employees came up to Jennings, two of them women with tears running down their faces. They thanked him for his vote in support of the Manager. One department head, in thanking Jennings, referred to Singer as "the best boss I ever worked for."

Black, quickly shaking Singer's hand after the session, told him, "Jack, I think I can do it. . . ."

"You'll have to do it without me," Singer shot back.

Within an hour after the close of the meeting, both Singer and the Assistant City Manager had submitted their resignations, effective in thirty days. Singer said to obey the order would have put him in an "untenable position." During the month he was still to be on duty, he would take no responsibility for the Police Department. He declared that administrative authority had been badly undermined, that the effect was one of electing a Chief to office by a "small minority of skillfully influenced people," and would result in the creation of an "autonomous police department." Actually, Singer was saying a considerable portion of this for public consumption. He was still hopeful that his departure from Valley might be averted and consequently handed his resignation to the Mayor, rather than the City Clerk. If it had been given to the latter, it would have been official. As it was, the resignation simply lay in the Mayor's hands until Singer desired to pass it on to the City Clerk.

The Council decision caused the *Times* to editorialize at considerable length the next day on Singer and his approach to his job. It pointed out that Black had become a symbol of impartial but firm law enforcement and therefore his potential support had not been recognized by the Manager and the Council.

> It was Mr. Singer's ideal of professional conduct, however, that finally put him in an untenable position. He felt that it was only necessary to do what he sincerely believed was right. He did not believe that it was incumbent upon him to justify to the people the correctness of his action. This left many individuals who dealt with the manager's office with the feeling that they were not getting a sympathetic hearing, that the city was being run "by the book." When this same philosophy was applied to the Black affair, it proved to be fatal to the manager.
>
> Black had a large public following—as subsequent events proved—and any plan for his dismissal had to allow in advance for answering to that public. Without that planning, a public clamor ensued and Mr. Singer took the position that it was not up to him to give a prompt and full accounting to anyone other than the five members of the council.
>
> In Utopia it may be possible for city managers to remain silent to the public they serve, but here and now a manager can continue in office only so long as he is understood by the public. . . .

The Prospect of No Government

BY THE NEXT MORNING the condition of Valley's government approached complete chaos. Not only were the resignations of the two top administrative officials submitted, but Mayor

Simpson called in the press at 11:00 a.m. to announce that he was quitting, too. (Jennings had made desperate efforts to dissuade him.) Simpson characterized the previous day's action as "a step backward to ward-heeling days" and said that he and Councilman Rodriguez had "diametrically opposite opinions and standards as to methods and approaches to the solution of city problems." He said he wanted "no part of that system."[12]

Unknown to Simpson, Councilman Jones had also made up his mind to resign. He appeared two hours after Simpson's press conference at the City Clerk's office to make the action official, in contrast to the Mayor's presentation of his resignation only to the press. His wife said he had been awake and sick all the previous night. The Councilman declared he could not "take any more of it. I retired from business because of nerves many years ago. . . . My position on the Council has been a lot worse than I thought." That left the city with three councilmen. One was Councilman Jennings, who had applied for a Fulbright Fellowship in The Netherlands the previous September and was expecting to hear at any time about whether he would get it.

Administrative operations, too, were in a state of turmoil. For weeks little work had been done at City Hall. Thirty-five employees signed a statement registering their confidence in the City Manager, and the Planning Director publicly announced he would resign with Singer. In his statement he made an obvious reference to the Lemon Street Gang and its involvement in the situation, saying,

> In the past few years there has developed in Valley a small political group that works under cover—a group that follows the old line—Stir up unrest, grasp any incident to create situations that appeal to the emotions, disorganize government. To create these situations they work through the weakest member of the Council [an apparent reference to Councilman Rodriguez] with the hope of weaving a web dragging the sincere members of the Council into a trap from which it is difficult to extricate themselves. This was demonstrated in the Kelly episode. Fortunately for Valley trying as it was, those undercover artists were sent back to their holes.
>
> Now the same old strategy is being used—this time they have succeeded in disorganizing city government. However, I believe there is still time for the sincere Councilmen to extricate themselves from the present trap. In spite of the acute proportions to which this grandstand play has developed, I believe the good citizens of Valley will rally and again bring organization out of chaos.

Black's status, too, was up in the air. He had gone back to work. Yet Singer, who was still Manager and still Black's boss, had told the Council he would not take the responsibility of putting Black back on the job. He did not order Black back on the payroll. Insofar as Singer was concerned, Black still was fired, Council confirmation or not. Singer took further steps. He said he had checked with the city's insurance carrier, and there was some question as to the municipality's liability should Black make an arrest or get involved in an accident while driving a public vehicle. Therefore, he ordered that Black do neither of these things.

In the atmosphere of crisis, the *Times* again inserted its editorial voice, suggesting that the council-manager form of government was perhaps at fault.

> In theory, the police department is just another department of government, along with cemetery, streets and water. The manager can supposedly deal with the water superintendent and the police chief alike.
>
> But law enforcement is by its nature a highly controversial subject. . . .
>
> The oldest question in the book is: Who shall police the police? And the way our municipality is presently set up the answer is: "the City Manager shall." At least that's what the citizens thought who constantly ran to Jack Singer in an effort to make Chief Black change his policies or his ways.
>
> This puts the city manager in the political position of having to interpret the wishes of the people and to supervise the police department accordingly. Political decisions are for elected officers—not appointive ones, and that's where our city managers have found themselves in hot water that was not of their own choosing.

A Meeting of Some Leading Citizens

It appeared that a resolution of the conflict would depend in great part on the future com-

[12] Before the Black affair, Mayor Simpson had not given any consideration to resigning from the Council, even though he had been planning a six-week trip to Hawaii for some time. He felt, however, the time had come for a change. "If I couldn't get the job done, we needed some people who could," he said later. A secondary reason, Simpson declared, was his disinterest in "taking any more punishment."

to the police department, or any of its members, shall first be submitted in duplicate to the office of the city manager for approval. No order or instruction by you shall be effective unless it has such approval. (2) In the absence of the city manager or the assistant city manager you shall submit such orders to the assistant chief of police for approval. (3) In the case of emergency all orders will be issued by the assistant chief of police or that officer who is in charge of the current shift. . . .

In response Chief Black signed and posted the following statement: "Since I am unable by this directive to issue any orders I suggest to all members of the police department that they comply."

Providing his own kind of harassment, Black followed the order scrupulously, sending something for approval to the Manager "every fifteen minutes," with a duplicate to each Councilman. Furthermore, as the *Times* reported, Black's strategy was to suggest three orders covering "certified hot potato issues." He proposed that the Department return to one-man patrol cars instead of the Singer-ordered two-man cars; that a selective enforcement program be reinstituted; and that an officer be reassigned to a regular parking enforcement beat. About the last item, Black commented, "They took the parking patrol man off his beat in May and gave him other duties . . . parking has become commonly improper throughout the city."

To these proposals, the Assistant City Manager responded for Singer with just eight words. "Not approved. Present procedures will remain in effect." The next day Black came back with the same type of proposals, and so the battle went.

A Challenge to the "Old Guard"?

As Black and Singer continued their tug of war, the *Times* on June 7 published an editorial that stirred many in the community. Provocatively titled, "Who Owns Valley?" it fed fuel to Black's claim that he was fired for enforcing the law equitably. The editorial declared:

What is being challenged is the Old Guard—the people who have been here for decades, if not generations, by the people who have only been here for years (not decades).

This controversy is being waged with symbols. As the elephant is the symbol of the Republican party, City Manager Jack Singer has been cast as the symbol of the Old Guard. As the donkey is the symbol of the Democratic party, Police Chief Bill Black has become the symbol of the challengers.

. . . As the *Times* had noted before the storm ever blew up, Valley was trying to make up its mind as to how much traffic law enforcement it wished to have. As the publication in the *Times* of the weekly "honor roll" of traffic violators showed to all, there were no sacred cows in the book of Bill Black. North side, south side, speeders, and stop jumpers all looked alike to him.

. . . Sympathetic to the Council, many citizens interpreted the pro-Black movement as a junior-grade revolution. They did not understand that what was wanted was fair play for all hands. And they began to fan the very flames which they sought to put out.

They used such terribly ill-advised words as "rabble." They implied that only long-time residents are true citizens of Valley and that newcomers are like children—not really entitled to vote. Some who should know better even used epithets which in a bar room would be strong enough to start a free-for-all brawl.

. . . The calm will finally come when the people generally, are convinced that equality before law is truly the settled policy. It will quiet when the newer citizens finally demonstrate that they are a constructive force in the community—as they are. It will be history when all of the older residents say—and mean it—that Valley belongs to everyone who lives in it.

The editorial, penned by the *Times* editor himself, was bitterly criticized. The newspaper was accused of stirring up controversy. City Manager Singer did not feel that these were the real issues, and most of the councilmen were resentful. (However, Councilman Simpson did say the community was "sensitive" and Carter that it was "clannish.") On the other hand, the *Times* editorial provided aid and comfort to the Black forces. The point was almost exactly that which Black had been making. The *Times* editorial helped to keep the Black controversy fierce and flaming. This in itself caused the *Times* to be severely criticized by (1) those concerned with the ugly spectacle of a fiercely divided city, and (2) those who supported the Manager.[13]

[13] Asked in 1958 if he had any second thoughts about the editorial, the *Times* editor said he considered it to be generally valid. He reported that there was no question the "somebodys" were treated differently than the "nobodys," as he thought was true in every community. In the editorial he had sought to point out to the "somebodys" that privileges carried responsibilities as well.

One councilman has labeled the editorial "hogwash." The "Old Guard vs. New Guard business was a nice simple

A few days later Professor Jennings learned that he had received a Fulbright grant. He was to go to The Netherlands for a year, leaving in August. Jennings got the announcement on Saturday, June 9, and immediately informed the newspapers that he would submit his resignation to the City Clerk on Monday. He pointed out that his resignation would not come as a surprise to his colleagues. He had told them the previous September of his application for the grant. "While we shall not be leaving immediately," he said, "I feel it is imperative that a full council be able to consider a replacement in the near future. Beginning soon one or perhaps occasionally two members at a time will be away on vacation."

Resignations and a Dismissal

THE NEARNESS of summer made it necessary for Valley's Council to settle the Black case quickly. Councilman Carter was to be gone throughout July, and Mayor Simpson had scheduled a trip to Hawaii for six weeks in June and July.

Two days after Professor Jennings had announced his resignation, the Council filled his position. The new appointee was suggested by the same group of citizens (convened by Cassius Bolt) that had put up Chandler. He was a resident of 37 years, Allen Campbell, a former Councilman and a real estate man. (Black said sometime later that of the groups who opposed him, none was so powerful and bitterly antagonistic as the real estate people.) The nomination of Campbell, who by his background certainly seemed to fit the Old Guard mold described by the *Times,* was made by new Councilman Chandler. The nomination was seconded by Carter, and these two were joined by Mayor Simpson in the vote. Councilman Rodriguez was absent because of the death of his father-in-law. If he had been present, however, Rodriguez would not have opposed Campbell's appointment. He had grown up with Campbell, talked to him about Council problems, and privately felt that Campbell might be on his side.

The supporters of Black again did nothing to advance a candidate of their own. It happened that Black was the personal leader and symbol of a new and hastily organized group of people who were not really close to the city government's power centers. As one Councilman recalled, "I had never seen the people who supported Black at a Council meeting before. I think that was the first time they had ever thought about city government." Some of these persons were the new commuters.

answer, but far too simple. . . . I think the *Times* bears a good deal of responsibility for the way this whole thing developed. I don't blame them for breaking the story when they got it. I do blame them for deliberately promoting community divisions with this kind of talk, north versus south, etc."

The Pressure on Rodriguez

Who could provide the leadership for the Black supporters that would enable them to rival the Council majority? Rodriguez was the most conspicuous possibility. However, there were two reasons why he was not particularly interested in assuming such responsibility. In the first place, he was not as heavily committed to the Black cause as his public utterances might have suggested. He thought the method of dismissing Black was wrong and was prepared to support his opinion with his vote. Having professional responsibilities outside Valley, however, he was not interested in waging the all-out fight necessary to keep Black in his position. "If they had simply taken the vote to dismiss at the public hearing, I would have voted my way and that would have been that," he later commented. "I wouldn't have made a further fight."

Second, Rodriguez himself was feeling tremendous pressures from the other side. "People I had never seen before in the community told me I was public enemy no. 1," he recalled. His wife, a city school teacher, felt a change in her treatment. And the Xerxes land title firm for which he worked was visited by a delegation of Valley's real estate men threatening to withdraw their business unless Rodriguez was dismissed. He was not fired. The firm's President had said, "I won't *ask* you to quit." But there were no salary increases.

That left Black the obvious man to take the leadership. However, he was still an administrative officer of the city. Even though he was involved in one of the biggest political fights of the town's history, this status imposed certain restraints on his behavior. He could not, he believed, engage actively now in a struggle over Council appointments, and he did not.

Singer Resigns

The Black affair was resumed shortly after Allen Campbell assumed his seat on the Council at 2:14 p.m., June 13. City Manager Singer reopened the problem himself when he reminded the Council that Black's status was not yet legally clear. The City Attorney then said that it would be necessary for the Council to take a definite action on the Manager's recommendation of dismissal, either approving or disapproving. He felt that the Carter compromise ought to be rescinded and direct action taken.

Singer then reported to the Council that the situation in the Police Department was "unhealthy" and that a "material split within the Department" was developing. He said two officers would be willing to appear before the Council and that there were rumors six planned to turn in their badges. "I don't enjoy making this request again, nor do I enjoy anything about this whole situation. I do not take this as a stand or a pressure move, but I am seriously concerned with what is happening to the Police Department," he continued. He said that he and the Assistant City Manager were resigning again.

Singer did not feel physically capable of continuing. Furthermore, the controversy was having an effect on his entire family. His child had been threatened in school; and he was not prepared to make further personal sacrifices, though he was still reluctant to leave Valley. In his formal statement, Singer declared that it was "evident" that no effort was to be made to resolve the "personnel problem that exists and becomes more serious with passing of time." He said his work could be of "little effect or benefit under existing circumstances." The Assistant City Manager simply asked that his resignation be effective in thirty days.

However, the request for definite Council action got nowhere. Mayor Simpson declared that any decision would have to await the return of Councilman Rodriguez. Speaking to Singer, Councilman Chandler said he had hoped the Manager would give the Council "a little longer—at least until all the Council members return from their vacations." But Singer said, "I live with this 24 hours a day. The phone is busy all day at the office and doesn't stop even after I go home. I cannot physically or constitutionally live with it any longer." Newly-seated Councilman Campbell said he and others had appreciated Singer's efforts. Would it be possible, he asked, for the Manager to take a month or six-week vacation and let the Assistant assume responsibility? Singer said he wished he could accept but he felt that the budget and other items of business had been delayed too long. Furthermore, he declared that he could not ask the Assistant City Manager to stay. The Assistant, he reported, had been "literally living on dietary supplements and high potency shots—he has not been able to eat or sleep for some time."

Thus the session ended with no decision. This time Singer and his Assistant filed their resignations with the City Clerk.

Black Challenges Singer

Police Chief Black lost no time issuing a statement the next day. He denied that there was a significant split in the Department and said, "Even assuming the accuracy of Mr. Singer's statement, more than eighty percent of my department is solidly behind the policies which I have attempted to institute. . . ." Black went on to say that he had begun again a training program with "police courtesy" a part of the curriculum, had gotten in contact with the president of the local insurance adjusters association to straighten out the records problem, and had attempted to be "co-operative" with the City Manager and "obedient to every order."

The next day, Thursday, Singer was completely discouraged, and he began to clean out his desk at City Hall. During the day he had gotten a phone call telling him his eighth grade daughter had been slapped and roughed up by boys in a school bus coming home on the final day of school.[14] She was near hysteria but uninjured. For Singer this was a final straw. His main interest was simply to get away and forget the whole affair. That included a budget session of the Council, which was scheduled for Friday night. Budget preparation was about six weeks behind schedule, but neither Singer nor his Assistant had any desire to participate further in city matters.

On Friday City Manager Singer did not go up to his office. During the day, however, he was visited at home by a group of citizens, led by new Councilman Allen Campbell. The meeting was relatively brief. Campbell said, "Jack, we don't ask for anything more right now. We just want you to be at the Council meeting tonight. That's all. Will you do that?" Singer remonstrated but finally agreed to go to the meeting.

Final Decision

The extent to which the new appointments had been decisive in settling the Black affair was seen at the Council meeting that night. Mayor Simpson was insistent that there be a final resolution of the problem, as he was leaving the next day for his month and a half in Honolulu. No elaborate preparations had been necessary. Simpson, Chandler, and Campbell met briefly before the session, as Mayor Simpson recalls; the principal question was who would introduce the resolution supporting the Manager. Chandler said he would do so. Campbell said he would second. Councilman Carter, who had nominated Chandler and who seconded Campbell's nomination, was not consulted and knew first about the changed outlook when Chandler spoke in Council meeting.

That night the Council Chamber was filled to capacity. Police guards turned away others who sought to enter.

As planned, Councilman Chandler took the initiative. After explaining that he lived on the "north side" and that his interest was in preserving Valley, he declared that he had come to conclude that the real issue, "regardless of who the Manager is," was the council-manager form of government in Valley. He emphasized that he brought little personal emotion to the situation, as he had seen neither the Manager nor the Police Chief before the previous week. Primarily he felt that the council-manager form was worth fighting for, as it was the only kind of government "capable of handling an area that is growing rapidly like Valley is." Chandler reminded the audience that he had served as Mayor in a town operating under the commission form of government, "and you wouldn't want it."

The Council's duty was reasonably clear, Chandler continued. As in a business, the Council held the Manager responsible for the operation of city affairs. As long as the Council had confidence in its Manager, it had the obligation to stand behind his handling of personnel matters. "The Council," he said, "approved the Manager's recommendation before—please, let's have no applause or boos—I think the Council should ratify the Manager's recommendation." He then made the formal motion endorsing the dismissal of Police Chief Black, who was in the audience with his attorney.

The new cut of the Council was indicated when Councilman Campbell, the man who had led the delegation to Singer, took the floor. Declaring his great respect for Councilman Chandler, Campbell went on to say that he too felt the Council had an obligation to back the office of City Manager, regardless of the occupant. He said he recognized the effectiveness of the Police Department's work in protecting "lives and property" in Valley. Yet, Campbell stated, "I don't believe . . . in the Chief of Police telling the Council what to do," an obvious reference to Black's oratory in the earlier hearings. "I'm sure Black is making every effort to do his best, and I believe he's a man who will probably go far—somewhere but not in Valley. . . . I'm going to second the motion." Campbell's second sealed the Police Chief's defeat. Mayor Simpson's vote would give the Singer

[14] Chief Black says this did not happen. "An investigation by the Assistant Chief . . . showed that this was not the case. Singer's daughter had been one of several children struck on the head by books in the hands of other youngsters celebrating the last day of school. . . . This is an example of the great distortion which took place. . . ."

position a three-to-two majority in the Council.

Before the vote was taken, however, Councilman Carter again stated his feeling that he wanted to keep both the Manager and the Chief. The Council had agreed to dismissal, Carter said, "only if . . . Black failed to mend his ways. So far there has been nothing but improvement," he asserted. The City Attorney again emphasized that the Carter compromise had not been satisfactory in that it neither ratified nor rejected the Manager's action.

Black's attorney then spoke. The lawyer declared that there was no need for Council action, because the Manager had not formally dismissed the Chief but had merely appointed an acting Chief. At the very least, he said, new hearings were required because of the change in the membership of the Council and the new allegations made against Black. The City Attorney responded that since personnel rules in the city were not formalized by law, it was unnecessary for the Manager to follow any specific procedure, and on the same grounds it was not required that the Council hold further hearings. Some of the conflict might have been avoided, the Attorney observed, if the dismissal steps had been spelled out in greater detail. Nevertheless, "we must operate within the framework of these laws."

In the two votes that were taken, the Singer victory was complete. First, the ratification of Black's dismissal was voted by Mayor Simpson and the two new members of the Council; then, by the same majority, the resignations of Singer and his Assistant were refused.

After the meeting, Black commented that "the city government of Valley now consists of Jack Singer."

Aftermath

ALTHOUGH the three-to-two decision of the Council marked the end of Black's tenure as Valley's Police Chief, it was almost a year before the issue—and the former Chief—receded from public attention.

Almost immediately after Black's dismissal his supporters began to organize formally a Better Government League, which was to be a "nonprofit continuing citizen group." As the president of the League later said, the organization was created as a counter-balance to the "very few" who held political power. The president also said:

> New people have come to our town who owe no allegiance, social or otherwise, to the families long entrenched. A few efforts have been made to right some of the wrongs, but they lacked the proper organization to accomplish anything.
>
> The incident which triggered the formation of the Better Government League was the dismissal, rehiring and again dismissal of William Black as chief of police. It is not important whether Black was a good or bad chief—it was the manifest injustice of the whole thing which made a few people band together in an honest effort to bring about a better government. Our name means exactly what it says.

Perhaps the best-known personality in the new League was former Mayor Crispin Lloyd, who was named Chairman of the Board. The membership of the new organization included a number of the newer residents and some older residents who had taken the lead in circulating petitions for Black when his dismissal had first been announced.

The core members of the group had little connection with either of the local political party organizations. Most had taken little part in civic affairs before. One of the members was an automobile salesman; another had a soft-water service route. Several wives were active in the group.

The League embarked on a strenuous program to secure its first objective, "fair treatment" for Black. It retained an attorney to press the case for the deposed Police Chief in the courts. At the attorney's suggestion, the League also went directly to the people by circulating petitions for an initiative election on a civil service ordinance. The ordinance would have established a standard merit system requiring formal charges and procedures for employees, whose dismissal could only be effected on specified grounds. Such civil service protection against discharge was to be conferred on all city department heads who had been in office on May 1, 1956, the day Black's dismissal had first been raised with the Council by the City Manager. The proposed legislation would thus have the effect of putting Black back in office and giving him the job security of civil service rules and procedures.

The ordinance proposed was one modeled after that in operation in Bakersfield, California, whose Chief had taken a special interest in Black's problem. He appeared before the League, explained what he considered to be civil service advantages, and urged the League membership to push for its adoption. However, it was two months after Black's dismissal before the circulation of petitions finally began. Since direct legislation procedures in California require that fifteen percent of the registered electorate sign petitions for an election on such a proposal, it was anticipated that 1,300 signatures would be needed. Later, the total registrations proved to be 10,456 and 1,569 signatures were necessary. There was hope that the required number could be obtained quickly, inasmuch as about two months were required to arrange for the actual election once the petitions had been certified. However, it was six months later, the middle of January, before the Better Government League finally qualified the measure for an April 2, 1957 ballot.[15]

Meanwhile the circulation of the petitions was not lost on the City Council. During August it had the City Manager conduct a secret poll of Valley's 204 municipal employees to find out their attitudes about the Better Government League's proposed ordinance. While the League argued that "the public should decide," the councilmen said the people most concerned were the employees themselves. The councilmen opened the ballots and found that an overwhelming majority of the 174 voting opposed the ordinance. Twenty-nine favored it. Later, a Municipal Employees Association was formed. Its Board of Directors campaigned actively against the proposed ordinance.

In the intervening months, Bill Black played an active role in the initiative campaign. Shortly after his return from a trip East, he made the first of several appearances at the Council, speaking as a "private citizen." He made several efforts to secure the election of new councilmen (to replace the three appointees). He made speeches at Council meetings for the dismissal of City Manager Singer. On one occasion he accused Singer of lying, spreading false rumors, committing felonious acts, and of incompetency. The statement was so hot that the newspapers would not print it for fear of libel. Nevertheless, the former Chief did have many of his statements published in the local press. He was by all odds the most quoted man before the April 2 election. The Manager made no statements on the election. As to the reasons Black stayed in Valley to fight, he said in statements that he did not want to be a "deserter." He continued:

> The Better Government League came into being to promote fair government for the citizens; I did not give birth to the BGL, but I have nurtured it since it came into our midst because it is the tangible expression of the minds of people for impartial government.
>
> A Chief of Police is a public figure; he can do things to improve a city, to help the citizens; that is the reason, and only that, for my remaining in Valley. I am not asking for benefits or privileges; I am asking for myself and the people only the rights guaranteed by the Constitution of the United States. To obtain, guard, and defend these rights, our just heritage, I have stayed in this City.

As long as Black stayed in Valley and carried much of the fight for the passage of the initiative ordinance, it was almost inevitable that opposition should center on him.[16] Two organizations were created specifically to fight the proposal. One, the April Second Committee, included

[15] The *Times* published the names of all the signers and made an analysis of their residences. "The Country Club might be considered the center of social status and power in the community," the *Times* editor has said, "and as one moved north from that point, the number of signers picked up from zero proportionately with the distance traveled. There were some modest exceptions, of course, but we were very much struck with the relationship we discovered."

[16] Many people in Valley, incidentally, felt that Black lost a great deal of community support because of his free-swinging political activity. Among these people was Councilman Rodriguez, who did not participate at all in the campaign.

three ex-Mayors in its membership and was well financed. The other, coming into battle later and playing a lesser role, was the Young Guard.

Both groups declared the issue was the former Police Chief and that the proposed ordinance was in his interest and not those of the city employees. The Chief, furthermore, was characterized as a "demagogue." In the frenzied activity, the anti-Black groups did pick up temporarily the support of Councilman Andy Carter. Friend of Black on both the critical votes in the Council, Carter said a few days before the election that he had changed his mind and was no longer on the side of the former Chief. He said Black's "wild and intemperate utterances" had demonstrated that he was "unfit to lead any City Department, let alone a quasi-military organization such as the Police Department." He would vote against the ordinance, Carter declared, first, because he had no confidence in Black, and second, because "our present form of Council, City Manager government is the best for our city."

By April 2, 1957, the charges and countercharges were flying thick and fast. Many on both sides were extreme, emotional, and provocative. But there was no question of citizen apathy. The newspapers ran thousands of inches of argument, dutifully quoting any of the principal spokesmen and printing scores of letters, the majority of which seemed to be in opposition to Black. So saturating was Valley's first experience with direct democracy that the *Times* commented on election eve that the experience had been "exhausting." Yet the newspaper also said that the consequence had been a complete discussion of the issues and "nothing like it could have been had in any other way." The editor added that the people were now "ready for the question."

The election brought the largest turnout in the city's history in a purely local contest, with 62 percent of those eligible voting. No other proposition or office was contested. The civil service initiative was defeated 4,312 votes to 3,090, with the Better Government League winning in only one of seven precincts. An analysis of the votes in the city again suggested that, in political terms, the split between the north and the south had some significance. How much of it had been caused by the election campaign and by Black's resistance was impossible to determine. At any rate, one of the north side precincts which had its polling place in a public housing project was the lone supporter of the proposition by a margin of 425 to 319. The initiative's worst defeat occurred in a distinctly south side precinct where the vote was 627 against, 108 for. Another south side precinct registered a four to one vote against, whereas the four other precincts in the city were more evenly divided.

The former Chief's own feeling was that the election occurred too late to provide any accurate index of the nature of his support at the time of dismissal. "If the election had been held within ninety days or so of my final discharge, I think I would have won. As it was, the matter dragged on, and interest and indignation deteriorated," he commented later.

The Court Fight

In the latter part of August 1956, the attorney for the Better Government League obtained a writ of mandate from the Superior Court demanding that Black be reinstated or that a proper hearing be granted. To that the city filed a demurrer. A series of lengthy court actions ended with a decision favorable to the city. Black decided in 1959 "to let the matter drop since it would cost a considerable amount of money to press it further, and, too, one of my ardent [Valley] sponsors passed away . . . her will was never found, yet I took her to her attorney so she could make some changes in it. An interesting and mysterious case well fitting into the intrigues of the community as I so well knew it."

Later Events

Manager Singer's appointee as Acting Police Chief continued in charge of the Department until the defeat of the civil service proposal provided assurance that Black would not be returned to his job. Singer then moved rapidly to select a new Chief. Again he went outside the Department, appointing a man who had been serving as Assistant Chief in a neighboring city of 50,000. Singer said he believed the second recruitment program had yielded a better group of men. As with the Black appointment, a Screening Board was used. This time, however, the Council joined the interviewing sessions and thus participated directly in the selection of William Black's successor.

In June 1962 the new Police Chief was still serving in Valley, and so was City Manager Singer. Things were calm in the Police Department, and the Manager's record of getting along well with city employees—and almost everyone else—was more conspicuous with the passage of six more years.

The Better Government League had disappeared. Following the high point of community conflict over Black in 1956, there had been six changes on the City Council in eleven months, all vacancies being filled by appointment. Chandler became Mayor and proved to be somewhat stronger in his management of Council meetings. When the former Chief made one of his later "private citizen" appearances before the Council to read a lengthy prepared statement, Chandler, after a few minutes, gaveled for silence and told Black to file the rest of his prepared statement with the Clerk. It was the first time that Black's oratory at Council meetings or hearings had been treated this way. Occupying the seat of former Mayor Simpson was the operator of a service station "across from City Hall" who was also a director of the Chamber of Commerce, a member of a Protestant congregation, and a member of the Elks and Rotary. He had been appointed against the wishes of the Better Government League, which, making its first effort to advance a candidate for appointment, had suggested former Mayor Lloyd.

Realtor Campbell, a Rotarian like Chandler and like Simpson's successor, announced his resignation as Councilman in April 1957, after the civil service initiative proposal had gone down to defeat. Council membership had been too great a drain on his time, he said. Campbell emphasized that he was leaving the city in sound condition again and in the hands of three good men in whom he had "all the confidence in the world." Specifically omitted from his statement was the name of Councilman Joe Rodriguez.

Within a week Councilman Rodriguez submitted his resignation. Senior member of the Council by virtue of three years service, Rodriguez said that the pressures directed against him and his family had been too great. "People in Valley, and I suppose other towns as well," he observed, "tend to let a man's actions in the role of councilman influence their relationships toward him as an individual and toward his family. This creates hardship on a councilman's family and affects friendships of long standing." Shortly after his resignation, Rodriguez received a promotion. Appointed to succeed Rodriguez and Campbell were another Mexican-American and a retired resident of the north side. In April 1958 regular municipal elections were held. The Better Government League supported a slate against the appointed incumbents. Its slate was defeated by three to one. Shortly after this, the Better Government League, dwindling in size, became involved in a divisive controversy over a freeway location. By 1962 it no longer existed.

Lasting Scars

Some of the leading supporters of Black in 1956 would carry lasting scars as a result of Valley's most intense civic controversy. It was considered unlikely that the attorney who had acted for the Better Government League would ever develop a substantial practice in the city. The automobile salesman's prominent connection with the pro-Black forces apparently raised the possibility that some citizens would be less inclined to buy cars from his employer, and he lost his job and left town for a time. The pro-Black leader who operated a soft-water service route ran into difficulties at the height of the controversy when one or two south side housewives reported to his employer that they would not let such a man as he enter their homes.

Black himself reported troubles in finding another job. In May 1958 he commented: "I'd be working right now if I had signed that resignation paper at the Hollywood Knickerbocker. Chiefs who have been complete busts on their jobs and have resigned have been appointed in other cities at higher salaries. I know because I have competed against them . . . and lost. I chose to fight something I considered wrong and now no manager wants to touch me." He finally got only a six-months' temporary assignment in a California city of 10,000 to reorganize a small department. The City Manager there later praised his work highly. "He did everything I asked of him, and we had a most pleasant relationship," he said. In 1959 Black accepted a professorship of police science at a state college in the west.

By June 1962 Valley's turbulent days seemed far away. But many leading citizens of Valley still shuddered when they recalled the 1956 controversy about Chief Black. Even to men who had not been strongly active on either side, it seemed in retrospect as if the community and its government had been threatened with disintegration by the intensity of the fight and by the nature of the charges and counter-charges. People who had lived together and accepted one another for years had begun to look at one another with hostility and suspicion, it was claimed. Even the small, comradely reportorial staff of the *Times* had felt the impact of the community's split on the issue, some reporters treating others with the reserve necessary when associating with a member of an enemy force.

Some citizens maintained that the editor and publisher of the *Times* had also felt the whip of public indignation from the affair that the newspaper had had a hand in creating. Originally "playing" the controversy for all it was worth in news value, the *Times* had drawn increasing criticism from the pro-Manager side for irresponsibly encouraging a bitter community dispute that at times had seemed about to lead to outbreaks of violence. The newspaper's treatment of the later phases of the matter had been more subdued, and some former councilmen said in 1962 that the editor and publisher had never since sought to whip up unnecessary controversy about governmental affairs.

City Manager Singer believed that some of the leading citizens of Valley had also learned something from the Black controversy—something about the cost of keeping silent on controversial public questions and letting the Manager and the Council bear alone the brunt of running the government. Singer reported in 1962:

> The Chamber of Commerce is now working in active cooperation with the City Council and the City administration, and has stated to the public several times that it would never again allow such a thing to happen in this community. It would stand in support of the City and the administration to prevent a recurrence.

Appointed by the Mayor

William N. Kinnard, Jr.

Editor's Introduction

THIS CASE DESCRIBES a selected handful of appointments made by a part-time Mayor of a city of 30,000 which had a "weak mayor" form of government and an annual operating budget of about two million dollars. The story is told to shed some light on appointment processes. But there are several factors the reader should consider in assessing the extent to which these events may be representative of appointment-making in other situations. Bridgeton had one of the weaker varieties of weak mayor government. By and large, its Mayor nominated to the unpaid policy posts, while boards and commissions nominated the paid administrative officials. Because of this limitation, and because of staggered term arrangements in many of the unpaid policy posts, the Mayor, on assuming office, did not have the opportunity to staff key positions with men of his own choosing.

The structural weakness of the Mayor's office may account for the notable absence of evidence that the Mayor marshaled his limited appointment powers in behalf of any coherent long-range strategy, a situation one might, perhaps optimistically, expect to find in the case of stronger chief executives who make most of their appointments on assuming office. It may have seemed pointless to Mayor Jackson to formulate long-range policies beyond his power to carry out, particularly since he served as a part-time amateur and did not expect to remain permanently a resident of his city or state.

This is not an autobiographical account. But the reader is cautioned that it has been necessary to rely principally upon the recollections of those in the Mayor's office, not least the Mayor himself. These same events may have had a different appearance to those in other vantage points.

The Setting

The scene is Bridgeton, a small city on the northeastern seaboard. It is a fairly old town, first settled in the mid-seventeenth century. Once it was a port with shipbuilding and trading ventures to the Far East. It is a factory town with the brick establishments of the nineteenth century. It is also almost a suburb for two industrial cities. Finally, it is also a college town. The college, a few sea captain's cupolas on Chestnut Street, and a number of early nineteenth century houses of grace and distinction remind one of the town's old days of prestige, high thinking, and cosmopolitan wealth.

Socially and politically, these facts have produced here, as in so many small cities of the northeast, a remnant of resentful Protestant Yankees who remember their past, maybe a bit too fondly, and who feel engulfed by the several waves of immigration. The newer groups are mostly Catholic. In Bridgeton, the largest number of these are Italian. Next are the Irish, who arrived earlier and became Democrats and politicians. Third are the Poles.

Much of the politics of such cities is determined by the procession of ethnic groups, each succeeding the other up the ladder of cultural assimilation and worldly accomplishment in the order of arrival in the New World. Public offices of different rank constitute conventional steps in this stately dance. Party identification depends a bit on the accidents of chronology. The Irish came first, became Democrats, and eventually became masters of the political craft. Later groups in these northeastern cities sometimes found the Irish no less difficult than the Yankees and so flirted with Republicanism, as do the Italians in Bridgeton.

But at the time of this study the city was, as one would expect in the northeast, more Democratic than Republican. The registration in 1952 showed 39 percent Democratic, 28 percent Republican, and the rest "independent," or not formally committed. Undoubtedly the college staff and the upper middle class made a practice of formal independence, though the unaffiliated or shifting voters also existed among Italians and Poles. The Democrats had elected the mayor in three out of the five previous elections. In 1952 they elected Mayor Jackson, whose appointments will be described. While Adlai Stevenson carried the city by several hundred votes, Mayor Jackson won a plurality running against two almost equally strong Republicans.

Like most northeastern factory towns, then, this was a Democratic town, but in this case by an exceptionally close margin. The population was not that of large scale, mass production industry. Of 14,000 locally employed, 4,800 were in manufacturing, and these were divided among 65 factories. Two thousand residents commuted out of town daily and three thousand commuted into town. Only ten percent of the residents had moved into town within the decade—not very dynamic when upward of twenty percent of Americans were moving their place of residence, if not their town, every year. Like small cities generally, there were more people in retailing and the service trades than in manufacturing. Bridgeton was not a strong labor town, and trade unions did not dominate political organization. The fact that the parties alternated in office set a good many of the rules of the game.

The Democratic Party, under these conditions, was a bundle of ethnic groups. Its slate of candidates, and the Republicans' too, had to represent the several self-conscious elements of the community. The leader of the Democratic Party was a sixty-year-old Irishman named Patrick O'Gorman. Tax Assessor for some years, he was a man slow in movements, careful in speech, a shrewd listener, a family man with great pride and satisfaction in the status he had laboriously achieved, a strong sense of party loyalty, and a genuine concern for public improvement. Unlike many of his kind, O'Gorman had learned to live at peace with the Yankee elite. He scorned the low-grade Yankee Republican machine politicians and the Italian Republican wheel horses and party bosses as well. He was intensely a party man. But he had earned the support of a good many normally Republican Yankees who could not always stomach Republican party politics. The leadership group of the Democratic organization besides O'Gorman consisted of an Italian lawyer, a Jewish lawyer, a Polish real estate-insurance man, and an Irish contractor.

In 1952 the Democrats planned to capitalize on a split in the Republican camp and recapture the office of Mayor. O'Gorman decided to run Professor Jackson, a political scientist on the local college faculty. Jackson demurred. He had lived in Bridgeton only six years. During these years he had been away a great deal, off and on, as a braintruster for the state's Democratic Governor, and for over a year in Washington in a staff capacity with the Democratic regime. His wife had helped the local party in campaigns, and Jackson knew O'Gorman well from patronage contacts at the state level. As a teacher of government he was fascinated by, and respectful of, the skilled practitioners of politics. Jackson was not anxious to continue his schedule of overwork, and he doubted his usefulness as a candidate in a community where he was not well known. But to O'Gorman, Jackson was an excellent candidate: free of entanglement with local faction, a Yankee with reliable liberal values, a strong party man, and in addition a vigorous man in his thirties with a silver tongue.

Jackson demurred until a month before election, then agreed when the alternative presented was an innocent Irishman locally described as a pinhead. Jackson was clear from the first that he was not embarking on a career in politics via local office. He agreed to run because it would be fun, because the party needed him, because of a sense of duty to his community, and because of a family tradition of useful public service. Like almost all teachers in America, he would find the supplementary salary helpful. Jackson had no personal obligations in local politics, no immediate local political ambitions, no dependence on the party or the job. In fact, late in his term as Mayor he accepted a university appointment in a different state.

Though the office of Mayor was habitually only a part-time job, and though Jackson continued with a full teaching schedule, he was a vigorous Mayor, putting in forty to fifty hours a week, launching new development programs for the city, and making for the party new political contacts with neglected groups, including the poorest Yankees.

The Architect for City Hall

Almost before he was settled in office, Mayor Jackson was confronted with the problem of selecting two building committees, one for a new grammar school and one for a new high school. These committees would determine the design and structure of the buildings, choose architects, and let the construction contracts. Ordinarily, the appointment of a school building committee was a matter of major concern for the party in power. A "proper line-up" of members was required to see that the contracts went to the "right" people. The choice of the architect was especially important to the party. The state architects' guild had established a flat percentage fee. For the two new schools the fees would come to $130,000 over three or four years, by local standards a substantial piece of public spending. Probably no other profession was so well rewarded by local political affiliation. Even the judge of probate in Bridgeton averaged only $18,000 a year in fees.

There were three architects in the town. One of them was inactive in politics and received no public building work. The other two were respectively Democratic and Republican, and each was normally expected to get the city business when his party was in power. But when Jackson took office, the Democratic architect, Salvatore Bartolotta, was out of favor with his party. Since World War II he had averaged $30,000 a year in fees from city business, but he had contributed to the last campaign only "a lousy four hundred bucks." The Democratic leaders did not advise Mayor Jackson on the customs of the party. He did not, therefore, know that if the business did not go to Bartolotta, at least it should go to the Republican, an understanding fellow who had been properly generous across party lines. The Mayor made the committee appointments without attention to partisan considerations, except for the chairmen, where he chose Republicans so that any future unhappiness with the committees' decisions would not fall on the Democratic Party alone. One school building committee decided on the local Republican architect. But the other went out of town for an architect, robbing the Bridgeton Democrats of any hope of grateful donations.

By this time, a third architectural contract impended. Since 1942 there had been a somnolent City Hall Building Committee. Jackson woke it up and proposed that the city needed its new city hall right away. Further, the Mayor decided that Bartolotta, the negligent Democrat, was the best qualified technically to do the city hall job. He did not know that Bartolotta was out of favor. Together with the chairman of the City Hall Building Committee, he called upon Bartolotta and requested preliminary sketches of a city hall on a new site. This constituted in effect an informal commitment to Bartolotta. The chairman of the Building Committee, himself a former Democratic Mayor, made inquiries about Bartolotta's work and joined Mayor Jackson in favoring Bartolotta for the job. Finally, Jackson filled the vacancies on the 1942 committee, bringing the membership to eight Democrats and three Republicans. The committee was ready to act.

Only at this late juncture did the Democratic Party leaders learn the nature and extent of Mayor Jackson's commitment. They were most unhappy. They urged delay. They proposed that Bartolotta must get things "straightened out" with the party before he received any contract. Mayor Jackson gave the matter earnest thought. He found that, to him, there was a difference between rewarding the faithful and demanding a kickback guaranteed in advance. To some this may have seemed an artificial distinction, presuming all those concerned had the normal intelligence to perceive cause and effect, sometimes known as the law of anticipated reaction. It is a nice point whether a more seasoned office holder would have felt the same distinction.

Mayor Jackson called a meeting of O'Gorman and his two chief party lieutenants. He found that besides the pain over the party war chest there was distrust of Bartolotta because he associated at coffee breaks with a lawyer in the same office building who had once led an unsuccessful palace revolt against O'Gorman. After long discussion, Jackson was able to get agreement that the City Hall Building Committee could make its choice of architect before Bartolotta made his peace with the party. Jackson then dissociated himself entirely from both the Building Committee proceedings and the negotiations between party and architect. Bartolotta was chosen on a straight party vote in the committee, eight to three. But no contract was signed until he had re-established himself in party favor, a delay of over two months enforced by the City Attorney, one of the three party leaders who had conferred with Mayor Jackson.

In retrospect, Jackson influenced an appointment that was beyond his legal jurisdiction. The party ran into temporary cross purposes from failure to communicate fully with the new Mayor in advance. In the mind of Mayor Jackson, there was a sharp and painful conflict between the legitimate needs of party finance and the demands of professional competence.

The Jury Selection Committee

Appointed by the Mayor with the consent of the Council, the Jury Selection Committee had three members. The job took two days or so every two years, and the pay was $10 a day. The work was selecting the names from which jury panels were drawn. The talents required were not specialized or rare, the work was easy, the rewards slight, the prestige minor.

The party leaders presented Mayor Jackson with a slate of three names, all women. One, for example, was Ellen Borkowski. She was the wife of a newly-elected young councilman. She was an energetic worker for the party among Polish voters. She would not be eligible, in all probability, for an important public office. The Jury Selection Committee was appropriate recognition for past service to the party and a stimulus for future services.

Mayor Jackson took no interest in the appointments and was expected to have no voice in the nominations, though legally the appointments were made by the Mayor. The appointments were easy because the job was easy. People would agree to serve. No skill or experience was needed. No policy decisions were involved. No large rewards were at stake.

The Parking Commission

There had been agitation in Bridgeton for additional off-street parking facilities, led by the Chamber of Commerce and the Main Street merchants. The Chamber, represented by Dr. George Becker and a few store owners, had been calling for a professional parking survey to determine needs and outline a program. Mayor Jackson, early in his administration, decided to appoint a Mayor's Committee on Parking, and he appointed Dr. Becker as chairman. Becker was a physician who had been very active in civic and fraternal organizations and particularly in the Chamber. He was a Republican and active in the party, once seriously considered as Republican candidate for Mayor. To O'Gorman he was, therefore, not a "good" Republican, being too closely identified with the regular party leadership. Early in his term of office, Jackson did not fully sense O'Gorman's opposition to people like Dr. Becker, and O'Gorman did not object to the appointment to a committee which would be without permanence or authority.

The Committee recommended a bi-partisan parking commission to administer the existing on-street meters and to construct off-street facilities. This would require legislation approved by the Council and passed by the State Legislature. Both houses of the Legislature and the Governor were Republican in 1953. Legislation for Bridgeton would therefore have to have the strong endorsement of the local Republican caucus. A bill would have to be submitted in the Legislature before February 1. Early in January a bill was prepared. The Republican Party leadership informally announced its opposition prior to the local party caucus.

Mayor Jackson called a meeting in his office, including Dr. Becker, the City Attorney, and Jason, a leading Republican critic of the administration. The Mayor had been active in stimulating the interest of Main Street merchants in the proposed legislation. Amendments to the bill were drafted in his office. Dr. Becker then proceeded to the Republican caucus, where he vigorously presented the case for the original bill. Jason, backed by the Main Street Republicans, then vigorously demanded the rejection of the bill unless amended as agreed at the Mayor's meeting. Dr. Becker then agreed to the amendment, with a show of reluctance, and the caucus approved the amended bill. The same procedure was used in the Council: the original bill, the Republican demand for the amendments, and the final approval by both parties. The Mayor was able to thank the minority party for its valuable and well thought out suggestions. The State Legislature passed the bill in April.

The bill established a commission of six members, bi-partisan, with six-year staggered terms. Prior to action by the Legislature, Jackson asked the Chamber of Commerce for suggestions of names, and they presented a list of four, with Dr. Becker at the top. The Mayor proposed to appoint Dr. Becker as chairman. O'Gorman and the Democratic leaders were vigorously opposed. Jackson argued that, in the eyes of the public, Becker was the leader of the parking movement. He argued that Becker would do a good job, would be energetic and forceful. Further, he wanted a Republican for Commission chairman.

Buying private property with public money, spending relatively large sums, providing facilities that would necessarily serve some more conveniently than others, getting the job done fast enough to suit the merchants: all these were activities that necessarily would stir criticism, and very likely become political issues in the 1954 election. It would be expedient to have a prominent Republican defend the detailed actions of the Parking Commission, while the Democratic administration could be credited with getting a positive program underway. The Democratic Party leaders finally agreed.

On the other appointments, Mayor Jackson exercised less influence. He yielded immediately to O'Gorman's veto of a Republican Chamber of Commerce nominee, though he took the trouble to phone the man and explain the need for a "balanced ticket." The second Republican chosen was Ralph Jones, a bank president of recognized financial knowledge, who could help with a bond issue. He carried wide personal prestige and was a Chamber of Commerce nominee. He was to be secretary of the Commission and with Dr. Becker would make an all-Republican executive committee. The third Republican was Angelo Marino, president of an Italian club. He was well known in the neighborhood where the Commission would have to acquire real estate. Further, he was a union plumber and could "represent" labor.

For Democratic members, it was agreed to appoint one of O'Gorman's lieutenants, the Jewish lawyer, Myer Field. He would be the Democratic party watchdog on the Commission. He had been City Attorney, knew bond financing, and would be useful as well as a forceful member for the party. The second Democratic member was a Chamber of Commerce nominee, Fred Schwartz, a large Main Street retailer, long an advocate of public parking facilities. He had not made parking provision for his patrons, as had his biggest competitor, but despite this possible self-interest in public parking he could represent an important segment of merchant opinion. Third was Eugene Satagaj, owner of a small shop on Main Street, who could represent little business, but who also was a loyal party worker and was relied on to do what the party leaders told him to do.

In the staggering of the terms, Field was given the one-year appointment so that he could surely be reappointed while the Democrats still held the office of Mayor. Jones was given the two-year term. He was a Republican who could be continued if the Democrats wanted him and won in 1954, and who would probably be reappointed if the Republicans won. Dr. Becker was given the three-year term, but only over O'Gorman's protest. The party leaders would have preferred him to have the two-year term and then drop him if they won the 1954 election. Marino received the four-year term, while Democrats Satagaj and Schwartz received the five and six-year appointments. The Democrats thus were assured of the maximum tenure: five, six, and seven years, regardless of future elections.

Mayor Jackson's arguments for Dr. Becker proved to be not only persuasive but accurate forecasts. The Commission was delayed by condemnation proceedings, and the first parking lot was not even under construction at the time of the 1954 campaign. The Republican candidate for Mayor singled out the Parking Commission for his attack on the Democrats. Dr. Becker made an impassioned defense and rejected all partisan arguments. The result was a minor split of the Republicans and no discredit to the Democrats, who swept the election.

Mayor Jackson was able to appoint the man he wanted to the chairmanship and for a three-year term. This he considered the most important appointment. He was willing, and indeed had to bargain with the party leaders about the other appointments, but was not dissatisfied with the Commission as a group. He was able to include three of the four nominations of the Chamber of Commerce, not in itself of large importance, but a contribution to harmony and to the Mayor's base of personal leadership in the community of Bridgeton.

In this, as in several other situations reported here, Mayor Jackson appeared to have acted with reference to a somewhat longer time frame than O'Gorman. Jackson was not necessarily less concerned with the welfare of the Democratic Party, its organizational strength, or the importance of rewarding loyal party workers. But his formal intellectual training may have shaped different ways of asking questions of the situation, and certainly as Mayor he had a different constituency than the organizing leader of the local party.

Reappointing the Water Commissioner

The Board of Water Commissioners of Bridgeton was treated by custom as a virtually autonomous and nonpartisan body. It operated the city water system, set rates, planned and constructed new mains, condemned land, and levied assessments. It was said in town that if the Board started playing partisan politics, or were used to reward incompetent party hacks, the headaches, or perhaps the bellyaches, would be intolerable. It is not always clear why and how certain public services come to be accorded this status. In other places and services the same arguments have not prevailed.

In July 1953 the term of one of the Water Commissioners expired. The Commissioner, J. J. Tarbell, was president of a local bank, an active man in civic causes, a man of note and status in the community. He was a Republican, but not close to the party leadership. He had served with distinction on the Water Commission.

Mayor Jackson discussed with O'Gorman his intention of reappointing Tarbell. O'Gorman immediately agreed, but he stipulated that it be O'Gorman who phoned Tarbell and asked him to serve again. Mayor Jackson approved this procedure, which was the standard practice of O'Gorman with each Democratic Mayor. O'Gorman was to make the initial informal announcement by phone on all nominations and appointments. Thus O'Gorman remained visibly the party leader in each administration and by inference the determining voice in all appointments, whether in fact he had had his way or not, or had even participated actively in the selection.

Interim Appointment of the Second Selectman

Being a town as well as a city, Bridgeton had three elected selectmen. The first selectman, as is common in many town governments, was an administrative officer of major responsibility. In Bridgeton he was in charge of highways and charities in one district of the township. The second and third selectmen had only residual functions, limited to sitting with the first selectman at infrequent intervals to swear in new voters.

In July 1953 the second selectman, a Democrat, resigned his office when he moved out of town. Mayor Jackson had to make an interim appointment. A few minutes before entering the Council meeting, where the appointment was to be made and confirmed, he was given the name Stanley Szemplinski, which was to be placed in nomination. The Mayor stumbled over the name and the following discussion ensued:

Councilman Giles [Republican]: Can you tell me something about him?

Mayor Jackson [after whispering with the Clerk of the Council]: He lives out on Jefferson Circle, and works at Schwartz's Department Store.

Councilman Giles: I have nothing against this man, but I think someone should know something about him.

Mayor Jackson: All I know is he is a man of good reputation. He works for Schwartz's and he lives in the Second Ward.

Councilman Welsh [Democrat, curmudgeon]: I also would like to know something about him. I am unwilling to vote.

Councilman Murphy [Democrat]: I know him. I am well acquainted with him. He is a fine young man. The selectman now spends time only in making voters, and I am sure he is qualified for that. He's worked at Schwartz's for many years, and he is a steady worker. He also worked at the Polish Club.

Mayor Jackson [reading note passed to him]: He is thirty-eight years old. He has three children.

Councilman Welsh: Well, that is the first information I have had.

Councilman Murphy: This is the first I have heard of him being mentioned for this post, but I am sure the Council can't go wrong. He is well educated, not a college man, but he doesn't have to be. There are two other members of the Board.

Councilman Giles: My only comment is that we should know something about him, but as long as someone knows something about him, I have no opposition.

The appointment was unanimously approved.

Reappointing a Member of the Board of Finance

The Board of Finance in Bridgeton was a body of eight members, appointed by the Mayor and Council for four-year staggered terms, two appointments being made each year. Members could not be reappointed after serving a full term. The Board prepared the city budget, and while no court decision confirmed its powers, in effect the Board had a virtual veto over all municipal expenditure. In recent years, the Board's budget had been approved in the Council by unanimous vote.

The administration's plans and programs were therefore dependent upon favorable action by the Board.

In January 1954, the second year of Mayor Jackson's two-year term, two members of the Board completed their terms of appointment, but both had been filling unexpired terms and were eligible for reappointment. One member was chosen for reappointment without discussion. Sebastian Marino was a Democrat and a labor representative. He was a loyal and reliable party man, and the Mayor was anxious to keep him on as a matter of policy, to increase labor participation in municipal affairs. Democratic Party leaders supported him strongly as a party man.

The other member, Jonathan Tompkins, was a Republican and for more than one reason O'Gorman opposed his reappointment vigorously. First, Tompkins was identified with the "dyed-in-the-wool Republicans," a category in O'Gorman's mind that easily provoked him to anger. In discussions between O'Gorman and Mayor Jackson, there had developed rule of thumb limits of tolerance. On the one hand, Jackson would not have "blackguard" Democrats, however industrious and loyal to the party. On the other hand, O'Gorman would not, if he could help it, have dyed-in-the-wool Republicans. And he usually could help it, since a Democratic administration, needing an independent or a Republican for an appointment, had a wider range of choice among the professionally trained upper middle class independents and Republicans than did a Republican administration seeking a minority Democrat for an appointment.

But his Republicanism was not the only count O'Gorman held against Tompkins. The man had not only been active in Republican politics, he had been Tax Assessor before O'Gorman, and was outspokenly critical of the way O'Gorman ran the office. This criticism had continued for a full twenty years, though O'Gorman had achieved a competence, reputation, and prestige in the job which gave him virtually a tenure appointment in the eyes of both parties. Tompkins had also served in state financial administration and brought his considerable familiarity with public finance to bear on Bridgeton fiscal administration in a fashion calculated to irritate departments of city government, mostly Democratic. Along with this criticism went a sharp eye for saving a penny, even to questioning how many times carbon paper was re-used.

Mayor Jackson was interested in other qualities displayed by Tompkins. He saw Tompkins as a man of considerable ability, unusual experience, willingness to serve and to serve vigorously and faithfully. He also had come to understand that while Tompkins pinched pennies, he was altogether outstanding in his enthusiasm for large, forward-looking plans for the betterment of Bridgeton. Tompkins carried the other Republicans on the Board of Finance in support of Jackson's large and constructive programs. He made it possible to get a unanimous Board. Further, Tompkins had the qualities of status and known experience which would make the appointment popular in a broad sector of the Bridgeton community.

Finally, Jackson had tried in vain to find a qualified Democrat who would serve as chairman. While the appointment in itself did not carry the chairmanship, which was elected by the Board, the Mayor could negotiate the choice through his appointments and contacts with the Board. Other things being equal, he would have preferred a Democrat. But the Board of Finance held regular and special meetings, many of which required home work and careful scrutiny of financial records. It was not a routine or an easy job. It exposed the members to many community and governmental tensions, since the Board's decisions increasingly determined public policy and "who got what."

In this case Mayor Jackson stood his ground against party pressure. He believed that Tompkins was important to the carrying through of the major policies of his administration: sewer extension, urban redevelopment, new schools, new city hall, new parking areas, new wage scales, and so forth. He believed the Tompkins appointment would add prestige to the Democratic Party and broaden its base. Though by now Jackson knew that he was himself leaving Bridgeton at the end of his term, he believed that Tompkins could be managed by Jackson's successor, hopefully also a Democrat. The burdens of his program would be financially heavy in the coming few years, and it would be well to have a strong and able Republican visibly committed in advance to the need for the expenditures.

Mayor Jackson yielded to O'Gorman on a series

of minor appointments, re-introduced Tompkins' name just before the December 1953 Council meeting, when appointment was scheduled, and won O'Gorman's grudging agreement. "Well, I think we'll live to regret it, but if you want him—O.K." Tompkins turned out to be an asset to Jackson's and succeeding Democratic administrations. With Tompkins' appointment, Jackson took a much firmer line than in the early months of his term with Dr. Becker's, and he took this stand against stronger and more explicit party opposition.

The Sealer of Weights and Measures

By act of the 1953 Legislature, Bridgeton found that it must, as a city of over 25,000 population, provide its own Sealer of Weights and Measures. The duties had previously been performed by the County Sealer on a fee basis. Bridgeton could, of course, employ the county officer on a part-time salary basis and satisfy the law. But County Commissioners and their appointed Sealer were Republicans and it seemed a pity to overlook the new patronage opportunity. The new job required a minimum of intelligence and a modicum of honesty.

Three candidates made their interest known, a Pole, an Irishman, and an Italian. The Pole did not interest Mayor Jackson one way or the other. The Irishman was a constable, a city hall hanger-on, vaguely unsavory, a town character. Jackson was determined that he would not get the job. The Italian, Salvatore, was a member of the Park Commission, and he was a harmless nuisance. He contributed little or nothing constructive and he had an embarrassing genius for sounding off to the local press. In the balance of party appointments it was appropriate to reward an Italian. Mayor Jackson persuaded the party leaders without too much trouble, stipulating that Salvatore must resign as Park Commissioner. He then was able to appoint to the Park Commission a high school athletics coach who was a prominent leader in youth programs, an inveterate after-dinner speaker, and a constructive force in organized recreation. Here the game of musical chairs worked smoothly, partly because the Mayor had become acquainted with all the nooks and crannies of his organization and the disparate qualities of his personnel.

A Director of Recreation

More complex and much more satisfying was the shuffling of personnel involved in appointing a Director of Recreation. Early in his administration Mayor Jackson concluded that the city was not doing all that was needed in a recreation program for young people. The Park Department ran parks and playgrounds, but almost entirely as a business of construction and maintenance rather than of recreation and use. Jackson proposed to establish a separate recreation program with its own director within the Park Department. He also proposed to move City Treasurer Fitzpatrick into the new job. None of the steps in these proceedings, creating a new job, appointing the new director, and dislodging the City Treasurer, were within the Mayor's authority, and he had to move informally.

While Jackson's concern for improved recreation was altogether sincere, his desire to dislodge Fitzpatrick was ardent. Fitzpatrick held the elective office of City Treasurer as a good Democrat, but not as an insider in party affairs. He was impregnable as a vote-getter because he was a universally known and popular personality. He had been a star athlete at Bridgeton High, then a sports reporter on the local newspaper. During the war, he had sent a news letter on local sports doings to the city's servicemen all over the world. He was a baseball umpire, a basketball referee. He was prominent in establishing the Little League in the state. He loved every minute of his work with young people and with athletics. And he won every election, even in the 1948 Republican sweep of local offices. The Democrats recognized the strength of his "kiddie vote." But he was weeks behind in counting parking receipts. His office was a nuisance to orderly city administration.

Mayor Jackson first cleared his scheme with O'Gorman, who told him to go ahead at his own risk. He then sounded out Fitzpatrick, found that he would accept the job, and at what salary. Then he approached the Park Commission, a body of five members, who had a tradition of working outside of "politics." The chairman was the football coach at Jefferson High. There were two overtly "political" members, one Democrat and one Republican. There were also two "non-political" members, a teacher at Bridgeton High and the newly appointed coach who replaced Salvatore. The three school men were overtly nonpartisan and brought to the Commission some of the traditional distrust of "politics" that is ingrained in American public school and public library affairs.

During budget discussions in January 1954 Mayor Jackson won the Park Commission's enthusiastic support for the plan of establishing a recreation director. Jackson advised the commissioners to advertise for applicants, and at the same time he talked with the two athletic coaches on the Commission and allowed it to "occur to him" that Fitzpatrick, right here in Bridgeton, was a well-qualified man for the job. The coaches knew Fitzpatrick well, liked him as a referee, admired his Little League work. The Mayor hastened to advise them against precipitate action. He would ask Fitzpatrick to submit an application, but the Commission must encourage open competition for the job.

It was at this point that the Republican commissioner began to smell what he thought was a political pay-off. In a way he was right. But he was wrong in thinking it was a pay-off. Either way, the coaches and the teachers were greatly alarmed at the thought of becoming embroiled in politics. An informal meeting with the Mayor was called at the home of the Commission chairman, with all present but the Democratic member. Mayor Jackson was forthright. This was no pay-off. The Commission had the sole authority to make an appointment, and that only *if* the position were established. If Fitzpatrick were chosen, his appointment would be welcomed in the community. Advertising the job would assure fair competition. He urged only that they not be prejudiced against Fitzpatrick because he was in politics. The Mayor emphasized that the Park Commission was universally esteemed as above politics.

The Park Commission allowed itself to be convinced of its own integrity. It voted to request the establishment of the position of recreation director. The Personnel Board had to set the rating and salary. The Board of Finance had to recommend the appropriation for salary. The Council had to establish the position and appropriate the salary. The Park Commission took the initiative at each step. The Mayor remained in the background, informally helping the Commission with its presentations. Fitzpatrick was duly appointed, resigned as Treasurer, and was replaced by a freshman councilman who later won re-election. The affair was pleasantly and expeditiously executed, and local editorials were highly laudatory.

Concluding Comments

There were 199 appointments made during the two years of Jackson's administration. Of these, 100 were formally initiated by the Mayor, 70 by the various boards and commissions, and 29 were Council Committee assignments. Speaking very generally, the Mayor nominated to non-remunerative policy posts, the boards and commissions nominated the paid officers of administration. As revealed in the selected cases above, the weak mayor form of government did not restrict the influence of the Mayor to the appointments that were formally within his jurisdiction.

This brief analysis of selected cases suggests that the executive operated with many themes which were by no means mutually exclusive. Appointment policy required a sense of the appropriate and the practicable as well as a theme or theory of administration. There were many such themes. There was the matter of purity: getting the best man, free of any partisan considerations; the best man in terms of intelligence, technical knowledge, or broad administrative experience. There was the theme of social awareness, sensitivity to community needs and aspirations. There was the theme of building *esprit de corps,* rapport on the job: engineering human relations to achieve a working team. There was the theme of representing fairly the self-conscious ethnic, religious, economic, and social groups. Closely allied to this was the constant need to build the political party by rewarding the faithful party workers and assuring a constant flow of contributions into the party war chest. And there was always the problem of finding people to serve. (The attractions of public office are not overwhelmingly tempting.) There was the question of building a program and getting it into execution, of finding people who shared the executive's goals with enthusiasm and would further them with determination.

In various proportions these considerations operated in Mayor Jackson's appointments. Some jobs went to the party workers without question of ability. In some jobs, party finances by custom had to be carefully tended. Some went to Republicans in order to share responsibility, to broaden the base of public support, or to strengthen administrative programs. Appointments often generated tension. Old party war horses wanted recognition. Young men on their way up were eager to show off their talents. The Mayor had to bargain with party leaders who had different sources of strength than his, different career aspirations, different concepts of party as an instrument of government. The bargaining was most often between himself and O'Gorman as individuals as well as representatives of different perspectives. O'Gorman had his little black book of names that were eligible, and his own priorities. Jackson had a sense of program and more than a touch of idealism about the public image of the Democratic Party. There was enough mutual respect between the two and enough sense of their respective lines of political influence so that bargaining never broke down. At times it was hard to dredge up a name that was appropriate to the situation as conceived from the two perspectives. At times one or the other made concessions about which he was uneasy. The underlying condition of the relationship was Mayor Jackson's growing influence in the community joined with his strictly amateur career pattern as an elective official of the city of Bridgeton.

The Florida Milk Commission Changes Minimum Prices

Harmon Zeigler

Introduction

IN THE 1950s Florida had a state milk commission with statutory powers to regulate the industry and to set price controls for its producers, distributors, and retailers. The Florida Milk Commission had been set up during the Depression of the 1930s in response to pleas from the various elements in the industry that cutthroat competition was forcing many to the wall. For the next 22 years the Commission maintained price controls and relied heavily on industry representation in making its decisions. In particular, it was often responsive to arguments and technical data put forth by the single trade association for the industry in Florida.

In 1954 a new Governor, LeRoy Collins, began an effort to do away with the Commission and with all milk price controls. Elected with strong support in big cities, he felt that free competition would benefit consumers, and he believed that the Commission had become, in effect, an instrument of the industry. The Governor, at least formally, had substantial power to influence the Commission, since he could appoint most of its members. After some earlier efforts to achieve his purposes had failed, he secured as chairman Brailey Odham, a man who believed intensely in free competition and who had often called for the abolition of the Commission because he believed it was dominated by the industry it was supposed to regulate.

Synopsis

This case study describes the efforts of the Governor and of Odham to end milk price regulation and to overcome the influence of the single industry trade association over Commission policies. Under Odham's leadership, the Commission countered the monolithic industry association by encouraging the divisive interests of its component groups: producers (dairy farmers), distributors (dairies), and retailers. In a four-year struggle, under encouragement from the anti-control faction of the Commission, a new producers' association was formed. It opposed the older trade association on price controls and on other matters. The larger distributors made strenuous efforts to keep dairymen from joining the new association, but Odham and the Commission Administrator sought a Commission order and even state legislation to strengthen its standing and its recruiting campaign.

In the course of the struggle, Chairman Odham became progressively familiar with the problems of the milk industry in Florida. By 1959 it seemed to him that the free and unregulated competition that he prized might lead to the destruction of small distributors and retailers and to the domination of the industry by the few larger—and competitively stronger—distributors and retailers. The Governor, who retained his devotion to the absolute abolition of price controls—at least when they were set and administered by a body often susceptible to industry influences—had seen such changes take place in some of his earlier appointees to the Commission; he hoped that Odham, as a believer in free competition, would resist similar tendencies to develop excessive sympathy with the industry.

The conclusion of the case study finds Odham, as a result of his long and generally successful efforts at countering industry influences, in a position to decide whether to end a substantial portion of controls or whether to keep them and bolster the position of the weaker "competitors." In describing how Odham finally achieved the ability to cast the decisive vote, after having begun four years earlier with a Commission strongly oriented toward a monolithic industry association that had influential support in the Legislature, the case takes the reader through many dimensions of the politics, administration, and economics of state regulation of an industry.

Background

In the late 1920s and early 1930s Florida, like the rest of the nation, faced the problem of coping with economic depression. Its industrial capacity was not very advanced. For years the primary source of revenue had been tourism, and the state was only gradually developing other resources.

The milk industry was typical of this youthful commercial structure. By 1930 Florida's own dairy produce was still insufficient to meet the needs of a growing population, and milk imports from established dairy states presented a serious challenge. Some milk distributors (the dairies that processed raw milk for sale to retailers and for sale and delivery direct to homes), competing strenuously for what little consumer buying power existed during the Depression, began to lower prices. A drop in price by one distributor was met by a corresponding drop by competitors. Eventually prices fell so low that below-cost selling became prevalent. Distributors, anxious to retain large retail accounts, offered to such clients discounts, which they hoped to make up in part by reducing the price paid to the producers, the dairy farmers.

Creation of the Florida Milk Commission

For about three years Florida's dairy industry suffered from the effects of recurring price wars. Finally the industry took its problems to the state government. It urged the government to undertake the responsibility of establishing the exact price to be paid to dairy farmers for milk and the minimum prices at which milk could be sold at wholesale and retail. In June 1933 the State Legislature passed an emergency milk control law to be administered by a Milk Control Board. Originally located in the state Department of Agriculture, the Board was established on an independent, permanent basis in 1939, and became the Florida Milk Commission.

Under the milk control law, the Commission was responsible for the supervision and regulation of all economic levels of the milk industry—production, transportation, delivery, and sale. To carry out the task the Commission was given statutory powers (1) to investigate the production, processing, transportation, and distribution of milk; (2) to issue rules and orders, and to institute suits or take other actions necessary to enforce them; (3) to examine the accounts and records of milk producers, distributors, and dealers; (4) to establish health and sanitary requirements; (5) to issue licenses, which were required of all dealers for purchase, sale, or distribution of milk.

The heart of the Commission's regulatory power—and its justification in the eyes of the depressed milk industry of the 1930s—was its authorization to maintain stability in the marketing of milk by setting prices for every phase of the production and distribution processes. Prices that could be regulated included those paid to producers by distributors and maximum and minimum wholesale and retail prices. (In practice, the Commission was to set only minimum prices, since minimum and maximum tended to converge.)

The Commission did not regulate prices for the state as a whole. Rather, the law instructed it to set up a system of milk marketing areas. *Producers* in each area had the right to petition for Commission control and to petition for withdrawal from Commission control. In determining prices, a "reasonable return" had to be assured to producer and distributor, and the Commission was required to consider cost, operating expense, and farming conditions in the area. Thus milk prices could vary from one marketing area to another. Price schedules could be revised or amended after an investigation and a public hearing.

Seventeen marketing areas were established at the time of the Commission's creation. Eight of them chose to accept Commission control. In 1956 the seventeen were consolidated into six, all under controls. At no time were all the counties of the state included in the milk marketing areas.

Commission operations were financed not by legislative appropriations but by an industry tax placed upon each gallon of milk produced and distributed. The tax was paid by producers and by distributors "for the privilege of continuing in or engaging in the business of" producing or distributing milk. (Chapter 501, Florida Statutes.)

Two provisions of the milk law made the Commission, in practice, dependent for its authority on the good will of its clientele. First, because of the optional character of the milk marketing areas, the extent of the agency's jurisdiction was contingent on acceptance by the producers. Second, most of the membership established by statute for the Commission consisted of milk industry personnel or persons with a professional interest in the industry.

Commission Membership

When it was first established, the membership of the Commission included an Administrator, who could vote, and six members: a producer, a distributor, a producer-distributor, a representative of the state Board of Health, a representative of the state Department of Agriculture, and a representative of the consuming public. The Department of Agriculture and the Board of Health designated their representatives; the Governor appointed the industry and consumer members. Actually, the Governor could freely choose only one appointee, for it became accepted practice for the producers and distributors to recommend slates of three to five names, leaving to the Governor only the final selection. Governors usually accepted the judgment of the industry. A Governor's influence over the members from the two state agencies was also limited, for in Florida the heads of at least six state departments—including the Department of Agriculture—were elected at large to serve the same four-year term that the Governor enjoyed. Candidates for department heads ran independently of candidates for the governorship and had separate political organizations. Unlike the Governor, the elected department heads could succeed themselves. (In the mid-1950s the incumbent Commissioner of Agriculture had held his post for almost thirty years.) Milk Commission members served for four-year, staggered terms.

The Commission staff was small—in the early 1950s about ten persons. It was headed by an Administrator, selected by the Governor for a four-year term. About half the staff consisted of clerical workers; the rest were deputy administrators who were either regional or subject specialists. The discretion of the Administrator was wide. Although he could (and did) consult with active and interested members of the Commission between meetings, he was not legally required to confer with them except at regular sessions. Section 501.04 of the law, however, provided that "no official act shall be taken, rule or regulation promulgated, or official order made or enforced [by the Administrator] without the approval of a majority of the Commission." The Commission met upon the call of the chairman or at regular monthly meetings; as was true of most Florida commissions or boards, members received only *per diem* compensation and had no office space in the agency's headquarters.

The Clientele of the Commission

Within the milk industry the Commission had a three-fold clientele: producers, distributors, and retailers. From the time of the agency's creation until the mid-1950s, all three segments of the dairy industry publicly supported price controls at all levels, according to oral and written testimony presented before the Commission during that period.

Producers were the dairy farmers who supplied raw milk to be processed. They believed that, without controls, the prices received by distributors might drop, thus lowering the prices paid to them as producers. If controls were eliminated at the distributor level, they thought, price wars might result. If distributors lost part of their markets through such intense competition, producers would also suffer.

Distributors were the dairies which purchased raw milk from producers, processed and packaged it, and delivered it to the market. Although all distributors advocated controls, their reasons differed, and some difference in interest existed between large and small distributors. Large dairies supported either total controls or absolute free enterprise. They were thought to be less vulnerable to the effects of price wars, since losses in one area could be recouped by raising prices in another. Large distributors, however, called this assumption a myth, pointing out that, while they could hold out longer during price wars, their local plants would suffer. And, in fact, large dairies seldom initiated price wars. (The largest of these in Florida were the so-called Big Three—the Borden Company, Foremost Dairies, Inc., and the Sealtest Company.)

Small distributors usually had an intense concern with protection against declines in prices. Since they marketed milk in only one locale, a drop in prices there could not be offset by profits in other markets. Small independent distributors thus wished protection against selling below cost, although they did not always favor complete regulation of prices, since they felt they could compete successfully with large distributors in their particular locale if some fluctuation were allowed.

A complicating factor here was the "cash-and-carry" operation: a farm on which milk was produced, processed, and sold, without ever passing through a distributor's plant. Cash-and-carry establishments were not regulated by the Milk Commission; farmers could sell below the going price because of the simplicity of their operation. They supported regulation for others, because any drop in general prices would reduce, or even destroy, their advantage.

The division of the Florida market between large and small distributors varied from area to area. In the state as a whole, the Big Three national dairies held slightly under fifty percent of the market in the mid-1950s.

Retailers contracted with distributors for the purchase of processed milk and sold it to the public. Here again, difference in size meant a difference in interest. Some large chain supermarkets favored a free market, since it allowed them to negotiate with distributors for discounts and to pass savings along to the consumer. Smaller retailers, like small distributors, felt that they needed protection against sales below cost.

After its creation the Milk Commission instituted complete price control over the marketing areas which had elected to accept its authority. In the following years the dairy industry was able to make a recovery from the chaotic conditions of the price wars. With protection against extreme competition, the industry underwent a period of concentration and specialization. Nation-wide dairy chain distributors increased their percentage of the Florida market. Economic decision-making tended to shift to the larger corporations, particularly Sealtest, Borden's, and Foremost.

A parallel development was an intensified movement toward the specialized dairy farm. Although milk had never been merely one of many sources of farm income, as in some other states, the dairy farm now became specialized, producing milk to meet the demands of only the large distributor. This development was of great significance for the structure of the industry. Since milk is a highly perishable product, it must be marketed immediately, or the farmer faces a loss. A dairy farmer with an investment of $75,000 to $500,000 naturally sought out the distributor who could handle his entire supply of milk. Thus the producer became economically dependent on the continuation of satisfactory relations with a single distributor (although a distributor bought milk from more than one producer). A system of dependence developed. Farmers became identified with the distributor who purchased their milk, e.g., Borden producers.

The Rise of the Florida Dairy Association

Before the creation of the Florida Milk Commission, the milk industry had formed two statewide trade associations. Distributors were organized into the Florida Dairy Products Association, while producers belonged to the Florida State Dairyman's Association. These groups were not active, however, and few attempts at industry-wide communication were made.

The existence of a government agency that required a great amount of technical information and that was capable of influencing the profit structure of the industry, made the existence of an active state association more desirable. The distributors' organization was the first to revive after 1933. In 1941 it hired a veteran trade association representative, E. T. Lay. (Lay had represented the Associated Industries of Florida, the Retail and Wholesale Merchants Association, and several other commercial groups. He was a familiar figure at sessions of the Florida Legislature.) On Lay's initiative, a merger between the two milk trade groups was effected in 1946, and the Florida Dairy Association (FDA) was born.

The FDA sought to present a united, industry-wide front in defense of the activities of the Milk Commission. It also kept an eye on the Commission itself, making certain that all members were informed of industry problems. Lay, who became executive secretary of the FDA, followed the activities of the Commission closely and also kept a check on the development of potential opposition to price controls in the Legislature. His relations with the Commission assumed such a degree of stability that he once referred to himself in these words: "I have had to give so much thought to the Milk Commission . . . that I possibly think I am on the Milk

Commission staff." At public hearings the FDA frequently was the only nongovernmental organization in attendance and took part in Commission deliberations. (Any other group could have done so, but the FDA was the only group that could be expected to attend regularly.)

The FDA's relations with the Milk Commission caused criticism by some observers of the agency's activities. One charge was that the influence of the FDA was so great that the Commission preferred to depend primarily on it for information about the milk industry, even though there were other sources of data—state and federal departments of agriculture, for example. The FDA and its representative, however, took pride in being able, consistently, to supply information quickly and efficiently.

Another cause for criticism arose from the fact that, since the entire Commission membership conferred infrequently, the day-to-day problems of the industry had to be met by the permanent, paid staff. It appeared to some observers that basic decisions were reached by consultation between the FDA, the Administrator, and the industry members of the Commission. Commission meetings often approved and adopted orders and regulations previously drafted at these consultations.

The FDA maintained close relations with the Commission for the dairy industry as a whole, but distributors were dominant in the milk industry's marketing process, and some Floridians felt that this prominence was reflected in the FDA and in the activities of the Commission. A former Commission member described his impression of the situation:

> The Commission readily sought information from any and all sources and naturally a good bit of it came from the Florida Dairy Association, which included distributors, producers, and producer-distributors. I recall that the distributors seemed to be predominant in the leadership of the Association.

The FDA pointed out, however, that its board of directors was divided evenly between producers and distributors (seventeen of each) and that the office of president rotated annually, a producer serving in that office one year, and a distributor the next.

Governor Collins and the Milk Commission

FOR ABOUT TWENTY YEARS the Milk Commission operated beneath the level of general public awareness. Although public hearings were held, little mention of its activities was made in the press. Since no public funds were involved, the State Legislature tended to approve routinely any Commission recommendations. No legislation seriously altering the functions of the Commission ever reached the floor of either the state Senate or House of Representatives, and only rarely were any such bills introduced.

In the late 1940s and early 1950s, however, the operations of the agency became the subject of some public controversy. Occasional grumblings were expressed by temporary and hastily organized consumers' groups. Two newspapers, the *Miami Herald* and the *Tampa Tribune,* criticized the agency in their editorial pages. The Commission became an issue in local campaigns in several metropolitan areas where there was pressure for reduction in consumer prices. (From 1944 to 1948 Florida retail milk prices were the highest, or among the highest, in the nation. Costs were also high. Grain and dairy feeds had to be imported via long and expensive hauling. Also, Florida, with its many seasonal enterprises, had a high milk consumption in winter, while in summer many dairymen had a surplus.) Aldermanic candidates who had promised to work for removal of retail controls in their areas were elected in Miami and Tampa.

In 1953 the milk industry, after conferring with Governor Dan McCarty, agreed to support legislation

(1) increasing consumer membership on the Commission from one to three;

(2) dropping the producer-distributor member; and

(3) removing the Administrator's right to vote. This amendment to the milk control law was passed by the Legislature. It gave the agency a total of seven members: two from the dairy interests, two representatives from state agencies, and three consumer members all appointed by the Governor. The legislation was the only major revision in the milk law since 1933. It was designed to forestall any further development of consumer opposition and, in the words of dairy industry leaders, to "educate" consumers through their representatives on the Commission.

The 1954 Democratic Primary

The activities of the Milk Commission were brought sharply to public attention during the 1954 Democratic primary.

Florida's one-party, Democratic politics has been characterized as "every man for himself." The size of the state, its dramatic population growth through immigration from other states, the high proportion of its residents who live in urban areas, its diversified economy—all appear to have contributed to a political climate unlike that elsewhere in the South. The outstanding features of this climate in 1954 were a multiplicity of factions and a dispersion of leadership. Candidates for state and local offices usually ran separately and individually, without forming the informal "slates" found in some other Southern states.

Urban-rural divisions played a part in the Florida situation. In 1940 over forty percent of the population lived in five large urban areas: Pensacola, Jacksonville, St. Petersburg, Tampa, and Miami. At the same time, the sparsely settled, rural counties dominated the State Legislature. To some observers, including V. O. Key in his book, *Southern Politics,* Florida politics often seemed, at least superficially, to be issueless, short-term, and individualized, with success going to the most personable and most effective campaigners.

One of the candidates for the Democratic nomination for governor in 1954 was Brailey Odham. Odham was a businessman-politician, a frequent combination in Florida public life. A native of Sanford, Florida, he had worked his way through Louisiana College, graduating in 1941. After serving in World War II he was connected with a variety of commercial enterprises in Sanford until, in 1951, he entered the construction business. By a series of unorthodox but carefully-planned financial moves, he soon built up a $500,000-a-year business. Odham's political career started in 1947 when he was elected to the state House of Representatives. Re-elected in 1949, he gained a reputation as a crusader by charging repeatedly that "gamblers control this Legislature." Odham was intensely committed to a laissez-faire economic philosophy. Until 1951 he had been one of the many state legislators who routinely approved the operations of the Milk Commission. That same year, however, Odham had an experience with the milk industry that had served, at least in part, to change his views. As president of the state Junior Chamber of Commerce, he had become interested in legislation requiring bread manufacturers to add vitamins to their product and to advertise the addition. The Florida Dairy Association had worked against this legislation in the state capital, and it had been defeated.

In 1952 Odham became a public critic of milk price controls and of the Commission, which he regarded as "controlled" by its own clientele, especially the large national dairies. Odham ran for governor in 1952 largely on a platform of reducing milk prices and abolishing the Milk Commission. He was defeated in the second, or run-off, primary by Dan McCarty, considered by some to be friendly to milk price regulation. McCarty was elected, died in office, and in 1954 a special election was held to fill the remaining two years of his term.

In his 1954 primary campaign Odham again called for the abolition of the Milk Commission. The Commission became the most frequently repeated issue in his race and represented, he said, "a symbol of the fix where the special interests used the people's power, their laws, to serve themselves instead of the public interest." Odham's stand was given considerable publicity by the *Tampa Tribune* and the *Miami Herald,* which ran editorials demanding abolition of the Commission.

Dairy interests waged a strenuous battle in opposition. The president of the FDA, Wilmer Bassett, wrote a series of letters to producers, distributors, feed dealers, and equipment company executives urging them to vote against Odham. E. T. Lay said of FDA efforts: "We opposed him in any way we knew how. Everything we could do to keep him from being elected, we did. He had a grudge against our organization and our industry."

The primary was held on May 4, 1954. Odham ran last in a field of three, receiving 187,782 votes. The other two candidates, Charley Johns and LeRoy Collins, received 255,787 and 222,791 votes respectively.

In the campaign for the run-off primary between Johns and Collins to be held on May 25, Odham supported Collins and campaigned in his behalf. LeRoy Collins, a native of Tallahassee and a lawyer, had been active in state politics for twenty years. For six years he had represented Leon County (Tallahassee) in the lower house of the Legislature. From 1940 to 1954 he had served in the state Senate. Collins' voting record was generally considered to be "liberal" with respect to racial issues and government spending, likely to appeal to urban voters. As a legislator, Collins, like Odham, had supported the continuance of the Milk Commission. In fact, he had once introduced legislation to extend milk price controls. As a candidate in the first 1954 primary election, Collins, in response to Odham's speeches, had defended his record of supporting the Milk Commission while a member of the House and Senate.

Odham's support of Collins in the run-off primary fit into the general pattern of the latter's public appeal. Collins was popular in the large, heavily populated counties—the areas from which consumer protests over the activities of the Milk Commission had come. (Odham had also run well in metropolitan areas: Tampa, Miami, and Orlando, his new home town.) In the 1953 session of the Legislature members from these urban counties had opposed milk price controls, while members from the small counties, many of them "dairy milksheds," had formed the backbone of Commission support. Some members of the FDA, remembering Collins' voting record in the Legislature, were unhappy that he had accepted Odham's backing. They tried to telephone the candidate to urge him to repudiate Odham's support, but they could not reach him. Other members, however, were less concerned, relying on what they believed to be Collins' personal assurance that he was sympathetic to their problems. Most distributors were relieved at Odham's defeat. They did not regard Collins as an enemy; in fact, many, including the president of the FDA, continued to support him.

No immediate consequence of Odham's support appeared in Collins' platform for the run-off primary. It did not mention the Milk Commission or price controls.

Collins won the second primary (and thus for all practical purposes the governorship), receiving 380,323 votes to his opponent's 314,198. Members of the milk industry were somewhat apprehensive, even though they had supported him. They did not know what the new Governor intended to do about the Milk Commission issue.

Governor Collins' Citizens' Committee

Collins was inaugurated on January 5, 1955. He offered a program that appealed to the urban counties, which had supported him in the primaries. It soon became evident that Collins' views on milk prices were now similar to Odham's and that removal of all milk price controls was to be very much a part of the gubernatorial program. The assumption in Collins' statement was that regulation by an "industry-dominated" Commission kept prices high.

The increase of consumer membership on the Milk Commission in 1953 had not altered the basic pro-controls posture of the agency. The industry personnel could not be expected to change, nor could the members from the state departments. The Department of Agriculture usually supported controls because of fears that farmers could not survive without price stabilization. Unless controls were maintained, its argument went, price wars would disrupt the entire Florida milk industry and distributors would purchase from out-of-state sources. (The Milk Commission had no authority to prevent the importation of milk from other states.) The Board of Health regarded price controls as part of a comprehensive regulatory program to insure that the sanitary quality of milk remained high.

The votes of the two industry members combined with the two members from Health and Agriculture constituted a majority of the seven-man Commission even if all three consumer representatives voted solidly in opposition. (Up to this point they had not always done so.) As constituted, therefore, the Milk Commission offered little hope to Collins for the removal of controls. Furthermore, Collins was handicapped by his inability to appoint new members. All members appointed by the previous Governor had at least one year remaining in their terms.

Collins had no choice but to work through other channels. On January 12 he appointed a Citizens' Committee, composed entirely of non-industry members, to study the milk pricing situation and report its findings to him. The Committee conducted one public hearing (it was held in the Miami area) at which the audience was provided principally by representatives of the Florida Dairy Association. Only fifteen or twenty non-industry people appeared, and only two consumer spokesmen registered opposition to price controls. The Committee concluded its study in February. It recommended that all controls *above the producer level* be abolished. (The Citizens' Committee apparently began with the intention of recommending the abolition of the Milk Commission in its entirety but modified its views before formal presentation.) Milk industry leaders had no doubts in their own minds that the Governor had expected such a report from the Citizens' Committee.

Retail Controls in the 1955 Legislature

Collins advocated removal of *all* controls, but he accepted the Citizens' Committee recommendation as a realistic first step. He announced that he would incorporate the Committee's proposals as part of his message to the Legislature. Meanwhile, the consumer members of the Commission, heartened by the Governor's attitude, began to take action indicating agreement with his goals. At a February Commission meeting consumer member William Imand proposed that a fifteen-cent fluctuation in retail price be allowed. A certain amount of resentment existed on the part of the old members to what they regarded as the "fixed ideas" of the new consumer members, whom they considered "outsiders," and Imand's motion served to strengthen the basis of the cleavage. Ordinarily such a motion would be doomed to certain defeat. However, an unusual circumstance at this time made it possible for the consumer motion to be adopted. Alex Shaw, the new Department of Agriculture member, had been appointed in January 1955 but, being out of the state on business, had not yet actually joined the Commission. Thus one member of the pro-control group was temporarily lost. Also, the producer member, Ben Waring, was thought to have given some indication that he would not object to a fifteen-cent fluctuation as long as it remained at the retail level. Actually, Waring had been misquoted by some over-enthusiastic newspapers and had no intention of supporting the Imand motion.

The Governor was optimistic: the Legislature was considering his recommendation to remove most price fixing from the authority of the Commission; the Milk Commission itself showed signs of flexibility; and the issue was being publicized by the sudden uprising of consumers' groups, such as the Emergency Consumers Milk Committee of Miami. In April 1955, however, the three consumer members of the Commission again faced an unyielding four-man majority in favor of controls. The Commission voted not to alter the existing structure of controls. Producer member Waring held to his position, while Shaw, the new state Department of Agriculture member, voted with the industry members. Furthermore, the consumer members themselves were not united. Only two of them voted for Imand's motion.

There was still hope for the Governor's legislation to abolish controls above the producer level. Members of the Dade County (Miami) delegation to the House introduced legislation requiring the Milk Commission to institute the changes on retail prices called for in the Imand motion. Both attacks on the *status quo* were met by a determined counterattack from the FDA, which distributed literature to every member of the House and Senate. Although the *Miami Herald* waged an extensive editorial campaign in favor of the Governor's program, and consumers' groups made their first attempt at lobbying, neither bill got out of committee.

Collins' Next Move: the Moratorium

In September 1955 Collins tried a new approach. Conceding for the time being the impossibility of making permanent changes in the Milk Commission law, he began to consider the idea of suspending price controls on a temporary basis. On September 7 the Governor asked the Commission to meet with him in Tallahassee and requested that the members consider a one-year moratorium on controls above the producer level. The Commission agreed to consider the proposal at its September 19 meeting.

Support for the Governor's position was spreading, especially among the large producers of the Miami area, who wanted to withdraw from the Commission marketing area to enter a federal marketing area. They had the option of leaving the Commission's jurisdiction and entering a federal marketing area because they exported milk to other states. (One hundred producers in this Southeast Florida area produced 38 percent of the state's milk.) These farmers were not in sympathy with the FDA, which many of them felt was dominated by large distributors. They wanted federal control, since they exported milk. The Miami area producers believed that they could prosper under a more competitive system and wished more freedom to negotiate with distributors. (They later petitioned out from Commission jurisdiction and entered the federal marketing area jurisdiction.) The Mayor of Miami and other local government officials in the area who were interested in lowering retail prices urged the Commission to accept the Governor's plan. The FDA remained adamantly opposed to any change in the price control system. Four days before the Commission was scheduled to meet, the FDA held a public meeting at which it expressed the belief that the proposed moratorium was illegal. The organization warned that a suspension of controls would be contested by means of an appeal to the Florida Supreme Court.

The vote on the Imand motion suggested what would be required for Collins to win his point on the moratorium. He would first have to be sure that the three consumer members could be relied upon. Then, if just one member of the opposing bloc could be persuaded to change his position, the vote could be won. The producer member, Ben Waring, had occasionally shown some willingness to deviate from the industry point of view. At the same time, Waring was a Borden producer, and both he and the Borden Company were active members of the FDA. The distributor member was a Foremost executive. Alex Shaw of the Department of Agriculture was a relatively unknown quantity, but he had voted to keep controls when he opposed the Imand motion at his first meeting. This left only the Board of Health member, Fred Ragland. He had generally favored the retention of controls and had mobilized the opposition to the Imand motion.

At its executive session on September 19 the Commission voted four to three to drop all controls above the producer level for a period of one year. The results of the Governor's diligent personal persuasion were reflected in the solidity of the consumer bloc. All three consumers declared in favor of the moratorium. The fourth vote was provided by Ragland, who decided to support the moratorium because of its temporary nature. As long as the Commission retained the authority to return to the control system, he had no objections. The vote represented the first tangible success after eight months of sustained effort on Collins' part, and was regarded as the first fissure in the hitherto impregnable defense of the dairy industry.

The Reconstitution of the Commission

The vote on the moratorium, establishing free competition in the milk industry at the retail level for the first time since 1933, was the last action taken by the Commission as then constituted. The three consumer members' terms expired in May and July of 1956, and Collins was given his first opportunity to appoint people who could be expected to share his attitude. He selected three men who had been active in his campaign for the governorship and who supported his position on price controls: Howard Walton, H. G. Cochran, and Dexter Lowry (who became Chairman). Walton, a young labor organizer from Miami, was perhaps firmest in his opposition to controls above the producer level. Born in White Plains, New York, Walton had moved to Florida in 1937. He had worked as a telephone lineman and later had become a business agent for the Communications Workers of America. His background in organized labor had made him suspicious of the activities of large businesses such as Sealtest, Borden's, and Foremost. The year before, he had appeared at the public hearing of the Citizens' Committee on behalf of organized labor to oppose the continuation of controls.

In addition to the three new consumer appointments, producer member Ben Waring resigned prior to the expiration of his term and was replaced by Wilbur Casey. (Waring's resignation was not unplanned. Collins had sounded out Waring about his position on controls sometime before, and Waring, after thinking the matter over, had decided to remain committed to his pro-controls point of view. At the time of the moratorium vote, Waring had submitted a resignation which had not been accepted. In the meantime, Waring had made it clear that he wanted to reinstate controls, and returned home one day to find his resignation suddenly accepted.) The Governor did not consult the industry in selecting Casey as the successor producer member. He acted on the advice of one of the consumer members, expecting that Casey would not support controls. Casey came from the Clearwater-Tampa area. He was a producer for Hoods Dairy, Inc., a sizeable distributor but not one of the Big Three. Like his distributor, he was an active member of the FDA.

Only three members who had participated in the vote on the moratorium remained: Henry Schneider (a distributor member), Ragland (Health), and Shaw (Agriculture). They formed a sort of conservative element against the three new consumer members, who entered the Commission intending to pursue the Governor's program with vigor.

The FDA Urges Return to Controls

Meanwhile, the milk industry began a campaign to return the Commission to its price control policies. In March 1956 the FDA held a special meeting in Orlando to urge that the moratorium be abandoned. This was followed by a petition from Foremost Dairies to the Commission declaring that price controls were necessary to avoid serious price wars. With the reconstitution of the Commission, industry efforts intensified. The Florida Dairy Association, in support of a suit by some of its members, instituted legal action to upset the moratorium vote on the ground that it had not been taken after a public hearing as required by law. In addition, the distributors sought to have the Commission reverse itself by means of the four-vote majority. This meant winning back the support of Ragland, who had voted with the consumers on the moratorium proposal. The support of Casey, the new producer member, also would be needed.

However, the effects of a temporarily free market produced evidence of a difference of opinion between producers and distributors within the FDA. Without wholesale and retail controls, the price paid by the retailer to the distributor dropped as much as two cents a quart in some areas, while the producer price, still under Commission control, did not fluctuate. In the past, producers had publicly supported regulation of prices at all levels. Now, realizing that the moratorium had not affected them, some producers—particularly a number of younger ones—began to express a desire to form an organization independent of the distributors in support of the Commission's vote. Impetus for this movement was provided by the Central Florida Milk Producers Association, a regional group not connected with the FDA.

The Court Invalidates the Moratorium

In July the Florida Supreme Court ruled on the suit brought by some FDA members. It held that the moratorium order was not valid. Price controls had to be re-established exactly as they had been in the past. The decision was a severe blow to the new consumer members and to the Governor. The loss was made more bitter by uncertainty over how the newly-constituted Commission would divide when the issue of controls came up again. The Supreme Court decision made it imperative that some action be taken if the Governor's wishes were to be enacted.

The new consumer members on the Commission began a campaign of persuasion both inside and outside the Commission designed to take advantage of the emerging industry discord. Howard Walton, for instance, followed a course of encouraging cleavages within the industry. He urged producers to think in terms of their own interests and tried to persuade them to attend Commission meetings. He announced that he would never oppose price controls at the producer level. Walton also scouted for allies within the Commission. He ascertained that Ragland (the Board of Health member) had "firmed up" and was once again committed to controls at all levels. Ragland's vote for the moratorium had been based on the conviction that the moratorium was temporary and experimental. The drop in distributor prices convinced him that removal of controls was an improper solution. Schneider, the distributor member appointed by the previous Governor, was firmly committed to controls, as was Shaw (Agriculture). The best hope for a split seemed to be Casey, the new producer member, since he had been selected without prior consultation with the industry. He became the focus of a campaign of persuasion which Walton later described as follows:

> In every contact we had with Casey we pointed out that the history and status of the producer is to be in a position of economic dependence upon the distributor. We tried to show him that the best way to better the situation of the producer was to think independently and help us achieve equality with the influence of the distributors. However, Casey was also approached by producer and distributor members of the FDA.

Walton believed that Casey might vote with the consumers.

He was ready to test this conviction at a Commission meeting the following October. He offered a motion that all controls above the producer level be renounced by the Commission *without* a time limit. Even as he made the motion he did not know how Casey would vote. It turned out that Casey felt a sense of overriding responsibility to dairy interests and could not accept the arguments of the consumers, whom he regarded as "outsiders." He voted against the motion, which was defeated four to three.

A year's strenuous effort had netted no results. The situation was exactly the same as when Collins became Governor. The industry was as powerful as ever in the Commission, nullifying hope that price controls could be abolished. Success had depended upon the good will of some member of the pro-milk industry group. If one member of this majority switched to side with the Governor, as had Ragland on the moratorium vote, the consumer/Collins position could prevail. If not, the consumer members and the Governor were defeated. The arithmetic of the Commission appeared even more unpromising following the October rejection of Walton's motion. Time after time Walton repeated his motion, only to be met with a cohesive and determined four-vote pro-controls majority. It seemed unlikely that any of these four members would alter his position.

The Appointment of Brailey Odham

THE OPPONENTS of price controls faced another threat besides the cohesion of the industry majority. The consumer members of the Commission were exhibiting a tendency to be impressed by the arguments of E. T. Lay, executive secretary of the Florida Dairy Association. This was particularly true of one of Collins' recent appointments, Chairman Dexter Lowry. Although he voted with the other consumer members, Lowry continually expressed pleasure at what seemed to him to be the well-marshaled evidence in support of controls offered by the FDA primarily on behalf of the distributors. (The distributors were taking the brunt of the Governor's attacks.) It seemed unlikely that Lowry would continue as a consistent opponent of controls. After winning an election in 1956 for a full four-year term (his previous election had been to fill the remaining unexpired term of the late Dan McCarty) the Governor began looking for a Chairman who would make more determined and persistent efforts to end the price control system. Collins had performed the unusual feat of securing a majority of votes against four other Democratic candidates in the *first* primary. A run-off primary had not been necessary. The campaign had centered largely on a university desegregation issue, with Collins running on an "anti-integration but obey the law" theme against a more extreme segregationist field. Collins would not be able to succeed himself when his new term expired in 1960.

Odham Considers the Job

At about the same time, the *Miami Herald* and the *Tampa Tribune* were printing frequent editorials criticizing the inability of the Milk Commission to cope with the power of the distributors. (The Miami newspaper kept up its campaign in favor of Collins' milk policies even though producers in the Miami area had left the Commission's jurisdiction by voting to join the federal marketing area system. Miami prices were therefore no longer affected. The *Miami Herald's* persistence on the milk issue has been explained on two grounds: (1) it was a strong supporter of Collins; and (2) it was always possible for the Miami milk producers to change their minds and switch back from federal to Florida Milk Commission price jurisdiction.) Brailey Odham, inactive politically since 1954, had not lost his interest in the Commission and was extremely popular with those newspapers that opposed price fixing. Odham also had close personal friendships with members of the editorial staffs. Early in 1957 he was asked by the *Herald* and *Tribune* if he would object to editorials urging that he be made Chairman of the Milk Commission. Odham did not object. He encouraged the two newspapers to bring up his name.

The idea of Odham as the new Chairman appealed to Governor Collins. The situation in the Commission was extremely discouraging. Odham had run two political campaigns on the alleged evils of price fixing in the milk industry. The industry itself had once regarded him as an arch enemy. A more conspicuous opponent of the Milk Commission could not be found. To a Governor fresh from an election victory but still with the sour taste of a year's frustration with the Commission, Odham's firm views and aggressive personality presented an attractive combination. Collins decided to appoint Odham without seriously considering any other candidate. He dispatched his former law partner to discover if Odham would take the job.

The distributors and the other members of the FDA literally could not believe that the Governor was serious. Most of them, especially those who had supported Collins in the 1954 campaign, thought he was joking when he casually mentioned his intentions to them. Some of the Commission's consumer members, especially Howard Walton, were also apprehensive, fearing that Odham could not be made to see their point of view on producer price controls, which they no longer opposed.

When the FDA heard that Odham was under consideration, its leaders sought a conference with Collins in the hope of changing his mind. Repeated efforts by the FDA to confer with the Governor—efforts supported by the Florida Farm Bureau Federation and the state Chamber of Commerce—met with failure. Meanwhile individual distributors arranged private conferences with people close to the Governor and persuaded some of his political friends to telephone his office to pass along the message that Odham's appointment would be considered an affront to every dairyman in the state.

Finally, in response to its requests, Collins wired the FDA that, although his decision had been reached, he would meet with the group prior to the formal announcement of Odham's appointment. At this meeting FDA leaders told the Governor how disturbed they were about his selection, but they could not change his mind.

Collins appointed Odham as a consumer member of the Commission (and helped him get the votes to be elected Chairman) effective July 1957. At the same time a statement from the Governor's office declared candidly that the Governor and the FDA had "come to a parting of the ways."

Distributor members of the FDA reflected bitterly on Collins' first election campaign in 1954 and the lack of any indication in Collins' platform that he had shared Odham's views on the Milk Commission. Moreover, they noted that Odham was a complete stranger to the milk industry. The new Chairman, they thought, would not be interested in their problems and would tear down all that the Commission had built up.

Other Changes in Commission Personnel

With Odham as Chairman, Collins hoped to make progress toward the final goal of free competition in the milk industry. However, the appointment of a new Chairman would have offered little reason for optimism had it not been for the opportunity to make other changes. Especially useful was the expiration on May 30, 1957 of distributor member Henry Schneider's term. Schneider, a Foremost executive, had been a consistent leader of the opposition to any changes in the system of controls. To replace him, Collins wanted a distributor whose views were less firmly fixed. Basically, this meant that Collins needed a distributor of non-Big Three environment, a smaller distributor of more "progressive" views. Wilmer Bassett became the leading candidate. Bassett operated his own small dairy a few miles from Tallahassee. Although he was a former president of the Florida Dairy Association, he was not convinced that complete price control was the only solution to the problems of the dairy industry. As FDA president, he had led an unsuccessful effort to replace L. K. Nicholas as Commission Administrator, although this effort had not reached the level of open controversy. When asked by Governor Collins to serve, Bassett mentioned his efforts to defeat Odham in the 1954 primary and expressed doubts that they could co-operate. However, Bassett was willing to try. Again, as with the Casey appointment, Collins did not rely on industry recommendations.

Another chance to increase his following was offered to Collins in the case of Fred Ragland. Although Ragland's term had not expired, Collins requested that he resign and suggested to the director of the Board of Health that some "new blood" would be welcome. The Board responded by naming Robert Carter to replace Ragland. Carter's entire professional life had been spent in the field of public health. After graduate study he had worked on the county level in Florida. He had been with the state Board of Health since 1938. Until his appointment to the Commission, Carter had had no connection with the dairy industry. But he was the sort of person who would devote a great deal of time and effort to do justice to matters that sparked his interest, even if they were not directly in the public health field. Like Ragland, he believed that some form of market regulation was necessary, but he did not believe that it need necessarily include total price control.

At this point the Commission had five members acceptable to the Governor. The only persons whose views he could have reason to doubt were Alex Shaw from the Department of Agriculture and Wilbur Casey, the producer member he had appointed in 1956. There was reason to hope that controls over the milk industry could be abolished.

Odham Reorganizes the Commission

Odham thought that the man who had been replaced as Chairman, Dexter Lowry, would retire, even though his term had not expired. However, through his personal friendship with the Governor, Lowry was able to obtain the salaried post of Administrator. (He was replaced as consumer member by Jackson Logan, a realtor and insurance man from Tampa, who had acted as manager of Collins' campaigns in the Tampa area.) L. K. Nicholas, long-time permanent staff head, became Assistant Administrator. It soon became apparent to Odham that this arrangement could not be tolerated. Nicholas was strongly committed to the industry's point of view and, since he had long been dedicated to enforcing controls through existing law, was not prepared to relinquish his opinions. Furthermore, even though he had been a consumer member, Lowry was leaning in what Odham saw as the direction of the distributors: i.e., continuation of resale price controls. Especially important from Odham's point of view was the fact that Lowry depended to a great extent on the FDA, which he regarded as a reliable source of information. Odham felt that the administrative staff of the Commission operated in such a way as to keep him from getting information except through "accepted" channels. There was a definite, although restrained, difference of opinion between the Chairman and his new Administrator. Odham later described the situation in the following way:

> I shall not soon forget my first meeting with Lowry, who was to serve as my Administrator, and his discussion of the complexities of bases, pricing systems and formulas for skim milk. Indeed, it sounded so complex that it frightened me. I asked Mr. Lowry where he had learned all of his information. His reply to me was that it was a very complex industry and I needn't worry about it, he knew the answers and I could simply turn to him.

Odham felt he could not operate in a situation in which he was asked to depend upon unfriendly sources for his information. He believed that his position was extremely precarious because of the hostility of the Administrator and the necessity of dealing with an Assistant Administrator who had long been sympathetic to the industry. He decided to try to remove both Nicholas and Lowry, and to move consumer member Howard Walton, the former trade unionist, to the position of Administrator. With Nicholas, all that was necessary was a telephone call to the Governor's office. To remove Lowry took two months of persistent effort before the "necessary change in Administrators" was accomplished. Lowry resigned, Walton replaced him, and the Governor named Mrs. Charlotte Tomlinson of Lake Wales —she had been active in his campaigns—to take Walton's place as consumer member.

Odham's First Move: The Rebate Investigation

When Odham became Chairman, he believed that he could accomplish the job of abolishing controls in about six weeks. However, he soon realized that this goal would require preparatory groundwork.

Much to the pleasure of Walton as the new Administrator, Odham displayed a sympathy toward the producer. One of the first actions of the Commission under its new Chairman was to make the control of producer prices more comprehensive. Previously the Commission had regulated producer prices only for Class I (retail) milk. About twenty percent of Florida dairy farmers' production was given to Class II and III milk (surplus milk used for by-products). Although prices for Class II and III milk had not been regulated, Odham supported the extension of Commission supervision into this area. A Commission order to this effect was strenuously opposed by distributors on the grounds that prices were excessive when compared to those of equivalent products on the open market. Borden's and Foremost informed the Commission that they would refuse to buy surplus milk at prices set by the Commission. Odham quickly warned them that refusal to buy would result in a suspension of licenses. Also, a thorough audit performed under Odham's guidance revealed that some distributors were charging producers excessive rates for hauling milk. The Commission issued an order requiring these distributors (mostly "contract" haulers) to charge more reasonable rates. The order later was contested by Superior Dairies but was upheld in the Florida courts.

However, none of these clashes with the distributors was as serious or as spectacular as the investigation of rebates. A study of the Commission's pricing structure was made in August and September of 1957 by a private C.P.A. hired by the Commission. It revealed that there was no differential between prices paid at stores and the price of milk delivered to the home, although the cost of delivering a quart of milk was estimated by Odham at six cents. (The industry men active in the FDA maintained that home delivery costs were much less.) Store prices were kept up to the level of delivered prices, whereas, Odham claimed, a differential would allow the consumer who carried his own milk to save six cents. The study indicated that distributors delivering to retail accounts were building additional profits and using them as "kick-backs" to large retail stores. In exchange for volume accounts and continuing contracts, some distributors rebated chain retailers as much as fifteen percent of purchase price.

Rumors of rebates had been fairly common in the past, but no previous Commission had unearthed evidence to suggest that the practice was as extensive as Odham now implied. Odham himself did not have enough evidence to constitute proof, but he released a statement charging distributors with spending $15,000,000 a year in rebates.

Distributors were quick to state that only three or four percent of the business was involved in rebates. Still, retailers and, especially, distributors were alarmed. Rebating was a violation of the Robinson-Patman Act, and violators were subject to fines of triple damages in federal courts. One distributor frankly stated: "He [Odham] could have ruined us and the retail chains if he had wanted to." Soon after issuing his statement, Odham was approached by the president of a large retail chain who inquired about the possibility of avoiding public disclosure.

To the relief of the chain retailers and distributors, Odham seemed to retreat. While preparing for a public hearing on the price of milk, he agreed not to ask distributors or retailers if they had actually given or received rebates, but merely if they had "heard of" such practices. This would avoid actual incrimination of particular firms or individuals. The agreement was satisfactory to all parties, including Odham, because it made possible the insertion in the record of evidence that might have been difficult to obtain under the threat of legal reprisal. In return, Odham extracted an important concession: the rebate system would be admitted to be a "prevailing practice."

The November 1957 Hearings

Assured that the existence of rebates would not be denied, Odham arranged a public hearing at which the entire price situation was to be discussed. He hoped the hearing would show that the best way to correct the evils of rebating was to allow free competition. A group of distributors asked Odham to meet with them at a Tallahassee hotel on November 18, the night before the hearing was to begin. Odham agreed to attend, hoping to show the distributors that he was not an unreasonable man and hoping also to forestall an organized show of bitter opposition at the coming hearing. He asked Robert Carter to accompany him. Carter was fast becoming his close ally. Although he represented the Board of Health, Carter showed no tendency to vote for controls at all levels. He had been studying the rebate system with Odham, and had concluded that the best solution lay in guaranteeing a home-store price differential. There had been a close exchange of ideas between the two men. When they went to meet the distributors, they were generally agreed on the line they would take.

At the hotel meeting the distributors tried to find out what sort of treatment they could expect at the public hearing. Odham told them that an effort would be made to establish a five cents per quart store-home differential. He also said that he would not support the abolition of controls until some method of assuring the differential was established. Carter said he was willing to accept a three-cent differential. The distributors indicated that they would oppose anything above a one-cent differential. Neither side would compromise. Odham and Carter withdrew, giving the distributors until midnight to change their minds. At 10:30 p.m. Odham received a message asking for another conference on the basis of a two-cent differential. The Commission Chairman refused.

At the public hearing the next day, all the testimony concerned the rebate system. The tense negotiations of the evening before were reflected in open hostility between Odham and distributor member Bassett. The testimony of the distributors, as expected, stated that rebating had been practiced, but each witness offered only hearsay evidence. Observers were struck by the bitterness of the distributors, who for years had been the Commission's staunchest defenders. A puzzling note was added by the testimony of E. T. Lay. When asked whether the FDA favored price controls, Lay simply refused to give a direct answer.

On the second day of the hearing, November 20, Odham made a firm commitment to the premise upon which he had accepted the position as Chairman:

> I disapprove of any law that regulates your business . . . and hope the day is not far . . . when there will no longer be a law that will be charged with the responsibility of regulating your business.

Odham did not mean that he was going to translate his disapproval into immediate action. Since joining the Commission he had formed an informal discussion group with Carter and Walton, whose views on price controls were less adamant. He had been impressed by their reasoning. Thus he was prepared to support Carter when the latter made a motion that a schedule of price floors be established: 20 cents per quart platform price; 22 cents cash-and-carry price; 23 cents wholesale price; and a retail price not to exceed the wholesale price by two cents. The plan was an attempt to establish differentials between the various distribution processes. Odham agreed with the principle behind it. He hoped that this price schedule would create in consumers an expectation that store-bought milk would be cheaper than delivered milk. He intended to wait until a differential had been firmly established, and then, in the following months, to move to end all controls.

A Surprise Move

Odham was arguing with Carter about increasing the differential when distributor member Wilmer Bassett asked to be recognized. Bassett offered (as a substitute for Carter's motion), a motion that all price controls above the producer level be abolished. Casey, the producer member, seconded.

Odham and Carter were taken completely by surprise. Having been appointed Chairman to achieve free competition against the stubborn opposition of the industry, Odham did not expect that there would come from his ostensible opponents a motion which he himself was not yet prepared to make. As Bassett expected, Odham and the consumer members had no choice but to support the substitute motion. Bassett's proposal passed by a vote of six to one. It was opposed only by Carter, who was not committed to the complete removal of controls.

The precise reasons behind Bassett's motion were complex. The distributors, for whom Bassett spoke, were extremely dissatisfied with the trend of the Commission under Odham. They had been angered by the extension of producer controls to Class II and Class III milk and the requirement that they buy surplus milk at Commission prices. They had failed to reach any agreement with Odham at the Tallahassee hotel meeting. As explained by E. T. Lay:

> The distributors decided that with such a man to administer price controls the dairy industry could be ruined. We were better off with no controls than with controls under Odham. It was certainly highly unethical to appoint him, because he was opposed to the law he was supposed to enforce. Impeachment proceedings should have been brought against the Governor for advocating and demanding non-compliance with a state law that he was sworn as Governor to uphold.

Lay's reluctance to assert opposition to price controls the day before now appeared somewhat more explicable. Odham later believed that Bassett's motion was part of a well-developed plan, a surprise attack. According to Odham, "[Bassett] did this on orders from the milk industry." Bassett, on the other hand, seemed less concerned with the course of the Commission and more interested in the possible results of Carter's motion. Odham's restraint on the rebate question had impressed Bassett. He had been alarmed, however, over Carter's floor price plan. He reasoned that the floors that had been proposed were below cost and, if established, would not only have created a differential but would also have enabled price wars to begin again. Bassett realized that, with Odham and the other consumer members supporting it, Carter's motion had at least four votes. His strategy then became to offer a substitute which could not fail to pass. He chose to offer the proposal which the consumer members had been trying for since 1955. Bassett thought that removal of controls without a differential would be preferable to Carter's program. His motion, as Bassett later explained it, was purely a defense against the Carter proposal and was not directly related to the meeting with the distributors or the general deterioration of relations.

Odham had achieved his goal, but he had not been the initiator. In fact, he had been caught completely off-guard. He had faced his first major hearing on price control prepared to listen to the Carter plan to keep a form of controls, in spite of his frequent statements against controls in any form. However, Bassett's motion, which granted everything Odham originally demanded, forced Odham into a position more extreme than he would have preferred at that time.

Splits Occur in Industry Forces

ALTHOUGH THE NOVEMBER 20 motion was interpreted by Odham as a hostile reaction by the large distributors to his chairmanship, upon reflection he was pleased with the results. He knew that the dairy industry was at last operating free of controls above the producer level.

During the winter and spring following the removal of controls, the market remained reasonably stable in most of the state, although there was a slight decline in price. In northeast Florida, however, especially in the Jacksonville area, there was a considerable disruption of price structures. It was here that independent distributors gave the Big Three their most persistent competition. On a state-wide basis, the market was divided about evenly between the small distributors and the Big Three, but in Jacksonville independents had nearly 65 percent of the market. In this area of intense competition, milk prices dropped sharply. By May 1958 most supermarkets were selling milk at or below cost, as they passed distributor discounts along to the consumer.

The independents could not long compete in this battle of discounts. They asked the Commission for a special hearing. Smaller distributors were now asking for help against their larger competitors. (The larger distributors had not begun the war, but merely had met the prices dropped by the cash-and-carry operators.) Although the small independent distributors belonged to the FDA, they did not work through that organization. They believed that by appealing to the Commission on their own, as *small* operators, they would get a more sympathetic hearing from the Chairman. Therefore, a number of independent dairies petitioned on behalf of the Jacksonville independents and indicated a clear difference of interest with the large national distributors. Their petition was supported by a letter from the National Association of Independent Dairies, an organization with a Washington office to which a number of independent Jacksonville dairies belonged.

The Jacksonville price wars presented Chairman Odham with a dilemma. Accustomed to thinking in terms of producers versus distributors, he was now given evidence that lack of controls could seriously harm a substantial number of small distributors. He was impressed by the arguments of the Jacksonville petitioners that below-cost selling could drive them out of the market, thus lessening competition and concentrating economic power in the hands of the few large distributors. Odham was clearly opposed to controls, but he also favored the freest kind of competition.

The No Tie-in, No Limit Order

Unwilling to return to any form of regulation, Odham developed and presented to the Commission a plan that he hoped would help the independents yet still allow the price of milk to be determined by competition. This was the "no tie-in, no limit" plan. It stated that no Jacksonville retailer could limit the amount of milk sold to any customer when offering at a reduced price; nor could he make the sale of cheap milk conditional upon the purchase of other goods. The object of the plan was to enable the independent distributors—or, legally, anyone else—to enter a retail establishment and purchase the entire milk supply, thus destroying the advertising appeal of the "loss leader." The order was passed unanimously by the Commission on May 16, 1958. Earlier, Odham had exhibited some sympathy for the problems of producers. This was his first demonstration of concern for distributors.

The Rise of a New Federation

Meanwhile, the cleavage in the milk industry between producers and distributors, which had begun to emerge with the ill-fated moratorium, was growing. As noted earlier, there was a divergence of interest within the FDA. This divergence was enhanced following Odham's appointment because of Commission actions that indicated a concern for producer interests.

In its hearings the Commission began to see a rising independence on the part of producers. In the past the testimony of dairy farmers had not deviated from that of distributors. Now local producers' groups began to declare publicly in support of Odham's program of scrutinizing the activities of large distributors. Many distributors and producer-distributors, unwilling to consider the vote of November 20, 1957 as final, were seeking a return to controls. Some producer groups, on the other hand, were satisfied with the Commission's policy, since prices paid to the farmers by the distributors were still controlled. The shift in producer attitudes frequently translated itself into support, by these producers, of Commission orders hostile to distributors. Early in 1958 the agency brought suit against the Borden Company for failure to pay Tallahassee, Pensacola, and Tampa producers in accordance with established price schedules. Several producer groups offered testimony helpful to the Commission's case.

Operating for the first time under a Commission which they thought was not easily influenced by the distributors—particularly by the large distributors—some of the younger producers began to work for the formation of a separate, state-wide, producers organization outside the FDA. At private meetings, convened sometimes before or after FDA gatherings, these younger dairy farmers argued with their elders (in some cases their fathers) that the interests of producers and distributors were distinctly separate and that prosperity of producers was not dependent on price regulation for distributors, since the Milk Commission was not going to do away with minimum producer prices under any circumstances. Moreover, the Commission was clearly receptive to separate representations by producers, thereby lessening the grounds for the traditional dependence of producers on the particular distributors who regularly bought their milk. The existence of an independent force of producers became conspicuous at the annual meeting of the FDA in July 1958, when a producer element vigorously opposed a distributor request for the sale of surplus milk at sub-minimum prices to enable distributors to compete with out-of-state bidders for unregulated contracts to supply milk to federal military installations.

In August 1958 a separate producer group was created: the Florida Dairy Farmers Federation. The nucleus for the new Federation came from the Central Florida Milk Producers Association, one of several regional associations that had existed for some time. The Federation quickly incorporated other local producer groups that asked to join. Some of its membership was drawn from producer members of the FDA. Within a year the Federation included producers of sixty to seventy percent of the state's milk. It included the Miami producers' association which alone accounted for about thirty percent of Florida milk production. (The Federation, however, was able to claim only about 35 percent of the milk produced under the control of the Milk Commission, since much of the Miami production was under the jurisdiction of the federal marketing area.)

The new organization was vigorously anti-large distributor and pro-Odham from the start. The Federation's attitude toward the FDA was summarized in the remarks of one of its officers.

> [The formation of the Federation] came about because Mr. Lay had been accused of changing minutes of meetings to serve his own purpose. He had been accused of being for or against policy before it was determined by the joint board. It was felt by our present leaders that Mr. Lay was being directed by distributors to lay traps for producers.

Lay denied these charges, attributing them to the jealousy of Federation leaders.

The FDA Reorganizes

Distributors did not take long to react. The FDA members voted to disband the FDA and to reorganize again into the two groups that had merged to form it originally (in 1946). The two reconstituted groups were the Florida Dairy Products Association (FDPA), exclusively a distributor and producer-distributor group; and the Florida State Dairyman's Association (FSDA), formed of those producers who were in the producer division of the old FDA and who refused to join the new Federation. E. T. Lay, who had initiated the original merger, took the lead again in the reorganization. The new associations, although separate, operated in close liaison, holding joint conventions and issuing a joint publication. Lay became executive secretary of the FDPA.

Relations between the Federation and these two organizations grew increasingly hostile. The Federation condemned members of the Florida State Dairyman's Association as "captive" producers. By this term it meant, the organization said, "those producers who are not able to determine for themselves what direction should be taken by the dairy farmers. They are the farmers who are . . . the leaders of the other state organization." The leaders of the FSDA were equally vigorous in their attack on the Federation, which they regarded as "radical." They pointed out that the economic fate of the producer was tied to the distributor and maintained that any organization designed to "protect" the producer must co-operate with the distributors.

Odham was delighted with the formation of the Federation. He felt he had achieved an element of support within the industry. When he had first become Chairman, he had been hampered by the inability or unwillingness of many producers, who privately supported his position, to provide active, public backing. With the Federation operating as a friendly pressure group, he hoped these problems would be less severe.

The Commission Encourages Producer Independence

Distributors did not accept the creation of an independent producer association without a struggle. Many of them would not give Federation member groups access to the "dues check-off plan." Under this plan, local producer groups arranged to have distributors deduct membership dues when farmers were paid for their milk. Now, however, Federation-affiliated producer groups were denied this convenience, while the dues check-off plan was continued for the FSDA. Lack of a check-off system could seriously harm the growth and survival of the Federation, since it did not have another "automatic" method of collection.

To prevent the disintegration of the newly-created friendly group, Odham supported a Commission order requiring that the dues check-off plan be made available to all producer groups without discrimination. The order stated that any producer group meeting certain standards established by the Commission could qualify for dues check-off. The order was passed by the Commission by a four to three margin on February 19, 1959. (It was appealed to the state Supreme Court by distributors, but was upheld.) Without a producer-distributor split on the Commission, the motion would have failed, since Jackson Logan, a consumer member, voted with Shaw and Bassett against the motion. But the producer and distributor members of the Commission voted against each other. The producer member was now a member also of the Federation. Dr. James Acree, a director of the Northeast Florida Milk Producers Association (affiliated with the Federation) had been persuaded by Odham and Administrator Walton to replace Wilbur Casey, whose term had expired in the summer of 1958. Prior to his appointment, Acree had been active in support of Chairman Odham. By the time of the dues check-off vote, he was a vice president of the Federation.

The staff of the Commission also acted to encourage producer independence and support. It will be recalled that during his tenure as a Commission member Howard Walton had urged producers to speak for themselves. As Administrator, acting independently of Odham but in consonance with the Chairman's goals, Walton found ways to encourage the Federation. He was aided by the aggressiveness of the new organization. When hurricane damage caused property losses on Florida dairy farms, the Commission exercised its authority to determine hardship cases and provide assistance. It notified all producer groups to help in compiling a hardship list. Donald Conkey, an officer of a local producer group and of the Federation, became the primary source of information for staff members making the list. Distributors who tried to have more producers added to those chosen to receive assistance were encouraged to work through Conkey.

In nurturing the Federation, Odham and Walton hoped to develop an alternate industry source of information that could compete successfully with distributors and the Florida State Dairyman's Association before the Commission. With the establishment of a strong producers' association, the agency would no longer have to cope with united, industry-wide opposition. Some years later, evaluating the success of the Commission's efforts on behalf of producers, Odham observed:

> Needless to say, when we continued to show examples like these to the milk producers of Florida, who had for years been forced into silence and had no voice of their own,[1] suddenly they began to realize that the producers' interest and the distributors' interest were not necessarily one and the same.

The FSDA Encourages Producers To Withdraw from Commission Rule

It soon appeared that Odham was going to need all the help he could get to deal with increasing distributor hostility. The large dairies began a new campaign to weaken the authority of the Commission.

It will be recalled that the milk control law gave producers within a marketing area authority to petition in or out of the jurisdiction of the Commission. In late 1958 the local affiliates of the FSDA (the producers' group reconstituted by

[1] The accuracy of this clause is disputed by E. T. Lay.

the FDA reorganization) began trying to persuade producers to exercise their option to withdraw. The movement met with some success. Producers in the Pensacola area passed a withdrawal petition, and a similar petition was circulated in Jacksonville. In these areas distributors, in various ways, encouraged sympathetic producers to take the lead in circulating the petitions. In Jacksonville a few selected producers were asked to meet in the Sealtest plant. It was claimed that they were given a withdrawal petition and asked to help get rid of the Commission.

The withdrawal campaign reached its climax in the Tallahassee area in January and February of 1959. Distributors were working through local groups affiliated with the FSDA to induce producers to sign a withdrawal petition. At the same time the FSDA and the Federation were holding membership drives in the area. The two simultaneous activities made the issue unusually clear-cut, for the Federation, in seeking members, defended the Commission and made a particular point of indicating satisfaction with Chairman Odham. The local FSDA groups, on the other hand, made it clear that signing the withdrawal petition was an essential part of their program.

The Fight in Lafayette County

The conflict soon centered in Lafayette County, midway between Jacksonville and Tallahassee and home of a large number of dairy farmers. All of these producers were affiliated with Borden's under Commission base-fixing agreements. The Federation claimed that the producers were offered eighteen-month contracts with Borden's —coincidental with the remainder of Odham's term—if they would petition for withdrawal. The distributors conceded that they "entertained overtures," but said that the initiative, including the suggestion of the contract, came from the producers. The struggle was seen as fierce by all parties concerned. The Federation believed the battle to be crucial to its existence. One Federation official later said:

> When we first got wind of it [the petition] we were right in the process of getting Lafayette County producers interested in the Federation, but they were hesitant because they were Borden's producers and Borden's can be plenty rough. The distributors were trying to strike at the heart of our membership [drive] by forcing the Tallahassee area producers to withdraw from Commission jurisdiction.

There were reports at public hearings of the Commission of possible economic sanctions against producers who did not sign the withdrawal petition. Distributors vigorously denied these allegations. It was alleged that farmers were presented with the petition by the local producers' group connected with the FSDA, told that enough signatures had been gathered, and warned that when there was no longer a Milk Commission their economic status would be precarious with no contracts. It was rumored that Foremost Dairies would close its Tallahassee plant if the Commission were not rejected. One producer said that he was told the petition's purpose was to "do away with Brailey Odham" and that if he did not sign he could "sell his cows on the market." He concluded, "I'm a poor man. If they cut me off, I'd be ruined. I'd be ruined if I hadn't signed the petition."

To combat these efforts, Administrator Howard Walton went to Marianna, a town in the same marketing area as Lafayette County, to speak to producers. He explained that the Commission intended to investigate and dispute any petition. He pointed out that once the marketing area had withdrawn, the Commission would no longer be able to exercise its power to enforce contracts between producers and distributors. Also, the Commission was developing plans for a "just cause" order stating that producers' contracts could not be terminated without just cause as defined by the Commission.

The Federation offered Lafayette producers legal help in loss-of-contract suits. It also promised legal and financial help if they refused to sign the petition and if retaliation by Borden's were attempted. This never proved necessary. Borden's offered all producers the same contract whether or not they had signed the petition.

The FSDA local association proved to be the stronger. Eighty-six producers in the Tallahassee area signed the withdrawal petition, which was presented to Chairman Odham at the February 19, 1959 meeting of the Commission. The document was drafted with the help of some distributors, including the distributor member of the Commission, Wilmer Bassett. Bassett's main contribution was in keeping the petition's language as moderate as possible. Following the formal introduction, the withdrawal petition read as follows:

> The management and control of the Milk Commission by its present chairman, J. Brailey Odham, is destructive of Florida's Dairy Industry and is harmful to the consumers. The Chairman's arbitrary and vindictive manner makes it impossible for either the producers, the distributors or the consumers to counsel with the Commission in a calm and constructive effort to attain a fair and reasonable objective.
>
> The undersigned urge that the Milk Commission Law be retained on the Statute Books because it has served in the past and can in the future, under other administrations, serve the public welfare. We reserve the right upon a change of chairmanship, to request that we may again be permitted to work with the Commission for the common good of the dairy industry.

Odham's reaction to the vehemence of this personal rebuke was tempered by what he perceived to be a larger issue:

> This was done prior to the 1959 session of the Legislature . . . to convince the legislators that the Commission, operating under me, was no good.

The Tallahassee petition represented the end of a phase in Odham's career. Deeply involved in intra-industry conflicts, he had become identified with what he thought to be "underdog" elements of the milk industry—producers and independent distributors. The prime antagonists, in Odham's eyes, were now the Big Three dairies, the largest, national-size distributors. With the divisions in the industry institutionalized by means of rival organizations and the conflict defined in terms of the Chairman, Odham, angered by the withdrawal tactic, was more determined than ever that the Commission should never again become dominated by large distributors.

The industry itself was divided over the issue of Odham's performance of his duties. The FDPA and the FSDA returned Odham's antagonism with interest and accused him of splitting the industry. They referred to the "bias" of the Commission in favor of the Federation as "sickening."

While sympathy with small distributors had guided Odham to sponsor the "no tie-in, no limit" order, he could not extend this sympathy to support any kind of distributor or retail price controls. To him, price controls and chain distributor domination were nearly synonymous.

The Fight Goes to the Legislature

THE WITHDRAWAL of the Tallahassee producers was only one of several problems faced by the Commission in early 1959, prior to the session of the State Legislature. A new and vigorous attempt was being made to abolish Odham's agency.

An interim committee of the Legislature studying reorganization of the state Department of Agriculture had drafted a report suggesting that the Milk Commission be abolished and its functions transferred to the Department of Agriculture. The chairman of the committee, state Senator Tom Adams, had supported the position of the Governor on milk in the previous legislative session.

Governor Collins, who had consistently favored abolition, supported the Adams Committee report, believing that its recommendations would be linked with a request for legislative repeal of all milk price control laws. The Governor had praised and vigorously defended Odham when his Chairman had been so severely criticized during the Tallahassee conflict, but this did not cause the Governor to lose sight of his more fundamental goal, the abolition of the Commission and all controls. It was better, in his view, to have no Commission than to face the possibility that the agency might again become, under a new Chairman appointed by the Governor who would succeed him in 1961, an instrument of industry regulation in industry interests. The recommendations of the Adams Committee were also supported by the newspapers which had for so long attacked controls: the *Miami Herald* and the *Tampa Tribune*.

In recommending the abolition of the Commission and the transfer of its functions to the Department of Agriculture, whose directly-elected Commissioner had held office continuously for many years, Senator Adams was joined by the FDA's successor distributor organization, the Florida Dairy Products Association. In the words of E. T. Lay, its executive secretary, FDPA support was based on the conviction that the milk pricing laws could function better under a director responsible to the Commissioner of Agriculture than under a commission appointed by the Governor. Lay cited experience in California and some other states. The FDPA further argued that abolishing the Commission was logical in view of the recent attempts to remove marketing areas from Commission control. With the loss of Pensacola and Tallahassee, the FDPA said, the Commission now served only 55 percent of the producing areas. The FDPA did not envision, as the Governor did, that the Adams recommendations would be attached to proposals for eliminating all milk price legislation. Sometime later, the Adams Committee lost the support of the FDPA when Lay learned that the Committee's final recommendation would include the elimination of resale price control laws.

The Federation, the recently-formed independent producers' group, was the only association to oppose the Committee immediately. It argued that dairy farmers had prospered more under Odham's chairmanship than at any other time in their history. Recalling the misfortunes of producers under previous Commissions, the Federation urged no change in the agency's status.

On February 18 (the day before the Tallahassee petition was formally presented) the Milk Commission voted unanimously to oppose the Adams Committee proposals. The only member who might have favored abolition was Odham. However, he reasoned that controls might be reinstated if the Commission's functions were transferred to the Department of Agriculture.

The Commission Makes Recommendations to the Legislature

The next day, February 19, the Commission met again to decide what proposals it wished to submit to the Legislature in April. It was known that the Governor, in spite of Commission opposition, would include termination of the agency in his 1959 legislative program. Although, as it turned out, the final report of the Adams Committee omitted any mention of the Department of Agriculture or transfer of functions, Collins chose to send a separate recommendation for abolition of the Milk Commission. The Commission, on record against its own abolition, now had to decide what sort of legislation it would recommend.

A major conflict had been developing on this point. Odham was anxious to have the milk law rewritten to have *all* price control authority above the producer level removed from the Commission. (Making it legally impossible for the Commission to set prices was Odham's most extreme recommendation since becoming Chairman.)

Opposition came from a variety of sources, including the Federation, which Odham had nurtured. Within the Commission, it was led by Robert Carter, the Board of Health appointee. In 1957, when he had offered a differential floor price plan as an alternative to controls, he and Odham had worked together. In 1959 Carter still believed in the necessity of a retail floor, while Odham was once again set against controls in any form. (Unlike the controls in effect before Collins—those to which the distributors wanted to return—Carter's floor plan did not set specific prices which could not fluctuate. Moreover, it called only for a basic minimum, or floor, which could keep competitive prices barely above a ruinous level.)

At the February 19 meeting, Odham moved that the Commission recommend to the Legislature that all price control language except that establishing producer prices be stricken from the existing law. Carter was absent, leaving six votes to decide the issue, and Odham was apprehensive when he saw that one of the consumer members, Jackson Logan, seemed to favor retaining authority for controls. A vote was called, and Logan declared against the Chairman's motion, as did Acree, Shaw, and Bassett. Odham reminded Logan that retention of controls would leave a potential avenue for distributor influence in the future. When Logan indicated that he would change his mind, Odham quickly called for a new vote, asking "Jackson, is there a second?" The vote on the motion was three to three, forcing a postponement until the next meeting but avoiding a defeat for the Chairman.

The following month, with Carter present, the question was taken up again. When Odham repeated his motion, Carter voted with the consumers, and the proposal was carried, four to three. The Commission would recommend that all price control authority above the producer level be removed from the milk control law.

In providing the winning margin, Carter had not abandoned his floor price plan, but he was accustomed to agency politics. Also, he had learned something from Bassett's tactics during the 1957 attempt to promote his plan. Carter had examined the attitudes of his colleagues and had found a clear division. Odham and consumer members Logan and Tomlinson favored killing the price control authority. Acree, Shaw, and Bassett were just as firmly committed to its retention. Neither side could win without Carter's support. Carter felt that his floor price plan offered a middle ground between the extremes and, as the swing man, he was in a position to influence the direction of the Commission.

By siding with Odham at the March meeting, Carter intended to indicate to the price control faction that it would have to accept his version of price controls or do without any. If his floor plan were not adopted, he would continue to throw his weight toward the consumer position. In Carter's words:

> Having first got the recommendation to throw out all controls, the producers and distributors would be more amenable to a lesser evil, and we could argue from a position of strength.

Carter's Strategy Succeeds

Carter's strategy achieved a certain amount of success. At the same March meeting, following the adoption of Odham's motion, producer-member Acree asked for a special committee to be created to consider further the question of legislative recommendations. A committee was set up, chaired by Administrator Walton and consisting of Logan, Bassett, representatives of the Federation, and several small distributors. This membership suggested the kind of report that might be expected. The Federation appeared to favor keeping the legal power to institute controls to prevent ruinous price wars above the producer level. Walton had come to agree with the principle of Carter's floor price plan and could be expected to support it. Bassett, as the distributor member, desired to keep some form of price schedules. He now favored Carter's scheme, even though in 1957 he had been the prime actor in frustrating it. Several factors were involved in Bassett's change of attitude. First, he understood Carter's strategy and was unable to counteract it. Second, he hoped that a floor price plan would be an effective alternative to Governor Collins' recommendation for abolishing the Commission and all controls. As Bassett explained it later:

> If we got behind Carter . . . we would have an escape and be able to steer the Commission away from the Governor's way of thinking.

Finally, Bassett believed that Carter had altered his proposal to conform more fully to the realities of pricing to the point where it now allowed a profit.

The committee reported to the Commission on April 2. Its report stressed the degree to which "loss leaders" were harming independent distributors. As for the promotion of competition within the milk industry—a favorite Odham cause—the report pointed out that the Big Three dairies now held 50 percent of the total market as compared to 48 percent in 1957 when most controls had been removed. The committee recommended that the Milk Commission law be rewritten to provide that the retail price of milk not be allowed to drop below 150 percent of the producer price.

The Commission took up the proposal. As the meeting progressed, Odham realized that he had lost Carter's vote, and he vigorously condemned the floor plan. A retail floor, he said, meant merely "price fixing at a lower level." Either there were controls or there were none. Contrary to his earlier attitude, Odham did not seem impressed with the plight of independent distributors. Granting that the Big Three had half the market, and adding the share held by large independent distributors, only fifteen percent remained for small independent dairies. The well-being of so small a segment of the economy could not justify protection, Odham said.

Carter's arguments in favor of a floor plan were supported by independent distributors. They emphasized that the retail floor was not a plan devised by Borden's or Foremost, but one written for independents. It set a floor at a minimum profit level above which prices could fluctuate. It was not the pre-Collins Commission practice of setting inflexible prices for each phase of the milk marketing process. Still, Odham would not agree.

By the time a vote was reached, both Odham and Bassett perceived what Carter had been trying to do. Odham acknowledged defeat. He announced regretfully that, since his personal philosophy and that of the majority of the Commission were no longer compatible, he would soon resign.

At the same meeting the Commission drafted other recommendations to make to the Legislature. It urged that many of its orders, such as the dues check-off order, be enacted into law. The inclusion of the "just cause" contract termination proposal (see page 416 above), which had been urged by the Federation to remove a weapon of the distributors at the time of the Lafayette County petition fight, was designed to bolster the Federation. The Federation regarded the "just cause" rule as a necessary protection for its members and itself.

The Odham faction on the Commission had hoped that the Federation would become a healthy competitive force against the FDPA and FSDA. The recommendations of the Commission to the Legislature suggested that the Federation was fulfilling this function. In fact, the entire legislative program was formulated with the co-operation of the Federation and in the face of opposition by the other two organizations formed from the former FDA. At the April meeting, the Chairman called for a formal vote on each suggestion from the producers' group. Thus the Commission in effect ratified the program of the Federation. In contrast, the FDPA representative, E. T. Lay, so powerful in past years, no longer took an active part in Commission meetings. Lay said he considered it useless to waste the time to try to persuade Odham and his majority following from their "biased and pre-determined views."

The Commission Tries to Move Its Program Through the Legislature

With the recommendations decided on and the opening of the State Legislature approaching, the leadership of the Commission shifted to Administrator Walton. Odham was still the Chairman; his threat to resign had been the result of temporary discouragement. But, although he supported much of the Commission program, he was still convinced that the evils of the retail floor far outweighed the good points (legislation for dues check-off, "just cause" contract termination) in the total package. He did not take a part in mobilizing support for the Commission's recommendations.

Almost immediately after the April 2 vote Walton began to devote his full energies to building support for the Commission's program in the Legislature, which was due to convene on April 7. His major source of strength was the Federation. It had hired as its representative a former state senator, W. E. Bishop, who worked closely with Walton. They were aided by Bassett, who was actively supporting the Commission's legislation. As a small distributor, a former president of the old FDA, and still a director of its distributor off-shoot, the FDPA, he was a valuable ally.

The formidable opposition was led by the FDPA. While it had lost access to the Commission, the FDPA was still influential in the Legislature. E. T. Lay, speaking for the distributors, argued strenuously their dissatisfaction with the repeal of price control, their lack of enthusiasm for the substitute retail floor, and their distaste for the "just cause" amendment. Lay himself resented the fact that his organization had not been consulted in preparing the Commission program. He wanted the milk law left as it had been since 1953 (the last revision) and he was especially opposed to the "just cause" provision, which, he felt, strengthened the independence of producers. While conceding the need for change, Lay wanted to wait for a more favorable climate.

In their course through the Legislature, amendments to the milk control law would have to be passed on by the House Public Health Committee. This Committee was regarded as the locus of milk industry power. Its members were appointed by the Speaker of the House, who came from one of the rural, "pork chop" areas traditionally sympathetic to the dairy industry and the law as it existed. The Speaker had formerly been a producer-distributor from North

Florida, a stronghold of FSDA membership. Advocates of the Commission's legislative program believed that the Committee membership, influenced by Lay's FDPA through the Speaker, was overwhelmingly friendly to the milk industry. It was unlikely that a bill unacceptable to the old FDA's successors, FDPA and FSDA, would ever be reported out.

Walton faced the task of, at the very least, neutralizing the joint influence of FSDA and FDPA in the conflict over the Commission's program. There seemed some hope of this, in view of the fact that the distributors were not united. Some smaller distributors and producer-distributors were trying to form their own trade association, separate from the FDPA. Also, Bassett was actively working for the legislation. Walton's most active antagonist, Lay, seemed to him now to be speaking primarily for the Big Three. Lay would not accept this description of his organization. Only six of the seventeen members of the FDPA board of directors were from the Big Three, he pointed out.

By the time the Legislature convened, hope of getting the Commission amendments through the House seemed dim. Every sign indicated that the bill, when it was introduced, would not get out of the House Public Health Committee. Bishop said, "We were up against a stone wall." Lay agreed, with the comment that: "Walton and Bishop thought they'd draft themselves a bill and ignore the rest of us, and they just didn't get anywhere with it."

The bill reached the House Public Health Committee on April 17. Normally, the Committee could have been expected to hold public hearings the following week, since it was allowed to hold the bill for fourteen days. The sponsors of the legislation, fearing its defeat, agreed to a ten-day extension during which time a substitute would be considered.

A meeting was arranged in Walton's office on April 29 in an effort to break up distributor opposition. Attending were representatives of the three dairy industry organizations: the Federation, the FDPA, and the FSDA. Walton fought to gain distributor support. He suggested that, in addition to the revisions already proposed, the milk law be amended to stipulate that full controls might be re-established for a period of six months upon determination by the Commission that an emergency existed. The Commission was to establish its own definition of an emergency, but price wars would certainly be included. Walton hoped that this concession to the principle of price controls would cause the distributors to alter their objections to the "just cause" amendment. He was not sure about the constitutionality or legality of such a provision, but was willing to try it in the hope of saving the rest of the legislative package.

Lay and an associate, for the distributors, reluctantly agreed to sound out their membership about Walton's compromise proposal. It was that in exchange for the emergency controls provision, their side would go along with "just cause," the dues check-off plan, and the other points in the Commission program. When key distributors throughout the state were informed of the terms of the proposed agreement, their reaction was unfavorable. The FDPA indicated that it did not consider the compromise proposal binding at this stage. It did not, however, repudiate its intention to continue negotiations.

An Appeal to Sealtest

The next step for Bishop and Walton was a public relations campaign to persuade FDPA members to accept the compromise legislation, and to counter the activities of Lay, who appeared to be less enthusiastic about the compromise than some of the members of the organization he represented. Lay was in touch with milk distributors and state legislators, arguing against both the "just cause" provision and Walton's emergency proposal. Whenever possible, Walton got in touch with the same people and tried to refute Lay's criticisms of the milk legislation. Particular attention was given by Walton and his colleagues to the Sealtest Company, smallest of the Big Three. While Foremost and Borden's were adamant in opposing any milk law revision, Sealtest seemed to be less so. (The president of the FDPA at that time was a Sealtest officer.) Bishop, in particular, spent considerable time talking to Sealtest representatives. Eventually, the company indicated that it would support passage of the compromise legislation.

In winning over Sealtest, Walton and Bishop succeeded in temporarily breaking the unanimity of the Big Three. Lay did not attach as much importance to the development as did Bishop, but he realized that unanimity was lacking.

In a further attempt to gain unqualified support by the FDPA, Bishop arranged alliances with independent grocers and, surprisingly, with the largest retail food chain in Florida, Winn-Dixie. Winn-Dixie's lobbyist, a close friend of Bishop, agreed to help in return for support for legislation giving a retail grocer membership on the Milk Commission. Walton was agreeable, but Lay objected to such an amendment at this time, and the project seemed about to fail. However, Winn-Dixie agreed to help Bishop immediately and to wait for the membership amendment until the next session of the Legislature. Another alliance was cemented.

The Milk Commission compromise legislation was introduced on May 6 but was not immediately referred to committee. (The same day, the House Public Health Committee began hearings on the bill embodying the Governor's plan to abolish the Milk Commission and all milk price controls.) Although support for the Commission's compromise was growing, the FDPA was not yet officially committed in its favor. Strong vocal opposition to the compromise package now appeared from another quarter. During the time that Walton had been leading Commission efforts to build support for the milk law amendments, Chairman Odham had been at home in Orlando. But he had not divorced himself entirely from the activities in the state capital. Walton had agreed to a retail grocer member in exchange for Winn-Dixie's support only after clearing it with Odham by telephone. However, Odham took the position that Walton, by making concessions, was being "conned," and he was opposed to the efforts to compromise with the distributors.

Odham Opposes the Package

Thus, when the House Public Health Committee opened hearings on the Governor's proposal, Odham came to the capital and publicly urged defeat of the Commission's legislative program. On several occasions he testified instead in favor of the Governor's bill to abolish the Commission, although he had formerly opposed the recommendations of the Adams Committee. However, the FDPA and its supporters prevailed before the House Public Health Committee, and the Governor's bill was abandoned.

Walton and his allies continued to press the FDPA to abandon its opposition. They saw that there were still no signs to indicate that the Public Health Committee would report out a Commission bill. A second meeting between Walton and distributor representatives was arranged for May 7 at the Cherokee Hotel in Tallahassee. As the conference proceeded, it appeared that Lay and the FDPA were still not ready to give their support to enable the bill to clear the Public Health Committee. The compromise offered by Walton at the earlier meeting in April, always shaky, seemed about to collapse. At this point Wilmer Bassett, as distributor member of the Commission, urged Lay and his colleagues to call a special meeting of the FDPA in Tampa on May 11. In Tampa Bassett led the fight for a compromise against sharp opposition. Lay was anxious that these differences of opinion be resolved and a definite and united FDPA policy be adopted. Otherwise, he believed, "our hands will be tied in Tallahassee." After a long session, Lay and a delegation were authorized to pursue the policy of compromise.

With united milk industry support—or at least approval—the Commission's milk legislation package was referred to the House and Senate Public Health committees on May 13. It easily cleared both committees. The House passed the Commission program on May 22, the Senate on May 27. By June 4 the amendments to the milk law were ready for the Governor's signature.

Governor Collins Considers a Veto

All the parties involved in the passage of the compromise legislation waited anxiously for hints as to whether Governor Collins would sign or veto. He could no longer hope to abolish the Commission. The FDPA and FSDA had been successful in killing the Governor's bill to abolish the Commission and price control legislation. On the basis of his past opposition to price controls, Collins could be expected to veto the milk legislation. Publicity, there was considerable opinion in favor of a veto. The *Miami Herald* and the *Tampa Tribune,* still battling against controls, were joined in their stand by several South Florida supermarket chains. On the other hand, E. T. Lay, who had talked with the Governor's assistant, believed that the compromise legislation had "the unofficial approval of the Governor." During the negotiations for a compromise, the FDPA had insisted that "an important condition of the agreement . . . is that the Governor will . . . agree that he will allow it to become law if passed." While the bill was in the Legislature, Bishop had sought Collins' commitment that he would not veto any legislation agreed to by the entire industry. This assurance had not been forthcoming, but Bishop believed that the Governor's executive secretary was sympathetic to the Commission's program, and he hoped this might be a factor in favor of the alliance effected in support of the compromise.

Odham's closeness to the Governor and his stand on the milk law revisions did not provide the waiting participants with a thoroughly reliable clue to the Governor's intentions. It was clear that Collins valued the Chairman's advice, but he also consulted with other members of the Milk Commission. When Odham arranged a conference with the Governor to convey his recommendation, Carter and Walton were invited to present the opposing side. Each point of view was heard, and Carter left thinking that the pro-legislation forces had an even chance.

On June 19 Collins vetoed the bill. The language of his veto message revealed how closely the Governor shared Odham's attitudes.

> I see behind this bill the same influences that were too long in control of the Commission setting unfair retail prices. . . and giving unlawful kickbacks to retail outlets in amounts estimated by the Chairman of the Commission at between seven and ten million dollars per year.

Collins ended his message by pledging to continue to work for abolishing the Commission.

Odham later recalled his reactions to the legislative struggle as follows:

> There were many of the reforms that we had created through regulation that we felt should be incorporated into the law. . . . The Legislature considered such reforms, but the milk industry, controlled by the distributors, was able to effect a compromise within the Legislature that required the Governor to veto. . . .

As far as Lay was concerned the veto was not a disappointment. He had entered the compromise reluctantly and had never thought that the legislation was satisfactory.

Now, in the summer of 1959, Odham had been Chairman of the Commission for two years. During those years there had been no resale price control in the Florida milk industry—a record which Collins and Odham were determined to protect. Collins' attitude toward the Commission had remained unchanged. Odham, however, had become more intimately concerned with the problems of the milk industry. At times he had been prepared to make concessions to the demands of producers and small distributors that they be protected, but he eventually had returned to absolute opposition to price controls. Although he had been unable to control the Commission, Odham's access to the Governor had enabled him to encourage Collins to veto the retail floor plan package.

Odham Casts a Decisive Vote

SHORTLY AFTER THE GOVERNOR'S veto, milk price wars again became serious in Jacksonville. Foremost dropped its price to 37.5 cents per half gallon—far below cost—to meet the price of Superior Dairies, an independent. The independent distributors renewed their pleas for help from the Milk Commission. Often the independents were larger than the chains in a given area and could compete on even terms or perhaps at an advantage. However, by cutting the independents' local market by use of loss leaders, the chains could gain the advantage over the long run. This was the problem of the Jacksonville independents. They urged the Commission to do by order what it had failed to do by legislation: establish a floor price. Chain distributors, on the other hand, argued either for total control with fixed prices or for a free market. But there were indications that they would take a floor price if it was all they could get.

In September 1959 the Commission met to consider a motion by Bassett (the distributor member) that a retail floor price of 150 percent of the producer price be adopted for the Jacksonville area. Carter, the Board of Health man, voted with Odham and the consumer members, thus defeating the motion. Bassett demanded that another meeting be held on the same subject. On September 19 the Commission met in Jacksonville and again took up the question of a retail floor. The issue centered around the competing aims of Bassett and Carter. Carter once again had a chance of achieving his floor price plan, this time by action of the agency. But he had been advised by the Commission attorney that, as a Commission order, the plan was legally precarious. (The basic legislation authorized the Commission to set fair prices. The low floor proposed by Carter was vulnerable to suits on this ground, and favorable judicial decisions could not be counted on.) Carter wished to provide an incentive for independent distributors to fight for a retail floor again in the next session of the Legislature. By prohibiting the independents the use of the Commission as a protective agency, Carter hoped to have his plan achieve later the sound legal footing of a legislative enactment. Therefore, when Bassett renewed his motion for a 150 percent retail floor, Carter offered a substitute providing for a retail floor of 140 percent of the producer price, a level considered insufficient for adequate protection. Thus, the choice presented to the Commission was between the 140 percent floor and no protection at all for the independent distributors. Over the strenuous objections of its Chairman, the Commission voted four to three to establish the floor for the Jacksonville area.

Odham Develops an Alternative

The establishment of the floor for Jacksonville did not solve the problems of independent distributors in other areas in the state. Complaints against loss leaders from the Tampa Bay and Central Florida regions poured into the Commission's offices. The complaints placed the blame for price-cutting on the retail chains, which were allegedly demanding discounts and playing one distributor off against another. However, smaller producer-distributors were also cutting prices. The size of the discounts offered to retail chains was growing, and sales below cost were prevalent. In exchange for large discounts, the complaints maintained, the dairy chains were allotted favorable space in store display cases. Advantageous display positions, it was alleged, invariably went to the large distributors who could afford to give rebates.

Out of this situation emerged a willingness of independent distributors to take action on their own behalf. They formed the Independent Dairy Distributors Association. Making it clear that it was not asking the Commission for a return to total control, this group warned that continuation of the discount system would result in the eventual concentration of the entire market in the hands of the Big Three. The Independent Dairy Distributors Association suggested that a *wholesale floor* would alleviate the situation. Under a wholesale floor, all distributors would be paid identical prices, irrespective of retail price. The Big Three dairies received the suggestion coolly and publicly showed little interest in becoming involved.

Odham once more became interested in the plight of the independents. The activities of the Independent Dairy Distributors Association symbolized to him a difference of interest within the distribution segment of the industry that he had previously not recognized. The difference, however, was not as deep as Odham may have imagined. The Independent Dairy Distributors Association never developed as much more than a "letterhead organization." In fact, the larger distributors, realizing the appeal these independents had for Odham, as contrasted with his hostility toward big distributors, had encouraged the independents to act on their own. The large distributors were pleased to let the independents "carry the fight" and allowed FDPA offices to be used for meetings of the independents' organization.

Odham was particularly impressed by the argument that the retail market was rapidly being dominated by chain supermarkets. In his view, this meant that a handful of purchasing agents of the retail chains could, by using the discount power, monopolize the dairy industry. He had entered the Commission determined to break distributor control and stimulate genuine competition. He now saw all of his objectives being subverted by the retail side of the industry, and, as he saw it, the motives of the retail chains were exactly the same as those of the Big Three distributors. He began to consider seriously the idea that free and unregulated marketing might destroy rather than stimulate competition.

Odham began to re-examine his position in the light of this newly-learned phenomenon of the milk industry—the discount system practiced between retail chains and large distributors. He saw three choices: (1) he could continue his opposition to any form of price regulation; (2) he could consider returning to the old system of comprehensive, inflexible prices set by Commission order; (3) he could adopt a middle ground between the two extremes. Since the large distributors were urging a choice between the two extremes, it was unlikely that Odham would accept either of those alternatives. His own phrasing of the issue revealed the degree to which he had abandoned his "either-or" perception of the situation: "Do we leave it uncontrolled and let only the big survive, or do we modify total control?"

The Adoption of the Wholesale Floor

Sometime in the fall of 1959 Odham began to accept the premise that a middle ground could be reached. It was only half a year or so after he had tried to have the Commission stripped of all price control authority. However, the Commission did not take up the question of partial protection for independents until almost a year after the protests from Central Florida and Tampa Bay.

During this time Odham displayed a growing tolerance of the principle of the wholesale floor. His altered views did not bring him closer to Carter, however, for Odham was beginning to think that Carter's proposed retail floor system would provide insufficient protection against excessive influence of the strong. A wholesale floor, on the other hand, would require distributors to charge the same price to retailers regardless of fluctuations in volume of sales or of display privileges granted. Retail prices would still be set by market conditions. Odham believed that a retail floor would leave the independent distributor still subject to rebating practices.

Carter, on the other hand, still thought that a retail floor would be adequate. He felt it futile for a state agency to try to regulate big interstate distributing companies by establishing a wholesale floor. Furthermore, a retail floor would be easier to enforce. Since his concern was mainly to prevent "loss leaders," he did not object to distributors selling at whatever price they could get.

During late 1959 and early 1960 the informal discussions between Odham, Carter, and Walton were the scenes of frequent and uniformly unsuccessful attempts by the Chairman to change Carter's mind. Finally, on August 3, 1960 the Commission was ready to act on the question of some kind of partial price regulation. By this time, all the Commission members appeared willing to abandon the kind of free market which had been in effect since 1957. Carter once again offered a 150 percent retail floor. His motion was carried by a four to three margin, and it appeared that only the vehement opposition of the Chairman prevented passage by a larger margin. Then Bassett presented a motion to establish a wholesale floor for milk of 43 cents per half gallon. The Chairman not only seconded but asked the other consumer members to help carry the motion. It passed by a six to one margin, with Carter as the lone opponent.

The Governor Intervenes

Governor Collins was disappointed with the outcome of the August 3 meeting, since the Commission had now established price floors at both wholesale and retail levels. Collins was also disappointed that Odham, his ally against controls, had agreed to one of these price floors. It appeared to Collins that Odham was undergoing the same process of identification with the industry that had affected many of his other appointees. In an effort to persuade the Commission to reconsider its action, Collins asked Odham and Carter to meet with him. He hoped to induce Odham to agree to call another meeting of the Commission in order to rescind the retail and wholesale floor orders. While the Governor objected to both types of control, he was particularly anxious that Carter's retail floor be repealed. The retail floor would affect the consumer directly, whereas the wholesale floor would still allow fluctuations in retail price. Odham and Carter agreed to reconsider, but neither made any commitments. The FDPA and FSDA, pleased with the Commission's action, were angry that Collins was not willing to let the decision stand. The *Florida Dairy News* (their joint publication) said: "Such dictation by the Governor to an agency of the state is nothing less than a threat to democratic constitutional government."

This meeting was not Collins' only effort to reverse the decision of the Commission. He did not depend solely on Carter switching his vote on the retail floor. He needed some degree of insurance. The member over whom he had the most influence at this time was Alex Shaw of the Department of Agriculture, a consistent supporter of controls. Shaw had served for nearly thirty years in the Department of Agriculture and expected to be eligible for retirement in two years. Nathan Mayo, the long-time Commissioner of Agriculture, had died. Collins had wanted to replace Shaw after his first term expired, but Mayo had stuck by Shaw and Collins had yielded. Mayo, as a directly-elected (and repeatedly re-elected) official, had had sufficient independent political power to keep pressure off his staff. (Ragland, whose state Board of Health was less independent than the Department of Agriculture, had been replaced while Shaw had remained.) However, Mayo's death in 1960 had given Collins the right to name an acting successor to serve until the next election. Collins informed the acting Commissioner that Shaw should carefully evaluate all available evidence before the next vote was taken. Whether or not Collins threatened Shaw's job is not clear. It is possible that the overzealousness of the acting Commissioner resulted in an exaggeration. Whatever the source, Shaw was given to understand that a change of attitude was required if he was to remain in the Department of Agriculture. Unwilling to serve under what he felt to be political pressure, Shaw submitted his resignation but was persuaded by his Commissioner to attend the next Milk Commission meeting.

The Commission Reconsiders Its Action

On August 12, 1960 the Commission faced the question of whether to rescind its orders of August 3 and satisfy the wishes of the Governor, or whether to continue the price controls which it had established nine days before. Odham summarized the Governor's strenuous objections to controls and recalled that he and several other members were appointed because they reflected Collins' attitude. He gave no indication of the direction he intended to take.

Carter then made a motion to rescind both orders of the last meeting. But, as part of this motion, Carter included the establishment of a 46 cents per half-gallon retail floor. At this point Odham and Carter engaged in the expected argument over retail controls, and Carter was persuaded to divide his original motion into two separate motions, so that repeal of the previous meeting's orders would not automatically result in adoption of the retail floor. On the first Carter motion, to rescind the orders of August 3, Shaw switched to the position of the consumers, leaving only Bassett and Acree in opposition. The Commission had repealed controls. It looked as though the Governor had won.

While the meeting was still in progress, however, Odham learned the reason for Shaw's change of mind. Although Odham had been through nearly three years of Milk Commission politics, he still shared the popular aversion to "pressure" and thought the Governor's alleged action improper. He also felt some concern for Shaw's personal situation after thirty years' service. A marked change in Odham's statements now occurred. He began to speak more favorably of the retail floor and drew a careful distinction between the floor system and total control. The basic difference was "whether you are guaranteeing these people a profit or you are guaranteeing them that milk will be so priced that they will not be destroyed through unregulated, ruthless, dishonest, corrupt competition."

The immediate question before the Commission at this point was the second part of Carter's motion: to establish the retail floor of 46 cents per half gallon. Since Shaw had voted to rescind the previous floor regulations, it was apparent that he was abiding by the Governor's wishes. This meant that, if Odham chose, he could defeat retail controls. With Shaw voting in alliance with the consumers, Odham had the four votes necessary to defeat retail control. He had waged a long and bitter struggle against such controls.

The inclusion of retail controls in the Commission's legislative recommendations had been the main reason that Odham had recommended a veto. Only nine days earlier Odham had voted against Carter on this same point. Now he had the decisive vote. But with victory within reach, he decided to reverse a consistent pattern of three years and to vote for the retail floor.

In explaining this decision later, Odham said he believed that the Governor was unable to understand the situation. If Collins had been through the same experiences that he had undergone, he reasoned, Collins' opposition to any controls would have been reduced. Odham later attributed his "conversion" neither to his reaction to the alleged pressure on Shaw nor to his awareness of the crisis of the independent distributor, but to a combination of these factors. His opposition to retail controls was not as intense as it had been at the August 3 meeting, and he simply was unwilling to use Shaw's pressured vote for a purpose in which he no longer devoutly believed. He also was convinced that the wholesale floor, to which he had already committed himself, would be more effective if controls were extended to the retail level. Both floors would result in protection for the weaker distributors and retailers and would promote the continuation in business of a large number of competitors.

Therefore, Odham decided to oppose the Governor. He moved that the Commission adopt an order establishing floors at both wholesale and retail levels. Since the Chairman himself had made this motion, producer-member Acree suggested that the Commission merely vote again on the motion to rescind the orders of the last meeting. An hour earlier the Commission had voted to rescind by a five to two margin. On this second vote the motion, which endorsed the decision of August 3, passed four to three. The opposing votes were cast by Carter, who was still opposed to the wholesale floor, and the two other consumer members, who could not accept the retail control provisions. With the Chairman now supporting partial controls, Shaw reverted to his earlier position and supported them, too.

Odham's conversion was clearly a major factor in the Commission's decision to continue controls. Having once voted to rescind its action, the Commission appeared to have conformed to the Governor's desires until Odham announced his intention to vote for the retail floor.

Conclusions

The Governor was extremely disappointed with Odham's dramatic shift. His feelings were echoed in the editorials of the metropolitan newspapers that had long opposed any form of controls. It seemed to them that Odham had made a sudden and unexpected reversal of position. The conclusion they drew was that Odham had given in to industry pressure. Those closer to Odham had a different explanation of the process by which his attitudes were changed. Robert Carter, perhaps the person most intimately involved in the decision process, was not surprised in the least when Odham announced his support for the retail floor. He had watched Odham's gradual absorption with the problems of the industry. To Carter, it was not a question of sudden reversal, but rather a slow evolution of attitudes.

To the FDPA and FSDA, Odham's action was a vindication of their position that the law required controls and that to take a contrary course of action would be not only unwise but illegal. Ideally, they wanted the full range of Commission-ordered prices that had prevailed before Collins, but they were content with the floor-price vote as representing all they could get while Collins and Odham continued in office.

Odham himself did not feel that he had been pressured by the independent distributors. What had happened, Odham explained, was simply that he had replaced one set of values with another. He had had no alternative but to support price floors. To have done otherwise, he said, would have been to allow the large to destroy the small.

Appendix

EDITOR'S NOTE: The following comments on this case study have been offered by Mr. E. T. Lay, executive secretary of the Florida Dairy Products Association, Inc., in a letter of July 24, 1962:

"Instead of making heroes of the Governor, the Chairman and the Administrator of the Milk Commission, it seems to us they should have been shown in their true role as elected and/or appointed officials of the government sworn to enforce, administer, and carry out a law of the state . . . yet officials who not only refused and failed this duty so far as the Florida Milk Commission was concerned, but officials who openly and publicly stated they did not agree with and opposed the law they had accepted the duty and responsibility to enforce.

"We feel this story should point out that the Florida Milk Commission law provides, (Section 501.13 (2)), 'The Commission, after making such investigation shall fix by official order the minimum wholesale and retail prices to be charged for milk handled within the state for fluid consumption. . . .'

"And further, the law states, (Section 501.13 (3)), 'It is the intention of the legislature that the public emergency requires that the producers and milk dealers receive a fair return for their products.' The Governor, the Chairman, and the Administrator of the Milk Commission stubbornly ignored the 'shall' indicated by the legislature. They could be likened to a policeman who refuses to enforce the law. These three Florida state officials refused to carry out the provisions of the Florida Milk Commission Act.

"In addition, we feel the story should briefly cover what has happened to the Commission's Chairman and Administrator. . . . In the campaign and election of Governor Farris Bryant [who succeeded Collins in January, 1961], neither the issues of the Florida Milk Commission, milk prices, and the setting of minimum retail and wholesale prices for milk, were made issues by any of the five gubernatorial candidates![2]

"Neither were any of these issues raised in the 1961 Florida campaigns for election to the legislature race! It would appear that political candidates in general realized the milk issue was not one in which the public was at all interested.

"As to the Collins appointed members of the Milk Commission, Chairman Brailey Odham resigned the day Governor Bryant took office. Walton was replaced as administrator about four months after Odham's resignation.[3] The term of an Odham-oriented and consumer Commission member, Jackson Logan of Tampa, expired early in 1962. . . . Wilmer Bassett requested that he not be reappointed when his term expired in 1961.

"The new Commission, which in recent weeks achieved a majority of non-Collins, non-Odham, and non-Walton committed members, seems uncommitted to any one segment of the dairy industry. It is beginning to show a sympathetic and understanding attitude toward the enormous problems created for the entire dairy industry by its predecessors. The new Commission appears to be endeavoring to carry out the law and its provisions for stabilizing the dairy industry."

[2] *Editor's Note: The major issue in the 1960 gubernatorial elections was segregation and how to deal with Negro "sit in" demonstrations, which had led to violence in Tallahassee a few months before the primary elections. A strong segregationist and conservative, Farris Bryant, won easily, defeating the more moderate candidate supported by Collins. A number of milk distributors in the organization Lay was working for supported Bryant.*

[3] *Editor's Note: Administrator Walton did not mollify the distributors after the change of governors, working in the spring 1961 legislative session for a package similar to that Collins had vetoed in 1959. After some intense infighting, he was fired by Governor Bryant in May 1961. He became executive secretary of the Florida Dairy Farmers' Federation, the independent producers' group whose formation and growth the Commission had encouraged in the Odham period.*

The Shredded Wheat Property

Howard F. Miller

Editor's Introduction

IN THE FALL OF 1956 there appeared on the desk of Governor Averell Harriman of New York letters and conflicting recommendations about a matter that might at first have seemed trivial to an outsider. It was whether the State Division of Parks should be permitted to purchase about four acres of property in the City of Niagara Falls. (The four acres were known as "the Shredded Wheat property" because a breakfast food plant of the National Biscuit Company had formerly operated there.)

The Governor of New York does not ordinarily concern himself with minor land purchases, but there were several reasons why it was necessary for him to give attention to this one. First, the State Division of Parks wanted the property for a parkway which was part of a larger beautification and development plan for the United States side of Niagara Falls. The parkway was an objective of both the Division of Parks and the Power Authority of New York State. Second, the Chairman of the State Council of Parks and the Chairman of the Power Authority was Robert Moses, chief of a number of state and city agencies (many of them independent authorities), a vigorous and widely respected administrator who was not in the habit of accepting delays to his projects with stoic resignation. Third, the State Budget Division recommended against releasing funds for the purchase of the property largely because the City of Niagara Falls opposed the action. The city had authorized construction on the land of a first-class motel. Fourth, the Director of the Budget Division was Paul Appleby, whose experience and stature in budget matters equaled those of Moses in the parks and public construction fields.

In the main this story illustrates the conflicting values and the differing recommendations that were passed to the Governor for decision. It also depicts the manner by which the conflicts were resolved. But in addition, the case study shows a strong state central budget agency using some of the powers in its armory of financial controls on behalf of a municipality which, standing alone, would have had little hope of opposing successfully the state agencies that wanted to build the parkway. Like most cases, this story raises many questions. Two which do not appear on the surface are: (1) Was this use of financial controls by the central budget agency justifiable, and if so how? (2) If, as seemed likely at the end of 1959, the results of the dispute caused park and power agency officials to lose enthusiasm for improving and beautifying the United States side with their funds, had the Budget Division's intervention resulted in a net gain for the state? Was solicitude for the municipality worth the cost of Moses' withdrawal from Niagara beautification?

There are two parts to this story. The first describes how the Shredded Wheat property issue was propelled to the Governor's level. The second describes what the Budget Division and the Division of Parks did to settle the issue after it came to the attention of the Governor. The story is told from the perspective of the Budget Division by one of the budget director's aides. While the writer has attempted to present an objective account, the reader will note that he was a party at interest.

How the Issue Got to the Governor

IN 1951 the Legislature gave the Power Authority of New York State, of which Robert Moses was chairman, the authority to develop the power resources of the Niagara River and "to preserve and enhance the scenic beauty of the Falls." The Authority had been created in 1931 with the mission of co-operating with Canadian agencies in the development of power and navigation along the International Rapids section of the St. Lawrence River.

That the scenic beauty of the American side of the Falls needed enhancing was not open to question—at least to United States planners who had chafed for years over the failure to improve the American bank as much as the Canadians had improved theirs. The Canadians had not permitted excessive commercialization. Instead, they had built a parkway system and had created garden-type parks. United States residents of the Niagara frontier area invariably took guests to the Canadian side of the Falls. The view was more impressive from Canada. The Canadian parkway and parking facilities made it easier to reach the viewing area. And the colorful gardens made an attractive setting.

The New York State Division of Parks had developed a plan to correct this neglect of the American side. Organizationally, the Division was part of the Conservation Department. It exercised the powers and duties of that Department as they related to parks, parkways, lands, grounds, reservations, and structures and buildings of scenic and recreational interest. But the State Council of Parks rather than the Conservation Department controlled the Division of Parks. The Council had authority to pass on new park projects and to prepare the annual budget for the Division. The ten-man Council included the unpaid presidents or chairmen of nine park commissions in the state. Robert Moses, president of the Long Island State Park Commission, had long been chairman of the State Council of Parks, and he was generally regarded as the man who "ran" the park and parkway programs of the state.

Moses had been a figure in New York state and city administration since 1919—and since the late twenties an increasingly prodigious one. In addition to being chairman of both the Power Authority and the State Council of Parks, and president of the Long Island State Park Commission, he was Park Commissioner of the City of New York (the only post from which he drew a salary), chairman of the Triborough Bridge Authority, New York City Construction Coordinator, and head of the Bethpage and Jones Beach State Parkway authorities. Moses' extraordinary accomplishments in developing parks, parkways, beaches, and other construction programs in the state and city had gained him, locally and nationally, a reputation as a vigorous administrator who got grand things done. He had an independent income, and his appointments as head of the various independent authorities and commissions were for fixed terms and were invariably renewed by governors or New York City mayors whatever their parties. Moses had an independent status in the eye of the public, and a reputation for singeing with caustic public statements those who stood in the way of his undertakings.

In the eyes of leaders of the Budget Division, Moses had always received a generous amount of state funds for his park and parkway programs. His projects were well advanced, in part because of his aggressive efforts in obtaining "his" share of the state dollar. But to a person of Moses' energy and imagination, the money that had been spent on these programs had never been sufficient. This had been especially true in the Niagara region.

The Master Plan

In 1952 the Niagara Frontier State Park Commission had approved a master plan for the development and further beautification of the

Niagara Frontier State Park area. The plan had been prepared by the eminent firm of Clarke and Rapuano, consulting engineers and landscape architects. It was regarded as an exciting aesthetic conception which would place United States planners far ahead of their Canadian "rivals." One of the keys to the plan was the construction of the Niagara Parkway, which would proceed along the river from the North Grand Island Bridge into the City of Niagara Falls and then on to the vicinity of the Falls. From this point it would continue to Fort Niagara State Park. The parkway would provide a scenic vehicular rim for the entire Niagara park area. The plan included boat basins, a golf course, a swimming pool, restaurants, picnic areas, an amphitheatre, and other features. Much was to be done to improve facilities next to the Falls themselves. At 1952 prices, the total construction estimate was $63,600,000, of which $42,000,000 was for the parkway.

It was never clear in the Budget Division how much of the Niagara master plan the State Division of Parks was prepared to support. It had never had to commit itself because of the unavailability of funds for major construction. However, the 1951 amendment to the Power Authority Act, which authorized the Power Authority to preserve and enhance the beauties of the area in addition to developing hydroelectric power, seemed to permit Moses to use Power Authority funds. (These funds would be derived from the sale of Niagara power bonds which would be repaid from electricity revenues.) Wearing his Power Authority hat, Moses undertook to build the first section of the proposed Niagara Parkway from the North Grand Island Bridge to the Niagara Reservation in the City of Niagara Falls.

According to the master plan, a good part of the first section of the parkway along the Niagara River was to be built on rock fill that would extend the existing shoreline outward. In the center of the city and approaching the rapids, the parkway was to be constructed primarily on existing shoreline. In the opinion of the designers,

> The present approach to the Niagara Reservation from North Grand Island Bridge via Buffalo Avenue is extremely unpleasant. The proposed parkway would offer a pleasant approach. To many persons the broad expanse of the magnificent upper Niagara River has qualities as attractive in their way as the more dramatic ones of the Falls themselves. We propose that the parkway should take every advantage of the stirring scene. Accordingly, we recommend that the outer roadway be at a safe elevation above high water and that the inner roadway, except at structures, be at least 5 feet above it. With this arrangement, people in cars proceeding down-river would have a clear view over the tops of the cars moving along the outer or up-river driveway.[1]

The Parkway was thus to have two separate roadways. The outer or river side roadway was to carry traffic away from the center of the city and from the Falls area itself. The inner roadway was to carry traffic into the city and to the Falls.

At the time the master plan was prepared, the state already owned a strip of land in the City of Niagara Falls adjacent to the river and the rapids. (See Map A.) An inadequate roadway was already in existence, and it was on this strip of land that Clarke and Rapuano proposed to build the new parkway from Sixth Street west to First Street. The consultants also believed that the privately owned land south of Buffalo Avenue between Sixth and First streets should be purchased by the state for beautification or for use as a park, even though it was not to be used for actual parkway purposes. The consultants assumed this would be done in the case of the property south of Buffalo Avenue between Sixth and Fourth streets. This property was completely undeveloped at the time the report was written, and the plan indicated that a portion of it was to be used as part of the Y that would provide ingress to both of the parkway's drives from Sixth Street. This was the Shredded Wheat property. For the property south of Buffalo Avenue between Fourth and First streets, on which many fine old homes were located, the consultants recommended:

> This area, although an intrusion into a very cramped park, is in itself a pleasant residential development that has been a good neighbor to the park. We understand that there are, however, signs of coming de-

[1] Clarke and Rapuano, "A Master Plan for Niagara Frontier Parks and Parkways, State of New York" (Unpublished report drawn for the Niagara Frontier State Park Commission), p. 11.

MAP A

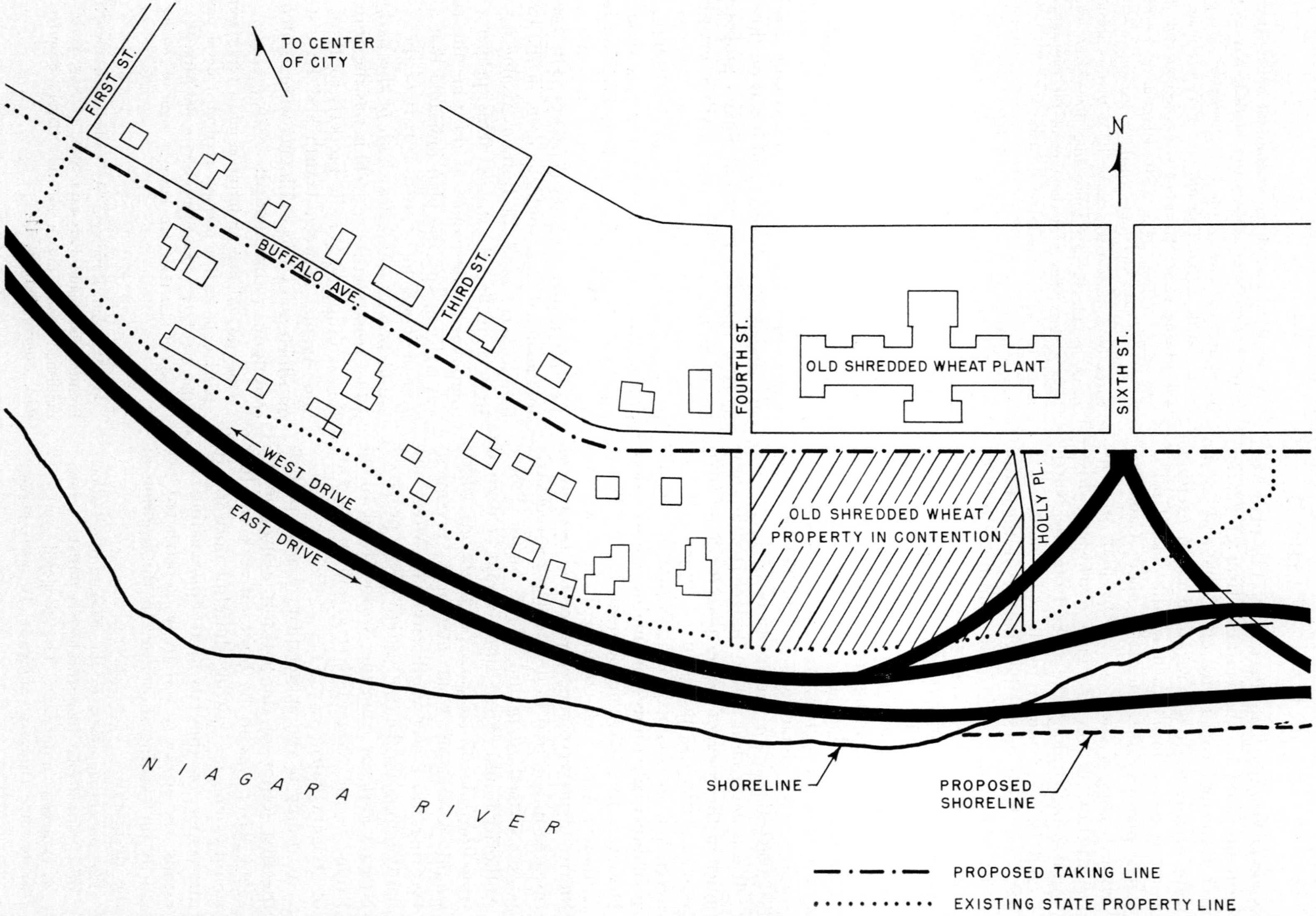

TO CENTER
OF CITY
N
FIRST ST.
BUFFALO AVE.
THIRD ST.
FOURTH ST.
OLD SHREDDED WHEAT PLANT
SIXTH ST.
WEST DRIVE
EAST DRIVE
OLD SHREDDED WHEAT
PROPERTY IN CONTENTION
HOLLY PL.
NIAGARA RIVER
SHORELINE
PROPOSED
SHORELINE
PROPOSED TAKING LINE
EXISTING STATE PROPERTY LINE

preciation in this vicinity, and we recommend that the Commission include in their master plan the ultimate acquisition of these properties. Perhaps it would be possible to enter into negotiations with the owners of these properties to the end that the Commission might be assured of first opportunity to buy when the present occupants no longer require these homes. It would be tragic if, as these properties are gradually sold off, the land should be put to commercial use. In the case of enterprises serving the tourists, there can be no doubt whether proximity to the park would be of real value, but the park too serves the tourist and in this location is the more urgently needed facility.

The sense of the Clarke and Rapuano recommendation to purchase lands on or adjacent to the proposed first section of the parkway when they became available or when commercialization threatened was accepted both within the Division of Parks and the Power Authority. Ordinarily, the Power Authority would make the purchases when it had a workable charter for the Niagara project and was able to float bonds. Until that time, it had no funds for this purpose, and purchases would have to be made by the state from its Capital Construction Fund. They could either be direct purchases or in the form of first instance advances to the Power Authority, to be repaid to the state by the Authority when its Niagara bonds were sold.

A Request for Money

Such was the background of the situation when action began on the Shredded Wheat property early in 1956. Plans were afoot to commercialize the property, and the Division of Parks, under its director, James Evans, sought to have funds included in the 1956-57 supplemental budget to permit purchase by the state. On the basis of recommendations by Budget Division examiners, the $150,000 request was not approved. The recommendation to disapprove the request was made not because the examiners were out of sympathy with the idea of purchase, but because an additional appropriation was unnecessary. The regular 1956-57 budget contained $20,000,000 for parkways, including land acquisition, and, in the judgment of the examiners, the purchase could be financed from this appropriation. Probably unaware of the reasons for Budget's disapproval, Evans tried other means and sought a special bill from the Legislature appropriating $150,000.

At this point, a word about Evans is necessary. Evans was self-confident, personally charming, intelligent, and an able and devoted state civil servant. No one ever doubted his dedication to the park and parkway program of the state, but because of his roguish air, new acquaintances were sometimes surprised at the details he had at his command. He and Paul Appleby, the Budget Director, respected each other, but they were somewhat different in their approach to a problem. Whereas the Budget Director might ask, "Where are your workload data?" Evans might have been expected to respond in an entirely principled way, "What kind of compromise can we make?"

Evans had started with the State Department of Public Works in 1915 while still in high school. He had been selected as the first Director of State Parks in 1938 after having been engineer for Moses' Long Island Park Commission. He had long been the top-paid state civil servant. Someone was once heard to remark that "with Jim Evans' interest and personality, it's too bad he never went into politics." Another person responded, "Jim Evans has been in politics for years; he's just never bothered to run for office." For a number of years, he had been at home with the Republicans in the Legislature who traditionally controlled both houses. For an equally long time, he had been Moses' representative at the Legislature, cajoling legislators and steering Moses' bills through both houses. This was not light work, since it was accepted practice that at least a half-dozen times during the legislative session, Republican legislators would rise to condemn Moses for his arbitrariness, his inflexible personality, his autocratic nature, and the like, and to say that they would not be bound by his refusal to make payments to municipalities in lieu of taxes for local land used in his projects. Democratic legislators, always in the minority, seldom bothered to join in this criticism. The sixth Republican speech on Moses was usually one of the signs to old Albany hands that the legislative session was nearing an end.

Moses was impervious to these attacks. They did not seem to trouble him personally, and his term appointments to state authorities were not affected. But it was Evans' job to pour oil on troubled waters and to see that the Moses bills were passed. He did this successfully—as he did most things. And it was therefore not surprising to anyone that Evans steered the special $150,000 bill through the 1956 Legislature after the Budget Division had turned down his request to have the item included in the Governor's 1956-57 supplemental budget.

Inevitably, a copy of this bill was forwarded from the office of the Governor's Counsel to the Budget Division for recommendation before the Counsel made a final recommendation to the Governor on whether to sign or veto. Apparently knowing that this was standard practice, Evans dispatched the following letter to the Budget Director:

April 2, 1956

Hon. Paul H. Appleby
Director of the Budget
Capitol
Albany 1, New York

Re: Senate Int. 3469, Print 4231

Dear Paul:

We submit the following in support of the above captioned bill which appropriates $150,000 to the Division of Parks.

This appropriation is intended for the purchase of land adjacent to the Niagara Reservation. The particular parcel is a piece of vacant land formerly owned by the National Biscuit Company, a part of the old Shredded Wheat Plant. It contains 4.23 acres and occupies the block between Buffalo Avenue and Riverway from Fourth Street east nearly to the line of Sixth extended. . . .

The National Biscuit Company recently sold their entire holding, including the factory site on the north side of Buffalo Avenue, as well as this parcel, to a local realty syndicate. It is clear from zoning applications, press reports and information received from the purchasers that they intend to lease a part of the land for the construction of a motel. The lower vacant land would be most desirable, being closer to the river and requiring no clearing. The Niagara Falls Zoning Board has approved the designation of this parcel as "commercial."

You will note on one of the attached plans (plate 5 from the 1952 Clarke and Rapuano report) [see Map A] that this parcel is involved in the connection from Buffalo Avenue and Sixth Street to the proposed Niagara Parkway. The hatched section on this plate also outlines the entire residential area between Buffalo Avenue and the Reservation lands. In this connection we have attached a copy of an extract from the above-mentioned report by Clarke and Rapuano.

We believe that this is a fair statement of desirable policy, and that this purchase is a good example of the policy—namely, not to commit the State to a hasty or all-inclusive program of expensive land acquisition, but to take individual parcels as they become available, and by all means, keep this section from becoming a commercial encroachment on the Reservation.

This is a desirable acquisition and an urgent one. We are firmly convinced that next year will be too late. Whatever the method, and we hold no brief for special bills in general, we ask your assistance in making it possible.

Cordially,
JAMES F. EVANS
Director of State Parks

The Budget Division recommended to the Governor's Counsel that the bill be vetoed. The reason for the veto recommendation was that the bill would have permitted an executive agency to "make budget" outside the regular process. This opinion was reinforced in the minds of Budget Division leaders by the fact that the purchase could be made by the Division of Parks if it used funds that had already been appropriated by the Legislature in the regular budget. The Budget Division was not then opposed to the idea of purchase itself. The Budget Director turned Evans' letter over to the Deputy Budget Director with the note: "I think the bill should be disapproved, but the purchase may be o.k. Please handle."

The Governor vetoed the special bill. Budget Division officials did not know that other voices had spoken to the Governor's Counsel recommending veto. The City Manager of Niagara Falls had written a strong protest, noting that permission had been given for the construction of a first-class motel on the property. Other city officials had also voiced objections. The State Comptroller, who was always asked to comment on bills affecting local government because his Department included the Division of Municipal Affairs, had also reported to the Governor's Counsel that the special bill was opposed by local officials. Budget Division officials, not knowing of these communications or of the local protests, assumed merely that the bill had been vetoed because of their administrative objections.

Late in May and early in June, Evans requested the Budget Division to release, for the purchase of the Shredded Wheat property, parkway funds, which had been appropriated as a lump sum in the Capital Construction budget. (Under the law, before money appropriated from the Capital Construction Fund could be spent for land acquisition, the Budget Division had to issue a certificate of availability certifying that the moneys were available and that the purpose was proper.) The responsible budget examiners recommended release of the money, and approval was granted by top Budget Division officials. During the month of June a certificate of availability in the amount of $150,000 was issued to the Division of Parks.

No one in the Budget Division had occasion to think much about the Shredded Wheat property in June. It was assumed that the Division of Parks was now in a position to purchase it. Actually, the owners of the property appeared willing to sell. On July 13, Jack E. Gellman, their legal representative, wrote to A. M. Anderson, executive secretary and chief engineer of the Niagara Frontier State Park Commission indicating readiness to negotiate:

July 13, 1956

Mr. A. M. Anderson
Executive Secretary and Chief Engineer
Niagara Frontier State Park Commission
320 Riverway
Niagara Falls, New York

Dear Mr. Anderson:

Pursuant to a directive that you have received from Albany, you have advised us that the State Parks plans to appropriate the 4 acres of land that we have between Buffalo Avenue and the river.

At the present time, we are building a hotel on this site.

I know that the State is eminently fair in the disposition of these matters and I am confident that rather than appropriate this property, representatives of the Parks Commission would much prefer an amicable purchase of this property.

If this could be negotiated with you then we would have an opportunity of going over our actual figures, our various appraisals and the amount of moneys that we have spent for architect's fees, building construction and other fees pertaining to the construction of this hotel.

I would be very glad to prepare a complete brochure of our appraisals and costs, and I would appreciate an opportunity of sitting down with your representatives in order to settle this matter. Thanking you for your courtesy in this matter, I am,

Sincerely yours,
JACK E. GELLMAN

Appleby and his top aides were only vaguely aware of the Clarke and Rapuano master plan and the relationship of the Shredded Wheat property to it. A copy of Gellman's letter was not made available to the Budget Division until months after it was written, and the Division had not been told of the motel construction that had recently begun on the property. Nor was the Division aware of the opposition of Niagara Falls city officials to the purchase. Budget officials were surprised, therefore, when they began to receive telegrams and telephone calls from Niagara Falls urging that construction of the motel be permitted to continue. On July 16, the City Manager sent the following telegram to John Tiesler, Chief Engineer of the Budget Division and head of its engineering-planning unit:

July 16, 1956

John Tiesler
Budget Department
Albany, New York

The Planning Department of the City of Niagara Falls and the City Council have approved the plans for a hotel now in actual construction which the Conservation Department now plans to appropriate for an alleged State park.

In addition, a building permit was granted and foundations have been poured and the land cleared. Construction is well on its way.

This proposed construction means thirty to forty thousand dollars in annual tax revenue to the City of Niagara Falls plus its ability to be of great benefit to the City of Niagara Falls. Accordingly, we wish to be continued on record that we want this hotel constructed in Niagara Falls at its present site.

Please advise.

CHARLES B. WRIGHT
City Manager

Tiesler immediately notified Appleby. The City Manager wished to be "continued on record" in favor of the hotel construction, and the Division up to this point hadn't known he was on record in the first place or that a hotel was planned. The Budget Director telephoned Evans and then suspended the $150,000 certificate of availability. Next he telephoned the City Manager and asked that hotel construction be halted so that the state would not incur further charges if it ultimately purchased the land. Late that afternoon Appleby wrote Evans:

July 16, 1956

Hon. James F. Evans
Director
Division of Parks
Conservation Department
Arcade Building
Albany, New York

Dear Jim:

This confirms our conversation of this afternoon in which I notified you that we are suspending the Certificate of Allocation under which the purchase of the Shredded Wheat property in Niagara Falls was in preliminary state by the regional park authority. I asked that the taking be not proceeded with, and you agreed that you would issue this order.

I have now talked to the City Manager at Niagara Falls. He tells me that construction on the site has been suspended and he will get to me from the owners a telegram saying that the construction will be suspended pending interchanges between the Parks Division, the Park Authority, and the City of Niagara Falls.

Sincerely yours,
PAUL H. APPLEBY

After several days during which further information was rounded up, the Budget Director reported to the Governor's office, which had become interested in the affair:

July 19, 1956

MEMORANDUM TO MESSRS: Bingham
Gutman
Stewart[2]

This is a memorandum designed to bring the Governor's Office up-to-date on what has been transpiring in my orbit in regard to the proposed purchase of the old Shredded Wheat Company property for park and parkway purposes.

Request for funds for this purpose was not approved when this year's budget was made on the general ground that we were uncertain about the wisdom of the necessity for acquisition and because another general appropriation would be available for the purchase of the land in case during the fiscal year it was decided that it was a necessary outlay.

Jim Evans succeeded in getting a bill passed by the Legislature which appropriated $150 thousand for the purchase of this land. I opposed permitting an executive agency to make budget in this roundabout way and recommended a veto, not knowing that at the time there was on file in the Counsel's Office a letter from the City Manager of Niagara Falls vigorously opposing the purchase, and not knowing that the Comptroller in reporting on the bill also reported that officials of Niagara Falls opposed the bill. On the basis of the information in the Counsel's office and my own recommendation, the Governor disapproved the bill. So far as I then knew this disapproval was based wholly on the fact that such appropriation was not needed and that the decision should be arrived at in normal executive decision-making fashion. Consequently, during the last month Budget Division yielded to Jim Evans' arguments and issued a Certificate of Availability of funds for the acquisition of the tract. When word of the prospective taking of the property got out in Niagara Falls, protests began to come into the Governor's Office and to us. We immediately suspended the Certificate of Availability and instructed Jim Evans not to let the taking proceed until after the City of Niagara Falls had adequate chance to be heard and the matter could be considered by all concerned in the State Administration. This suspense order was duly relayed, and the matter has been held in abeyance.

Just before the suspense order was issued, it was brought out that the owners of the property in question entered into an arrangement with the Treadway Inns for the construction of a motel on the site. The site and the motel construction were estimated to involve an investment of about $1 million, and with the development of part of the tract by a metallurgical company, the City of Niagara Falls foresees here a loss of $30,000 or $40,000 a year in tax revenue if the State takes the property. At this stage, the cost to the State for the property will undoubtedly be a good deal more than it would have been if the motel proposition had not been developed to the point it was. The ground has been cleared and 75 feet of concrete has been poured for the foundation. The general contract for construction has been let. In addition the sale of the portion of the property that went to the metallurgical company complicated the problem somewhat, although the State had no intention of retaining all the property to be taken, and this latter may prove to be a small part of the problem.

While Evans and the Park Commission have good ground for insisting that what they intended to do is of interest to Niagara Falls as well as to the State at large, it is also true that the City of Niagara Falls is warranted in seeking time in which the matter could be more thoroughly explored by both sides,

[2] Jonathan Bingham was Secretary to the Governor. Daniel Gutman was the Governor's Counsel. Milton Stewart was Executive Assistant to the Governor's Counsel.

and negotiated. Jim Evans is now engaging in the job of meeting with the Niagara Falls people and trying to work out a mutually satisfactory solution.

PAUL H. APPLEBY

Other telegrams from Niagara Falls reached the Budget Director during the next several days. One from Gellman indicated that the corporation's expenses to date had been approximately $150,000 but went on to say:

We are most anxious to continue construction for we feel that this hotel would be a great asset to the entire area. We have engaged a manager. We have made our arrangements with personnel. We will have our building constructed and finished for next season and there will be a very attractive place for many visitors that come to Niagara Falls. Even if the State Park owned this property nothing could be more suitable for the location of the proposed hotel.

Another telegram from the City Manager further illuminated the city's opposition to the state's intended purchase. It read:

Re Shredded Wheat property problem this hotel building was passed by the Planning Board as a zoning change and approved by the City Council despite the appearance of A. M. Anderson in opposition. When the news reached us that funds were available the City Council authorized me as City Manager to oppose the State taking this property. This was done in a meeting of the council as a committee of the whole. This is our official position. Study of the master plan of the Park Commission indicates little usage of this land in the dim distant future. Niagara Falls needs this hotel and it needs the tax revenue therefrom. We again reiterate that we strongly oppose the discontinuance of this progressive move to improve the City of Niagara Falls.

These and other communications were persuasive but by themselves would not have caused the Budget Director to rule in favor of continued hotel construction. Appleby was seeking a sense of the feeling among leading city officials and private citizens. Had there been evidence of a lack of unanimity—meaning the existence of some support for the position of the Division of Parks—Appleby probably would have decided in favor of the Division of Parks. In the absence of any such support, he felt obliged to decide in favor of the official city position in the interest of the principle of local responsibility. Appleby had asked Evans to go to the city and sound out opinion. But Evans decided not to make the trip—probably, some Budget officials believed, because he felt he would not be able to find any support for the Park Division's position.

On August 13, the Budget Director dispatched the following telegram to the City Manager:

Mr. Charles Wright
City Manager
City Hall
Niagara Falls, New York

The suspension of funds for the purchase of the Shredded Wheat property has been changed to a revocation of funds. This means that the State has no present intention of taking the property, and that private construction on the site may proceed. We trust, of course, that construction plans will be of a sort which will contribute to the good appearance at the river front so that when the parkway is built the surrounding improvements will be appropriate in kind and appearance.

PAUL H. APPLEBY

Moses Acts

Shortly after Appleby announced revocation of the certificate of availability, Robert Moses came to the defense of the Division of Parks:

August 28, 1956

Mr. Paul H. Appleby
Director of the Budget
State Capitol, Room 113
Albany 1, New York

Dear Dean:

May I ask you to read the attached letter carefully. We have been working on a Niagara Frontier improvement program for many years. I have been at it since 1924 and gradually, very gradually, we are making progress. Gilmore Clarke in one capacity or another, has been our top consultant.

It seems now as if we are on the eve of a coordination of power, park, parkway and thruway plans. The acquisition of the Wheat property is no hit or miss, spot protection and zoning matter. It is an integral part of the essential comprehensive program, and should not be neglected or passed up because private developers have been allowed to go so far. I must say frankly that the Power and Arterial features of our program will have to be modified very considerably if there is no genuine cooperation on immediate acquisition of threatened key parcels.

I have asked Jim Evans to present this letter to you personally.

Cordially,
ROBERT MOSES
Chairman

MAP B

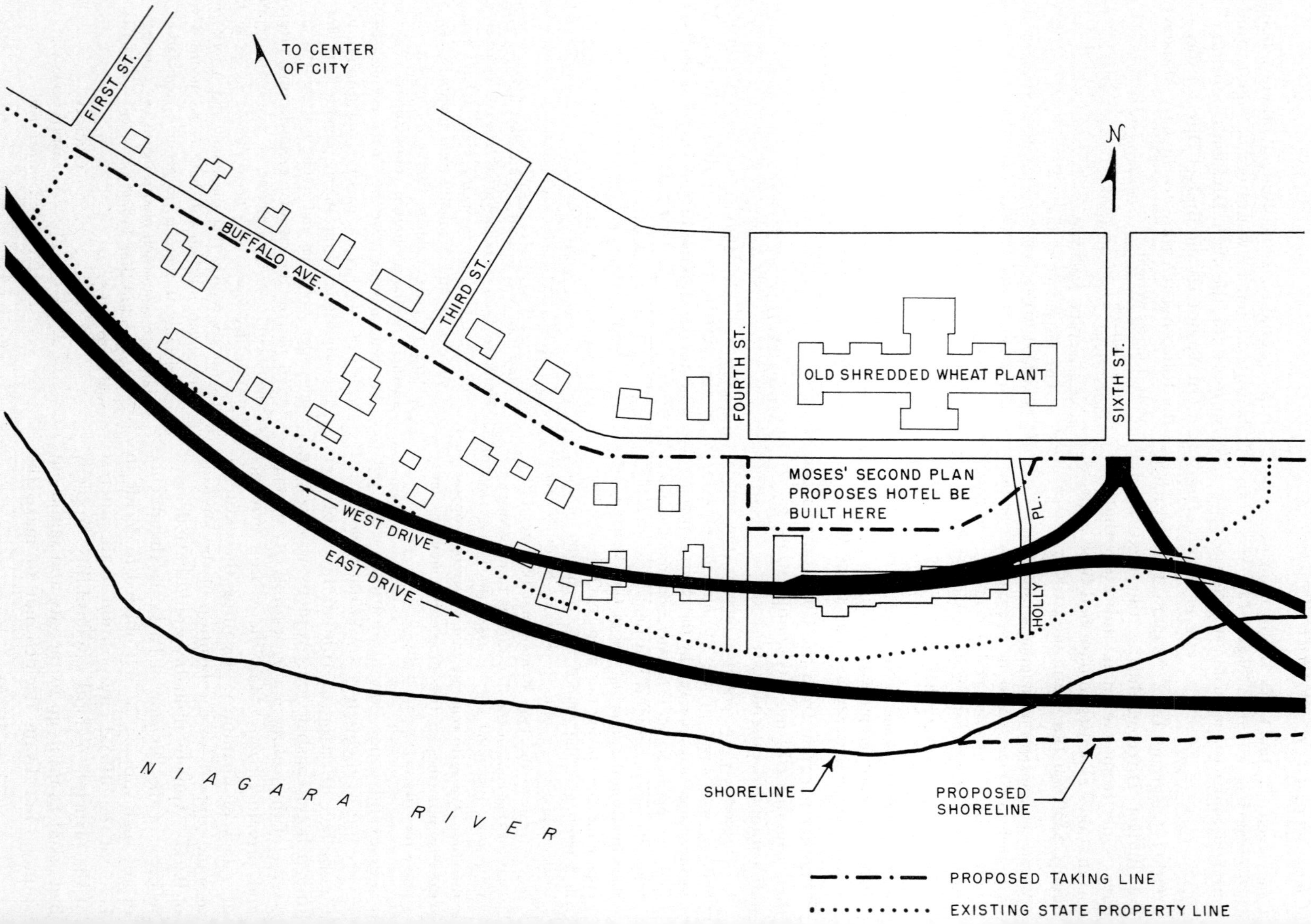

TO CENTER OF CITY
FIRST ST.
BUFFALO AVE.
THIRD ST.
FOURTH ST.
OLD SHREDDED WHEAT PLANT
SIXTH ST.
N
MOSES' SECOND PLAN PROPOSES HOTEL BE BUILT HERE
PL.
HOLLY
WEST DRIVE
EAST DRIVE
NIAGARA RIVER
SHORELINE
PROPOSED SHORELINE
PROPOSED TAKING LINE
EXISTING STATE PROPERTY LINE

The attached letter referred to in Moses' communication was an exposition by Gilmore Clarke of the desirability of having a generous right-of-way in the vicinity of the Shredded Wheat property. Clarke also described the need for the Shredded Wheat parcel if the connection to the parkway from the area of Sixth Street was to be maintained. The letter reiterated some of the statements made in the 1952 Clarke and Rapuano report about holding back commercialization and closed with the following comment: "I urge that every possible measure be brought to bear to keep this area, available for park and power development, of a quality that for once will not call for apologies and invidious comparisons with the Canadian side."

Appleby was away from the office when the Moses letter arrived, but he returned in approximately a week and replied as follows:

September 13, 1956

Hon. Robert Moses
Chairman, State Council of Parks
270 Broadway
New York 7, New York

Dear Bob:

I have been out-of-town for a few days and this has delayed my reply to your letter of August 28, handed to me by Jim Evans.

I feel that I understand your interest in this river front property in Niagara Falls, but my own feeling is that as long as the City of Niagara Falls is taking a position wholly opposed to acquisition, and as long as there seems to be no showing of substantial difference of opinion in the community the State should go slow about exercising its sovereign powers and make sure that each acquisition has a high priority in a program of developing the Niagara area from a scenic and tourist-accommodation aspect. Since the property acquisition in question has not at any time been presented in terms of any kind of development other than beautification, it has seemed to us that the parkway right-of-way will be wide enough in any case to provide good highway ingress and egress and at the same time to have appropriate planting on the sides that would be somewhat adequate without extending it all across the property in question.

I am slow to make myself party to an entirely arbitrary slapping down of a position taken by a local governmental unit which certainly should have some perception of the scenic and tourist values that are important to it as well as to the State and country. Only because these considerations weigh so largely with me have I felt confident in my own mind about the position I should take.

Very secondarily I have felt that we do not have the funds available for purchasing the entire area and at the same time meet commitments of many other kinds already made. Your own interest in acquiring rights-of-way on Long Island is just one example of the many items that compete for the limited State dollars, and we in the Division have not been persuaded up to now that this particular item is one that has such a priority that we ought to do fiscal violence in order to put it through over a firm local objection. I have no question of its desirability. I do have questions about its essentiality; these questions underscore questions of State dollar priorities.

Sincerely yours,
PAUL H. APPLEBY

Moses, having found that he could not reverse Appleby's judgment, next carried the argument to Governor Harriman in a series of letters. In addition, to counteract the Appleby arguments, he changed the plan for the parkway. The 1952 Clarke and Rapuano plan showed the construction of both roadways of the parkway on existing state land in front of the Shredded Wheat property and in front of the houses standing between Fourth and First streets. Thus, the primary reason for buying the Shredded Wheat property was beautification. Under the new Moses plan, shown in Map B, the outer or river side roadway was to be located approximately where the inner roadway had been on the 1952 drawings, while the new inner roadway was to proceed directly through the center of the area on which the hotel was being constructed. It also was to be located on a considerable portion of the land possessed by the private homeowners between Fourth and First streets, thus eventually necessitating the purchase of these properties. With regard to the Shredded Wheat property under contention, the hotel was now directly in the way of the parkway itself; therefore, the property would have to be purchased for the parkway to be built.

(Moses built a suggested compromise into his second plan by leaving a small area upon which the hotel could be built. The depth was only 150 feet. This proved unacceptable to the hotel interests for the following reasons: (1) The hotel plan was too large for the reduced plot. (2) The reduced plot would eliminate any parking facilities for the hotel. (3) The City Planning Commission would not issue a permit for such construction on reduced area. (4) Hotel construction had advanced too far to begin again.)

Moses may have discussed the first parkway design with the Governor in his early communications with him, but within a short time he was concentrating on the second plan. For an equally short time, the second plan was the framework for discussion in the Governor's office while it was still unknown to the Budget Division.

The Governor's Position

From a program point of view, the Governor might well have been in sympathy with Moses' ideas of beautification. For years, the Governor had been a park and parkway enthusiast. His family had given much land to the state for park purposes. As a working member of the Palisades Interstate Park Commission for years before becoming Governor, Harriman had taken a keen interest in park development in that region of the state. In his budgetary decisions during his term of office, he was inclined to allocate to Moses as much money as he possibly could for park and parkway purposes.

With Moses and Appleby as protagonists, the Governor was dealing with two strong personalities who had clashed before. There was no lack of mutual respect between Appleby and Moses, but they were quite opposite in outlook. Appleby believed strongly in integrated financial management and administrative teamwork. Moses was principally interested in getting as much money for his projects as he could and in being left alone to do his various jobs. For example, one of the issues between the two had been the repayment of first instance advances which the state had made on occasion to various authorities which Moses headed, such as the Power Authority and the Jones Beach State Parkway Authority. The previous administration had made a number of such advances without any schedule of early repayment being required. To pinpoint this, at the time the Harriman administration came into office, the state had advanced $15,900,000 to the Jones Beach State Parkway Authority with no foreseeable early repayment. The Governor's first Budget Message commented on the situation in general as follows:

> The picture of the development of the Capital Construction Fund is incomplete if we examine only the income and the expenditures of the Fund. The practice has been to make cash advances from the Fund to certain of the State's authorities, pursuant to 'first instance' appropriations. These advances are made without interest and with the date for repayment left indefinite or subject to agreement negotiated between the Director of the Budget, representing the State, and the authority concerned. In at least one instance, unless a new agreement can be reached, repayments to the State will not begin before 1980, or be completed prior to the year 2000.

To Appleby's way of thinking, this was highly irresponsible fiscal management, and he early insisted upon first instance agreements being negotiated with the proviso that repayment to the state be made from the first sale of bonds by the recipient authority. This proviso was included in future advances made to any of Moses' authorities. In the second year of the Harriman administration, the Legislature was persuaded to support this approach and passed a law requiring first instance advances to be repaid out of first bond sales.

Harriman was himself a strong personality and was not in any case going to decide the issue on the basis of the strength of the personalities of Appleby and Moses. Nevertheless, the way the problem was handled was a reflection of his relationships with each. Harriman had personally selected Appleby as his Budget Director. When Appleby, then Dean of the Maxwell School at Syracuse, had demurred somewhat for reasons of health, Harriman had insisted that he needed him. The two had a keen mutual respect as a result of having worked together in the federal government under Presidents Roosevelt and Truman, including a time when both were in London during World War II. As Governor, Harriman relied heavily on Appleby's fiscal and program judgments, but between the two there was complete understanding of their respective roles. When a decision had to be made, it was the responsibility of the Budget Director to provide the Governor with as much information on the subject as the Division could develop, and if called upon, to recommend a line of action. The Governor had to make the decision, and, once made, it immediately became accepted policy within the Budget Division regardless of what the Division's recommendation had been.

Moses was a slightly different proposition. Technically, he was not a member of the "team" although he and the Governor were friends from earlier years. His various term appointments to different authorities had carried him into the Harriman administration and made him independent in that sense. Moreover, he was something of an administrative "loner." He did not take kindly to interference in his work by any agency, including the Division of the Budget, and early in the Harriman administration he established a working pattern whereby he directed almost all his recommendations and requests to the Governor personally.

In addition, Moses was an acknowledged expert in his field. He had an outstanding reputation in planning and administering parkway and other projects. Those who wished to criticize him had always been confronted with the fact that he had produced tangible things that could be seen and appreciated. Because of his considerable abilities, any Governor would want to give his recommendations every consideration.

Finally, except for Appleby, there was a semblance of an "eggshell" attitude within the administration in dealing with Moses. There was always the possibility that he might "sound off" in public if too many of his recommendations were turned down, and because of his public reputation this was to be guarded against. In comparison with other administrators, he was regarded as having a low boiling point. Therefore, in dealing with him it was considered especially necessary to be sure of one's reasons for any decision contrary to his liking.

Whatever his reasons for doing so, the Governor reopened the question of the Shredded Wheat property after Moses wrote him. One of his first moves was to ask Appleby for the background of the issue. Appleby responded as follows:

October 9, 1956

MEMORANDUM TO THE GOVERNOR:

On the Shredded Wheat property, this is the story. At the time Evans came to us for a release of funds, they had a plan of development indicated on the enclosed map, which at the time did not contain the green lines. The area outlined in red is the Shredded Wheat property. The plan at that time was for the parkway to be located at the site of the two parallel wide blue lines with a Y for ingress and egress. At the time this presentation was made Evans said that for the Y alone, it was not necessary to acquire the Shredded Wheat property. At that time we were being bombarded with telegrams and telephone calls from Niagara Falls officials demanding that we not release funds for the purchase of this property and saying that both the Planning Commission of Niagara Falls and the City Council of Niagara Falls had approved the zoning of the tract so as to provide there for a motel. Since Evans was unable in the course of several weeks to engender any public support in the community, and since the City held rigidly to its position, and since it seemed to us that Evans was proposing to take more land than was required for the beautification along the parkway, and since the whole property involved would ultimately cost the State a million or two, we said no. In the course of all this I went over the matter in detail with Jonathan Bingham and he shared in our judgment.

Now the Division of Parks has redesigned the parkway along lines indicated in green pencil on the map so as to traverse all of the property along the river front, and with roadside planting requiring about 60% of the entire Shredded Wheat tract. This is an entirely new plan and was unknown to Jim Evans and unanticipated by him at the time he was pushing for the release of funds. Consequently, what Bob Moses has been talking about recently is something quite different from what was discussed earlier. The difficulty facing me, and to an extent, you, is in the fact that at the time we made the decision in August, we notified the City of Niagara Falls that the funds were not being made available and indicated that the State had at the time "no present intention of taking the property," and to be given the green light to the advancement of private construction on the site. Actually, while the construction was not resumed, we would now have to pay not only the value of the land but damages suffered by the contractor, but worse than that, we would be greatly irritating the City government of Niagara Falls. If we are going to reverse ourselves, it seems to me we ought at least to indicate to the City of Niagara Falls officials that we are favorably considering this action before we do in fact act. Even then, I think they will be pretty angry. The Parks people have never told the City of Niagara Falls officials the extent of their plans, and Jim Evans is very reluctant to do this. The City will be even more offended at the intention of taking the cross-hatched property adjoining the Shredded Wheat property than they will be about the Shredded Wheat tract. However, Moses now promises that if we use State money to take the Shredded Wheat tract they will not ask us to put up State funds for any of the other adjoining land or for the parkway within the City but will use Authority funds when they become available. It must be said, too, that the redesigned parkway plan is a distinct improvement in that the upper road will be elevated so that people on both sides of the parkway will have a fine view of the river and the points of interest round about.

As far as I am concerned, my pride will not suffer in any way if in your judgment the revised parkway plan justifies a reversal of judgment, but I do think the relationship with the City of Niagara Falls needs to be considered and some kind of friendly overture made before any public decision is announced. On the other hand, if action is going to be taken, action ought not be much longer delayed or we would run the risk of having heavier damages to pay for.

PAUL H. APPLEBY

Despite the fact that Appleby's memorandum suggested that he was quite willing to withdraw his objections to the state's purchase of the Shredded Wheat parcel, the Governor refused to make this easy decision. Instead, he suggested to Appleby that he send some of his staff to Niagara Falls to make an on-the-spot examination of the property to analyze afresh the wisdom of the Moses recommendation. Accordingly, Appleby dispatched his chief engineer, Tiesler, and his administrative deputy, Howard Miller.

Tiesler and Miller toured the site with the deputy chief engineer of the Niagara Frontier State Park Commission and with the district engineer of the Department of Public Works. On the basis of their examination, both Tiesler and Miller concluded that the 1952 Clarke and Rapuano plan was reasonable. This called for building both sections of the parkway on existing state property. In their opinion, there was sufficient land between the extreme southern line of the Shredded Wheat property and the river for this to be done. The Department of Public Works' district engineer concurred in this judgment, as did the Niagara Park Commission's deputy engineer, who was if anything confused because he had never heard of the second Moses plan. Subsequently, the district engineer of the Public Works Department sent a long letter to Appleby supporting the stand that the existing state property was sufficient for the intended parkway. Part of that letter follows:

There is merit in the idea of having traffic lanes in one direction at a different elevation than those in the opposite direction. We have generally tried to provide this treatment along the New York State Thruway. It tends to relieve the monotony of a standard construction section and promotes safety by more positive evidence of the separation of traffic.

However, the park lands in this area contain many full grown trees, the foliage of which would be at about the level of traffic on the upper highway. This would interfere with the sight distance of people riding in cars on that highway, and thus preclude their seeing the river and rapids unless the trees were removed.

I do not have any detailed maps available for study, but it was indicated to me that the northerly right-of-way line of the existing park lands is at the top of the existing slope. From my field observations I can conclude that there is plenty of space on the existing park right-of-way to provide a divided highway of 24 or 36 foot pavements in each direction, and the northerly lane could be elevated 3 or 4 feet which would provide the desired vision for traffic on those lanes, without obstruction. At about the center of this stretch of proposed highway the existing park lands may be rather limited in width, but a variable mall treatment, a small retaining wall, or a rise in elevation could easily solve this situation. Also, at the easterly end opposite Eighth and Ninth Streets the proposed rock fill for the parkway to the east would have to be continued to this area. In either case, if a connection is made to the Erie-Highland arterial highway, which is proposed to run north and south between Eighth and Ninth Streets, the acquisition of a few pieces of private property would be necessary.

Appleby summed up the Tiesler-Miller recommendations in a memorandum to the Governor:

October 18, 1956

MEMORANDUM TO THE GOVERNOR

Shredded Wheat Property

I spoke to Jim Evans about the impression you got from Moses that there is now still a third plan for the Parkway route in Niagara Falls for which the Shredded Wheat property was desired. Jim had heard of no such plan, and talked to Moses, who confirmed Jim's statement that there is no new plan.

Howard Miller of my office and John Tiesler, head of our Works Unit, spent Monday in Niagara Falls looking over the site, talking to local officials, to the Department of Public Works Regional Engineer, the Deputy Chief Engineer of the Niagara Park Commission, etc. Moses' chief engineer in that district had been invited to join them, but did not. The Public Works Department now officially concurs in my team's view that the original parkway plan is adequate and perhaps preferable. Scenically, the second plan would destroy many fine trees, and open no significant vista. In other words, they recommend against any change in our position on the Shredded Wheat property matter because of any important Parkway considerations. The Deputy Chief Engineer of the Niagara Frontier Parks Commission had never before seen the second Parkway plan, and had no argument for it.

The two men uncovered no evidence that Moses had persuaded anybody in Niagara Falls; rather the contrary. [City] Officials returned from their New York conference with him in no way mollified. Jim Evans tells me that the Shredded Wheat property had been mentioned only briefly in passing and makes no claim that there was any shred of agreement on it; he said the principal talk was about Authority payments in lieu of taxes.

The people who are building the hotel were interviewed, and their blueprints reviewed. The construction cost is $1.2 million, and total cost will be about $2 million. There is a lease with the Treadway Inns, and a subordinate management lease has been given to a man who has quit another job to take this on. It will be a good development at about the only location Niagara Falls has for such facilities, which eventually will spread over adjoining tracts which the second Parkway location would eliminate from that kind of tourist-facility development.

My judgment is that we should emphatically reaffirm the earlier decision not to release the money for the purchase of the Shredded Wheat property. I shall be quite happy to assume the responsibility, but send you this memo to clear up the point about a new, third Parkway plan. We need to send word to Niagara Falls promptly, and word will be sent in my name as soon as Mrs. McCray [the Governor's private secretary] gives me the green light.

PAUL H. APPLEBY

Contrary to Budget Division expectations, the issue was not decided by the Tiesler-Miller report and by Appleby's positive recommendation. For on October 20, Moses again wrote the Governor:

October 20, 1956

Honorable W. Averell Harriman
Governor of the State of New York
Executive Chamber
Albany 1, New York

Dear Averell:

I gather from Jim Evans that, on top of all the trouble we have had with Dean Appleby, on the Niagara Certificate of Intent and other matters, he has come to the conclusion that he will not approve the acquisition of the so-called Wheat Company-Motel property for the parkway improvement at the Niagara Reservation. This is on the basis of the modified plan which leaves enough land for the building of the motel on a strip approximately 550 feet long and 150 feet deep. Apparently the Dean sent a couple of his boys up to Niagara. They redesigned the parkway and decided that it could be built nicely without taking this strip.

Let me point out to you again where this leaves us. It means that the State refuses to acquire the only piece of right-of-way on which building started due entirely to State neglect. This is all the State has to do in anticipation of construction with power funds of an enlightened, integrated, comprehensive program of power and park development analogous to what has been done in Canada. We anticipated the development of the Wheat company land last fall and when the item was not included in the budget, a special bill was put through the Legislature appropriating $150,000 for the property, in order to emphasize the importance of the acquisition. Appleby advised you to disapprove this bill. This was before there was any development. With a reduction in the size of the plot it is very unlikely that the award will exceed $150,000 available out of parkway funds.

Obviously if this Wheat-Motel strip is not acquired, it is useless to acquire adequate frontage and protection beyond and below on the basis of our new revised plans. In fact I see no purpose in spending any power funds whatever for any comprehensive program if this is the spirit in which the problem is being approached by the State, and if we are going to have constant interferences by the Budget Division. [Emphasis added.]

If this is your intention, the only course I can possibly take is to advise all those concerned with the power program to drop all but strictly technical requirements of power development, and leave out everything that has to do with conservation, neighborhood improvement, esthetics, landscaping and incidental features. This would mean that we have learned nothing from our own and from Canadian experience.

Let me point out also that I am individually fed up with attempting to work with Appleby. You may recall that I was asked to help on the numerous problems related to the establishment of three state hospitals in New York City and more recently an additional one east of the City line on Long Island. This is no part of any duties or responsibilities I am required to perform, and the same applies to my top assistants in the City. All of us went to work on this subject vigorously in the face of obstacles Appleby does not seem remotely to comprehend, to be helpful and spent hours in anticipating and quieting opposition of City officials who have to run for office next year, etc. I have kept your office informed continuously on this subject.

Apparently the State administration is represented in such hospital matters primarily by the Budget Director and the other officials concerned, that is, those in Mental Hygiene and Public Works, take only a minor part. No doubt the Chief Engineer of the Budget Division, John Tiesler, can inform you on this subject. I have not had so much as a word of thanks from Appleby. Cooperation seems to be a one-way street where he is concerned. Under the circumstances I am turning over what remains of this problem in and outside of the City to other officials, including the matter of having the City chip in the property it owns within these hospital sites. No doubt this can be arranged by others.

We have at Niagara confronting us seemingly endless problems of local opposition as to taxes, land acquisition and incidental improvements. We have the radical REA and COOP people from other states to contend with. We have trouble getting rates down to where the existing basic frontier industries and the transmission company can afford to pay them in the light of conversion to sixty cycle operation. We have to buck tremendously increased construction costs. We have the conservation, park and protection possibilities to consider. If we are going to have to take on petty opposition and sniping in the Budget Division, it looks, as Governor Smith used to say, like too much corned beef and cabbage. I therefore ask for your personal support.

Sincerely

ROBERT MOSES

The Governor Suggests a Solution

ON OCTOBER 29, the Governor convened a meeting in his office to discuss a compromise. Present were Appleby, Evans, and Tiesler. The basic compromise suggested by the Governor was to permit the Division of Parks to take a small parcel of the Shredded Wheat property on the easterly side to allow for entrance to the parkway from Sixth Street. Although Moses had warned that the entire beautification and improvement plan would be stultified if the motel property were not acquired, the Governor stated that he wanted a solution that would meet essential parkway requirements but that would take a minimum of property from the site of the projected motel. The Governor also wanted someone to go to Niagara Falls to further examine leadership opinion with regard to the desirability or undesirability of the hotel's construction. Miller was already in the Niagara Falls area on other business, and Appleby was able to reach him to give him this assignment.

The State Consults City Leaders

Miller's findings were contained in the following memorandum to the Budget Director which he wrote after his return to Albany and which Appleby then forwarded to Governor Harriman:

MEMORANDUM

October 31, 1956

To: Paul H. Appleby

From: Howard F. Miller

Subject: Interviews at Niagara Falls Relative to the Parkway

Yesterday at the Falls, I interviewed eight persons to get their reactions and opinions on the controversial hotel construction at the old Shredded Wheat property south of Buffalo avenue and on park and parkway development in this area in general. The persons interviewed were: (1) Ernest Kremers, a former chairman of the City Planning Board, now semi-retired and seemingly mostly occupied with his duties as an official of the Niagara Hotel Corporation; (2) Tom Barrigan, who I believe is managing editor of the *Niagara Falls Gazette;* (3) Hamilton Mizner, who I believe is city editor of the *Gazette*. In any event, both Barrigan and Mizner are leading figures on the paper . . . (4) Alpheus Phelps, a leading lawyer in the City, presently a member of the Planning Board, a person who would logically be referred to as a leader in both civic and business affairs in the community; (5) Clarence Greenwald, City Corporation Counsel, a Republican wise in ways relevant to survival through the intra-party arguments and ranklings to the extent of his having approximately twenty-five years of municipal service; (6) Calvin Keller, Mayor of the City and a member of the Council; (7) Charles Brown, a former councilmanic leader and now something of a wise elder statesman on community matters although no longer taking an active part; (8) Daniel Collins, formerly executive secretary of the Planning Board, who appears to have been recently removed from that position to head up the Housing Division so as to make room in the Planning unit for someone more acceptable to the present majority coalition on the Council.

All of these persons struck me as intelligent individuals and as having substantial interest in the community. None of them was especially dogmatic in his opinions. As a matter of fact, I was impressed by the general lack of positive thinking on the subject, by the general lack of explicit knowledge of what was intended by way of park and parkway development, by the general belief that Bob Moses would tell them what was to be done or what needed to be done, by the feeling that the "State" would get its way in any event, and by the lack of unified thinking on the subject. There seems to be little in the way of a community position among the leadership group, although several of the persons interviewed expressed the belief that the typical citizen was in favor of the hotel construction because of what is regarded as the future tax problem of the City. The subject of the hotel construction, etc., is definitely not an inter-party squabble. . . . To the extent that friction exists, it is among Republicans within the party. There is [some feeling toward] . . . Jack Gellman, the Republican lawyer for the hotel interests. It is believed that Gellman and two of the Republican councilmen . . . represent one element of the Republican Party in Niagara Falls and that they . . . are influential with the City Manager . . . and that the Mayor and other Republican councilmen represent another element of the party. . . .

Before outlining the positions taken on the subject by the several residents with whom I talked, it might be useful to comment on the area under discussion and explain compass directions so that you can more easily visualize what is involved as you read the rest of this memorandum. As you know, the land on which the hotel is being constructed lies on the South side of Buffalo Avenue towards the river and is bounded by Fourth Street on the West and Holly Place on the East. It is either through the hotel property, or just below it, nearer the water's edge, that the parkway is projected. Also on the South side of Buffalo Avenue and immediately to the West of the hotel property, nearer the center of the Falls and nearer the rapids, is another strip of property approximately 400 yards in length on which are located many of the old fine homes of the City, including the Tone residences. These face on Buffalo Avenue and back on the present strip of State property along the river. In this memorandum, I shall use the terms, "all property South of Buffalo Avenue" and "the property West of the hotel site." The first of these terms encompasses the hotel site property and all the old homes immediately to the left of it, as one would describe it looking at a map, from Fourth Street down to First Street and the Niagara Reservation. The second term refers to all these properties except, of course, the hotel site property. On the North side of Buffalo Avenue, directly opposite the hotel site, is the old Shredded Wheat plant which is in the process of being demolished. Immediately West of it on the same side of Buffalo Avenue, from Fourth down to First Streets, is another group of old but less pretentious homes than those across from it. It is this area that is referred to in the memorandum when it is suggested that hotel and other construction be limited to the North side of Buffalo Avenue.

Turning now to the particular comments of the individuals with whom I talked, I found as follows:

1. *Mr. Kremers:* . . . He welcomed the high-grade competition of the Treadway people. He believes the general community reaction is in favor of continuing with construction of the hotel. He believes, however, that all property South of Buffalo Avenue should be reserved for park and parkway development, including the property where the hotel is being built. And he believes that commercial, including hotel interests, should concentrate on the North side of Buffalo Avenue, with hotels and apartment houses facing the park. Whether these properties could be acquired easily from present residents he was unprepared to say. He indicated that if the present shoreline could be extended so that the parkway were more than a ribbon, he would probably have no objection to commercial development of the South side of Buffalo Avenue, but this was only a secondary thought with him. He looks at the development of the parkway and the possible commercialization of the North side of Buffalo Avenue as a long-range, gradual thing, not to come about in the immediate future. My impression was that he was a bit vague about a potential time schedule and that he was in effect saying that this beautification and development project had been lying dormant for so long that it was only useful to think about it in general terms. He had once seen a copy of the original plan for the development of the parkway, but he had no knowledge of what we in Budget have been calling the second plan.

2 and 3. *Mr. Barrigan and Mr. Mizner:* Both men

were impressed with the fact that this was to be a Treadway operated enterprise and were in favor of it. Their position was that the City no longer had desirable properties available for industrial and business commercialization. They felt that the properties South of Buffalo Avenue were too valuable to take for parkway purposes, having in mind of course the serious tax losses the City would suffer from the power project and the taking of many thousands of dollars off the tax rolls by the development of the parkway. They appreciated and were sensitive to the need for beautifying the area near the river but were of the opinion that the price was too high to pay in view of their tax situation and the lack of land for expansion within the City; they were in favor of a "ribbon-type" parkway along the river and saw the rest of the land South of Buffalo Avenue used for commercial purposes. In their opinion, Moses has built "ribbon-type" parkways in the New York City area, and the Falls was no place for him to satisfy his desires for an expansive parkway system. Their only information on the subject of what was intended for the Falls came when the Governor and Moses visited there some weeks ago [on Power Authority business]. They knew nothing of the proposed second plan. They said the people of the community were in favor of continuing with the hotel construction because of the tax situation.

4. *Mr. Phelps:* He had substantially the same attitude as Mr. Kremer, although he was more actively interested in the subject and slightly more positive in his opinions. His attitude was that all property South of Buffalo Avenue should be reserved for the parkway development and that commercial construction should proceed on the North side of the street. He talked about the long-range nature of the project but had in mind its completion within a five or ten-year period. As a member of the Planning Board, he was in attendance when the Gellman interests submitted their request for rezoning of the Shredded Wheat property, but did not attend the meeting when it was voted. The vote of the Planning Board, incidentally, was 5-1 in favor, with Mr. Phelps not voting. He said he would have voted against it had he been there. He is not concerned with the loss of tax revenue to the City by not using the Shredded Wheat and other properties along the river for commercial purposes. When asked about the possibility of extending the shoreline outward to accommodate both commercial and parkway development in modified form, he was interested in it as a compromise plan, all the while admitting that it had not previously occurred to him. He impressed me as having a rather mild-mannered preference for ruling out commercial development except for the North side of Buffalo Avenue.

5. *Mr. Greenwald:* He expressed preference for parks as well as parkway development of the entire property South of Buffalo Avenue. He was of the opinion that the first Moses plan was ideal because it ostensibly provided for a park area between the parkway and Buffalo Avenue. He was opposed to the second plan to the extent it would provide for beautification of the area but not for actual park facilities alongside the parkway. He had no comment on the loss of tax revenue. He had only a vague understanding of what was projected for park or parkway facilities since he had only a minor booklet on the subject which was printed some time ago. He said that Moses discussed the parkway briefly with the Republican leaders when they met with him in New York City several weeks ago to discuss the question of financial payments in lieu of taxes relating to the power project, but he had not heard of the second parkway plan until we discussed it. It is difficult to assess the depth of his feeling on the subject. . . .

6. *Mr. Keller:* The Mayor was one of the two Republicans voting against the Council resolution for hotel construction. He indicates he favors full park and parkway development South of Buffalo Avenue. He, too, was only vaguely aware of what was projected for the area and mostly confined himself to agreeing with Mr. Greenwald. He has no answer to the loss of tax revenue. While Mr. Greenwald declared himself opposed to the second Moses plan, the Mayor would not go that far. Since he mentioned his previous vote on the subject, I gathered he was saying he wouldn't know how to switch sides at this time. He is openly opposed to the Republican majority and to Gellman. He mentioned that he had tried to work with Gellman once but that they couldn't get along. The point I am obviously laboring is that while both Greenwald and the Mayor may be quite sincere in their commitment to the beautification of the Falls area by the establishment of parks and parkways, they are unable to discuss the subject or assess the situation much beyond the point of being for something in the abstract, and I am unable to assess how much their feeling is based on their opposition to the "new" Republican majority coalition and the fact that this group is for modified commercialization of the entire South side of Buffalo Avenue. Incidentally, both Greenwald and the Mayor alluded to the "influence" this group backing the hotel construction had in Albany. This, of course, is nonsense, but it might be suggested that part of the proof that this is fantasy lies in the fact that George Donahue, the Niagara County Democratic Chairman, who lives on Buffalo Avenue just North and West of the hotel site, was an active member of a so-called neighborhood association which opposed the granting of an application to

build to the hotel interests. George, by the way, was mildly unhappy over the continued hotel construction, but his also was seemingly a lack of preoccupation with the question.

7. *Mr. Brown:* He was not in favor of using the entire area South of Buffalo Avenue for park and parkway development. His judgment is that the parkway can be built on presently state-owned land below the hotel and below the residences to the West. If it could not, he suggested, without my raising this with him, moving the shoreline out by the use of rock fill. . . .

8. *Mr. Collins:* He was in favor of either of the Moses plans, particularly the first one. . . . With respect to the second plan, he recommends the combining of park and parkway facilities by the use of overhead walks so that pedestrians might avail themselves of park facilities between the East-bound and West-bound sections and between the West-bound section and Buffalo Avenue.

It is difficult to generalize on what is the proper position for us to take on the basis of the opinions expressed above. It is agreed that majority sentiment in the City would be in favor of continuing with hotel construction. Some of the leaders I talked with are also of that opinion. Others favor discontinuance of hotel construction and reserving the entire area South of Buffalo Avenue for park and parkway facilities. I am impressed with what appears to me to be a lack of depth of feeling on either side. I am impressed also with the fact that it seems to be uniformly accepted that the decision to permit continuation of the hotel construction is final. In my opinion, to reopen that question at this time is not good judgment. . . .

The Engineers Meet on the Spot

At the October 29 meeting in his office, Harriman had also brought about an agreement that the engineers for both sides would make a last trip to the site to determine how much of the hotel property was required for the Y through which Sixth Street would enter the parkway. The result of the engineers' on-the-spot conference was described in a memorandum to Appleby by Chief Engineer Tiesler:

MEMORANDUM

To: Paul H. Appleby, Director
From: John A. Tiesler, Chief Engineer
Date: November 8, 1956

In accordance with instructions from Governor Harriman and you, as a result of our meeting in the Governor's office on October 29, I accompanied Jim Evans to Niagara Falls on Wednesday, November 7, to attempt to work out the Governor's compromise proposal in relation to the hotel property on the Niagara River Parkway. Meeting with Mr. Evans and me yesterday in Niagara Falls were the following:

Messrs. Elmer Youngman, District Engineer, Department of Public Works; Gilmore D. Clarke, Consulting Architect for the proposed parkway; Frank Seigfried, Deputy Ch. Engr., Niagara Frontier Park Com.; Arthur Williams, Commission's new designee for title of Ch. Engr.; William Leathem, Chief Engineer, N. Y. S. Power Authority.

Governor Harriman's proposal at the Monday, October 29 meeting had to do with working out a minimum taking from the hotel property in order to provide for the access drive to Buffalo Avenue. Since the October 29 meeting in the Governor's office it is quite apparent that the Park Commission and its consultant had given a great deal of attention to the whole problem of this parkway for Mr. Gilmore Clarke presented a revised plan in connection with the Parkway development and park use of land along the Niagara River from Bridge Street easterly to the hydraulic canal.

A number of significant changes have been made in this proposed plan:[3]

1. The access drive in the vicinity of Sixth Street, which previously required a portion of the hotel property, has been deleted. This access has now been moved easterly and will no longer require any of the hotel property for this purpose.

2. The consultant proposed a minimum 50 ft. strip to be acquired from the hotel property along the parkway frontage.

3. A revision of the land required for parkway and park purposes, between First Street and Fourth Street, is indicated in the new plan.

By reference to the map you will note it is now the Commission's intention to leave a strip of land along Buffalo Avenue varying from 150 ft. in depth at the westerly end to 100 ft. in depth at Fourth Street. This last proposal would seem to be a compromise and probably acceptable to the City Council of Niagara Falls, although the idea was not checked with City officials during my visit.

Field Inspection

After a general discussion in administration headquarters the party made a survey of the site in the vicinity of the proposed hotel in order to determine the need for the 50′ strip proposed to be acquired from the hotel ownership. Mr. Clarke stated that the area was tight in width requirements and that he felt that for adequate parkway pavement and a reasonable amount of landscaping a strip should be acquired from the hotel ownership as well as exten-

[3] These are shown in Map C.

MAP C

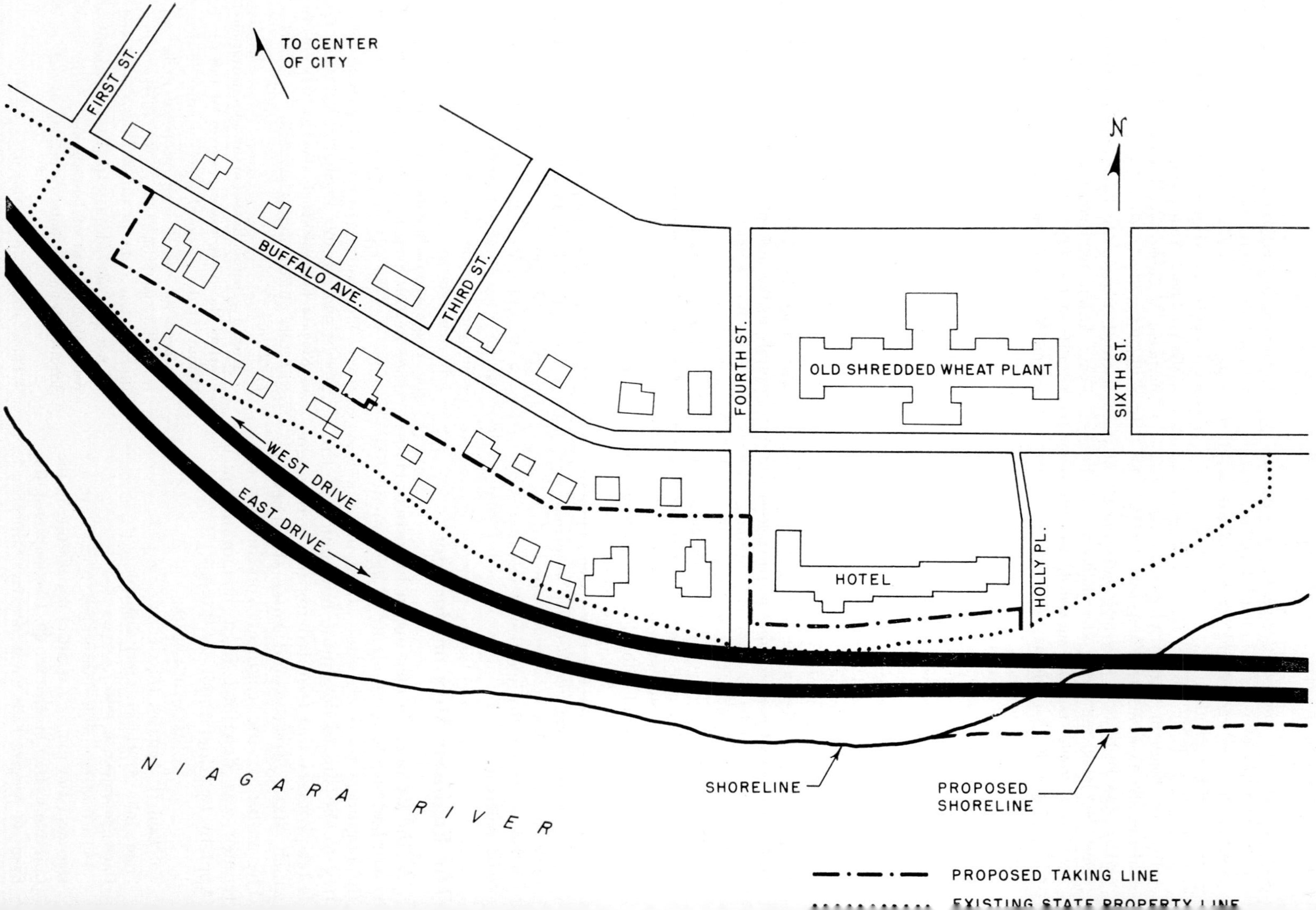

TO CENTER OF CITY
N
FIRST ST.
BUFFALO AVE.
THIRD ST.
FOURTH ST.
SIXTH ST.
HOLLY PL.
OLD SHREDDED WHEAT PLANT
HOTEL
WEST DRIVE
EAST DRIVE
NIAGARA RIVER
SHORELINE
PROPOSED SHORELINE

PROPOSED TAKING LINE
EXISTING STATE PROPERTY LINE

sion of the shore line in this vicinity by the placement of rock fill. It will be noted by referring to this new plan that the west bound parkway drive is located along the present hotel property. Mr. Clarke argued that additional width must be provided in order to landscape and protect the west bound drive. The conference decided after this inspection that the plan submitted would satisfy all requirements involved in good parkway construction. I felt that the 50 ft. strip indicated by Mr. Clarke was not entirely necessary and, after some discussion, he revised his preliminary sketch to show a strip along the hotel property 50 ft. wide at Fourth Street and 25 ft. wide at Holly Place. This suggestion was accepted by all present.

Meeting with Hotel Owners

Following our general meeting and inspection, Mr. Evans and I met with Mr. Jack E. Gellman and Mr. Harold A. Dautch to present this new plan to them. First of all, I told Mr. Gellman that Governor Harriman had taken a personal interest in this matter and was most anxious to see the hotel constructed following as nearly as possible the owners' original intention and that we had met in Niagara Falls again at the Governor's instruction to work out a final solution of the parkway problem. I explained first that we were able to eliminate the access drive to Buffalo Avenue in the vicinity of the hotel. By this decision there would be no requirements to redesign the hotel itself or to require land at the southeast corner of this property for such access purposes. I then explained to Mr. Gellman that the consulting architect and the party had visited the site that morning endeavoring to minimize acquisition requirements of the hotel property. I then presented him with a large scale map prepared by Mr. Clarke at our morning meeting which indicated a strip of land 50 ft. in depth at Fourth Street narrowing to 25 ft. at Holly Place. The strip of land so required would be used entirely for landscaping purposes and would in effect appear still to be hotel property. The immediate reaction was that the acquisition of this property would probably eliminate a parking space for twenty cars now proposed to be constructed at the southwest corner of the building. This he indicated would present something of a problem for the parking area proposed is to service a rear entrance to the dining room and bar. He thought, however, that he would be able to solve this parking problem working with the City officials for the use of Fourth Street for parking, if the City would agree to their use of Fourth Street for parking. (Under the parkway plan Fourth Street would become a dead end street when the new parkway is constructed.) Mr. Gellman and Mr. Dautch, after considerable discussion, said that they felt that the State's proposal was very fair.

They were most pleased that they would not have to redesign the hotel itself at Holly Place for the access drive. The new proposal would affect them far less than the previous proposal. They further stated that they would have to talk to the bank in regard to mortgage release for this part of the property but did not believe this presented much of a problem. General acceptance of the State's new proposal was indicated and Mr. Gellman stated that he would write a letter indicating his approval of this plan. As a last reservation he asked Mr. Evans whether he could continue to park on this proposed State strip until the new parkway had been constructed. Mr. Evans said that he would have no objection to its temporary use. The parcel of land to be acquired comprising less than one-half an acre and damages should be not greater than $20,000 by Evans' and my calculations. As we left this meeting Mr. Gellman said to tell Governor Harriman that he was most pleased to cooperate in regard to this matter and felt confident that complete agreement would be forthcoming.

Conclusions:

Our direct instructions by Governor Harriman in regard to this matter were to negotiate a friendly settlement in regard to any necessary land acquisition at the southeast corner of the hotel property which might be necessary for access purposes. In effect Mr. Evans and I exceeded our authority in taking back this new proposal in relation to the narrow strip along the parkway and obtaining the owner's preliminary approval. However, we both felt that for good public relations purposes it was in the State's best interest to explain the entire situation to Mr. Gellman while we were in Niagara Falls. I believe the settlement reached at our meeting yesterday is entirely satisfactory and would recommend your approval of our actions. Attached to this memorandum is a clipping from the *Buffalo Evening News*, Wednesday, November 7, in which Commissioner Davis of the State Park Commission defends the Moses proposal in relation to the entire development plan for Niagara Falls. This release has reference to the narrow strip of land we discussed with the owner. At the time we met with Mr. Gellman, I did not know that Mr. Davis was going to make the press release in regard to this narrow strip of land. It would, therefore, indicate that our decision to reveal the plan to Mr. Gellman yesterday afternoon was most timely for I am sure he would have been disturbed had he seen this proposal in the newspaper for the first time.

JOHN A. TIESLER

Final Decision and its Consequences

With a final settlement finally worked out between Budget Division and Division of Parks officials, it remained only for the Budget Director to advise the Governor and to obtain his official concurrence. Evans had gone directly to New York to report to Moses. He telephoned to report Moses' acceptance. Appleby advised the Governor to approve the arrangement, concluding, "So in the end I think everybody will be happy." The Governor signified his approval. The Budget Division continued to negotiate with Gellman over the price to be paid for the parcel; the final settlement was for approximately $5,000.

But was everybody to be happy with the Shredded Wheat property decision? In his October 20 letter to the Governor, Moses had stated flatly that unless the motel property were acquired, it would be "useless to acquire adequate frontage and protection beyond and below. . . . In fact, I see no purpose in spending any power funds whatever for any comprehensive program if this is the spirit in which the problem is being approached by the State." Three years later, by the end of 1959, neither the Parks Division nor the Power Authority had made any move to acquire the properties west of Fourth Street, which had figured prominently in the master plan. It appeared that the Shredded Wheat property decision might have resulted in the scrapping, or at best the long postponement, of the exciting, comprehensive program that was to develop and beautify the United States side of the Falls.

HOW MUCH TO SPEND AND WHO WILL PAY?

"To tax and to please, no more than to love and be wise, is not given to men."

Burke

Governor Freeman and the Minnesota Budget

Thomas Flinn

Introduction

IN THE FALL OF 1954 the Republican Party in Minnesota lost a gubernatorial election for the first time since 1936. Along with the governorship, it lost every other statewide office except that of state auditor. Control of the lower house of the Legislature slipped from the hands of the Conservative Caucus (allied with the state Republican Party) into the hands of the Liberals (allied with the Democratic-Farmer-Labor Party). The State Senate withstood political change and remained under control of the Conservatives. However, a sharp break had occurred in the development of Minnesota politics.

The incoming Governor was the 36-year-old Orville L. Freeman, the first member of the Democratic-Farmer-Labor Party to be elected to that office.

This case study, written from the perspective of the Governor's office, describes the preparation and passage of Freeman's budget. Since the Governor's term was for two years only and the Legislature would meet only once in that two-year period, this was the only budget and tax program for which Freeman would be responsible during his term.

The first section of this study describes the efforts of Freeman and his aides to prepare a budget and a fiscal program for presentation to the Legislature. They had less than two months for this task—from shortly after Freeman's election in November 1954 to the opening of the legislative session in January 1955. Their first examination of the state's finances revealed that existing taxes would not even pay for continuing state services at the level set by the previous administration, much less permit the increase in state services which Freeman and his party had pledged during the campaign. The Governor-elect had to make some hard decisions about what level of state services should be sought and who would have to pay the tax bill.

Putting together a coherent fiscal program in less than two months did not complete the task for Freeman and his aides. They still had to steer the Governor's program through the Legislature. The second section of this study describes Freeman's four-month negotiations with the members of the Legislature and the decisions made by that body. The Governor's proposed fiscal program became the most controversial issue in the 1955 session. Soon the Legislature was debating not only specific fiscal proposals but different theories of taxation and different views about the future shape of Minnesota's tax system.

The author, who had assisted the Governor in his campaign, was in the Governor's office (but not a paid member of his staff) during the period described here. Much of the information on which the study is based was gained by direct observation of staff meetings, executive-legislative conferences, partisan legislative caucuses, and informal discussions of all kinds. Many events are omitted; conferences of several hours duration are summarized in a few paragraphs. But crucial decisions and debates are retained. If the reader gains the impression that some important decisions were made quickly, without protracted discussion or argument, it is the same impression the author had while the events were taking place. If a multitude of events seem to be flashing past in the space of a few days, this is the reality of a Governor and a Legislature trying to shape fiscal policy for a large state in a short span of time.

The State

Minnesota in the early 1950s was about half urban and half rural (slightly more rural than the national average). More than one-third of the state's three million people was concentrated in and around the St. Paul-Minneapolis metropolitan area. Only one other city—Duluth—had more than 30,000 population.

The state enjoyed a fairly well-balanced economy, although it depended more on agriculture than did most states. Dairy products, corn, and hogs were the most important agricultural commodities. Iron mining, meat packing, and flour milling led the state's industries. There was a variety of manufacturing in the St. Paul-Minneapolis area, the transportation, financial, and commercial center for a large region extending east and west of Minnesota. In general, the state was neither unusually rich nor poor; its 1954 per capita income of $1,642 placed it twenty-sixth in the nation.

The DFL Party

Minnesota's Democratic-Farmer-Labor Party of 1954 was a result of the merger of the Democratic Party and the Farmer-Labor Party. The Democratic Party had never enjoyed much success in Minnesota, although its candidates had won the governorship several times between 1900 and 1916. The Farmer-Labor Party, in turn, had grown from the Non-Partisan League, an agrarian protest movement which began in North Dakota and spread to Minnesota about 1918. From that time until the middle 1940s, the Democrats had run a poor third in state contests. Farmer-Labor Party strength was strongest in the mid-1930s, when it had captured the governorship several times, but during its later years in power the party had developed a reputation, among some Minnesota voters, for radicalism and corruption.

The new coalition party, the Democratic-Farmer-Labor Party, was formed in 1944. The first four years of its existence were spent settling factional disputes between left-wing Farmer-Laborites and a right wing led by Democratic Senator-to-be Hubert Humphrey and Governor-to-be Freeman. The wrangling was settled decisively in 1948, with the defeat by the Humphrey-Freeman group of the left-wing supporters of Henry Wallace, the Progressive Party candidate for President. Freeman became state chairman, followed in 1950 by Karl Rolvaag.

The DFL remained weak organizationally. Although by 1950 the party had committees in all but one of the state's 87 counties, in most cases the organization consisted of a handful of dedicated partisans and a slightly larger number of hangers-on. Even by 1954 the party was still far from having a committeeman in every precinct, and many of those whom the party had enrolled were virtually inactive.

Party finances continued to be shaky during this growth period of the 1950s. Although efforts were made to establish local clubs with year-round programs and to develop a dues-paying membership, the collections were not enough to finance campaigns. At best they helped stabilize the state party headquarters.

Until it won office, the DFL could not attract party members by patronage, and, in fact, there was little profit to be made in Minnesota government even for the winners. Since 1940 the state government had been covered almost completely by the merit system. Only top positions were political appointments, and the qualifications for these jobs were stiff enough to make them of little value as political prizes. Local elections were legally non-partisan, and practice frequently coincided with the law. When the parties did intervene in city and county contests, their intervention was often ineffective. Furthermore, merit systems were common in Minnesota local government.

The DFL could not count on strong press support. The big dailies in St. Paul and Minneapolis, which circulated through most of the state, were Republican, although the morning *Minneapolis Tribune* seemed more sympathetic to the DFL cause than the others. The daily press in Duluth was Republican, as was the overwhelming majority of the weekly newspapers in the state.

One strength the DFL Party did have was a close association with organized labor.[1] The chairmen of the Ramsey and Hennepin County DFL organizations (St. Paul and Minneapolis) were veteran A. F. of L. officials. Trade unionists held party office in other counties, too, and there were several union leaders on the state executive committee.

Also strengthening the DFL was its relation-

[1] In 1954-1955 organized labor in Minnesota claimed 325,000 members. (The urban labor force numbered approximately 700,000.) About half the trade union membership was in the Twin City area. The other large center of trade union membership was in the Iron Range, where the miners were well organized.

ship with the liberal farm organization, the Farmers' Union. Some state officers of the Farmers' Union were cautious about too open identification with the DFL, but in many counties DFL leaders were also Farmers' Union leaders, and most political observers counted Farmers' Union members as probable DFL voters. In 1954-1955 the Farmers' Union claimed as members 30,000 to 35,000 of the 170,000 Minnesota farm families, and it also claimed to be the largest Minnesota farm organization in terms of farm membership.[2]

Despite the diversity of its membership, the DFL by 1954 was a relatively united and harmonious party. Perhaps the most serious intra-party difference was conflict between labor and non-labor elements in Minneapolis. But even this was occasional and limited to that city, since labor groups outside the area tended to side with the non-labor faction. Both labor and DFL farmer delegates organized caucuses at state DFL conventions, but the caucuses were not important in the making of convention decisions. There were, of course, personality conflicts, but for the most part a substantial majority of active DFLers in 1954 seemed satisfied with the Humphrey-Freeman-Rolvaag leadership. Party platforms and the statements of party candidates were consistently liberal, and conservative points of view in the party were hard to find.

In short, the DFL had its strengths and weaknesses. Important for this case study is the fact that the Governor and other DFL leaders were acutely aware of the weaknesses. Especially prominent in their minds was the thought that the DFL did not enjoy widespread public confidence. It had never before controlled the state administration, and its legacy from the Democratic and Farmer-Labor parties did not include the ingredient "public confidence."

[2] This was a new status. Although the Farmers' Union had been active in the state for many years, its membership had been largely restricted to northern and western Minnesota. Other parts of the state were organized by the more conservative Farm Bureau. But Minnesota farmers, hurt by worsening economic conditions and angered by the Eisenhower-Ezra Benson farm program, had turned in large numbers to the Farmers' Union during 1953 and 1954.

The Governor-elect

Freeman had entered politics after World War II by joining the Democratic-Farmer-Labor Party. Before that time he had been an honor student at the University of Minnesota, a member of Phi Beta Kappa and the Law Review. He had served with the Marines in the South Pacific and had been seriously wounded. He was elected DFL Party secretary in 1946, one of the few right-wingers to win party office that year. In 1948 he became party chairman, and in 1950 he sought convention endorsement for Governor. Failing to get the endorsement, Freeman ran instead for Attorney General; he was defeated with the rest of the ticket. In 1952 he easily won party endorsement for Governor but was defeated in the general election. In 1954 his friends again endorsed him for Governor, although his chances did not seem bright at the beginning of the campaign. This time Freeman won, with 52.9% of the two-party vote—about the same proportion gained by the other successful DFL candidates. His climb upward had been made exclusively on the ladder furnished by the DFL Party.[3]

The Platform and the Campaign Promises

Occasionally espousing efficiency but never economy, the DFL had endorsed virtually every proposal advanced on the national level by both the New Deal and Fair Deal administrations of Presidents Roosevelt and Truman. It was equally liberal in its approach to state policy. The 1954 DFL platform on which Freeman won election recommended that annual state basic aids for public schools be increased from $80 per pupil unit to $100. The same platform favored removing the $60 per month ceiling on old-age

[3] The career of Karl Rolvaag, the new Lieutenant Governor, was similar in some respects to Freeman's. Rolvaag had been a Phi Beta Kappa member at St. Olaf College. During the war he rose to the rank of captain in the Army, and he was wounded in Germany. Returning to Minnesota, he ran for Congress twice on the DFL ticket in the rock-ribbed Republican First District. In 1950 he took Freeman's place as DFL state chairman, and served in that post until mid-1954. In 1952 he ran unsuccessfully for Congress against Walter Judd in the Minnesota Fifth District.

trim departmental requests and on the publicity the operation was receiving. Nearly everyone was in favor of holding the line on expenditures as far as possible.

Senator Schultz, who in the first meeting had recommended "slashing," renewed his recommendation with vigor. He represented a St. Paul district in which organized labor was strong, and he judged his constituents were worried more about taxes than about any government services. "They just don't want any more taxes," he said flatly. (After the meeting Freeman told him that he was right, that the people were tax conscious. But, Freeman added, "Organized groups are program conscious.")

The discussion turned again to the possibility of diverting the costs of the state teachers' colleges to relieve the pressure on the General Revenue Fund. Sentiment was unanimous: it was politically impossible. Alfred Johnson, the Liberal candidate for Speaker of the House, and Ed Chilgren, the Liberal Chairman-designate of the House Tax Committee, both warned Freeman of trouble from the Republican-controlled Senate. They feared that the Senate would agree to diversion but that it would reject any program sponsored by the Governor to strengthen the Income Tax School Fund. Thus an increase in school aids would be impossible, and the DFL would be blamed for diversion without being able to claim credit for increased state aids to education.

Finally the Governor-elect demanded, "Just who is it that fights diversion anyway?" Laughter greeted Ed Chilgren's reply, "We've done fairly well." Chilgren, Johnson, and other members of the DFL legislative group had worked closely with education interests in preceding sessions. Johnson added that any surplus in the education fund was due to their efforts in the past. He went on to say, however, that they would "go along" on diversion if Freeman wanted to recommend it.

Freeman then asked for suggestions for increasing revenue in the General Revenue Fund. He got some random replies about present taxes but few suggestions beyond the favorite one that increases should be spread over existing sources. It was clear to the Governor and his aides that this was not a topic about which the legislators felt much enthusiasm. As one legislator pointed out, increases in General Revenue Fund taxes would be, in effect, sales taxes by the back door. Johnson suggested that all present taxes be increased a little; Popovich suggested that the needed revenue be raised by raising one or two taxes sharply. "Our majority is so small, and the Senate is hostile," Popovich pointed out. "Orv can't control; so why take on everybody? We want to get re-elected."

Johnson, the prospective Speaker, disagreed; that would not be a genuine program, he felt. Tempers began to rise, and Freeman changed the subject. Later he explained privately to Johnson that he agreed that putting all increases on a few taxes would be an abdication of executive responsibility.

There was some discussion of the Income Tax School Fund. Freeman presented the idea he had been discussing with Heller since the previous June: to revive the DFL-sponsored bill of the 1953 session which provided for a withholding system of collecting state income taxes. This move would mean collection of three years' income taxes in two years, a substantial "windfall."[9] Another advantage of the plan was that it would improve compliance and make payment of income taxes (and tax increases) less painful. The legislators reacted favorably to Freeman's suggestion. Representative Mosier, Chairman-to-be of the House Appropriations Committee, said it was a good idea, and Representative Chilgren added that he thought it could be passed at the coming session.

A few days later Freeman directed a memo to Spaeth, asking him to submit: (1) figures on the level of compliance with the present state income tax; (2) an examination of the problems which would be encountered in setting up a withholding system, including a comparison of various state systems then in operation.

Freeman was still not convinced that diversion was dead. He saw it as the relatively easy

[9] Inauguration of a pay-as-you-go system on July 1, 1955 would result in collection of one-half of the 1955 tax bill during that year while all of the 1954 income tax bill was also being paid. In 1956, taxes due that year would be collected, as well as that half of the 1955 taxes not withheld.

way to solve the problem of the General Revenue Fund shortage and he was loath to abandon it. On December 16 he invited in a group of DFL leaders: Alfred Johnson, who would become Speaker of the House; Fred Cina, prospective Majority Leader; Arthur Hansen, newly-elected DFL state treasurer; and Hjalmar Petersen, one-time Farmer-Labor Lieutenant-Governor, now elected Railroad and Warehouse Commissioner.

The group resisted Freeman's suggestion for diversion. Johnson repeated that in the past DFL representatives had fought hard to protect the surplus in the Income Tax School Fund; Freeman was asking them now to load that Fund with a new burden, the state teachers' colleges. Cina stood firm on his counter-proposal that the General Revenue Fund deficit should be met instead by an overall increase in existing General Revenue Fund taxes. Petersen pointed out that a previous attempt at diversion had brought immediate reactions from constituents. After considerable discussion, Speaker-designate Johnson told Freeman: "It would be a hard pill to swallow, but we'll support you." But Freeman had been persuaded of the legislative hazard, and he gave in. "I couldn't do that to you," he replied. The next morning Freeman told Johnson diversion was definitely out.

Demands on Freeman's Time

A frantic cramming of facts and figures into a viable program was not the only task which was filling Freeman's time during this fifty-day period. He had just gained new importance as a public figure, but he was relatively unknown to the people of the state. Requests for speeches arrived in unusually large numbers from civic and business groups whose members Freeman had not met before. It seemed that the time was ripe for consolidating and increasing support. Freeman accepted a very heavy speaking schedule for the month of December, and he maintained it throughout the legislative session that followed. In addition, large numbers of well-wishers wanted the opportunity to say a few words to the new Governor. He found it hard to say no.

The making of appointments also sapped his time. There were not many, but the posts he had to fill included the top positions in the state government. Freeman decided against hasty replacement of incumbents, but he did want to install his own top administrators as soon as he could identify suitable candidates.

Furthermore, Freeman intended to take a position on many issues in the forthcoming legislative session. He asked organized labor groups for their ideas. With no guarantee of acceptance, but with assurance of a friendly hearing from the Governor, the labor groups submitted a long list of proposals dealing with workmen's compensation, unemployment compensation, and existing state laws in the field of labor-management relations. Freeman also wanted to effect a general administrative reorganization of the state government, and he created an informal committee to work with him and Naftalin in preparing a plan. He also created an informal group to consider changes in state election laws. One particularly troublesome problem was presented by the Highway Department which, over the years, had gained a semi-autonomous position, although it was formally subordinate to the Governor. Freeman meant to get it into line. These and a host of other problems and obligations competed with the budget for a share of Freeman's time in the busy December days before he took office.

Outside Formal Channels

During the month of December Freeman met frequently with groups of leading businessmen in St. Paul and Minneapolis in what he called "get-acquainted meetings." He renewed his promise to seek ways to bring new industry to Minnesota. A few of his listeners renewed their argument that taxes handicapped Minnesota in the competition for new business, but they did not suggest cutting government costs.

In the same period a few delegations came to Freeman in support of specific appropriations. One group, for example, sought a larger appropriation for the mental health program. The Governor-elect and his aides agreed that the budget allotment for mental health was austere, but, like leaders of the retiring administration, they saw no way of increasing it greatly. The director of the program was reported willing to get along as best he could.

But in that same month the Mental Health Advisory Committee, an official body, invited the Governor-elect to a state conference on mental health which it had organized. As a result of conversations in connection with the conference, Freeman became convinced that marking time would injure prospects of improved state mental health service in the future. He therefore directed a slight upward revision of the budget to finance a psychiatrists' training program which the Mental Health Advisory Committee had urged. This was one of the rare instances of informal representations made to influence the hectic budget-drafting work being carried out by the Governor-elect and his aides.

Also, during this busy December period, Freeman appeared as an impressive figure to those who were working most closely with him. It seemed, at least to Naftalin and Heller, that the assumption of the executive responsibility was bringing to the fore qualities of decision and leadership only hinted at during the campaign. They saw him now as the Governor. And they were increasingly impressed by his ability to absorb information rapidly and to think beyond the mass of facts to a coherent program. Heller was delighted by Freeman's adherence to progressive tax principles and by his willingness to accept sophisticated economic advice in planning the state's fiscal program. Both Heller and Naftalin were moved to long hours of intense work, not only by the coming deadline but by a sense of enthusiasm for the value and freshness of the new fiscal program which the Governor would present.

The Figures Come Piling In

On December 17 Tax Commissioner Spaeth completed a ten-page memorandum answering, as well as could be answered at that time, the questions raised by Freeman on November 30. Freeman met that day with Naftalin, Heller, and George Selke, former president of St. Cloud State College, who had returned recently to Minnesota after service with the American occupation administration in Germany. (Selke later became a special assistant to the Governor and then Commissioner of Conservation. Having passed normal retirement age, Selke was enjoying a new career.) Heller came prepared with a check list of tax alternatives for the General Revenue Fund. The most important variables were taxes on iron ore and taxes on consumer items. The plan with the highest iron ore tax was necessarily the plan with the lowest consumer taxes. Freeman decided to put the heavier burden on the iron ore industry. The problem was now to construct the tax program around that decision.

A few days later Heller gave Freeman a memo which listed all the proposed General Revenue Fund taxes in order of what Heller conceived to be their equity and their probable political acceptability. The "least objectionable taxes" were the iron ore taxes, insurance taxes, and inheritance and gift taxes. "More objectionable taxes" were the beer tax, broadening the base of the property tax, and gross earnings taxes. "Most objectionable or questionable taxes" were cigarette and tobacco taxes, new special utility taxes, and an admissions tax. Heller's memorandum is reproduced below:

December 20, 1954

To: Governor-elect Orville L. Freeman
From: Walter W. Heller
Subject: General Fund Revenue Program for 1955-57

1955-57 Revenue Increases

I. LEAST OBJECTIONABLE TAXES

A. *Iron ore taxes* — $10,000,000

1. *Rate increases:* On royalty and occupation taxes combined, each point of increase will yield roughly $2,000,000 additional revenue in 1955-57 for the General Fund (assumes 65 million tons). An increase of 5 percentage

points (from 12 to 17 per cent) would bring in $10,000,000 additional in the biennium. It would be an increase of just over 40% in the present rate.

Here are a few facts to keep in mind with respect to the iron ore tax increase:

(a) As a percentage of pig iron and steel prices, the ore taxes that vary with output (i.e., the occupation and royalty taxes) are lower today than they were in 1929, 1941, and 1950. Rising steel prices and a falling ratio of ore to steel have more than off-set the increase in taxes. The two taxes today represent only about ¾ of 1% of the Bessemer pig iron price per ton, and less than ⅓ of 1% of the price of sheet steel. Raising the tax to 17% would push the tax to just over 1% of the Bessemer pig iron price and about ½ of 1% of the sheet steel price. (Adding in the *ad valorem* tax, which does *not* vary with output, would raise these figures to a total of about 1.5% and ¾ of 1%.)

(b) The occupation taxes are in lieu of corporate income taxes.

(c) The increase to 17% would also increase the amount available to the income tax school fund in the 1957-59 biennium and thereafter if the necessary constitutional amendment is enacted.

2. *Labor credits:* Narrowing the scope of labor credits as discussed would produce about $750,000 for the General Fund in the next biennium. 750,000

B. *Insurance taxes*

1. *Annuities:* After a discussion with A. H. Nelson, I am strongly inclined toward including annuities in the base of the tax. The Insurance Department says 28 states do this. About 90% of the annuities business in Minnesota is written by foreign companies, and only 10% by Minnesota companies. The yield would be close to $400,000 a year. 615,000

2. *Mutual and fraternal companies:* There seems to be no reason, in terms of equity, why the premiums of these companies should not be included in the base of the present tax. Information on other states' practices is not yet available. Including the mutual companies (i.e., the property mutuals; life mutuals are already in) would add another $750,000 revenue for the biennium; including fraternals would add $500,000 more. However, the political implications of this move should be examined very carefully. 635,000 / $ 1,250,000

3. *Rate Increases:* One has to proceed here with extreme caution because of the retaliatory provisions in other states that would hurt Minnesota companies. (An increase of ¼ *of 1%* would add about $1,500,000 of revenue biennially.) (1,600,000)

C. *Inheritance and gift taxes*

1. We are clearly below the national average here, and are exceptionally liberal as to deductions, and as to rates in the lower and middle ranges.

2. A 30% increase as indicated, carefully worked out structurally, which will yield $2,000,000 in a biennium. But in the 1955-57 biennium, an optimistic estimate for this change would be $1,000,000. $ 1,000,000

II. MORE OBJECTIONABLE TAXES

A. *Beer tax*

This is of course a "selective sales tax," but our beer tax and prices are so 1,700,000 (50¢)

low relative to other states that a tax increase seems very much in order. [2,500,000 (75¢)]
Our other liquor taxes are in general very high relative to other states, and it seems that we should hold the line on these. A tax of 50¢ per barrel (increase on both 3.2 and strong beer) would increase our revenues $1,700,000 biennially.

B. *Property tax*

1. Leaving the General Fund mill rate *where it is* would yield about
$1,750,000 more than the current figure in the General Fund estimate and 1,750,000
would leave an accrued "cushion" of over $3,000,000 at the end of the 1955-57 biennium.

2. This would leave a little lee-way for the building fund (.11 mills in 1955; .34 in 1956) without going above the 9.15 mill state levy this year.

3. Spreading the General Fund levy on *all* property, including homesteads, 1,200,000
would add about $1,200,000 to the biennial yield of a 2.96 levy. The recent 3 mills
Minnesota Tax Study Commission study gives considerable indirect aid ($30.00)
and comfort to this move. . . .

C. *Gross earnings taxes*

It still appears, though we are following this up in more detail, that we are well above the national average in taxing gross earnings of utilities. However, circumstances alter cases. It may be that the nine-city plea for an addition to the gross earnings taxes to be distributed back to them makes a case for an increase in these taxes, especially if at the same time one wants to go into a personal property reclassification which would cost them money.

III. MOST OBJECTIONABLE OR QUESTIONABLE TAXES

A. *Cigarette and tobacco taxes*

A 1¢ increase on cigarettes would raise $5,500,000 biennially: $4,125,000 for $ 4,125,000
the state and $1,375,000 for local governments. The best opinion I have 2,062,500
been able to get so far is that, apart from the fact that no other state uses ($687,500)
the ½¢ break, such an increase might result in a 1¢ increase in the price of cigarettes for a great proportion of the total sales. Machine sales seem to be less than ¼ of the total.

We are still investigating the other tobacco products.

B. *New special utility taxes*

1. *Natural gas distribution:* Further investigation of this possibility leads to the following misgivings about this revenue source, which ought to be considered: (1) It singles out one source of BTUs and raises the question of taxing electricity, coal, oil, etc. (2) A good part of the tax would fall on industrial users and worsen their inter-state position. (We will try to get a break-down on use of gas.) (3) This tax would be on top of the tax which is imposed in some localities, and there would be the perennial problem of the municipally owned gas utilities. (4) The new gas pipeline from Alberta might possibly be affected (for example, as to ICC approval) by the imposition of the tax on natural gas. (5) It is worth remembering

that Duluth and the Iron Range are just on the verge of getting natural gas. (6) Like other taxes of this sort, this is a "selective sales tax."

A tax of 1¢ per thousand cubic feet on natural gas deliveries would yield $2,100,000 biennially. 2,100,000

2. *Electric transmission:* A tax of 10¢ per thousand KWH of electricity generated in Minnesota (not transmission) would yield $1,150,000 biennially. Some of the objections listed under natural gas would also apply to this tax. On both of these taxes, we are attempting to get further information and analysis as a basis for final decision. 1,150,000

C. *Admissions tax*

Just for information, a tax of 5% on admissions would raise about $2,500,000 biennially. Although this has a very low rating for state revenue purposes, it might be kept on the back burner for possible use at the local level, either by enabling legislation or by state collection and local distribution. Again, this is relevant in connection with possible state action to reduce the taxes on personal property. 2,500,000

Freeman now had just ten days in which to get the estimates of General Revenue Fund revenues from different combinations of taxes and to make his final decisions. He had decided that he would have to close the program-making process by January 2 in order to leave time for the actual writing of the budget message and the printing of it in time for the January 18 legislative session.

The Income Tax School Fund

Information was also piling up on prospects for the Income Tax School Fund. Early study of the financial situation had shown that maintenance of a program of state aids, including $80 basic aids, during the 1955-1957 biennium would require about $5,000,000 additional income and would exhaust the $30,000,000 balance available at the beginning of fiscal 1956. Maintenance of basic aids at the $80 level in the following (1957-1959) biennium would require at least $30,000,000 in new revenue to fill the gap left by disappearance of the surplus. Probably more than that would be needed, since the school population of the state was growing.

Information collected by Naftalin during December indicated that expenditures for an education program with basic aids fixed at $80 per pupil unit would be $158,000,000 instead of $151,000,000. But Naftalin had also discovered that the amount of money actually paid out in school aids regularly fell below estimates. It was possible to introduce a "cancellation" factor of about five percent, which left the problem much as it had been before.

However, in his campaign Freeman had pledged support for $92 basic aids per pupil unit. The education lobby had taken the same stand, and the DFL platform called for $100 basic aids. It was estimated that each hike of $1.00 in the level of basic state aids would cost an additional $1,250,000 for the biennium. An increase to $92 would cost about $15,000,000 over the $5,000,000 needed to maintain the $80 aid level for 1955-1957.

Freeman honored his campaign promise. There was no discussion of the decision; there was no indication that he ever seriously considered any other course. Freeman would have to find $20,000,000 in new income for the Income Tax School Fund in the 1955-1957 biennium. He was under no obligation to recommend ways to raise the money that would be needed to pay aids in the 1957-1959 biennium, but he told his advisers in his December 17-18 staff meetings that there would be little chance to get $92 basic aids for the coming biennium unless he could also offer the Legislature a solution for the problem that would have to be faced in the 1957 session.

Figuring in all discussions of the Income Tax

Income Tax School Fund, 1955-1959
(In Millions of Dollars)

Basic School Aid at $85	1955-57	1957-59
Expenditure	$156	$156
Income		
Existing Taxes	116	116
Withholding	31	. . .
Iron Ore Tax Amendment	. . .	20
Balance Brought Forward	30	21
	$177	$157
Balance	$ 21	$ 1

Basic School Aid at $92	1955-57	1957-5
Expenditure	$166	$165
Income		
Existing Taxes	116	116
Withholding	31	. . .
Iron Ore Tax Amendment	. . .	20
Balance Brought Forward	30	11
	$177	$147
Balance	$ 11	—$18

ore tax constitutional amendment. As shown in the table above, the Fund would be in balance at the end of four years if basic aids were fixed no higher than $85. The $92 program advocated by the Governor would produce a deficit of about $18,000,000. (He had suggested elimination of federal deductability as a solution to the problem in the 1957-1959 biennium. Support for this idea had not developed, and Freeman had decided it would be wise not to force the issue.)

Johnson and Cina told the Liberals on the Education Committee to report an $85 basic education aid bill. Some committee members were dissatisfied, but they could not hope to pass a $92 basic aid bill without the help of the leadership. Freeman was disappointed, too, but he did not challenge the strategy advocated by the Liberal leaders. The amended bill came out of committee on a vote of seventeen to seven; the "no" votes were cast by Conservatives. On April 1 Freeman sent a memorandum to all members of the House Education Committee, which had already acted, and to all members of the Senate Education Committee, which had not acted, supporting the $85 program and demonstrating that the program could be financed for the next four years without any tax increases, assuming passage of withholding and of the iron ore tax amendment.

The Legislative Deadline Nears

By the time the school aid bill cleared the House, there was less than a week left of the ninety legislative days in the session. Adjour ment would be mandatory on April 21. The las day for the passage of bills would be April 2(since the Constitution prohibited passage c bills on the last day of a session.

Of the three big appropriation bills (stat departments, welfare, and education), only th state departments bill had been passed by th House (April 11). But welfare passed on Apri 15, and education followed on April 18. Th effect of the various cuts and increases was t cut about $6,000,000 off the Governor's Genera Revenue Fund appropriation request. Tota General Revenue Fund appropriations in th House bill were $156,000,000. Despite the Gov ernor's dissatisfaction, which was shared by the leadership, the big money bills were enacted without significant amendment or protest. The tradition of the House was to accept the work of the Appropriations Committee, and it was expected that the Senate would restore some House cuts, a practice it had followed in past sessions.

Once the total appropriation figure was known, the omnibus tax bill for the General Revenue Fund was pushed through. Every Liberal voted for passage; so did sixteen Conservatives. It provided about $17,000,000 in new revenue instead of the $19,000,000 the Governor had sought. However, the House had reduced the needs of the General Revenue Fund by $6,000,000, so it was in the position of supplying about $5,000,000 more than was needed to balance the General Revenue Fund budget. Consequently the leadership, with Freeman's approval, decided to allow the General Revenue Fund property tax to expire (it would provide about $7,000,000), a course of action which had not seemed possible when the Governor had been preparing his budget. While this meant that the House was providing slightly less than estimated General Revenue Fund expenditures, the deficit was small enough to be risked. Actual receipts might exceed estimates, or, at worst, the next session of the Legislature could be asked for emergency action to permit the state to get through the biennium.

House Changes in Governor's Proposals
General Revenue Fund Taxes
(In Millions of Dollars)

TAX	GOVERNOR	HOUSE
Property	$ 6.8	. .
Fees	3.3	2.0
Gift and Death	1.0	1.0
Beer	2.1	2.1
Tobacco	2.0	2.0
Annuities	.6	.6
Telephones	1.5	.9
Iron Ore, Increased Rates	8.0	8.0
Reduced Labor Credits	.75	.75
	$26.05	$17.35

Senate Action

Senate hearings on the important administration bills began much later than House hearings. They were shorter but similar, with no changes in the ranks of defenders or critics who appeared to testify.

Freeman attempted to win support for his legislative program, including the budget, from the Senate's Conservative rank-and-file members. He met them and the entire membership of the Senate in equal installments at three dinner meetings on March 22, 24, and 28. The Governor described his position with care and in detail. No Conservative present offered any alternative, nor did any of the Governor's guests criticize seriously any of his major policy recommendations. They listened politely and then commented amiably on safe topics.

Senate action came later than House action and then in a rush. During April 14-16, it passed an old-age assistance bill, the omnibus fee bill, the iron ore severance tax constitutional amendment (to use ore taxes for current needs instead of using them to swell the bulging trust funds), and a school aid bill. All were in a different form than that requested by the Governor and passed by the House. The Senate version of the severance tax amendment provided that all the revenue currently assigned to the trust funds would go to the General Revenue Fund. (The House had decided that the forty percent of current receipts being deposited up to that time in the Permanent School Fund would go to the Income Tax School Fund.) While the House had cut the Governor's school aid recommendation from $92 to $85 per pupil unit, the Senate school aid bill held to the $80 level already in effect. The small band of Liberals in the Senate made a few attempts to amend these bills on the Senate floor, but their motions were brushed aside.

Disposition of Revenue from Iron Ore Severance Tax

	AT START OF SESSION	FREEMAN'S PROPOSAL	HOUSE PROPOSAL	SENATE PROPOSAL
Permanent School Fund	40%	....	....	....
Permanent University Fund	10%	....	....	....
General Fund	50%	60%	60%	100%
Income Tax School Fund	....	40%	40%	...

The necessary conference committees were formed. The House was able to insist successfully on its version of the old-age bill. The fee bill presented few serious difficulties, but the iron ore severance tax constitutional amendment got drawn into the clash of rival plans for supplying needed revenue for the General Revenue and Income Tax School funds. Finally, in the second week of April, with only a week left of the constitutional length of the session, unhappy House conferees accepted an $82 basic school aid bill, thus ending the issue for this legislative session.

The Senate also passed its big General Revenue Fund appropriation bills during the mid-April flurry. As anticipated by the Governor and the House leaders, the Senate restored some of the cuts the House had made in the Governor's appropriation recommendations. Senate figures were about $2,000,000 above what the House had accepted and about $4,000,000 less than what the Governor had recommended. A compromise was worked out in the next few days. The House conferees were able to insist successfully on their more expensive old-age assistance program, while the Senate conferees insisted on their appropriation decisions. The net result was a figure slightly above the original Senate total. Now, with appropriations agreed upon, the Legislature faced the need to agree on a tax program.

General Revenue Fund Appropriations and Revenue Needs
(In Millions of Dollars)

	Governor	Mid-April House	Mid-April Senate	Final
Expenditures	$167	$161	$163	$164
Less Cancellations and Transfers	— 5	— 5	— 5	— 5
Net Expenditures	162	156	158	159
Revenue from Existing Taxes[a]	137	137	137	137
Amount of New Revenue Needed	$ 25	$ 19	$ 21	$ 22

[a]The income of $7,000,000 from state property taxes is not included in revenue from existing taxes. It will be recalled that the Governor assumed their continuation while the House specifically decided to let them expire.

When the Senate reconvened Monday, April 18, after its Sunday recess, the administration's withholding plan for the Income Tax School Fund still rested in the Senate Tax Committee, where it was soon joined by the House-approved omnibus tax bill for the General Revenue Fund.

During the preceding week Freeman had tried to encourage friendly action. He had had several meetings in his office with the Senate leadership for discussion of the tax issues; he found the Conservatives unwilling to reveal their hand or to bargain with him, although they were uniformly courteous.

On Tuesday, April 19, Senator Donald Wright, Chairman of the Senate Tax Committee, revealed his own tax program. He proposed balancing the General Revenue Fund budget by imposing for two years a $5.00 tax on every person filing an income tax return regardless of income and number of dependents. (This head tax was in addition to the head tax imposed several years before to help pay for the state veterans' bonus. The first head tax was to expire at the end of 1958.) Wright's new project would raise $10,000,000 in the next biennium. Wright also suggested some token and some genuine increases on business taxes, which he replaced the next morning by a five percent surtax on corporation income taxes and on iron ore taxes.[14] They would raise another $6,000,000 or $7,000,000. Wright's committee decided to increase the iron ore surtax to six percent. Its small show of opposition to the will of the chairman was unusual. The bill was then voted out, withholding having been dismissed with contempt, at least by Senator Wright.

The Governor's reactions to the events of the week are revealed by a memorandum he dictated on Tuesday evening after Senator Wright had unveiled his head tax plan. This memorandum was not prepared for circulation or public delivery. It was literally the Governor thinking out loud in a complicated and rapidly changing situation. (A few comments that would not be clear without additional information are omitted.)

1. The Governor can immediately take the initiative, castigate the Conservative Senate, proclaim their failure to adopt a Liberal, sound tax program, and set the state finances in order as done by the House of Representatives. This would involve a long-term battle with the necessity of placing the responsibility on the Conservatives relative to the fact that this is, after all, a drive for a sales tax and an intentional way of getting the state in such a mess that a sales tax is inevitable.

2. The Governor can sit tight and if the House and Senate fail to reach an agreement on a tax program, the Legislature will then be forced to adjourn without any decision with a special session to be called at an appropriate time, facing the necessity of raising the funds to meet current state expenditures. In the event this is done, a consistent program of moderation can be followed by the Governor, to the effect that he submitted a sound tax program, the

[14] A surtax is, of course, a tax on a tax. In the case of the iron ore severance tax, a five percent surtax would be five percent of the normal eleven percent on the value of ore brought to the mouth of the mine, or an actual increase in the rate of about one-half of one percent. Freeman had proposed an increase of four percent in the basic rate.

House passed it, the Senate rejected it, the two failed to reach a conclusion, and, as such, he, the Governor, has performed his function and he is calling them back again to re-advocate his program with the necessity of reaching a solution for the bills must be paid.

3. The weakness of carrying on a vigorous fight and placing the sales tax label on the Conservative forces is as follows:

a) While it is true that the Liberal program in the omnibus tax bill would only represent a burden of approximately 62¢ on the average taxpayer per year as opposed to the $5.00 which is represented in the "Head" tax, the fact remains that withholding will involve a temporary doubling up of payments in becoming current which, figured on the basis that the average taxpayer's income tax totals $42.00, works out at the figure of $21.00 for the biennium. It will be difficult to convince the average taxpayer that he is benefiting when he will not get the advantage of becoming current until the end of his income tax life. Therefore, the Conservatives will be able to say that their program presents the alternative of $5.00 head tax plus 62¢ of general revenue taxes, or a total of $5.62 a year as compared to an increase which our program would involve of $22.00 per year plus the 62¢ figure. It is true that our proposal would place the state finances on a sound basis and would provide the needed revenue for increased basic aid for a four-year period and generally would withstand the financial crisis which will result in a sales tax. This, of course, is in part speculation and difficult to convey to the average citizen.

b) The conclusion then seems one worthy of consideration that the issues to be presented in the event of a special session are going to be difficult to convey with simplicity. The immediate situation will be one where the administration tax program actually costs more money immediately. The sales tax proposition is one step removed, for none of the Conservatives have advocated a sales tax. The "head" tax, as proposed, is to be limited to a two-year period when the "head" tax presently in effect will be available, because the bonus is paid off and it could then be argued that the state could move ahead on a basis which would prevent additional taxes. This, of course, completely ignores the factor of where we will be two years from now, facing a $30,000,000 deficit in education in order to maintain $80 basic aid. This again, however, is thinking two years ahead and not in terms of immediate alternatives of immediate tax payments. . . .

4. The alternative is not to have anything to say immediately, to leave the decision as to whether there will be a solution reached at this session up to the respective bodies of the Legislature and then upon the end of the session with no decision reached, to work out the public relations involved preparatory to the calling of a special session. [But] if a special session comes about in terms of these almost natural means without any action by the Governor, the question is what issues are there to . . . activate people in such a fashion that any different result can be anticipated when the special session is convened.

Deadline Day

Senator Wright, Conservative Chairman of the Tax Committee, presented his head tax plan on the Senate floor before noon on April 20, the deadline day for legislation. The Liberal minority leader immediately rose to denounce it. When he had finished, the Senate recessed for lunch. During the recess Conservative Senator Gordon Rosenmeier suggested as a substitute for the head tax an ungraduated income tax levy at a very low rate. There had been no previous public discussion of this proposal, but it was in keeping with the report of the 1953-1955 Minnesota Tax Study Commission. That predominantly Conservative and Republican body had concluded just a few months before, in the fall of 1954: "Every person making a living in this state will have to make a direct contribution through the application of a broad-based tax measured by a flat rate applied to what he buys or what he earns."

When the Senate reconvened, Senator Wright moved to amend his own plan in the direction of Senator Rosenmeier's suggestion. He inserted a tax of one-half of one percent on net taxable income, individual and corporate, to replace every other tax in his bill except the six percent surtax on iron ore taxes. His amendment prevailed, as did a motion to increase the iron ore surtax to thirteen percent (which would have the effect of raising ore taxes by 1.4% compared with the Governor's proposed four percent). The Senate plan provided about $27,000,000 for the General Revenue Fund, $6,000,000 more than Senate appropriations required. It was not necessarily the aim of the Senate to supply a surplus. The bill was going to conference, where bargaining would take place and where adjustments could be made.

The new plan was preferable to the first Wright proposal, but in the eyes of the Governor it was certainly not a progressive plan, since the proposed income tax was ungraduated and allowed no credits for dependents.

Freeman had expected all along that the Senate majority would act to force a Conservative revision of the state tax structure. Early in February he had written of his anticipation that the Senate Conservatives might pass appropriations bills and then balk at the tax measures in the hope of confronting the Governor with a choice of (1) a long drawn-out "civil war" between the Senate and the executive branch that would be politically embarrassing to the new administration, or (2) passing a general sales tax. Throughout February several teams of administration aides had been deployed to study alternative tax possibilities should a showdown emerge, but no outstanding alternatives had been found. At one point there had been consideration of a "woodchuck" strategy: namely, encouraging the introduction by individual legislators of tax bills (on advertising or chain stores, for example) that would be offensive to some Conservatives and cause them to come to the support of administration measures. Now in April Freeman assumed that the Conservative Senate leadership had decided that a sales tax would be impolitic and impossible. (The Wright head tax had met loud and vigorous Liberal opposition from the moment it was announced.) But the Rosenmeier (ungraduated supplementary income tax) plan was still regressive, if less obvious than the Wright measure. It was complicated enough to create protective confusion for the Conservatives. As the Governor saw it, the decision of the Senate leaders showed determination, flexibility, ingenuity, and fundamental opposition to his progressive tax policy.

SENATE VERSION OF GENERAL REVENUE FUND TAX PROGRAM
(In Millions of Dollars)

TAX	GOVERNOR	HOUSE	SENATE
Property	$ 6.8	..	..
Fees	3.3	2.0	2.0
Gift and Death	1.0	1.0	..
Beer	2.1	2.1	..
Tobacco	2.0	2.0	..
Annuities	.6	.6	..
Telephones	1.5	.9	..
Iron Ore, Increased Rates and Reduced Credits	8.75	8.75	..
13% Surtax on Iron Ore Tax	..	..	2.8
½ of 1% on Net Taxable Income[a]	..	..	20.0
½ of 1% on Corporation Income	..	..	2.0
	$26.05	$17.35	$26.8

[a]In addition to existing income tax for Income Tax School Fund.

The House immediately rejected the Senate tax program, and a conference committee was organized a few hours before midnight, the constitutional deadline for legislation. Only Liberals were chosen for the conference from the House side. Four Conservatives and one Liberal were selected by Senate leaders, the Liberal being one who did not stand with his caucus or party on tax issues.

The Conference

In the few hours between passage by the Senate of its program and the convening of the conference committee, the House conferees met with the Governor and emerged with a compromise to offer the Senate. (See the accompanying table.) All the House tax increases to meet the General Revenue Fund deficit would be scaled down. The tax on telephones would be omitted altogether. The 1953 property levy would be reimposed at a slightly reduced rate, and the cost of the teachers' colleges put over to the Income Tax School Fund, where it could be supported easily if withholding were passed. It was decided to make the offer on a take-it-or-leave-it basis. Senators were told that, if the Senate refused to accept the House compromise, the House would adjourn as required by the Constitution, and the Governor would call a special session to pass a satisfactory tax bill.

The Senate did not accept the House compromise, and the House did not adjourn. The Governor and the House leaders decided it would be unwise to allow themselves to appear unreasonable and intransigent. The clock in the Senate was stopped, and after a futile attempt to stop the House clock, it was hastily covered. The Legislature went into overtime after midnight, Wednesday, April 20.

However, legislative action would have to be completed by midnight, Monday, April 25. The clocks might be stopped in the chambers of the Legislature, but they kept ticking in the Governor's office, and, constitutionally, he had only three days after April 21, Sundays excluded, in which to sign any bills which might be passed by the Legislature.

Negotiations between the two Houses continued intermittently on Thursday and Friday. Little progress was made the first day, but by Friday evening, the second full day of the conference, the Conservatives were ready to offer a modification of their own plan. The income tax levy was altered to provide that incomes under $4,000 would be taxed at one-fourth of one percent, and those over, at one-half of one percent. While not yet in their eyes a progressive tax, the modification made the tax more acceptable to House Liberals. The corporation tax increase was raised from one-half percent to one percent. The ore surtax would be fifteen percent instead of thirteen percent. An interim committee would consider withholding, and the House version of the severance tax constitutional amendment would be passed. The House conferees took the proposal to the Governor and to the Liberal caucus.

House and Senate Offers on General Revenue Fund Tax Program Compromise (In Millions of Dollars)

Tax	Governor	House	Senate	House Offer	Senate Offer
Property	$ 6.8	. .	. .	$ 5.4	. .
Fees	3.3	2.0	2.0	2.0	2.0
Gift and Death	1.0	1.0	. .	.7	. .
Beer	2.1	2.1	. .	.9	. .
Tobacco	2.0	2.0	. .	2.0	. .
Annuities	.6	.6	. .	.6	. .
Telephones	1.5	.9	. .	. .	. .
Iron Ore, Increased Rates and Reduced Credits	8.75	8.75	. .	4.4	. .
13% Surtax on Iron Ore Tax	. .	. .	2.8	. .	. .
½ of 1% on Net Taxable Income[a]	. .	. .	20.0	. .	. .
½ of 1% on Corporation Income	. .	. .	2.0	. .	. .
Transfer of Teachers' Colleges to Income Tax Fund	. .	. .	. .	6.2	. .
¼ of 1% on Net Taxable Income under $4,000, with ½ of 1% on Income above	. .	. .	. .	. .	13.6
1% on Corporation Income	. .	. .	. .	. .	4.5
15% Surtax on Iron Ore Tax	. .	. .	. .	. .	3.9
	$26.05	$17.35	$26.8	$22.2	$24.0

[a]In addition to existing income tax for Income Tax School Fund.

During this hectic week advisers had been moving in and out of the Governor's office. What role was the Governor to play in this legislative deadlock? Should he capitulate to the Senate program? Should he allow the session to end in deadlock, appeal to the public to justify his program, and call a special session? Or were there any further pressures, short of this drastic action, which the Governor could bring to bear on the senators? Among the factors the Governor and his advisers had to take into consideration were these:

1. Failure to enact some new taxes would leave the state without sufficient revenue to finance current operations; sustained, bitter dispute might tend to discredit all parties. In either case, where would the public fix the blame? It might be on the Governor since he was most visible.

2. The DFL had just returned to office after sixteen years in the wilderness. Surely the public would not be impressed by a return to power which resulted in governmental impotence and a degree of bitterness in politics unknown since the last days of the Farmer-Laborites.

These considerations pointed to capitulation. However, many DFL legislators and leaders felt their position was right and believed they could best their political opponents in an open appeal to the people in the next election.

Whether or not the Senate could actually be defeated in a special session was a problem to which the Governor gave urgent consideration during this last week of the Legislature. He consulted some key labor leaders in St. Paul and Minneapolis to find out whether the public would understand the issues and support him in a long fight with the Senate. Without exception they urged caution. All felt it would be very difficult to acquaint the rank and file of organized labor with the relatively complicated facts and to arouse mass support for the Governor's tax position. Times were good; interest in politics was low. An all-out fight would enlist little support. These comments confirmed what the Governor feared.

Freeman, nevertheless, went on television Friday afternoon—just before the Monday, April 25 deadline—and launched an attack on the Senate and the interests that he felt were supporting the Senate position. A full report of the Governor's speech was carried in the afternoon newspapers. Included in the Governor's speech were a number of strong statements, such as:

> Behind the two-day deadlock in the conference committee lies the conflict between the people as a whole and special privilege, upon the solution of which depends the future of our state.
>
> . . . .
>
> The maintenance of special privilege for the U. S. Steel Corporation and for the beer interests is now endangering the future of Minnesota, and threatening the education of every child in the state.
>
> . . . .
>
> The Senate proposals reflect an attitude of no concern for the fact Minnesota schools would be left destitute two years from now. . . .

Accept the Senate Offer?

Despite growing bitterness, the Governor and the House conferees sat down for about an hour immediately after dinner Friday evening to consider the Senate offer. The Governor and a majority of the House team were not willing to reject the Senate plan immediately, but at least two members of the conference group refused to have anything to do with it. The Liberal Caucus was asked for an opinion the next day, Saturday, and it flatly refused to accept the Senate offer.

Very early the next Monday morning, with the midnight deadline in everyone's mind, the conference committee reached an agreement after an all-night session. It was essentially a further modification of the Senate plan. Persons earning less than $4,000 would not be subject to the new income tax levy if they were not already paying the regular income tax.[15] Withholding would be enacted, although it was not clear that Senator Wright, the leader of the Senate conference, had agreed to this. The House version of the iron ore severance tax constitutional amendment was accepted. All that resembled the original House omnibus tax bill (and the Governor's recommendation) was the fifteen percent surtax on iron ore, and this raised $3,900,000 from the ore companies in place of $8,000,000 in the original Freeman-House program. The House leaders informed the Governor of the tentative agreement, and he gave his support. Representatives Karth and Wozniak (Liberal House conferees) were reluctant to accept the product, which they felt was a regressive program. A meeting of the House Liberals was convened in the Governor's reception room to discover what the group would do. Liberal senators were admitted if they appeared.

Fred Cina, Majority Leader, led off with an explanation of the agreement. He said little in its defense and concluded with the statement, "We can't hold you to this, I suppose." He was followed by the Governor, who took a slightly more vigorous, although still very cautious, position in favor of the compromise. He acknowledged that the compromise was not everything they would like but asserted that it did contain some good things. He pointed out that they had succeeded in getting the biggest increase in ore taxes obtained in a long time. He said the one percent tax on corporations would not have had a chance if the Liberals had proposed it. Business spokesmen would have complained that the DFL was out to ruin business, but now the Senate had offered an increase in corporation taxes.

Freeman continued that he was very proud of the way they had stuck together, no matter what the outcome, and he thanked all of them for their patience and for the part they had played in the things which had been accomplished. Turning to the alternative of a special session, he emphasized that it would be a very tough fight and that everyone would have to do his

[15] Under Minnesota income tax law there were some persons who were required to file returns but escaped payment of an income tax by virtue of deductions and credits. However, as was pointed out earlier, the plan devised for payment of the Minnesota veterans' bonus included the stipulation that every person filing an income tax return must pay a $5.00 head tax.

COMPROMISE PROPOSAL GENERAL REVENUE FUND PROGRAM
(In Millions of Dollars)

TAX	GOVERNOR	HOUSE	SENATE	HOUSE OFFER	SENATE OFFER	APRIL 25 FIRST COMPROMISE[b] FROM CONFERENCE COMMITTEE
Property	$ 6.8	..	..	$ 5.4	..	..
Fees	3.3	2.0	2.0	2.0	2.0	2.0
Gift and Death	1.0	1.0	..	.7	..	..
Beer	2.1	2.1	..	.9	..	..
Tobacco	2.0	2.0	..	2.0	..	..
Annuities	.6	.6	..	.6	..	..
Telephones	1.5	.9	..	..	..	..
Iron Ore, Increased Rates and Reduced Credits	8.75	8.75	..	4.4	..	..
13% Surtax on Iron Ore Tax	..	..	2.8	..	..	..
½ of 1% on Net Taxable Income[a]	..	..	20.0	..	..	..
½ of 1% on Corporation Income	..	..	2.0	..	..	..
Transfer of Teachers' Colleges to Income Tax Funds	..	..	..	6.2	..	..
¼ of 1% on Net Taxable Income under $4,000, with ½ of 1% on Income above[c]	..	..	..	..	13.6	11.4
1% on Corporation Income[a]	..	..	..	..	4.5	4.5
15% Surtax on Iron Ore Tax	..	..	..	..	3.9	3.9
	$26.05	$17.35	$26.8	$22.2	$24.0	$21.8

[a]In addition to existing income tax for Income Tax School Fund.
[b]Includes the withholding tax as well as items below.
[c]Persons paying only the bonus tax were exempted from the proposed new surtax.

part. He stated, "I can't do it alone. We would have to put on a real campaign all over this state." He then asked the assembled Liberals to express their opinions concerning the proposed compromise.

Representative Don Wozniak, one of the conferees, stated simply that he could not sign the report. Nor could Representative Joe Karth, another conferee. Representative Popovich of St. Paul said that he had stood outside the door of the conference room the previous night with Representative Vlad Shipka and had listened to what was going on. He reported, "You wouldn't believe the violent, abusive language they [the Senate conferees] used." Ed Chilgren, another conferee, reported:

> The Senate is backing down on their agreement to accept the House occupation [severance] tax amendment. We've had agreement after agreement, and they've broken them about as fast as they were made. I can't sign this now. There's not an ounce of honor among them.
>
> *Representative Podgorski:* I've seen some of the people in my district. They come up to me, and tell me they don't want any increase in income taxes. [Podgorski represented a low-income, working-class district in St. Paul.]
>
> *Representative Halsted:* I don't know about everyone else, but I can't come back here and stand the heat for two months. [Halsted, DFL candidate for Governor in 1948, was in poor health.]
>
> *Representative Mosier:* [Gentle, courteous chairman of the Appropriations Committee, angry at allegations the Senate conferees were arguing that the man who doesn't earn much isn't much good and should pay his share of the taxes.] They are talking about the people I represent. I would take that as an insult to myself. No foul-mouthed, petty self-appointed Caesar could say that to me. I would slap his face.
>
> *Representative Cina:* We weren't too kind to them either, Leo.

Representative Yetka: I come from a liberal district. If I vote for a bill like this, they might as well have elected my opponent.

Then, one after another, representatives rose to denounce the Senate and the compromise tax measure. No one defended the settlement until Halsted rose again to say, "I was here in 1937 when we had a special session of 44 days. We didn't come out very well."

Representative Kording: Is there a chance for a change in the Senate leadership in a special session?

Majority Leader Cina: I have it from a sound Liberal member that there isn't a chance. They've been telling us in conference that if we come back we'll be sitting down with them again.

Representative Wichterman: We should wait a while for a special session. Some of us have about two weeks work in the fields before we can do any campaigning.

Majority Leader Cina: [Concluding] Well, we just brought this agreement back for discussion. It's pretty clear where we stand.

Final Agreement

The conference between House and Senate members was resumed in desultory fashion until a new approach was started in the corridors. A Liberal senator asked several leading Conservatives if they would favor a five percent surtax on the existing individual income taxes, in place of the one-fourth of one percent on net taxable income under $4,000 and the one-half of one percent on income above $4,000. It was now five hours before the absolute midnight deadline, and the Conservative senators were agreeable. Wozniak and Karth from the House group were consulted. They said they would "go along." The conference began moving toward agreement. About 8:00 p.m. Speaker Johnson and

SUMMARY OF GENERAL REVENUE FUND TAX PROPOSALS
(In Millions of Dollars)

TAX	GOVERNOR	HOUSE	SENATE	HOUSE OFFER	SENATE OFFER	APRIL 25 FIRST COMPROMISE FROM CONFERENCE COMMITTEE[b]	FINAL
Property	$ 6.8	..	..	$ 5.4	..	..	$ 7.0
Fees	3.3	2.0	2.0	2.0	2.0	2.0	2.0
Gift and Death	1.0	1.0	..	.7	..	..	..
Beer	2.1	2.1	..	.9	..	..	..
Tobacco	2.0	2.0	..	2.0	..	..	1.5[c]
Annuities	.6	.6	..	.6	..	..	.6
Telephones	1.5	.9	..	..	..	..	..
Iron Ore Increased Rates and Reduced Credits	8.75	8.75	..	4.4	..	..	..
13% Surtax on Iron Ore Tax	..	..	2.8	..	..	..	..
½ of 1% on Net Taxable Income[a]	..	..	20.0	..	..	..	..
½ of 1% on Corporation Income[a]	..	..	2.0	..	..	..	..
Transfer of Teachers' Colleges to Income Tax Fund	..	..	..	6.2	..	..	..
¼ of 1% on Net Taxable Income under $4,000, with ½ of 1% on Income above	..	..	..	..	13.6	11.4	..
1% on Corporation Income[a]	..	..	..	..	4.5	4.5	4.5
15% Surtax on Iron Ore Tax	..	..	..	..	3.9	3.9	3.9
5% Surtax on Net Taxable Income	..	..	..	..	..	..	4.6
	$26.05	$17.35	$26.8	$22.2	$24.0	$21.8	$24.1

[a]In addition to existing income tax for Income Tax School Fund.
[b]Includes the withholding tax as well as items below.
[c]Late revisions in revenue potential of tax.

Majority Leader Cina advised Freeman that an agreement seemed likely but that it could not be completed before midnight. The Governor agreed to issue a proclamation calling a special session to meet the following day.

The second compromise agreement was accepted without much discussion by a weary House and Senate. The bills finally enacted bore little resemblance either to the Governor's tax program or to the Senate plan. Parts of the Governor's program had been accepted: agreement on increased fees was fairly general. The Senate accepted the tobacco tax, the new tax on annuities, and an increase in the iron ore severance tax less than half as large as the Governor's proposal. The taxes on beer and telephones were lost as were the gift and inheritance tax increases. An interim committee was established to study withholding. There was some feeling the Liberals might have been able to pass the withholding tax if they had made one last fight for it, but they didn't. The ungraduated or slightly graduated income tax that the Senate had sought was replaced by a five percent surtax on existing individual income taxes. Income tax structure was not changed. The increase in corporation income taxes was significant. The property tax was reimposed, and the iron ore severance tax constitutional amendment, providing for transfer of part of the receipts to the Income Tax School Fund, was offered to the voters of the state for approval by referendum. (It was passed in November 1956.)

Curiously, no last effort was made to supply additional revenue for the Income Tax School Fund for the 1955-1957 biennium. Estimates indicated that an aid program with $80 basic aids would create a deficit in the Fund of about $5,000,000. Increasing basic aids to $82 would add $2,000,000 or $3,000,000 to the deficit. The contestants were too exhausted, and their differences too great. Rather than try to solve the problem, they decided to hope that expenses might be less than estimated or that revenues might exceed what was anticipated. On balance, the Governor and the House Liberals felt they had won a limited victory: even though almost all of the details of the original program had been changed, the progressive tax structure had been retained. Newspaper reaction was mixed. The *St. Paul Dispatch* editorialized on April 27:

> Considering the wide differences in views of Governor Freeman and the House Liberals on one hand and the Senate Conservatives on the other, the closing atmosphere of the Legislature was surprisingly amicable. Both sides compromised on important matters, recognizing that to do so was in the public interest.
>
> However, the Senate proved that it could not be stampeded by political attack and held fast against the more drastic and undesirable features of the Liberal finance program. The realities of the money problem may produce a more sensible attitude toward a general sales tax two years from now.

The *Minneapolis Tribune* said in an editorial on April 28:

> The tax compromise finally approved by the Minnesota legislature was the product of too-little and too-much. There was too little time and too much pressure to do a first-rate job and so the legislature, with partisan emotions running deep and strong, did a patchwork job. . . .
>
> But the needed revenues are in sight and that is something to be grateful for.
>
> There is at least a possibility that the next legislature will arrive at a thorough, carefully considered and objective solution of the state's financial problems.
>
> Or are we dreaming?

A news story in the April 28 *Minneapolis Star* was more sympathetic:

> The new DFL governor drew the battle line in the legislature principally on fiscal matters.
>
> He asked for an income tax withholding plan. Like other key plans in his program, it squeaked through the Liberal-controlled House, 71-56.
>
> Then it banged head-on into stubborn, unyielding Senate opposition that touched off Freeman's own break from the patience and restraint he had shown —publicly—through the session.
>
> . . . .

Later Events

Governor Freeman was re-elected in the fall of 1956 with 53 percent of the vote. All but one of the incumbent DFL state officers were re-elected, and the Liberals increased slightly their majority in the House. There were no Senate elections. The victory was not sweeping, but Freeman interpreted it as a vote of confidence. He had won against the national trend and in spite of Eisenhower's 54 percent victory in Minnesota. Revenues in the two years following the 1955 session were higher than had been estimated.

Seattle Seeks a Tax

Robert L. Peabody

Introduction

THIS IS THE STORY of the City of Seattle's progressive search for additional tax revenues culminating in its attempt in 1955 to secure from the Washington State Legislature a city sales tax enabling act. The act would have empowered Seattle and other Washington municipalities to levy a sales tax of up to one percent, in addition to the three percent retail sales tax levied by the state. The chief protagonist in this story—and a person who felt prime responsibility for solving Seattle's tax problem—is David Levine, Finance Committee Chairman of the Seattle City Council.

Urban Tax Problems

Approximately two-thirds of all Americans live in urban areas. Urban populations are expanding, the demand for city services is increasing, the costs of operating a city continue to rise, and more capital improvements are needed and demanded by the citizens. Cities responsible for providing adequate police, fire and health protection, proper streets, sewers, recreational facilities, and many other services—remain creatures of the states. In order to finance these services most cities are dependent upon the states for authorizations to impose local taxes.

However, as federal and state governments have expanded their activities, *their* tax needs have also increased. The great revenue-producing fields of sales, income, and excise taxes have, in the main, been dominated by either the state or federal governments. Although the amount of city revenues has remained fairly constant, the cities' share of the total tax dollar has been diminishing. In 1932, for example, cities received approximately 55 percent of the total tax dollar; in 1955 cities were receiving less than fifteen percent—a serious drop even though these calculations do not reflect state aid to local governing units.

Many municipal finance experts agree that the property tax is no longer an adequate means of supporting counties, cities, school districts, and other local districts. Twenty years ago, property tax collections totaled more than all other taxes (federal, state and local) combined. In 1955 only eleven percent of all tax revenues sprang from this source, income and excise taxes having increased with the expansion of state and federal government responsibilities. Rising costs have brought about several marked changes in municipal revenue patterns, including increased demands for greater shares of state-collected taxes, for direct state grants, and for the adoption of a variety of locally-administered taxes to supplement the property tax. In spite of their declining importance in relation to total tax revenue, property taxes furnished U. S. municipalities with three-fourths of their total tax collections in 1955.

The Property Tax in Washington

The property tax is the basic source of municipal revenue in the State of Washington.[1] Here, its use has been curtailed and complicated by the forty mill property tax limitation, sustained by the initiative process since 1932 and adopted as a constitutional amendment in 1944. By this amendment the voters decided that no more than forty mills in taxation may be applied against their property during any one year unless a higher amount is approved by the voters at a special election. The amendment also requires that the "assessed valuation shall be fifty *per centum* of the true and fair value of such property in money."

Property taxation is fixed by two processes—assessing and levying. Assessing, the function of evaluating property, is done by the local county assessor. Levying, the process of setting

[1] The situations described in this case are those existing in 1955-56.

tax rates in mills (after the amount of revenue needed has been determined in dollars), is done primarily by local governing bodies such as city councils, boards of county commissioners, and school boards. Millage is used as a multiplication factor against assessed value to determine the amount of tax to be paid. A rate of ten mills, for example, would mean that for every $100 in assessed valuation, $1.00 of tax would be paid.

In Washington State millage ceilings of the various units of government within the forty-mill limit have been determined by state law. For example, Washington's cities may levy up to fifteen mills for general city operations—one of which must be used for firemen's pensions—plus an additional mill for firemen's pensions if necessary, a total of sixteen mills. Counties may levy up to eight mills, school districts up to fourteen mills. Although a city or county need not levy up to its limitation, most units—particularly in metropolitan areas—levy the full limit and rely on special elections for additional levies. These special elections have proven unwieldy, and voters frequently reject appeals by local government units for additional millage.

Washington's property tax picture is further complicated by the fact that assessments have not approached the "fifty *per centum* of the true and fair value" of the property. Not only have assessments been fractional in amount, they have been unequal as well. In a state-wide survey it was shown that assessments throughout the state averaged 19.6% of actual sales figures. Furthermore, counties varied from 13.3% to 37.5%, and the inequalities prevailed not only between counties but within counties between different classes of property and within the same classes of property.

Bearing the brunt of the criticism for the low and uneven assessments are the county assessors. Property tax revenues are subject to the ability and willingness of the assessors to perform the constitutional duty of assessing property at fifty percent of the true and fair value of the property. The assessor must face the electorate every four years and thus is confronted with a conflict of interest between concern for his own re-election and the demands of the local units of government for added revenue.

As a consequence of low and unequal assessments and the millage limitation, the amount that Washington cities and other local units of government received from the property tax had not by 1955 kept pace with the increased costs of providing added services. Property taxes represented 80 percent of all state and local taxes in 1931, 46 percent in 1936, 32 percent in 1941, and 28 percent in 1955. Seattle received $3,000,000 less from real property taxes in 1953-55 than it had in 1929-31.

Home Rule and the AWC

The State of Washington has been considered a "home rule" state since its inception in 1889. Municipal home rule to the extent that it does exist is based upon Article XI, Section 10 which authorizes any city of 20,000 or more inhabitants to frame a charter for its own government consistent with the State Constitution and the general laws of the state. In addition, Article XI, Section 11 empowers cities and towns to make and enforce within their limits all such police, sanitary, and other regulations as are not in conflict with general laws. Although the Legislature has no power to impose taxes for municipal purposes upon municipal corporations or their inhabitants or property, by general law it determines the taxes that counties, cities, and towns may assess and collect, and imposes ceilings on both taxation and municipal borrowing. Strict judicial interpretations of the home rule powers and legislative enactment have further limited the fiscal scope of municipalities.

In order to strengthen home rule powers and advance the cause of the cities in general, the municipalities of the state formed an organization known as the Association of Washington Cities.[2] Representing all but about ten of the State of Washington's 252 municipalities, and speaking for over 1,900 city officials throughout the state, the primary mission of the Association of Washington Cities is to secure state legislation beneficial to the municipalities.

In its lobbying activity, the Association usually works through city officials, who meet with

2 By 1958, all but four of the 48 states had formed similar municipal associations and these organizations in turn had united at the national level to form the American Municipal Association.

state legislators from their own areas before and during legislative sessions. Most Association bills are drafted well in advance of the legislative session to allow time to secure maximum acceptance from legislators and to build up interest group support where possible. Early drafting also enables the Association to analyze the effect of proposals on *all* cities and towns prior to the session.

Although the Association works within the framework of policy that is formulated and adopted by its annual, state-wide convention during early summer, the focus of power is its Executive Committee. This Committee, which is virtually self-perpetuating, is composed of eight city officials evenly divided between the western and eastern parts of the state, plus the President of the Association, also a city official. The Executive Committee selects the nominating committee which in turn presents a single slate of candidates to the convention to be ratified. Floor opposition to the slate is rare but occasionally successful. The state's three major cities—Seattle (555,000), Spokane (182,-000), and Tacoma (156,000)—are invariably represented on the Executive Committee. The other positions are usually rotated among the other first-class cities of the state (over 20,000 population), with a scattering of small city representation. The larger cities pay a sizable share of the Association's $36,000 annual budget and retain most of the power. The Association is represented at sessions of the State Legislature by its legislative committee, which is essentially the Executive Committee plus the paid staff of the Association and several key officials from the larger cities.

Illustrative of the Association's legislative strength is its record at the 1955 legislative session. A total of some 1,388 bills, resolutions, and the like, were introduced, of which 430 became laws. Of that number, some 25 bills sponsored or favored by the Association were enacted, and twelve failed to pass. Some nineteen bills considered detrimental to cities were defeated; only one bill was passed against Association opposition.

The City of Seattle

Seattle's 1955 population of 555,000 formed roughly one-fifth of the total population of the state and was larger than that of the next eight largest Washington cities combined. A port city with varied industrial enterprises, by far the largest being the Boeing Airplane Company, Seattle extends over 91 square miles. King County, in which Seattle is located, accounts for almost one-third of the state's population.

In common with many rapidly growing urban and suburban areas, Seattle and King County were in 1955 proportionately under-represented in both houses of the State Legislature. At the 1955 legislative session, King County was represented by seven Democrats and five Republicans in a Republican-controlled Senate (24-22), and by twelve Democrats and twelve Republicans in a Democratic-controlled House of Representatives (50-49).

"Weak Mayor, Strong Council"

Seattle's form of government is best categorized as "weak mayor-strong council" government, despite the fact that under the city's 1946 Charter, the Mayor has a veto power over city ordinances and considerable control over the city's departments through his appointive powers. However, in the crucial area of fiscal policy, the Mayor's power is practically nil. The City Council consists of nine members elected at large for four-year terms, staggered so that either four or five councilmen come up for re-election every other year. Each councilman receives an annual salary of $7,200 and is expected to work full-time. The political status of a city councilman is somewhat above that of the typical state legislator partly because the former has a full-time, year-round position. Incumbent councilmen are almost invariably re-elected, with the voters seeming to pay small attention to the individual merits of particular councilmen. Most councilmen view the position as a career, and several have succeeded in making it one. At the time of this case two of the councilmen had been in office for over twenty years, several others for more than a decade.

Although Seattle's municipal elections are non-partisan, not infrequently undercurrents of party affiliation rise to the surface. Thus, it was no secret to most citizens of Seattle in 1952 that Allan Pomeroy, the newly elected Mayor, was a Democrat and that most of the councilmen were linked with the "Devin crowd." This group, a "good government" organization named after the Mayor unseated by Pomeroy, consisted essentially of civic-minded business leaders with Republican affiliations in state and national party contests.

Although councilmen are elected at large, the major geographical sections of the city are usually represented by one of their own. Thus, the Ballard section had its councilman, M. B. "Mike" Mitchell, owner and publisher of the *Ballard Tribune* for over twenty years, while West Seattle had long been represented by Bob Jones, owner of a men's clothing store.

The Council's Fiscal Powers

In Seattle the budget is *prepared* by the City Council—not by the chief executive. Under the provisions of its own budget law enacted by the State Legislature at the 1925 session, the City Council is responsible for the preparation and adoption of the annual budget for all city departments except the transportation system. Thus, department heads, though appointed by the Mayor, must submit their budget requests directly to the Council.

Seattle's budget law requires that all expenditures must first be appropriated for in the budget. Briefly stated, the budget process is as follows: on or before the tenth day of July of each year, the heads of all departments submit an estimate of their probable expenses for the ensuing year to the Finance Committee of the City Council. The Council then reviews these estimates in the light of foreseeable revenue and, after hearings, adopts a preliminary budget on or before the first Monday in September. On or before the first Monday in October, the Council further revises the preliminary budget, the result being the final budget, which is adopted together with the necessary implementing tax ordinances. During this four-month period the Council alternates between public hearings and closed executive sessions.

Seattle, in common with most cities, makes use of a general fund "into which shall be paid all revenues of the city, except as otherwise provided by law, and from which shall be paid all expenses and liabilities not required to be paid out of some special or other fund." The general fund finances the operation of most of the city's departments with the exception of park, library, city transportation, light and water. The general governmental budget is made up of the general fund, plus the park fund, library fund, city-county health fund, bond interest and redemption fund, and six miscellaneous funds, which include city employee pensions and retirement funds. Not included in the general budget (also known as the total tax-supported funds budget), are various other funds, including the public service enterprise funds which cover the operations of the municipal light and water utilities. Whereas the tax-supported funds budget approached $27,000,000 in 1955, the total budget including the city-owned-and-operated utilities was well over $60,000,000. The average citizen and taxpayer is rarely confronted with the total amount; he remains most concerned with the tax-supported functions of government. This story as well is primarily concerned with the tax-supported functions of government, particularly the Council's attempt to balance the general governmental budget of $27,000,000 for 1955.

The Search for Revenue Begins

SEATTLE'S BUDGET had been increasing at an annual rate of from one to two million dollars since 1950. During the war years and up to 1954, Seattle's annual budgets were balanced, and the city government was able to finish each year with a substantial cash surplus.

In July 1954 the City Council was presented with 1955 preliminary budget requests from the various city departments totaling $30,090,000, some $5,000,000 higher than the 1954 budget. After cutting departmental requests, 1955 estimated expenditures were reduced to $26,900,000, an amount which exceeded foreseeable revenue by about $1,500,000. Was the city to cut services or raise taxes? If the latter, where was the city to find an additional one and one-half million in revenue?

Councilman Levine's Dilemma

Councilman David L. Levine, Chairman of the City Council Finance Committee, felt that his was the primary responsibility for answering these questions. That a member of a legislative body, rather than the chief executive or a department head of the executive branch, should have ultimate responsibility for fiscal policy is uncommon but by no means unique in U. S. local government. In Seattle the Mayor may confer with department heads and make suggestions before the budget requests are submitted to the Council, but the City Council prepares the final budget in closed session. Councilman Levine assumed his position of responsibility partially as a result of the weak mayor-strong council form of government under which Seattle operated, and partially because of his personality and because he had had previous experience.

Only one other member of the Seattle City Council had served longer than Councilman Levine. After a recall election had disposed of the Mayor in 1931, the councilman who was appointed Mayor by his colleagues in turn appointed Levine to fill his vacant position on the Council.

Born of Jewish parentage in Russia in 1884, Levine had lived in Seattle since 1900. As a retail jewelry worker he became active in the Seattle Jewelry Workers' Union, serving as secretary of Local 30 since 1918 and as president since 1939. In a city long noted for its union strength, Levine rose rapidly in local labor activities. He had been president of the Seattle Central Labor Council for five years prior to his appointment to the City Council in 1931. During the thirties, Levine and the man who appointed him were considered union labor's representatives on the City Council. At first associated with a group in the City Council that opposed substantial cuts in the city budget, Levine aroused the wrath of a reform movement in Seattle politics, the Order of the Cincinnatus, a group which sponsored Republican Arthur B. Langlie's candidacy for the Council in 1935 and was instrumental in his successful mayoralty campaign in 1938. Although Langlie and Levine found themselves on opposite sides in their first political encounter, they found common ground in their mutual dislike of John F. Dore, Mayor from 1932 to 1938. What was at first grudging respect developed into mutual toleration and later into friendship as Levine and Langlie came to hold similar ideas on municipal fiscal policy. As the perennial president of the Seattle Jewelry Workers' Union, which became an A. F. of L. affiliate, Levine was elected vice president of the International Jewelry Workers' Union in 1947. Although casual observers might have labeled Levine a Democrat (despite his claim of nonpartisanship) because of his long-time labor affiliations, his fiscal policies accorded more with Southern Democratic conservatism than with the liberal spending associated with New or Fair Deal Democrats. Never completely cold to city employee demands for salary increases and pension benefits, Levine by 1955 had nevertheless achieved a reputation for being a hard bargainer in his dealings with city employee groups. Since the late thirties Levine had consistently stressed tight fiscal control, a balanced budget, and efficiency.

Levine maintained his political and personal associations with Langlie after the latter became Governor in 1941. Since the early 1940s Levine had been associated with, and benefited from the financial backing and organizational support of the so-called "Devin reform crowd." Although in substantial agreement with the philosophy of this group, Levine was by no means exclusively dependent upon it for political support.

Because he had become a familiar figure to Seattle citizens Levine was able to play a considerably independent role in the conduct of the city's fiscal affairs. His opponents considered him honest and firm in principle, although several criticized him for ruthless tactics and some thought that he was too rigid in his convictions.

Councilman Levine had gradually assumed primary responsibility for city fiscal policy. For 24 years he alternated between the positions of Council President and Chairman of the Finance Committee. In either position he had the final word on financial matters. His long service; his shrewdness in dealing with employee groups, department heads, and members of the Council; and his reputation for personal integrity encouraged other councilmen to concur in almost all of Levine's decisions on fiscal matters and to be wary of clashing with him on any matter.

With mayors holding a similar fiscal philosophy, such as Langlie or Devin, Levine worked co-operatively towards a common goal of a balanced budget. These mayors worked closely with department heads to draft an overall budget that would win Council approval. But Mayor Pomeroy, who defeated Devin in 1952 by 78,000 to 75,000 votes, had his own ideas about the way the city should be run. Before becoming Mayor, Pomeroy had been an active Democrat. As 45-year old Pomeroy took office in June 1952, he was confronted with councilmen whose average tenure in office was over twelve years.

The clash between Pomeroy and the "old guard" on the Council began when the new Mayor requested $103,490 for the Mayor's office in the 1953 preliminary budget, including the purchase of a new Lincoln for his own use. (The former Mayor's Lincoln had over 35,000 miles on it.) The total amount sought was eighty percent over the previous budget allocation. When the Council, under Levine's direction, drastically slashed the Mayor's request, the battle started. Pomeroy criticized Council policy at public appearances and through the press. The Council retaliated by ignoring his suggestions on fiscal matters and by refusing to approve Pomeroy's appointments of key department heads. This hostility between the new Mayor and the majority of the nine-man City Council was to continue throughout Pomeroy's four year term.

One result of this conflict was the bolstering of Levine's role as spokesman for the Council and as its policy maker in fiscal matters. By 1954 Levine, as he approached his seventieth year and his twenty-third year in office, had some of the attributes ordinarily associated with the executive branch. These included a sense of overall responsibility, virtual permanence in office, and the chief executive's technique of resorting to a direct appeal to the people for support of his policies.

The Revenue Raising Problem

The task of somehow cutting the 1955 budget or raising an additional $1,500,000 presented complicated problems for Levine and the other members of the Council. Departmental requests had already been cut substantially to the accompaniment of vigorous and public protests from department heads. No further cut in the budget was deemed possible. Early in August 1954 Levine made the Council's position clear: "One, we shall not add any additional services; two, only urgent and unavoidable salary increases will be considered; and three, we will insist that the budget be balanced."

The Council considered four possible sources of added revenue: (1) increasing existing taxes; (2) utilizing revenue sources as yet untapped by the city, such as a charge on sewer or garbage collections; (3) appealing to the State Legislature for new taxes; or (4) resorting to a combination of several of these.

Levine's experience with Seattle's fiscal problems led him to conclude that there was little hope of increasing the existing tax rates. The property tax which furnished the city with over one-third of its revenue was already being used to the limit allowed under the State Constitution. It would bring no revenue to criticize the Assessor by pointing out that in per capita property tax collections Seattle was far below other cities of a similar population classification. To lift the property tax limitation would require action by the Legislature, at best a long-range hope.

Another major source of municipal revenue was Seattle's share in three state-collected, locally-shared taxes—liquor profits from state-owned stores, the automobile ownership excise tax, and the gasoline tax. These, too, could not be increased without action by the Legislature. The portion of these revenues that could be used for Seattle's general fund would amount to over $3,000,000, but it had already been included in anticipated income. The Councilman estimated that the business and occupation tax (one-tenth of one percent on gross revenue) could not be increased without arousing substantial opposition from the business interests of the community. Most other revenue sources—licenses, fines, parking meters, admissions taxes, and departmental income—were already giving close to their maximum return.

The second broad possibility was to open new sources of revenue. There appeared to be at least two—a sewer service charge and a garbage collection fee. The Legislature had authorized cities to levy these charges and over 100 were already using either one or both.

On the other hand, councilmen felt that sewer and garbage fees were apt to be extremely unpopular with Seattle's voters. Four incumbent councilmen faced an election in eighteen months. Agitation about sewage pollution was already underway, and the councilmen felt that the sewer service fee would eventually be needed to pay for new sewage-treatment plants. The Council decided to postpone either a sewer service charge or a garbage collection fee and settled for the enactment of five local tax ordinances which it believed would cause less controversy but still provide sufficient revenue to balance the budget. Although several of the councilmen were critical of doubling the business and occupation tax on service professions (lawyers, teachers, and the like) while leaving the tax rate of most business and occupation taxpayers unchanged, this measure would bring in an additional $300,000. The Council also approved ordinances which increased the licensing tax on amusement devices, increased the tax on city-owned utilities to five percent, created a fee system for garbage disposal at the city dumps, and established fees for street uses or "private uses of public places." These five measures together with an additional $80,000 anticipated revenue from use of the Metropolitan Building Tract Company tract would yield an estimated $1,238,000. All five ordinances were passed on September 13, 1954 and received Mayor Pomeroy's signature. Together with overall tightening of the budget, this anticipated income would result in a balanced budget for the coming 1955 fiscal year.

Raises for Firemen and Policemen?

Levine and his fellow councilmen were fairly satisfied with the proposed budget for 1955 despite some signs of opposition to the five local tax ordinances, referred to as "nuisance taxes" by several of the affected interests. Looking ahead to the city's planned co-operation with the Association of Washington Cities, there even appeared to be some possibility of securing additional revenue at the coming legislative session.

Just as the councilmen were congratulating themselves on a job well done, the Police Advisory Committee, formed by Pomeroy of interested civic and business leaders, appeared before one of the final open budget hearings of the Council and asked it to raise the salaries of policemen. The firemen were quick to echo the demands of the police. These two demands, which would have cost between $500,000 and $700,000, were supported by Mayor Pomeroy.

The Mayor suggested a tax conference between himself, the Council, and various civic-minded interest groups to study revenue-raising measures. Under Levine's direction the Council rejected the Mayor's tax pleas and voted to put the police and fire increases up to the public. To pay for the wage increases, the business and occupation tax of one-tenth of one percent of gross revenues of all businesses, not just services, was doubled, and the ordinance was placed on the November 2, 1954 municipal ballot as Proposition Five. Policemen and firemen were promised a wage raise of the measure passed. Pomeroy rapped the Council for putting Proposition Five on the November ballot but could come up with no alternative plan to raise the necessary $700,000.

The shrewder members of the Council, Levine included, gave Proposition Five little chance of passing. The decision to double the business and occupation tax and place this ordinance on the November ballot was first, an attempt to arouse the business interests of the community to an awareness of the city's financial plight; second, a further means of antagonizing Mayor Pomeroy and opposing his policies. Levine regarded Pomeroy's request for wage raises as politically motivated. Pomeroy's actions, coming at a late date in the budget process, were contrary to the expressed policy that Levine had voiced at the beginning of the budget period. Levine felt that the Mayor too often was guilty of seeking higher expenditures without accepting responsibility for raising the offsetting revenues. This was contrary to Levine's general fiscal philosophy in which what was spent had to be equated with what was coming in.

Mayor Pomeroy was caught in the awkward position of being for the wage raises but against Proposition Five. Business interests of the community, organized and led by the Chamber of Commerce, flooded the newspapers and airwaves with attacks on the measure. The campaign was led by the Citizens' Committee Against Proposition Five, which had been organized by the Chamber. Much was made of the fact that although only $700,000 was needed for the wage raises, doubling of the business and occupation tax would bring in an estimated $2,500,000. Proposition Five was defeated by over two to one despite active support of the measure by both firemen and police.

The day after the election, the Chamber's *ad hoc* committee renamed itself "The Citizens' Committee for Police and Firemen's Wage Raises." In part this committee represented the same interests which had promoted the original agitation for raises. The Council had tossed the problem directly back to these business interests by placing Proposition Five on the ballot. Feeling some responsibility after the election, this group initiated a research project to investigate less drastic means of obtaining new revenue.

The Search Resumed

The overwhelming defeat of Proposition Five stimulated intensified protest by the individuals and groups directly affected by the five ordinances passed in September and slated to go into effect in January. The most controversial of these measures was the ordinance which doubled the business tax on service and professional people. Three thousand notices had been mailed to those in "service" professions and occupations warning them that the municipal occupation tax on this category of businesses would be raised to one-fifth of one percent of their gross incomes. It had been estimated by the Council that this tax increase would bring an additional $300,000 to the general fund. Those affected complained that they were being unfairly singled out. Groups such as the Seattle Music Teachers Association began to explore the possibilities of circulating petitions to bring this measure to public vote. The ordinance requiring payment of fees for use of the city's refuse dumps was also generating opposition from groups such as the Building Owners and Managers Association, the Retail Grocers and Meat Dealers Association, the Retail Trade Bureau, and the Chamber of Commerce. Partly to ameliorate public discontent, the Council began a series of public hearings on these five tax measures which had not been placed before the public for acceptance or rejection though they had already been passed by the Council and signed by the Mayor.

Adding further to the Council's mounting problems were demands for wage raises from the Joint Crafts Council representing 21 A. F. of L. unions with members employed by the city, including some 2,000 City Light workers. On November 23, 1954, the Joint Crafts Council rejected wage adjustments offered by the City Council and submitted several revenue proposals of its own. In late November, Levine issued a public warning: "The city's finances are perilously low. . . . The sources of new revenue available to the city are limited to those permitted by the State Legislature while a Constitutional Amendment restricts the millage rate of property taxes that can be levied." With an outward show of assurance that he did not really feel, Levine added that the five new tax ordinances would not be revoked, that budget estimates would be further slashed in order to insure a balanced budget, and that all requests for pay increases would be refused. Levine had no illusions about the eventual necessity of granting the wage requests and the demands for added pension benefits by various city employee groups. Although balancing the budget was foremost in his mind, he felt that many of the wage demands were justifiable and long overdue.

Levine and the AWC

Some hope lay with the Association of Washington Cities and its legislative plans for alleviating city revenue problems on a state-wide basis. Although never a member of the Association's ruling body, the Executive Committee, Levine had long been active in determining Association fiscal policy. Seattle mayors and councilmen had always been prominent in the leadership of the Association. In 1954 Councilman Bob Jones, who had been president of the Association in 1952-53, was serving as chairman of its Executive Committee, and he kept Levine informed on key policy decisions.

At its annual convention in June, the Association, with Levine playing an active role, had drafted a policy statement advocating two major financial measures for aiding municipalities. One called for applying the same distribution formula to the state liquor tax that then governed the distribution of profits from state liquor stores, namely: cities forty percent, counties ten percent and the state fifty percent. It was estimated that this measure alone would result in $500,000 to $600,000 additional revenue for Seattle. The second measure approved by the Association in convention was a bill which would have exempted municipal governments or any of their agencies from paying state sales and excise taxes. Levine hoped that these two measures would pass the Legislature and would provide at least a temporary solution to the growing pressure in Seattle and in other Washington cities for wage increases for municipal employees.

In October and November Levine represented the Association in negotiations with state representatives of Washington's municipal fire departments over the firemen's proposed amendments to the State Firemen's Pension Act. These proposed amendments called for higher municipal contributions to the firemen's pension fund. After reporting on the progress of his negotiations to the Association's Executive Committee in November, Levine was authorized to continue to act on behalf of the Executive Committee in the negotiations with the firemen's representatives.

Levine's hopes for aid from the Association's two fiscal bills aimed at the coming legislative session were dampened when he heard a report of the discussion between the Association's Executive Committee and Governor Langlie which took place in Olympia on December 9. The Governor, who sixteen years earlier as Mayor of Seattle had led Washington cities in demanding a larger share of the state gasoline tax, was generally sympathetic to the Association's proposals for sharing the state liquor taxes and for securing exemption for cities from paying state taxes. However, the Governor pointed out to the members of the Executive Committee that the state itself was also in a severe financial plight. It seemed unlikely to the members of the Executive Committee that the Governor would give strong support to their proposals.

Levine Rejects Sewer and Garbage Fees

Public agitation in Seattle over city fiscal affairs intensified during December. Petitions were circulated to bring about a vote on the doubling of the business and occupation tax on services. The Committee for Police and Firemen's Wage Raises had still not met with the Council, although several attempts had been made to bring the two groups together. Just as one meeting had been scheduled, Levine called it off because two of the newer councilmen had publicized a revenue scheme of their own before taking up their proposal with the rest of the Council. The Chamber of Commerce was circulating an independent report among its members which recommended either a sewer service charge or a city-wide garbage collection fee. The Municipal League of Seattle and King County had also suggested further investigation of these two possibilities.

Levine, at this point, could have given in to what were essentially business group suggestions and gone along with either a sewer service charge or a garbage collection fee. From the Chamber of Commerce and other interest groups, he could have obtained considerable support in generating public acceptance for these measures. Each of these suggested revenue proposals would have brought in an estimated revenue of over $2,000,000. Although it would probably have been necessary to earmark the sewer service charge for construction of needed sewage treatment plants, the garbage collection fee would have certainly resulted in a direct increase in the general fund. Currently, the city was paying over $2,000,000 to a private concern for garbage collection.

Several members of the Council were opposed to either proposal. The Council members coming up for re-election did not want to be associated with either of the two increases. In any event, most councilmen felt that the proposals should be put before the voters for approval or rejection. In the light of experience with Proposition

Five and with several bond proposals that had been rejected at the same time, Council members were not optimistic about the chances of either measure passing. Finally, such a special election could not be held before spring, and the financial crisis appeared to be immediate and pressing.

Taking care not to antagonize the groups advocating a garbage and sewer charge, Levine nevertheless quietly delayed active consideration of these suggestions, relying on the two Association revenue bills aimed at the State Legislature. Levine was now in almost daily contact with one or another of the Association's leaders or with Chester Biesen, the Association's Executive Secretary. Throughout the fall the Association had been priming its members at a series of regional meetings which state legislators had been urged to attend. In addition, the mayor of the largest city in each region of the state was encouraged to arrange a special dinner for city officials and state legislators just prior to the opening of the legislative session on January 10. These meetings, considered effective in rural areas, were regarded with condescension by many big-city legislators, especially those who acted regularly if unofficially as spokesmen for one or more interest groups in the state. These men were firmly committed for or against the cities before the legislative session began. As the opening of the session neared, copies of the Association's municipal policy statement were mailed to key legislators together with personal letters from the Executive Secretary or members of the Executive Committee. City officials were urged to keep in close contact with their legislators and to be prepared to deluge them with letters, telegrams and/or personal contact when the proper time came. Levine and other Seattle councilmen took an active part in these preparations for the session. On December 28, it was publicly announced that Seattle would work with the Association of Washington Cities in all of its major legislative proposals. Among their collective goals would be a larger measure of home rule, a broader tax base, and new sources of revenue, particularly a share in the tax on liquor profits.

The Search Leads to Olympia

FRUSTRATED IN LOCAL EFFORTS to resolve its financial problems and faced with increasing agitation for wage raises, Seattle turned for help to the 34th Legislature of the State of Washington. With the Republicans holding a slim majority in the Senate and the Democrats in control of the House by one vote, neither party was able to put any lasting lawmaking coalitions together. Matters were further complicated by factional fights within both party delegations, particularly in the Senate.

Conditions did not appear auspicious for Seattle. In his budget message Governor Langlie, now serving his third term, requested an additional $40,000,000 in new taxes just to balance the *state* budget. With the Democratic leadership on record as favoring higher expenditures for education and public welfare, it was apparent that much more than $40,000,000 would eventually be needed.

In 1955 more than four out of every five dollars of tax revenues collected by the State of Washington came from various sales taxes, including a retail sales tax, a use tax for out-of-state purchases, the business and occupation tax (on the gross sales), and miscellaneous sales taxes on items such as cigarettes, alcoholic beverages, and insurance premiums. Seattle, seeking aid from the state, had to take into account the fact that local units and the state were competing for much of the same revenue, and that the state was already taxing certain choice fields including retail sales.

Another handicap confronting Seattle's leaders was that several legislators had reiterated their intention not to open new revenue sources or to give a larger share of state-collected taxes to the cities until they had made full use of already authorized revenue sources.

Councilman Levine was well aware of state financial needs and of the critical attitude of many legislators toward Seattle's failure to use either the sewer service charge or the garbage collection fee. When, on the eve of the new session of the Legislature, Levine convened representatives from various Seattle groups to form what became known as the Citizens' Advisory Committee on Municipal Finances, he had a number of reasons for doing so. First, Levine needed advice. He hoped to identify a revenue measure which would be acceptable to the state legislators and still bring in enough to enable Seattle to grant the wage demands of its various employee groups. Second, Levine knew that it was necessary to build community support for the bills of the Association of Washington Cities and any other municipal revenue proposals that might be forthcoming. Third, Levine was somewhat annoyed with several of the groups that had voiced interest in a sewer service charge as a solution; he wished to harness the energies of these organizations before they created more trouble, and, if possible, convert them to more "acceptable" approaches. Finally, Levine hoped to use the citizens' body as a sounding board for assessing the political feasibility of several other revenue measures which he had been mulling over in his mind. The most notable of these was a city sales tax enabling act.

A City Sales Tax?

A city sales tax had been suggested in prior years but had been met with little enthusiasm. The incumbent Governor had made such a proposal to the Legislature four years earlier but no action had been taken. A state law reserved the retail sales tax for state use only. Such was not the case in at least ten other states across the nation. Municipal sales taxes, unknown in the U. S. 25 years earlier, were being used in 1954 by some 900 cities in ten states including New York, Chicago, Los Angeles, San Francisco, Washington, Denver and New Orleans. Levine considered California experience particularly significant. Here, as in Washington, there was a three percent state sales tax. However, California municipalities were authorized to levy an additional sales tax of up to one percent. The 170-odd California cities which had taken advantage of the sales tax had realized from it approximately $50,000,000 during fiscal 1954. Not yet convinced that the California success could be transplanted or that the sales tax would be the least objectionable means of raising revenue, Levine felt nevertheless that the method was certainly worth discussing with Seattle groups.

Levine contacted representatives of various Seattle groups including the Chamber of Commerce, the Central Labor Council, the Seattle and King County Municipal League, the Apartment House Operators Association, and the Seattle Parent-Teachers Association. Forming the nucleus of the Citizens' Advisory Committee on Municipal Finance were the leaders of the Citizens' Committee for Police and Firemen's Wage Raises. The first meeting of the new group was held in closed session on January 7, 1955 with Mayor Pomeroy and the entire Council in attendance. Sharp differences of opinion arose immediately as to the least objectionable form of taxation. Representatives of the Chamber of Commerce and the Municipal League suggested a sewer service charge. But the Apartment House Operators Association aggressively opposed that proposal. The first meeting produced few concrete conclusions, but those attending agreed to sound out their organizations before meeting again the following Friday. Three days after the first meeting, the legislative session began.

As the second meeting of the Citizens' Advisory Committee opened on January 14, Levine reviewed the alternatives in his mind before taking the plunge. Although the sewer service charge proposal had received considerable vocal support, it had also aroused bitter opposition both within and without the Council. Feeling that the time was not ripe for either the sewer service charge or the garbage collection fee, Levine considered the other major possibilities. The city was already committed to backing the Association of Washington Cities program. But Councilman Jones had cautioned him that morning that these bills were already beginning to arouse considerable controversy in Olympia. Levine thought it best not to bank on these measures alone. Municipal income taxes had to be ruled out on the basis of previous State Supreme Court decisions on the unconstitutionality of state income taxes. Other city taxes seemed exhausted. The proposed doubling of the business and occupation tax on all businesses in the city had been defeated as Proposition Five two months earlier. The business and occupation tax on services was being bitterly criticized by affected groups at this very meeting. On the other hand, a city sales tax of one percent would bring in more than enough to meet the pressing demands for wage raises. Such a tax would provide a means whereby persons working and shopping in the city, but living in the suburbs, would contribute to the support of various municipal services from which they benefited. Experience in California and other states had shown that cities could administer sales taxes effectively. As long as the rate was one percent or below, the burden on lower income groups would not be too heavy, Levine believed. Finally, the act was enabling only. Seattle voters could be offered the choice between a sewer service charge or the city sales tax.

As the meeting started, the advantages of a city sales tax seemed to Levine to outweigh the disadvantages. Opponents would claim that a sales tax was regressive. But Levine believed that objection could be met by exempting food purchases. There were other potential problems. Would not a city sales tax on top of a state sales tax result in administrative difficulties and create serious bookkeeping problems for retailers? Would these taxes drive shoppers outside the city limits? California cities had not suffered too much. Convinced finally to the point of action, Levine waited for a lull in the proceedings of the Citizens' Advisory Group and took the plunge.

Reaction ranged from vigorous opposition on the part of several labor representatives to a lackadaisical willingness to explore the merits of the idea on the part of the businessmen. A few persons at the meeting, and several councilmen whom Levine had sounded out earlier, gave an enthusiastic endorsement. Most of the persons present preferred to withhold judgment until they could confer with their respective organizations.

Levine Goes to Olympia

For Levine, however, time was running out. Some agreement had to be reached on a revenue proposal if it were to be introduced at the State Legislature with any hope of passing. As he re-examined the advantages and disadvantages of the city sales tax enabling act, Levine became more and more convinced that the City of Seattle should sponsor such a bill. As he himself became sold on his own proposal, Levine began to assume on the part of others a determination equal to his own which few actually felt. Those organizations whose representatives had remained neutral at the January 14 meeting would, he believed, ultimately support it. Those in opposition he belittled. The firemen and policemen had a pressing interest at stake, reasoned Levine. His proposal was a means by which they could obtain their raises. A sales tax enabling act could secure the powerful support of these groups as well as that of the Association of Washington Cities. He and Councilman Jones could win Association support for the bill; possibly the Association could be brought to sponsor it. A major consideration remained unresolved, however: could a city sales tax enabling act be gotten through the Legislature? On January 19, two days before the third meeting of the Citizens' Advisory Committee, Levine journeyed to Olympia with Councilman Charles M. Carroll, Chairman of the Council's Legislative Committee. Levine wanted to consult leaders of various interest groups at Olympia, particularly officials of state-wide groups of municipal employees. He also wanted to sound out key legislators. If the results of these conversations seemed promising, he hoped to secure from Governor Langlie a public reaffirmation of the merits of a city sales tax enabling act.

Levine was considerably encouraged by the response he received in Olympia. Leaders of the various municipal employee groups, although cautious about committing support early in the legislative session, gave Levine reason to believe that they could be counted on to work for a city sales tax enabling act. In part, these leaders were willing to support any measure that would ensure their Seattle brethren a wage raise. Also, the state-wide officials of municipal fire and police groups could not afford to antagonize Councilman Levine, a ranking member of the City Council of the state's largest municipality and the chairman of the Firemen's Pension Committee of the Association of Washington Cities. At this stage of the legislative session it cost them little to say "yes" to Levine's proposal.

Levine turned to legislators in both parties. Well known by all but the most inexperienced legislators, he had no difficulty in arranging for conferences with key committee chairmen and other influential leaders of both houses. He avoided those legislators whom he expected to be antagonistic to any municipal sales tax bill. Levine found much more enthusiasm for his proposal among Republicans than among Democrats. The 1954 State Democratic Convention had gone on record opposing any increase in the retail sales tax. Aware that the House of Representatives had a Democratic majority of one, Levine nevertheless felt reasonably sure that several Democratic legislators could be converted. He recalled having watched a Democratic Legislature, aided by a Democratic Governor, enact the state's first sales tax in 1935.

Encouraged by the lack of opposition among interest groups and favorable response from several key legislators, particularly Seattle Representative R. Morton Frayn, a Republican, who had served as Speaker at the previous legislative session, Levine took his proposal to the Governor. Langlie, familiar with Seattle's needs because of his previous experience as Mayor, was more than sympathetic. Levine's bill was in line with the Governor's fiscal policy that local jurisdictions should accept financial responsibility and face revenue problems at home, not turn them over to the state. Another feature which commended the bill to the Governor was that it was an *enabling* act: each city would have to accept responsibility at the local level for its use.

An Embarrassing Leak

After these talks in Olympia, Levine was certain that Seattle should sponsor a city sales tax enabling act. The decision reached Seattle citizens in a round-about way. Several of the legislators Levine had talked with let slip to reporters that they had been approached about the possibilities of Seattle sponsoring a city sales tax enabling act. When questioned by reporters on the morning of January 20, Councilman Carroll (in charge of Council liaison with the Legislature) confirmed reports that a move to get such enabling legislation was "taking shape." He added that the bill had not yet been drafted. The decision was out in the open: Seattle *would* sponsor a city sales tax enabling act. Levine had made his decision at Olympia with most Seattle councilmen unaware as to just how far they had been committed. In Seattle, Council President M. B. "Mike" Mitchell was surprised and indignant. "I immediately contacted Chairman Levine at Olympia by phone and asked for an explanation," Mitchell told reporters inquiring about the Olympia report. "I was told that the initiative was being taken by the Council's Legislative Committee."

Several councilmen echoed Mitchell's sentiments, but the majority of the Council reacted more favorably. Questioned by reporters the day that the news reached Seattle, Councilman Alfred R. Rochester confirmed the fact that the Citizens' Advisory Committee had discussed the possibility of a city sales tax at a recent closed session. As far as Rochester was concerned, Seattle *wasn't* sponsoring such legislation; but if such a measure were passed in Olympia there was every likelihood that the Council would vote to put the tax to use. Councilman Bob Jones cited favorable California experience and observed that "undoubtedly the Association of Washington Cities will be in favor of any sound measure which will broaden our cities' taxation base." Council President Mitchell, however, stressed the fact that the Council had never taken any position on a sales tax, although such a tax had been discussed as one of various possibilities which the Council would welcome. When pressed for comment about the next day's meeting of the Citizens' Advisory Committee, Mitchell remarked that the Committee might continue discussing possible revenue measures, but that it should reach definite conclusions since time was getting short.

Later that same day, Governor Langlie publicly endorsed a city sales tax enabling act: "I recommended such legislation four years ago, and my feelings haven't changed. Cities and counties should have as broad latitude as possible to meet their needs."

Opposition Develops

Levine returned from Olympia on the evening of January 20, a Thursday. The release of the news story before all Council members could be consulted had opened a definite rift on the Council. However, by the time the Citizens' Advisory Committee meeting opened on Friday Levine had managed temporarily to placate Mitchell; the meeting ran smoothly, though it closed without definite action being taken. Most of those present withheld commitment, wanting to consult further with their own organizations. While these persons temporized, Levine was working himself up to greater enthusiasm. The more he spoke in favor of the measure to the group representatives and to other city councilmen, the more convinced he became. What had been at first but one of a number of alternatives had now become to him a shining single cause. Levine's vigor soon won most of the councilmen to his side.

The next Monday, January 24, the Council, under Levine's urging, unanimously endorsed a city sales tax enabling act. The bill, as drafted by the Corporation Counsel, exempted food sales. Cities were authorized to levy a tax of up to one percent in addition to the existing three percent sales tax already levied by the state on all retail sales including food. Aside from the food exemption, which applied to food sold for human consumption off the premises, the other exclusions in the bill resembled those in the state sales tax and included liquor bought in state liquor stores, motor vehicle fuels, certain livestock sales, and sales made in interstate and foreign commerce.

The first reaction to the Council's bill came in a lead editorial in the conservative, home-owned *Seattle Times* on January 26. The bill, said the editorial, would drive business to nearby shopping districts outside the city limits; it would present costly bookkeeping problems to retail establishments that sold food and other items. A more likely solution, said the *Times*, would be for the Legislature to increase the state sales tax, partly to solve the state's own fiscal problems and partly to gain revenue for municipalities.

Despite the Council's unanimous endorsement, there were still some bruised feelings about the bill. On January 27, Council President Mitchell visited Olympia and gave his approval to a rival legislative proposal sponsored by several independent Democratic legislators: if the Legislature had to raise the state sales tax from three to four percent to meet *its* mounting spending, this proposal provided that one-fourth of the one percent increase would go to Washington cities on a population basis. It was estimated that a one percent increase would provide over $40,000,000 a year in additional revenue, with Seattle's share amounting to $2,000,000.

When Mitchell returned to Seattle for the Monday Council session, Levine charged that he had spoken out of turn, that the statements he made conflicted with the unanimous stand taken by the Council the previous week, and that they would hamper the efforts of the Council's Legislative Committee in Olympia. Councilman Carroll, head of that committee, agreed that Mitchell's statements in Olympia had hurt the chances of Seattle's bill and had disturbed the city's relations with the police and firemen, who were supporting the city's bill to get their raises. Mitchell replied hotly that he wasn't against an *enabling* act; he just didn't like the idea of a city sales tax. Mitchell finally agreed that a united front was needed. Although still not in complete agreement, he agreed to keep his doubts to himself.

An ominous indication that Levine had not convinced all the organizations represented on the Citizens' Advisory Committee came in the February 5 edition of *Municipal News*, the organ of the Seattle and King County Municipal League:

> The League recommends that the City Council appoint a committee of citizens who will study the city's finances and frame a long-range program to raise the needed additional revenues. If necessary, as a short-range plan it is recommended that the Council might utilize the sewer or garbage tax. The Municipal League is not in favor of a city sales tax right now pending more study of its effect on the city's economy.

Undaunted, the Council unanimously adopted a resolution on February 7 appealing to the Legislature for a municipal sales tax enabling act. Copies were sent to Governor Langlie, the President of the Senate, the Speaker of the House, and the representatives and senators of King County, most of whom had already been contacted in person.

The next step was to secure sponsorship for the bill. For a time Levine considered introducing it in both the Senate and the House but he finally settled on the latter alone. There was an element of boldness in Levine's decision to introduce the bill in the Democratic House rather than in the Republican-controlled Senate. Despite the dangers that with Democratic House leadership the bill might never get out of committee, Levine thought it best to concentrate Seattle's legislative efforts first in an all-or-nothing attempt in the lower house. If the measure got through the House, chances were good that it would win Senate and gubernatorial support. Early in February Levine concluded arrangements for the bill's co-sponsorship by a member from each political party. On February 9, 1955, House Bill No. 501 (H. B. 501), the Seattle-sponsored city sales tax enabling act, was introduced by Representatives Dr. James L. McFadden, Clallam County Democrat, and R. Morton Frayn, Republican from Seattle and King County's 43rd District. Dr. McFadden, a freshman Representative, was sympathetic to Seattle's financial plight, having served two previous terms as City Councilman for Port Angeles, a city of 12,000 on the Straits of Juan de Fuca. Frayn, owner of a Seattle printing firm, was serving his fifth consecutive term including service as Republican Speaker of the House during the previous session. Following its introduction and first reading, the bill was referred to the House Committee on Revenue and Taxation.

For the next two weeks, both before and after the Committee hearing on February 19 and up to the time the bill was voted upon the floor of the House on February 25, Levine and other city officials worked assiduously to secure support among legislators and interest groups. For the most part, but by no means exclusively, Councilmen Levine, Jones, Mitchell, and Carroll concentrated on Republican legislators, while Councilman Rochester and Mayor Pomeroy sought to convert Democratic representatives to the city's point of view. In addition, the Mayor and councilmen urged city employees to write to their state representatives.

Association Endorsement

Fundamental to the success of any legislation affecting the municipalities of Washington is the support of the Association of Washington Cities. When Levine had first voiced his intention to work for a city sales tax enabling act to Association staff members, the response had been one of uneasiness. Both Chester Biesen, Executive Secretary of the organization, and Paul Schiffner, the Association's influential Legislative Consultant, were wary of any bill which might diffuse efforts to push through the Association's own two municipal revenue measures. However, Levine and Councilman Jones, the Vice-Chairman of the Association's Executive Committee, were able to convince Biesen and Schiffner that Association support for Seattle's bill would not materially affect the Association's own program.

Levine and Jones arranged for endorsement of the bill at the afternoon session of the Association's Executive Committee meeting on February 15 in Olympia. Although Biesen and other Association officers had been present in Olympia since the opening of the session, this was the first full meeting of the Executive Committee since its meeting with Governor Langlie in December. Occupying the Committee's attention were police and firemen's pension bills as well as the status of the Association's own revenue measures. As Councilmen Jones and Levine enlarged upon Seattle's financial plight and explained the workings of the sales tax enabling act, they spoke to a sympathetic but not particularly enthusiastic audience. Although most of the mayors present had municipal financial problems of their own, a city sales tax did not offer their cities a particularly appealing solution. The administrative machinery needed to collect the tax would be too complex for all but the largest municipalities. Cities on the border of the state, in competition, as it were, with cities of other states with no sales tax or less sales tax, had no desire for such a measure. Nevertheless, on the motion of Mayor Robert Stobbs of Enumclaw, with a second by Mayor Harold Tollefson of Tacoma, the Association went on record favoring Levine's bill. With only Seattle really interested in the bill, the Association endorsement was essentially an honoring of Seattle's heavy financial contribution to the AWC budget and a recognition of devoted past service to the Association by Levine and Jones.

Association leaders reasoned along the following lines: the bill was enabling only; the cities not immediately interested might be glad to have the authority in the future. City sales taxes were widely used in California, Illinois, and other states. Why not attempt to secure this additional revenue for Seattle? The only possible reason for withholding Association support was that another municipal revenue request might act as a drag upon the passage of Senate Bill 104, AWC's measure to obtain a share of the state liquor tax for Washington cities. However, Seattle's influence in the Legislature was judged to be powerful enough to enable it to get its own bill through without lessening the support for AWC's liquor tax bill.

Following endorsement of Seattle's city sales tax bill, the Executive Committee moved on to other important municipal legislation, including the Firemen's Pension Bill. Levine and his committee were again given power to meet with the representatives of the firemen and act on a compromise measure less costly to the municipalities. Levine's chairmanship of this Association committee aided him in securing support for Seattle's city sales tax enabling act. When a public hearing on Seattle's sales tax measure was held by the House Committee on Revenue and Taxation four days later, among those speaking in favor of the bill was Earl Brower, Vice President of the state's International Fire Fighters' Union. However, Levine later complained that most of the support gained from city employee groups was limited to passive "lip service."

The Committee Hearing on H.B. 501

Reflecting the 50-49 Democratic majority in the House of Representatives, its 23-man Committee on Revenue and Taxation, to which Seattle's bill had been referred, had a Democratic majority of one. The Democratic Chairman, Wilbur G. Hallauer, serving his fourth term as representative of the eastern Washington counties of Okanogan and Douglas, was a fruit rancher and manager of an apple evaporating plant in Oroville, a town of about 1,500 population just south of the Canadian border. Unlike many eastern Washington legislators, Hallauer had considerable interest in and familiarity with Seattle's problem, being the owner of several apartment houses there. Despite the implications for his own property holdings, Hallauer in his role as legislator felt that the best solution to Seattle's financial troubles could come only from revitalizing the property tax by bringing assessments in line with state constitutional requirements. Recognizing that this was at best a long-range program, Hallauer nevertheless opposed the sales tax enabling act because he felt certain it would result in the city officials lessening their pressure on county assessors for stringent assessing and thereby further weaken the property tax structure. As Chairman of the Revenue and Taxation Committee, moreover, Hallauer's primary concern was with state financial requirements; only secondarily was he interested in city fiscal needs.

On the Revenue and Taxation Committee were six representatives from King County, three from each party, including several with ambition and potentially bright political futures. One was Andrew Hess, 31, an aggressive, liberal Democrat, a representative from the 31st District, which included a portion of south Seattle and extended into a wide area of suburban King County. In this district, which contains many working-class families including a high proportion of the Boeing Airplane Company's 40,000 employees, Democratic nomination was tantamount to election.

In addition to Hallauer's concern for state fiscal needs and Hess's strong feeling of obligation to a working-class constituency, both men were opposed in principle to a sales tax increase of any kind. In line with the State Democratic Party Platform of 1954, they argued for a reduction of the state sales tax because they considered it regressive; they favored a graduated income tax instead. In the early 1930s an initiative measure for a graduated net income tax had been passed, but it had been held unconstitutional by the State Supreme Court. An amendment to the Constitution permitting a graduated net income tax had been submitted to and defeated by the voters four times, the last vote coming in 1942.

Proceeding with caution, Hallauer, Hess, and other Democratic Party leaders decided to hold the Seattle bill in committee until they felt confident that enough votes had been lined up to defeat it on the floor of the House.

As Levine waited for the public committee

hearing, he continued to seek organizational and legislative support. He intensified his efforts among representatives of municipal employee groups. He, Jones, and the other councilmen continued to persuade legislators and gained promises of votes should the bill reach the floor. During the week preceding the public hearing, Levine and Jones concentrated on the 23 members of the House committee. After a week's effort Levine felt reasonably certain the bill would reach the floor and would pass the House.

The Hearing

By the time the public hearing opened on February 19, Levine had arranged for a large number of group spokesmen to appear in behalf of the bill. Councilman Jones spoke first. He introduced Levine almost immediately. Levine described at length the financial difficulties that cities were facing, pointing out that unless the sales tax were allowed Seattle would have to lay off some of its policemen and firemen as well as curtail services. The only other alternative that Levine could see was deficit financing and, "we're dead set against deficit financing." Levine went on to mention that a civic advisory committee had decided that a sales tax would work the least hardship on the average wage earner and would eliminate the necessity of garbage and sewer charges. When asked by a Committee member why Seattle did not make use of either a sewer service charge or a garbage collection fee, Levine replied that these were only temporary measures that would not greatly add to the general fund and that a sales tax would be easier to collect. He preferred to reserve the sewer service charge for financing sewage treatment plants and trunk sewage lines. A sales tax would have the further advantage of bringing in money from those making use of city facilities but living outside the city, including tourists.

Following Levine, Jones introduced a series of speakers, all of whom stated that their groups had endorsed the city sales tax. Among those testifying in behalf of the bill were Chester Biesen, Executive Secretary of the Association of Washington Cities; Mayor Tollefson of Tacoma; J. McClooney, representing the Washington's Peace Officers' Association; Councilmen Carroll, Mitchell and J. D. Braman of Seattle; Robert Heweth, representing the Building Owners and Managers Association of Seattle; Earl Brower, International Fire Fighters' Union vice president; Al O'Brien, Chairman of the Joint Crafts Union representing some 21 A. F. of L. unions in Seattle; Captain Corning of the Seattle Police Department, representing the Chief of Police; Donald Hass of the Apartment House Owners Association of Seattle; and several business representatives of Seattle locals of various unions. Representative Frayn, perhaps the House's most influential Republican legislator, completed the list.

After this presentation, a smaller group spoke against the bill. John Current of the Washington State Research Council, formerly the Washington State Taxpayers Association, opposed it, agreeing with Chairman Hallauer that Seattle should bear its financial troubles until the property tax revenues were increased through more equitable and higher assessment of property. Instead of the $3,000,000 to $4,000,000 that Levine had predicted the sales tax would bring in with food exempted, Current estimated it would net nearly $6,000,000. Representatives of the Retail Trade Bureau of Tacoma, the Retail Grocers Association, the Associated Grocers of Seattle, and the Retail Food Dealers Association also testified against the bill. These spokesmen for the groceries and supermarkets protested that the exemption of food would result in increased overhead and additional bookkeeping headaches. They felt that as the state sales tax did not exempt food, neither should this bill.

The Committee Reports

At the close of the public hearing the Committee on Revenue and Taxation went into executive session. Democrat Ralph Purvis of Bremerton moved that the bill be amended to remove the food exemption. His motion was seconded by Lester Robinson, a Republican from Walla Walla, and the motion carried. This motion was less a partisan action than an effort to make the bill more workable, in accordance with the wishes of the food merchants. The eleven members of the Committee still present voted eight to three for the bill as amended.

By February 23 when the bill was passed to the Committee on Rules and Order for the scheduling of the second reading on the floor of the House, a total of twelve members had signed the "do pass" Committee report, while eight representatives, including Chairman Hallauer and Representative Hess, had signed a minority report recommending its defeat. Levine and Jones had been successful up to this point in preventing a strict party vote. Five Democrats—one from Seattle's 35th District and the others from western Washington—were among the majority recommending passage. On the other hand, three Republicans, all serving their first term in the House—Representatives Harris and Weitzman from Spokane and McDermott from Seattle's 37th District—were in the minority.

As Levine waited for the Committee on Rules and Order to place House Bill No. 501 on the calendar for the second reading, he calculated the number of votes for and against the bill as best he could. It became increasingly apparent to him that action taken by King County's 24 legislators, including twelve from each party, would make or break the bill. If Levine could win over all of the Republicans and convince even one-third of the Democrats that they should vote for the bill, he felt assured that the rest of the House would divide fairly evenly, and the bill would pass.

With an aggressiveness unimpeded by tact, Levine intensified his efforts to win the support of recalcitrant King County legislators. To several he suggested that unless they supported the bill he would speak to community clubs in their districts and say that they had been against wage raises for Seattle police and firemen. These threats had a negative effect on some representatives. As one King County representative put it: "Levine may be a dictator in the City Council but he can't come down here and tell us what we should or shouldn't do. When we draw $5.00 per day for a lot of hard work and very little glory, it's not very difficult to remain independent from such threats."

While the Seattle councilmen, Mayor Pomeroy, and Mort Frayn were trying to win last minute support, Democratic party opposition to the measure began to congeal. Partly because of suspicion of Levine's intentions in introducing the bill, partly because of his vigorous tactics, but primarily because they felt sales taxes were regressive, Democratic leaders spread the word that H. B. 501 should not pass. The opposition was led by Chairman Hallauer of Oroville, Floyd Miller of Seattle, and Andy Hess and Ed Munro of the 31st District. As the afternoon session began on Friday, February 25, the Chief Clerk rose to read H. B. 501 for the second time.

Defeat

After the bill was read, Democratic Speaker John O'Brien recognized Chairman Hallauer, who moved the adoption of the committee amendment removing the food exemption from the bill. This was passed by a voice vote.

Then Mark Holliday, Vancouver Democrat, moved that the bill be indefinitely postponed. Long debate ensued. The climax of the heated session came when Hess, the Seattle Democrat, paused in the middle of his speech, pointed a finger at Levine sitting above him in the gallery, and angrily accused him of insulting the integrity of the members of the House of Representatives by threatening political reprisals against those members who refused to vote for the bill. Holliday's motion to postpone H. B. 501 indefinitely carried by 53 to 45 with a few members of both parties crossing over in what was primarily a party vote. To make sure that the bill was not revived, Hess moved that the House immediately reconsider its vote. Representative Frayn made several attempts to adjourn the House, hoping to gain enough votes to save the bill, but Speaker O'Brien overruled these attempts and called for a vote on the reconsideration. The bill was irrevocably lost.

Of the seven Democrats voting to reconsider, one, Dr. McFadden, was one of the bill's original sponsors; two others indicated that they would vote against the bill, although they voted to reconsider out of courtesy to Frayn. Of the remaining four, two were from Everett, a city some thirty minutes driving time north of Seattle. At least one of these representatives was motivated in part by the retail sales advantage this bill might provide local Everett merchants should Seattle enact the one percent tax. Among the Republicans voting against the bill in contrast to the great majority of their party were several representatives from border communities and a number who felt that the measure was too regressive with food sales no longer exempted.

Democratic disenchantment with any form of sales tax increase seemed the main reason for the bill's defeat, and yet, somewhat paradoxically this same Legislature subsequently voted an increase in the state sales tax. Also, the fact that Seattle had not yet made use of either a sewer service charge or a garbage collection fee led some representatives to believe that Levine was not facing up to political or economic reality. Several envisioned Levine's bill as an attempt to "pass the buck" for raising Seattle taxes to the Legislature. Once the city sales tax had been enacted, Levine could have put the measure up to the people of Seattle in a referendum. If the sales tax passed, then the people and the Legislature would have to bear responsibility for increased taxes. If the measure failed, then the people, not the Council, would be to blame for not raising wages of police and firemen.

From Levine's point of view the defeat of the city sales tax bill was deplorable but not disastrous. He and the city had met legislative defeat before, and this was not the first time Seattle had faced a financial difficulty. Wage raises would be postponed. As an elected representative charged with the responsibility of keeping the city operating on a sound financial basis, he would not resort to deficit financing. His biggest regret, he said, was that the same people who elected him also elected legislators who would not permit him to manage the city's affairs properly.

Aftermath

Although this case ends with the defeat of Seattle's bill there is no beginning or ending to the story of the city's relationships with the Legislature or to its search for a solution to its fiscal difficulties.

Several days after the defeat of Levine's bill the Association of Washington Cities' liquor tax bill was passed by overwhelming majorities in both houses. Governor Langlie withdrew a threatened last-minute veto as the state's financial problems were temporarily solved by the increase in the state sales tax from three to three and one-third percent. Every city in the state received approximately $1.00 per capita of new revenue through the passage of the liquor tax bill. With this increase together with added revenue from several existing taxes, Seattle collected $1,000,000 more from sources other than property taxes in 1955.

During the summer of 1955, however, Seattle was once again faced with a budget crisis. Firemen, policemen, and other city employees were still demanding wage raises. In August, after much debate, the Council passed a sewer service charge of $1.00 per month for single family residences and additional fees for other larger installations. The Apartment House Operators Association led a successful drive to secure enough signatures to force the Council to submit the sewer service charge to the voters at a municipal election. Following repeal of the ordinance increasing business and occupation taxes on services (with the backing of some seventy business, labor, and civic groups, including a contribution of over $30,000 for publicity) a "stop pollution" campaign was successful. On March 13, 1956, by a vote of over two to one, the ordinance was passed, thus providing Seattle with an additional annual income of $2,600,000 to $3,000,000. At this same municipal election two of the four incumbent councilmen, Robert Harlen and Al Rochester, and Mayor Pomeroy went down to defeat. One of the two new councilmen was former state legislator Floyd Miller, who campaigned on the basis that he had helped defeat the city sales tax enabling act.

The Council, in approving the 1956 budget, had included over $1,000,000 in wage raises, including $25 per month across the board for firemen and police. Part of the million dollars became available because the sewer charges would help to absorb some $400,000 in sewer-operation costs previously paid from general tax revenue.

Meanwhile, Councilman Levine, looking forward to the 1957 legislative session, met with the Subcommittee on Revenue and Taxation of the Interim Legislative Council to discuss the financial plight of Washington cities. After discussing the failure of House Bill No. 501, among revenue possibilities mentioned was a two-thirds of one percent increase in the state sales tax to be distributed to the cities on the basis of population. At its 1956 convention in May, the Association of Washington Cities adopted a program for municipal action which urged that "the state government, just as have many other progressive state governments nationally, should authorize cities to levy a municipal sales tax and other types of taxes which individual cities may believe are essential to best fit their economy and other local conditions." The Association's Executive Committee began to lay plans for drafting and securing the passage of permissive legislation allowing cities to enact a sales tax up to two-thirds of one percent.

Taxing the Southern Railway in Alabama

Valerie A. and Chester B. Earle

The Preliminaries

THIS CASE DESCRIBES an administrative decision to raise the assessed valuation of the property of a big taxpayer. The decision was taken within one state; the property of the taxpayer extended over fourteen states. The initial decision and the subsequent issues involved sharp differences of opinion about valuation technique, but they also exemplified fundamentally different views about the proper distribution of the tax burden.

The story of Alabama's dealings with the Southern Railway also illustrates some of the administrative and tactical considerations that affected the strategy of both sides in the controversy.

The Setting

In 1947, the Alabama Department of Revenue notified the Southern Railway that the assessed valuation of its Alabama properties would be increased by $7,000,000 over the tax base of the preceding year—an increase of almost forty percent. This increase was the result of a decision of the Department of Revenue to systematize procedures for assessing railroad property and to equalize railroad assessments. The Railway appealed the decision, and the ensuing controversy was carried through informal and formal administrative steps, through the Circuit Court, to rest before the Alabama Supreme Court for nearly three years.

Powers of the Department

The Alabama Department of Revenue was charged with the responsibility for assessing all public utility property within the state. In fixing the true value of both tangible and intangible property, the Department was required "insofar as the other evidence and information does not make it appear . . . improper or unjust . . . to do so, . . . to consider as a factor the net earnings, averaged over a period of five years, and also take as a basis therefor the aggregate average market value, or true value, for the preceding year of all its shares of stock and add thereto the average market or true value for the preceding year of all indebtedness secured by any mortgage, lien, or other charge" upon the company's assets, "and the sum or sums so produced shall be treated and considered a factor in ascertaining the true value of said entire property, tangible and intangible for purposes of ad valorem taxation."

Where information was obtainable, "and has or may have any bearing on the values of such property, the tax assessing authorities shall consider the average market or actual value of the stocks and bonds of such companies during the preceding year and also shall take into consideration the estimated investment as returned by the duly authorized officer or employee of such company to the Public Service Commission, or to the Interstate Commerce Commission, Tennessee Valley Authority, the Reconstruction Finance Corporation, or the Railroad Credit Corporation," or other similar agencies "of the State or of the United States, or value stated in folders, schedules, or prospecti. . . . Also, any valuation made for rate-making or other purposes of the Public Service Commission of the State, the Interstate Commerce Commission, or other state or governmental bodies shall be considered."

The Department could also consider such factors as original cost, reproduction cost less depreciation, recent sales of contiguous property, the nature of the property, its location, gross or net income for the preceding year or years, market value of stocks and bonds, loans or mortgages upon the property, and the amount of insurance carried.

In addition to the bases for determining the true value indicated in the preceding paragraphs, the Department could "likewise consider the value of individual units or items of property, and the sum of the values of such units or items." In cases where the property of a utility extended beyond the boundary of the state, the Department was required to "ascertain and fix the value of the entire property, tangible and intangible, in this State by taking such proportion of the value of the entire property . . . which is specifically used in its business . . . as its total lines or business within this State bear to the total lines or business both inside and outside the State, or as its total receipts from within this State, bear to its total receipts from both within and without the State."

To perform this assessment function, the Department of Revenue could require all utilities to report on all properties both within and beyond the state. In the case of railroads, such reports had to include information on the total length of the road, and total length within the state and within each county, city, school district, or other special tax district; the number of engines or other units of motive power; the number of passenger, freight, construction, and other cars for the entire system and for the state; and had to indicate the allocation formula used, as well as holdings of real estate, fixtures and appliances, and buildings and structures. The Department could also compel additional testimony and records necessary for the intelligent discharge of its duties.

After the process of setting true value (or 100 percent assessment) was completed, the law provided that both the state and local tax be levied on sixty percent of this true valuation. (Local assessors were formally required to use the sixty percent ratio in assessing all local property as well.) The final duty of the Department was, therefore, to notify local tax assessors of the amount of the valuation of public utility property within their jurisdictions, since local assessors could not evaluate any public utility property.

Notices of tentative valuation were then sent by the Department of Revenue to each utility taxpayer with a notification that, on a specified day, the taxpayer could appear to protest the valuation. Should the taxpayer not appear, the valuation became final. If, after a departmental hearing, the taxpayer did not accept a valuation figure, an appeal could be taken to the Circuit Court of Montgomery County. In such appeals the Department of Revenue was represented by the Attorney General.

The statute had this to say with respect to the scope of review by the Court:

> The assessment made by the Department of Revenue shall *prima facie* be correct, and where the appeal is taken by the taxpayer, the burden shall be on the appellant to show that such assessment is incorrect. The Circuit Court in equity, or the Supreme Court of Alabama on appeal to it may, if it be of the opinion from all the evidence that the assessment as made is either too high or too low, fix the amount of such assessment. The Court shall hear such appeals according to its own rules and methods or procedure so far as practicable and shall decide all questions both as to the legality of the assessment and the amount thereof.

The Judge of the Montgomery Circuit Court had held consistently that this statute required *de novo* review.

Public utilities were the only properties for which the state bore responsibility for initial assessment. Other properties were assessed locally, but, in the interest of equalization, the Department of Revenue could set aside any local assessment, and, after notice and hearing to the taxpayer affected, reassess his property. An appeal from these reassessments could then be taken to a circuit court. The Department could also instruct any local board of equalization to readjust and re-equalize any class or classes of property the assessment of which the Department had investigated and found to be disproportionate to the fair and reasonable market value.

These were the salient provisions of the Alabama tax law in 1947 when the Southern Railway joined issue with the Department of Revenue.

The Property Tax in Alabama

In 1947 Alabama was facing a decline in the proportion of state revenue yielded by the *ad valorem* property tax. In 1943-44 the tax had produced seven percent of the state's revenues. By 1949 this figure would drop to 3.8 percent. Approximately fifty percent of property tax revenues was earmarked for education, a function which required more than one-third of annual state expenditures. Nearly 37 percent of property tax receipts went into the General Fund and were thus at the disposal of the Legislature. The property tax was the largest single source of the General Fund, since only about ten percent of all state revenues were paid into that account. Local governments depended even more than the state on the property tax.

Although the rate of the property tax was consistently set at the constitutional maximum, the burden upon Alabama property owners was comparatively light, because valuation procedures had tended to be hit-or-miss and had resulted in assessments not only well below market values but considerably below the sixty percent of total value required by statute. As of 1947 the state had done little to improve assessment techniques, either by setting a good example in its own assessment processes or by providing expert assistance to local tax assessors.

Public utility property provided about twenty percent of Alabama's assessed values. Because they were big taxpayers, the utility firms were continuously concerned with how the property tax was administered. The utilities' interest was quickened when several tax authorities revealed that the level of assessment on non-utility property throughout the state was not only below the sixty percent ratio required by statute, but considerably below the assessment level imposed by the Department of Revenue on utility property, even though the Department had made no consistent effort to assess utilities at the full sixty percent ratio.

Believing that they were already paying at a disproportionately heavy rate, the utility companies were ready to resist any increase in valuations or in the level of assessments.

Lean Years, Tax Decreases

Alabama's effort in 1947 to increase the taxes paid by the Southern Railway disturbed several existing arrangements that had originated during the depression of the thirties.

In 1932 most of Alabama's Class I railroads —that is, those with the highest operating revenues—protested their assessments. Several appealed to the Circuit Court. The essence of the protest was that while the depression had lowered both the incomes and property values of the railroads, their Alabama tax assessments had remained nearly as high as in the preceding years. The Governor, concerned by dwindling tax revenues, had instructed the Commissioner of Revenue (who was appointed by the Governor) to hold the line on taxes wherever he possibly could and to leave any reduction to the courts. The Circuit Court of Montgomery County subsequently ruled that the railroad assessments should be reduced by twenty to fifty percent, and the Governor, alarmed at the substantial tax losses entailed by the reduction, became more willing to compromise with major utility companies rather than have them appeal to the courts.

The Southern Railway, one of the largest taxpayers in Alabama, was one of the railroads appealing to the courts for a reduced assessment in 1932. Before the case could go to trial, the administration invited the railroad to send representatives to Montgomery in order to work out a compromise. The Southern sent to Montgomery *its* Tax Commissioner, Haddon Johnson, who represented the railroad in all Alabama tax matters except income tax. After some negotiation, the 1932 assessment was set at $17,347,953, and the same assessment was agreed to for 1933. This represented a reduction of almost $5,000,000 from the 1931 assessment and was about $4,250,000 less than the protested 1932 tentative assessment.

From 1933 through 1939 the Southern's assessments were continuously reduced; in 1939 the amount was down to $13,633,844. During the war years, which brought heavy traffic to the railroad, Southern's assessments were increased gradually to $18,251,496 in 1946, almost $1,000,000 more than the 1933 figure. The 1946 assessment was 21 percent above the 1938 assessment and 9 percent above the 1942 assessment.

From 1933 through 1946 there was comparative harmony between the Department of Revenue and the Southern Railway. But two events occurred during that period that contributed to the conflict of 1947.

The "Gentlemen's Agreement"

The first of the events was a so-called "gentlemen's agreement" between state officials and representatives of the Southern Railway. The Southern had discovered late in 1942 that the Department of Revenue's interpretation of a statute levying a gross receipts tax was probably unconstitutional. Johnson, the Southern's tax specialist, informed the Commissioner of Revenue that the railroad would bring suit to recover its gross receipts tax payment for the preceding two years. Such a suit, if successful, would have forced the state to pay a considerable sum to the Southern, and inevitably other railroads would also have brought suit. For these reasons it seemed important to the Governor, Chauncey Sparks, to arrange a settlement that would persuade the Southern to drop its court action.

Haddon Johnson was invited to Montgomery and bargained with state officials over the *quid pro quo* that would induce the Southern to drop its suit. Johnson promised that the railroad would drop the suit, and, in addition, support legislation to amend the gross receipts statute so as to clear up any question of its constitutionality, if, in return, the state would pledge to keep its tax hands off Southern's war-swollen earnings.

The Southern believed that taxes should not be increased at a rate commensurate with the wartime increase in profits and property values, because the increased revenues and values resulted from unusual and temporary circumstances. If taxes were to reflect war prosperity at all, the increase in taxation should be spread over a fairly long period of time. The Southern professed itself willing to increase its property tax payments as it acquired new holdings, but it did not believe that assessment of old holdings should be increased at the same rate as the war-inflated values. Moreover, the Southern pointed out, its long-run profit and loss position had been distorted because it had been unable to maintain its usual repair and replacement policy. At the end of the war, like all railroads, it would have the accumulated expense of bringing equipment and roadbed back to prewar standards.

Accordingly, Johnson asked that the state hold off on all tax increases except those based on new acquisitions. The state had no statutory authority to give such assurance formally. But Johnson wanted no written agreement, simply an understanding among gentlemen. Although the moratorium seemed to deal only with the war years, Johnson probably thought of it as covering any postwar years in which the railroad continued to receive swollen earnings directly or indirectly due to the war. Believing that the Southern would win its suit if it chose to contest the gross receipts tax, the state officials entered into the agreement early in 1943. For four years the Commissioner of Revenue of Alabama made no substantial increase in the Southern's property tax assessment—despite continued demands for such action from the chief of the Department's Franchise and Public Utility Division.

Two Appointments—Dowling and Hamilton

The second event contributing to the 1947 conflict occurred later in 1943. Dr. Henry Dowling, ex-Superintendent of Schools of Tuscaloosa, was appointed by Governor Sparks to be the new Commissioner of Revenue. Dowling's training and experience were primarily in the field of school management. But he was well liked, and, in the estimate of Haddon Johnson, a fine and capable gentleman.

Early in 1944 Dowling appointed Peter B. Hamilton as assistant to the veteran chief of the Franchise and Public Utilities Division, Henry Knight, who had been ill for some time. Hamilton served under the state merit system which had been introduced in 1939. It had brought stability of employment to the division. Hamilton was a member of an old Alabama family. He had graduated from the University of Alabama Law School in 1926 and had practiced law in Mobile. From 1929 to 1934 he was employed with various banks in Mobile, and for the next four years he was attorney for a Mobile lumber company. In 1939, the first year of an administrative reform program sponsored by the Governor, Hamilton entered state employment on a part-time basis, valuing shares of domestic corporations. He also served as chairman of the Personnel Board (Civil Service Commission) of Mobile County. The words "erudite" and "theoretical" were sometimes used to describe him. In his leisure time he studied philosophy.

Knight, the long-time head of the Public Utilities Division, had been a railroad employee for many years before coming to state government. He had held many kinds of jobs, ranging from construction work to accounting. He was proud of his intimate knowledge of railroad operations and of the fact that this permitted him to consider, in his work for the Department, many factors not included in most valuation formulas.

Hamilton did the major share of public utility assessment in 1944 and 1945. During a part of those two years, Knight was on the job and made his own calculations of assessments. However, Dowling relied primarily on Hamilton, asking the latter to check the calculations made by Knight. In 1946, Knight retired, and Hamilton became chief of the Public Utilities Division.

Dowling, the former educator, believed that salvation in tax matters, as in most others, lay in study and education. Accordingly, his Department prepared a manual for local tax assessors and distributed it widely. He expanded the Revenue Department's program of advice and assistance to local officials within the limits of the Department's small staff and heavy work load. He also played a leading role in getting a task force of experts to study Alabama's revenue system and to recommend improvements.

Results of a Survey

Dowling and Hamilton began in 1944 to review the procedures used by the Utilities Division for assessing large firms. They quickly concluded that Knight's staff of three "southern gentlewomen" was not adequate for administering the public utility property and license taxes. They also discovered that the procedure for utility valuation was open to question on many counts, and they came to believe that procedural weaknesses might have been a major reason for the state's uniformly unsuccessful showing in the courts in 1932 and 1933.

Dowling and Hamilton learned from their reading that assessment procedure ordinarily considered three factors in determining the value of utility property: reproduction cost less depreciation, capitalized earnings, and the value of stocks and bonds. Railroad reproduction costs were usually determined from figures submitted by the railroad to the Interstate Commerce Commission. Capitalized earnings and the value of stocks and bonds could be taken from tax returns and market reports.

There was wide agreement among tax authorities, and among most railroad officials, that in making an assessment, it was desirable first to ascertain the value of the entire railroad system and then to determine what fraction of total system value lay within a state. Only in this way could the stocks and bonds and operating income be used as bases of valuation. Stock and bond figures obviously applied only to a system as a whole, and net earnings had to be allocated, since railroads did not record operating expenses on a state by state basis. Moreover, Dowling and Hamilton learned, most tax experts agreed that assessment should be done largely by formula, with enlightened judgment tempering the results in special circumstances.

Formula or Personal Judgment?

Dowling and Hamilton discovered that Knight, by contrast, took pride in the fact that personal judgment played a considerable part in his assessments, and that he had been supported in this by previous commissioners of revenue. In dealing with railroad valuation, his forte, Knight made no independent effort to determine system value, although railroads were free to submit their figures for system values to him. Apparently, little or no use was made of Interstate Commerce Commission figures on reproduction cost, this being determined in Alabama on the basis of the railroads' own estimates and the "informed judgment" of Knight. Company figures for Alabama earnings were accepted with little or no investigation of the method by which they had been determined, although Knight had once made a tour of neighboring states to learn whether the earnings figures submitted to the several states added up to the total earnings as reported by the firms.

To determine the going value of stocks and bonds, Knight usually averaged the highest and lowest quotations of a railroad's stocks and bonds during the preceding year. Most authorities with whom Dowling and Hamilton were familiar appeared to agree that valuation by use of stocks and bonds, always tricky, was unrealistic with the method Knight employed.

Knight usually tried to fix assessment rates of all railroads at 45 to 50 percent of what he considered to be the value of their Alabama assets. His own estimate of the rates set by local assessors on non-utility property was 40 to 45 percent, but the exact rate was unknown, since no studies of the local assessment levels had been made.

Data preparation on railroad cases was apt to vary in direct proportion to the amount of controversy anticipated. If relationships with a particular railroad were good, Knight usually submitted very meager data to the Commissioner of Revenue. On the other hand, if disagreement was expected, considerable time was spent in compiling material to substantiate an assessment. Actually, from 1933 to 1947 few disagreements had reached a serious stage, and no appeals were made to the courts. This harmony may have been related to the fact that company reports, along with the assessment made the preceding year, formed the major basis of assessment.

Dowling and Hamilton soon concluded that these assessment techniques had resulted in many inequities. Hamilton, in particular, distrusted the emphasis placed upon personal judgment. Even unintentional misuse of discretion, he felt, could produce gross cases of over or under taxation. To protect themselves in such situations, taxpayers, especially large corporate taxpayers, were likely either to insist on more reliable procedures or to seek to exercise control over the assessor. Hamilton and Dowling concluded that to be fair to the taxpayer and to protect revenues of the state, it would be necessary to establish scientific criteria by which equitable and consistent assessments could be made. They decided to revamp the state's assessment methods.

As a first step, Hamilton, at Dowling's suggestion, consulted C. M. Chapman, a Wisconsin tax official accepted as an authority in tax assessment by the National Association of Tax Administrators. He then obtained the views of George Mitchell, tax economist for the Federal Reserve Bank in Chicago and president of the National Tax Association. Hamilton also conferred with experts of the Interstate Commerce Commission. He began to take an active role in the National Association of Tax Administrators, becoming a member, and eventually chairman, of the Association's Committee on Railroad Allocation. Later he was appointed to the Association's Committee on Valuation.

Raising the Assessment

IN 1945, very shortly after his discussion with Chapman, Hamilton, with Dowling's approval, announced that henceforth his Department would ascertain system value before it attempted to determine the Alabama value of public utility property. Each railroad would be required to file information about its system value. The Department would use data compiled by the ICC on reproduction costs, and information provided by other public and private agencies on stock and bond value. The railroads grumbled at first—arguing that it would be difficult to compile the information that Hamilton required—despite the fact that in the 1933 litigation they had advocated use of system value to prove the declining worth of their property. However, since most of the information was already required by the ICC, it was not long before the railroads acquiesced. This did not mean that the companies accepted Hamilton's methods of determining system value which included the three factors: reproduction costs less depreciation as reported in ICC figures; capitalized earnings over a period of the preceding five years; and stocks and bonds as determined by averages of high and low monthly quotations over the preceding year.

Shortly after he announced he would use the system value approach, Hamilton decided that his division also would use the allocation formula then being developed by the NATA Allocation Committee. This formula reflected the pattern of railroad use in a state—that is, the relation between terminal business and hauling business and costs. Still quite elementary in 1944 and 1945, the formula was later polished and improved until, in early 1947, the NATA Committee on Allocation felt ready to recommend it to the Association. The Association itself on June 25, 1947, recommended its adoption to tax officials.

Hamilton felt that the formula, even as it

stood in 1945, offered substantial advantages, as it would permit accurate allocation to each state of the value of railroad property within that state. For example, through use of this formula, Alabama, which was not predominantly a terminal state, would receive its fair share of terminal values. Under the old assessment procedure, it might have received almost nothing. Widespread adoption of the formula would induce uniform railroad assessment among the states, Hamilton believed, and it would make for equitable treatment for the railroads as well. Despite the fact that the allocation formula was controversial, Hamilton and Commissioner Dowling were convinced that it represented a step in the right direction.

Startling disparities appeared immediately after Hamilton instituted the procedure of first determining system value, then using the NATA allocation formula to determine the proportion of system value in Alabama. He discovered that there was no real equalization among railroad taxpayers. The percentage of Alabama value upon which the railroads were paying taxes ranged from 34 to 72 percent, the average being 45 percent. He found, further, that the Southern, one of the two most valuable railroads in the state, was paying taxes on a lower percentage of its Alabama value than any other railroad. To Hamilton it seemed imperative that all railroad assessments should be equalized and set at the average level.

Hamilton believed that the first step toward equalization was, necessarily, raising the rate of assessment on the Southern, since it was farthest out of line. After this had been done, Hamilton felt, he could proceed to raise and lower other assessments to bring them into line with the average. Accordingly, he sent to the Southern in the Commissioner's name notice of a 1945 tentative assessment twelve percent higher than the assessment for 1944.

Equalization vs. "Gentlemen's Agreement"

The Southern protested Hamilton's assessment to the Commissioner of Revenue. Haddon Johnson came to Montgomery to remind Dowling that the "gentlemen's agreement" of 1943 had not been rescinded and that its terms precluded a raise of twelve percent. Dowling had never heard of the agreement, and he assigned a member of the Department's legal staff to investigate. The following morning, the Commissioner received a memorandum substantiating Johnson's statement. Dowling then said that he would consider himself bound by the agreement and would increase the Southern assessment only by the taxable value of its new acquisitions. He and Johnson agreed on a 1945 assessment two percent higher than that of 1944.

Hamilton did not attend the conferences between Dowling and Johnson, but Dowling told him of the decision and of the "gentlemen's agreement" still in force. Hamilton protested that the state ought never to have made such an arrangement and certainly ought not to continue it. Dowling, however, took the position that however doubtful the origin of the agreement, it had been entered into by the Administration still in office and the Department must therefore observe it.

Throughout 1946 Hamilton contended in vain that the state could not validly make an agreement not to raise taxes. He sent the Southern notice of a tentative assessment approximately twelve percent higher than the assessment for 1945 and fifteen percent higher than that for 1944. Again Haddon Johnson visited Montgomery. Dowling had meanwhile resigned, but Acting Commissioner Pitts, an old employee of the Department, reaffirmed the 1943 agreement. This time, Pitts and Johnson set the assessment at 0.8 percent higher than for 1945, and three percent higher than for 1944.

The Folsom Administration

In 1946, the voters of Alabama elected James E. Folsom Governor. Folsom's campaign theme was one of concern for the little man, as opposed to the "Big Mules," as he termed the wealthy landholders, industrialists, and the big corporations.

Folsom appointed as Commissioner of Revenue Philip J. Hamm, a school teacher from a small town in southern Alabama. Hamm's political views and his ideas concerning the common man and the "Big Mules" were substantially the same as Folsom's. He was inclined to be idealistic and came to his new job with a sense of mission. (Folsom later chose Hamm to run as his successor, Alabama governors being forbidden to succeed themselves.)

Compared with the two most recent commissioners, Hamm had little experience in taxation. He was more interested in implementing a broad philosophy of taxation than in overseeing the details of departmental organization and procedure.

When Hamm became Commissioner, Hamilton almost immediately obtained an appointment with him. Hamilton briefed his new chief on events of the preceding two or three years as they pertained to the Franchise and Public Utilities Division. He described the "gentlemen's agreement," and also told Hamm that for the preceding two years he had been barred from the assessment conferences between the Commissioner of Revenue and the Southern's representative. Hamilton added that in the future he wished to be present at these conferences if only to give his argument. To this the new Commissioner readily agreed.

Hamilton's knowledge of public utility assessment impressed Hamm. Moreover, the conclusions which Hamilton had derived from application of expert techniques happened to coincide with Hamm's philosophy of taxation. Hamilton believed that the Southern assessment had to be raised in the interest of equalization, and Hamm agreed, for somewhat different and more diffuse reasons. Hamm was much interested in Hamilton's statements that, judged by systematic criteria, several railroads—the Southern in particular—were being assessed too low. Hamm agreed heartily that all "low" roads should be raised, but he was not so sure that it was desirable to lower the rates for railroads then paying above the 45 percent average rate. Here Hamilton's procedures and Hamm's philosophy parted company, but the split was of comparatively little significance at this time.

Attempts at Compromise

As the time drew near for making out 1947 tentative assessment notices, Haddon Johnson decided to come to Montgomery to talk with Hamm and Hamilton. In previous years, the Southern had not sent a representative until the notice of tentative assessment had been received. (The Southern had fallen into this habit during Henry Knight's illness, when it had seemed more sensible to wait until the appeal stage and thereby talk directly with the Commissioner concerning the final or permanent assessment.) Johnson explained his departure from custom by saying that he had known personally the previous commissioners but had not yet met Hamm. He may also have had some uneasiness about the status of the 1943 "gentlemen's agreement" under Folsom's anti-big-business administration.

Any such uneasiness was warranted. Hamilton informed Johnson that the Southern's 1947 assessment would be $25,000,000. Hamilton had arrived at this figure by applying the NATA's newly refined allocation formula to what he had determined to be the system value. The tentative assessment was 26 percent higher than the tentative assessment for 1945 and 23 percent higher than the tentative assessment for 1946. Twenty-five million dollars represented an increase of 38 percent over the actual 1945 assessment and nearly 37 percent over the actual 1946 assessment of roughly $18,000,000.

Johnson countered with an offer of $20,000,000. He declared that the proposed $25,000,000 figure was completely unreasonable. After hours of discussion, Hamilton suggested that he might recommend to the Commissioner a compromise assessment figure of $21,750,000, roughly half the difference between the preceding year's assessment and the $25,000,000.

Hamilton's decision to recommend a compromise to the Commissioner was based on three considerations. One was that the sizable jump to $25,000,000 might justifiably be considered a hardship for the Southern. Second, an increase to $21,750,000 for 1947, with an understanding that the assessment would probably be raised to $25,000,000 in 1948, would achieve the necessary first step toward equalization of railroad assessments. Third, Hamilton thought that the Railway would accept the $21,750,000 assessment, in view of the fact that it did not greatly exceed Johnson's proposed figure of $20,000,000. If the Southern could be persuaded to accept the compromise, the Department would avoid considerable administrative work as well as a probable lawsuit.

Johnson Rejects an Offer

However, Johnson would not accept the compromise. He asked Hamilton to recommend to the Commissioner the Southern's offer of $20,-000,000. Hamilton did not feel that he could. It would not come sufficiently close to the $25,000,000 figure that he considered to be the just and reasonable assessment, and moreover, a $20,000,000 assessment would put him in a less strategic position to reach the $25,000,000 goal the following year.

Hamilton and Johnson conferred with Hamm the following day. According to Hamilton, Hamm was much interested in the valuations the Southern had filed with the Public Service Commission for rate-making purposes and with the Department of Revenue for purposes of income tax. Three times Hamm stated that he thought the tax value of the Southern, as indicated by rate-making and income tax figures, was closer to $30,000,000 than to $25,000,000. Johnson noted during this conference that Hamm appeared highly excited and that the climate in the Department had become one of hostility toward the Southern.

Hamilton then recommended the compromise figure of $21,750,000. Hamm appeared to consider this very carefully. He asked to see the black loose-leaf notebook that Hamilton had brought with him. According to Hamm, this notebook contained Hamilton's formulae. According to Hamilton and Johnson, however, it contained the record of previous Southern assessments. Hamm scanned these data, and pointing to the 1932 assessment, $21,550,252, selected that amount as the tentative assessment for 1947. It was an unfortunate selection, because the 1932 tentative assessment was the one that had been reduced after protest to $17,347,000; apparently the Department's records in the "black book" had never been amended to show the actual rather than the tentative figure.

Hamm's action in ending the discussion with the figure from the black book later provided the Southern with a colorful instance of alleged "crystal ball" assessment. Actually, however, Hamilton later persuaded Hamm to send formal notification of a tentative assessment at his original compromise figure of $21,750,000. Hamilton interpreted the black book episode as Hamm's effort to show Johnson that he, not Hamilton, exercised the power to set the assessment.

At the close of the conference, Johnson asked Hamilton what would happen next. Hamilton inferred that this question meant the railroad planned to accept the compromise figure. He replied that he would send out a notice of tentative assessment for the amount set by the Commissioner. Johnson seemed to acquiesce, and Hamilton thought it unnecessary to obtain any more formal expression of acceptance, oral or written, at the conclusion of the conference.

Upon receiving the tentative assessment, the Southern returned a notification of contest and a request for hearing, the granting of which was mandatory. Hamilton was surprised. Protests and appeals to the Commissioner were not unusual, but Hamilton had thought that the railroad knew in this instance exactly where the Commissioner stood. However, the Southern was looking to an appeal to the courts, which would not be possible until all administrative remedies had been exhausted.

Appeal to the Commissioner

The Southern's decision to appeal to the Commissioner placed the Department in an embarrassing position. It was settled practice that tentative assessments were never increased at a protest hearing. In fact, in nearly all cases, protested tentative assessments had been lowered.

These precedents presented a problem to Hamilton. He could not agree to lowering the tentative assessment. He was convinced that, should an appeal be taken to the court, the Department could not go into court with the $21,750,000 assessment because it could not justify the figure on the basis of any system of valuation or allocation. The method Hamilton had employed and which he could lay before the court had yielded a figure of $25,000,000. To go in with the $21,750,000 assessment would be a damaging blow against the very techniques he had been trying to promote.

Hamilton recalled the state's weaknesses in the 1933 controversy. He believed that these weaknesses sprang primarily from assessment procedures that had been unscientific. He did not want to go into court unable to demonstrate that his assessment was the product of anything but the most precise calculation, tempered, perhaps, by a modicum of informed judgment.

Hamilton also knew that the whole compromise episode would be taken as another instance of the horse trading approach to taxation from which he wished to disassociate himself completely.

The possible Southern plea that the $25,000,000 assessment would excessively increase a taxpayer's burden was answered in Hamilton's thinking by his belief that the Southern had successfully avoided justified increases for two years under the continuation of the "gentlemen's agreement."

There were two other problems in fixing $25,000,000 as the permanent assessment. Was it legal to increase a tentative assessment during the protest hearing before the Commissioner? The Department's legal staff produced the answer that there was no legal bar to raising a tentative assessment. The remaining problem seemed to Hamilton to be an ethical question. In the taxation appeal, he regarded Hamm, his Commissioner, as a judge. He saw himself as an advocate whose job was to present for his side as persuasive an argument as he could muster—but during, and not prior to, the hearing. Hamilton had decided that the final assessment to be set by Hamm should be $25,000,000. But how was he to communicate to the Commissioner the process of reasoning by which he had reached this amount? To put it bluntly, how could he be sure that the Commissioner would set the "right" assessment, one defensible in the probable court tests?

Hamm was new to the job and could quite easily connect an upward revision to the Folsom administration campaign objectives regarding the "Big Mules." Hamilton could be fairly certain that Hamm would not lower the tentative assessment and that he would be tempted to raise it. But Hamm had already spoken on three occasions of $30,000,000 as a possible assessment. To Hamilton $30,000,000 would have been as indefensible a figure to take into court as $21,750,000.

Later, before the Circuit Court, Hamilton testified that he had made no effort to communicate his position to the Commissioner prior to the hearing, and that the Commissioner had scrupulously avoided discussing the forthcoming hearing with him.

As for Hamm's considerations before the hearing, he knew the substance of the legal department's opinion on the legality of a permanent assessment higher than the protested tentative assessment. He said later that he had concluded before the hearing that the Department should not be taken into court with any assessment but one higher than the $21,750,000 compromise. How much he knew of Hamilton's line of thought is uncertain. Of course, the offices and desks of all the chief officials in the Alabama Department of Revenue are located together in a comparatively small section of the Capitol, and conversations over coffee, as in most public offices, are frequent and often concern shop matters.

The Hearing

On the morning of August 6 the Commissioner's hearings began. They were, in many respects, novel proceedings. Not since 1933 had a major utility taxpayer been involved with the Department in a serious controversy. Moreover, Hamm had invited Montgomery and Birmingham newspapermen to attend, a precedent-breaking move that convinced the Southern's representatives that Hamm planned to put on a big show and make as much political capital as possible. Press reports appeared subsequently in newspapers throughout the state and even in the *Wall Street Journal*. Frontis Moore, an Alabama lawyer retained by the railroad, later questioned the legality of having newspapermen present, on the grounds that the value of a taxpayer's property was a private matter; but no formal protest was entered.

Although Hamilton regarded himself as an advocate and Hamm as the judge, Hamm certainly did not view himself as the objective and impartial judge. As in the tentative assessment hearing, Hamm again exhibited great interest in the income tax figures the Southern had filed. Although Johnson explained that his office had nothing to do with income tax matters, Hamm pursued this line of questioning relentlessly, clearly implying that Johnson was deliberately withholding information.

Hamm's questions to Hamilton on the 1943 agreement and the pre-1944 assessment practices of the Department were clearly intended to bring out the past "bad" practices in the state's dealings with the Southern. These questions indicated that in his seven months as Commissioner, Hamm had learned Hamilton's point of view very well, was sympathetic to it, and knew what to expect from Hamilton.

Finally Hamm set the assessment at precisely $25,000,000. Formal notices were served on the Southern without any accompanying findings of fact. All efforts of the Southern Railway to obtain copies of the hearing record and of Hamilton's calculations were unsuccessful. The Department's explanation was that the record as transcribed from the shorthand notes of two departmental stenographers was incomplete, inaccurate, and highly confusing. Although Hamilton began revising it, he never got beyond page two.

Hamilton regarded it as bad strategy to let the Southern's agents see his exact computations, part of which he had described in some detail at the hearing. He felt that the Railway had demonstrated in the past that it was completely capable of defending its interests, and he had no wish to arm it further. There was now no doubt that the Southern was going to appeal to the courts; Johnson had remarked that Hamilton had won one round but had not yet gotten the final decision.

Reaction to the $25,000,000 assessment was mixed. To Haddon Johnson, litigation was always unfortunate. In this instance, however, he felt there was no alternative but to appeal to the courts from the Commissioner's ruling which, he felt, had set an indefensible assessment at the conclusion of a highly partisan hearing. Johnson believed that Hamilton had also been surprised and disappointed at the outcome, since in Johnson's opinion, Hamilton could not have believed $25,000,000 to be a fair assessment. But actually Hamilton was greatly relieved. Johnson believed that Commissioner Hamm was not interested in equalization but only in raising corporate taxes as part of the Folsom program.

Frontis Moore said later that he had been shocked at the highly unjudicial nature of the hearing, and that never before, except in cases of error by the taxpayer, had the final assessment been higher than the tentative assessment. Moore was affronted by statements that "pull" had been used to keep the Southern assessment unjustifiably low. Both Johnson and Moore felt that the final assessment might have been raised as punishment to the Southern for protesting the compromise amount.

Legislative Repercussions

The hearing and the Commissioner's ruling had noticeable repercussions in the Legislature, which was then in the midst of the first session of the Folsom administration. The Governor's leadership was being challenged by a large group of legislators who opposed Folsom's political objectives. To the Folsom opposition, the Southern case was but part of a larger drive to exercise state power to set aside and raise assessments of business and industrial firms made by local assessors. The Southern case took place during the same period as reassessment actions against the B. F. Goodrich Company at Tuscaloosa, the Goodyear Tire and Rubber Company at Gadsden, the Goodyear Mills at Decatur, two plants of the Robbins Tire and Rubber Company, the Colbert Hotel Company, Alabama Hosiery Mills, Ingalls Ship-Building Company, Nebraska Consolidated Mill Company, and Cooper Wells and Company. The proposed reassessments on these companies provided for increases ranging from 83 percent to 1,700 percent, with a median increase of 300 percent.

The administration's foes charged that these reassessments were not aimed at equalization, but were merely the product of an anti-big-business philosophy. Commissioner Hamm defended his Department against this charge by stating that with the inadequate staffing resulting from skimpy appropriations, he could not begin a comprehensive reassessment program; he was attempting to deal first with large taxpayers in order that their reassessments might set an example for local tax officials on all other property.

In the closing weeks of the 1947 legislative session the anti-Folsom forces introduced a bill to strip the Department of Revenue of its power to set aside local assessments. The bill purported to be a measure to prevent the Folsom administration from driving industry from the state and from discriminating against certain classes of taxpayers. It was placed on special order but lost the race against adjournment and was recommitted for action in the next session.

While these legislative reactions to the whole assessment fight were given a good deal of newspaper publicity, the Southern case itself received little coverage throughout its entire course. None of the parties involved made a serious effort to present to the general public the basic issues of the case, such as the concept of equalization.

The Southern Prepares Its Case

It was in this environment of legislative hostility and public ignorance that the Department began to prepare its case for the Circuit Court. It sought to defend the full $25,000,000 assessment and to win court approval of the valuation procedures and allocation formula used to compute that figure.

The first step was to retain special counsel to prepare the Department's case. Francis Hare, a Birmingham attorney, was selected. The decision to employ a special counsel rather than the Attorney General was apparently made by Hamm, Hamilton, and Attorney General Albert A. Carmichael. Carmichael was a political independent. Although Attorney General during the Folsom administration, he was elected on his own political strength. (His family was old and respected in the state.) He had never identified himself closely with Folsom's brand of "liberalism" although he was considered neither reactionary nor conservative. He was not on particularly good terms with Commissioner Hamm or with the legal staff of the Revenue Department, even though that staff was composed of lawyers on detached service from his own office. Carmichael was an ardent opponent of the Dixiecrats in Alabama, where President Truman and the "regular" Democrats were barred from the ballot in 1948. This campaign was already brewing at the time the state's case against the Southern Railway was being prepared, and Carmichael's interest in national politics may have overshadowed his interest in the Southern litigation.

The Special Counsel himself thought he had been retained primarily because, as an attorney in private practice, he would be immune to political pressures. He had had no particular experience in public utility work, although at one time he had represented the trucking companies in the state. The fact that these companies were natural rivals of the railroad might, he thought, have influenced his selection.

Hare insisted, as a condition of taking the case, that "politics" must be kept out and that the case must not be turned into the kind of political show that the hearings had provided. In his conduct of the case he avoided bringing into it any of the central political figures concerned. Commissioner Hamm was never called to testify for the state, and his name was mentioned only infrequently by the state, although he was a target of the Southern's attorneys.

A second decision made by the state was to secure three expert witnesses: C. M. Chapman, in charge of railroad assessments in Wisconsin and a leading member of the National Association of Tax Administrators' Committee on Allocation; George Mitchell, tax economist for the Federal Reserve Bank in Chicago and president of the National Tax Association; and Harold M. Groves, professor of economics at the University of Wisconsin, author of several books on public finance, and tax consultant for the United States Treasury. All three had been concerned with the development of the allocation formula, and the experience of all three lay on the side of public tax authorities rather than on the side of the taxpayers.

The Southern's Strategy

The Southern was also building its case with the help of tax experts, principally that of James W. Martin. At the time of the trial, Martin was professor of economics and director of the Bureau of Business Research at the University of Kentucky. He had served as a consultant on tax problems for nearly twenty years, advising, at various times, the United States Government and a number of states, counties, and municipalities as well as the Southern Railway. He had served for over three years as Kentucky's first Revenue Commissioner, and he had been president of three national tax associations and president of the Southern Economics Association. He was the author of a Virginia report on railroad evaluation.

The Railway's other two witnesses were E. R. Oliver, vice-president of the Southern in charge of traffic; and Dr. Herbert R. Simpson, professor of public finance at Northwestern University, and a former member of President Herbert Hoover's committee on taxation and home ownership.

The Trial and the Appeal

COMMISSIONER HAMM'S FINAL assessment and the Southern's administrative appeal both occurred in August 1947. The case came to trial in the Circuit Court of Montgomery County in April 1948 and lasted two weeks.

The presiding judge of the Circuit Court was Walter B. Jones, member of an old Alabama family, and son of a distinguished former state legislator and Governor, Thomas Goode Jones. He had served on the Montgomery City Council, the State Highway Commission, and in the State Legislature before his appointment to the Montgomery Circuit Court in 1920.

Because he presided over the chief court with general original jurisdiction in the capital city, Judge Jones had, over the years, reviewed many state administrative decisions. In fact, he seemed almost a part of the administrative process. As noted on page 518, the Judge believed that on utility assessment matters he was empowered by existing statutes to review cases of this kind *de novo;* he did not have to confine his decision to the legality of previous proceedings. And he had the power to set whatever assessment he thought fair. Judge Jones' concepts of utility tax law were not an entirely unknown quantity, for he had decided the 1933 cases which had lowered railroad assessments. Since then, there had been no significant utility property tax litigation.

The Southern's Case

The Southern's case was handled by J. T. Stokely, a former judge, as principal counsel, together with Frontis Moore and several others. The railroad followed two lines of attack: first, to hammer at defects in the valuation and allocation techniques; and second, to object to defects in the Department's administrative procedures. The state filed a demurrer to this second set of charges, and the Circuit Court sustained the demurrer. Thus attacks on the procedures were not admitted as relevant to the question at issue, and the argument was restricted to the substantive matters of the allocation formula and the three elements of system value.

Some years later, in recollecting the handling of the trial, Frontis Moore attributed the Southern's avoidance of the procedural questions to instructions given him and Judge Stokely by the president of the Southern, who had been disturbed by the publicity given the charges of political influence in earlier administrations, and who was concerned about the railroad's public relations. Robert G. Pruitt, also a counsel for the railroad, could recall no instructions. But it appeared likely that Moore and Stokely would have been guided by their knowledge of the president's attitude, whether or not he had given them formal instructions.

Another reason for the railroad's neglect of the alleged defects in administrative procedure was Haddon Johnson's view that the manner in which the administrative agency operated was not a matter of great concern, since any assessment could be appealed to the courts for *de novo* review. And in the courts the requirements of due process were certain to be met.

The Southern set forth the heart of its position in its subsequent Reply Brief on appeal to the Alabama Supreme Court:

> Reproduction cost, while perhaps under the statute may be considered, is not a factor of value. To consider a factor is not to give it weight if it appear not relevant in the circumstances. The bloodlines of an unraced thoroughbred gelding might immensely influence his market value, but fall into utter insignificance after his hundredth race. So, in respect to valuing a brand new railroad, untried in operation, cost or cost of reproduction might cut some figure, but in the minds of practical people investing their money in the plant after years of operation it would be obliterated as a factor by proved capacity for making profits or incurring deficits. Moreover, the State, while its own witnesses testified that the Bureau of Valuation figures (ICC) for the cost of reproduction of railroads by States, and the actual figures for Alabama were available, nevertheless took, or at-

tempted to take, a percentage of the entire reproduction cost as representing reproduction cost in Alabama. Moreover, Mr. Hamilton weighted these figures in some way known only to himself, and the figures that he used are not any official figures of the Bureau of the Interstate Commerce Commission.

Second, the chief and practically the only support which the State had for its case, is based on net railway operating income, which, as we all know, was very high during the war years. Every one of the witnesses both for the State and for the taxpayer, with the possible exception of Mr. Hamilton, testified that war earnings were not normal. Mr. Chapman said that neither abnormally high nor abnormally low earnings should be considered. Yet the State in order to support its case, made its chief criterion the high earnings of the war years, ignoring completely the earnings for 1946, the year involved, and for 1947, which figures were available at the time of the trial. The taxpayer, to the contrary, in an effort to arrive at some period recognized by all as being an average period, chose the years 1936-1939, which the Government of the United States used for the purposes of the excess profits tax. The State repeatedly refers to the taxpayer's using the low income years.

. . . While the year 1938 was low, the four years average represented average income; 1936 was good, 1939 was very good. Moreover, the Federal Government, as was brought out in the bulletin of the Bureau of Internal Revenue, did not pick these figures out of a hat, or even a "black book," but by exhaustive study showed that those years were almost exactly the same as the average for the preceding eighteen years. Therefore we submit that the years used by the taxpayer as being average years are based on long and detailed studies by the Government of the United States and are as nearly official as any that could be had. Even, however, combining those years with 1946 and 1947 would make an average income far below that used by Mr. Hamilton and by the State's experts.

In the trial of the railroad cases in 1932 and 1933, the State attempted to use a five-year basis, going back to the high income years of 1928 and 1929. This was rejected as not being a proper criterion for the depression years of 1932 and 1933. Actually there was less difference in net railway operating income for the Southern between the year 1933 and 1939, the peak, than between the year 1942, the peak war year, and the year 1946, the last year under consideration here, and practically the same difference exists if 1947 is used. We submit that any figure or combinations of figures which would use the high war years as a basis is highly objectionable. . . .

Nowhere, . . . is there any support for the argument made by the State that the assessment of a utility is a scientific thing to be determined by a group of so-called experts by putting certain figures together, taking the average of them, and declaring the result to be the proper valuation of the property.

The State's case is built up entirely on formulae which we think and will hereafter argue are based on wrong premises, but regardless of the selection of years or other points of dispute between the experts and between the State and the taxpayer, the State's primary position that an assessment of a utility is a simple matter of collecting certain statistics, averaging certain figures, using certain formulae evolved by some group of so-called experts, and that the result *ipso facto* IS THE CORRECT VALUATION OF THE PROPERTY, IS, WE SUBMIT, IN VIOLATION OF THE STATUTE, contrary to common sense, and its establishment would make any such assessment invalid. Valuation of properties, whether simple or complex, is not a mere matter of mathematics.

The Southern's Reply Brief also indicated, in some detail, the objections of Martin, principal expert for the railroad, to Hamilton's valuation and allocation methods.

While Dr. Martin in reaching his conclusions perhaps used ultimately a formula, he nevertheless applied his knowledge and judgment, based on consideration of a great many factors, to determine the proper elements to be put in that formula. Among other things which Dr. Martin pointed out and relied on was the trend of freight and passenger revenues, both up and down. He showed that freight revenues held up from 119 million in 1941 to 190 million in 1944, while passenger revenues rose from 21 million to 71 million in the same period. From 1944 to 1946 freight revenues declined to 168 million while passenger revenue fell from a high of 71 million to 44 million. He also pointed out that percentage-wise, freight revenues of the Southern in recent years have been a smaller proportion of the total revenues than that of other railroads in the Southeastern District. He emphasized that while freight revenues continued in the black through 1946 and 1947, passenger revenues fell from a profit of 12 million to a deficit of 9 million in 1947 and the prospect was that such deficits would continue. He stated, which everybody knows to be a practical fact, that a railroad cannot control passenger business as they cannot remove passenger trains, however great the loss may be, without the permission of the Interstate Commerce Commission or the State public service body, and usually on account of local political conditions, the removal of any train is very difficult.

Dr. Martin stated that the maintenance on the Southern was slightly lower than other Class 1 railroads in the Southeastern District. He pointed out that costs had gone up with extraordinary rapidity; materials and supplies were far more expensive; but that the greatest increase was in wages and salaries, payrolls having been increased 31 million, 573 thousand against rate increases of 23 million. He pointed out, however, that rate increases often were made at the cost of business.

Dr. Martin pointed out that the net profit in 1938 on a dollar's worth of earnings meant 21¢ of net railway operating income; whereas in 1946 the figure was only 9¢. This is a striking illustration of the difference between gross and net existing at the time this great increase was made.

Dr. Martin stated that the Southern has lost more ground than its competitors since the war; the abandonment of camps and other war plants which have been favorably situated contributing to this fact. He mentioned obsolescence and explained in answer to the court's question that obsolescence as applied to a railroad particularly meant the dry-up of the territory which it served; that originally many of the Southern lines, particularly branch lines, served the timber industry and the cutting down of the timber had left these lines practically obsolete. He pointed out that a third approximately of the Alabama lines of the Southern produce a freight traffic density of only 17.5% of the system's traffic density. With reference to the reproduction cost he said it would be ridiculous to say that when net operating income fell 28%, the value increased 12%, as use of reproduction cost did.

In a letter written by Martin to the authors of this study in 1952 he advocated the proposition that utility valuation should be neither a formula, however intelligent, nor guesswork:

In my own judgment as I think I made clear in the record, the better choice is one which abandons both approaches and places the valuation on a definitely professional scale. . . . It is conceivable that an attorney, in determining whether a particular action is or is not constitutional, could set up a guesswork system and get an answer. Alternately, he could devise a formula for arriving at an answer. Neither of these answers would be particularly defensible. The intelligent constitutional lawyer would actually accumulate as much evidence from the constitution, the record of constitutional debates, and especially the decisions under the constitution [as he could], and from the wealth of facts bearing on the decision he would apply a professional judgment. . . . In making an appraisal of any property of any consequence, the intelligent appraiser does a substantially identical thing; that is, he brings to bear all the evidence, marshals it in as effective fashion as possible, and then expresses a professional judgment. . . .

It is, of course, fair to say that an appraisai formula can be designed in such a manner as to represent a distinct improvement over sheer guesswork. . . . The wisdom of the formula depends completely on whether or not the ingredients in the formula are designed to measure the value of all of the properties appraised. Thus, the ingredients in a formula must be applicable to all railroads within the jurisdiction; otherwise, the existence of the formula tends to introduce inequalities.

Dr. Martin went on to criticize Hamilton's allocation formula:

When the early stages of the Southern case were enacted, nobody was aware of the fact that the NATA allocation formula operated badly in the case of the Southern Railway because it was so unusual and consequently had the effect in application to this line, in the light of practices in other states, of apportioning a total equal to more than 100 per cent. It is a fact, however, that in the later stages of the controversy there was a good deal of feeling on the part of the railway company that, in addition to the basic objections to the formula, it was peculiarly objectionable in the particular case because no other Southern Railway state was in practice actually applying the formula and because it operated to make the total (in the light of other states' practices) more than 100 per cent.

Alabama's Pleading

The state's position on Hamilton's formula was quite different. In its Brief on Appeal to the Supreme Court, it presented these statements concerning valuation:

1. The market value of the stock and bonds of the Southern Railway System during the year preceding October 1, 1946, is a matter of record in standard financial publications and all factors in this calculation should be constant. There should be no room for difference of opinion.

2. "The average net earnings is averaged over a period of five years" prior to October 1, 1946, and is taken from the records of the taxpayer itself. The figures used by the State for these five years are the same figures used by the taxpayer for these five years. It is possible to differ about the rate of capitalization, for instance whether it should be 4%, 5%, or 6%. The State's exhibits demonstrate that at any rate which could be reasonably selected, the resulting valuation more than sustains the assessment.

This objective approach throws into bold relief an important fallacy in the taxpayer's calculations. Instead of taking the average net earnings for the five years commanded by the statute, the taxpayer selects certain other years when its earnings were far less. As a matter of law, we are all forbidden to accept those years as the basis. It is not necessary to point out that abnormal depression years were selected, and that if the statutory "five year next preceding" rule makes for a higher valuation in one taxable year, it makes for a lower assessment following lean years. It would be possible for the value indicated by the capitalization of the five year average to be discounted if the earnings for the period covered be considered high. This is possible but the mandate of the statute is plain. The previous five years is the period provided for the averaging of earnings.[1]

3. The valuation made for rate-making purposes by the Interstate Commerce Commission is a matter of record from its own reports and admits of no difference of opinion. The parties stipulated the correctness of the figures as such. The statute in this instance states that we must include this factor.

The second conspicuous fallacy of the taxpayer is thus brought to light. In bill and brief and in expert testimony the taxpayer contends that the Interstate Commerce Commission figures are entitled to no weight, and they received no consideration in the exhibits of the taxpayer calculating the assessment according to their contentions.

Again, it is not necessary for the State to point to the beautiful accuracy of the Interstate Commerce Commission figures, which the railroad stoutly asserts are too little if anything when rates are to be made, nor need we here stress the court decisions supporting the contention that the Interstate Commerce figures are valuable aids to assessments.

The State's position on Hamilton's allocation formula is summed up in the following excerpts from its brief:

The determination of allocation of the percentage of the value of the railroad which lies in Alabama involves the evolution of the all important "allocation fraction." It does admit of dispute. The position of the State here is that when its "allocation fraction" is analyzed and compared with that employed by the taxpayer, the State's allocation fraction is plainly and clearly sustained by logic, authority, and expert testimony, and that used by the taxpayer will not withstand any of these three tests.

[1] Actually, the statute did not specify the *preceding* five years, but the state maintained this was the legislative intent.

The statute says that the allocation shall be upon the basis of the proportion of the "total lines or business within this State" . . . "to the total lines of business both inside and outside of this State" *or* on the proportion of its total receipts within the state to the total receipts of the entire railway system.

Both of the words "lines" and "business" admit of construction and the statute cannot be translated into a precise formula without expert testimony.

For example, if a railroad had total lines of five thousand miles of which seven hundred fifty miles consisted of a track running across some barren state (called in the vernacular a "bridge State") where little or no freight was received or discharged and little or no business done, the experts agree on both sides that valuation giving to that State 750/5000ths of that railroad would be unfair. Likewise, "business" may refer to receipts or to expenses or to line haul activity or to terminal activity.

The evolution of the allocation fraction is a highly specialized scientific problem. Alabama's P. B. Hamilton who made this assessment has received national recognition for his work on this subject and is regarded as an expert in the field. For the trial the State brought to Montgomery two men who were elected for the sole reason that they are the two foremost authorities on this subject in the United States, and their testimony in the record, while it will take study to get a grasp of it, will then disclose with the unmistakable ring of truth that the Alabama allocation fraction is right and that the taxpayer's allocation fraction is a shabby attempt to evade Alabama's taxation.

For illustration, we sought in vain to have the taxpayer test his mathematical problems by giving us the proportion of the railroad which lay in each of the other states where it is found to see that if we added together the percentages in each of the states the total would be 100% as it would necessarily be if correct, and the question was never answered.

The taxpayer made a contention that only the second factor mentioned by the statute, "total receipts," should be considered and they construed "total receipts" to mean gross revenues which according to their "green sheet" (the allocation data furnished by the taxpayer on its report to the State) happens to produce a smaller allocation fraction. Among other fallacies of this contention it ignores the statute which commands us to consider "total lines or business within the state" and it is in our judgment erroneous to construe "total receipts" as synonymous with the figure furnished by them as "gross revenues." Gross revenues as reflected by the taxpayer's bookkeeping system is partially sound, that is to the extent of intrastate revenues, but the important figure of interstate revenues for Alabama is itself developed by them with allocation procedures not disclosed by the report; and the Welch report which was cited by both the taxpayer and the State as a recognized authority on railroad assessments states that the gross revenue, for the reason that we have mentioned, is a "dull" factor. In other words, the taxpayer begs the question involved, in this: To determine the correct allocation fraction it *allocated* to Alabama arbitrarily a percentage of the interstate gross revenues while the "green sheet" report does not disclose how the figures are determined.

A Defeat for Both Parties

Commissioner Hamm's final assessment and the Southern's appeal both occurred in August 1947. The case came to trial in April 1948, and the trial lasted some two weeks. On September 27, 1948, Judge Jones handed down his decision. It was brief—three and a quarter legal size, double-spaced, typewritten sheets—and it primarily consisted of a formal recital of the facts of the tentative and final assessment, and of the statutory assignment conferred upon the court to give *de novo* review and to alter the Department's assessment in the event that assessment was considered too low or too high. The one substantive paragraph read as follows:

> After full consideration of the record on this appeal, the Court has come to the conclusion that the final assessment of $25,000,000 made in this case on August 6, 1947, by the State Department of Revenue, is too high; and, now proceeding to its statutory duty of fixing the amount of such assessment the Court is of opinion that a proper assessment of the properties of the Southern Railway Company in Alabama, for the year 1947, as of October 1, 1946, is the sum of $21,250,000.

The amount thus fixed by the Court was approximately $5,000,000 less than the Department's tentative assessment, and nearly $4,000,000 less than its final assessment, but it was about $3,000,000 more than the assessment for the previous year and more than the railroad had said it was prepared to accept when it began negotiations. In no way did the decision indicate the process by which the figure $21,250,000 had been reached; but it was observed by the litigants that the reduction was precisely fifteen percent of the $25,000,000 fixed in the final assessment.

The Southern did not appeal from this decision. Attorney Moore said he opposed making an appeal, since, by law, the Supreme Court could not overrule the Circuit Court unless the lower court's findings of facts contained palpable errors. In view of the brevity of the Circuit Court's opinion, it would have been difficult to prove (or disprove) a palpable error.

The State Appeals

The Department, however, decided to carry an appeal to the Alabama Supreme Court. This decision appears to have been made almost exclusively by Hamilton and Hare, with Hamm and Carmichael giving consent. Hamilton wanted to appeal, first, because he felt he would be satisfied with nothing less than the $25,000,000 assessment which was the product of "precise" calculation; and second, because he strongly hoped to see the Supreme Court approve his valuation and allocation techniques. Hare felt that since the Circuit Judge had reached his decision without revealing any of the grounds on which it was based, the state might have a good chance of winning its appeal.

The state was taking a gamble in appealing. The Court might sustain the Circuit Court, it might remand the case to the Circuit Court for further findings of fact, or it might grant the state's request and raise the assessment. It might, however, lower the assessment. This would lose money for the state and might also constitute a repudiation of Hamilton's methods. For that matter, if the Supreme Court were to fail to give express approval to Hamilton's methods, its omission would be a more severe blow than was the same failure in the Circuit Court. However, it was decided to take the gamble in the hope of winning high stakes.

Hamilton and Hare carried the burden of preparing the state's appeal, and Hamilton, in effect, served as author of the state's reply brief. The appeal brief assigned error to the opinion of the Circuit Court, urging that Judge Jones had merely taken the state's assessment of $25,000,000 and reduced it arbitrarily by fifteen percent. The following paragraphs from the Brief indicate the tenor of the state's argument:

> We vigorously insist that the assessments made by this Department ought not to be repudiated upon a record and a circuit court opinion which do not demonstrate any error in the State's method of procedure or point out how the State could fix such

an assessment in any better manner and upon a record and opinion which do not demonstrate that the State's findings were in any way opposed to the weight of the evidence. No greater mistake in public policy could be made than one which in effect confides to the court the intricate and voluminous duty of central tax assessment and particularly so where there is substituted for the measured and accurate statutory assessment of a department created for and experienced in that specialized work, a circuit court review which after three weeks of trial arrives at its result by cutting a Gordian knot which the law says must be untied, by a process no more judicial or accurate than substituting the toss of a coin for processes which are required to be highly complex in order to take into consideration economic, scientific and mathematical factors essential to accuracy and equality. . . .

If the $25,000,000 assessment made by the State is upheld by the Supreme Court of Alabama, the meaning of the decision is plain. We uphold an assessment made by trained men in conformity to statutory procedures, working where discretion and judgment are involved according to modern authorities. We uphold an assessment which is sustained by the expert testimony of expert witnesses brought to Alabama for the trial by the State who testified that they went through the entire process of making the assessment themselves, auditing the State's facts and methods, and these men testified that the assessment was conservative and correct.

If we reduce the $25,000,000 assessment and uphold the $21,250,000 assessment fixed by the Circuit Court, what law have we made, what principles have we established for the future guidance and the future information of this and other public utilities? The answer is simply that without a correcting of the personnel, methods or statistical data employed by the Department of Revenue, this public utility assessment, and presumably others in the same category, must be reduced by an arbitrary 15%.

The result of this trial in the Circuit Court of Montgomery County has shocked the central tax authorities all over the country and if allowed to stand it will produce chaos in this important state department. Modern advances will be nullified. Use of patient and scholarly work and study by career personnel are held for naught. Crude and primitive methods will be substituted for statutory and scientific procedures. Guess-work and inaccuracy will be forced into the place of equality and uniformity and millions of dollars of annual revenue will be jeopardized and placed upon an insecure and uncertain status.

We cannot say too forcibly that it is the duty of this court not to shrink from the difficult task of studying and understanding this case and rendering an opinion which will put Alabama's important central tax assessment procedures where its remarkably fine public service can put it, in line with the best and most modern in the country.

And, finally, the state's Reply Brief charged the court as follows:

We respectfully point out to this court that though the Administrative Agencies should be eager to correct their procedures, they cannot very well be expected to do so unless they know wherein their approach is wrong. The Department of Revenue should, and we are sure will, welcome any specific correction in any particular case, as well as any correction of its procedures which is capable of application generally to its assessment problems.

BUT IF THE DEPARTMENT OF REVENUE IS SIMPLY TOLD BY THE COURTS TO USE A PARTICULAR ASSESSMENT FIGURE, THE *RESULT* ARRIVED AT BY THE APPLICATION IN AN UNDISCLOSED MANNER, OF NUMEROUS UNMENTIONED PROCEDURES AND PRINCIPLES, THEN THE COURTS NOT ONLY HAVE SUBSTITUTED THEIR JUDGMENT FOR THAT OF THE DEPARTMENT OF REVENUE, AND HAVE ACTUALLY BECOME THE ASSESSING AUTHORITY, BUT THE DEPARTMENT OF REVENUE IS LEFT IN THE DARK AS TO WHAT PRINCIPLES IT, AS A SUBSIDIARY BODY, SHALL USE IN ITS FUTURE ASSESSMENT WORK. THERE WILL BE THE KNOWLEDGE THAT IF A TAX ASSESSMENT IS NOT REDUCED UPON STRONG OBJECTION THAT THERE MAY BE AN APPEAL. THE VEHEMENCE OF THE OBJECTION AND NOT ITS CONTENT OF SENSE WILL BE THE MOST PRACTICAL CRITERION. "GOVERNMENT BY LAWS" WILL BE IN RETREAT BEFORE THE ANIMAL INSTINCTS OF MEN. AND THIS CASE WILL BE AUTHORITY FOR THE PROPOSITION THAT THE WILL OF THE POWERFUL IS MORE IMPORTANT THAN OUR DEMOCRATIC INSTITUTIONS.

To protect its interests, the Southern filed a cross-assignment of errors, again attacking the assessment method used by Hamilton, and criticizing the stoic experts as being biased in favor of public tax authorities. The railroad argued that since the decision of the Circuit Court was not palpably wrong, even though there was a sharp conflict in evidence, the Supreme Court, under its own rules, could not upset that decision.

Although the appeal was filed in the late

summer of 1948, the final briefs, counter-briefs, and so on, were not filed until October 1950, and it was another year before any decision was forthcoming.

The Case Is Settled

BEFORE THE SUPREME COURT could decide on the state's appeal in the Southern case, two major developments occurred which radically changed the outlook for the Department of Revenue's position, both legally and politically. First, the Supreme Court ruled on the Alabama Power Company case; and second, the 1950 election brought a new Governor into power.

Effect of the Alabama Power Case

In 1949 and 1950, the Commissioner set all utilities assessments at the statutory sixty percent of total Alabama value, as calculated by approximately the same assessment procedure and allocation formula used during the preceding years. This constituted a considerable increase over the 45 percent level previously used. This sixty percent level was appealed to the courts by nearly all the utilities, including the Southern, with the Alabama Power Company taking the lead. The utilities argued that regardless of the statute they should not be assessed at a rate they claimed was far above that assigned by local assessors to non-utility properties.

Before any argument had established what assessment ratio was actually being applied in the various counties, the Alabama Supreme Court ruled, on an appeal from a demurrer, that the state could not apply a higher assessment ratio to the utilities than was generally being applied by local assessors to other property in the state. This meant that classification of property for tax purposes was not permissible, and that the state would certainly lose in any test of its power to tax the utilities at a sixty percent ratio. Furthermore, it did not seem likely that even the 45 percent ratio could be maintained. Such evidence as was available to the Department and to the utilities indicated that, while the local assessment ratios varied greatly, they were substantially below the 45 percent figure. Informally, the utilities indicated that they were no longer willing to accept the 45 percent ratio.

Before any further court action could be taken, the regular quadrennial change in state administration occurred.

Persons Settles the Alabama Power Case

In the summer of 1950, Gordon Persons was chosen the new Governor of Alabama. Second in the field of fifteen was Commissioner Philip Hamm, who had run with the help and blessing of Governor Folsom.

Although as head of the state's Public Service Commission Persons had had various controversies with the utilities, he announced soon after his nomination that he planned to give the state a "conservative administration," and he followed this announcement with public assurances that the state's attitude toward industry would be favorable during his term.

Persons appointed as the new Revenue Commissioner J. M. Edwards of Tuskegee, a graduate of Alabama Polytechnic Institute. An automobile dealer who had served as president of the Automobile Dealers' Association of Alabama, Edwards had had no particular experience in the field of public finance. The new Attorney General was Silas Garrett, chief assistant to Carmichael during the previous administration.

The new Governor soon set about to find a compromise on the utility assessment ratio in order to cut through the tangle of litigation over corporate assessments and to forestall developing legislative activity.

By mid-summer 1951, the Alabama Power Company case was settled by agreement among the parties. The compromise, embodied in a consent decree of the Montgomery Circuit Court, set the assessment ratio at forty percent of calculated Alabama value. Since there was reason to believe that non-utility property had been assessed on the average at 28 to 30 percent, an overall ratio of 40 percent did not represent too unfavorable a settlement, from the point of view of immediate state revenue. The effect on the Southern Railway of this lower equalization rate was a net assessment not much greater than that set by the Circuit Court in 1948.

Attached to the settlement in the power company case was an unpublished agreement, not incorporated in the consent decree but accepted by all the utilities, including the Southern: for the duration of the Persons administration, the utilities would abide by the Department of Revenue's techniques for reaching unit and Alabama value. One of the Southern's counsels, Robert Pruitt, interpreted the agreement regarding techniques to mean "that for the four years of Governor Gordon Persons' administration, there would be no changes in techniques or methods of approaches merely to increase railroad assessments." Furthermore, Mr. Pruitt stated that this was not an agreement but an understanding.

The Settlement of the Southern Case

In late September 1951, the state and the Southern Railway agreed upon a 1947 assessment of $21,750,000. This, it will be recalled, was the original figure set in the tentative assessment.

The 1948 assessment was set at $22,000,000, modifying a previous agreement between the state and the Railway. When the controversy over the 1947 assessment reached the courts, and it became clear that there would be no resolution for some time to come, both parties agreed that the 1948 assessment would be $500,000 higher than the amount of the 1947 assessment. The Southern, however, now felt that it had already made a concession to the state in settling for 1947 at $21,750,000, a figure $500,000 higher than the $21,250,000 set by the Circuit Court. It was therefore unwilling to give the entire $500,000 increase for the next year.

The state offered to start from scratch on the 1948 assessment, but the Southern stated it was "bound by sentiment" to the original agreement. The agreement had been entered into in behalf of the Southern by Judge Stokely, long-time counsel for the railroad, who had died after the trial in the Circuit Court was concluded. The Railway wished to hold to Stokely's agreement as the point of departure for a sensible compromise. Finally, both parties agreed to split the difference on the $500,000 proposed increase and to round the 1948 assessment off at $22,000,000.

Although the Governor, the Commissioner of Revenue, and the Attorney General all participated in making the settlements discussed above, Attorney General Garrett seemed to play the most important role. Under a court decision during the preceding administration, the Attorney General's office had full authority to settle any tax case.

In reviewing the settlements later, Garrett believed that the 1947 and 1948 assessment rates were the best that could be obtained. After the Alabama Power ruling, it appeared to him that the state had lost almost all hope of assessing public utilities at sixty percent of Alabama value, at least for the present. Nonetheless, he had tried to save the statutory ratio of sixty percent. During the negotiations with the Alabama Power Company, he had pointed out to the utility companies that there were two variables in property tax assessment: the ratio of assessment and the value of the property. If the utilities would accept the sixty percent ratio of assessment, there was the possibility that their valuations could be lowered to equate their taxes with taxes on other properties. Thus both the Constitution and the statutory requirement of sixty percent could be satisfied. The utilities did not agree to this. For his part, Garrett was unwilling to accept an assessment ratio explicitly lower than the statutory sixty percent. Consequently, in the settlement of the Alabama Power Company case no assessment ratio was mentioned, only an assessment figure. (An assessment ratio of forty percent could be derived from this, but no official announcement of a ratio was made.)

On the plus side for the state, Garrett felt, the settlement obtained was a half million dollars more for Alabama than the Circuit Court had allowed. He considered it very probable that the Supreme Court would have upheld the decision of the Circuit Court.

Garrett said he had decided that the state

would never have offered the compromise tentative assessment of $21,750,000 if this figure had not been "right"; i.e., reached by defensible procedures. To him, the final assessment of $25,000,000 had been nothing more than an expression of the Folsom spirit of state administration.

Moreover, the Southern, along with the other utilities, had agreed to abide by Hamilton's methods in valuation for the next four years.

Hamilton's reaction to the Southern settlement was very different. He believed that the $25,000,000 assessment had been completely defensible in terms of scientific evaluation and a 45 percent assessment ratio. He said that he had emphasized repeatedly to the Attorney General's staff during the settlement negotiations that the tentative assessment figure was not based on professionally justifiable assessment procedures. Hamilton also doubted that his valuation methods were sufficiently protected by an agreement that was not public and that had an assured life-span of only four years.

It was apparent that Hamilton believed that an actual judicial trial and decision by the Supreme Court might have cleared the air, either by explicitly affirming his principles or by openly striking them down. For this reason, the state's appeal briefs had pressed the Supreme Court to do more than simply name an assessment figure. Hamilton's court strategy had consistently been aimed at narrowing the issues to certain significant points, so that the courts could in no way escape a decision concerning them. As matters stood after the settlement, Hamilton believed that the entire matter of utility ad valorem taxation was clouded and in doubt, and that temporary acceptance of procedures could easily be lost. He thought that Garrett's negotiations had gained nothing by way of establishing lasting principles of sound taxation action.

To the publicly elected and politically responsible Attorney General, the important thing was to reach an agreement representing the best attainable financial settlement for the state, without being unfair to the taxpayer. He reasoned that the business of the state must go forward, that prolonged controversy was burdensome for all, and that the results of court battles might prove satisfactory for none.

To Hamilton, the career tax administrator, relatively removed from the pressures for compromise felt by the man in active political life, the primary objective was to secure vindication and complete endorsement of his administrative techniques and principles. He believed that while rigid adherence to principle might have entailed the loss of a battle and in this instance, a temporary diminution of tax revenues, only thus would the war have been won.

Others noted that the Southern case illustrated some of the reasons for the decline of the general property tax as a source of revenue in state and local government. In contrast to newer taxes —for example, the sales and use tax, the gasoline tax, the income tax—the property tax is slow to adjust to changing conditions; it necessitates the exercise of a considerable amount of judgment in its administration; and it affords the taxpayer an opportunity to invoke an appeals procedure which may delay tax collection for an indefinite period. And though it might be argued that a higher ad valorem property tax on utilities than on other properties is fundamentally no more a breach of "equal treatment" than, say, a one-cent cigarette tax and a five-cent gasoline tax, the practice of Alabama courts held otherwise. Efforts to improve the property tax system thus ran into the court-sustained bulwark of tradition. And some raised the question whether the state, in its drawn-out fight with the Southern, had been fighting the right war.

ADMINISTRATION IN LOCAL GOVERNMENT

"... for all eminent Governments ... have a great burden, huge care, infinite business, little rest, innumerable fears."

Jeremy Taylor

The County Buys Dunwoodie Golf Course

Robert T. Daland

The County Buys Dunwoodie Golf Course

IN 1956 WESTCHESTER COUNTY, New York, purchased the privately owned Dunwoodie Golf Course located in the City of Yonkers. The reason for the purchase was to add another public golf course to the four already owned and operated as part of the park system by the Westchester County Park Commission. The course had been operated for many years as a private golf club which numbered among its original members such luminaries as John Barrymore, Flo Ziegfeld, and George M. Cohan. In 1952 it had been acquired by real estate investors.

Purchase of a golf course as such did not raise important issues of policy, since Westchester County had operated public golf courses in its parks since 1927. The issues which surrounded the decision were concerned with competing potential land uses proposed for the site. They involved land development policy for the county (population 630,000) and the City of Yonkers (population 153,000). The decision was not unique, dramatic, or highly controversial. The purchase represented the almost routine discharge of the responsibility of the Westchester County Park Commission to keep its program abreast of the increasing needs of the people of Westchester. It was one of a continuing stream of decisions which cumulatively influenced the physical development of the county for better or for worse. Such decisions have a quiet drama of their own.

The purchase of Dunwoodie was not entirely devoid of conflict. Whenever governments seek to acquire land in a heavily built up urban area, they must compete with prospective alternative users. This study centers on the techniques by which Westchester County succeeded in obtaining the golf course—despite the opposition of a number of local and private interests.

Westchester County lies just north of New York City and contains six cities, twenty-two incorporated villages, and eighteen towns. Of the eighteen towns, sixteen have organized governments, the remaining two being coterminous with the boundaries of the incorporated villages. In addition there are various special districts, the most notable of which is the County Sewer District.

The county government was until recent decades typical of the New York county. As such it had, and still retains, the supervisory system of representation. Each town has one representative on the Board of Supervisors. Each city has a number of supervisors, roughly prorated according to population. The total membership of the Board is 45. In 1937 the county received a new charter which "modernized" the county government in various respects. The major break with the past was the establishment of an elected chief executive officer known as the County Executive. This office formalized and perpetuated a relatively centralized control over the county administration which had been in the hands of the Republican "boss" of the county, William Ward, for the three previous decades. Under the charter the County Executive appointed virtually all of the department heads, boards, and commissions of the county government, with the exception of the several judicial and law enforcement agencies, which were constituted of elected officials or their appointees. The County Executive was frequently the county Republican leader.

Westchester's Park Planning

Long-range park planning in Westchester County was initiated by "Boss" William L. Ward, whose control of the political affairs stretched from 1898 to 1933. Ward was wealthy, as were substantial numbers of his constituents in this elite suburban area. He was free to pursue, with considerable devotion, major county-wide civic projects. One of the earliest of these was to get the sewage out of the Bronx River, which bisects southern Westchester and the Bronx, northernmost of the five boroughs of New York City. To do this a system of trunk sewers was built to take sewage to the Hudson.

The interest in cleaning up the river, however, was strongly reinforced, if not in fact initiated, by the City of New York. While rural Westchester of 1900 could tolerate a polluted river, growing New York could not. In 1895 a commission was appointed to look into Bronx River pollution. Westchester County was little interested, and nothing was accomplished. In 1905, however, the New York Zoological Society stimulated legislation which resulted in the appointment by the Governor of a state commission to study and report. The state thereby took cognizance of a "metropolitan" problem affecting Westchester. The commission reported that the only practicable solution to the problem was public acquisition of the "low and practically valueless" river bottom lands. This necessity arose because the river contained sewage—soon to be abated—and because it was a repository for every form of junk, waste, refuse, and filth from the surrounding area. Particular offenders were the stables and barnyards. The commission recommended that these lands be used as parkway reservation.

In 1907 the Legislature acted on the report by creating a permanent Bronx Parkway Commission, also appointed by the Governor, to acquire the lands and construct the parkway. New York City was to provide 75 percent of the necessary funds, and Westchester County 25 percent.

At this point New York City developed a reluctance to furnish its share of the finances, while Westchester became ever more eager for the project. By 1912 little had been done, though $35,000 for planning had been provided. Headquarters for the project were in the New York City Hall. The 1912 report of the commission revealed New York's attitude: "It is practically assumed that the entire section traversed (from the Bronx to Kensico Reservoir in Central Westchester) will be absorbed by the City in the not distant future."

In 1913, however, the commission received authority and funds for property acquisition, and by 1916 two-thirds of the total of lands needed had been acquired. Though the World War slowed the project, substantial road construction began in 1920. In 1922, despite the necessity to sue New York City for failure to provide its share of that year's funds, land acquisition had been virtually accomplished. The construction was completed in 1925 at a total cost of $16,500,000. Total area of the Bronx River Parkway was about 1,100 acres.

Before the completion of the county sewer and the parkway, William L. Ward created a mechanism for the planning of a county-wide system of parks to be connected by parkways similar to that along the Bronx River. For this purpose the Westchester County Park Commission was established in 1922. The experience of collaboration with New York City had not been a happy one, and in 1926 the portion of the Bronx River Parkway in Westchester County was turned over to the County Park Commission.

By 1924, as a result of Ward's stimulus, the Park Commission had projected a major system of parks and parkways and had spent more than $1,500,000 on land acquisition. During the next six years thousands of acres of land were acquired by purchase, gift, and condemnation. In 1925 three new parkways were in planning or under construction: the Sawmill River, Hutchinson River, and Cross County parkways. By 1927 over 15,000 acres of land were devoted to park and parkway uses—roughly half of them for park lands. During the next three years a few hundred more acres were acquired, so that in 1930 the county owned over 17,000 acres, including the Bronx River Parkway and its extension, on which a state parkway was later constructed.

This program of 1924-1930 resulted in a park acreage of 9,700 acres in 1930, which was 18.6 acres of park land per 1,000 population. During the next three decades, however, county purchases were offset by sales, so that the net acreage remained about the same. The population increase since 1930 has reduced the park acreage per 1,000 population to 12.6 acres. The forward looking park planning of the 1920s was by no means abandoned in 1930. The initial conception of a park and parkway system had been substantially achieved, including the advance acquisition of lands on which highways were still being constructed in 1960. The link of the New York State Thruway connecting the Connecticut Turnpike with New York City, for example, was built in 1959 on lands acquired during the 1920s. On maps of the Westchester parkway system there appear strips of county-acquired lands connecting the county-owned Blue Mountain Reservation with the parkway system to the south. According to plan, highways will be built on these lands when Blue Mountain is needed for development as a county park at some future date. When the Depression of the 1930s arrived, then, it was with no thought of abandoning long-range park planning that further land acquisition was halted. World War II continued to delay park development, so it was not until the postwar years that active attention was again turned to the expansion of park facilities.

The interest in county planning did not wane with the retirement of Ward. In the new charter adopted in 1937 provision was made for a Planning Commission and a Planning Department. The Planning Commission was not to replace the Park Commission in park and parkway planning. For many years the Park Commission had operated in substantial autonomy from the County Executive and the other county agencies. It had ample legal powers to maintain this position. When the Planning Commission arrived on the scene, it did not seek to assume leadership in park planning; rather, over the years it established an increasingly high level of communication with the Park Commission's staff. The Planning Commission was provided an official voice on matters involving capital projects by a provision in the charter requiring a report of the Commission to the County Executive and the Board of Supervisors on all such projects. Since the charter officially recognized Planning's role, the two commissions co-ordinated their positions on capital projects through communication between their technical staffs.

The Planning Commission in the 1950s did not prepare advance plans for park development and would not have presumed to do so except after agreement with the Park Commission. It did, however, have firm ideas on park development policy. These were generally consistent with those of the Park Commission. In simplified form they could be stated as follows: More park lands must be acquired to meet the needs of the future. These should be located in such a way as to preserve as far as possible the rural aspect of the county. Existing park lands should not be alienated from park use or developed to the degree that they lose their rural character. The purchase of Dunwoodie Golf Course, on its face, was consistent with all of these ideas. In this situation the participation of the Planning Commission and staff was confined to giving support to the initiative of the Park Commission.

Growth Brings Pressure for More Parks

By the early 1950s the growing population of Westchester had placed added demands on the sorts of recreational facilities in the parks to which citizens of the county had become accustomed. These facilities included golf courses, swimming pools and beaches, picnic areas, playfields, winter sports areas, and others. Additional demands had resulted from growing populations in neighboring parts of the metropolitan area. Park users began to press the Park Commission and their local delegates to the Board of Supervisors for expansion of park facilities. These pressures provided the stimulus which caused the Park Commission to activate again its long-range policy of park acquisition.

Within the broad policy of park expansion the Park Commission had opened four golf courses between 1925 and 1931. Three of these were located in the heavily populated southern portion of the county at Sprain Lake, Saxon Woods, and Maple Moor. The fourth was in northern Westchester at Mohansic Park. Over the years Westchester's public golf courses had bred many an ardent golfer to add to the even larger number of patrons of the private golf clubs scattered throughout the county. The public courses were open to all comers, including residents of New York City, at the same fees. During the post-World War II years the golfers increasingly complained that they were being denied the pleasure of their own golf courses. More and more it became necessary to arrive at the county courses in the early dawn in order to avoid an excessive wait before teeing off. Golf appealed to New Yorkers as well as to Westchesterites, and the three south-county courses were easily accessible to residents of the Bronx and Manhattan. For many low-income residents of New York City, the Westchester courses were the closest on which they could afford to play. On weekends the practice arose of sending a New York cab driver to hold a place in the waiting line so the golfer could appear at a reasonable hour and take his place in the lineup. Westchester golfers resented the presence of these "outsiders." When assaults and other delinquencies were reported in the parks, they were attributed to undesirables from New York City.

These irritations were pressed on the members of the County Board of Supervisors, particularly on those from the towns and cities near the three south Westchester courses. A proposal that the courses should be restricted to residents of the county was questioned as possibly illegal, but in December 1954 the county attorney stated that the county had the right to restrict parks to county residents. The demand for restriction was not confined to the golf courses; it applied to the parks generally. However, some types of park facilities could absorb overcrowding more readily than others. The golf courses were the least expansible of the parks' recreational assets. The problem of overcrowding was so obvious that it did not require proof. The Park Commission seized the opportunity to convert the interest in restriction into an interest in acquiring one or more new golf courses.

The Parks Superintendent

The prime mover in the purchase of Dunwoodie was George Haight, who served under the Park Commission as Superintendent of Parks. Haight had been trained as a civil engineer at Cornell University and had been employed by the Park Commission in 1925, when the great land acquisition program was getting under way. He had played a key role in planning and designing the park and parkway system, and in 1938 he was appointed General Superintendent. Much of the land had been acquired by negotiation rather than condemnation, and Haight was widely credited with the success of the acquisition program. Haight was quick to point out, however, that a good share of the credit must go to active and influential members of the Park Commission.

During the 1920s and early 1930s, when most of the park land was being acquired, the political regime of "Boss" Ward was in full sway, and the parks and parkways were his favorite project. Crucial decisions on land acquisition could be made during this period with dispatch and without extended public debate or controversy. This situation, together with the fact that real estate transactions were traditionally conducted in private, molded Haight's method of operation, which carried over into the 1950s, long after William Ward had retired as county leader. Haight conducted the affairs of the Park Commission without drawing into the process anyone not vital to the decisions concerned. Whenever possible, secrecy was considered preferable to publicity. This attitude extended not only to the acquisition of property but also to other Park Commission business. Within the county government Haight earned the reputation of "an operator." His position in the county government after his promotion to the superintendency was buttressed by the full confidence of the Park Commissioners, from whose hands he received ample delegated authority. Business was usually brought to an advanced stage of maturity before it was necessary to check with the Commission in any formal way. Informally Haight was perceived as speaking with the authority of the Commission. During the period of negotiations for Dunwoodie Golf Course, the President of the Park Commission was Evans Ward, treasurer of the county Republican organization and son of William Ward. The Vice President was Colonel John Stilwell of Yonkers, brother of "Vinegar Joe," who as a vice president of the Consolidated Edison Company had a long experience in handling large real estate transactions. The Commission and its staff, in short, constituted a powerful, experienced, autonomous administrative organization with a high degree of strategic skill in adjusting to its political arena. Moreover, it knew precisely what it wanted to achieve.

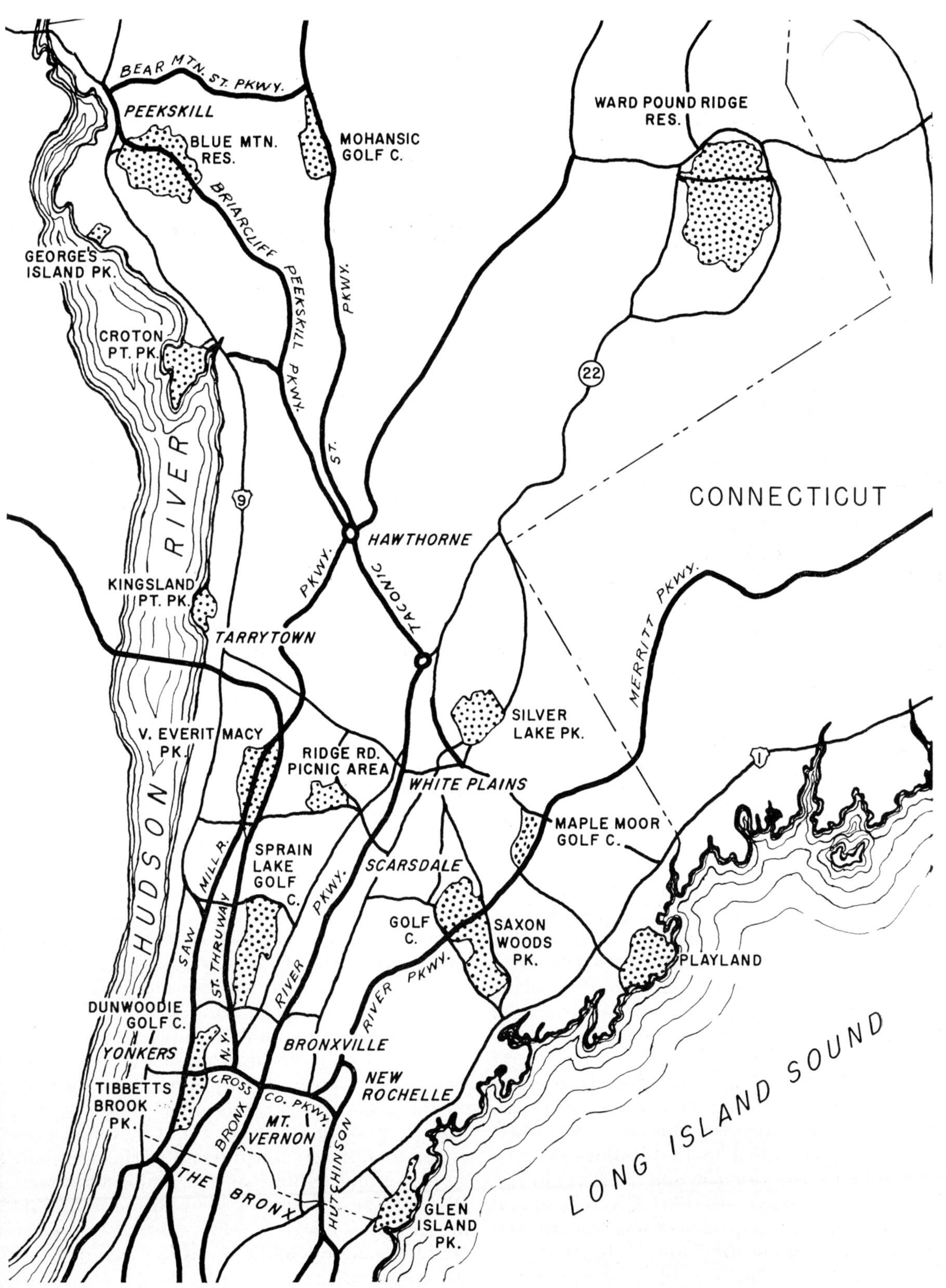

BEAR MTN. ST. PKWY.
PEEKSKILL
BLUE MTN. RES.
MOHANSIC GOLF C.
WARD POUND RIDGE RES.
BRIARCLIFF PEEKSKILL PKWY.
GEORGE'S ISLAND PK.
CROTON PT. PK.
22
TACONIC ST. PKWY.
HUDSON RIVER
9
CONNECTICUT
HAWTHORNE
KINGSLAND PT. PK.
MERRITT PKWY.
TARRYTOWN
SILVER LAKE PK.
V. EVERIT MACY PK.
RIDGE RD. PICNIC AREA
1
WHITE PLAINS
MAPLE MOOR GOLF C.
SAW MILL R.
SPRAIN LAKE GOLF C.
SCARSDALE
N.Y. ST. THRUWAY
GOLF C.
SAXON WOODS PK.
PLAYLAND
RIVER PKWY.
BRONX RIVER PKWY.
DUNWOODIE GOLF C.
YONKERS
BRONXVILLE
LONG ISLAND SOUND
TIBBETTS BROOK PK.
CROSS CO. PKWY.
NEW ROCHELLE
MT. VERNON
HUTCHINSON
THE BRONX
GLEN ISLAND PK.

Site Selection

George Haight took the initiative in the search for a new golf course site as early as 1950. During the next few years he reviewed "probably a hundred" different sites in various parts of the county. While undeveloped areas suitable for golf courses were much more numerous in the northern part of the county, the demand for courses was primarily in the heavily populated southern section. The disparity of population distribution in Westchester was extreme. Eighty percent of the population was south of the narrow "waistline" of the county as marked at a major traffic intersection known as Hawthorne Circle; ten percent was distributed along the shore of the Hudson River north of the waistline. The remaining ten percent of the population occupied the sixty percent of the county remaining in northern Westchester.

The selection of Dunwoodie was a result of a strategic calculation by Haight and the Park Commissioners that the Westchester park program would be advanced farther by seeking an available site than by resorting to condemnation and the possibility of sharp controversy. As a result, two sites, Dunwoodie and Saxon Woods, were uppermost in the thinking of the park staff by 1953. Up to this point the intentions of the Park Commission had been aired only within the staff.

The Park Commission's vice president, Colonel Stilwell, had long had his eye on Dunwoodie as a possible addition to the park system. He was approached by the Brown Realty Company of New York City, which hoped to sell Dunwoodie to the county. With the interest of the county confirmed, Brown Realty sent a formal letter to the Park Superintendent offering Dunwoodie Golf Course for sale at $650,000, subject to a two-year lease to a golf club then operating the course. The firm happened to offer the property for sale at just the moment when the county was actively interesting itself in the site. The participants later explained this as coincidence. What is known is that in 1945 Dunwoodie had been sold by the original golf club to Joseph LoCascio of Yonkers. In 1949 LoCascio leased the course to a group of Yonkers golfers who had organized a private golf club. Whatever the reasons for LoCascio's interest in the course, he sold it in 1952 to William J. Sherry and Abraham Dreier, who purchased it as a real estate investment. At this point the lease to the golfers still had two years to run. The price of the sale was $400,000, of which half was cash and the remainder a mortgage with the First National Bank of Yonkers. It was widely believed later that the funds for purchase had come largely from Dreier. William Sherry was an active real estate broker as well as a leader in the Yonkers Democratic organization.

Dunwoodie Golf Course was located in the center of the City of Yonkers between the Sawmill River Parkway and the New York State Thruway. It was bounded on the south by the Cross County Parkway. It was, therefore, highly accessible from any direction. In 1953 Dunwoodie, comprising 124 acres, was the largest undeveloped acreage in Yonkers other than the existing county park and parkway lands. Yonkers was the largest and most densely developed city in the county. These facts made Dunwoodie a prime object for virtually any kind of development. A real estate firm handling the transaction, even with a minimum understanding of county operations and policies, could easily see that the golf course would fit the pattern of county park development. It met the requirement of access to a parkway, and it was adjacent to the existing county park at Tibbetts Brook. In view of current complaints about overcrowding at the Sprain Lake Golf Course just to the north of Dunwoodie, here was a location which might go far toward solving the local golfing problem. It would have been very easy for an alert real estate agent to have picked up the hearsay which circulates around governmental offices that the Park Commission had been making a survey of possible golf course sites. Whatever the degree of information or suspicion that the county would be interested, nothing would be lost in offering the tract to the county. Sale was not urgent in any event, since the lease to the golf club had some time to run. It was safe to think that a buyer could be found even if the county were not interested. However, sale to the county would have one major advantage: it would be a cash sale, and the profit would accrue immediately. The existing mortgage could be paid off, and a profit upwards of $250,000 was in prospect.

From the point of view of the Park Commission there were several advantages in Dunwoodie as a county park and golf course. The fact that a course already existed on the site would minimize development costs. The purchase would represent a substantial increase in park acreage in line with the historic policy of acquiring more park lands. Existing park lands would not have to be alienated from their undeveloped state to create a new golf course. The Park Commission had several times resisted efforts to provide additional recreation facilities on the park lands due to a real concern for maintaining park areas in a wilderness state.

The Planning Department, whose role at this stage was entirely informal, agreed with the Park staff. It was particularly interested in the Dunwoodie purchase because it lay in an area already highly developed. The new park would keep this key part of southern Westchester from becoming "improved." The acquisition of additional open areas throughout the county had been, and remained, a major objective of the Planning Director, Hugh Pomeroy, and the Planning Commission. Purchase of Dunwoodie by the Park Commission would further that policy. Now that the site was in the hands of real estate speculators, it was clear that this might be the last chance to acquire the acreage. Moreover, something of an understanding had grown up among the officials of the county to the effect that whenever a private golf course was put up for sale, the county would attempt to purchase it in order to preserve the undeveloped space which already existed in the county, lending it an open character. This understanding alone might have been enough to suggest to the buyers that the county was the prime prospect for the sale.

Saxon Woods was an alternative site for a new golf course. It offered the advantage of being owned by the county so that no purchase cost would be involved. However, other factors made it seem less desirable in the thinking of the Park staff. While it was accessible from the Hutchinson River Parkway, Saxon Woods was north of the main concentration of population. It was just a short distance south of the existing Maple Moor Golf Course operated by the county. Moreover, a golf course already existed in Saxon Woods, and, while ample room was available for another, the resulting concentration of golfing facilities was not deemed desirable by the Park Commission. The site was also less desirable in the view of both Park and Planning Commissions because it would reduce the acreage of wilderness area in the park, while adding nothing to the total park area or the county's capital of open space. Since a new course would have to be built, some of the financial advantage of holding ownership to the site would be lost.

While the ultimate construction of a golf course at Saxon Woods was by no means rejected at this point, George Haight definitely decided to pursue negotiations for the purchase of Dunwoodie following the official offer of the site to the county by the realty company. Other lines of action were not closed by this tentative decision, but it proved to be crucial in determining the actual site. In a sense it remained only for the decision to be sold to the various county officials whose consent would be necessary to implement it. The existing two-year lease seemed to give Haight plenty of time to prepare his campaign for acceptance of the project and to negotiate with the owners. Since no public revelation of the decision was made, and since no formal decision of any kind could be pointed to, the entire project could be kept secret until it became useful to reveal it.

Negotiating the Price

During the summer of 1953, subsequent to receiving the offer from Brown Realty, Haight pursued the negotiations over price by letter, phone, and private conference. In July Brown Realty reported that the owner would take $630,000 for the site. In September Haight reported to Brown Realty that the Park Commission was waiting for the "rock bottom price." The response of Brown Realty was a letter indicating that the owner, Mr. Dreier, had come down to $600,000 cash. Thereupon the Park Commission took its first formal action on the matter at a meeting of October 23. It was decided not to recommend purchase to the Board of Supervisors at this price and to advise Brown Realty to this effect.

The reasons for the Park Commission's decision were never disclosed, but the major elements in the situation were not obscure. Since the lease was still in effect, there was no urgency.

Another buyer would not be likely to spend over half a million dollars without getting control of the property for two years. Conceivably the sellers might come forth with a still lower offer. Apart from these considerations, however, there was the basic fact that the Park Commission then had no funds with which to make the purchase. It knew approximately what the price would be; now it would be necessary to arrange for getting an appropriation for the purchase. This was a subject of some delicacy. The approach of Haight and the Park Commission was not to employ routine administrative methods for this purpose, but rather to operate more informally as had been the tradition in the past. Haight had often before sought funds for park expansion without success, and he fully intended to maintain as flexible a position as possible in the existing circumstance.

Westchester County had had a capital budget procedure since the charter was adopted in 1937. As it existed in 1953, this procedure involved departmental requests for capital funds, review by a technical subcommittee of a capital projects committee, review by the full capital projects committee including the County Executive and leading members of the Board of Supervisors, and finally action by the Supervisors in the appropriation process. The capital budget request for 1954 was prepared in May 1953, the same month during which Haight was negotiating the price which might be paid for Dunwoodie. Nevertheless, he chose not to insert in the capital request a sum to cover the purchase of Dunwoodie. Another administrator might have thought that the timing was ideal for a capital request for this purpose, since an actual site was potentially available. Haight decided that there would be a strategic loss in requesting funds at that time. In the first place, the proposed transaction would be made public. This could alert other potential buyers to the availability of the site. (One Yonkers real estate developer, in fact, had had his eye on the property as early as 1952. His part of the story is told below.) Publicity regarding the county's intention could also lead to other forms of opposition to the purchase or competition for available funds. Moreover, to insert an item in the capital budget would have weakened Haight's negotiating position with respect to price. With funds earmarked for the purchase, it would be difficult for the county to plead lack of funds in the interest of reducing the price.

Several months now passed without any apparent activity looking toward purchase of the property. If any negotiations occurred, they were entirely off the record. The Park staff, however, was still interested in the project. An appraiser was hired to establish the value of the site. His report was transmitted on June 11, 1954. It stated that the highest and best use of the land was for subdivision purposes, for which it would be worth $1,000,000. Continued in use as a private golf club, it would be worth no more than $300,000. Everything considered, the appraiser valued the property at $618,000.

Up to this point there was still no assurance that funds for the purchase would be forthcoming, even if the Park Commission should request them. During October, however, decisions on county fiscal policy were made which completely changed the prospects of the purchase. These decisions and their sources will be described below. Suffice it to say that George Haight was informed by the Budget Director that he would be given $2,400,000 to spend on golf courses and swimming pools. He immediately began to press in earnest for the purchase of Dunwoodie.

It was with considerable difficulty, Haight reported later, that he convinced the owners to sell. By October 4 the impression had been circulated in the county that the property was in imminent danger of being sold for subdivision, either for residential or commercial development. One of the owners, Sherry, reported later that while there was some interest among real estate men in the area in various types of development, he and Dreier had not been approached with a specific offer by any of them. In any case, Haight spent much effort convincing Dreier to sell to the county rather than to seek a higher price from a subdivider. Haight now offered $600,000 and soon raised the figure to $650,000. His appeal for sale at this price included two chief points. First, the civic interest required preservation of the site for public use. Second, the county could condemn the property and acquire it in any case.

Dreier and Sherry, who were in a position to make a substantial profit on the course at the offered price, gave the county an option to buy on November 8, 1954, pending completion of the county's official commitment to purchase. In addition to avoiding the problems of condemnation, Dreier and Sherry recognized that the sale would be a cash sale, which would eliminate any mortgaging of the property. The negotiations leading to the option were conducted in secrecy. The matter was officially known only among those immediately concerned: the two owners, their real estate representatives, the County Park Commission and its staff, and the appraiser. But secrecy would soon have to be broken, for the Board of Supervisors would have to vote an appropriation. This last and public stage of the Dunwoodie decision was prefaced by a series of other decisions which eventually led the county administration to agree to budget the funds needed for the purchase.

The Role of the Budget Process

Budgeting in Westchester County was carried out with sophisticated techniques in the manner of advanced executive budgets elsewhere in the United States. But Westchester's Department of the Budget (commonly known as the budget office) did not act independently on proposals, or base its decisions purely on budgetary techniques. As in many jurisdictions where the executive budget is in effect, preparation and submission of the budget to the Board of Supervisors was by charter a function of the elected County Executive. He appointed the Budget Director, who reported to him directly. The contact between the two was constant and intimate. Through this interchange political judgments, including consideration of traditions of long standing in the county and subjective evaluations of what people wanted from county government, could come to bear on budget decisions. On the other hand, budgeting as a technical process was an influential force in making decisions, as the following brief summary of county fiscal trends will show.

A survey of the budget experience of Westchester County for eighteen years was made by the writer to determine the cumulative effects of the budget process in terms of the accuracy of estimates, the relationship of revenues to expenditures, and the practices with respect to treatment of surpluses. The consequences of these practices in 1954 had an important effect on the decision to purchase Dunwoodie Golf Course.

During the eighteen-year period (1940-1957) the adopted operating budget varied from actual expenditures only from .1% to 5.5%. In only seven of the eighteen years was the variation more than 2.0%. The period covers World War II, the postwar readjustment, and the Korean conflict—times which did not ease the situation for the budget estimators. This is substantial evidence that the budget process bore an intimate relationship to decisions to spend. Revenues, always more difficult to predict, varied slightly more, from .1% to 9.3%, but only during a six-year period from 1944 to 1949 was the variation more than 3.5%. In only two years was the revenue estimate slightly below, rather than above, budget estimates. In every one of the eighteen years, revenues were more than actual expenditures by amounts varying from .2% to 6.8%.

The decision as to what to do with the surplus represented a real policy decision of a different magnitude than a decision merely to maintain existing programs at prevailing levels. A surplus could be appropriated to the following year's operating budget, thus tending to reduce the tax rate; it could be appropriated to capital projects, an action less likely to affect the tax rate; or it could be retained in the treasury for future use. Under New York state law controlling county fiscal operations, the deliberate maintenance of a surplus as such was not authorized. The budget office thus had to be on guard against the development of money balances which would constitute a surplus. This factor played a role in the purchase of Dunwoodie Golf Course.

The county's excess on January 1 of each year amounted to an average of 6.1% of total expenditures. The excess fluctuated considerably from year to year, depending on factors only partly under control of fiscal officers. In 1945 the excess had grown to 10.3% of expenditures during that year. This growth was typical of many state and local governments during that period. By 1952 the excess had been reduced to 3.7%, to a large extent by appropriating a large share of the excess each year to the budget for the following year. In 1952, 1953, and 1954, however, only small portions of the excess were so appropriated. The reasons for this were associated with the adoption of a capital budget program in 1952 and the prospects of imminent parkway reconstruction.

In County Executive Gerlach's budget message of 1952 a capital improvements program was announced with the suggestion that, if the tax rate could be pegged at about $8.52 per thousand, it appeared that roughly $3,000,000 would be available for each year of a capital improvements program. This tax rate was substantially adhered to in following years. In 1956 County Executive Hopkins made reference to the "constant tax rate" of $8.52, indicating the desire to continue that policy.

Thus in a sense it may be said that by 1954, when Haight turned to the task of seeking a budget item for the purchase of Dunwoodie, the finances were ahead of the programmers and engineers of public works. A major objective of a capital improvements program is to stabilize both the rates of taxation and expenditures for public works. Therefore, an extreme tax reduction in the face of a temporary treasury excess would defeat the purposes of the program, which is intended to contemplate financing from a longer-than-annual point of view. The budget office was well aware that there was no real excess of funds, since it was clear that major expenditures for parkway reconstruction were imminent, in addition to other needed public works. The parkways had been built to standards of the 1920s and were becoming dangerously inadequate for current traffic loads. The excess of income over expenditures was to be used for parkway reconstruction even though no formal decision to this effect had moved to the level of the Board of Supervisors. This situation illustrated one of the dilemmas of administration. Sound management implied long-range planning. Long-range planning implied policy decisions which only the legislative body had authority to make. At what stage should plans-in-the-making be checked with the governing body? As it turned out, no answer was needed to this question because of a tangential decision made by the Board of Supervisors. A Westchester County Parkway Authority was created to finance reconstruction of the parkways exclusively through tolls. Thus revenue excesses would not be spent on modernizing parkways.

At this point, 1954, the county's excess stood at 10.4% of expenditures. By January 1 of the following year it had risen to 12.5%. Since the county was required by state law to prevent an unauthorized surplus, and since a bumper surplus was anticipated in 1955, the financial situation was favorable for Haight's Dunwoodie request. The budget office and the County Executive were aware of the Park Commission's need for additional facilities, and, at a conference in the County Executive's office during late October, the tax rate and budget were set. At the suggestion of the Budget Director a sum of $2,400,000, which was available for capital expenditures, was inserted in the capital budget. These funds were put in two items: $1,900,000 for "additional golf course facilities," and $500,000 for "additional swimming pool facilities." It was with these funds that Dunwoodie was ultimately purchased. The final report of the Capital Projects Committee to the County Executive on November 4 contained these items, not considered previously in the regular capital projects budgeting process which began in May and ended in November. Before insertion of these items, they had been approved informally by the majority party steering committee, a normal procedure for major expenditures. They were appropriated by the Board of Supervisors in due course and, to a large extent, were responsible for the reduction of the excess to 7.6% of expenditures as of January 1, 1956, a figure only slightly above the average. The budget office had successfully averted the creation of an illegal surplus, without jeopardizing the stability of the tax program. Incidentally, George Haight got his money for Dunwoodie Golf Course.

Opposition to County Purchase

Up to the time of the administration's decision to provide funds for "additional golf course facilities" the entire negotiation for Dunwoodie had been conducted in secrecy. Despite this, however, news of the county's interest in Dunwoodie became public a few days before the option was secured by Haight. The news got out in the form of a rumor whose source is unknown. In the face of the rumor, the administration stuck to its secrecy policy until the decision could proceed still further. During October, while the details of the option were being negotiated, the Park staff responded to a letter from a Yonkers citizen who urged the county to acquire Dunwoodie to prevent the rumored subdivision of the property. The Park Superintendent replied: "We are going into the matter." At this point began a conflict between the county, represented by its Park Commission, and various groups in Yonkers over the question of whether the land should become a county park or be subdivided for residential or commercial purposes.

When the difference of view over proper use for Dunwoodie became public in October, the press, through representatives of the Macy chain of newspapers published in the county, sought confirmation of the county's intention to secure Dunwoodie. On November 3, 1954, just five days *before* the option for purchase was transmitted to the county, both the Park Superintendent and Sherry stated to the press that the county had no plans for the purchase of Dunwoodie Golf Course. Their statements were technically correct only in the sense that it was necessary for the Board of Supervisors to make the final decision, and it had not yet been called on to do so. The Board could not be called on to do so on November 3, because the county had not yet received an option to purchase at any definite price, and no funds had yet been appropriated for the purpose. Pending the taking of these steps, Park Commission strategy was to keep the negotiations confidential. On November 8, the option was secured.

In October, meanwhile, the forces of opposition to county purchase of Dunwoodie began to organize. All they had to go on was the rumor that the county was about to purchase and the denial from both principals that this was the case. The opposition groups had no notion of the degree to which the decision had matured. In fact, the large institutional and political resources of the county government were by now strongly committed, privately, to the decision. All that remained was to make formal and official ratification through constitutional processes. The decision was not inevitable. It could be changed should publication of the county's intent arouse such a storm of protest that the Board of Supervisors would refuse to act.

Just as Dunwoodie was ideally located from the point of view of park development, it was a prime location for commercial development. Not only was it located at an intersection of major highways, but it was bordered by the Putnam Division of the New York Central Railroad. These facts were well known to Yonkers developers. Whatever dreams others may have had for the site, one real estate man in particular had conceived a definite plan of development for Dunwoodie prior to its sale by LoCascio in 1952. This man was C. Van Ness Wood. Wood was then engaged in one of Westchester's major real estate promotions, which was culminating in the creation of the Cross County Shopping Center near the intersection of the Cross County and Bronx River Parkways. His involvement with the shopping center during this period left little time for developing his plans for Dunwoodie. Accordingly in 1952 he had no definite commitments of funds, tenants, nor a detailed plan of development for the Dunwoodie site. He had, even prior to sale of the property in 1952, interested an architect and a land planner in the potential for development of the site, and had presented some preliminary ideas to some life insurance companies, including United States Life and Guardian Life. When the sale became imminent in 1952 an official of the First National Bank of Yonkers informed Wood of the Sherry-Dreier plan to purchase the property and suggested the possibility that Wood might become a co-broker on the sale. The bank had been in close touch with Wood on matters relating to attracting new business enterprises to Yonkers.

Wood rejected this idea since his primary interest was development, while he regarded the Sherry-Dreier interest as speculation. This being the case, the land would still be available for development, and Wood proceeded with his development plans for the site despite the sale. Wood reached the decision that the best development would provide for the creation of an office center of major proportions, comparable to a Rockefeller Center adapted to suburban conditions. In addition to offices, the center would contain a band of warehousing and related facilities stretching along the railroad.

This feature was of particular importance because of the poor financial condition of the Putnam Division of the New York Central Railroad. A warehousing center with several dozen carloads of traffic each day would give a financial shot in the arm to a rail line that would be of considerable importance to any economic expansion of Yonkers—an objective ardently hoped for by much of Yonkers' business community.

During the summer and fall of 1954, Wood continued his search for funds to purchase the site and for prospective tenants. He was making progress toward both goals at the time that the county was coming to a definite understanding with the owners. When, in October, it became known that the county might buy, Wood became active in developing and communicating his alternative theory of proper land use for the site.

The major issue raised by Wood and other opponents of county purchase concerned the effect of removing the acreage from the tax base. Wood argued that, with the sort of development he had in mind, the annual tax return to the City of Yonkers could be three or four hundred thousand dollars. He suggested that the existing parks and parkways in Yonkers already constituted an excessive amount of tax-exempt land. To forego the tax returns on a developed Dunwoodie would adversely affect Yonkers' ability to support municipal services, particularly public education.

In a closely related contention it was argued that an office center development would strengthen the Yonkers economy materially by providing jobs. It would also strengthen the economy of Yonkers in indirect ways. It would represent Yonkers as a growing commercial and financial center and thus tend to attract other new business. The advertising value of the site, which thousands of motorists passed each day, would further contribute to Yonkers' commercial growth. These factors were particularly important because of the recent loss by Yonkers of the Alexander Smith (Carpet) Company and the possibly imminent loss of the Otis Elevator Company, it was asserted. Both of these firms had substantial manufacturing payrolls. A suburban Rockefeller Center at Dunwoodie might well reverse Yonkers' economic decline. The envisioned development, it was claimed, would guarantee an additional twenty to forty carloads a day for the Putnam Division of the New York Central and would prevent the further decline of this portion of the railroad.

Looking further into the implications of the choice, Wood argued that the consequence of removing Dunwoodie from the tax rolls would be to necessitate the establishment of sales or other "nuisance" taxes. This turn of events would give the *coup de grace* to any prospect of Yonkers maintaining a satisfactory competitive position as compared with such adjacent commercial centers as White Plains, the county seat.

In addition to the economic need for the suburban Rockefeller Center, Wood argued that the county did not in fact need to put a county golf course at the Dunwoodie site. He noted that little gain to Westchester golfers would accrue unless the course were restricted to county residents, and that this could be done, he asserted, was nothing more than a pious hope. He said that a better golf course location could be found at either the Ridge Road Picnic Area, miles to the north, or the Vernon Hills Country Club, which could be condemned for a county park. Moreover, if, as Wood doubted, Yonkers did need another course, this could be built on county-owned lands at Grassy Sprain, toward the south end of the city.

In a final argument, on which Wood placed little emphasis, it was noted that the planning process had not been adequate, in that there was not sufficient co-ordination of long-range park and school planning. That is, even if the best site for the golf course proved to be Dunwoodie, the economic considerations and the related tax outlook for Yonkers public schools would no doubt weigh in the balance more heavily for the office center than for the golf course in the long run. It was possible to make this point, Wood noted, because neither the County Planning Department nor the Yonkers City Planning Department had been consulted by the Park staff prior to its decision to seek purchase of Dunwoodie.

In addition to arguing the case on its merits, Wood questioned the validity of the basis on which the county's decision was made. He asserted that the decision was partly the result of partisan politics. White Plains, unlike Demo-

Dunwoodie Golf Course. The course is in the foreground, and New York City is far to the south.

cratic Yonkers, was a citadel of the dominant Republican county machine. The business, and particularly the banking, leadership of White Plains, he alleged, was determined to prevent a threat to the leadership of the White Plains area with respect to office centers and commercial activity generally. To this end they were seeking to remove the possibility of competition in Yonkers by purchasing (for a county golf course) the last potential office center site in Yonkers. No evidence was ever adduced to support this contention, which was later denied and discounted by county officials and by Sherry.

Wood reported having made an unofficial, that is, unwritten, offer of $650,000 to Sherry and his partner. (Sherry denied having received such an offer.) In accounts to newspapers, Wood sought to explain why Sherry, a leading Yonkers Democrat, was willing to go along with the alleged White Plains plot against Yonkers. He alleged that county officials had used both the carrot and the stick. The carrot, he claimed, was the promise of county "co-operation" in some real estate matters. The stick, Wood alleged, was the threat that there might be difficulties in gaining the re-zoning of Dunwoodie which would be necessary for any development other than residential. No proof of either allegation was offered by Wood. And it is worth noting that the county had no zoning authority whatever, and that zoning control was exercised over the property by the City of Yonkers. Also, Sherry denied the existence of any carrot. He explained that county officials had mentioned that they had the "ultimate weapon" in their right to condemn the property. This "stick" was all they needed. (Actually the County Executive later told the writer that the county would never have resorted to condemnation; it would have looked for another location. But the threat of condemnation was apparently used.)

Wood used a number of instruments and channels for presenting his case and his charges. He was in frequent contact with the banks of Yonkers, which were concerned with the tax-base question and, more specifically, with the accounts which a suburban Rockefeller Center might bring. Bank officials made private efforts to get the owners to sell Dunwoodie for development; they issued public protests against purchase by the county. They were prepared to use their influence with Yonkers officials to get Dunwoodie re-zoned from residential to commercial.

Other elements of the business community of Yonkers were concerned primarily with the tax rate and opposed county purchase because of the tax exemption which would follow. The Chamber of Commerce was the first to act, sending a unanimous resolution of its Board of Directors condemning the prospect of county purchase to the County Board of Supervisors. This action was taken five days after receipt of the still secret option by the county. It served to bring the problem forcefully to public attention. Almost immediately, the Yonkers Council of Civic and Taxpayers Associations sent a similar protest to county officials, followed by the Yonkers section of the Westchester County Realty Board. Triggered by these substantial signs of community opposition, the *Yonkers Herald Statesman* began to cover the story of the controversy and, on November 3, 1954, elicited the denial from the Park Commission that the county had any intention of buying Dunwoodie.

Six days later, the Yonkers City Council, apparently unconvinced by the statement of the Park Commission, formally resolved to oppose acquisition of Dunwoodie by the county. At this point a major portion of Yonkers business interests as well as the Yonkers city government were on record as opposing an action which the county denied any intention of taking. It would be two months before the county would publicly take action looking toward acquisition of Dunwoodie. In the meantime, the voices in support of county acquisition were confined to two or three letters from single individuals urging the county to preserve Dunwoodie as a park. When, on November 18, the County Executive seemed to indicate in a statement to the press that the decision would not be made in opposition to the wishes of Yonkers, there seemed to be little chance that any barrier to the suburban Rockefeller Center would develop. Wood became very active in promoting his plan. The illusion did not persist, however. Just before the Christmas holidays the Board of Supervisors appropriated the $2,400,000 for golf and swimming facilities. Just after the holidays, on January 6, 1955, the Westchester County Park Commission made its formal recommendation to the Board of Supervisors that Dunwoodie Golf Course be purchased, using money from the newly-appropriated fund.

Wood then turned his attention to the press. He solicited the editorial support of the Macy chain of newspapers, particularly the *Yonkers Herald Statesman*. (The Macy chain owned all of the dailies published in Westchester.) He presented his case to the Kiwanis Club. He provided the *New York Herald Tribune* and the *New York Times* with his interpretation of the issue, suggesting that they investigate his charges of political "influence." These moves were only partly successful. Early in February the *Herald Tribune* published a major story on the situation. On March 4 the *Yonkers Herald Statesman*, in an editorial, strongly supported county purchase of Dunwoodie despite Wood's campaign.

As a final effort, Wood turned to the New York offices of several major retailers operating in Westchester County with the plea that they send their local representatives to urge the Macy papers to oppose county purchase. This move brought response from the retailers, but none from the Macy chain. Its editorial support for county acquisition continued.

While some of the issues raised by Wood seemed spurious, others appeared to go to the heart of county development policy. What were the relative advantages of more public golf courses as against increased tax revenues for schools? Was added protection against "Bronxification" more important than stimulation of business activity? Would the increase in tax income resulting from a suburban Rockefeller Center be offset by declines in tax values of adjacent property? Would the purchase of Dunwoodie prevent decline of neighboring property values? These and other questions were never subjected to intensive research by either side. The county's position rested on assumptions as to the relative value of the park as an amenity and the stimulation of business. The assumptions took the form of the long-range park development policy. No research was deemed necessary. While facts and figures might have helped the opposition forces, Wood was in no position to conduct the extensive research that would have been necessary to measure exactly the gains and losses of various lines of action.

Other weaknesses plagued the opposition cause. As a result of conflicts in goals, elements of opposition never organized effectively to urge the defeat of the county's proposal. Some wanted alternative park uses, some wanted residential subdivision, while some wanted a suburban Rockefeller Center. Wood, the most energetic protagonist of an alternative use of the site, was several weeks or months behind the county in the development of a detailed alternative plan for two reasons. He was almost fully occupied with other business and, through lack of information on the county's project, he had no sense of urgency.

Informal channels of communication with the individuals in the county government responsible for the decision were exploited only to a very limited extent. There was little personal contact attempted between the opposition and county officials, despite the fact that the period between discovery of the project and the formal announcement might have been used for behind-the-scenes effort rather than for the public blasts of the Yonkers Chamber of Commerce, Realty Board, and City Council. It was later suggested by knowledgeable persons both in Yonkers and at the county seat in White Plains that this lack of intimate communications was a symptom of an historic gulf which separated the Westchester which had been "Bronxified" from the Westchester of upper middle class rural estates. Yonkers, the most Democratic of Westchester's communities, was at a disadvantage in exploiting the lever of the Republican Party to influence the county administration. It was quite possible that Wood could find no Republican channel to use. Only one Republican Supervisor from Yonkers, Christian Armbruster, ultimately opposed the county administration's position, and he was not willing to push his opposition to the extreme of joining the Democratic minority on the Board of Supervisors against purchase of Dunwoodie.

The Political Management of Formal Ratification

It remains to turn back the clock to late October 1954 and follow the story of formal ratification from the perspective of the county officials.

When Park Superintendent Haight had been informed that funds for additional park and swimming facilities would be made available, the decision had already been cleared by the County Executive with the steering committee of the Board of Supervisors. This was normal practice for all major decisions on policy and expenditure. When the steering committee met, the leadership of the Republican Party on the Board, as well as several leading members of the administration, sat in attendance. While technically the administration's representatives were not members, they usually participated fully in deliberations and influenced decisions, which were usually arrived at by consensus. The deliberations of the steering committee have always been secret.

Having received clearance from the County Executive through the Budget Director, George Haight had proceeded to obtain the option to buy Dunwoodie on November 8, 1954. On the same day the Park Commission had addressed to the Board of Supervisors an official request for approval of the golf and swimming pool items in the capital budget. Two points supported the request. The congestion of existing facilities was cited. Moreover, the Commission asserted it was studying the restriction of the facilities so that they might be enjoyed "without . . . a tremendous overload from outside the county." There had been no doubt that the Board of Supervisors would not approve these items without such an assurance. On November 15 the County Executive's budget message had singled out these items and had strongly recommended that they be adopted. In due course the Board's Committee on Budget and Appropriations had recommended the adoption of the entire budget with no change, and on December 20 the Board had adopted it in toto by a vote of 36 to 7. This action had not committed the county to the purchase of Dunwoodie Golf Course, but merely to the expansion of golf and swimming pool facilities.

When the item for golf courses had been placed in the capital budget, it was quite clear to everyone involved, including the leadership of the Board of Supervisors, that Dunwoodie was the golf course to be purchased with the money. This fact had been concealed, however, so that the minimum of controversy would arise before the actual appropriation of the funds, and in order to deal with certain elements of the opposition which were already manifesting their strength. Under questioning from the press the County Executive had implied, on November 18, that the wishes of Yonkers in the matter of the site would not be overridden. The *Yonkers Herald Statesman,* assuming the county was no longer considering the Dunwoodie site, had begun to inquire where the new course would go. This was the situation on December 20 when the appropriation was made by the Board.

Immediately following the Christmas holidays, on January 6, the Park Commission formally and publicly requested the Board of Supervisors to approve the purchase of Dunwoodie for use as a public golf course. The Commission stated that the greatest need for golfing facilities was in the southern portion of the county. The site should be readily accessible and adjacent to other park and parkway facilities. Dunwoodie met these qualifications and should be acquired at once. For the proponents of another course at Saxon Woods, it was noted that this project would be recommended in the future, but the present need was to acquire Dunwoodie.

Now, for the first time, it became clear to everyone concerned that the county was going to try to acquire Dunwoodie. But, since the request had come from the Park Commission, a relatively autonomous agency, there was still a question as to the position of the county administration. The County Executive did not hasten to affirm his support for the project. Only a few weeks before, he had indicated that Dunwoodie would not be purchased over Yonkers' opposition. But how was the position of Yonkers on the matter to be determined? Up to this time most overt activity in Yonkers had registered opposition to the purchase of Dunwoodie by the county. It now seemed time to wait for a further crystallization of sentiment.

The announcement of the Park Commission's request unleashed a flood of activity for and against county purchase. Opposition to purchase, however, was now confined almost entirely to C. Van Ness Wood and his allies, the bankers. Few others felt that there was any hope of balking the county. The Yonkers City Manager and Council remained opposed but inactive. In contrast, support for the Park Commission arose on all sides. No little of this support was attributable to the personal activity of the Park

Superintendent, George Haight, and of the two commissioners who had been the most interested in Dunwoodie, Evans Ward and John Stilwell. Early support came through party channels, from Yonkers Republican clubs. By now, community associations were afraid of residential subdivision of Dunwoodie. The Yonkers Council of Civic and Taxpayers Associations met and rescinded its opposition to county purchase. Composed of neighborhood associations, the Council had hoped for Yonkers to acquire Dunwoodie for a park. With this hope gone, the Council moved to forestall the danger of development by supporting the Park Commission's plan for county acquisition.

In February the Yonkers Recreation Commission backed county purchase. In early March, the Independent Republican Macy-chain press came out for county acquisition. The Board of Supervisors still failed to act. The opposition of the Yonkers Council still seemed important. County Executive Hopkins agreed to meet with the Yonkers Council to hear its views. While the Council remained opposed after this meeting, the strength of its opposition lessened, as did any hopes that the county could be thwarted. Some councilmen privately told Hopkins that they failed to support county purchase only because of certain political commitments.

If the county's Republican leadership was waiting for the results of the campaign for approval, it seemed to have been satisfied by March 25. On that date the County Executive formally recommended approval of the purchase of Dunwoodie to the Board of Supervisors. When the Board met on March 28, this message was received, together with the approval of the County Planning Commission. The Planning Commission's approval was required by law for capital projects and had been obtained in a telephone call made just before the meeting of the Board of Supervisors. The Planning Director reported the Commission's approval to the County Executive, who reported it to the Board.

The recommendation for purchase of Dunwoodie had been referred to the Board's Committee on Budget and Appropriations. In Committee the pros and cons of purchase of Dunwoodie had been discussed at length but without a sharp division of opinion. The decision to recommend purchase was arrived at by consensus. When the Committee reported favorably on the request of the Park Commission, the Board of Supervisors voted for purchase of Dunwoodie by a vote of 33 to 5, and authorized the Board of Acquisition and Contract to proceed with the purchase. The five opposing supervisors were all members of the Democratic minority. Rather than join this minority on the floor, Armbruster, the only Republican Yonkers supervisor who opposed purchase, took this time to plead his cause in the County Executive's office.

Throughout the formal process of ratification the usual routine had been followed. Just prior to the final vote by the Board it had been necessary to wait several weeks in order that the campaign for public support of the county's purchase could be developed. Just as the secrecy policy had prevented premature opposition, it had also prevented the organization of support by proponents of county purchase. Once this job had been accomplished sufficiently to produce visible signs of public support in Yonkers for the project, the final vote was taken. There was no evidence that more citizens of Yonkers opposed the purchase than supported it. The total number of actors was small throughout the process.

The purchase was actually closed on January 11, 1956. The delay in closing represented the time during which the existing lease was still in effect.

The Trenton Milk Contract

Robert Golembiewski

A Reformer Is Elected

THIS IS THE STORY of the cancellation and the reinstatement of a contract to supply milk to a city hospital in Trenton, New Jersey. The events occurred in the summer of 1955. The account describes the efforts of a "reformer" recently elected to the Trenton City Commission to press for improvements in the administration carried on by a majority of his fellow commissioners who had been in office for many years. Under the commission system of city government the commissioners collectively act in a legislative capacity while individually they serve as the heads of the major city departments. When Arthur Holland, the reform-minded commissioner, acted in a legislative capacity and criticized paving contracts and similar matters at Commission meetings, he violated a custom under which commissioners supported the decisions and recommendations made by each individual commissioner for his own department. Inside *his* own department, which among other things was responsible for the operation of city hospitals, Holland found himself limited, in his attempt to gain real as well as formal departmental control, by dependence on, and early resistance from, civil servants who had been appointed by his predecessors.

It was while he was keeping his eyes on opportunities for reforms in other departments that Commissioner Holland came a cropper when he canceled the milk contract. He acted quickly when the technical aides in his Department reported to him that a dairy was delivering milk with butterfat content below contract specifications. The upshot of his action was that Holland soon found himself confronted with legal claims that he had acted without due process, upon inadequate evidence, and on the basis of staff advice that was not, from the standpoint of the technology of milk testing, first class. To Holland's surprise, and to the delectation of his foes, he found himself depicted not as a hero but as a capricious tyrant, not as a supporter of administrative reform but as someone who had acted either incompetently or from base and reprehensible motives.

This story raises a number of issues. There is, first, the role of the administrator in making and canceling city contracts—particularly the manner by which he balances consideration of government interest, on the one hand, against the right of the contractor to due process on the other. To what extent must the executive, responsible for administrative justice, familiarize himself with the technological details that may underlie the most minor decision? From one standpoint this is the story of an administrator who, en route to civic improvement, kicked at a pebble and found, when he picked himself up, that it was really the protruding tip of a boulder.

Trenton's Commission Government

Although Trenton, New Jersey's capital, has about 130,000 citizens, it has some qualities of a smaller city: a "local booster" atmosphere, local heroes, and its own peculiar political tradition.

The formal structure of the city government in 1955 was set by New Jersey's Walsh Act of 1911. Trenton had a five-man Board of Commissioners chosen at four-year intervals in non-party elections. The Board had the full legislative power allowed to municipalities, and the Board itself decided by majority vote which of the five city departments each commissioner was to administer. In Trenton the three "big" departments were Public Safety, Public Works, and Public Affairs. Their 1956 budgets ranged from $4,000,000 to $1,500,000. The other two departments, Parks and Finance, spent $700,000 and $300,000 respectively.

The full Commission selected one of its members as Mayor who "shall be president of the Board, and shall preside at its meetings, supervise all departments and report to the Board for its action all matters requiring the attention of the Board or any department . . . but shall have no power to veto any measure." A commissioner was paid $7,500 a year in 1955. The Mayor received $8,250.

Trenton was one of the earliest New Jersey cities to adopt commission government. One of the major attractions of the new form was the promise of ridding municipal government of party machine politics. (Non-party elections were required by the Walsh Act.) As has happened in other cities using this form of government, however, Trenton commissioners sought to insure their re-election by using their departmental powers and perquisites to develop personal followings which cut across party lines. With each commissioner preoccupied with his own department and his own following, the city Democratic organization only sporadically exercised control over county government despite the fact that predominantly Democratic Trenton comprised three-quarters of the population of Mercer County. For commissioners this meant little opportunity to climb higher than their municipal posts.

The Dead End of Trenton Politics

In the early thirties Crawford Jamieson, a lawyer, managed to bypass Trenton politics and capture control of the Mercer County Democratic organization. He was elected to the State Assembly, later to the State Senate; then he became acting Democratic State Chairman. A number of Jamieson men gained elective or appointive posts in county and state government.

In 1939, seeking a city base for his county organization, Jamieson backed a four-man slate for seats on the City Commission. One of his candidates, Donal J. Connolly, appeared to have an especially bright political future. But none of the Jamieson men were elected.

Jamieson and his associates then ran head-on into the powerful Democratic organization of Mayor Frank Hague of Jersey City. Jamieson led a successful fight to defeat a state sales tax bill supported by Hague; he supported state constitutional revision against Hague opposition; and he tried to keep the Mercer County Democratic organization free from Hague influence. In 1942 Jamieson and Connolly were appointed by Democratic Governor Charles Edison to state administrative posts, Jamieson to the Public Utilities Commission, and Connolly (through Jamieson's intervention) to the State Beauty Board, as its Secretary. The appointments were designed to serve mixed purposes, one of which was to protect Jamieson and his associates from Hague retribution at the next election.

Hague succeeded in replacing Jamieson with a more friendly Democratic State Chairman, and he blocked appointment or reappointment of other members of Jamieson's faction to state and local government positions. This reinforced the separation of city and county politics. Jamieson retired to private law practice in 1945, and most of his other associates also withdrew from active politics. Connolly, through a local arrangement, was appointed to a vacancy on the Trenton City Commission in 1946. A year later, however, he was indicted for allegedly conspiring, while working for the State Beauty Board, to violate the state beauty culture laws for financial gain. Connolly was acquitted, but the fact that he had been indicted would have handicapped any immediate advance beyond a municipal political career. Municipal elections thus took on a special importance for Connolly. Like other Trenton commissioners, he was able to use his departmental position to develop and solidify a personal following. Like other commissioners, he was successful. From 1943 until 1955, only one incumbent Trenton commissioner was unseated by a candidate who did not have the support of one of these personal followings. The man who accomplished this feat was Arthur Holland, the central figure of this story.

The Majority Coalition of 1955

Three of the five Trenton city commissioners standing for re-election in 1955—Mayor Donal Connolly, George W. Rieker, and Andrew J. Duch—presented a united public front and had pretty much their own way in municipal politics. Thus the three could—and did—control departmental assignments and the selection of the Mayor.

Connolly—by now commissioner for nine years and Mayor for eight of them—was the most powerful of the three men. His preeminence was in part explained by and reflected in his selection as Mayor and his administrative control of the important Department of Public Works with its extensive program of street development and improvement. Described locally as the "Salesman for a Greater Trenton," Connolly sought "polite" government (his reactions to public criticisms of himself or his Department were strong) and "private" government (the Commission majority refused to permit evening public sessions in 1951, "to save on the light bill," as Connolly said).

The Mayor's position was also a result of the congenial meshing of his "political character" with that of the two other majority commissioners. Rieker, 57 in 1955, had been a commissioner for a little less than twelve years but was content as director of the Department of Parks, generally regarded as a low-pressure, low-patronage post. Duch, at 60, on the other hand, had three consecutive terms behind him, including one as Mayor. He headed the city's large Department of Public Safety. He had not attempted to use the potential political leverage of that Department against Connolly in any continuing fashion.

The other two commissioners had held office since 1951. Warren W. Orpen, once deputy director of the large Public Affairs Department, was treated well by the majority, which made him director of that Department. The other minority member, Sido L. Ridolfi, had been more of an "outsider." Educated at Princeton and the Harvard Law School, he received the tiny Finance Department. Ridolfi was able to use the post to snipe at practices of other commissioners in letting some city contracts.

The 1955 Election

On the eve of the 1955 election, the Commission presented to the outside world a study in harmony. (Internal differences were settled privately. Criticisms from outside were few and unpublicized.) The incumbents preserved this picture in the election. They ran as a "team."

The opposition field did not seem likely to disturb the status quo. Only four challengers filed petitions for the five Commission seats. And only one of the candidates who filed to oppose the "team" did not fit the categories into which Commission candidates usually fell: that is, he was not an incumbent, he was not coopted, he was not regarded by insiders as a political eccentric, and he was not hoping to parlay a substantial "also-ran" showing into a political appointment. That man was Holland. Young—36—and perhaps the most prominent "joiner" in the county, Holland was something of a new type in city politics. For one thing, he laid heavy emphasis on the need to improve municipal government from the "point of view of both efficiency and moral outlook." Many explained these aims by noting that Holland had spent six years in preparation for the Roman Catholic priesthood. Also somewhat unusual—since most Trenton political figures were lawyers or businessmen—was the fact that Holland had worked for five years as a field supervisor and research analyst for Opinion Research Corporation. In 1949 he switched to part-time executive work with another firm in the field in order to complete an A.B. at the Rutgers University evening college and, if possible, to begin a local political career.

Holland had been mentioned as a possible Commission candidate in the relatively fluid election of 1951. But on December 31, 1950, he had accepted the $4,300-a-year post of deputy director of the Department of Public Affairs, the position from which Orpen had resigned to run for a Commission seat. Holland was the senior executive present in the Department for four months during the fatal illness of the director. In 1952 Holland was appointed deputy director of Rieker's Parks Department at $4,960 (later increased to $5,700)—a testimony to his ability and to the strength of a City Hall tradition that the deputy of a commissioner who died in office was always retained. Regarded as a more-than-likely candidate for the Commission in 1959, when two incumbents were not expected to run, there seemed to be no place for Holland in the "certain" 1955 race. But rather than wait his turn, Holland announced his candidacy for a Commission seat and resigned his Parks Department post.

Early in the campaign Holland seemed to have little chance of winning. His releases alone could not create a campaign—the newspapers paid them little notice—and no other candidate was anxious or perhaps able to stir up brisk public interest. But shortly before the election a chance event gave Holland notoriety. He had criticized the Commission team for splitting contracts into lots of less than $1,000 and distributing them without competitive bidding.[1] To follow up, he dropped in to see Orpen to ask for access to his Department's files to check certain purchases. Orpen exploded. He swung at Holland and kept swinging as Holland retreated some fifty feet out of Orpen's office through a crowded corridor, protecting himself but not striking back.

Front-page stories of the incident kindled public interest in the campaign and in Holland. He began receiving extra newspaper attention. For example, the newspapers devoted ten inches to Holland's charge that Orpen purchased ten $14.10 bedpans when, Holland said, a purchasing agent at a private hospital told him that $7.00 was the top price for bedpans. "He has strong moral convictions," wrote one reporter. "He is inclined to get mad when he thinks something is morally wrong, and excited in his youthful way when he thinks he can rectify the matter."

Many seemed to feel that Trenton needed a political crusader, and Holland suddenly found himself with what he called the "greatest voluntary organization the city ever saw." Enthusiasm for Holland increased even though the remaining twenty days of the campaign did not see many of his charges proved in any strict sense. In the case of the bedpans, for example, the other side retorted—though their report certainly did not definitely settle the question—that $14.10 was the price of lifetime stainless steel pans, and that the $7.00 price quoted to Holland had been for less durable models. Nevertheless Holland won a commissionership in the election by running a strong third. At 36 he was the youngest commissioner-elect in Trenton's history.

Holland on the City Commission

Old hands in city politics waited for Holland to get his come-uppance at the hands of the incumbent commissioners, but his first experience on the City Commission was a pleasant one. In the distribution of administrative departments, he was given Public Affairs, Orpen's old department. The Commission majority had planned to give Holland the low-budget Department of Finance, but incumbent Ridolfi declined to advance to Public Affairs. He had been elected to the State Senate, and only the relatively light work load of the Finance Department would permit him to serve in the Legislature, to continue his private law practice, and also to hold city office.

"His immediate objective . . . is to improve the city's purchasing practices," a city newspaper reported after Holland's election, adding that he "also intends to carry on his investigation of the city's paving program. . . ." But inside his own sprawling Public Affairs Department, Holland had much to do, and in his early days in office he encountered a number of obstacles.

First, civil service regulations limited the appointments he could make to one deputy, one secretary, and one clerk or one stenographer. Also, there was some early antagonism to the new director within the Department; many of the permanent officials owed their jobs to previous directors and to the Commission majority.

Second, Holland had trouble filling even the key appointment available to him, that of deputy director. His preference, James H. Davidson, had managed Holland's publicity campaign. But Davidson finally decided he could not resign his $15,000 job with National Dairy Products Corporation to accept the $5,700 deputyship.

Third, Public Affairs was a catch-all Department with health and welfare its major functions. This meant that Holland had to master a wide range of procedures and expertise. The Department was responsible for Donnelly Memorial Hospitals; the office of the City Clerk; Weights and Measures; Health (including the City Chemist's office); Public Welfare (which handled social work and assistance); Marine Terminal; and the Municipal Farmers' Market. Many of these units had traditions of autonomy and traditional ways of doing things.

However, Holland did not let these departmental difficulties slow down his zeal for reform of all city departments. By the second week after his election he was stirring up Commission meetings, supported by Ridolfi. On May 26 Holland

[1] State law requires that contracts for amounts exceeding $1,000 be awarded competitively. Two $500 contracts, however, may be awarded without advertising for bids—a practice which could easily be used to discipline local businessmen and solidify a commissioner's following.

took up the attack on purchasing and paving practices which had formed a large part of his election campaign. When Mayor Connolly offered a resolution to award a $32,000 street paving contract, Holland argued that the city could save $2,200 if it utilized a different method of calling for bids. He cited City Engineer Joseph R. English as his authority. Unfortunately for Holland, English told the commissioners that he had since revised his thinking after checking with the contractors. However, if abortive from Holland's standpoint, the paving incident had significance for one of the city papers:

> An era ended at City Hall yesterday. The City Commission, which for the last four years regularly put up a united front whatever differences it had in private, split 3 to 2 and 4 to 1 on two votes yesterday with the promise of further open dissension.

It was clear to the majority commissioners that Holland was not going to play by the established rules. Over the years, the courtesy of allowing an individual commissioner freedom within his department was normally honored by all commissioners, or at least disputes were settled in conference before the public meetings, which could give them city-wide attention.

The Contract Is Canceled

ONE OF THE MORE routine acts of Commissioner Holland immediately after his election was to submit a resolution to the full Commission on June 2 authorizing the City Clerk to advertise for competitive bids on sixteen varieties of milk products. The milk was to be supplied to Donnelly Memorial Hospitals for the three-month period beginning July 1. Donnelly, chiefly for tuberculous patients, was a division of Holland's Department and had a 1956 budget of approximately $750,000. The resolution was adopted unanimously without discussion on June 2.

There was no review of the milk order in the Public Affairs Department prior to the submission of the resolution. Holland's deputy did not take office until June 15, and Holland himself had been preoccupied with other duties. Moreover, Holland had no special competence in dietetics or tubercular diseases. He recalled from his previous experience in the Department that one of the major problems in tuberculosis treatment was loss of appetite. Hence the need for foods like milk, which have a high food value per unit consumed.

After the Commission's approval of bid advertisement, individual bids for each of the sixteen items—a purchasing innovation by Holland—were submitted directly to the Purchasing Office, a service agency for all city departments. No one in Holland's office had any contact with the contract-letting until June 23, 1955, and then it was a casual one. Commissioner Holland formally presented a resolution to the full Commission on that date to award the several contracts. The resolution was adopted unanimously.

Ryan's Dairy of Trenton won the bid on seven items and made the first delivery on July 1. On July 5, Assistant City Chemist Arthur R. Bartolozzi of the Bureau of Health, Department of Public Affairs, conducted the first routine biweekly test of the milk Ryan delivered. He reported that samples taken from deliveries to Donnelly's two patient wings, Madden and Klempner, contained 3.25 and 3.5 percent butterfat, respectively.

The test for butterfat was important for two reasons. First, the proportion of butterfat is a measure of a milk's dietetic utility for tuberculous patients. Second, the proportion of butterfat is *the* qualitative measure of milk and is invariably used as the basis of payment for such supplies. Milk with a fat content of four percent or more is labeled Grade A and that with a content between 3.5 and 4.0 percent is Grade B.

The butterfat contents Bartolozzi reported for the first test were significant to him and to his immediate superior, City Chemist Michael A. Lettiere, for they understood that only Grade A (four percent butterfat) milk was to be supplied to Donnelly. Lettiere reported the test results directly to Commissioner Holland because Lettiere's immediate superior, part-time Bureau of Health head Dr. Elmer J. Elias, was in South America on vacation. Holland told Frank Mara, a long-time city employee with the title of Milk Inspector, to inform Peter A. Ryan of the low fat content. Mara did so. Holland also recalled that Ryan's Dairy had had a similar difficulty with the Public Affairs Department during the administration of his predecessor.

On July 6, Bartolozzi made another pair of tests and reported fat contents of 4.5 and 3.3 percent for the two Donnelly wings. Lettiere once again went to Holland, and the commissioner told Lettiere to act himself if he thought the matter so important. The chemist explained that he could act through Dr. Elias' office only in a criminal prosecution for a violation of state law, which sets a three percent fat content minimum for salable milk. Since Ryan's milk tested above that minimum, the Bureau of Health could not act, Lettiere held. But he did promise to call Ryan and tell him about the butterfat values. Mara also complained to Holland about the fat contents, with similar results.

Assistant City Chemist Bartolozzi next tested samples of the Ryan milk on July 12. He reported that both samples were from Grade A milk since the fat contents were 4.15 and 4.2 percent. Holland was not told of the results personally, although a report did cross his desk. Lettiere performed the tests on the July 13 milk. He reported that both samples tested 3.5 percent. The chemists told Holland of the test results late the next morning.

While Lettiere and Bartolozzi were with Holland, Anthony Thein walked in. He was the City Hall correspondent of one of the local newspapers. Holland announced to Thein that he was canceling the Ryan Dairy contract. He explained that the milk met the State Health Department requirements, so it was not a matter for Health Bureau action; but tuberculous patients needed the high butterfat milk in their diets. Therefore, Holland stated, he was going to transfer the contract to the Delaware Valley Dairy, the next lowest bidder.

Thein suggested that Holland first contact City Counsel Louis Josephson whose office was in the building. Holland telephoned, but the City Counsel was not in his office. Accounts differ as to what happened after the call. Thein claims Holland asked him to break the story "big." Holland agrees, but with the qualification that he asked Thein to hold the story until Ryan's Dairy received a letter of notification. In any event, the cancellation story barely beat the deadline for the city edition, and it was on the streets early that afternoon. Holland was still news in Trenton, and from this point on unusually vigorous and extensive reporting by Thein and others expanded the cancellation into a major local affair.

While the presses turned, Holland was involved in a stormy City Commission meeting. To illustrate the subjects of contention, Mayor Connolly offered a resolution to advertise for competitive bids for fire hydrants. The specifications restricted the bids to the products of one manufacturer. Holland—in the negative all afternoon—voted "Pass" (the equivalent of checking in poker), and Ridolfi voted "No." The Mayor exploded at this public display of dissent. "You're trying to run all five departments," he said. "Why don't you stick to your own department?"

When Holland returned to his office after the meeting, he reports that he found a telephone message from Peter A. Ryan, owner of Ryan's Dairy, asking that he call him. The first thing Ryan allegedly said was, "Arthur, will you give me another chance?" At that moment Holland's secretary placed before him a copy of the *Trenton Times* which carried a front-page story announcing the contract cancellation. "I'm afraid it's too late for that now," Holland told Ryan.

Holland Checks the Law

Holland immediately called Louis Josephson, the City Counsel, with whom he had always had cordial relations. (Josephson had been active in local politics before his appointment in 1944. He, Commissioner Duch, and the late Commissioner Waldron had run as a team for Commission seats in 1943. Duch and Waldron had been elected, Duch had been named Mayor, and shortly thereafter, Josephson had been appointed City Counsel.) When Holland told Josephson of the cancellation, the Counsel was surprised; he could not recall a similar action. Josephson was even more surprised when Holland mentioned that Ryan's Dairy had not been formally warned (Mara and Lettiere had given verbal warnings), and that a notice of cancellation had not yet been prepared. Josephson agreed to write the letter of cancellation. Before he did, he consulted his *Annotated Statutes of New Jersey* and jotted these notes on the back of the foolscap on which he wrote the draft of the cancellation letter:

1. "After the various powers of government in commission controlled cities have been distributed among the several departments and the appointment of the director has been made, the executive and administrative powers are to be exercised by the respective commissioners presiding over the several departments and not by the whole body of commissioners." *Rubenstein v. Board of Commissioners of City of Bayonne,* 121 N.J.L. 97.

2. "A contract can be cancelled by an individual commissioner for 'good cause,' on evidence that would lead 'reasonable men to the same conclusions'." *Peluso v. Board of Commissioners of Jersey City.*

The cancellation letter which Josephson wrote, and Holland signed, referred to "the contract you now hold with the city to furnish homogenized Grade A milk for the Donnelly Memorial Hospitals."

Holland also received some unsolicited advice. That evening Mayor Connolly issued a statement to the press declaring that he personally would see to it that the city re-advertised for bids to re-award the contract. The newspapers reported that the Mayor could not understand Holland's actions, for he was certain that the young commissioner was aware of the relevant state law. Moreover, he noted pointedly, it was customary to bring such matters up at the informal commissioners' conference held each Thursday morning just before the public meeting. There, seasoned advice was available.

Ryan Protests

The day after the cancellation, Peter A. Ryan publicly challenged the City Chemist's contention that the milk his firm supplied to Donnelly Memorial Hospitals was below specifications. The milk had "at all times met specifications," he wrote. Every batch of Ryan's milk had been tested by a resident technologist, Ryan went on, and every test showed a butterfat content of four percent or more. Moreover, Ryan's statement continued, Public Affairs Director Holland had acted illegally in canceling the contract for provisions in the State Food and Drug Act required that samples of any milk to be tested and later used in terminating a supplier's contract, had to be taken in the presence of a representative of the dairy concerned, who was given a part of the sample so that the dairy could also test it. This procedure for protecting the supplier from arbitrary government action was not followed in this case, Ryan noted. In fact, Ryan added, he had not known of the cancellation or of the tests until he read the news story. Thus, the City Chemist's test results did not constitute legal grounds for the cancellation of the contract. Ryan added a parting shot in the direction of both Holland and Lettiere:

> If we were notified the tests were to be made and if we were furnished with a sample as the law directs, we would have had a disinterested chemist available to make a test simultaneously with that being made by the city official under the direction of Mr. Holland. He must have realized that such a test would indicate that our milk fully met all requirements of the contract. Obviously, there is no way we can verify the city's alleged test when it is done surreptitiously, and in direct violation of the procedure established by the law of New Jersey.
>
> We shall, of course, expect the city to honor its contract with us and shall expect Mr. Holland to make public admission that legal procedure was not followed in this case.

Ryan's allegation that Holland had acted contrary to provisions of the State Food and Drug Act discomfited Holland. As he later explained:

> I never heard of a "legal sample." Ryan's charge that one was necessary to cancel the contract made my action seem pretty arbitrary. I was still morally convinced I was right. But I was worried about whether or not I had the legal right to do it. That was the only worry I had in the beginning.
>
> Somebody should have told me about the "legal sample," though. My Department let me down.

The members of Holland's Department were not eager to accept the responsibility for the slip. "That wasn't my job," City Chemist Lettiere later noted. "I just test the milk." Milk Inspector Mara, on the other hand, could only express surprise that Holland had canceled the contract, since such a thing had never been done before. At any rate, it was clear that the City Chemist's office only infrequently (once since 1947) used the legal sample. The procedure normally followed was more casual. Milk Inspector Mara would make the rounds and collect samples of various milks, supposedly on an irregular basis to prevent dairy "anticipation" of tests. The samples collected were not "legal," and when a dairy failed to meet certain requirements—butterfat content, for example—it was notified informally of the deficiency. Though the state law provides for prosecution for failure to meet standards, Lettiere could remember no cases in which that formal remedy had been applied.

Two explanations were offered to Holland for the general failure to take legal samples. First, the taking of legal samples in all cases would have imposed an impossible burden on Milk Inspector Mara. Second, records in the City Chemist's office showed that the overwhelming majority of milk samples tested were above state standards. When the City Chemist conducted "special" tests such as the higher butterfat Donnelly milk, Lettiere explained, the "normal" procedure was followed.

The City Counsel's Opinion

To Holland, these explanations were sufficient. But they did not contradict Ryan's contentions that a legal test was necessary. For aid on this score, Holland contacted City Counsel Josephson. The City Counsel was also unfamiliar with the law concerning legal tests. And he again repaired to the *Annotated Statutes*. The section of the New Jersey Food and Drug Act to which Ryan's letter had alluded, Josephson discovered, did provide for legal samples:

> At the time of the delivery or the taking of the sample . . . it shall be divided in the presence of the [supplier] or before a witness, into two or more parts and each part shall be sealed in a suitable package. One part shall be . . . delivered to the person of whom the request or demand was made with a statement in writing that such sample is taken for the purpose of examination, issued in the name of the department and signed by the person taking the same.

But the statute is limited in two ways: it requires legal samples only where state standards are in question; and it requires that legal samples be submitted as evidence only in cases of criminal prosecution for the violation of state standards.

The law, Josephson noted, was not applicable to the Ryan cancellation on either count. For the Ryan contract was not canceled for the violation of any state standard, and the city did not contemplate any criminal prosecution. He wrote a formal opinion—which has the force of law until overruled by a court—to this effect. It stated in part:

> . . . that if any of said milk did not meet . . . specifications, [Commissioner Holland's] action in cancelling said agreement was entirely proper and in all respects valid. Whether it did or not is a question of fact and not of law. I may add that based upon the facts submitted to me, there was a violation of the agreement.
>
> The contention of the seller that State law requires [a legal sample] . . . has no application in this instance.
>
> [Commissioner Holland's] action is not based upon or for the purpose of prosecuting a violation of law. It is merely . . . a remedy for breach of an agreement, which any party thereto may assert and establish by competent evidence in the event of litigation. If the seller feels that he has complied with the agreement, he may sue for breach of the contract and [the City] can present the evidence to the court and the jury.

Not included in his formal opinion, but communicated to Commissioner Holland some time after Josephson learned of the cancellation, was one other piece of legal advice. Although a single commissioner could terminate an agreement for good cause, contracts for sums over $1,000 could be awarded or permanently transferred only after competitive bidding. Thus, Holland would have to advertise for bids for the remainder of the three-month period covered by the canceled Ryan's contract since the value of the milk products was approximately $1,700.

Holland, however, could not simply advertise for bids and award the contract. Now that new bids had to be solicited, the matter was within the jurisdiction of the full Board of Commissioners. For in New Jersey only a majority of the full Commission may authorize public advertisement for bids; and only a majority of the full Commission may determine who in fact is a "responsible bidder." Holland accepted Josephson's advice concerning re-advertisement. As for the sudden and permanent transfer of the contract to the Delaware Valley Dairy, Holland explained: "Somebody had to supply the milk. I wasn't clear in my own mind then whether I had to re-advertise for bids or not. But I went ahead anyway."

Before Holland acted publicly on Josephson's advice, however, he waited for the file on Ryan that he had asked City Chemist Lettiere to prepare early the same day. Part of that file confirmed Holland's moral conviction about the cancellation. It contained a list of eight instances over a two-month period in 1952 in which Ryan's Dairy milk supplied to the Donnelly Hospitals allegedly had fallen below the four percent specification. Another section of the file listed seven occasions over a two-month period in 1952 when another Trenton-area dairy—Johanna Farms, Inc.—had also allegedly failed to meet the required four percent butterfat specification. Also included were letters to Johanna Farms from the City Purchasing Agent and from Warren W. Orpen, then Director of Public Affairs, warning Johanna that unless future samples met specifications its contract would be canceled. Ryan apparently had not received a formal warning.

The documents on Johanna were not included by mistake. Johanna, Lettiere explained to Holland, supplied the milk products which Ryan's Dairy delivered to the Donnelly Hospitals in 1955. In 1952, Ryan had operated his own dairy, but in 1955 he was merely a distributor for Johanna Farms. Holland had been unaware of this relationship, important because Johanna, the largest independent dairy in the area, was in a far better position to fight any city action than the smaller Ryan's Dairy. (Peter Ryan was one of his own salesmen.)

Holland immediately released to the press the file which Lettiere had compiled. Three points received prominent mention in the next day's city newspapers: (1) Josephson's upholding of the legality of the cancellation; (2) the records of the 1952 butterfat deficiencies of both Ryan's Dairy and Johanna Farms; (3) Holland's announcement that he would follow the advice of City Counsel Josephson and re-advertise for bids for the remainder of the three-month period, a decision, as the newspaper noted, which Holland claimed to have made "prior to the demand by Mayor Connolly . . . that new bids be sought."

The Johanna-Ryan Defense

EXCEPT FOR THE PUBLISHED criticisms by Ryan and Connolly, the cancellation had raised little public reaction.[2] To Holland this was reassuring. But Johanna Farms and Ryan's Dairy were preparing a counter-case. Indeed, later arguments employed against the cancellation were based on preparations Johanna claimed to have made early in July, nearly two weeks before the cancellation by Holland.

The first element in the Johanna-Ryan defense—and the only element of which Holland was aware—was a letter to Commissioner Holland from Attorney Lloyd Fisher. Fisher's letter was dated the day after the cancellation and was apparently written before Ryan had received Holland's formal letter of cancellation. The letter complained of blatant disregard of due process and stated that Ryan's only notice of the action was through the public press. The bulk of Fisher's letter rephrased the points in Ryan's protest. One paragraph immediately caught Holland's eye:

> My *clients* deny emphatically that there was any deficiency of butterfat but, on the contrary, allege that each and every shipment of milk made to the Donnelly Hospital under their contract was tested by a duly accredited technologist immediately before it left the premises of my *client* and that each and every shipment contained 4% butterfat or in excess of that figure. [Emphasis added.]

Fisher's reference to his "clients" was a signal that Johanna's management had decided that it would associate itself with the Ryan case. Since the milk had been tested at the Johanna plant and found above specification there, Johanna might have kept out of the case, for it might

[2] The material in this section is organized topically and the sequence of topics does not always follow actual chronological development.

have been argued that its obligation ended with the transfer of milk to Ryan. Johanna could not be absolutely certain just what milk Ryan had delivered to the hospital. But Johanna did not choose to remain in the background.

Fisher's letter also expressed the desire of Johanna-Ryan for the restoration of the contract. "This is a matter of great urgency to my client," the letter concluded. "They will suffer inestimable damage if [the contract is not immediately restored], damage far beyond the loss they will suffer by reason of the cancellation of the contract. They will suffer damage . . . because people will be led to believe that the charges you make are true and that my client handled an inferior product." If Holland failed to act, the letter warned, "action will be immediately instituted against you and the city to compel a restoration to my clients of the rights which are theirs."

Fisher sent a copy of the letter to each of the five commissioners. The copy that reached Holland's office was quickly relayed to City Counsel Josephson for an answer. Underlying Fisher's letter was a web of evidence which could not be dismissed lightly.

Mara's Visit to Johanna

Fisher's letter said that Johanna-Ryan had received no previous notice that cancellation proceedings were being considered by Commissioner Holland. But Johanna-Ryan had had notice that the Donnelly milk had tested low on several occasions. Lettiere claims to have phoned Ryan, and both sides agree that Milk Inspector Mara, on orders from Holland, informed Johanna of the low fat contents on at least one occasion early in July 1955. The manner in which Mara allegedly delivered the information became, in the public arguments of Johanna-Ryan against the cancellation, the first strand in an alleged possible conspiracy on the part of some city officials against the dairies.

Mara reported the test results of July 5 to Kurt Goldman, the manager of Johanna. Goldman had better "get on the ball," the droll Mara advised, "because there are a lot of milkmen around City Hall now." The "milkmen" referred to were James Davidson, Holland's chief campaign aide and district sales representative for National Dairy Products Corporation; Holland's deputy director, who had been associated with a national dairy firm with a plant in Trenton; and Holland's step-brother, Edward E. Atwood, who was a salesman for Meadowbrook Dairy, a local firm. Mara did more than tell Goldman of the City Hall milkmen. "Watch yourself," he said, "someone is out to get you." And though this was later denied, Mara was alleged to have mentioned names: that "someone" was Meadowbrook Dairy. Although no evidence was ever offered to support these charges, some could understand why Goldman became alarmed, for in addition to Holland's step-brother, as salesman, Meadowbrook Dairy could claim a long-time friendship between the City Chemist and its owner.

Forewarned is forearmed, and Goldman apparently prepared for the worst. He contacted Dr. David Levowitz, the owner of a large private milk-testing concern and a national authority on milk products. "On being consulted," Levowitz recalled, "I instructed that samples of all shipments [from Johanna] be taken and labeled in the presence of witnesses, then frozen and stored against the possibility that they would have to be tested. This, Goldman said, he did himself. Thus, in addition to the normal butterfat tests performed by the resident technologist at the Farms, Johanna claimed to have a number of samples of its product whose test results could be compared with tests made by Holland's department.

Goldman's caution was reinforced by another factor. City Chemist Lettiere had for some time run a private milk-testing service "on his own time." He had done Ryan's milk-testing work until 1954. After that date, Ryan operated only as a distributor for Johanna. Since all Ryan's testing was then done on Johanna's premises by the Dairy's own full-time employee, Ryan no longer required Lettiere's private services. It was alleged, however, that Lettiere had unsuccessfully solicited work from Johanna twice in the months immediately preceding the cancellation. The fact that, when the contract actually was canceled, Holland awarded the contract to the Delaware Valley Dairy, did not end the suspicion of a conspiracy that existed in the minds of Johanna officials. Delaware Valley was an affiliate of the National Dairy Products Corporation, the firm with which Holland's erstwhile campaign aide, James Davidson, was associated.

Discourse on Method

The release to the press of the memo on the alleged 1952 butterfat deficiency records of both Johanna and Ryan on Donnelly milk further incited the suspicions of officials of the two firms. For to Johanna the 1952 test data were not conclusive. The City Chemist's memorandum contained fifteen cases in which Johanna and Ryan Grade A homogenized milk supplied to Donnelly in 1952 tested below the four percent city specification. The then-independent Ryan's Dairy—if informed of the deficiencies—had made no effort to contest the results. Johanna was informed of the reported deficiencies, however, and the firm entered an immediate protest. Dr. Levowitz, whose testing firm was doing Johanna's control work, arranged to see City Chemist Lettiere. "I brought my organization's file [for Johanna] with me," Levowitz said of his 1952 visit, "and an abstract detailing the fat tests of 'A' Homogenized Milk [over the relevant period]. None of these samples showed values below 4.10 percent."

Moreover, Levowitz learned during the meeting that Lettiere had used a butterfat test which in the doctor's opinion could have accounted for the difference between Lettiere's and Levowitz' results. In 1890 a Dr. S. M. Babcock developed a relatively quick and economical test which approximated the values obtained by the "solvent extraction" test of raw whole milk. The Babcock test, like all butterfat tests, "unzips" the membranes which cover butterfat globules. The light fat is then free to rise, the butterfat content being determined by the height of the butterfat column at the top of the milk being tested. The test was unable to recover small globules of butterfat in whole milk. But these unrecovered globules were estimated to constitute only five percent of the butterfat in any milk sample. Babcock advised a rough rule-of-thumb to compensate for the unrecovered butterfat, and quickly the Babcock method became the method of determining butterfat content for the buying and selling of milk products in the United States.

Experts in the 1950s seemed to believe that growth in sales of homogenized milk had limited the usefulness of the Babcock test. For in homogenization, the butterfat globules in whole milk are broken up into very small particles which remain suspended in the liquid and do not rise to the top. Moreover, the Babcock test is not suited to high-sugar, flavored milk drinks (like chocolate milk) which have become increasingly popular.

In the same year that the Babcock test was developed in America, Nicholas Gerber in Europe developed a technique which many experts today believe to be useful in testing homogenized and chocolate milks as well as other types. The Gerber test was quickly adopted in most of Europe, but its reception in the United States was not enthusiastic. American testers tended to develop modifications of the original Babcock technique. New Jersey law reflected both strains of milk testing development. It established two standard techniques. One was the Gerber test and the other a modification of the Babcock test, the Lucas-Trout Modification. Since 1943, all licensed milk testers in the state had been required to establish competence in at least one of the two official techniques. It was a violation of the law to use as a basis for payment for milk, butterfat values which were not obtained by either the Gerber or the Lucas-Trout tests.

When Levowitz learned during his visit to Lettiere in 1952 that the City Chemist had used an unmodified Babcock test on Johanna milk and all other milk tested since 1947, he felt he understood why Lettiere had obtained low butterfat values. The Babcock test, Levowitz told Lettiere, had simply failed to recover all of the small-diameter fat globules in homogenized milk. Levowitz explained the relative merits of the Gerber test and the Lucas-Trout Modification and advised Lettiere to obtain a copy of the *Manual for Milk Testers in New Jersey*—whose technical sections Levowitz had written. Lettiere agreed to employ the Lucas-Trout Modification for testing homogenized milk butterfat content in the future.

When the milk Ryan delivered ran afoul of City Chemist Lettiere's results again in July 1955, one of the Johanna representatives telephoned Levowitz. Levowitz was asked to obtain from Lettiere a detailed description of the test he had used that year. Levowitz contacted Lettiere and learned that the Lucas-Trout Modification had been used. Levowitz posted this information to Johanna.

Johanna's Butterfat Values

Johanna Farms, Inc., is not a dairy in the ordinary sense of the word: it has only a few cows of its own. The bulk of the Johanna milk is shipped from the Dairymen's League Cooperative Association, Inc., of Delhi, N. Y., to Johanna's Flemington, N. J., processing plant. Johanna is thus a subcontractor which further subcontracts part of its milk to distributing concerns like Ryan's Dairy. The 3.25 and 3.3 percent butterfat contents for Ryan's milk reported by the Chemist's Office were not credible, Johanna argued, because no milk of less than 4.2 percent butterfat had been purchased by Johanna in the first two weeks of July. Further Johanna claimed that transfer and shipping reports of the Delhi terminal established that point, and the tank receipts of Johanna Farms confirmed it. Since Johanna made payment for the milk on the basis of its butterfat content, it was argued that there was no obvious reason for Johanna to certify that it had received milk of 4.2 percent butterfat or more if Johanna tests showed it to be 3.25 and 3.3 percent butterfat. As for the claim that any of the milk which left Johanna was under four percent butterfat, the "Laboratory Reports of Daily Fat Tests" filed with Johanna by the resident technologist indicated that no milk destined for Ryan's Dairy contained less than the required four percent butterfat after processing at Johanna. The Johanna technologist used the Gerber test.

To strengthen the Johanna-Ryan position further, Johanna manager, Kurt Goldman, sent to Levowitz' laboratory in New Brunswick the frozen samples of the milk Johanna had sent to Ryan—the samples which Goldman had allegedly reserved in the event of trouble. Levowitz reported that Gerber tests of these samples averaged above 4.35 percent butterfat, the lowest sample being 4.25.

And so Goldman, armed with the tests of the Delhi terminal, of the Johanna resident technologist, and of one of the best known milk experts in the country, was ready to defend Johanna.

Enter Crawford Jamieson, Esquire

Johanna-Ryan also engaged the legal aid of Crawford Jamieson. The arrangement was not unusual. Johanna's lawyer, Fisher, was a partner in a firm in Hunterdon County. The contract cancellation and any subsequent litigation, however, were within the jurisdiction of neighboring Mercer County. In such cases, it is advantageous to engage a law firm from the county-of-jurisdiction. Fisher's firm and Jamieson's firm had cooperated before on such occasions.

Even if the matter did not get into Mercer County courts, the choice of Jamieson seemed apt. Holland had to present a resolution to the City Commission to re-advertise for bids on the remaining portion of the canceled Ryan's Dairy contract. Jamieson had long associations with Connolly and Rieker; and Ridolfi, the most independent of the other commissioners, had clerked in Jamieson's office. But Jamieson insisted:

> I don't like to think that the only reason I was retained was because of my influence with the Commission. It certainly was a factor, but this influence business is exaggerated. We are an established firm and handle considerable administrative law and civil trial work. We have lost many cases before the City Commission, too, you know.

Jamieson's hiring brought immediate and unexpected benefits. Shortly after it became publicly known that he was representing the Johanna-Ryan interests, a person allegedly in the Department of Public Affairs leaked information to Jamieson's office that Lettiere had been promoted to City Chemist without examination. Jamieson sent an assistant to the nearby Civil Service Commission office to check the rumor. The aide allegedly learned that Lettiere had been promoted in 1947 to City Chemist without examination under Civil Service Rule 24, which provides that ". . . if there are not more than three persons eligible to take [a] promotion exam . . . the Commission may, in its discretion, authorize such promotion without competitive test." Lettiere had been the only employee left in the Chemist's Office after the departure of the former Chief Chemist, and the Commission had authorized his appointment under Rule 24. Jamieson's aide also reported a rumor that Lettiere allegedly had finished only three years of college. Lettiere denied this. The

State Civil Service Commission, after considerable prodding, revealed that no records on Lettiere had been preserved. While a college education is not required for milk testers in New Jersey, the Johanna-Ryan technical experts—Dr. Levowitz and Miss Avice Dickson, the resident technologist at Johanna—had both done graduate work in the milk-testing field.

The Dairies Get a Hearing

IN THE Department of Public Affairs, the Ryan's contract cancellation was just another item in a large day-to-day operation. And during the week of July 18, it seemed like a rather unimportant item. There had been little public controversy over the cancellation, and Holland was unaware of the preparations being made by the representatives of Johanna-Ryan. Moreover, Holland had deflated to his satisfaction one of the main contentions in Ryan's protest and in the Fisher letter: he had City Counsel Josephson's opinion that a legal test was not necessary. And Holland had already publicly announced that he would advertise for new bids on the canceled milk order. Holland thus devoted himself to the more pressing task of preparing an attack on the Mayor's paving program for the Commission meeting of Thursday, July 21.

The July 21 Commission Meeting

The July 21 Commission meeting opened in what had become usual fashion. Six resolutions to award paving contracts were offered by Mayor Connolly, all six were accepted by the Commission, and all six times Commissioner Holland voted "No." When the Mayor offered other resolutions to award paving contracts totaling $120,000, Holland introduced a counter-resolution calling for new bids on the projects since the paving firms had quoted the same prices for both gravel and crushed stone, which Holland claimed normally have different quarry prices.

Holland had unsuccessfully raised the same objection before. But offering a resolution for new bids was a more obvious thrust at the Mayor, and it stung Connolly. Holland's resolution was "perfectly asinine" and just another example of "stupid departmental interference," the Mayor charged. Holland retorted that when $500,000 was being paid by the city for work that should cost only $400,000, the question "transcends departmental interests." Holland insisted on calling several witnesses to support his contention. He first called City Engineer Joseph English. "[He] told me himself that the city was paying at least $2 a ton too much [for paving material] and I am prepared to take an oath," Holland stated. English did not support the Commissioner. Holland referred to two other witnesses. Their complaint: they were "shut out" of bidding on city work. However, one was a building contractor who had never paved a street and the other was a contractor who could not obtain a letter from a supplier guaranteeing delivery of stone because, as the attorney for the supplier firm noted, "he already had us hooked for $26,000 and the Lord knows when we will get it." After watching the witnesses' performance, Jamieson, acting as attorney for one of the paving companies, invited them to bid rather than to carry on "a campaign in the papers." Holland retorted: "I pledged to try and save the city money in my campaign and I am going to try and carry it out!" Attorney Jamieson did not see it quite Holland's way. "It's a campaign for good publicity, you mean," he countered. Holland's attempt to do something was unsuccessful: the resolution awarding the contracts was passed three to two, Holland and Ridolfi voting "No."

The Contract Cancellation

Holland had expected no opposition to his resolution to advertise for bids on the balance of the Donnelly Hospitals order, temporarily being filled by the Delaware Valley Dairy Company. He was wrong.

Immediately after Holland offered his resolution Jamieson asked to be heard, this time as counsel for Ryan's Dairy. Holland was surprised by Jamieson's appearance for Ryan, and he was even more surprised by Jamieson's long statement, which touched off an hour-and-a-half-long Commission squabble. Before he finished his rambling presentation, Jamieson had hit most of the elements in the Johanna-Ryan store of evidence described above: the "leak" to Johanna of an impending attempt to "get" the dairy; Lettiere's private testing service; his 1952 tutoring in the testing of homogenized milks by Dr. Levowitz; his alleged attempts to get work from Johanna; and Davidson's relation to Holland and to the Delaware Valley Dairy to which Holland had given the canceled contract. Jamieson also made a passing reference to "more reliable" test data than those of the City Chemist which "proved" that the Donnelly milk had been above the four percent minimum butterfat requirement.

Whether Holland (or anyone else) fully understood Jamieson's statement and its implications is questionable. The technical matters involved certainly were not familiar to the Commissioner. Holland, in fact, requested Lettiere's aid midway through the discussion, but the City Chemist was unavailable. However, Jamieson's trump card was still to come:

> Mr. Mayor, you have to sign all contracts, and I wonder if you should sign milk contracts for another supplier when we contend that [Ryan's] contract is validly in effect. . . . No formal opinion was given to the press or to you Commissioners that [Lettiere's] tests [were] proper and valid, and I submit that the [tests were] not proper and valid and we can prove it if we are given a fair hearing. We can prove that the milk contained 4 percent butterfat, unless someone tampered with it. . . . If you Gentlemen, as a body . . . permit someone else to supply [the milk], you do so at the risk of having it cost the City . . . a lot of money.

The Commissioners sent a hurry-up call for City Counsel Josephson. He made his position clear:

> It is my opinion that under commission government, a Director of a Department has full executive and administrative authority in his Department, and if materials are being supplied which he feels do not meet the specifications of the contract—and he can establish that fact—he can terminate the contract. The resolution [offered by Holland] is based upon the theory that the other contract is terminated. That is why bids . . . for the balance of the contract are being advertised. The issue whether or not the contract can be terminated by the Director is a factual and legal question—not for this body to decide.

Nevertheless, the other commissioners entered protests against Holland's action, which threatened to upset traditional practice on city contracts. Commissioner Duch, for example, admitted amazement at the Holland cancellation. "In twelve years on the Commission," he said, "I have never known one Commissioner to take so much on his shoulders. The cancellation sets a dangerous precedent and could get us into a lot of trouble." As far as anyone knew, Mayor Connolly was right when he said that the city had never broken a contract before. But although the commissioners, according to Josephson, had no legal power over the cancellation itself, their influence was not limited to public criticism. For if the Commission passed Holland's resolution to advertise for new bids, Josephson told the Commission in answer to a question by Ridolfi, the contract would go to the lowest responsible bidder (which might be Ryan's Dairy). The determination of the lowest responsible bidder also was by law a function of the full Commission. "Then why don't we have the right to decide if the old contract is to be broken?" Commissioner Duch wondered aloud. That, by law, was a departmental matter, Josephson replied.

The Majority Suggests a Hearing

After thrashing around in the technicalities of commission government law, all the commissioners except Holland huddled in a corner of the meeting room. Capitalizing on their legal power, as Ridolfi recalled, the commissioners decided that Jamieson should get the hearing he requested. But there was disagreement over whether it should be a departmental hearing under Holland or a full Commission hearing presided over by the Mayor. Ridolfi objected to a hearing by the Commission, and Rieker's firm support over the long run was problematic because of his friendly relations with his ex-deputy. Thus, after recess, Duch made a motion that action on Holland's resolution be postponed for one week. Jamieson quickly defied Holland to introduce a resolution to cancel the contract and to hold a public Commission meeting on the cancellation. Holland, without conferring with the other commissioners, then announced that he would give Ryan a public departmental hearing. On the basis of that agreement, Duch's resolution passed, five to zero. Holland's sudden action is explained by Ridolfi in this way: "I don't think overt threats were made. Even if they were, I doubt whether they would have done any good. Holland is independent. But he knew what he had to do; the majority had him." Holland explained his actions differently:

> I was vitally interested in the welfare of the patients of Donnelly . . . and milk is medicine to those people. City Counsel had stated that I had the authority to cancel the contract [without notice], but in conscience, I really began to think I had been unjust to Ryan in the way the cancellation was announced. I was certain he was in the wrong, but the notification was undemocratic and un-American.

The next afternoon Holland set the Ryan contract hearing for the coming Monday, July 25. Two factors apparently influenced this decision. First, Holland felt the pressure of the week of grace which the Commission had granted before voting on the resolution to re-advertise for bids. City Counsel Josephson had also assured Holland that it was only necessary to show that the cancellation had been made in good faith on the basis of reasonable evidence and that this could easily be done. Second, the only charges clearly made by Jamieson that were new to Holland—the contentions that Lettiere ran a private testing service, that he had once had Ryan's Dairy as a client and recently lost its work, and that he had twice recently solicited Johanna Farms for business—were cleared up to Holland's satisfaction the morning after the Commission meeting.

Lettiere affirmed that he did in fact operate a private milk-testing service and that Ryan had been one of his clients until late 1954, contributing an average of approximately $125 monthly to Lettiere's income over a period of years. But, Lettiere argued, the work was done on his "own time." Moreover, the work—which consisted of butterfat-content tests to serve as the basis of payment for milk sold by small dairy farmers to independent dairies—was normally done for dairies which did not bid on city contracts. Ryan's Dairy and another small local dairy were the only ones for which Lettiere had done such work while they held city contracts. Lettiere also argued that the City Chemist's salary of $5,720 was by itself insufficient to attract and retain able personnel, especially since the workload had roughly doubled while Lettiere had been with the city while the pay scale was unchanged. Giving up his private practice, Lettiere said, would force him out of city government. Holland decided to allow Lettiere to continue his private work.

As for soliciting work from Johanna, Lettiere denied it. He claimed to have sufficient work. Moreover, any charge of falsification of tests to gain work from Johanna, Lettiere claimed, was nonsense. It required that he jeopardize his source of livelihood for a relatively small gain which was especially hazardous because of Johanna's size and its independent testing facilities. Finally, Lettiere told Holland that the Lucas-Trout Modification was only "a hair less accurate than the Gerber." He had an article from a technical journal to document his point. He added that the Modification required only the equipment already in the Chemist's Office, while a change-over to the Gerber test would require about $2,000 worth of new equipment.

Departmental Hearing—the City's Case

Over the weekend, reporters whipped up sufficient interest in what was called the "city's raging milk dispute" to crowd the Commission meeting room, unusual under any circumstances and extraordinary considering the afternoon hour, the 97 degree temperature, and the high humidity. The hearing was also noteworthy for what it proposed to do. City Counsel Josephson, the chief city participant in the hearing, set the theme at the outset. "By the showing of evidence," he said in a preliminary statement, "it is up to [Commissioner Holland] to decide, sitting in an administrative capacity, whether or not there [were] sufficient facts to warrant [the decision] Director [Holland] made."

The case presented by Josephson to Commissioner Holland for his judgment of the actions of Department Director Holland was simple and straightforward. As the City Counsel outlined that case:

> The City of Trenton has a contract [which] provides that the successful bidder supply 4.0 percent butterfat homogenized milk. [Ryan's Dairy] either did or it did not. If it did, the cancellation of the contract was

unlawful and improper. If it did not, it was proper. That is a question of fact and not of law. . . . I shall present the evidence, the records, the tests made by witnesses who will present the facts to show that Ryan's Dairy did not supply such milk.

Josephson called only three witnesses for the city: Frank Mara, Milk Inspector; Arthur Bartolozzi, Assistant City Chemist; and Michael Lettiere, City Chemist. Mara briefly described his collection of the milk samples and his trip to Johanna Farms to deliver news of the test results reported for July 5. Mara admitted advising Kurt Goldman to "get on the ball because there are a lot of milkmen at City Hall now," but he denied naming any specific milkmen "out to get" Johanna. Bartolozzi and Lettiere testified equally briefly that tests conducted by them showed that the Ryan's Dairy milk was under the four percent specification on several occasions. Josephson also introduced the 1952 documents citing the butterfat deficiencies of Ryan's and Johanna milk supplied to Donnelly and the 1955 record of tests publicly released in full for the first time:

Date 1955	Hospital Destination	Description Test Container	Butterfat Percent
7/5	Klempner	Johanna Farms Homo A	3.25
7/6	"	"	4.5
7/12	"	"	4.15
7/13	"	"	3.5
		Average	3.85
7/5	Madden	Johanna Farms Homo Paper Bottle	3.5
7/6	"	"	3.3
7/12	"	"	4.2
7/13	"	"	3.5
		Average	3.6

The city rested its case.

The Johanna-Ryan Case

The Johanna-Ryan case was developed largely by Jamieson, although attorney Fisher was also present. Jamieson sought to establish that the dairies were the objects of a conspiracy fomented by Public Affairs Department officials. The strands in the web of evidence may be briefly summarized: Johanna manager Goldman testified that Mara's warning of the City Hall "milkmen" had been taken seriously and all precautions had been taken by Johanna should "worst come to worst." Thus, Johanna-Ryan was now prepared to meet the city's charges. Dr. Levowitz' report on butterfat values and those of Johanna's supplier and resident technologist as well were offered to establish the Johanna contention that no milk supplied by them to Ryan contained less than 4.2 percent butterfat, let alone the 3.3 or 3.5 percent which city tests reported. Moreover, Jamieson emphasized that Lettiere's private interests constituted a sufficient reason to regard the City Chemist's test reports with reservation. Lettiere's alleged solicitations of Johanna for work underscored those reservations. And, Jamieson continued, Dr. Levowitz' testimony concerning his 1952 meeting with Lettiere at least diminished the usefulness of the 1952 documents the city had offered, even if they were relevant.[3]

The Cross-Examination

The rough-and-tumble of cross-examination revealed new aspects of the controversy, but it was a one-sided revelation. The Johanna witnesses were unshakable, while the Public Affairs' representatives most qualified to dispute their testimony, Lettiere and Bartolozzi, were subdued. Chemist Bartolozzi, a recent college graduate, new to his job and not anxious to dispute the claims of the more experienced Johanna witnesses, contributed little to the Department's case. City Chemist Lettiere was quite upset, a fact reflected by his appearance at the hearing with counsel. On the political level, the city position was also a defensive one. Holland had to explain that his deputy, Faherty, had only driven a truck for a local dairy during college vacations some years before. Moreover, Holland continued,

I didn't know about Faherty's connections until last week, and I didn't know until [Jamieson] brought it out at the last Commission meeting that Delaware Valley was a subsidiary of Davidson's company. And as for my brother, he knows me well enough to realize nothing irregular could ever happen.

3 Lettiere notes that the 1952 data were offered to prove his honesty rather than to show that Ryan's milk was below specification. Ryan's Dairy was then a Lettiere client and the City Chemist felt the reported results established his integrity. Apparently Lettiere did not make the point to Holland or Josephson.

The Department's position, however, was vigorously attacked. For example, Jamieson noted in cross-examination that Lettiere had conducted the tests of July 13, while Bartolozzi had conducted the previous tests. The fat values reported for July 12 were 4.2 and 4.15 percent, Jamieson asked, so why did the City Chemist perform the tests on July 13? Lettiere answered: "Because I wanted to check and see that everything was right." Jamieson similarly handled the question of the test results of the Delaware Valley milk supplied to Donnelly after the cancellation, which reported a uniform four percent for twelve tests. "Most unusual," was Dr. Levowitz' opinion, "and I have been testing the products of many plants for many years." Jamieson also noted that the Delaware Valley report card had been roughened by erasures and "4.00" had been written in. The Ryan's Dairy report card showed no erasures.

City Milk Inspector Frank Mara's testimony was also closely scrutinized. Mara testified that he had taken samples from the two Donnelly wings, Madden and Klempner. The Klempner milk was in steel cans stamped "Grade A," Mara revealed, and he always took a sample carton full of milk from one of those cans, selected at random. Milk delivered to the Madden wing, however, was in quart cartons because Madden did not have the refrigerating equipment to handle the twenty-gallon steel cans. The Klempner milk was always designated as "Johanna Farms Homo A" on Lettiere's lab reports, and the milk cartons from Madden were identified as "Johanna Farms Homo Paper Bottle." Jamieson noted that the latter designation did not tell whether the milk was Grade A or Grade B, or in butterfat terms, 4.0 or 3.5 percent milk. When Mara produced one of the cartons he had taken from Madden, the carton was not stamped "4% butterfat" as Johanna contended all of its Grade A cartons were labeled. Since Ryan's supplied both Grade A and Grade B milk to Donnelly under the terms of the canceled contract and since some Grade B milk was also supplied under an order for "extras" not covered by the contract, what Mara did, Jamieson argued, was mistakenly take Grade B milk from Madden which he thought was Grade A milk. Thus, when Lettiere's office tested the milk, Jamieson argued, it naturally contained less than the four percent butterfat required for the Grade A.

Mara agreed it was possible he had done just that, since he had not known that any milk but Grade A was being delivered to the Madden wing by Ryan's Dairy. City Chemist Lettiere reported that he also had assumed that Ryan's Dairy was delivering only A milk to Donnelly and that all samples Mara had gathered were from A milk.

After five hours, perhaps the longest public session in City Hall history, Commissioner Holland "guessed" that he had heard enough testimony. "It is possible that Grade B milk was confused with the regular premium [four percent butterfat] milk supplied to Donnelly patients," Holland noted. "[I] will discuss with hospital officials *the specifications of the milk contract* and whether the two grades of milk possibly were mixed." [Emphasis added.] And Holland adjourned the meeting. Hearing the evidence had not suggested to him another possibility, one which he thought of only after this incident was over: it was logically possible that while Johanna might have bought Grade A milk and shipped Grade A milk to Ryan, the milk delivered to Donnelly need not have been of Grade A standard.

Reinstatement

THE QUESTION Jamieson raised about Grade B deliveries to Donnelly by Ryan's Dairy was a crucial one. On the morning following the hearing, Holland met with officials at the Donnelly Hospitals to "trace every quart of milk that comes into these buildings." The task was not an easy one for, as Holland learned, sixteen different milk products were used at Donnelly. Although Ryan's Dairy had contracted to supply three kinds of milk products, including Grade B milk, Holland reported that no Grade B milk—contract or "extra"—should have gone to Klempner or Madden wings. Moreover, the contract B milk was bulk packaged. At the hearing Mara had claimed (without challenge) that he took samples of milk from Klempner only from bulk containers stamped "Grade A." That milk had tested low on two of four occasions.

Holland Reinstates the Contract

This resolved to Holland's satisfaction the question of any possible mix-up of Grade A and Grade B milk in the samples Mara had collected for the City Chemist. After his personal investigation and a call to Ryan, Holland contacted Jamieson and advised him that the Department would henceforth take legal samples when it contemplated any action against dairies. But in this case, Holland continued, the cancellation would have to stand. His investigation of the milk situation at Donnelly and Ryan's alleged inability to explain how B cartons got into the Madden wing, Holland said, left him "no moral choice." Jamieson recalled his reaction to the call in these terms:

> Holland kept repeating what some nurse or purchasing officer or someone else had said about the milk delivered to Madden. I told him it was very unfair to accept such information and not give us an opportunity to cross-examine those people. If he wanted to rely on their say-so, I told him, have another hearing and trot those people out so we can have a crack at them.

Jamieson added that "his side wanted another crack at Lettiere anyhow." Moreover, if Holland did not rescind the cancellation or grant a second hearing, the matter would be taken to court.

The conversation made Holland want more than ever to stand firm on the cancellation. But there were factors which led him to change his mind. Holland had seen his witnesses in action, and, compared to Johanna's experts, they were not impressive. The week-long moratorium granted Holland by the City Commission was about to run out. There was little reason to think that he would be treated gently at the next Commission meeting. In fact, Holland claimed that "reliable informants" in City Hall had warned him that the Commission majority would "get him" at the coming Thursday public meeting, apparently by voting to hold a full Commission hearing on the cancellation. The purpose would be to discipline Holland because of his trans-departmental criticisms of city policies, especially paving. Jamieson denied any such connection:

> It was coincidental that I was concerned both with the Ryan's case and the paving controversy. I will admit that the papers certainly made the connection. And I guess even Holland may have done the same thing.

To make matters worse, the press, as one local observer noted, "was beginning to sour on Holland, and without it he's dead."

Holland was thus pulled in two directions. The letter of reinstatement that Holland finally wrote revealed this tension:

> On July 14th, I . . . cancelled the contract with Ryan's Dairy. . . . I was convinced at that time that on the basis of past performance and on the reports immediately at hand, that my action was justified in the interests of the patients at Donnelly. . . .
>
> A review of all of the evidence and facts available at the time of the cancellation and presented to me since then, convinces me that there have been a number of violations by Ryan's Dairy, that the agreement was breached, and the contract cancellation . . . was justified.
>
> In view of certain extenuating circumstances presented at the public hearing on the matter, however, I have decided that the cancellation be revoked and the Ryan Dairy be given another opportunity to fulfill its existing agreement in strict accordance with its terms.

Holland contacted Jamieson and told him of his decision and of the use of the unelaborated term "extenuating circumstances." The full text of the letter was not read to Jamieson, but Holland did agree to explain publicly what he meant by "extenuating circumstances" if either of the dairies requested it. Jamieson OK'd the term and the statement was immediately released to the press. A letter was sent to Ryan confirming a telephone order to resume supplying milk to Donnelly, and notice was served to the Delaware Valley Dairy that its temporary agreement with the Department of Public Affairs was terminated.

Compensation?

Neither Jamieson nor Fisher was completely pleased by the way in which the contract had been reinstated. Jamieson asked Holland to withdraw his statement about the guilt of Ryan, and Fisher asked for compensation for his clients for the loss they had suffered. Holland replied to Jamieson—on the City Counsel's advice—only that he considered the question closed. Mayor Connolly who had been sent copies of the Fisher and Jamieson letters released them to the press where they appeared in front page stories. Josephson then drafted an answering letter to Fisher which set out the city's final position:

> . . . the facts are as clear as the noonday sun, that your client delivered milk to the hospital which did not meet the butterfat requirement. . . . [This] is established by the test made of the bulk milk in the metal containers. The fact that a celebrated expert . . . testified that he examined samples of milk . . . [which] contained 4 percent butterfat does not establish that the milk delivered to the hospital by Ryan met the required standards. Neither does it matter that two or more kinds of milk were delivered to the hospital.
>
> [As for your criticism of the use of the term "extenuating circumstances" in Commissioner Holland's cancellation letter], it should be borne in mind that your client was found guilty, and you are aware of our legal procedure, whereby a person after conviction can be placed on probation, based if upon no other reason, than a belief in his future good conduct. That is what happened in this instance.
>
> [As for awarding compensation to your client], upon what legal principle could a city enter into such an arrangement for giving away the taxpayer's money?
>
> It is my opinion that your client should be more than glad that he received the break he did, and show his thankfulness for it by complying with his contracts in the future. If, however, he feels otherwise, the courts of the state are always open to him.

Josephson's letter was released to the press in "view of the release of [Fisher's] communication to the press [although it] does seem a bit childish," the City Counsel noted, "since the trial of such matters should be referred to the proper tribunals, and not to the newspaper columns, unless it is done for the purpose of laying the groundwork for the suit by preparing the public mind in your favor."

Fisher replied by denying again that Ryan was "in a probation situation." As for Josephson's invitation to settle the question of compensation, Fisher noted, "I can only repeat that it is my honest belief that Ryan should be compensated for the loss suffered because of the hasty action of Holland, and I shall take up with them the question of whether they will take advantage of the fact that . . . the courts are always open. . . ." Mayor Connolly, who received a copy of the letter, once again released it to the press.

Case Closed

Ryan's Dairy never did take advantage of the fact that the courts of the state were open, although a suit was considered. The controversy which had surrounded the cancellation and the subsequent reinstatement of the contract died down as suddenly as it had started less than a month before. The "Ryan Cancellation" file was closed in the Department of Public Affairs. And Commissioner Holland moved on in his crusade.

rill senior supervisor without any increase in pay. He also announced that the Personnel Board had agreed that Byrum, while remaining on the payroll as street superintendent, would be temporarily assigned to expediting city WPA projects. Merrill would therefore assume many of the duties of street superintendent, but he would receive neither the title nor the salary. In recognition of these increased responsibilities, Morgan obtained permission from the Personnel Board to pay Merrill an additional $25 a month. This raise brought Merrill to the top pay level for district supervisor.

On March 4, 1940, Morgan wrote the Personnel Board requesting another $25 per month increase in salary for Merrill. Justifying such action on the grounds of Byrum's "transfer" to the position of WPA expediter, Morgan said that "there was an extreme need for someone to take the responsibility of general field supervision. Merrill's record proved beyond a reasonable doubt that he was more capable of taking on this added responsibility." After a detailed description of Merrill's duties, Morgan declared that he already depended on Merrill for more or less general supervision over the other district supervisors.

This time the Personnel Board did not agree. At its meeting of March 13, the board accepted the recommendation of its Director of Personnel that Morgan's request be denied, since Merrill had already reached the top of the salary range for district supervisor. As an alternative, the board suggested that Morgan might create a new and higher-salaried position of general superintendent. In this event the board would be glad to hold an examination to fill the new position.

Morgan did not act upon the board's suggestion. Instead, seven months later, on October 30, he sent a second letter to the board, renewing his request for a salary increase for Merrill and again citing Byrum's WPA assignment and Merrill's qualifications and present performance of many of the duties in question. To support his case, Morgan cited Rule 2 of the board's rules and regulations, permitting the Director to recommend to the board that a position be reclassified whenever he believed that the duties and responsibilities of the position had changed sufficiently.

The board decided that a reclassification of the position of district supervisor was not in order and recommended that the Commissioner establish a new position, that of general superintendent, to be filled by competitive promotional examination.

Again Commissioner Morgan ignored the board's suggestion. From October 1940, then, until June 1941, the Merrill-Byrum situation remained as it was, although during this period Morgan took one more step that seemed clearly related to his efforts to promote Merrill. On February 12, 1941, the Commissioner appeared before the Personnel Board to request that the board not revoke its Rule 10.6 (see Appendix, p. 607) permitting it to make promotions, under specified conditions, without competitive examination. The Commissioner asked that, in any case, the board permit certain promotions in his Department before repealing the rule. The board replied that none of the promotions Morgan proposed came within the purview of the rule, since the policy of the board had been to suspend promotional examinations only where no competition for the position existed.

The board then repealed the rule, stating that although it permitted a justifiable flexibility in making promotions, it had already provoked some litigation and seemed likely to cause more misunderstanding in the future.

The Situation in 1941

Although there are differing estimates of Byrum's effectiveness as street superintendent, Byrum himself candidly admitted that his tastes and his talents disinclined him to the work involved. Morgan spoke highly of Byrum as a "desk man" but expressed doubts about his ability to handle the men on the street-cleaning details.

But in early 1941 the significant question was not why Byrum was being eased on to other things but rather why the Personnel Board had consented for two years to an informal arrangement for replacing him, which, in effect, constituted promotion without examination.

Members of the Personnel Board claimed later that they permitted the arrangement because they wished to give the Commissioner as much freedom as possible in running his Department.

On the other hand, the board had frequently declared that it would not permit promotions without competitive examination. It reiterated this view, ignoring the fact that Morgan had come to speak of Byrum's assignment as a "transfer" and of Merrill as the new street superintendent.

Morgan's reasons for selecting Merrill as a replacement for Byrum were reviewed many times in his letters to the Personnel Board. Merrill had first attracted his attention in the Ensley District by suggesting changes for greater efficiency and economy. As time went on, he found that Merrill dealt well with subordinates and showed more drive and capacity than the other three district supervisors, although they had been employed very nearly as long and had received efficiency ratings nearly as high.

Morgan would admit no other reason for championing Merrill's cause. Prior to his election he had had only the barest acquaintance with Merrill. Merrill himself said that he had supported Morgan's opponent. Merrill's disinterestedness was questioned by J. T. Waggoner who asserted that Merrill had supported Morgan in both his 1933 and 1937 campaigns and had solicited support for Morgan from Waggoner's father-in-law, then judge of the Ensley District Inferior Court.

According to Waggoner, in January 1941 Morgan asked District Supervisors Waggoner, Johnston, and Branyon to inform the Personnel Board that they had no interest in competing for the post of general superintendent. They would not do so, Waggoner said later, because they feared it might preclude their competing at some future time for a higher position. Morgan denied this.

The Wartime "Promotion" of Merrill

IN MAY 1941, Byrum, who held a reserve commission, was ordered to active duty and was granted military leave. According to the rules, the Personnel Board recognized the claim to reinstatement of all employees called to the armed services, provided they returned within forty days after discharge. During his Army service from 1941 to 1947, Byrum was carried on the city payroll as "Street Superintendent, Absent on Leave."

In October 1941, Morgan wrote the Personnel Board asking that it again consider Merrill's case:

> Nearly two years ago a vacancy occurred in the Street Superintendent's job. I called in Lem D. Merrill to fill the place in addition to the District of which he had charge, and his work has proved to be very satisfactory in his dual capacity of District Superintendent and General Superintendent.
>
> In view of the fact that he has taken on additional duties and assumed greater responsibilities, I respectfully recommend to the Board that Mr. Merrill be given the place permanently as General Superintendent, or whatever classification you might see fit to give him, and pay him accordingly.

At this point, Morgan was assuming that the position of street superintendent had been vacant since the assignment of Byrum to WPA projects. Moreover, he was recommending that Merrill be promoted to a position that had not yet been created, a position which the board had consistently asserted could be filled, once it was created, only after a promotional examination.

The board agreed "to permit Mr. Merrill to perform the duties of Street Superintendent and to receive the salary fixed for the person occupying that position during the time Mr. Byrum, the Street Superintendent, was absent on military leave." According to Howard Yeilding, then Chairman of the Personnel Board, the board knew in 1941 that Merrill was not actually performing all the duties of street superintendent; that Morgan and his personal staff were doing much of the supervisory work and that a good bit of the rest had been parceled out to the other district supervisors. Yeilding thought that Merrill was conscientious and hardworking but not able to organize himself or others, with the result that morale was lower than during Byrum's superintendency. The board was willing to overlook all this because the war had made it difficult for the city to recruit personnel. To keep Merrill, the board had not made an issue of his temporary boost in salary and status.

The PAS Survey

In October 1941, Public Administration Service presented the Personnel Board and the City Commission with its completed position-classification and compensation plans for Birmingham city employees. These plans, later to prove of considerable importance in the Merrill case, were the result of several months' study undertaken at the joint request of the board and the City Commission. From the start, Morgan had been very doubtful of the usefulness of such a study, but he went along when he learned that the Personnel Board could authorize it without the consent of the City Commission. His doubts increased when, as he claimed, the PAS staff failed to consult him during the study.

The classification and compensation plans covered more than 95 percent of those employed by the city. Two joint meetings and several public hearings were held by the board and the commission to consider the plans; on October 22 both bodies unanimously adopted them, and on November 1 they were put into effect.

Byrum's name did not appear in these plans. Merrill's current class title was listed as district supervisor. In the column for "Recommended Class Title," there appeared opposite his name the words "Street Superintendent," with "Present Salary" listed as $200 per month, and "Recommended Salary" of $225. There was nothing to indicate anything temporary about Merrill's occupancy of the post of street superintendent, despite the fact that symbols indicating provisional or temporary appointments (*P* and *T*) were attached to some other positions in the classification plan.

At the close of 1941, then, there was considerable confusion about Merrill's status. Morgan was writing and speaking of the street superintendency as if it had been vacant for nearly two years, and by the end of the year he concluded that Merrill had become street superintendent. Nothing was said about Byrum.

The Personnel Board, on the other hand, seems to have believed that everyone understood that the position of street superintendent still legally belonged to Byrum and that Merrill's occupancy was temporary. During the years that followed, according to the Personnel Director, he informed the four supervisors several times that Merrill did not have a permanent claim to the office and that an examination would be held if Byrum should not return.

This ambiguous state of affairs continued, apparently without disturbing anyone, for the entire period of Byrum's military leave. In 1946 Byrum was injured in line of duty and, after a long period of hospitalization, received a medical discharge from the Army. He returned to his job on July 22, 1947 and was formally reinstated in his position as Superintendent of Streets by the City Commission on August 12. Merrill, in turn, resumed *his* old position as district supervisor of the Central District, with a reduction in pay from $355 per month, top level pay for street superintendent, to $275 per month, top level pay for district supervisor. But, as the city stated later in a brief to the State Supreme Court: "During the period from July 22, 1947, until February 1, 1948, Byrum discharged none of the duties of Superintendent; these duties continued to be discharged by Merrill, all with the knowledge of the Personnel Board and without any objection by the Board."

Byrum's war injury made him seek less arduous duties than those of street superintendent. He wanted a desk job, and Morgan was eager to co-operate. Early in July, before Byrum's actual return to the city, Morgan had proposed to the board that Byrum be transferred to a job that would combine an existing position, Chairman of the Board of Adjustment, with a new position, Technical Advisor to the Birmingham Planning Board. This combination of duties would make it possible to pay Byrum a salary equal to the salary of street superintendent, thereby protecting the essence of his reinstatement rights. Morgan requested the Personnel Board to transfer Byrum to the new position without examination.

On July 12 Personnel Director Mullins wrote Morgan:

> . . . I do not think that Mr. Byrum's assignment could be approved as a transfer. I do not see how

such a position could be put in the same classification as Superintendent of Streets, since there would be little, if any, similarity of duties and responsibilities. I think, therefore, that it will be necessary for us to give an examination to permanently fill the position you have in mind.

Sometime between July and November, however, the board decided that Byrum *could* be transferred without examination. Morgan began to prepare for this transfer which was not actually effected until February 1948 since the incumbent chairman of the adjustment board did not resign until then.

Streets Employees Petition the Board

Early in December 1947, employees of the Streets Division became aware that the position of Superintendent of Streets would soon become vacant. They became alarmed that the vacancy would be filled without competitive examination. Their alarm may well have been stimulated by the fact that during the preceding August the Legislature had amended the civil service law so as to reinstate Rule 10.6.

On December 10, 59 employees of the Streets Division, including three district supervisors, but not Merrill, addressed a petition to the Personnel Board:

We, the undersigned, with Commissioner Morgan's full knowledge, do hereby petition the Civil Service Board to hold a promotional examination for the position of Superintendent of Streets and in every instance where promotions are to be made.

The Personnel Board scheduled a hearing on this petition for December 17. A hearing was not required by law, but members of the board were apparently uncertain as to whether they would give to the newly-enacted legislative amendment the same interpretation that the board had formerly given to its Rule 10.6: that promotional examinations could be suspended in the absence of competition for the promotion. Moreover, a hearing would serve to acquaint a new board member, John Black, with the background of the case.

Present at the hearing were Board Chairman James C. Lee, Board members Thomas T. Huey and John Black, Personnel Director Ray Mullins, Board Attorney Frank Bainbridge, and Attorney Chester Austin representing District Supervisors Waggoner and Johnston. Morgan was aided by Ervin Jackson, Birmingham real estate dealer, and Maurice Bishop, Birmingham lawyer, both close friends.

Morgan opened the hearing by giving an unfavorable evaluation of Byrum's performance as street superintendent, contrasting this with what he called Merrill's excellent work. He urged the "reinstatement" of Merrill to the job he had done so well and cited the new legislative amendment as giving the board the power to make this promotion without examination. Furthermore, he charged that some of the employees had been coerced into signing the petition.

Attorney Austin, speaking for the petitioners, took the position that the promotion of Merrill without examination would violate and undermine the civil service system. He cast no aspersions on Merrill's performance but maintained that Merrill ought to have no fears of the examination if he were as well qualified as Morgan represented.

Waggoner for his part disclaimed any animosity against Merrill but claimed his right to compete in the examination for the street superintendency. He denied that any coercion had been used to secure signatures to the petition.

Chairman Lee summarized the board's past policy in dealing with requests for promotion under the 1947 amendment to the law. He stated that, in his opinion, the board should conduct promotional examinations in all cases where competition existed.

The decision was announced on December 18. Director Mullins informed Morgan that "in the event of a vacancy occurring in the position of Street Superintendent, it will be necessary that the position be filled as a result of a competitive promotional examination."

Morgan Protests the Board Decision

Commissioner Morgan's unwillingness to accept this decision was quickly evident. He began to marshall public opinion in support of his position in public speeches and press releases, stressing the savings to the taxpayers of retaining an experienced man on the job.

Morgan also began enlisting the support of

several of his friends, one of whom, an automobile dealer from the western section of the city, wrote to Board member Black urging that Morgan's request be granted:

> My interest in this is solely on the ground that Merrill has been on the job and has done a good job for the past nine years. I believe he gave both other gentlemen [Waggoner and Johnston] jobs under him and you know it just won't work out when you take men who are against Jim Simpson and for Folsom and the CIO and put them in charge of Merrill who I believe is one of our kind. . . .
>
> I know that you are trying to do the right thing but let's don't lean so far backward that we will do the wrong thing. I am personally interested in Lem Merrill and will appreciate seeing him retain the job he now occupies and not upset this section of the city's business that is functioning so well at the present time.

The letter suggests that in Alabama's political tussle Merrill was an anti-Folsom man. James Folsom had been elected Governor of Alabama in 1946 on a platform which promised to soak the "Big Mules," as he termed the wealthy industrialists.

On December 29, Morgan complained to the City Attorney's office that contrary to the wording of the petition, he had not been told of its circulation. He added:

> . . . Since the case has taken the course that it has, several of the employees who signed the petition have told me that they did not know that the thing was aimed at Mr. Merrill and would gladly withdraw their names from the petition if they had the opportunity.

This charge was reinforced shortly after when 75 employees of the Streets Division sent another petition to the Personnel Board:

> We, the undersigned employees of the Street and Garbage Department of the City of Birmingham, heretofore signed a petition addressed to the Civil Service Board requesting the Board "to hold a promotional examination for the position of Superintendent of Streets and in every instance where promotions are made." . . . We did not intend that the petition should be used in support of a request that L. D. Merrill be required to stand an examination for the position of Superintendent of Streets and Garbage. We did understand and intend that the petition would apply to vacancies occurring in the future in the Street and Garbage Department. We would like to go on record at this time as stating that we have no objection to the confirming of L. D. Merrill in permanent status in the position of Superintendent of Streets and Garbage without requiring an examination. We feel that Mr. Merrill is fully qualified and entitled to hold this position without examination.

Since the signers of the original petition numbered only 59, and since not all of these signed the second petition (Branyon, Johnston, and Waggoner, for example, did not) at least twenty persons whose names appeared on the second petition clearly had not "heretofore signed a petition addressed to the Civil Service Board."

Morgan Invokes Other Rules

Morgan's next move was to request a rehearing by the Personnel Board on its decision of December 17. This hearing took place on January 9, 1948. In addition to the board, the Personnel Director, and the board's attorney, there were present Commissioner Morgan, City Attorney Willis, Attorney Maurice Bishop, and Lem Merrill. Also present were District Supervisors Branyon, Johnston, and Waggoner with their attorney, Chester Austin.

Attorney Willis' statement was concerned this time with Merrill's legal claim to the position of street superintendent. His claim was based largely on the fact that the board, in adopting the PAS classification in 1941, allegedly recognized the promotion of Merrill and his right to the position of street superintendent, which, it was claimed, could be pre-empted only by the reinstatement rights of George Byrum. Moreover, Willis argued, the board, in adopting its rule concerning the reinstatement rights of employees on military leave, Rule 9.8 (b), admitted that only two persons had any claim to a position vacated for military service: first, the employee on military leave; and, second, the person who took his place while he was away. If the first failed to claim his reinstatement rights, then the second was the legal holder of the position. Willis suggested there were two reasons for Rule 9.8 (b). The first was to recognize "appropriately the dictates of patriotism" by protecting the rights of those employees who were serving their country in the armed forces; the other, which bore directly on Merrill's situation, was to assure efficiency in local governments during absence of those to whom military leaves . . . were granted. The obviously *best mode* of assuring efficiency in local government during absence of those vacating positions to enter the armed forces was for the Board to permit such a vacated position to be filled by the City Commission by promoting thereto, without competitive promotional examination, such in-line-for-promotion employee as might be deemed best qualified to perform the duties thereof, and, as a means of *retaining* such promotee in such position *during absence* of the military person vacating same, as against higher wages in industrial plants during such absence, for the Board to assure such promotee of "permanency" in such position *as to all except the person vacating same to enter* the armed forces.

Finally, Willis contended that Merrill's rights were governed by the board's rule on reduction in force. The pertinent part of this rule states:

A person laid off from a classification or grade shall have the right, so long as he, or she, is in the service or on the lay-off list to return to the position from which he, or she, is laid off, in the event such position is refilled.

Maurice Bishop chose other ground. He based his argument on the recent amendment to the civil service law, permitting promotions without examination. He contended that the board was under an obligation to apply this revision of the law to Merrill, and he pointed to instances in which promotions had been made under Rule 10.6 prior to its repeal in 1941.

On behalf of Johnston, Waggoner, and Branyon, Attorney Chester Austin agreed with Bishop that the crux of the case lay in the board's power under the 1947 revision of the civil service law. He stated that the real question was whether the amendment conferred discretionary or mandatory powers on the board, and hence whether or not the board could insist on holding an examination for the job of street superintendent.

Chairman Lee said that he believed that the first issue to be determined was whether Merrill had ever acquired permanent status in, and therefore legal right to, the position of street superintendent. He suggested that the various attorneys file briefs with the board dealing with this question. He recommended that the board withhold its decision pending these briefs. The other two members of the board accepted this recommendation, and the board adjourned.

On February 18, the board attorney gave the board his opinion. He held that Merrill had not acquired permanent status in the position of street superintendent. He advised the board that the 1947 amendment to the civil service law would permit, but did not *require,* the board to promote Merrill without a competitive examination.

The board then notified Morgan (1) that Merrill had no claim to the position now vacant by reason of Byrum's transfer, and (2) that the board would not change its policy of promoting without examination only when there was just one qualified candidate. Since all the district supervisors had the necessary lengths of service and efficiency ratings, all were qualified to compete for the position of superintendent. The board therefore announced its intention of holding an examination to fill the position.

The City Commission, at Morgan's request, responded by adopting a resolution on February 24, 1948, *promoting,* not reinstating, Merrill to the position of Superintendent of Streets at the top salary of $365 per month. The following day this resolution was disapproved by the Personnel Board and the city's action promoting Merrill was disallowed.

Litigation

ON MARCH 19, 1948, Personnel Director Mullins reported to the board that he had been notified by the City Attorney representing Commissioner Morgan, and by Attorney Maurice Bishop representing Lem Merrill, that the city would file suit in the Alabama Circuit Court to determine the legality of the Personnel Board's refusal to promote Merrill without competitive examination. The board responded by voting that unless the city acted at an early date, the board would hold a promotional examination to fill the street superintendent vacancy.

Four days later, Morgan wrote the Personnel Board that the city's case would be filed next week. He continued:

> I cannot understand the haste of the Civil Service Board in preparing an examination for superintendent without a request from this office. I do not consider the Superintendent's position vacated as yet, and I still wonder what disposition will be made of the several hundred changes in classification and salary schedules that were adopted in 1941. Many of Birmingham's leading citizens are wondering about the same thing.

Thus Morgan indicated that the city would claim before the court that the Personnel Board had recognized Merrill's promotion when it accepted the survey of the Public Administration Service in 1941.

The Trial

The trial began on September 29. Merrill intervened as petitioner. Branyon, Waggoner, and Johnston intervened as defendants. Frank Bainbridge acted for the board, and Chester Austin acted for the defendant interveners. Before summarizing the litigation that extended over more than three and a half years, it will be helpful to review the personalities and relationships involved in the case at this state.

For the city, Morgan was clearly the moving force. When the case first entered the courts in the spring of 1948, Morgan had been twice re-elected to his commissionership, each time by a larger vote. His determination may have been reinforced by the feeling that none of his opponents had submitted themselves to an election or received such a strong token of endorsement by public opinion.

There was no indication that the other two city commissioners were unwilling to support Morgan in the Lem Merrill affair. In fact, there was very little public questioning by any commissioner of the decisions of his two colleagues. The commission usually closed ranks and stood as a unit when any one of its three members became involved in a dispute over an official action. All steps in the Merrill case were taken in the name of the entire commission, with unstinting support from the City Attorney's office.

Morgan frequently warned the other commissioners that the Merrill case was a bellwether. He implied that if the Personnel Board were permitted to break faith with its 1941 action, the other commissioners might also expect trouble with the board.

Merrill himself played a decidedly minor role in the court battle and in the newspapers; Morgan remained the center of attention.

Merrill's attorney, Maurice Bishop, had entered the case first as a friend of Commissioner Morgan. A well-known Birmingham lawyer with substantial behind-the-scenes influence in Birmingham politics, he professed an interest in the case not only because of his friendship for Morgan, but because of his "sincere belief that Merrill was the best qualified man for the job." He decried any insinuation that he was opposed to the principle of the merit system, pointing to the fact that his father, while president of the county governing board, had been one of the principal advocates of the merit system in 1935, and that his family had contributed to the support of the Personnel Board when the County Treasurer refused to pay salaries to the director's staff pending judicial review of the civil service law. As he put it, "The first money to campaign for a merit system law and to pay salaries for the Director of Personnel came off my family breakfast table."

Two members of the Personnel Board, James C. Lee and Thomas T. Huey, had been on the board since its inception in 1935. Lee was a Birmingham businessman, and Major Huey a spry septuagenarian and attorney from Bessemer, a community near Birmingham. Both appeared to be dedicated to the cause of "good government," and both were acquainted with the Merrill case from the beginning. Black, the third board member at the time the suit was filed in March, was killed in an auto accident before the trial opened and was replaced by Francis Hare, also a Birmingham lawyer. Before the conclusion of the case in early 1952, Lee died (in 1950) and was replaced by James A. Head, Birmingham businessman.

Both Hare and Head were extremely busy men and were prevented from giving all the time to the board's affairs that each would undoubtedly have liked. There were several occasions in 1951 when the board could not transact business because only Major Huey was present.

Personnel Director Mullins had served as assistant director for six years before becoming director in 1941. Before 1935 he had been employed in the state comptroller's office. Throughout the case Mullins acted on the premise that he and the Personnel Board were fighting for a principle. He believed that Morgan's main purpose was to get his own way regardless of the damage done to the merit system. During Mullins' early years with the board, there had been strong and highly articulate enemies of the merit system, and even those who paid it lip service had seemed determined to evade the law. Mullins had come to the conclusion that hostility to the merit system was the natural order of things among operating officials and that the Personnel Board could not hope to put aside its watchdog role.

Of the defendant interveners, Waggoner and Johnston were by far the more active. Branyon joined the other two supervisors in order to strengthen their case. But he was nearing retirement, and he had only a limited personal interest. Moreover, Branyon failed both promotional examinations for the street superintendency held during the course of the case.

Of Waggoner and Johnston, Waggoner, the more aggressive, was the younger and apparently the more ambitious. It was generally assumed that he intended at some point to run for commissioner against Morgan. The position he took in the present case was explained as follows: between 1941, when he was willing to yield his rights to the promotion to Merrill, and 1947, when he began his fight to make certain that a promotional examination would be held, his friendship and admiration for Merrill fell off very sharply. Merrill, he claimed, did not actually perform the work of street superintendent but, except for the purchasing, divided the duties of superintendent among the district supervisors. For these reasons he could not support Merrill's willingness to concur in statements that Merrill had been performing the work of the superintendency when it was commonly known that he had not. Moreover, Waggoner argued that Merrill's living habits had changed: that Merrill became extravagant and a frequent party-goer, and had since left the circle of friends which the two of them had shared. In sum, by 1947, Waggoner had become more conscious of his own rights and more desirous of protecting them.

Johnston, at this point, believed that Merrill's advancement had come about largely for "political" reasons, and he discounted statements that Merrill's superior abilities accounted for his rise in the Department. He believed that Merrill would have difficulty in passing an examination despite the advantage of experience. Johnston claimed that his sole interest during the whole of the conflict was in upholding the civil service system.

While the contenders were preparing their cases and filing briefs with the Circuit Court, the Merrill story was beginning to reach the community of Birmingham. On March 11, a well-known feature writer for the *Birmingham News,* the city's evening paper, wrote a factual account of the case, summarizing Morgan's position and that of the board.

In June 1948, employee groups outside the Streets Division grew alarmed at "attempts being made to fill positions with disregard to competitive examinations. . . ." The Birmingham Firefighters Association addressed a resolution to the Personnel Board asking it to campaign actively for repeal of the legislative act re-inserting Rule 10.6.

The City's Case

The principal arguments advanced by the city have already been suggested. The core of the city's case seemed to be the claim that the Personnel Board had accepted Merrill's promotion in November 1941, when it accepted the PAS classification and compensation plans. The city also argued that Section 24 of the Civil Service Act provided that promotions should be based upon merit, competition, and the superior qualifications of the person promoted, as demonstrated by his records of efficiency. Certainly, the City Attorney maintained, Merrill had shown merit, not only as district supervisor, but as street superintendent; his efficiency ratings had consistently been higher than those of the other three supervisors. The city stated that "in a very real sense Merrill was in constant competition with the three other interveners from the dates they first began discharging the duties of District Supervisors."

With respect to the examination, the city contended that the law instructed the director to "prepare and conduct examinations to determine the merit, efficiency, and fitness of applicants for positions. Such examinations shall be thorough and practical and shall relate to those matters which fairly test the relative capacity and fitness of the person examined to discharge the duties of the position he seeks." The city's interpretation of these words was that there was certainly no need for *written* tests, and that even if the board should insist that there be a written examination, the detailed questionnaires filled out by each of the district supervisors during the PAS classification survey would certainly fulfill this requirement.

Finally, the city argued that the board was estopped, as were the interveners, from contending at this late date that Merrill's promotion in November 1941 was other than permanent in nature, except for the rights of Byrum. The city cited the board's acceptance of the classification plan, which, although it indicated that some persons were holding temporary, or provisional, appointments, made no such indication for Merrill. It also cited the board's assent to the payrolls submitted by the city during the 1941-47 period of Byrum's absence, upon which Merrill was carried as street superintendent. With respect to the interveners, Branyon, Waggoner, and Johnston, the city contended that it was their duty to have recognized in November 1941 that Merrill had been promoted and would, after a year's probation, acquire permanent status excepting for Byrum; they should have raised immediately the issue of their rights to compete for the promotion. Since they had "slept on their rights for over seven years," they could no longer take any formal action.

The Board's Case

Arguments for the board and for Branyon, Johnston, and Waggoner were built upon contentions that Merrill had never been regularly promoted, that he had therefore never acquired permanency in the position of street superintendent, and that he could, in consequence, make no claim to the position. The board stated that from February 1941, when Rule 10.6 was repealed, until August 1947, when the Legislature had in effect written this rule into the civil service law, there had been no way for the board to make promotions of a permanent nature without the holding of competitive examinations. While the board had suspended the holding of examinations during the war, appointments or promotions made without examination had been designated as temporary or provisional in nature. The board, moreover, rejected completely the city's assertion that the plain intention of its rule on military leave had been to confer an exclusive right of accession to the position left vacant by military leave upon the employee who had held the position during the war.

As to the estoppel, Merrill's right to the job had never been established; there could therefore be no question of the board being estopped from filling the position by competitive examination at this time.

The board claimed that the classification plan was intended only to describe positions and not to confer rights upon the individuals who happened to occupy the positions at the time the plan was drawn up. Moreover, the board asserted that Merrill's tenure in the position of street superintendent was governed by its rules on military leave rather than by its rules on provisional or temporary appointments; that with Byrum's military leave a matter of record, Merrill's appointment to the superintendency was not provisional or temporary in the way such terms are defined in the civil service rules, and hence the symbols *P* and *T* by his name would have been inappropriate.

The Circuit Court Rules

After two days of testimony, the trial was concluded. Nine months later, on June 7, 1949, the Circuit Court handed down a decision in favor of the Personnel Board. In a brief one-page decision, the Court held that Merrill was not legally entitled to hold the position of street superintendent after July 22, 1947. The decision did not examine the nature of Merrill's tenure in the position from the date of Byrum's departure in 1941 to his return in 1947. The city immediately took an appeal from this decision to the Alabama Supreme Court.

Efforts to Compromise out of Court

Throughout the summer of 1948, after the case had gone to the Circuit Court, no extra-legal efforts seem to have been made by either side to resolve the dispute. So far as the Personnel Board knew, Commissioner Morgan and his personal staff were performing the duties of street superintendent. Throughout the case Morgan's statements were inconsistent on this point. In a letter to the Personnel Board dated October 13, 1949, Morgan stated that he was managing very well without a Superintendent of Streets and did not need an examination to fill the position. On other occasions he insisted that Merrill was serving as street superintendent but was receiving only a district supervisor's pay.

From October 1948 to June 1949, while awaiting the Circuit Court's decision, both sides made moves to try to reach an out-of-court settlement. On December 15, 1948, Morgan attended the regular meeting of the board and asked for Merrill's promotion under Rule 10.6. His objection to Merrill taking a promotional examination, he indicated, was that he "feared that an examination prepared by the Personnel Office would be of such nature that Mr. Merrill could not make a passing grade." Chairman Lee then suggested that the board consent to the preparation of an examination by a committee of engineers, in order to make sure the examination would be practical. Morgan did not accept this suggestion. He was then informed that, pending the outcome of the case in the Circuit Court, the board would decline to approve Merrill's promotion without competitive examination.

As soon as the decision of the Circuit Court was announced, the Personnel Director was instructed to hold a competitive examination for the position of street superintendent. The city then obtained a temporary injunction on the grounds that such action should not be taken until the decision of the Alabama Supreme Court had been given. This injunction was dissolved on September 8, 1949, and the board again instructed Mullins to hold the examination.

Before the date of this examination was announced, however, the possibility of asking a committee of Birmingham engineers to prepare the examination was revived, apparently largely at the insistence of Merrill's counsel, Maurice Bishop. Bishop and Morgan both appeared at the board's August 31 meeting. Bishop stated that while Morgan had not agreed to an examination prepared by professional engineers, he was hopeful that the Commissioner and the board could work something out along these lines. Chairman Lee said the board was willing to turn the examination over to a committee of engineers, provided Morgan agreed (1) to make his appointment from the register established by this examination, and (2) to drop all further litigation.

Morgan flatly rejected these conditions. He would not bind himself to appoint from a register established by a promotional examination, nor would he commit himself to appoint anyone but Merrill, even after the Supreme Court had ruled in the case. The board could certify, he noted, but only he had the power to appoint or not to appoint a street superintendent.

From this time on, relations between Morgan and the board and its director steadily deteriorated. Shortly after the dissolution of the injunction, Commissioners Morgan and Green swore to this affidavit:

> The City Commission of Birmingham has not requested any examination, promotional or otherwise, for the position of Superintendent of Streets or for the purpose of establishing a list for this position. We did not request the examination advertised by the Personnel Board to be held June 28, 1949. The Commission of the City of Birmingham will not request this examination or any person to fill this position until a final disposition is made of the case on appeal to the Supreme Court of Alabama.
>
> This Commission has no intention of filling such position with any person other than Lem D. Merrill unless the Supreme Court of Alabama should affirm the case now pending on appeal.
>
> . . . We consider it a useless expenditure of public funds and city money to hold any examination that would serve no useful purpose.

Despite the failure of effort at compromise, Bishop made two more moves to negotiate an agreement between Morgan and the board on the basis of an examination prepared by engineers. On September 14 and October 5, Bishop again appeared at board meetings, still of the opinion that something could be worked out.

The board would not depart from its stipulated conditions and told Bishop on October 5 that it would wait no longer to make arrangements for the examination unless he could secure the necessary commitments from Morgan by the following day. These commitments were never forthcoming.

At almost the same time that Bishop was appearing before the Personnel Board, Morgan was swearing out his affidavit and writing Francis Hare, new board member, protesting the immediacy of the examination:

> . . . I appeared before the Board and appealed to them to not hold the examination until the case was settled by the State Supreme Court. My reasons were given very clearly, I thought, because I stated that, if an examination was held at this time, I would make no appointment, that I still thought we might be favored by the State Court in my last opportunity and there would be some confusion; and, further, if the case was decided against us, we could hold an examination immediately, thereby saving further embarrassment both to the Civil Service Board and the City. No good could come from an examination being held at this time, and such action would further harass me in carrying on my work. There is a lot of personal feeling being engendered in the thing that could be eliminated, and it has almost reached the point whereby my department, which has functioned very satisfactorily for many, many years, is being slowly but surely torn to pieces. Much more bitterness exists between the men in the department than ever before.
>
> Just why such a determined effort is being made to hold the examination for street superintendent at this time is mysterious to me and to lots of other people. There is no telling just what might happen if I am forced into doing something that I don't want to do, all of which could be avoided and the examination held at the expiration of the trial. I told the men involved when the thing started that there would be no feeling on my part toward them, and we would carry on as usual, awaiting the outcome of the case, but, if an examination is held (which would be absolutely useless at this time) considerable changes in our personnel will result, and the outcome can be harmful to the taxpayers of Birmingham. If adequate reasons were pointed out to me why the examination should be held now and how it could result in good, I am not so obstinate that I might not see eye to eye with those in favor of such action. We are getting along all right without a superintendent. I am acting in that capacity, and I am satisfied for matters to continue as they are until the thing is over.
>
> . . . I have never done [anything to harm the civil service laws] and do not propose to, because I am an advocate of civil service and want the civil service laws to continue in force. As in court trials, there can be a difference in the interpretation of the laws, and I am sincerely hopeful that the due course of the law will be pursued at this time and that we can simply let the Supreme Court decide whether or not Merrill is entitled to the job. Then, should it be necessary, an examination can be held without bitter feelings prevailing.

Copies of this letter were sent to Chairman Lee of the Personnel Board; to Major Huey, board member; and to Maurice Bishop, attorney for Merrill.

Thus, while Bishop, Merrill's attorney, was continuing to try for a compromise to end the litigation, Morgan was making it increasingly plain that he intended to fight to the finish.

The Board Examines

ON OCTOBER 7, Mullins announced that the examination would be held on October 15. Notice was mailed to the four eligible district supervisors. Merrill declined to take the examination on the ground that by doing so he might prejudice his appeal. His letter of refusal to Mullins indicated that he and Morgan felt they were being singled out for discriminatory treatment by the Personnel Board. Among other things Merrill said:

> . . . I could never understand why you and the Board would pick me out of over a hundred and sixty-five persons whose classifications were changed by the Public Administration Service survey and make a guinea pig out of the case. I will cite you one in particular in your own office. You refused consistently to reclassify Mrs. Matlock while she was employed in Mr. Morgan's office, without an examination, but, when she resigned her position with the City and was employed in your office, after serving several months in a lower bracket, she was

reclassified by you and the Board to a higher rating. This was done without examination.

If time would permit, I could point out many people, not only in your own office but employed by both the City and County, that you have reclassified and given promotions without examination. If there is anything fair about that, I want to know what it is.

I sincerely hope that I will be given an opportunity to take the examination for Street Superintendent should the case be decided against me in the Supreme Court.

Copies of this letter were sent to Lee, Huey, Hare, and Bishop.

Up to this time Morgan had not attacked Mullins directly in the waging of his case, although some of his public comments implied that his confidence in the Personnel Director was limited. The board took this into account when it stated that its willingness to have a special examination prepared by a local engineering committee was not to be taken as a lack of faith in the director. Mullins himself took these implications into account in his reply to Merrill. After dispensing with Merrill's charges of unfair treatment with the answer that all these charges had been considered and thrown out by the Circuit Court, Mullins continued:

As you know, the Personnel Board has been told that one of the reasons you do not want to take the examination is because you feel that I am prejudiced and would not give you an equal chance in the examination. Naturally, I resent, and the members of the Board resent, an accusation that I would be dishonest in any of my official duties. However, I wish to remind you that the Board, with my consent, agreed to have the examination prepared and conducted by a committee of civil engineers to be appointed by the Engineering Council of the Engineers Club. . . . The Board negotiated with your attorney, Mr. Maurice Bishop, for several weeks on this question, and Mr. Bishop was unable to secure any satisfactory agreement from you or Mr. Morgan; therefore, our only choice was to schedule and hold the examination in the regular manner.

My only interest in this entire proceeding, which has continued since back in 1938, is to carry out the provisions of the civil service law and to protect the rights of the other three men who are eligible to compete with you for promotion to Street Superintendent. Your contention has always been that you are entitled to the position without regard to the rights of the other three men eligible to compete with you. . . .

It is my opinion that if you refuse to take the examination on the scheduled date you will not be given an opportunity to take the examination after your case has been ruled on by the Supreme Court of Alabama.

On October 15, Branyon, Johnston, and Waggoner were given the examination, and Johnston and Waggoner passed. During the first part of November, Mullins three times notified Commissioner Morgan that Johnston and Waggoner were ready to take the oral examination. The oral examination counted 25 percent. As usual it was to be given and graded by the Department head, in this case Morgan. When Morgan made no reply, Mullins proceeded, as provided by law in event of failure of the Department head to act, to hold the oral examination himself. In due time he notified Morgan that a register had been established with Waggoner in first place and Johnston in second.

Morgan Carries the Fight to the CSC

Morgan's next move was to appeal to the Citizens Supervisory Commission. The commission appointed board members and, as noted, had the power to recommend to the board. The commission chairman, Tom Garner, rather hesitantly agreed to call a special meeting to consider the Merrill case after Morgan rounded up the required number of members to request the special session. Prior to this meeting, Morgan had written the members of the commission urging that each be present, because he expected to present "facts relative to certain rulings of the Civil Service Board which are contrary to the spirit and purpose of the Civil Service Law and render it difficult to effect economy in certain operations of your city government."

It was a stormy session. Morgan was given one hour to state his case before some fifteen members of the Citizens Commission. He closed with the assertion that in the interest of good government, fair play, and the taxpayers, the commission should recommend to the Personnel Board that Lem Merrill be *restored* to the position of superintendent.

A member raised the issue whether the commission could make recommendations to the

Personnel Board. The commission attorney at first replied that he did not know. After some thought he concluded that, although the commission could remove board members, it could not instruct them on board action. In spite of this opinion, another member then rose to introduce a resolution that the commission request the board to recognize Merrill as street superintendent. The chairman decided that this resolution could not be introduced until the Personnel Board had had an opportunity to present its case, but this decision was overruled by a voice vote.

In the ensuing free-for-all, lawyer Frank Bainbridge presented the argument for the Personnel Board. Yet another member then advanced the argument that the PAS survey was binding in the same way as a union contract and that the Personnel Board had acted in bad faith in failing to permit Merrill's promotion when Byrum was transferred. Then a motion to defer all action by the commission until the Supreme Court had rendered its decision was defeated by a vote of eight to seven.

Finally, the sponsor of the first resolution got the floor to press for action on his motion for the commission to put itself on record as requesting the board to recognize Merrill as street superintendent. After considerable debate, the resolution was passed by a vote of seven to six, with one member voting "present."

The Personnel Board met the following day and voted not to heed the commission action. A letter from the board went out to all commission members setting forth the board's intention to abide by the decision of the Circuit Court as long as that decision stood unreversed by the Supreme Court. The letter reflected the high feelings of the board:

> Frankly, we were amazed at the manner in which developments at this meeting transpired. We have always felt that the Commission members came to the meetings with unbiased minds and prepared to act upon issues presented on the basis of evidence submitted at the meeting. It is very evident that this was not true at your meeting yesterday, inasmuch as a member of the Commission brought with him to the meeting a prepared resolution to reverse the rulings of this Board and the decisions of the Circuit Court of Jefferson County. This member of the Commission insisted upon getting the resolution before the Commission without even hearing the Board's answer to Mr. Morgan's charges. We have now learned, also, that Mr. Morgan, prior to the meeting, mailed to all members of the Commission copies of his attorney's brief filed in the Merrill case. This could have been for no reason except an effort to influence the members of the Commission. It is significant to us that after the Commission members received the materials from Mr. Morgan, no member contacted any member of this Board, nor did any member visit the Personnel Office where all of the official records in the Merrill case are on file.

The Citizens Supervisory Commission took no further action on the Merrill case until after the Supreme Court decision in the fall of 1950. However, the sponsor of the resolution adopted by the commission resigned within two weeks of the issuance of the Personnel Board's reply.

City Employees Rally Against Morgan

The Personnel Board's answer to the commission resolution was released to the press. Shortly after this, the Fraternal Order of Police and the Birmingham Firefighters Association, two strong employee groups in the city, passed resolutions commending the Personnel Board and vigorously criticizing Morgan for "dissipating the dignity and prestige of his office and perverting the confidence placed in him as a public official by the use of cunning, misrepresentation, sheer deception, and political pressure on Supervisory Commission members. . . ." The Firefighters' resolution went on to say, ". . . Commissioner Morgan is unquestionably using Lem D. Merrill as a monstrous tool, veiled in innocence, to force the resignation of Messrs. James C. Lee, Thomas T. Huey, and Francis Hare and destroy civil service."

Two weeks after these statements, the Birmingham Municipal Employees Association, the general organization of city employees, adopted a similar resolution against "vicious efforts being made to destroy civil service and throw our jobs back into politics." Prior to the Merrill case the Municipal Employees Association had been virtually moribund, but the issues in the case and the example of the policemen and firemen stirred it to unprecedented activity. So high was the feeling among municipal employees that several pro-Morgan members of the Association, including some of Morgan's office staff, resigned from the Association to form a separate group backing Morgan's attempts to advance Merrill.

Morgan's strategy of appeal to the Citizens Supervisory Commission boomeranged since these reverberations seemed to have strengthened the Personnel Board's determination not to change its decision unless the Supreme Court should rule against it. Furthermore, the entrance of employee groups reinforced the impression that Morgan was fighting the civil service. The public image of himself as a champion of the merit system, which Morgan had sought to create, was being seriously endangered by the backlash of his actions in the Merrill case. He became extremely sensitive to press coverage of the case, on several occasions charging reporters and editors with bias or failure to report the facts.

He also redoubled his efforts to tell his side of the story to the public. He never failed to state that his support of the civil service system was a proved fact, and that since Merrill was the man best suited for the job, there was no essential conflict between his promotion and the merit principle. On occasion, Morgan implied that the conflict lay between himself and the Personnel Board and Personnel Director, who were, for some reason, bent on thwarting him in the job he had been elected to do.

In this charged atmosphere, the summer of 1950 passed, with Morgan awaiting the Supreme Court decision. In July, the Alabama League of Municipalities filed an *amicus curiae* brief with the Supreme Court, asserting its devotion to the civil service principle, but stating that in the Merrill case it thought that Morgan had selected the best man for the job. The brief contended that a municipality should be permitted to retain permanently in an important position a man who through eleven years had demonstrated his fitness. The League added that Merrill had been appointed a district supervisor four years before Morgan became a city commissioner, and that there could not be, therefore, any question of the spoils system being a factor in the case.

The Supreme Court Upholds the Board

On October 12, the Alabama Supreme Court upheld the Circuit Court and the Personnel Board. Its opinion dealt not merely with Merrill's status after February 1, 1948, the date of Byrum's transfer, but also with his status and any rights which he might have established during the 1939-48 period. The Court held that the promotion from district supervisor to street superintendent could have been made only after a competitive examination; that since Merrill had taken no such examination he could not possibly have been promoted; and that since the position of street superintendent had not been vacant from the date of Byrum's appointment to the date of his transfer, nobody could have been promoted to the superintendency in any way or by any procedure during this time. On the city's argument that Merrill had acquired permanent tenure as against all except Byrum while Byrum was in the Army, the Court ruled that permanent tenure is a concept which is not compatible with such an exception. Finally, the Court held that the state or its municipal subdivisions could not be estopped from doing that which they had no authority or right to do. Consequently, since the Personnel Board had no right to promote Merrill during Byrum's military leave, it could not be estopped from holding examinations by the argument that it *had promoted* him.

The various parties reacted differently to the decision. The Personnel Board debated whether or not to have the decision and the briefs printed for public distribution. Deciding that the expense would be too heavy, it had copies mimeographed and sent to members of the Citizens Supervisory Commission, to department heads, and to interested citizen groups.

Morgan investigated the feasibility of a rehearing before the Supreme Court, but was informed that the City Attorney did not believe that there was sufficient ground for an appeal. His chances of being successful in this litigation would be poor "for the simple reason that any court deciding in his favor would be vulnerable to the charge that such decision struck a blow against the merit system." Concluded the City Attorney:

> Under the circumstances, it is our recommendation that Merrill take the examination with the hope that he will be successful in outranking the other three who have already taken same. If so, he will of course receive the position and pay of Superin-

tendent. If not, he is in no worse position than he is at present. It is also our view that the exam should be held under the exclusive auspices of the Personnel Board.

The Rule-of-One

At this point, Merrill's promotion began to hinge on a new factor, the so-called "rule-of-one" governing promotional examinations. By this rule, the appointing authority may not choose from the top three, but must take the top man in the examination. The City Attorney believed that the rule was invalid.

Whether Morgan had been aware of the operation of the rule-of-one in the early stages of the Merrill case is uncertain. The Personnel Board and the director insisted that they had notified the Commissioner concerning the rule-of-one at an early point in the case. Subsequently, Morgan stated that his concern over the board's insistence that Merrill could not be promoted without an examination kept him from considering the rule-of-one until the later stages.

Publicly, Morgan continued to express his indignation at board action and to express doubts about the approaching examination. As late as January 1951 he issued a statement to the press in which he said:

> Legally, they have defeated the city.
>
> Morally, they are wrong, and I say what was supposed to have been an honorable agreement entered into in 1941 was broken in 1948.
>
> The conspiracy on their part is a real blow below the belt to the taxpayers. Any citizen or group of citizens who doubt this can see the truthfulness of what I say by looking at the records. I have them.
>
> It's a shame.

In October 1951, after the decision of the Supreme Court, Morgan wrote to Henry L. Freeman, chairman of the Engineering Council and member of the Citizens Supervisory Commission, "If an examination was set up for Merrill by the powers that be to determine his qualifications to perform the many varied duties connected with the job, he wouldn't have as much chance as the proverbial snowball in hell." Morgan complained further that he had never been consulted in the construction of any examination to fill the jobs in his Department.

Merrill Takes the Examination

In November, the Citizens Supervisory Commission urged the Personnel Board to offer another examination for street superintendent and to give Merrill an opportunity to participate. The board agreed, and at its December 11 meeting, voted to abolish the existing register and to invite all district supervisors to participate in a new examination, to be held as soon as possible.

This decision drew Morgan's fire. On December 13 he wrote the board:

> I have learned from the newspaper that an examination is to be held for Street Superintendent.
>
> Ordinarily, the requests for examinations to set up eligible lists to fill jobs in my department, particularly where just one position is involved, would come from this office.
>
> There is a possibility that I may reorganize the Department, and for that reason I will ask that the examination referred to in this letter be held up until my plans are completed, at which time I will acquaint the Board with the study I have made.

The Personnel Board declined to postpone the examination, replying that the Citizens Supervisory Commission had recommended that the examination be held and the Personnel Board had agreed to do so. Morgan fired back on January 5, 1951 that the willingness of the board to comply with the suggestion of the commission was surprising:

> I am going to remind you of a recommendation made previously by the same Commission, during the hearing in Judge Garner's courtroom, which was that you reinstate Merrill to his position. This you failed to do.
>
> It so happens that you choose in every instance in the Merrill case to do the things that will carry your point. This is your privilege. The appointing of a superintendent, however, will be my privilege.
>
> Hold the examination whenever you please.

The examination was scheduled for February 6, 1951. On that day, all four district supervisors appeared. All but Branyon passed. On February 7 Morgan was requested to set a time for the oral examinations for the three successful candidates.

Morgan Gives an Oral Examination

BETWEEN JANUARY 5 and February 7, Morgan had apparently decided that since Merrill could not avoid taking an examination, and since he, Morgan, could not avoid filling the position of street superintendent from the register, the resolution of the whole case depended on the rule-of-one. If Merrill were not top man on the register, what could be done to make it possible to appoint him?

There were three possible ways to deal with the rule-of-one. First, the city might take legal action to contest the validity of the rule which the City Attorney felt was questionable. If the city should invalidate the rule, Morgan would be free to choose any one of the three men on the register.

Second, if the city should decide not to contest the rule-of-one, and if Merrill were not first man on the register, Morgan might exercise his power to appoint and demote until he reached Merrill. The regulations of the Personnel Board permitted the appointing authority to demote during the probationary period of one year, and such demotion was not reviewable. Mullins recalled that during the Circuit Court trial in the fall of 1948, it was suggested to Morgan that he use this authority to demote to reach Merrill on the list. Morgan replied that he was reluctant to use this power because he thought it would make for bad morale in the Department if he demoted a man only to make it possible for him to get to Merrill.

The third possibility was the use of the oral examination grades to insure Merrill's position as top man on the register. These grades counted 25 percent of the total score, and as appointing officer, Morgan alone would be responsible for oral evaluation of the three candidates.

Morgan chose the third way—at least at first. It promised to eliminate the necessity for further litigation and to maintain the appearance of staying within civil service regulations, while giving least cause for disturbance to employees of the Department.

Morgan's Ratings

Morgan held the oral examinations on February 7. According to Mullins, on the following day, Bishop, Merrill's attorney, telephoned the office of the Personnel Director and requested that the written examination grades of the three men be released to him. When Mullins declined, Bishop came to see him.

When he arrived at the office, Bishop asked Mullins to demonstrate how the board weighted the grades for the written and oral parts of the examination to get the final grade. Mullins used hypothetical figures to show Bishop how the calculation was done. According to Bishop and Morgan, Mullins demonstrated how any one of the three men could be guaranteed top position on the register by figuring the oral grade at various levels. Bishop left Mullins' office with the remark, "Morgan can do about anything he wants."

On February 9, Morgan notified the Personnel Director that he had assigned oral grades to the three men. The full meaning of Bishop's parting remark was revealed when Mullins discovered that Morgan had rated Merrill at 100, and Waggoner and Johnston at 9 each. Even though Waggoner had ranked first on the written examination, these grades of 9 resulted in both men receiving total grades which were below passing. Thus Merrill had become not only the top man on the register, but the *sole* man on the register.

Morgan admitted that his ratings were intended to give the job to Merrill and were calculated as follows: Merrill had made at least 70 on the written examination, because 70 is the minimum passing grade. Assuming that Merrill had done no better than to make the lowest passing grade, 70, and that Waggoner and Johnston had each made the highest possible grade, 100, an oral examination of 100 would give Merrill a final grade of 78.50, while grades of 9 each would give Waggoner and

Johnston total grades of 77.25. Thus, Merrill would certainly rank first on the register.

Morgan justified his grades by explaining that Merrill's ten years of experience as street superintendent were each worth about ten times as much as Johnston and Waggoner's experience as district supervisors during those years. Consequently, for each year that Merrill received ten, the others should receive one. Actually, this does not result in 100 to 9 but in 100 to 10. Morgan felt that his principle was sound, even though his arithmetic was slightly defective.

Morgan contended that the rule-of-one really meant that the power to appoint had been taken from the appointing authority and given to the Personnel Director who prepares, conducts, and grades 75 percent of the examination. He asserted, therefore, that the appointing authority should have full freedom to assign any grade he saw fit within the 25 percent of the examination grade that he controlled.

Morgan and Bishop both maintained that the Personnel Board and the director had in effect promised Morgan that his use of the oral grade would not be contested if Morgan would yield on the matter of Merrill's submitting to examination in competition with the other district supervisors. Both claimed that Mullins had instructed Bishop how Morgan might rate the three to make certain that Merrill would come out first. Members of the Personnel Board and Mullins consistently denied that they had ever suggested that Morgan might use his control over the oral grade to guarantee Merrill the appointment.

Immediately after receiving the oral grades Mullins informed Morgan that both Waggoner and Johnston had failed the examination for street superintendent.

The Board Revises the Orals

The next action was taken by Waggoner and Johnston. On March 5, they submitted a petition asking the Personnel Board to set aside the Commissioner's oral grades and re-rate the three contestants.

This petition was strongly worded. It accused Morgan of attempting to thwart the civil service law, but it also contended that the attempt to promote Merrill was not based on consideration of merit but was due rather to Morgan's "sole desire to achieve and to insure continued achievement of personal gain." This was the first time that a public statement had been made to the effect that Morgan's interest in Merrill might possibly be rooted in alliance between them for some sort of personal gain. The charge came from employees of long standing and of fairly high rank in the Department, though these employees were not devoid of personal interest in the case.

The charge that Merrill and Morgan were joined in an effort to enrich themselves was never substantiated. Waggoner was inclined to accept as proof of such an alliance the fact that three grand juries, within a period of ten years, had been moved to investigate the Department of Public Improvements. No indictment, however, was ever returned.

Waggoner was also disposed to think it unlikely that Morgan and Merrill would not have known of the activities of one employee of approximately the same rank as the district supervisors, who had resigned in October 1945 shortly after an investigation into his conduct in office had turned up a number of irregularities. Again, however, there was no tangible evidence or proof that Merrill and Morgan were in any way involved. Members of the board were divided in their conclusions, some being satisfied that Merrill and Morgan were above suspicion, some remaining skeptical. Morgan himself denied vigorously the charges and insinuations of wrongdoing in the Department and in his conduct of office.

Aside from its thinly-veiled hint of wrongdoing, the petition presented by Waggoner and Johnston raised a question for the Personnel Board for which no precedent existed. The petitioners argued that the rule by which department heads were authorized to give oral ratings was void because it constituted a delegation of power vested in the Personnel Board. They further argued that the rule could be saved only by the board's having power to review and annul these ratings.

According to Johnston, his interest in the conflict lay not in any hope of obtaining the job of street superintendent, for he was content with being district supervisor, but rather in his and had not slept well since. Morgan suggested that Johnston come to his office. A day or so later the two men spent an hour together in Morgan's office "renewing their friendship and praying together for strength and guidance."

The second event was the re-grading of Merrill's oral examination by Mullins. After the Circuit Court decision denying department heads the power to give and grade the oral part of the examination, the city's attorneys and Maurice Bishop asked the Personnel Board to re-grade Merrill, as Mullins had already re-graded the other two men. The board granted the request and instructed Mullins to examine Merrill orally and to grade him. Mullins did so, and Merrill remained second on the register.

Demotion

ON JANUARY 21, 1952, Waggoner was appointed street superintendent. Two weeks later, on February 2, he was demoted, clearing the way for the certification and appointment of Merrill.

Morgan's letter demoting Waggoner to his old position as district supervisor of the Ensley District charged that Waggoner could not "direct the activities of the department and . . . work harmoniously with [the Commissioner] and with other employees of the department." This incapacity was defined by Morgan as follows:

> So far as I am aware, you have taken no steps to present to the Solicitor of Jefferson County or to the various grand juries which have sat in this county since March 5, 1951, any facts within your knowledge tending to establish any violation of law on my part. Such was your duty as a citizen and as an employee of the City of Birmingham. Your failure to do so constitutes serious neglect of duty on your part.
>
> Your attitude during the period of time since you became Superintendent, as exemplified by your failure to withdraw your baseless charges and to state either publicly or privately to me that same were without foundation, convinces me beyond all doubt that your retention of the position of Superintendent is intolerable and is not in the best interest of sound public service.

The letter omitted the facts that Waggoner had attempted to support his charges at the Personnel Board hearing on the oral grades, and that, at the time the letter was written, he was under summons from the Grand Jury then poised to investigate the Department of Public Improvements. As it turned out, this Grand Jury did not pursue its investigation of Morgan's Department, much of its time being taken with bringing in an indictment against another of the city commissioners on a morals charge.

It was R. L. Sims, Morgan's executive secretary, who gave Waggoner the letter of removal. Waggoner kept a memorandum of his conversation with Sims on this occasion. Sims asked Waggoner whether his failure to withdraw his charges against Morgan indicated that Waggoner still believed them. Waggoner replied that that was not relevant at the moment. Then Sims stated, "Jab, I have been here a long time, and I pride myself on keeping in close touch with the operations of this Department, particularly the actions of Commissioner Morgan, and the Superintendent of Streets, and I don't believe it could be possible for anything dishonest or dishonorable to occur in these offices without my knowledge." Waggoner's response was, "Bob, if you were in the darkness, the light might dawn later." Waggoner then indicated that he had been expecting his removal and turned over the keys to the office of street superintendent.

Merrill Becomes Street Superintendent

The final moves in the Merrill case followed quickly on Waggoner's demotion. Merrill was duly certified and appointed early in February 1952. A few weeks later, Morgan requested the Personnel Board to raise Merrill to top pay as superintendent, in view of his long experience with the job. The Personnel Board readily agreed.

At long last Lem Merrill was Birmingham's Superintendent of Streets—in name, in fact, and by due process of the civil service law.

Postscript

ALTHOUGH IT TOOK MORGAN twelve years to get Merrill formally recognized (and paid) as street superintendent, Merrill's tenure in the post was comparatively short. Three years after his appointment, Lem Merrill was retired for disability. By this time Morgan had been elected Mayor of Birmingham. Waggoner remained as district supervisor until he resigned in August 1953. To fill the vacancy left by Merrill in 1955 the Personnel Board held an examination for the three incumbent district supervisors. Personnel Director Mullins conducted the oral interviews. Two supervisors were certified; the leading candidate, Neil McRae, was promoted; and at the beginning of 1959 McRae was serving as street superintendent.

In April 1956, an election was held to fill a vacancy on the City Commission. One of the candidates was Eugene Connor, who had been City Commissioner approximately as long as Morgan, but who had resigned in 1955 to run unsuccessfully for Sheriff of Jefferson County. Connor had supported Morgan throughout the Personnel Board controversy, and the two men had always worked closely as commissioners. One of the candidates who opposed Connor in the 1956 election was J. B. Waggoner. In the course of electioneering, Connor branded Waggoner a troublemaker because of his fight against Morgan in the Merrill case. In a close race, Connor received more votes than Waggoner. Since there were other candidates, however, Connor did not receive a majority, and a run-off election was necessary. In the run-off, Waggoner was elected Commissioner. In the regular election in 1957, both Mayor Morgan and Commissioner Waggoner were re-elected, and Connor secured the third commissionership.

Appendix

Rule 10.6

In case of a vacancy in a position which requires peculiar and particular training and experience which, in the judgment of the Board, may be properly and sufficiently acquired in the office or department in which the vacancy exists but not elsewhere, and it can be shown to the satisfaction of the Board that there is in such office or Department an employee who was regularly appointed and who is serving in a lower or different class or position following regular appointment, and whose familiarity with the duties of the position vacant and whose ascertained merit in performing or assisting in such work make it desirable for the best interests of the service to suspend competition, the Board may, after a public hearing, approve the promotion of such employee, either without examination or with such tests or evidence of fitness as the Board may see fit to require. Notice of the public hearing held under this section shall be posted publicly in the office of the Board for at least three days prior to said hearing, and all such cases shall be fully set forth in the Minutes of the Board.

The New York City Health Centers

Herbert Kaufman

Early Efforts To Effect Change

IN THE YEAR 1915, the Commissioner of Health of New York City decided to make a change in the way the work of his Department was carried on. Theretofore all its work had been handled by its specialized bureaus; thereafter, while the bureaus would be retained, work in the field would be carried out through district health offices, each under the supervision of a district health officer with general responsibility for health operations in his district.

The decision was made and announced; but the decision was, in an important sense, still being made 44 years later, in 1959, and new announcements concerning the underlying decision were still being issued. At first glance, this may seem astonishing; but any decision that involves fundamental changes in working habits and relationships, that affects status and power, usually can come into effect only through a continued process of adjustment. The process may be long or short, easy or hard, successful or abortive, but all that the initial order can do is start the chain of action. This study illuminates some characteristics of the process.

Growth Along Functional Lines

The New York City Health Department, in 1915, had behind it a long-established and highly-respected tradition. For more than a century, departmental work had been divided along functional lines—i.e., according to the major end-products of the Department, the major services provided, and the clienteles served. Within the major functional components of the agency, one could often find territorial units; immediately below the Commissioner's office, however, there were only functional bureaus.

This was less conscious design than the product of circumstance. For four generations after the Revolutionary War, the main object of public health authorities in the city was to prevent epidemics. This was to be accomplished by keeping the city clean, since it was recognized that dirt and disease were somehow connected, even though a century was to elapse before the discovery of the significance of bacteria. For two decades, the city experimented with administrative techniques for the discharge of this responsibility; not until 1804 did a relatively stable agency, the City Inspector's Department, make its appearance.

In addition to his sanitation duties, the City Inspector was also charged with keeping statistics of births, deaths, and marriages. As time went on and the city grew, he began to increase his staff. By 1852, the Department was divided into two bureaus, one for Sanitary Inspection and one for Registry and Vital Statistics, both reporting to the City Inspector. This division of work on the basis of the major end-products of the agency was to constitute its organizational framework for many years. Even when the City Inspector's Department gave way in 1866 to a Metropolitan Board of Health (operated by the state of New York as a result of inefficiency under the Tweed administration in the city), the two bureaus continued in the new organization, and they survived another change four years later when the responsibility for health administration reverted to the city government and the present Department of Health was organized under the newly established municipal Board of Health.

In the last quarter of the 19th century, social, economic, and scientific developments compelled administrative readjustments. In the first place, the stream of immigrants swelled. Frequently penniless refugees from abroad, often brought over by employers for purposes of exploitation, these hapless people were forced to move into the oldest, most crowded sections of New York. Jammed into overcrowded, rickety, poorly lighted, and unventilated tenements, they were easy prey to disease. The water supply was growing short, and sewage disposal and drainage facilities were heavily taxed. So the efforts of the Health Department's Bureau of Sanitary Inspection to avert epidemic by enforcing sanitary regulations had to be redoubled, and the staff grew with the workload.

In addition, as the population grew, the whole pattern of social and economic life underwent rapid alteration. Factories replaced craftsmen and small shops; new processes of packing, transporting, and preserving food made their appearance; drugs and patent medicines appeared on the counters of local drug stores in large numbers. No man could master all of these problems, and the sanitary inspectors were finding it necessary to concentrate on specific aspects of their field; a new type of specialization, of division of labor, was taking place along the lines of the new functions created by circumstances.

While these changes were taking place, Pasteur and Koch made known their findings about the bacterial origin of many diseases and thus revolutionized medicine, surgery, and the protection of the public health. In addition to general sanitary measures, the attack on specific diseases, on individual micro-organisms, began. Diagnosis sometimes became a problem for the laboratory instead of for the attending physician alone. New techniques of administrative control of disease were called for, and inspection demanded medical training in the new theories and methods in addition to common sense and industry. Physicians began to specialize in pathology, bacteriology, and in the diagnosis and treatment of specific diseases. In the medical profession as in sanitary regulation, the field was being divided by new developments, and new specialties were appearing.

Consequently, the Bureau of Sanitary Inspection began to subdivide.[1] By 1896, it comprised five new functional divisions; fifteen years later, seven.[2] (The Bureau of Records, on the other hand, while it expanded along with the city and the Department, remained organizationally intact.)

It became a case of the tail wagging the dog, for the divisions were indeed outgrowing the Bureau of which they were part. Most of them embraced individual medical specialties. Many of them had field organizations of their own. They owed their status and size in part to the vigorous leadership of their respective directors, several of whom achieved professional standing equaling, if not exceeding, the reputation and influence of the bureau chiefs. Structurally, the divisions were still subordinate to the Bureau, and the work of the Department continued nominally to be divided solely between Records and Sanitary Inspection, but it was clear that this fiction could no longer sustain itself. In 1913, the Department underwent a thorough reorganization.

When the units had been split, combined, and recombined, eight bureaus emerged. There was still a Sanitary Bureau, but it was now shorn of all its functional divisions and all its duties except those relating to inspection of buildings, complaints, and nuisances. The Bureau of Records came through relatively unchanged. The former divisions of Food Inspection, Child Hygiene, Infectious Diseases, Laboratories, and Hospitals were elevated to bureau status, with chiefs reporting directly to the Commissioner. In addition, a Bureau of General Administration in charge of departmental housekeeping duties was set up.

The following year, 1914, a ninth bureau, Public Health Education, was added. When World War I broke out, the Health Department thus consisted of nine bureaus, each performing a single function (one, Child Hygiene, serving a specific clientele; one, General Administration, carrying on a process; the rest devoted to specific end-products of the organization), each operating

[1] In 1873, the responsibility for street cleaning was transferred to the Police Department. After another eight years, it was lodged in a separate department.

[2] In 1896, the constituent divisions were Contagious Diseases and Medical Sanitary Inspection (manned by medical inspectors); General and Special Sanitary Inspection (covering non-medical matters); Food Inspection, Offensive Trades and Mercantile Establishments (calling for specialized knowledge of these industries); Pathology and Bacteriology; and Medical School Inspection. By 1911, after going through a number of internal changes, the Bureau consisted of a Division of General and Special Inspection; a Division of Child Hygiene; a Division of Communicable Diseases (handling those diseases at that time not classified as contagious); a Division of Laboratories; a Division of Hospitals (bringing together for the first time the contagious disease hospitals of the Department); and the old Divisions of Pathology and Bacteriology and Medical School Inspection.

throughout the whole city, and each having its own field setup, the whole brought together at only one point in the entire agency, the Commissioner's office.

From many points of view, this arrangement for the division of work in the Department was a highly satisfactory one. The fight against disease seemed to be succeeding, for the general death rate was falling, the incidence and fatality of epidemic infections were shrinking, and the prospect of new and greater victories seemed good. Yet there were some who claimed to discern, beneath the reassuring exterior, serious weaknesses that spelled danger to the health program of the city and to the institutional existence of the Department itself.

Challenge to Function: 1914

The first public challenge to the functional organization of the Department was issued by Dr. S. S. Goldwater, Commissioner of Health during 1914 and 1915, and his assistants, Dr. Haven Emerson (Commissioner from 1915 to 1917) and Dr. Alfred E. Shipley (Secretary of the Department). They presented a six-count indictment.

First, they maintained, the Department had in effect been split into units so separate and distinct from one another that its operations were almost completely uncoördinated and the leadership of the Commissioner had become all but nominal. The bureau chiefs were specialists of such stature and repute in their respective fields that the Commissioner was doubtless reluctant to interfere with them, and policy making, the definition of program, the hiring and assignment of personnel, the location and duties of field installations, and many similar key decisions fell into their hands. The activities of each bureau frequently bore so little calculated relationship to those of its sister bureaus, it was held, that

> The system of administration of the Health Department has been the growth of a series of kingdoms, within an empire, each to a great extent independent and with its function's sphere of influence sharply defined; each bureau was served by a staff of employees more or less specially trained and independent of the other bureaus, in thought, action, and method of work. There was no opportunity or desire for conference or comparison of the records and results or for consultation for the sake of obtaining joint action between the different bureaus. There was no place in the city where investigation was being carried on in respect to the effectiveness of the existing or other possibly desirable methods of health administration.

Secondly, it was contended, under the established system of administration, "The Director of a bureau is too far removed from those who do the field work of the bureau." With the head of each unit located in departmental headquarters, the organization was apparently thought to be growing over-centralized.

Thirdly, the intense specialization of departmental personnel, while it had undeniable advantages, had one very severe shortcoming in the eyes of the three critics of the prevailing practice:

> Where there is a high degree of differentiation of function, the individual worker ceases to see things in their true proportion, and fails to grasp or apply the broad principles by which the department is governed. Mental and professional developments are inhibited by the repetition of detail work of a monotonous character.

Fourthly, there was said to be costly and irritating duplication in the existing procedures: "Various bureaus sent their representatives into the same districts, often into the same houses, which results in undue expenditure of time and energy and in annoyance to the individual citizen." For example, if a nurse assigned to tuberculosis work visited a home and found, in addition to the patient she had come to see, a child suffering from measles, she could take no measures in the case; that was the task of another bureau, and a different nurse would be dispatched to the same home upon notification of the proper authorities by the first nurse. As far as the family was concerned, there was sometimes a bewildering stream of representatives of the Department passing through its door, none of them having any idea that the others had been there or any interest in what the others had done.

Fifthly, it was declared that the city-wide statistics produced by the system of city-wide bureau operation cloaked alarming contrasts between various sections of the city. While some areas would almost eliminate a disease, others would lose dreadful numbers to it, yet the average for the municipality often showed nothing that warranted concern. Consequently

> Anyone who attempted to analyze the results of health organization as set forth by the Bureaus of the Department of Health would be struck by the fact that no officer of the Department was familiar with all the needs and phases of civic health work in any given borough or district of the city. The general death rate, the infant mortality rates or incidence of the different communicable diseases in the community as a whole, were known to the Health Department, but as soon as one came to analyze the rates he found that he was dealing with too large groups to make these statistics applicable to any one district.

Finally, the philosophy of public health administration was held to have changed. Originally, it reflected a negative, police point of view that confined it to abatement of nuisances and suppression of infectious diseases. Now, it aimed at bringing to each individual in the community the medical means and general knowledge with which he could achieve good health—i.e., the organic, functional, and social conditions which enable individuals fully to enjoy, participate in, and contribute to life. "Old methods of administration do not secure these results and the attempt to modify present procedures to meet new conditions, in many cases, has been like putting new wine in old bottles," argued the complainants, and what was needed was "new ways of organizing and administering health work."

All the counts in this list of changes—the second and fifth most of all—reflected two circumstances that were rendering inadequate many of the traditional methods of conducting all types of business, whether public or private, in the city (though this point was implicit in the argument rather than expressed). One of these was the tremendous increase in the city's population, especially at the turn of the century. The other was the geographical expansion of the city (which meant, quite naturally, a sudden and substantial addition to the number of people being served as well as the acquisition of territory) through the consolidation of 1898 which resulted in the establishment of the present boundaries of the city.

The way to meet the new conditions and eliminate the enumerated defects of administration, concluded Drs. Goldwater, Emerson, and Shipley, was to modify the system of dividing up the work of the Department. Specifically, they proposed that the operating responsibilities be lodged in a number of new officers, all physicians, each of whom would be in charge of one of the districts into which the city would be partitioned, and each of whom would supervise within his district the activities of not only one bureau but, eventually, of all, or, at least, of most of them.[3] These district health officers and their staffs would actually do the work of the Department while the bureau chiefs would become a "faculty" of distinguished specialists furnishing assistance to the districts in a consultative capacity and advising the Commissioner in the formulation of broad policy. They would also inspect the districts to see that technical standards were maintained, but, instead of ordering particular corrective measures or innovations, they would make recommendations: execution would be entirely in the hands of the district officers. These arrangements were described as putting into practice the line-and-staff concept advanced by Frederick Taylor, the specialist on administration and efficiency, then at the height of his fame, and with whose work Dr. Shipley was quite familiar:

> The general principles of "line and staff" organization have been applied. . . . for the line or routine work of the district, the Health Officer is responsible; his business is to see that the current work of his district is efficiently performed and to him that the district staff is responsible and by him that they are assigned to duty, as he may deem best [sic]. The staff is represented by the Bureaus. . . .

The Bureaus' Reply

As one might expect, the bureau chiefs did not take kindly to the suggestion that they surrender their command authority over their staffs to another group of officers and content themselves with a planning and advisory role. While

[3] The district officers would report to five borough officers, who would in turn report to the Commissioner through a central division of health districts. This was apparently designed to prevent overextension of anyone's span of control. (New York City is subdivided for certain governmental purposes into five boroughs.)

they did not leave in the record as complete a presentation of their side of the case as did Goldwater, Emerson, and Shipley on behalf of their thesis, it is possible to reconstruct their arguments.

In the first place, the accomplishments of the New York City Department of Health for a generation past, and they were noteworthy, were the accomplishments of the individual functional bureaus. Admittedly, there might be certain weaknesses in the bureau system, but, they argued, was it wisdom to scrap great achievements to eliminate relatively minor administrative problems? On the basis of past performance, the bureaus needed to apologize to no one, and the proposed reorganization would do municipal health more harm than good if it devitalized them.

In the second place, the bureau chiefs were for the most part medical specialists; they were experts in their respective fields. Could any district health officer (though a physician himself) responsible for all their specialties compete with the bureau chiefs in their own spheres of special competence? To them it seemed obviously impossible, and the adoption of a type of organization built on this proposition would sacrifice the technical excellence of the whole Department.

In the third place, their argument ran, no bureau head could fairly be required to assume responsibility for the technical quality of his service if the personnel who carried out the program were under the direction of another officer.

In the fourth place, what need was there of dividing the city into districts when, in those days, a five-cent telephone call could reach almost every corner of it and a five-cent ride on the subway put every field agent never more than 45 minutes or an hour away? In a large jurisdiction where communications were expensive and travel slow and difficult, district organization might be justifiable, but hardly in New York City.

In the fifth place, it might very well have been contended that it would prove no easier to co-ordinate a large number of district health officers than a smaller number of bureau chiefs. If field co-ordination did break down, the Department would suffer all the administrative handicaps of which its critics now complained without enjoying the advantages of which it could boast. Departmental policy would be fragmented and communications between headquarters and field vastly complicated.

There was doubtless an element of power in the situation, too. The bureau chiefs wielded great influence in the operations of the Department, and they supervised substantial staffs including professional and semi-professional personnel. They consequently enjoyed high status in the Department and in general medical circles. All this must have seemed at stake, and was in fact at least partially involved, and the bureau chiefs would have been more than human if they had willingly and cheerfully relinquished so much. Furthermore, the proposed changes would have disrupted the whole pattern of personal relationships established within the bureaus and between them, tearing up the fabric of existing informal organization.

The Experiment: 1915-1917

In the face of this natural and substantial opposition, Commissioner Goldwater decided to test the district idea in order to find out once and for all, as he thought, the answer to the question, "How far can the work of the Department be improved by the substitution of a system of local or district administration for the present purely functional administration? Can field workers be trained to perform, and can they actually perform in a satisfactory manner, a variety of functions?" On January 1, 1915, therefore, a single district was set up on an experimental footing, with entreaties from the Commissioner to the bureau chiefs to give it a fair chance. (This experiment, it should be noted, was aided by the general atmosphere of the reform administration in office in the city at the time.)

Health District Number 1, as the experimental area was officially designated, comprised one complete federal census tract, an area of 21 city blocks (63 acres) in the lower East Side slum section of the city with a population of 35,000. It was headed by a district chief in whom was vested jurisdiction over the bureau personnel engaged in field work in that area. The funds for the undertaking were drawn by Dr. Goldwater from other parts of the departmental budget; no special appropriations were made. The District operated at the start as a special unit directly under the supervision of the Commissioner and his two assistants; everywhere in the city except inside that 21-block pocket, the work of the Department went on as before.

In a short time, the three proponents of the plan, who were obviously not altogether unbiased judges, were convinced of its feasibility and of its advantages over the old system. They claimed the people reacted much more enthusiastically to this general-purpose installation than to the minutely specialized field stations, of the functional bureaus, and they thought the staff developed an enthusiasm for, and knowledge about, the community that did not exist before. Settlement of inter-bureau affairs at the local level, eliminating reference back to central headquarters, allegedly became the rule. The health program of District No. 1 was better adapted, it was said, to local needs, and civic organizations showed an interest in building a community health program. Nurses proved they could perform generalized service, and greater effectiveness was achieved through shifting them from function to function as conditions warranted. And all this improvement in the quality of service, it was said, was achieved at lower cost as a result of reduction of overhead organization at central headquarters and increased flexibility of staff. All in all, Goldwater, Emerson, and Shipley were convinced they were on the right track.

When Commissioner Goldwater resigned to return to his work as private consultant in hospital management, Dr. Emerson succeeded him, and, on May 1, 1916, opened four new health districts in Queens (one of the city's boroughs) and set up a Division of Health Districts to which all health officers were to report. The line of command now ran from the Commissioner through this Division to the health officers, to whom the bureau chiefs bore an advisory relationship without formal authority to direct or prohibit action. In 1917, the list of activities for which the health officers were responsible was lengthened, and plans were drawn for operating at least three additional districts in the Borough of Brooklyn in 1918. Eventually, it was contemplated that the city would be partitioned into from forty to fifty districts of about 100,000 people each.

Collapse: 1918

Just when the district plan seemed well on the way to full adoption, it collapsed, and almost overnight. The Department's annual report for 1917 is full of vision and expectation; the report for 1918 contains not a single word on health districts, which simply and quietly disappeared from sight. Except for the records, not a trace of them remained.

Two factors contributed to this development. One was the resounding defeat that swept Mayor John Purroy Mitchel and his reform administration out of office and brought the Democratic machine back to power. The new Mayor, John F. Hylan, was liberal in matters of patronage and suspicious of the reforms undertaken during the administration of his Fusion predecessor. Under a hostile chief executive, with some of the top departmental posts occupied by political appointees, there was no one left to fight for the district system.

Furthermore, the organized medical profession then opposed the establishment of district health centers, despite the assurances of advocates of the plan that the centers would not encroach on the legitimate sphere of the private practitioner. Some more emotional physicians cried that it was just a predecessor to socialist "institutions telling us where to eat, what to eat, how much to eat, and how to have it cooked." "Shall we," asked one in the course of an address on health centers, "have our ideas and religions supervised and regulated by public agencies?" In calmer, more restrained tones, but unequivocally all the same, the New York Academy of Medicine reported against the proposed system, and the county medical societies withheld their approval.

Under these conditions the position of the bureau chiefs in their opposition to the plan was greatly strengthened. In addition, America's entry into World War I drew off into military service many of the physicians from the Department, and no one who remained could be spared for the continuation of the experiment even if it could have been revived. So it simply vanished.

The abortive step toward district health administration in the Health Department was actually part of a widespread movement taking place throughout the country. Private health agencies had been experimenting with health service on a neighborhood basis from 1910 on, and health centers were springing up all over the country. In New York City, even before the war, health and social work leaders had begun to discuss the possibility of using this device to eliminate the overlapping and duplication in the operations of their agencies. Voluntary societies dedicated to fighting specific diseases such as tuberculosis and cancer went about their business without reference to public relief and welfare agencies, to one another, or to the Health Department. Their personnel crossed paths in the same sections and even in the same homes without knowing it. They maintained separate quarters, separate secretarial staffs, separate clinics, separate field organizations. They saw the possibility of cutting costs and increasing the effectiveness of their work if they could group their services physically and administratively through health centers.

The American National Red Cross gave this trend strong support when, at the end of the war, casting about for a peacetime program of sufficient scope and vitality to hold its membership and local chapters together, it elected to promote, in addition to a number of other things, the creation of neighborhood health centers throughout the country. The New York City Chapter thereupon instituted a plan for a neighborhood health center demonstration to show how health and welfare work in a given area could be co-ordinated, and to initiate such services as might be wanting. The chapter put up the funds for three years, with the understanding that the executive committee of the center would raise the money to keep it going at the end of that time. Quarters were rented, and the East Harlem Health Center commenced operations in the fall of 1921. A total of 23 voluntary health and welfare agencies participated in the enterprise, including the Department of Health, which agreed to locate some of its local clinics in the building. The project has been described as the first "department store" of health and welfare, in which clients could find under one roof almost every health and welfare service they needed.

In 1926, another such co-operative demonstration was undertaken in mid-Manhattan under the sponsorship of the Milbank Memorial Fund. The Bellevue-Yorkville demonstration, as it was called, was larger in scope than the East Harlem Center; it served an area with a population of 200,000 and the number of participating agencies and institutions was about 65. With larger resources than were available to the East Harlem Center for testing and improving district health procedures and activities, it became perhaps the most important proving ground in the country. The Commissioner of Health took an active part in directing the affairs of the demonstration, and the Department co-operated with it extensively.

A small group of leaders in the private health and welfare field figured prominently in the metropolitan health center movement from its very beginning. They appeared in the smaller neighborhood centers that sprang up in the city before World War I, and they were among the moving spirits at both East Harlem and Bellevue-Yorkville. With the two big demonstrations going so well, they began to visualize a system of neighborhood health centers throughout the city, the buildings to be provided and maintained by public funds, in which their private agencies would have both space and a voice in local planning. When Dr. Shirley W. Wynne, who, as an official of the Health Department, displayed a keen interest in Bellevue-Yorkville, became Commissioner of Health in 1928, they carried their ideas to him and urged him to do whatever was necessary to turn the ideas into reality.

Under this pressure, Commissioner Wynne, in 1929, appointed a Committee on Neighborhood Health Development for the express purpose of drawing up blue-prints for such a project. The Committee was composed of the representatives of 25 medical, health, and welfare agencies, with the Commissioner as chairman, who were "to study the city and work out plans for dividing it into districts for health centers." The members of the body secured the funds for the study from the Milbank Memorial Fund, for the Commissioner could not furnish public money. After considering the current population of the city, its characteristics, and the trends of the period 1920 to 1930, they concluded that 200,000 was the optimum population for a district. On this basis, they recommended that the city be divided into thirty such districts, each of which was to contain a health center building erected by the city and serving as a local headquarters for both private health and welfare agencies and for the field installations of the Health Department. In order to get things moving, an appropriation of $1,000,000 a year, to cover the cost of constructing four centers, was proposed for the succeeding four years.

Renewed Official Backing: 1930-1933

The recommendations of the Committee on Neighborhood Health Development impressed Mayor James J. Walker, and in 1930, he secured an appropriation of $1,000,000 for the first four centers. Before work could be started, however, the depression struck in earnest, and the city, in financial straits, had to withdraw the funds. Nevertheless, the measure indicated the growth of renewed interest in the possibilities of area administration.

At the same time that the plans for the first million-dollar program were being enacted, a health center operated entirely by the Health Department was opened in rented quarters in Central Harlem. This neighborhood had such a poor health record that it was deemed an emergency area; the general death rate was fifty percent higher than the rate for the city as a whole, the infant mortality rate about twice as high, and tuberculosis mortality some three times as high. Without waiting for the construction of new buildings, the Department launched an attack on this situation by means of a local health center.

While the center was under the direction of a district health officer, he was not equipped with anything like the powers Goldwater, Emerson, and Shipley had proposed for him. Four of the functional bureaus operated facilities in the center, but the district health officer was given no authority to direct any of their activities; the personnel of the center took orders only from the bureau chiefs for whom they worked. The district health officer was a kind of moderator who presided over a group of independent, almost autonomous agencies with no control over them other than what he could exert informally. Whatever the reason, Commissioner Wynne chose to proceed far more cautiously than Commissioner Goldwater fifteen years before. Nevertheless, the selection of a district approach to the health problems of Central Harlem was further indication of the increasing acceptance of the idea in official health administration circles.

Adoption of the District Program: 1934

Encouraged, the Committee on Neighborhood Health Development continued its efforts to obtain a city-wide, city-operated system of district health centers. In 1931, the medical profession relaxed its earlier opposition; the Coordinating Council of the five county medical societies in the city went on record as favoring in principle the establishment of neighborhood health centers, provided they were primarily for educational purposes, and each of the county societies appointed representatives to serve on the Neighborhood Health Development Committee.

In 1933, the new administration of President Franklin D. Roosevelt embarked on a nationwide public works program to bolster the flagging economy; part of its program included provision of federal funds for local civic improvements. The Committee on Neighborhood Health Development, seeing a golden opportunity, requested the staff of the Milbank Memorial Fund to conduct another study of the feasibility of district health administration. This report confirmed the desirability of the plan and recommended the installation in the Department of Health of a Director of Health Centers and the appointment of full-time district health officers at least in those areas badly in need of prompt assistance. Before the end of the year, Commissioner Wynne succeeded in having inserted in the budget an item providing funds for the establishment of centers in rented quarters in seven of the municipality's worst "sore spots," and he dispatched to Washington a request for federal emergency funds for the construction of specially adapted buildings. He also caused an examination for health officer to be given, and set up a register of potential appointees to the position.

Fiorello H. LaGuardia took office as reform mayor in 1934. He took an active interest in public health, not only because of his strong humanitarian instincts, his liberal social philosophy, and his political acumen, but also out of deep personal conviction. For his first wife lay dying in 1921 when he, then President of the Board of Aldermen, represented city government at the ceremony marking the opening of the East Harlem Health Center. LaGuardia believed his wife was the victim of lack of medical care during a childhood of poverty, and he declared with fervor as the health center was opened: "We are going to have other health centers all over the city because the people have learned they have a right to be healthy."

LaGuardia brought in his own appointees to take charge of municipal affairs, and Wynne, despite his leadership in the district health program, was replaced. The new mayor selected as Wynne's successor Dr. John L. Rice, Health Commissioner of New Haven, whose city had just won the award of the American Public Health Association, and who assured the Mayor of his deep interest in district health administration. The new Commissioner assumed his place at the head of the Health Department, and the machinery which had been set up by Wynne was set in motion. Dr. Margaret W. Barnard, former medical director of the Bellevue-Yorkville demonstration, was brought in to direct the district system, the seven district health officers were appointed, and area administration was on its way. True, the work of the Department was not completely reorganized, for it continued to be divided among the functional bureaus everywhere outside the seven sore spots. On the other hand, in these areas, it was to be assigned to the district officers. This, at least, was the intent of the decision.

Progress Despite Discord: 1934-1951

THE BUREAU CHIEFS were no more won over to the district plan in 1934 than they had been in 1914. All their earlier arguments were still valid, they maintained, while the chief objections to the bureau system had been overcome by the institution of generalized nursing as a standard Department-wide practice in 1928. (At that time, a separate Bureau of Nursing had been established and all the nurses in the agency instead of being attached to individual bureaus, now operated as a general pool at the head of which was their own director; this, it was asserted, made possible the benefits of functional expertise without the penalties of duplicated, uncoördinated operation.) From the bureaus' point of view, district health administration was entirely unnecessary. Conflicts thus developed between the bureau chiefs and the district health officers over health work in the seven centers.

Each center was the local headquarters for the activities of the Department. Clinics were maintained for assisting the local population in maternity and child health, for tuberculosis control, and for control of venereal diseases. The physicians servicing the schools in the neighborhood also worked out of the centers. The control of acute contagious diseases was a district responsibility, and home visits were made by nurses based in its center. The centers also kept district health statistics. Not all of the departmental activities were assigned to district administration, for some of them were better kept at central headquarters. But a very substantial portion of the agency's program in those neighborhoods having district health centers was handled through the centers.

Each of the activities carried on in the centers had previously been conducted by a functional bureau, and, in fact, outside these seven districts, still was. This meant that the field personnel actually doing the work outside the centers took all their instructions from, and reported to, their respective bureau chiefs or authorized representatives, were hired and assigned by the heads of the functional bureaus, and drew their pay from the bureaus. The bureaus supervised them to ensure that they maintained the proper standards and put in the required time.

Inside the districts, these relationships changed as soon as the districts were introduced. If the reorganization had followed the pattern recommended in 1914 by Goldwater, Emerson, and

Shipley, the district health officers (all of whom were physicians) would have been in command, taking over all the command authority exercised by the bureau chiefs with respect to personnel in the field. The bureau chiefs would have acted only in an advisory capacity without authority to issue orders, instructions, or directions to the personnel in the districts; they could only have made recommendations to the health officer. On the other hand, if the relationships had been arranged as some of the bureau chiefs desired, the health officers would have been advisory, and the bureau chiefs would have continued to exercise all the powers they had exercised up to then. In this case, the health centers would have brought the field activities of the various bureaus physically together, but, administratively, the local services would have remained arms of the bureaus and nothing more.

Neither of these plans was followed even in theory. Neither the health officers nor the bureau chiefs were reduced to advisors. Both were granted authority to direct personnel in the centers. But they were to direct different phases of the activities of those persons. The health officers would have charge of all matters of administration; the bureau chiefs would have charge of all technical matters. Each would be supreme in its own sphere, and the operating personnel in the centers were to take orders from both and report to both.

This distinction between technical and administrative authority was not invented by the New York City Health Department. It was, for example, part of the organization doctrine of the contemporary Federal Emergency Relief Administration. Whether the decision was wise or not, (and the reasons for picking this particular formula are unknown), its prospects for easy and effective operation were in considerable part dependent on an atmosphere of general agreement.

Such was not the atmosphere in the Health Department. With disturbing frequency, bureau chiefs and health officers disagreed on how to meet particular situations. Thus, for example, when a health officer wanted to close the doors of his center for a while for what seemed to him good and sufficient reasons, one of the bureaus objected vehemently that such a step would unnecessarily disrupt its service. When a health officer decided to suspend a service pending completion of a new building, the bureau chief concerned protested and made his own arrangements for continuing the service. When a health officer restricted one of his clinics to a single population group because of its special needs, the head of the bureau affected took angry exception. When a health officer channeled through his own office all contacts of a certain kind between field personnel and one of the bureaus, a hue and cry was raised by the bureau concerned. In all these instances, the health officers appealed to their chief, the Director of District Health Administration, Dr. Barnard, who, as an officer of equal standing with the bureau chiefs, presented to the latter the point of view of the district officials. When no agreement could be achieved on this level, and this, too, was annoyingly common, the dispute would go to a Deputy Commissioner or even to the Commissioner himself.

Furthermore, there was little accord on what was administrative and what was technical. To be sure, there were broad areas in which no confusion was possible; no health officer would challenge a bureau chief on the length of a hypodermic needle, the method of conducting a pneumothorax refill, or the type of medication to be used, and bureau chiefs did not interfere in the distribution of paychecks or the allocation of office furniture. But when it came to deciding how many clinic sessions of a particular kind would be held in the district, or whether a particular type of service would be expanded or contracted, or if the time of some of the field personnel could be redistributed to better advantage, each felt the matter was within his own sphere. In general the bureau chiefs gave a rather broad interpretation to the term "technical," while the health officers were liberal in their understanding of the term "administrative." So these differences went to the bureau level for discussion, and, if they were not resolved there, continued upward even to the Commissioner's office.

The field personnel in the districts, having looked to the bureau chiefs for leadership in every respect for so many years continued to do so despite the inauguration of area administration. District health officers were simply circumvented as the technical personnel maintained direct contact with their bureau headquarters and neglected to send the district chiefs even information memoranda. In one instance, a health officer was unaware of the outbreak of a disease in almost epidemic proportions in his district because the personnel fighting it had taken the matter to the bureau concerned and were working under bureau supervision without even mentioning the incident to him. The bureau chiefs did not seem at all anxious to discourage this state of affairs; partly from force of habit, partly for other reasons, they kept in direct touch with the field and rarely bothered to go through the district officers. There was little the district health officers could do, for the hiring, assigning, and disciplining of professional functional personnel remained a power of the bureau rather than of the district organization. So district health officers complained to Dr. Barnard, who took the matter up with the bureau chiefs for them, and with higher echelons when necessary.

First Efforts at Resolution: 1934-1942

Commissioner Rice believed in the district system, but he also believed that it could not be made to work except under the direction of a strong central departmental office. And he believed that the bureaus had lost too much of their power to the members of the Committee on Neighborhood Health Development, who had come to wield considerable authority over the internal affairs of the Department though they themselves were not actually in the Department or on the public payroll. So it seemed to him that the best way to quiet the clashes constantly flaring up between the bureaus and the districts was to build up the central office, which to him meant strengthening the bureaus.

This he attempted to do by means of an order issued in 1935. In general, it repeated the formula for division of operating responsibility between technical and administrative supervisors, but it also authorized the bureau chiefs to ignore the district health officers whenever they thought they were acting on a matter within their respective provinces. "Bureau directors," he decreed, "on matters specifically within their functions [which they were to decide for themselves] may deal directly with their representatives. Such communications will be marked 'Personal' and will not be opened by the Health Officer." He made it clear, too, that he meant to take personal charge of the situation until the conflicts were eliminated, or, at least, considerably reduced:

> It must be borne in mind that the Commissioner of Health is the only final authority in the Department on all matters of policy and administration. During the early period of health district management, whatever rules or regulations may be adopted, many points of doubtful interpretation and doubtful desirability will inevitably arise, as to which there will be difference of opinion between the other bureau chiefs and the director of district health administration, or between the bureau directors and their local representatives in the districts. It is desirable that when such differences of opinion are entertained, and when frank discussion fails to resolve them, they should be reported to the Commissioner in person, for his consideration and decision, in order that he may have an opportunity to take a hand in the development of policies and methods for which he is, in any case, responsible. The development of the health districts is certainly the most important of the new subjects arising, thus far, in his administration. It will need and should have his personal attention on all strategic points.

But neither his backing of the bureau chiefs nor his determination to intervene personally in the disputes between areal and functional officers was enough to end the disturbances in the department. So Dr. Rice invited Professor Ira V. Hiscock of the Department of Public Health at Yale University to study the situation and report on what could be done to improve it.

Hiscock confirmed the existence of the conflict, urged that some plan be devised to bring the central office and the health officers into closer contact, and recommended that a manual on district health administration be prepared as soon as possible. In accordance with his findings, the Director of District Health Administration was given more assistance to free her for contact work, and work was begun on a manual. The manual endeavored to explain in detail which matters were to be treated as administrative and which as technical. A tentative draft was prepared and circulated, but it had an indifferent reception and no effect. It never got beyond the first-draft stage, and was never used. The problem of working out satisfactory relationships between the functional and area officers remained unsolved; the conflicts went on.

Nevertheless, the district system expanded. With funds from the federal Public Works Administration, health center buildings were erected in the seven original districts. New districts were organized. By the end of 1936, twelve of the thirty districts projected in the original proposal of the Committee on Neighborhood Health Development were in operation. In 1937, the entire city was divided into districts, but, since it was not possible to staff all thirty at once, they were grouped into twenty administrative units of which eleven were individual districts and nine consisted of groups of two or three districts under a single officer.

Time brought some relief as the area people and the functional people learned to live with each other in a kind of uneasy, intermittent truce. But the growth of the district system at the same time provided more occasions for clashes between them, and the difficulty, after several years of sputtering, again claimed the attention of the Commissioner in 1941.

On this occasion, he took a drastic step. He abolished the office of the Director of District Health Administration completely and directed that "District Health Officers will take up matters relating to a bureau activity in their district directly with the Director of the Bureau concerned." Dr. Barnard was named Consultant in Local Administration, in which capacity she had no authorization to command; her role was strictly "advisory and instructive." The swing away from the Goldwater doctrine was now almost complete.

This move did not directly diminish the powers of the health officers, for the familiar administrative-technical dichotomy remained intact. But it did leave them without any representative on the bureau level to take their part against the bureau chiefs. The district officers were neither in a position, nor could they take time from their operating duties, to do this job adequately themselves. Rice's action was consistent with his belief that the way to strengthen the districts was first to strengthen the rest of the Department, and the result was to increase greatly the influence of the bureau chiefs over the activities of the health centers. The situation approached that of the original Central Harlem Health Center in which the health officer was little more than a moderator presiding over, but not commanding, branches of the functional bureaus operating as independent tenants in one building. This was the state of affairs when Rice resigned in 1942.

A Different Approach: 1943-1945

Rice's successor, Dr. Ernest L. Stebbins, apparently was not favorably impressed with the way the Department was functioning. Transferring the former Director of District Health Administration to a purely advisory position, he felt, did nothing to eliminate the source of controversy, which was in the operation of the health centers themselves. The district health officers continued to try to assert what they thought was their grant of authority over administration, and the bureau chiefs continued, with greater effectiveness than ever, to ignore them. The conflict persisted, though it was now somewhat more one-sided.

So Stebbins set out to improve administration. But he took a completely different tack. Where Rice had sought to further district administration through building up the bureaus, Stebbins attacked the problem by building up the headquarters representation of the district system itself. This he did in 1943 by establishing a new position of Assistant Commissioner for District Health Administration, which was above the bureau level, and by appointing Dr. Barnard to the post. Among her duties in this capacity was "General supervision over . . . relationships between district and bureau activities." The Health Officers thus again had someone above their own level to champion their point of view, and they found her in a considerably stronger position than had originally been the case. She continued to function as Assistant Commissioner for more than three years; in 1946, a new city administration directed that all officials of the municipal government use their official civil service titles instead of the titles granted by departmental order, and she assumed once again the designation of Director of District Health Administration.

Report to the Mayor: 1947

In the course of time, the area of understanding between the bureaus and the district officers expanded a good deal, but the clashes were not eliminated by any means. Mayor William O'Dwyer, shortly after taking office in 1946 and appointing Dr. Israel Weinstein to replace Dr. Stebbins as Commissioner when the latter resigned, instituted a thorough survey of the Health Department. To this task he assigned his administrative secretary, Paul L. Ross, who spent nine months on the job and conducted more than seventy hearings before rendering his report in the early part of 1947. Ross found the same "fundamental conflicts of attitudes, philosophies, and purposes within the Department" that had plagued it since the introduction of the area plan of administration:

> There has . . . been a lack of cooperation on all sides. There has also been an unwillingness to compromise and make things work, as well as an undue willingness to find fault with others' work and procedures. As a result, District Health Administration has been marked by continual conflicts over trifles. Items which should have been handled routinely have become major problems, requiring undue time and attention on the part of high executives.

In a sense, the district system was on trial, for many of these difficulties had arisen only after it was installed, and they persisted despite every effort to end them. Some of the bureau chiefs seized the opportunity to attack it vigorously, and its representatives were on the defensive a good part of the time. Yet, though the author of the report admitted that "the role of District Health Administration and its lack of proper integration within the Department has been the cause of frequent conflicts and impasses," he denied categorically that the remedy lay in abandonment. On the contrary, he concluded that the districts were the core of the Department.

The fundamental reason for the conflicts, in his judgment, was the failure of the departmental leadership to define the agency's changing objectives. To be sure, he allocated much of the blame to both the bureau chiefs and the district health people, whose disposition to circumvent and battle each other contributed substantially to the difficulties of the organization. But underneath it all, he added, was the lack of understanding at every level of what the Department was trying to do and how it was trying to do it.

No longer, ran the argument, was the negative, police work of the health agency its central objective. Mere suppression of outbreaks of disease was no longer enough, for the whole pattern of disease and ill health was changing. The goal now was to reach each individual with a new idea of health conservation through local community organization of health services. It meant renunciation of the effort to separate preventive medicine from curative medicine. It required a positive neighborhood approach.

Before the problems of the Department could be solved, the report continued, it therefore had to be brought home to everyone that the "objectives of District Health Administration must be accepted as those of the Department itself." This was the *sine qua non*. Once it had been accomplished by a forthright, unequivocal statement by the top leadership, a series of conferences might be undertaken at every level to effect a reconciliation among the contending parties, and the necessary reorganization of the departmental structure could take place.

The proposed reorganization would have made the district health officers "the primary line organization of the Department." As far as these officials were concerned, said Ross in his report,

> If the policy is community health, then the district Health Officer should be the line officer and the functional specialists the staff consultants, the planners, and the guides. . . .
>
> There has been a lack of understanding and agreement as to whether District Health Administration is to be a 'vertical' organization with Central Office bureaus exercising direct control of programs in the Health Centers, or a 'horizontal' organization with the District Health Officer responsible for all district activities and personnel.

In this language, reminiscent of the recommendations of Goldwater, Emerson, and Shipley a generation earlier, the report to the Mayor urged what it termed the "horizontal" type of organization.

For reasons not entirely clear, the report was shelved. Some two years afterward, when the administrative secretary was no longer with the city government, his assistant on this job drew the assignment of preparing a study of Health Department organization for the municipal Bureau of the Budget. In this roundabout fashion, many of the recommendations of the report found their way into practice. But the key one, the new statement of objectives and the corresponding reorganization of the whole Department around the district health system, was never carried out.

A Big Step: 1948

When Dr. Harry S. Mustard became Commissioner late in 1947, he found his Department still hampered by wrangling between the two major factions. He determined to introduce gradually a series of directives aimed at putting an end "once and for all" to this situation. An emergency, however, thrust upon him the opportunity—indeed, the necessity—to take drastic action much sooner than he had anticipated.

The day after Christmas, 1947, New York was smothered beneath 26 inches of snow that had fallen in 24 hours and paralyzed the entire city. For days, the city fought to extricate itself from the results of the blizzard. Meanwhile, the Health Department was bombarded by urgent telephone calls for all kinds of help, and especially by frantic appeals from desperate citizens whose oil deliveries had been held up and whose homes were beginning to freeze.

Mustard seized the chance to see how his field units functioned under stress. He was appalled to find his health officers virtually helpless to mobilize the forces at their disposal. Field personnel, instead of looking to the district chiefs for leadership in the crisis, sought direction from their respective bureaus, and, in place of action, were wasting precious time in calls for instructions to a central headquarters that had little idea of local conditions. The Commissioner returned to his office grim and resolute, and on New Year's Day, 1948, promulgated a drastic order.

It contained four principal provisions. First, the district health officer was made "responsible for all localized activities of the Department of Health in his district . . . which heretofore were directed by the respective bureaus in central office, and will have authority to make any necessary decisions and allocation of personnel. Such decisions are to be binding on all members of the Department in the District . . . concerned."

Secondly, all communications, without exception, including technical instructions, were to pass through the office of the Director of District Health Administration, and only her office was authorized to issue administrative instructions.

Thirdly, the Director of District Health Administration was granted power to hold up for 24 hours any technical instruction with which she disagreed, during which time she and the bureau director concerned were to try to work out a solution to their differences. In the event that no agreement was reached, the case was to be referred to the Deputy Commissioner, but, Mustard warned, "It is not believed that many such references should be necessary, and as Commissioner of Health, I shall watch this with interest."

Finally, field personnel taking exception to an order of a district officer were *nevertheless to obey such order,* challenging it meanwhile in a written message to the appropriate bureau chief and submitting a copy of the protest to the district chief. Furthermore, "Field personnel under the direction of the District Health Officer will not, in the future, telephone to Bureaus for confirmation of District Health Officer's orders, nor will Bureau Directors or others in the Central Office convey orders other than indicated above."

Put out to cover the emergency situation created by the big snowfall, this order was to remain in effect "until further notice," and, except for a later order removing responsibility for building maintenance from the health officers, no revision or rescission was ever issued. It furnished the health officers with the strongest authorization they had ever enjoyed, and some of them were more successful in gaining control over their district organizations after this than they had been in the previous ten years.

More Difficulties and a Fresh Approach: 1951-1958

But the Mustard directive did not solve the problem. Emboldened by the order, district health officers grew more aggressive in the assertion of their reinforced authority, and the bureau chiefs became correspondingly more resistant. The Commissioner's attention was drawn away by other public health issues, and he was unable to follow up his order as vigorously as he had intended. By the time he resigned in 1950, there was almost as much turbulence in the Department as ever.

Dr. John Mahoney replaced him, and district health administration went into a new decline. For one thing, much of the responsibility for the program during his period of service devolved upon his deputy, Dr. Samuel Frant; the Deputy Commissioner's sympathies lay with the bureau chiefs and the proponents of centralization. Secondly, Dr. Barnard retired in 1951, and the post of Director of District Health Administration was left unfilled. The district health centers continued to function, but the position of the district health officers was considerably weaker; field personnel of the bureaus went on circumventing all but a few, who, by force of personality, were able to achieve a measure of influence. A new study of the Department, part of a larger study of the city government by the Mayor's Committee on Management Survey, was conducted in 1951, and the report, released in 1952, strongly recommended (1) that major responsibility and authority for field services be vested in the district health officers, and (2) that direction of district health administration be lodged in a single, top-level administrator. The report, however, had no immediate effect; the district health officers remained in an underdog position.

In 1953 Robert F. Wagner took office as Mayor and promptly appointed Dr. Leona Baumgartner Health Commissioner. Dr. Baumgartner had served in the Department for almost twenty years in a variety of capacities, including district health officer, Director of the Bureau of Child Hygiene, and Assistant Commissioner for Maternal and Child Health. She, in turn, appointed to the First Deputy Commissionership Dr. Roscoe P. Kandle, then Field Director of the American Public Health Association and one of the authors of the report to the Mayor's Committee on Management Survey two years earlier.

The new leaders of the Department adopted a fresh approach to the long-standing controversy. One of their first steps was to make it clear throughout the Department that the district health officers were no longer to be regarded as an inferior breed. Next they attacked the organizational problem at the borough level rather than at the city headquarters or district levels as their predecessors had done. Since the mid-1930s there had been in each of the city's five boroughs a Borough (or "Regional") Director of Health Services. His task was to supervise the district health officers in his jurisdiction. The borough posts were originally established to reduce Dr. Barnard's span of control by interposing an additional level between her office and the district officers. The positions, however, had always been filled by ordinary district health officers, who carried the borough responsibilities in addition to their own district obligations. Consequently, the borough positions had never been administratively important even before the departure of Dr. Barnard.

Baumgartner and Kandle proposed to resolve the conflict between the bureaus and the districts by making the boroughs important administrative centers. In 1954, the Commissioner issued an executive order making the Borough Director in Brooklyn, "in co-operation and consultation with, and under the technical direction of, the Directors of the Department's bureaus," directly responsible to the First Deputy Commissioner for co-ordination of virtually all the departmental services in that borough, including the activities of the health centers and relationships with other city departments and voluntary agencies. At the same time, each bureau was directed to designate one of its members to be its Brooklyn representative and to delegate to him substantial administrative discretion. The representatives of the bureaus were to work with the Borough Director "to have as many decisions as possible for Brooklyn . . . made in Brooklyn, on the basis that they are apt to be sounder than when made in the Central Office." Within a year, a similar arrangement was decreed for Manhattan and Richmond (Staten Island) together, under a single Borough Director, and for the Bronx.

The borough emphasis represented a conviction on the part of the Commissioner and the Deputy Commissioner that the old concept of a neighborhood pattern of health administration was no longer applicable to New York City. When the concept was originally advanced it was probably appropriate, they believed, but many factors—the cessation of large-scale immigration, the rise in the standard of living and in levels of education, the continual movement of the city's population, the tapering off of the rate of population increase within the city, the aging of the populace, the decline of acute diseases and the consequently greater relative significance of chronic and degenerative ailments, and other developments—had rendered the districts unsuitable as service areas, and had made undesirable the adoption of one set of service areas for all departmental functions. "The borough is chosen . . . ," the order said, "because it is believed that the best service units may vary for different services and that deliberate experimentation on the size and kind of service units is needed." There was a bow in the direction of the neighborhood idea: "It is also intended to decentralize further the administration to the districts." This, however, was clearly not where the chief stress would be placed; the borough offices had become the real hope for co-ordination. For the Deputy Commissioner, this was a drastic modification of policy, since he had played a prominent role in formulating the strong recommendations of the Mayor's Committee on Management Survey; from the perspective of his official position, he had come to doubt the wisdom and applicability of some of his earlier proposals. (It was possible, he believed, that each type of health problem required a different administrative area for most efficient treatment.) For the Commissioner, a former bureau chief as well as a former District Health Officer, this was an appealing compromise between the contending factions. The synthesis, the two leaders hoped, had been discovered.

Less than a year later, they elevated the old Office of District Health Administration (renamed the Office of District Services) from status as an ordinary bureau to a unit in the office of the First Deputy Commissioner, and appointed a Director of District Services to fill the post, vacant since the resignation of Dr. Barnard. The line of communication now ran from the district health officers through the borough directors directly to the high command of the Department, a symbolic as well as an administrative adjustment, the significance of which was presumably not lost upon the personnel of the agency. The first Director of District Health Services, it is true, was also a Borough Director and a District Health Officer simultaneously, so he could not give his new position his undivided energies. But this only permitted—indeed, obliged—the First Deputy Commissioner to exercise active supervision of the program, and thereby tended to strengthen the borough directors. The Commissioner and the Deputy took pains to impress upon the members of the bureaus and on the district services people that differences were to be resolved as far as possible at the borough level or below. They declared that they realized the relationships would have to "evolve gradually," but they made it clear the borough directors, and the district health officers under them, once again had friends at court. Eventually, it may be predicted from all current indications, the neighborhood districts will be allowed to languish; the present leaders of the Department have placed their bets on the borough directors, working in co-operation with the borough representatives of the bureaus, to achieve the elusive objective of co-ordinated field activities and to discover the optimum area for each major health problem that the Department now faces. The borough directors can count on top-level support as long as these leaders are in office.

Whether this will do the job remains to be seen. In form, at least, except for the emphasis on boroughs rather than districts as the units of areal administration, the old conditions obtain. "The intention," says the order of 1954, "is to have the Bureaus serve as staff to the line activities in the Borough," yet borough directors are placed under the "technical direction" of the bureaus. This was the very language of Goldwater, Emerson, and Shipley two generations ago. On the other hand, the determination of the high command that the borough directors shall not be ignored, circumvented, or arbitrarily overruled by the bureaus, and (perhaps more importantly) the active implementation of that determination by the Deputy Commissioner, is a development of considerable significance. One Borough Director has grasped this opportunity and has succeeded in settling differences between himself or his district officers and bureau officials by a forceful exercise of his authority which has won the respect of all those involved. Another has been reluctant and hesitant to use his power, and the usual conflicts continue unabated. At the end of 45 years, it is conceivable that a viable form of areal administration is at last emerging, but the experience of 45 years compels the observer with any training in administration to be cautious, if not skeptical.

Concluding Comments

THAT PART of the story that is already past raises a number of questions to a student of administration. Why did so many attempts to achieve understanding and co-operation miscarry or yield such limited success? What measures might have had more success? What stood between the pronouncement of the decision and its effectuation?

The problems behind these questions are not peculiar to the Health Department, or even to the field of public health, alone; on the contrary, they often seem generic to organization. In any agency that conducts field operations, there is usually a conflict, potential or actual, between areal officials and functional officials; there is almost always some practical distinction, however ambiguous, between technical and administrative responsibilities; and over a period of years there are almost inevitably some shifts in the relative status of areal and functional officals. The situation in the New York City Health Department was thus a compound of perennial difficulties.

Yet the situation described in this case differs from many others in degree if not in kind; the shifts were more violent, the exacerbations sharper, the time required to reach a workable equilibrium longer.

There is no single or simple cause for this unfortunate situation. A number of factors combined to make the problem particularly difficult, or at least to give an unusual quality to it from the very beginning; among these are:

(1) The bureaus of the Health Department had a long and distinguished tradition that permeated the staff of the Department. It was already firmly established as early as 1915, when Commissioner Goldwater undertook his reforms.

(2) Specialization is a relatively new phenomenon in the field of medicine, but has quickly become an accepted part of the profession. Regardless of the form of departmental organization, therefore, field work in the Health Department must be done to a considerable extent by specialists. The specialists in the districts naturally tended to be responsive to their counterparts in central headquarters no matter what the formal organization charts showed. Professional bonds within each area of medicine, as well as hierarchical bonds, tied organization members to each other.

(3) The ease, cheapness, and rapidity of communications within New York City facilitated unofficial contacts between specialists. And at the same time, the introduction of district offices tended to complicate somewhat the channels of official communication.

(4) Though the boundaries of the districts tended originally to coincide roughly with neighborhoods, the areas encompassed were not unified or politically articulate for the most part. Thus, the areal officers lacked such support and prestige as might have been provided by regions with greater coherence and articulateness.

(5) The inherent problem of defining the difference between technical and administrative matters was affected by the fact that the district health officers were (and this was perhaps inevitable) themselves doctors and therefore possessed of technical competence. Their technical competence enlarged the area in which jurisdictional disputes could easily arise, even though no conscious attempt to enlarge their jurisdiction was involved.

For all practical purposes, these factors could not be manipulated by the administrative leaders of the Department. Perhaps in the long run, some of them might be modified, but it seemed clear that they could not be changed in time to alter the immediate setting of the problem. They could only be taken into account.

The attack on the problem therefore had to proceed on other lines, through those factors that *could* be manipulated. Caution is necessary here, for we know only the highlights of the story. While we, with the advantages of hindsight, can identify the factors that seem important in the light of what did happen, it is not easy on the basis of available knowledge to evaluate them in terms of actual situation at the time or to appreciate fully the considerations that led to stress on one rather than another.

But it is apparent that primary emphasis was placed on changing in various ways the formal hierarchical relationships between the functional and areal officers. There was little or no attempt to modify attitudes and win compliance by education or other means, partly because the pressure of other official business prevented successive commissioners from giving their full attention to this possibility, and partly because there was a fundamental lack of agreement on—perhaps even understanding of—the objectives of the Department.

In view of the many alternatives untried in this case, any conclusion that situations of this kind cannot be relieved is probably unwarranted and certainly undemonstrated. If one analyzes the hypothetical alternatives in this case, it is clear that the successive commissioners had various choices open to them in a number of different fields: in relation to education and indoctrination, in relation to the organization of the central office, in relation to the definition of "technical" or "administrative," in relation to assigning responsibility for the initial decision—good unless repealed. However, in the course of such analysis, no easy, pat solution is likely to be revealed.

The Reorganization of the California State Personnel Board

Frederick C. Mosher

Editor's Note

This study was made with the full co-operation and assistance of the Personnel Board and its staff. Professor Frederick C. Mosher was given access to official and personal files. Following individual interviews, several group interviews and meetings were arranged. The manuscript has also benefited from careful review and criticism by members of the staff of the Personnel Board. Professor Mosher wishes to record his thanks to the staff for their co-operation and hospitality. He also acknowledges the assistance at every stage of his wife, Edith. He of course assumes sole responsibility for the contents of this study.

Introduction

THE BUDGET REQUEST of the California State Personnel Board for the fiscal year 1955-56 stated, in typically succinct terms:

> The budget also reflects a major change in organization effective July 1, 1954. *The new organization provides for an Operations Division to handle classification, pay, and examinations on a generalist basis in lieu of three separate divisions, each specializing in its respective field for day-to-day activities.* A Standards and Surveys Division will handle the detailed classification and pay surveys. The examination unit will conduct oral interviews and establish examination standards and techniques. [Emphasis added.]

This study is an attempt to recapture the process by which this "major change in organization" came about, the reasons for it, the forces that impinged upon it, the problems generated by it. Unlike most reorganizations, this one necessitated changes in the duties, the work habits, the skills, the procedures, and in the personal as well as official relationships of most of the supervisors and professional workers in three major divisions of the Board—about 55 people in all. It was no mere shifting of boxes on a chart.

Like other administrative reorganizations, this one covered a considerable span of time. It was announced as "effective July 1, 1954." But the first formal step had been taken in November 1952 after many months of gestation. The final formal step did not take place until October 1954. And the process was still going on as this was written in July 1955. The major phases of the reorganization covered three and one-half years, from January 1952 to July 1955.

Of primary interest in this story is the content of the reorganization—the substitution of the so-called "generalist" pattern for the traditional "functional" or "specialist" structure. The forward march of specialism and professionalism has long been an object of interest to students of western society, many of whom have noted a danger of losing the whole in efforts to lend perfection and dignity to the parts. Frequently deplored in public administration has been the shortage of generalists capable of an overall point of view. The problem is acute at the level of management where there is concentrated the responsibility for integrating diverse specialisms and for continuously relating goals to techniques.

Public personnel administration has enjoyed no immunity from this trend or from misgivings about it. Its various functional fields—examinations, classification, training, placement, employee relations, and others—have each provided the basis for occupational specialties, each relatively sufficient unto itself, each lending to a professional self-consciousness. Many feel that this segmentation impedes the performance of the total personnel job and retards the development of *compleat* personnel workers. In the past fifteen years, a number of public personnel agencies have begun grouping specialist functions to try to counteract the trend toward specialization.[1]

The reorganization of the California State Personnel Board, reflecting these anti-specialism considerations, was not without precedent. Yet it was in many respects a bold and forward-looking step. The state's civil service system, one of the oldest in the country, had been organized on traditional functional lines for many years. The reorganization was the first modern effort by a large public personnel organization to integrate within the same units and the same individuals the responsibilities for both examining and classification—two of the most important and virile personnel specialties.

[1] In 1954-55 the Civil Service Assembly of the United States and Canada conducted a nation-wide survey of generalist programs in public personnel administration. The findings of this study were summarized and analyzed in an article, "Personnel Generalist: Experience and Advice," by Lyman H. Cozad and Kenneth O. Warner, *Public Personnel Review,* July 1955. This study disclosed that, of its sample of 119 federal, state, and local personnel agencies in the United States and Canada, 58, or nearly half, operated partially or completely on a generalist basis.

CALIFORNIA STATE PERSONNEL BOARD

BEFORE

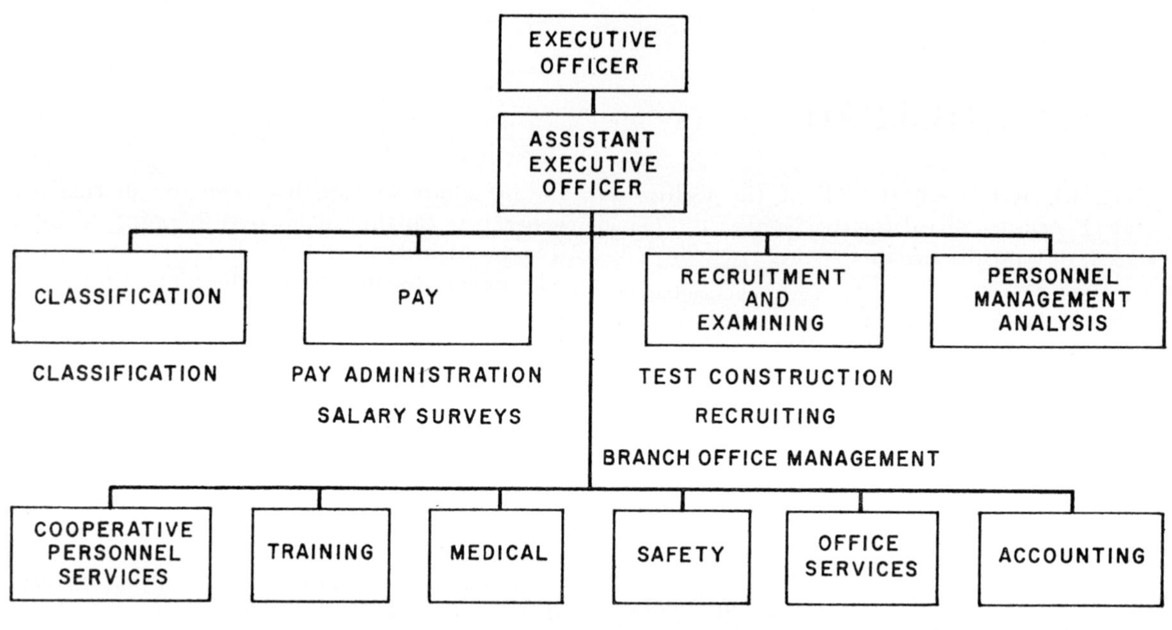

AFTER OCTOBER 1, 1954

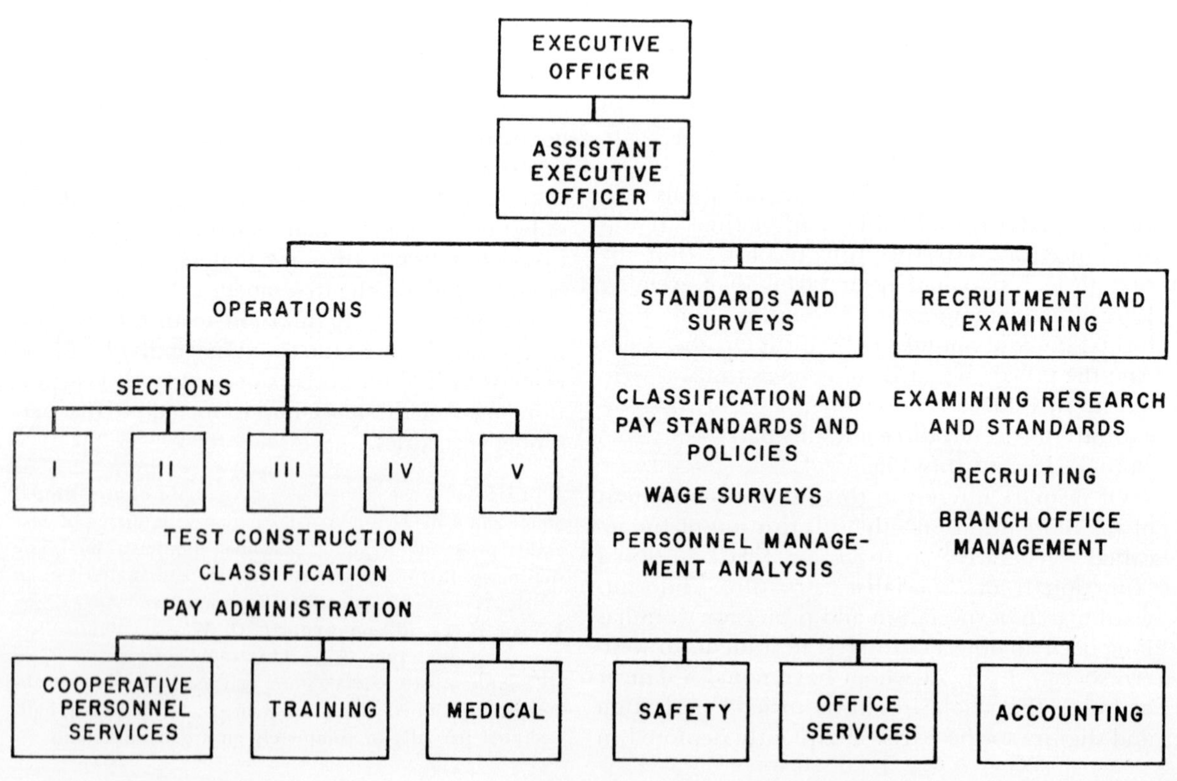

The Personnel Board and its Staff

THE TWO KEY DATES in the evolution of California's civil service are August 15, 1913 and November 6, 1934. The earlier date marked the passage of the state's first Civil Service Act, a landmark to governmental reformers of that era and one of the many progressive contributions of Governor Hiram W. Johnson. The later date was the day on which the people of the state endorsed, by an overwhelming margin, Article XXIV of the State Constitution, which established the legal framework for the present personnel system. Both actions were conceived and adopted to counteract political pressures in the selection and management of the state service. As in many other jurisdictions, California's merit system developed as part of the popular crusade against spoils.

The 1913 legislation provided a three-man Commission, appointed by the Governor, with powers over examining and selection comparable to those of contemporary civil service agencies. In spite of strong early appointments to the Commission and the development of a competent examining staff, the Commission declined in prestige during the twenties and came itself to be increasingly responsive to political forces, particularly from the Governor's office. In 1929, by the last of several reorganizations, the Commission became the Division of Personnel and Organization within the Department of Finance, then as in 1952-54 perhaps the most powerful of all state administrative agencies.[2] But, in the face of political inroads, the stature of the merit system continued to decline:

> Exemptions from civil service became continuously more numerous. By 1932 over half of all the state employees were either in exempt or "temporary" positions, or holding other quasi-political appointments. Violations of the Civil Service Act were common.[3]

It was this reversion toward patronage which gave rise to the new drive in 1934 to safeguard the merit system by a constitutional amendment:

> The constitutional amendment was intended primarily to correct three evils: (1) political control of the administration of civil service, (2) exemption of employees from the civil service law by either the Legislature or the Commission, and (3) the unreasonable use of temporary appointment authorizations to evade the intent of the Civil Service Act.[4]

In the best anti-spoils tradition, the constitutional amendment of 1934, Article XXIV, established an independent, virtually autonomous body. The State Personnel Board, which replaced the old Civil Service Commission, was to comprise five members appointed by the Governor with the consent of the Senate. Except for deaths or resignations, one member was to be appointed every biennium for a ten-year term. Normally, no Governor could select a majority of the Board within a single term. (The amendment did not stipulate that the Board be bi-partisan, and in 1955 all the members were apparently of the same political party. Party affiliation, however, did not appear to influence their deliberations.)

The amendment reaffirmed the principles of the merit system in unequivocal terms: "Permanent appointments and promotion in the state civil service shall be made exclusively under a general system based upon merit, efficiency, and fitness as ascertained by competitive examinations."[5] It defined the "state civil service" to include "every officer and employee of this State except. . ."—and it proceeded to list a limited number of exempt positions, principally elected officers, officers ap-

[2] For a picture of the political and administrative forces in a similar evolution in another state, see Peter Bart and Milton Cummings, Jr., *The Transfer of the Kansas State Civil Service Department,* No. 31, The Inter-University Case Program (University of Alabama Press, 1956).

[3] *Twenty-First Biennial Report of the California State Personnel Board* (1952-54), p. 9.

[4] *Ibid.,* p. 10.

[5] *Constitution of the State of California,* Article XXIV, Section 1.

pointed by the Governor with Senate confirmation, employees of the Legislature and of the Governor's office, employees of the University and state colleges, and a few others. It locked the door against other exemptions. Further, it restricted to a period of months (now nine) the tenure of any temporary appointment. The Board received all the powers of its predecessor Commission, and new ones were subsequently added. The Board's powers were to be exercised by an executive officer appointed by the Board and himself a member of the state civil service.

Neither the political sterilization of the Board nor the eradication of its subservience to the Governor was accomplished overnight. During the terms of Republican Governor Frank F. Merriam and Democratic Governor Culbert L. Olson, political forces continued to operate upon and within the Board. They contributed to the voluntary departure in 1938 of the Board's first Executive Officer, William Brownrigg, and to the dismissal in 1941 of his successor, Louis J. Kroeger. Kroeger's dismissal sparked the organization of a statewide group to defend him and to protect the merit system from the Board itself. Kroeger withdrew to a war-agency job in Washington, but enthusiasm for merit system reform was once again ignited.

The picture changed two years later following the first election of Governor Earl Warren, who apparently determined to insulate state civil service from politics. Enabled through retirements and other separations to make several Personnel Board appointments during his first years, Warren named a group of men of high, and not necessarily political, reputation. Three of these, appointed in 1943, 1944, and 1945 respectively, were still on the Board in 1955. Subsequent appointments by Warren and his successor, Governor Goodwin J. Knight, maintained a high standard, and, from 1945 to the time of this case, patronage played a minor, almost irrelevant, role in the operations of the Board. By 1952 most employees of the Board and of the rest of the state service were professional career personnel. Many department heads had "come up through the ranks," and the Personnel Board itself was increasingly called upon to set salaries, classification standards, and rules to govern the relatively few employees still in the exempt category.

The reorganization of 1952-55, which is the subject of this study, was affected by two important conditions. One was the Personnel Board's high degree of independence. The reorganization was to be "an inside job," uninfluenced by political parties, the Legislature, or the Governor. The single formal external control over the Board throughout the reorganization was the annual budget. The way in which the reorganization was carried out was also influenced by the Board's desire to provide the best possible service to the state departments that constituted its "using agencies." It should be noted, incidentally, that while the Board endeavored to stress service rather than control in dealing with state departments, its authority to exert control in defense of the merit system was universally accepted and frequently exercised.

A second important condition affecting the reorganization was the relationship between the Board and its staff head, the Executive Officer. During the troublesome thirties, the Board, or part of it at least, had participated frequently in staff operations—a source of many of the difficulties of the first two Executive Officers. The constitutional amendment of 1934 provided that the Executive Officer "shall perform and discharge all of the powers, duties, purposes, functions, and jurisdictions hereunder or which hereafter by law may be vested in the Board except that the adoption of rules and regulations, the creation and adjustment of classifications and grades, and dismissals, demotions, suspensions, and other punitive action . . ." required a majority vote of the Board.[6]

Following its renaissance of 1943, the Board, by tacit agreement, had removed itself from operations. Since then there has been almost complete delegation of responsibility for internal administration to the Executive Officer. The decision to carry out the 1952-55 reorganization was his. He apprised the Board of the projected change, and the Board members had the opportunity to voice their views. Had they opposed, he would have reconsidered. But the question of his legal authority was not raised, nor had it been raised on similar issues in previous years. One Board member maintained that no one knew where the legal authority for such a decision lay and that it would

[6] *Ibid.*, Section 2.

probably have taken a court decision to find out. At any rate, by 1952 the Board usually met in an open session for about a day and a half every two weeks. Its calendar was prepared under the direction of the Executive Officer. Its meetings were taken up with new or amended class specifications, new or changed pay schedules, broad policy matters, and appeals. In addition to the official meeting, the Board met informally with the Executive Officer and a few top staff to discuss plans and policy questions. All Board members served part-time only, and they had few contacts with the regular staff other than through these scheduled sessions.

The Growth of the Staff

The Personnel Board's staff developed by expanding in scope, function, and size. Like other civil service agencies, the original Commission had been concerned primarily with examining. The first classification plan had been completed in 1922 and had been greatly improved after a survey by a private firm in 1930-31. A salary standardization program had been begun in 1934 and had been thoroughly revised following a survey in 1937-38. Since that time, administration of the state salary plan has been one of the Board's principal responsibilities. An entirely new civil service law, adopted in 1937, still provided the statutory base for most of the Board's operations in 1952. Also in 1937, the Legislature gave the Board authority to provide technical personnel services on a cost basis to local governments and counties. In 1952 a separate and quite independent unit of the Board, the Cooperative Personnel Services Division, carried out these assignments under contract with local governments.

The postwar period witnessed sizable expansion of existing activities as well as enlargement of the Board's functions. In 1948 the Board established a Recruiting and Veterans Personnel Section. This unit was known in 1952 simply as the Recruiting Section, and it operated two field offices. The special postwar problems of pay administration were similarly recognized in 1946 by the establishment of a separate Pay Division. Also in 1946, a new office of Personnel Management Analyst was created. The Personnel Management Analyst was to develop improved personnel practices, systems, and organization structures.

Of more consequence for the reorganization of 1952-55, however, was a vast growth in the workload of the central personnel functions, examining and classification. The increase in these duties, performed respectively by the Recruitment and Examining Division and the Classification Division, was largely a consequence of the growth of the state service.[7] Until 1930, the primary production function of the Board had been the preparation and administration of examinations. This work required six professionals in a total staff of 23. Classification actions were then handled incidentally by the examining staff in what was, in fact, a generalist organization. During the thirties, when classification became a separate division, and during the forties, when pay matters were extracted from classification as a third major division, examining remained by far the largest single production job of the Board. The growth of these personnel functions, rapid in the thirties, became astronomical after the war, when the requirement that wartime appointees be replaced by permanent appointees necessitated a gigantic examining program. The number of civil service employees doubled in the forties. During the fifties, staff growth leveled off, continuing gradually with the enlargement of the state service.

A striking element of the Personnel Board's work in the fifties was the staggering load of examinations. By 1955 it was conducting about 1,500 examinations a year, or an average of about six each working day. About two-thirds of these were regular written examinations, and about half involved oral interviewing by qualifications appraisal boards. The work involved in preparing examinations and in selecting, supervising, and participating in the oral examination boards was enormous. In the fiscal year 1953-54, in the midst of the reorganization process described by this case the Board received more than 127,000 applications for examinations, tested over 77,000 persons, and interviewed more than 16,000 competitors.

The Staff Before the Reorganization

The professional staff of the Personnel Board in 1952-55 was largely the product of two distinct

[7] In the rest of this study, the Recruitment and Examining Division is sometimes referred to simply as Examining.

THE STATE SERVICE AND THE PERSONNEL BOARD STAFF[a]

	1930	1935	1940	1945	1950	1952	1955
Total Civil Service Employees in State (in thousands)	11	20[b]	25	29	50	56	60
Civil Service Commission or Personnel Board Staff, Total	23	41	142	175	319	323	339
Professional Personnel Staff, Total[c]	6	17	24	23	68	69	76
Recruitment and Examining	6	10	14	14	42	42	[d]
Classification	[d]	7	10	9	16	17	[d]
Pay	[d]	[d]	[d]	[d]	10	10	[d]

[a] Average filled positions in the Personnel Board staff for the fiscal year except 1955 for which are shown positions authorized in the budget. This difference accounts for much of the indicated increase in 1955.

[b] Figure shown is for 1936; 1935 figure is not available.

[c] Only professional staff in the three activities shown is included.

[d] Figures not applicable because of organization structure.

waves of recruitment. Most executive and supervisory employees had joined the Board during the late thirties and early forties. For most, the Personnel Board was their first personnel job, and a few had joined it directly after leaving college. Most of these officials had studied public administration in undergraduate and graduate courses at the University of California. Relatively few, even of those in Examining, had had any psychological, psychometric, or industrial relations training. Most of the executive and supervisory officers joined one of the military services during the war and returned after discharge. The continuity and homogeneity of the senior group were thus rather striking. Virtually all were between forty and fifty, energetic, and dedicated; and all were men. Almost all top supervisory jobs were filled by promotion, assuring continuity.

On first joining the Board, men in this first wave had been assigned to the Examining or Classification divisions. Until the reorganization there was almost no movement of staff between these two divisions, so that the officials were for the most part firmly oriented to their original functional field. Later, when the Pay Division was established, a number of classifiers moved into it, and there was some later interchange between Classification and Pay. But functional or specialist allegiance remained strong. Almost none of the top officials had had significant experiences in all three functional divisions, Examining, Classification, and Pay.

The second wave of recruitment occurred after World War II, when a large number of persons was hired to meet the bulging workload. Most of the journeymen professional staff at the time of the reorganization fell into this category; a few had advanced to supervisory posts. This second wave was, of course, larger, and the men in it were younger (for the most part, 25 to 40 years old), though it included a few older men who had had considerable outside experience, even some outside the personnel field. Most men in the second wave, like men in the first group, came from university programs in public administration. They exhibited characteristics of energy and dedication similar to those of their Seniors. Although a few, when hired, progressed through orientation programs that took them for a few months into all aspects of the professional work of the Board, all were assigned to one of the functional divisions where most remained until the reorganization. The new men, like the old, identified themselves strongly with their respective specialties and with the divisions which carried on these specialties.

The two top officials of the Board's staff were, in certain respects, exceptions. John F. Fisher, the Executive Officer, came to the Board as its first Assistant Executive Officer in 1944, and succeeded to his top post in 1947. Fisher had, a decade before, studied public administration at Syracuse University. He went into personnel work in the East and in 1939 joined the staff of the Los Angeles City Civil Service Department as head of classification. He served briefly during the war as classification director for the OPA in Washington, then returned to Los Angeles as Acting General Manager of Civil Service. At the time of the reorganization he had been with the Board a shorter time than most of his senior colleagues, and he was one of the few who had not come up through the ranks.

James R. Bell had been Assistant Executive Officer since 1947. For some years before joining the Board he worked with the Highway Department and subsequently served as personnel officer for the State Relief Administration. He came to the Board in a supervisory rank just before the war. For some years, he directed office services and administrative activities, and he then served as first Personnel Management Analyst before succeeding to the post of Assistant Executive Officer.

Fisher and Bell directed the staff and were responsible for relationships with the Board and with the rest of the state service. They themselves were not overtly affected by the reorganization.

At the time of the reorganization the staff was as shown in the following table:

DIVISION	PROFESSIONAL STRENGTH [a]	TOTAL STRENGTH
Classification	19	50
Recruitment and Examining	41	98
Pay	10	12
Training	4	6
Medical	0	6
Office Services	0	107
Cooperative Personnel Services	7	16
Administration	4	14
	85	309
Board Secretariat and Hearing Officer	1	15
Total (Rounded)	86	324

[a] Includes executive, supervisory, journeymen, and trainee personnel in professional work. Does not include professional personnel in other fields such as doctors, nurses, accountants, and the like.

Only the Classification, Recruitment and Examining, and Pay divisions were to be significantly involved in the reorganization. They included the bulk of the professional personnel and had responsibility for most of the substantive, non-clerical personnel work.

The *Classification Division* was responsible for classifying positions, developing job specifications, and servicing state agencies on all matters relating to classification. In addition, the Division included a group which, every five years, surveyed all positions in all the departments. Normal classification matters were handled by two groups, totaling twelve analysts and supervisors, and were assigned on an *organizational basis* with each analyst responsible for a group of state agencies. The relatively large clerical staff consisted principally of 27 people responsible for maintaining the roster of state employees. This task and all the personnel were to be transferred to the Office Services Division as a result of the reorganization of the Board.

The *Recruitment and Examining Division* was responsible for test construction, test scheduling, the management of oral boards, test research, the preparation of bulletins, review of applications, and the like. Nearly thirty examiners and supervisors, the largest bloc of professionals in the Board, engaged in this work. Most of the other professionals in this Division worked for the Recruiting Section and its branch offices in Los Angeles and San Francisco. This Section was quite independent of the rest of the Division, and it was not to be directly affected by the reorganization. Much of the clerical staff was engaged in certification and the management of the Test Pool.

The *Pay Division* administered the pay plan for the state. It handled all individual requests for pay changes or new pay levels, making recommendations to the Board on each one, and it conducted at least two "community" pay surveys a year. It also was responsible for prevailing rate studies for manual and trade jobs, for overtime compensation, and for related matters. Smaller than either Classification or Examining, Pay exercised the responsibility for the state salary plan which had been delegated to the Personnel Board by the Legislature. The Board determined the salary range for every class of position within only the most general statutory guide-lines, and its decisions were final. On the basis of its periodic surveys of pay levels of other employers, private and public, it annually recommended to the Governor and the Legislature the lump sums to be appropriated for salary increases. It then administered these appropriations. For this work, probably its most crucial and potentially its "hottest" assignment, the Board relied heavily upon the staff of the Pay Division.

All the divisions were hierarchically organized with a Chief and an intermediate supervisory group over the operating personnel. The professional personnel were classified in two series of classes—as Personnel Analysts in the Classification and Pay Divisions, and as Personnel Examiners in the Recruitment and Examining Division. Separate classes were recognized for Engineering Examiners and a Legal Examiner. The Division chiefs carried the rank of Principal—Principal Personnel Analyst or Principal Personnel Examiner. Their immediate assistants were Seniors. The journeymen operators were Associates, Assistants, Juniors, and Trainees in that sequence downward. Since California controlled its budgets on a line item basis, the number of positions in each of these classes, especially those in the higher ranks, would be of dominating importance in the consideration of any organizational change. The major executive and supervisory titles, their salary ranges, and the numbers authorized in 1953 were:

TITLE	MONTHLY SALARY	TO BE AFFECTED BY REORGANIZATION	TOTAL IN BOARD
Executive Officer	$1,050-1,150	0	1
Assistant Executive Officer	821-1,000	0	1
Assistant Secretary to Board	821-1,000	0	1
Principal	745- 905	3	5
Senior	613- 745	9	10

The five Principals included the heads of the three divisions described above, the State Training Officer, and the Chief of Cooperative Personnel Services. Four of the Seniors supervised examining work and a fifth headed the Recruiting Section in the Recruitment and Examining Division. The Classification Division had two Seniors and the Pay Division one; another was the Personnel Management Analyst, who at that time reported directly to the Executive Officer; and the last was in Cooperative Personnel Services. With the exception of one Senior vacancy in Examining, all these positions were filled when the reorganization began.

California Government

This description of the Board, its development, and its staff has provided only small clues to the total atmosphere in which the reorganization was to occur. California's burgeoning population of the last few decades, a mobile population making ever-rising demands on government, had created a strong force for change which would not be contained either by venerable institutions or revered traditions—especially when change appeared to mean growth, improvement, or progress.

The movement for public managerial reform had found fertile soil in California. Most middle-sized cities there had already moved over to the council-manager plan. Even the two largest cities had gone far in the direction of professionalized administration. Nowhere in the United States did state and local public services enjoy higher prestige and nowhere had public administrators developed a higher sense of professional self-consciousness.

In aspiration and performance the California State Personnel Board typified the oft-quoted California sentiment that "good government is good politics." The Board aimed at providing the best possible service to the using agencies. At the same time it treasured its independence. Maintaining a crusading spirit, it nevertheless endeavored to spread the good-government gospel through a gradual educational process rather than through the iron hand of disciplinary authority. Its staff was energetic, youthful, ambitious, and it desired to establish a pre-eminent professional reputation in the personnel field. At the time reorganization was first considered, the Personnel Board ranked among the largest and strongest of all public personnel agencies. One may reasonably wonder: why did it reorganize? The program was operating well; there were no outward signs of need to change. Why, then, disrupt such an organization by an internal upheaval?

Birth of an Idea January-November 1952

EVEN IN 1952 the generalizing of functions and skills was being widely discussed in the personnel world. Staff members of California's Personnel Board had participated in national professional conferences on this subject. For many years, they had talked among themselves about the potential advantages and disadvantages of a generalist form of organization. The Board's Division of Cooperative Personnel Services offered a demonstration of generalism at work; it had been organized so that each staff member worked with localities in all personnel specialties. Thus the field was already fertile when 1952 opened. And while immediate practical problems came into sharper focus that year, it is probable that they provided less of a stimulus for a generalist reorganization than did the "theoretical" and "professional" considerations, which had been under discussion for several years. These practical problems, which are described below, provoked no crises and were not particularly unusual. They provided part of the context and some of the incentive for organizational change, but they alone were not decisive.

Co-ordination Among the Divisions

One of the "practical" reasons for organizational change was the need for continuing co-operation and co-ordination among the three divisions, Pay, Classification, and Recruitment and Examining. This problem, endemic in personnel organizations organized on a functional basis, had grown more acute when the three units expanded after the war. In personnel work, many of the decisions of one functional unit affect the work of the others. Co-ordination of general policy at the top level is not enough; actions of the lowliest examiners and analysts require close co-ordination with actions of other units. In the Board, these operators had fewer regular opportunities than did their superiors for reaching meetings of the mind through arrangements such as inter-divisional staff meetings.

Some operating officials and many of the supervisory staff were aware of these difficulties. In fact, some of the initiative for organizational change came from the operating staff. In January 1952, Jane Carmack, then a junior member of the Classification Division, wrote a memorandum proposing a study of the problem of inter-divisional communications and suggesting a new plan of organization. The memo was addressed to her Senior, who forwarded it to Roy Stephens, Chief of Classification; Stephens sent it on to the Assistant Executive Officer, James Bell. The proposal elicited a good deal of discussion. Miss Carmack was asked to prepare a second memo, and this later document, dated March 7, 1952, elaborated on existing difficulties and on the new organization pattern which she had in mind.

Miss Carmack has disavowed any originality in her memoranda; they were an attempt to put down on paper ideas that had been discussed for some time by a few of the analysts in Classification. Her organizational proposal was a partial generalist plan, but it fell considerably short of the scheme that was ultimately to be adopted. She proposed that specialists in Classification, Pay, and Examining continue to pursue their specialties, but that they be brought together, organizationally and physically, in a number of groups. Each group would cover a sector of the state service. It would be headed by a Senior, who would thus have to be a generalist, and the Senior would be responsible to one of two Principals, both generalists. The Carmack proposal was apparently not seriously considered in the subsequent discussions. But the memorandum helped to trigger the self-examination and give-and-take which ultimately led to reorganization. In September 1954, after Stephens came across the second Carmack memorandum while clearing his files, he returned the document to her with the penciled notation: "For your memoirs. Look what you started."

The Carmack memoranda are particularly interesting in retrospect because they reveal what problems were seen under the old system by workers at the operating level. In her second memorandum, she wrote that the new pattern of organization was "proposed as an approach to the perennial problems of coordination and communication. These problems are more basic to the proposed study than the suggested organizational structure." Among them, she said, were:

Relations with the Departments: "Departments have expressed confusion with the number of contacts required in their working with the Personnel Board Staff." "These contacts [with Classification, Examining, Recruiting, Pay] frequently require repetition by the department of information previously given to another representative." "The [proposed new] organization of our staff could reduce the number of communication channels for the department."

Co-ordination within the Board: "There would be better 'follow-through' on problems affecting more than one personnel function." "Problems of timing that occur when a staff member of one division commits the Board to work involving other divisions, might be alleviated." "Departmental problems that may overlap several divisions . . ." would become the "shared problems of [one] group."

Staff Development: "Individual staff members thus could gain broader knowledge of our total personnel management program and more effectively relate their specific specialties to over-all Board objectives and would be more aware of the total problem. . . ."

Departmental service and convenience were accorded only minor weight in the subsequent discussions, but inter-divisional co-ordination and staff development and morale were given central attention. Dissatisfaction with co-ordination was strong in Classification, and it later emerged even more markedly in Examining. The classification specialists believed that the Pay Division could hardly set the pay of a class of positions without understanding the responsibilities of, and the qualifications for, these jobs, which were determined by Classification. These data obviously affected recruitment and selection as well. Examiners had to relate their tests to the job content of positions for which the classifiers were primarily responsible; if the classifiers did not have, or did not provide, such information, duplication of field work and research was inevitable. In fact, virtually every major personnel problem of the Board involved, directly or indirectly, all three functional elements, and many also affected a fourth—recruiting. The necessity for continuing co-operation and co-ordination was evident; the locus of decision-making responsibility was crucial; the possibilities of conflict were many. Problems that might occur included:

Two or more staff members of different divisions might work on the same problem from different angles without knowing that someone else was also working on it.

Examinations might be announced and given needlessly, since examiners might not know of related classifications that were going to be revised.

Pay proposals might go to the Board without adequate review of their implications for Classification or Examining.

"Using" departments might play off one division of the Board against another.

Proposed new or revised job specifications, including proposed minimum qualifications, might be sent to the Board before there had been adequate review by affected examiners.

The last example—specifications and minimum qualifications—had been a problem of long standing which assumed crucial importance during the discussions of 1952. The classifiers, the examiners felt, often merely went through the motions of co-ordinating "specs" and allowed only a few minutes for appropriate review by examiners. Some examiners felt that authority to give final approval to minimum qualifications should rest solely with the examiners, who were ultimately responsible for selection. Some also felt that specifications could be greatly improved if examiners were consulted in writing them. The classifiers, on the other hand, felt that the responsibility for specifications was theirs and that examiners' opinions were, at best, advisory. The question of timing, mentioned by Miss Carmack, was central to much of this difficulty. The classifiers frequently made commitments to departments as to the time when an action would go to the Board. This resulted in a number of "crash" actions, requiring rapid review by other divisions. The examiners complained that they were allowed insufficient time to consider such proposals and that too often their comments were ignored.

Problems of this kind were not unique to the Personnel Board, but they were compounded by the Board's large size. In a smaller organization employees of different divisions might have maintained daily contacts, informally resolving co-ordination problems before they came to a head. The size of the Board's divisions, especially its examining group, made it difficult for personal relationships to budge divisional jurisdictions. Functional divisional loyalties were strong.

The problem was further aggravated by the fact that the three divisions were organized on different bases. Classification's internal structure was on a departmental basis—each analyst was responsible for all classification matters within a group of state departments. In Examining and Pay, the basis was occupational—each analyst or examiner had responsibility for a cluster of occupational classes, the majority of which crossed departmental lines. And the clustering within Examining did not parallel that in Pay. More hampering than the jurisdictional and mechanical difficulties which these functional arrangements presented were the subtle differences they bred in outlook, in approach to the job, and, indeed, in conception of the overall mission of the Personnel Board. The departmental grouping in Classification contributed to an organizational type of outlook—a desire to service each using agency well or to control it effectively (or a little of each). The occupational view, on the other hand, saw the state service as a number of series and classes—of clerks, or social workers, or engineers—and its emphasis was upon interdepartmental relationships, upon consistency in treatment regardless of organization, and upon the logic of occupational patterns.

The Pay Division

A unique aspect of the general co-ordination problem was the separate existence of the Pay Division. Until 1946, pay had been the responsibility of Classification. In that year, the pay group was given divisional status co-equal with Examining and Classification. The new Pay Division was staffed largely with personnel transferred from Classification. It was established partly to emphasize the importance of the function which, many felt, had theretofore been subordinated to classification. It was also a response to the tremendous need for pay studies and adjustments in the unsettled years after the war. The Board's concern to establish a logical salary alignment was shared by the California State Employees Association (CSEA), the influential spokesman for the state's organized employees. The CSEA lent vigorous support to the establishment of a separate Pay Division in the State Personnel Board, and it subsequently acted as a watchdog to protect the Division's status.

Another element that may have contributed to the establishment of the Pay Division was the desire to bring in a highly qualified man to direct pay matters and to provide him with appropriate salary and status. Carl Richey, widely known classification and pay expert, was hired as the first Chief. He resigned shortly to accept another job and was replaced by Kelvin D. Sharp, who, in turn, was replaced in 1948 by R. Permin Everett when Sharp became Assistant Secretary to the Personnel Board.

Under these three leaders, the Pay Division became a highly effective organization. It blazed new trails in its field and developed an extremely advanced system for pay determination and control. Yet the senior staff of the Board felt that the permanent separate existence of the Pay Division presented something of an anomaly, principally because of the overlap with Classification. This problem was thrown into public focus by a report of the State Assembly's Interim Committee on Governmental Efficiency and Economy in the late forties. The Committee had retained the consulting firm of Louis J. Kroeger and Associates (the same Kroeger who seven years earlier had been forced out by the Personnel Board) to make a "thorough and impartial survey" of the Personnel Board and its practices. The Kroeger study was published in its entirety by the Committee in 1949. It included 157 specific recommendations, and one of the most significant of these was that the Pay Division be abolished. "We see no logic in a separate Pay Division. Much of the information required to set the salary range is identical with that which determines the classification of the job. To do this work twice imposes a double burden upon the departments, delays decision, and adds to cost." Kroeger proposed that the entire function be merged with classification and that a new unit be provided in the Classification

Division "to gather and analyze salary data."[8]

In June 1949 the Assembly called upon the State Personnel Board to report on progress in implementing the Kroeger recommendations. On December 16, 1950 the Personnel Board submitted its report—as long as or longer than Kroeger's original one—in which it discussed each recommendation and expressed agreement with a great many. But it rejected the proposal to abolish the Pay Division. It pointed to the dominant importance of the pay function, to the fact that seventy percent of the state budget was spent on salaries almost all of which were determined by the Board, and to the costliness of errors in judgment in this field. Finally, it wrote:

> In the opinion of the Board, the collection and analysis of information on which salaries must be based is still too important a function to be made the part-time responsibility of individuals assigned to a combined pay and classification division.

The Board's own position on the matter was somewhat less emphatic and unanimous than its report implied. It had given much attention to its pay responsibilities. But some Board members felt that Pay should logically be merged with Classification, sooner or later. The principal question was one of timing. The majority of the Board felt that the special postwar pay problems which had warranted the establishment of the separate Division were still sufficiently important to warrant its continuation. The majority was reinforced by continuing support for the Pay Division from the State Employees Association. Another factor militating against the consolidation at that time was that it would have entailed relinquishing one position at the level of Principal—and the Board had only five of them. This was seen as a serious loss of high supervisory positions; it would require demoting one person from this level—presumably the head of either Classification or Pay—and perhaps the chain demotion of another Senior, and subsequently possibly even others at lower levels.

The Board's firm refusal inhibited further discussion at the lower staff levels about abolishing the Pay Division, and this potential argument for generalist organization was not expressed during the months that reorganization was under consideration. Yet, even submerged, it was one of the decisive background factors.

Morale, Status, and Development

Although some thought it inevitable, most Pay Division officials, even those who later became enthusiastic supporters of the generalist program, were opposed to amalgamation with Classification. The Pay Division, the smallest of the three operating units, was considered by some the "elite" professional corps of the Board. It had developed high morale. Promotion had been relatively fast. A number of its people had accepted positions as personnel officers for state departments. Its contacts with the departments were frequent, important to the departments, and at high level. Most of its work culminated in Board consideration and action, and this meant that the individual analysts had frequent contacts with the Board itself, a privilege virtually denied the examiners. Some staff members thought pay analysts were casual about intra-Board co-ordination. These attitudes toward the Pay Division added to the co-ordination problem and at the same time contributed to another of the Board's problem areas—morale.

A good deal of attention had been given for some time to the individual development of staff members. A staff personnel committee had been functioning; a grievance system had been set up; a house organ known as the *Espe Bee* was being published. The management, interested in opportunities for employees to broaden themselves and to prepare for advancement, had long favored a system for rotating personnel from one division to another. In good part, this policy emanated from the members of the Board. For years they had insisted upon greater delegation of authority. Soon after Fisher became Executive Officer, the Board had practically directed him to delegate responsibility to his staff; he had been advised not to attempt to answer personally all the questions the Board might raise. Subsequently, the Board urged that the analysts concerned, not their division chiefs, present cases before the Board. Further, the Board encouraged rotation among the supervisory staff, partly so that these officials would gain broader experience, partly so that they

8 Assembly, California Interim Committee on Governmental Efficiency and Economy, *Partial Report of the Study of the Personnel Board and its Operation,* p. 29.

would look at problems from an overall, organizational point of view. Under law, the Board had one position to fill that was exempt from civil service regulations, its Assistant Secretary. (The Executive Officer was the Secretary.) This job was consistently filled with career men from Recruitment, Pay, and Classification.

Efforts of management to develop temporary rotation of assignments among the operating professional personnel met with varying success. There was a good deal of rotation between Pay and Classification. In fact, for some time most of the pay analysts came from a classification background. But rotation made little headway between the Recruitment and Examining Division and the other two divisions. Most of the pay and classification analysts did not want assignments in Examining, even temporary ones. Some referred to them as "assignments to Siberia." Also, supervisors hesitated to release good men on rotation assignments; a division chief would willingly release his weakest man, but the chief of the recipient division would, of course, resist such movements.

Reluctance to move to Examining may be understood in terms of the background and leadership of that Division. The oldest unit in the Board, it had been headed for many years by only two Chiefs. Nova Beal had served in examining work since the establishment of the Civil Service Commission in 1914. She retired as Chief of the Examining Division in 1944, and she was succeeded by Edwin A. Abeel, himself an "old-time" examiner. An engineer by training, he had joined the staff in 1931. Both he and his predecessor were strong-willed, effective leaders of unquestioned and sometimes fearsome integrity. Their Division was an impregnable citadel against political pressure and a prodigious producer of examinations, but it was never closely integrated with the rest of the Board. Abeel, strongly oriented to maintaining production, was reluctant to rotate assignments even within his own Division. After one of his men had developed into a capable journeyman in a subject matter area, he considered it wasteful to sacrifice know-how and training time for rotation to another job. Former staff members of Examining recall that Abeel severely reprimanded an associate who had asked for a rotation assignment outside the Division. Thereafter, requests virtually ceased. The bulk of the professionals on the Board's staff, especially those specialists whom the "front office" believed to be most in need of a rotation program, were thus kept out of it.

The Attitude Survey

Rotation was one element of a larger morale problem that was brought to everyone's attention, and perhaps exaggerated, by an attitude study which the staff conducted during May and early June of 1952. It was apparently a coincidence that the study was made at about the same time that the generalist idea was germinating. Fisher had had the idea of making such a study for some time. He saw it as a means of improving the effectiveness of the Board and its staff. Also, Robert Gray, a Board member, was deeply interested in attitude surveys and had directed a number of them in private industry. Since no other state agency had made such studies, Fisher thought the Board might set a good example to other departments in the matter of gauging and improving employee morale.

The results of the survey—which covered attitudes toward pay, working conditions, management, status and recognition, and the like—indicated generally favorable attitudes. In a memorandum report to all staff members on August 11, 1952 Fisher stated that seventy percent of the employee responses were favorable; fifteen percent were unfavorable; and fifteen percent were "don't know." The overall results were distinctly above the normal pattern of responses in industries using the same survey forms. Fisher indicated gratification at finding "the strong sense of friendliness among the people of the SPB and that a high percentage of the staff are proud to work for this agency. . . ."

On the other hand, the Executive Officer noted that the survey had pinpointed certain trouble spots including the need for "better training and more of it, better communications, better working conditions, closer cooperation between divisions, and better job instructions and performance standards." The survey indicated considerable dissatisfaction with general working conditions. (At that time the Board occupied an old building, noisy, poorly equipped, and greatly overcrowded.) The study also indicated misunderstanding and resentment between the clerical and professional staffs—a longstanding problem in this agency. Most important for the reorganization story, the survey indicated to Fisher the existence of problems among the professionals—problems about which the survey statements themselves were insufficiently explicit. Fisher asked the heads of his three principal professional divisions to take up the results of the survey in staff meetings and to attempt to identify the sources of trouble. There followed a series of conferences in Examining and Classification during August and September 1952, and reports on these meetings went to Fisher, who made them the basis of discussion meetings of all Principals and Seniors. These discussions contributed substantially to the thinking that led to the generalist reorganization.

The survey and the discussions that came after it brought to light the following problems in Examining and Classification:

In Examining the survey showed three areas in which the responses of the examiners were significantly lower than those of other professional personnel: "confidence in management"; "effectiveness of administration"; and "opportunity for growth and advancement."

The subsequent discussions among the examiners revealed that there were serious morale problems, most of which involved feelings about "status." Said a summary memorandum dated August 22, 1952:

> Members of the examining staff do not enjoy status or receive recognition comparable to technicians in other divisions; examiners feel that they are an "out group."
>
> There is some feeling also that examination problems do not receive the weight of consideration [by management] that the problems of other divisions receive.
>
> Members of the examining staff do not have either the formal or informal contacts with management above the divisional level that other divisions have.
>
> Its accomplishments are not recognized by other divisions.
>
> . . . examiners do not have occasion to participate in matters before the Board.
>
> That there is insecurity with respect to status was voiced with specific reference to contacts with the classification staff about specifications, the pay staff, the executive office, and the Board itself.
>
> General exception was taken to the fact that there is not the same chance in the Examining Division to move to other agencies or transfer to other sections as is enjoyed by others on the same grade level.

A common sentiment in Examining was, "You will never be Executive Officer if you are an examiner." It was felt that top positions in the Board went predominantly to classifiers, almost never to examiners. It was a fact that every Executive Officer in the history of the Board had had a classification background; none had been examiners. Nor, in spite of the fact that examiners had always constituted the largest number of professional employees, were any former examiners incumbent in the three ranking staff jobs of the Board.

A further thorn in the examiners' sides was the fact that the many state departments which had set up new jobs for personnel officers seemed always to hire analysts from Pay or Classification. Hence, advancement was fairly rapid in those divisions, particularly in Pay. Most of the examiners had been hired by the Board during the first two postwar years to meet emergency problems. The absence of any movement upward or out of the Division had virtually halted promotion for half a decade.

Discussions with the examiners also emphasized problems of co-operation and co-ordination with Classification and Pay. There were also complaints against the clerical staff and its service; it was said that the clerical tail was wagging the dog. But the basic morale problems in Examining appeared to be concerns about status and advancement.

In Classification the attitude survey indicated that "the morale of the technical staff of the Classification Division is 'average' as compared to the general industrial norm on which the inventory is based. As compared to the technical staff of the agency as a whole, it indicates that the morale in the Classification Division is lower."[9] But the nature of the complaint was quite different from that in Examining. Here was no mention of status. There was reference to some of the problems of co-ordination and communication suggested earlier in the Carmack memorandum. Considerable stress was also placed upon the need for more adequate training. But most of the criticism in Classification was directed at management and

9 From a memorandum from the Classification Division, September 19, 1952.

supervision. Emphasis was laid upon such needs as: clearer understanding of objectives; more explicit policies and standards; assurance of support against protesting state departments; and firmer support in general, from the Executive Officer on down. Much dissatisfaction in Classification derived from the feeling that supervision was too close; that too much time was spent in reviewing details and in rewriting documents.

The difficulties of classifiers—unlike those of the examiners—could not be remedied by changes in the *form* of organization. But the awareness of these dissatisfactions and internal tensions rendered the climate more favorable to organizational change, even though morale of the staff as a whole was distinctly above the industrial average and the overall morale picture was neither desperate nor critical.

The Conception of the Pilot Unit

Exactly what the reasons were for establishing a generalist pilot unit it is impossible to say; it probably would have been impossible to identify them precisely at the time in 1952 when the decision was made. Fisher, who initiated the idea and who ultimately decided to establish the pilot unit, was later inclined to attribute the decision to three factors: (1) his decision that the time had come to merge Classification and Pay; (2) the difficulties of the rotation program; (3) the problems of inter-divisional co-ordination. The results of the attitude survey and of the conferences which had followed it contributed to the final decision to go ahead, but the idea had been launched before these results were known.

An important, perhaps a dominant, factor in the decision was Fisher's own predisposition. Long experienced in personnel work, both in classification and as director of personnel programs, he was thoroughly familiar with the problems of functional specialism. Even before coming to California, he had entertained the idea of a generalist personnel organization. He now wanted to give the idea a try. But in this matter, as in others, he avoided imposing a change upon his staff until it had been thoroughly discussed.

Internal communication in 1952 was accomplished principally by staff meetings. Every two weeks the Executive Officer and his Assistant met with all the Principals and Seniors on the staff. These officers likewise met with their divisional staffs on a weekly or biweekly basis. There were occasional meetings of the entire professional staff, and official announcements (usually about important personnel changes) were infrequently issued from the Executive Office. The Board was quite informal in making decisions about its internal operations, and no formal records of these meetings were kept. Informal notes were sometimes made by participants, but by 1955 these were incomplete and fugitive. For factual data, the chronicler has had to rely upon the fallible memories of participants.

During the spring of 1952 some of the problems discussed above, particularly inter-divisional co-ordination, were often considered in Principal-Senior meetings. They were attacked on a number of fronts: improvement of procedures (such as that for the review of specifications by examiners), review of forms, rotation of personnel, grouping of workers from different divisions in common geographic locations, and the like.

In May or June Fisher suggested setting up a pilot unit, organized on a generalist basis, in which each analyst would have complete responsibility for all personnel functions in a segment of the state service. Response to the proposal was mixed. All three of the Principals in Examining, Pay, and Classification were opposed or at least skeptical. A few Seniors were enthusiastic, but some, perhaps the majority, were cool. Had the proposal been submitted to a vote at that time, it probably would have been decisively rejected.

Chopson's Memorandum

Fisher nonetheless pushed his proposal. He asked E. W. Chopson, a Senior Examiner then serving under Fisher as Personnel Management Analyst, to prepare a plan, or alternative plans, for a generalist pilot unit. Chopson, an enthusiastic advocate, produced a plan on July 9, 1952.[10] Indeed, he also prepared a plan for reorganizing the entire Board on a generalist basis. The latter plan was not circulated and was never seriously considered, but Chopson's proposal for the pilot unit became the basis of all further discussion on

[10] Memorandum from Chopson to Fisher, Subject: Recommended Pilot Unit Assignments.

the subject, and the unit ultimately established resembled in basic respects the first alternative outlined in the proposal.

Chopson's memorandum stipulated certain requirements for the proposed unit: its personnel "should all be volunteers, or people sincerely interested in trying out the plan"; they should "insofar as possible be persons with broad experience"; they should be in or near the class "which would normally be used in staffing later such units." Specifically, he thought the pilot unit should be headed by a Senior and should include two Associates, one or two Assistants, one or two Juniors, and one Trainee. These officials would be drawn as follows: three from Examining, two from Classification, and one each from Pay and Recruiting or two from Pay and none from Recruiting. Not stated was an understood requirement: each person should know the subject matter or service area that the pilot unit would handle.

Chopson further stipulated that the unit, "at least during the early phases of its operation," should have responsibility only for examining, classification, and pay. He obviously contemplated a possibility of its moving later into recruiting, training, and perhaps other fields. To remove the unit from the control of any of the functional Principals, Chopson proposed that its head be made directly responsible to the Assistant Executive Officer.

From the standpoint of timing, Chopson proposed that the unit become fully operational within fifteen days after its activation. He assumed that it would take three months to bring it to full efficiency and another three to six months to test its operation. Still another three to six months might be necessary to make changes and to evaluate the changes. "At the end of not more than one year a final decision should be reached as to whether the new organization should be adopted on an agency-wide basis or whether the project should be dropped."

Chopson calculated that if the new unit included six workers, this would comprise twelve percent of the professional staff in the three divisions.[11] Therefore, it should assume about twelve percent of the workload, or about 250 of the state's classes and about 6,000 of its employees. The area of coverage which he proposed comprised the Departments of Mental Hygiene, Corrections, Youth Authority, and the Division of Special Schools and Services of the Department of Education. From these he suggested excepting agricultural, clerical, and mechanical trades classes, leaving a net of 277 classes and 10,720 employees. If this grouping proved impracticable, he suggested a grouping of Agriculture, Natural Resources, and Fish and Game. For each grouping he suggested the staff members who should be assigned.

Behind Chopson's choice of the first group lay two main factors. First was the basic and as yet unresolved question as to whether the generalist unit should be structured on a departmental or an occupational basis. Some of the staff thought that the unit, and within it each analyst, should have responsibility for all personnel matters in a department or a group of departments; others favored occupational groupings which might or might not cross departmental lines. While the Classification Division was structured on a departmental basis, Pay and Examining were organized by occupation. Decision on this question was crucial to the nature of the entire generalist pattern.

But Chopson did not want his proposal to be bogged down in this argument. He therefore proposed for the new unit an area of coverage in which departmental and occupational lines were basically similar; that is, most of the classes to be covered were largely confined to a limited number of departments.

A second factor in Chopson's choice of the Mental Hygiene-Corrections group was his desire to secure the assignment of enthusiastic personnel to the pilot unit. During his work on the proposal, fifteen persons had asked Chopson if they could be assigned to the pilot unit. Three whom Chopson suggested for assignment were Robert Lawson (then on a temporary appointment as Senior in the Examining Division), whom Chopson proposed as Chief of the new unit, and Kay Groff and Jane Carmack (both in Classification), two of the most ardent advocates of generalism. All three had had experience with the occupations and departments which would be involved in Chopson's first group.

In the following months, Chopson's memoran-

[11] In calculating this percentage he counted the five workers in Recruitment, even though he specifically opposed transferring recruiting functions at that time.

dum furnished the basis for spirited conversation but little else. It was discussed in the Principal-Senior staff meetings, in the divisional staff meetings, in corridors, and over the lunch table. Reactions were mixed, although opposition to the proposal was never well organized or well articulated. William Popper, Senior Engineering Examiner, wrote Fisher early in July proposing a committee system to solve the inter-divisional coordination problem. In another memorandum to Fisher, Alden Brock, then a Senior Examiner, proposed a gradual system of grouping staff and of broadening responsibilities rather than the all-or-none technique implied in the pilot program.

Further argument ensued about the occupational versus the departmental approach. But it became evident that if Examining were to be included in the generalist program, the occupational approach was inevitable. The great majority of state employees were in classes that were employed in several different departments; in fact, the largest group, the clerical employees, occupied classes common to all the departments. This was also true of some other categories—administrative, fiscal, legal, custodial, and some trades. To have set up duplicating or competing examining systems in different units for the same classes would have been wasteful and self-defeating. In retrospect it appears that the argument for a departmental system was, consciously or not, an argument against any generalizing plan that included the examining function.

Eventually the occupational basis prevailed. In spite of Chopson's efforts at compromise, his proposal essentially accepted an occupational basis for the pilot unit. Many of the classes in the departments assigned to the pilot unit were common to the entire service, and these were excluded from the unit's responsibilities. On the other hand, the unit was given responsibility for the custodial classes, which overlapped most of the state departments.

The period during which Chopson's plan was being discussed—late summer and early fall of 1952—was also the period during which the conferences and staff meetings were held about the attitude survey. During these months the Board was handling its normal workload in normal fashion. Never did the idea of the pilot unit carry more than a minor importance in the deliberations of the staff. The delay in decision was a source of restiveness among some of the more enthusiastic supporters of the plan. It seemed that much of the original interest in and enthusiasm for the plan was being frittered away for want of quick decision. But this was a characteristic method of management in the Board. Everyone was given time to digest the idea and ample opportunity to express his views. Insofar as a meeting of minds could be reached through deliberation and discussion, this was done.

The pilot unit idea was put forth only as an "experiment." Any commitment as to future action was disclaimed. If it did not work, it would be easy to return to the old system; if it did, there would be ample opportunity to discuss what the next step would be. It is always difficult to oppose an experiment.

After a final discussion of the proposal in a Senior-Principal meeting in October, Fisher asked for a show of hands. One participant recalls that the vote came out about even. In general, the Principals of the three divisions all had reservations about it, and the Seniors were split. Members of the operating staff, had they been called upon to vote, would probably also have split but with a clear majority in favor. Their feelings, and those of many of the supervisors, would perhaps have been swayed less by arguments of principle than by personal desires to broaden their experience, to enlarge promotional opportunities, or, in some cases, to escape difficult local supervisory situations. A few felt that "it's time for a change"—whatever the change might be.

Following the vote, Fisher announced simply that he would go ahead. Thus was revealed what may have been the most crucial decision in the whole reorganization process. A few days later, Fisher told the Personnel Board that the staff was going to experiment with a generalist unit, and subsequently he informed the state departments to be serviced by the new unit.

On October 21, the following announcement was posted on the bulletin board in the Personnel Board building:

> Pilot Program for Generalist Approach to
> Examining, Classification, and Pay Activities
>
> The above program which has been discussed with members of the various technical staffs will be started on or about November 17, 1952. The program is being organized on an experimental basis to determine the

feasibility and practicability of individual staff members carrying out the examining, classification and pay activities with respect to a specified group of classes. We hope to learn whether or not it is desirable to extend this generalist activity.

Classes to be handled: medical and allied services; regulatory; public safety inspection; social security and rehabilitation; custodian and domestic services.

Persons assigned: Bob Lawson in charge; Kay Groff; Jane Carmack; Betty Walton; Wiley Hartley.

The Trial Run November 1952-October 1953

ALTHOUGH FISHER'S announcement stated the pilot unit's responsibilities strictly in terms of occupational classes, and although there were some important changes from the earlier proposal, the unit as it went into operation was similar to the one proposed by Chopson. The positions covered were confined to a relatively small number of agencies—Social Welfare, Mental Hygiene, Public Health Education, Youth Authority, and Veterans Affairs—many of which operated institutions. In no case did the new unit cover all positions of any department, nor even a majority of the classes in a department, but its problems were somewhat simplified by the fact that its departmental contacts were relatively limited.

The key members of the staff assigned to the unit were those proposed by Chopson, but its total size was smaller: one supervisor and four workers as against his proposal of six. In February 1953 a new member was assigned from the Pay Division, and for most of its history the pilot unit staff remained one supervisor and five operators. The staff consisted of three from Examining (Lawson, the Chief, Walton, and Hartley), two from Classification (Groff and Carmack), and later on, one from Pay (Specht).

The group was fortunate in its Chief. Lawson was one of the few supervisors with experience in both examining and classification. Before he joined the Board in 1949, he had done graduate work in personnel administration and had served with civil service agencies in Detroit and Alameda County, California. Though most of his work had been in examining, he had done classification. Further, he was young, enthusiastic about the generalist idea, and determined to make it succeed. His enthusiasm was abetted by that of the Misses Groff and Carmack. Soon the entire staff was imbued with a will to prove that the new system would work—and work better.

Lawson, as the Senior in charge of the unit, assumed the responsibilities of a Principal in the three fields of pay, classification, and examining. His decisions were not subject to review by other Principals, although he called upon them for guidance from time to time—particularly in pay matters, in which he had had no experience. In examining, he largely steered his own course. He was responsible directly to Bell, the Assistant Executive Officer, but Bell encouraged him to make his own decisions.

During the period of the pilot unit's separate operation, from November 17, 1952 until January 1, 1954, the other parts of the Board continued as usual. Pay, Classification, and Examining simply lost their responsibility for the classes assigned the unit.

Preparation

None of the unit's members, aside from its Chief, came with any prior training or experience in more than one functional field. Training in the other fields was, therefore, the first order of business. The mornings of the first two weeks were devoted almost exclusively to a fairly formal training program. Examining was the subject the first week. Most of this course was given by Lawson himself, but separate sessions were also conducted by representatives of the Recruiting Section and the Scheduling Unit of the Recruitment and Examining Division. The mornings of the second week were devoted to classification (three days) and to pay (two days). The sessions were conducted by various Seniors and journeymen from the two divisions concerned. The nature of the sessions is suggested by the following list of subjects covered by the Classification representatives, each having one hour for presentation and discussion:

Document Review and Processing Transfers
Job Survey Techniques
Classification Plan and Principles
Definition and Typical Tasks (in Specification Writing)
Minimum Qualifications and Knowledges and Abilities
Board Memoranda
Survey Principles and Methods
Allocation Standards

There was obviously too little time for complete coverage of the techniques of examining, classifying jobs, and making pay analyses. In fact, a considerable proportion of the allotted period was consumed in learning procedures, mechanics, and relationships. Some difficulty was encountered, for example, in the use of forms calling for signatures by one or more of the division chiefs; in general, it was decided not to develop and print new forms but to adapt the old ones to the new type of organization, giving Lawson signing authority which was comparable to that of the three Principals.

But questions of a great deal more substance also engaged the new unit during this period. There was a great deal of discussion of the varying usages of class specifications, of the differing significances of statements of minimum qualifications, and of the degree to which class requirements, determined by classifiers, had to be taken literally by examiners in the preparation of examinations and the review of applications. In general, those with examining background held for a liberal and flexible usage, with more room for discretion in the appraisal of individuals seeking employment and advancement. Though rather few solutions were agreed upon, these discussions exposed differing points of view and made one group more sympathetic to the problems of the other. Many of the problems discussed were unique to the operations of the new unit, but others were central to the whole problem of interdivisional co-operation and understanding. As such, the discussions served as a kind of catharsis. In January Lawson wrote Fisher a six-page, single-spaced memorandum on the problems that had been discussed during the training period.

During the initial period the new unit also discussed a name for itself, bearing in mind the significance of its title should the whole Board be reorganized on a generalist basis. It arrived at "General Personnel Operations Unit," and thereafter was referred to simply as the GPOU. In this and in its other actions described above the unit acted without direction by the Executive Office.

Although the formal training program had been completed by the end of November, a good part of the working time in December was also, in effect, training time. The members worked closely with each other, reviewed documents, and studied the groups of classes to which they were assigned. There were frequent discussions about methods and problems. Much of the necessary business was handled as a device for further training, enabling the staff to "learn by doing."

One of the first problems was to decide how work should be assigned within the unit. The group determined to proceed on a generalist basis from the start, so that each person would begin work in both classification and examining. There was further discussion of the old problem of occupational versus departmental assignments, and again it was decided to assign each individual a group of occupations and classes comparable to his prior occupational assignments, but to group the classes so as to maximize departmental concentration. The analysts were arranged in teams of one classifier and one examiner, so that they might learn from each other and review each other's work. It was agreed that the unit would not perform any work in the pay field until the Pay Division was able to assign one of its men. This occurred in February, and thereafter the unit gradually took over pay responsibilities. However, it was not until the following June that the GPOU could properly be considered a full-fledged generalist unit.

The Unit in Operation

Although the training aspects of its work continued for many months, the unit became fully operational by January 1953. The nature of its activities thereafter is suggested by its report for March, a representative month:

prepared 15 examinations, of which four were form tests, 4 were tests provided by the American Public Health Association, one was for transfer, and 6 were regular; the regular tests involved 181 new items, or 17% of the total items in these tests; also prepared 188 other new items for future use;

acted as chairmen of oral boards for 8 classes and 74 candidates;

reviewed 113 classification documents;
prepared 15 examination bulletins;
reviewed 297 applications for examinations;
conducted field trips to a state hospital and to laboratories in Agriculture and Public Health;
completed a new procedure for the checking of medical licenses.

The unit was able to keep up with its schedule of work requirements—an achievement most necessary in the field of examinations.[12] Although there may have been some slow-down in classification work, the using departments made little complaint. Pay studies and adjustments for the new fiscal year occupied much of June.

The analysts felt that their more intimate acquaintance with a smaller number of classes than they had handled previously provided information which made possible more adequate and quicker handling of individual actions. The knowledge they gained from pay studies, or classification transactions, or preparing examinations was, they felt, transferable. And the absence of the need for inter-divisional clearances increased the speed of the work process and added to job satisfaction. Even in its first month, December, Lawson was able to point with pride to the elimination of an examination due to the unit's acquaintance with another usable list—an accomplishment he felt would not have occurred under functional organization. The relatively high morale of the group was raised by its practice of holding informal evening staff meetings at the home of one of the members. Discussions were directed primarily at the objectives and the philosophy of the unit, and at ways by which its advantages could be maximized.

The analysts of the new unit were especially eager to undertake projects for which their generalist-occupational type of organization made them especially suited. Two of them worked part time for several months on a thorough survey of all the classes in the food service series, taking into account pay, classification, and to a lesser extent, examining considerations. Other studies—smaller, but similarly comprehensive from a functional standpoint—were also carried out.

But the unit also had its problems. One was keeping its activities and standards up to date and co-ordinated with the policies and programs of the three functional divisions.

Another difficulty was the organization and scheduling of work. The combination of pressures and deadlines on the shoulders of a single analyst, factors which neither he nor his supervisor could control, resulted in heavy peak loads. This difficulty was partially alleviated by the team arrangement and by the flexibility which enabled assignments to be temporarily transferred.

Problems of co-ordination with other divisions arose, although they were of a somewhat different type than previously. Positions and classes closely related to the occupational assignments of the unit but not included in them sometimes fell "between desks." Departmental reorganizations and other developments often affected not only some of the unit's classes but also a good many classes beyond its jurisdiction.

In a six-month progress report to Fisher, dated June 25, 1953, Lawson mentioned some of these advantages and disadvantages and concluded: "It would appear that the practicality of such an organization as this has been sufficiently established. It cannot be claimed, however, that at this stage, we have demonstrated any substantial or clearcut advantages over the more conventional type of organization. We do feel that substantial progress has been made. . . ."

Evaluation

From the very beginning, the senior personnel of the Board had recognized the necessity of an objective appraisal of the effectiveness of the pilot unit. As early as July 1952 Chopson had proposed a list of objectives of the unit, which he thought would furnish a basis for appraising its effectiveness. Most of these criteria, however, were too general to permit direct measurement. Shortly after the unit was established, the Executive Office asked the heads of each of the three functional divisions to prepare a set of criteria for measuring the unit's effectiveness. A good deal of work went

[12] Under the California system, the Board has little discretion as to the timing of examinations. When a vacancy occurs for which there is no "current eligibles" list available, the department fills it with a temporary appointment or promotion. But, under the Constitution, such an appointment must expire at the end of nine months. During that period, an examination must be prepared and administered and an eligible list produced.

into this in November and December 1952, particularly by R. W. Stephens, Chief of Classification, who prepared an elaborate set of devices and indices for comparison and appraisal. These were forwarded to Lawson for comment, and subsequently Bell, the Assistant Executive Officer, called a meeting to discuss them. The criteria fell into four main categories: (1) quantity of work, (2) quality of work, (3) reaction of using departments, and (4) satisfactions of individual staff members.

But in spite of these early steps, little effort was made during the months that followed to gather data that might be evaluated systematically. The difficulties in doing so were great and perhaps insurmountable.

For *quantity of work,* the Board had no universal system of work measurement, and there was little agreement as to the work units that might be used to reflect performance. Lawson, during his tenure as the unit's Chief, tried three different methods of measuring work output and was not satisfied with any of them. Even had he been, the measurements would not have been useful for comparison purposes unless the same methods were used in other divisions. A second difficulty of quantitative comparison was that the unit's work content was not comparable with that of any of the divisions. It was like comparing the whole of a stew with the beef, onions, and potatoes which had gone into it. There was no standard time for the writing of an examination or the writing of a class specification. This problem was confounded by the fact that the classes assigned the unit were in many ways not typical—and this would undoubtedly have been true of any assortment of classes. For example, the examining load of the unit was thought to be fairly easy, because it used tests developed by the American Public Health Association for many of the medical classes. On the other hand, those in the unit thought many of the classes to which they were assigned were unusually difficult from a classification standpoint.

Comparison of *quality* was even more ephemeral. Perhaps the best device for comparing would have been a review of all or a substantial part of the work product of the unit by the Principals in the functional divisions. Variations on this method were proposed, but little was done systematically by any of the division chiefs, and the unit would probably have resented such an effort, as it was not completely convinced of the impartiality of the division chiefs toward its operations. In the field of examining, Lawson himself could make some evaluations, although his position precluded perfect objectivity; but in the other fields, he did not feel himself capable of making qualitative appraisals. Abeel, Principal in Examining, did not review any of the examining work, and no other review of completed examinations was conducted in the Board. For pay and classification recommendations sent to the Board there did exist a basis for qualitative evaluation by the Executive Office. But evaluation was not done systematically.

A further difficulty in evaluation was that the unit was still learning its job. At first, it would have been clearly unfair to compare it with the long-experienced divisions. Subsequent experience has led some to feel that it takes at least a year and a half for a unit to attain its full potential. There was little agreement during 1953 on when the unit had attained sufficient maturity to warrant a fair comparison.

Because of these difficulties, little was done in the first half of 1953 to provide a basis for objective appraisal. During the summer, however, Bell decided to evaluate the unit in order to determine its future and that of the rest of the organization. The three principal criteria upon which the evaluation ultimately rested were: the job satisfaction of the unit's employees; the reaction of the using departments; and the opinions and feelings of the principal officers of the Board's staff.

Job Satisfaction: There could be no equivocation on this criterion. Members of the unit were enthusiastic. Their reasons were set forth at some length in a memorandum written by Kay Groff on October 5, 1953. Miss Groff had been asked by John McKay, who had become Personnel Management Analyst, to write him a frank memo on her reactions to the new unit. She was then about to leave the Board in order to be married, and she dictated the memo on her last day of work. She wrote that she was "just as enthusiastic" about the unit after eleven months in it as she had been at the start, and that all of its staff felt the same way. In Classification, she had been "constantly . . .

frustrated" by the way responsibilities were divided among divisions, by the time-consuming requirement of clearances, by the reliance that had to be placed upon representatives of the departments and upon the examiners for job information. She was impressed in the pilot unit by the tremendous increase in her knowledge about the jobs and classes to which she was assigned, by the usability of this knowledge in all the personnel functions, by the ease and speed of clearance, by the nearness of the Senior to advise and to act quickly on problems. She attributed part of this to the personal capability of Lawson. She felt that the increased morale and the increased knowledge about jobs were contributing to better work performance. She acknowledged certain problems of co-ordination but thought they were far less serious than such problems under the old organization. Finally, she expressed the hope that "even if the decision is made not to reorganize the entire board along generalist lines, that at least one or two units will be continued for the purpose of intensive review of classes in schematic groups, which is only possible in this kind of organization, and that it also be kept for the purpose of staff training."

This memo was written and broadly circulated shortly before the decision was reached to generalize the entire organization, and it may have provided a final push in that direction. But several weeks before, Bell had already become convinced that feeling within the unit was favorable. In fact, he had determined that the unit should be maintained, if only for this reason, regardless of the decision about the rest of the organization.

Departmental Reaction: In September 1953 Bell and Lawson arranged a series of meetings with the heads, the personnel officers, and certain other officials of each of the departments principally serviced by the unit. In these one to two-hour conferences, they elicited the frank reactions of the using agencies. Fisher attended some of these meetings.

The views expressed at the meetings ranged from mildly affirmative to enthusiastic.[13] Some felt that it was still too early to express a confident judgment; some were reluctant to recommend, at that time, that the entire Board be reorganized; some wished that the unit were on a departmental rather than an occupational basis—that each department have one man to deal with. But none suggested that the old form was preferable or that the new system was not. And some officials were vigorously in favor of generalism, both as an idea and in practice. Among the advantages seen by the using agencies were:

Personnel workers have improved understanding of jobs and of departmental problems.

Personnel staff is better able to perceive relationships between jobs and classes.

Staff views personnel problems as a whole, not as segments.

Service, particularly in pay and classification, is faster.

Strengthens position of personnel officer in the departments since Personnel Board now presents more unified front.

Better solution of interdepartmental problems—analysts in position to settle such differences rather than leaving up to departments to fight it out.

Makes it impossible for departments to operate with the technical divisions of the Board on the basis of "divide and conquer."

Single contact with Board on any given job problem rather than several (but the obverse of this was also stated—that a number of different contacts are necessary for each department under the occupational scheme).

Generalist is able to make and express a decision—the specialists are more hesitant and slower.

The specialist background of staff members was at first obvious, but deficiencies disappeared in six months.

The time and work of the agency on personnel problems were reduced.

Qualifications of individual personnel of staff have improved as result of getting out more and seeing problems.

Less buck-passing within the Board.

Relationships between Board and departments are "more comfortable."

May have effect of changing whole approach of Board from that previously of umpire and arbitrator to one of participant and assistant to better management.

The verdict of the departments, then, was favorable to the generalist program. But it may be noted that there was virtually no comment upon its effect on examining—still the largest single segment of the Board's workload.

Reactions of Officers within the Board: On August 26 Bell met with Lawson, the Principals,

[13] These comments are based on Bell's penciled notes.

and some of the Seniors in the three functional divisions to discuss the effectiveness of the unit. The meeting produced a fairly systematic review of most aspects of the unit's work.[14]

From the standpoint of production, both R. P. Everett, Chief of Pay, and the representatives from Examining seemed to feel that the unit had successfully carried its share of the workload in their fields. Stephens, Chief of Classification, thought it had fallen considerably short of a full job in his area. He said that regular analysts on his staff would have produced more new specifications and specification revisions. Lawson acknowledged this but called attention to the fact that many of his staff had been in a semi-training status for the first six months.

With regard to quality, Everett thought the unit had done a satisfactory job on pay, but reported that some of his staff felt the unit as a whole was not attaching sufficient importance to pay matters. There was little basis for judging the quality of examinations, since they had not been reviewed in Examining. E. V. Williams, a Senior from Classification, commented that some of the classification materials prepared by inexperienced analysts on the unit's staff were not up to normal standards, and Stephens said he saw some danger that the unit "may be drifting apart" on standards. Lawson said that his analysts felt that they were doing better jobs in their original fields.

Some expressed the sentiment that the unit's staff was exceptionally able and that not all personnel could handle this triple job. Both Stephens and A. L. Brock of Examining expressed a fear of over-specialization in regard to classes, over-identification with "special interests," and a resultant overall lack of co-ordination and consistency. There was little support for extending the new system to the entire staff, but representatives of both Pay and Classification felt that the unit should be continued and the experiment broadened to include another unit. Some endorsed the idea of trying out a unit on a departmental basis.

Thus, staff reactions in August were mixed, inconclusive, and on balance, slightly negative. But when Bell, in early October, reported to the general meeting of Seniors and Principals on the favorable responses of the using departments, the resulting verdict was clear consensus that, for whatever reasons, the pilot unit had been a success.

Reorganization November 1953-October 1954

AT THE BEGINNING of October 1953, Personnel Board executives faced a choice of four possible steps:

1. Drop the pilot unit and revert to the old organization.
2. Retain the pilot unit temporarily, or even permanently, without extending the idea.
3. Keep the present unit and set up a second pilot unit, either as a further experiment or as a step in the direction of complete generalization at some unspecified future time.
4. Prepare for a complete change-over to the generalist pattern.

The first possibility was precluded by Bell's report. It would have been like saying: "We tried the idea; it worked; so we dropped it."

[14] These comments are based on Bell's penciled notes taken at the meeting.

The second choice seemed somewhat more practicable, but the forcefulness of Bell's report militated against it. The original idea had been to give the pilot unit a year's trial. The year was almost up.

The third possibility had been suggested in Bell's meeting with the Seniors and Principals, some of whom had proposed that a second unit be set up and tried on a departmental rather than an occupational basis. For a while it appeared that this course would be followed. In September Fisher instructed John McKay, who had become Personnel Management Analyst in May, to prepare a plan for a second generalist unit. But McKay's plan, which was released on October 19, stated explicitly that its purpose was not the further testing of the effectiveness of the generalist approach. Nor was it designed to answer the "larger problem of determining the practical limits of the generalist form of organization. . . . This matter requires a great deal more study and discussion." McKay appeared to assume that the generalist idea would be extended, but that there was as yet no commitment to a Board-wide decision.

The establishment of a second unit without first deciding about the total future pattern of organization was vigorously opposed by Stephens, Chief of Classification. He held that the difficulty of operating the Board on two different organizational bases was already great enough with one generalist unit. The time had come to decide whether or not to go the full way. This view evidently was supported by others, and the choice was reduced to one of two alternatives: dropping the unit or changing the organization of the entire California State Personnel Board to a generalist pattern.

Certain other considerations probably entered into the decision and its timing. One was that in late September the Civil Service Assembly of the United States and Canada had held its annual conference in Los Angeles. One of the panel sessions had been on the subject, "The Generalist vs. the Specialist." Bell, the Board's Assistant Executive Officer, had been a member of that panel and had spoken about the Board's experience with the pilot unit. Fisher had attended the Assembly sessions, as had a fairly large number of other staff members. The subject of generalism, and of the California experience in particular, had generated considerable attention and discussion at the conference. This focusing of national professional interest on the subject, plus the enthusiasm the Californians had developed in describing their innovation at the conference, may have contributed to a feeling of greater urgency when the Board employees returned to Sacramento.

A second consideration was that Abeel, for a decade the Chief of the Recruitment and Examining Division, had retired during the summer of 1953. Abeel had paid little attention to the pilot unit experiment. Some staff members felt that he disliked the generalist idea and might have opposed it actively had he not been close to retirement.

A third consideration was that there still remained some of the inter-personal and supervisory problems discussed in the attitude survey conferences held many months before.

There is no record of the decision to proceed—as to exactly how or when it was reached and announced—and the memories of participants provide only vague clues. During October there was a great deal of consultation and, as in the year before, discussions were held, particularly in the Principal-Senior meetings. No special effort was made to probe staff opinions beyond the customary reports of supervisors. The decision itself was made by Fisher in close collaboration with Bell, apparently toward the end of October. The first written evidence of it occurs in the October monthly report of Personnel Management Analyst McKay, written on November 3, 1953:

> a. *As of January 1, 1954:* After detailed study and discussion it has been decided, as the next step toward a generalist form of organization, to consolidate the Classification and Pay Division staff functions. This combined unit together with Generalist Unit Number 1 would become a new Division of Operations. At the same time a Division of Technical Services would be established with responsibility for policy and standards relating to the classification and pay functions as well as the specialized services of wage surveys, departmental classification surveys, classification and pay transactions, etc.
>
> b. *As of April 1, 1954:* A Second Generalist Unit would be established on this date to undertake the technical work for the groups Agriculture and Conservation, and Regulatory and Public Safety. This second unit would report to the the Chief of Operations.

Even this decision seemed somewhat tentative, and it left unanswered a number of questions about the future. (It may be noted in passing that the occupational assignments for the second generalist unit were exactly those McKay had proposed in his memorandum of October 19.)

Planning the Change

Central responsibility for developing a specific plan for change-over was assigned to McKay. During the closing months of 1953 he worked closely with the various officers principally concerned. Much of the planning process was one of negotiating, identifying the principal points at issue, and bringing to a higher level any unresolved disagreements. A number of disputed points were discussed at meetings of Principals and Seniors, and some were taken up in private meetings with Fisher and Bell. During this period McKay was seeking to maintain objectivity and thus tried to avoid taking sides.

Within the Board at this time it was generally understood that reorganization was aimed at two objectives: first, to enlarge the challenge of work to staff, thus providing greater job satisfaction and greater opportunities for development and promotion; second, to improve the quality of the personnel work from the standpoint of the Board and from the standpoint of the departments which it serviced. The second goal, it was hoped, would result in part from achieving the first. But it was also anticipated that other elements of the generalist pattern would contribute to improved performance: the approach to individual problems from a broad rather than a segmental basis; greater knowledge of the job; more direct lines of supervision and control and therefore the possibility of greater delegation of authority for making decisions; fewer requirements for intra-Board clearance, and therefore greater speed of service; and, finally, the opportunity for the development of better standards and policies by a clear cut separation of operations from staff responsibilities.

Two possible purposes were definitely *not* considered. First, the reorganization was not viewed as a means of bringing about any basic change in the broad purposes and policies of the State Personnel Board. It was seen as a new arrangement for doing fundamentally the same things. Some anticipated that it would accelerate the trend toward greater delegation of personnel authority to the departments, but this was at most an incidental purpose. Second, the reorganization was not prompted by considerations of economy. Some hoped that there would be savings in operations which would make possible greater attention to some of the staff-type work which had been relatively neglected. But no one anticipated that any positions would be dropped as a result of the change. In fact, there was assurance that this would not be the case.

In short, Board officials hoped that by reason of the generalist plan, the Board would do essentially the same things at the same cost—but do them better than before and provide more satisfaction to those doing them.

One "formal" element of decisive importance in planning the reorganization was the budget of the Board and the positions it authorized. Early in the planning stage Fisher and Bell conferred with officials of the state's Budget Division, including members of its organization and methods section. At this meeting, they agreed that no increase in funds or in authorized positions would be sought as a result of the reorganization. (This agreement constituted the totality of Budget Division participation.) Virtually all the Board's professional positions, particularly those at supervisory levels, were filled by persons who had had several years experience. Therefore, the reorganization had to be accomplished within the framework of the existing positions, ranks, funds, and personnel.

These budgetary, classificatory, and status considerations provided "givens" within which the new organization had to be framed. In the old organization there were three Principals, each the head of a functional division. The rank of Principal required division-head responsibilities. Therefore, there had to be exactly three divisions under the new plan, each capable of supporting the classification of Principal. This might have been accomplished by dividing the operations work between two divisions, each headed by a Principal, and providing a third consolidated staff division. Since this possibility would have created difficulties of co-ordination between the two operating divisions, it was not seriously considered. The other possibility was that of a single operations division and two staff divisions, one for Examining and Recruitment, the other for the combined residuum of Pay and Classification.

The decision was made to proceed on the latter basis: there would be a single, generalist Operating Division and two staff divisions. This meant, among other things, that responsibilities would have to be distributed among the three in such a way as to warrant divisional status—and a Principal job—in each.

Nine Senior positions were potentially involved: the Personnel Management Analyst; the Chief of the pilot unit; two in Classification; one in Pay; and four in Examining, including three examiners and one head of the Recruitment Section. Unless he had a special or unusual job, such as that of Personnel Management Analyst, a Senior Analyst headed a section or group of professional workers and reported to a Principal. The head of Recruitment and Examining would need to retain the Senior in charge of recruiting and at least one other to take charge of whatever examining work was left. The head of the classification-pay staff work would need at least one Senior. The Personnel Management Analyst job was to be retained. This left, at an absolute maximum, five Seniors to head up sections in the new Operating Division. In view of the supervisory responsibilities involved in directing all operating activities, five also appeared to be the minimum. Thus, there was early agreement on having five sections in the new generalist Operations Division.

Within the basic organizational design already decided (three divisions and five sections in the Operations Division), McKay pursued his intensive study. His work was directed at the delineation of responsibilities of each division and section, the interrelationships of the units, the number and grades of positions to be assigned to each, the names of individuals to be reassigned, and the timing of the various changes.

Classification and Pay Functions

One of his more difficult tasks was to determine how responsibilities should be divided between the two projected staff divisions and the generalist Operations Division. McKay made a detailed inventory of all the functions of the existing divisions. After conferring with the division chiefs, he prepared memoranda for the front office proposing allocations of responsibilities on which he and the division chiefs had agreed, and stating the differences of view on disputed matters. Part of this discussion went on before the division chiefs yet knew what their new assignments would be.

The fundamental criterion in McKay's allocations was that work which applied directly to groups, classes, positions, and individuals would be assigned to the Operations Division. Developmental, research, and survey work would go to the two staff divisions, which would provide technical and advisory service to the generalists in Operations. In the fields of classification and pay, this meant that the Operations Division would have responsibility for:

The classification plan

The pay plan

Preparing virtually all classification documents for Board review (except those delegated to departments)

Providing contact and service to departments on all classification and pay matters

Developing and applying new salary scales to classes

The new Standards and Surveys Division (to be formed from the old Pay and Classification divisions) would have responsibility for:

Community wage surveys—planning, supervision, and reporting; but the Operations Division would lend personnel to participate in data collection

Special salary studies—for groups of classes as required

Studies of overtime practices, and advice to Operations Division on overtime problems

Conduct of periodic departmental classification audits

Development of classification and pay techniques—such as improved format for specifications, minimum qualification patterns, standardized terminology, work measurement techniques, improved classification and wage survey methods

Interpretation and application of the law and rules in these fields and formulation of new policies where necessary

Prevailing rate studies for manual jobs

Supervision and direction of the Board's statistical and reporting activities

Training in classification and pay for the entire agency

Preparation of the Board's reports to the Governor and the Legislature, including recommendations on appropriations needed for wage adjustment purposes

Development and maintenance of technical manuals on pay, classification, and transactions.

To this new Division was also assigned the Personnel Management Analyst, theretofore responsible directly to the Executive Officer, on the grounds that his job was essentially a research function and that the Standards and Surveys Division would become the principal research agency of the Board. Another consideration was that this shift would strengthen the staff and responsibilities of the new Division and its Chief. For operational purposes, this officer continued to report directly to the "front office." It was decided to transfer the maintenance of the employee roster, the large clerical task of the Classification Division, to the Office Services Division.

There was little disagreement in principle with

these assignments. But there were loose ends, some of which later rose to plague the divisions when they began to work under the new arrangements. For example, how were the findings and decisions of the staff studies made in Standards and Surveys to be communicated to the generalists in the Operations Division? How were the mis-classifications discovered in the departmental surveys to be corrected? How many analysts, and which ones, were to be loaned to Standards and Surveys for wage surveys? The jurisdiction of the staff division, Standards and Surveys, over legal and procedural questions on individual transactions was certain to cause confusion for the operating sections, themselves presumably responsible for the transactions. One general question, which was discussed but not permanently resolved, was that of staff-line relations in assuring that standards in classification and pay were maintained by the generalists in the Operations Division. There was no provision for technical inspection or review of the operators' work by the staff unit; and it was agreed that one device that might have served this purpose, the periodic classification audit, was to be used only to correct current position misallocations without any investigation as to how they might have occurred.

Examining Functions

Little change was anticipated for the recruiting function, which would remain intact within the Recruitment and Examining Division. But the distribution of responsibilities for examining was a difficult proposition, perhaps partly because there had been so little previous understanding of Examining's activities. In theory, the allocation was quite clear. The Operations Division would take over test preparation and the review of applications; the staff division would schedule the interviewing boards, conduct research in examining, maintain the library of testing items (the Testing Pool), provide training and technical guidance on the preparation and conduct of tests, and see that testing standards were maintained and, if possible, improved.

But one difficulty arose from the fact that the Board had done little in the research and development of testing technique *as such*. It had been predominantly production oriented. How could development of technique be divorced from the development of tests? And how could one division be held effectively accountable for technique when another was fully responsible for the tests themselves? What role could a staff division fill, and through what means, to assure the maintenance of standards in examining? This question was particularly pertinent since the head of Operations was to be a man relatively unversed in testing and since some of his Senior supervisors and operators would also have had no testing experience.

A further problem arose from the need to centralize some of the examining functions in the hands of one or two people. For example, the scheduling of examinations and of oral interview boards had to be centralized, and to maintain uniform standards it appeared desirable also to centralize the determination of passing marks and of residence requirements. Under the personnel limitations already discussed, it seemed that it would not be feasible to staff the Chief of the new Operations Division with technical assistants able to perform such jobs.

After extensive study and discussions with Brock, head of Recruitment and Examining, and Everett, who by this time had become the head of Operations, McKay prepared a detailed nine page memorandum, describing points of agreement and, most particularly, points of disagreement. This document, dated January 28, 1954, formed the basis for a meeting of Everett, Brock, McKay, Bell, and Fisher at which detailed decisions were reached about the assignment of functions. In general, these officials agreed to the allocation of research studies and developmental work to the new staff division, although they had no clear definition of what these kinds of work should consist of in practice. They also agreed that the new Recruitment and Examining Division was to prepare instructional and training material, conduct training in examining, check examinations for compliance with standards, supervise the Testing Pool, supervise investigations of applicants, and the like. Some of the key points of disagreement at the meeting are listed in the following table together with the decisions Fisher made to resolve them:

FUNCTIONS	ASSIGNED TO
Handling and recommending to Board on appeals from written examinations	Operations
Handling and recommending to Board on appeals from oral interviews	Examining
Determination of need for examinations	Operations
Scheduling of examinations	Operations
Scheduling, selecting outside members, and handling correspondence on oral interview boards	Examining
Determining examination bases: open, promotional, nationwide, and the like	Operations, but Examining will determine waiver of residence
Determining promotional eligibility for examinations	Operations
Setting and approving passing marks on examinations	Operations, subject to Examining review (temporary)

These determinations made it clear that, in addition to research and development, the examining unit in the Recruitment and Examining Division would continue to keep its hand in certain operational aspects of testing. It would continue to maintain the library of testing materials, the principal resource in the preparation of examinations; it would continue to co-ordinate and schedule the oral interviews for tests, a very substantial and time-consuming job. It would handle and make recommendations on all appeals from the oral interviews, by far the largest category of examination appeals.[15] Finally, it was agreed that for the first year its Chief should review and decide upon the passing marks of individual examinations.

Assignments to the Five Operating Units

Determining the assignments of the five sections of the Operations Division was simplified by the experience of the pilot unit. The old issue of departmental versus occupational approaches was now—perhaps inevitably—decided definitely in favor of the latter. Although effort was made to align departmental with occupational groupings in the case of some sections, the occupational scheme was clearly the dominant one "across the board."

At this stage of the planning several requirements came into focus: (1) the distribution in terms of workload and staffing requirements should be equitable; (2) occupational assignments for each group would, where possible, have to be logically related and homogeneous; (3) the assignments should correspond as nearly as possible with the occupational divisions already developed within the functional divisions, in order to take maximum advantage of existing staff familiarity with classes.

The method of allocation employed was similar to that used by Chopson the year before—counting the numbers of different classes and of total positions in each occupational grouping, and then attempting to divide them logically and also equally between the five sections. At the time, there were 2,160 classes and 56,228 employees in the state service. The pilot unit, which was to become Operations Section I, had about 300 classes and 10,600 employees in its jurisdiction. It was left largely intact but given some additional classes. McKay had already (October 19) proposed a second unit which would cover about 310 classes and 8,700 employees. A third unit was clearly indicated for the Engineering and Allied group, which already was separately handled by a small group of specialized Engineering Examiners and a Senior Engineering Examiner. A related group, Mechanical and Construction, was added to bring the totals for this section to about 550 classes and 11,800 employees. This was somewhat larger than the other projected sections, and the section had a heavy examining load. On the other hand, the majority of jobs were in the mechanical and trades fields, generally somewhat easier for classification purposes.

McKay had earlier suggested, as an alternate plan for a second generalist unit, the group of Fiscal, Management, and Staff Services. Added to these to form Section IV were the Legal group and

[15] The Board received few appeals from written tests, perhaps partly because its response was expected to be negative. Most appeals were handled at the staff level by deletions of items and modifications of scoring. Appeals from the oral rating boards were frequent.

parts of the Social Security group not assigned to the pilot unit. The totals of about 480 classes and 7,600 persons were somewhat smaller than some of the other sections, but these groups were considered most difficult for examining, classification, and pay. Personnel in many of these classes were employed by all departments and agencies, and here no specialization in departmental contacts was possible.

This left two groups (for the fifth section in Operations), the large Clerical and Allied, and the Education and Library categories. These comprised about 320 classes and 15,600 employees—most of whom were clerical. Like the fourth section, this unit would have to deal with every department and agency, and clerical positions were considered among the most difficult to classify. Also, some staff members, perhaps most of them, considered the clerical category an unstimulating, dull field in which to work.

Though there were some subsequent adjustments, these occupational assignments went into effect the following year. The basic scheme was as follows:

SECTION I: Custodian and Domestic; Medical and Allied; part of Social Security and Rehabilitation
SECTION II: Agriculture and Conservation; Regulatory and Public Safety
SECTION III: Engineering and Allied; Mechanical and Construction
SECTION IV: Fiscal, Management and Staff Services; Legal; part of Social Security and Rehabilitation
SECTION V: Clerical and Allied; Education and Library

Allocating Positions

Assignment of positions to the divisions and, within them, to the sections proved more difficult. Early in the planning stages McKay attempted to make an analysis of the worker man-years and fractions thereof currently being utilized on each activity in the three divisions, and of the time required for handling the operational work for each occupational group in the state service. There were many difficulties. Complete time records were not available for all operations, and some of the figures had to be estimates or even guesses. In many cases, individuals worked on a variety of activities. Further, assignments and workloads varied from month to month during the year; in some cases, as in the periodic pay surveys, the fluctuations were extreme. And the little jobs, such as correspondence and record-keeping, which one large examining unit had been able to absorb, now loomed as a heavy burden. Another of McKay's problems was that his man-year estimates had a disturbing tendency to add up to a larger sum than the number of positions authorized. For example, his earliest analysis of the staff needs of the various occupational classes (in October 1953) showed a total requirement for the operating sections of 33 professional positions below the Senior level, not counting the five already assigned to the pilot unit. This would have left only twelve for assignment to the other two divisions. A later projection markedly reduced this first estimate. He proposed a total of 32 journeymen in the Operations Division, including six in Section I (an addition of one), five in Section II, seven in Section III, eight in Section IV, and six in Section V. This left eleven in Standards and Surveys and seven in Examining. This was approximately the breakdown finally adopted.

Staffing needs of the two non-operating divisions were not determined until much later. In June 1954 McKay worked up a detailed analysis of the functions remaining in these divisions. Discussions were held, particularly about examining, and following these discussions tentative agreements were reached. McKay's new analysis showed a total of 33 journeymen positions in Operations, the 32 indicated above and one person for the scheduling and control of written examinations. The continuing responsibilities of Standards and Surveys were expected to require ten positions, and those in Recruitment and Examining five positions, as shown in the table on the following page.

This left unassigned two positions (of the grand total of fifty). Fisher, at a meeting on June 24, 1954, decided to assign one each to Standards and Surveys and to Examining for the new research work. In addition, he decided that the Operations Division should assign one analyst on a rotating basis to the examining group to work on the preparation of test materials. It had already been decided that the Operations Division would detail staff members to the Standards and Surveys Division to participate in the spring and fall wage surveys. A year later these arrangements were still unchanged.

STANDARDS AND SURVEYS	WORKING LEVEL STAFF REQUIREMENTS
Classification surveys	4
Personnel transactions matters	2
Wage surveys (general and special)	1.5
Personnel management research	1
Policy, standards, and developmental	.5
Prevailing rates, pay transactions, and Governor's report	.5
Special projects (overtime, fringe benefits, and the like)	.5
Total	10.0
RECRUITMENT AND EXAMINING	
Investigations	.6
Oral board arrangements, deferred examinations, physical and performance tests	1.7
Oral board appeals and correspondence	.6
Test Pool supervision	.4
Application review activity	.1
Test scoring activity	.1
Test research	.2
Special projects and reports (great variety)	1.3
Total	5.0

Assigning People

The first task in assigning personnel was choosing the new division chiefs. After talking privately with each of the three Principals directly involved, Fisher decided to appoint Everett, then Chief of Pay, to head the new Operations Division. Stephens, Chief of Classification, was chosen to head the Standards and Surveys Division. Brock, who had recently assumed leadership of Recruitment and Examining, would remain in that title. Fisher's decision was announced only a few weeks before the new divisions were to start work.

The filling of the Senior positions was determined in part by the prior responsibilities and the wishes of the officials concerned. Chopson, a Senior in Examining, desired an assignment in the Operations Division. In January 1954 he traded jobs with Lawson, who had been head of the pilot unit; Lawson returned to Examining temporarily and was subsequently transferred back to Operations as Chief of its Section V when that unit was activated in October. Popper, the Senior Engineering Examiner, was the obvious choice for Section III. This left one Senior in Recruitment and Examining.

It was determined at a fairly early date that Clarence Burger, a Senior in Classification with long experience, should head Operations Section II, and McKay himself was expected to take over Section IV on completion of his Personnel Management Analyst assignment. These plans were changed in September 1954, when Stephens became Assistant Secretary to the Personnel Board, and McKay was named acting chief of Standards and Surveys. It was then decided that E. V. Williams, the other Senior from Classification, should head Section IV. As his Senior Assistant in Standards and Surveys, McKay brought in C. Heldebrant, who had previously worked in the Pay Division. After Lawson left the Personnel Board in March 1955, Section V was headed by Frank Taffet, a former pay analyst.

Many staff assignments to Operations sections were also determined on the basis of previous experience. The pilot unit became Operations Section I without staff changes. The Engineering Examiners were obviously slated for Section III. There was no systematic effort to ascertain the wishes of staff members, but all had an opportunity to express their desires, and in some cases adjustments were made. One examiner, long in clerical examining, was transferred to another operating section, partly to strengthen its examining staff and partly to give him a change and broadening of scene. The Legal Examiner, who had long had responsibility for all legal tests, asked to remain in Recruitment and Examining so that she would have no responsibilities for classification and pay matters. Her request was granted, and the preparation of legal examinations remained in Examining, though all other activities in the legal field were assumed by Operations Section IV.

Most operating personnel wanted to go to the Operations Division. In part, they sought broader experience, but even more enticing was the belief that in the new Division lay the most promising road to increased responsibility and to promotion. Thus a major problem was how to keep people in the two remaining staff divisions. Discussions of a rotation program began anew, and it was agreed that such a program should be undertaken after the new organization had time to "jell."

Phasing the Change-over

Fisher and Bell had decided at the start that the transition would be made over a period of months, thus avoiding any abruptness that might cause confusion in the office or inconvenience to the using departments. Preparatory training could then be scheduled, and the experience of the staff could be enlarged gradually. Furthermore, problems that developed during the process could be handled one at a time before they became office-wide stumbling blocks. The transition period thus served as a training period and as a "shake-down cruise."

On November 27, 1953, Fisher announced the schedule in the first two stages of change-over:

Stage 1 (Effective January 1, 1954)

1. Creation of the Operations Division, to include:
   a. Operations Section I, the former pilot unit;
   b. Full responsibility for pay and classification operations throughout the state service;
   c. Two Classification and Pay Sections, one to handle these functions for the occupations later to be assigned Operations Sections II and III, the other, those later to be IV and V; each of these sections to be headed by a Senior (Burger and Heldebrant) and to be staffed by analysts from the Classification and Pay Divisions; each staff member would handle classification and pay matters on a generalist basis for an assigned group of occupations roughly similar to his subsequent assignment.
2. Creation of the Standards and Surveys Division with the same responsibilities and staff as it would have in the future.
3. Elimination of both the Classification and Pay Divisions.
4. No change in the Recruitment and Examining Division.

Stage 2 (Effective April 1, 1954)

1. Establishment of Operations Section II in the Operations Division under Burger by transfers from Examining and from Classification and Pay.
2. The remainder of the Classification and Pay Sections would continue under supervision of Heldebrant.

The schedule for the last two stages was not announced until the spring of 1954:

Stage 3 (Effective July 1, 1954)

1. Establishment of Operations Section III by further transfers from Recruitment and Examining and from the Classification and Pay Section.

Stage 4 (Effective October 1, 1954)

1. Establishment of Operations Sections IV and V, similarly by transfers.
2. Elimination of the remaining Classification and Pay Section.
3. Heldebrant to return from his Operations Division assignment to the Standards and Surveys Division, and Williams to move from that Division to head Operations Section IV.

The schedule enabled the analysts from the Classification and Pay divisions to benefit from a partial generalist experience for a period ranging from three to nine months before they assumed any examining responsibility. A reshuffling of desk assignments was made to enable staff members to develop familiarity with future associates as well as with the occupational groupings for which they would soon become responsible. The examiners and the analysts who were to work together in Operations sections were assigned to adjacent desks for several months before the new sections started to operate.

On December 17, 1953 Fisher sent a letter to all state agencies announcing the changes through Stage 2. This letter described the basic features of the reorganization plan and expressed the hope that better service would be the result.

After the reorganization was formally complete, on October 29, 1954, Fisher sent a second memorandum to all state agencies describing in detail the assignments of each section. The memorandum identified the proper staff members for the agencies to consult about the different kinds of personnel problems.

Formal Training

The Board could not allow its current work to be interrupted by the change-over. The pay analysts could not drop their current assignments for a month to learn how to write an examination any more than the examiners could stop examining to learn how to write specifications. Formal training sessions had to be sandwiched into the regular working day. Many of the sessions were held between 12:30 and 1:30, and the employees were asked to bring box lunches. Under these conditions training could not be very intensive. It was expected that training would continue on the job and that there would be additional formal instruction on technique and method after the Operations sections were activated.

It was necessary that the staff of each new section receive its formal training before, but not too long before, its unit was activated. This meant that training had to be carried out in four stages, each just prior to a corresponding stage in the reorganization. The first training period, held in December 1953, consisted of training in classification and pay for all analysts in the Classification and Pay divisions as well as for members of the examining staff who would be assigned to Operations Section II. The principal topics and the instructors are shown below:

SUBJECT	LEADER
General Introduction	Bell
Collection of Data (Pay)	Heldebrant
Analysis of Data (Pay)	McKay
Review of Typical Pay Cases (two sessions)	Heldebrant
*Specification Writing	Williams
*Classification Survey of a Position	Price
*Decisions Involving Status Determinations	Stephens
*Personnel Transactions	Thomas
*Process of Establishing a New Class	Williams
*Classification Tools	Burger
*State Employees, State Agencies, and the State	Fisher

*Relate to Classification

These one-hour sessions were conducted on about half the working days in December. During the same period the staffs of Classification and Pay also discussed problems of the new organization at weekly joint staff meetings. By early December the Personnel Management Analyst had developed a three-page bibliography of readings in classification, pay, and examining. Copies were distributed to the staff members involved, with instructions as to which items were required reading and which were "additional desirable." Each staff member was instructed to check off the items after reading them and to return the list to his supervisor when he finished.

The second training stage dealt with examining. It began late in February and ended in April. It was attended by all the classification and pay personnel who were to transfer to Operations Sections II and III.

SUBJECT	LEADER
Description of Examining Functions	Brock
Principles of Testing and Examination Planning	Chopson
Items—Use and Construction	Lawson
Scheduling and Recruiting Bulletin Preparation	Carney, Spelbring
Application Review	Swabey
Test Pool; Consultants and Source Material	Smith
Test Assembling	Popper, Taylor
Passing Marks	Brock
Performance and Physical Tests	Walton

The third training stage, in May, was substantially a repetition of the classification and pay syllabus for all the examiners to be assigned to Operations Sections III, IV and V. It was followed during the summer by the fourth and final stage—a repetition of the examining syllabus for the classification and pay personnel who were to be assigned to Operations Sections IV and V.

In the judgment of staff leaders, the exchange of information and ideas within the various sections before and after they were activated proved as helpful as formal training. Also beneficial was the ability of the staff to collaborate on problems as they arose. Each section was organized on a team basis following the technique explored by the pilot unit. Thus each examiner and analyst, though individually responsible for a category of occupations, had a partner in his section from one of the other former functional divisions, and he could call on this partner for consultation and advice.

Shake Down November 1954–July 1955

IT WAS NOT EASY for the new Operations sections to work up to full effectiveness. No longer present was the twin spur of challenge and of pioneering zeal that had fired the pilot unit in its early months. Some sections—notably IV and V—found that maintaining contact with "client" agencies was much harder than it had been before reorganization; these sections had to work with many different agencies in dealing with the personnel matters of the occupations that had been assigned to them.

Each section seemed to develop in a unique manner. Some inherited special projects and special problems. Each had a different supervisor with his own particular background, point of view, and concern for the new system. The same was true of the respective staffs.

Even Section I, the old pilot unit, did not start off at full steam. Chopson, who became supervisor of Section I, said later that it took the Section eighteen months (through the summer of 1954) to achieve full effectiveness. As of July 1955, it was too early to appraise how generalism had worked out in the other sections. None had been operating more than fifteen months; two had had only nine months experience. It was clear that in some sections the full generalist ideal would not soon become a reality. This was partly because both supervisors and staff were inclined to direct more attention to the specialist fields in which they had greater experience and confidence—and, frequently, greater interest. For example, Everett, Chief of Operations, devoted his primary efforts to pay matters for which he had previously had responsibility. Similarly, some of the Senior examiners and classifiers heading generalist sections devoted their principal attention to their former specialties and delegated to others much of the supervisory responsibility for other functions.

The perpetuation of individual functional specialisms among the staff was greatly encouraged by the pressures of work. Supervisors were reluctant to assign important rush jobs to "green hands," when time did not permit either training or close supervision. It was far easier, sometimes imperative, to use the best-trained people available. An example of this was a "big push," in May and June 1955, to develop a new pay plan for the entire state service. To supervise and co-ordinate this program, Everett designated a committee consisting of one representative from each Operations section. Taffett, the Chief of Section V and the only pay man among the section chiefs, was named to head the committee, and its other members were former pay men, one from each section.

Perhaps inevitably, some examiners had little inclination and small professional respect for pay and classification work. The disdain was reciprocated by a few of the classification and pay analysts. In one or two of the sections such preferences were supported and even encouraged by the supervisors, who assigned examining work to former examiners and classification work to former classifiers.

Brock, the Chief of Recruitment and Examining, supervised an analysis of the new test items developed in the Operations sections and submitted to the Testing Pool during the months from October 1954 to January 1955. Former examiners made up slightly less than half the working-level staff of the five Operations sections at that time. This group produced nearly four-fifths of the new test items—1,985 out of 2,682 multiple-choice questions and 410 out of 436 true-false questions. Only five members of the Operations Division wrote no new items and all five were of non-examining background.

By July 1955 progress toward generalism appeared to be accelerating. A former analyst, assigned to that Operations section in which generalism was thought to have made the slowest headway, was in 1955 preparing two of the most important examinations. Virtually the entire staff worked on the 1955 pay adjustments, even though leadership in that work had centered in former pay analysts. And by July 1955 most men in the Operations sections had had some experience in all three functional fields.

Reactions: Staff Development and Morale

With respect to one of its initial objectives, that of broadening the scope of the professional staff, the reorganization had already borne fruit by 1955.[16] In general the staff seemed glad for the opportunity to gain experience in other personnel fields; and it appreciated management's concern for employee development, a concern which the change-over had demonstrated. Opportunities for advancement within and without the state service appeared to have enlarged for some of the staff. (A case in point was the appointment of Lawson as personnel officer of one of the state departments; another was the 1955 examination for personnel director of Sacramento County, in which Personnel Board employees gained two of the first three places on the eligible list.) In addition, the reorganization caused greater delegation of responsibility and decision-making authority to Seniors and their operating personnel. In many cases, probably in most, this increased job satisfaction. The old complaint of the examiners—that they had no direct contact with the Personnel Board—was largely corrected. Virtually all professionals in the Operations Division were making periodic appearances before the Board by mid-1955.

The change-over to functional generalism was not without cost. Generalism focused upon individual staff members a great variety of pressures, deadlines, and interruptions. As illustrated in the accompanying cartoon (originally published as

THE GENERALIST

VOLUME VII FEBRUARY, 1954 NO. 1

the cover sheet of the "Espe Bee," the Board's house organ), each analyst was continually forced to juggle a variety of different problems. Some, but certainly not all, complained that the accumulation of different demands interrupted the sustained concentration necessary to do a good job on any one assignment. They missed the satisfaction of doing a single job well. This reaction appeared to be strongest among former examiners who had been accustomed to a scholarly pace and to shelter from interruptions while constructing a test.

As Lawson had noted with the pilot unit, the problem of multiple pressures and interruptions was accentuated by the fact that it was so difficult to schedule or balance the work load. It was impossible to prevent peak periods when demands exceeded the eight-hour day capacity of the individual. These peaks were alleviated somewhat by flexibility in work assignments within sections and even between them. The team arrangement also helped. There was frequent detailing of indi-

[16] Most of the material that follows is based upon meetings and interviews by the author. These included a meeting with the Personnel Board itself and individual discussions with some of its members; meetings with groups of the executives of the staff as well as individual interviews with all of them; individual interviews with the majority of supervisors in the professional divisions; and individual interviews with about one-quarter of the professional staff in the Operations Division. No claim is made as to the "scientific" validity of these observations. There has been no attitude survey since 1952. Also, the author undertook no appraisal of the reactions of the using departments.

viduals from one section to another to handle particular jobs.

One of the more annoying sources of interruption in 1955 was the recurring requirement that the analysts serve on, and chair, oral interviewing boards. These boards might take a man from his desk for periods lasting from one day to several weeks; meanwhile his normal work was either held up or handled by his team partner or by someone else in his or another section. For example, a member of Section III, normally assigned to mechanical and trade classes, had to serve on an oral board for several weeks. In his absence, an examination had to be prepared for a certain class of printers. A former classifier in Section IV, assigned to work on administrative and staff-type occupations, had to prepare the examination, even though he had had no experience with this type of position.

A further cost of reorganization was that functional generalism necessarily resulted in a greater degree of occupational specialism. Both the former examiners and the former pay analysts found that the occupational groups over which they had cognizance were considerably narrower than they had been before. The former classifiers, previously organized on a departmental basis, lost their department-wide orientation and scope. One complained that while he had once known all that was going on in a number of different state departments, he now lacked a complete picture of any department. He felt that his sources of organizational information had dried up and that with them had gone much of the interest and challenge of his job.

The reorganization did not, and could not, eliminate specialism in individual assignments. It had, it seemed by 1955, substituted one kind of specialism for another.

To some of the staff, generalism seemed to bring with it a loss of status. The examiners had complained previously of their relatively low status within the organization. But status had more than one connotation. In the eyes of some of the former examiners, the examining function had higher *professional* status than any other personnel work. A few would have maintained that examining was the only truly professional activity of the Board. Classification and pay they tended to regard as involving merely common sense plus negotiation and compromise. On the other hand, some former classifiers took the opposite line: that the first need in examining was knowledge of the requirements of the job for which the test was being designed; that once these were fully understood, putting together a selective test was easy.

Some staff members were asked in 1955 whether they thought it was harder for a former examiner or for a former classifier to become a generalist. The answers followed a consistent pattern. The former examiners thought the classifier had the harder time because he had to learn much more before he could construct a good examination. And the former classifiers thought the examiners had the tougher road since they had to acquire skills in penetrating job situations, in negotiating, and particularly in saying "no." A few, skeptical of the generalist idea, expressed the view that the two types of jobs called for different personality types: examining called for a creative, studious mind and inclination; classifying and pay work required ability in, and satisfaction from, frequent dealings with people. Still other staff members, favorable to the reorganization, discounted this argument and emphasized the wholeness of the personnel job.

By mid-1955 there were differing views about the extent to which the reorganization was aiding the professional development of personnel. Some employees, particularly from examining, questioned whether former classifiers or new trainees could be developed into truly qualified examiners within generalist units. However, others held stoutly that it was possible to develop *compleat* personnel men "from scratch" in much faster time than might have been expected. One supervisor expressed the view that a three-field generalist could be trained in about one and one-half times the period required to train a specialist in a single field.

Finally, reorganization brought morale problems to those remaining in the two staff-type divisions, Recruitment and Examining, and Standards and Surveys. The increase in the responsibility of the Operations staff resulted in some loss of responsibility for the other two divisions. In 1955 many of the non-Operations personnel looked forward to a transfer to Operations.

Reactions: the Staff-Line Problems

The reorganization resulted in a division between line and staff-type responsibilities that had not existed before. This division created new possibilities, but it also brought new problems of inter-divisional relationships. Virtually all the problems were familiar staff and line difficulties, but they were complicated somewhat because the heads of the staff and line divisions were coequal and because the head of the line division had virtually no staff assistance of his own. The major staff and line problems are described below:

1. *How should the programs and priorities of the staff units be developed?* The principal clients of the staff units were the line sections in the Operations Division. These sections naturally expected to have some influence on the work of the staff units. Yet, there was a risk that the staff divisions would assume merely a servicing role to the line division, rather than the role of equals as implied by the structural plan. The Standards and Surveys Division at an early date undertook to develop for itself a program and priority system and to obtain from the Operations Division an expression of its views and needs. But the system fell into disuse, partly because Operations could not predict far in advance the special studies that it would need to cope with future operating problems. When it needed a study it often needed it urgently. It would not be practicable to delay a request for an urgently needed study until it could be discussed by the two division chiefs, or sent to higher authority for a decision about whether or not Standards and Surveys should be asked to make the study. On the other hand, officials in the staff divisions feared that if they simply responded to the requests of the Operations sections, they would become Operations' subordinates and would forsake the functions of bolstering standards and conducting independent studies. The reorganization had left the Chief of the Operations Division with no staff of his own, requiring him to lean heavily on the two apprehensive staff divisions.

2. *What may be done to assure that staff findings are communicated to the line operators and are used by them?* While they are useful, written communications have their limitations. Some time after it issued a new procedural instruction, the Standards and Surveys Division discovered that many in Operations were not following it; some had forgotten that it had ever crossed their desks. Joint meetings were held from time to time, usually with the Chiefs and the Seniors of the divisions concerned. But not all staff matters warranted such high-level meetings in a busy office; and even high-level staff meetings could not always assure adequate communication of staff advice to officials down the line at the operating level.

3. *Where is the line between "staff" and "operations"?* The work of the Transactions section in Standards and Surveys in interpreting laws and rules and applying them to individual cases was indeed very close to operations. So were the departmental classification surveys. How were the changes indicated by these surveys to be put into effect? Were the classification surveyors to act themselves or were they simply to provide their findings to the line officials in the Operations sections? Thinking on this question in 1955 was that changes in individual allocations should be handled by the surveyors; changes in the classification plan should be transferred to the operators to handle. Questions like this one were being worked out as they arose.

But for written examinations the responsibility was unclear in 1955. Should the examining specialists prepare examining materials? A major project conducted during 1954-55 was the development of testing materials in the manual and trade fields and the results were highly approved on all sides. By mid-1955 the examining groups appeared to have insufficient staff for such test development work, and there had been little follow-up on the program. There were also further problems: Who should determine what kinds of test materials to develop? And who should ultimately be responsible for the content of such tests as long as the responsibility for individual tests lies in the Operations Division?

4. *Where lies the responsibility for maintaining and developing quality in work product?* The Chief of the Operations Division, in 1955, had neither the time nor the staff to check work quality on any but the most important types of jobs and these did not include examinations, which amounted to nearly half the total workloads of his sections. Pre-audit by another division would have caused severe internal stresses. And the me-

chanics of post-auditing by another division, and making its findings effective, had not been thoroughly worked out by mid-1955. The staff divisions were reluctant to become inspectors and tended to assume that responsibility for maintaining quality lies within the line organization. In the Personnel Board, Standards and Surveys was careful to avoid letting its classification surveys take the guise of audits on the work of the operators. As of 1956, Examining had not developed a system for the post-audit of tests, nor had it mobilized its potential resources to make statistical analysis of examination questions or to make studies of the validity of test results in relation to job performance.

Furthermore, in handling appeals from oral tests and in reviewing passing grades on written tests, Examining was certainly close to an inspection role. But since neither of the staff divisions was in the position to act on findings (other than communicating them to the Chief of Operations), they felt that they could not assume responsibility for the quality of the Operations Division's product.

Reactions: Production

By mid-1955 opinions of supervisors and staff varied on how the transition had affected output. Some felt that increased familiarity of staff members with the occupations they handled had greatly increased productivity. Knowledge gained for one purpose could be used for other types of assignments. Thus the total output of the analyst was increased, and the greater understanding he brought to his occupational classes appeared to assure higher quality work. These persons also felt that productivity would continue to grow as job familiarity increased. They also expected that the segregation of the line from staff functions would increase productivity. Finally, a few stressed that people were working harder; the supervisors were busier, and some said the workers were spurred by greater incentive as well as heavier work loads.

On the other hand, some supervisors and workers stated that per capita quantity and quality of output in their sections was lower than before. The principal complaint was of lost time from interruptions and from repeated transfers of attention. Since much of the work had to be turned out, the principal sacrifice was in quality, not quantity. The major deficiency was felt to be the quality of examinations. A number of references were made to "cover-page" examinations—that is, old tests pulled out of the files and used again without change. One or two former examiners alleged they had to rely largely on examining materials built up over previous years, since they lacked the necessary time it would take to develop new materials.

The overall evidence about quantity and quality was pretty thin as of mid-1955. Such clues as existed, however, did not suggest that there had been any significant changes as a result of reorganization. Throughout the transition period, the Board met its examining schedule, though apparently with increasing difficulty. The number of tests declined somewhat during 1954-55. It was hard to say how much of this should be attributed to reorganization.

The Board completed on schedule its various pay projects, including that of June 1955. There was a noteworthy decline in the number of actions taken before the Board itself, much of it due to extraneous factors. The statistical record maintained by the Operations Division did not indicate any significant change in the speed of processing departmental requests for classification and pay actions.

As of June 1955 there had been no systematic appraisals of the effects of reorganization upon quality of output. However, some impressionistic data were available, since many classification and pay projects normally went up through channels to the Board. In spite of a few slips and mistakes, officers in the higher echelons felt that the quality of work had been maintained. Furthermore, a few broad studies were made of pay and classification of entire occupational series; these probably would not have been made under the old form of organization.

Insofar as output of examining could be judged, it did not appear, overall, that there had been marked change. The new materials submitted by the Operations staff to the Testing Pool during the early period of October 1954 to January 1955 totaled only slightly under the average for the same four months during 1950-54. During the same period, a project for developing trade tests, conducted by the Recruitment and Examining Division, produced a large number of new items, bringing the Board's total considerably higher than the four-year average. Of course, the number of new items furnished little evidence about quality.

Finally, as a result of reorganization, two new positions for performance of developmental work were created and assigned to the two staff divisions. These two divisions subsequently made significant contributions. Standards and Surveys developed manual material and conducted a survey of overtime and fringe benefit practices. Recruitment and Examining developed instructional material on oral interviewing and trade testing materials.

All in all, the results did not appear unfavorable to the new plan of organization, particularly since the period to July 1955 had been one of transition when some decline in output was expected.

However, the maintenance and improvement of quality, in the examining field especially, appeared to present a challenging problem. No system existed for appraisal of examining work, nor even for informed scrutiny of many examinations. A large proportion of the more important pay and classification projects went up through channels to the Board; review was possible, and necessary, at a number of levels. Most examinations, on the other hand, were prepared by examiners with only general guidance from their Seniors. The Seniors approved the examinations for printing after reviewing them, sometimes in a rapid and superficial manner. No examination went above the Senior level; none was reviewed by a technician from Recruitment and Examining; and more than half of the staff analysts and the Seniors in the Operations Division had had little or no prior examining experience.

Reactions: Service to the Departments

One of the avowed intentions of the reorganization was to speed up and improve services to the users. It was hoped that it would reduce the number of contacts individual agencies would have to maintain within the Board, and that it would minimize internal clearances and opportunities for conflict among the divisions. But the decision for an occupational basis rather than a departmental basis of assignment, however inevitable, meant that every state agency had to deal with at least two different sections in the Operations Division; some of the larger departments must deal with as many as four or five.

There were offsetting advantages. The new system assured that, in any problem affecting a single series of positions or classes, an agency dealt with only one Personnel Board representative—a representative who was equipped to handle all aspects of the question. While the department head or his personnel officer might have a variety of Board contacts while handling his multifarious problems, most departmental executives and supervisors, with more restricted scope, usually found it necessary to deal with only one or two officials in the Board.

Personnel matters that cross occupational lines, and reorganizations affecting a variety of positions, raised special problems of co-ordination within the Operations Division. An effort at a solution was made by designating each section in Operations as primary liaison contact for specified using departments. This device was not widely used, but multifaceted problems had not been especially difficult for the Board to handle as of July 1955.

Postscript

AS THIS WAS WRITTEN in the summer and fall of 1955, it was too early to draw from the California experience any conclusions about the desirability of the generalist plan. On the other hand this case study does afford some observations about the reorganization process which are neither premature nor inappropriate.

One is that a reorganization of this kind is a considerable job and a long one. Synthesizing plans, preparing men's minds, staging the formal changes, and getting accustomed to new responsibilities are matters of years. In fact, the task of readying the California staff for this reorganization, though probably not consciously conceived as such, probably began many years before 1952 with the concern about staff development and rotation. To the outsider, the movement toward change-over, after the idea was first broached in the spring of 1952, may appear hesitant, deliberate, and cautiously experimental. The avoidance of hasty commitment on the part of management and the drawn out discussions were probably tactically wise and strategically essential. It is interesting that one of the criticisms voiced by two staff members was that the reorganization was too fast—that insufficient time was allowed for planning and adjustment. The success of the plan depended upon the understanding of the professional staff, upon the support of most of them, and upon the co-operation of all of them. It could not be dictated from above. It took time to elicit such participation and to bring about change, when the scope and habits of work of all the individuals were affected.

It is therefore noteworthy that no organized opposition ever developed within the staff. Some staff members were conscientiously opposed to reorganization, and a few felt personal threats and hurts. A few scars seem to be the inevitable consequences of major organizational change. The degree to which these pains were minimized was probably due to the skill and to the gradualness with which the reorganization was brought about. Also, the staff members—even those who opposed the principle of the reorganization—entered wholeheartedly into the program once it was decided.

This was voluntary reorganization. There was no pressure or compulsion from outside the organization. Consequently there was a greater need for staff support, if not for complete unanimity, than would have been true if there had been external pressure for change.

Nor was the change-over forced by internal conditions. In the words of James Bell, Assistant Executive Officer of the Board: "It was not prompted by a break-down or change in administration, but rather was a conscious, studied, experimental effort simply to see if by this type of operation a better job could be done." The Board had its problems before it reorganized, and some of these undoubtedly contributed to the desire to try the new plan. But the problems were not critical; they in no way dictated so drastic a change as that which was undertaken. Management's decision to change is perhaps best understood as a fusion of a belief in the generalist principle, an awareness of certain existing problems, and a restless desire to experiment and improve.

One may ask: Was this truly management's decision? Or was it rather forced upon management by the staff itself? One participant described the reorganization as a grass-roots movement in which the initiative and drive for change came up from below. So blunt an interpretation, however, does not seem to square with the events. There was much interest in, and support of, the generalist idea from the operating staff and, through the variety of meetings and discussions and through the experience of the pilot unit, the staff contributed much to the shape and the timing of the change. There was also democratic participation in planning and preparing for decision. But the initiative, the leadership, and the quiet persistence of top management were present almost from the beginning. The decisions themselves were clearly those of top management. The momentum for change came largely from the Executive Office and from the operating professional staff. The intermediate supervisory staff, with few exceptions, were skeptical or "had reservations."

This story, unlike some other case studies in administration, contains little drama. Yet it relates no less authentic workings of dynamic administration—normal people trying to do their jobs and do them better over the long run. It may give pause to those who are prone to deplore the "dead hand" and conservatism of bureaucracy.

Unlike a case study, which fortunately may come to a close, administration is an ongoing process. So is reorganization. The episode described in the foregoing pages had its origins many, many years ago, and its ramifications may never end. Even as this case study was being written, the staff in Sacramento was re-examining itself, studying some of the problems mentioned in the preceding chapter and discussing possible further organizational changes. As a result, a further reorganization was put into effect in October 1955. It evolved from the reorganization described in this study but did not amend the basic generalist pattern.

Appendix

Executive and Supervisory Officers of Personnel Board Staff Involved in Reorganization

NAME	RANK [a]	POSITION *Before*	POSITION *After*	MAJOR OR GRADUATE (G) EDUCATIONAL BACKGROUND	MAJOR FIELD OF PERSONNEL EXPERIENCE	FIRST CAME TO BOARD
Fisher, J. F.	Executive Officer	Executive Officer	Executive Officer	Public Administration (G)	Classification; General	1944
Bell, J. R.	Assistant Executive Officer	Assistant Executive Officer	Assistant Executive Officer	Public Administration (G)	General Personnel Management	1939
Sharp, K. D.	Assistant Secretary, SPB	Assistant Secretary, SPB	Assistant Secretary, SPB	Public Administration (G)	Pay; Classification; General	1937
Brock, A. L.	Principal [a]	Senior Examiner	Chief, Recruitment and Examining Division	Public Administration (G)	Examining	1936
Everett, R. P.	Principal	Chief, Pay Division	Chief, Operations Division	Economics; Public Administration	Pay; Classification	1942
Stephens, R. W.	Principal [a]	Chief, Classification Division	Chief, Standards and Surveys Division	Personnel Administration (G)	Classification	1936
Abeel, E. A.	Principal	Chief, Recruitment and Examining Division	Retired	Engineering	Examining	1931
Chopson, E. W.	Senior	Examining Division [c]	Supervisor, Operations Section I	Psychology (G)	Examining	1938
Burger. C. L.	Senior	Classification Division [d]	Supervisor, Operations Section II	Public Administration (G)	Classification	1936
Popper, W.	Senior	Engineering Examiner	Supervisor, Operations Section III	Engineering	Examining	1946